International Directory of
COMPANY HISTORIES

International Directory of
COMPANY
HISTORIES

VOLUME 82

Editor

Tina Grant

ST. JAMES PRESS
An imprint of Thomson Gale, a part of The Thomson Corporation

Detroit • New York • San Francisco • New Haven, Conn. • Waterville, Maine • London

International Directory of Company Histories, Volume 82

Tina Grant, Editor

Project Editor
Miranda H. Ferrara

Editorial
Virgil Burton, Donna Craft, Louise Gagné, Peggy Geeseman, Julie Gough, Linda Hall, Sonya Hill, Keith Jones, Lynn Pearce, Holly Selden, Justine Ventimiglia

Production Technology Specialist
Mike Weaver

Imaging and Multimedia
Leslie Light, Michael Logusz

Composition and Electronic Prepress
Gary Leach, Evi Seoud

Manufacturing
Rhonda Dover

Product Manager
Jennifer Bernardelli

LIBRARY OF CONGRESS CATALOG NUMBER 89-190943

ISBN-13: 978-1-55862-586-0   ISBN-10: 1-55862-586-0

This title is also available as an e-book
ISBN-13: 978-1-55862-630-1   ISBN-10: 1-55862-630-0

BRITISH LIBRARY CATALOGUING IN PUBLICATION DATA

International directory of company histories, Vol. 82
I. Tina Grant
33.87409

Printed in the United States of America
10 9 8 7 6 5 4 3 2 1

Contents

Preface

The St. James Press series *The International Directory of Company Histories* (*IDCH*) is intended for reference use by students, business people, librarians, historians, economists, investors, job candidates, and others who seek to learn more about the historical development of the world's most important companies. To date, *IDCH* has covered over 8,000 companies in 82 volumes.

INCLUSION CRITERIA

Most companies chosen for inclusion in *IDCH* have achieved a minimum of US$25 million in annual sales and are leading influences in their industries or geographical locations. Companies may be publicly held, private, or nonprofit. State-owned companies that are important in their industries and that may operate much like public or private companies also are included. Wholly owned subsidiaries and divisions are profiled if they meet the requirements for inclusion. Entries on companies that have had major changes since they were last profiled may be selected for updating.

The *IDCH* series highlights 10% private and nonprofit companies, and features updated entries on approximately 50 companies per volume.

ENTRY FORMAT

Each entry begins with the company's legal name; the address of its headquarters; its telephone, toll-free, and fax numbers; and its web site. A statement of public, private, state, or parent ownership follows. A company with a legal name in both English and the language of its headquarters country is listed by the English name, with the native-language name in parentheses.

The company's founding or earliest incorporation date, the number of employees, and the most recent available sales figures follow. Sales figures are given in local currencies with equivalents in U.S. dollars. For some private companies, sales figures are estimates and indicated by the abbreviation *est*. The entry lists the exchanges on which the company's stock is traded and its ticker symbol, as well as the company's NAIC codes.

Entries generally contain a *Company Perspectives* box which provides a short summary of the company's mission, goals, and ideals; a *Key Dates* box highlighting milestones in the company's history; lists of *Principal Subsidiaries, Principal Divisions, Principal Operating Units, Principal Competitors*; and articles for *Further Reading*.

American spelling is used throughout *IDCH*, and the word "billion" is used in its U.S. sense of one thousand million.

Users of the *IDCH* series will notice some changes to the look of the series starting with Volume 77. The pages have been redesigned for better clarity and ease of use; the standards for entry content, however, have not changed.

SOURCES

Entries have been compiled from publicly accessible sources both in print and on the Internet such as general and academic periodicals, books, and annual reports, as well as material supplied by the companies themselves.

CUMULATIVE INDEXES

IDCH contains three indexes: the **Index to Companies**, which provides an alphabetical index to companies discussed in the text as well as to companies profiled, the **Index to Industries**, which allows researchers to locate companies by their principal industry, and the **Geographic Index**, which lists companies alphabetically by the country of their headquarters. The indexes are cumulative and specific instructions for using them are found immediately preceding each index.

SUGGESTIONS WELCOME

Comments and suggestions from users of *IDCH* on any aspect of the product as well as suggestions for companies to be included or updated are cordially invited. Please write:

The Editor
International Directory of Company Histories
St. James Press
27500 Drake Rd.
Farmington Hills, Michigan 48331-3535

St. James Press does not endorse any of the companies or products mentioned in this series. Companies appearing in the *International Directory of Company Histories* were selected without reference to their wishes and have in no way endorsed their entries.

Notes on Contributors

M. L. Cohen
Novelist, business writer, and researcher living in Paris.

Ed Dinger
Writer and editor based in Bronx, New York.

Paul R. Greenland
Illinois-based writer and researcher; author of two books and former senior editor of a national business magazine; contributor to *The Encyclopedia of Chicago History*, *The Encyclopedia of Religion*, and the *Encyclopedia of American Industries*.

Robert Halasz
Former editor in chief of *World Progress* and *Funk & Wagnalls New Encyclopedia Yearbook*; author, *The U.S. Marines* (Millbrook Press, 1993).

Evelyn Hauser
Researcher, writer and marketing specialist based in Germany.

Frederick C. Ingram
Writer based in South Carolina.

Bruce Montgomery
Curator and director of historical collection, University of Colorado at Boulder.

Carrie Rothburd
Writer and editor specializing in corporate profiles, academic texts, and academic journal articles.

Christina M. Stansell
Writer and editor based in Louisville, Kentucky.

Frank Uhle
Ann Arbor-based writer; movie projectionist, disc jockey, and staff member of *Psychotronic Video* magazine.

Ellen Wernick
Florida-based writer and editor.

A. Woodward
Wisconsin-based writer.

Suzanne Clark York
Writer and researcher based in Michigan.

List of Abbreviations

¥ Japanese yen
£ United Kingdom pound
$ United States dollar

A
AB Aktiebolag (Finland, Sweden)
AB Oy Aktiebolag Osakeyhtiot (Finland)
A.E. Anonimos Eteria (Greece)
AED Emirati dirham
AG Aktiengesellschaft (Austria, Germany, Switzerland, Liechtenstein)
aG auf Gegenseitigkeit (Austria, Germany)
A.m.b.a. Andelsselskab med begraenset ansvar (Denmark)
A.O. Anonim Ortaklari/Ortakligi (Turkey)
ApS Amparteselskab (Denmark)
ARS Argentine peso
A.S. Anonim Sirketi (Turkey)
A/S Aksjeselskap (Norway)
A/S Aktieselskab (Denmark, Sweden)
Ay Avoinyhtio (Finland)
ATS Austrian shilling
AUD Australian dollar
ApS Amparteselskab (Denmark)
Ay Avoinyhtio (Finland)

B
B.A. Buttengewone Aansprakeiijkheid (Netherlands)

BEF Belgian franc
BHD Bahraini dinar
Bhd. Berhad (Malaysia, Brunei)
BRL Brazilian real
B.V. Besloten Vennootschap (Belgium, Netherlands)

C
C.A. Compania Anonima (Ecuador, Venezuela)
CAD Canadian dollar
C. de R.L. Compania de Responsabilidad Limitada (Spain)
CEO Chief Executive Officer
CFO Chief Financial Officer
CHF Swiss franc
Cia. Companhia (Brazil, Portugal)
Cia. Compania (Latin America [except Brazil], Spain)
Cia. Compagnia (Italy)
Cie. Compagnie (Belgium, France, Luxembourg, Netherlands)
CIO Chief Information Officer
CLP Chilean peso
CNY Chinese yuan
Co. Company
COO Chief Operating Officer
Coop. Cooperative
COP Colombian peso
Corp. Corporation
C. por A. Compania por Acciones (Dominican Republic)
CPT Cuideachta Phoibi Theoranta

(Republic of Ireland)
CRL Companhia a Responsabilidao Limitida (Portugal, Spain)
C.V. Commanditaire Vennootschap (Netherlands, Belgium)
CZK Czech koruna

D
D&B Dunn & Bradstreet
DEM German deutsche mark
Div. Division (United States)
DKK Danish krone
DZD Algerian dinar

E
EC Exempt Company (Arab countries)
Edms. Bpk. Eiendoms Beperk (South Africa)
EEK Estonian Kroon
eG eingetragene Genossenschaft (Germany)
EGMBH Eingetragene Genossenschaft mit beschraenkter Haftung (Austria, Germany)
EGP Egyptian pound
Ek For Ekonomisk Forening (Sweden)
EP Empresa Portuguesa (Portugal)
E.P.E. Etema Pemorismenis Evthynis (Greece)
ESOP Employee Stock Options and Ownership
ESP Spanish peseta

Et(s). Etablissement(s) (Belgium, France, Luxembourg)
eV eingetragener Verein (Germany)
EUR euro

F
FIM Finnish markka
FRF French franc

G
G.I.E. Groupement d'Interet Economique (France)
gGmbH gemeinnutzige Gesellschaft mit beschraenkter Haftung (Austria, Germany, Switzerland)
G.I.E. Groupement d'Interet Economique (France)
GmbH Gesellschaft mit beschraenkter Haftung (Austria, Germany, Switzerland)
GRD Greek drachma
GWA Gewerbte Amt (Austria, Germany)

H
HB Handelsbolag (Sweden)
HF Hlutafelag (Iceland)
HKD Hong Kong dollar
HUF Hungarian forint

I
IDR Indonesian rupiah
IEP Irish pound
ILS new Israeli shekel
Inc. Incorporated (United States, Canada)
INR Indian rupee
IPO Initial Public Offering
I/S Interesentselskap (Norway)
I/S Interessentselskab (Denmark)
ISK Icelandic krona
ITL Italian lira

J–K
JMD Jamaican dollar
KB Kommanditbolag (Sweden)
Kft Korlatolt Felelossegu Tarsasag (Hungary)
KG Kommanditgesellschaft (Austria, Germany, Switzerland)
KGaA Kommanditgesellschaft auf Aktien (Austria, Germany, Switzerland)
KK Kabushiki Kaisha (Japan)

KPW North Korean won
KRW South Korean won
K/S Kommanditselskab (Denmark)
K/S Kommandittselskap (Norway)
KWD Kuwaiti dinar
Ky Kommandiitiyhtio (Finland)

L
LBO Leveraged Buyout
Lda. Limitada (Spain)
L.L.C. Limited Liability Company (Arab countries, Egypt, Greece, United States)
L.L.P. Limited Partnership (United States)
L.P. Limited Partnership (Canada, South Africa, United Kingdom, United States)
Ltd. Limited
Ltda. Limitada (Brazil, Portugal)
Ltee. Limitee (Canada, France)
LUF Luxembourg franc

M
mbH mit beschraenkter Haftung (Austria, Germany)
Mij. Maatschappij (Netherlands)
MUR Mauritian rupee
MXN Mexican peso
MYR Malaysian ringgit

N
N.A. National Association (United States)
NGN Nigerian naira
NLG Netherlands guilder
NOK Norwegian krone
N.V. Naamloze Vennootschap (Belgium, Netherlands)
NZD New Zealand dollar

O
OAO Otkrytoe Aktsionernoe Obshchestve (Russia)
OHG Offene Handelsgesellschaft (Austria, Germany, Switzerland)
OMR Omani rial
OOO Obschestvo s Ogranichennoi Otvetstvennostiu (Russia)
OOUR Osnova Organizacija Udruzenog Rada (Yugoslavia)
Oy Osakeyhtiot (Finland)

P–Q
P.C. Private Corp. (United States)
PHP Philippine peso

PKR Pakistani rupee
P/L Part Lag (Norway)
PLC Public Limited Co. (United Kingdom, Ireland)
P.L.L.C. Professional Limited Liability Corporation (United States)
PLN Polish zloty
P.T. Perusahaan/Perseroan Terbatas (Indonesia)
PTE Portuguese escudo
Pte. Private (Singapore)
Pty. Proprietary (Australia, South Africa, United Kingdom)
Pvt. Private (India, Zimbabwe)
PVBA Personen Vennootschap met Beperkte Aansprakelijkheid (Belgium)

R
REIT Real Estate Investment Trust
RMB Chinese renminbi
Rt Reszvenytarsasag (Hungary)
RUB Russian ruble

S
S.A. Société Anonyme (Arab countries, Belgium, France, Jordan, Luxembourg, Switzerland)
S.A. Sociedad Anónima (Latin America [except Brazil], Spain, Mexico)
S.A. Sociedades Anônimas (Brazil, Portugal)
SAA Societe Anonyme Arabienne (Arab countries)
S.A.C. Sociedad Anonima Comercial (Latin America [except Brazil])
S.A.C.I. Sociedad Anonima Comercial e Industrial (Latin America [except Brazil])
S.A.C.I.y.F. Sociedad Anonima Comercial e Industrial y Financiera (Latin America [except Brazil])
S.A. de C.V. Sociedad Anonima de Capital Variable Mexico)
SAK Societe Anonyme Kuweitienne (Arab countries)
SAL Societe Anonyme Libanaise (Arab countries)
SAO Societe Anonyme Omanienne (Arab countries)

SAQ Societe Anonyme Qatarienne (Arab countries)

SAR Saudi riyal

S.A.R.L. Sociedade Anonima de Responsabilidade Limitada (Brazil, Portugal)

S.A.R.L. Société à Responsabilité Limitée (France, Belgium, Luxembourg)

S.A.S. Societá in Accomandita Semplice (Italy)

S.A.S. Societe Anonyme Syrienne (Arab countries)

S.C. Societe en Commandite (Belgium, France, Luxembourg)

S.C.A. Societe Cooperativa Agricole (France, Italy, Luxembourg)

S.C.I. Sociedad Cooperativa Ilimitada (Spain)

S.C.L. Sociedad Cooperativa Limitada (Spain)

S.C.R.L. Societe Cooperative a Responsabilite Limitee (Belgium)

Sdn. Bhd. Sendirian Berhad (Malaysia)

SEK Swedish krona

SGD Singapore dollar

Sdn. Bhd. Sendirian Berhad (Malaysia)

S.L. Sociedad Limitada (Latin America [except Brazil], Portugal, Spain)

S/L Salgslag (Norway)

S.N.C. Société en Nom Collectif (France)

Soc. Sociedad (Latin America [except Brazil], Spain)

Soc. Sociedade (Brazil, Portugal)

Soc. Societa (Italy)

S.p.A. Società per Azioni (Italy)

Sp. z.o.o. Spólka z ograniczona odpowiedzialnoscia (Poland)

S.R.L. Sociedad de Responsabilidad Limitada (Spain, Mexico, Latin America [except Brazil])

S.R.L. Società a Responsabilità Limitata (Italy)

S.R.O. Spolecnost s Rucenim Omezenym (Czechoslovakia

S.S.K. Sherkate Sahami Khass (Iran)

Ste. Societe (France, Belgium, Luxembourg, Switzerland)

Ste. Cve. Societe Cooperative(Belgium)

S.V. Samemwerkende Vennootschap (Belgium)

S.Z.R.L. Societe Zairoise a Responsabilite Limitee (Zaire)

T

THB Thai baht

TND Tunisian dinar

TRL Turkish lira

TWD new Taiwan dollar

U

U.A. Uitgesloten Aansporakeiijkheid (Netherlands)

u.p.a. utan personligt ansvar (Sweden)

V

VAG Verein der Arbeitgeber (Austria, Germany)

VEB Venezuelan bolivar

VERTR Vertriebs (Austria, Germany)

VND Vietnamese dong

V.O.f. Vennootschap onder firma (Netherlands)

VVAG Versicherungsverein auf Gegenseitigkeit (Austria, Germany)

W–Z

WA Wettelika Aansprakalikhaed (Netherlands)

WLL With Limited Liability (Bahrain, Kuwait, Qatar, Saudi Arabia)

YK Yugen Kaisha (Japan)

ZAO Zakrytoe Aktsionernoe Obshchestve (Russia)

ZAR South African rand

ZMK Zambian kwacha

Alfesca

Alfesca hf

—■—

P.O. Box 20
Fornubudir 5
Hafnarfjoerdur, 222
Iceland
Telephone: (354) 5508000
Fax: (354) 5508001
Web site: http://sifgroup-e.ecweb.is/

Public Company
Incorporated: 1932 as Sölusamband íslenzkra fiskframleiðenda (SIF) (Union of Icelandic Fish Producers)
Employees: 3,500
Sales: EUR 554.7 million ($695 million) (2005)
Stock Exchanges: IcelandTicker Symbol: SIFI
NAIC: 311712 Fresh and Frozen Seafood Processing; 311711 Seafood Canning

■ ■ ■

Alfesca hf is one of Europe's leading producers of high-end and "festive" foods. Formerly known as fresh and frozen seafood SIF, the Iceland-based company's transformation into a processed foods leader was largely completed through its acquisition of European festive foods leader Labeyrie Group. That purchase, made in December 2004, added the highly respected Labeyrie brand of foie gras and smoked salmon. Labeyrie also includes the Blini brand, a producer of blinis (a sort of pancake) and seafood spreads; Scotland's Farne smoked trout and salmon brand, the number two in the United Kingdom; and Vensy, the leading smoked salmon brand

in Spain. Alfesca also controls the U.K. seafood group, Lyons, a leading processor of shrimp and other specialty seafood products; Delpierre, a producer of smoked herring, salmon, and other fish, in France; and Christiansen Partner, based in Norway, active in the sourcing and trading of fresh salmon and salted seafood. In keeping with its new focus on the processed foods market, Alfesca spun off its fresh and frozen fish trading operations, creating Iceland Seafood International for its Iceland-based business, which, together with its U.S. operations, were sold off in 2005. The company has continued seeking buyers for its other non-core units, such as its Delpierre frozen seafood operation, which was sold to Icelandic Group in July 2006. Alfesca is listed on the Iceland Stock Exchange and is led by chairman Ólafur Ólafsson and managing director Jakob Oskar Sigurdsson.

BUILDING ICELAND'S SEAFOOD INDUSTRY IN 1927

Iceland's emergence from Danish domination following World War I prompted the newly independent country to seek a strong economic base through the development of homegrown industry. With few natural resources on the island itself, the country turned to the ocean, and its fishing and shipping industries, for economic growth. Indeed, the country's fishing industry quickly emerged as the veritable motor for Iceland's economy, and by the end of the 1930s Iceland already enjoyed the status as one of Europe's most important fish exporters. In the absence of refrigeration and freezing technology, the majority of the country's fish exports at the time remained in the form of salted fish.

COMPANY PERSPECTIVES

The role of Alfesca is to create value for its stakeholders by operating a market driven European food, marketing and manufacturing company of ready-to-eat products, that bring convenience and festivity to its consumers. The vision of Alfesca is to be a leading food-processing and marketing company, as measured by return on equity and marketshare in the markets and categories it competes in.

Nonetheless, the difficult economic period at the beginning of the 1930s placed the country's many small, largely independent fishing companies under intense pressure. In response, the country established Sölusamband Islenzkra Fiskframleidenda (SÍF, for Union of Icelandic Fish Producers) in 1932. The company became the exclusive exporter for the country's salt fish production. As such, SIF served not only as an exporter, but also provided the country's fish industry with marketing and sales support. SIF's monopoly on the saltfish export market remained in place until the market's deregulation in 1992. By then, however, the company had already begun its expansion into the larger continental European market.

That market, however, was made difficult by significant import fees and other trade barriers. In order to skirt heavy import tariffs, SIF made its first international acquisition in 1990, buying up France's Nord Morue. This foothold into continental Europe gave the company the base from which to establish a strong European presence, and by the end of the decade, the company had also added sales operations in Spain, Greece, Italy, and Norway. The company further supported its international sales network with a series of new acquisitions, including Canada's Sans-Souci Seafood Ltd., a seafood trader, and Norway's SIFTOR, which operated both in the fishing and processing markets. The company also expanded its presence in Spain, forming Copesco-SIF as a sales and distribution business.

ACQUIRING SCALE AT THE END OF THE NINETIES

The movement toward the modern Alfesca began in earnest toward the end of the 1990s, with the acquisition of France's Jean Baptiste Delpierre. That company was a leading producer of processed, fresh fish products, including smoked salmon and haring, marinated herring, mackerel and haddock, and salted codfish. The addition of Delpierre formed the core of a new subsidiary, SIF France. Soon after the Delpierre acquisition, the company expanded its target to include the South American region, opening a subsidiary in Brazil. SIF also took steps to increase its sourcing operations, taking over Norway's Christiansen Partner A/S that year.

SIF leapt at a new opportunity in 1999, when it acquired the newly privatized Iceland Herring hf. That company had been founded in 1935 as the government-owned Iceland Herring Board. Herring had long been a staple food in Iceland, as well as the country's core export product. Through the 1960s, salted herring remained the country's largest single export product and the Iceland Herring Board grew into the world's leading herring exporter. A growing part of the organization's business was also supplied by the development of domestic fish farms. With the disappearance of herring from Iceland's territorial waters in the late 1960s, the Herring Board's fisheries became its main source of salted herring exports. After the Herring Board was restructured into a limited liability company in 1998, the company agreed to be acquired by SIF. That merger was completed in March 1999.

By the end of the year, SIF's drive to acquire greater scale in the European seafood industry reached a new milestone. In December 1999, SIF announced that it had agreed to merge with another major Icelandic seafood group, Iceland Seafood hf. That company stemmed from the Samband íslenskra samvinnufélaga, or the Federation of Cooperative Societies, which was founded in 1902 to group the interests of Iceland's cooperative movement. Samband grew into Iceland's largest commercial concern, operating in a wide variety of sectors. In 1952, Samband created a dedicated seafood arm, Samband Seafood.

By 1965, Samband had begun its own overseas expansion, starting up a subsidiary in the United States, called Iceland Seafood. Originally based near Harrisburg, Pennsylvania, that company moved its operations to larger facilities in Newport News, Virginia, in 1997. Later, Samband expanded into a number of continental European markets, starting with the United Kingdom and the creation of Iceland Seafood Ltd in Hull in 1980. By 1986, the company had launched operations in Germany, and then in France, establishing its presence in the three largest European markets. The new offices were placed under the oversight of Iceland Seafood Ltd.

By the early 1990s, Samband Seafood was the largest and most profitable part of the larger Samband federation, with sales of more than $160 million per year. This led the federation to spin off Samband Seafood as an independently operating limited liability company, called Iceland Seafood hf. The company continued

marketing groups, boasting total sales of nearly $700 million. The new group, which also became Iceland's largest company, retained the SIF name, and renamed its overseas subsidiaries accordingly. Nonetheless, the Iceland brand remained one of the company's key brands.

REFOCUSED ON LUXURY FOODS FOR THE NEW CENTURY

SIF continued to build up its international seafood interests into the early 2000s. In 2002, the company bought the fisheries operations of failed French company Fecamp, based near Le Havre. SIF next attempted to consolidate its position in Iceland, entering merger talks with Icelandic Freezing Plants Corporation in March 2003. Those talks eventually broke down, however.

Instead, SIF found a new international target. In October 2003, the company further consolidated its position among the European leaders with the purchase of Lyons Seafood, based in the United Kingdom. Founded in 1958, Lyons had become part of the Allied Domecq group, before being spun off in a management buyout in 1994. The addition of Lyons positioned SIF as one of Europe's top producers of processed shrimp and other shellfish, and further boosted the company's turnover by some $75 million.

However, the Lyons acquisition, which gave SIF a significant position in the market for high-end value-added products, soon appeared to be the inspiration behind a dramatic change in the company's direction. The company's new interest in processed foods over its traditional fresh and frozen fish sales, led it to bid for Financière de Kiel, the holding company for France's Labeyrie Group. Then controlled by Industri Kapital, Labeyrie, a specialist in high-end foie gras, smoked salmon, and other "festive foods"—so-called because their largest sales came during holiday periods—was the European leader in that segment.

The Labeyrie acquisition was completed in 2004, costing SIF more than EUR 330 million. The addition of Labeyrie, which also included Blini, a French producer of blinis and seafood spreads, among other products, and Farnes, the major Scottish salmon and trout producers, boosted SIF sales significantly by the end of that year.

Following the integration of Labeyrie, SIF's management, led by chairman Ólafur Ólafsson and managing director Jakob Oskar Sigurdsson, decided to organize the group around a new core focused on the luxury foods sector. In keeping with its new strategy, the company restructured its operations, placing its Iceland-based fresh and frozen fish operations, including Tros,

KEY DATES

1902: Samband íslenskra samvinnufélaga (Federation of Cooperative Societies) is founded in Iceland, with both fresh and salted fish operations.
1932: Sölusamband Islenzkra Fiskframleidenda (SÍF, for Union of Icelandic Fish Producers) is created and becomes the exclusive international sales and export arm for saltfish.
1935: The Icelandic government creates the Iceland Herring Board as the exclusive exporter for the country's herring exports.
1952: Samband establishes the dedicated seafood wing, Samband Seafood.
1965: Samband Seafood launches its first international operation, establishing a subsidiary in Harrisburg, Pennsylvania, called Iceland Seafood Corporation.
1980: Samband Seafood opens a sales subsidiary in Hull, England.
1986: Samband Seafood creates sales offices in Germany and France.
1990: SIF acquires Nord Morue, in France, beginning the company's expansion into continental Europe.
1991: Samband spins off Samband Seafood as an independent company called Iceland Seafood.
1998: The Iceland Herring Board is privatized as Iceland Herring Hf.
1999: SIF and Iceland Herring merge, followed by a merger with Iceland Seafood.
2003: SIF acquires Lyons Seafood in the United Kingdom.
2004: SIF acquires the Labeyrie Group and becomes a European leader in the luxury foods sector.
2005: SIF sells off its frozen and fresh fish operations to refocus on the luxury food sector.
2006: Company adopts the new name, Alfesca.

building its international presence, adding a sales office in Japan in 1996, then entering Spain in 1997. The company also boosted its fresh fish division with the purchase of export group Tros that year, then moved into France, buying up that country's Gelmer S.A., a producer and distributor of processed seafood.

The merger between SIF and Iceland Seafood created one of the world's leading seafood sales and

into a separate company, Iceland Seafood International, in 2004. That company was subsequently sold to a consortium led by Ker Ltd, B. Benediktsson Ltd, and Benedikt Sveinsson. SIF also sold its U.S. operations, which were acquired by Sjovik hf that same year. SIF continued its streamlining into 2006, selling off the frozen fish business of Delpierre to Icelandic Group.

In keeping with its transformation into a processed foods leader, SIF changed its name in February 2006, becoming Alfesca—the name was based on the Greek "alpha" and the Latin words "festiva" and "esca." With a new name and a new direction, Alfesca had successfully completed its transformation as a high-end festive food products leader.

M.L. Cohen

PRINCIPAL SUBSIDIARIES

Nord Ocean ehf; Christiansen Partner AS (Norway); Zilia Holding NV (Netherlands); SIF Prime Foods Ltd (U.K.); SIF France sas; Lyons Seafoods Ltd (U.K.); Financiére de Kiel SAS (France); Labeyrie SAS (France); Pierre Guéracague SAS (France); Gueradis sarl (France); Blini SAS (France); Farne Salmon and Trout Ltd (Scotland); Vensy Espana S.A. (Spain); Vensy Portugal LTDA (Portugal); Labeyrie Norge AS (Norway); Palmitou sas (France).

PRINCIPAL COMPETITORS

Alpesca S.A.; Primlaks Nigeria Ltd.; Antarktika Fishing Company; Hanwa Company Ltd.; Orkla ASA; Mukorob Fishing Proprietary Ltd.; Aker ASA; Maruha Corporation.

FURTHER READING

"Iceland's SIF Brings Lyons Seafoods into Group," *Quick Frozen Foods International*, October 2003, p. 47.

"Merger of SIF and Iceland Seafoods Creates Largest Company in Iceland," *Quick Frozen Foods International*, January 2000, p. 588.

"New Name for Samband as Part of Reforms," *Seafood International*, January 1991, p. 15.

"PPM Ventures Offloads Seafood Business," *Acquisitions Monthly*, August 2003, p. 55.

"SIF Changes Its Name to Alfesca," *just-food.com*, February 10, 2006.

"SIF hf Changes Strategy, in Final Talks to Acquire Labeyrie Group," *Nordic Business Report*, October 26, 2004.

"SIF hf Divests 40% Holding in UK Trading Company Icebrit Ltd.," *Nordic Business Report*, December 21, 2005.

"SIF, Parent Company of Lyons Seafoods and Farne, Changes Name to Alfesca," *Hugin*, February 10, 2006.

Tieman, Ross, "Icelanders After French Salmon," *The Daily Deal*, October 26, 2004.

American & Efird, Inc.

22 American Street
Mt. Holly, North Carolina 28120
U.S.A.
Telephone: (704) 827-4311
Toll Free: (800) 453-5128
Fax: (704) 827-2060
Web site: http://www.amefird.com/

Wholly Owned Subsidiary of Ruddick Corporation
Incorporated: 1891 as Nims Manufacturing Company
Employees: 2,900
Sales: $319.7 million (2005)
NAIC: 313113 Thread Mills

■ ■ ■

A subsidiary of Ruddick Corporation, American & Efird, Inc., (A&E) is a Mt. Holly, North Carolina-based company that manufactures and distributes sewing thread to the industrial and consumer markets.

Industrial products include heat resistant thread with high tensile strength; thread packaged on bobbins for use in making bedding, furniture, footwear, leather products, and other industrial applications; cotton threads used in garment sewing; thread with a polyester core and cotton wrapped for garment sewing; thread spun from Tencel fiber for garments that will be over-dyed and enzyme washed; abrasive-resistant thread used in automotive trim, quilts, furniture, and footwear; polyester-based threads for applications that require resistance to chemical treatment, ultraviolet radiation, mildew, or abrasion; and specialty engineered yarns. The

industrial products division also offers the Anesyst Web-based order management system to help customers order thread and track shipments. A&E's consumer product division produces thread for home sewing, and notions, including zippers, hook and loop tape, and polypropylene webbing.

The company maintains eight manufacturing plants in North Carolina, two in Pennsylvania, and one in New Jersey, with operations in 18 countries around the world and majority-owned joint ventures in the Dominican Republic, Haiti, and China.

19TH CENTURY ORIGINS

American & Efird was founded by Charles Egbert Hutchison, born in North Carolina in 1860, the son of a farmer who after the Civil War decided to keep a general store in the town of Woodlawn, North Carolina. The younger Hutchison joined his father in business but became increasingly interested in the textile industry that was emerging in the area. When he was 29 he took the jump, acquiring the Mt. Holly Knitting Factory in 1890, renaming it Albion Manufacturing Company and converting the plant from knitting to spinning. A year later, in May 1891, he arranged a meeting of some of the area's most prominent businessmen to discuss the formation of a new cotton mill corporation. Six of them became principals in what would be called Nims Manufacturing Company, so named because the water-powered plant was to be built at Nims Shoals On Dutchman's Creek one mile north of Mt. Holly. In addition to Hutchison, the investors were Luther Nims, R. Kel Davenport, Martin R. Dewstoe, J. Alonzo Abernathy, and John C. Rankin.

Initially the Nims Mill produced seine twine, hawser, and cable cords, all crude products, but the business grew ever more sophisticated. A second mill was built in Woodlawn in 1905 and began producing spun yarns. A third operation was acquired in 1910, the Mountain Island Mill, which manufactured a variety of twines, powered by the Catawba River. The deal also included a cotton gin, grist mill, and an entire village. Unfortunately, all would be swept away several years later in a massive flood. Nims continued to grow, however. In 1916 the first of a pair of manufacturing plants flanking a railroad track in Mt. Holly opened. The "Adrian" plant was followed by the "Madora" plant in 1922. Together they would process raw cotton to produce combed yarns. In between their construction, Nims acquired the Alsace Manufacturing Company in 1918 and renovated it, and in that same year built another plant in town, the American Processing Company. It was one of the first facilities in the United States, and the first in North Carolina, to mercerize yarns, shrinking them to add strength and improve the ability to receive dyes by immersing them in a cold solution of caustic soda. In the 1930s the plant would add other processing capabilities, including gassing, bleaching, and tinting.

AMERICAN YARN AND PROCESSING COMPANY FORMED: 1920

In 1920 Hutchison and some investors acquired Maiden, North Carolina-based Union Cotton Mills to add further combed yarn production. Hutchison decided to consolidate all the mills in which he held investments. Because he was the only common investor in all of them, they had become known as the Hutchison Group of Mills. In July 1920 they were combined together to form a new corporation, American Yarn and Processing Company, as Hutchison and three investors bought all the stock of the six different Hutchison mills. As a result,

decision making was streamlined and the accounting of the businesses was consolidated. Moreover, Hutchison could leverage the size of American Yarn to forge plans to open offices outside of North Carolina, as well as expand beyond the production of combed cotton yarns to the manufacture of fabrics and knit goods.

Within a few years, thoughts of expansion would be replaced by concerns about mere survival, as the great Depression ushered in by the stock market crash of 1929 led to the closure of many textile mills. American Yarn was in better shape than most and was able to scrape by, but not without being forced to shut down the original Nims plant, which was no longer economically viable to operate. Like most of American industry, textiles did not recover until the advent of the United States' entry into World War II in late 1941 when military spending spurred the economy. Less than a year later, American Yarn would have to contend with an upheaval of a different sort: the death of its long-time leader, Egbert Hutchison.

Well aware that his health was failing, the 82-year-old Hutchison took steps to ensure the future of American Yarn and protect its investors and employees. He traveled to Charlotte, North Carolina, and met with several investment bankers before settling on one to purchase his controlling interest in the company, which he sold to R.S. Dickson Company for $2.5 million. In the process he also handpicked his successor: the head of the investment bank, 47-year-old Rush Smith Dickson. Born in South Carolina, Dickson grew up on a farm but turned to a business career rather than take up the plow like his father. He worked as a bookkeeper for mill owners and began making investments in the textile industry. This led to his development as an investment banker specializing in textiles. Well connected in North Carolina, he was able during the Depression to supply New York bond houses with the kind of information they needed to determine credit worthiness. As a result, he was greatly responsible for the survival and growth of the textile industry during this difficult period.

With the war driving demand for textiles of all types, A&E operated its plants at capacity and resumed expansion. Under Dickson's leadership, the company became more than a knit yarn company, adding the manufacture of thread yarns to its capabilities. The two plants of the Whitnel Cotton Mill Company were acquired in 1943. They were almost entirely devoted to the production of socks and underwear for the military. In that same year, American Yarn completed its first acquisition outside of North Carolina, buying Lawrenceburg, Kentucky-based Dean & Sherk, a former customer that produced industrial threads used to make boots for soldiers. In order to produce outerwear using the yarns

KEY DATES

1891: Charles Egbert Hutchison forms the Nims Manufacturing Company.

1920: Hutchison mills merge to form American Yarn and Processing Company.

1942: Hutchison dies.

1952: American Yarn merges with Efird Manufacturing to form American & Efird, Inc.

1968: Ruddick Corporation becomes A&E's holding company.

1978: Grove Thread Company is acquired.

1993: A&E begins producing home-sewing thread.

2003: Foreign sales exceed domestic sales for the first time.

its plants produced, American Yarn in 1944 opened the Holly Knit Plant in Mt. Holly. To dye the knitted goods produced by this operation, in 1946 the Holly-Knit Finishing Plant was added.

The demand for textiles was so great during the war years that the old Nims plant, shuttered for 14 years, was put back into use by Efird Manufacturing. The relationship with Efird would become even closer in 1947 when American Yarn acquired a controlling interest in the company to further expand its yarn offerings. Efird had been founded in 1896 in Albemarle, North Carolina, by brothers Polycarp Efird and John Efird, who grew the business to include five mills. In May 1952 American Yarn and Efird were formally merged to create American & Efird, Inc.

The 1950s brought a period of expansion and modernization. The Albion Knitting company was acquired in 1950, and shortly after the Efird merger, the five Efird plants were consolidated and upgraded, and at the end of the process three plants remained. By the close of the 1950s, A&E was operating 15 plants. Working together they were capable of turning raw cotton into finished goods. The business was divided among three divisions: the Sales Yarn Group, the Thread Division, and the Finishing Division.

HOLDING COMPANY FORMED: 1968

A&E's growth continued into the 1960s as sales grew to more than $40 million. Expansion was fueled by the financial backing of R.S. Dickson Company. A&E reached another turning point in September 1966 when Dickson died. Control of the investment firm passed to Dickson's oldest son, Stuart Dickson, while another son, Alan Dickson, assumed control of A&E. Because two of the A&E shareholders wanted to sell out and A&E was in need of capital, the Dickson brothers considered merging A&E with a Philadelphia investment firm, but in the end decided to join A&E with R.S. Dickson Company, the latter to provide the company with the necessary capitalization. Thus, in 1968 the Ruddick Corporation was created to serve as A&E's holding company. Ruddick soon gained a listing on the New York Stock Exchange, and in addition to A&E it added a second subsidiary in 1969 by purchasing the Harris Teeter supermarket chain.

The 1970s were a time of change in the textile industry, which experienced a period of consolidation and increasing competition from foreign companies. One of A&E's long-time customers, Union Underwear, began buying its own mills and then made an offer for the Efird mills in Albermarle. It was at this point that A&E's management realized it had to focus its resources in order to ensure future growth, and it elected to cast its lot with the production of thread, an area in which it had always been a bit player. Company personnel visited all of the major thread plants in the country and A&E then began to convert some of its plants to thread production, counting on A&E's workforce to find ways to improve productivity and give the company an edge over the entrenched competition. A&E also gained much needed expertise in 1978 through the acquisition of Grove Thread Company. Around this time, A&E received a major break when Levi-Strauss, a minor customer over the years, decided to contract with A&E to supply the thread it needed in Hong Kong. The deal was facilitated by Levi's new director of international operations, a close friend of A&E's Director of Thread Sales. This contract opened the way for further expansion overseas, as A&E began supplying thread to a Levi's plant operating on the Chinese border, followed by Scotland, Brussels, Australia, and New Zealand operations. Initially A&E established warehouses as it followed Levi's, but factories would follow, as would distribution centers. A&E then began supplying other manufacturers doing business in foreign countries. To fill out its capabilities overseas, A&E began making acquisitions. For example, the Little Box Company, a Hong Kong thread company, was purchased. A distribution point established in England to serve Levi resulted in the 1980 acquisition of H. Greenberg, Ltd., a thread dye business located close to Manchester. Other foreign investments in the 1980s included a joint venture in

Singapore, the purchase of Canada's second largest thread company, Allied Thread, and the building of dyeing and finishing plants in Korea.

A&E did not neglect its domestic operations in the 1980s, however. Business was thriving, and an increase in production requirements led the company to replace its traditional manual winding operation with new automated sewing thread winders. A&E also beefed up its capabilities by acquiring the Delta Thread dyeing plant from SCT Yarns, Inc., in 1988. By 1990 the company was generating nearly $200 million in sales.

INTO THE FUTURE: 1990 AND BEYOND

A&E continued to improve productivity and streamline its operations while expanding its product offerings. In 1991 the company's dyeing and finishing divisions were consolidated into a single manufacturing division. The company also continued to rely on the input from workers to improve production, following what management called "the 20-foot rule." Simply put, it meant that anyone working within 20 feet of a process was deemed an expert on that particular subject, regardless of formal education, and took part in any decision related to it.

In 1993 A&E moved into the home-sewing thread market, taking on the dominant player in the field, Coats & Clark, which enjoyed an 85 percent market share. A&E's Signature line of consumer thread was not an immediate threat to Coats & Clark, but management was hoping to carve out a 15 to 20 percent share of the $60 million-a-year home-sewing market. The new business helped A&E to approach $300 million in sales in 1995.

A&E continued its pattern of growth as the second half of the 1990s began. In July 1996 it completed the acquisition of Dixie Yarns Inc. and its four manufacturing plants in Gastonia, North Carolina. A&E then expanded its product range, global reach, and client base in 1999 with the acquisition of Hicking Pentecost PLC, a United Kingdom company that produced thread in the United States, China, Northern Ireland, Italy, Hong Kong, and South Africa. However, A&E also elected in 1999 to shut down its operations in Korea, where business conditions had deteriorated. Business was soft elsewhere in the world as well, leading to a dip in sales after the company had posted a record $355 million in revenues in 1997.

A difficult environment continued into the new century. The U.S. apparel, textile, and home furnishings industries suffered from foreign competition that enjoyed lower labor costs, and as a result A&E's domestic sales eroded, forcing the company to look for opportunities overseas, in particular, Latin America, the Caribbean basin, Africa, China, and other Asian countries. In fiscal 2000 34 percent of A&E's total revenues of $349.9 million came from overseas, as opposed to 29 percent in fiscal 1999. Although net sales were less than the $351.6 million posted the year before, A&E was still able to maintain operating profits. That situation would not hold true in 2001, however, when sales continued to slide to $326.5 million and operating profits fell from $47.4 million to just $21.6 million.

To meet the challenge, A&E began closing U.S. plants and reducing jobs while continuing to expand its overseas' business. Net sales continued to fall, reaching $294.5 in fiscal 2002 and bottomed out at $293.1 million a year later. Fiscal 2003 also marked the first time that foreign sales accounted for more than half of total revenues at 52 percent. The trend continued in fiscal 2004 when sales improved to $296.2 million. To grow its foreign business, A&E forged joint ventures in China in 2003 and Brazil in 2005.

A&E was not, however, giving up on domestic sales. Instead, it looked to increase the non-apparel thread business. In 2004 A&E acquired Synthetic Thread Company, Inc., maker of threads and specialty engineered yarns used in the production of canvas products, leather goods, luggage, and bedding. In 2005 A&E added Ludlow Textiles Company, Inc., another manufacturer of threads and non-apparel yarns used in the production of non-apparel goods. Further diversification in non-apparel fields included the August 2005 acquisition of Robison-Anton Textile, Co., maker of value-added embroidery threads sold in the United States and throughout the world. A&E was clearly on the rebound as sales jumped to $319.7 million in 2005 and operating profits improved to $113.6 million.

Ed Dinger

PRINCIPAL DIVISIONS

Industrial Products; Consumer Products.

PRINCIPAL COMPETITORS

Coats Holdings Ltd.; Coats North America, inc.; Stowe-Pharr Mills, Inc.

FURTHER READING

"American & Efird Merges Two of its Divisions," *Daily News Record*, October 24, 1991, p. 9.

Clune, Ray, "An Educated Work Force Is American & Efird's Best Tool," *Daily News Record*, November 25, 1998, p. 12.

McAllister III, Isaaca, "American & Efird Winds Up A Winner," *Textile World,* November 1994, p. 47.

Snow, Katherine, "American & Efird Expands," *Business Journal Serving Charlotte and the Metropolitan Area,* November 23, 1992, p. 1.

Yockey, Ross, *A Century of Quality,* Charlotte, North Carolina: McMillan and Associates, 1991, 144 p.

American Media, Inc.

1000 American Media Way
Boca Raton, Florida 33431-1000
U.S.A.
Telephone: (561) 997-7733
Fax: (561) 272-8411
Web site: http://www.americanmediainc.com

Private Company
Incorporated: 1991 as Enquirer/Star Group, Inc.
Employees: 2,181
Sales: $560 million (2006 est.)
NAIC: 511120 Periodical Publishers

∎ ∎ ∎

American Media, Inc., (AMI) was incorporated as The Enquirer/Star Group, Inc., in 1991 to serve as a holding company for the best-selling supermarket tabloids in the United States. Since then the company has acquired its main tabloid rival, the *Globe.* A line of mini-magazines rounds out the company's supermarket checkout offerings.

Tabloids are not the whole story at AMI, however. The company has amassed a number of top-selling consumer magazines relating to active lifestyles. AMI claimed a monthly readership of more than 35 million even after the proposed sale of five special interest titles in 2006. A number of mainstream publishers use the company's Distribution Service Inc. (DSI) subsidiary to get their magazines into supermarkets.

NEW YORK ORIGINS

The *National Enquirer,* the Group's flagship publication, traces its history to 1926, when newspaper magnate William Randolph Hearst lent his protégé William Griffin money to found the *New York Evening Enquirer.* This Sunday afternoon paper was distributed throughout New York City. As partial payment of his loan, Hearst asked to use the *Enquirer* as an experimenting ground for new ideas. Hearst used the good ideas in his successful publications; the less successful ideas stayed with the *Enquirer,* and as a result the *Enquirer*'s sales never soared. They were further undercut during World War II, when Griffin wrote such fiery editorials against U.S. military involvement in the war that he was indicted for subverting the morale of U.S. troops. (Charges were later dropped.) By 1952, circulation had dropped to 17,000 copies.

In 1952, Generoso Pope, Jr., son of the founder of New York's Italian language daily newspaper *Il Progresso,* purchased the *Enquirer* for $75,000 (financed by the Mafia, his son later said). Pope planned to gradually change the format of the paper to that of a national news-feature weekly. He dropped the paper's Democratic partisanship, increased its staff, and added a new, anonymously written "world-wide intelligence column." Although Pope initially said the newspaper would not convert to the tabloid format, the paper became a tabloid in 1953.

The greatest change Pope instituted, however, was in the paper's editorial content. Gory stories of murder and mutilation became regular features. Confessions such as "I'm sorry I killed my mother, but I'm glad I killed my father," appeared. Headlines declared: "I say 'no' to passionate potentate and he has his half-men beat me into submission!" The *Enquirer*'s content was so salacious that New York City Mayor Wagner frequently voiced his displeasure, which eventually led to Pope's resignation from the city's Board of Higher Education in 1954. At that time, Pope also announced that he was handing control of the publication over to former general manager Roy Moriarity, although he did not disclose whether he still owned all or part of the paper.

In 1957, the paper was renamed the *National Enquirer*. Pope broadened its focus to include national stories of sex and sadism and also expanded its distribution. Sales grew steadily, despite content so offensive that the Chicago Transit Authority temporarily banned its sale at station newsstands. By 1966, however, sales had reached a plateau at 1 million copies per week, prompting Pope (who had once again taken control of the publication) to clean up the paper's image. "There are only so many libertines and neurotics," he told *Newsweek* in 1969. In defense of his earlier editorial choices he declared, "Every publication starts out by being sensational. I intended to make it a quality paper all along."

FINDING A PLACE IN THE SUPERMARKET

Analysts cited the declining number of newsstands as the real reason for the paper's stagnation. As mom and pop grocery stores and corner newsstands were gradually replaced by supermarket chains, outlets for the *National Enquirer* diminished. Pope sought to clean up the paper's image in order to tap into the enormous market of women who frequented supermarket check-out lines. He hired seasoned journalists, paying them some of the best salaries in the business. In keeping with the publication's new pristine image, company headquarters were moved from New York to Lantana, Florida (population 8,000), where the *Enquirer* soon gained acceptance in the com-

munity by sponsoring Little League teams and purchasing a new ambulance for the local fire station.

Pope also hired a vice-president for corporate planning and a public relations firm to broadcast the paper's new content. Stories such as "Poor Italian Immigrant's Son Starts Chinese Food Business in a Bathtub" were more zany than distasteful. The new *Enquirer* also began covering politics, albeit with its own special bent. Senator Edward Kennedy's much-publicized accident at Chappaquiddick, in which he survived a watery car crash that killed his female companion, received thorough coverage in the *Enquirer*. The paper even went so far as to hire clairvoyant Jeane Dixon to foretell the Senator's future.

Despite its improved image, supermarkets were initially reluctant to sell the *Enquirer*. Pope courted them by promising the supermarkets 22 percent of the cover price. Free subscriptions were given to wives of supermarket executives, and endorsements from Hubert Humphrey, Barry Goldwater, and Joan Crawford were made into a promotional film narrated by a well-known newscaster. When that did not work, Pope claims that he enlisted the help of a friend, Melvin Laird, Secretary of Defense during the Nixon administration, who took supermarket executives on a private tour of the White House and allowed them to meet with the President for half an hour.

Within three years, the *Enquirer* was available in most supermarket chains across the United States. By 1969, circulation had climbed to 1.2 million copies per week, and the *National Enquirer* ousted *Reader's Digest* from the newsdealer's top-five bestseller's list. Sales continued growing to just below 4 million a week by 1974. Gross revenues in 1973 were $17 million; the next year they hit $41 million. Advertising sales were so good that the company allegedly turned down accounts, and analysts were calling the publication "outrageously successful."

In 1978 circulation reached 5.7 million copies, but slid to just under 4.6 million by 1981. The decline was attributed to the growing number of competing supermarket tabloids, including one created by Pope. In 1979, Pope launched *Weekly World News,* a black-and-white tabloid that published unusual stories similar to those found in the early days of the *Enquirer,* printed at the *Enquirer*'s printing plant in Pompano Beach, Florida. Within two years of its debut, *Weekly World News* began making a profit, with a circulation of over 700,000. By 1984, Australian media mogul Rupert Murdoch introduced the *Star,* a four-color gossip sheet, to take advantage of consumer desire for naughty news.

KEY DATES

1926: *New York Evening Enquirer* is formed by William Griffin, protégé of William Randolph Hearst.

1952: The *Enquirer* is acquired by Generoso Pope, Jr., for $75,000.

1957: The increasingly sensationalistic paper is renamed the *National Enquirer.*

1966: The *Enquirer* has weekly sales of one million copies.

1969: The *Enquirer* is available in most supermarket chains.

1971: Headquarters are relocated from New York to Lantana, Florida.

1974: Annual revenues reach $41 million in a sales boom.

1975: *Star* rival tabloid is formed in New York by Rupert Murdoch's News Corp.

1978: The *Enquirer's* circulation reaches 5.7 million copies.

1979: Pope launches *Weekly World News.*

1982: An advertising campaign and a price increase help lift revenues 54 percent to $140 million.

1989: GP Group Acquisition LP buys Pope's business for $413 million following his death.

1990: GP Group buys the rival, *Star,* in a $400 million deal.

1991: The Enquirer/Star Group, Inc., holding company is formed and soon goes public.

1993: *Weekly World News* TV show debuts.

1995: The Enquirer/Star Group is renamed American Media, Inc. (AMI).

1999: A group led by David Pecker acquires AMI for $850 million.

2001: AMI is among the media organizations targeted by anthrax letters; the company relocates to Boca Raton.

2006: AMI announces it is selling off five specialty magazines to focus on celebrity weeklies and active lifestyle magazines.

WOOING CORPORATE ADVERTISERS

In 1982, Pope raised the *Enquirer's* cover price by 20 cents, to 65 cents an issue. Circulation, fueled by an enormous advertising campaign, rose by 11 percent. Gross revenues climbed 54 percent to $140 million.

Pope also sought to improve the bottom line by luring blue-chip companies such as General Motors, Procter & Gamble, and Sears to purchase advertising space in the paper. Until the early 1980s, approximately 12 percent of revenues came from advertising. Most were small, mail-order companies offering everything from biorhythm charts to seeds for growing six-pound tomatoes. Calculating that revenues could increase by 25 percent if these small ads were replaced by full-page ads from major corporations, Pope began an all-out effort to woo advertisers, using the tag line, "You may not like the *Enquirer,* but 14 million people do."

Luring respectable advertisers prompted another change in editorial content, as Pope directed cutbacks in the gossip columns in an attempt to become "a service and entertainment publication for middle America." Pope used the same strategy he developed to get the *Enquirer* into supermarkets, giving free subscriptions to the wives of advertising executives, recording celebrity endorsements, and courting the approval of decision-makers. His strategy worked. By 1986, color ads for cigarettes, clothing, brand-name foods, and household products had replaced many of the smaller ads. Advertising revenues for 1985 were $31.1 million, up from $29.2 million in 1984.

NEW OWNERSHIP IN 1989

Generoso Pope, Jr., passed away in October, 1988. Several of the world's leading publishing companies bid for the family-owned business, including Diamond Communications, Maxwell Communications Corp., and Hachette S.A. In June, 1989, GP Group Acquisition Limited Partnership (a partnership created by Boston Ventures Limited Partnerships III and IIIA and Macfadden Holdings, L.P.) purchased the operations for $413 million in cash.

GP Group Acquisitions instituted a number of reforms to boost revenues and cut costs. The *Enquirer's* outmoded printing plant in Pompano Beach, Florida, was closed, television advertising was discontinued, and editorial expenditures were reduced. In addition, mail order and classified advertising rates were increased substantially and the cover price of the *National Enquirer* was boosted to 85 cents in the United States, and 89 cents in Canada.

In early 1990, GP Group purchased the *Star,* *National Enquirer's* rival publication, from Rupert Murdoch's New America Publishing Inc. for $400 million in cash and stocks. At the time of purchase, the *Star's* 3.6 million weekly circulation was just below *National Enquirer's* weekly circulation of 4.1 million. That year, the company took the name Enquirer/Star Group, Inc. The

Enquirer/Star Group went public in July 1991, with an initial offering of 13 million shares of Class A Stock. Also that year, the group launched *Soap Opera Magazine,* a weekly publication that provided in-depth coverage of daytime soap opera and was sold at supermarket checkout lines for $1.19 in the United States and $1.29 in Canada. Distribution of the *National Enquirer* and *Weekly World News* soon spread to the United Kingdom, Europe, and Asia.

Circulation declined across the publishing industry in the early 1990s, due to increased competition from television celebrity news programs. The Enquirer/Star Group responded by expanding its overseas market. The Group also entered into a number of other ventures in the early 1990s, including trademark licensing, story syndication, and the launch of *What People Are Wearing,* a monthly spin-off of the *Star* devoted to celebrity fashion and beauty. In 1993, the company entered into a joint venture with Brandon Tartikoff (former chairman of Paramount Studios) to begin production of a one-hour television program produced by the staff of the *Weekly World News* to be aired on network television. Stories on the one hour pilot included the usual *Weekly World News* fare, including a faith healer/mechanic who fixed cars by laying his hands on them and photos proving "beyond a doubt" that humans lived on Mars.

Although the Enquirer/Star Group churned out some questionable stories, the company's bottom line remained solid. Net income grew by 15 percent to $19.4 million in 1993. With a strong cash flow and bold expansion strategies, Enquirer/Star Group's future as the world's primary news source on alien sightings and celebrity romances seemed strong.

NEW NAME IN 1995

The owners of GP Group, which held 53 percent of Enquirer/Star's common stock, proposed buying out the remainder and taking the company private again in 1994. However, the offer was withdrawn as a number of major tabloid stories helped push the company's share price far beyond the price suggested for the buyout. Instead, Enquirer/Star underwent a recapitalization, issuing $200 million in junk bonds to reward its shareholders with a $7 per share dividend. The company's name was changed to American Media, Inc., (AMI) in 1995.

The largest celebrity story of the day was the O.J. Simpson trial, and AMI's *National Enquirer* covered it closely. Some of its exclusives were grudgingly acknowledged in the mainstream media, conferring, some said, a new level of respectability on the tabloid. This did not stop the *Enquirer's* circulation by slipping by a third, to about two million readers, from 1994 to 1999. At the same time, mainstream magazines were devoting increasing attention to celebrity gossip stories.

PRIVATE AGAIN IN 1999

A group led by David Pecker, including the investment firm Evercore Partners, acquired AMI in May 1999 for $850 million. Pecker, an accountant by training, had previously tried to buy Enquirer/Star as CEO of Hachette Filipacchi Magazines but was outbid by GP Group. One of Pecker's first projects after acquiring AMI was to buy its nearby rival Globe Communications Corp., which published the *Globe, National Examiner,* and the *Sun,* for $105 million. The *Star* was relocated from New York to the *Globe's* Boca Raton offices; AMI soon moved its own headquarters nearby. At the same time, the *Enquirer* and *Star* were given makeovers and bolstered by a $50 million TV campaign. In fiscal 1999 AMI had revenues of $275 million, the bulk of which came from newsstand sales rather than advertising.

2001 ANTHRAX CRISIS

AMI was one of the news outlets targeted by anonymous letters containing anthrax in 2001. The spores killed a photo editor and sickened another employee. AMI had to evacuate its 63,000-square-foot headquarters near Boca Raton following the incident, and ultimately abandoned the building—and an archive of five million photographs collected over 50 years (it was able to save many that had been scanned into digital files).

The company's papers were in a sales slump. By 2003, the *Enquirer, Star,* and *Globe* combined were selling fewer than three million copies a week. In a move to broaden its consumer base, AMI bought Weider Publications from Weider Health & Fitness for $350 million. Weider's health-oriented magazines included *Muscle & Fitness,* which dated back to 1940, and *Shape.* About one-fifth of Weider Publications' 400-strong workforce was cut after the buy. The acquisition helped lift AMI's revenues from $315 million $515 million in fiscal 2004.

A new partner was brought in to AMI in 2003. Thomas H. Lee Partners invested $250 million as AMI's was valued at $1.5 billion. Evercore Partners participated in the restructuring with a new fund. AMI's revenues were up to $375 million for the year.

HIRING A STAR EDITOR IN 2003

Also in 2003, *Star* magazine was relocated back to New York. To lead it, Pecker hired editor Bonnie Fuller away from the celebrity-oriented *US Weekly* she had helped revitalize. (Her resumé also included the editor's spot at *Cosmopolitan* and *Marie Claire*.) The next year, *Star* was relaunched as a glossy magazine. AMI had also moved its mini-magazine business, valued at $40 million a year, to New York, where it was easier to recruit staff and meet advertisers.

Other titles, including the *Enquirer,* and *Men's Health,* were being retooled. The company also tested new concepts, such as magazines produced with Sylvester Stallone and Latina singer Thalia Sodi. A shelter magazine called *Happy Home* was aimed at young women. *Looking Good Now* was a cut-price health and fitness title originally distributed exclusively at Wal-Mart.

In June 2006, AMI announced it was selling off a handful of specialty magazines to focus on celebrity weeklies and active lifestyle magazines. The titles for sale were *Muscle & Fitness, Flex, Muscle & Fitness Hers, Country Weekly,* and the Spanish-language celebrity magazine *Mira!* Together, they represented sales of $84 million a year. AMI was keeping *Shape* magazine and *Men's Fitness.*

AMI's remaining titles had a total monthly readership of 35 million. Pecker told *Business Week* the company was expecting revenues of $560 million for 2006. The *Star* was being moved back to Florida yet again in the name of cutting costs.

Maura Troester
Updated, Frederick C. Ingram

PRINCIPAL SUBSIDIARIES

American Media Operations, Inc.; Distribution Services, Inc.

PRINCIPAL DIVISIONS

Celebrity Journalism; Health & Fitness; New Media/Brand Development; Distribution Services Inc.

PRINCIPAL COMPETITORS

Bauer Publishing USA; Rodale Inc.; Time Inc.; Wenner Media LLC.

FURTHER READING

Abrams, Bill, "National Enquirer Starts Drive to Lure Big-Time Advertisers," *Wall Street Journal,* March 18, 1982.

Byrne, John A., "Slugging It Out in the Supermarkets," *Forbes,* March 14, 1983.

Calder, Ian, *The Untold Story: My 20 Years Running the National Enquirer,* New York: Miramax Books, 2004.

Carr, David, "A Tabloid King Looks Beyond Elvis," *New York Times,* Bus. Sec., June 30, 2003, p. 1.

——, "Tabloid King Seeks Makeover from Sassy to Stable," *New York Times,* Bus. Sec., April 19, 2004, p. 1.

Case, Tony, "Check-Point Bonnie," *American Demographics,* October 1, 2003, p. 22.

Donaton, Scott, "'Enquirer-Star' Team to Bring Both Clout," *Advertising Age,* April 2, 1990, p. 2.

"Enquirer/Star Junk Bond Deal Reminds Some of 1980s Excess," *Mergers & Acquisitions Report,* November 21, 1994.

Fine, Jon, "Inquiring Minds Want Results; Times are Tougher for David Pecker's Empire," *BusinessWeek,* October 3, 2005, p. 28.

"From Worse to Bad," *Newsweek,* September 8, 1969, p. 79.

Goodnaugh, Abby, "Exclusive: It's Doom for Tabloid Archives!" *New York Times,* August 21, 2003, p. A14.

Hopkins, Brent, "Weider Staff in Local Office Is Cut by 60; Move Comes After Purchase," *Los Angeles Daily News,* January 30, 2003, p. B1.

Leonard, Devin, "The Tabloid King's Dilemma: Can David Pecker, Publisher of the *National Enquirer* and *Star,* Turn His Company Into a Glossy-Magazine Bigfoot?," *Fortune,* November 1, 2004, p. 164.

Lunsford, Darcie, "Taming the Tabloids," *American Journalism Review,* September 2000, p. 52.

Macintyre, Ben, "Mafia 'Bankrolled' Paper's Founder," *Times* (London), November 11, 1999.

Melcher, Charles, Valerie Virga, and David A. Keeps, eds., *The National Enquirer: Thirty Years of Unforgettable Images,* New York: Talk Miramax Books, 2001.

Meyer, Meghan, "'Enquirer' to Jettison New York for Boca," *Palm Beach Post,* April 6, 2006, p. 1A.

Pappu, Sridhar, "Argh! Pecker the Pirate," *New York Observer,* August 4, 2003, p. 1.

Peer, Elizabeth, "The Enquirer: Up Front Smut," *Newsweek,* April 25, 1975.

Pondel, Evan, "American Media to Buy Woodland Hills, Calif.-Based Weider Publications," *Knight-Ridder Tribune Business News,* November 28, 2002.

"Pope Quits Board of City Colleges," *New York Times,* September 28, 1954, p. 26.

Rose, Matthew, "Evercore Revamps American Media—Lee Invests $250 Million as Co-Owner of Publisher Now Valued at $1.5 Billion," *Wall Street Journal,* February 25, 2003, p. B13.

Sheridan, Terry, "AMI Building Would Be a Tough Sell If Abandoned," *Broward Daily Business Review,* October 11, 2001.

Sheridan, Terry and Anika Myers, "Sticking Around," *Broward Daily Business Review,* October 18, 2001.

"Tabloid Publisher Moving Mini-Mag Operations to New York," *Associated Press Newswires,* December 24, 2003.

Tartakoff, Joseph M., "Makeover Has 'Star' Publisher Shining," *Palm Beach Post,* August 28, 2005, p. 1F.

Washburn, Mark, "Schlock Value? With the O.J. Simpson Case, the National Enquirer Is Earning Some New Respect," *Knight-Ridder Newspapers,* January 28, 1995, p. 5.

Wayne, Leslie, "Market Place," New York Times, May 3, 1993, p. C4.

Wyatt, Edward A., "Tabloid Account," *Barron's,* June 13, 1994, p. 17.

———, "Tabloid Turnabout: Why Investors Withdrew Bid for Enquirer/Star Group," *Barron's,* July 18, 1994.

Asatsu-DK Inc.

1-13-1 Tsukiki
Chuo-ku
Tokyo,
Japan
Telephone: (81) 03 3547 2111
Fax: (81) 03 3547 2345
Web site: http://www.adk.jp

Public Company
Incorporated: 1999
Employees: 2,850
Sales: ¥424,705 million ($3.78 billion) (2005)
Stock Exchanges: Tokyo
Ticker Symbol: 9747
NAIC: 541810 Advertising Agencies; 541870 Advertising Material Distribution Services

■ ■ ■

Asatsu-DK Inc. is the third-largest advertising agency in Japan, trailing only Dentsu and Hakuhodo DY. Formed in 1999 by the merger of Asatsu and Dai Ichi Kikaku, Asatsu-DK also ranks in the global top 10, with consolidated billings of ¥424,705 million ($3.78 billion) in 2005. The company is active in every advertising segment, including magazine, radio, internet, newspapers, and digital media, although its sales remain driven by its television division, which alone accounts for nearly 50 percent of the group's annual revenues. In addition to its television operations, Asatsu-DK has long been itself a producer of television content: the company operates two production subsidiaries, and its past efforts included the creation of such popular cartoon series as *Doreamon* in the 1970s and the global success *Yu Gi Oh!* in the 2000s. In 2004, the company led the creation of Sesame Street Partners in order to create a localized version of the popular television program for the Japanese market.

Asatsu-DK has long played the role of maverick in the traditionally rigid Japanese advertising industry, which has long been heavily dominated by Dentsu. Asatsu was the first Japanese advertising agency to go public in the late 1980s, and the company has also been one of the most active in developing an international network. In addition to its subsidiaries in Japan, the company is present in 15 other countries in the Southeast Asian region, with a particular focus on the mainland Chinese market. Asatsu has formed a partnership with the United Kingdom's WPP GRoup—the two companies swapped stock in 1999, in an agreement that gave WPP a 20 percent stake in Asatsu. In addition, Asatsu has set up alliances with a number of global agencies, including JWT, Young & Rubicam, Ogilvy & Mather, and RedCell, in order to provide services to the international operations of its largely Japanese clientele. Asatsu-DK also founded the Drill joint venture partnership with Dentsu, in order to provide integrated advertising campaigns. Listed on the Tokyo Stock Exchange, Asatsu-DK is led by chairman and Asatsu founder Masao Inagaki, and president and CEO Koichiro Naganuma.

JAPANESE ADVERTISING UPSTARTS IN THE FIFTIES

The rise of radio and television broadcasting in Japan in the post-war era opened up new opportunities for the

COMPANY PERSPECTIVES

What do we mean by "Management by All"? This philosophy simply means that, at ADK, everyone shares a management perspective and is encouraged to make full use of their individual talents. By doing so, we aim to contribute as much as possible to the success of our clients. Our long-term vision is to create a New Wave Agency. In other words, we don't cling to traditional thinking or try to maintain the status quo. We go all out to achieve maximum client satisfaction through the creation of next-generation advertising and communications. The "Management by All" philosophy and vision to create a New Wave Agency are infused with the challenger's spirit we've embodied since our founding. ADK refuses to be boxed in by conventional wisdom or become complacent because of past successes. Our raison d'etre as an advertising agency is to constantly create unique solutions for our clients.

country's advertising industry. Although the field was already dominated by a small number of giant companies—and especially by Dentsu, which continued to control a large portion of the country's radio, television, and newspaper advertising markets through the end of the century—the post-war period and the resulting economic boom nonetheless provided a fertile bed for a number of new players in the market.

Unlike Dentsu and Hakuhodo, which were independently owned companies, many of the new advertising companies were established by the country's industrial and distribution groups. These included Tokyu Agency, formed as part of the Tokyu retail group, and Saison, owned by another retailer. Other agencies, including Daiko, Yomiko, Asahi, and Nihon Keizaisha, were all formed in conjunction with the country's major newspaper publishers.

In 1951, the Mitsubishi company, on its way to becoming one of Japan's and the world's largest corporations, formed its own advertising unit, called Dai-Ichi Kikaku Senden Co. Founded in Tokyo by Naoya Sakai and Saburo Hotta, Dai-Ichi's initial focus was on the radio advertising market. The 1950s were to see a dramatic boom in radio advertising, particularly following the introduction of the first transistor radios. The new radio market also inspired an entirely new type of advertisement, which became highly popular with

Japanese consumers. As a result, the country's advertising market quickly grew into the world's second-largest, trailing only the United States.

The strong growth of the market was reflected in Dai-Ichi Kikaku's own expansion during the decade as it followed the spread of local radio markets across the country. Dai-Ichi opened its first branch agency as early as 1953, setting up shop in Osaka. The company added a new office in Nagoya in 1955, followed by a branch in Fukuoka in 1958. In that year, Dai-Ichi Kikaku moved its headquarters to a new, larger site in Tokyo.

Dai-Ichi moved again in 1961, to larger headquarters in Tokyo. The company changed its name to Dai-Ichi Kikaku that year as well, and opened a new branch office in Hiroshima. By the end of 1962, the company had begun its ascent into the country's top ten, merging its operations with two other Tokyo-based advertising companies, Futaba Kigyou and Keishin-sha Co.

While the radio advertising market grew rapidly through the 1950s, the booming economy and increased leisure time in the country also inspired a boom in the country's magazine publishing industry. The fast-rising number of magazine titles provided another foundation for the new generation of advertising companies in the country. One new entrant into the market was Asatsu, created as part of the Asahi Tsushin publishing group in 1956.

Led by Masao Inagaki, who served as the company's CEO before becoming its chairman—a position he continued to hold into the mid-2000s—Asatsu initially focused on the magazine advertising market in the Tokyo area. The launch of Japan's national public television broadcasting network in 1958, however, provided the company with a springboard to a national level. Asatsu quickly began adding branches, opening offices in Osaka and Fukuoka in 1958, and then in Sapporo and Nagoya in 1959.

The development of the Japanese animation industry in the early 1960s provided a fresh opportunity for Asatsu, as the company became one of the only advertising agencies in the country to launch its own television production operations. The company's content creation effort, and especially its knack for developing popular animated characters, soon earned the company the nickname "cartoon Asatsu." An example of an early success of the company's programming unit was its Doreamon character, created in the early 1970s.

By then, the company had moved to larger headquarters in Tokyo, and had continued its national expansion. In 1970, for example, the company opened a branch in Sendai, followed by an office in Hiroshima, opened in 1974. By the beginning of the next decade,

```
┌─────────────────────────────────────────────────┐
│                                                 │
│              KEY DATES                          │
│                    ■                            │
├─────────────────────────────────────────────────┤
```

1951: Dai-Ichi Kikaku Senden Co. is founded as part of Mitsubishi in order to provide advertising services for the radio market.

1956: Masao Inagaki leads the creation of the Asatsu advertising company as part of Asahi Tsushin, focusing on the magazine advertising market.

1976: Dai-Ichi forms an international partnership with DDB.

1984: Asatsu forms an international partnership with BBDO.

1987: Asatsu becomes the first Japanese advertising agency to list shares on Tokyo Stock Exchange.

1993: Asatsu forms its first joint venture subsidiary in China.

1996: Dai-Ichi goes public with a listing on the Tokyo exchange.

1999: Asatsu and Dai-Ichi merge, forming Asatsu-DK, then forming a partnership with WPP Worldwide, which takes a 20 percent stake in Asatsu-DK.

2002: Asatsu-DK acquires animation company Eiken Co. Ltd.

2004: Asatsu-DK forms Drill, a joint venture partnership with Dentsu.

2006: Asatsu-DK adds a new subsidiary in Fujian, China.

the company had added offices in Okayama and Takamatsu as well.

INTERNATIONAL EXPANSION IN THE SEVENTIES

Dai-Ichi continued its own growth into the 1970s as well, expanding its range of advertising markets, and moving to still larger head office facilities in 1974. In that year the company also led the creation of DIK Network Partners, providing the company a link with the operations of a number of local agencies throughout the country.

The mid-1970s, however, marked the beginning of a new era for the Japanese advertising industry. The country's rise as an industrial and economic powerhouse, and its growth into a major exporter of increasingly sophisticated products throughout the world had transformed many of the country's top advertisers into globally operating companies. As a result, Japanese advertising agencies were increasingly called on to provide support for their clients' international operations. Rather than extend their own businesses, Japanese advertising companies began seeking out international partners to provide them with a presence outside of Japan. At the same time, the world's largest advertising groups had begun making an effort to enter the huge advertising market in Japan.

Dai-Ichi became one of the first Japanese groups to engage in a successful partnership with a foreign agency when it signed an agreement with Doyle Dan Bernbach, more commonly known as DDB (and later as DDB Needham Worldwide Inc.), in 1976. Dai-Ichi's initiative was followed by that of Asatsu, which formed its own partnership with BBDO International (later known as BBDO Worldwide) in 1984. That partnership was to last more than 15 years.

Asatsu made industry history in 1987, when it became the first Japanese advertising agency to go public, listing its shares on the Tokyo Stock Exchange. The company's shares initially traded on the TSE second section, before being transferred to the main board in 1990. Dai-Ichi's own public offering followed in 1996.

Asatsu continued to play the role of maverick in the traditionally rigid Japanese advertising industry. Despite the increasing number of international partnerships established among the country's largest advertising groups, their focus remained largely fixed on the domestic market. Asatsu, however, began developing its first international interests in the early 1990s, entering the mainland Chinese market with the formation of a partnership with the Xinhua News Agency. By 1994, the company became the first Japanese agency to establish its own base in the mainland market, forming a joint venture with the People's Daily group in Beijing.

Asatsu rapidly expanded its interests in the Chinese market, forming some 16 subsidiaries in markets including Shanghai, Guangzhou, Chengu, and Fuzhou, among others. Through the end of the decade and into the mid-2000s, Asatsu continued to develop its international network, adding subsidiaries in Thailand, Malaysia, Hong Kong, Taiwan, Malaysia, the Philippines, Singapore, Vietnam, and Korea.

MERGING FOR THE NEW CENTURY

The late 1990s represented a new era for the Japanese advertising industry. While Dentsu remained the market's dominant player, the major international groups had increasingly begun to make an effort to establish direct operations in the country. At the same time, the domestic industry was on the verge of a consolidation phase, which culminated in the creation of Hakuhodo DY in a merger among Daiko, Hakuhodo, and Yomiko. In order to solidify its number three ranking, Asatsu turned to Dai-Ichi in 1999. The two companies agreed to merge that year, becoming Asatsu-DK. Both companies shared a common client, in the form of Mitsubishi. Yet, Mitsubishi, rocked by scandal at the beginning of the 2000s, surprised the advertising industry, and especially Asatsu-DK, by announcing it was moving its account to Dentsu. Asatsu put a brave face on the sudden loss of its major client, pointing out that the move would enable it to begin building a relationship with other automotive companies.

The period was also marked by the end of Asatsu's relationship with BBDO. Instead, Asatsu turned to the U.K.'s WPP Group, forming an initial partnership in 1998. Following the creation of Asatsu-DK, the two companies moved to strengthen their partnership. In a stock swap, WPP acquired a 20 percent stake in Asatsu-DK, while the Japanese company received an equivalent stake—of approximately five percent—in the larger British company.

The deal encouraged Asatsu-DK to explore expansion beyond its Southeast Asian stronghold in the 2000s. In 1999, the company established a subsidiary in France, then strengthened its European presence with the creation of Knots Europe BV in the Netherlands in 2001. Asatsu-DK also added a liaison office in New Delhi, in a first move into the vast Indian market, in 2000. By then, the company had also added a subsidiary in Vietnam as well. In 2004, the company moved to boost its operations in China, in the face of stiffening competition from Dentsu and Hakuhodo, creating a new in-house unit to coordinate the advertising operations of its various Chinese subsidiaries.

Back in Japan, the company strengthened its programming production operations through the acquisition of the Eiken Co. Ltd. animation studio in 2002. The purchase brought Asatsu-DK Eiken's library of more than 6,000 cartoon titles, including its popular *Eightman* and *Sazaesan* series. Asatsu-DK, which saw new success with its *Yu Gi Oh!* cartoon series in the 2000s, also led the formation of Sesame Street Partners, which acquired the license to produce a localized version of the popular children's television program, in 2004.

Asatsu-DK continued to form new relationships into the mid-2000s. In 2004, the company launched a joint venture with Dentsu. Called Drill, the new company was meant to provide Western-styled communications planning services for the Japanese market. Asatsu-DK's part of the joint venture stood at 40 percent. At the same time, the company deepened its relationship with WPP, forming a partnership with that group's J. Walter Thompson Japan subsidiary to explore cooperation agreements not only in Japan, but elsewhere in Asia and into the United States as well. On its own, meanwhile, Asatsu-DK broadened its presence in the mainland China market, launching a new subsidiary in Fujian in 2006. Asatsu-DK not only claimed a clear position as Japan's third-largest advertising agency, it had also grown into one of the new century's top 10 global advertising groups.

M.L. Cohen

PRINCIPAL SUBSIDIARIES

ADK America Inc.; ADK Arts Inc. ADK International Inc.; ADK Asia Regional Center (Malaysia); ADK BOYS Inc.; ADK Deutschland GmbH; ADK Europe (Netherlands); ADK France S.A.S; Asatsu (Thailand) Co., Ltd.; Asatsu Advertising Co., Ltd. (China); Asatsu-DK Hong Kong Ltd.; Asatsu-DK Inc. Seoul LG (South Korea); Asatsu-DK Malaysia Sdn. Bhd.; Asatsu-DK Singapore Pte. Ltd.; Asatsu-DK Vietnam Inc.; ASDIK Ltd. (Thailand); Dai-Ichi Kikaku (Thailand) Co., Ltd.; Dai-Ichi Kikaku Advertising Co., Ltd. (China); Dai-Ichi Kikaku Fortune Advertising Co., Ltd. (China); Digital Advertising Consortium Inc.; Drill Inc.; DS Public Relations Consulting Co., Ltd. (China); Eiken Co., Ltd.; KNOTs Europe B.V. (Netherlands); Kyowa Kikaku Ltd.; Motivation Marketing Inc.; Neo Shobo Inc.; Nihon Ad Systems Inc.; Nihon Bungeisha Co., Ltd.; Nippon Information Industry Corp.; PT. Asta Atria Surya (Indonesia); Right Song Music Publishing Co., Ltd.; Scoop Ad World Pte. Ltd. (Singapore); Super Vision, Inc.; Tiexu Advertising Co., Ltd. (China); TRI Communication Inc.; United-Asatsu International Ltd. (Taiwan).

PRINCIPAL COMPETITORS

Dentsu Inc.; Hakuhodo DY Holdings; Gendai Agency Inc.; Shinken-AD Company Ltd.; Tokyo Electron Agency Ltd.; Catalina Marketing Japan K.K.; Nippon Oil Trading Corp.

FURTHER READING

"Asatsu, DIK Fine-Tune Post-Merger Moniker," *Advertising Age*, November 2, 1998, p. 48.

"Asatsu-DK Acquires Majority Stake in Animation Company Eiken," *Japan Toy and Game Software Journal*, October 25, 2002.

Garrett, Jade, "Japan's Advertising Giants," *Campaign*, February 25, 2000, p. 30.

"Japan's Asatsu-DK Forms China Coordination Body to Win Ad Deals," *Asia Pulse*, June 8, 2004.

Kilburn, David, "Asatsu Pays for Mitsubishi Mess," *Marketing Week*, September 13, 2001, p. 31.

Madden, Normandy, "Dentsu, Asatsu Form Joint Venture," *Advertising Age*, December 6, 2004, p. 14.

"Poor YU-GI-OH! Sales Hit Japan's Asatsu-DK FY05 Profit," *AsiaPulse News*, December 22, 2005.

Yan, "Confucianism to Benefit the Whole World," *People's Daily*, April 5, 2006.

ATA Holdings Corporation

7337 West Washington Street
Indianapolis, Indiana 46231
U.S.A.
Telephone: (317) 247-4000
Toll Free: (800) I-FLY-ATA; (800) 435-9282
Fax: (317) 282-7091
Web site: http://www.ata.com

Private Company
Incorporated: 1973 as Ambassadair Inc.
Employees: 6,900
Sales: $1.53 billion (2004)
NAIC: 481211 Nonscheduled Chartered Passenger Air
Transportation; 481212 Nonscheduled Chartered
Freight Air Transportation; 481111 Scheduled Pas-
senger Air Transportation; 481112 Scheduled
Freight Air Transportation; 56152 Tour Operators

∎ ∎ ∎

ATA Holdings Corporation owns ATA Airlines, Inc., a major low-cost airline in the United States. Formed in 1973 as an offshoot of the Ambassadair travel club, ATA outlasted most of its pre-deregulation peers to become America's largest charter carrier. ATA then developed a low-fare scheduled network and achieved $1 billion in sales by the end of the 1990s. Unfortunately, an ambitious refleeting plan left the company vulnerable to the falloff in traffic and rising fuel costs in the early years of the new millennium.

Following a wave of airline bankruptcies in the U.S., Amtran, Inc., ATA's former corporate parent, ultimately applied for Chapter 11 protection and a new holding company was formed. During the restructuring, the airline scaled back drastically at its Indianapolis home town to focus on its hub at Chicago-Midway, while developing its codeshare arrangement with Southwest Airlines. The Ambassadair Travel Club, which by then accounted for just a fraction of sales, was divested in the restructuring. ATA retained a substantial military and commercial charter business.

EARLY GROWTH

Airline founder J. George Mikelsons was born in Riga, Latvia, and moved with his family first to Australia, then to Germany, and finally to Indianapolis, Indiana, in 1960. There he trained as a pilot, and in 1965 he took a position as a DC-7 copilot for a local travel club known as Voyager 1000.

In 1973, Mikelsons started his own travel club, Ambassadair Inc., taking out a second mortgage on his home to fund the venture. For Ambassadair, Mikelsons not only flew the plane, a leased Boeing 720 dubbed "Miss Indy," but he also drove the passengers to the airport in a second-hand school bus, loaded their baggage, and took them sightseeing once they reached their destination. As a travel club, Mikelsons' start-up could not publish rate or schedule information; it could only serve its members. A second plane, acquired by Ambassadair in 1978, the year of deregulation in the American airline industry, was named "Spirit of Indiana."

During this time, another entity, known as American Trans Air (ATA), was set up by Mikelsons to manage Ambassadair's flight and travel operations. In 1981, however, ATA received its certification as a charter carrier and added eight Boeing 707s to the fleet. It began flying charters for the U.S. Department of Defense. Employees numbered 320 in 1982, when revenues were $30.5 million.

Mikelsons next formed Amtran, Inc., a holding company for Ambassadair and ATA, in 1984. ATA ditched the 707s in favor of 727s during this time and began operating wide-body aircraft as well, in the form of McDonnell Douglas DC-10s and Lockheed L-1011s. By the mid-1980s, Amtran had become the largest charter operator in North America and, according to Inc. magazine, the seventh fastest-growing private company in the United States.

In 1986, ATA launched its first scheduled service, between Indianapolis, Indiana, and four destinations in Florida. As a scheduled passenger carrier, ATA sought to distinguish itself by keeping its fares low and imposing few restrictions on travel times. Mikelsons remained involved in tour packages, and in 1987 created the ATA Vacations, Inc., subsidiary to oversee these operations.

The broader scope of Amtran's operations necessitated a move to new corporate headquarters in Indianapolis, as well as construction of ATA's own maintenance center at Indianapolis Airport. Amtran's annual revenues had multiplied eight times in six years, reaching $254 million in 1988 and involving a workforce of 1,800. In 1989, ATA began operating four Boeing 757s, formerly owned by Singapore Airlines, and soon thereafter created ATA ExecuJet, a corporate jet and helicopter charter service. A freight handling subsidiary was created in 1991.

During the Persian Gulf War, ATA carried more troops (108,000) for the U.S. military than any other civil airline. These flights contributed some $50 million in revenues. However, as Operation Desert Storm ended, ATA was forced to lay off some of its workforce. The company posted its first loss, $2 million, in 1990. Between 85 and 90 percent of the company's business at the time came from civil and military charters.

In the early 1990s, consolidation was expected to thin the ranks of independent carriers willing to deal with tour operators, much to ATA's benefit. The company sought to raise the public perception of charter flights during this time by offering top-notch wine, food, and cabin service. In 1993, in addition to its considerable military transport duties, Amtran offered an around-the-world flight on an L-1011 priced at $45,000 a ticket. The trip reportedly took in $1 million for the company.

When it began flying out of Midway Airport in 1992, ATA carried 500,000 passengers out of Chicago alone. Operating revenues at this time reached $422 million and the workforce had increased to 2,400. ATA operated 12 L-1011s and seven 727s. The Ambassadair Travel Club had 27,000 members in 1992. Another club, Ports of Call, had also been established, and both clubs offered installment payment plans to their members.

GOING PUBLIC IN 1993

Amtran completed an initial public offering (IPO) on the NASDAQ in May 1993. Until that point, founder George Mikelsons had been the company's sole shareholder; after the IPO he still retained a 73 percent stake in Amtran. The $40 million Amtran raised through the IPO helped strengthen its debt-heavy balance sheet after a couple of unprofitable years, while about half the money was earmarked for buying new planes. ATA also opened a new reservations center in Chicago and began flying out of Milwaukee. John Tague, a former Midway Airlines executive who joined ATA in 1991, was promoted to president and chief operating officer in 1993.

Scheduled flights accounted for between 25 and 30 percent of ATA's revenues of $468 million in 1993. Vacation traffic accounted for 80 percent of ATA's revenues, and the carrier soon began renewing its focus on vacation travelers. In alliance with tour operator Pleasant Hawaiian Holidays, ATA began flying to Hawaii from Los Angeles, San Francisco, and Chicago. (In 1992 ATA had become the first airline certified for extended—180 minute—flights over water in the Boeing 757.) The company soon acquired another Lockheed L-1011 and Boeing 757 aircraft to keep up with demand for seats.

KEY DATES

1973: Pilot J. George Mikelsons starts his own tour company, Ambassadair.

1981: American Trans Air (ATA), another Mikelsons entity, begins flying military charters.

1984: Amtran, Inc., holding company is formed.

1993: Amtran goes public.

1996: High fuel costs, competition, and the ValuJet crisis produce ATA's worst year ever.

1998: An invigorated ATA takes on United and American at their own hubs, and thrives.

1999: Revenues exceed $1 billion.

2001: Ambitious fleet renewal program is launched.

2004: Holding company and seven subsidiaries enter Chapter 11 reorganization, battered by rising fuel costs.

2006: ATA emerges from bankruptcy with new ATA Holdings Corporation as ultimate parent company.

By the mid-1990s, Amtran was retaining a workforce of 3,200. Membership at its Ambassadair travel club had reached some 90,000, and ATA was the largest charter carrier and the tenth largest airline in the United States. ATA carried more than five million passengers on its 25 jets in 1995. After the city of St. Petersburg, Florida, courted ATA to relocate its headquarters there, Indianapolis assembled a $40 million incentive package to keep the carrier at home. Much of the tax credits in this plan, which ATA accepted, hinged on the airline's planned expansion in Indianapolis.

Also during this time, ATA became a global concern. A weak dollar and lower labor costs helped make ATA attractive in Europe, where charter airlines already enjoyed a better public perception. ATA opened a sales office in Frankfurt and began operating seasonal routes to Ireland (Shannon and Dublin) from New York's JFK International Airport. The company also opened another maintenance hangar at Midway to service its fleet there and launched the ATA Connection in conjunction with Chicago Express, a shuttle service that linked Chicago, Grand Rapids, Des Moines, and Dayton. Lansing, Michigan, and Madison, Wisconsin, were soon added to the ATA Connection route. Amidst this expansion, Tague, the company's president and COO, left the Amtran executive team to start his own consulting practice.

TROUBLED TIMES: 1996

The year 1996 marked the beginning of increased competition from a major player in the industry. In January 1996, Southwest Airlines, the king of budget carriers, entered ATA's Florida markets. This was just the beginning of the bad news. Like most budget carriers, ATA saw a dip in bookings after the ValuJet crash in the Everglades on May 11, 1996. Although ATA should have clearly been differentiated from the flock of start-up airlines at the time, being a well-established company with a good safety record, one of the company's jets suffered a decompression incident on May 12, 1996, that was widely reported in the immediate aftermath of the ValuJet disaster. With its reputation suddenly under media scrutiny, the company also experienced financial stress in the form of rising fuel costs.

A change in leadership was imminent. Mikelsons stepped down as CEO of Amtran in August 1996, remaining active as chairman. Stanley L. Pace, leader of a consulting team dispatched by Boston-based Bain & Co., was named CEO and president, filling the vacancy left by Tague. Pace brought considerable experience to Amtran, having helped develop a turnaround strategy for Continental Airlines.

Competitive pressure from Southwest Airlines and Delta Express forced ATA to retrench from the scheduled market. Increased sales on this side had not led to increased profits. Amtran trimmed its route structure, cutting scheduled service to Boston entirely. It also canceled leases on five Boeing 757s. In the fall, the company announced plans to lay off 1,000 of its 5,300 workers. Amtran lost $27 million in 1996, its worst year ever. Positive developments for the year were few and included the launch of ATA's new web site, which began offering special bargain fares on the web, and was able to take and record reservations online.

Stanley Pace left the company in May 1997, returning to his home state of Texas. Ironically, the $2 million it cost to pay off his contract wiped out the company's second quarter earnings. Before he left, he had recommended that Amtran merge with the beleaguered ValuJet, a proposal Mikelsons promptly vetoed. ValuJet eventually merged with AirWays Corporation to form AirTran Holdings, Inc., and Tague returned to Amtran in the roles of president and CEO.

A STERLING 25TH ANNIVERSARY IN 1998

Nevertheless, at the company's 25th anniversary in 1998, there were plenty of reasons to celebrate. From origins as a simple travel club, the company had nearly achieved major carrier status; it was the 11th largest in the country in that capacity, as well as the country's largest charter operator. The airline began to post record results in a booming economy with lowered fuel costs. ATA carried more than six million passengers in 1998, and revenues reached $919 million.

In this optimistic environment, ATA ordered more planes and reserved a dozen gates at a new terminal at Midway Airport. Only Southwest Airlines had a larger presence there. ATA boosted flight frequencies at Midway 50 percent in the summer of 1998 and announced plans to hire 500 workers in the area. ATA also began competing with United Airlines on the route between that major airline's two largest hubs, Chicago and Denver. It also took on American Airlines, offering connections from that airline's biggest hubs, Dallas and Chicago. The two majors soon cut fares in response to ATA's threat. Still, the risky bet seemed to pay off in record earnings for Amtran. Mikelsons had once told *Air Transport World*, "If there is a cornerstone to our philosophy it is cowardice."

Amtran postponed a planned stock offering in August 1998 due to a general softening among airline stocks. Amtran's stock originally sold for $16 a share, slipped to $9 in 1996, and rose to $28 in July 1998 before falling to $23. The offering would have brought in $37 million and reduced Mikelsons' holding to a minority.

Acquisitions characterized the late 1990s at Amtran. In March 1999, Amtran bought out T.G. Shown Associates Inc., which owned the other half of its $13 million a year Amber Air Freight venture. A few weeks later, it announced plans to sell at least part of its stake in Chicago Express Airlines. The unit operated nine turboprop planes and brought in $9 million a year in sales. Amtran also bought Chicago Express, Key Tours, and Travel Charter.

BECOMING A MAJOR AIRLINE

Total revenues exceeded $1 billion in 1999 and ATA was soon recognized as a major airline. A fleet renewal program was launched in 2001. It leased new, stretched versions of the Boeing 737 that featured leather seats to cater to the more lucrative business travel market.

In 2002, the company began operating from new gates at Chicago-Midway Airport. ATA's ambitious plans met with a general slowdown in the aviation industry following the September 11, 2001 terrorist attacks on the U.S., however. Amtran, Inc., was renamed ATA Holdings Corp. in 2002, while subsidiary American Trans Air, Inc., was renamed ATA Airlines, Inc., in 2003.

Revenues were about $1.5 million. Military charters typically made up about 20 percent of business. A number of industry conditions complicated ATA's recovery, including the effects of the war in Iraq. The largest problem was rising fuel prices. In 2003 the company managed its first profit in four years, thanks to extensive cost-cutting at the hands of Mikelsons, who had again taken the role of CEO. However, ATA ultimately followed a similar path to many carriers after 9/11.

IN AND OUT OF BANKRUPTCY: 2004–2006

ATA Holdings Corp. and seven subsidiaries entered voluntary Chapter 11 reorganization in October 2004. The company operated 82 aircraft at the time, all but six of them leased. As part of its restructuring, the company cut its fleet nearly in half. Its new Boeing 737-800s were traded in for older, shorter models that held fewer passengers but were less expensive to lease.

A number of airline companies, including America West Holdings, reportedly showed an interest in acquiring ATA or its assets, which included more than half a dozen gate leases at Midway. Some of these went to Southwest Airlines, which would play a large role in the restructuring.

John Denison, Southwest's retired CFO, was hired as the new CEO of ATA Airlines in February 2005. He became CEO of the holding company as well following the retirement of Mikelsons a few months later. Part of the plan included ATA's first codeshare agreement, signed with Southwest Airlines, which had lacked its own long-haul aircraft certified to operate over water. ATA was able to give Southwest a connection to Hawaii.

A new holding company, ATA Holdings Inc., was formed in early 2006 as the airline prepared to emerge from bankruptcy. Southwest had loaned ATA about $50 million to keep it flying, and took a stake in the new corporation. A private group, MatlinPatterson, invested $120 million while employee groups agreed to concessions to keep ATA's operating costs down. The bankruptcy wiped out the value of the former holding company's shares, of which 70 percent had been held by Mikelsons.

A once-central business, Ambassadair Travel Club Inc., was sold to Grueninger Cruises and Tours, Inc. At the time of the sale, it accounted for just 5 percent of its parent company's revenues.

During the restructuring, ATA had reevaluated its network to focus on routes with little discount carrier competition. Notably, it scaled back at the Indianapolis home base in favor of its hub at Chicago-Midway. It did sell off its Chicago Express commuter airline, however. Operations at heavily competitive Denver were closed in 2006; services to a number of cities including San Juan, Puerto Rico, were ended as well.

The airline was flying directly to New York, Dallas, Washington, Guadalajara, and Cancun from Chicago. It also flew between Houston and New York and operated routes to Hawaii from several points in the Southwest and California. Connections to dozens more domestic destinations were available through Southwest Airlines. The charter service for military and civilian clients continued, though its relationship with tour operator Pleasant Holidays ended.

Frederick C. Ingram

PRINCIPAL SUBSIDIARIES

ATA Airlines, Inc.

PRINCIPAL COMPETITORS

AMR Corporation; Continental Airlines, Inc.; Northwest Airlines Corporation; UAL Corporation; US Airways Group, Inc.; World Air Holdings, Inc.

FURTHER READING

Compart, Andrew, "Southwest Wins Battle for ATA's Midway Assets: Sets Stage for Carrier's First Code-Sharing Arrangement," *Travel Weekly,* December 20, 2004, p. 25.

Dinnen, S.P., "Future Location of Indiana Charter Flight Company Headquarters Uncertain," *Indianapolis Star,* September 13, 1996.

———, "Seven-Year Search for New Amtran CEO Ends; Pace to Head Indianapolis Airline," *Indianapolis Star,* August 13, 1996.

Eckert, Toby, "ATA Faces Incentive Deadline," *Indianapolis Business Journal,* September 23, 1996, p. 1.

———, "Mikelsons: Pace Left for Personal Reasons; Ex-CEO Gives No Explanation for Leaving," *Indianapolis Business Journal,* June 2, 1997, p. 4A.

Edelhart, Courtenay, "Airways-ValuJet Merger Announcement Came After Amtran Talks Failed," *Indianapolis Star,* July 22, 1997.

Flint, Perry, "Back in Chartered Waters," *Air Transport World,* January 1997, pp. 39-40.

———, "Jack of All Trades," *Air Transport World,* June 1992, pp. 54ff.

———, "Schedule Change," *Air Transport World,* January 1994, pp. 71ff.

Gross, Daniel, "The Great State Giveaway," *CFO: The Magazine for Senior Financial Executives,* January 1996, pp. 24-29.

Hayes, John R., "Penny-Pincher," *Forbes,* September 12, 1994, pp. 96f.

Horgan, Sean, "Parent Firm May Sell Chicago-Based Commuter Carrier," *Indianapolis Star,* May 12, 1999.

Jonas, David and David Meyer, "ATA Cultivating Deeper Connections to Corp. Market," *Business Travel News,* October 20, 2003, pp. 6f.

Kjelgaard, Chris, "IPO Heralds New Era for American Trans Air," *Airfinance Journal,* August 1993, pp. 8ff.

Lacey, Peter, "J. George Mikelsons," *Chief Executive,* June 1994, p. 20.

Leonhardt, David, "Small Airline, Tricky Flight Plan," *Business Week,* June 22, 1998, pp. 96-98.

O'Malley, Chris, "American Trans Air Has Grown But Kept Low Fares," *Indianapolis News,* February 1, 1998.

———, "Amtran Stock Rises on Good Season, Changes in Service," *Indianapolis News,* April 6, 1998.

———, "ATA Chief Joins List of Creditors: Mikelsons' Betaco Files Claim for Charter Helicopter Lease," *Indianapolis Business Journal,* March 7, 2005, pp. 3f.

———, "ATA Ills Point to Breakup: Airline Talking to Suitor; CEO Puts Home on Market," *Indianapolis Business Journal,* October 18, 2004, pp. 3f.

———, "ATA May Fly Solo Again, Exec Says: Restructuring Officer Sees Opportunities Ahead," *Indianapolis Business Journal,* February 7, 2005, pp. 3Aff.

———, "Fuel Hike Might Ground ATA Plan," *Indianapolis Business Journal,* September 5, 2005, pp. 3f.

———, "Travel Firm Says Aloha to ATA Deal: Hawaii Pact with Southwest May Ease Loss of Business from Pleasant Holidays," *Indianapolis Business Review,* July 11, 2005, pp. 3f.

———, "With Cash Light, ATA Trading New Planes for Old," *Indianapolis Business Journal,* April 18, 2005, p. 6.

———, "Indianapolis Airline Amtran Inc. Delays Stock Sale," *Indianapolis News,* August 4, 1998.

Ott, James, "Recovering ATA Plans on Midway Expansion," *Aviation Week & Space Technology,* February 23, 1998, p. 53.

Schoettle, Anthony, "ATA Airlines Leads Industry in Cost Cuts," *Indianapolis Business Journal,* March 1, 2004, pp. 6f.

The Babcock & Wilcox Company

20 South Van Buren Avenue
Barberton, Ohio 44203-0351
U.S.A.
Telephone: (330) 753-4511
Toll Free: (800) 222-2625
Fax: (330) 860-1886
Web site: http://www.babcock.com

Wholly Owned Subsidiary of McDermott International
Founded: 1867 as Babcock, Wilcox and Company
Employees: 10,800
Sales: $1.37 billion (2004)
NAIC: 332213 Plate Work Manufacturing; 331210 Iron and Steel Pipes and Tubes Manufacturing from Purchased Steel; 333412 Industrial and Commercial Fan and Blower Manufacturing; 333994 Industrial Process Furnace and Blower Manufacturing

■ ■ ■

A subsidiary of McDermott International, The Babcock & Wilcox Company (B&W) provides boilers, steam generators, and related equipment and services to the conventional and nuclear power generation market; process recovery boilers and services to paper mills; and equipment used for environmental purposes, to reduce emissions created by the burning of fossil fuels as well as equipment to convert waste products into energy. Furthermore, B&W manufactures "package boilers" used by a wide variety of customers, including manufacturing plants, hospitals, and universities, to produce steam to generate energy or for use in industrial processes. The

company also offers a complete range of field construction, construction management, installation, and maintenance services for the boilers it sells. In addition to its headquarters in Barberton, Ohio, B&W maintains operations in Lancaster, Ohio; West Point, Mississippi; Cambridge, Ontario, Canada; and Beijing, China. All told, the company employs more than 10,000 people.

MID-19TH CENTURY ORIGINS

The men behind the Babcock & Wilcox names were childhood friends, George Herman Babcock and Stephen Wilcox. Born in Rhode Island in 1830, Wilcox was two years older than Babcock. He was a talented inventor who, after a common school education and an apprenticeship, began improving existing machines and developing new ones. He received the first of 47 patents at the age of 23 when he created a hot-air engine that he tried to sell to the United States Lighthouse Board as a way to produce fog signals. Wilcox soon turned his attention to a field that had far greater commercial potential: steam boilers. In 1856 he and partner O.M. Stillman, a Babcock relative, received a patent on an improved water tube boiler, one that applied water circulation theory to produce a safe boiler, not prone to explosion like earlier versions. The device was not without flaws, however, and 11 years later Wilcox teamed up with Babcock to perfect the water tube boiler.

Babcock was the son of a successful inventor, and his mother's family also boasted a large contingent of mechanics. Born in New York State, he moved to Rhode Island when he was 12 and became friends with Wilcox. At the age of 19 he launched his own newspaper and printing company and, working with his father, invented

COMPANY PERSPECTIVES

For more than 135 years, The Babcock & Wilcox Company (B&W) has been supplying innovative solutions to meet the world's growing energy needs. With power generation systems and equipment found in more than 800 utilities and industries in over 90 countries, we are truly generating powerful solutions.

a pioneering Polychromatic printing press. Babcock then turned his attention to engineering and during the Civil War worked as the chief draftsman of the Hope Iron Works in Providence, Rhode Island. It was in Providence that he was reunited with Wilcox. The two men worked together to improve Wilcox's water tube boiler, which they knew would find a receptive market because of the post-war demand for steam-powered locomotives and engines for manufacturing. In 1867 they received patents for the "Babcock & Wilcox Non-Explosive Boiler" and the "Babcock & Wilcox Stationary Steam Engine." In that same year they formed Babcock, Wilcox and Company, along with Joseph P. Manton, the founder of Hope Iron Works, to manufacture the new boiler.

The boiler was well received and found a new major source of customers in the 1880s with the growth of the industry that arose to generate electricity. In 1878 famed inventor Thomas Edison bought a B&W boiler for his work on electricity and a year later made a successful public demonstration of incandescent lighting, ushering in a new era of electric power. In 1881 four B&W boilers were installed in the first central electrical station in the United States, which was owned by the Brush Electric Light Company of Philadelphia, Pennsylvania. That same year, the B&W partnership was incorporated as The Babcock & Wilcox Company, funded by $225,000 and headed by Babcock as president. It was not long before the company opened its first international office, located in Glasgow, Scotland. A future B&W president, Nathaniel W. Pratt, headed the operation and began selling boilers to process industries throughout Europe. A year later, in 1882, Edison brought electric street lighting to New York City, powered by four B&W boilers in the Pearl Street Central Station in lower Manhattan.

B&W also developed other new markets for its boilers, in particular marine power. In 1889 Babcock fitted his yacht with a specially design boiler that became an immediate sensation. Five years later the company created a Marine department and soon a number of

U.S. and British naval vessels would be equipped with B&W marine boilers. In fact, until the advent of the nuclear age, virtually all U.S. Navy ships and a large portion of America's merchant fleet were powered by B&W boilers. Even with the introduction of reactor power, Navy ships continued to rely on B&W pressurizers and heat exchangers. Moreover, B&W designed and built the power plant for the United States' first nuclear-powered merchant ship, commissioned in 1959.

COMPANY FOUNDERS DIE: 1893

In November 1893 Wilcox died. Just 19 days later Babcock passed away as well, and Pratt took over, beginning a period of turnover in the top ranks of B&W management. Pratt died in 1896 and was replaced by Edwin H. Bennett, who died two years later. His replacement, Edward H. Wells, would have a long tenure, however, and would lead B&W well into the 20th century.

The early years of the new century brought a number of developments. In January 1901, B&W opened its first manufacturing plant, located in Bayonne, New Jersey. A year later, the area's first subway system opened in nearby New York City, powered by B&W boilers. Then, in 1903, Chicago's Fisk Street Station power generation plant installed 24 B&W boilers to become the first utility to rely solely on steam turbines to produce electricity. To meet the demand for its products in the power generating, marine, and industrial markets, B&W expanded its operations through acquisitions. In 1904 it bought the Pittsburgh Seamless Tube Company operation in Beaver Falls, Pennsylvania, and two years after that B&W acquired the Stirling Consolidated Boiler Company plant in Barberton, Ohio. Not only did this latter deal expand its line of marine and stationary boilers, it provided B&W with its future corporate home.

As the century progressed, B&W remained in the forefront of boiler technology. Whereas generating plants had once increased capacity by simply adding more boilers, they turned to massive single boilers, some weighing as much as a Navy destroyer, to meet the escalating demand for power. In this way the duplication of expensive hardware was eliminated, resulting in more economically produced electricity. Larger boilers also led to B&W to become involved in the use of pulverized coal for fuel, which increased the amount of heat generated per unit of coal. In 1926 B&W acquired a maker of pulverized coal equipment, Fuller Lehigh Company. The new fuel, however, led to the accelerated deterioration of a boiler's firebrick refractory. To address this problem, B&W led the way in the development of a water-cooled furnace, and in 1933 resulted in the introduction of B&W's Integral Furnace boiler, combin-

KEY DATES

1856: Stephen Wilcox invents an improved water tube boiler.
1867: Wilcox and George Herman Babcock form Babcock, Wilcox and Company.
1881: The partnership is incorporated as The Babcock & Wilcox Company.
1893: Wilcox and Babcock die within 19 days of each other.
1906: The Stirling Consolidated Boiler Company plant is acquired in Barberton, Ohio.
1933: B&W introduce the Integral Furnace boiler.
1956: The Atomic Energy Division is formed.
1978: The company is sold to J. Ray McDermott & Co., Inc.
1982: B&W begins settling asbestos liability claims.
2000: Due to asbestos claims, B&W seeks Chapter 11 Bankruptcy protection.
2006: B&W emerges from bankruptcy.

ing a boiler and water-cooled furnace, capable of burning pulverized coal, as well as any combination of oil and gas. In that same year, B&W introduced Junior Firebrick for marine boilers, offering a service life as much as four times longer than the material the in use. Another important development during this period was the 1935 installation of the first "black liquor" recovery boiler in the United States, using a byproduct of the pulping process as a fuel. A year later the company introduced the Radiant boiler and Open-Pass boiler.

Although the U.S. economy was mired in the decade-long Great depression of the 1930s, B&W continued to find sufficient need for its equipment to keep its plants running. One of the notable contracts of the period was the manufacture of the penstocks, water-carrying steel pipes, used in the Hoover Dam project in 1932. With war clouds developing over Europe and the Far East, the United States built up its Navy in preparation for another World War, and once the country entered the war in December 1941 the pace of construction of vessels of all types increased dramatically. Hence, B&W sold the government a large number of water-tube boilers, water-cooled furnaces, superheaters, air heaters, pulverized-coal equipment, chain-grate stokers, oil burners, seamless tubes and pipe, and refractories. It was not just the marine market that relied on B&W equipment; there was also healthy demand from power plants needing to increase capacity to meet electricity demand from war industries, which in turn needed B&W equipment as they ramped up production.

The war effort having jumpstarted the U.S. economy, B&W prospered during the post-war economic boom. Demand was strong for both industrial and heating boilers, but because of escalating field construction costs, B&W in the late 1940s introduced the package boiler, built in B&W shops and shipped to the customer for installation. It was also during the post-war years that B&W became involved in the nuclear power field. In 1953 it supplied many of the key components used in the U.S. Navy's *Nautilus* submarine, the first nuclear-power ship in history. Revenues rose steadily during this period, from $64.2 million in 1949 to $170.7 million in 1949 and more than $305 million in 1953. The company included three divisions. Boilers still accounted for the bulk of its business. The Tubular Products Division, which made carbon and alloy steel tubing used in making boilers and sold to other industries, contributed about 30 percent. A third division, generating about 5 percent of sales, produced refractories, insulating firebrick, and other furnace materials. Another 10 percent of revenues came from a pair of subsidiaries acquired in the 1920s: Bailey Meter Co., a Cleveland-based boiler control and metering equipment maker, and Diamond Power Specialty Co., a Detroit-based mechanical boiler cleaning equipment manufacturer.

B&W continued to expand its product lines and capabilities during the rest of the 1950s. It acquired Milwaukee-based Globe Steel Tubes Company in 1955 to bolster its Tubular Products Division. A year later the B&W formed a fourth unit, the Atomic Energy Division, to produce cores, nuclear fuel elements, and other reactor parts. In 1957 B&W introduced the coal-fired Universal Pressure boiler, the first commercial, supercritical pressure steam cycle unit. Also of note, in 1958 the Boiler Division moved its headquarters from New York to Barberton, which would eventually become B&W corporate headquarters as well.

B&W IMPACTED BY 1979 THREE MILE ISLAND DISASTER

B&W continued to make advances in boiler technology and grew its nuclear power business in the 1960s and 1970s. Among the most important milestones of this period was the 1969 development of a construction technique that allowed a nuclear power plant to erect a complete outer shell before the major components were installed. Another was the 1973 installation of the world's largest electrical generating unit, a 1,300-megawatt, pulverized coal-fired plant for the Tennessee Valley Authority. Unfortunately, B&W was also connected to the first case of melted fuel in a full-scale commercial nuclear power plant when, in March 1979, one of the units at the Three Mile Island nuclear power facility in Pennsylvania came perilously close to causing a catastrophic nuclear accident. As it was, Three Mile Island was the United States' worst commercial nuclear accident, and because B&W designed the nuclear steam supply system and built the reactor, it found itself at odds with the plant's operator, General Public Utilities Corporation, each side blaming the other for the incident.

Shortly before the Three Mile Island incident took place, ownership of B&W changed hands, as J. Ray McDermott & Co., Inc., a Louisiana maker of production platforms for the offshore oil industry, acquired the business. McDermott paid $750 million for B&W and less than a year later found itself facing $4 billion in lawsuits related to the Three Mile Island accident. McDermott had internal problems of its own to contend with, including a political bribery scandal that resulted in several of its executives going to prison. The combined company had to endure a rough patch as a new management team took over, but the addition of B&W soon began to pay dividends for McDermott, whose fortunes were bolstered by B&W at a time when the production platform business was in a down cycle. In addition, the two companies proved to be more compatible than might appear at first glance: B&W's tubular products were not only suitable for boilers but could also be sold to oil companies by McDermott for drilling activities as well as pipelines and other transport needs for oil and gas.

After B&W emerged from the Three Mile Island difficulties, it found itself dealing with another problem, asbestos claims. Although it never manufactured asbestos, B&W had for many years used the material—at the behest of government agencies—as insulation in power-generation projects in order to protect both people and equipment. This came to an end in the early 1970s when asbestos was phased out, but B&W found itself the recipient of asbestos liability claims, which it would be saddled with for the next 20 years. Starting in 1982 B&W began quietly settling claims out of court, dispatching with about 340,000 of them by the end of 1999 at a cost in excess of $1.6 billion, an amount borne by both B&W and its insurer.

Even with the asbestos suits hanging over its head, B&W carried on business. It looked to countries where so many of the world's manufacturing operations were moving, resulting in a rising demand for electricity. B&W expanded its international operations through joint ventures established in Mexico in 1985, Indonesia and the Peoples' Republic of China in 1986, India in 1989, Turkey in 1990, and Egypt in 1994. The company also opened a new division in 1988, the Energy Services

Division, to perform repair and upgrade services on fossil-fueled power plants as well as industrial units. In 1995 B&W opened the Clean Coal Environmental Development Facility, an Alliance, Ohio-based combustion and emissions testing facility that kept the company on the cutting edge of modern power generating technology.

The asbestos problem only grew worse with time, however, as plaintiffs' demands escalated, despite the total number of claims having been whittled down to about 45,000. In March 2000 B&W elected to file for Chapter 11 Bankruptcy protection in order to work out a comprehensive solution to the asbestos liability claims. The company remained in Chapter 11 until early 2006. During that time the number of asbestos personal injury claims swelled to more than 222,000. Part of the company's reorganization plan, approved by a federal court in late 2005, called for the creation of a $1.9 billion fund to settle these claims. The company's business was thriving, as demonstrated later in 2006 when B&W signed a deal in excess of $1 billion to supply Texas power plants with eight coal-fired boilers and related equipment, the largest North American boiler order in several decades. With the burden of asbestos claims about to be lifted, the company hoped to resume a history of continued and steady growth.

Ed Dinger

PRINCIPAL SUBSIDIARIES

Babcock & Wilcox Canada; Babcock & Wilcox Vølund ApS.

PRINCIPAL COMPETITORS

Ducon Technologies Inc.; Foster Wheeler Ltd.; Mitsubishi Heavy Industries, Ltd.

FURTHER READING

"Babcock & Wilcox Profits Work Up Head of Steam," *Barron's National Business and Financial Weekly,* July 22, 1963, p. 19.

Blueprints For Success: 125 Years, Barberton, Ohio: The Babcock and Wilcox Company, 1992, 31 p.

Cook, James, "Two of a Kind," *Forbes,* July 5, 1982, p. 168.

Haberman, Alan and Richard Abrons, "Babcock & Wilcox: It Is the Nation's No. 1 Boiler Maker," *Barron's National Business and Financial Weekly,* May 3, 1954, p. 13.

Lawrence, Herbert, "News and Views on Investments: Babcock & Wilcox," *Barron's National Business and Financial Weekly,* June 14, 1943, p. 1.

Prial, Frank J., "3 Mile Island Owners and Builder Fault Each Other for '79 Accident," *New York Times,* November 2, 1982, p. A11.

Thomas, Dana L., "New Head of Steam," *Barron's National Business and Financial Weekly,* March 9, 1964, p. 3.

Trottman, Melanie, "McDermott Unit Seeks Protection Under Chapter 11," *Wall Street Journal,* February 23, 2000, p. 1.

Zipf, George G., "Babcock & Wilcox Power for Tom Edison—and the Nuclear Navy," *Nation's Business,* January 1973, p. 42.

Bacardi & Company Ltd.

65 Pitts Bay Road
Pembroke, HM 08
Bermuda
Telephone: (441) 295-4345
Fax: (441) 292-0562
Web site: http://www.bacardi.com

Private Company
Incorporated: 1919 as Compania Ron Bacardi, S.A.
Employees: 6,000
Sales: $2.9 billion (2002 est.)
NAIC: 312130 Wineries; 422820 Wine and Distilled
  Alcoholic Beverage Wholesalers

■ ■ ■

Bacardi & Company Ltd. is one of the largest wine and spirits groups in the world, shipping upwards of 200 million bottles of rum blends annually to approximately 200 countries worldwide. As the first distiller to produce smooth, light-colored rum in the mid-1800s, Don Facundo Bacardi turned his blending process, called the "marriage of rums," into a reported billion-dollar empire. Some of the company's other brands include Bombay Sapphire gin, Martini & Rossi vermouth, Dewar's Scotch whisky, and DiSaronno Amaretto.

FROM RUM SALES TO MANUFACTURING: 1830–1875

Bacardi, the giant liquor conglomerate, began with the emigration of Facundo Bacardi y Masso from Spain in 1830. Born in Sitges, Catalonia, Bacardi arrived in the Caribbean port city of Santiago de Cuba, then a Spanish colony populated by many fellow Catalans. There the 14-year-old Bacardi began importing and selling wine. While working for an Englishman named John Nunes who owned a local distillery, Facundo started tinkering with ways to upgrade the quality of aguardiente (fire water), which was also known as rumbullion. Facundo hoped to "civilize" the dark liquor from its early incarnation as a coarse, harsh liquid swilled by buccaneers. As rum production had changed little in the previous 200 or so years, Facundo decided it was time to elevate the spirit into something smoother and more refined.

In 1843 Facundo married a young woman named Amalia, the daughter of a French Bonapartist fighter, and soon began a family. Around this time his rum experiments had paid off and he offered samples of his newfangled light rum to relatives and friends. Facundo's secret formula enabled him to ferment, distill, and blend from molasses a rum one could drink straight, almost like wine, without mixers or additives. Since molasses was a byproduct of processing sugarcane, Cuba's largest export, there were ample quantities around the island. On February 4, 1862, Facundo, his brother Jose, and a French wine merchant joined forces to buy Nunes' tin-roofed distillery for $3,500. The facility had the necessities (a still of cast-iron, fermenting tanks, and aging barrels) for creating and selling a Bacardi brand of rum. Buying the old distillery lock, stock, and barrel, Facundo also received an added bonus in the deal—a colony of fruit bats that later came to represent the Bacardi name.

The Bacardi enterprise was a family affair. As Facundo's three sons—Emilio, Facundo (Jr.), and Jose—came of age, they joined the company and learned their father's secret formula for making what was fast becoming the Caribbean's finest rum. Emilio, the oldest, worked in the office; Facundo Jr. worked in the distillery; and Jose, the youngest, eventually sold and promoted his father's products. Facundo Jr., in honor of his father and to celebrate the new family business, planted a coconut palm tree just outside the distillery. As the Bacardi boys learned their father's trade, a young man named Enrique Schueg y Chassin, who was born in 1862, the same year Don Facundo purchased the Santiago distillery, was maturing and would soon join both the business and the family, by marriage. In the ensuing years, as the business thrived, young Facundo's coconut palm did, too. The tree became an enduring symbol of the Bacardi family and its spirits operation.

Not long before Don Facundo and his partners bought the Nunes distillery, an Australian named T. S. Mort had perfected the first machine-chilled cold storage unit. Three years after Bacardi was established, Thaddeus Lowe debuted the world's first ice machine. Although these two inventions seemed completely unrelated to Don Facundo's premium rum, they later helped Bacardi conquer the social drinking marketplace by making ice and cold mixers commonplace. Yet such thoughts were far from Don Facundo and his family's minds, for they had no idea how widespread the appeal of their smooth, fine rum would one day become. Instead, they greeted Bacardi's increasing popularity in Santiago and the neighboring villages as a pleasant surprise.

As was the custom of the day, customers brought their own jugs and bottles to the distillery; the Bacardi family members promptly filled and returned them. With business booming, Don Facundo decided the current method of distribution was not good enough and set out to find an alternative. Meanwhile, back in Spain, Queen Isabella, who ascended the throne in 1843 at the age of 13, was deposed. For Bacardi and his family, as

with most Catalans living on the Spanish-controlled colony of Cuba, the insurrection mirrored their own growing unrest. As civil war raged in Spain in 1872, Emilio, who had become a Cuban freedom fighter, was caught and exiled to an island off the coast of Morocco. During his absence, hostilities grew and a rebellion swept through Cuba, although the family business was unharmed. Emilio returned to Cuba four years after his capture and learned Bacardi rum had earned a gold medal at the Philadelphia Exposition of 1876.

A CHANGING LANDSCAPE: 1877 TO 1931

As the 1880s dawned, Don Facundo retired and turned Bacardi over to Emilio, Facundo Jr., Jose, and Enrique, who was now his son-in-law. The company's distribution problems had been solved with the suggestion from Dona Amalia that Bacardi products be sold with a distinctive, easily recognized label. As many of Santiago's residents could not read, Dona Amalia recommended using a symbol to represent Bacardi. The Bacardi logo was then born, sporting a most unlikely mascot, the fruit bat.

Before the turn of the century, as Bacardi flourished, Cuba was again engaged in battle to gain its independence from Spain. Emilio, fighting for his country, was banished a second time and Enrique went with him into exile. The United States joined the fray after a mysterious explosion on the U.S. battleship Maine sparked the Spanish-American War in 1898. After the defeat of the Spanish fleet at Manila, the U.S. and Spain signed the Treaty of Paris, which ceded Cuba, Guam, the Philippines, and Puerto Rico to the U.S. for $20 million. In 1901 Cuba became an independent republic, and Emilio returned home to the Bacardi family and business.

Emilio was elected mayor of Santiago while Bacardi continued buying sugarcane fields and expanding its operations through several bottling facilities. In 1906 Emilio was elected to the Cuban Senate and the next year Jose, the youngest Bacardi son, who had represented the company's interests in Havana, died. Though the family mourned his loss, the business continued to prosper and in 1910 Emilio returned to his father's homeland to begin Bacardi's first international venture: a new bottling facility in Barcelona, Spain. Less than a decade later, on May 2, 1919, Compania Ron Bacardi, S.A. was incorporated with Emilio as president, and Facundo Jr. and Enrique as vice presidents.

As Bacardi set out to conquer the world—especially the United States—with its premium rum, a roadblock called Prohibition stood in its way. Though temperance

KEY DATES

1830: Facundo Bacardi y Masso emigrates from Spain to Santiago de Cuba.

1862: Facundo, his brother Jose, and a French wine merchant jointly purchase a distillery for $3,500.

1919: Compania Ron Bacardi, S.A., is incorporated.

1934: Bacardi sells over 80,000 cases in the U.S.

1944: Bacardi Imports is established in New York City.

1960: The government of Fidel Castro seizes most of Bacardi's assets; Bacardi shareholders reconstitute the company as Bacardi & Company Limited; Bacardi International Limited is also formed.

1977: Approximately 12 percent of company stock is sold to an outsider, Hiram Walker.

1986: Chairman Alfred O'Hara and president Manuel Luis Del Valle buy back and convert shares from Bacardi's IPO in 1962 as well as those sold to Hiram Walker in 1977.

1993: Bacardi buys a majority interest in Martini & Rossi.

1998: The company acquires Dewar's Scotch whisky and Bombay gin brands.

2002: Tequila Cazadores is purchased.

2005: Facundo Bacardi—great grandson of the company's founder—is named chairman.

had been gaining ground for several years, the Prohibition amendment was officially ratified less than four months earlier on January 16, 1919. However, although Bacardi could not sell their spirits to the U.S., nothing stopped Americans from coming to Cuba for liquor. Havana soon became known as "the unofficial U.S. saloon" and Bacardi rum was one of its biggest attractions. Bacardi's international sales were also strong in a world whose population topped 1.8 billion by 1922. This same year, both the family and the business suffered the loss of patriarch Emilio, followed two years later by Facundo Jr. Enrique, though not a family member by blood, took the reins of the burgeoning company and served as its president.

The dawn of the 1930s brought further international expansion for Bacardi as its bottling operation in Spain was a huge success. Realizing that Bacardi rum could be distilled and sold from any facility with the appropriate equipment, Enrique began to open what soon became a network of distribution points. In 1931 came the establishment of a new subsidiary in Mexico, which was nearly bankrupt through a severe recession. Enrique's son-in-law, Jose Bosch, intervened and kept the operation afloat until the economy improved and the small company turned profitable.

AFTER PROHIBITION

When Prohibition was repealed in the United States in December 1933, Bacardi was ready to start serving the thirsty market. Enrique promptly sent his son-in-law Jose to New York City to pave the way for Bacardi's distribution in the United States. Back in Cuba the political climate was once again boiling as Fulgencio Batista y Zaldivar, the country's army chief of staff, became Cuba's de facto ruler after a military coup. Unfettered by its tropical roots, Bacardi entered the U.S. marketplace in a bang—selling over 80,000 cases in 1934. To save the company the United States' expensive import duty tax (nearly $1 per bottle), Jose Bosch decided to open another Bacardi facility in Old San Juan, Puerto Rico. Under American control since the Treaty of Paris in 1901, Puerto Rico was considered U.S. soil and its exports duty free. Under the name Bacardi Corporation, the new company soon moved to larger accommodations across the bay in Catano.

The 1940s brought several milestones for Bacardi, both in expansion and brand recognition. Much of the company's U.S. business had begun through word-of-mouth praise from visitors to the Caribbean, especially those flying Pan American Airways, which used Bacardi in some of its ads, "Fly Pan Am to Cuba and you can be bathing in Bacardi in hours." To capitalize on Bacardi's growing reputation and enhance its brand at the same time, Enrique and Jose initiated advertising that focused on Bacardi's excellent qualities as a mixer. Two of the more popular variations were the Daiquiri, named after a Cuban village where an American mining engineer mixed Bacardi, crushed ice, and lime juice in 1896; and the Cuba Libre or Rum & Coke, created by an American army lieutenant in honor of Cuba's new independence. The latter concoction gained widespread attention when the Andrews Sisters made "Rum & Coca-Cola" a hit in 1944.

The same year "Rum & Coca-Cola" sailed up the charts, Bacardi Imports was established in New York City to coordinate the increasing demand for Bacardi, and both Cuba and the United States joined the Allied war effort. By the end of the decade, however, challenges loomed for Bacardi. In the United States, where whisky was reintroduced in 1947, rum sales plummeted 47 percent in a one-year period. Next came the death of Enrique Schueg in 1950, at which time Jose Bosch assumed the role of CEO. By 1953, drinkers had become concerned over the caloric content of liquor. In response to consumer concerns, Bosch introduced a new advertising campaign, comparing the calories of a Daiquiri with those in a glass of milk. This successful spin was soon followed by ad campaigns directed toward blacks and Hispanics, and in 1956 the company broke cultural gender barriers by featuring a woman in its ads, advising homemakers to serve a Daiquiri with the evening meal.

It was around this time (there were two dissenting versions) that the first Pina Colada was mixed in Puerto Rico, using Bacardi rum, varied fruit juices, and coconut milk. As the 1950s came to an end, Cuba was once again seized by revolution—this time to unseat Batista, who had returned to power in 1952. Regarded by many as a puppet of the United States, whose continued interference in Cuban affairs spawned guerrilla uprisings, Batista ruled until 1959 when rebels led by Fidel Castro and Che Guevara overthrew his dictatorship.

THE NEW BACARDI: 1960–1989

Bosch, no fan of Batista, was shocked when the new Castro government seized Bacardi's assets, valued at $76 million, in 1960. Luckily for Bacardi, it not only had its Mexican, Puerto Rican, New York, and recently established Brazilian operations to fall back on, but its registered trademark, as well, which Castro tried to seize, to no avail. Bacardi's shareholders, all descendants of Don Facundo, reconstituted the company in 1960 as Bacardi & Company Limited, headquartered in Nassau, the Bahamas. Another company, Bacardi International Limited, was also formed and headquartered in Bermuda. In 1962 the company sold 10 percent of its shares in an IPO (initial public offering).

Trying to stave off competitors with Bacardi's reputation as a mixer, the company launched a new advertising campaign once again expounding its rum's versatility. "Enjoyable always and all ways" was supposed to be taken literally, to use Bacardi's light-colored rum as a substitute for anything, even vodka in heavyweight drinks like highballs. The formula worked and Bacardi's sales grew by 10 percent annually throughout the 1960s, when the company finally broke into the top ten of distilled spirits brands. In 1964 Bacardi sold over one million cases of rum; this figure doubled by 1968.

During 1970, 2.6 million cases of Bacardi were sold. Aiming to further dominate the U.S. spirits market, Bacardi aggressively campaigned its rum as the mixer of choice, featured in joint promotions with Coca-Cola, Canada Dry Ginger Ale, Dr. Pepper, 7Up, Pepsi, Perrier, and Schweppes' tonic water. In a well-played game of one-upmanship, Bacardi won the battle against Smirnoff

vodka as the nation's biggest-selling distilled spirit. After a dispute with the Bacardi family, Jose Bosch resigned as president of the company in 1976. The following year Bosch and a group of his supporters sold their company stock (amounting to 12 percent or so) to an outsider, Hiram Walker. Unfortunately, this break with family tradition was the first in a series of squabbles that rocked the Bacardi empire over the next decade-and-a-half.

Bacardi's rums sold just shy of 8 million cases in 1978 and by 1980 Bacardi reigned as the number-one liquor brand in the United States. During this period, consumers were once again weight-conscious and accordingly, Bacardi relaunched its status as a low calorie diet drink mixer. By 1985 Bacardi was selling over 18 million cases a year, with old rival Smirnoff selling less than 14 million. In 1986, three years after Bacardi Capital was created to manage and invest company funds, a group of inexperienced brokers lost $50 million speculating in the bond market. Regrouping, Bacardi chairman Alfred O'Hara and president Manuel Luis Del Valle (non-family members brought in to run the company in the 1970s) commenced a controversial stock buyback, which divided the company and inspired a storm of controversy. Many of the 500 family shareholders cried foul, several Bacardi family members were ousted, and O'Hara and Del Valle—despite the ruckus—succeeded. Spending more than $241 million, they bought back or converted shares from Bacardi's IPO in 1962 as well as those sold to Hiram Walker in 1977.

THE BACARDI OF THE 1990S

When the 1990s began Bacardi was once again a private company. Having weathered the Bacardi Capital scandal and increasing family discord, the company was faced with falling market share and sales. In an effort to jazz up its image, the company introduced Bacardi Frozen Tropical Fruit Mixers and Bacardi Breezers to wide acclaim. Two years later came Rum & Coke in a can, and a majority interest in Martini & Rossi for $1.4 billion. Bacardi hoped the diversification would help its European operations; as a result of the purchase, Bacardi became the fifth largest wine-and-spirits company in the world. Before the Martini & Rossi acquisition, Bacardi was bringing in close to $500 million annually, yet was nowhere near complacent. Its next new product launch, Bacardi Limón, was aimed at younger drinkers of flavored liquors like Absolut's Citron and Stoli's Limonaya. Introduced in 1995 with an $11 million advertising campaign, Bacardi Limón took off and was considered one of the hottest high-proof new brands of the year.

By the mid-1990s Bacardi had bottling facilities located in Australia, Austria, France, Germany, New

Zealand, Switzerland, the United Kingdom, and the United States, while its spirits were still manufactured in the Bahamas, Mexico, Puerto Rico, and Spain—with Brazil, Canada, Martinique, Panama, and Trinidad added to the list. The company's brands, of which Bacardi Breezers and Bacardi Limón were the latest newcomers, had grown to accommodate virtually all tastes. First and foremost were Bacardi's four premium rum blends: Bacardi Light, the original, comparable to gin and vodka as a mixer; Bacardi Dark (full-bodied, its amber color achieved by blackening the inside of wooden aging barrels) and Bacardi Black (charcoal-filtered just once before extended aging; later renamed Bacardi Select), which competed with whisky and bourbon; Bacardi Anejo, a golden rum blend named for the Castillian word meaning "aged" that appealed to upscale brown spirits-drinkers; and Bacardi Reserve, a twice-filtered blend for brandy and cognac drinkers.

By 1996 all of Bacardi's products were given a more hip look with updated labels and bottle caps as Bacardi Spice (to compete with Seagram's Captain Morgan) made its way to the market with several more prototypes in the works. By now, Bacardi was once again a family-run empire, with Don Facundo's heirs calling the shots. Manuel Jorge Cutillas and brother Eduardo occupied the top posts, while the company created alliances with partners in Hong Kong, Japan, Malaysia, the Philippines, Russia, Taiwan, and Thailand to introduce its products. Another global project was the debut of Club Bacardi, the company's web site. Well-positioned for the future, the name Bacardi conjured up far more than a refined, dry rum; Bacardi was not just a premium spirit but an institution here to stay.

BACARDI HEADS INTO THE NEW MILLENNIUM

As Bacardi headed into the 21st century, the company continued to expand its business in the highly competitive liquor industry. In 1998 it added Dewar's Scotch whisky and Bombay gin to its arsenal. Bacardi then set its sights on Seagram Company's alcohol beverage segment, which was up for sale as a result of the impending Seagram and Vivendi SA merger. In 2000, Bacardi teamed up with Brown-Forman Corp. of Louisville, Kentucky, to bid for Seagram's prized liquor business that included brands such as Chivas Regal Scotch whisky, Crown Royal Canadian whisky, and Captain Morgan. A bidding war ensued and in the end, Bacardi and Brown-Forman lost out to Diageo PLC and Pernod Ricard S.A.

Undeterred, Bacardi forged ahead with its growth plans. In 2002, the company purchased Tequila Cazadores, a premium reposado tequila. Bacardi also added tequila infused rum Ciclon, Turi vodka, and malt bever-

age Bacardi Silver to its brand portfolio that year. Bacardi chairman Ruben Rodriguez commented on the cutthroat nature of the liquor industry in a December 2002 *Calgary Herald* newspaper. "It's a very competitive environment, and we have to get bigger in order to be able to effectively compete," claimed Rodriguez. He went on, "It's important to be the first one in the marketplace giving consumers what they want. If you don't do it, your competition is going to do it for you." Indeed, this mind-set remained at the forefront of Bacardi's strategy. In 2004, the company acquired Grey Goose vodka. It continued to launch new products and also redesigned some of its packaging.

Despite the company's successes, family squabbling, management changes, and failed plans to take the company public were taking a toll on morale at company headquarters. At the same time, Pernod Ricard's takeover of Allied Domecq left Bacardi well behind competitors Diageo and Pernod Ricard. The company reported a 21 percent drop in net profits for 2004 due in part to falling demand for its ready-to-drink cocktails.

Facundo L. Bacardi, great-great grandson of the founder, was named chairman in 2005. Under his leadership, the company took steps to secure its position in the industry. In 2006, Bacardi launched a new marketing strategy designed to take advantage of online social networks and blogs. It also launched Bacardi B-Live, an online and mobile radio station, and offered a sweepstakes on its Web site that tied in with the 2006 debut of the Miami Vice movie. Later that year, Bacardi U.S.A. relaunched its Havana Club brand in limited supply after winning a decade-long legal battle with the Cuban government and Pernod Ricard concerning the rights to market the brand. Back in 1960, Castro had seized Arechabala's Havana Clubs assets. The rum was then exported by the Cuban government's Cubaexport company and Pernod Ricard—but was not sold in the U.S. due to the embargo on Cuban products. In the mid-1990s, Bacardi bought the family recipe and the Havana Club name from the Arechabala family. The Havana Club product was pulled from store shelves however, after Pernod Ricard and the Cuban government cried foul. Havana Club's reinstatement in the United States in August 2006 was a sweet victory for not only the Arechabala family, but for Bacardi as well.

Taryn Benbow-Pfalzgraf
Updated, Christina M. Stansell

PRINCIPAL SUBSIDIARIES

Bacardi & Co. (Bahamas); Bacardi Corporation (Puerto Rico); Bacardi U.S.A. Inc.; Bacardi y Compania

(Mexico); Bacardi-Martini Ltd. (United Kingdom).

PRINCIPAL COMPETITORS

Allied Domecq plc; Diageo plc; Pernod Ricard S.A.

FURTHER READING

"Bacardi Branding Out Beyond Just Rum," *Calgary Herald*, December 29, 2002.

"Bacardi Has Long-Term Plans for Spice Market," *Grocer*, August 12, 1995, p. 25.

"Bacardi Signals Shift with Global Digital Ad Campaign," *Marketing Week*, July 20, 2006, p. 3.

"A Bat, with a Coat of Arms," *Financial World*, November 22, 1994, p. 80.

Behar, Richard, "Hangover," *Forbes*, July 14, 1986, p. 33.

"Diageo and Pernod Near a Seagram Deal," *Wall Street Journal*, December 19, 2000, p. A3.

Farrand, Tim, "Switching Brands Bacardi Buys Dewar's, Bombay Gin," *Rocky Mountain News*, March 31, 1998, p. 2B.

Grant, Jeremy, "Bacardi Scion to Become Group's Chairman," *Financial Times*, September 27, 2005.

Holleran, Joan, "Bacardi Breakthrough," *Beverage Industry*, July 1996, p. 32.

Hornik, Richard, "Rum Deal in an Old Family Farm; the Bacardis Tussle Over Taking Their Liquor Company Private," *Time*, May 25, 1987, p. 56.

Khermouch, Gerry, "Bacardi's Proof Positive," *Brandweek*, March 11, 1996, p. 30.

Rushe, Dominic, "Feuding Leaves Bacardi on the Rocks," *Sunday Times*, April 24, 2005.

Simley, John, "Bacardi," *Encyclopedia of Consumer Brands*, edited by Janice Jorgensen, Detroit, St. James Press, 1993, pp. 24-26.

Walker, Elaine, "Bacardi to Re-Launch Havana Club Rum Label," *Knight Ridder Tribune Business News*, August 8, 2006, p. 1.

Whitefield, Mimi, "A Renovated Bacardi Plans New Generation of Snappy Niche Beverages," *Knight-Ridder/Tribune Business News*, March 26, 1995.

Baptist Health Care
Corporation

1000 West Moreno Street
P.O. Box 17500
Pensacola, Florida 32522
U.S.A.
Telephone: (850) 434-4011
Fax: (850) 469-2307
Web site: http://www.ebaptisthealthcare.org

Not-for-Profit Corporation
Incorporated: 1951 as Baptist Hospital
Employees: 4,000
Sales: $400 million (2004 est.)
NAIC: 621493 Freestanding Ambulatory Surgical and Emergency Centers; 621498 All Other Outpatient Care Centers; 621610 Home Health Care Services; 621999 All Other Miscellaneous Ambulatory Health Care Services; 622110 General Medical and Surgical Hospitals; 623110 Nursing Care Facilities; 623311 Continuing Care Retirement Communities

■ ■ ■

Baptist Health Care Corporation operates medical facilities in the Florida Panhandle and Gulf Coast and Alabama. The company's flagship Baptist Hospital in Pensacola was a pioneer in controlling costs through incentive programs in the 1960s and 1970s. It grew through acquisitions and new buildings in the 1980s, but emerged with substandard facilities and an abysmal customer service reputation. Its new leader focused the organization on better customer service through employee empowerment, and soon BHC was winning prestigious awards. BHC has leveraged its much-vaunted corporate culture with a side venture that provides customer service presentations to staff from other organizations.

OPENED IN 1951

Pensacola's Baptist Hospital opened in 1951. Its founder was Earl R. Gaston. Funds for the $1.25 million hospital included a federal Hill-Burton grant and $600,000 raised from the local community.

Baptist originally had 95 beds, according to Dr. Pat N. Groner's revealing 1977 tome *Cost Containment Through Employee Incentives Program*. It was considered large at the time, he later told the *Health Care Management Review*. Groner served as administrator of the Baptist Hospital in Pensacola for decades. Groner's father and brother had led the Baptist hospitals in New Orleans and Memphis. "We've not been opposed to nepotism in this organization," he explained.

After a couple of additions, by 1963 Baptist's bed count was 325, and the hospital had an outpatient surgery center and an intensive coronary care unit. In the late 1960s, the Hillhaven Convalescent Center across the street from the hospital was acquired and converted into the Specialty Care Center, a facility for mental health and substance abuse treatment.

Baptist's first capital campaign raised money for another addition in 1972, bringing the hospital to 520 beds. There were roughly 900 full-time employees, paid an average annual salary of $6,664, which was relatively generous for Florida but still less than the national average.

COMPANY PERSPECTIVES

Baptist Health Care's mission is to provide superior service based on Christian values to improve the quality of life for people and communities served. While quality in health care can be defined in many different ways, at Baptist Health Care quality means recognizing the diverse clinical needs of the customers we serve and aligning our corporate goals and objectives to continually exceed them.

According to data in *Cost Containment,* in 1964 the hospital had operating expenses of $3.1 million and payroll expenses of $2.0 million. Ten years later, these figures had increased to $12.3 million and $7.7 million. Baptist admitted 15,000 patients in 1964 and almost 20,000 in 1974.

CONTAINING COSTS

The hospital's management addressed rising healthcare costs through incentive programs in areas ranging from the operating room to the coffee shop. The program was officially launched in 1965. In a foreshadowing of things to come, in the 1970s the hospital began hosting visiting administrators eager to learn the secrets of their efficiency; this resulted in the development of a three-day workshop to present its principles of incentives. In 1974 Baptist hired consultants from the Medicus Systems Corporation to improve its methods even more.

Capital requirements rose dramatically. The hospital's budget for new equipment had been $8,000 in 1954, according to *Cost Containment.* In the mid-1970s, the hospital spent $1 million in one year to keep up with improving technology.

Baptist also faced soaring insurance premiums due to a wave of malpractice suits sweeping the industry. To save money, it shifted its coverage to a newly formed offshore carrier called Multi-Hospital Mutual Insurance Company Ltd. In 1981, following several years of growth in its insurance business, Baptist acquired American Continental Insurance Company (ACIC).

Another ancillary venture was the 1975 conversion of an apartment complex (Mallory House) into senior housing. A few years later, this was followed with construction of the Azalea Trace life care facility in 1981.

Baptist Hospital was a charter member in the Voluntary Hospitals of America cooperative which was launched in 1977. Baptist Regional Health Services began leasing the nearly defunct Jay Hospital in Santa Rosa County in 1979.

RESTRUCTURING

The parent company, Baptist Care Incorporated (BCI), was formed in 1983. In the same year Jim Vickery took over the organization from Pat Groner and Mizell Memorial Hospital became an affiliate of the group; Mizell soon underwent a massive renovation. BCI became known as Baptist Health Care Corporation (BHC) in 1989.

BHC grew through mergers and new building projects in the 1980s. It ventured into the home healthcare market and added a standalone urgent care facility. New retirement homes were added in the mid-1980s while the original hospital was expanded yet again and the Gulf Breeze Hospital built. Some of the senior-oriented facilities were expanded towards the end of the decade.

Not all plans came to fruition right away. A plan to add a satellite to BHC affiliate St. Joseph's in Tampa failed to gain the necessary approval from the state in 1986, though it was revived years later.

Originally called Baptist Hospital, the legal name had changed over the years. As the corporate structure evolved, the entity became known as Baptist Hospital Inc. (no comma), Baptist Regional Health Services, Inc., and Baptist Hospital, Inc. (with a comma). The parent Baptist Health Care Corporation was formed in 1989.

The system was reshaped through mergers and downsizing in the early 1990s. BHC teamed with Sacred Heart Hospital to run some programs of University Hospital after it was shut down. However, said future CEO Al Stubblefield, its home market of Pensacola was left with one too many hospitals. BHC then had two local rivals, and was saddled with an inconvenient location next to the worst part of town.

ENGINEERING A TURNAROUND

By the mid-1990s, the system had five hospitals, as well as a nursing home and a mental health center; it employed 5,500 people. It had also expanded its family medicine practice. In 1995, BHC's flagship, the Baptist Hospital in Pensacola, ranked as one of the worst in the country in terms of customer satisfaction.

Part of the reason was unhappy employees. Annual turnover was 33 percent. Al Stubblefield, chief operating officer at the time, set out to improve customer satisfaction by raising employee morale and focusing the

<table>
<tr><td colspan="2">

KEY DATES

■

</td></tr>
<tr><td>1951:</td><td>Baptist Hospital opens in Pensacola, Florida with about 100 beds.</td></tr>
<tr><td>1963:</td><td>An addition increases the number of beds to 325.</td></tr>
<tr><td>1969:</td><td>A neighboring nursing home is acquired to house a mental health unit.</td></tr>
<tr><td>1972:</td><td>The largest expansion to date leaves the hospital with a total of 520 beds.</td></tr>
<tr><td>1975:</td><td>Multi-Hospital Mutual Insurance Company is set up in Bermuda to avoid skyrocketing malpractice premiums.</td></tr>
<tr><td>1977:</td><td>Baptist Hospital is a charter member of the Voluntary Hospitals of America cooperative.</td></tr>
<tr><td>1981:</td><td>American Continental Insurance Company is acquired; the Azalea Trace nursing facility is built.</td></tr>
<tr><td>1992:</td><td>BHC partners with Sacred Heart Hospital to run programs of the recently closed University Hospital.</td></tr>
<tr><td>1995:</td><td>Baptist Hospital is ranked one of the worst in the country in terms of customer satisfaction.</td></tr>
<tr><td>1997:</td><td>"Baptist University" leadership development program for managers is launched.</td></tr>
<tr><td>1999:</td><td>The Baptist Healthcare Leadership Institute established.</td></tr>
<tr><td>2002:</td><td>BHC begins appearing on *Fortune*'s annual listing of "Best Companies to Work For."</td></tr>
<tr><td>2004:</td><td>BHC gets a Baldrige National Quality Award.</td></tr>
<tr><td>2005:</td><td>CEO Al Stubblefield publishes a book of BHC's organizational insights.</td></tr>
</table>

organization on service excellence. The process included soliciting employees for ideas. BHC also sent groups to benchmark other healthcare institutions across the country.

In 1997, BHC introduced a leadership development program for management dubbed "Baptist University." It used tools such as the Myers-Briggs Type Indicator (MBTI) test to accommodate work style preferences. Two years later it set up the Baptist Healthcare Leadership Institute, through its for-profit Baptist Health Ventures unit, to impart its motivational insights to other healthcare organizations. In its first few years the institute claimed to have assisted staff from 1,600 hospitals.

50TH ANNIVERSARY IN 2001

Meanwhile, Vickery retired as CEO and was replaced by Stubblefield. Also, Mizell Hospital's longstanding affiliation with BHC was terminated in 1999. In 2000, Baptist opened ambulatory care facilities in Escambia and Santa Rosa counties. The next year, the group's celebrated its fiftieth anniversary by having staff perform 50 community service projects.

Following a practice CEO Al Stubblefield observed at New York's famous Ritz-Carlton Hotel, in February 2001 BHC began mandating ten-minute daily meetings for staff. These briefings were considered the equivalent of 40 hours a year in training. *Fortune* noted BHC's employees averaged 60 hours of professional training a year in all.

BHC began appearing on *Fortune*'s "100 Best Companies to Work For" list in 2002. In other recognition, the group's Baptist Hospital Inc. unit received a Malcolm Baldrige National Quality Award in 2004.

All was not sunny. The organization was hit with three hurricanes in the space of the year. One of these, Hurricane Ivan, caused a reported $50 million worth of damage to BCH. However, most of this was covered by government and insurance funds.

BHC's revenues were $443 million in 2004, according to *Fortune;* however, Moody's reported the figure to be about $65 million less. Three facilities—Baptist Hospital, Inc. (which included Gulf Breeze Hospital), Baptist Manor (nursing home), and Lakeview Center, Inc. (mental health and substance abuse)—made up about 60 percent of total system revenues, noted Moody's in its press release. BHC had roughly 19,000 admissions a year.

Nurses were making an average of $53,000 a year. With the staff turnover rate reduced to the low teens, the six jobs BHC created during the year reportedly attracted more than 19,000 applicants, according to *Fortune.*

In 2005 CEO Al Stubblefield published a book called *The Baptist Health Care Journey to Excellence: Creating a Culture That WOWs!* At the time, BHC was looking for financing to open a $30 million sports medicine institute.

Frederick C. Ingram

PRINCIPAL SUBSIDIARIES

Baptist Health Ventures; Baptist Hospital Inc.; Baptist Manor; Baptist Medical Park; Lakeview Center.

PRINCIPAL OPERATING UNITS

Andrews Institute; Atmore Community Hospital; Baptist Hospital; Baptist Leadership Institute; Baptist Manor;

Baptist Medical Park–Navarre; Baptist Medical Park–Pensacola; Gulf Breeze Hospital; Jay Hospital; Lakeview Center; Portofino Medical Spa.

PRINCIPAL COMPETITORS

Sacred Heart Health System; West Florida Healthcare.

FURTHER READING

"The 100 Best Companies to Work For," *Fortune,* January 24, 2005, p. 72.

"Baptist Hospital Cornerstone to Be Laid Saturday," *Panama City News-Herald,* November 9, 1950, p. 3.

Consilvio, Jean, "Speedy Recoveries: Quick Turnaround on IT Help Desk Calls Boosts Employee Satisfaction at Baptist Health Care," *Computerworld,* May 26, 2003, p. 46.

"Contented Employees Mean Satisfied Customers at Baptist Health Care," *Training,* January 2005, p. 11.

"Employee-Centered Focus Sets This System Apart: 'The Best Health System in America,'" *Occupational Health Management,* March 2003, p. 32.

French, Liz, "The Show Must Go On: While Competitors Had More Money and Better Locations, Al Stubblefield Chose to Concentrate on Patient Satisfaction," *Health Executive,* October 2005, p. 27.

Groner, Pat N., *Cost Containment Through Employee Incentives Program,* Germantown, Maryland: Aspen Systems Corp., 1977.

———, "Hospital Administrative Services: How Hospitals Gain by HAS Comparison," *Hospitals, JAHA,* May 16, 1964, pp. 54–58.

"HCMR Interview: Pat N. Groner," *Health Care Management Review,* Fall 1992, p. 85.

"Health Care Organization Shares the Wealth with 'Benchmarking Days'," *HealthCare Benchmarks and Quality Improvement,* March 2003, pp. 25ff.

"Hospital Trustee Institute Meeting Said Valuable," *Panama City News,* June 16, 1953, p. 1.

"Hospital Trustees Air Problems with Panel Discussion," *Panama City News,* May 22, 1954, p. 1.

"It's All About Connection," *Training,* October 2003, p. 18.

Leering, Robert, and Milton Moskowitz, "The 100 Best Companies to Work For: In a Tough Year These Companies Tried to Do Right By Their Employees," *Fortune,* February 4, 2002, p. 72.

"Moody's Affirms A3 Rating Assigned to Baptist Hospital Inc. (Pensacola, FL) with Stable Outlook: Approximately $116 Million of Total Debt Outstanding," *Moody's Investors Service,* May 25, 2005.

Runy, Lee Ann, "The Dynamics of Satisfaction," *H&HN Hospitals & Health Networks,* November 2002, p. 57.

"St. Joseph's Has Big Plans for Hospital," *Tampa Tribune,* January 6, 2001, p. 1.

Solovy, Alden, "The Baptist Shuffle," *Hospitals & Health Networks,* April 1, 2006, p. 36.

Stubblefield, Al, *The Baptist Health Care Journey to Excellence: Creating a Culture That WOWs!* Hoboken, N.J.: John Wiley & Sons, 2005.

"Training Rx'es," *Training,* July 1, 2006.

"Within Reach: Baptist Health Care's Al Stubblefield Says Strong Commitment, and the Right Tools, Are All It Takes to Get Hospitals to a State of Enviable Customer Service," *Health Executive,* September 2005, p. 8.

Best Kosher Foods Corporation

3944 West Morgan Street
Chicago, Illinois 60609-2511
U.S.A.
Telephone: (773) 650-5900
Fax: (773) 650-5968
Web site: http://www.bests-kosher.com

Wholly Owned Subsidiary of Sara Lee Corporation
Founded: 1886
Employees: 400
Sales: $55 million (2005 est.)
NAIC: 311612 Meat Processed From Carcasses

■ ■ ■

Based in Chicago, Best Kosher Foods Corporation is a subsidiary of Sara Lee Corporation, specializing in the preparation of kosher meats, including all-beef frankfurters and sausage links, bagel dogs, deli meats, low-fat meats, meat snacks, and pickles. In order to meet Jewish dietary laws, kosher (meaning clean, fit, or proper) meat can come only from healthy split-hooved animals, including cattle, goats, sheep, and deer. They must be killed humanely and the blood drained from the forequarters of the animal (chuck, rib, navel, brisket, and shank)—the only section suitable for kosher processing. In addition, the main arteries and fats deemed unacceptable are removed. At this stage the actual koshering process begins. All traces of blood are removed by soaking the meat in water for 30 minutes, then thoroughly salting and allowing it to drain another hour before a complete rinsing. Because dairy products may not come in contact with kosher meat products, the use of milk powder as a sausage filler is forbidden. Every step of the way, from inspection of the living animal to packaging, requires full-time rabbinical supervision. Moreover, all food ingredients and manufacturing equipment must be certified as kosher. At one time, Best Kosher catered almost exclusively to Jewish customers, but the high quality of kosher meats has attracted an increasing number of non-Jewish customers.

The company's brands include Best's Kosher and Sinai 48; Oscherwitz, offering a higher standard of glatt kosher meats; and the Shofar and Sinai Kosher labels for meats that are double inspected. All Best Kosher products are made at the company's Chicago USDA-inspected plant. In addition to grocery stores and warehouse clubs, Best Kosher sells to the food service channels. Its hot dogs are especially popular in Chicago, a city known for its distinctive style of serving frankfurters. Best Kosher is, or has been, the official Kosher Hot Dog of local professional sports teams: Major League Baseball's White Sox and Cubs, the National Basketball Association's Chicago Bulls, the National Hockey League's Blackhawks, and Soldier Field, home of the National Football League's Bears. Best Kosher also exports its products to Canada and Mexico, as well as to Venezuela, Panama, Aruba, Hong Kong, and Taiwan.

COMPANY FOUNDED: 1886

Best Kosher was founded in Cincinnati in 1886 by a Jewish German immigrant named Isaac Oscherwitz, who opened a small butcher shop and began making kosher

---

COMPANY PERSPECTIVES

Today, as it has been for over 100 years, Best Kosher Foods Corporation is committed to producing the highest quality kosher meat products.

---

sausage. His five sons—Sam, Max B., Israel W., Phillip, and Harry (from eldest to youngest)—joined him as they came of age in the early years of the 1900s. Together they expanded the sausage business and sold their products throughout the Midwest. The family outgrew the small plant Isaac had established on West Sixth street in Cincinnati, and in 1909 the operations were moved four doors down the street to a newly constructed plant. Also in 1909 a partnership was established: I. Oscherwitz & Sons Co.

Isaac Oscherwitz died in 1925, the same year that his youngest sons, Harry and Philip, moved to Chicago to establish a sister company called Best's Kosher Sausage Company. The two family companies operated separately for the next 40 years, successfully negotiating the Great Depression of the 1930s and the food rationing of World War II in the early 1940s that led to meat shortages. Sam Oscherwitz died in 1925, followed by Israel in 1959. Max remained active with I. Oscherwitz & Sons until 1973 when at the age of 81 he retired. By this point a third generation was in charge, but most of Isaac Oscherwitz's grandsons sought livelihoods unconnected to meat processing. Israel's two sons, for example, became doctors, one shortening his name to Dr. Stanley Osher, and moving to Oakland, California. Harry Oscherwitz's only son also became a doctor and assumed the Osher name, Dr. Eugene Osher, as did one of Max's sons, Dr. Daniel Osher. Another of Max's sons, Millard S. Oscherwitz, followed him into the family meat business and eventually became president. He would be joined by his cousin, Philip's son, Jerry Oscherwitz.

The Cincinnati and Chicago companies mostly catered to Jewish customers, who, according to Best Kosher marketing research, accounted for three-quarters of all sales in the 1950s. In the first decades of operation in Chicago, Best Kosher focused on making hot dogs, salami, and knackwurst, but a second generation of management would change that. Millard Oscherwitz assumed the presidency, while his cousin, Jerry, nine years younger, headed the company's marketing department after earning a degree in marketing from the University of Illinois. It was the younger Oscherwitz who, in the 1950s, was responsible for pushing Best Kosher into

lunch meat packaging. Also of note, he was later responsible for McDonald's decision to add Best's hot dogs to the menu of its Japanese restaurants.

NEW HIGHWAY FORCES CINCINNATI CLOSURE: 1962

The Cincinnati and Chicago companies were forced by circumstance to join forces in 1962 when the Cincinnati meat processing plant found itself in the path of a new highway, The Mill Creek Expressway, I-75. As a result, I. Oscherwitz and Sons merged with Chicago's Best Kosher, where all meat production took place. A distribution plant was subsequently opened in Cincinnati to supply that community with the Oscherwitz products. The consolidated business operated under the Best Kosher name and continued to grow and expand its product lines. With Jerry Oscherwitz serving as the driving force, in 1972 Best Kosher, according to *Crain's Chicago Business*, "took the hot dog industry by surprise when it introduced a lower-fat frankfurter. It took that idea one step further in 1984 when it began marketing a low-fat brand with no sugar and less salt than in regular hot dogs."

Best Kosher also grew through expansion. In 1983 it merged with another Chicago business, Sinai Kosher Sausage Co. The combined company took the name of Bessin Corp. Harry Oscherwitz, well into his 80s, stayed on as chairman with nephews Millard remaining as president and Jerry serving as director. They continued the effort to introduce products that were not traditionally Jewish as a way to appeal to an increasingly non-Jewish customer base. By this point less than 40 percent of Bessin's customers were Jewish, as a growing number of non-Jewish consumers were willing to pay a higher price for kosher products because of their careful production and the use of few additives. The company introduced Italian and Polish sausages, and in 1986 went far afield to introduce kosher chili and corn beef hash. Nevertheless, hot dogs remained the company's best selling product, accounting for 30 percent of sales. Chicago, famous for its love of hot dogs, provided about 20 percent of the company's revenues. Bessin also did well with its kosher salami, trailing only Hebrew National as the top seller in this category across the country. Bessin's growth as a purveyor of national kosher brands was enhanced in the late 1980s and early 1990s by its ability to successfully sell into the growing warehouse club channels.

There were changes in the family composition of Bessin during this period. Harry Oscherwitz died at the age of 87 in 1987, followed two years later by 68-year-old Millard. Then, in November 1993, Jerry Oscherwitz died at the age of 63. By the time of Jerry's death, however, ownership of Bessin had passed out of the family's hands. In February 1993 Chicago's Sara Lee

KEY DATES

1886: Company is founded in Cincinnati by Isaac Oscherwitz.

1909: I. Oscherwitz & Sons Co. is formed.

1925: Oscherwitz family launches Best's Kosher Sausage Company in Chicago.

1962: Sister companies merge as Chicago business.

1983: Company becomes Bessin Corp. after a merger with Sinai Kosher Sausage Co.

1993: The Sara Lee Corporation acquires Bessin.

1999: Bessin is renamed as Best Kosher Foods Corporation.

Corp. acquired Bessin, and its $85 million in annual sales. The reported purchase price was in the $70 million to $100 million range. The Oscherwitz family remained involved in the running of the business, however, as William S. Oscherwitz served as Bessin's chief operating officer.

The move into processed kosher meat was hardly a surprise for Sara Lee. In the 1980s, according to *Crain's Chicago Business*, the processed meats industry was growing at a rate of less than 3 percent while Best Kosher was enjoying sales increases that exceeded 15 percent. In addition to growing sales, kosher meats also commanded a higher price, providing greater profits. At the same time Sara Lee was wooing Bessin, ConAgra Inc. and its Armour Swift-Eckrich unit announced that it was acquiring New York's National Foods Inc., the parent company of America's leading kosher meat processor, Hebrew National. With two corporate giants backing the top two kosher meat processors, the kosher category was expected to enjoy even greater growth as Sara Lee and ConAgra exerted their hefty marketing prowess to elevate kosher meats beyond niche status. Instead of being strong in urban markets with high concentrations of Jewish consumers, kosher meats began to gain acceptance with a broader range of consumers across the country.

Its new corporate parent folded Bessin into the Sara Lee Meat Group, which included such packaged meat brands as Ball Park, Bryan, Hillshire Farm, and Jimmy Dean. Bessin got off to a poor start under its new ownership, as the Chicago Rabbinical Council withdrew its approval and Bessin products were removed from supermarkets until the problem could be rectified.

With Sara Lee's backing, Bessin expanded on a number of fronts in the 1990s. The Shofar Kosher trademark was acquired in 1995 and Bessin began offer-

ing products under that label and built up distribution for Shofar Kosher on both the East Coast and West Coast. A year later Bessin launched a line of 97-percent fat-free products. While kosher meats were regarded as healthier because of their careful preparation and lack of additives, they did not necessarily contain less fat, a factor of concern for many dieters and health-conscious consumers. This new line of products was intended to appeal to these potential customers and take advantage of a national trend toward low-fat, healthier eating. The new low-fat hot dogs, salami, and bologna were packed under the Best's Kosher, Sinai Kosher, and Shofar Kosher labels.

To expand its product offerings, Bessin reintroduced the Oscherwitz brand name in 1997 for a line of fresh and cooked glatt kosher meats, including a line of sausage products. Bessin looked to take advantage of another trend with consumers: a renewed interest in meat snacks. From 1993 to 1996, the category enjoyed double-digit sales increases, according to the Snack Food Association, while food sales in general had been relatively flat since the start of the 1990s. In August 1997 Bessin introduced, under the Best's Kosher brand, Beef Salami Sticks. It enjoyed strong sales, and in February 1998 Best's Kosher added a second product, Lean Beef Jerky, a low-fat, low calorie, high in protein snack, available in both original and Teriyaki flavors. Furthermore, Bessin looked to take advantage of the long-time presence of its hot dogs at Chicago sporting events held at Comiskey Park, Wrigley Field, the United Center, and Soldier Field. The company developed a grocery-store version of these popular franks, christened Best's Kosher Sports Dogs. It became available in Chicago grocery stores in the early months of 1997.

NEW CENTURY, OLD NAME

Bessin ended the 1990s by changing its name to Best Kosher Foods Corporation. The Oscherwitz family remained very much involved, with William Oscherwitz taking over the chief executive officer position. As the new century began, the meat industry underwent changes that had the potential to impact the future of Best Kosher. Companies such as Sara Lee relied on meat packers—Tyson Foods Inc, Smithfield Foods Inc., Swift & Co., and Cargill Inc.—to supply them with raw material. The slaughtering facilities of Best Kosher were about the extent of Sara Lee's holdings in this area. The packers, meanwhile, had been consolidating, growing larger, and starting to process and market their own brands of packaged meats, which produced greater profits than raw meat. In effect, the packers were becoming competitors to the likes of Sara Lee and Kraft, which were strong on branding but lacked meat-packing assets.

As a result, it appeared that these companies would either have to sell out to a meat-packer or align themselves with one. *Crain's Chicago Business* in a 2004 article quoted industry analyst Timothy Ramey, who commented, "What has historically been a 10% margin business for Sara Lee could easily start to erode." He added, "Every pound of meat Smithfield processes themselves is a pound Sara Lee can't sell." Nevertheless, Sara Lee indicated that it had no intention of exiting the meat business, which was continuing to grow and accounted for 21 percent of the company's $19.6 billion in sales in fiscal 2004. But in November 2004, Sara Lee executives were telling the press that while they planned to remain in the packaged meat business they might concentrate their efforts on a select number of brands, in particular Jimmy Dean, Ball Park, and Hillshire Farm. According to *Crain's Chicago Business*, this left uncertain the future of Best Kosher.

Best Kosher was still in the Sara Lee fold in 2005 when Hebrew National encountered problems with a new processing plant that resulted in curtailed production and shortages of kosher meats on the market. Best Kosher and other rivals rushed in to take advantage of the situation and gain market share at their rival's expense. In 2006 Sara Lee was pursuing a strategy of building its packaged meats business, looking to grow sales by about 5 percent by 2010, part of a greater effort to grow Sara Lee. Where Best Kosher fit into those plans was uncertain, but there was no indication that Sara Lee planned to sell the business.

Ed Dinger

PRINCIPAL COMPETITORS

Hebrew National; Empire National; International Glatt Kosher Inc.

FURTHER READING

Commins, Patricia, "Going Kosher: Marketing Giants Eye Mass Audience," *Crain's Chicago Business,* February 15, 1993, p. 4.

Jargon, Julie, "Must Kraft, Sara Lee Go Meatless?," *Crain's Chicago Business,* October 11, 2004, p. 3.

"Meat Firm, in Path of X-Way, To Merge With Chicago Concern," *Cincinnati Post Times Star,* January 29, 1962, p. 3.

Reyes, Sonia, "Shortage Prompts Rivals to Dog Hebrew National," *Brandweek,* February 21, 2005, p. 11.

Slutsker, Gary, "The Naked Truth," *Forbes,* August 16, 1993, p. 94.

Snyder, David, "Best Spicing Up Kosher Menu With Chili Debut," *Crain's Chicago Business,* March 3, 1996, p. 8.

Stewart, Janet Kidd, "Appetite Growing for Food That's Kosher," *Chicago Sun-Times,* May 6, 1997, p. 43.

Blue Ridge Beverage
Company Inc.

———————■———————

4446 Barley Drive
Salem, Virginia 24153-8542
U.S.A.
Telephone: (540) 380-2000
Web site: http://www.blueridgebeverage.com

Private Company
Founded: 1938
Employees: 250
Sales: $180 million (2004)
NAIC: 424810 Beer and Ale Merchant Wholesalers;
    424820 Wine and Distilled Alcoholic Beverage
    Merchant Wholesalers

■ ■ ■

A private company based in Salem, Virginia, Blue Ridge Beverage Company Inc. is one of the largest wholesale beverage distributors in the state of Virginia, selling a wide variety of beers, wine, soft drinks, and bottled water to more than 3,500 customers in 36 counties in southwestern, central, and southern Virginia. The company's four warehouses are located in Salem, Waynesboro, Lynchburg, and South Boston, Virginia. Blue Ridge is an authorized distributor of the Miller Brewing Company, a relationship that has been in place since the early 1950s, and one that has been the lifeblood of the company. In addition, Blue Ridge offers a wide range of imported beer brands, including Becks, Corona, Fosters, Grolsch, Molson, and Sapporo. Blue Ridge also always carries the products of Miller's Plank Road Brewery; micro craft brews from the likes of Samuel Ad-

ams, Rolling Rock, and Sierra Nevada; and malt alternatives such as Twisted Tea, Mikes Hard Lemonade, and the Hoopers Hooch products. Blue Ridge prides itself on an extensive portfolio of wines, which includes fine wines from around the world and California, as well as wines from Virginia and North Carolina. Blue Ridge also sells sparkling wine and champagne, fortified and dessert wines, table wines, kosher wines, non-alcoholic wines, coolers, and hard ciders. The company distributes bottled water, primarily Evian and Perrier, soft drinks such as RC Cola, Diet-Rite, 7-Up, Canada Dry, Hires, and Nehi; and the Arizona and Mistic brands of ready-to-drink tea products. Blue Ridge also sells new age beverages as well as miscellaneous beverages like Orangina, Stewart's specialty sodas, and Yoo Hoo chocolate drink. Furthermore, Blue Ridge offers a variety of services to its customers, including customized wait staff training, wine list consulting, and party planning assistance. Blue Ridge is owned and operated by the Archer family.

POST-PROHIBITION ROOTS

While the United States outlawed the consumption of alcoholic beverages in 1919, Virginia imposed its own Prohibition three years earlier, and in Salem, Virginia, alcohol had been outlawed since 1893. Virginia's prohibition was far from a successful effort, however, due to neighboring "wet" states, and it proved even more problematic because of Virginia's long coastline that made smuggling easy. Moreover, in the mountainous region of Southwest Virginia, especially in Franklin, County, adjacent to Salem, there was a tradition of "moonshining," the illegal distillation of alcohol in hidden makeshift stills. Even when Prohibition went into

COMPANY PERSPECTIVES

Blue Ridge Beverage Company's successful growth strategy and strong competitive position are directly attributable to the quality of its employees. Without experienced, hard-working and dedicated individuals, none of the Company's achievements would be possible.

effect around the country, Virginia had to contend with neighboring Maryland, which was notorious for not enforcing Prohibition, reasoning that enforcement of a Federal law was the Federal government's responsibility. It was not surprising that by 1933 Virginia, like the rest of the country, was eager to repeal Prohibition. In 1934 Virginia established the Department of Alcoholic Beverage Control and many of the state's breweries that had been forced to close in the 1910s were reopened and began to produce beer once again, albeit with a lower alcohol content of 3.2 percent. Demand for legalized beer and spirits led to the creation of distributorships and wholesale operations across the country. It was no different in the Roanoke area, which included Salem, even though Franklin County moonshiners continued to ply their trade. The Blue Ridge Beverage Company was founded in 1938 as a small wholesaler of beer and soft drinks to the Roanoke valley.

Fifteen years later, in 1953, the company took a major step forward when it became a Miller Brewing Company distributor. In business in Wisconsin since 1855 when a German immigrant bought the Plank Road Brewery (now the name of the company's craft beers), Miller did not expand beyond its regional status until the years following World War II, when the founder's grandson took the helm. By 1952 Miller products became available in all 48 states as well as Hawaii. In many ways, Blue Ridge Beverage would hitch its wagon to Miller's rising star.

The Archer's family involvement with Blue Ridge dated to 1958 when James M. Archer, Jr., moved to Salem with his wife Regine. He came from the Virginia town of Saltville, which, not surprisingly, was a major salt producer. It had served as the main supplier to the South in the Civil War. His wife, on the other hand, had been born in Belgium and because of their Jewish heritage she and her family was forced to live under assumed names during the occupation of Belgium by Nazi Germany. The war also brought her into contact with James Archer, who was serving in the United States

military. The two were wed in 1945, she came to the United States with him, and together they ran Blue Ridge Beverage, buying into the business in 1958 and becoming full owners in 1960.

Under the management of the Archers, Blue Ridge enjoyed steady expansion, both in terms of markets and product offerings. The company began selling wine in 1961 when it was able to pick up the franchised rights of a distributor from Alexandria, Virginia, that was abandoning the Roanoke market. Beer remained the backbone of Blue Ridge's business, however, and the company continued to benefit from the growth of Miller, which by 1968 had become the eighth largest brewer in the United States. When it was acquired by the Phillip Morris Corporation a year later, Miller took advantage of the deep pockets of its new corporate parent to launch highly successful national marketing campaigns to build awareness of the Miller brand and support the launch of new products, such as the popular seven-ounce "pony bottle." There was also the highly successful Miller Light launch, supported by countless commercials anchored by former athletes taking sides over the seemingly unsolvable question: was Miller Lite good because it was less filling or because it just tasted great? While the answer was hashed out in a myriad of permutations, Miller Brewing rose to become America's second largest brewer, trailing only Anheuser-Busch. As the distributor of Miller products in the Roanoke Valley, Blue Ridge shared in the success of the brewer.

JAMES ARCHER DIES SUDDENLY: 1972

In 1972 James Archer died suddenly at the age of 51, the result of a heart attack. His wife assumed the presidency of Blue Ridge, assisted by their son, Robert A. Archer. Born in 1947 in Saltville like his father, the younger Archer also served in the military. After graduating from Virginia Tech with a degree in marketing in 1969 he served in Vietnam with the 82nd Airborne until early 1972 and remained in the U.S. Army Reserves until eventually retiring as a colonel in 1999. When he came back from the war to help his mother, Blue Ridge Beverage was still a small business, employing just ten people. This situation would soon change, however, as the family business—which was becoming one of the leading distributors for Miller Brewing—enjoyed strong growth, thanks to its top supplier. In addition, more members of the Archer family became involved, until four of the children of James and Regine Archer held top positions at Blue Ridge.

In a matter of five years, employment increased to more than 30, and included the youngest of the Archer children, Paul, who took over as operations manager in

KEY DATES

1938: The Blue Ridge Beverage Company is founded.
1953: A Miller Brewing distributorship is added.
1958: James and Regine Archer acquire the company.
1972: James Archer dies and is succeeded by his wife as president.
1984: The Archer family acquires the Cavalier Beverage Company.
1985: New company headquarters and a new warehouse open.
1997: Blue Ridge and Cavalier merge.
2002: Regine Archer steps down as president.

1975. Having outgrown its warehouse space, Blue Ridge also opened a new facility just outside of Salem. It, too, was soon overwhelmed by a surge in business, and just two years later the company expanded its new facilities. Blue Ridge also began investing in technology, introducing computers to handle accounting and inventory chores and becoming the first area distributor to take orders with new hand-held computers.

Blue Ridge expanded on a number of fronts in the 1980s. To keep pace the business opened a new warehouse in 1985, a 78,000-square-foot structure that would become home to the company's present-day headquarters. Another Archer sibling, James E. Archer, joined the family business in 1983. He also graduated from Virginia Tech, earning a degree in industrial engineering, and then joined the Army. While on an Army fellowship he earned a master's degree in business administration at Emory University and then went on to serve in Germany. When he came home, Blue Ridge was too small to employ another family member, and so he went to work for Corning Glass in Pennsylvania. In the early 1980s he decided to return home to Salem and thought about starting his own engineering consulting firm, but because of the strong growth at Blue Ridge, joining the family business was a viable option. He took over as marketing manager and spearheaded the effort to broaden the distributor's product lines. He oversaw the addition of imported beers and a broader slate of wines. The wine business was greatly enhanced in 1987 with the acquisition of a Roanoke Valley rival, picking up its portfolio of brands to effectively double Blue Ridge's wine business. Blue Ridge also grew its soft drink offerings, adding bottled water like Evian and Perrier, and new age beverages from Snapple, Arizona, and Mistic that were becoming popular with consumers.

Miller products continued to be the heart of Blue Ridge's business, however, and the Archer family built upon this foundation in the 1980s through acquisitions. In 1984 the Archers bought Charlottesville, Virginia-based Cavalier Beverage Company, to add a second Miller distributorship, and dispatched Paul Archer to run the new business as general manager. Four years later, Cavalier made an acquisition of its own, adding a Miller distributor located in Harrisonburg, Virginia.

SISTER COMPANIES MERGE: 1997

Both Blue Ridge and Cavalier continued to expand their territories and broaden their product mix in the 1990s. In 1996, Cavalier acquired the RC Cola franchise and began distributing Canada Dry products, Hawaiian Punch drinks, and Snapple ice tea products. In that same year, Blue Ridge also gained a local 7-Up franchise. Several months later, in June 1997, sister company Cavalier was merged into Blue Ridge to create a larger, leaner operation. It would then add to its core Miller Brewing business by acquiring distributorships in Danville and Keysville, Virginia. Then, in February 1998, Blue Ridge added Lynchburg, Virginia, to the markets for which it held the rights to distribute Miller products.

Blue Ridge was a much larger operation now, employing more than 250, a far cry from the ten-person business it was when James Archer passed away. It required an experienced person to serve as the chief financial officer, and the family was fortunate to have such a person in the family, the youngest daughter, Jackie, who had spent the previous 11 years working in the banking industry in Chicago.

In 2002 Regine Archer, approaching 80 years of age, stepped down as president of Blue Ridge and turned over the post to her son Robert. Nevertheless, she stayed on as chairwoman of the company. In 2005 her efforts in growing the business after losing her husband were recognized when she was inducted into the Junior Achievement of Southwest Virginia's hall of fame, becoming only the second woman to receive the honor. Even as she was stepping back her involvement with the family business, Blue Ridge was continuing to grow. The company was especially active in supporting new Virginia wineries, representing ten of them. It was also looking to add other new products, such as Hooper's Hooch and its popular alcoholic lemon brew, and over beverages. Nevertheless, it was the distribution of Miller Brewing products that remained the foundation of the business and key to its ongoing growth.

Ed Dinger

PRINCIPAL COMPETITORS

PA Short Distributing; Valley Distributing Corporation.

FURTHER READING

Adams, Duncan, "Archer Heads Va. Chamber of Commerce," *Roanoke Times,* February 5, 2004, p. C8.

————, "Survivor of Nazi Germany Honored," *Roanoke Times,* January 21, 2005, p. C8.

Carter, Emily Paine, "Tech Grad Becomes Major General," *Roanoke Times,* March 3, 2005, p. 2.

Bourbon Corporation

—◼—

4-2-14 Matsunami
Kashiwazaki,
Japan
Telephone: (81) 0257 23 2333
Fax: (81) 0257 22 2005
Web site: http://www.bourbon.co.jp

Public Company
Incorporated: 1924 as Kitanihon Seika
Employees: 2,790
Sales: ¥91.79 billion ($806.6 million) (2005)
Stock Exchanges: Tokyo
Ticker Symbol: 2208
NAIC: 311821 Cookie and Cracker Manufacturing; 311320 Chocolate and Confectionery Manufacturing from Cacao Beans; 311330 Confectionery Manufacturing from Purchased Chocolate; 311340 Non-Chocolate Confectionery Manufacturing

◼◼◼

Bourbon Corporation is a major Japanese producer of candy, confectionery, snacks, beverages, bottled water, and other food products. The company's product range includes rice crackers, bean snacks, wheat crackers, tea-based soft drinks, and fresh and frozen deserts. Approximately two-thirds of the company's sales, which neared ¥92 billion ($800 million) in 2005, come through the company's Biscuit division, which includes its cookie, candy, chocolate, and bean snack product lines. The rice cracker division adds 28 percent, while beverages, water, cocoa, tea, and chewing gum combine for 5 percent of group sales. Bourbon distributes its products under a variety of brand names, including Bonbure, Veneti, Sepiart, Chotos, Mini Bit, Paribre, Cres, and Petit. The company has increasingly targeted the fast-growing "healthy snack" market in Japan, and operates a research and development facility that focuses on producing foods that promote health and help to prevent disease. Bourbon operates through 11 manufacturing subsidiaries throughout Japan. Listed on the Tokyo Stock Exchange, Bourbon was founded in 1924 by Kichizo Yoshida and is led by President Yasushi Yoshida.

FILLING A CONFECTIONERY GAP IN 1924

Bourbon Corporation was founded in the aftermath of the Great Kanto Earthquake, which, in 1923, had destroyed much of Tokyo, Yokohama, and other heavily populated areas in the Kanto plain region of Japan. More than 100,000 people were killed in the earthquake, which was measured at as high as 8.4 on the Richter scale at its epicenter. The earthquake, and the rioting and looting that followed, also had destroyed a great deal of Tokyo's industry as well, and many goods remained in short supply for some time afterward. These shortages were felt particularly strongly in Japan's rural areas.

The confectionery industry was already an important part of Japanese life in the 1920s. Among those hit hard by the disruption in confectionery production and delivery was the well-known Mogamiya, a Japanese-style confectionery shop in Kashiwazaki, in Niigata Prefecture. In order to supply the Mogamiya

COMPANY PERSPECTIVES

"Resonance" is our watchword, and we at Bourbon aim to contribute to society by enhancing our customers' physical and mental well-being and the lives of their families through our original, high-value products and services, which are responsive to changes in consumers' basic needs and lifestyles. Moreover, we have added the concept of enjoyment to our basic principles of promoting health and ensuring safety, convenience, and affordability.

store, as well as other stores in the area, Kichizo Yoshida decided to set up his own factory to launch mass production of Mogamiya's biscuits and other confectionery. In 1924, Yoshida established a new company, Kitanihon Seika, which set up operations next to the city's railroad station that year.

Before long, Kitanihon Seika became Yoshida's main business, and the company began expanding its range of products. In 1925, for example, the company began production of Japanese-style candies. The fast-rising demand for the company's products led it to increase its production capacity. In 1927, the company doubled its biscuit production capacity, and also added a second candy line. Into the early 1930s, the company extended its range to include other candies and confectionery, including chewing gum and candy cigarettes, and by the end of the decade had begun producing rice crackers, miso powder, and sweeteners. The company also began supplying the Tokyo market during this time. In 1933, the company launched direct sales in Tokyo, opening its own retail store.

The Japanese war effort prompted the company to develop more diversified operations during the war, with the addition of livestock farming and fishing operations, and a new subsidiary, Kitanihon Shoji Corporation, founded in 1940. By 1942, all of the company's production had been converted to wartime supplies. It was only in 1945 that the company was granted permission to return to its civilian production, at which time the company began producing flour and crackers. By the end of the 1940s, the company had added food items such as baby biscuits, soy sauce, and caramel.

GOING PUBLIC IN 1954

Kitanihon changed its name to Kitanihon Shokuhin Kogyo Corporation in 1952, then went public in 1954,

listing its shares on the Niigata Stock Exchange. The company continued adding new products through the decade, such as candy confetti and "China Marble" candies. In the late 1950s, Kitanihon invested in expanding its production capacity. The addition of the company's first biscuit band oven in 1957 was a particularly significant moment, enabling the company to begin continuous production of its popular biscuits. In 1963, Kitanihon opened a new factory in Arahama, near Kashiwazaki. That facility also became the site of the company's headquarters in 1968.

In another expansion, the company added an automated rice cracker production line in 1966, becoming the first in Japan to do so. The company added several new product categories through the 1960s, including Haroromo style crackers and white crackers. In 1962, the company filled a gap in its production when it launched its own line of confectionery based on beans—a traditionally important confectionery ingredient in Japan.

Kitanihon began building a national presence in the 1960s as well. In 1967, the company opened an office in Tokyo, which was shortly followed by the end of the decade by offices in Osaka, Nagoya, Kobe, and Yokohama. The company also built new factories, in Maki in 1969, in Ogata in 1973, and in Wajima in 1975. The expanded production helped support the launch of one of the company's most successful products ever, the Lumonde waferlike cookies, introduced in 1974. The new product helped double the group's sales in just a year, to more than ¥50 billion by the end of 1975, compared with the company's revenues at the start of the decade at just ¥8 billion. Part of the credit for the group's strong growth was a restructuring of its operations, launched in 1971. By 1976, the company had expanded its network to more than 60 offices across the country. That figure was raised to 100 offices by the end of the decade.

With its expanded presence and increasing demand, Kitanihon invested in new production facilities at the start of the 1980s, building a factory in Tsukigata in 1981. This was followed by the construction of the company's Murakami factory in 1989. During this period, the company launched a number of successful brands, including its award-winning Pikkara crackers, and other sweet cracker brands, such as Cheese Okaki, Elise, and Ajigonomi.

HEALTHY IDENTITY FOR THE NEW CENTURY

The year 1989 marked another major milestone in the company's history when Kitanihon merged with another

KEY DATES

1924: Kichizo Yoshida founds a confectionery factory, Kitanihon Seika, in order to ensure supply to the Kashiwazaki market.

1952: The company name is changed to Kitanihon Shokuhin Kogyo Corporation.

1954: The company lists shares on the Niigata Stock Exchange.

1966: An automated rice cracker production line, the first in Japan, is added.

1974: The launch of Lumonde cookies helps double the company's sales in just one year.

1989: The company acquires the Bourbon confectionery brand and changes the company name to Bourbon Corporation.

1995: Bourbon launches diversification into food and beverage production, including the first bottled mineral waters.

1996: Yasushi Yoshida takes over as company president and leads diversification into healthful foods and snack production.

2000: Bourbon lists shares on the Tokyo Stock Exchange.

2004: The company launches a tomato-based biscuit as part of a drive to introduce nutritional foods.

2005: Company sales near ¥92 billion ($800 million).

popular confectionery brand, Bourbon. As a result the enlarged company adopted the Bourbon name as its own. Bourbon then entered a new confectionery market that year, launching production of its High Chocolate line of chocolate confectionery products.

Bourbon built a new factory in Haguro in 1993. The expanded production helped support that company's move into a new product category, wheat flour crackers, the following year. At the same time, Bourbon laid plans to expand beyond the confectionery market. The aging of the Japanese population, which could be expected inevitably to lead to a decline in candy and confectionery sales, had nonetheless stimulated the growth of a new market devoted to healthful and health-promoting foods. Bourbon's entry into this segment came in 1995, when the company launched its own brand of mineral water, as well as its Alkaline brand of ionized water. Marketed as healthful alternatives, the launch of the group's bottled waters coincided with the Kobe earthquake of that year.

In response, the company's initial production, launched that same day, was shipped immediately to the Kobe region as part of the relief effort. In another product extension in the mid-1990s, the company, which traditionally had remained focused on the snack categories, added its first dessert products.

A new generation, under Yashushi Yoshida, took over at the head of the company in 1996, and stepped up the group's product diversification. In that year, for example, the company began selling cocoa powder; the following year, the company began marketing its own tea brands. Closing out the decade, the company added a new subsidiary, Reman Seika Co., in 1998. In 2000 Bourbon added its shares listing to the Tokyo Stock Exchange's secondary market.

Into the middle of the 2000s, Bourbon continued its effort to expand its development of healthful snacks. The company became caught up, however, in the controversy surrounding genetically modified foods. In 2002, for example, the company was among those forced to recall their potato-based snacks after becoming tainted with the genetically manipulated New Leaf Plus potato variety. That year, as well, the company was forced to recall some 19 products that had become contaminated with unauthorized flavoring ingredients.

Despite these setbacks, Bourbon's sales remained high, nearing ¥92 billion ($800 million) by 2006. The company also had made progress in its development of health-promoting foods. In 2004, for example, the company began marketing a new line of tomato-based cookies—the presence of lycopene, found in condensed tomato paste, enabled the company to label the new snack as a nutritional product. Bourbon's determination to build a healthful identity promised robust growth in the increasingly health-conscious Japanese market.

M. L. Cohen

PRINCIPAL SUBSIDIARIES

Bonbisco Co., Ltd.; Kitanihon Haguro Shok Co. Ltd.; Kitanihon Maki Shokuhin Co., Ltd.; Kitanihon Murakami Shokuhin Co., Ltd.; Kitanihon Ogata Shokuhin Co., Ltd.; Kitanihon Tsukigata Shokuhin Co., Ltd.; Kitanihon Washima Shokuhin Co., Ltd.; Nishikan Beika Co., Ltd.

PRINCIPAL COMPETITORS

Japan Tobacco Inc.; Yamazaki Baking Company Ltd.; Morinaga Milk Industry Company Ltd.; Warabeya Nichiyo Company Ltd.; Ezaki Glico Co. Ltd.; Kameda Seika Company Ltd.; First Baking Company Ltd.; Nakamuraya Company Ltd.; Imuraya Confectionery Company Ltd.; Morozoff Ltd.; Kotobuki Seika Company Ltd.

FURTHER READING

"Bourbon Corporation to Add Niigata-Based Confectioner As Its Special Subsidiary," *Reuters Key Development,* March 31, 2006.

"Illegal Flavouring Agents Prompt Food Recall," *Dairy Reporter.com,* April 6, 2002.

Jae, Hur, "Japan's Snack Recalls Exacerbate Biotech Fuss," *Reuters News Service,* June 25, 2001.

"Japan Confectioner to Stop GMO Sweetener Use," *Food & Drink Weekly,* June 19, 2000.

"Tomato Cookies," *Food Engineering & Ingredients,* December 2004, p. 21.

WORLD'S LARGEST CHRISTMAS STORE

Bronner Display & Sign Advertising, Inc.

25 Christmas Lane
P.O. Box 176
Frankenmuth, Michigan 48734
U.S.A.
Telephone: (989) 652-9931
Toll Free: (800) 255-9327
Fax: (989) 652-3466
Web site: http://www.bronners.com

Private Company
Incorporated: 1945
Employees: 530 (2006)
Sales: $28 million (2004 est.)
NAIC: 453220 Gift, Novelty, and Souvenir Stores; 327215 Glass Product Manufacturing Made of Purchased Glass; 335129 Other Lighting Equipment Manufacturing; 339999 All Other Miscellaneous Manufacturing

■■■

Bronner Display & Sign Advertising, Inc., operates Bronner's Christmas Wonderland, the largest Christmas-themed store in the world. Open 361 days each year, the Frankenmuth, Michigan, retail outlet offers more than 50,000 different ornaments, trims, lights, and gifts as well as large-scale decorations for use by shopping centers and municipalities. More than 2 million people visit Bronner's each year, and the firm also wholesales to smaller stores and sells its goods through mail-order catalogs and a Web site. The family-owned company is run by the children of founder Wally Bronner, who continues to serve as its chairman.

BEGINNINGS

Bronner's origins date to the 1940s, when teenager Wallace "Wally" Bronner founded a sign-painting business in his parents' basement in Frankenmuth, Michigan. Bronner started working as a clerk at his aunt's grocery store at the age of 12, and then began painting signs at 16. Upon graduation from high school in 1945 he went into business full-time, making signs and creating window displays for commercial accounts in Frankenmuth and nearby towns.

Bronner's first major Christmas-related assignment came in 1951, when several merchants in Clare, Michigan, asked him to produce decorations for lampposts. The work gained him notice, and Bronner and his lone employee soon found themselves busy creating Christmas decorations for other cities, shopping centers, and stores.

In 1952 Bronner rented temporary quarters in Frankenmuth to display his signs and decorations, and the response was so strong that he decided to build a permanent location there. In 1954 his father, a stonemason, built a new showroom on land owned by his mother's family.

The town of Frankenmuth (population 4,000) had been founded in 1845 by Lutheran missionaries from Bavaria, and its older residents still spoke a 19th century version of the German Bayerish dialect. Though known locally for this heritage and the German-style chicken dinners served at its restaurants, most visitors stopped

---

COMPANY PERSPECTIVES

The Bronner motto is "Enjoy CHRISTmas, It's His Birthday; Enjoy LIFE, It's His Way."

there because it was located on a busy state highway between the larger cities of Flint and Saginaw. When a new interstate superhighway that bypassed Frankenmuth was completed in the late 1950s, several local businessmen put their heads together to find ways to lure customers back to the town. With guidance from Wally Bronner, a Chicago architect, and members of the Zehnder family (who operated one of the most popular restaurants), Frankenmuth began to make itself over as a "quaint" Bavarian-style town.

Meanwhile, Wally Bronner's sign-painting business continued to grow, and he also began to sell Christmas decorations for homes. In 1960 a mail-order catalog and personalized gift items were introduced, and three years later the company's building was expanded.

In 1966 a second location was opened in the former Frankenmuth Bank Building. Dubbed Bronner's Tannenbaum Shop, it featured items for the home like glass ornaments, lights, artificial Christmas trees, garlands, and wreaths. A third location was added in 1971 when the closed Hubinger Grocery store was bought from the family of Bronner's wife Irene and renamed Bronner's Bavarian Corner.

BRONNER'S CHRISTMAS WONDERLAND OPENS IN 1977

Business continued to grow each year, and the firm's three stores soon began to require doormen on fall weekends to control crowds. Urged on by his wife, Wally Bronner decided to consolidate operations into a single new building on 45 acres of farmland south of town, and in 1977 Bronner's Christmas Wonderland opened at 25 Christmas Lane. The firm capitalized the first half of the word "Christmas" to emphasize the fact that, despite the many Santa Claus decorations and other non-religious products offered, its devout Lutheran owner recognized the birth of Jesus Christ as the central reason for celebrating the holiday. The company also enclosed a religious tract in each bag and mail order shipment, and Wally Bronner himself served as an elder in his church and frequently spoke to groups around the state about his faith.

As the retail business grew, the company's sign-

making unit, which had become known as Bronner Screen Printing, receded into the background. With the development of the membrane switch printing technology in the early 1980s, it became Memtron Technologies, and in 1984 Bronner sold the business to the unit's long-time manager Don Fischer and his wife.

By the mid-1980s Bronner's was offering more than 30,000 decorative trim items and gifts, which ranged in price from less than $1 to $11,000 for a life-size ceramic Hummel figure. With a retail showroom that featured 260 decorated trees and hundreds of animated figures, and with the half-mile long Christmas Lane illuminated with thousands of lights, the company paid $150 for electricity each day. The firm had also introduced an annual dated ornament series and begun personalizing ornaments with a team of artisans by this time. To keep up with escalating demand, in 1991 Bronner's doubled the size of its retail space.

"SILENT NIGHT" CHAPEL ADDED IN 1992

In 1992 Wally Bronner built a full-scale replica of a chapel in Obendorf, Salzburg, Austria, that had been constructed to honor the Christmas song "Silent Night," which was first performed there. Dedicated that November, the distinctive octagonal building housed religious artifacts from Germany as well as plaques with the song's lyrics in dozens of languages. It was illuminated brightly at night and featured audio recordings of "Silent Night" both inside and out.

The more than 2,000 busloads of tourists arriving each year had made Frankenmuth one of the top ten bus tour destinations in the U.S., and the town was also home to two of the ten largest restaurants in the country, both operated by the Zehnder family. Bronner's was selling 580,000 ornaments, 520,000 feet of garland, 75,000 light sets, and 130,000 post cards to nearly 2 million customers annually. Other offerings included collectible figurines, Nativity sets, and Bibles in 30 different languages. Half of the goods were priced at $10 and under, with the typical customer spending between $20 and $40.

With Bronner's business tied to a single holiday, it followed a changing schedule throughout the year. During the first several months buyers traveled the U.S. and Europe looking for new products, and during the spring and summer shipments began arriving as the company built up stock for the busy Christmas shopping season. Sales were slow but steady during late winter and spring and then increased with the start of Michigan's summer tourist season, peaking Thanksgiving weekend (when 50,000 customers filled the store) and in the remaining

KEY DATES

1945: 18-year-old Wally Bronner founds a sign painting company in Michigan.
1954: The company's first permanent location selling Christmas decorations is built.
1960: Catalog sales begin.
1966: Bronner buys the Frankenmuth Bank building and opens the Tannenbaum Shop.
1971: The Hubinger Grocery becomes Bronner's Bavarian Corner.
1977: Company operations are consolidated at new Bronner's Christmas Wonderland store.
1984: The sign-painting and screen-printing unit is sold to management.
1991: A new addition doubles the size of the store.
2002: The company's facilities are expanded to a total of 320,000 square feet.

days before Christmas. No matter what the season patrons could always buy Christmas ornaments, and Bronner's stocked a limited supply of items for other holidays as well.

Though the focus was on its retail store, the firm also distributed 1 million printed catalogs, wholesaled merchandise to more than 1,000 retailers worldwide, and operated a commercial division that sold displays to cities and shopping malls. Bronner's employed a year-round staff of 250 that was supplemented in the fall and winter with seasonal workers to top 400. Sales for 1995 were estimated at more than $20 million.

The company's success was due in no small part to Wally Bronner's marketing skills and canny use of advertising. In addition to relying on direct mail, the firm also rented more than 70 highway billboards in Michigan and other states to promote "The World's Largest Christmas Store," with the furthest-distant one located near Orlando, Florida, on I-75, the interstate freeway which passes close to Frankenmuth more than 1100 miles northward.

WEB SITE DEBUTS IN 1997

To capitalize on its existing mail-order operation, in 1997 Bronner's added a Web site designed by its in-house graphics department. It was strictly informational at first, but the following year a limited number of items were offered for sale. Creation of the site had been spearheaded by the Bronners' eldest son Wayne, and in

early 1998 the 45-year-old was named president and CEO of the company, with Wally continuing as board chairman. His wife Irene was also on the board, with two of their three other children serving as vice presidents and their spouses and children involved as well. Though he had relinquished a day-to-day management role, founder Wally Bronner continued to be the firm's public face, clad in his trademark outfit that included a red blazer, colorful suspenders and tie, and a button that simply read, "Originator."

The firm's growing reputation brought it business from around the world and from a few high-profile customers. In 1976 movie legend John Wayne called to order a Santa Claus suit for a television appearance, and in the early 1990s the company began boosting efforts to market goods to filmmakers, with the producers of holiday-themed movies like *Jingle All The Way* and *The Grinch* using Bronner's to supply set decorations. Other clients ranged from NBC's "Saturday Night Live" to makers of television commercials. In 1999 Laura Bush, wife of then-presidential candidate George Bush, also visited Bronner's and left with ornaments engraved with family members' names.

In 2000 the firm began construction of a new $3 million, 37,000-square-foot addition to its shipping department, which was already so large that employees used bicycles to navigate it. The expansion included two 1,900-square-foot bins for storing foam "peanuts," which were used to pack some 4,000 orders per day by a staff of 60 in peak season. The company also had 17 employees who added personalization to ornaments, a shop where fiberglass outdoor decorations were custom-painted and refurbished, and a telephone call center with a staff of more than 15 operators on two shifts to take calls during the business hours of all U.S. time zones. Orders from the 1.75 million catalogs mailed out and the firm's expanded Web site had grown by 50 percent the year before to make up 8 percent of total sales.

While combined mail-order and retail sales accounted for 85 percent of revenues, the firm also continued to wholesale products to smaller shops; supply decorations to commercial accounts like cities, shopping centers, and churches; and produce custom-decorated ornaments for use in fundraisers. By this time the third most popular tourist destination in Michigan, Bronner's sales were estimated at between $27 and $30 million per year.

The exuberant Wally Bronner enjoyed his success, and had long sought ways to share his good fortune with others. In 1965 he and his wife founded the Walter and Irene Bronner Foundation, which annually made some 400 grants to organizations like the United Way, the Salvation Army, and the Saginaw Community Foundation. In 2000 the Bronners also donated $1 million to build a 500-seat auditorium at Frankenmuth High School.

RETAIL SPACE EXPANDED IN 2002

In 2001 the firm began a $7 million addition that would increase its total building size to 320,000 square feet. Completed in May of 2002, the work boosted the retail salesroom to 92,000 square feet. The store had 33 checkout lanes and a parking lot that could hold 1,250 cars and 50 tour buses. Despite the U.S. economic downturn after the September 11 terrorist attacks, Bronner's sales were continuing to increase as Americans returned to traditional themes of family and patriotism. For its part, the company added new items like a patriotic-themed tree ornament and Santa Claus suit.

Bronner's extensive outdoor displays were sometimes a tempting target for vandals, typically local high school or college students, and in July of 2002 $10,000 worth of damage was caused to fiberglass statues near the store. It was one of the worst in a long string of such incidents, most of them minor.

In 2003 small additions were made to the store's south entrance and checkout area which enabled Bronner's shoppers to use shopping carts for the first time. Two years later the firm supplied ornaments for the debut episode of ABC reality television program "Extreme Makeover: Wedding Edition," and on Christmas Day of 2005 ABC-TV's "Good Morning America" aired a segment taped at Bronner's.

The firm's 2.1-acre retail store boasted 350 decorated trees, 500 nativity scenes, 700 animated figures, and nearly 100,000 individual lights, resulting in an electric bill that averaged $900 per day. The company was sending out more than 3 million catalogs and shipping 100,000 packages each year, and its retail offerings included a huge selection of decorative figures, lights and trims; dozens of Santa Claus suits; 150 different nutcrackers; extensive collections of Hummel and Precious Moments figurines; and 6,000 styles of ornaments, half of which were designed in-house. Founder Wally Bronner continued to greet visitors at the store, where a two-minute shower of soap-flake "snow" fell at the main entrance every half hour.

More than 60 years after the company's founding, the Bronner's Christmas Wonderland store of Bronner Display and Sign Advertising, Inc., had become the leading retail outlet of its type in the world. Tied to a holiday that was celebrated by Christians, some members of other faiths, and even the non-religious, the firm continued to expand its eye-popping showroom and grounds, extensive inventory, and service offerings each year, with no end in sight.

Frank Uhle

PRINCIPAL COMPETITORS

Wal-Mart Stores, Inc.; Meijer, Inc.; Target Corp.; The Christmas Dove; ChristmasDepot.com, Inc.; The Christmas Place; Rogers' Christmas House.

FURTHER READING

Asimakoupoulos, Greg, "Mr. Christmas: Wally Bronner Wants to Wish You a 'Merry Christmas'—365 Days a Year," *Today's Christian*, Nov-Dec., 2004, p. 38.

Azizian, Carol, "Bronner's Shares Holiday Magic with Hollywood," *Flint Journal*, November 19, 1998, p. B1.

Bott, Jennifer, "Bronner's Christmas Wonderland Uses the Internet to Peddle Decorations Around the World," *Detroit Free Press*, December 5, 2000, p. 1C.

Brennan, Mike, "A Town that Means Business," *Detroit Free Press*, November 6, 1995, p. 6F.

———, "The Christmas Store," *Detroit Free Press*, November 6, 1995, p. 8F.

Chu, Dan, "Stocking Up for Christmas? Yule Love Wally Bronner's Massive Michigan Store," *People Weekly*, December 24, 1990, p. 75.

Coleman, LaNia, "Bronner's Replacing Statues," *Saginaw News*, July 25, 2002, p. 1B.

Crumm, David, "Behind All of Frankenmuth's Glitter: Faith," *Detroit Free Press*, December 24, 2004, p. 1A.

Finkel, David, "Sweat and Sparkle at Recovery's Dawn; Behind Job Numbers, Some Messy Realities," *Washington Post*, December 14, 2003, p. A1.

Hughes, Mike, "It's Where Christmas Never Ends," *Lansing State Journal*, December 22, 2005, p. 1D.

Karoub, Jeff, "Bronner's Recipe: Happy Customers, Attractive Pricing," *Flint Journal*, October 9, 1997, p. D7.

Murray, Dave, "Ornamental Decisions—Pressure at a Feverish Peak at Bronner's," *Flint Journal*, December 15, 1997, p. A1.

Ross, Philip E., "Frankenmuth Journal: Shopping, All Year Round," *New York Times*, January 8, 1988, p. A12.

Rossiter, Maggie, "Always the Tinsel Season," *Saginaw News*, January 6, 1999, p. 1A.

Sanders, Rhonda S., "Bronner's Brings Christmas to Wedding," *Flint Journal*, May 3, 2005, p. B1.

Schlossberg, Caroline Kennedy, "Building a Bigger Wonderland," *Gifts & Decorative Accessories*, May, 2002, p. 246.

Spenner, Jean, "Business Boom Boosts Bronner's," *Saginaw News*, May 4, 2000, p. 1A.

Tasker, Greg, "Bronner's Renovates Shoppers' Wonderland," *Detroit News*, December 10, 2003, p. 3B.

Windsor, Shawn, "Christmas, Cheer For Sale—Bronner Says Faith More Vital This Year," *Detroit Free Press*, December 10, 2001, p. 1A.

Carlisle Companies Inc.

13925 Ballantyne Corporate Place
Suite 400
Charlotte, North Carolina 28277
U.S.A
Telephone: (704) 501-1100
Toll Free: (866) 869-0474
Fax: (704) 501-1190
Web site: http://www.carlisle.com

Public Company
Incorporated: 1986
Employees: 11,000
Sales: $2.2 billion (2005)
Stock Exchanges: New York
Ticker Symbol: CSL
NAIC: 326299 All Other Rubber Product Manufacturing; 326199 All Other Plastics Product Manufacturing

∎ ∎ ∎

Carlisle Companies Inc. is a diversified global manufacturing firm with three main operating groups: Construction Materials; Industrial Components; and Diversified Components. Some of its products include commercial roofing, specialty tires and wheels, industrial belting products, foodservice products, motion control systems, specialized heavy-haul trailers, high performance wire and cable, and climate controlled truck bodies. The company's customers include consumers, original equipment manufacturers, and distributors. The present day Carlisle Companies Inc. was incorporated in 1986 as a holding company for the original company, Carlisle Corporation, founded in 1917 as a manufacturer of inner tubes. Later it became a major manufacturer of bicycle tires, brake linings, and rubber roofing. In the 1970s the company also diversified into the manufacture of electronics components.

A NEW STRATEGY LEADS TO SUCCESS

For years, Carlisle had tried to compete with the big rubber companies for the automobile tire market, but in 1980, a new strategy began to pay off for the company. Carlisle simply decided not to compete with the big tire companies for the automobile original equipment market. Instead, the company sold half its products to the replacement market and also concentrated on specialty products such as snowblower, tractor, motorcycle, and dirt-bike tires. Carlisle chairperson George Dixon told *Forbes* that the company's new resolution was "not to get trampled by the elephants." So while the economic recession hurt such big tiremakers as Firestone and BF Goodrich, Carlisle's net earnings were $26 million, representing a 38 percent improvement over the year before, and its stocks were soaring.

During this time, Carlisle was also very successful in the rubber roof market, which accounted for most of the company's earnings and brought in 43 percent of its profits for 1980. The rubber roofing market was strong, having become a popular and effective alternative to the traditional felt and asphalt coverings of flat roofs, and Carlisle led the market with 40 percent of its sales. Furthermore, Carlisle's best-selling Sure-Seal and other

COMPANY PERSPECTIVES

Carlisle Companies Incorporated is a diversified global manufacturing company focused on providing above average returns to our shareholders through profitable growth. We allocate resources carefully to our businesses that have or can obtain leadership in their markets. We strive to consistently grow these businesses by increasing market share, improving manufacturing processes and targeting new markets with expanded product lines.

construction materials helped make up for any losses in other divisions of the company. Although growth in the rubber roof industry was attracting competition from larger rubber companies, Carlisle was confident in its ability to compete with "the elephants" in this market, because of its years of experience in production of the single-ply rubber sheeting. Its president, Malcolm Myers told *Forbes*, "When it comes to single-ply roofing, we're the giants." He also commented that it would probably take some time before the other companies could even begin to produce a product as good as Carlisle's. To further secure its lead, Carlisle opened a new plant in Greenville, Illinois, to manufacture single-ply rubber roof sheeting. The Greenville plant, as well as a plant in Carlisle, Pennsylvania, were equipped with special machines to automate the manufacture of the huge rubber sheets, measuring 40 feet by 100 feet or larger.

Another market in which Carlisle held a unique niche was in providing contractors with complete roofing systems, including the rubber sheeting, all pipe seals, flashing, metal fasteners, edging, and adhesives. Contractors installing Carlisle roofs were required to learn proper installation from Carlisle representatives, who then inspected installations before guarantees could be issued. Other areas in which Carlisle dabbled included the manufacture of specialty wire and cable for data communications, magnetic computer tapes, and magnetically coated plastics for floppy disks.

CARLISLE COMPANIES IS FORMED IN 1986

Carlisle's strength in its market niches earned it a place among the Fortune 500 companies in 1985 with sales of $527 million. The following year, a holding corporation, Carlisle Companies Inc., was incorporated to oversee operations at Carlisle and the other companies that were being added to the group, such as Data Electronics,

purchased in 1986 for $33.4 million in cash, and Hardcast, Inc., which was acquired the following year. In 1988, Carlisle bought Ivan software, a developer of utility software, while selling its International Wire Products Company. Shortly thereafter, Carlisle decided to sell its interest in Graham Japan Ltd., a joint venture in Japan that sold computer tapes made by Carlisle.

Carlisle's corporate headquarters, which had been based in Cincinnati since 1971, were moved to Syracuse, New York, in 1989. President and CEO Stephen Munn maintained that its new location would provide more convenient access to the country's major financial institutions. Headquarters were eventually moved to Charlotte, North Carolina. Munn, a former executive of Carrier Corporation, an air conditioning manufacturer based in Syracuse, welcomed E. Douglas Kenna, former president of Carrier, as Carlisle's new chairperson.

In 1990, Carlisle became one of only 170 U.S. companies to form joint ventures with the Soviet Union. Carlisle's subsidiary, SynTec Systems, had a 49 percent share, and the Soviet Union retained a 51 percent share of the Moscow-based Krovtex, which sold and installed rubber roofs in the Soviet Union. The roofing materials were manufactured in the United States by Carlisle Syn-Tec Systems, the largest company in the corporation's construction materials division. The Soviet Union was a complicated place to conduct business and it became even more complicated when the country broke into separate republics in 1992. Krovtex continued to operate as a joint venture following the breakup, despite chaotic conditions, and the company foresaw strong long-term potential in Russia and other Eastern European markets.

As part of its plan to grow 15 to 20 percent yearly, in 1990 Carlisle purchased Brookpark Plastics Inc. of Lake City, Pennsylvania, and Off-Highway Braking Systems, a division of BF Goodrich Aerospace based in Bloomington, Indiana. Brookpark, a compression molder of diversified plastics products, became part of Continental Carlisle, Inc., while Off-Highway, a maker of braking systems for off-highway vehicles, with manufacturing facilities in The Netherlands and Brazil, became part of Carlisle's Motion Control Industries Inc. With the addition of the former Goodrich division, Carlisle was for the first time capable of manufacturing a complete brake system, as it already manufactured brake linings, pads, and other brake system components.

In September 1991, Carlisle purchased SiLite Corporation, a maker of reusable mugs, cups, and dishes for restaurants and cafeterias, with manufacturing facilities in California, Illinois, and Wisconsin. Carlisle already had plastic foodware production facilities in Oklahoma and Pennsylvania, and SiLite, with sales of $37 million in 1990, was a welcome addition.

KEY DATES

1917: Carlisle Corporation is incorporated as a manufacturer of inner tubes.
1980: The company adopts a new strategy to focus on the replacement market and specialty parts.
1986: Carlisle Companies Inc. is incorporated as a holding company.
1990: Carlisle becomes one of only 170 U.S. companies to form joint ventures with the Soviet Union.
1993: Goodyear sells its roofing products business to Carlisle.
1999: Johnson Truck Bodies is acquired.
2005: The company sells Carlisle Engineered Products.
2006: Carlisle Process Systems is sold.

Due to the effects of recession on the automobile and truck industries, Carlisle's profits fell substantially in 1991, due to a decline in sales of its plastic parts for interior and exterior trim, as well as brake components for the heavy trucking industry. The company also suffered losses in the one-half inch computer tape market.

RESTRUCTURING IN THE NEXT DECADE

Consequently, the company began a restructuring strategy designed to consolidate or sell parts of its slumping data communications and electronics businesses. Carlisle had entered the electronics industry in the 1970s, seeing a need to diversify into these potentially profitable and growing new product lines since its current product lines and markets had already reached maturity. By the 1990s, however, the electronics competition was stiff, the market and prices were slumping, and Carlisle was losing money.

Carlisle Memory Products group, which manufactured and marketed cartridges for backing up main memory tapes of small and mid-sized computer systems, was sold to Verbatim Corporation in 1992. The company also sold the rest of its magnetic tape business. Having divested itself of its unprofitable, peripheral divisions, Carlisle began to strengthen its core businesses, acquiring ECI Building Components Inc., a manufacturer of components for metal roofing and siding. ECI had sales of $32 million in 1991, and its acquisition strengthened Carlisle's marketing position,

particularly in the Southwest and West, as metal became an accepted roofing material for many nonresidential buildings.

Carlisle also consolidated some plants. Carlisle Tire and Rubber, which mainly manufactured tires for use on lawn and garden equipment, relocated its Indianapolis wheel plant to Aiken, South Carolina. Two Continental/SiLite factories were closed and their operations were moved to other plants.

Internationally, Carlisle acquired a brake shoe factory in Canada in order to increase its share of the heavy-duty after market. Because shipping of these heavy assemblies was very expensive, the market for these brake shoes was regional. Carlisle continued to expand its foreign sales with more than 40 percent of its off-highway braking systems for heavy machinery and other vehicles being sold outside the United States. Furthermore, the company entered a joint venture with Rutgerswerke, a large German manufacturer, in Mexico, producing brake pads and truck brake linings for the small but growing Mexican truck market.

During this time, the company's Tensolite division began moving away from the commodity wire market and into the aerospace and electronics markets. Its line of precision-coated wires and cables was selected for use in Boeing's 737s and 757, representing the first time Boeing, the leading airframe maker, used a single wiring system in its planes.

In 1993, Goodyear sold its roofing products business to Carlisle Companies Inc., strengthening Carlisle's position as the number one supplier of nonresidential roofs. Carlisle also became the leading supplier of pneumatic tires and specialty wheels to makers of riding mowers, garden tillers, and other lawn care equipment such as utility carts. With plans to expand its market for wheels and tires to include the golfing industry, the company also began manufacturing and marketing Soft-pave, shock-absorbing, bonded rubber crumb tiles for use on golf practice ranges and walkways. A related product, Playguard tiles, provided a soft, shock-reducing surface for use on playgrounds. These products were manufactured from recycled scrap from Carlisle's tire-making plants, as well as from used tires and rubber bought from other suppliers who first removed the steel belts. The use of recycled material helped reduce the company's costs and was good for the environment.

Despite its success with roofing materials and other rubber products, however, Carlisle's food service market represented the largest segment of its business in the early 1990s. Carlisle's Continental/SiLite International division manufactured more than 6,000 different plastic products and was a leader in the market for plastic permanentware, having captured a large share of the market in cafeterias of schools, colleges, and correctional institutions. The division dominated the growing market for display food containers in deli departments and salad bars of supermarkets, which were upgrading their counters. Although fast-food restaurants had represented a growing market for Carlisle in the 1980s, that market stabilized in the 1990s while mid-priced family-type restaurants became a growing market for the company's kitchen products as well as dinnerware, beverage dispensers, and salad bar containers. Also a manufacturer of acrylic gift and table accessories sold in major department stores, Continental/SiLite expanded its lines, adding high quality pewter items.

Carlisle intended to continue its focus on its core industries as it approached the late 1990s, emphasizing its strategy in its mission statement: "to serve customers worldwide by building on our strengths in rubber, plastics, friction and precision coating products, and other technologies in which we can develop a competitive advantage."

INTO THE NEXT CENTURY

As Carlisle prepared to enter the new millennium, the company continued its long-standing history of growth through acquisition and joint ventures. In fact, from 1990 to 2005, Carlisle purchased over 50 companies. In 1996, the company acquired five companies and secured record sales and earnings. Global Manufacturers, Johnson Truck Bodies, Innovative Engineering Ltd., Marko International Inc., and Cragar Industries Inc. were added to the company fold in 1999. Over the next two years, 17 companies were purchased.

MiraDri, a waterproofing firm specializing in commercial and residential applications, was Carlisle's single acquisition during 2002. Net income nearly tripled that year as revenues climbed to $1.97 billion. Net income rose even higher in 2003, reaching $88.9 million.

During this time period, the company's acquisition activity slowed significantly. Flo-Pac, a manufacturer of brooms, brushes, and cleaning tools, was purchased in 2003. Trintex Corp., North America's leading manufacturer of semi-pneumatic tire and wheels for lawn and garden and industrial markets, was added to Carlisle's holdings in 2004. Zhejiang Kete and Arvin-Meritor were purchased in 2005.

By now, the company was looking to strengthen its core operations. Its construction materials arm was experiencing steady growth as demand for its products remained strong, however, sales and profits in its automotive segment were sluggish due to a downturn in the auto industry. As such, the company decided to exit the automotive business and set plans in motion to divest

Carlisle Engineered Products in 2005. One year later, Carlisle Process Systems was sold to Tetra Pak AB. In addition, several smaller Carlisle companies were consolidated into its Diversified Components group. When the dust settled on the restructuring strategy, Carlisle Companies consisted of three main business segments including Construction Materials, Industrial Components, and Diversified Components.

Carlisle's overall strategy in the early years of the new millennium was to create opportunities in underserved markets. The company's SynTec business set plans in motion to open a new roofing manufacturing facility in Tooele, Utah and an insulation plant in Terrell, Texas. These plants enabled Carlisle to serve new customers in the western U.S. as well as Canada. Carlisle also continued to operate with a decentralized management structure, which allowed each individual company to make quicker business decisions.

Looking to the future, Carlisle was focused on organic sales growth. Its business strategy also included four main focal points: cost, service, quality, and innovation. As a company with a record of solid sales and profits, Carlisle appeared to be on track for success in the years to come.

Wendy J. Stein
Updated, Christina M. Stansell

PRINCIPAL SUBSIDIARIES

Carlisle China Coatings & Waterproofing, Inc.; Carlisle China Stainless Equipment, Inc.; Carlisle Coatings & Waterproofing Incorporated; Carlisle Corporation; Carlisle Engineered Products, Inc.; Carlisle Flight Services, Inc.; Carlisle FoodService Products Incorporated; Carlisle Insurance Company; Carlisle Intangible Company; Carlisle International, Inc.; Carlisle Management Company; Carlisle Power Transmission Products, Inc.; Carlisle Process Systems, Inc.; Carlisle Roofing Systems, Inc.; Carlisle SPV, Inc.; Carlisle SynTec Incorporated; Carlisle Tire & Wheel Company; Johnson Truck Bodies, Inc.; Kenro Incorporated; Motion Control Industries, Inc.; Tensolite Company; Trail King Industries, Inc.; Trail King of S.D., Inc.; Versico Incorporated; Walker Stainless Equipment Company, Inc.; Carlisle TPO, Inc.; Hunter Panels, LLC.

PRINCIPAL COMPETITORS

ArvinMeritor Inc.; Pirelli & C. SpA; Wabash National Corporation.

FURTHER READING

"Carlisle Companies Announces Plans to Exit the Automotive Business," *Business Wire*, January 6, 2005.

"Carlisle Companies Have Record 1996," *Business Journal—Central New York,* March 31, 1997.

"Carlisle Companies Prepare to Acquire Titan International," *Business Journal—Central New York,* August 20, 1999.

"Carlisle Makes It the Hard Way," *Fortune,* April 29, 1985, pp. 320-27.

"Carlisle Sells Unit to Tetra Pak in Ongoing Shake-up," *Reuters News,* April 10, 2006.

Flax, Steven, "Where the Rubber Meets the Roof," *Forbes,* April 13, 1981, pp. 58-61.

"TetraPak Buys U.S. Co Carlisle Process Systems," *Dow Jones International News,* April 11, 2006.

Charles Vögele Holding AG

Postfach 58
Gwattstrasse 15
Pfaeffikon SZ, CH-8808 CM13 3EN 2
Switzerland
Telephone: (41) 055 416 71 11
Fax: (41) 055 410 12 82
Web site: http://www.voegele-mode.com

Public Company
Incorporated: 1955
Employees: 7,258
Sales: CHF 1.35 billion ($1.10 billion) (2005)
Stock Exchanges: Switzerland
Ticker Symbol: VCH
NAIC: 448140 Family Clothing Stores; 315222 Men's and Boys' Cut and Sew Suit, Coat, and Overcoat Manufacturing; 454113 Mail-Order Houses; 551112 Offices of Other Holding Companies

∎ ∎ ∎

Charles Vögele Holding AG operates a cross-European chain of nearly 800 clothing stores. The company, based in Pfaeffikon, Switzerland, operates stores primarily in Switzerland, Germany, Austria, the Netherlands, and Belgium. The company also operates a store in Slovenia, opened in 2005. Since 2006, the company has begun testing its retail format in Hungary, Poland, and the Czech Republic as well. Germany remains the company's largest single market, with nearly 340 stores. In Switzerland, the company is the market leader, with 159 stores in operation. The company has been expanding quickly in Belgium and the Netherlands, with more than 150 stores in 2006. The company also operates 144 stores in Austria. Vögele designs nearly all of the clothing it sells, but operates no production plants itself. Instead, the company contracts its manufacturing to third parties. European contractors account for 40 percent of the group's business, with the bulk produced in Asian markets. Women's wear forms the group's largest sales segment, averaging more than 55 percent of sales in each of the company's markets. Men's clothing adds some 30 percent to sales, while children's clothing accounts for more than 12 percent of sales. Charles Vögele has traditionally targeted a somewhat older, low-fashion market. However, in 2006 the company launched a new, more modern store design to target a more fashion-oriented clientele. Listed on the Swiss Stock Exchange, Vögele is led by chairman Bernd H. J. Bothe and CEO Daniel Reinhard. In 2005, the company posted revenues of CHF 1.35 billion ($1.10 billion).

MOTORCYCLE MODE IN 1955

Charles Vögele (alternatively Voegele) was a successful race car pilot, who, together with his wife Agnes Vögele-Antig, opened a store selling motorcycle clothing in Zurich, Switzerland, in 1955. Although Vögele continued racing with some success through the 1960s, and even sponsored his own racing team, his real fortune came from his clothing sales. The success of the company's motorcycle fashions encouraged the company to expand its operations, and by 1957 Charles Vögele GmbH had acquired an expanded range of sportswear designs. The company then launched a new, larger store in Winterthur.

The new store was followed by a steady string of store openings, and by 1958 the company had already begun to eye operations on a national scale. Vögele's timing seemed perfect, as the retail clothing market in Switzerland remained dominated by small stores. Few large retail groups existed, and most retail clothing groups operated only a handful of stores. Yet the rising Swiss economy, and particularly the country's emergence as one of the world's wealthiest, encouraged the development of the retail clothing sector. Consumers not only possessed greater purchasing power, and more leisure time, but the spirit of the period also encouraged greater individual expression through clothing choice.

Through the 1960s, Vögele continued expanding its network of retail stores. In 1970, the company moved its headquarters to a larger facility in Rapperswil. The company had also been developing a larger, city-center retail format, launched with the opening of an eight-story store in Berne in 1969. Vögele also began experimenting with other formats, particularly a small format store. The new format not only allowed the company to enter smaller towns, it also proved the perfect fit for the newly developed shopping mall format. The first shopping mall in Switzerland opened in Spreitenbach in 1970, and included a Vögele store among its first tenants.

Through the 1970s, Vögele achieved national penetration with its retail network. The company also launched a mail order business, enabling the company to reach markets not yet covered through its retail stores. In support of its growing clothing sales, the company opened an office in Hong Kong, taking advantage of the lower production costs in the Asian region. Meanwhile, Vögele added new operations, including real estate development. In 1974, for example, the company built its own shopping mall in Pfaffikon, Charles Vögele's hometown. Pfaffikon also became the site of the company's headquarters in 1985.

By then, Vögele had already begun to look beyond

Switzerland's borders. In 1979, the company entered Germany, through the acquisition of Josten-Joka, based in Sigmaringen. That acquisition provided Vögele with a base of 22 stores with which to launch its international expansion. Germany quickly became the company's most important market, and by the mid-2000s represented more than one-third of the group's total retail network.

PUBLIC OFFERING IN 1999

Vögele began testing a new large-scale store format, dubbed Moderama, which featured selling space ranging from 4,000 to 6,000 square meters. The first Moderamas opened in Volketswil and Oftringen in 1984, and featured an extended clothing selection, including evening wear. The new format was destined exclusively for the Swiss market.

Nonetheless, Vögele's interest in foreign expansion remained strong through the decade. The company added a new Southern Germany retail group, Kurz, soon after the Josten acquisition. In 1988, the company expanded its German holdings again with the purchase of the 34-store chain of Cosmos Mode S.A. and Willy Korn AG. By then, too, the company had expanded its mail order operation, acquiring Germany's Braun & Goll in 1987. That purchase also brought the company additional retail operations based in Pforzheim.

Vögele, which had acquired an art gallery and auction house, Stuker, in the 1970s, targeted a new area of diversification in the late 1980s, founding its own travel agency, Vögele Reisen, in 1988. The company remained active in the travel market for more than a decade, before selling that business to TUI.

Retail remained the group's primary business, and in the early 1990s, Vogele, which had long targeted a relatively older, low-fashion-oriented clientele, attempted to expand its range of retail offerings. In 1991, the company bought 80 percent of the Dyckhoff Group, based in Cologne. The move was intended to bring the group into the high-end clothing sector. However, by 1995, the company had decided to abandon that effort, selling off its Dyckhoff stake in order to refocus itself on its core clothing market.

Vögele also added to its international operations, buying up Austria's Moden Muller GmbH in 1994. That purchase placed Vögele among the leaders in Austria's retail clothing sector, with a network of 57 stores. Back at home, Vögele stepped up its presence with the acquisition of rival Kleider Frey, adding 22 new stores to its Swiss network in 1995.

That year Charles Vögele also retired from the company, turning over its direction to sons Marco and

KEY DATES

1955: Race-car driver Charles Vögele opens a shop in Zurich to sell motorcycle clothing.

1957: The company extends its range to general sportswear and begins building a retail network throughout Switzerland.

1979: The company's first international expansion occurs with the acquisition of the Josten-Joka retail network.

1991: Vögele attempts to enter the high-end retail clothing market with the purchase of majority control of Dykhoff.

1994: The company enters the Austrian market with the purchase of Moden Muller GmbH.

1997: The Vögele family sells majority control to Schroder Ventures.

1999: Vögele goes public with listings on the Zurich and Frankfurt exchanges, and adds Belgium and the Netherlands to its international markets.

2005: A Vögele store opens in Slovenia.

2006: The company launches operations in Hungary, Poland, and the Czech Republic.

Carlo. (Charles Vögele died in 2002 at the age of 79.) By then, Vögele counted nearly 330 branches, more than half of which were outside Switzerland. Under its new direction, the company decided to exit its flagging mail order business, which had become unprofitable in the first half of the 1990s. Instead, the company concentrated on revamping its retail network, revising its store design while investing in a new IT network to connect all of its branches to the headquarters.

The second half of the 1990s, however, presented a new challenge to the company. Faced with a growing number of rivals, such as H&M, Zara, The Gap, and others, Vögele recognized the need to expand its own network in order to remain competitive. For this, the company turned to Schroder Ventures, selling a majority of its shares to the investment group in 1997 in a deal worth more than $900 million. Under Schroder Ventures, the company continued to streamline its operations, selling off all non-core operations in order to focus exclusively on retail clothing sales.

By 1999, Vögele was prepared to launch its next phase of expansion. In support of this, the company went public, listing its shares on the Swiss and Frankfurt stock exchanges. The listing on the Frankfurt exchange proved only temporary, and the company removed its listing on that exchange in 2003.

NEW MARKETS FOR A NEW CENTURY

In the meantime, Vögele had targeted new international markets. In 1999, the company entered Belgium and the Netherlands, acquiring 27 stores formerly operated by P&C Groep. The company further expanded its Benelux presence with the purchase of the Kien Group, adding 106 stores, as well as a warehouse facility, in 2001. Vögele paid NLG 126 million ($65 million) to acquire the chain from parent Vendex KBB, the Dutch retailing powerhouse. At the same time, the company added to its German holdings, buying Hannover-based Mac Fash Textil, with 40 stores, in 2000. By the end of that year, the company total retail network numbered more than 570 stores.

Vögele's rapid expansion in the early 2000s, however, cut deeply into its profits. By 2002, the company was forced to undertake a major restructuring of its operations, streamlining its organization structure, while also rolling out a new store design across its network. The new "jazzier" interior was developed in order to help the company attract a younger clientele. As part of the process, the company adopted the new store brand and logo, Charles Vögele Switzerland.

With its restructuring underway, Vögele began developing new expansion goals for the middle of the decade. With further growth limited in the Swiss market, and with its presence already well developed in Germany, Austria, Belgium, and the Netherlands, Vögele turned its attention to the developing Eastern European markets. In 2005, the company entered this emerging market, opening a store in Slovenska Bistrica, in Slovenia.

The successful launch into that market led the company to expand its Eastern European ambitions. In 2006, the company began testing the waters elsewhere in the region, opening pilot stores in Hungary, Poland, and the Czech Republic. Charles Vögele hoped to replicate its history of success in these new markets, setting the pace for its next 50 years as a European retail clothing leader.

M.L. Cohen

PRINCIPAL SUBSIDIARIES

Charles Voegele Ceska s.r.o. (Czech Republic); Charles Voegele Polska Sp. z o.o. (Poland); Charles Vögele (Austria) AG; Charles Vögele (Belgium) B.V.B.A.; Charles Vögele (Netherlands) B.V.; Charles Vögele

Deutschland GmbH; Charles Vögele Fashion (Hong Kong) Ltd. (Hong Kong); Charles Vögele Hungária Kereskedelmi Kft. (Hungary); Charles Vögele Import GmbH (Germany); Charles Vögele Mode AG; Charles Vögele Store Management AG; Charles Vögele Trading AG; Charles Vögele trgovina s tekstilom d.o.o. (Slovakia); Cosmos Mode AG; Mac Fash GmbH; Prodress AG.

PRINCIPAL COMPETITORS

Asda Group Ltd.; Hennes and Mauritz AB; Royal Vendex KBB N.V.; NEXT PLC; Arcadia Group Ltd.; C and A Mode KG; Vivarte; Stockmann Oyj Abp; Gruppo Coin S.p.A.; Peek and Cloppenburg KG; Cortefiel S.A.

FURTHER READING

"Charles Vogele Opens First Shop in Hungary," *Hungarian News Agency*, March 17, 2006.

"Charles Vogele Textiles Group Invests in the Netherlands," *European Report*, November 29, 2000, p. 600.

"Expansion Will Hurt Earnings at Voegele," *Wall Street Journal Europe*, January 23, 2002, p. 7.

Freeborn, Tim, "Is Swiss Giant Ready to Try on New Look?," *Daily Mail*, October 1, 1999, p. 81.

Hall, William, "Swiss Offering Fails to Excite," *Financial Times*, June 7, 1999, p. 30.

———, "Vogele Cuts IPO Range," *Financial Times*, June 1, 1999, p. 27.

"Higher Profit at Voegele," *Swiss News*, April 2004, p. 17.

"Losses in Germany for Swiss Vogele," *Suddeutsche Zeitung*, March 9, 2005.

"Vogele Profits Double After Sales Edge Up," *just-style.com*, March 8, 2006.

"Vogele to Make Acquisition," *Textil Wirtschaft*, June 24, 1999, p.13.

Chicago Bridge & Iron Company N.V.

Polarisavenue 31 2132 JH
Hoofddorp,
The Netherlands
Telephone: (31) 23-5685660
Fax: (31) 20-5789589
Web site: http://www.cbi.com

Public Company
Incorporated: 1889 as Chicago Bridge & Iron Company
Employees: 11,000
Sales: $2.26 billion (2005)
Stock Exchanges: New York
Ticker Symbol: CBI
NAIC: 234930 Industrial Nonbuilding Structure Construction; 234990 All Other Heavy Construction; 332313 Plate Work Manufacturing; 332420 Metal Tank (Heavy Gauge) Manufacturing; 551112 Offices of Other Holding Companies

■ ■ ■

Chicago Bridge & Iron Company N.V. is a global leader in the engineering, procurement, and construction (EPC) business. While no longer a maker of bridges or iron products, the company has decades of experience fabricating large steel vessels for water, chemicals, and gases. It has grown into a vertically-integrated supplier for all phases of oil and natural gas production.

The company is known for its fixed-price bids that offer clients security from cost overruns while providing an incentive for CB&I to control costs. Another distinction is its preference for using its own traveling project specialists rather than local subcontractors. CB&I maintains sales, engineering, and fabrication operations at more than 60 offices around the world. About 90 percent of revenues were derived from the hydrocarbons industry in 2005.

FROM BRIDGES TO WATER TANKS

The Chicago Bridge & Iron Company, forerunner to CBI Industries, was established in 1889 through the merger of two companies. One of these companies was a Minneapolis-based engineering concern run by Horace Ebenezer Horton, who had distinguished himself by building some of the country's first metallic span bridges over the Mississippi River. The other was the Kansas City Bridge and Iron Company, operated by George Wheelock and A.M. Blodgett. In the three years before the merger, this company built more than 500 structures across the United States.

The new company relocated to Washington Heights, Illinois, a suburb of Chicago, which provided easy rail transportation to the foundries and steel mills in the area. Though it took several months to relocate machinery from Kansas City, Chicago Bridge & Iron immediately began accepting jobs to build bridges.

In 1890 Chicago Bridge & Iron absorbed the operations of the Des Moines-based George E. King Bridge Company. King was an established bridge builder in Iowa, a market that Horton and his new partners had been unable to crack. Meanwhile, King was attracted to an interest in his new partners' reliable metal fabricating facility.

COMPANY PERSPECTIVES

CB&I is a global engineering, procurement, and construction (EPC) company specializing in lump-sum, turnkey projects for customers that produce, process, store and distribute the world's natural resources. We serve a number of key industries, including oil and gas, petrochemical and chemical, power, water and wastewater, and metals and mining. For more than a century, we've built upon our technical capabilities, our expertise and our financial strength to develop a comprehensive package of EPC services and technologies. Our in-depth knowledge of our customers' business and our history of proven results have made CB&I a trusted name in the industry.

The demand for bridges at this time was extraordinary. In the decades after the Civil War, railroads helped to establish burgeoning rural communities. As commerce grew, demands on transportation followed. Between so many points, there were rivers, streams and gulleys, and each route required its own span.

Until that time, wooden bridges were the order of the day. While these were sturdy, they were susceptible to rot and structural failure. The answer was in iron bridges, which few foundries were equipped to design or manufacture. With demand high, Chicago Bridge & Iron won contracts to build several hundred bridges by 1893. Other structures they were contracted to build included the first metallic water towers and standpipes and a Horse Exchange Amphitheatre for the Chicago stockyards.

That year, however, irregularities in railroad financing, shoddy banking practices, and the failure of agricultural crops caused a severe four-year economic depression that nearly closed Chicago Bridge & Iron. Then, in 1897, a devastating fire destroyed nearly the entire operation. Faced with the tremendous task of rebuilding, King opted to leave the corporation to concentrate on his more profitable banking and agricultural interests. While it took Horton nearly six years to pay King off, he did emerge as the company's sole shareholder.

As the Washington Heights plant was rebuilt, work under contract was gradually brought back from other factories working under subcontract. Also, the company's water towers became extremely popular after Horton's son George Horton perfected a hemispherical tank bottom that eliminated the need for a complex tank deck. This business helped the company weather an extremely difficult period in which all sales offices outside of Chicago were closed.

By the turn of the century the company was once again on its feet and taking on its first ventures in Canada. However, a covert trade dispute waged by Canadian firms and the government convinced Horton to abandon Canada and never again do business there. His son George, however, succeeded in winning several important contacts on his own, purchasing the materials from his father's company.

The company entered 1907 on strong growth, with contracts for several hundred water tanks, hundreds of bridges, and miscellaneous structures. Later that year a second financial panic sent the American economy into a tailspin. Public funds, which municipalities used to purchase water tanks and bridges, evaporated almost over night. Contracts were canceled and, once again, Chicago Bridge & Iron was forced into retrenchment.

These conditions were made more difficult by the fact that all steel products at this time were subject to artificial shipping costs from Pittsburgh, regardless of where they were made. This prevented Chicago Bridge & Iron from competing effectively in the East. In an effort to open this new market, the company established a second facility in 1911 at Greenville, Pennsylvania, outside Pittsburgh. Horton died on July 28, 1912, leaving the business to his wife and five children. The eldest son George later emerged as leader of the company. Unencumbered by his father's anti-Canadian prejudice, George Horton quickly merged his own Canadian operations with Chicago Bridge & Iron, establishing a new factory at Bridgeburg, Ontario, near Niagara Falls. Other business arose in Cuba, where the demand was for tanks to hold molasses, water, and, later, oil. Soon afterward the company was asked to build water tanks in the shapes of a milk bottle, a pineapple, and a "peachoid." Diversifying further, Chicago Bridge & Iron was asked to build water pumping facilities for the City of Chicago.

By 1914, as the war in Europe began to heat up, the countries involved began to purchase more and more war material from American manufacturers. This energized the American economy and drastically assisted Chicago Bridge & Iron's growth. Only three years later, after the United States entered the war and many of the company's employees left for the army, Chicago Bridge & Iron received hundreds of war-related orders, including one to build 150 5,000-ton barges.

KEY DATES

1888: Liquid Carbonic founded to supply carbon dioxide gas to soda fountains and soft drink bottlers.
1889: Chicago Bridge & Iron is founded through the merger of two Midwest bridge-building businesses.
1893: The company makes its first standpipe.
1923: The Hortonsphere® pressurized vessel debuts.
1966: The company builds its first offshore oil storage structure, the Molly Brown.
1972: The Chicago plant is relocated to Kankakee, Illinois.
1976: CB&I builds storage tanks for the trans-Alaska oil pipeline.
1977: The company goes public on the New York Stock Exchange.
1979: The CBI Industries, Inc., holding company is established.
1984: CBI acquires Liquid Carbonic, a leading global supplier of carbon dioxide.
1996: CBI is acquired by industrial gasses giant Praxair Inc.
1997: Chicago Bridge & Iron Company N.V. (CB&I) is spun off in a public offering; U.S. fabrication operations are consolidated in Houston.
2001: CB&I acquires rival fluid tank construction unit of Pitt-Des Moines Inc.
2003: The corporate identity is updated; John Brown Hydrocarbons Ltd. is acquired.

A SHIFT TO THE PETROLEUM INDUSTRY

At the close of the war in 1919, George Horton decided not to involve his company in the reconstruction of Europe. Governments there, he was told, were not as creditworthy as Central and South American governments. This decision paid off when Chicago Bridge & Iron began taking large orders for huge oil storage tanks, first in the United States and then in Cuba, Venezuela, Aruba, and Mexico. Additional orders later came from the Dutch East Indies, Malaya, India, and China. The tremendous tank business also prompted Horton to phase out the company's bridge building business in favor of plate steel structures.

Horton made an important discovery during this time. Noting how his engineers spent so much time boring rivet holes with templates, Horton conceived of a 12-hole rivet punch, capable of boring a dozen perfectly placed rivet holes at once. This "Chi bridge Spacer" shortened production schedules, enabling the company to secure more business. Later, Horton abandoned rivets altogether, favoring leak-proof welded seams.

Meanwhile, the company experienced a brief labor strike in October 1919 when, soon after organizing, workers walked out. Queried as to why they went on strike, workers replied that their union was seeking a closed shop and better benefits. The strike was resolved after 18 days.

In 1922 Chicago Bridge & Iron purchased the rights to a "floating roof" storage system patented by a Bureau of Mines engineer named John H. Wiggins. The design allowed the tank's roof to float on the stored product, trapping the contents within and preventing losses to leakage or evaporation. Another major product for the oil industry, intended for natural gas storage, was the Hortonsphere, a spherical steel vessel capable of holding gas under great pressure.

In December 1923 the Horton Steel Works in Bridgeburg suffered a debilitating fire. During reconstruction of this plant, Chicago Bridge & Iron merged the Horton plant with another Canadian firm, Des Moines Steel. In 1929, on the strength of its tank business, Chicago Bridge & Iron absorbed the large Reeves Brothers plant in Birmingham, Alabama. Later that year, however, a stock market crash plunged the world into the Great Depression. Once again, Chicago Bridge & Iron's orders were either deferred or canceled, profits took a nosedive, and employees were laid off.

But, surviving on a trickle of work from the oil industry—namely, in the Middle East, the Dutch East Indies, and Italy—Chicago Bridge & Iron forged ahead with plans to incorporate new electric arc welding technology into its products. This new process allowed entire structures, rather than just tank bottoms and roofs, to be welded. This greatly reduced the weight of the structures, resulting in more efficient designs.

The company once again faced labor trouble in 1930 when new labor laws lifted certain restrictions on union organization of workers. When the matter came up before unrepresented workers at Chicago Bridge & Iron, the employees rejected outside labor representatives and established their own independent union. Still, the company's nomadic tank builders were left unrepresented. Local Boilermakers unions incited battles with the company's "tankees," and killed many during gun fights. The Boilermakers later agreed to negotiations which led to the establishment of an associated union for transient tank builders.

Chicago Bridge & Iron entered several new fields during the 1930s. While the Canadian plant began building heat exchangers and welded ships, the repeal in 1933 of Prohibition led to massive brewery contracts for the American plants. Once again public works projects, including work on the San Francisco Bay Bridge and the Tennessee Valley Authority, provided much needed income. Layoffs were reversed in 1934 and in the following year the company began taking on new hires. Later work included barge building and work on chemical and infant nuclear plants.

BUILDING LANDING SHIP TANKS DURING WORLD WAR II

The outbreak of war in December 1941 put Chicago Bridge & Iron on a war footing. By agreement with the government the company was assigned to build drydocks and ships, for which it purchased land in Morgan City, Louisiana. In January of 1942 Chicago Bridge & Iron took control of a Pacific yard at Eureka, California, and later established facilities in Newburgh, New York, and Seneca, Illinois. As construction commenced at these sights, entire families were relocated from the company's other locations. Employment ballooned from 4,000 employees in 1941 to 20,000 the following year.

The company's first contract was for 40 Landing Ship Tanks, or LSTs, which were designed to deliver heavy mobile machinery from ships to beachheads. Construction began on LSTs immediately. In fact, ships were built as the yard was built, and few of the employees were trained shipbuilders. Many learned their jobs as they went. The company also built drydocks, capable of lifting 100,000-ton ships out of the water for repairs, and underground fuel storage facilities at Pearl Harbor and, near the end of the war, in Subic Bay in the Philippines.

As the war drew to a close, Chicago Bridge & Iron was highly regarded for its excellent production schedule and cost control. After building 157 LSTs, George Horton reminded employees in February of 1945 that war production was ending and that, "a contractor without contracts does not amount to much." A month later, Horton was killed in a car accident. The company's directors, eager to prevent ruinous disorganization, elected George Horton's younger brother Horace president of the company, and career engineer Merle Trees chairman of the board.

Later that year, John Wiggins announced that he was terminating his design and consulting agreements with Chicago Bridge & Iron and going to work for a rival, the General American Transportation Corporation. This threatened to knock the company out of its most profitable peacetime line at precisely the wrong moment. Trees issued a challenge to his engineers to develop an improved floating roof technology free of Wiggins' patent. Operating under a short deadline, the engineers succeeded in designing an original Horton model.

POSTWAR CHALLENGES

The company entered the postwar period in very solid financial condition, holding no bank loans. Market conditions were favorable for strong growth, owing to pent-up demand for public works and industrial projects. Chicago Bridge & Iron received orders for a variety of its standard products—water and oil tanks—but also was asked to construct pressure and containment vessels for the emerging nuclear testing and power industries.

But the company faced two serious impediments to postwar business. First, few companies could find enough skilled draftsmen to design these products. While some talent could be hired away from competitors, the company's design offices still could not keep up. There also was a shortage of experienced construction engineers. And, secondly, CB&I, as it had become known, was faced with recurrent shortages of steel, which was still being rationed in monthly allocations. During the war, however, the Geneva steel mill that had been established at Salt Lake City lacked a large local customer base. Seeing it as the perfect supplier, the company immediately began construction of a full-scale fabricating plant at that site.

By March 1946, the company encountered a boat glut. The company's shipbuilding unit, which employed 12,000 workers during the war, was down to 12 employees. However, growth in overseas markets more than made up for this loss. With tax incentives to invest in Latin America, as part of the Roosevelt Administration's "Good Neighbor Policy," CB&I established subsidiaries in Venezuela and Brazil. Later, the company decided to aggressively pursue foreign licensing to boost sales and protect patent rights. Licensees were established throughout the world, including France, Germany, Japan, and Australia.

In 1948, the first year of postwar profitability, CB&I won a contract to modernize U.S. Steel's massive South Chicago Works. A few years later the company was invited to build an enormous tank farm in Aden for British Petroleum, which later led to the establishment of a British subsidiary.

Employees ran on nine-hour days and six-day work weeks. As the job backlog lightened up, this was scaled back to eight hours and five days, avoiding layoffs. By 1953, however, the backlog had disappeared, forcing the company to institute layoffs and a "necessary absence" plan.

SERVING EMERGING INDUSTRIES IN THE ATOMIC AGE

By 1954 CB&I had become involved in cryogenics, hydroelectric and nuclear power, and liquified natural gas, and, later, built wind tunnels and vessels for the space program. Returning to bridgework after nearly 40 years, the company built caissons for the construction of the Mackinac Bridge in Michigan which would connect the Upper and Lower Peninsulas of the state for the first time.

Also in 1954, Merle Trees died. He was replaced as chairman by Horace B. Horton, who was himself replaced as president by E. E. Michaels. Michaels was well suited to lead the company at that time. He was an experienced corporate diplomat, capable of maintaining a balance between two opposing ownership forces within the company. He was also, however, a good manager, unafraid to assert his own views.

With the discovery of oil in Western Canada, CB&I established a facility in North Lethbridge, Alberta, where it manufactured vessels for the oil, gas, pulp, and fertilizer industries. In 1957 the company became involved in sewage projects. In 1958, as international expansion continued, the company established an Argentine subsidiary, Cometarsa, which failed to perform well and was sold nine years later. Still, massive water desalinization projects, particularly one in Kuwait, were undertaken in partnership with G. & J. Weir Ltd. of Glasgow. Building on its aeronautical business, CB&I acquired an interest in the Minneapolis-based FluiDyne Engineering Corporation.

In September 1959 Horace B. Horton died and was succeeded as chairman by his son Arthur. Later, in 1962, E. E. Michaels resigned to run, unsuccessfully, as a Republican for the U.S. House of Representatives. He was replaced by Josh Clarke.

In 1960 the company established subsidiaries in Germany and Holland and, later, in Mexico. The company also restructured its Australian interests, forming Chicago Bridge Lennox with its Australian licensee, but later dissolved it in favor of a wholly owned company called CBI Constructors. Additional operations were later established in the Philippines, Italy, and Japan. Back home, in 1961, CB&I broke ground on a new headquarters building in Oak Brook, Illinois. Two years later, recognizing the tremendous growth the company had experienced, the Board of Directors decided to take the company public.

In 1963 CB&I won a contract to build major sections of the large Mangla Dam in Pakistan. This successful project led to work on a second, the Tarbela Dam, in 1971. In 1964 CB&I acquired three engineering companies, Rebikoff Oceanics, Copeland Process, a specialist in industrial waste disposal, and Walker Process, which built equipment for water and sewage plants. And, to keep up with the growing volume of nuclear plant projects, CB&I opened a new facility specifically for supplying nuclear reactors in Memphis. The company continued to bolster its engineering ranks in 1967, when it set up a new research lab at Plainfield, Illinois, and staffed it with some of the best engineers in the world.

During the 1960s, the liquified natural gas (LNG) business began to take off. As a pioneer in engineering these projects, CB&I became the industry leader in vessel manufacturing, both for land storage and on ships. In 1969 the company formed a gas transportation subsidiary called American LNG. That year CB&I also built an enormous oil storage and loading device designed to sit on the seafloor. This project, Khazzan Dubai, was built for the Gulf Sheikdom of Dubai, and was nominated for honors by the National Society of Professional Engineers. Unfortunately the project's competitors were the Apollo space program and the Boeing 747.

John Horton, son of Horace B. Horton, who succeeded Josh Clarke as president in 1968, stepped down after only 11 months in office to pursue personal interests. He was replaced as president by Marvin Mitchell, a career CB&I engineer. Early in 1973 Arthur Horton, who had been inflicted with polio as a boy, died after a long illness. Mitchell succeeded him as chairman of the company.

The Arab oil embargo in 1973 and 1974 was a tremendous boon to the company. Oil consumers, used to frequent oil deliveries, had little storage capacity for oil, which was available only when you could get it. With sales up 80 percent in 1973, CB&I was again awash in a backlog of orders. The energy crisis caused by the embargo set into motion plans to exploit huge oil reserves in Alaska. Here, too, CB&I was asked to supply equipment and storage tanks for the Alyeska Pipeline Company between Barrow and Valdez. The company also opened a new facility at Prairieville, Louisiana, to service projects in the Gulf of Mexico and train underwater welders.

But, after the embargo ended, Mitchell grew weary of the cyclical and unpredictable nature of the energy business. He moved to diversify the company and in 1975 purchased Virginia-based Fairmac Corporation, a real estate developer. In 1977, however, CB&I unveiled a more economical process of extracting carbon dioxide from LNG, called Cryex. This patented process only helped to push CB&I further into the energy business. In 1979 CB&I took control of Circle Bar, an oil drilling company based in New Orleans.

GOING PUBLIC IN 1977

CBI became a public company in 1977 with a listing on the New York Stock Exchange. Management affected a corporate reorganization two years later, creating a holding company called CBI Industries, which took ownership of Chicago Bridge & Iron. The name change was deemed necessary because the company was no longer based in Chicago, did not build bridges, and had not used iron for decades.

CBI won new contracts for large petroleum projects in the North Sea and in Abu Dhabi and, in 1983, once again tried to diversify. Its search ended in 1984 when the company purchased Liquid Carbonic, the world's leading supplier of carbon dioxide, from Houston Natural Gas for $407 million. Liquid Carbonic had been founded in 1888 to supply carbon dioxide gas to soda fountains and soft drink bottlers. In 1926 the company began commercial sales of solid carbon dioxide, or "dry ice." After World War II, Liquid Carbonic branched into frozen food technologies and commercial sales of oxygen, nitrogen, and argon which, unlike carbon dioxide, are extracted from the atmosphere.

Marvin Mitchell resigned as chairman of CBI upon turning 65 in 1981 and was replaced by Bill Pogue. Pogue served as chairman until 1989 when he, too, turned 65. Pogue was succeeded by John Jones, a former vice-chairman and chief operating officer.

After a difficult period of adjustment during the mid-1980s, caused primarily by cyclical retrenchment in the energy construction business, CBI entered the 1990s with a stronger, revitalized organization built on more than 100 years of successful projects. While Liquid Carbonic had helped to insulate CBI from the ups and downs of energy development, it remained to be seen whether the company would continue to pursue additional businesses that were equally stable.

In fact, CBI thrived under an aggressive diversification strategy led by Jones, noted *Forbes*. It began supplying equipment for a number of different industries while regaining some of its old dominance in the steel water tank market. It also invested heavily to increase capacity at Liquid Carbonic while developing new agricultural applications for carbon dioxide.

With a booming demand for carbon dioxide, particularly in South America, the Liquid Carbonic unit made a tempting acquisition target for rivals. Airgas unsuccessfully tried to buy it for $1.5 billion in 1994. In spite of numerous anti-takeover defenses instituted since the late 1980s, CBI itself was taken over in 1996 by industrial gasses giant Praxair Inc.

By this time, CBI had annual sales of $2 billion. An interesting sideline launched in the mid-1990s was the construction of giant floating casino vessels, drawing on the company's experience with steel-plate fabrication.

SPUN OFF IN 1997

Praxair was primarily interested in the gasses business and sold the other units. Statia Terminals, N.V., which CBI had acquired in 1986, was sold to an investor group. In 1997, CBI was spun off in an initial public offering on the New York Stock Exchange. At this time, a Netherlands corporation, Chicago Bridge & Iron Company N.V. (CB&I), was created as the parent company for the U.S. business, still called Chicago Bridge & Iron Company, and international operations under the name Chicago Bridge & Iron Company B.V. The Kankakee, Illinois, plant was shut down as fabrication operations were consolidated in the oil industry center of Houston. The North American administrative offices were relocated from Plainfield, Illinois, to the Houston area in 2001.

As the energy industry struggled in the late 1990s, CB&I invested in high tech industries in 1999. It acquired XL Systems, Inc., a designer and builder of thermal vacuum test facilities. It also created a new UltraPure Systems business unit to provide high purity process piping systems, but it left this business after a couple of years following the burst of the tech bubble.

VERTICAL INTEGRATION PATH IN 2000 AND BEYOND

CB&I's 1999 revenues were $675 million. The company added another digit to its top line when it acquired Howe-Baker International, L.L.C. in December 2000. This Texas-based engineering and construction firm had been established in 1947 to produce dehydrators and desalting equipment for the refining industry. In the 1960s it branched out into process design and plant fabrication. By the time of the acquisition, Howe-Baker employed 2,000 people and had annual revenues of $308 million. CB&I's total annual revenues exceeded $1 billion after the deal. The combination promised to take Howe-Baker to new international markets, while giving CB&I access to its process engineering and modular construction strengths.

In February 2001, CB&I purchased the Engineered Construction and Water divisions of Pitt-Des Moines Inc. for $84 million in cash and stock. The acquired units, based in Houston and Pittsburgh, respectively, together employed 1,000 people and had combined revenues of $244 million a year.

A series of subsequent acquisitions extended CB&I's reach into all phases of petroleum and gas production as the energy industry recovered from its late-1990s trough. The 2003 purchase of London-based John Brown Hydrocarbons Limited, which was involved in the onshore, offshore, and pipeline sectors, was a crowning achievement in the vertical integration strategy. CB&I also acquired the U.S. subsidiary of another British engineering and construction firm, Petrofac Limited, which it folded into Howe-Baker.

CB&I announced a new corporate identity in July 2003. Its new logo retained a spheroid shape in use since the 1950s. The widely used acronym "CB&I" was adopted as a master brand.

Revenues exceeded $2 billion in 2005. About 90 percent was derived from the hydrocarbons industry. One new line of business was retrofitting petrochemical plants to meet increasingly stringent emissions requirements.

The company's legal life was becoming complicated. In January 2005, the Federal Trade Commission upheld an earlier administrative law judge ruling that its four-year-old acquisition of units from Pitt-Des Moines Inc. had violated antitrust law. The FTC said it would require CB&I to spin off some of its assets to restore domestic competition. The decision surprised some observers, as it related to a merger that had closed four years earlier after passing the usual regulatory review. CB&I appealed the ruling.

The SEC launched an accounting investigation in the last half of 2005. The CB&I board later terminated CEO Gerald Glen, citing no official reason for the dismissal. Glenn had led the company since its 1997 IPO. The company's chief operating officer was also let go.

Revenues were expected to be $2.8 billion for 2006. In an environment of soaring oil and natural gas prices, CB&I continued to focus on energy infrastructure. Among its projects around the globe were a couple of very large contracts to design and build two separate LNG import terminals in the U.K. A $1 billion LNG terminal was being built in Texas.

John Simley
Updated, Frederick C. Ingram

PRINCIPAL SUBSIDIARIES

Chicago Bridge & Iron Company B.V.; Chicago Bridge & Iron (Antilles) N.V.; Chicago Bridge & Iron Company (USA); Lealand Finance Company B.V.

PRINCIPAL DIVISIONS

Process & Technology; Low Temperature/Cryogenic Tanks and Systems; Pressure Vessels; Standard Tanks; Specialty and Other Structures; Repairs and Turnarounds.

PRINCIPAL COMPETITORS

Denali Inc.; Kingspan Group plc; Matrix Service Company.

FURTHER READING

Block, Donna, "Across the Bow," *TheDeal.com*, January 17, 2005.

"Companies to Watch," *Fortune*, November 5, 1990.

The Bridge Works: A History of Chicago Bridge & Iron, CBI Industries, Inc., Mobium Press, Chicago, 1987.

Hensel, Bill, Jr., "Fired Head of CB&I May Still Be CEO; Ousted Leader's Lawyer Says Dutch Judge Backs Client," *Houston Chronicle*, Bus. Sec., February 17, 2006, p. 1.

Palmeri, Christopher, "Rebirth," *Forbes*, August 31, 1992, pp. 45f.

"Praxair Launches Takeover of CO2 Maker CBI Industries," *Chemical Marketing Reporter*, November 6, 1995.

Schmeiser, Lisa, "Chicago Bridge Excels with Fixed-Price Bids; Engineering Firms' Tack Forces It to Keep a Close Watch on Costs, Schedule," *Investor's Business Daily*, May 9, 2005, p. A12.

Seiberg, Jaret, "A Bridge Too Far?," *Corporate Counsel*, January 2003.

"Superior Turnkey EPC Services: CB&I's Decades of Expertise Mean Customers Can Depend on the Company's Products, Technology and Services," *Chemical Week*, September 18, 2002, p. 24.

mabe

Controladora Mabe, S.A. de C.V.

Palmas 100
Mexico City, D. F. 11000
Mexico
Telephone: (52) (55) 9178-8200
Web site: http://www.mabe.com.mx

Private Company
Founded: 1946
Employees: 18,000+
Sales: $2.82 billion (2005)
NAIC: 335211 Electric Houseware and Fan Manufacturing; 335221 Household Cooking Appliance Manufacturing; 335222 Household Refrigerator and Home and Farm Freezer Manufacturing; 335224 Household Laundry Equipment Manufacturing; 335312 Motor and Generator Manufacturing

■ ■ ■

Controladora Mabe, S.A. de C.V., is the third largest manufacturer of large household appliances in the Americas, located in Mexico but serving the Western Hemisphere from Alaska to Argentina. In Mexico, it accounts for almost half of all refrigerators, stoves, and washing machines sold, and it also holds about one-quarter of the U.S. market for these products. In Latin America south of Mexico, Mabe has plants in five South American countries. It exports its products to over 70 countries and sells more than 13.5 million appliances a year, some 75 percent outside of Mexico. Mabe is 48 percent owned by General Electric Company, which is its exclusive distributor in the United States.

MABE ALONE AND MABE PLUS GE: 1946–92

Luis Berrondo Martínez was a young Spaniard when he arrived in Mexico City in 1944 to play jai alai. His brother Francisco owned, along with an Egyptian, Egon Mabardi, an importing company located in the city. In 1946 the two founded a tool-and-die firm that also manufactured lamps. They named it Mabe for the first two letters of their surnames (Mabardi-Berrondo). In the beginning Mabe only had 20 employees, but it soon received backing from the Saíz Sánchez brothers and the following year began making kitchen furnishings. Mabe also made special lamps for government offices and other customers.

Mabe was employing 150 people in 1953, when it began making gas stoves. It founded its first branch outside Mexico City, in Monterrey, Nuevo Leon, in 1955, added ovens and toaster-broilers to its kitchen line in 1959, and established its first distribution center in 1961. This facility was in Mexicali, Baja California, on the border with the United States. The following year Mabe opened an assembly plant for its products in Venezuela. By 1966, the company was building entire modular kitchens and had distribution centers in other parts of the Caribbean and in Central and South America. Luis Berrondo became chief executive in 1965 on the death of his brother and also went on to found other businesses, most notably Grupo Financiero Bital, S.A.

Mabe joined with three other companies—IEM,

KEY DATES

1946: Controladora Mabe is founded in Mexico City.

1947: The firm begins making kitchen appliances.

1953: Mabe starts producing gas stoves.

1960: The company starts overseas production with an assembly plant in Venezuela.

1977: Mabe begins making refrigerators, under the Astral brand name.

1987: General Electric Co. buys 48 percent of Mabe.

1991: Full production begins in a new Mabe factory making one million gas ranges a year.

1994: Mabe and Sanyo Electric Co. Ltd. open a plant to make compressors for refrigerators.

1997: Mabe is the leading white goods manufacturer in Mexico and has 13 plants.

2001: Mabe opens a Mexican plant designed to export 500,000 refrigerators a year to the United States.

2005: Mabe buys Camco, Canada's largest manufacturer of home appliances.

Supermatic, and Acros—in a consortium formed in 1969 to manufacture compressor motors. In 1974 it was a firm with 1,000 employees and annual sales of $20 million. Three years later it opened a plant in Querétaro to manufacture refrigerators under the Astral brand name.

Mabe was making more refrigerators in Mexico than any other company when, in 1987, it formed a joint venture with General Electric Co.'s Major Appliance Business Group. GE acquired 48.42 percent of Mabe and immediately began putting into effect a plan to construct and operate a factory in Mexico that would turn out one million gas ranges a year, chiefly for the U.S. market, under four labels, including GE and Hotpoint. Ground was broken for the plant in San Juan Potosí in 1988, and full production began in 1991, with the facility quickly supplying one-third of all gas stoves bought in the United States. It was the world's largest facility for making gas stoves, but 80 percent of the components were made in the United States.

THRIVING AND GROWING: 1992–99

General Electric provided Mabe with technology, channels of distribution, and access to raw materials. With the support of so powerful a company, Mabe had the wherewithal to make major acquisitions. In 1988 it purchased the washing machine business of Grupo Industrial Saltillo, S.A. de C.V., the Mexican leader in this field (and also allied with GE), and in 1993 it acquired Polarix, a Colombian manufacturer of refrigerators. Mabe also signed a strategic alliance with the Dutch firm Ceteco, manufacturer of washing machines and stoves in Venezuela. By means of the Regina brand, Mabe exported its products to other South American countries. In 1994 it opened a research and development center in Querétaro and joined with the Japanese company Sanyo Electric Co., Ltd. to produce compressors and motors in San Luis Potosí for refrigerators and washing machines. The following year it acquired Durex, a producer of home appliances in Guayaquil, Ecuador. Mabe was able to raise $100 million in a private placement and was the first private sector Mexican company to receive an investment grade rating from Standard & Poor's LLC. Moreover, the rating did not require explicit credit guarantees from General Electric.

These were Mabe's golden years, in which it invested $60 million a year on average and its goods were exported to 70 nations. By 1997 Mabe had become the most important manufacturer of white goods in Mexico—and not only from its factories in Mexico, since one-fourth of its sales volume was coming from its three South America plants. The company had long sent executives to South America to identify the places that offered the best conditions to build a production facility. They also sought out white goods manufacturers that were still small but had good prospects for growth. With those that qualified, Mabe would offer to buy a minority stake but insisted on control of the operation. Mabe had the capacity to produce four million units of various appliances a year, a distribution system thought superior to its competitors in arriving at major population centers, advertising to back its products, and post-sale service rarely found elsewhere in the region. In 1997, its sales of refrigerators, washing machines, gas ranges, and compressors came to eight million units, with 40 percent of its revenue in Mexico, 35 percent in the United States, and 25 percent in Latin America outside Mexico. GE provided Mabe in Mexico with its top-of-the-line electric ranges, washing machines, and refrigerators of 14 or more cubic feet. To serve its diverse markets, Mabe had created a distribution system suitable for third world conditions where roads are poor and retail chains are technologically backward. Developed by Hewlett-Packard Co., the system's function was to place virtually all of Mabe's goods in containers and trailers.

The following year, 1998, was an extremely active one for Mabe. An agreement with the Spanish company

Fagor brought it two plants in Spain and Argentina. The company purchased the Inresa brand in Peru and combined Madosa with Ceteco in Venezuela, where it acquired the Condesa and Admiral brands and management of the GE brand. Mabe also entered Brazil in collaboration with General Electric's Brazilian subsidiary, forming the GE Dako brand. In 1999 Mabe initiated work on a $280 million Quantum plant in Celaya, Guanajuato, with the objective of producing 500,000 refrigerators a year for export to the United States, where they replaced the output of a GE plant in Bloomington, Indiana. This facility, opened in 2001, covered the equivalent of 15 football fields and cost $300 million to put into operation.

MABE IN THE 21ST CENTURY

Mabe's sales in 2000 came to about $1.32 billion, almost twice as high as the $721 million registered in 1995. With the opening of the Celaya plant the following year, its number of its factories came to 18. The company was exporting its goods to more than 30 countries, and export accounted for 60 percent of its revenue. It now enjoyed 53 percent of the white goods market in Mexico, 50 percent in Central America and the Andean region of South America, and 25 percent of the market for ranges in the United States. However Standard & Poor's LLC pointed out that the company's debt—believed to be nearly $500 million—was increasing faster than its cash flow. There were rumblings within General Electric itself. In 2002 the company combined its lighting and appliance businesses into a single division to reduce backroom and administrative costs. An investment analyst reported that both GE and Mabe were beginning to shift appliance production from Mexico to Asia, where costs were lower. Another analyst predicted that GE would exit "nonperforming industrial segments, including motors, lighting and appliances," according to Kathryn Krandeld of the *Wall Street Journal.*

The competition was indeed growing stronger. Mabe's sales stagnated in 2002, as two companies based in Mexico—Whirlpool and Electrolux—and three from South Korea—LG, Samsung, and Daewoo—stepped up their efforts with sales campaigns based on low price and an eye on the U.S. market as well as Mexico. By late 2004 Mabe had shifted its strategy, spending heavily on an advertising campaign intended to target distinct segments of the market, including the high-end sector, to take advantage of consumer interest in space-saving and energy-saving appliances. Some of Mabe's marketing in Mexico was being aimed at housing developers, construction firms, and architects, with the company offering to provide custom-designed appliances at added cost. For developers of luxury apartment complexes in

beach resorts such as Puerto Vallarta, Ixtapa, and Cancún, Mabe was providing a combined kitchen with refrigerator, microwave, and washer/dryer. The company prices ranged from about $125 for its cheapest ranges and washing machines to about $3,500 for its highest-end stove and about $9,500 for its highest-end institutional refrigerators.

To meet explosive growth in luxury items, Mabe was importing GE's Profile and Monogram brands, as well as producing its own in Celaya under the GE brand. It was also planning to introduce an intermediate line called Platinum for apartment dwelling affluent young couples who wanted good design but did not have sufficient kitchen space for a Profile, Mabe's most expensive brand. One product of Mabe's research-and-development facility was its "Id System"—computerized intelligence that allowed its washing machines to run more efficiently, clean clothing better, and practically rule out the possibility of damage.

In 2004 Mabe manufactured about ten million units, with 40 percent of production from its six plants in Mexico and the rest in Brazil, Colombia, and Ecuador. Of its sales of $1.8 billion that year, Mexico accounted for only $700 million. Of the rest, direct exports from Mexico accounted for $800 million, and goods made as well as sold abroad for $300 million. "If you buy a washing machine or stove or refrigerator anywhere from Alaska to Brazil," wrote Kelly Arthur Garrett for *Business Mexico,* "there's a pretty good chance Mabe made it. That's true even if it's not called Mabe or GE. About a dozen other brands sell Mabe manufactured units."

Throughout Latin America, the GE label on Mabe's production indicated appliances in the premium segment. The Mabe brand sold in the highest volume and was aimed at the middle and upper-middle classes. Smaller local brands in the various countries indicated lower prices for a lower-income clientele. Serviplus was the name for a network of 100 company workshops, plus 200 concessionaires, dedicated to serving customers. The shops provided 15,000 replacement parts that could be called up electronically in response to orders, arriving from any of Mabe's 14 or 15 plants.

A commercial accord between Mabe and General Electric would not expire until 2012 and was automatically renewable for periods of four years unless either party gave notice two years in advance. The alliance allowed Mabe to acquire raw materials for the same cost and with the same conditions as GE subsidiaries. It also allowed Mabe to benefit from GE's distribution network and technical advantages. Mabe continued to supply all gas stoves sold by GE in the United States. It was also providing a large percentage of electric stoves and two-door refrigerators sold by GE in the United States.

Mabe consolidated its Brazilian operations in 2003, creating Mabe Itú Electrodomésticos S.A. by buying out Dako (washing machines) and CCE (refrigerators). In 2005 Mabe purchased Camco Inc., the largest Canadian manufacturer, marketer, and servicer of home appliances, for $70.4 million. Camco's product lines included GE, Profile, and Hotpoint, and it was the primary supplier of clothes dryers to General Electric in the United States. The company was manufacturing clothes dryers and dishwashers in Montreal, and its acquisition extended Mabe's line of products to these appliances for the first time. In order to finance the purchase of Camco, which was renamed Mabe Canada, Inc., the company issued a ten-year, $200 million bond. Also in 2005, Mabe opened a new corporate headquarters and introduced improved packaging design. In 2006, it opened a showroom to display its new products, plus a gourmet center with culinary workshops and an area for potential suppliers to present their wares.

Besides washing machines, gas and electric ranges, clothes dryers, dishwashers, and refrigerators, Mabe was producing electric and gas space heaters, smoke exhausts, ovens and oven/ranges, microwave ovens, and toaster-broilers. Mabe's president and chief executive officer was Luis Berrondo Ávalos. The 52 percent of the company not held by General Electric was owned by the Berrondo, Saíz, and Esteve families, with Luis Berrondo Ávalos the largest individual shareholder.

Robert Halasz

PRINCIPAL SUBSIDIARIES

Mabe, S.A. de C.V.; Mabe Canada, Inc.; Mabesa, S. de R.L. de C.V.

PRINCIPAL COMPETITORS

Daewoo Electronics de México, S.A. de C.V.; Electrolux de México, S.A. de C.V.; Industrias Acros Whirlpool, S.A. de C.V.; LG Electronics Mexico, S.A. de C.V.; Samsung Electronics Mexico, S.A. de C.V.

FURTHER READING

Butler, Robert J., "A Project Milestone Bonus Plan," *National Productivity Review,* Winter 1991/92, pp. 31–39.

DuPont, Tom, "GE Confirms Joint Venture to Make Gas Ranges in Mexico," *HFD,* July 3, 1987, p. 18.

Fuentes, Valentín, "Del frontón a Mabe," *Expansión,* May 1–15, 2002, pp. 68.

García, María Eugenia, "Hasta la cocina," *Expansión,* July 25–August 8, 2001, pp. 83–84.

Garrett, Kelly Arthur, "Mabe: At the Vanguard in Household Appliances," *Business Mexico,* April 2005, p. 27.

Guerrero, Maurizio, "Anclados al exterior," *Expansión,* June 25–July 9, 2003, pp. 247–48.

Krandeld, Kathryn, "GE Appliances Don't Wash with 'Growth,'" *Wall Street Journal,* April 3, 2003, p. C3.

"Mabe Offer for Camco Successful," *CNW Group,* September 23, 2005.

Millman, Joel, "GE Boosts Mexican Output As Labor Talks in U.S. Near," *Wall Street Journal,* January 5, 2000, p. A17.

Ramírez, Fernando, "De polo a polo," *Expansión,* 2006 (accessed from Mabe Web site).

Ramírez Tamayo, Zacarías, "Hasta la cocina," *Expansión,* December 17, 1997, pp. 54–55, 58–59, 61–62.

Rosas, Ana María, "Un paso al lujo," *Expansión,* November 10–24, 2004, pp. 153–54, 156, 159.

Smith, Geri, "This Venture Is Cooking with Gas," *Business Week,* November 8, 1993, p. 70.

Coppel, S.A. de C.V.

Calle Republica 2855 Poniente
Culiacán, Sinaloa 80100
Mexico
Telephone: (52) (667) 759-4200
Fax: (52) (667) 759-4223
Web site: http://www.coppel.com

Public Company
Incorporated: 1965 as Almacenes Coppel S.A.
Employees: 28,412
Sales: MXN 19.61 billion ($1.8 billion) (2005)
Stock Exchanges: Mexico City
Ticker Symbol: ALMACO
NAIC: 531100 Department Stores; 448210 Shoe Stores

■■■

Coppel, S.A. de C.V, specializing in household goods and clothing, is one of the largest department store chains in northern Mexico. It is the second-largest chain in Mexico for the sale of furniture and articles for the home. The Coppel chain operates more than 300 stores in every Mexican state under the Tiendas Coppel name and almost 200 shoe stores under the name Tiendas Coppel-Canadá.

FIFTY YEARS IN NORTHERN MEXICO: 1941–90

The enterprise initiated activities in 1941, when Luis Coppel Rivas decided, along with his son Enrique Coppel Tamayo, to move from Mazatlán, Sinaloa, to Culiacán, the capital of the state, and establish a small gift shop that later specialized in selling radios and watches. According to family lore, business did not go well until Coppel Rivas' wife took control of the purse from her husband. "She measured even the water in which he bathed," a grandson recalled to Adolfo Ortega of the Mexican business magazine *Expansión.* Later the enterprise obtained more financing, renamed itself Comercial Coppel and shifted its specialty to household goods, especially furniture. Over the course of time, its goods came to include electronic products, household appliances, toys, calculators, travelers' items, auto accessories, optical goods, and jewelry. The enterprise was incorporated in 1965 as Almacenes Coppel. (*Almacen* is the Spanish word for warehouse). It would later reincorporate as Coppel, S.A. de C.V. in 1992.

Coppel owed its success to its policy of making sales on credit, secured by weekly payments. In 1970 it began selling clothing and household appliances under a revolving credit scheme. The company had no competition in this field during the decade, since, as a practical matter, clothing could not be repossessed for nonpayment. During the 1970s the company added perfume, shoes, and tennis clothing and accessories to its range of products. The large volume of Coppel's business and the complexity in managing inventory resulted in a system that allowed the company to maintain optimal quality control in the operation of such distinct areas a sales, credit, collection, promotion, finance, and human resources.

A grandson of the founder, Enrique Coppel Luken, became chief executive and chairman of the board of the firm in 1983. Although Coppel began listing its common stock on Mexico's stock exchange in 1988, it

COMPANY PERSPECTIVES

Our Mission: To be the favorite store of the great majority of the popular market that buys on credit, offering, in an easy manner, a wide supply of products and services for all the family at good prices.

remained almost totally a family-owned firm, which reincorporated in 1992 as Coppel, S.A. de C.V.

EXPANSION THROUGHOUT MEXICO: 1990–2005

Coppel had 22 stores at the beginning of 1990, when it initiated an expansion program. As the decade progressed, the chain expanded its reach beyond its base, entering cities such as Guadalajara, Monterrey, Puebla, and Tijuana. There were 143 Coppel stores in 21 Mexican states in 2002, when the company bought the Calzados Canadá footwear chain. Canadá, once the largest producer and retailer of shoes in Mexico, had fallen on hard times by the 1980s, but 178 stores remained in almost all parts of the country, and its Guadalajara factory was still turning out 4 million pairs of shoes per day. The seller was Grupo Financiero BBVA Bancomer, S.A. de C.V., which had taken over the heavily indebted chain and wanted to divest itself of nonperforming assets. The Canadá stores were remodeled and continued operation under the name Tiendas Coppel-Canadá.

The Canadá stores were little more than one-tenth the size of the Coppel stores, which were divided into 16 specialized departments by line of product. The number of Coppel stores was growing by an average of 20 percent a year during the first years of the 21st century. Coppel was planning, in 2002, to open units in areas where the chain had no prior presence, such as the southeastern states and Mexico City. Each new store opened represented an investment of about $2 million.

Interviewed for the Mexican business magazine *Expansión* by Raúl Curiel, one investment analyst questioned whether, given a clientele of modest means and the need to extend credit to them, opening new stores was worth the expense. A Standard & Poor report echoed these concerns. Coppel's finance director told Curiel, however, that "The popular market protects its credit rating because thanks to credit it has access to articles that it can't acquire otherwise; that, and the ease with which we extend loans are our competitive advantages."

One believer in Coppel was the International Finance Corporation, the private credit arm of the World Bank, which extended the enterprise a $30 million loan in 2002 as a means of expressing its interest in financing profitable private long-term projects in Mexico with a strong social impact. The IFC granted Coppel a new 10-year loan of $35 million in 2005. On this occasion, an IFC press release declared, "This loan conforms to IFC's strategy of aiding the Mexican private sector to obtain more access to foreign private finance and to facilitate the growth of local enterprises, better their competitiveness, and create new employment."

A staff of 2,000 was dedicated to keeping credit risks low, with only 5 to 6 percent of all accounts in arrears of payment. More than 90 percent of all credit applications were authorized automatically, with decisions on the rest made in less than five minutes. Credit sales carried installment periods of 12 or 18 months for furnishings and five months for clothing. Coppel's credit charges came to about 15 percent of net sales in 2005. Its total debt was 56 percent of total assets at the end of the year—about the same as the previous year, although operating expenses grew 27 percent, mainly because of the cost of opening new stores.

Enrique Coppel and his brothers were not disposed to raise money for the firm's expansion by selling stock to outsiders. Disgusted by the high rates and short terms of bank loans, Enrique Coppel turned to local capital markets in 2003, raising $97.6 million from a peso-dominated bond sold to insurance companies, private banking clients, and company-run pension funds at a cost not much higher than the Mexican interbank rate. Coppel was hoping to issue bonds of even longer term to closely related local pension funds known as *afores*, which were required to invest mainly in government paper or investment-grade corporate securities. Only one agency had given the company an investment-grade rating, however. Meanwhile, Coppel was having success in shifting its short-term debt to longer terms and lowering its finance costs.

Coppel shrugged off the cost of opening stores, inaugurating 38 new ones in 2003, 44 in 2004, and 52 in 2005. Its formula for financing growth remained the same. Each store opened represented an increase in sales and assets, supported by new loans and reinvestment of profits. In 2004 the company secured a credit line of MXN 1 billion (about $90 million), about half of which it earmarked for the first half of 2005. "We believe that we can continue growing at this rate for another decade," Augustín Coppel, a younger brother of Enrique, told Ortega. He was in charge of the expansion program that could take the chain to 2,000 stores in 2012—a

KEY DATES

1941: Luis Coppel Rivas establishes a small gift shop in Culiacán, Sinaloa.
1965: The enterprise is incorporated as Almacenes Coppel, S.A.
1970: Coppel begins selling clothing and household appliances under a revolving credit scheme.
1983: Enrique Coppel Lukens, a grandson of the founder, takes over direction of the firm.
1992: Almacenes Coppel is reincorporated as Coppel, S.A. de C.V.
2002: The Coppel chain has 143 stores in 21 Mexican states; Coppel buys the Calzados Canadá footwear chain, once the largest in Mexico.

goal that Enrique told Ortega was "not a plan but a desire. ... It isn't an obligation or a task, but it can be a result."

Coppel was in a hurry to grow because it saw a great opportunity in selling goods on credit to people of slender resources. There were over 20 million Mexicans without financial services whatever and 50 million who needed loans to buy merchandise because they were living on less than $600 a month. To tap this market, however, Coppel needed an alliance with a bank—or its own bank. The company, along with two others, had joined with Banca Afirme, S.A. to share credit information and extend loans, but Enrique Coppel was not satisfied with the experience. Coppel had already begun offering its customers cash loans of up to about $1,000, life insurance, a service that would send money from one city to another, and a bill paying service for public utilities such as water, light, and telephones. Coppel also began operating a retirement fund, Afore Coppel S.A. de C.V., in 2005.

The company was not sufficient to consume all the energies of Enrique Coppel, who was in the process of founding a 2,500-acre self-financed model community in Culiacán that was named La Primavera and was seen as the embryo of a larger one to be called Ciudad Coppel. Built around an artificial lake, the gated community would ultimately consist of 100,000 people, all carefully selected from the best elements of northwestern Mexico, living in well designed large houses or apartment towers. There were spaces reserved for commercial and industrial zones, offices, schools, a Catholic church and small chapels, a hospital, a university, a hotel, an extensive park and canal system, sporting clubs, and an artificial beach—even a race track and a casino or amphitheater. Coppel said, however, that non-Catholics should not look to him for contributions to the purchase of land or erection of buildings for their denominations or faiths.

COPPEL IN 2005–06

At the end of the first quarter of 2006. Coppel was operating 306 Coppel stores and 176 Tiendas Coppel-Canadá in 134 cities and every state. Some 40 percent of the properties on which these stores rested belonged to the company; the rest were rented. The company also had a network of 74 distribution centers and ten warehouses and maintained a fleet of 241 trucks, plus smaller vehicles, in order to fill, and, if necessary, install, 20,000 home delivery orders a week without charge to the customer. All the stores, distribution centers, and warehouses were connected by computer, which also stored information on credit customers.

Coppel's furnishings division consisted of electric home appliances; other articles for the home and for personal use; electronic items, such as television sets and cellphones; household appliances; furniture; tires and other automobile accessories; bicycles; toys; watches; jewelry; and optical goods. All merchandise in this division was guaranteed for two years, even when the manufacturer did not offer said guarantee. In the case of failure of an essential appliance such as a refrigerator, stove, or heater, Coppel, at the option of the customer, could provide a substitute during the period of repair. The clothing division included boys' and men's clothing, girls' and women's clothing, sheets and pillowcases, shoes, and perfume. The furnishings division was accounting for 72 percent of sales and the clothing division for 28 percent. In all, Coppel was selling about 14,000 items and was stockkeeping 44,295 units.

Some 88 percent of Coppel's 2005 sales were made on credit. The other sales were made in cash or by credit or debit card. Coppel's credit charges allowed it to gain a profit from this form of sales beyond covering its own finance costs and other costs related to credit sales, such as administration and absorbing bad debts. The company had about 9.9 million customer accounts, of which 4.3 million were active, and its own proprietary credit card. Coppel saw as its market the 57 percent of the Mexican population with monthly incomes between 4 and 45 times the minimum wage. The company was initiating 19 sales promotion campaigns a year and publishing a promotional monthly with a circulation of 10.1 million. Advertising on radio and television was continuous and was in the form of 20- and 30-second spots. Print advertising was geared to the 19 campaigns a year and special times of the year such as St. Valentine's Day and Christmas. Coppel's suppliers were covering about 30 percent of the company's advertising expenses.

Considered as a department store chain, Coppel's sales volume was not as high as that of Wal-Mart de México or El Puerto de Liverpool but was superior to such well established rivals as El Palacio de Hierro and Sears Roebuck de México. Elektra and Famsa were considered the competitors most similar in the socioeconomic segment at which Coppel aimed. Elektra had some 850 stores, sales 60 percent higher than Coppel, and a tie-in to bank services, but it did not sell clothing or footwear. Famsa, which was smaller, had 250 stores in Mexico and United States and had begun selling clothing in some of its stores for the first time. The records of a federal consumer agency showed fewer customer complaints against Coppel than Elektra or Famsa in 2003–04; moreover, Coppel had resolved a higher proportion of the complaints than Elektra or Famsa.

Coppel's line of merchandise included such household appliances as stoves, washers, dryers, refrigerators, air conditioners, irons and ironing boards, blenders, hot plates, toaster-ovens, and grills. It was also selling luggage, portable coolers, tires and batteries, audio components, cameras, telephones, television sets, radios, videocassette and digital video recorders, and personal care items.

Coppel's common stock remained almost exclusively in the hands of the five Coppel Luken brothers who were grandsons of the founder. They owned 99.9 percent of the shares in 2006.

Robert Halasz

PRINCIPAL SUBSIDIARIES

Coppel Corporation (United States).

PRINCIPAL DIVISIONS

Clothing Division; Furnishings Division.

PRINCIPAL COMPETITORS

Grupo Elektra, S.A. de C.V.; Grupo Famsa, S.A. de C.V.

FURTHER READING

Castellano Gutiérrez, Ángeles, "Ciudad Coppel," *Expansión,* August 3–17, 2005, pp. 74–78, 80.

Curiel, Raúl, "A la conquista de México," *Expansión,* July 24–August 7, 2002, pp. 294–95.

Galloway, Jennifer, "Gridlock in the Bond Market," *LatinFinance,* March 2004, pp. 27, 30.

Monroy, Pedro, "Buscará Coppel socio conocedor de calzado," *Reforma,* April 15, 2002, p. 12.

Ortega, Adolfo, "Mi gran plan," *Expansión,* February 2–16, 2005, pp. 40–45.

D.F. Stauffer Biscuit Company

360 South Belmont Street
York, Pennsylvania 17405-1426
U.S.A.
Telephone: (717) 843-9016
Toll Free: (800) 673-2473
Fax: (717) 843-0592
Web site: http://www.stauffers.net

Wholly Owned Subsidiary of Meiji Seika Kaisha, Ltd.
Founded: 1871
Employees: 500
Sales: $125 million (2005 est.)
NAIC: 311821 Cookie and Cracker Manufacturing

■ ■ ■

A subsidiary of Japanese pharmaceutical and confection company Meiji Seika Kaisha, Ltd., D.F. Stauffer Biscuit Company is a York, Pennsylvania, baker of value-priced sandwich cookies, sugar wafers, and other cookies, including ginger snaps, lemon snaps, oatmeal, chocolate chip, shortbread, snickerdoodles, and iced cookies. The company also offers cracker items such as oyster crackers; "whales" in a variety of flavors; Cheddarfetti, a cheese snack in a variety of shapes; Chicken Snack crackers; and cracker crumbs for cooking and toppings. Stauffer's signature product, however, is animal crackers, which come in 13 shapes and are made from the same recipe the company has been using for well more than 100 years—albeit the equipment used to make the crackers has been modernized a number of times. Animal crackers are less sweet and also healthier than their cookie counterparts, containing half the fat, one third the so-

dium, and 15 percent fewer calories. Stauffer's animal crackers are available in graham, chocolate, cinnamon, and iced versions. Stauffer also does contract baking, primarily at its new Santa Ana, California, plant. In addition, Stauffer operates its main plant in York, another plant located in Cuba, New York, and maintains an outlet store in York.

19TH-CENTURY ROOTS

The company was established by David F. Stauffer, the son of a Mennonite minister. Rather than follow in his father's footsteps, he initially worked as a millwright and was involved in the construction of a number of flour mills before deciding to try his hand as a baker. In 1871 he came across a small bakery operating out of the back of a house in downtown York, the site of a present-day McDonald's restaurant. It had been in business since 1858 and its founder, one Jacob Weiser, was looking to sell. Stauffer bought the business, put down his millwright tools, tied on an apron, and began producing 750 pounds a day of unseasoned water crackers, biscuits, and pretzels. When baking for the day was done, he sold his wares out of the shop and was known to make door-to-door deliveries in a wheelbarrow. Around the start of the 20th century, Stauffer was looking to expand his product line and began experimenting with animal cracker recipes until he found one he liked. It would prove to have enduring appeal, as animal crackers become the cornerstone of the company's success.

In the beginning, Stauffer and his family lived in an apartment above the bakery, but as the business grew over the years, the bakery expanded around the original site, and the Stauffer clan moved out. It was very much

COMPANY PERSPECTIVES

Each day, thanks to sixteen oven lines, the Stauffer Biscuit Company produces more than 250 tons of animal crackers, cookies and snack crackers in every imaginable form. Today you'll find Stauffer cookies and Animal Crackers all over the United States and beyond.

a family enterprise, involving Stauffer's four sons. When he died in 1921, his eldest son, Calvin, took charge. By this point a third generation also was involved in the business. A year earlier David E. Stauffer, Sr., born in 1901 to Calvin and his wife, joined the company after graduating and serving an apprenticeship at S. Morgan Smith Co. He always expected to join the family business. Often as a child he accompanied his father to work on Saturday, the bakery's pay day when workers making more than $5 were handed paper money and those making less were given silver dollars. On one of those occasions his grandfather presented him with a silver dollar. "Oh boy," Stauffer recalled on the eve of his 100th birthday in an interview with the *York Daily Record,* "I thought I was a millionaire."

When David Stauffer, Sr., went to work at the bakery, he was trained on how the hearth ovens, reel ovens, and other baking equipment worked, but being the owner's grandson (and later the son of the owner) did not ensure that the old hands at the bakery were forthcoming in sharing their secrets with him. "The foremen would walk around with their recipe books in their hip pockets," he told *Snack Food & Wholesale Bakery,* in November 2000. "They would seldom give information out to anyone. It was their job security, their power over management." David Stauffer found another way to gain access to formulas, however. He began attending industry conferences where he could network with other independent bakers and pick up recipes and learn about new technologies. As a result, the company in the 1920s began to add new lines of chocolate, creamy, and marshmallow confections that helped Stauffer to better compete and survive, unlike other regional bakeries that fell by the wayside as national concerns like National Biscuit Company drove them out of business.

CROSSROADS: 1960

In 1954 Cecil Stauffer died and David Stauffer, Sr., became president. By 1960 the company reached a

crossroads. The bakery had grown to be five stories high, but its downtown location made further expansion impossible. In order to keep the family business viable, one that could be passed to the next generation, the company had to make a move to a new location. It was not an easy plan to execute, however. Just a regional business with sales of less than $2 million, Stauffer had a difficult time arranging for the $250,000 loan it needed. When the money was secured, a new manufacturing and headquarters was built at a new site, where future expansion was possible. When the new 64,000-square-foot facility opened with a 115-foot cookie oven and a 75-foot pretzel oven, it seemed that further expansion might not be necessary or was at least a distant dream. In time Stauffer ran out of room. In 1970, 25,000 square feet of space was added, followed by another 10,000 feet in 1977, and a 78,000-square-foot warehouse addition in 1995. The operation totaled 244,000 square feet, situated on 17 acres of land.

In 1964 David Stauffer, Sr.'s, cousin Neil P. Stauffer assumed the presidency. He held the position until his retirement in 1981 and David E. Stauffer, Jr., took over. Before this transition, Neil Stauffer and his daughter, Susan Stauffer, decided they were interested in selling their half of the business, valued around $3 million, and he lined up several major corporations interested in buying the company. David Stauffer, Sr., and David Stauffer, Jr., an executive vice-president, wanted to keep the business in the family and convinced Neil Stauffer to agree to a preliminary sales agreement. It would expire before they could arrange the necessary financing, and as a result the terms of the sale were changed to include a provision that called for Neil Stauffer to receive a percentage of any amount exceeding $3 million should the business be sold within the next ten years. In this way, the David Stauffers would be prevented from putting the company on the block in the near term and potentially achieve a windfall that did not benefit the other family members. Thus, in June 1981, the David Stauffers paid their cousins $1.5 million, as well as $50,000 to Neil Stauffer for his services that year, to acquire 100 percent control of D.F. Stauffer Biscuit Company.

Neil Stauffer moved to Florida to pursue other interests while the family bakery in Pennsylvania came under control of David Stauffer, Jr. He took over a company that was still very much a regional business, but he was interested in expanding Stauffer's geographic reach. Because the York plant was not operating at capacity, he looked to pursue contract baking. In 1985 an opportunity arose to forge a joint venture with Meiji Seika, which had been working with the Pennsylvania Department of Commerce to line up a baking concern interested in being acquired or in working in a joint ef-

```
┌─────────────────────────────────────────────┐
│                                               │
│              KEY DATES                        │
│                  ■                            │
│                                               │
│   1871:  David F. Stauffer buys a York,       │
│          Pennsylvania, bakery.                │
│   1921:  Stauffer dies.                       │
│   1960:  The company is moved from the        │
│          original site.                       │
│   1981:  David Stauffer, Sr., and David       │
│          Stauffer, Jr., buy out family        │
│          members.                             │
│   1990:  Meiji Seika Kaisha acquires          │
│          control of the company.              │
│   1999:  Laguna Cookie and Dessert Co. is     │
│          acquired.                            │
│   2001:  A new Santa Ana, California,         │
│          plant opens.                         │
│   2005:  Stauffer family involvement ends.    │
│                                               │
└─────────────────────────────────────────────┘
```

fort to produce specialty breadsticks. The two companies agreed to work together, an arrangement that allowed Stauffer to fill out the bakery's capacity. For the next five years Stauffer produced the breadsticks, but its sales force struggled to grow sales. In 1990 the arrangement was terminated, but Meiji Seika was comfortable with its working relationship with Stauffer and offered to buy control of the company while allowing the Stauffer family to continue to run the business.

The Meiji Seika offer was a tempting one, as David Stauffer, Jr., explained to *Snack Food & Wholesale Bakery:* "It became clear to us that, as a strictly family company, we were fairly limited as to what we could do. The industry was becoming much more capital intensive, particularly as relates to the rising costs associated with automation and technology. We felt that Meiji Seika would be able to assist us with the technological advances in the industry." In addition, David Stauffer was interested in expanding the company's cracker business, which he believed offered more growth potential than cookies, but lacked the funds to beef up cracker production. Later he would also testify in court in litigation related to the sale that the company had experienced some "financial reversals" in addition to being undercapitalized.

MEIJI SEIKA ACQUIRING CONTROL: 1990

In January 1990 Meiji Seika bought a 51 percent controlling interest in Stauffer for $2.3 million and gained a seven-year option to acquire the remaining stake for $2.2 million, an amount subject to change, pending the determination of a fair market value of the company at the time of purchase. In addition, David Stauffer, Jr., received a four-year employment contract to serve as chief operating officer. Five months later Neil Stauffer sued his cousins, maintaining that because the sale took place between the eighth and ninth years of his sales agreement with the David Stauffers, he was entitled to 20 percent of the deal's value over $3 million. He contended that the structure of the Meiji Seika transaction, which fell below the $3 million threshold until his ten-year provision had expired, was "a subterfuge to get around my original intent of sharing in the future sale of the business." In December 1992 the matter went to trial at the York County Common Pleas Court where David Stauffer, Jr., maintained that the terms of the sale to the Japanese company were purely coincidental, and a board member also testified that he was involved in the negotiations with Meiji Seika and had not even been aware of the provisions in the 1981 agreement. The jury took just 30 minutes to decide that Neil Stauffer was entitled to $224,058, an amount that included interest over the three years it took to settle the matter.

With the family conflict finally resolved, Stauffer began a period of strong growth, as sales tripled over the course of the next two years, leading to the major expansion of the warehouse. The company was especially successful in accommodating the new warehouse clubs as well as other retail outlets in addition to supermarkets, including mass merchandisers, discount stores, dollar stores, and drugstore chains. Although owned by Meiji Seika, it remained a family business in many respects. David Stauffer, Jr.'s, sons served in top executive posts while his wife was on the board of directors and ran the outlet store at the warehouse and at a York location. However, the backing of the Japanese parent corporation was key to the company's expansion in the second half of the 1990s. In 1997 Stauffer acquired Fleetwood Snacks and its manufacturing plant in Blandon, Pennsylvania. The following year it bought Farnsworth Cookie, adding a production plant in Cuba, New York. Stauffer closed the decade with an even more significant acquisition, buying Laguna Cookie and Dessert Co. and its Tustin, California, manufacturing facility. Stauffer was able to gain a presence on the West Coast while broadening its product line, adding Laguna's gourmet mini-cookie line and fruit bars. In addition, Laguna enjoyed strong club business, bolstering that segment for Stauffer, had a contract business producing private-label items, and provided Stauffer with entry into the competitive in-store bakery channel. Stauffer elected to keep the Laguna brand—changed from Laguna Cookie to Laguna Bakery—and apply it to the more upscale, in-store baked goods.

At the start of the new century, Stauffer was generating annual sales of about $125 million. The company was especially optimistic about the potential of the Laguna operation and invested $20 million in building a new 217,000-square-foot plant in Santa Ana, California, which opened in the summer of 2001 to replace the 50,000-square-foot plant in Tustin. The new facility took on the production of animal crackers, which remained Stauffer's top-selling product, and added a line the company had not offered since the early 1980s: sandwich crème cookies. It was an item especially popular with Hispanic consumers, and Laguna's location was ideal for serving this market.

In March 2005 David Stauffer, Sr., died at the age of 103. Shortly thereafter, Meiji Seika announced that no Stauffers would be employed there by the end of the month, thus bringing to an end the 134-year involvement of five generations of the Stauffer family in the operation of the business founded by David F. Stauffer. In April 2006 the company closed its Blandon, Pennsylvania plant.

Ed Dinger

PRINCIPAL COMPETITORS

Kellogg Snacks Division; Kraft Foods North America, Inc.; Parmalat Finanziaria S.p.A.

FURTHER READING

Cecil, Andra Maria, "Stauffer's Past President Dies at 103," *York Daily Record,* March 22, 2005, p. 6.

Malovany, Dan, "West Coast Offense," *Snack Food & Wholesale Bakery,* December 2002, p. 16.

Pacyniak, Bernard, "Taming the Cookie/Cracker Market," *Snack Food & Wholesale Bakery,* November 2000, p. 20.

Rauhauser-Smith, Kate, "Businessman's Century: David E. Stauffer Sr., Former President of Stauffer's Biscuit, Is Turning 100," *York Daily Record,* April 14, 2001, p. B06.

Scott, Melanie D., "Family's Crackers a Staple of the Stauffer Business," *York Daily Record,* December 27, 1999, p. C01.

Wise, Dean, "Ex-Head of Stauffer Sues Over Sale," *York Daily Record,* December 17, 1992, p. 1.

———, "Jury Gives Stauffer Share of Proceeds," *York Daily Record,* December 18, 1992, p. 4.

DeVry Inc.

One Tower Lane, Suite 1000
Oakbrook Terrace, Illinois 60181
U.S.A.
Telephone: (630) 571-7700
Fax: (630) 571-0317
Web site: http://www.devry.edu

Public Company
Founded: 1931 as DeForest Training School
Employees: 5,700
Sales: $781.3 million (2005)
Stock Exchanges: New York
Ticker Symbol: DV
NAIC: 611310 Colleges, Universities and Professional Schools; 551112 Offices of Other Holding Companies

■ ■ ■

DeVry Inc., one of the largest publicly held, international, higher education companies in North America, is the holding company for DeVry University, Ross University, Chamberlain College of Nursing, and Becker Professional Review. DeVry operates one of the largest for-profit groups of business and technical schools in the country, offering associates, bachelor's, and postgraduate degrees in subjects ranging from engineering and electronics to accounting and business administration. DeVry University operates 23 campuses that offer undergraduate programs in technology—and business—related fields, as well as seven master's degrees through Keller Graduate School of Management. Several undergraduate and graduate programs are also offered online. Ross University runs a medical school and a veterinary school in the Caribbean. Chamberlain College of Nursing, previously Deaconess College of Nursing, offers an associate of science in nursing degree (ASN), an ASN degree program for licensed nurse practitioners and a bachelor of science in nursing degree (BSN). Becker Professional Review, which includes Stalla CFA Review, provides preparatory coursework for the certified public accountant and chartered financial analyst exams. Becker operates at about 300 locations worldwide.

BEGINNINGS: CONVERGENCE OF KELLER AND DEVRY

The origins of DeVry can be traced to the 1931 establishment of the DeForest Training School in Chicago. The school's founder, Dr. Herman DeVry, was an engineer and inventor who had, among other things, developed a motion picture projector and become involved in the production of educational and training films. He set up the school to offer training in the repair of movie and radio equipment and the curriculum eventually expanded to include training in the repair of televisions and other electronics.

In 1953 the school changed its name to DeVry Technical Institute, and four years later it was granted accreditation to bestow associate's degrees in electronics. DeVry eventually branched out into computers and accounting, and built more campuses in the Chicago and Toronto areas. In 1967, the Bell & Howell Company, best known perhaps for its role in inventing movie cameras, completed its acquisition of the school, and a fast-paced, nationwide expansion program ensued. The following year, the school underwent another name change, to DeVry Institute of Technology. In 1969 DeVry was authorized to award bachelor's degrees in electronics.

Throughout the 1970s Bell & Howell developed a technology-based curriculum which focused on preparing students for careers in the burgeoning engineering and computer industry. By 1983 DeVry had an enrollment of 30,000 students nationwide.

The real success of DeVry during this time was owed to two men who met while working for the company in the early 1970s. Dennis Keller, a Princeton and University of Chicago graduate, and Ronald Taylor, who earned degrees from Harvard and Stanford, were working for DeVry in Chicago when they decided in 1973 to form their own postgraduate school of business. After raising just over $150,000 dollars from friends and family, the two entrepreneurs opened a non-accredited day school which offered certificates (not degrees, as the school was not accredited) in business administration. Calling the business the Keller Graduate School of Management, Keller and Taylor at first performed all the work the school required themselves, from moving furniture into a rented school room to teaching and balancing the books. By the end of 1974, the company had a staff of five, fewer than 30 students, and almost no money in the bank. Unless a new track could be found, Keller and Taylor knew they would be bankrupt within the year.

Because the school was unaccredited and ineligible for federal loans many potential students could not afford to enroll, even though Keller and Taylor kept tuition lower than other nonprofit institutions. So, instead of continuing to compete with such schools as a full-time day school with a traditional student body, the company switched its focus and began offering evening classes to working adults. By offering evening classes, the school's students had the option of continuing to concentrate on

their careers while at the same time attending classes, a formula which has become increasingly effective to a broad range of students over the prior decades. The new emphasis proved to be quite profitable for the fledgling business: within two years the school was offering M.B.A. certification, and the year after that, in 1977, the Keller Graduate School was fully accredited.

Accreditation was traditionally a contentious issue between the academic establishment and for-profit institutions. According to Leslie Spencer, writing in Forbes magazine, the "educational establishment has long thrown roadblocks in the way of for-profit schools by withholding accreditation—the seal of approval required for a school to receive student loans and grants. Any school seeking to make a profit was automatically denied the seal." Because of the Keller Graduate School's success with its students, however, the company was able to throw over that tradition. Spencer, in the same article, noted that the "Keller Graduate School was the first for-profit school the North Central Association of Colleges & Schools ever accepted for membership."

Being granted accreditation enabled the school to overcome many obstacles: the school's academic reputation automatically and dramatically improved, making competition with other schools more feasible; federal loans became available to the school's students; and, most importantly, the school could offer degrees instead of certificates. By 1987, the Keller Graduate School was a true financial success, grossing $5 million a year with an enrollment of about 1,300 students.

While the Keller Graduate School saw increases in both profits and enrollment in the 1980s, DeVry Institutes was facing just the opposite: after its peak year of enrollment in 1983, the business began losing students as more and more people began looking towards business education, as opposed to technological training, to increase their career opportunities. As a result of this negative turn in DeVry's financial outlook, Bell & Howell, having owned DeVry since 1967, decided to divest its 85 percent stake in the company.

1987: DEVRY INC. IS BORN

Keller and Taylor, buoyed by the steady growth of the Keller Graduate School, realized that acquiring the company owned by their former employers presented a unique and somewhat risky opportunity for expansion. Many analysts in the industry questioned why a small but vibrantly successful company like the Keller Graduate School would choose to saddle itself with a business which, despite being many times the size of the Keller Graduate School, was slowing in growth and losing profits. Keller and Taylor, however, saw that if DeVry's

KEY DATES

1931: Dr. Herman DeVry establishes DeForest Training School in Chicago to prepare students for technical work in electronics, motion pictures, radio and later, television.

1953: School's name changed to DeVry Technical Institute.

1957: DeVry Institute achieves associate degree granting status in electronics engineering technology.

1966: DeVry is purchased by Bell and Howell Education Group.

1968: Name is changed to DeVry Institute of Technology.

1969: DeVry is authorized to grant bachelor's degrees in the electronics and computer fields.

1987: DeVry merges with Keller Graduate School of Management after it completes a leveraged buyout of DeVry Institutes from Bell and Howell.

1991: Company goes public on the New York Stock Exchange.

1996: Becker CPA Review is acquired and becomes the Becker Professional Review division.

2000: DeVry begins offering its bachelor's of science degree in business administration online.

2002: DeVry Institutes and Keller Graduate School of Management became DeVry University.

curriculum could be changed to meet the needs of the modern computer and technological industry, the two schools combined could benefit one another, offering training and educational services to an even broader range of students.

However, Keller and Taylor did not have the financial backing necessary to make such an acquisition. Thus, in 1987, the two men approached Citicorp, and a group of insurers headed up by Massachusetts Mutual Life Insurance Company, and borrowed the necessary funds to purchase the DeVry Institutes. Equity investors, Frontenac Venture Company of Chicago among them, also contributed to the effort, loaning Keller and Taylor over $16 million dollars. By the year's end, Keller and Taylor had purchased both Bell & Howell's 85 percent stake in the school as well as the 15 percent that was publicly owned for about $182 million dollars.

The two businesses, the Keller Graduate School and the DeVry Institutes, were combined under DeVry Inc., with Keller acting as chairman and CEO and Taylor acting as president and COO. Until its acquisition of DeVry, the Keller Graduate School was a Chicago institution, where five of its six campuses were housed. Suddenly, as leaders of DeVry Inc., Keller and Taylor had to contend with a cluster of DeVry campuses sprinkled around the United States and in Canada. Such tremendous overnight growth offered not only an opportunity for the Keller Graduate School's expansion, but also presented many organizational and bureaucratic challenges. Keller and Taylor soon found that they needed to amend the DeVry Institutes' curriculum. They also had to face a potentially crippling debt.

To attract more students, Keller and Taylor treated the DeVry Institutes in much the same manner as they had handled the Keller Graduate School's needs: they began offering not only engineering and technical training to the Institutes' undergraduates, but added a business curriculum which complemented the postgraduate programs at Keller as well. Recognizing that most students who attended the DeVry Institutes in all likelihood needed to work while in school, Keller and Taylor expanded the hours and availability of DeVry's courses, making it possible for students to attend part time and during the evening. Another important feature which helped to attract students, and draw them away from more traditional higher-education institutions, was the development of the year-round school year. Offering classes year-round enabled students to complete their programs in a fraction of the time it would otherwise take them, an important factor when considering that the typical DeVry student was attending courses for reasons of practical career advancement.

The curriculum at the DeVry Institutes in the late 1980s and early 1990s branched out to include a wide range of educational services, including courses on electronics engineering technology, computer information systems, telecommunications management, accounting technical management, and business administration.

Most DeVry students were first generation students, coming from low-income households and eligible for both federal and state student loans. To appeal to potential students, DeVry Institutes developed ways in which to make payment plans flexible and less rigid than those at rival institutions, allowing people previously priced out of the higher-education establishment an opportunity to earn degrees.

Keller and Taylor's efforts to turn the DeVry Institutes around worked; by 1992, after only five years of debt, DeVry Incorporated had paid off its creditors and was in the black, claiming a net worth of $1.3

million. It was not only DeVry's increased growth that saved the company, however. In 1991, DeVry Incorporated went public, with an initial public offering of 20 million shares of stock, priced at $1.25 per share. Since then, DeVry's stock has continued to increase in value, with initial proceeds from the offering being used to pull the company out of debt.

EXPANSION: TAKING ADVANTAGE OF EDUCATIONAL TRENDS

By the early 1990s two things became clear to analysts in the educational industry: students were graduating from high school in record numbers, and, of those graduates, more and more individuals were seeking training in higher education which would put them on a fast track to technological or business-oriented careers. DeVry Inc. was in the right place at the right time, offering undergraduate training in technical fields and graduate programs for business people. Moreover, in doing away with such traditional collegiate frills as secluded, landscaped campuses and sports teams, DeVry managed to keep costs low, further bucking the higher educational trend of skyrocketing tuition.

As DeVry Institutes was shaped in the late 1990s into a school well-equipped for the needs of both the business and technology student, Keller and Taylor continued to refine the Keller Graduate School's curriculum. By 1999, the school was offering master's degrees in business administration, project management, human resource management, telecommunications management, accounting and financial management, as well as information systems management. The goal of having each school complement the other was complete, making Dennis Keller's 1988 prediction that "DeVry will be the brand name for our undergraduate degrees and Keller the brand of our postbaccalaureate degrees" a reality.

DeVry's positive reputation grew from several sources, the most powerful of which was the fact that a DeVry graduate in all likelihood was not going to be left upon graduation with a degree and no job. According to DeVry sources, in the 1990s, "of the more than 44,000 graduates who actively pursued employment or were already employed, more than 93 percent held positions in their chosen field of study within six months of graduation." The company also aggressively advertised its success, sending more than 300 recruiters annually to businesses and high schools across the country.

While tuition was lower at DeVry than at private colleges, many public universities still offered similar degrees for less money. What kept DeVry's enrollment up was the company's promotion of the fact that an individual with a DeVry degree could almost be guaranteed a position in his or her desired area. Taking into consideration DeVry's flexible payment plans and class schedules, DeVry's steadily increasing enrollment figures, almost every year in the 1990s, was not surprising.

The company did, however, have its detractors. Some in the education industry questioned the quality of DeVry's instructors, claiming that because most of them did not have PhD's in their fields that they were less qualified than professors found at more traditional universities. DeVry instructors were also usually hired part time, in order to keep costs down, and had jobs outside of teaching, making one-on-one student-teacher interaction something of a rarity on DeVry campuses. DeVry responded to this criticism by pointing out that their instructors had the most important quality a DeVry student needed to complete meaningful training: hands-on experience in technological or business fields.

Continuing to diversify and follow job trends, in 1996 DeVry Inc. acquired Becker CPA Review, a company which helped students prepare for accounting certification. With over 150 locations across the United States, the Middle East, Canada and the Pacific Rim, Becker truly represented to DeVry an international expansion. In 1998 Keller Graduate School of Management received approval from the North Central Association to offer its master's degree programs online, and DeVry Institutes followed, offering its bachelor's of science in business administration online, in 2000.

The early 2000s brought a period of acquisitions. In 2003 DeVry acquired Ross University, one of the largest medical and veterinary education schools in the world based in the Caribbean. Ross was the single largest provider of physicians in the United States. Focused exclusively on professional medical and veterinary education, the university awarded both doctor of medicine (M.D.) and doctor of veterinary medicine (D.V.M.) degrees. Students completed their basic science curriculum at the medical and veterinary school campuses in the Caribbean countries of Dominica and St. Kitts/Nevis, respectively, and they completed their clinical rotations in U.S. teaching hospitals and veterinary schools throughout the United States.

In 2005, DeVry acquired Chamberlain College of Nursing, previously known as Deaconess College of Nursing. Chamberlain offered associate degrees (ASN/AND and LPN/ASN) and bachelor of science degree (BSN) nursing programs at its St. Louis, Missouri, campus as well as an ASN degree online. Additionally, Chamberlain offered a "Fast Track" online bachelor of science in nursing (BSN) degree completion program that provided registered nurses across the country the opportunity to advance their careers by earning a BSN degree in 12 months.

In addition to broader course offerings, DeVry shifted away from large campuses to smaller learning centers in downtown office buildings, which proved more convenient for working students. This turnaround strategy, in response to the drop in computer training enrollment, brought about an enrollment spike of 46 percent.

During this time, DeVry Institutes and Keller Graduate School of Management became DeVry University, following the approval of The Higher Learning Commission of the North Central Association. DeVry offered undergraduate programs in business and technology and graduate courses in business at 22 campuses and 55 satellite centers and operated about 300 sites worldwide. With an enrollment of over 49,000 students, the company was one of the most successful and high profile for-profit schools in the nation.

Rachel Martin
Updated, Suzanne Clark York

PRINCIPAL DIVISIONS

DeVry Institutes; Keller Graduate School of Management (KGSM); Becker CPA Review; Ross University; Chamberlain College of Nursing.

PRINCIPAL COMPETITORS

Apollo Group Inc.; ITT Educational Services Inc.; Strayer Education, Inc.

FURTHER READING

Blumenstyk, Goldie, "An Exception to the For-Profit Rule," *Chronicle of Higher Education,* April 22, 2005.

Byrne, Harlan S., "Trends Favor Chain of Job-Training Schools," *Barron's Investment News & Views,* February 8, 1993.

Cho, Hanah, "For-Profit Education Sector Struggles to Avoid Decline," *Knight-Ridder/Tribune Business News,* February 28, 2006.

Hofmeister, Sallie, "A Touch of Class," *Venture,* January 1988.

Levine, Daniel Rome, "The Best and Worst CEOs: Ronald L. Taylor," *Crain's Chicago Business,* May 29, 2006.

Manor, Robert, "DeVry CEO to Exit in November: Turnaround on Track, Taylor Says," *Knight-Ridder/Tribune Business News,* February 25, 2006.

Murphy, Lee H., "DeVry's Classes Go Online: Competition, Convenience Push Internet Offerings," *Crain's Chicago Business,* November 30, 1998.

———, "New Degrees, Sites Back on the Books at DeVry," *Crain's Chicago Business,* November 14, 2005.

Ryan, Kate, "Community Colleges Beat For-Profits on Price," *Crain's Chicago Business,* January 31, 2005.

———, "Spotlight: Daniel Hamburger, DeVry Exec to Become Its CEO in November," *Crain's Chicago Business,* May 8, 2006.

Slania, John T., "DeVry Aims to Score with Games Degree," *Crain's Chicago Business,* April 25, 2005.

Spencer, Leslie, "Competition? Heaven Forbid," *Forbes,* January 2, 1995.

———, "Good School Story," *Forbes,* May 27, 1991.

VandeWater, Judith, "DeVry Deal Will Close This Week," *Knight-Ridder/Tribune Business News,* March 17, 2005.

Distrigaz S.A.

Rue de l'Industrie 10
Brussels, B-1000 46120 61131
Belgium
Telephone: (32) 02 557 30 11
Fax: (32) 02 557 30 02
Web site: http://www.Distrigaz.be

Public Company
Incorporated: 1929
Employees: 120
Sales: EUR 3.8 billion ($4.87 billion) (2005)
Stock Exchanges: Euronext Brussels
Ticker Symbol: DIST
NAIC: 221210 Natural Gas Distribution; 486210
Pipeline Transportation of Natural Gas

■ ■ ■

Distrigaz S.A. is one of Europe's top ten natural gas sales and trading companies. The company provides transit, transport, and delivery services for natural gas via pipeline, as well as in liquefied form via tanker vehicles and ocean-going vessels. The company's customers include industrial companies, natural gas re-sellers and distribution companies, and power generation companies. Distrigaz's largest market remains Belgium, where it controls as much as 80 percent of the resident and corporate/industrial markets. The company has also taken advantage of the liberalization of the European energy market to launch sales in other countries, including France, Germany, the Netherlands, Luxembourg, Spain, and the United Kingdom. In addi-tion to gas sales, the company is one of the Europe's leading provider of arbitrage services, enabling the transfer of excess natural gas capacity among the differ-ent national markets. In support of its operations, Dis-trigaz has put into place a highly diversified supply portfolio, with long-term contracts from the Netherlands, Algeria, and Norway, excess capacity from the United Kingdom, and, starting in 2007, from Qatar. Distrigaz also holds a 16.4 percent in the Interconnector pipeline project connecting the UK to the continent at Zeebrugge. Distrigaz is itself majority held by Suez Tractebel, which controls more than 57 percent of the company. Publigaz owns more than 31 percent of the company, while the Belgian government retains a "golden share" in the formerly state-owned business. Listed on the Euronext Brussels Stock Exchange, Distrigaz posted revenues of EUR 3.8 billion ($4.87 billion) in 2005.

COKE GAS BEGINNINGS IN 1929

Distrigaz was founded in 1929 by the United Kingdom's Imperial Continental Gas Association, which had long been an active player in the continental European gas market. Distrigaz's initial operations consisted of transporting gas generated by the country's coke ovens. In support of that, the company began constructing its own pipeline. By 1932, Distrigaz was operational, hav-ing completed some 143 kilometers of pipeline. Dis-trigaz was later taken over by the Belgian government.

The rising gas demand in the years following World War II required the company to find new sources for its gas needs. The development of the natural gas industry during this time offered the company the promise of the capacity it required. The period also saw the discovery of a number of large-scale natural gas fields in the 1950s, such as the Hassi R'Mel gas field in Algeria's Sahara Desert region, which came under the control of that country's government-owned Sonatrach.

Distrigaz's first shift toward natural gas came in the early 1960s, when a natural gas field was discovered close by, in Slochteren, in the Netherlands. Distrigaz negotiated its first large scale supply contract, and by 1966 the company had received its first shipment of gas from the Netherlands.

Into the 1970s, Distrigaz set itself an objective of further diversifying its gas supply agreements, in an effort to ensure a stable and steady supply of gas to the Belgian market. The company began negotiating with Sonatrach to receive gas from the Hassi R'Mel field. In 1975, the two sides reached a 20-year agreement for Sonatrach to supply 100 billion cubic meters to the Belgium gas group. Two years later, the company reached a new supply agreement with Ekofisk, which had begun exploiting the huge natural gas fields discovered in the North Sea near Norway. In support of both contracts, Distrigaz constructed a new transmission network in western and southern Belgium.

The Distrigaz focus on developing its transmission and transit capacity led the company to begin construction of an LNG terminal complex in Zeebrugge. With a capacity of 135,000 cubic meters, the new facility became the largest in Europe, and helped position Belgium as a hub of the future inter-European gas market. Started in 1978, the company's LNG terminal was fully completed by 1987, accepting its first tanker delivery that same year. Much of the technology behind the Zeebrugge complex came from Distrigaz's own long-term research and development efforts.

The European natural gas market remained confronted with heavy competition from the continent's coal, oil and nuclear power industries. In 1986, however, the gas producers at the Sleipner and Troll gas fields in Norway agreed to ship more than 10 billion cubic meters of natural gas per year to the European market. The promise of this abundant gas supply helped the natural gas market position itself as a low-cost energy provider. By the 1990s, natural gas had largely outpaced coal gas in Belgium and elsewhere.

GAS HUB FOR THE NINETIES

By the early 1980s, Distrigaz had not only developed a diversified gas supply portfolio, it had also developed its own cutting-edge gas technologies. The company's strengths lay particularly in gas storage, pipe protection technologies, transmission control systems, and the like. In 1983, the company adopted a new strategy of becoming a technology services provider, and accordingly created an international consulting division.

Yet the movement toward European trade unity, and the prospect of the liberalization of the European gas market offered a new prospect for Distrigaz. By 1989, the company had begun to downplay its consulting operations in favor of a new strategy of becoming the major gas transmission hub for the European market. The company's Zeebrugge complex was ideally suited for this role, offering the continent's largest and most modern transmission facility, while its location placed it at the center of the continental European gas transmission grid.

A major step toward Distrigaz's new ambition consisted of the launch of construction of the new Zeepipe pipeline linking the Sleipner and Troll gas fields in Norway to the Zeebrugge complex in 1989. That pipeline was completed in 1993. In the meantime, the company had launched construction on a new pipeline linking Belgium to Luxembourg. The company also added a new 145-kilometer pipeline to the French border. Completed by 1995, the new pipeline connected to the Zeepipe pipeline, offering the potential of transporting natural gas from the Norwegian gas fields as far as to Spain.

Also in 1995, Distrigaz joined in the Interconnector gas pipeline project linking the United Kingdom to the European continent. The new pipeline proposed a link between Bacton in England and Distrigaz's Zeebrugge complex. While the bulk of the project was meant to transmit over-capacity in the United Kingdom to the European continent, the new pipeline also offered reverse flow capacity, offering European producers access to the U.K. market, where gas prices remained higher. Distrigaz's ambitions to become the single largest gas transmission hub in Europe suffered a setback, however,

NEW STRUCTURE FOR THE NEW CENTURY

With an increasing percentage of its revenues coming from its transmission services, Distrigaz also moved to widen its own gas delivery markets. Focused on the Belgian market through the 1990s, the company began targeting the international market in the early 2000s. Among the company's early international clients was France's Rhodia, with first deliveries slated for early 2002. By the middle of the decade, Distrigaz had added gas sales to Germany, Luxembourg, the Netherlands, the United Kingdom, and Spain as well.

In the meantime, Distrigaz joined the unbundling effort among the European natural gas market, as new European Union rules came into effect. As a result, Distrigaz split up its operations into two separate companies: the newly created Fluxys, which took over the company's transportation and Zeebrugge hub services, as well as its storage facilities; and Distrigaz, which became a purely commercial company focused on gas sales, purchasing, and transit agreements. Distrigaz went public in 2002, but remained controlled by majority shareholder Suez-Tractebel, itself a 100 percent subsidiary of French energy giant Suez. Another large shareholding belonged to Publigas, while the Belgian government retained "golden shares" in both companies.

Distrigaz stepped up its international sales portfolio in 2003 with an agreement with Energie de Rhône, in France, giving the Belgian company access to the industrial market in that region. The following year, the company added Russia to its list of operations, signing a transit agreement with Gazprom subsidiary Gazexport. Also in 2004, Distrigaz became a shareholder in the second phase of the Interconnector project.

Distrigaz continued to seek a diversification of its gas suppliers. This led the company to reach an agreement with the RasGas II gas facility in Qatar to supply the company with some 2.75 billion cubic meters of gas per year, starting in 2007. The company began lining up new customers for the increase in capacity. In 2005, for example, Distrigaz deepened its penetration of the French market, signing its first industrial supply contract in the Gironde region near Bordeaux. Also in 2005, Distrigaz made its first gas delivery to the United Kingdom.

The planned merger of Suez and Gaz-de-France at mid-decade placed new pressure on Distrigaz and its dominant position in the Belgian gas market. The merger threatened to place as much as 90 percent and more of the Belgian market under the control of combined operations, and brought Distrigaz under scrutiny by European Commission antitrust authorities in 2006. With the liberalization of the European gas market under

when the company lost out on the bid for a new pipeline connecting the continent to the Norwegian gas fields. Instead, that pipeline went to Dunkirk, in France.

As part of its commitment to the Interconnector project, Distrigaz commissioned a new pipeline connecting the Zeebrugge site with Germany. That pipeline was completed in 1998. Not only did it connect the company to the German market, it also offered access to the Eastern European markets and to the Russian market. Meanwhile, the first phase of the Interconnector pipeline was completed in 1998 as well, with the first shipments of gas taking place in October 1998. In March of the following year, Distrigaz raised its stake in Interconnector to 10 percent.

full swing, however, Distrigaz promised to remain a major player not just in Belgium but throughout the region.

M. L. Cohen

PRINCIPAL SUBSIDIARIES

Distri RE S.A.; Distrigaz & Cie SCA; Etac BV; Finpipe GIE; Huberator S.A.; Interconnector (U.K.) Ltd.; Interconnector Zeebrugge Terminal SCRL; Sofipar S.A.; Transfin S.A.

PRINCIPAL COMPETITORS

Royal Dutch/Shell Group; RWE AG; ENI SpA; E.ON AG; Repsol YPF S.A.; SUEZ; Centrica plc; E.ON Ruhrgas AG; ENDESA S.A.; SHV Holdings N.V.; Electrabel N.V.

FURTHER READING

"Belgium Casts Eyes on Bigger Role in European Natural Gas Operations," *Oil and Gas Journal,* May 9, 1994, p. 29.

"Belgian Distrigaz Split into Distrigas, Fluxys," *World Gas Intelligence,* December 5, 2001, p. 1.

"Belgian Gas Storage Site Gets Direct Drive Compressor," *Oil and Gas Journal,* May 15, 2000, p. 60.

"Distrigaz Confirms Demerger," *Gas Connections,* December 6, 2001, p. 8.

"EU Targets Distrigaz," *Gas Connections,* May 25, 2006, p. 4.

Jones, Huw, "Belgium's Bid to Be the Focus for European Gas," *Gas World International,* December 1989, p. 41.

Jones, Simon, and Trevor Loveday, "Belgium's Warning on French Mega-Merger," *Utility Week,* March 17, 2006.

Mollet, Paul, "Belgium Consolidates Its Position as Europe's Transit Hub," *Gas World International,* March 1995, p. VI.

Dobrogea Grup S.A.

Str Celulozei 1
Constanta,
Romania
Telephone: (40) 0241 512 195
Fax: (40) 0241 639 944
Web site: http://www.dobrogea-ind.ro

Private Company
Incorporated: 1961 as Dobrogea Milling and Baking
    Plant
Employees: 2,100
Sales: EUR 75 million ($95 million) (2005)
NAIC: 311211 Flour Milling; 311330 Confectionery
    Manufacturing from Purchased Chocolate; 311423
    Dried and Dehydrated Food Manufacturing;
    311514 Dry, Condensed, and Evaporated Dairy
    Product Manufacturing; 311812 Commercial
    Bakeries

■ ■ ■

Dobrogea Grup S.A. is one of Romania's largest and
fastest-growing bakery products group. The Constanta-
based company produces a wide range of baked goods
and bakery ingredients. Dobrogea Grup is Romania's
leading miller and supplier of wheat flour, flour-based
ingredients (including premixes), and gluten and other
enzyme-based "improvers" to the baking industry.
Among the latter category, the company has developed
and patented its Dan-Do-Pan bread improver range, created to address specific characteristics of Romanian
breads. The company also produces pasta, cereal breads,

pastries, cookies, breakfast cereals, including the Captain
Crantz brand launched in 2003, and other fresh, frozen,
and prepared foods. In addition, Dobrogea operates its
own chain of 32 retail shops, including 15 revamped
Fresh stores, largely in the Constanta region.
International expansion has played a role in the
company's development in the 2000s, with initial efforts
to export a limited range of finished products, including
cookies, to markets including France, Italy, the United
States, and Spain. In the mid-2000s, the company
adopted a new strategy of contract production for
multinational food groups. In July 2005, for example,
the company signed a contract to produce cookies for
Unilever. By the end of that year, contract manufacturing represented as much as 35 percent of Dobrogea's annual sales of more than EUR 47 million ($58 million).
Formerly a state-owned enterprise under the Ceausescu
regime, Dobrogea Grup has been privately held since
the early 1990s. Fotini Teodorescu, who joined the
company in 1968, is president of the company and chief
architect of its transformation from a small, local
company into a national leader.

MILLING AND BAKING IN 1961

Dobrogea Grup was established in 1961 in order to
provide wheat flour and bread products to the Constanta area. Comprised of two wheat mills, as well as
production facilities manufacturing bread and cookies
and other pastries, the company was originally called
Constanta Milling and Baking Plant. A state-owned
company, the Constanta plant grew into the region's
main supplier of breads and bread flour, with production facilities in five cities: Constanta, Navodari, Har-

COMPANY PERSPECTIVES

Dobrogea is an integrated manufacturer that provides its clients and consumers with a complex range of brand products in the following fields: milling, bakery, pastry and confectionery, premixes and complex improvers for bakery and pastry, pasta and sugary products, prebaked and frozen foods, as well as a large range of services of highest quality. By its commitment to R&D, innovation, and raising consumer knowledge about healthy, natural and highly nutritive products, Dobrogea ranges among the world's biggest players in the bakery industry.

sova, Medgidia, and Eforie Nord. From the start, the Constanta factory also developed its own network of retail shops. By the end of the 1980s, the company also branched out into pastries, added a corn mill, and also launched production of pasta.

The Constanta group's bread production remained barely industrialized—baking remained a highly manual process dependent upon small bread ovens with only limited capacity. Because of this, the company's total bread production remained at just 20 tons per day into the mid-1980s. However, in 1987, the company was allowed to invest in new equipment, installing a number of new continuous baking ovens. In this way, the company was able to raise production to more than 50 tons of bread per day.

Yet the company's true development came especially after the toppling of the Ceausescu regime and the installation of a more democratic, liberalized market. Following the change of government, the Constanta operation was renamed as Dobrogea Milling, Baking and Pastes Enterprise. The change of name reflected the company's growth from a local operation to the Dobrogea (or Dobruja) region's top milling and baked products group.

In 1991, the company reincorporated as a limited liability company, called Dobrogea S.A., as a step towards its future privatization. Fotini Teodorescu, who had joined the company as an intern in 1968, and had risen to a management position by 1979, took charge of restructuring the company for the new economic realities of the post-Communist Romanian market. The management team under Teodorescu was noteworthy in that it was composed nearly entirely of women.

Teodorescu's first task was to change the company's

corporate culture. As she told *Bucharest Business Week*: "Changing mentality was the hardest process I had to accomplish. People expected to receive but they gave little in return. It was like somebody else had to think for them. I changed mentalities by reorganizing the system, but in a smooth way. We put all the elements in balance, we settled mid and long-term strategies, but we also made them flexible, because at that time the Romanian market was changing and we had to adapt."

Dobrogea increasingly began investing in its production capacity. In the early 1990s, the company added new mixing technology, as well as spiral mixers in order to step up its dough preparation. The company also earmarked a large part of its investment program to expand its milling operations. As such, in 1994, the company turned to Buhler, based in Switzerland, to upgrade the company's milling equipment. Buhler also provided Dobrogea with invaluable technical assistance. The technical partnership and modernized equipment enabled the company to branch out into the production of new flour types. This in turn allowed the company to extend its own range of bread and pastry products.

Importantly, Dobrogea also invested in its own research and development capacity. This effort was quickly rewarded with success in 1992, with the development of its first "improving agent," a process for activating yeast. Dobrogea received a patent for the process. Encouraged, the company set up a dedicated research and development department the following year.

PRIVATIZED IN 1995

By 1994, the company had developed a new and more important improver, called Dan-Do-Pan. The new enzyme-based process was developed specifically for the professional Romanian bakery market, helping to overcome variations in flour quality and in baking conditions to produce a more consistent and higher quality of bread. The company was later awarded a new patent for the Dan-Do-Pan agent.

Dobrogea's research and development efforts led to the company's extension into new product categories as well. In 1995, the company became one of the first in Romania to enter the frozen, prepared foods market, with the launch of its "dose" or ready-to-eat pastries. Developed entirely in-house, the new pastry products were made available both through the retail consumer channel as well as through the professional sector, including in Dobrogea's own network of retail shops.

Dobrogea's emergence as a profit-driven and increasingly profitable, modern business was highlighted in 1995 when the company completed its privatization

KEY DATES

1961: The Constanta Milling and Baking Plant is founded in Constanta in the Dobrogea region of Romania.

1991: The company reincorporates as Dobrogea S.A. and becomes a limited liability company owned by the Romanian government.

1995: Dobrogea is privatized in a management buyout led by company president Fotini Teodorescu.

1998: The company launches its Fresh retail bakery chain and acquires 43 percent of Bucharest-based Lujerul S.A.

2000: Dobrogea builds a new high-capacity wheat mill and becomes the largest milling group in Romania.

2004: A new investment program is launched to expand capacity in milling, baking, frozen foods and other areas of operation.

2005: The company begins contract manufacturing operations for Unilever and opens a new, large-scale biscuit manufacturing factory.

process. In that year, Teodorescu led the company's management, together with its employees, in a management-buyout of the company. Teodorescu then steered the company into a new phase of investment. The company stepped up its pasta operations with new equipment suppled by Italy's Fen Food Enterprise, stepping up the quality of its pasta production as well as increasing its range of pasta types. Previously, the company had been limited to short pasta shapes using Romanian wheat. The new equipment enabled the company to begin production of long shapes based on higher quality semolina in 1997. At the same time, Dobrogea launched an upgrade of its bread-making facilities, adding new packaging technologies, and extending its range of bread types.

Backed by an increasing line of patented improvers, Dobrogea became a full-service provider to the professional baking, catering, and restaurant industries in 1998, supplying its own range of basic ingredients, improvers, and other additives, as well as supplying technical and commercial services. Yet Dobrogea had also continued to develop its own retail operations. The following year, the company began converting a number of its stores to a new retail store format, called Fresh, featuring a modern interior design. By the mid-2000s, the company operated some 15 Fresh stores.

Dobrogea had also developed a new line of frozen foods and half-baked baked goods in the late 1990s. The company then added a new factory for this product segment, which launched production in 1999. By then, the company had made its first move to enter the Bucharest market. Already dominated by a number of bakery companies, the Bucharest market had long proven out of reach of the Constanta company. The privatization of another government-owned bakery group, Lujerul, in 1998, provided Dobrogea with its opportunity, and in 1999, the company acquired 43 percent stake in the Bucharest-based company.

While the purchase remained more or less on the investment level—that is, Dobrogea did not gain access to the Bucharest market for its own baked goods—the purchase provided the company with the possibility of expanding its milling operations. This was especially true after Lujerul shut down its own milling business in 2000. Dobrogea built a new, high-capacity flour mill that year, boosting its production to 800 tons per day. The company thus became the largest milling operation in Romania.

INVESTING FOR GROWTH IN THE NEW CENTURY

In 2001, Dobrogea formed a new partnership, this time with Denmark's Palsgaard Industri, creating the 50/50 joint venture Ro Credo Srl. The new company enabled Dobrogea to extend its product list with a range of cake and other premixes, as well as ingredients such as chocolate and vanilla creams and the like.

Dobrogea also continued to roll out its own product innovations. In 2001, the company began fortifying its bread products with vitamin and mineral additives. The company also launched Romania's first probiotic bread brand, Activa. Similarly, the company added to its range of functional foods with the Dieta line of pasta and flour mixes in 2003. By then, the company had also expanded its range of pastas with the new Pasta Magica brand, and had begun producing the Matina brand of breakfast cereals. The company boosted its cereal range in 2003 with the launch of the popular children's breakfast cereal Captain Crantz. This was joined in 2004 with the "Funky" brand of breakfast cereals.

Into the mid-2000s, Dobrogea stepped up its investments efforts, taking advantage of the new opportunities in financial assistance and capital backing available in the run-up to Romania's joining the European Union later in the decade. The company spent some EUR 2.5 million to renovate and modernize its

Constanta milling plant in 2004. This was followed in 2005 by the construction of a new EUR 3.8 million automated facility for the production of cookies and biscuits. Also that year, the company announced an additional spending effort of EUR 6 million, eyeing expansion in its bakery, frozen products, logistics, and milling operations.

Increasingly, Dobrogea had begun investigating the possibilities of international expansion. The company began test marketing a number of its products, primarily finished goods, in the early 2000s. As a result, the company developed limited exports to Spain, Italy, France, and the United States.

A more promising market for the company, however, was the contract manufacturing sector. The company began acquiring contracts to produce branded products for a number of international markets, including Spain and Austria. In July 2005, the company landed a still bigger contract, when it began producing biscuits for consumer products giant Unilever. By the end of that year, the company's contract manufacturing operations already accounted for nearly 35 percent of its total production. With its sales topping EUR 75 million, Dobrogea had emerged as one of Romania's leading and most international milling and bakery groups.

M.L. Cohen

PRINCIPAL SUBSIDIARIES

Lujerul SA (43%); Rocredo Srl (50%).

PRINCIPAL COMPETITORS

Kamps Brot- und Backwaren GmbH and Company KG; General Organization for Food Industries; LU France S.A.; Geest Ltd.; Royal Cebeco Group Cooperative U.A.; Ferrari Ghezzi Ltda.; Liral Group; Jowa AG; Milch-Union Hocheifel eG; Harry-Brot GmbH; M-Preis Warenvertriebsges mbH; Glockenbrot Baeckerei GmbH and Company oHG; Businovskiy Meat Processing Plant Joint Stock Co.; Kharkov Biscuit Factory Joint Stock Co.; Conditorei Coppenrath and Wiese GmbH and Company KG; Roncadin S.p.A.

FURTHER READING

Ariton, Claudia, "Flour Power," *Bucharest Business Week*, June 23, 2006.

Bodeanu, Teodora, "Dobrogea Improves Facilities," *Bucharest Business Week*, July 7, 2005.

Negrea, Stelian, "Dobrogea Grup Starts Biscuit Production for Unilever," *Ziarul Financiar*, July 1, 2005.

——, "Dobrogea Grup Investeste 2,5 mil. Euro Pentru o Moara Mai Buna," *Ziarul Financiar*, December 16, 2004.

——, "Dobrogea Grup Posts 72m-Euro Revenues," *Ziarul Financiar*, May 23, 2005.

——, "Dobrogea Retools Mill," *Ziarul Financiara*, December 17, 2004.

——, "Dobrogea Aiming at 75m-Euro Market Slice," *Ziarul Financiara*, July 26, 2004.

Yoruk, Deniz Eylem, "Role of Network Development in the Growth of Firm: The Case of a Romanian Bakery Company," *Economic and Social Research Council*, February 2002.

Earle M. Jorgensen Company

10650 Alameda Street
Lynwood, California 90262
U.S.A.
Telephone: (323) 567-1122
Toll Free: (800) 336-5365
Fax: (323) 563-5500
Web site: http://www.emjmetals.com/

Wholly Owned Subsidiary of Reliance Steel and Aluminum Co.
Founded: 1921
Employees: 1,712
Sales: $1.6 billion (2005)
NAIC: 423510 Metals Service Centers and Other Metal Merchant Wholesalers

■ ■ ■

One of the largest steel distributors, Earle M. Jorgensen Company (EMJ) sells more than 25,000 metal bar, tubular, sheet, and plate products made from carbon, alloy, stainless steel, iron, nickel, copper and brass, and aluminum through 39 distributorships and service facilities in the United States and Canada. EMJ also offers such value-added processing services as saw cutting, Blanchard grinding (rotary surface grinding), plate burning, honing, end finishing, skiving and roller burnishing, and facing and centering. Based in Lynwood, California, EMJ maintains approximately three dozen service and processing centers spread across North America. The company has a long-standing reputation for timely and reliable deliveries, instituted well before just-in-time delivery practices. For decades, exceptional customer service has been a key element in the company's ability to enjoy steady growth despite the cyclical nature of the metal services industry, allowing EMJ to command higher prices than the competition. The company's slate of 35,000 customers come from the machine tools, industrial equipment, transportation, fluid power, energy, fabricated metal, construction, and agricultural equipment industries. Run for most of its history by its founder, Earle M. Jorgensen—who, until a few days before his death in 1999 at the age of 101, continued to come into the office nearly every day—EMJ is a subsidiary of Reliance Steel and Aluminum Co.

FOUNDER SURVIVED THE 1906 SAN FRANCISCO EARTHQUAKE

Earle M. Jorgensen was born in San Francisco in 1898, the only son of a Danish immigrant sea captain, who plied the South Pacific routes out of the city. It was a profession that came in handy during the 1906 earthquake that leveled and set San Francisco ablaze. The family took to the sea, where, from the safety of his father's ship, the young Jorgensen witnessed the calamity onshore. His father died when he was just 13, forcing him to quit school and go to work. Although he never attended college, Jorgensen completed his high school education at night. He was a hard-working, ambitious young man, inspired by the era's inspirational self-help literature that promoted the virtues of pluck and industry in getting ahead. At the age of 16 he came across a magazine article titled, "Hustle—That's All!" It became a lifelong creed for Jorgensen and a motto for

COMPANY PERSPECTIVES

From top to bottom, everyone in our company is imbued with the spirit of our founder whose motto "Hustle, That's All" motivates us to meet the needs of our customers every single day.

the company he founded. Years later he came across a book, *The Go-Getter: A Story That Tells You How to Be One*, which in many ways mirrored his own story, about a young man who turned himself into a successful businessman. Jorgensen bought the rights to the book and made a practice of giving away signed copies to visitors.

When the United States became involved in World War I in 1916, Jorgensen served in the Army Tank Corps. After his discharge he tried his hand in New York City, taking a job with a novelty toy company, but he never got paid because the company soon went bankrupt, forcing him to borrow $200 to make his way back to California, where he settled in Los Angeles. Unable to land a job, Jorgensen was undeterred: The young go-getter simply went into business for himself with barely a shirt on his back in 1921. In fact, he pawned a suit to raise $2.50 to rent a desk from a public stenographer named Anna Moore in the Douglas Building in Los Angeles. He lacked the full $15 a month rent, but fortunately she trusted him. After learning that the U.S. Navy had scrapped steel shafts from submarines no longer needed, he took advantage of an oil boom in Southern California, where wells were being drilled on the beaches and eventually moved offshore, and convinced oilmen that the shafts could be retooled for drilling. With sales in hand he was able to buy the shafts and begin scouring the shipyards for other scrap metal to sell to the petroleum companies at less than the cost of newly milled steel.

TAKEN PUBLIC: 1957

In 1923 Jorgensen raised $20,000 in venture capital and spent half of that to acquire one acre of land in nearby Lynwood, California. He also bought equipment and built his first warehouse. In 1924 he incorporated Earle M. Jorgensen company and became involved in the steel warehousing business, graduating from scrap to handling steel taken on consignment. He steadily grew the business, moving beyond oil companies to service the emerging aerospace industry in Southern California as well as other industries. He also expanded outside of

California and across the country. He added aluminum to the product mix in 1950, and took the company public in 1957 as Earle M. Jorgensen Steel Company. The offering managed by Blyth & Co Inc. was well received by investors and, according to the *Los Angeles Times,* heavily oversubscribed.

The money raised was used to expand the company's capabilities as well as to acquire and open new warehouses. As customers demanded more services the steel warehouses became metal service centers, and Jorgensen added such processes as slitting coiled steel, shearing steel into sheet and plate, cutting plate, roller leveling, and cutting into shapes. Because service centers were non-union—or, if they were unionized, had contracts less costly than those negotiated by the steelworkers—they could process steel more profitably than a good number of mills. Between 1958 and the summer of 1961, EMJ expanded from 8 service centers to 13, opening facilities in Denver, Honolulu, Phoenix, Seattle, and Wichita. They carried steel and aluminum produced by 60 domestic mills. EMJ opted not to carry foreign products, due to problems that incurred during a period of short supply when quantity and price proved too unreliable. By this time, EMJ had established itself as a dependable supplier, able to provide next-day shipping, and the company was loathe to compromise its chief competitive advantage. At this stage EMJ's service area included the West Coast and Hawaii, the Southwest, and portions of the Midwest. Customers were small companies that did not need or could not afford to buy the carload-size quantities sold by steel mills and needed fast delivery, as well as larger companies that required special services not offered by the mills. In 1960 annual sales topped the $50 million mark and continued to climb, spurred to a large degree by acquisitions. The most significant of these was the $4.2 million purchase of the Isaacson Forge division from Seattle-based Isaacson Iron Works in 1965. EMJ added the ability to produce such basic forms as steel slabs and ingots, and was no longer dependent on mills for these items.

The 1960s also saw Jorgensen's son, John W. Jorgensen, become president and chief operating officer in 1967. The younger Jorgensen was also a veteran, having served in the Navy during World War II. He then graduated from Pomona College in 1948, joined his father's company, and worked his way up through the executive ranks for the next 20 years. Also in the 1960s, Earle Jorgensen became involved in politics. He had been introduced to the Hollywood social scene by his second wife, Marion, who had been previously married to a Hollywood producer. Jorgensen and his wife became friends with actor Ronald Reagan and his wife Nancy. In 1966 Jorgensen and auto dealer Holmes Tuttle urged Reagan to run for governor in California, and they then

KEY DATES

1921: Earle Jorgensen begins selling scrap metal.
1924: Jorgensen incorporates his warehousing business.
1948: Son John W. Jorgensen joins the company.
1957: The company is taken public.
1965: Isaacson Forge is acquired.
1986: John Jorgensen succeeds his father as CEO.
1990: John Jorgensen dies and the company is merged with Kilsby-Roberts and taken private.
1999: Earle Jorgensen dies.
2004: The company is taken public again.
2006: Reliance Steel acquires the business.

lined up political consultants for him and raised funds. After Reagan's successful bid, the two men became part of Reagan's "kitchen cabinet" of businessmen advisors. Jorgensen and his cohorts continued to support Reagan's political aspirations, backing him in his 1976 effort to become president of the United States, and his successful run in 1980. Reagan made a tradition of watching his election returns after dinner at Jorgensen's house. Reportedly, the president's staunch support for the free enterprise system was very much influenced by his friend's success story, that of building a major company from $2.50 raised from a hocked suit. While Jorgensen accepted an appointment to the State College Board of Trustees in California, when Reagan became president he had no interest in joining many of his friends who moved to Washington to take government posts. Asked why by one of his stepsons, Jorgensen explained, "That's not my business. I need to stick to what I know best."

EMJ cracked the $100 million level in annual sales for the first time in 1966, posting revenue of $116.8 million. That number increased to $124.4 million by the end of the decade before a down cycle led to a dip in sales to less than $110 million in 1971. Business rebounded and revenues topped $200 million. Then, sales and earnings fell off once again in 1975 and 1976 because of a depression, before surging to $241.9 million in 1977. Nevertheless, by the end of the decade EMJ maintained 19 service centers, two forge operations, a pair of sheet and strip plants, and a blade plant producing parts for construction equipment.

In 1986, Jorgensen, now 87, finally promoted his son, who was himself 60 years old, to the post of chief

executive officer. Nevertheless, the elder Jorgensen remained chairman of the board and continued to come into the office on a daily basis. The younger Jorgensen's tenure as CEO was destined to be brief, however. In April 1990 he was forced to retire and within the month died from stomach cancer at the age of 64. Despite his presence at headquarters, Earle Jorgensen, over 90 years old, was no longer able to run the company. Even before his son's passing, a deal was in the work to sell the business to the New York buyout firm Kelso & Co., which agreed to pay about $265 million. EMJ was then merged with Kilsby-Roberts Holding Co., control of which Kelso acquired at the same time. The surviving entity assumed the Earle M. Jorgensen Company name.

Kilsby-Roberts was comprised of steel and aluminum supply companies founded by entrepreneurs in the vein of Earl Jorgensen himself. The oldest, launched in 1921, was the C.A. Roberts Company. In 1981 the Chicago-based company merged with Kilsby Tubesupply, a Los Angeles business established in 1946 by Perry Kilsby, to form Kilsby-Roberts. Employees of the company bought it from Flour Corp. in 1984, backed by Kelso, and two years later Kilsby-Robert acquired A.B. Murray Company, which had been in business since the 1890s.

The new Earle M. Jorgensen company boasted an asset base of $550 million and annual sales in excess of $900 million, making it America's largest independently-owned metals distributor. The EMJ and Kilsby-Robert combination appeared to be an excellent fit, featuring a minimum of overlap in business. The former did less than 3 percent of its sales in tubing and pipe, while the latter did about the same amount of business in rod. Since 1987, in fact, the two companies had maintained an informal alliance to help one another serve customers who needed a full range of products. Although the company consolidated branches and eliminated redundancies as much as possible, integrating the two companies proved extremely difficult. According to *Forbes,* "The new management handled the merger clumsily. Expenses hit 90 cents of every $1 grossed." There were also cultural differences to contend with, much of which were traceable to Earle Jorgensen, according to *American Metal Market,* which opined: "A hands-on executive who for years insisted that all his male employees wear white shirts and ties and answer the telephone within three rings, Jorgensen engendered a fierce personal loyalty that still exists today among his former employees. … In fact, many of his former employees, as well as outsiders, believe that this strong corporate culture built by Jorgensen was one of the factors that initially made it difficult to mesh the company with the former Kilsby Roberts specialty tubing chain."

Earle Jorgensen stepped down as chairman in 1994, although he stayed on as a director and chairman of the board's executive committee. The company continued to struggle, its plight highlighted by the botched installation of a new computerized information system intended to replace the two incompatible systems inherited from the 1990 merger. Business was disrupted, leading to a loss of $29.3 million in fiscal 1996. A year later the company lost another $25.4 million. By this time Kelso was looking to unload the company but found no one interested in the asking price, or in taking on EMJ's heavy debt load.

FOUNDER DIES AT 101 IN 1999

With EMJ on the verge of bankruptcy, Kelso convinced David Roderick, the former chairman of U.S. Steel to take over as chairman. Roderick said he only agreed to take the position if Earle Jorgensen remained as chairman emeritus, once again demonstrating how much beloved Jorgensen was in the industry. Roderick then recruited a new chief executive, hiring 58-year-old Maurice "Sandy" Nelson, who had recently quit the top post at Inland Steel Co. and was about to begin an extended trip to France with his wife, both of them fluent in French and avid art collectors. *Forbes* reported, "Nelson says it was Jorgensen's example that convinced him he was too young to retire. 'I said to myself, 'Look at Earle,' says Nelson." While Nelson set about the task of restructuring EMJ, Jorgensen continued to come into the office. At one point he asked Nelson if it was okay to take a week off. Nelson told *Forbes* that he replied, "I don't know, Earle, that's pretty excessive." Following his week-long Caribbean cruise, the company founder showed up for work, according to Nelson, "in a crisp three-piece suit" early Monday morning. He continued to come into the office regularly, even after he reached 101 years of age, ceasing his regimen only weeks before his death in August 1999.

Nelson took over a company that was saddled with excessive overhead expenses. Not only was EMJ too paper-intensive, it had too many high-salaried people in its headquarters. He soon reduced the number of vice presidents from 22 to just 5, and also closed down some underperforming operations while beefing up the moneymakers. He also invested in technology to improve efficiencies. Nelson was able to complete the turnaround of EMJ well before Earle Jorgensen's passing. In recognition of his efforts, Nelson was named *Metal Center News'* as its Service Center Executive of the Year in 2001.

Under Nelson, EMJ increased revenues to $1.88 billion in 2004, and then in April 2005 took the company public. Investors were far from enthusiastic about the offering, unlike the IPO of the original EMJ in the 1950s. Rather than being oversubscribed, this sale fell far short of its $300 million target, netting just $176 million. Many of its shareholders were also less than happy with the company's initial performance. EMJ's public status lasted just two years, however. In April 2006 the company was sold to Reliance Steel and Aluminum Co. for $984 million, a price that included the assumption of close to $300 million in debt. Based in Los Angeles, publicly-traded Reliance was one of the United States' largest metals service center companies. By acquiring EMJ, Reliance broadened its product offering, bolstered its presence in the Midwest, and expanded its geographic reach into New England and Canada. Upon completion of the transaction, Nelson was finally able to retire, staying on briefly to help in the transition to new ownership.

Ed Dinger

PRINCIPAL SUBSIDIARIES

Earle M. Jorgensen (Canada) Inc.; Stainless Insurance Ltd.

PRINCIPAL COMPETITORS

Allegheny Technologies Inc.; Russel Metals Inc.; Ryerson, Inc.

FURTHER READING

Bry, Barbara, "Jorgensen: Industry's 'Steel Supermarket,'" *Los Angeles Times*, May 7, 1978, p. V3.

"Century of Hustle Ends for Earle M. Jorgensen," *Metal Centers News*, October 1999, p. 12.

"Expanded Facilities and Services Aid Results at Earle M. Jorgensen," *Barron's National Business and Financial Weekly*, July 3, 1961, p. 19.

"Jorgensen Agrees to Kelso Purchase for $41.50 a Share," *Wall Street Journal*, January 31, 1990, p. A4.

Lorincz, Jim, "Earle M. Jorgensen Company Merger Combines Great Bloodlines," *Purchasing World*, June 1990, p. 43.

Marsh, Ann, "A Legend in His Own Time," *Forbes*, June 15, 1998, p. 80.

Petry, Corinna C., "Service Center Executive of the Year: Sandy Nelson of EMJ," *Metal Center News*, December 2001, p. 16.

Pollack, Andrew, "Earle Jorgensen, Reagan Adviser, Dies at 101," *New York Times*, August 13, 1999, p. A19.

Eastland Shoe Corporation

---

4 Meetinghouse Road
Freeport, Maine 04032
U.S.A.
Telephone: (207) 865-6314
Toll Free: (888) 988-1998
Fax: (207) 865-9261
Web site: http://www.eastlandshoe.com

Private Company
Incorporated: 1955
Employees: 55
Sales: $35 million (2006 est.)
NAIC: 316213 Men's Footwear (Except Athletic) Manufacturing; 316214 Women's Footwear (Except Athletic) Manufacturing

■ ■ ■

Eastland Shoe Corporation is a leather casual shoe company based in Maine. Founded in 1955, the company was one of the last large-scale shoemakers to produce footwear in the United States. Ultimately, price competition caused it to succumb to the allure of the Orient and begin importing shoes in the late 1990s; in 2001 it closed its last plant in Maine. Since then, Eastland has continued to strive to sell quality products in classic styles at affordable prices.

FREEPORT ROOTS

Eastland Shoe Corp. of Freeport, Maine, was formed in 1955. (It has also been known as Eastland Shoe Manufacturing Corp.) Jonas B. Klein was one of the co-

founders of Eastland, which would remain controlled by the Klein family through the end of the 20th century.

According to *Footwear News* and *Footwear News Magazine,* daily production began at 540 pairs and Eastland was soon making 900 pairs of moccasins a day by hand. It then progressed to manufacturing penny loafers, boat shoes, and other casual leather footwear for men and women—Yankee styles pioneered by Maine rivals G.H. Bass & Co. and Sebago, Inc. Another perennial competitor for the company would be the Dexter Shoe Co. of Massachusetts.

The original Eastland factory was located a few blocks from the famous L.L. Bean store in Freeport. In 1964, the company opened a plant in the largely agricultural western Maine town of Fryeburg. This site was dubbed "Northland"; it produced golf shoes, other sport shoes, and casual shoes. Though about 60 workers staged a brief walkout over stagnant wages at the Freeport plant in 1965, the company remained non-unionized.

A BRAND OF ITS OWN

Eastland originally produced shoes for sale under other brands. It introduced its own "Easysteps" label in the mid-1970s before trading this for the Eastland name. It continued to make private label shoes for discount chains, though by the mid-1980s its own brand accounted for 70 percent of sales.

The removal of quotas in the early 1980s led to a flood of cheap, imported shoes in the U.S. market. This

COMPANY PERSPECTIVES

Since 1955, Eastland Shoe Mfg. Corp. has made classic American styled footwear reflecting our Maine heritage and casual style of living. While the seasons may change and shoe styles follow with them, Eastland Shoe remains constant—committed to creating classic styles, contemporary and durable designs. Our commitment to our customers is to continue making quality leather shoes with the finest workmanship, long lasting value and comfort. Today, our line of men's and women's footwear is specifically designed to meet the demands of daily life and weekend activities—where comfort, style and function merge.

had caused 94 U.S. footwear manufacturers to close in 1984, reported the *Christian Science Monitor;* 32 of these were in Maine, the country's largest shoe-producing state. An industry spokesman told the *Christian Science Monitor* that foreign manufacturers had increased their share of the domestic market from 50 percent to 71 percent. Eastland's workers were still hand-sewing 6,000 pairs of shoes a day, according to the *Monitor.* This was down 25 percent from the previous year.

While Eastland was one of the survivors, it was vigorously cutting costs and scaling back its manufacturing operations. The company shut down stitching rooms in Fryeburg and Lewiston in 1984. Overall employment had been cut back nearly in half, to 325 workers. According to company president Jonas Klein, Eastland was committed to its domestic manufacturing, investing in such things as new computer equipment and stitching machines. In fact, the company did not even use imported components at the time, an official told *Footwear News Magazine.*

In spite of the industry woes, Eastland grew rapidly in the last half of the 1980s and the early 1990s. A 1987 story in *Footwear News Magazine* said that after an upturn the previous year, the company had 500 workers making 3,100 pairs of shoes a day. "Made in America" was becoming an important selling point again, and buyers praised Eastland's quality and affordability. "There's a very serious and renewed interest in domestic manufacture," said executive vice president Bernard Kazon in the *Southern Maine Business Digest.* At the time, Eastland had four factory outlet stores around Freeport, but was focusing on the manufacturing end.

BROWN SHOE BONANZA

According to *Footwear News,* the Eastland brand was little known on the West Coast until the early 1990s. However, with its heritage of making traditional loafers, Eastland was well positioned for the brown shoe mania that was sweeping aside sneakers as the preferred casual shoe of young people. The company emphasized the "rugged dependability" of Maine in its marketing and merchandising materials. The Falmouth camp moccasin was a fashion hit for the company, noted *Footwear News.*

At the time, women's shoes were the largest segment of business; the company also made men's and children's shoes. It had reintroduced duty shoes after a six-year absence from that market.

Eastland was building a considerable export business. Its greatest success was in Canada and Japan, where the brand had been active for several years. The brand was introduced to Great Britain, France, and Italy in the early 1990s, prominently displaying "Made in Freeport USA" on the shoe boxes. In the midst of the Americana boom, Eastland opened a plant in tiny Lisbon Falls, Maine, in 1994. This was soon employing 170 people.

Eastland advertised in high-fashion magazines such as *GQ* and *The Source* in the late 1990s. Company president Jim Klein told *Footwear News* the target audience was "someone who is going to set the style, not follow it." He added, "We were doing brown shoes before they were a category," referring to the footwear sales phenomenon driven by Timberland and others.

Unfortunately, Eastland's domestic retail sales were slowing, thanks largely to continued price competition from abroad. By this time, the U.S. was importing 90 percent of its footwear. The company closed its Fryeburg factory in 1998, letting go 95 of its approximately 650 total employees. Klein said the move would help strengthen the remaining plants in Freeport and Lisbon Falls. (This was also the year that the venerable G.H. Bass & Co. decided to stop making shoes in Maine after 122 years.) In 1999, Eastland began sourcing some of its shoes abroad, while earning environmental kudos at home for reducing hazardous chemicals at its domestic plants.

Eastland closed its Lisbon Falls plant in the fall of 2000. Some of its workers were relocated to Eastland's remaining manufacturing facility in Freeport. By this time, according to the American Apparel and Footwear Association, 96 percent of the shoes sold in the U.S. were coming from overseas—Asia and China in particular. Eastland could no longer continue to bear the

KEY DATES

1955: Maine's Eastland Shoe company is founded in Freeport to make private label shoes.
1964: The Fryeburg plant (Northland) opens.
1976: The company begins developing its own brand.
1994: The Lisbon Falls plant opens.
1998: The Fryeburg plant closes.
1999: Eastland begins sourcing some shoes abroad.
2000: The Lisbon Falls plant closes.
2001: The Freeport plant closes.
2005: Eastland produces 1.5 million pairs of shoes in its 50th anniversary year.

brunt of the huge price differential of U.S. labor. The company itself had already started to sell some imported shoes.

LAST U.S. PLANT CLOSED IN 2001

Eastland closed its last U.S. manufacturing plant, in Freeport, in September 2001. About 150 jobs were cut, though the company's administrative and distribution operations continued to employ 50 to 75 people. The Freeport factory building and its surrounding five acres were put up for sale at $1.5 million.

The town of Freeport considered buying the property for use as government offices and talked the building's four owners down to $900,000, reported the *Portland Press Herald*. However, they walked away from the deal after ascertaining it would cost $6 million dollars to convert the property. The site was later slated for construction of a new 99-room Hilton Hotel.

Eastland brought out a new line of comfort-oriented footwear under the Camden Rock brand in 2004. It was aimed at providing independent retailers with a distinct product line from that carried by national chains, an executive told *Footwear News*.

50TH ANNIVERSARY IN 2005

The company passed an important milestone in 2005: its 50th anniversary. By this time, James B. Klein had taken over as president from his father and company co-founder Jonas Klein, who remained chairman. "We want retailers to remember we've been around," said Jim Klein in *Footwear News*. "Our stability is good." At the same time, Eastland worked to keep its traditional styles

updated. The company was then producing 1.5 million pairs of men's and women's footwear annually.

Frederick C. Ingram

PRINCIPAL COMPETITORS

Dexter Shoe Co.; G.H. Bass & Co.; L.L. Bean Inc.; The Rockport Company, LLC; Sebago Inc.

FURTHER READING

Bell, Tom, "Freeport Council Gets New Offer to Buy Building," *Portland Press Herald,* June 25, 2002, p. 1B.

———, "Freeport Declines to Buy Factory," *Portland Press Herald,* July 27, 2002, p. 1B.

———, "Freeport Looks Into Buying Shoe Factory," *Portland Press Herald,* June 22, 2002, p. 1B.

"Eastland Back in the Duty Shoe Business," *Footwear News,* November 11, 1991, p. 21.

"Eastland Links Image with Maine," *Footwear News,* May 13, 1991, p. 17.

"Eastland Shoe Closing Lisbon Falls Plant," *Associated Press State & Local Wire,* September 12, 2000.

"Eastland Shoe Corp: A Classic Brand Capitalizes on Comfort," Case Study, *Imago Creative,* http://www.imagocreative.com.

"Eastland Shoe to Close Fryeburg Plant," *Bangor Daily News,* October 2, 1998.

Hyde, Christopher, "Shoe Stores Spring Up Everywhere," *Southern Maine Business Digest,* January 1, 1988, p. 51.

"King Gives Out Awards for Environmental Efforts," *Portland Press Herald,* September 22, 1999, p. 7B

Lunt, Dean, "Eastland Shoe to Shutter Fryeburg Plant," *Portland Press Herald,* October 2, 1998, p. 1A.

Murphy, Edward D., "Eastland Closing Last Maine Plant," *Portland Press Herald,* July 20, 2001, p. 1A.

Nacelewicz, Tess, "Crane Topples at Hotel Site, Cutting Power in Freeport," *Portland Press Herald,* December 3, 2004, p. A1.

"Negotiations Hanging, But Workers On Job," *Kennebec Journal,* August 28, 1965, p. 7.

"Obituary: Bernard Kazon, 79," *Footwear News,* December 1, 2003, p. 18.

Pulda, Ellen, "Eastland: Driven to Patriotism," *Footwear News Magazine,* November 1987, pp. 26, 28.

Purcell, David, "Maine's Shoe Industry Struggles to Survive," *Christian Science Monitor,* April 4, 1985, p. B1.

"S.D. Warren Employs Most in Portland Area; The Other Top Employers Range from Shoemakers to Computer-Chip Manufacturers," *Portland Press Herald,* March 8, 1998, p. 16.

Schneider-Levy, Barbara, "Breaking Tradition: Eastland Is Giving the Young and Hip a Taste of Its Classic Styles," *Footwear News,* August 10, 1998, p. 70.

——, "Maine Attraction; Eastland Shoe Is Still a Family Affair—Even as It Celebrates the Big 5-0," *Footwear News,* February 7, 2005, p. 66.

"Shoe Manufacturer Plans Expansion," *Bangor Daily News,* August 26, 1994.

Tedeschi, Mark, "A Brand Takes Hold—It's No Longer Eastland Who?," *Footwear News,* November 11, 1991, p. 23.

——, "Americana Firms on Safe, High Ground," *Footwear News,* September 24, 1990, p. 28.

——, "'More for the Buck' Credo Brings Eastland Big Gains," *Footwear News,* February 10, 1992, pp. 22f.

"U.S. Style and Quality in High Demand," *Footwear News,* September 9, 1991, p. S3.

GROUPE
EDIPRESSE
Edipresse S.A.

---

33 Ave. de la Gare
Lausanne,
Switzerland
Telephone: (41) 021 349 45 00
Fax: (41) 021 349 45 40
Web site: http://www.edipresse.com

Public Company
Incorporated: 1988
Employees: 3,734
Sales: CHF 894.39 million ($673.30 million) (2005)
Stock Exchanges: Swiss
Ticker Symbol: EDIN
NAIC: 511110 Newspaper Publishers; 511120 Periodical Publishers; 551112 Offices of Other Holding Companies

■ ■ ■

Edipresse S.A. is the dominant media group in French-speaking Switzerland, and one of the country's top three newspaper publishers. The Lausanne-based company controls all three major French language dailies—*Le Matin*, *24 heures*, and *Tribune de Geneve*—and publishes a long list of other newspaper and magazine titles, including free daily *Le Matin Bleu*, *Tvguide*, *Tele-Top-Matin*, *Bilan*, *femina*, *terre&nature*, *Optima*, and *Journal de la Broye*. The company also holds a 41 percent stake in *Le Temps*, in partnership with German-language rival Ringier. Edipresse's position in the already saturated Swiss market has provided the company with the foundation (and cash flow) to build an international

network of magazine holdings. In Spain, the company owns such titles as *Lecturas*, *Clara*, *Mujer 21*, *Habitania*, *Tu Bebe*, *Rutas del Mundo*, *Top Auto*, *Todo Plantas*, and *Comer y Beber*, among others. The company's Portuguese operations, in a joint venture with Abril, include *Telenovelas*, *Cosmopolitan*, *TV Mais*, *Activa*, *Caras*, *Super Interessante*, and *Exame*, as well as several other titles. Edipresse has generally avoided larger markets in favor of smaller and emerging markets less served by its large scale multinational competitors. In this way the company has established operations in Poland, Ukraine, Romania, and Russia, in Eastern Europe, and China, Hong Kong, Malaysia, Singapore, the Philippines, and Thailand in the Far East. Many of the company's acquisitions in these markets have been of smaller, family-owned companies—a reflection of the company's own status as a public company still under the control of the founding Lamunière family. Pierre Lamunière is company chairman, while Tibère Adler is the group's CEO. Edipresse is listed on the Swiss stock exchange. In 2005, the company posted revenues of CHF 894.39 million ($673.30 million).

18-CENTURY ROOTS

While Edipresse was officially founded in 1988, the company stemmed from a company set up in the 1920s, which itself had roots reaching back to the turn of the 20th century—and as far back as the eighteenth century. The oldest member of Edipresse's newspaper portfolio was *La Feuille d'Avis de Lausanne*, which was published for the first time in 1762. That newspaper became a daily in 1872; in 1907, the newspaper operation was reorganized into a new company, Société de la Feuille

COMPANY PERSPECTIVES

The Edipresse Group is active in Switzerland, France, Spain, Portugal, Russia, Ukraine, Poland, Romania and several countries in Asia including China and Hong Kong. It publishes over 160 titles and has more than 3,800 employees, of whom slightly under half are based in Switzerland. The group's development strategy centers on three simple principles. The first of these is to concentrate resources, both human and financial, on activities and countries where the company can achieve significant market share. The second principle expresses the corporate desire to publish quality titles, which clearly meet the needs of both readers and advertisers. The third principle concerns the special responsibilities involved in the publishing profession. In this regard, the Edipresse Group has created its own code of ethics and practice. Thanks to these rules, the Group's media pursue their role in a spirit consistent with the interests of democracy, while respecting the fundamental principles of the press: independence, freedom of expression and diversity.

d'Avis de Lausanne. The company by then owned its printing press, which was joined to the newspaper group as Imprimeries Réunies S.A. that same year. In 1911, Société de la Feuille d'Avis de Lausanne et des Imprimeries Réunies acquired a second newspaper, the daily *Tribune de Lausanne*, which had originally been published as *L'Estafette* in 1862, but which adopted its new name in 1893. Both newspaper grew into French-speaking Switzerland's largest newspapers.

In 1925, Jacques Lamunière, together with Samuel Payot and Charles Patru, founded the holding company Lousonna S.A. in order to acquire Société de la Feuille d'Avis de Lausanne et des Imprimeries Réunies. Lousonna became French-speaking Switzerland's first press-based holding company, and soon grew into the region's dominant publishing group, with operations in book publishing, printing, graphic arts, and distribution. In the 1930s, Lousonna added to its distribution operations, acquiring 50 percent stake in LESA S.A., which was then renamed as Kiosk S.A. In 1942, Lousanna acquired the third major French-language daily in Switzerland, *La Suisse*, through the purchase of a 40 percent in that paper's parent company, Sonor S.A.

Throughout the post-war period, Lousanna continued to build up its holdings, extending a dominant position over French-speaking Switzerland's newspaper market. In 1964, the company, by then led by Marc Lamunière, son of the company's founder, built a new 12-story headquarters building in Lausanne. The company also entered magazine publishing on a limited basis, with titles including *femina*, launched in 1962, and the business-oriented *Bilan*, launched in 1989.

The 1970s marked a period of new growth for the company. In 1972, Lousanna converted *Le Tribune de Lausanne* into a morning edition newspaper, renamed as *Le Matin*. The move proved successful, and *Le Matin*'s circulation topped 65,000 by the end of the century.

Lousanna acquired Librarie Payot and Editions Payot Paris, the bookstore and publishing concerns owned by the Payot family, in 1973. In 1977, the company acquired Financière de Presse, which owned Naville S.A. In this way, the company gained control of the de facto monopoly of newspaper and magazine distribution in French-speaking Switzerland.

Into the early 1980s, the founding families behind Lousanna began the process of separating their interests. The Lamunière family bought 50 percent of Lousonna in 1982, while the Nicole family bought up the other half of the holding company, including the stake held by the Payot family, which in turn bought back control of Librarie Payot. The restructuring process was largely completed with the breakup of Lousonna into its printing and publishing halves. The latter was then taken over by the Lamunière family's holding company, Lamunière S.A. In order to ensure control of its newspaper and magazine distribution, Lamunière acquired a 51 percent stake in Naville S.A. in 1987. Finally, after Lamunière sold its 50 percent of Lousonna to the Nicole family, the Lamunières renamed their newspaper and magazine business as Edipresse S.A. in 1988.

INTERNATIONAL EXPANSION STARTS IN 1990

Edipresse took full control of Financière de Presse in 1988, and acquired control of Librarie de Payot, as well as another distributor, Office du Livre Fribourg. These three were merged into a new entity, Payot Naville Distribution in 1990. In that year, Edipresse sold a 65 percent stake in Payot Naville to Hachette as the group prepared to embark on a new strategic direction.

By 1990, Edipresse had become the dominant newspaper group in French-speaking Switzerland. Yet that market, with a population of just two million, offered only limited future growth for Edipresse. Rather than attempt an entry into the larger German-Swiss market (dominated by the Ringier family), Edipresse adopted a new international growth strategy.

KEY DATES

1762: La Feuille d'Avis de Lausanne newspaper is first published.

1862: L'Estafette newspaper is launched in Lausanne.

1893: L'Estafette becomes Le Tribune de Lausanne.

1907: The Société de la Feuille d'Avis de Lausanne et des Imprimeries Réunies is created.

1911: The Société acquires Le Tribune de Lausanne.

1925: Lousonna is founded as a press holding company to acquire the Société de la Feuille d'Avis de Lausanne et des Imprimeries Réunies.

1982: The Lamunière family acquires 50 percent control of Lousonna, which spins off its printing operations.

1988: Lamunière takes control of the Lousonna newspaper and magazine publishing business, which is renamed Edipresse.

1990: Edipresse launches an international expansion, acquiring majority of HYMSA in Spain.

1992: The company enters the Portuguese market.

1995: Edipresse acquires a 50 percent stake in Helvetica Sarl in Poland.

1998: The company enters Greece with the purchase of a stake in Liberis Publications, and Romania through the purchase of the Romanian Publishing Group.

2000: The company launches Edipresse Ukraine and acquires Edinstvennaya magazine.

2003: Edipresse acquires a majority stake in Kone Liga Publishing House to enter Russia.

2005: Edipresse Asia is founded; control of Communication Management Ltd. extends operations into Hong Kong, China, Thailand, Malaysia, the Philippines, and Singapore.

Edipresse's first move beyond Switzerland came that same year, when the company acquired 75 percent of Spain's El Hogar y la Moda S.A. (HYMSA) publishing group. Founded in 1909, HYMSA, was, like Edipresse, a family-owned group. HYMSA brought Edipresse one of Spain's top magazine publishing groups, forming the basis of a portfolio that grew to more than 20 titles by the mid-2000s.

From Spain, Edipresse entered the Portuguese market, buying majority control of two companies in

that country, Publiçaçoes Projornal and Reporteres Asociados, both based in Lisbon, in 1992. Also that year, the company established its first operations in France, creating the subsidiary Presse Publications France S.A.

Yet through the mid-1990s, Edipresse's primary international growth focus was on the Iberian peninsula. The company continued seeking new acquisitions in both Spain and Portugal. In 1994, the company acquired 70 percent of Family Circle S.A. in Spain. The company also added to its portfolio through a number of successful launches, including the women's magazine *Clara*, in 1992, parenting magazine *Tu Bebe* in 1993, the needlework monthly *Labores del Hogar Ideas y Puntos*, and cooking magazine *Comer Bien*, in 1994.

Edipresse acquired full control of its Portuguese operations in 1996, and boosted its holding in Family Circle S.A. to 100 percent. The company also boosted its stake in HYMSA to nearly 85 percent in 1997. By then, the company had successfully reduced its reliance on the Swiss market. Between 1990 and 1995, the share of foreign revenues on the group's total had risen from zero percent to 23 percent. By the end of the decade, Edipresse's international operations already provided more than 40 percent of the company's total sales.

In the meantime, Edipresse had begun to target expansion beyond Spain and Portugal. The company entered Poland in 1995, buying up a 50 percent stake in Helvetica Sarl, based in Warsaw. Edipresse acquired full control of that company in 1998, renaming it as Edipresse Polska. At the same time, the company entered a 50-50 joint-venture with the Marie Claire Group, forming MC Press Sarl in Warsaw.

MULTINATIONAL FUTURE IN THE NEW CENTURY

By the end of 1998, Edipresse had extended its operations to Romania, buying a 50 percent stake in the Romanian Publishing Group, and Greece, where the company acquired 50 percent of Hellenic Printing S.A. and Liberis Publications. Through Liberis, which went public in 2000, Edipresse also gained control of another Greek group, Desmi Publishing.

Back in Switzerland, Edipresse merged its title *Le Nouveau Quotidien* with prominent Geneva title *Le Journal de Genève*, creating the new title *Le Temps*. Launched in 1998, *Le Temps* quickly become one of French-speaking Switzerland's leading newspapers. In 2001, the company purchased the advertising sales agency Senger Media, which was subsequently renamed as Edipub. The company also acquired an additional 20 percent of *Le Temps* that year. Despite the crowded Swiss newspaper market, in 2005, the company achieved success with the launch of a new free daily newspaper, *Le Matin Bleu*.

Yet international growth remained a company priority. Edipresse entered the Ukraine market in 2000, creating a subsidiary in that country and acquiring the women's monthly magazine *Edinstvennaya*. Over the next five years, the company built that title into a leader in the market, while expanding its portfolio of titles to 10 by 2006. The company also continued adding to its holdings in Poland, buying up *Przekroj*, *Pani*, and *Urod* in 2001.

In 2003, Edipresse moved into Russia, buying majority control of Moscow's Kone Liga Publishing House, founded in 1993. That company, renamed as Edipresse-Konliga ZAO, added its portfolio of more than 20 magazine titles to Edipresse's growing international list.

As it turned toward mid-decade, Edipresse began searching farther abroad for its next growth effort. In 2005, the company formed a new subsidiary in Hong Kong, called Edipresse Asia Limited. That company then acquired 70 percent of Hong Kong's Communication Management Limited, one of the Asian region's leading magazine groups. The purchase not only gave the company a strong portfolio in the Hong Kong market, it also gave the company a range of titles in mainland China. Thailand, Malaysia, the Philippines, and Singapore. The purchase helped boost the company's sales to nearly CHF 895 million ($675 million) and cemented the company's transformation from a French Swiss-focused newspaper publisher to one of the world's fastest-growing international publishing groups.

M. L. Cohen

PRINCIPAL SUBSIDIARIES

Agedip S.A.; Center d'impression Edipresse Genève S.A.; Center d'impression Edipresse Lausanne S.A.; Communication Management Ltd (Hong Kong); Edimpresa-Editora Lda (Portugal); Edipresse A.S. SRL (Romania); Edipresse Asia Ltd (Hong Kong); Edipresse Hymsa S.A. (Spain); Edipresse International Sàrl (Luxemburg); Edipresse Livres S.A.; Edipresse Polska S.A.; Edipresse Publications S.A.; Edipresse Publiventas S.A. (Spain); Edipresse Ukraine LLC; Edipresse-Konliga ZAO (Russia); Edipub S.A.; Focus Ediciones SL (Spain); Illustrated Magazine Publishing Company Ltd (Hong Kong); Imprimerie Corbaz S.A.; IRL–Imprimeries Réunies Lausanne SA; Libedi S.A. (Luxemburg); Office Share Lda (Portugal); Presse Publications SR S.A.; SA de la Tribune de Genève; Semana SL (Spain); Servicios de Edición México SA de CV; Sucesores de Rivadeneyra S.A. (Spain).

PRINCIPAL COMPETITORS

Ringier AG; Edipresse S.A.; Tamedia AG; AG fuer die Neue Zuercher Zeitung; Basler Zeitung AG; Espace Media Groupe; LIMMATDRUCK AG; AZ Medien AG; St Galler Tagblatt AG; Suedostschweiz Mediengruppe; LZ Medien Holding; Zollikofer AG; Huber and Company AG; Der Bund Verlag AG; Zuerichsee Medien AG; Buechler Grafino AG.

FURTHER READING

"A Certaines Conditions, Edipresse lorgnera du Côté de la Suisse Allemande," *Press Suisse*, January 17, 2005.

Arnould, Valerie, "Strategie newsdesk chez Edipresse," *Campus XML*, November 2005.

Depommier, Joël, "Vive la Concurrence, Version Edipresse," *Gauche Hebdo*, February 2005.

"Edipresse Reveals Strategy," *Media Finance*, December 2004.

Hirel, Serge, "Groupe EDIPRESSE: La Réussite d'une Dynastie Familiale," *La Gazette*, August-September 2002.

Marquis, J.F., "Concentration et Hiérarchisation dans la Presse en Suisse," *A l'Encontre*, January 2002.

Rodger, Ian, "Edipress Fails to Follow Fashion," *Financial Times*, January 10, 1996, p. 21.

Whelpton, Eric, "The Writing is on the Wall for Dwindling Swiss Press," *European*, July 3, 1997, p. 32.

Fired Up, Inc.

7500 Rialto Boulevard
Suite 250
Austin, Texas 78735
U.S.A.
Telephone: (512) 263-0800
Fax: (512) 263-8055
Web site: http://www.carinos.com

Private Company
Incorporated: 1997
Sales: $375 million (2005 est.)
NAIC: 722110 Full-Service Restaurants

■ ■ ■

Fired Up, Inc., is the Austin, Texas-based parent company of the Johnny Carino's Italian restaurant chain. Johnny Carino's offers full service and a menu inspired by Southern Italian country recipes, including Italian pot roast, spicy shrimp and chicken, Tuscan ribeye steak, grilled Sicilian meatloaf, and angel hair with artichokes. The chain also offers such favorites as lasagna and pizza, and appetizers include oven-baked pepperoni bread, hand-breaded calamari, and Italian nachos. Johnny Carino's offers alcoholic drinks like Italian margaritas and sangria, as well as Italian sodas and creams, and espresso, cappuccino, and latte. Desserts include tiramisu, Italian chocolate cake, and cannoli. The interior of a Johnny Carino's restaurant features wood and stone walls, mismatched chairs, Italian ceramics, and an open kitchen to emulate an Italian farmhouse. Fired Up owns about half of the more-than-150 Johnny Carino's restaurants

located in some 30 states and the Middle East, and has plans with 21 franchise partners to open another 500 restaurants by 2020, at which point 70 percent of the units will be franchised.

FIRED UP FOUNDED: 1997

Fired Up was incorporated in 1997 by Creed L. Ford III and Normal Abdallah, both veterans of Dallas-based Brinker International, developer of casual-dining concepts, best known for the Chili's restaurant chain. In 1976, when he was 24, Ford went to work as an assistant manager at the first Chili's Grill and Bar, founded just a year earlier, and began working his way up through the ranks of the organization. Seven years later restaurant veteran Norman Brinkley gained an equity stake, took charge, and transformed Chili's from a small Dallas-area burger chain into a national full menu, casual restaurant chain. He also served as a mentor to Ford and others who became top food-service executives. Ford became chief operating officer at Brinker, overseeing all of the company's restaurant concepts, while Abdallah, who had joined Brinker in 1987, held a number of management positions before becoming Vice President of Franchise Operations and Development. Brinker launched a reorganization effort in 1996. In that same year, Abdallah left to become president and chief executive officer of Red Hot Concepts, a Chili's licensee of Chili's restaurants in Australia, New Zealand, and the United Kingdom. In early 1997, as it announced less than expected earnings that resulted in a major erosion of the company's stock price, Brinker eliminated 20 jobs in its corporate headquarters and Ford resigned. He planned to remain involved with Brinker as a consultant and to

---

COMPANY PERSPECTIVES

Johnny Carino's Italian is a casual, full service Italian concept with an innovative menu featuring "Grandioso" platters and "Wine Harvest" dinners catering to families and dining parties of all sizes.

---

serve as a franchisee of Brinker's new airport concept, Chili's Too.

Instead of devoting his time to franchising the new Chili's format, Ford turned his attention to a pair of other Brinker concepts, the Kona Ranch Steakhouse, a Hawaiian cattle ranch concept Ford had developed several years earlier, and Johnny Carino's Italian Kitchen, which had superseded Spageddies, Brinker's child-oriented Italian restaurant concept. Ford recruited Abdallah, who quit his job in May, and in June they incorporated Fired Up, Inc., and acquired the Kona Restaurant Group Inc. from an investment group headed by Red Hot Concepts' chairman Colin Halpern. They received one Kona Ranch, located in Oklahoma City, and seven Carino's, located in El Paso, Houston, Lewisville, and Lubbock, Texas; Fort Collins, Colorado; Scottsdale, Arizona; and Little Rock, Arkansas.

Ford and Abdallah leveraged their real estate to raise $6 million in seed money by selling one Carino's property and engineering a sale/leaseback arrangement on three others. They also wasted little time in revamping Carino's, which had done little to distinguish itself from Spageddie's, other than remove the bocce ball courts. The lasagna was frozen, the meatballs prefabricated, and the tiramisu ready made. All this was scrapped in favor of having everything made fresh, from scratch, everyday. To convey the freshness of ingredients and the nature of the menu, Ford and Abdallah decided to insert the word "country," in the restaurant name, making it Johnny Carino's Country Italian. In keeping with this idea, the décor was changed to include the country farmhouse look and the open kitchen where customers could see how the food was prepared. It was an interior Ford and Abdallah were familiar with. While at Brinker in the early 1990s they had visited Tuscany, Italy, and became interested in transferring the look to the United States.

Within the first year, Fired Up added two Kona Ranch Steakhouses, in Texas and Arkansas, and grew Carino's to 11 units. Revenues for the fiscal year sales totaled $23 million. In early 1998 Chili's founder, Larry Lavine, agreed to a joint venture to franchise Carino's,

and Fired Up reached an international development agreement with Abdulghani Khalid Al-Ghunaim of Kuwait, a Chili's franchisee, to develop Carino's locations in ten countries of the Middle East. The company also planned to open a 5,000-square-foot restaurant on the ground floor of Austin's historic Brown Building, which LBJ Holding Co. was converting into loft-style apartments. LBJ was an investment firm with interests in real estate, radio stations, and other companies but was new to the restaurant business. Management was impressed by Ford and Abdallah, and decided to invest more than $1 million in Fired Up.

SECOND CONCEPT ADDED: 1999

From the start, Ford and Abdallah planned to build out the Carino's to a certain territory and rely on franchising to spread it further. By the spring of 1999, Fired Up signed up a franchisee group to develop New Jersey, Pennsylvania, and Maryland, and another to serve the Western part of the country. The company soon added a third restaurant concept: Gumbo's, a Louisiana Style Café, acquired from St. Gumbeaux Inc., the owner of the single location in Round Rock, Texas. The acquisition resulted from a chance meeting of Ford with one of Gumbo's founders, Michael Amr. Ford was dining at Gumbo's with his wife, a restaurateur in her own right, when their waiter made the mistake of neglecting to serve the appetizer before the entrée. Michael Amr paid a visit to the table to apologize, and struck up a conversation with Ford, who had become a regular customer and had heard the owners were interested in developing the Gumbo's concept. Ford was impressed with Amr and decided Gumbo's would be a good complement to the Kona and Casino's concepts. A second Gumbo's was opened in the Brown Building space, and Fired Up also opened the Brown Bar to handle overflow crowds at the restaurant.

By the end of fiscal 2001 in June of that year, Fired Up had built the Carino's chain to 33 units—26 were company owned, and seven were franchised operations. New units were to be found in California, Georgia, Montana, New Mexico, and Oklahoma, as well as in Egypt and Bahrain. By the start of the next calendar year new units would also open in Idaho and Oklahoma. In April 2001 Fired Up reached an agreement with Food & Life Trading LLC, a division of the Al Abbas Group, to develop a Carino's presence in the United Arab Emirates with the help of Al-Ghunaim. In addition to the Carino's chain, Fired Up owned two Kona Ranch Steakhouse restaurants, the pair of Gumbo's cafes in metropolitan Austin, and the Brown Bar. The company also devoted some time in moving to new corporate offices in 2001, finally graduating from the converted

KEY DATES

1997: The company is founded.
1999: The Gumbo's concept is acquired.
2002: Rosewood Capital acquires a stake in the company.
2003: Other restaurant concepts are spun off to focus on Johnny Carino's.
2004: Johnny Carino's opens its 100th unit.

house that had served as the initial headquarters and had been periodically expanded with trailers.

In 2002, in order to fuel further growth, Fired Up secured a private equity partner in Rosewood Capital, a San Francisco-based investment firm that specialized in consumer growth companies. Other restaurant investments included Jamba Juice, Noah's Bagels, and Rubio's Fresh Mexican Grill. Fired Up received $15 million from Rosewood and another $1 million from U.S. Bancorp Piper Jaffray Venture Capital. At the time of the investment, the Carino's chain numbered 42 units, of which 28 were company owned. Franchised operations would take on increasing importance, as reflected by a bevy of franchise development deals Fired Up completed in 2002 and 2003.

In March 2002, Fired Up reached an agreement for franchise operation in Kentucky and southern Ohio with Thomas & King, Inc., owner and operator of 80 Applebee's restaurants. Two month later Zenzations, Inc., another major Applebee's operator, signed up to develop Carino's in Virginia, North Carolina, and South Carolina. Also in May 2002, Fired Up signed an agreement with TLC South, LLC, which owned 42 Applebee's restaurants, to open Carino's in Northern Florida. Next, in July 2002, JC American, LLC became a franchise partner, contracting to open Carino's units in Indiana and Northern Ohio. Although a small operation that owned and operated three Panera Break Bakery Cafes and three specialty restaurants, JC American was headed by Donald Strang and a team of executives that had formerly run Apple American Group, which operated 64 Applebee's restaurants. Also in July Carino's opened its 50th unit, in Spring Hill, Florida, and Fired Up struck a deal with Tomatto Grotto, LLC to develop the Carino's concept in Michigan. Tomatto's managing partner, Rob Bruce, was a former Chili's executive, who had been working with Ford and Abdallah since the founding of Fired Up. He had been a vice-president at Captec Financial Group, which bought three of the old Spageddie's sites in the sale/leaseback arrange-

ment that provide Fired Up with its seed money. Fired Up closed 2002 by reaching an agreement with Neighborhood Pasta Company to open Carino's restaurants in Western Pennsylvania and West Virginia.

CARINO'S OPENS 100TH UNIT: 2004

In the early months of 2003, Fired Up added Prairie Pasta, Inc., as a Carino's franchise partner to develop restaurants in North Dakota, South Dakota, and Northern Nebraska. The principals of Prairie Pasta owned six Applebee's units, four Papa John Pizza operations, and one Rio Bravo Fresh Mex restaurant. Late in the year, Fired Up signed an agreement with Allegro Restaurants to develop 15 Carino's restaurants in Tennessee. One of Allegro partners, Tom Root, was already quite familiar with the Carino's operation, having served as chief operating officer at Thomas & King. By this point the Carino's chain totaled 98 units. The 100th restaurant would open in January 2004 in Howell, New Jersey. Revenues totaled $126 million and system-wide sales exceeded $235 million. It was clear that Carino's was the primary engine for growth at Fired Up, and so in 2003 Kona Ranch Steakhouse, the Gumbo's restaurants, and the Brown Bar were spun off to allow the management team to focus solely on Carino's. Growth was so strong that the company was soon moving to larger offices, trading in 11,000 square feet for 26,000 square feet in southwest Austin.

The executive ranks were bolstered in March 2004 by the hiring of Jerry Deitchle as president. He was the former president of The Cheesecake Factory Incorporated, a public company which during his tenure increased its market capitalization ten-fold, from $250 million to $2.5 billion. His arrival was part of a plan to take Fired Up public. Abdallah told *Nation's Restaurant News,* "The public market is looking pretty good right now; Jerry is the last piece to bring in." An IPO was an obvious exit strategy for Ford and Abdallah, aside from the option of selling the company. No timetable was set for an initial public offering of stock, and in fact it was not to be forthcoming. Several months later, in January 2005, Deitchle resigned as president, although he stayed on as a director of the company and retained his equity stake in Fired Up. He maintained that he was leaving because he wanted to relocate to California, where he had lived while employed at Calabasas Hills, California-based The Cheesecake Factory.

The Carino's chain continued to grow and new franchise partners were brought on board. In one such deal, a plan was made to develop 18 restaurants in Washington and Oregon with Northwest Johnny Carino's, LLC, headed by Gary Hubert, a 26-year veteran of the restaurant business who had once been the president of the Red Robin restaurant chain. Carino's reached the 150 unit level in 2006 with plans to possibly open another 500 units. As of mid-decade, the company had not yet made a move to go public.

Ed Dinger

PRINCIPAL COMPETITORS

Brinker International, Inc.; Darden Restaurants, Inc.; OSI Restaurant Partners, Inc.

FURTHER READING

Breyer, Michelle, "Fired Up Again," *Austin American-Statesman,* June 16, 1998, p. D1.

Monroe, Dennis L., "Financing Tools From Those Who Have Don't It," *Franchise Times,* April 2003.

Peters, James, "Johnny Carino's Ignites Growth of Ex-Brinker Exec's Fired Up Inc.," *Nation's Restaurant News,* February 12, 2001, p. 26.

Rogers, Monica, "Big Country," *Chain Leader,* October 2001, p. 31.

Ruggless, Ron, "Former Brinker Execs to Buy Kona," *Nation's Restaurant News,* June 30, 1997, p. 6.

———, "Regional Powerhouse Chains: Johnny Carino's Country Italian," *Nation's Restaurant News,* January 28, 2002, p. 110.

Spector, Amy, "Deitchle Departs Cheesecake Factory to 'Fire Up," IPO at Johnny Carino's Chain," *Nation's Restaurant News,* March 29, 2004, p. 1.

Forbes

Forbes Inc.

———■———

60 5th Avenue
New York, New York 10011
U.S.A.
Telephone: (212) 620-2200
Toll Free: (800) 242-8786
Fax: (212) 620-2245
Web site: http://www.forbesinc.com

Private Company
Incorporated: 1917
Employees: 750
Sales: $370 million (2004 est.)
NAIC: 511120 Periodical Publishers

■ ■ ■

Forbes Inc. has enjoyed a long history as one of the most successful and recognized publishers of financial news and information and ranks as one of the top 15 highest-grossing magazine publishers. *Forbes* magazine and international editions are read by more than five million people. In addition to the flagship magazine, the company produces *Forbes.com,* which claims to be the Web's leading business site. Other publications are *ForbesLife* (formerly *Forbes FYI*) and *American Heritage,* as well as local language editions produced by affiliates in several foreign countries. Forbes Conference Group and Forbes Custom Media are newer parts of the business.

The architect behind much of Forbes's growth was Malcolm S. Forbes, who oversaw the company from the 1960s until his death in 1990. Since that time, Mal-colm's son Steve and Caspar Weinberger have chaired the company. Privately owned, Forbes Inc. continues to be family-run, with Steve Forbes serving as CEO of Forbes Inc. and editor-in-chief of *Forbes* magazine. His brothers also are involved in Forbes Inc.: Timothy Forbes as COO, Christopher Forbes as vice-chairman, and Robert L. Forbes as vice-president, as well as head of *ForbesLife.*

ORIGINS

Bertie Charles or "B.C." Forbes was born in Buchan, Scotland, in 1880, the son of a tailor and later beer shop owner. Persuaded by a teacher that he had a knack for words, young B.C. landed a job as a type compositor with the *Peterhead Sentinel,* mistakenly assuming that compositors "composed" the news stories that would launch his journalistic career. Eventually, B.C. did get a chance to prove his reporting skills and won a cub reporter's job with the *Dundee Courier and Weekly News,* where he covered everything from murder trials to swimming contests. Forbes's taste for work was insatiable, and he quickly rose to senior reporter, only to leave Scotland for South Africa in 1902 to assume a senior reporter's position with the *Johannesburg Standard and Diggers' News.* Two years later, B.C. was back in Scotland with a nest egg, a growing interest in business stories, and the ability to engage the people who wrote and made the news. Because New York City was, in B.C.'s words, the "greatest newspaper town in the world," it seemed only logical that an ambitious business reporter would establish his career there, and in August 1904 Forbes left Scotland for good.

COMPANY PERSPECTIVES

Forbes is a privately held publishing and new media company. Its flagship publication is *Forbes,* oldest of the nation's major business magazines, which will celebrate its 90th Anniversary in 2007. In an industry increasingly dominated by public conglomerates, Forbes remains one of the largest and most successful family businesses of its kind. In recent years the company has expanded to include Forbes.com, Forbes Conference Group, Forbes Custom Media, and American Heritage.

"DEVOTED TO DOERS AND DOINGS": 1904–29

By promising to "work for nothing," Forbes convinced New York's *Journal of Commerce and Commercial Bulletin* to hire him as a reporter on the dry goods industry, where he showed an unusual ability to report not just on business news but the personalities behind it. His reputation was growing, and when a London paper offered him a job he turned it down on the condition that the *Journal of Commerce* make him a financial editor. In addition to these new duties, he also was offered the chance to write a regular editorial column for the *Journal,* which soon led to an opportunity to write another column for a rival New York paper (a practice not unheard of in the period). Thus when newspaper mogul William Randolph Hearst sought to give his *New York American* paper a better financial page it was natural that the prolific Forbes seemed the most likely candidate. As a Hearst writer, Forbes enjoyed even greater readership, more venues in which to print his stories, and real power as the most prominent business journalist of his time.

Though increasingly well paid by Hearst (more than $185,000 a year in today's terms), in September 1917 Forbes decided to leave the position behind to pursue the only journalistic rung he had not yet seized—running his own publication. By relying on his continued income from a column for Hearst's paper as well as loans from the many businessmen he had met as a reporter, Forbes established *Forbes* magazine to profile the "doers and doings" of the growing American business scene. Published every two weeks for 15 cents an issue, the early *Forbes* was written in large part by B.C. himself and offered an unusual combination of assertive, biting prose; unabashed cheerleading for business success stories; and a moralistic streak that excoriated companies when they demonstrated corruption or exploitative labor practices.

In the boom years of the 1920s, *Forbes* had the business magazine front to itself, which it served well by popularizing the world of business through revealing glimpses at the personalities behind the numbers and products. To his credit, B.C. Forbes seemed to sense that the great bull market of the late 1920s was getting out of hand, and in the months before the crash of October 1929 he warned his readers that "this is the ideal time to get out of debt," that is, close out their highly leveraged stock portfolios and abandon speculative investing. Forbes thus escaped the terrifying free-fall in stock prices in the fall of 1929, but he mistakenly assumed the worst was over and prematurely bought stocks at their new bargain-basement prices. When stocks continued their descent in the months that followed *Forbes* magazine joined the rest of the country in hard times. Because B.C. himself continued to write for Hearst's paper, however, he could use his still sizable writing income to keep the magazine afloat.

THE GREAT CRASH AND NEW COMPETITION: 1929–45

The crash, however, was not the only source of trouble B.C. faced as the 1930s began. In 1929 and 1930, respectively, two new competitors, *Business Week* and *Fortune,* joined the business magazine market. Each took a different approach to business news. By publishing twice as often as *Forbes, Business Week* embraced a news-oriented approach, and the monthly *Fortune* built a reputation for long, in-depth analyses of corporations. *Forbes*'s highly subjective style and businessman-as-hero slant suddenly seemed less than cutting edge. By 1939, *Forbes*'s advertising had fallen from 1,216 pages in 1929 to 269, and its paid circulation of 102,000 ran a distant third to *Fortune*'s 248,000 and *Business Week*'s 192,000.

To keep Forbes afloat, B.C. tried to innovate and diversify. He published books with titles such as *The Salesman's Diary* for 1938 and *Daily Pep Pellets,* hired and fired a series of managing editors, and shifted the magazine's focus from financial and stock market stories to a more nuts-and-bolts industrial beat. Although by 1943 B.C. could still claim an income of $50,000 and holdings of half a million dollars, his longtime safety valve, his column for the *New York American,* disappeared when Hearst canceled it.

POSTWAR "REBIRTH": 1945–64

Like the U.S. economy after World War II, things started to look better for *Forbes* magazine as the postwar boom began to take hold. After winning the Bronze Star and

KEY DATES

1917: *Forbes* is launched in New York by business reporter B.C. Forbes.

1945: Malcolm Forbes, son of the company founder, begins to revitalize the namesake magazine.

1964: Malcolm Forbes becomes majority owner following the death of his brother Bruce.

1982: *Forbes* launches its annual ranking of the world's wealthiest individuals.

1984: *Forbes* is the second most profitable magazine in the United States.

1986: Forbes Inc. buys *American Heritage.*

1990: Steve Forbes inherits control of the company following the death of his father, Malcolm.

1995: Steve Forbes makes the first of two consecutive bids for the U.S. presidency.

1996: Former Reagan defense secretary Caspar Weinberger is named chairman of Forbes Inc.

1998: *Forbes Global* is launched.

1999: Jim Michaels retires as *Forbes* executive editor after 37 years.

2002: Forbes.com introduces a money-back guarantee for larger advertising customers.

2003: Local languages editions are being established in China and other countries.

2005: *Forbes Asia* replaces *Forbes Global.*

Purple Heart in World War II, B.C.'s second oldest son, Malcolm, began to shake things up at the magazine, insisting that it hire its own staff and stop relying on commissioned pieces and scrapping B.C.'s insider's stock tip service in favor of the much more lucrative Forbes Investors Advisory Institute, which by 1950 would be generating $51,000 a year in net profit. In 1946, *Advertising Age* reported that *Forbes*'s circulation had leaped by 26,000 in the space of four months, and by 1948 Malcolm had launched the magazine's annual January 1st ranking of U.S. corporations, which eventually became a profitable source of advertising revenue (and anticipated the *Fortune* 500 list by five years).

Malcolm also made mistakes, however. His attempt at a coffee-table celebration of American history, *Nation's Heritage* magazine, may have been, as it was billed, "the most beautiful magazine in history," but its expensive inks, deluxe coated paper, and hefty newsstand price taxed Forbes Inc.'s coffers and it quickly folded in 1949. While Malcolm's older brother Bruce ran *Forbes*

magazine's business operations, in the 1950s Malcolm pursued another quixotic and doomed pursuit that distracted him from his duties at the magazine: running for election to Congress. When B.C. died in May 1954, Forbes's postwar bloom had begun to fade, and with the magazine's ownership divided between Malcolm, Bruce, and two other brothers (who shared one-third of the company's equity) it was unclear who would lead *Forbes* back to battle against *Business Week* and *Fortune*. When a new managing editor, Byron "Dave" Mack, began hiring researchers to verify writers' facts, however, *Forbes* began to become a more reliable source of information, and this seemed to free its writers to write more confidently. *Forbes*'s circulation once again began to climb. By the late 1950s, with Dave Mack shifted to editor and James W. Michaels hired as managing editor, *Forbes* was winning a larger and larger readership among business executives and investors. Between 1954 and 1958 alone, circulation grew by more than 100 percent to 265,000, and in 1957 Forbes Inc.'s revenues stood at an estimated $3.5 million annually.

MALCOLM TAKING OVER: 1964–90

In June 1964, Bruce Forbes, whose advertising and business savvy had helped strengthen Forbes's bottom line, died of cancer at 48. Malcolm stepped into the breach, buying out the 30 percent stake of Bruce's widow to become the majority owner of Forbes's stock. He then pressured his brothers Gordon and Wallace to sell their shares and eventually gained total control of Forbes Inc. His ultimate goal was to make *Forbes* the highest circulation business magazine on the market, and his aggressive, award-winning "Forbes: Capitalist Tool" ad campaign paid immediate dividends. Positioning *Forbes* as the bold and adventurous interpreter of the story behind the news, the message of the new ads was mirrored by Malcolm's own personal promotions: local publicity visits to major advertising markets in which potential *Forbes* advertisers were wined and dined on the family yacht, *Highlander.*

By the third quarter of 1966, *Forbes*'s circulation had passed *Fortune,* and by the end of 1967 it stood at 500,000, ahead of *Fortune* by 25,000 but still trailing *Business Week* by 30,000 readers. There were still false steps, however. An Arabic-language version of the magazine folded in 1979, and a weekly *Forbes Restaurant Guide* folded after two years. Moreover, Malcolm had begun buying expensive mansions, ranches, and even a Pacific island to offer getaways for businessmen seeking to live the *Forbes* life. These projects lost money, however, until Forbes decided to break up his Denver-area ranch into five-acre parcels to be sold to the public through

Forbes magazine and its newsstand competitors. The stratagem worked, and the Sangre de Cristo ranch eventually returned $34 million for the company on a $3.5 million initial investment. Meanwhile, by the end of 1972 *Forbes*'s circulation had climbed to 625,000 (75,000 higher than *Fortune*), and subscriptions alone were generating $4.5 million a year. Advertising was bringing in $20 million a year by 1976, and the income from the Forbes Stock Market Course and from renting its Manhattan office building further padded the bottom line.

Forbes's competition was only growing fiercer, however. In 1978 *Fortune* switched to a twice-monthly format, which would triple its revenues over the next six years, and a year later a new magazine, *Inc.*, materialized to seize the small business market. By 1984, *Forbes*'s circulation of 770,000 trailed *Business Week* by 120,000 and led *Fortune* by only 22,000 readers. Worse, in gross advertising revenue *Business Week* and *Fortune* led with $156 million and $101 million, respectively, with *Forbes* trailing at $84 million. Still, *Forbes* had made enormous progress since 1964: It could boast that "one in five of our readers is a millionaire," and it remained the second most profitable magazine after *Playboy* because it produced no international or regional U.S. editions and maintained only a slim global network of journalists and a comparatively smaller U.S. editorial staff.

In 1982 Malcolm undertook the first of several international "Friendship Tours," in which an army of "Capitalist Tool" motorcyclists and hot-air balloonists descended on countries such as China, Pakistan, Japan, Germany, Turkey, and Spain spreading goodwill and the Forbes name. The same year, *Forbes* launched its notorious "Forbes Richest 400" list, which helped to raise the magazine's net worth to about $250 million (with another $150 million coming from real estate and other property). By 1983, Forbes ranked eighth among *Ad-Week*'s "ten hottest" magazines (ranked by ad revenue). Since 1970, *Forbes* had expanded from an 18 percent share of the total ad revenues of Big Three business magazines to 33 percent, and it was *Business Week* that bore the brunt. In 1984, therefore, it hired a new editor to stave off the *Forbes* threat, but new magazines including *Manhattan Inc.*, *Financial World*, and *Crain's* were making the business newsstand an increasingly crowded, cutthroat place. In 1986, the gloves came off in the business magazine ad wars when *Forbes* ran a confrontational ad under the words "Business Weak."

STEVE FORBES AND THE TECHNOLOGY CHALLENGE: 1990–99

By the late 1980s Malcolm's son Malcolm S. "Steve" Forbes, Jr., who had started at the magazine in 1971,

had risen to president and deputy editor-in-chief. He had been giving *Forbes*'s editorial point of view a marked rightward tilt, which was underscored when Caspar Weinberger, Ronald Reagan's secretary of defense, was named the magazine's publisher in 1989. In February 1990, Malcolm died in his sleep at age 70, leaving 51 percent of Forbes Inc. to Steve and the rest to his three younger brothers. As his celebrated father was eulogized, Steve reassured the press that the *Forbes* style would not change. For the most part, it seemed to be doing things right. Circulation stood at 735,000, and only *Business Week* sold more ad pages. *American Heritage* magazine, which it had purchased in 1986, had been given a new look under Steve's brother Timothy, and its ad pages grew 20 percent in 1989 alone. A German edition, *Forbes von Burda*, had been co-launched with Germany's Burda Publications the month Malcolm died, and plans continued to launch a four-issue-per-year "lifestyle" magazine, *Forbes FYI*, in the fall of 1990. Only *Egg*, a self-styled "hip, urban" lifestyle magazine launched just before Malcolm's death failed to pan out and was shut down in early 1991.

Forbes Inc. worked hard to keep pace with the increasingly global and technology driven business climate of the 1990s. A Japanese edition was unveiled in March 1992; a Chinese edition was announced in 1993; and in 1998 *Forbes Global Business and Finance*, an English-language international edition, was launched under the leadership of former Canadian prime minister Brian Mulroney. Forbes Inc.'s *American Heritage* operations also expanded, entering the custom publishing market in 1993 and starting a quarterly African-American history magazine named *American Legacy* in 1996. In the same year, Caspar Weinberger was named chairman of Forbes Inc., and in both 1995 and 1999 Steve Forbes launched presidential campaigns that were reminiscent of his father's political crusades of the 1950s.

The challenge of the Internet was the real story, however. Forbes launched a new technology quarterly supplement, *Forbes ASAP*, in 1992, and in the mid-1990s Forbes moved rapidly to establish an online presence, christened "Forbes Digital Tool." As hip, new magazines, including *Wired*, *Fast Company*, *Business 2.0*, *Industry Standard*, and *Red Herring*, vied to become the business magazine for the Internet generation, *Forbes* opened a news office in Silicon Valley in 1997 and began to run more high technology cover stories (it was reporters from Forbes Digital Tool who exposed the Stephen Glass media scandal at the *New Republic*). When in January 1999 Jim Michaels stepped down as executive editor after 37 years at the helm, it was no surprise that his replacement, William Baldwin, had built a reputation as a committed technophile.

MORE WIRED, MORE GLOBAL IN THE NEW MILLENNIUM

Because of its emphasis on high technology, some observers believed the company was more exposed than its rivals to the tech slowdown. *Forbes* revenues fell 26 percent in 2001 to $363 million, according to *Advertising Age,* as the recession cut into ad sales. *Forbes ASAP* was shuttered in October 2002; it was one of several notable tech publications to close during the tech bust.

Nevertheless, the Internet remained a central part of the media empire. Jim Spanfeller was named CEO of Forbes.com in January 2001. He set out to exploit the advantages of the online product, such as the ability to target ads toward specific audiences. In September 2002, Forbes.com introduced its Brand Increase Guarantee for its larger advertising customers. Those spending six figures a month on online ads could claim a refund if their ad metrics did not rise after 60 days. Forbes.com experimented with linking ads to keywords in its editorial content in the summer of 2004. It dropped the practice due to a lack of acceptance from staffers.

Forbes was getting into media other than print and the Internet. It launched a show with cable television's Fox News Channel in 2001. In 2005 it began developing a syndicated weekly radio program in collaboration with TRN Enterprises.

The group was expanding its frontiers in the real world as well as in cyberspace. *Forbes* magazine introduced its Forbes 2000 survey of the world's largest companies in 2003. The next year, it dropped its list of the 500 largest U.S. companies to reflect the increasing importance of international business. Its rival's *Fortune* 500 list of domestic companies was outmoded, an executive said in *Campaign.* The larger, international listing also demonstrated a broader worldview to *Forbes Global* readers in Europe.

Forbes Global was closed in July 2005 as the company restructured its international offerings through more local titles. *Forbes China* had debuted in March 2003 in collaboration with Morningside Business Publishing of Hong Kong. Local language editions also were brought out in Korea (2002) and Russia (2004). *Forbes Asia* was launched in September 2005 to provide expanded coverage of the booming Asia/Pacific region. Editions based in Dubai, Israel, and Poland began publishing in 2004, followed by the launch of *Forbes Turkey* in 2005.

The lifestyle publication *Forbes FYI* was restyled as *ForbesLife* in April 2006. It had increased its publication frequency from quarterly to bimonthly the previous year.

Whereas Forbes was famous for its rankings of the world's largest corporations and wealthiest individuals, the privately owned company was less forthcoming about its own finances. Sales estimates in other media sources varied widely. *Advertising Age*'s 2004 listing of 100 leading media companies pegged Forbes Inc.'s sales at $370 million a year. Publishers Information Bureau ranked *Forbes* magazine number 14 among leading magazines. Its advertising revenues were down slightly in 2005 to $323 million, placing it between rivals *Business Week* (13) and *Fortune* (15) on the list.

At the same time, Forbes.com was logging more than nine million unique visitors every month. Its president, Jim Spanfeller, said at a media conference that the site would pass the print product's revenues by the end of 2006, reported *B to B.*

The *New York Times* suggested that the Forbes publishing empire may have been worth more than $1 billion. It remained 51 percent owned by Steve Forbes, with the rest held by others in the family.

Paul S. Bodine
Updated, Frederick C. Ingram

PRINCIPAL DIVISIONS

American Heritage; The Forbes Collections; Forbes Conference Group; Forbes Custom Media; Forbes Investors Advisory Institute; Forbes Magazine Group; Forbes Newsletter Group; Forbes Radio; Forbes Television.

PRINCIPAL COMPETITORS

Dow Jones & Company, Inc.; The Economist Group Limited; McGraw-Hill Cos.; Time Inc.

FURTHER READING

Aitken, Lucy, "International Business Magazines Bite the Dust," *Campaign,* January 13, 2006, p. 23.

Arnold, Matthew, "Incessancy Overcomes Intimidation in Winning Forbes' Respect," *PR Week* (U.S.), August 12, 2002, p. 14.

Callahan, Sean, "Jim Spanfeller, CEO, Forbes.com," *B to B,* July 19, 2004, p. 24.

Carr, David, "Now Steve Is Running to Revive Forbes," *New York Times,* August 26, 2002, p. C1.

Donaton, Scott, "Malcolm S. Forbes Jr.," *Advertising Age,* March 1990.

Fine, Jon, "Ad Pages Decline: Forbes Parent Feels Sting of Recession," *Advertising Age,* October 21, 2002, p. 1.

Forbes, Malcolm, "Cap Weinberger to Become Fourth Forbes Publisher," *Forbes,* October 3, 1998, p. 17.

Foroohar, Kambiz, "Tracking Lies," *Forbes.com,* May 11, 1998.

"Greater Expectations," *Forbes,* September 15, 1977, pp. 121+.

Griffin, Marie, and Ellis Booker, "As Digital Dollars Grow, B-to-B Publishers Debate Impact of Blogs," *B to B,* May 3, 2005.

Heller, Robert, "The Battle for U.S. Business," *Management Today,* August 1984, pp. 62+.

"In 2005, All Top 12 Magazine Ad Categories Exceeded $1 Billion," *MIN: Media Industry Newsletter,* January 23, 2006.

Jones, Arthur, and Malcolm Forbes, *Peripatetic Millionaire,* New York: Harper & Row, 1977.

Kuczynski, Alex, "Changing of the Guard and Coverage, at Forbes Magazine," *New York Times,* October 12, 1998.

Lehmann-Haupt, Rachel, "Egg (1990–1991)," *Folio: The Magazine for Magazine Management,* March 1, 2004.

Levere, Jane L., "Advertising: Forbes Hustles to Build Its Web Brand," *New York Times,* June 9, 1999, p. C8.

Mack, Ann M., "Forbes.com Nixes Ad Links in Editorial," *AdWeek Online,* December 2, 2004.

Maddox, Kate, "Forbes.com Offers Brand Guarantee; Advertisers Get Money Back If Campaigns Don't Produce Significant Increase in Brand Metrics," *B to B,* October 14, 2002, p. 14.

"A Magazine of His Own," *Forbes,* September 15, 1967, p. 13.

Motavalli, John, "Clash of the Titans," *AdWeek,* May 22, 1989, pp. 20+.

"The Rise of Consumerism," *Hub Magazine,* Spring 2006.

Rothenberg, Randall, "Forbes Clan Masters the Art of Keeping in Touch with Targets," *Advertising Age,* October 11, 2004, p. 26.

Sorkin, Andrew Ross, "Forbes May Seek Investment from Outside," *New York Times,* May 8, 2006, p. C2.

"Top Media Companies, 2004," *Advertising Age,* 100 Leading Media Companies (annual), August 22, 2005, p. s-4, *Business Rankings Annual,* online edition, Thomson Gale, 2006.

Tungate, Mark, "Forbes Broadens Its Scope with Top 2000 Survey," *Campaign,* April 2, 2004, p. 21.

Winans, Christopher, *Malcolm Forbes: The Man Who Had Everything,* New York: St. Martin's Press, 1990.

Frontier Natural Products Co-Op

3021 78th Street
Norway, Iowa 52318
U.S.A.
Telephone: (319) 227-7996
Toll Free: (800) 365-4372
Fax: (319) 227-7966
Web site: http://www.frontiercoop.com/

Cooperative
Founded: 1976
Employees: 250
Sales: $49 million (2006)
NAIC: 311423 Dried and Dehydrated Food Manufacturing

■ ■ ■

Based in Norway, Iowa, Frontier Natural Products Co-Op bills itself as the nation's largest supplier of organic herbs and spices, selling to natural products stores and specialty stores in the United States and Canada. The company manufactures products, sources agricultural products from around the world, and distributes the products of other companies. Frontier's offerings include a wide variety of non-irradiated spices, seasonings, and blends; natural and organic baking ingredients, including mixes sold under the Simply Organic brand name; supplement; loose-leaf teas; holistic and craft herbs; and the Aura Cacia brand aromatherapy and natural personal care products, such as essential oils, and body and bath products. Frontier prides itself on a progressive company culture and provides employees on-site childcare and meal programs in addition to traditional health care and retirement benefits.

KITCHEN TABLE ORIGINS: 1976

Frontier was begun in Eastern Iowa in 1976 by a young married couple, Rick Stewart and Colleen Greenhaw. While Rick was a student at Kirkwood Community College in Cedar Rapids, they belonged to an area food cooperative, where Colleen worked on a volunteer basis. One of her tasks was ordering the co-op's herbs and spices. Disenchanted with the quality of the merchandise and the poor customer service from suppliers, she began to suggest that she and Rick could do a better job. Thus, the idea was already in the air when chance intervened. In Iowa City some 30 miles away, their co-op's distributor, Blooming Prairie Warehouse, was on the verge of eliminating herbs and spices altogether because their supplier planned to stop selling five-pound bags in favor of ten-pound bags. At the same time, the customers of the warehouse were clamoring for one-pound bags. Stewart offered to repackage the ten-pound bags into salable one-pound bags. He began bringing home the warehouse's large bags of herbs and spices, and on their kitchen table he and Colleen bagged them into smaller quantities and labeled them.

Satisfied with the job the couple had done, Blooming Prairie hired them to handle the ordering and invoicing of its herbs and spices business. Sales were meager at first, totaling just $26 in August 1976, but the $3,000 in sales generated in March 1977 made the Stewarts realize how much work was involved as well as the business potential. "We knew that no one else was going to do this for fun like we were," Stewart told the Cedar Rapids *Gazette* in 1992. "We either had to make it bigger so it could pay people to work or we had to get rid of it altogether." They decided to become wholesalers of herbs and spices, calling the business Frontier Cooperative Herbs. Seeing little opportunity to break into the Iowa market, they drove around Wisconsin, Illinois, and Michigan to visit local food cooperatives in hopes of drumming up customers. Their perseverance paid off in September 1977 when the food cooperatives of Madison, Wisconsin, agreed as a group to use the Stewarts as their supplier. The initial order of $4,000 was twice as much inventory as the couple had on hand and jump-started the business. Soon, employees were being hired and, having outgrown the cabin, the business was moved to the basement of Cedar Rapids' Good News General Store Co-op.

FRONTIER INCORPORATED AS CO-OPERATIVE: 1979

Sales were growing so quickly, reaching $18,000 by the end of 1977, that within a few months Frontier was on the move again, taking over a former grocery store in Fairfax, Iowa, 5,200 square feet in size. Sales continued to build, fueled in part by an expansion in what Frontier had to offer. It added a variety of uncommon herbs and spices and developed a network of supplier contacts. In 1978 the company responded to customer requests and began bottling essential oils for resale, and a year after that Frontier began selling products from other manufacturers, again at the behest of customers. As a result of its responsiveness to customer needs, Frontier quickly developed a reputation as an excellent supplier, leading to even more business. In 1979 Frontier was incorporated as a cooperative and was now owned by its customers. A year later, in March 1980, Frontier cut the first profit-sharing checks to its member-owners.

To meet demand, Frontier had to lease more space in Fairfax as well as erect portable buildings. To keep up with orders, the company installed its first computerized system in 1980. (Five years later personal computers would be purchased as well.) As business approached the $1 million mark, Frontier bought ten acres of land in Norway, Iowa, in February 1982, and constructed a

22,152 square-foot-facility, which was ready to be occupied in October of that year. Soon after that, a day-care center was opened for employees. As Stewart explained to the *Gazette,* "We always brought our children to work and we felt it was perfectly natural for our employees to do the same."

To help in running the business Stewart returned to college in September 1982, enrolling at Coe College in Cedar Rapids to take courses at night and on weekends. Finally in 1990 he had accumulated enough credits to receive a degree in business administration and accounting.

When Stewart was not learning about business principles in the classroom, he was gaining a practical education running a fast-growing business in a changing landscape. The allure of food cooperatives had dimmed with the years, so that by the mid-1980s far more were shutting their doors as were opening them. As a result, Frontier sales stalled around the $3 million level and Stewart decided that the company needed to pursue the business of non-cooperatives. Customer-members then voted to amend the organization's bylaws to permit non-cooperative customers to buy on an equal basis. Stewart expected that Frontier's reputation would extend to this new market and prosper from it. To accommodate more business, Frontier expanded its Norway facilities to nearly 32,000 square feet in 1984. But gaining acceptance with these new customers took time, as well as money to be spent on advertising in trade publications. Frontier's reputation was also enhanced in 1986 when it became the first herb and spice manufacturer to receive United States Food and Drug Administration certification for organic processing. Frontier further helped its standing in the natural foods industry in 1989 when it became the first to eliminate chemical fumigants to achieve greater purity by employing a natural carbon-dioxide process to ward off infestation in herbs and spices. A year later, the company opened the Frontier Research Farm to develop new ways to conduct organic farming. In 1992 the company turned its attention to processing, introducing cryogenic grinding to help preserve product quality.

With sales growing at a 20 percent clip each year in the late 1980s, compared to a 5 percent annual growth rate of the natural food industry, Frontier again had to expand its Norway plant. To do so, the company bought another 46 acres of adjacent land to add 5,800 square feet of space in 1988 and nearly 20,000 square feet a year later. Some of that space would be needed because of the 1988 introduction of a line of package spices, again in keeping with the requests of customers. In 1990 Frontier unveiled a line of bottled spices. By the end of that year company revenues reached $9 million and

```
┌─────────────────────────────────────────────────┐
│                                                 │
│              KEY DATES                          │
│                    ■                            │
│  1976:  The company is launched in Iowa by Rick │
│         Stewart and Colleen Greenhaw.           │
│  1979:  Frontier is incorporated as a cooperative. │
│  1982:  Plant and headquarters are built in Norway, │
│         Iowa.                                   │
│  1988:  Frontier introduces packaged spices.    │
│  1992:  The first Herbfest is held.             │
│  1997:  The company's marketing office opens in │
│         Boulder, Colorado.                      │
│  1999:  Stewart resigns from Frontier.          │
│  2002:  Simply Organic product lines are introduced. │
│  2003:  Tony Bedard is named CEO.               │
│                                                 │
└─────────────────────────────────────────────────┘
```

business continued to grow steadily, spurred in July 1991 by the introduction of Frontier Coffee, a line of 100 percent certified organic, gourmet coffee. This business would soon be supplemented by the acquisition of a company that sold natural coffee filters. Frontier generated additional revenues in 1992 when it began to sell Frontier-branded products through natural food distributors, and continued to expand the coffee line two years later when a roasting plant was opened in Urbana, Iowa. In 1993 the company introduced organic Frontier beer and added a line of aromatherapy products by acquiring Weaverville, California-based Aura Cacia, founded in 1981. Frontier scored another first in 1995 when it became the first company to introduce a line of certified organic essential oils. As a result of product growth, the Norway facilities were expanded to more than 86,000 square feet in 1993, and by 1995 sales reached $29.6 million.

On other fronts in the mid-1990s, Frontier began hosting an August conference each year, starting in 1992, called Herbfest, a three-day event which attracted over a 1,000 people, who participated in seminars conducted by experts in herbs and spices and the natural living lifestyle, and also included farm tours, herb walks, and entertainment. In keeping with its family-friendly philosophy, Herbfest also included specialized activities for children. A botanical garden was created on the company's Norway acreage in 1993. Frontier launched the Goldenseal Project in 1996, its purpose to encourage the cultivation of goldenseal in order to prevent over-harvesting of the herb in the wild. Moreover, the project promoted alternative herbs as a way to protect the goldenseal population. In 1998, Frontier bought 68 acres of land in Meigs County, Ohio, part of the state's Appalachian region, and started the National Center for the Preservation of Medicinal Herbs to conduct research on the way to cultivate native herbs, many of which were at risk of over-harvesting.

COLORADO OFFICE OPENS: 1997

Frontier enjoyed continued growth in the late 1990s, elevating annual sales to the $40 million level, which led to a further expansion of the Norway facilities to more than 115,000 square feet. The company also opened a marketing office in Boulder, Colorado, in 1997 and soon moved its corporate headquarters there and assumed the name Frontier Natural Products Co-op. As the decade came to an end, Stewart announced that he was retiring after 23 years at the helm. He said that he was stepping aside as a way to encourage the board to recruit a CEO with the experience and skills needed to take the company to the next step in its development. He was replaced on an interim basis by Tony Bedard, who had been with Frontier since 1991.

Several months passed before the Frontier board chose, in November 2000, Steve Hughes, former CEO of Celestial Seasonings, as Stewart's successor. Hughes, who had 20 years of experience in the food and beverage industries, quickly began putting his stamp on Frontier, bringing in industry managers and mapping a strategy to position Frontier to take advantage of the growing market for natural and organic products in mainstream stores. To help raise capital to fund this effort Frontier sold its organic coffee brand to Vermont's Green Mountain Coffee Inc. for $2.7 million in the summer of 2001. Then, late in the year, Hughes secured approval from the Frontier Board to establish a subsidiary, Frontier Natural Brands, to break into the mass market with a line of organic products under the Simply Organic label, including culinary spices and add-meat dinnertime pastas, and aroma therapy oils, lotions, and shampoos under the Aura Cacia brand. The goal was to transform Frontier into a natural consumer packaged goods company. Not everyone on the board was convinced this was the right direction for Frontier to take, and the restructuring plan was approved by only a single vote from membership. Some members were also upset when herb researchers were fired and their research gardens mowed over to allow for warehouse expansion. Herbfest was also discontinued, no longer deemed necessary by the new management team.

Hughes' grand plan quickly fizzled, however. Simply Organic was launched in April 2002, but it was rushed to market and Frontier lacked the financial resources to stick to the plan when cash flow failed to meet expectations. Within a matter of weeks Hughes resigned, as did others in top positions, and the board's president, Andy Pauley, stepped in as acting CEO. Before the year was out the Boulder office was closed and the headquarters was reestablished in Norway, and steps were taken to return Frontier to its core business.

In May 2003 Bedard, who had left to become a production manager with Winnebago Industries, was reinstalled as Frontier's chief executive. In October 2003 he sold the Simply Organic boxed dinner product line to Annie's Homegrown, a Massachusetts company, but retained the Simply Organic bottled spice, seasoning mix, and flavor lines. In 2004 Frontier moved its Aura Cacia operation from California to Urbana, Iowa, making use of the old coffee roasting facility, which had been used for storage since the divestiture of the coffee business. Because of its proximity to Norway, the company hoped to expand the Aura Cacia business by taking advantage of the main facility's research and development and other resources. Later in the year Frontier introduced a line of alcohol-free, roll-on aromatherapy sticks.

By the start of 2004 Frontier had recovered enough from the missteps of 2002 to resume making dividend payments to its customer-owners. In August 2004 the company once again hosted Herbfest, something Bedard announced as a priority when he returned to the company. Almost 1,000 people attended the event, a strong showing after a two-year hiatus.

Frontier returned to its philosophical roots as well. In 2004 it began offering what it called Fair Trade teas, organic loose leaf teas procured from suppliers who met a standard in providing wages and working and living conditions for the workers who picked the tea. A year later Frontier established the CONVERT program to find socially responsible supplier partners around the world. The first of these partners was an Indian vanilla supplier.

Although Frontier no longer experienced a 20 percent annual growth rate, business was on the rise again. Sales reached a record $43.4 million in 2005. To accommodate demand, Frontier was once more looking to add to its facilities and hire additional people. In 2006 the company announced plans for a $3 million expansion that would add 30,000 square feet of space to the Norway facilities.

Ed Dinger

PRINCIPAL COMPETITORS

Aveda Corporation; Levlad LLC; Natural Selection Foods; United Natural Foods, Inc.

FURTHER READING

Brand, Rachel, "Natural Foods Firm Explores New Frontier," *Rocky Mountain News,* May 2, 2002, p. 4B.

Eykyn, Sarah, "Merging Organic Products and Social Responsibility," *In Business,* July/August 2000, p. 18.

Ford, George C., "A Growing Concern Frontier: From Kitchen Table to Big Business," *Gazette* (Cedar Rapids, Iowa), April 12, 1992, p E1.

"Frontier Herb Chief Resigns," *Gazette* (Cedar Rapids, Iowa), December 23, 1999, p. B7.

Gutknecht, Dave, "Co-op Devolution: North Farms Folds, Frontier Falters, Blooming Prairie Faces Funk," *Cooperative Grocer,* September-October 2002.

The Garden Company Ltd.

---

58 Castle Peak Road
Kowloon,
Hong Kong
Telephone: (852) 2386 42
Fax: (852) 2387 43
Web site: http://www.garden.com.hk

Private Company
Incorporated: 1926
Employees: 1,500
Sales: HKD 6.5 billion ($825 million) (2005 est.)
NAIC: 311330 Confectionery Manufacturing from Purchased Chocolate; 311520 Ice Cream and Frozen Dessert Manufacturing; 311812 Commercial Bakeries; 311821 Cookie and Cracker Manufacturing

■ ■ ■

The Garden Company Ltd. is Hong Kong's leading manufacturer of packaged breads and baked goods, supplying the retail, and restaurant and catering market. Garden's product range includes ready-to-eat packaged breads, biscuits and cookies, snacks, pastries, hamburger buns, rolls, candy and cakes. In the mid-2000s, Garden continued developing a new line of "healthy" foods, including calcium-enriched and other breads. The company also manufactures partly baked frozen products, as well as frozen dough products.

Garden operates from a 70,000-square-meter factory in Sham Tseng, Hong Kong, which includes eight automated biscuit production lines, three cake production lines and four continuous baking bread lines. The company's bread brands include the flagship Life brand, the Better Sandwich snack bread line, the Sweet Home brand, including raisin scones and oatmeal buns, and other specialty breads, such as the Satellite bun, pita bread, and sweet round rolls. Garden is Hong Kong's leading producer of packaged cake, primarily marketed under the Garden brand, as well as the Be Be cake mix line. Biscuit, cracker, and cookie brands include Gala, Vincenzi, Sisisic, Eggo, Zonee, and Pop Pan. The company's snacks line include Wizard oriental snacks and potato chips and Wow snacks. Lastly, the group's candy and confectionery range is marketed under various brand names, including Lucky, Hi G and Pernigotti, among others. Garden has made an effort to expand outside of Hong Kong—the company set up its first sales operations in mainland China in the 1980s—and markets a wide range of products for the international market. The company has also established a manufacturing presence in China through two joint venture subsidiaries in Dongguan and Yang Zhou. With an approximate 64 percent share of the Hong Kong bread market, Garden generates sales estimated at close to HKD 6.5 billion ($825 million). The company remains privately held and controlled by the founding Cheung family.

BAKED BREAD PIONEER IN 1926

The beginning of British domination of China and Hong Kong introduced many new types of food to the region, including Western-styled breads, biscuits and other baked goods. Traditional Chinese breads, often eaten for breakfast, generally took the form of steamed buns. The development of the British colonial administration and the growing taste for European style foods in Hong Kong encouraged the development of local production of a number of products, including breads.

In the early 1920s, two cousins, T. F. Cheung and W. O. Wong, launched plans to open their own bakery business. In 1926, the pair opened a shop in Kowloon. Cheung and Wong named their bakery The Garden Company, after the famed Hong Kong Botanic Garden. The new company met with quick success, and by 1927, demand for their baked goods led Garden to open its first bakery branch, in the Central area of Hong Kong island.

Demand continued to rise, and in 1931 the company moved to a larger facility, in Sham Shui Po, in the northwestern area of Kowloon. The company operated from a three-story building and had already launched a 24-hour production schedule. By then, Garden's range had expanded to include bread and biscuits. Yet, just a year later, the company was hit by a major setback, when its factory burned down. Uninsured, the company nonetheless managed to arrange the financing to buy new equipment and construct a new factory.

Garden was back in business by 1935, operating from a 475-square-meter plant on Kowloon's Castle Peak Road. The beginning of the Sino-Japanese war just two years later proved a boon for Garden, as it launched production of the so-called "Army Cracker" to support the Chinese war effort. Garden met the challenge: in one week, working round-the-clock for seven days, Garden produced some 200,000 pounds of army crackers. The experience convinced the company of the importance of investing in new equipment and machinery. The company promptly installed a new generation of mechanical baking equipment imported from Britain, becoming the first in Hong Kong to develop industrialized bakery facilities. By 1938, the company had opened a new 1,400-square-meter plant on Castle Peak Road. The investment played a major role in Garden being appointed by the Hong Kong government to be the primary producer of baked goods for the army.

Tragedy struck the company again, however, after the Japanese army occupied Hong Kong in 1941. The Garden factory was taken over by the Japanese occupational force, ending the company's production for the duration. By the end of the war, the factory and its equipment had been destroyed.

OVERCOMING ADVERSITY AGAIN AND AGAIN

The restoration of British control of Hong Kong enabled the Cheung family to restart their bakery business in 1945. By 1947, the company had once again returned to its position as one of the leading food manufacturers in Hong Kong, and in that year the company formally registered as a limited liability company under the name The Garden Company Limited.

The destruction of its factory during the war worked in the company's favor, as it was able to build a larger and more modern facility. The company also placed an order for its first fully automated biscuit production in 1949. Two years later, after receiving a supply contract for the Hong Kong military, the company completed the expansion of its factory, to 7,000 square meters, in anticipation of the new equipment. Finally installed in 1952, the new production line made Garden the first Asian company to launch automated biscuit production. The new equipment enabled the company to achieve production levels of some 5,000 kilograms per day. In 1954, Garden extended its automated production facilities to include bakery and confectionery as well.

Yet the peaceful times for Garden once again proved short-lived. When Hong Kong pro-nationalists began rioting in 1956, they attacked a number of factories in Kowloon, including The Garden Company. As a result, the company's equipment was once again destroyed. Nonetheless, Garden once again found triumph in adversity; by 1958, the company had not only rebuilt the factory, but had extended its total floor space to 10,000 square meters.

The rising affluence of Hong Kong during the 1960s provided new opportunity for the company. In 1960, Garden launched its famous Life brand white bread. The new bread brand claimed to provide a higher nutritional value than typical industrially produced

KEY DATES

1926: T. F. Cheung and W. O. Wong open a bakery business in Kowloon named after the Hong Kong Botanical Garden.

1931: Garden moves to a larger factory in Sham Shui Po and launches 24-hour daily production.

1938: The company moves to a new, 1,400-square-meter factory on Castle Peak Road.

1941: The factory is taken over by Japanese occupation force and production is stopped.

1947: The company registers as The Garden Company Limited.

1952: The company installs its first automated baking equipment, capable of producing 5,000 kilograms of biscuits per day.

1960: Launch of Life bread brand takes place.

1962: A 13,000-square-meter site is acquired in Sham Tseng for biscuit and confectionery production.

1969: A confectionery plant is completed at the Sham Tseng site.

1970: A dedicated production plant for Life bread is added at the Sham Tseng site.

1979: The company launches production of ice cream and snack foods.

1985: The first operation in mainland China is established through a joint venture.

1987: A factory in Dongguan, China is added.

1992: The company expands the Sham Tseng site to 50,000 square meters.

2000: Production at a new biscuit joint venture in Jiangsu begins, in partnership with Gong Yang Foodstuff.

2006: Garden is the largest baked goods company in Hong Kong with sales estimated at nearly HKD 6.5 billion

breads, while also boasting a longer shelf life. Life quickly grew into one of Garden's flagship brands. The launch also enabled the company to dedicate the Castle Peak Road factory to bread production. In 1962, the company began construction of a new factory in Sham Tseng, on a 13,000-square-meter site. The company then transferred its biscuit production to the new purpose-built facility, which launched production in 1963. The facility also enabled the group to expand its range of biscuits,

crackers and related snacks, leading to the launch of a new brand success, Pop Pan, launched in 1967.

By 1969, Garden had completed a new confectionery plant on the Sham Tseng site as well. At the same time, the company launched construction of a new dedicated facility for the production of the group's Life bread brand. That plant launched production in 1970. The Sham Tseng location continued to develop its role as Garden's main facility, and in 1974, the completion of a new production facility on the site enabled Garden to launch production of a new range of buns and other sandwich breads.

FEEDING HONG KONG—AND THE WORLD—IN A NEW ERA

Garden continued to seek new areas for its expansion. In 1979, the company launched a diversification effort, extending its range to include the production of ice cream. The company then entered the snack food category, launching the production of the Si-Si-Sic brand of snack foods, including sandwiches and convenience packs.

Into the 1980s, the company added to its production capacity, building a third bakery plant in 1982. Garden expanded its confectionery factory at the same time. Meanwhile, Garden began targeting further growth. The economic reform policies in mainland China and that country's new openness to foreign investment gave Garden a natural market for expansion. The company became one of the first foreign food companies to invest in the mainland, establishing a joint-venture, called Hua Jia Foodstuff Company, in Dongguan, Guangdong Province in 1985.

The prospect of serving the vast Chinese market prompted Garden to step up its interests in the mainland. In 1987, the company added a new subsidiary, LiHua Biscuit, again in Dongguan. By the mid-1990s, with the unification of Hong Kong with the Chinese mainland pending, Garden moved to expand its mainland operations again, reaching an agreement with Gong Yang Foodstuff Co. to form a new joint venture in Jiangsu. By then, too, Garden had carried out a massive expansion of its Sham Tseng operations. In the early 1990s, the company rebuilt its bakery factory, which was extended to 50,000 square meters and outfitted with new equipment in 1992.

The company's newest production facility, built as part of its joint venture with Gong Yang Foodstuff, was completed in 2000, with manufacturing of biscuits launched that year. The new facility enabled the company to begin developing a new range of products, such as a line of Garden-branded crackers launched in 2002, tailored to the tastes of mainland consumers. In this way, Garden positioned itself to reap the benefits of the rapid growth of the Chinese economy, and the growing affluence of its population, which in turn were expected to influence the country's eating habits.

At the same time Garden capitalized on another growing trend in Hong Kong and China. The appearance of the bird flu virus, and the panic surrounding the SARS epidemic, helped stimulate demand for a new category of "healthy" foods. Garden joined in this trend, launching its own line of healthy foods, such as calcium-enriched breads and the like. By the mid-2000s, the company looked back on 80 years as a family-owned Hong Kong bakery leader—and looked forward to gaining a strong position in the mainland Chinese market as well.

M.L. Cohen

PRINCIPAL SUBSIDIARIES

Gong Yang Foodstuff Co. Ltd. (50%; China); Hui Jia Foodstuff Co. (50%; China); Li Hua Biscuit Factory (China).

PRINCIPAL COMPETITORS

Cadbury Four Seas Company Ltd.; Cadbury Food Company Ltd.; Trebor Wuxi Confectionery Company Ltd.; Taiwan Sugar Corp.; Katokichi Company Ltd.; Chu Shui Che Foods Manufacturing Company Ltd.

FURTHER READING

Asprey, Donald, "Flour 'Explosion' Creates Snowscape," *South China Morning Post*, July 8, 2006.

"Garden Crackers," *International Product Alert*, February 18, 2002.

Redruello, Francisco, "Health Awareness Drives Bakery Market in Hong Kong and China," *Euromonitor*, April 7, 2005.

The Gatorade Company

555 West Monroe Street
Chicago, Illinois 60661-3605
U.S.A.
Telephone: (312) 222-7111
Toll Free: (800) 88-GATOR
Web site: http://www.gatorade.com

Wholly Owned Subsidiary of PepsiCo, Inc.
Incorporated: 1967 as Gatorade Inc.
Employees: 1,200
Sales: $1.22 billion (2004 est.)
NAIC: 312111 Beverages

■ ■ ■

The Gatorade Company makes the world's leading sports drink, Gatorade Thirst Quencher. Created in 1965 by University of Florida researchers interested in improving the school football team's performance in sweltering heat, the drink virtually invented the sports drink industry and continued to dominate the market for decades. The beverage's carbs and electrolytes are only part of its formula for success. Intensive marketing is another ingredient. Sponsorships across a wide range of top-tier sporting competitions, leagues, teams, and individual athletes keep the brand in the public eye. Gatorade has faced down dozens of competitors over the years and typically holds an 80 percent share of the U.S. sports drink market. Gatorade also makes Propel fitness water.

FLORIDA ORIGINS

Gatorade was developed in 1965 at the University of Florida; its name is a reference to the Gators sports teams there. In that summer, more than two dozen freshman players were hospitalized due to the effects of practicing in the sweltering heat. Dr. Robert Cade, a kidney specialist at the University of Florida, led the group of four doctors credited with inventing Gatorade. Others included Dana Shires, Cuban émigré Alex De-Quesada, and Jim Free. Drawing on research into rehydration, the team developed an electrolyte-carbohydrate solution, a mix of salts and sugars designed to provide the athletes with energy and necessary chemicals for physical and mental performance. Plain water could not move through the body quickly enough, nor restore its chemistry.

By replacing minerals lost in sweat, the players were able to outperform their exhausted rivals in the second half of games. The Gators won their first Orange Bowl in 1969. (In the same year the second Gatorade flavor, appropriately enough, orange, was introduced.) Gatorade was soon adopted by other football and basketball teams.

Gatorade was not the only sports drink brewing in collegiate football, notes Darren Rovell's *First in Thirst: How Gatorade Turned the Science of Sweat into a Cultural Phenomenon.* A New Jersey doctor named Gerald Balakian was plying the Rutgers team with his own "Sportade"; it failed, however, to attain the same level of success and legend.

The doctors who invented the brew realized its sales potential but tired of their initial attempts to

COMPANY PERSPECTIVES

Gatorade was born on the playing field in the 1960s by researchers at the University of Florida to help the Gators football team prevent dehydration when they played in the swamp-like heat. Since the Gators' 1967 Orange Bowl victory, Gatorade has grown to become an essential part of the equipment of sports, and can be found on the sidelines, in the locker rooms and on almost every field of play. Backed by more than 40 years of scientific research, Gatorade has proven rehydration and performance benefits over water. No other beverage or sports drink company has established such a strong expertise in rehydration and sports nutrition.

commercialize it. Canned food packer Stokely-Van Camp acquired U.S. rights to the drink in 1967, whereupon Gatorade Inc. was incorporated in Florida. Its start-up capital was reported as just $500. The doctors agreed to be compensated with royalties through the Gatorade Trust, which included a few other supporters, such as internist Eugene Tubbs and nephrologist Kent Bradley, who had transferred to the University of Indiana and was responsible for making the initial connection with Stokely-Van Camp.

EARLY MARKETING COUPS BEGINNING IN 1967

Stokely was quick to sign up Gatorade as the official sports drink of the National Football League in 1967. Distinctive orange and white coolers and green waxed paper cups, all branded with the Gatorade logo, took up a highly visible presence on the sidelines.

The formula was tweaked by one of Stokely's chemists to make the briny brew more palatable. After one of its ingredients, the artificial sweetener cyclamate, was banned in 1969 because of a link to cancer, Stokely quietly had the drink reformulated to replace it with more fructose, a natural sugar found in fruit. A number of other flavors were developed but set aside in favor of the original lemon-lime and the second flavor, orange. The company also toyed with dozens of other names before opting to preserve the brand recognition Gatorade had already attained.

Gatorade was marketed originally to sports teams and sold in 64-ounce metal cans. When it turned out that the salts in the drink made these cans leak, it was put into the 32-ounce glass bottles that would be the

standard for 25 years. But, writes Rovell, the teams soon convinced Stokely to produce a powdered concentrate so that they could mix it themselves in safer, nonglass containers on the field.

Stoked by profiles in leading regional and national sports publications, Stokely's own ads trumpeted the drink as "Gatorade, The Big Thirst Quencher for Active People!" Even Elvis Presley became a fan during a marathon series of performances in Las Vegas, notes Rovell.

Royal Crown Cola licensed a carbonated version of Gatorade but pulled the plug in the early 1970s. Gatorade's phenomenal early success had attracted the interest of another soda pop company, Coca-Cola, which announced its short-lived Olympade sports drink in 1970.

The federal government questioned whether the doctors were the proper owners of Gatorade's rights since they had been working on government grants at the time it was developed. The inventors considered it a side project. The University of Florida, too, was looking for a share of the fortune. Legal challenges were resolved in 1972 when a settlement gave the University of Florida a 20 percent share of Gatorade royalties; this would amount to nearly $100 million by the end of 2004, notes Rovell. To satisfy the federal government, the doctors were required to publish their Gatorade-related research.

ACQUIRED BY QUAKER OATS IN 1983

In 1983, Quaker Oats Company bought Stokely-Van Camp for $220 million. It promptly sold off most of Stokely's assets, keeping the famous pork and beans business, as well as Gatorade, which was the main reason for the deal.

The New York Giants are credited with starting the ritual of the "Gatorade dunk" —a postgame dowsing of the winning coach with the team's bucket of Gatorade—in 1985. Replicated at countless other sporting events, including the Super Bowl, it made for great TV, and was an unplanned marketing bonanza.

Gatorade expanded its international distribution under Quaker ownership. It became available in Canada beginning in 1984, followed by Asia in 1987, and Europe and South America in 1988. Australia followed five years later. By 1998, Gatorade was sold in 47 countries and was the market leader throughout North America and much of Latin America. The overseas products included dozens of flavors not available in the United States.

Gatorade virtually owned the $200 million sports drink market when Quaker acquired it, though this

KEY DATES

1965: University of Florida scientists formulate Gatorade.

1967: Stokely-Van Camp acquires the U.S. rights to Gatorade, which becomes the official sports drink of the NFL.

1969: Gatorade is reformulated with fructose after cyclamate is banned because of a cancer link; orange flavor is introduced.

1972: A lawsuit settlement gives University of Florida a 20 percent share of Gatorade royalties.

1983: Quaker buys Gatorade owner Stokely-Van Camp; fruit punch flavor is introduced.

1984: Gatorade enters the Canadian market; a partnership is formed with the NBA.

1987: Gatorade expands to Asia.

1988: Citrus cooler flavor is introduced; the European and South American markets are entered; Gatorade Sports Science Institute is opened.

1989: The first aseptic (box) and plastic packaging introduced.

1990: Gatorade signs a ten-year endorsement deal with Michael Jordan.

1993: Gatorade is introduced in Australia.

1997: Gatorade Frost is launched.

1999: The first of Fierce flavors debuts.

2000: Propel fitness water is launched; Pepsi acquires Gatorade parent Quaker Oats.

2001: Sports nutrition products such as energy bars and energy drinks debut.

2002: Propel fitness water and Gatorade Ice flavors are launched.

2005: Record heat and military use lead to a reported Gatorade shortage in the United States.

category still accounted for just one-tenth of 1 percent of total U.S. beverage sales. Net sales had been $90 million in 1982, but Quaker would nearly double this in a couple of years.

The new owners revisited the laboratory to study their new product. In 1988, the Gatorade Sports Science Institute (GSSI) opened in Barrington, Illinois, site of Quaker's other food labs. Gatorade claimed to be the most researched sports drink on the market.

Quaker brought the brand's marketing to a higher level. The company successfully tapped into a new interest in exercise in the United States by identifying and targeting different categories of active people, such as fitness buffs, competitive team players, and people working physically demanding jobs.

Net sales were about $170 million a year in the mid-1980s, notes Rovell. A hugely successful television campaign with the tagline, "Gatorade is Thirst Aid for that deep down body thirst," helped to drive sales to nearly $900 million by the end of the decade. Another firm, Sands, Taylor & Woods Co. (best known for King Arthur Flour), had already trademarked the "Thirst Aid" name for flavoring syrups and successfully sued Quaker for infringement, bringing the campaign to a court-ordered close in 1990.

One of Gatorade's inventors, Dr. Robert Cade, created a new sports drink containing glycerol and pyruvate in the early 1990s. Quaker bought the patent and shelved it, according to *First in Thirst*.

LIKING MIKE FROM 1990 TO 2000

A new approach followed the Thirst Aid campaign. In 1990, Quaker signed a ten-year, $13.5 million contract to make Michael Jordan its exclusive celebrity spokesperson. A catchy jingle urged millions of TV viewers to "Be Like Mike." Gatorade had previously oriented itself toward sponsorship of teams and leagues rather than individual sports stars, recalled a Quaker marketer in *First in Thirst*. Signing up Jordan, however, helped to deny Coca-Cola his services for its new sports drink, POWERade.

Gatorade switched to plastic for its larger jugs and introduced a 16-ounce sports bottle in the first half of the decade. These moves helped get the drink into new environments. At the same time, the U.S. sports drink market continued to grow, reaching $1 billion by 1994. In 1997, the hugely successful Gatorade Frost line was launched to reach beyond the sports drinks into the wider "active thirst" market. It had the same basic formulation as the original but lighter flavors.

There were some notable failures for the brand. The saccharine-sweetened Gatorade Light, introduced in 1990, failed to catch on with its target audience of women. Midnight Thunder, a black-colored, blackberry-flavored variant, also proved unappealing. The Gatorgum chewing gum of the 1980s was another flop. More short-lived side ventures that threatened to dilute the brand included the fruit juice–based Freestyle and the caffeinated Sunbolt energy drink. Gatorade also failed to build a significant presence in the energy bar business despite launches in 1994 and 2001.

Jordan's contract was extended through 2007. In the late 1990s, Gatorade increased its endorsement roster to include several star athletes. Introduced around 1999, the very successful "Is It In You" campaign featured weekend recreational athletes. The ads visualized the sweating process with computer graphics.

Coca-Cola and Pepsi sought to dominate the growing sports drink market with their new products (Pepsi's carbonated product being called Mountain Dew Sport, later All Sport). Gatorade, notes Rovell, helped stave off the attacks by a proliferation of flavors that the soda giants' distribution networks were not equipped to match. It also gave increased attention to growing convenience stores as a marketing channel. Another area of interest was the growing Hispanic market, for whom Gatorade rolled out a line of "Xtremo" tropical flavors in 2001.

Sports beverages had become a $2 billion market in the United States by 2000. Gatorade was so dominant, however, that it expanded its view of the competition to include bottled water and other beverages in addition to the sports drink category. Its own Propel fitness water was introduced regionally in 2000 and nationally two years later. (The Gatorade logo was displayed on the sub-brand's packaging.) Propel had very few calories and, unlike Gatorade, included vitamin additives, which Gatorade had always maintained did not enhance performance during athletic activity.

A PEPSI BRAND IN 2000

PepsiCo, Inc., acquired Gatorade's owner, Quaker Oats, in December 2000 in a stock deal worth $13 billion. Pepsi had also acquired the SoBe brand and to meet antitrust requirements subsequently sold its existing All Sport business to The Monarch Beverage Company, the Atlanta-based maker of Dad's Root Beer.

Endurance Formula, with more sodium and potassium, addressed the issues of cramping on extra hot days and tied in to the popularity of endurance sports. According to *First in Thirst,* the elixir was developed after some cramp-ridden football players were spotted quaffing Pedialyte on extra-hot days. Over the years, doctors had come to dispense Gatorade to dehydrated patients. Although Abbott Laboratories Ltd. embraced the medical setting with Pedialyte and Rehydralyte, Gatorade did not play up the connection due to regulatory and image considerations (it was one thing to be associated with the sweat of athletic exertion and quite another to be associated with illness and diarrhea).

Record heat and sales to the military overseas led to a shortage of Gatorade in 2005. The company was soon working on its ninth facility, in Pryor, Oklahoma. Gatorade also had plants in Indianapolis, Indiana; Atlanta, Georgia; Dallas, Texas; Mountain Top, Pennsylvania; Kissimmee, Florida; Oakland, California; Tolleson, Arizona; and Wytheville, Virginia. Gatorade remained the leading player in the estimated $3 billion market for sports beverages in the United States.

Frederick C. Ingram

PRINCIPAL COMPETITORS

Abbott Laboratories Ltd.; Cera Products, Inc.; The Coca-Cola Company; Energy Brands Inc.; The Monarch Beverage Company, Inc.

FURTHER READING

Amdur, Neil, "Florida's Pause That Refreshes: 'Nip of Gatorade,'" *Miami Herald,* November 30, 1966, p. 4D.

Donnelly, Scott, "Hot Weather at Home, War Abroad, Lead to Shortage in Sports Drinks," *Post-Star* (Glen Falls, N.Y.), August 10, 2005.

Flowers, Corey, "Gatorade Inventors Share Story at U. Florida Leaders Seminar," *Independent Florida Alligator,* February 26, 2001.

"Gotta Get That Gator," *Business Week,* November 27, 2000, p. 91.

Jaroff, Leon, "A Thirst for Competition," *Time,* June 1, 1992.

Lloyd, Barbara, "Gatorade Challenged," *New York Times,* December 24, 1990, p. 42.

Peugh, Peter H., "Gatorade's Fast-Growing Popularity Stirs Royalty Fight Involving U.S., University," *Wall Street Journal,* December 18, 1969, p. 13.

Rogin, Gil, "The Bottle and the Babe," *Sports Illustrated,* July 1, 1968, p. 54.

Rovell, Darren, *First in Thirst: How Gatorade Turned the Science of Sweat into a Cultural Phenomenon,* New York: American Management Association, 2006.

Whitford, David, "The Gatorade Mystique: It's Salty. It's Fluorescent. It's Wildly Popular," *Fortune,* November 23, 1998, p. 44.

Genesis Microchip Inc.

2150 Gold Street
Alviso, California 95002
U.S.A.
Telephone: (408) 262-6599
Fax: (408) 262-6365
Web site: http://www.infobox@gnss.com

Public Company
Incorporated: 2002
Employees: 476
Sales: $269.50 million
Stock Exchanges: NASDAQ
Ticker Symbol: GNSS
NAIC: 335999 All Other Miscellaneous Electrical
   Equipment and Component Manufacturing

■■■

Genesis Microchip Inc. is a leading designer, producer, and marketer of integrated circuits called display controllers that receive and process analog and digital video and graphic images for viewing on flat-panel display screens. The company's display controllers are used in an array of flat-panel display devices, such as flat-panel televisions and computer monitors. The company also is pursuing established display applications, including liquid crystal display (LCD) television, plasma television, digital cathode-ray tube televisions, digital television, and other display devices for the consumer electronics market. Headquartered in Silicon Valley, California, Genesis markets its products globally through a network of support centers in Taipei, Taiwan; Seoul, South Korea; Shenzen, China; Tokyo, Japan; and Singapore. The company operates two development sites in Toronto, Canada, and Bangalore, India.

BEGINNINGS

Genesis Microchip Inc. began as a Canadian company in 1987 and changed its domicile to become a Delaware corporation in February 2002. The company rapidly became a success story for its innovations in display controllers for the flat-panel display markets. In 1994, Genesis introduced a new technology called Acuity that could implement image resizing in a single signal processor (DSP) chip without losing crucial pixels. Although the technology was 30 years old, it presented hurdles to implement in hardware. The key, however, rested in developing an image processing capacity that could facilitate image resizing—reducing or enlarging the size of an image—without losing the quality of the image itself. Reducing the size of an image, for example, always required eliminating pixels or lines, while enlarging an image required adding pixels. Until the early 1990s, successful image resizing necessitated up to five image processing boards, costing thousands of dollars. Genesis, however, discovered a way to provide the same capacity in a single chip through its Acuity technology, which it offered in two chip versions. The technology could facilitate image resizing without losing crucial pixels. The company developed the Acuity technology's resizing algorithms and architecture in conjunction with North Shore Laboratories of Princeton, New Jersey.

COMPANY PERSPECTIVES

Technology is the primary driver of Genesis Microchip's leadership position in both the flat-panel TV and LCD monitor markets. Because of the breadth of its intellectual property, from the company's initial founding as well as strategic acquisitions that contributed mixed-signal integration, Faroudja video processing and DTV technologies, the company serves all of the display markets easily and cost-effectively. Our areas of technological expertise include: Scaling, Response Time Control, Advanced Color Management, Film Mode, Format Conversion, Motion Adaptive Deinterlacing, Directional Correlation Deinterlacing, Edge Enhancement, Cross-color Suppression, Noise reduction, Video Decoding, and the DisplayPort digital interconnect standard.

GENESIS PIONEERS ITS WAY TO GROWTH

In 1996, Genesis and National Semiconductor Corp. teamed up to showcase a breakthrough liquid crystal display driver aimed at the growing cathode-ray tube replacement market. The two firms began providing flat-panel producers a reference design that combined Genesis's video processing and National Semiconductor's low voltage differential signaling technology. The combination provided faster transmission of sharper full-motion video images. In the following year in 1997, Genesis continued its record of innovation by introducing the gmZ1 Advanced Image Magnification chip, offering crisper graphics and video on flat-panel displays. The company claimed that the chip could resolve de-interlacing, zoom scaling, display synchronization, and overlay control problems for liquid crystal and plasma displays as well as Digital Light Processing–based projector systems, and large screen TVs. The powerful gmZ1 chip found ready acceptance by a number of producers of flat-panel displays, including Apple Computer's Studio Display monitor, a new flat-panel active matrix LCD that offered images twice as crisp and bright as those of standard cathode-ray tube monitors.

In 1998, Genesis—already a leader in imaging, digital, and graphics processing integrated circuits (ICs)—announced that it was taking a $500,000 equity position in Toronto-based digital image chip specialist, Shamrock Semiconductor. The company aimed to expand its customer base in the video and graphics market, which already included such firms as Apple Computer, CTX Opto-Electronics Corp., Hitachi, Ltd., In Focus Systems, LG Electronics, Texas Instruments, and more than 180 other companies. In 1998, Genesis introduced two new ICs, the gmZ2 and gmZ3, which were improved low cost alternatives to the industry-leading gmZ1 integrated circuit for producing high-quality graphics and video. In addition to being designed for flat-panel displays, projection systems, home theater equipment, and other applications, the new chips provided effective auto-detection and auto-configuration support. The chips also offered Genesis's ImEngine de-interlacing process, used to convert interlaced television-style video for display on non-interlaced systems, such as personal computer monitors. At the end of fiscal year 1998, Genesis reported record revenues of 248 percent over fiscal 1997 to $15.7 million. The company's success was attributed to the introduction of the ImEngine product line aimed at both the projection system market and the emerging LCD monitor market in which Genesis already had an impressive list of customers manufacturing LCD monitors.

In June 1999, Genesis completed a merger agreement with privately held Paradise Electronics, Inc., of San Jose, California, a designer and manufacturer of highly integrated mixed-mode integrated circuits for the flat panel monitor market. Under the terms of the merger, 4.5 million shares of Genesis common stock, worth about $130 million, would be exchanged for all outstanding shares and options of Paradise Electronics. Genesis saw the merger as a way to gear up for what it anticipated would be an enormous surge in the flat-monitor market in the years ahead. In this regard, the deal also would strengthen its position in the race to capture the market for next-generation LCD monitors. Already, a host of start-ups had entered the market with integrated solutions that in some cases surpassed Genesis's own offerings. Paradise provided a means to both strengthen and advance Genesis's portfolio of products and ability to serve other markets such as digital displays, HDTV, projection systems, DVD players, and other applications. With the merger, Genesis believed it was positioned to be the premiere display chip player in the evolving digital display revolution. The merger, however, ignited some controversy as Genesis president and chief operating officer Stephen Solari left the company toward the end of the negotiations.

In August 1999, the company introduced an innovative new video decoder chip—the gmD2000, designed to enhance image quality of decoded NTSC/PAL video. Genesis also announced a $1.1 million minority equity investment in privately held Techwell, Inc., of San Jose, California, a designer of video decoder integrated circuit products. Company Chairman and

KEY DATES

1987: Genesis is founded in Canada.
1998: The company takes a $500,000 equity position in Shamrock Semiconductor.
1999: Genesis makes a $1.1 million minority investment in Techwell Inc.
1999: Genesis acquires Paradise Electronics, Inc.
2001: Genesis acquires Sage Inc. for $241 million in stock.
2002: The company is incorporated in the U.S. and acquires the assets of VM Labs Inc. for $14.2 million in cash.
2003: Genesis and rival Pixelworks call off their proposed merger; Genesis loses a patent infringement suit to Silicon Image.
2004: The company relocates its Taipei offices to larger facilities.

CEO Paul M. Russo said that the investment in Techwell would give Genesis new visibility in the consumer video electronics and television markets. In September 1999, Genesis's rapid pace of innovation led to the radical advancement of its video/graphic-processing technology with the gmZ4 integrated circuit. The new, third-generation chip further widened the image quality gap between the company and its competition. The chip was developed both to provide high visual quality and to reduce the cost of flat-panel displays, ultra-portable projection systems, home theater gear, and other pixilated display applications. In January 2000, Genesis introduced another new chip, the gmZAN1 LCD, a cost-effective, feature-loaded integrated circuit for LCD monitors.

In February 2000, Amnon Fisher was appointed as the company's new president and chief operating officer. Before joining Genesis, Amnon was senior vice president and general manager of the consumer products division at NeoMagic where he compiled a successful track record in managing the various aspects of the IC business. By April, however, Paul Russo turned over his day to day responsibilities as CEO to Amnon, in order to focus on strategic issues as a working chairman of the board of directors. With Amnon in place, the company looked forward to the next stage in targeting the high-volume markets including LCD monitors, digital CRTs, and the emerging digital video markets. Amnon joined Genesis at a propitious time as the company soon reported annual revenues of $53.3 million, a 37 percent jump from

fiscal 1999. The company was profiting from its synergy with Paradise Electronics, which led to the introduction of an array of innovative new products.

In July 2000, Genesis spun off its image warp technology and business into a separate start-up firm. Genesis's initial $2 million investment enabled the company to begin operations and focus on marketing its warp technology chip, which served to digitally manipulate real-time video images while maintaining image quality and detail. By the end of fiscal 2001, Genesis's 19 percent revenue growth reflected its ability to continue expanding and solidifying its leadership in the flat-panel monitor market and other high-growth markets of digital television. The company's sustained revenue growth put it among Deloitte & Touche's fastest-growing 500 technology companies in North America.

GENESIS STUMBLES AMID MERGERS AND ACQUISITIONS

In September 2001, Genesis announced an agreement to acquire rival Sage Inc. of Milpitas, California, a maker of chips used in flat-panel televisions, computer monitors, and Internet appliances, for $241 million in stock. The merger promised to create a technology leader with a history of innovation and a portfolio of products for the rapidly growing semiconductor industry. The transaction also was anticipated to greatly expand Genesis's global reach, giving the combined company significant research and development, and service and support operations in Canada, the U.S., India, Korea, and China. Moreover, with the acquisition of Sage, Genesis's share of the flat-panel market would jump to from 50 percent to 70 percent. The acquisition was completed in February 2002 for $402 million after shareholders approved the merger and the required change in domicile from Canada to the U.S., which was a condition of the acquisition of Sage.

In March 2002, Genesis won an auction in bankruptcy court to acquire the assets of VM Labs Inc. of Mountain View, California, including all patents, trademarks, and intellectual property for $14.2 million in cash. Genesis believed that VM Labs' decoder technology would expand its product offerings in consumer electronics, especially in the DVD market. Genesis also expected to benefit from the firm's relationships with major electronic companies, including Motorola, Samsung, and Toshiba. In the same month, Genesis aggressively moved to file a patent infringement suit against Taiwan's Media Reality Technologies, Inc. (MRT), SmartASIC Inc., and Trumpion Microelectronics, Inc., in the U.S. District Court for the Northern District of California and later with the U.S.

International Trade Commission (ITC). In the suit, Genesis sought monetary damages and a permanent injunction barring the companies from producing, using, importing, or selling the allegedly infringing products in the United States. MRT quickly responded to the legal action in April by suing Genesis in federal court in San Francisco seeking a declaratory judgment that it was not infringing on Genesis's patent. The complaint also charged that Genesis misappropriated confidential trade secrets from MRT and that Genesis used the trade secrets to interfere with its business operations, resulting in lost revenues. In August 2004, the ITC ruled that the companies had infringed on Genesis's U.S. patent titled "Method and Apparatus for Upscaling an Image in both Horizontal and Vertical Directions." With the ruling, the ITC issued an exclusionary order barring the import of their display controllers into the U.S., in addition to LCD monitors and boards containing these products.

In June 2002, Genesis anticipated that its first quarter 2003 revenues would range from $41 million to $43 million, compared to previous estimates of $60 million. The company attributed the decline in revenues to a drop in orders, stemming from losing business to competitors and panel manufacturing constraints that produced excess inventories. As demand for its chips began to slide, the company adopted a shareholder rights plan to ward off potential investors from acquiring significant shares of its common stock.

The company's sliding revenues and stock price, however, did not stop it from signing a March 2003 deal to acquire rival Pixelworks for about $584 million in stock. Under the terms of the agreement, the companies would finalize the deal as a reverse merger, with Pixelworks issuing 2.3366 shares of stock for each share of Genesis. The deal would give Genesis shareholders 62.5 percent of the new company with Pixelworks shareholders getting 37.5 percent. With the acquisition, Genesis added Pixelworks' 75 percent market share of the world's projector ICs to its own leading 60 percent share of LCD monitor chips. Because the two companies had been investing heavily in advanced television chips, the merger would enable the combined firms to better compete with major consumer electronics players such as Sony Corp. and Samsung Electronics Company Ltd., which developed their own chips.

The transaction, however, drew an antitrust review by the Federal Trade Commission (FTC). With the FTC's antitrust review underway, in July 2003, Genesis was ordered by a federal court in Virginia to uphold a memorandum of understanding with Silicon Image, a company that owned patents to part of a new display interface that gained rapid acceptance from the industry's

major consumer electronics manufacturers. The memorandum of understanding settled a patent infringement dispute and directed Genesis to pay for access to Digital Visual Interface (DVI) and High-Definition Multimedia Interface (HDMI) technologies owned by Silicon Image. The patent licensing dispute forced the ouster of Genesis chairman and chief executive James Donegan, who had verbally agreed to the MoU, allegedly without the authorization of the board, to resolve a patent lawsuit filed by Silicon Image. With few options other than to pay for the rights to a display interface that was on the verge of dominating the media industry, analysts predicted that Genesis' financial position would be considerably weakened. As a result, the stocks of both Genesis and Pixelworks began selling off as investors lost faith in the merger. In August 2003, Genesis and Pixelworks jointly announced an agreement to terminate the proposed merger in the interests of their respective shareholders.

With the termination of the merger, the company's hopes for immediately strengthening its market share in its core businesses collapsed. Genesis was facing intense competition and pricing pressures in its critical LCD monitor business, which declined by 11 percent in its fiscal 2004 first quarter. Indeed, a quarter of profit losses, a ruined merger, brutal price erosion, the ousting of the company's chief executive, and the rise of a number of competitors seemed to cast a shadow over Genesis's record of success. Still, the company had much going for it, including leadership in the fast-growing market for LCD-monitor controller ICs and a strong position in the rapidly expanding market for LCD TV chips.

GENESIS REGAINS GROWTH AND PROFITABILITY

By the beginning of 2004, the company seemed to be putting its difficulties behind it and trying to position itself to take advantage of the rapidly growing market for LCDs in desktop personal computers and televisions. In July 2004, Genesis relocated its Taipei offices into larger facilities, adding engineers and sales staff. In addition, in November, 2004, Genesis announced the appointment of Elias (Elie) Antoun as its new president and chief executive officer. Antoun brought more than 20 years of semiconductor and consumer electronics experience to Genesis. His prior experience included serving as president and chief executive officer of both Pixim, Inc., an imaging solution provider for the video surveillance market, and MediaQ Incorporated, a mobile handheld graphics IC company. He also had held a variety of executive positions with LSI Logic Corporation.

In June 2005, Genesis signed a strategic licensing

agreement with Meridian Audio Limited, a United Kingdom–based producer of high-end audio, video, and home theater systems and components. The agreement gave Meridian rights to integrate, manufacture, and distribute home theater solutions under Genesis's Faroudja brand name as part of Meridian's audio/video line of products. Under the terms of the agreement, Genesis would cease the production and distribution of its advanced Faroudja home theatre solutions, but would continue to develop advanced video processing technologies with Meridian for its Faroudja-based products. A sign that Genesis was back to profitability came with record revenues of $59.8 million for the first quarter of fiscal 2006. The company's profitable quarter stemmed from significant design achievements in both the LCD monitor and flat-panel TV markets. With continued improvement in the marketing of its products on a worldwide basis, in September 2005, Genesis opened a new regional sales and engineering facility in Singapore in close proximity to key customers, including Dell, Philips, TTE, and Toshiba. According to the company, the facility promised to support its local customer base as well as diversify its supply chain and provide new business opportunities in emerging markets such as Malaysia, Thailand, Indonesia, and Vietnam. Genesis closed out fiscal 2006 with a 32 percent surge in total revenue to $269.5 million compared to $204.1 million for fiscal 2005. The company attributed the financial results to a robust 81 percent growth in flat-panel revenues and a major improvement in earnings.

Bruce P. Montgomery

PRINCIPAL COMPETITORS

Pixelworks Inc.; Silicon Image Inc.; STMicroelectronics N.V.

FURTHER READING

Chin, Spencer, "Genesis Files Suit Against Taiwanese Competitors," *EBN,* September 23, 2002.

"Genesis Chip Used in Apple's Studio Display to Provide Smart Scaling Feature," *Business Wire,* March 27, 1998.

"Genesis Creates Startup Company," *InsideChips.Ventures,* July 2000.

"Genesis Extends Flat Panel Monitor Product Line; The Company Introduces gmZ2 & gmZ3," *Business Wire,* September 28, 1998.

"Genesis Microchip Adopts Poison Pill," *Daily Deal,* June 28, 2002.

"Genesis Microchip and Meridian Audio Announce Strategic Alliance," *Business Wire,* June 29, 2005.

"Genesis Microchip and Pixelworks Terminate Merger Agreement," *Business Wire,* August 5, 2003.

"Genesis Microchip Announces Opening of Expanded Facilities in Taiwan," *DVD News,* July 23, 2004.

"Genesis Microchip Appoints Elias Antoun as President and Chief Executive Officer," *Business Wire,* November 19, 2004.

"Genesis Microchip Expands with New Office in Singapore," *AsiaPulse News,* September 29, 2005.

"Genesis Microchip Files Patent Infringement Lawsuit," *Business Wire,* March 15, 2002.

"Genesis Microchip to Merge with Paradise Electronics," *Business Wire,* January 22, 1999.

"Genesis, Pixelworks in $584M Deal," *Daily Deal,* March 18, 2003.

Landriault, Gabriel, "Genesis Goes to Paradise," *Computer Dealer News,* July 9, 1999.

Lieberman, David, "Flat-Panel Chips Branch Out," *Electronic Engineering Times,* January 31, 2000.

———, "Genesis Eyes Virtues of Its Paradise Play," *Electronic Engineering Times,* February 8, 1999.

"Media Reality Technologies (MRT) Denies Patent Infringement, Sues Genesis for Misappropriation of Trade Secrets," *Canadian Corporate News,* April 23, 2002.

"NATSEMI, Genesis Team on Desktop Flat Panel Market," *Computergram International,* December 6, 1996.

Ojo, Bolaji, "Court Ruling Rocks Genesis Microchip—CEO Ousted in Patent Licensing Flap," *EBN,* July 28, 2003.

———, "$600 Million Deal—Merged Genesis, Pixelworks Say They're Ready for All Comers," *EBN,* March 24, 2003.

Shandle, Jack, "Image-Resizing IC Delivers Highest Possible Fidelity," *Electronic Design,* May 27, 1993.

Webster, John, "A Single Chip Brings Image Resizing Down to Size," *Computer Graphics World,* September 1994.

GF Health Products, Inc.

2935 Northeast Parkway
Atlanta, Georgia 30360
U.S.A.
Telephone: (800) 347-5678
Fax: (800) 726-0601
Web site: http://www.grahamfield.com

Private Company
Incorporated: 1946 as Graham-Field, Inc.
Employees: 2,000
Sales: $378 million (1998)
NAIC: 423450 Medical, Dental, and Hospital Equipment and Supplies Merchant Wholesalers

■ ■ ■

GF Health Products, Inc., doing business as Graham-Field Health Products, Inc., is a manufacturer and distributor of healthcare products, primarily for the home healthcare, rehabilitation, long-term care, and medical-surgical markets in North America, Central and South America, Europe, and Asia. Customers include physicians, hospitals, nursing homes, government agencies, drug stores, pharmacies, and catalogers.

Graham-Field manufactures and distributes more than 4,000 products. Major brands include Lumex, maker of specialty chairs, beds, walkers, and lifts; Everest & Jennings, offering manual and power wheelchairs; Basic American Medical Products/Simmons, one of the world's largest bed manufacturers; John Bunn and its line of respirator products; Labtron, maker of

stethoscopes and exam room supplies; Grafco, offering a wide variety of medical and surgical products, ranging from bandages to microscopes; and the Akros and Aquatherm lines of pressure management products.

Graham-Field is based in Atlanta, Georgia, and maintains distribution centers in New Jersey, Wisconsin, Denver, Missouri, California, and Mexico. Manufacturing plant are located in Denver, Wisconsin, and Rhode Island. Graham-Field has courted controversy since the late 1990s. The company's long-time chief executive, Irwin Selinger, has been indicted, tried, convicted, and sentenced to serve time in prison for securities fraud and conspiracy for inflating the value of Graham-Field's stock in connection to a merger. Nevertheless, Selinger continued to run the company well into the 2000s, pending an appeal.

GRAHAM-FIELD FOUNDED: 1946

Forty years before Selinger became involved in the company, Graham-Field was founded in 1946 in New York City as Graham-Field, Inc., by Samuel Graham Golub and Philip Field. They set up a medical equipment supply business in a loft on Pearl Street in a Manhattan neighborhood that is now known as TriBeCa (the "Triangle Below Canal"). A year after it opened, Graham-Field brought out its first product, Medicopaste, a bandage product the company still carries. It remained a relatively small, but well respected company, generating about $10 million in annual revenues when Selinger and his company, Patient Technology, Inc., bought it in 1986. Two years later Patient Technology adopted the Graham-Field name, becoming Graham-Field Health Products, Inc.

Selinger came to the medical supplies business with no experience in the healthcare field. In the mid-1960s he was marketing staplers for Swingline Inc. but was more interested in running his own company. Acting on the advice of a stockbroker who told him that the healthcare field held great potential, in 1966 he went to work for a small medical-supplies company as marketing director. Two years later he seized an opportunity to start his own business when he met a scientist who developed a way to measure sterilization levels in packages. Selinger bought the rights to the system and launched Surgicot, Inc., with little more than $3,000 and a garage. Over the next decade he built on the company, completing three acquisitions along the way. By the end of the 1970s Surgicot was generating $25 million in sales. It also caught the attention of healthcare giant Squibb Corporation, which made Selinger a offer too tempting to refuse: $28 million in stock and a position running Surgicot. Selinger soon grew disgruntled answering to his new corporate bosses, however. Having built his company on a shoestring budget, Selinger continued to fly coach, only to have his conduct criticized by a Squibb officer who told him that as an executive he was expected to fly first class. He ruffled feathers even more when he made an acquisition on his own. Such freewheeling put him at odds with Squibb management and he quit in 1980.

"I was an entrepreneur without a company to run," he told *Nation's Business* in a 1986 interview. It was a rude awakening. He began scouting for a new opportunity. During his time at Squibb he had learned about an electronic patient bedside monitor the company had turned down. Developed by a Long Island inventor, Survalent kept track of body temperatures. In April 1981, Selinger formed Patient Technology, Inc., (PTI) in Hauppauge, New York, and bought the device for $550,000 and a 38 percent stake in the company. He was able to sell 270,000 units in the first year.

PATIENT TECHNOLOGY
ACQUIRES GRAHAM-FIELD: 1985

PTI also began developing a patient bedside monitor, MedTake, which Selinger believed would be a high-tech way to cut down on nurses' paperwork. After spending $3.5 million to develop the product and still unable to get the product to market, Selinger sold the MedTake line in 1986. Along the way, in order to support the development of this and other high-tech devices, PTI went public, completing an initial public offering of stock in late 1983, and subsequently acquired numerous medical supply companies and other healthcare businesses, seven in all between March 1983 and October 1985. They included the 1983 acquisitions of Medical Specialists in Packaging, Inc.; Scientek Instrumentation, Inc,; and Labtron Scientific Corp. A year later PTI added Bio-Med Devices Inc. and generic drug manufacturer Newtron Pharmaceuticals, Inc. Selinger became disenchanted with Newtron and unloaded the property in 1985. At the same time he added sundries manufacturer Medisco Federal, Inc., as well as Graham-Field, for which PTI paid about $9.2 million in cash, stock, and notes. Coming over from Graham-Field was Peter Galambos, who became PTI's president and chief operating officer. Less than three years later, however, he quit, citing difficulties working at a public company.

PTI originally consisted of two divisions, medical devices and sundries, but company leadership soon elected to exit the medical device field and concentrate on the medical supply business. In keeping with this new strategy, PTI in May 1988 assumed the Graham-Field name, which was recognized in the field. Two months later the company resumed a growth-through-acquisitions approach when it acquired Bristoline Inc., importer and distributor of medical instruments and microscopes. In 1990 Graham-Field completed a pair of deals. In March of that year it spent nearly $3 million for M.E. Team, Inc., a distributor of medical and health care products for home use that had strong ties to retailers, in particular cable television home-shopping networks. Then, in November 1990, Graham-Field paid about $1.6 million in cash for the John Bunn Division of Omnicare, Inc., to add a line of respiratory aid products. Two more acquisitions followed in 1991. For approximately $2.4 million in cash International Health Care, Inc., was added. Formerly known as AquaTherm Products Corporation, the company manufactured and distributed pressure control products and deodorizers. TEMCO National Corp was bought in October 1991 for $5.8 million in cash. It made and distributed a variety of medical supply products, including geriatric seating units, ambulatory aids, and bath and shower accessories. Graham-Field then paid $369,000 in 1992 to add the bandage division of a Squibb subsidiary, ConvaTec, a

KEY DATES

1946: Graham-Field, Inc., is founded.
1981: Patient Technology, Inc., is established.
1985: Patient Technology acquires Graham-Field.
1988: Patient Technology takes the Graham-Field name.
1997: Fuqua Enterprises, Inc., is acquired.
1999: Graham-Field files for Chapter 11 bankruptcy protection.
2003: Graham-Field assets are sold to GF Health Products, Inc.

deal that brought with it a manufacturing facility in Rhode Island. Also in that year, Graham-Field paid $11.5 million for Diamond Medical Equipment Corp. and National Health Care Equipment Inc., manufacturers of patient aids and distributors of nutritional supplements, adult incontinence products, and other home healthcare products. To support its growing business, Graham-Field also opened a distribution center in Los Angeles in 1992.

In 1992 Graham-Field was generating $84 million (a marked increase over 1991's $57.1 million) on sales from 20,000 medical products, making it one of Long Island's largest public companies. The company was on the rise and able to secure a coveted listing on the New York Stock Exchange, moving over from the American Stock Exchange. However, as had been the case in the past, the company had trouble digesting its acquisitions. While sales continued to rise, to $92.5 million in 1993 and $94.5 million in 1994, the company lost money, $2.9 million in 1993 and $2.4 million in 1994. The company finally returned to profitability in 1995, netting $738,000 as sales topped the $100 million mark.

Graham-Field was quite active in 1996 and 1997, especially in the field of durable medical equipment, jump-started by the November 1996 acquisition of wheelchair manufacturer Everest & Jennings International Ltd. Selinger then fleshed out the new unit with the March 1997 acquisition of a pediatric wheelchair manufacturer, Kuschall of America, Inc., which also produced high-performance adult wheelchairs and other rehabilitation products. On another front in 1996, Graham-Field rolled out the Graham-Field Express program, which offered same-day and next-day delivery of certain products to home healthcare dealers. The company then beefed up the program through acquisitions, buying V.C. Medical Distributors Inc. in 1996 to add a distribution operation in Puerto Rico, and Bobeck Medical to gain an express facility in Dallas in early

1997. More facilities were opened in Baltimore, Cleveland, and Bowling Green, Kentucky, in 1997.

FUQUA ENTERPRISES ACQUIRED: 1997

Sales reached $127.2 million in 1996 and then soared to $263.1 million a year, due mostly to the largest acquisition in Graham-Field's history, one that held a great deal of promise but led to years of trouble. In the fall of 1997 Graham-Field agreed to acquire Fuqua Enterprises Inc. for $166 million in stock. Based in Atlanta, Fuqua designed and furnished the interior of nursing facilities, a business that was expected to benefit nicely when combined with Graham-Field's distribution network, which was already selling to Fuqua's customer base. Three months after the deal was completed in December 1998, Graham-Field's reported its fourth-quarter and year-end earnings: a pretax loss of $43.9 million in the fourth quarter and a $22.9 million net loss for 1997. The numbers were not at all what Fuqua's founder, J.B. Fuqua, an experienced deal-maker and Graham-Field's second-largest shareholder, had been led to expect. The price of Graham-Field stock quickly lost half of its value. Fuqua was not hesitant to express his displeasure about the turn of events, telling the *Atlanta Journal-Constitution*, "We just got snookered." He stopped short of claiming he was the victim of fraud, but added, "The fact is that we and our consultants and advisers and what-not depended on figures as of the end of last September, which was the third quarter, and all of these things couldn't have happened in the fourth quarter. And we were not told that the fourth quarter would be a disaster; we were told it would be profitable."

Fuqua was not alone in his concerns about the dealings at Graham-Field, which was immediately hit with shareholder lawsuits alleging a failure to disclose material information. Although these suits would be settled for $20 million in 1999, the company was engulfed in turmoil that would be difficult to escape, and the price of its shares tumbled to penny stock levels. Selinger resigned as chairman and CEO in July 1998, replaced by Rodney F. Price, chairman of Thistle Hotels who owned nearly one-quarter of Graham-Field's voting stock. He would stay until February 1999, when Graham-Field's chief financial officer and interim president, Paul Bellamy, replaced him as chairman and CEO. A month later an internal audit revealed a number of accounting irregularities, resulting in the reporting of a further $10 million in losses for 1997 and 1998. As the CFO during this time, Bellamy, along with the new CFO, was now replaced by a turnaround expert, John McGregor. The company explored the possibility of a sale, and as the losses mounted, it was delisted by the

New York Stock Exchange and had to resort to trading on the NASDAQ Over-the-Counter Bulletin Board. By the end of the year McGregor resigned and Graham-Field and each of its 24 subsidiaries filed for Chapter 11 bankruptcy protection from creditors. The company reported $182 million in assets and more than $201 million in debts.

While Graham-Field underwent restructuring, the corporate headquarters was relocated to Atlanta to the Fuqua offices. It also experienced further changes in the top ranks of management before finally emerging from bankruptcy in April 2003 following an auction of the company in which bondholders outbid Invacare Corp, a Cleveland wheelchair manufacturer, agreeing to pay $28 million. To make the acquisitions, GF Health Products, Inc., was formed. The following month Selinger was reinstalled as the company's chief executive, a move made more noteworthy given that several months earlier he had been indicted by the U.S. Attorney for the Eastern District of New York for propping up the price of the Graham-Field's stock prior to the Fuqua acquisition. He was accused of conspiring with an independent medical distributor, Marc Chapman, to create a phony contract and other documents that appeared to provide Graham-Field with $450,000 in cash and $700,000 in credit. The resulting inflated numbers on the company's balance sheet helped to increase the price of Graham-Field's stock, important because the acquisition agreement with Fuqua was based on a target price: Were the Graham-Field shares to fall below that price, Fuqua would receive more Graham-Field stock.

Chapman pleaded guilty but Selinger went to trial in 2004 while continuing to run Graham-Field. After a five-week trial, he was found guilty of securities fraud and conspiracy, and faced as many as ten years in prison. He told Long Island's Newsday that the jury's verdict was "an absolute outrage," adding, "There was zero evidence presented to the jury. I believe that over time I will be vindicated and I will be found innocent." In April 2005 Selinger was sentenced to 18 months in prison and three years of probation. However, at mid-year in 2006, he had not yet served any time and he continued to hold the top spot in the company. Despite the uncertainty surrounding the future of its chief executive, Graham-Field continued to operate, reintroducing the Everest & Jennings, LaBac, Simmons Healthcare, John Bunn, Grafco, Labtron, and Lumex product lines. Three new distribution centers, located in Atlanta, Los Angeles, and East Rutherford, New Jersey, opened in late 2004, and Graham-Field continued to introduce new products on a regular basis. But with its financial results no longer available to the public, it was difficult to determine the health of the restructured company.

Ed Dinger

PRINCIPAL SUBSIDIARIES

Graham-Field, Inc.; AquaTherm Corp.; Everst & Jennings International Ltd.; Kuschall of America, Inc.; Medical Supplies of America, Inc.; Basic American Medical Products, Inc.

PRINCIPAL COMPETITORS

Invacare Corporation; Medline Industries, Inc.; Sunrise Medical Inc.

FURTHER READING

"Graham-Field Chief Sentenced to Prison, Plans Appeal," *Home Care Magazine,* April 25, 2005.

Harrigan, Susan, "Graham-Field Health Products CEO Is Convicted of Fraud for Inflating Profits," *Newsday,* June 11, 2004.

Hyatt, Joshua, et. al., "The Inc. 100 Portfolio," *Inc,* May 1986, p. 51.

Saporta, Maria and Cynthia Mitchell, "Fuqua 'Snookered' in Stock Deal," *The Atlanta Constitution,* March 25, 1998, p. B1.

"Selinger Focused on the Future," *Long Island Business News,* February 28, 1994, p. S23.

Siwolop, Sana, "Problems at Graham-Field Cloud Future," *New York Times,* August 23, 1998, p. 12LI.3.

Wallach, Van, "Surgery For A Health Care Firm," *Nation's Business,* February 1986, p. 71.

Glazer's Wholesale Drug Company, Inc.

———————— ■ ————————

14911 Quorum Drive, Suite 400
Dallas, Texas 75254
U.S.A.
Telephone: (972) 392-8200
Fax: (972) 702-8508
Web site: http://www.glazers.com

Private Company
Founded: 1933
Employees: 5,500
Sales: $2.8 billion (2005 est.)
NAIC: 424820 Wine and Distilled Alcoholic Beverage
   Merchant

■ ■ ■

Despite its name, leftover from the days of Prohibition, Glazer's Wholesale Drug Company, Inc., is one of the largest distributors of wine, malts, and spirits in the United States, and the largest wholesaler in the state of Texas. Other states in which Glazer's operates are Arkansas, Arizona, Kansas, Illinois, Indiana, Iowa, Louisiana, Mississippi, Missouri, Ohio, and Oklahoma. Customers include grocery stores, package stores, membership clubs, convenience stores, restaurants, hotels, and specialty retailers. Based in Dallas, the company is still privately owned by the Glazer family and headed by a member of the third generation—with a fourth generation being groomed for eventual leadership.

GLAZER FAMILY'S MOVE TO TEXAS: 1909

The forebears of the Glazer family, Louis Glazer and his wife Bessie, were Russian Jews who emigrated to the United States around 1904. According to company documentation they moved to Dallas from Chicago in 1909, although Bessie's obituary published by the *Dallas Morning News* in 1944 indicates they lived in St. Louis for five years before relocating to Texas. The 1962 obituary of one of their sons, Max, however, referred to him as "a native of Chicago." In any event, the family came to Dallas and became involved in the beverage business, originally distributing flavored soda waters from horse-drawn wagons. They soon branched into bottling, running the Jumbo Bottling Company, which produced a variety of flavored soda water. The business was very much a family affair. Three of the couple's five children—Fritz, Max, and Nolan—joined the company and learned the bottling business. According to newspaper accounts, the family enterprise also included a beer bottling plant, established in the early 1910s. When the United States imposed Prohibition in 1919, banning the consumption of beer, wine, and spirits, this business came to a close.

Judging by newspaper articles from the period, the family apparently turned to a different business vehicle, the Real Juice company, owned by the three Glazer brothers. In September 1933, according to the company's official history, Max and Nolan formed Glazer's Wholesale Drug Company, looking to take advantage of the repeal of Prohibition that had taken place earlier in the year. For some 14 years Americans had been denied the legal right to drink alcoholic beverages, and only drug wholesalers and drugstores could carry consumable alcohol, hence the Glazer's Wholesale Drug Company name. Articles published in that month in the *Dallas Morning News* made no mention of the name, referring instead to the Schlitz Distributing Company of Dallas, which it said was headed by Max Glazer and had just begun to distribute "bottles and kegs of the beer that has served to make Milwaukee famous." Another article appearing two weeks later refers to Max and Nolan Glazer as "the owners of the Real Juice Company, 2201 Leonard, distributors for Schlitz beer." Until the 1940s Fritz Glazer also was mentioned as a principal of the company, and not until 1950 do *Dallas Morning News* articles refer to Glazer's Wholesale Drug Company.

Dallas residents, like people in the rest of the country, had found ways to satisfy their thirst for alcoholic beverages during the days of the "great experiment," but both quality and supply had been uncertain. The demand for legalized beer, wine, and spirits was strong, and Glazer's benefited, as the business enjoyed rapid success, steadily adding new brands and suppliers. For example, in the mid-1930s Glazer's began distributing Clark Bros. bourbon and rye whiskeys produced by Peoria, Illinois–based Arrow Distilleries. Glazer's also remained involved in the soda bottling business through a separate division that produced a line of flavored sodas called "Woosies." The brand was very popular in the area, known for the unusual six-pack it sold, consisting of a root beer, grape, strawberry, orange, lemonade, and cream soda. The division also acted as a distributor for other national brands of soda in Dallas and 20 other Texas counties when it acquired a Pepsi-Cola franchise in 1948, Pepsi-Cola Bottling of Dallas, a business that the family would continue to operate until the mid-1960s, operating out of the 2201 Leonard Street location.

ADDING A LOUISIANA OPERATION: 1943

The Glazers apparently had a falling-out with Schlitz in 1941, when the brewer sued the three brothers and Real Juice Company seeking $11,671. The two parties settled out of court when an agreement was reached on the disputed claims. Glazer's first expanded beyond the Dallas market in 1943, establishing an operation in Louisiana. In July of that following year, 70-year-old Bessie Glazer, her husband having long since passed away, died in a bathtub accident, succumbing to injuries received from scalding water. Glazer's expanded into Arkansas in 1946. It was also during this period that Max and Nolan played a prominent role in raising money to relocate displaced European Jewry to what would become Israel. They were also involved in a number of other humanitarian and philanthropic endeavors.

In 1946 a second generation of the Glazer family became involved in the business in the form of Max's son, Irving D. Glazer, who had just finished serving in World War II. In 1949 Robert S. Glazer, Max's 26-year-old son, also joined the company. Their father remained the head of the company until his death in late 1962. The following month his brother Nolan succeeded him as president. He took charge of a spirits distributorship that operated 13 branches in three states as well as the Pepsi franchise. By this time his sons, Robert L. Glazer (called "R.L.") and Bennett Glazer had joined the family business in the 1950s and 1960s.

With the second generation of the family assuming greater control, Glazer's continued to enjoy robust growth over the ensuing decades. The company bought out competitors in Texas, Arkansas, and Louisiana, and entered a new market in 1966 when R.L. launched an operation in Arizona. Five years later he returned to Dallas to become a vice-president in the corporate office. A short time later, in July 1972, Irving Glazer died at the age of 48. Nolan Glazer, on the other hand, lived until 1991 when he died from heart failure. Robert S. Glazer assumed the presidency of a company with 15 branches in four states.

In 1996 there was a major changing of the guard as R.L. Glazer became chairman of the board and treasurer, and Bennett Glazer was named president. There also were changes taking place in the beverage industry in the mid-1990s, as a wave of consolidation took place among suppliers as well as distributors. Doing business of $700 million a year, Glazer's was far from a small company, but given the industry trend the company clearly had reached a crossroads in its history. According to vice-president of corporate strategy Louis Zweig, management decided that it had three choices: "We could be the acquirer, we could retrench or we could be acquired... . The Glazer family made the decision that we would be a major player in the market, that we would start growing and that we would do it in a multi-faceted way." Bennett Glazer told *US Business Review,* "At that

```
┌─────────────────────────────────────────────┐
│                                               │
│               KEY DATES                       │
│            ───────────■───────────            │
│                                               │
│  1933:  The company is founded by Max, Nolan, │
│         and Fritz Glazer.                     │
│  1943:  The company expands to Louisiana.     │
│  1946:  Arkansas is added to Glazer's         │
│         territory.                            │
│  1962:  Max Glazer dies.                      │
│  1966:  Glazer's enters the Arizona market.   │
│  1991:  Nolan Glazer dies.                    │
│  1997:  Missouri's Boone Distributing is      │
│         acquired.                             │
│  2003:  Reliance Wine & Spirits Co. is        │
│         acquired.                             │
│                                               │
└─────────────────────────────────────────────┘
```

point, we had to either get in the game or get out." He added, "We realized we couldn't go on as the status quo. We became proactive and put together a vision." That vision would include acquisitions, internal growth, and joint ventures.

ADDING BEER DISTRIBUTION: 1997

In the final years of the 1990s Glazer's entered several new states, growing northward from its Texas base, and added new product lines. The 1997 acquisition of Longview, Texas–based Maxwell Distributing expanded the company into beer distribution, a field in which Glazer's had not been involved for many years. Late in the year the company moved into Missouri through the acquisition of Boone Distributing and its branches in Columbia, Springfield, and Joplin, Missouri. Several months later the Missouri business was bolstered with the acquisition of Griesedieck Imports, distributor of boutique wines and specialty beers in Kansas City and St. Louis. Also in 1998 Glazer's formed a joint venture with Chicago's Romano Brothers Beverage Co., named M&M Beverages L.L.C., to buy Olinger Distributing Co. Inc., the second largest wine and spirits distributor in Indiana. M&M was subsequently merged with a small Romano Brothers subsidiary, Miller Distributing. Also in 1998 Glazer's Arizona operation, Cactus Beverage, merged with Arizona-based Sunbelt Distributing's Arizona Beverage to form a 50-50 joint venture, Alliance Beverage Distributing Company, to conduct wholesale liquor distribution in Arizona.

In another 1998 move, Glazer's acquired Des Moines, Iowa–based Messer Distributing, forming the basis for subsidiary Glazer's of Iowa, adding yet another state to Glazer's reach. Glazer's also made a bid to enter Kansas in 1999 by acquiring Premiere Beverage of Lenexa and A.B. Sales of Wichita, which shared mutual

ownership. The deal was put on hold until 2001 because of a 52-year-old Kansas law that prevented out-of-state liquor wholesale companies from doing business in the state. The law had been put on the books as a way to make it easier to do criminal background checks on buyers, thereby limiting the chance of criminal elements becoming involved in the state's liquor industry. Given that nonresidents could acquire liquor licenses and even manufacture liquor in the state, and that modern technology and crime databases rendered the underlying premise of the law antiquated, it was only a matter of time before a federal judge issued a ruling that set aside the Kansas law and paved the way for the acquisition to be completed. Glazer's also looked to achieve internal growth in the final years of the decade. It established a subsidiary called Glazer's Domaines & Estates to work with fine wine producers to market their wines through the Glazer's network.

Glazer's entered the new century with momentum. Sales neared $1.5 billion in 2000, a 33 percent increase over the prior year, making the company the eighth largest beverage bottler/distributor in the United States. Glazer's took a step back to get a better grip on its increased size and scope, and in 2001 solidified its funding by securing $25 million by issuing notes arranged by Banc One Capital Markets. Those funds were used to help Glazer's acquire a 60,000-square-foot distribution center in Kansas in 2003 and open a business development office in Napa Valley, California, providing the company with a toehold in the state. A short time later Glazer's returned to the capital market with Banc One to raise another $75 million.

Glazer's forged another major alliance in 2003, joining forces with Indianapolis-based National Wine & Spirits to work together in Illinois, a state with an estimated $1.3 billion in annual business. As a result, Glazer's entered a new state with a sales force and infrastructure in place, while National, the largest wine and spirits distributor in the Midwest, gained access to Glazer's extensive portfolio of brands. Glazer's also grew through acquisition in November 2003, adding Tulsa-based Reliance Wine & Spirits Co., Inc., the largest distributor in Oklahoma. It was the eleventh state in which Glazer's operated. In early January 2004, Glazer's expanded its Oklahoma business by acquiring Hirst Imports Co., based in Oklahoma City, giving Glazer's the top two wine and spirits distributors in the state. Later in 2004 Glazer's acquired Wisconsin-based Capital-Husting Co. Inc. and its Nebraska sister company, Sterling Distributing Co. Although this move expanded Glazer's Midwest reach, the company chose not to extend the Glazer's name to these markets, preferring instead to allow the subsidiaries to do business under their established names. Capitol-Husting, for instance, had been in business for more than half a century.

The Glazers had worked hard over the years to work constructively to keep the family business together. A fourth generation was well entrenched in management positions. Mike Glazer was an executive vice-president and possessed more than 20 years of experience, and Barkley Stuart also had joined the company, becoming chief operating officer after 14 years of work for nonprofit corporation Change Inc. Whether Glazer's would remain independent and family owned and operated came into question in May 2006. The *Dallas Morning News* reported that Glazer's was talking to potential buyers. The United States's largest spirits distributor, Miami-based Southern Wine & Spirits, was reportedly talking to Glazer's about a possible purchase or merger. As had been the case for the past decade, the industry remained very much in a state of flux. "We're talking to everybody, and everybody is talking to everybody," Glazer's Zweig told the press. "This is a consolidating industry, and the speed of consolidation is increasing."

Ed Dinger

PRINCIPAL SUBSIDIARIES

Glazer's of Texas; Alliance Beverage Distributing Company; Glazer's Distributors of Arkansas; Olinger Distributing Co.; Glazer's of Iowa; Premier Beverage; Glazer's of Louisiana; Glazer's Companies of Mississippi; Glazer's Midwest; Glazer's of Ohio; Glazer's Oklahoma.

PRINCIPAL COMPETITORS

E&J Gallo Winery; National Wine & Spirits Inc.; Southern Wine & Spirits of America Inc.

FURTHER READING

Foote, Andrea, "Glazer's: Growing Strong," *Beverage World,* July 15, 2005, p. 40.

"Funeral Services for Max Glazer Scheduled Sunday," *Dallas Morning News,* December 20, 1962, p. 1.

"Local Leader," *Food and Drink,* March–April 2005, p. 166.

Robinson-Jacobs, Karen, "Florida Firm Says It's Looking at Glazer's," *Dallas Morning News,* May 10, 2006.

"Spirit of Change," *US Business Review,* March 2005, p. 66.

"Woman Dies from Scalding," *Dallas Morning News,* July 21, 1944.

Gosling Brothers Ltd.

17 Dundonald Street
Hamilton, HM CX
Bermuda
Telephone: 1441 295-1123
Fax: 1441 295-1775
Web site: http://www.goslingsrum.com/

Private Company
Founded: 1806
Employees: 87
Sales: $917.7 million (2002)
NAIC: 312140 Distilleries

■ ■ ■

Based in Bermuda, Gosling Brothers Ltd. is best known as the distiller of Black Seal rum, a blend of three-year-old rum made from a Gosling family recipe over 150 years old. Gosling also offers a less expensive light product, Gold Bermuda Rum, which combines rums produced from continuous stills and pot stills. The company also produces Family Reserve Old Rum, based on the same blend that produces Black Seal but allowed to mellow in oak barrels for at least 16 years. This upscale product comes in a numbered, hand-labeled bottle dipped in wax with an "Old Rum" seal impressed upon it, and wrapped with a metal band with "Old Rum embossed on it. The bottle is sold in a heavy wooden box with a Plexiglas slide front, resting on a bed of straw. Gosling also packages Black Seal Rum with cans of ginger beer, the ingredients for Bermuda's signature drink, the "Dark'n Stormy." In addition, Gosling has

introduced a line of gourmet products inspired by Black Seal Rum, including sauces, preserves, and a hot buttered rum toddy mix. As part of a branding effort, Gosling also sells t-shirts, ties, baseball caps, and other items with the Black Seal logo, featuring a seal balancing a barrel on its nose. These items are sold at the three company-owned stores in Bermuda—two located in Hamilton and another in St. George—which also sell beers, wines, and other spirits. Subsidiary Bermuda Duty Free Limited operates two duty-free stores at Bermuda International Airport. The company is owned and operated by the seventh generation of the Gosling family. It is Bermuda's oldest business and the largest exporter of a Bermuda-made product.

EARLY 19TH CENTURY ROOTS

Gosling traces its history to 1806 when English wine and spirits merchant William Gosling, head of the London concern, Gosling and Sons, decided to set up a business in the United States. He dispatched his eldest son James, along with employee John Till, to establish the outpost. With £10,000 worth of merchandise they set sail from Gravesend, Kent, on the ship Mercury. It proved to be an ironic name for the vessel because the winds were so calm the ship barely crept across the ocean. When the ship's charter expired after 90 days and the crew was short on provisions, the Mercury put into the nearest port, St. Georges, Bermuda. Discovered by the Spanish some 300 years earlier, Bermuda had been colonized in the early 1600s by the English after 150 colonists bound for Virginia had the misfortune of being shipwrecked there. Like those that came before, Gosling and Till decided to make the best of the situation and set up shop in St. Georges in December 1806 to sell their stores of wine and spirits.

A younger brother, Ambrose Gosling, then joined James sometime before 1824 and along with Till they established a partnership, Goslings and Till. With Bermuda's capital moving to Hamilton, the company opened a second outlet in that town, leasing a shop on Front Street for £25 a year, a site on which the company would operate a shop for more than 125 years. Ultimately Till returned to England, leaving the business solely in the hands of Ambrose, who changed the name to Ambrose Gosling and Son. More than just Ambrose's eldest son, William, joined the company, however. Edmund and Charles Gosling became involved, as well. (A fourth brother, named for his father, died at the age of two.) At the age of 70 Ambrose Gosling died in 1857, at which point his sons reorganized the business as a partnership called Gosling Brothers.

Around the time of the reorganization, perhaps as late as 1860, the company began to move beyond the mere distribution of wine and spirits to producing its own rum. The firm imported oak barrels of rum distillate—fermented molasses, a byproduct of sugar cane—and began experimenting with different blends and aging techniques until it developed a recipe for a smooth black rum, which included three independently aged distillates, three to six years in age, which were further aged in once-used charred American oak bourbon casks. The Gosling family simply called it "Old Rum." They did not bottle the product, instead selling it by the barrel or selling it to customers who brought their own bottles to the Gosling shop.

PARTNERSHIP INCORPORATED: 1929

A new generation took charge of the Gosling business by the end of the century. Edmund died in 1885, Charles passed away in 1893, and despite being the oldest, William was the last to go in November 1894. Another Ambrose Gosling, born in 1860, now headed the business. He would eventually be succeeded by his son Ambrose Tucker Gosling, born in 1897. In 1929 the partnership was incorporated.

The bottling of Old Rum and the change of name to Black Seal did not take place until after World War I. Bermuda housed an important base for England's Royal Navy because of its strategic location in the North Atlantic. Some 650 miles east of Newport, Rhode Island, it was a perfect way station between the United States and Great Britain. The rum proved popular at the officer's club, as did champagne. The club produced a considerable number of empty champagne bottles, which Gosling eventually took advantage of, washing and refilling them with Old Rum to sell to tourists who enjoyed the spirit while visiting the islands and were interested in taking some of the product home. Bermuda had been a tourist destination since the late 1800s because it was located close to the Northeast United States. Despite being situated in the North Atlantic, it enjoyed balmy weather due to the Gulf Stream, attracting the winter visits of such notables as Mark Twain, William Dean Howells, and Woodrow Wilson. Gosling corked the bottles of Old Rum and sealed the top with black wax. The distinctive look became a staple of the brand, even after it graduated from reused champagne bottles. People began calling the rum Black Seal, perhaps to distinguish it from other brands that sealed their bottles with red wax. It was not until 1950, long after the rum was commonly known as Black Seal, that Gosling officially adopted the Black Seal name. The company added a logo that was a visual pun: a black seal juggling a small barrel of rum on his nose.

The Royal Naval Officer's Club also played a key role in the creation of the trademark drink called the Dark'n Stormy. The club ran a ginger beer factory as a subsidiary to supply the needs of the officers, and it was not surprising that someone would eventually mix in some of Bermuda's most popular rum to see how it tasted. The resulting concoction received general approval, one that warranted its own name. According to lore, a sailor, whose name has been lost with the passage of time, gazed at his glass of ginger beer and rum held up to the light and pronounced that it was "the colour of a cloud only a fool or dead man would sail under." Hence, the drink took the name Dark'n Stormy.

Black Seal remained a Bermuda mainstay, a favorite of both tourists and inhabitants of the islands, and a required ingredient in Bermuda's national drink, Dark'n Stormy, a spice to add to the Rum Swizzle, as well as being used in local dishes such as the national dish, Bermuda Fish Chowder. However, Black Seal enjoyed limited outside distribution and the Gosling operation remained two spirit shops and a single brand of rum. In 1975 Gosling formed a subsidiary, Cosmopolitan Liquors, to act as a second distribution operation in Bermuda. It imported wines from California, Chile, New Zealand, Australia, Italy, France, and Germany, as well as beer and such spirits as Jim Beam and Absolut

KEY DATES

1806: The Gosling family establishes a wine and spirits shop in Bermuda.
1857: The Gosling Brothers partnership is formed.
1929: The Gosling business incorporated.
1950: Gosling adopts the "Black Seal" name.
1980: The company begins exporting to the United States.
2003: Gosling's Export is formed.
2004: Gold Bermuda Rum and Family Reserve Old Rum are introduced.
2005: Gosling-Castle Partners Inc. is formed.

Vodka. The Gosling family also trademarked the Dark'n Stormy name and attempted to branch out in the 1970s by introducing a canned version of Bermuda's signature drink, but it failed to catch on. The company had better luck in 1980 when it began exporting Black Seal to the United States. It soon became Bermuda's largest export.

Around the time Gosling made its entry in the U.S. market, the first female member of the family, seventh generation Nancy Lloyd Gosling, joined the business. Before going to college, she expressed her interest in the family business to her father, Malcolm Gosling, the company's chairman. He urged her to study accounting because the business was in need of a financial person. She then traveled to Canada where she studied accounting at Dalhousie University in Halifax. To gain seasoning she spent three years at Price Waterhouse and then went to work for the American International Insurance Co. Ltd. Offered a promotion 18 months later, she decided to make the transition to Gosling Brothers, rather than make a further commitment to American International. She started out as assistant treasurer in 1981 and over the next decade worked her way up through the ranks. In 1991 she became the firm's president and chief executive officer. She was especially aggressive in expanding the company's local offerings of beer, wine, and other spirits.

Nancy Gosling was joined by other members of her family as the seventh generation assumed greater responsibility. Her cousin Charles Richard Gosling was responsible for local marketing and the two duty-free stores at the airport. Her brother, Edmund Malcolm Gosling, a Boston College graduate with a degree in economics, carved out his own role on the export side of the business. He became a director of Gosling Brothers in 1985 and oversaw domestic product and sales operations, but he also recognized that Black Seal pos-

sessed untapped export potential and spent a great deal of his time nurturing overseas markets.

Rum had always suffered from an image in the minds of many consumers as a second class spirit. While vodka made great strides in the 1990s when a number of super-premium brands were introduced to the market, rum continued to be neglected. All that would begin to change at the end of the 20th century. Customers were looking for something different, and interest began to build in the aged rum and premium rum category. To take advantage of this growing interest, Gosling took a number of steps to better position itself as a premiere name in the world market for rum.

NEW CENTURY, NEW RUM PRODUCTS

In 2001 Gosling merged with its Cosmopolitan Liquors subsidiary to operate as a single entity and eliminate costly overlaps in staff and resources. In this way, the company would have more resources to devote to expanding the overseas business. Gosling also sought to develop new products to build the Gosling and Black Seal brand. It began work on a light rum, Gold Bermuda Rum, to appeal especially to the U.S. market, which generally preferred amber rums to dark rums. In addition, Gosling was pursuing a luxury cask-aged rum, which grew out of an earlier long-term experiment in which rum had been placed in oak barrels for a number of years to see what would happen. The company tasters were so pleased with the result that Gosling decided to launch a premium rum, cask aged between 13 and 16 years. As for the packaging, the company looked to its cellars where it stored some of the old black-wax sealed champagne bottles it had used decades earlier to contain Old Rum. As a result the new product, Family Reserve Old Rum, would use a champagne-style heavy green bottle.

While the final touches were being made to the two new products, Gosling formed Gosling's Export (Bermuda) Limited in 2003, with Malcolm Gosling serving as its president. Then in March 2004 Gosling introduced its Family Reserve Old Rum, followed a month later by the unveiling of Gold Bermuda Rum. While Gosling was able to distribute its products in all 50 states and every Canadian province (with the exception of Quebec), the brand still lacked recognition with consumers. To address this concern, Gosling joined forces with its U.S. importer, New York City-based Castle Brands Corp., to create a marketing joint venture, Gosling-Castle Partners Inc., which would hold the global export rights to Gosling rums. It would be headed by Malcolm Gosling. In order to better fulfill this role, he decided to move his family to Boston, a city familiar to him from his college days, and run the operation from there, although he planned to eventually return to Bermuda. Shortly before the joint venture was formalized, Castle Brands had already begun selling Gosling rums in the United Kingdom and would soon begin selling the products in Italy. New markets on the horizon included Germany, France, and Ireland.

The marketing push was supported by a multi-million dollar advertising and marketing program, centered on the theme of "Seven Stubborn Generations," and playing up the historic scarcity of the product to pique consumer interest. One somewhat controversial execution of this idea was a Boston billboard that declared that Gosling Rum was "Almost as hard to find as White Bulger." The reference, familiar to area residents, was to a notorious leader of Boston's so-called Irish Mob, a man who had been eluding the FBI since the 1990s. While billboards were leased throughout the United States, Gosling mostly focused on developing new customers through promotions at bars, where people were willing to give Black Seal a try for a few dollars, rather than spend more money for an entire bottle of an unknown brand.

To support increased sales Gosling added 20,000 square feet to its warehouse, and it also built upon its brand by introducing a line of gourmet cakes, sauces, and preserves, all of which used Black Seal rum as a base. The partnership with Castle appeared to be off to a strong start, as Castle reported a surge in sales of Gosling rum from 400 cases in 2005 to 13,500 cases in 2006. With the rum category growing at a strong clip, Gosling was well positioned to enjoy even greater success as it began its third century in business.

Ed Dinger

PRINCIPAL SUBSIDIARIES

Gosling's Export (Bermuda) Ltd.; Bermuda Duty Free Ltd.

PRINCIPAL COMPETITORS

Bacardi U.S.A, Inc.; Diageo North America; Cruzan International, Inc.

FURTHER READING

Arnot, Alison, "Rum Cocktail," *CGA Magazine,* September 1, 2003, p. 22.

"Gosling's Launches New Venture," *Royal Gazette,* April 8, 2005.

"Gosling's Reaches 200 Not Out!" *Royal Gazette,* February 10, 2006.

"Gosling's Toasts New Luxury Rum," *Royal Gazette,* March 5, 2004.

Menzies, Jeannine Klein, "Gosling's Looks to New Markets," *Royal Gazette,* July 5, 2006.

"Message in a Bottle," *Beverage Industry News,* July 2005.

Gould Paper Corporation

■

11 Madison Avenue
New York, New York 10010
U.S.A.
Telephone: (212) 301-0000
Toll Free: (800) 221-3043
Fax: (212) 481-0067
Web site: http://www.gouldpaper.com

Private Company
Founded: 1924
Employees: 500
Sales: $1.3 billion (2005)
NAIC: 424110 Printing and Writing Paper Merchant
Wholesalers

■ ■ ■

Gould Paper Corporation is a privately owned, New York City–based paper distributor, representing major domestic and offshore mills. The company's business is divided among 15 divisions, which offer newsprint, fine papers, and papers used in commercial printing, direct mail, and envelopes, as well as computer paper, copy paper, and multipurpose paper. Gould also offers fine art papers, handmade paper, gift wrapping, matte papers for framing, and archival digital papers. Gould's paperboard products are used in food-service applications, liquid packaging, corrugated boxes, and other packaging materials. In addition, the company provides related services, such as supply chain management, job costing, waste control, pressroom support, and consulting services. Gould maintains 20 domestic units and operates

in another dozen countries, including the United Kingdom, France, Finland, the United Arab Emirates, Hong Kong, Dubai, Singapore, New Zealand, the Philippines, and the People's Republic of China. In addition to paper, Gould is involved in nut harvesting and mowing equipment through its Weiss McNair Ramacher unit.

FOUNDING THE COMPANY IN 1924

Gould Paper Corporation was founded in 1924 by Harry Edward Gould, Sr., in New York City. The business sold both domestic and imported paper, mostly used in the making of greeting cards. The company grew internally over the next 20 years before completing its first acquisition in 1943, when it bought Reinhold Card & Paper, which had been doing business in New York City since 1906. By the end of the decade, Gould had expanded its product lines to include commercial printing paper, teabag paper, and nonwoven web products such as stencil paper. The company continued to grow steadily in the 1950s and 1960s. An import/export company called Caylye Paper was formed in 1955 as a joint venture between subsidiary Reinhold-Gould and Alfred Hernball. Another significant paper acquisition came in 1968 with the addition of Champion International, the New York unit of Whitaker Paper Company. Harry Gould's business interests were not confined solely to paper, however. Before the United States' entry into World War II, he and partner Francis Levien had the foresight to acquire a struggling steel manufacturer. The company, Steel Materials Corporation, thrived on Navy contracts. After the war, in 1950, the partners bought another steel mill

COMPANY PERSPECTIVES

Gould is both sales-oriented and customer-focused. It is currently operating at a sales level in excess of $1 billion.

in Ohio, and then traded it for Universal Laboratories, maker of printing inks. As Universal American, it became a holding company that would be merged with Gulf & Western Industries in 1968.

By the end of the 1960s Gould Paper was generating annual sales in the neighborhood of $16 million. It was at this point that Harry Gould convinced his son, Harry Edward Gould, Jr., to take the reins. The younger Gould, born in New York in 1938, earned an undergraduate degree from Colgate University in 1960 and also studied at Oxford University in England. He then entered the Harvard Business School and left to work in the finance department at Goldman Sachs & Co. before eventually earning a Master of Business Administration degree from Columbia University in 1964. He spent some time working at Universal American, followed by several years in Detroit at Young Spring & Wire Corp., where he worked his way up to executive vice-president and chief operating officer. In 1969 he left to become the president, chief executive officer, and chairman of Gould Paper.

Harry Gould, Jr., brought new energy and ambition to the company and quickly moved to expand the business, both in terms of product lines and geography. Over the next 30 years, he bought half-a-dozen paper distributors and added eight divisions. In 1978, for example, Gould Paper opened a Dallas sales office to become involved in the catalog business of high-end retailers like Bloomingdale's and Neiman Marcus. Another subsidiary controlled by Gould Paper was the Clifford-Gould Paper Corporation, assembled between 1982 and 1985 when the sales operations of New York paper distributor Majestic Paper Corporation were acquired, followed by the addition of another area competitor, Olympic Paper Company. Another New York City rival, Capital Paper Company, was acquired in 1989, the same year that Gould Paper shed an asset, Aldine Specialty Paper, sold to a stockholder.

FIRST NON-PAPER ACQUISITION IN 1969

Like his father, Gould did not limit his business interests to paper, making acquisitions in other areas, although he elected to fold them into Gould Paper rather than own them under a separate entity. His first acquisition outside of paper came in 1969 with the addition of Samuel Porritt & Co., an Illinois machine shop that Gould would own until it shut down in 1986. Next came the 1971 purchase of Ingalls Manufacturing, Inc., a California agricultural equipment maker, specializing in nut harvesting equipment. Over the ensuing decade, Gould expanded this business by acquiring other California companies: Weiss Manufacturing, Inc.; McNair Manufacturing, Inc.; and Vrisimo Manufacturing, Inc. These businesses were packaged into Chicago, California-based Weis McNair Division, which became Weiss Mc-Nair Ramacher in 1996 after it acquired one of its top competitors, Ramacher Manufacturing.

In the 1980s Gould became involved in the entertainment industry when he took charge of a struggling movie production company called Cinema Group, formed by Merrill Lynch. He soon turned around the company, releasing ten films, seven of them through the Paramount studio, from 1983 to 1986. The company was involved in the making of the hit film *Flashdance*, the profits of which made up for the losses accumulated by Gould's predecessors. Cinema Group also produced movies such as *Staying Alive*, the sequel to *Saturday Night Fever*, *Star Trek III*, and *The Philadelphia Experiment*. He also produced another film, *The Runestone*, with a different company in 1990. As a result of this sideline, Gould became a member of the Academy of Motion Picture Arts and Sciences and would each year vote on the Oscar Awards.

Gould was able to focus more of his attention to growing his paper company in the 1990s. Philadelphia, Pennsylvania–based Whiting-Patterson Company, purveyor of fine paper, was acquired from American Envelope in 1991. A year later, in May 1992, Gould Paper purchased a Richard Lewis Paper Corporation subsidiary to add operations in Miami and the Chicago suburb of Northfield, Illinois. The following month, Gould Paper acquired a longtime Mead Corporation subsidiary, now the Bermco Division of WWF Paper Company (Wilcox Walter Furlong). In July 1992 Gould Paper established a second Dallas-area subsidiary, BRW Paper Company, a paper merchant that would operate throughout Texas and Kansas, staffed primarily by the former salespeople of the Texas operation of Minneapolis-based Leslie Paper Company, which was in the process of being purchased by International Paper Company. To close out 1992, Gould Paper bought most of Select Paper Company from Buffalo, New York–based Sofco, creating the core of an Albany, New York division.

Expansion continued for Gould Paper in the mid-1990s. Willow Grove, Pennsylvania–based Total Busi-

```
┌─────────────────────────────────────────────┐
│                                             │
│            KEY DATES                        │
│                  ■                          │
├─────────────────────────────────────────────┤
│                                             │
│  1924:  The company is founded by Harry     │
│         Edward Gould.                       │
│  1943:  Reinhold Card & Paper is acquired.  │
│  1969:  Harry Edward Gould, Jr., is named   │
│         president, CEO, and chairman.       │
│  1978:  The Dallas sales office is opened.  │
│  1992:  Richard Lewis Paper Corporation is  │
│         acquired.                           │
│  2002:  WWF International UK Ltd. is         │
│         acquired.                           │
│  2004:  The Salehurst Group is acquired.    │
│                                             │
└─────────────────────────────────────────────┘
```

ness Papers was acquired in March of that year to bolster the company's Mid-Atlantic Division. Total Business distributed printing and office paper products in the Pennsylvania, Delaware, and New Jersey markets surrounding Philadelphia. Later in the year, Gould Paper acquired Miami, Florida–based Southern Paper Company through the Richard Lewis subsidiary acquired the previous year. In 1994 Gould Paper grew internally, in March of that year forming Legion Paper to distribute art paper products, and three months later opening a 70,000-square-foot warehouse in Edison, New Jersey to distribute its products throughout the United States.

Around the same time, Atlantic Paper group was established in Lyndhurst, New Jersey, staffed by personnel lured away from New Jersey's Milton Paper. Also in 1994, Gould Paper opened a sales office in Laurel, Maryland, to sell paper to commercial printers and other Mid-Atlantic corridor customers; the company's Florida business was beefed up by launching Gould's Paper House, to distribute paper products to the fast-growing Tampa-Orlando area; and Gould Paper subsidiary Fibreweb, producer of newsprint, reopened a Canadian paper mill. Gould paper opened a sales office in Spring Valley, Ohio, in 1996 to service printers and publishers across the United States. In May 1996 the company acquired Diamond Paper Corporation, a Sterling, Virginia–based distributor of copy and computer paper and other office supplies in the Washington, D.C., and northern Virginia area.

NEW CENTURY ADVANCES

Gould Paper ended the 1990s with nine divisions combining to generate annual sales of some $600 million. The company continued to expand with the start of the new century. In 2000 it established what it called the "MOM and POP" program to distribute coated paper from Mead ("Mountains of Mead") and

Consolidated Paper ("Pounds of Consolidated Paper"). By building up its inventories of these products, Gould Paper was able to provide printers with same- or next-day delivery on a wide variety of gloss, dull, or matte coated papers in most popular sizes. Other distributors, carrying lower inventories, could not provide the same service to printers, who either had to buy paper larger than needed and cut it down to size or wait for an order to be shipped direct from the mill.

Another 2000 initiative was a joint venture with Philadelphia's WWF Paper Corporation that was intended to create the largest independent distributor of fine papers in North America. The alliance was forged as a way for the two companies to keep pace in an industry experiencing consolidation on the supply side, as paper manufacturers merged to achieve economies of scale, and customers, who were growing larger to achieve greater buying power and other benefits that came with size. The Gould/WWF joint venture made sense because they were of similar size and filled in gaps in each other's business. For example, WWF had a presence in Canada and the United Kingdom that Gould Paper lacked. Although the semi-merger failed to materialize, Gould Paper was nevertheless able to achieve a major part of its goals in 2002 when it acquired WWF International UK Ltd. and subsidiary Paper Sales UK Limited, companies with more than 30 years of experience in selling fine papers to book and magazine publishers and greeting card companies. The most significant deal in the history of Gould Paper, it added some $300 million in annual sales and provided a foothold in Europe on which the company could make further acquisitions. Gould was in no hurry to expand the European business, however, opting instead to proceed with caution. "We're talking walking pace here, not running pace," he told *Printing World.* "We'll be looking more at brokerage rather than selling out of a warehouse."

On the domestic side, Gould Paper took a number of steps in 2002 and 2003. It formed a pair of new divisions. One of them, Gould North America, was established in the Boston area to service U.S. catalog, magazine, and newspaper publishers. Gould International Packaging, meanwhile, was formed in Greenwich, Connecticut, to sell paperboard used in the food-service, folding carton, and corrugated industries, as well as providing some plastic products used in the packaging industry. Later in the year, Gould Paper acquired the Town Paper Corporation division Paper Dynamix, which bought and sold mill closeouts, side trims, excess inventory, and other clearance items from major mills as well as other sources. In 2003 Gould Paper established a joint venture with New Jersey–based Siclar Corporation to operate a pair of rotary sheeters to provide contract paper converting services—such as sheeting, cutting and trimming, and cartoning—to paper mills, paper merchants, brokers, and end users in the New York City area. Also in 2003, the Miami operation bought a sheeter and launched a new subsidiary, Alliance Converting, to serve printing customers in south Florida.

Gould Paper made advances both home and abroad in 2004. Early in the year WWF UK completed a friendly takeover of Salehurst Group, a United Kingdom–based paper merchant. Not only did Gould Paper strengthen its position in the United Kingdom, it gained a French paper distributor, Gallium EURL, operating out of Paris. This was followed by the creation of a new subsidiary, WWF Paper & Board Limited, to add an operation in Brentwood, Essex, in the United Kingdom. Gould Paper's position in the country was further strengthened with the acquisition of Price & Pierce, a London Stock Exchange–listed paper merchant with a history that dated back to 1869. Price & Pierce also brought with it operations in Helsinki, Dubai, Singapore, Shanghai, Hong Kong, and Auckland. As a result, Gould Paper was well positioned to operate in an increasingly global marketplace.

In 2005 the company merged its business papers divisions to form Gould Office Papers. Gould Paper completed another acquisition in February 2006, buying Missouri-based Boone Paper company, which was folded into subsidiary BRW Paper Co. to supplement Gould's Midwest business.

Ed Dinger

PRINCIPAL SUBSIDIARIES

BRW Paper Co., Inc.; Price & Pierce International Inc.; Gallium EURL; WWF International Ltd.

PRINCIPAL COMPETITORS

Cascades Inc.; International Paper Company; Sappi Fine Paper North America.

FURTHER READING

Ackland, Bruce, "Harry's Game," *Office Products International,* May 2006, p. 30.

Clinkunbroomer, Jeanette, "Gould, WWF Join Forces to Achieve Critical Mass," *Printing News,* December 18, 2000.

Hays, Kathy, "Harry Knows Paper," *UPM Magazine,* June 2005, p. 14.

Larkin, Jim, "Gould Outlines Invasion Plans," *Printing World,* August 5, 2002, p. 13.

Perone, Michael T., "Gould Paper Corp. Proudly Rolls Out Innovative 'MOM and POP' Program," *Printing News,* August 28, 2000, p. 11.

Grupo Industrial Lala, S.A. de C.V.

Av. Lázaro Cárdenas 185
Gómez Palacio, Durango 35070
Mexico
Telephone: (52) (871) 7500101
Fax: (52) (871) 7500209
Web site: http://www.lala.com.mx

Private Company
Founded: 1949 as Unión de Productores de Crédito de Leche de Torreón
Employees: 24,000
Sales: $2.2 billion (2005)
NAIC: 112120 Milk Processing; 311511 Fluid Milk Manufacturing; 311512 Creamery Butter Manufacturing; 311513 Cheese Manufacturing; 551112 Offices of Other Holding Companies

■ ■ ■

Grupo Industrial Lala, S.A. de C.V., is Mexico's leading producer of fluid milk. Organized both horizontally and vertically, it is a holding company that embraces many enterprises, including a credit union and cooperatives. Lala maintains eight pasteurization plants located in the most important population centers of Mexico and the widest refrigerated distribution network in the nation. Lala also makes and sells butter, cheese, yogurt, and fruit juices. Its advanced technology includes artificial insemination, enriched feed for cattle, veterinary services, laboratories, and chemical and pharmaceutical materials.

PROVIDING BETTER MILK FOR MEXICO: 1949–99

Lala was founded in 1949 in Comarca Lagunera, also called La Laguna (hence the Lala name), and this region remains its principal production area. Located in eastern Durango and western Coahuila states, the region is fertile but hot and dry, requiring irrigation from rivers and underground aquifers. Cotton growing, once the chief agricultural activity, was abandoned, due to low prices, in favor of dairy farming. Green Revolution scientific and technical advances, and capital—including public and foreign funds—enabled Lagunera to develop the infrastructure required to become Mexico's leading dairy farming region. Pasteurization of milk, beginning in 1950, defeated the scourge of brucellosis (undulant fever), and the import of Holstein cows greatly fostered productivity.

Originally Lala was a cooperative credit union for milk producers in Comarca Lagunera who needed to pool their resources to obtain financing for the necessary infrastructure. The Unión de Crédito de Productores de Leche de Torreón was established in 1949 and transformed into the Unión de Crédito Industrial y Agropecuario de La Laguna, S.A. de C.V., in 1975. This enterprise began pasteurizing milk in 1950 and installing automatic milking machines in 1955. The growth of a modern dairy industry required a number of specialized enterprises, including those providing irrigation technology, veterinary services, and equipment and materials, generally imported, including fertilizers, seeds, semen, and antimicrobial products. It involved development of artificial insemination and transplant of embryos, the introduction of enriched feed to supple-

KEY DATES

1949: Founding of the enterprise, in Torreón, Coahuila.
1966: Lácteos Lala is founded to exploit the market in central Mexico.
A subsidiary is founded for the production and marketing of cheese and yogurt products.
1986: Ultra Lala is established to produce ultrapasteurized milk.
1996: Lala's producers have a combined herd of 128,218 cows.
2000: Some 220 dairy farmers, all Lala stockholders, are providing the enterprise with milk.
2004: Lala purchases Parmalat Finanzieria's Mexican subsidiary.
2005: Mexico's president, Vicente Fox, dedicates a new Lala plant.

ment alfalfa and corn silage, the use of chemicals and pharmaceuticals, automatic milking machines, farm machinery, milk processing equipment, cold tanks, and the bettering of conditions for the care and management of cattle. At the same time, it required vertical integration ranging from forage production to distribution and commercialization of the end products. By 1996 Lala's producers had a combined herd of 128,218 cows producing an average of 8,239 liters each per year.

Lácteos Laguna was founded in 1966 to exploit the market in central Mexico, beginning with Mexico City. A pasteurization plant was acquired in Acapulco in 1972 to serve cities in the states of Guerrero and Michoacán. Another plant opened in Mexico City in 1976 and in Monterrey in 1978. Lala Derivados Lácteos was founded in 1982–83 for the production and marketing of cheese and yogurt products. Lala Productos Químicos was established in 1983 to meet strict hygienic standards by employing detergents, disinfectant products, and germicides. In time, this unit diversified its production with veterinary medicines and household cleaning products. Pasteurizadora Lala del Norte was created in 1986 to sell Lala's products along the Mexican frontier with the United States, and Ultra Lala was established in the same year to produce ultrapasteurized milk in antiseptic containers that did not require refrigeration and had a shelf life of more than three months. A Durango pasteurization plant was acquired in 1992.

The federal government controlled pasteurized milk prices in Mexico from 1974 to 1989, and all controls did not end until 1996. While the dairy industry chafed at restrictions on the prices it could charge, it also received considerable subsidies in the form of below market credit and electricity rates. Nevertheless, it maintained during the 1990s that it needed help to compensate for the high cost of cattle feed (70 percent of total costs) and competition from subsidized farmers in the United States and Europe. "The government has to support the milk industry in Mexico," Jesús Raúl Villareal González, Lala's chairman of the board, told James Blears for an article in *Business Mexico*. Villareal, who was also head of Mexico's Milk Producers Association, added, "It's like the tortilla or frijoles [beans], part of the basic diet."

As of 1996, Lala was one of six Mexican enterprises that dominated pasteurized milk production. The industry was experiencing a shakeout in which companies were finding it hard to control costs and compete unless, like Lala, they were engaged in every area of production and services. Lala's extensive network of companies included Envases Especializados de la Laguna, S.A. de C.V. In 1998 this liquid packaging firm formed a joint venture with Elopak, a Norwegian company. Lala and Elopak shared ownership and operating control of the new company, Envases Elopak, S.A. de C.V. Also in the late 1990s, Lala added more new products, including various new yogurt flavors.

LALA IN THE 21ST CENTURY

In 2000 Grupo Industrial Lala consisted of 23 companies employing 10,500 people, and it controlled 26 percent of the fluid milk market in Mexico. Lala Transportadora was running 62 tank trailers to collect raw milk each day from the 220 dairy farms supplying the enterprise. These farms were owned by individual Lala stockholders. "You have to be a stockholder to supply milk to Lala; suppliers are the company's only stockholders," a Lala executive told Foss Farrar for an article in *Bulk Transporter*. The tank trailers delivered the milk to Lala Enfriadora, the company's headquarters and consolidation point for raw milk in Gómez Palacio. It was also the location of Lala's central laboratory, where the quality of the milk was tested before pasteurization. Another facility in Gómez Palacio housed a fleet of heavy-duty tractors and trailers, various work and repair stations, and a parts warehouse. Lala was selling its products to supermarkets, small grocery stores, and such food service accounts as McDonald's restaurants, to whom it provided private label cheese. It was also exporting ultrapasteurized milk and some other products to El Salvador, Guatemala, and Honduras.

Under Lala's chairman of the board, Eduardo Tricio, the company embarked in 2002 on a campaign to convince Mexicans to drink more milk, with the goal of raising the annual consumption per capita 50 percent, to the level of Argentina and Brazil. Using billboards and posters, Lala increased its advertising expenses threefold. The basic idea, as expressed by the company's marketing director, was to transform a traditional commodity into something more than a basic product, using colorful and modern images. The concept involved enlisting the support of young mothers looking for aid in the rearing of their children.

Grupo Industrial Lala purchased the milk and cheese operations of Grupo Latinlac, which was in receivership, in 2003 for MXN 802 million (about $75 million). Lala thereby added the milk brands Nutrileche, Mileche, and Plenilac, plus many local brands, to its own resources, raising the company's share of the milk drunk in Mexico to 28 percent. The purchase also included two cheese-making plants and the cheese brand Los Volcanes.

Financially troubled Parmalat Finanziara SpA, one of the world's largest producers of dairy products, sold its Mexican operation to Lala in 2004. The acquisition included a plant in Lagos de Moreno, Jalisco, three distribution centers, land, buildings, machinery, and inventory, but not the operation's debts, and it helped raise Lala fluid milk market share to 40 percent (and 48 percent in 2005).

At the same time, however, Lala reversed course, deciding that emphasizing milk sales was no longer good business because of the small profit margin per unit. The company could not even count on maintaining its volume, since many Mexicans continued to drink milk without any sanitation control, and Liconsa, a government-supported agency, was selling 1 million liters annually of powdered milk to the poor at a subsidized price. The new corporate viewpoint was that in any case milk had become a mature market and that for growth Lala had to look to specialized dairy products, which were increasing faster in sales than milk and yielding larger profit margins. These so-called functional products included not only yogurt and cheese but also oils—laced with omega-3 fatty acids—and even chewing gums that whitened the teeth and contained calcium.

A 2002 study by the World Health Organization reported that next to the United States, Mexico was the world leader in obesity. For Lala and other dairy products providers, this indicated a large market for healthy products to combat the medical problems of overweight people, such as diabetes and cardiovascular and digestive difficulties.

In early 2004 Lala began heavy advertising on television shows of its line of yogurts, under the slogan "The yogurt made from good milk." It was soon buried under competition from firms that stressed specialized ingredients and benefits such as fiber. Even so, Lala's volume of yogurt sales tripled during the year as another slogan seemed to question the quality of its rivals' yogurt: "Where did the milk from the other yogurts come from?" As a result, Lala rose from fifth to an estimated second place in liquid yogurt sales, trailing only Danone de México, S.A. de C.V. Yogurt was a rapidly growing market—one that grew 120 percent in both volume and revenue in 2004, according to one study. In early 2005 President Vicente Fox inaugurated a new $50-million Lala yogurt factory in Irapuato, Guanajuato, where Danone already had a presence. By the middle of the year the plant was rolling out the Lala Vive line, containing fiber, with the aim of targeting young women. Lala's yogurt portfolio also included Bio 4, with bacteria to improve the intestinal microclimate and carbohydrates and calcium.

Lala had 21 plants, including 3 for dairy product derivatives. With a fleet of more than 3,500 trucks and 128 distribution centers, it was visiting more than 200,000 clients daily, selling almost 4 million liters of milk and thousands of tons of diverse dairy products each day.

The company was offering four kinds of whole milk: Premium, Light, Semi, and Entera, and three kinds of specialized milk: Fácil Digestión, Desarrollo, and Silecta Plus. There were also two kinds of formulated milk products—Nutri Leche and Mileche—and four kinds of what the company called *saborizada*—Choco, Yomi, Licuado, and Shot. Lala's six cheeses were Parela, Oaxaca, Chichuahua, Manchego, Crema, and Americana. Its three butters were Untable Entera, Untable Light, and En Barra. Its yogurts were Batido, Para Beber, Natural, Licuado, Light, Yomi, Bio 4, and Petit Suisse. Lala also had a line of soft drinks enriched with Vitamin C.

Robert Halasz

PRINCIPAL SUBSIDIARIES

Envases Elopak; Industrias Lácteas de la Laguna; Lala Derivados Lácteos, S.A. de C.V.; Tecnopak de la Laguna; Ultra Lala, S.A. de C.V.

PRINCIPAL COMPETITORS

Asociación de Productores de Leche Pura (Alpura); Danone de México, S.A. de C.V.; Sigma Alimentos, S.A. de C.V.

FURTHER READING

Anderson, Bárbara, "La Lala leche," *Expansión,* April 30–May 14, 2003, pp. 96–102, 104.

Blears, James, "Land of Milk & Money," *Business Mexico,* June 1995, pp. 32–34.

"Concreta Lala compra de Parmalat," *Reforma,* July 16, 2004, p. 1.

"Domina LALA el 40 por ciento del mercado," *Palabra,* September 15, 2004, p. 4.

Farrar, Foss, "Lala Expands, Adds Shop, Upgrades Fleet," *Bulk Transporter,* August 1, 2000.

"Firman convenio Lala y JD Edwards," *Reforma,* April 11, 2000, p. 1.

García, Luis A., et al., "Dinámica del sistema lechera mexicana en el marco regional y global," in *La transformación de la actividad lechera en México.* Mexico City: Plaza y Valdés Editores, 1997, pp. 72–77, 80–81.

Vázques, Gisela, "La fórmula europea," *Expansión,* December 21, 2005–January 25, 2006, pp. 87–88, 90.

Guinot Paris S.A.

1 Rue De La Paix 75002
Paris,
France
Telephone: (33) 01 44 55 55 00
Fax: (33) 01 44 55 37 62
Web site: http://www.guinot.com

Private Company
Incorporated: 1963 as the Rene Guinot Company
Employees: 348
Sales: EUR 75.63 million ($100 million) (2004)
NAIC: 325620 Toilet Preparation Manufacturing

■ ■ ■

Guinot Paris S.A. is a world-renowned specialist in the development and production of skin and beauty care products. The company's product line, sold under the Guinot, Mary Cohr, and Master Colors brands, are exclusively available through professional beauty salons, and by beauty therapists. The company supplies its products directly, including through subsidiaries in Germany and Mexico, but especially through a global network of licensed distributors. The company has also developed a franchise system for its Guinot-branded beauty salons. As such, the company's products are available in more than 70 countries and some 9,000 salons worldwide.

The core Guinot Paris line features a lineup of company-developed spa treatments. These include the flagship Hydradermie, developed in the 1960s by founder Rene Guinot, which utilizes ionization in the application of the company's creams. Other treatments include Beaute Neuve, a one-hour, four-part facial treatment; Liftosome, a skin tightening treatment for mature skin; Aromatics, using essential oils; and Tres Homme, developed for men's skin. The company's treatments are backed up by a long list of skin care, body care, and sun protection creams and lotions for use in the customer's home. In addition to this skin care line, Guinot has developed the Mary Cohr brand of spa treatments and creams, which incorporate essential oils as their active ingredients. Guinot rounds out its product offering with the Master Colors professional cosmetics line. These are available exclusively through beauty salons and other beauty professionals. Guinot's production is centered at its main facility in Melun, near Paris. Guinot has been owned and led by Jean-Daniel Mondin since 1972. The company last reported revenues of more than EUR 75 million ($100 million) in 2004.

A BEAUTY CARE IDEA IN 1930

Guinot's origins lay in the work of chemical engineer Rene Guinot who began working with skin care and cleansing products in the late 1920 and 1930s. Guinot's chemical background allowed him to approach the skin and beauty care market from a scientific viewpoint. In 1930, Guinot achieved his first breakthrough by recognizing that deep cleansing the skin allowed the active ingredients in skin care creams to penetrate more deeply.

Over the next several decades, Guinot built up a list of more than 55 biologically active ingredients that could be used to treat various skin types. Guinot also began

COMPANY PERSPECTIVES

With over 30 years of experience Guinot's vocation is to beautify women. Our advanced research laboratories have created exclusive face and body treatment methods that have established the reputation of leading beauty salons and spas throughout the world.

experimenting with the use of electricity as a means of stimulating the action of the different substances incorporated into his creams. These innovations were supplied to his wife for use in her own Parisian beauty salon. By the early 1960s, Guinot's formulas had begun to attract interest from other salons and spas in Paris. To respond to the rising demand, Guinot founded his own company, Rene Guinot in Montreuil, a suburb of Paris. The company started out with a small staff, and a customer network of just 22 salons.

Guinot himself continued developing new formulas and treatments, and especially those involving the use of electrical current. Guinot's experiments began to orient themselves toward the use of ionization techniques. By 1965, Guinot had succeeded in finalizing his first breakthrough treatment, which he called "Cathiodermie" (alternatively "Hydradermie"). The treatment, lasting as long as 90 minutes, consisted of several steps, including an ionization step to cleanse the skin, followed by the use of special gels applied with the aid of roller electrodes. The use of electrodes, according to Guinot, allowed active ingredients to penetrate even deeper into the skin than the traditional manual massage technique. In a later phase in the treatment, a layer of gauze through which an electrical current was passed was placed over the face as a means of boosting the supply of oxygen to skin cells. The treatment ended with a more traditional massage using various creams and gels.

BUILDING A GLOBAL BRAND FROM 1972

Guinot's treatments proved popular, and they were soon embraced by a widening circle of beauty salons and their clientele. Nonetheless, the company operated on a decidedly small scale, posting revenues of the equivalent of roughly $300,000 into the 1970s.

The early 1970s, however, marked a new phase in the company's growth. In 1972, Dr. Jean-Daniel Mondin, a young chemist with a doctorate in pharmaceutical science, bought the Rene Guinot company. Under Mondin, Guinot quickly evolved into an industrial producer

with an international focus. For its international development, the company focused on building a network of local distributors. In the United Kingdom, for example, Rob Robson established a distribution company in 1972 for the express purpose of introducing Cathiodermie and the rest of the Guinot product line into the market. Mondin, who continued to lead the ongoing refinement of hydradermie/cathiodermie and related products, also set up a franchise system. As part of this system, prospective "beauty therapists" were required to receive training and certification from Guinot. Sales of the company's products were at the same time restricted to salons, helping the brand build an exclusive image.

Guinot also sought new product areas for its expansion. The company naturally turned toward cosmetics in the late 1970s, launching the Mary Cohr cosmetic brand. The Mary Cohr line, however, increasingly developed into a parallel spa and salon treatment, based on the use of essential oils. In 1987, the company debuted the Mary Cohr Catiovital facial treatment. The salon-based treatment was also backed up by a new range of products for home use sold exclusively through the growing number of salons in Guinot's distribution network.

With the growing reputation of the Guinot and Mary Cohr brands, Guinot's sales increasingly came from beyond France. In support of this growth, the company began developing its own globally operating distribution network, based on licenses and partnerships with local companies. The company established distribution relationships with two companies in the United States: Lachman Imports, on the East Coast, and Thibiant International, on the West Coast. In Australia in 1990, the company turned over the exclusive distribution for that market to John Pritchard International. In 1993, Guinot boosted its Japanese presence through a distribution agreement with Mandom Corporation, a leading producer of men's care and other beauty care products in that market. The company also established a number of its own subsidiaries into the early 1990s, notably in Germany and Mexico. By the mid-2000s, the company's distribution network had grown to include some 70 countries.

Supporting the company's growth was its main production facility in Melun, in the Val de Seine outside of Paris. In 1992, the company launched an expansion of the facility, increasing its space to 18,000 square meters. That expansion was completed in 1993. The increased capacity helped fuel strong growth for the company through the 1990s, and by 1998 the company reported sales of the equivalent of nearly EUR 42 million. In that year, the company expanded its product

KEY DATES

1930: Rene Guinot develops new skin care treatments based on deep-cleansing.

1963: Guinot establishes the Rene Guinot company to supply skin care treatments to Parisian beauty salons.

1965: The company introduces the Hydradermie skin treatment system.

1972: Jean-Daniel Mondin buys the Rene Guinot company and launches a major expansion of the company's production and distribution.

1977: The Mary Cohr line of cosmetics is introduced.

1990: Guinot begins international expansion, establishing distribution partnerships throughout the world.

1993: The company completes expansion of its Melun production facility to 18,000 square meters.

1998: Guinot opens a dedicated research and development department.

2000: The Guinot Paris Spa franchise format is launched.

2001: Guinot launches its Master Colors cosmetics line and repositions the Mary Cohr brand to emphasize aroma therapy and essential oil ingredients.

2003: A new expansion of the Melun facility is completed, bringing its size to 30,000 square meters.

2005: TechniSpa and Hydradermic Lift treatments are introduced.

2006: Guinot debuts a new active product ingredient, called Dermostimulines.

development with the establishment of a dedicated research center. The group's new research efforts quickly paid off, and by 1999 the company launched a new product, Epil Confort, a long-lasting depilatory system. The following year, the company launched another new product line, Longue Vie Cellulaire, with separate treatments developed for different parts of the body.

FRANCHISING THE BRAND IN THE NEW CENTURY

At the same time, Guinot began developing a new distribution model. In 2000, the company began testing a new franchise format, called Guinot Paris Spa. The first spas were test marketed in Paris that year, and featured beauty therapists trained by Guinot itself. The success of the format led to a larger rollout of the brand. By 2003, there were nearly 19 Guinot Paris Spas in operation, including the first spas opened overseas. In England, for example, the company opened a flagship spa in London in 2002.

By then, Guinot had launched a new cosmetics collection, called Master Colors. The launch enabled the company to reposition its Mary Cohr brand, which increasingly had developed as a parallel line of beauty treatments to the core Guinot brand. In order to differentiate itself from the Guinot brand, the Mary Cohr line adopted new formulas based on the use of essential oils and aroma therapy. In 2002, that line was relaunched as Aromatic Face Treatment. Meanwhile, Guinot continued developing new products under its own name. This resulted in the debut of a new slimming treatment, Absolue Minceur, introduced in 2003.

In support of its rising sales, the company expanded its production facility in Melun again, adding an additional 14,000 square meters of production and storage space to the site. That project was completed in 2003. The expanded facility helped back the launch of a new Guinot success in 2004, when the company introduced its "Youth Boost" anti-age treatment.

This was followed by an update of the group's flagship Hydradermie treatment, called Hydradermic Lift. The new treatment utilized micro-currents to simulate the effects of facelifts. By the end of 2005, the company had added another treatment, called Technispa, marketed as an anti-cellulite slimming treatment. At the same time as the company continued to develop new treatments, it also continued to seek out new active ingredients. In March 2006, for example, Guinot debuted a new complex, called Dermostimulines, which is derived from passion fruit. The product was meant to replace the retinol, or Vitamin A, found in many of the group's products. With sales at more than EUR 75 million, Guinot had established itself as a leading name in the beauty care market for the new century.

M.L. Cohen

PRINCIPAL SUBSIDIARIES

Guinot Mexico SA de CV; Laboratores Rene Guinot GmbH (Germany); Guinot distributes its products through a network of exclusive distributors in more than 70 countries worldwide.

PRINCIPAL COMPETITORS

Nestle S.A.; Sunstar Inc.; Procter and Gamble Co.; Unilever; Johnson and Johnson; E. Merck; Ipiranga Comercial Quimica S.A; Sanofi-Aventis; Abbott Laboratories; House Off Fuller S.A.; Wyeth; L'Oreal S.A.; Christian Dior S.A.; LVMH Moët Hennessy Louis Vuitton S.A; Consell S.A.; CP and P Inc.

FURTHER READING

"Caucasians Need Skin Whiteners Too," *Manila Times*, November 23, 2004.

Chee Kee, Raoul, J., "French Spa Brand Opens Local Branches," *BusinessWorld*, April 4, 2003, p. 11.

"Crowning Glory," *Health & Beauty Salon*, December 1, 2005, p. 22.

Evans, Matthew W., "Guinot to Inject Youth into Mix," *WWD*, April 4, 2003, p. 11.

"French Cosmetics Expert Launches New Enhancement Machine in Manila," *BusinessWorld*, August 9, 2005.

"French Skincare Company Guinot Has Formulated A New Ingredient to Replace Retinol (Vitamin A) in Its Anti-Ageing and Firming Face and Bodycare Products," *Health & Beauty Salon*, March 1, 2006, p. 12.

"Guinot Offers Skincare Solutions," *Cosmetics International*, June 25, 1995, p. 2.

James, Karen, "Guinot's Sun Care Code," *WWD*, May 4, 2005, p. 15.

"Jean-Daniel Mondin: Des Femmes et des Crèmes," *Le Point*, January 20, 2005, p. 17.

"The French Brand Guinot Has Reformulated Nucleic Defense, Its Collection of Self-Tanners, Sunscreens and After-Sun Products," *Household & Personal Products Industry*, June 2005, p. 34.

H&R BLOCK

H&R Block, Inc.

4400 Main Street
Kansas City, Missouri 64111
U.S.A.
Telephone: (816) 753-6900
Toll Free: (800) 829-7733
Fax: (816) 753-5346
Web site: http://www.hrblock.com

Public Company
Incorporated: 1955
Employees: 133,800
Sales: $4.67 billion (2006)
Stock Exchanges: New York
Ticker Symbol: HRB
NAIC: 541213 Tax Preparation Services; 51121 Software
Publishers; 522292 Real Estate Credit

■ ■ ■

The name of H&R Block, Inc., has become synonymous with the business of preparing income tax returns, and justifiably so. The company is far and away the largest in this field with more than 12,000 offices in the United States, the United Kingdom, Australia, and Canada. During the 2004 income tax filing season it served over 19.2 million clients. The company spent most of the late 1990s focused on becoming a provider of diversified financial services. The early years of the new millennium were spent battling class action lawsuits, a fraud suit launched by the National Association of Securities Dealers (NASD), and a suit filed by New York Attorney General Eliot Spitzer that claimed H&R Block defrauded

customers who purchased its Express IRA product.

TAX PREPARATION EVOLVED FROM ACCOUNTING SERVICES

H&R Block was founded in Kansas City, Missouri by Henry and Richard Bloch. The two brothers had followed slightly different paths: Henry Bloch had received his degree in math at the University of Michigan and served as a bomber crewman during World War II whereas Richard studied economics at the University of Pennsylvania's Wharton School of Finance. In 1946, while still in their early 20s, Henry and Richard teamed up and formed in their hometown a business services company called United Business. They offered bookkeeping, collections, advertising, and other forms of assistance to local businesses. Tax preparation was one of those services, but the Bloch brothers considered it so marginal that they offered it free of charge to their customers. Within eight years, they were running the largest bookkeeping firm in Kansas City. They also made a sideline out of preparing individual tax returns for people who worked in the building in which they were headquartered.

Preparing individual returns might have remained a mere sideline if the Internal Revenue Service (IRS) had not stopped offering such assistance to the public in 1955. Ironically, Henry and Richard Bloch wanted to get out of that line of work at the time, feeling that it was distracting them from their core operations for little profit. One of their individual clients, an advertising salesman for the Kansas City Star named John White, persuaded them to give tax preparation more of a try—

COMPANY PERSPECTIVES

H&R Block's Values: Client Focused. We are passionate about helping clients. Their success is a key measure of our success. Integrity. We are honest and ethical in everything we do. Excellence. We take pride in doing our best in everything we do. We embrace change to learn and grow. Respect. We treat each other with respect and dignity, recognizing that innovation springs from unique perspectives. Teamwork. Everyone's collaboration and full participation make us stronger and allow us to serve clients better.

and to take out two advertisements in his newspaper. On the first day that the ads ran, the Blochs found their office flooded with customers.

Thirty-two years later, Henry Bloch would recall: "I can distinctly remember thinking, 'This tax thing is tremendous—it is really going to help our accounting business, what with the advertising and the referrals and all.' But it had the opposite effect. ... Because my brother and I began devoting so much of our time and energies to the tax side, we didn't give our business clients the type of service they wanted. ... We found that they were quitting on us."

Therefore, the Bloch brothers divested their accounting business by selling it to their employees. They reincorporated in 1955, setting up shop under the H&R Block name, and devoted themselves to preparing tax returns for the "little guy" full-time. The Bloch brothers also chose to deliberately misspell their last name in christening their new venture. Two similar, though distinct, reasons for why they did this have been given. According to one story they dropped the "h" in favor of the more phonetic "k" to make sure people would not mispronounce the name; in another, they simply assumed that people would misspell it phonetically anyway.

However they felt about the new company's name, customers were quick to pony up for its services. In its first year H&R Block generated $20,000 in revenues, enough to pique the Blochs' interest in expansion. In 1956 they opened seven storefront offices in New York City to see if they could duplicate their success. These new offices generated $67,000 in revenues in their first year, but the Bloch brothers grew homesick for Kansas City and did not want to stay in the Big Apple or shuttle between the two cities to keep tabs on business in both. Anxious to sell, they agreed to hand over their New

York operations to two local accountants for only $10,000 and a percentage of future revenues. For that, H&R Block would be hailed as a pioneer in franchising, even though, as Henry Bloch later admitted, the company more or less backed into it. "When we first franchised," he said, "we didn't even know what the word meant."

The company's first experience in franchising also would turn out to be an unhappy one. Concerned by unscrupulous practices on the part of the New York franchisees, H&R Block would initiate legal action against them in 1964, charging violation of the company's pricing and advertising arrangements. The two parties settled out of court in 1966, and as a result H&R Block bought back the franchises for more than $1 million.

DAZZLING GROWTH

More immediately, however, the New York experiment proved to the Bloch brothers that tax preparation would be a viable business outside of their hometown. In 1957 H&R Block opened offices in Topeka and in Columbia, Missouri. The next year, it added offices in Des Moines, Oklahoma City, and Little Rock. From there, the company grew at a dazzling rate. It went public in 1962, and by 1967 it could boast of having nearly 1,700 offices in 1,000 cities in 44 states. During the 1967 tax season H&R Block estimated that it would prepare a total of 2.5 million tax returns by the April 15th filing deadline. The company operated only 35 percent of these offices itself; the rest were franchised. At first, franchises were granted for a mere two percent of gross receipts. "We didn't sell franchises; we gave them away," Henry Bloch would later recall. "An employee would come in and ask us to help him open an H&R Block office in Chicago or Detroit or someplace. We gave him a little spending money and loaned him enough to rent a store and buy some desks. These guys were on their own, and in almost every case they have become wealthy men." In the 1960s, however, H&R Block wised up and raised its price to ten percent, then about 30 percent of gross receipts.

Of course, the company needed legions of trained personnel to keep up with such rapid expansion. In many respects, this proved to be a more substantial problem than drawing customers. To cope with it, H&R Block set up its own training program, which operated more or less as a trade school for tax preparers. In exchange for a small fee, trainees would enroll in an eight-week course taught by company managers. At the conclusion of the course, trainees might receive employment with the company, but they were also free to work for competitors or use their expertise on their own

KEY DATES

1946: Henry and Richard Bloch form a business services company called United Business.

1955: The brothers reincorporate under the H&R Block name.

1962: The company goes public.

1967: By now, there are 1,700 H&R Block offices in 1,000 cities in 44 states.

1972: H&R Block opens outlets in 147 Sears department stores.

1978: Personnel Pool of America, a temporary personnel agency specializing in health care, is acquired for $22.5 million.

1980: The company purchases CompuServe.

1986: The IRS begins to allow electronic filing of tax returns.

1996: CompuServe is spun off.

1997: Option One Mortgage Corporation is acquired.

1998: H&R Block launches HRB Business Services, a national accounting and consulting business.

1999: Olde Financial Corp. and McGladrey & Pullen LLP are purchased.

2001: The company pays $21 million to settle an old fraud lawsuit brought against Olde Financial.

2004: The NASD charges the company with fraud related to the sale of Enron Corp. bonds.

2006: Accounting errors force H&R Block to restate earnings from the previous two years.

returns. In 1967, for instance, more than 10,000 students enrolled in H&R Block's tax school, but less than half of them went to work for the company at the conclusion of the course. Even so, H&R Block gained 5,000 new employees to staff its storefronts that year.

The tax preparers themselves were and still are seasonal employees, the demand for their services being limited to the first four months of the year. Many of them are housewives, retirees, or people with day jobs looking for a second source of income. In recent years, the company has drawn many working mothers, who like the flexible hours that come with the job. Despite the seasonal nature of the job, most of them return the next year for another round of grappling with the IRS. In 1987 Henry Bloch stated that 75 percent of the company's preparers come back the following year, no

doubt because the company rewards its veterans with higher commission rates.

With a virtual headlock on its market, no capital costs except for the leases on its storefront offices and a few dollars for furniture and coffee, and labor costs limited to a fixed percentage of revenues, H&R Block proved wildly successful in the 1960s. In an average year, profits increased by 50 percent over the previous year. In 1969 and 1971, however, changes in the federal tax code reduced the overall number of taxpayers, thus shrinking the company's customer base. Even worse, in 1972 the IRS went to war against tax preparation firms. It cracked down on fraudulent preparers, resumed helping taxpayers prepare their returns, and launched a massive advertising campaign encouraging them not to use commercial preparation services. The IRS campaign, aided by the press, succeeded in tarring legitimate preparation services like H&R Block as well as dishonest ones. That year, the company's profits fell for the first time in its history.

SOLIDIFYING THE COMPANY'S POSITION AND ACCUMULATING CASH RESERVES

The IRS campaign eventually collapsed after some public relations debacles of its own. After IRS Commissioner Johnnie Walters declared that the 1040 form was so simple a fifth-grader could complete it, his claim was subjected to various acts of scrutiny that proved it was far more complex than that. An experiment conducted by the Wall Street Journal also suggested that the IRS's preparers were no more reliable than most commercial services. H&R Block not only weathered the firestorm but came out of it in better shape than before, because the IRS's crusade had weeded out its weaker competitors. It was, in fact, the only profitable tax preparation firm of consequential size left in the nation. H&R Block solidified its overwhelming position in 1972 when it opened outlets in 147 Sears department stores—an entirely appropriate move for a company that Richard Bloch once had described as "the Sears, Roebuck of taxes."

Once the crisis had passed, the company found itself faced with a happy dilemma, one that the Bloch brothers had begun to contemplate in the late 1960s. Because its capital costs were so small for a business of its size, and because most of its revenues came in the form of cash, H&R Block had been able to accumulate vast cash reserves. It also found itself unburdened by long-term debt. Because the tax preparation business seemed ready to mature and slow its rate of growth, it was only logical that the company should diversify through acquisition to keep its revenues pumped up.

H&R Block spent most of the 1970s searching for likely acquisition targets, but it was limited by a lack of companies that were both available and potentially profitable as well as by Henry Bloch's reluctance to pull the trigger. "A guy told me that two out of three acquisitions fail," he said in 1974. "I just don't want to make a mistake the first time out."

DIVERSIFICATION AND ACQUISITION

H&R Block finally took its first major plunge in 1978, when it acquired Personnel Pool of America, a temporary personnel agency specializing in health care, for $22.5 million. The move seemed to make sense, as H&R Block already had some expertise regarding temporary personnel; after all, the core of its work force at the time was made up of temps. Indeed, the acquisition worked out well: In two years, Personnel Pool of America jumped from the sixth largest to the third largest company in the temporary help field.

The 1980 acquisition of CompuServe also proved quite successful. H&R Block paid $23 million for the information services company, which provided computer time-sharing for corporations and government agencies. Soon after it was acquired by H&R Block, however, CompuServe entered the burgeoning field of providing information services such as software forums, electronic bulletin boards, electronic mail, and interactive games for personal computer users. In doing so, it made its new parent company look positively brilliant. CompuServe's earnings tripled between 1983 and 1985, and its subscriber base quadrupled. It was growing so fast that CompuServe chairman and cofounder Jeffrey Wilkins resigned in 1985 when H&R Block refused to allow him and some of his managers to purchase CompuServe stock. Wilkins subsequently headed an investor group that offered to buy CompuServe for $72.5 million, but H&R Block refused to sell. Wilkins's departure may have seemed like a setback to H&R Block, which considered it wise to keep its acquisitions' existing management teams intact, but CompuServe continued to grow without him. In the early 1990s it was the largest commercial online service, with one million subscribers.

Also in 1980, the Bloch brothers entered into a joint venture with Ohio attorney and entrepreneur (as well as son-in-law of U.S. Senator Howard Metzenbaum) Joel Hyatt, who wanted to set up his own chain of discount law offices patterned after the Los Angeles-based firm of Jacoby & Myers. Hyatt's idea was to tap into the same middle-income market for basic legal services, but to stake out his own geographic territory before Jacoby & Myers could expand beyond its California base. He had opened nine offices between 1977 and 1980, when H&R Block approached him with the idea of partnership. For Hyatt, such a deal would provide him with the capital he needed for rapid and widespread expansion. The two parties set up a separate company called Block Management to operate Hyatt Legal Services to comply with American Bar Association rules forbidding anyone but lawyers to directly own a law firm. H&R Block took an 80 percent stake in the company, with Hyatt and his other partners taking the remaining 20 percent.

Both parties in this deal hoped that H&R Block's marketing resources would boost Hyatt Legal Services past archrival Jacoby & Myers. Before long, however, they realized that the synergies they had expected to create between tax preparation and legal services simply were not happening. In 1987 H&R Block sold its interest in Block Management to Joel Hyatt for $20 million in what was described as a friendly parting of ways.

The 1985 acquisition of Path Management Industries, a business seminar company, also proved that, for all of Henry Bloch's prudence, H&R Block's touch was not always golden when it came to acquisitions. The 1988 postal rate increase hurt Path Management by hiking the cost of its direct mail advertising, and the recession of the late 1980s depressed sales. Having paid $35 million for the company, H&R Block sold it to the American Management Association in 1990 for $20 million.

In the meantime, Richard Bloch had become less involved with the running of the company after he was diagnosed with lung cancer in 1978. Bloch battled his illness successfully, but after his recovery he devoted much of his time to sponsoring cancer research and treatment. He retired in the early 1980s and died in 2004. As the father reached retirement, Henry's son Thomas M. Bloch began to work his way up through the ranks. Thomas M. Bloch became president and COO in 1988, and in 1992 he succeeded his father as CEO. Henry Bloch remained as chairman.

Of course, the business of preparing tax returns remained profitable for the company. Tax preparation did in fact represent a mature line of business for H&R Block in the 1980s, and the company's rapid diversification reduced its contribution to the overall bottom line to just more than half of total earnings by the decade's end. When the IRS began allowing electronic filing of tax returns in 1986, it opened up a brand new opportunity for H&R Block. The opportunity to receive an early refund inspired many who prepared their own returns to come to H&R Block to file electronically. Providing the service was relatively easy for the company, because it used CompuServe's existing communications links to transmit the returns through cyberspace. H&R Block also began offering advances on refunds, or refund anticipation loans (RALs), through agreements with several different banks. In return for a service charge, a participating bank would loan the amount of the refund to an H&R Block client, accepting direct deposit of the refund check as repayment. Electronic filing gave the company's core business a needed boost; within five years it was handling an annual volume of 4.3 million electronic returns—nearly two-thirds of all returns filed electronically.

MORE ACQUISITIONS, DIVESTITURES, AND REFOCUSING

For all the adventures that it encountered in the 1980s, H&R Block entered the 1990s still in the market for acquisitions. In 1991 it purchased Interim Systems, a temporary personnel agency, for $49.5 million and merged its assets with those of Personnel Pool of America. The resulting merged subsidiary then was renamed Interim Services. Interim Services was spun off in January 1994 through an initial public offering (IPO). Net proceeds to H&R Block were $200 million, with an additional $28 million going to Interim. Block sold its interest in the temporary staffing firm to focus on its tax preparation and computer information service businesses.

With $400 million earmarked for further acquisitions, the company had three main businesses. For 1991 its tax preparation service accounted for $700 million in revenue, its temporary personnel company Interim Services had $385 million in revenue, and CompuServe brought in another $280 million. H&R Block entered the personal financial software market in late 1993 with the purchase of MECA Software, which was best known for its "Managing Your Money" program. Block decided, however, to sell MECA in March 1995 for $35,000, while retaining the right to publish tax preparation software under the name TaxCut. By 1998 its subsidiary, Block Financial Corporation, was the second largest publisher of personal financial software, with record sales of Kiplinger TaxCut, as more people were using their computer and the Internet to prepare their own tax returns.

In April 1994 Thomas M. Bloch resigned as CEO of H&R Block. He wanted to spend more time with his family and teach at an inner city school. In September 1995 Richard H. Brown, former vice-chairman of telecommunications company Ameritech, was named president and CEO of H&R Block to succeed Thomas M. Bloch. He became the first nonfamily member to head the firm. Brown, with his high-tech background

and interest in investing more in CompuServe, lasted less than a year. In April 1996 H&R Block spun off CompuServe with an IPO of 18.4 million shares that raised barely more than $500,000 and reduced H&R Block's ownership to 80 percent.

SERIES OF STRATEGIC ACQUISITIONS

In June 1996 Frank Salizzoni, formerly president and chief operating officer of USAir Group, Inc., was named CEO and president of H&R Block. Salizzoni's plan was to transform the company into an integrated financial services business offering not only tax preparation help, but also such services as mortgage loans, financial planning, and investment advisory services. Over the next two and one-half years Block acquired two of its franchises and 251 independent tax preparation firms as well as mortgage businesses and a string of accounting firms. As a result of acquisitions, the company's total assets increased from $1.7 billion in 1997 to $2.9 billion in 1998.

In June 1997 H&R Block acquired the California-based firm Option One Mortgage Corporation, which controlled more than 5,000 mortgage brokers in 46 states. During 1997 H&R Block launched its mortgage service, H&R Block Mortgage Company, on a trial basis in 31 offices in four states. The mortgage service began by selling only second mortgage loans, then it introduced new mortgage products at offices in 15 states. As a result, H&R Block Mortgage Company accounted for $135.8 million of the company's 1998 revenues of $1.307 billion, or slightly more than ten percent. In February 1999 the company acquired Assurance Mortgage Corp. of America to further enhance its mortgage-related product offerings.

During the 1997-98 tax season H&R Block experimented with offering a wider range of financial services, including auto insurance, mortgages, and investment advice. It had 14 "premium" offices that featured enclosed offices rather than cubicles and sold mutual funds, annuities, stocks, and bonds. Some 30 offices also sold mortgages. Throughout 1998 and early 1999 the company opened prototype financial planning centers on a trial basis. These centers included investment advisors and mortgage representatives in addition to tax preparers. The company also tested a telemarketing approach to sell other financial products to its tax service customers though telemarketing call centers located in Florida and California.

In January 1998 the company divested CompuServe, selling its 80 percent interest to Internet access provider WorldCom Inc. in a stock-for-stock transaction valued at about $1.3 billion. Following the transaction, World-Com sold CompuServe's online service and 2.6 million subscriber base to America Online (AOL) in exchange for AOL's ANS Communication division, which provided Internet access mainly for large businesses. AOL also committed to make WorldCom its largest network access provider.

As part of its strategy to provide a fuller range of financial services, H&R Block launched HRB Business Services, a national accounting and consulting business, in 1998. It had acquired several CPA firms during the year, including the Kansas City-based Donnelly Meiners Jordan Kline, Chicago-based Friedman Eisenstein Raemer & Schwartz and three of its affiliates, and Katz Sapper & Miller of Indianapolis. A fourth firm, Sigman Page & Curry, merged with Donnelly Meiners in September 1998, and two more firms were acquired by the end of the year. HRB Business Services was headed by Terrence E. Putney, the former president of Donnelly Meiners.

Block's strategy was to acquire CPA firms to strengthen its position in the tax preparation market. The addition of CPA firms was intended to attract more high-income individuals who would normally seek out their own CPA firm. One analyst estimated in 1998 that CPA firms controlled about one-fourth of the tax preparation market. H&R Block's share of the tax preparation market at the end of 1998 was 13 percent, and it could increase its share by acquiring CPA firms. By mid-1999, H&R Block was in the process of acquiring Olde Discount. It also added McGladrey & Pullen LLP, a Minnesota-based accounting firm, to its holdings that year. In 2000, the company began offering a host of financial services including brokerage services, annuities, mutual funds, and IRAs through its financial centers and its Web site. Henry Bloch retired that year and became honorary chairman.

Without a doubt, the business odyssey of the Bloch brothers was an astoundingly successful one. Richard Bloch once compared his company to Sears, and a journalist once called it "the McDonald's of tax preparation"; the fact that neither analogy seems absurd is a testament to H&R Block's standing in its part of the service economy. All three of these companies have dominated their respective markets so thoroughly that they have not only become synonymous in the public mind with what they sell, but their names have entered the annals of American popular culture.

It is also impressive that the company managed to maintain a steep earnings curve. A $10,000 investment in H&R Block stock when the company went public in 1962 would have been worth $12.3 million in 1992. In 30 years the stock had split 120:1, dividends and

revenues had increased every year, and earnings rose every year except one. With the company focused on becoming a provider of diversified financial services for an expanding market, H&R Block was expected to continue its stability and growth into the next century.

PROBLEMS IN THE NEW MILLENNIUM

Despite the company's longstanding record of success, the next chapter in H&R Block's history proved to be quite challenging and potentially damaging to its public image. Lawsuits filed by New York's Attorney General, the NASD, and by angry consumers threatened to tarnish H&R Block's good name. To make matters worse, accounting errors forced the financial services firm to restate its earnings for 2004, 2005, and part of 2006.

In 2001, the company shelled out $21 million to settle an old fraud lawsuit that had been filed against Olde Financial. Two years later, the NASD charged an H&R Block subsidiary with fraud in the sale of $16.4 million worth of Enron Corp. bonds between October 29, 2001 and November 27, 2001—Enron filed for bankruptcy on December 2, 2001. The suit claimed that the company's brokers received extra incentive for selling the bonds but failed to disclose the risks involved with buying the bonds. At the same time, the company was fending off lawsuits related to its refund anticipation loan (RAL) program. The suits claimed the company charged exorbitant interest rates for providing customers with early tax refunds.

By now, Mark A. Ernst—who was named president and CEO in 2001—faced an uphill battle. The company's financial advisors business segment had lost $330 million since its inception and its once stellar mortgage unit was experiencing a sharp decline in earnings as a result of interest rate increases. To make matters worse, the company's core tax business was losing customers. In fact, from 2003 to 2005, H&R Block lost more than one million clients due in part to long lines and wait times exceeding two or three hours at its tax preparation offices. To add insult to injury, H&R Block was forced to restate earnings for 2004, 2005, and part of 2006 due to miscalculations in its own state income taxes. Then in 2006, New York Attorney General Eliot Spitzer filed suit against H&R Block claiming the company sold individual retirement accounts (IRAs) that earned less money than what customers were charged in fees. The company denied the charges and planned to fight them in court.

The company celebrated its 50th anniversary in 2005 even as its share price plummeted. Despite the problems it faced related to the aforementioned lawsuits and increased competition brought on by the likes of Jackson Hewitt Tax Service Inc. and Liberty Tax Service, H&R Block remained dedicated to expanding the number of its U.S. offices. In 2005, the company opened over 600 company-owned offices, nearly 450 co-locations with partners including Wal-Mart and Sears, and 150 new franchise locations. While the company's foray into financial services had yet to pay off in the long-term, H&R Block remained optimistic about its success in the future.

Douglas Sun
Updated, David Bianco; Christina M. Stansell

PRINCIPAL SUBSIDIARIES

H&R Block Group Inc.; HRB Management, Inc.; H&R Block Tax and Financial Services Limited; Companion Insurance, Ltd.; H&R Block Services, Inc.; H&R Block Tax Services, Inc.; HRB Partners, Inc.; HRB Texas Enterprises, Inc.; H&R Block and Associates, L.P.; H&R Block Canada, Inc.; Financial Stop, Inc.; H&R Block Canada Financial Services, Inc.; H&R Block Enterprises, Inc.; H&R Block Eastern Enterprises, Inc.; The Tax Man, Inc.; HRB Royalty, Inc.; H&R Block Ltd.; West Estate Investors, LLC; H&R Block Global Solutions (Hong Kong) Ltd.; Black Orchard Financial, Inc.; H&R Block Tax and Business Services, Inc.; H&R Block Tax Institute, LLC; Block Financial Corporation; Option One Mortgage Corporation; Option One Mortgage Acceptance Corporation; Option One Mortgage Securities Corporation; Option One Mortgage Securities II Corp.; Premier Trust Deed Services, Inc.; Premier Mortgage Services of Washington, Inc.; H&R Block Mortgage Corporation; Option One Insurance Agency, Inc.; Woodbridge Mortgage Acceptance Corporation; Option One Loan Warehouse Corporation; Option One Advance Corporation; AcuLink Mortgage Solutions, LLC; AcuLink of Alabama, LLC; Option One Mortgage Corporation (India) Pvt Ltd; Companion Mortgage Corporation; Franchise Partner, Inc.; HRB Financial Corporation; H&R Block Financial Advisors, Inc.; OLDE Discount of Canada; H&R Block Insurance Agency of Massachusetts, Inc.; HRB Property Corporation; HRB Realty Corporation; 4230 West Green Oaks, Inc.; Financial Marketing Services, Inc.; 2430472 Nova Scotia Co.; H&R Block Digital Tax Solutions, LLC; TaxNet Inc.; H&R Block Bank; BFC Transactions, Inc.; RSM McGladrey Business Services, Inc.; RSM McGladrey, Inc.; RSM McGladrey Financial Process Outsourcing, L.L.C.; RSM McGladrey Financial Process Outsourcing India Pvt. Ltd.; Birchtree Financial Services, Inc.; Birchtree Insurance Agency, Inc.; Pension Resources, Inc.; FM Business Services, Inc.; O'Rourke Career Connections, LLC; Credit Union Jobs, LLC; RSM McGladrey TBS, LLC; PDI Global, Inc.; RSM Equico, Inc.; RSM Equico Capital Markets, LLC; Equico, Inc.; Equico Europe Ltd.; RSM Equico Canada, Inc.; RSM McGladrey Business Solutions, Inc.; RSM McGladrey Insurance Services, Inc.; PWR Insurance Services, Inc.; RSM McGladrey Employer Services, Inc.; RSM Employer Services Agency, Inc.; RSM Employer Services Agency of Florida, Inc.

PRINCIPAL COMPETITORS

Intuit Inc.; Jackson Hewitt Tax Service Inc.; Liberty Tax Service.

FURTHER READING

Butcher, Lola, "$400 Million in Hand, Block Hunts Deals," *Kansas City Business Journal*, September 4, 1992, p. 1.

Demery, Paul, "New Directions for H&R Block?," *Practical Accountant*, September 1995, p. 12.

Ellis, James E., "H&R Block Expands Its Base," *Business Week*, April 29, 1991.

Epper, Karen, "Block's Exit from Personal Finance Software Underscores Intense Competition in the Field," *American Banker*, April 6, 1995, p. 1.

"H&R Block Enters the Fray; AmEx Continues Acquisitions," *Practical Accountant*, July 1998, p. 8.

Hallinan, Joseph T., "NASD Charges H&R Block Unit," *Wall Street Journal*, November 9, 2004, p. C5.

Hallinan, Joseph T., and Paul Davies, "H&R Block Sued Over Fee Disclosure," *Wall Street Journal*, March 16, 2006, p. D1.

Hayes, David, "H&R Block Looks Ahead To Expand Financial Services," *Knight-Ridder/Tribune Business News*, September 11, 1997.

"A Jewel's Lost Luster," *Forbes*, March 24, 1997, p. 16.

Johnston, David Cay, "H&R Block's Risky Stab at Synergy," *New York Times*, September 19, 1999.

Karp, Richard, "The Bewilderment of Henry Bloch," *Dun's Review*, September 1974.

Mannes, George, "One of Three Firms May Buy Ailing CompuServe," *Knight-Ridder/Tribune Business News*, September 5, 1997.

Nicolova, Rossitsa, "Block Acquisitions Promote Goals," *Kansas City Business Journal*, December 25, 1998, p. 10.

——, "Block's CPA Empire Growing," *Kansas City Business Journal*, December 11, 1998, p. 1.

Palmeri, Christopher, "Watch Out, Merrill Lynch," *Forbes*, May 4, 1998, p. 45.

Norris, Floyd, "H&R Block Fumbles on its Own Tax Return," *New York Times*, February 25, 2006.

Phillips, Dana, "Interim Share Price Stays Up After January IPO," *South Florida Business Journal*, February 18, 1994, p. 19.

Razzi, Elizabeth, "This Job Is Less Taxing," *Kiplinger's Personal Finance Magazine*, February 1997, p. 134.

Serres, Christopher, "H&R Block's Venture Passing Test," *Crain's Cleveland Business*, August 10, 1998, p. 3.

Silverman, Robin, and Christine Riccelli, "Henry W. Bloch," *Ingram's*, September 1990, p. 27.

Stires, David, "Taxing Times at H&R Block," *Fortune*, March 21, 2005, p. 181.

Stodghill, Ron, II, "Tom Bloch's No. 1 Reason for Leaving the Field," *Business Week*, June 26, 1995, p. 127.

"Storefront Tax Service Earns a Good Return," *Business Week*, March 25, 1967.

"Taxman Henry Bloch," *Inc.*, December 1987.

Timmons, Heather, "H&R Block Still Hoping To Unlock Treasure Chest of Customers," *American Banker*, April 19, 1999, p. 23.

Wasserman, Elizabeth, "WorldCom Deal Brings Change to America Online as Well as CompuServe," *Knight-Ridder/Tribune Business News*, September 9, 1997.

Hampshire Group Ltd.

1924 Pearman Dairy Road
Anderson, South Carolina 29625-1303
U.S.A.
Telephone: (864) 231-1200
Fax: (864) 231-1201
Web site: http://www.hamp.com

Public Company
Incorporated: 1977
Employees: 370
Sales: $324 million (2005)
Stock Exchanges: NASDAQ
Ticker Symbol: HAMP
NAIC: 315191 Outerwear Knitting Mills

■ ■ ■

Hampshire Group Ltd. is an Anderson, South Carolina-based apparel company and North America's largest designer and marketer of branded and private-label men's and women's sweaters, which are manufactured mostly in Asia. The company also offers women's woven and knit related separates.

Hampshire divides its business among five operating divisions within its Hampshire Designers, Inc., subsidiary. The Women's Divisions produces sweaters under several labels: Designers Originals, Hampshire Studio, Babe, D.O., and Mercer Street Studio. Sweater brands of the Men's Divisions include Hampshire Brands, Geoffrey Beene, Dockers, Levis, Nick Danger, and Spring & Mercer. Hampshire's David Brooks Division produces women's sweaters, jackets, knits, wovens,

and bottoms in a category the company calls "better casual sportswear" or "country club chic," which it sells to specialty stores. At the other end of the market, the Shane Hunter division sells juniors' apparel to the mass market under the Aqua-Blues label as well as private labels. Finally, the Item-Eyes, Inc., Division designs and markets women's sweaters, shirts, pants, and blazers, sold under the RQT by Requirements, Requirements, and Nouveaux labels, and customer private labels.

Hampshire is a public company listed on the NASDAQ, and is 25-percent owned by its long-time chairman and chief executive officer, Ludwig G. Kuttner, who in 2006 was placed on administrative leave along with others at the company while an audit committee investigated allegations of misuse and misappropriations of assets for personal benefit.

COMPANY INCORPORATED: 1977

Hampshire was formed in South Carolina and incorporated in Delaware in 1977, the result of a merger between a hosiery company and a sweater company. The latter launched the Designers Originals label in 1956 in order to sell acrylic sweaters to the mass market. The divergent businesses were operated through a pair of subsidiaries: Hampshire Designers, located in Anderson, South Carolina, to produce sweaters; and Hampshire Hosiery, located in Spruce Pine, North Carolina, to manufacture pantyhose, tights, stockings, and thigh-high and knee-high stockings. A predecessor company had been engaged in hosiery manufacturing since 1917. Two years after Hampshire Group was founded, Kuttner became chairman and ran the business from offices in

New York City. Born in Munich, West Germany, in August 1946, he grew up in postwar Europe, earning a college degree from the University of Reyensburg before coming to the United States. His father, Dr. Ludwig Kuttner, owned Kuttner NAK Prints, Inc., a Lyndhurst, New Jersey-based fashion fabric printer that provided heat transfer prints for junior apparel and sportswear.

By 1987 Hampshire Group was a $100 million business, split equally between the hosiery and sweater units. Over the next four years, the company built up its hosiery assets while overall sales tailed off. In 1989 it spent nearly $2 million to add the production assets of hosiery company Trend Industries. Then, in February 1991, Hampshire acquired Belmont, North Carolina-based Vision Hosiery Mills, which made Christian Dior hosiery under a licensing agreement and did about $12 million in overall sales. Vision Hosiery became a third division for Hampshire Group. Its purchase was part of a strategy to sell higher-priced merchandise, items that retailed for $100 or more. In order to offer such high-end sweaters, Hampshire acquired five specialized knitting machines that could produce intricate patterns using lamb's wool, cashmere, and other expensive yarns, becoming the only North American sweater manufacturer to own this kind of equipment. At this stage in the company's history, however, hosiery accounted for most (54.4 percent) of Hampshire's $87.2 million in revenues in 1991. The addition of Vision Hosiery was the difference, the new unit by itself contributing 14.4 percent of sales.

IPO: 1992

In 1992 Kuttner took Hampshire public. With the investment banking firm of Legg Mason serving as book manager, Hampshire completed an initial public offering of stock in June 1992. The company hoped to receive $12 to $14 a share, but in the end had to settle for $9.50 a share. As a result, Hampshire netted about $8.3 million. The money was earmarked primarily to reduce debt, but some was also kept as working capital. About a week after the offering, Kuttner stepped down as Hampshire's chief executive, while remaining in New York to act as chairman. He was succeeded by Richard Owczarzak, a 20-year veteran of the apparel business,

who worked out of the company's Charlotte, North Carolina, offices. His tenure at the helm would be brief, however, as Kuttner soon took back the CEO post.

Sweaters became more important to Hampshire in 1993 when hosiery sales slumped due to softening demand, while Hampshire Designers was enjoying a record year. In response to conditions, Hampshire consolidated its hosiery operations, closing a finishing plant in Belmont, North Carolina, and another facility in Concord, North Carolina. The work done at these locations was moved to Hampshire's three other hosiery plants. The company pursued a private-label strategy, producing hosiery for mass merchants, chains, and high-end customers under their private labels.

Hampshire's sweater business, in the meantime, was not overly diversified and was mostly limited to two product lines: women's branded acrylic sweaters, a market that had matured and offered little opportunity for growth, and high-quality cotton sweaters sold through mail order channels. All were manufactured in the United States and Hampshire's only significant brand was Designers Original. Moreover, retailers were looking to buy from fewer and larger suppliers. All these factors essentially forced Hampshire to diversify its sweater segment in an effort to become something of a one-stop shop, capable of filling a customers' complete sweater needs, both men's and women's and at all price tiers. This effort would also require the company to expand Hampshire's manufacturing capabilities beyond the United States and embrace global sourcing.

In early 1994 Hampshire completed the $3.2 million purchase of San Francisco Knitworks, taking Hampshire into the men's and women's better sweater business. The new unit produced sweaters for designers Calvin Klein, Donna Karan, and Anne Klein. Despite the added business, revenues continued to dip to $83.6 million in 1994. In 1995 Hampshire began an effort to diversify beyond sweaters. Early in the year it acquired Seque, Ltd., maker of upper-moderate and better-price sweaters as well as women's blazers, blouses, skirts, and pants. The company had offices in New York and Hong Kong and generated annual sales in the neighborhood of $10 million. Later in 1995 Hampshire added designer Mary Jane Marcasiano and her signature line of knitwear to the fold, and added such high-end accounts as Barney's New York, Bergdorf Goodman, Saks Fifth Avenue, and Bloomingdale's. Also, in October 1995, Hampshire acquired The Winona Knitting Mills, Inc., of Winona, Minnesota. Founded in 1943, Winona did about $30 million in business each year in men's sweaters, mostly the result of private-label work for the likes of Woolrich, Lands' End, and L.L. Bean. It also produced men's sweaters under the Landscape, The Lake Harmony

```
┌─────────────────────────────────────────┐
│                                         │
│          KEY DATES                      │
│              ■                          │
│  ┌───────────────────────────────────┐  │
│  │ 1977: The company is incorporated │  │
│  │       as a hosiery and sweater    │  │
│  │       company.                    │  │
│  │ 1992: Hampshire Group is taken    │  │
│  │       public.                     │  │
│  │ 1995: Segue, Ltd. is acquired.    │  │
│  │ 1999: The hosiery business is     │  │
│  │       sold.                       │  │
│  │ 2000: Hampshire's manufacturing   │  │
│  │       plants are sold.            │  │
│  │ 2005: The company acquires the    │  │
│  │       David Brooks label.         │  │
│  └───────────────────────────────────┘  │
└─────────────────────────────────────────┘
```

Rowing Club, Berwick, and American Portrait brands. In 1997 Hampshire added another well known brand, Geoffrey Beene, to its men's sweater line.

As a result of its acquisition spree, Hampshire experienced a sharp rise in net sales, which reached $112.5 million in 1995 and $148.3 million in 1996. Net income also increased to $6.7 million in 1995 and approached $12 million in 1996 when Hampshire sold more than 10 million sweaters. Sweater sales in 1996 accounted for $117.6 million while hosiery sales totaled just $30.7 million. This disparity grew even wider in 1997 when sweater sales increased to $140.8 million and hosiery sales slipped further to $23.6 million for net sales of $164.4 million. Also of note, in 1997 Hampshire looked to gain further diversity in its business by forming Hampshire Investments, Limited. In the first year the venture invested about $8 million in publicly traded apparel and textile companies, as well as real estate, entertainment, industrial, and service businesses—areas that Kuttner had been investing in personally for the previous 25 years.

Hampshire faced strong competition in the sweater field in 1998, but its diversified offerings helped it to increase sales to $168.7 million and stave off a significant erosion in earnings. For the year, Hampshire netted $5.7 million. The Mary Jane Marcasiano label performed poorly enough that the company elected to sell it in 1998. Hampshire Investments made further investments in 1998, the value of which increased to $15.5 million, split 60 percent real property and 40 percent stock. The hosiery business, by this point, was no longer a core business and the Hampshire took steps to sell it to a management team. The buyout was completed in June 1999.

Poor market conditions continued in 1999. One bright spot was the signing of a license agreement with Levi Strauss & Co. to produce and market men's sweaters under the highly popular Dockers label. By this point

about half of Hampshire's sweaters were produced overseas. Due primarily to a significant drop in the sale of men's non-branded sweaters, Hampshire experienced a drop in net sales to $151.3 million in 1999, while earnings dipped below $5.2 million.

FACTORIES SOLD: 2000

Hampshire took the next step in its development in 2000 when it sold all of its manufacturing plants in favor of a worldwide sourcing network. The company also achieved greater diversity in 2000 by acquiring Item-Eyes, Inc., for $18.5 million. Item-Eyes added a broad line of women's coordinated sportswear, $100 million in sales, and major department stores accounts, such as Macy's and J.C. Penney Co. Hampshire added further breadth to its sweater lines in 2001 by signing licensing agreements with Levi Strauss and VF Corp. to produce and market men's sweaters under the Levi's, Wrangler, Wrangler Hero, and Timber Creek labels, and women's sweaters under the Dockers and Riders labels. As a result of these changes, Hampshire grew sales to $196.9 million in 2000 and to $263.5 million in 2001, while net income improved to $8.5 million in 2000 and $11.1 million in 2001.

With the apparel business doing so well, Hampshire Investments was no longer deemed an important factor in the company's business, and in 2003 it was sold to a management group. Hampshire devoted all of its attention to further growing its sweater and other apparel lines. In 2003 the company launched a new men's sweater collection, Spring + Mercer, an allusion to a pair of intersecting streets in New York City's trendy SoHo neighborhood. The line offered luxurious and fashionable, yet affordable, sweaters. The Nick Danger line of men's sweaters followed in 2004. Nick Danger was intended to be a casual wear design brand that could include other apparel.

Revenues topped $300 million and net income totaled $13.7 million in 2004. Hampshire focused attention on its women's offerings, especially in the upper end of the market. The David Brooks "country club chic" clothing line was acquired in 2005 to form its own division. Then, in 2006, the Marisa Christina brand was purchased for $4.8 million. An $18 million company, Marisa Christina offered a lifestyle apparel collection that appealed to a younger demographic than Hampshire's other lines. It was sold in specialty stores and upscale department stores. Hampshire also sought to appeal to younger customers by acquiring San Francisco-based Shane Hunter, Inc., which sold junior's apparel to mass merchant retailers, including Target and Mervyn's.

Hampshire was enjoying strong growth, with sales

reaching $324 million and net income to $12.8 million in 2005, but the company would also have to contend with controversy in June 2006. The company announced that a probe would be launched by an audit committee and the board of directors to investigate claims connected to the misappropriation of assets for personal benefit, certain related party transactions, tax reporting, internal control deficiencies, and the reporting and accounting of expense reimbursements. Until the matter had been fully examined, Kuttner was placed on administrative leave, as was the chief accounting officer, the former chief financial officer who now served as treasurer, and two personal assistants. The head of the Hampshire Designers unit, Michael Culang, took over as Hampshire's interim CEO.

Ed Dinger

PRINCIPAL DIVISIONS

Women's Divisions; Men's Divisions; David Brooks Divisions; Shane Hunter Divisions; Item-Eyes, Inc.

PRINCIPAL COMPETITORS

Capital Mercury Apparel, Ltd.; Kellwood Company; Oxford Industries, Inc.

FURTHER READING

Greenberg, Julee, "Hampshire's Multibrand Strategy," *WWD,* May 31, 2006, p. 12.

"Hampshire Group Starts Probe," *Wall Street Journal,* June 23, 2006.

"Hampshire Plans To Go Private," *Women's Wear Daily,* February 8, 1999, p. 12.

Macintosh, Jeane, "Hampshire Goes Public," *WWD,* June 19, 1992, p. 9.

Ozzard, Janet, "Hampshire Designers Division Acquires Mary Jane Marcasiano," *Women's Wear Daily,* October 27, 1995, p. 13.

"Sweater Demand Aids Hampshire QTR," *Women's Wear Daily,* March 13, 2002, p. 7.

GO THE DISTANCE.

The Holland Group, Inc.

∎

467 Ottawa Avenue
Holland, Michigan 49423
U.S.A.
Telephone: (616) 396-6501
Fax: (616) 396-1511
Web site: http://www.thehollandgroupinc.com

Private Company
Incorporated: 1910 as Safety Release Clevis Company
Employees: 1,400
Sales: $500 million (2006 est.)
NAIC: 336399 All Other Motor Vehicle Parts Manu-facturing; 336330 Motor Vehicle Steering and Suspension Components (Except Spring) Manu-facturing

■ ■ ■

The Holland Group, Inc., is the world's leading manufacturer of truck-to trailer couplers called fifth wheels, and also makes related products like kingpins and pintle hooks; truck landing gear; truck, bus, and RV suspensions; lift gates; and roll-formed metal parts. The firm's brands include the 3500 Series, FleetMaster, and Holland Simplex fifth wheels; Holland Neway suspensions; and Holland Binkley rolled metal parts. The Holland Group has operations in Canada, Mexico, Europe, and the Far East, with most manufacturing done in the United States.

BEGINNINGS

The Holland Group traces its roots to 1910, when a company called the Safety Release Clevis Co. was

founded in Corsica, South Dakota to make plow hitches. Dutch immigrants Gerrit Den Besten, Albert Hulsebos, and Henry Ketel had invented a new hitch that featured a pressure release which broke when the plow hit a hard object, preventing injuries to the animal pulling it and damage to the equipment. Over the next decade the firm grew to about ten employees.

Safety Release Clevis soon expanded its offerings to include coupling devices for trucks and trailers, and in September of 1920 the firm moved to the largely Dutch-immigrant community of Holland, Michigan, to be closer to the auto industry. Six employees moved north to help run the company's new factory at the closed Holland City Brewery on West 10th Street. In April of 1921 the firm's name was changed to the Holland Hitch Company.

Sales fell off during the Great Depression, however, and in the early 1930s the firm went bankrupt. It was revived in 1935 by co-founder Henry Ketel and Holland businessman Henry A. Geerds, who bought out the other founders. They were able to turn the company's fortunes around, and by 1940 annual revenues had grown to $1 million and employment to 86. Holland Hitch's product line included plow hitches, heavy truck fifth wheels, and pintle hooks for attaching trailers.

SHIFT TO TRUCK PRODUCTS DURING WORLD WAR II

The next decade saw many changes at Holland Hitch. In 1940 general manager Ketel developed a new heavy-duty pintle hook, and the U.S. government ordered 1,600 of them for military use. After the country entered

World War II late the following year, the firm ramped up production. In 1942 Holland Hitch began construction of a new factory and its workforce became unionized. By the war's end in August of 1945 the company had produced more than one million pintle hooks, as well as large numbers of truck landing gear and fifth wheels. Wartime production shifted the firm's focus away from plow hitches, and afterwards it would concentrate primarily on fifth wheels, pintle hooks, landing gear, and related equipment for the heavy trucking industry.

In the spring of 1946 Henry Geerds took over the job of general manager from Ketel. Three years later a new type of pintle hook was introduced, with the firm so busy that it needed two shifts to keep up with orders. In 1950 sales doubled again, with new 34- and 36-inch fifth wheels and plow hitches both selling strongly. The Korean War brought more military work, and in 1956 the company added a warehouse in Milpitas, California. Two years later tools and machinery were shipped from Holland and the site was converted into a manufacturing operation.

Growth continued during the early 1960s, with a Canadian subsidiary formed in 1963 to manufacture hitches in Woodstock, Ontario. The firm also added a new plant in Denmark, South Carolina, which was designated the Holland Atlantic Hitch Company.

The company expanded and modernized its facilities during the latter half of the 1960s, and in 1969 added another new plant at a nine-acre site in Holland. The firm also formed a subsidiary called the Holland Hitch Forwarding Company and opened a sales office in Germany during the year.

Holland Hitch continued to expand during the 1970s, in 1973 forming new subsidiaries Holland Hitch of New Jersey and Holland R.V.E. Ltd., which later became known as Holland Equipment, Ltd. Three years later Henry Geerds' son-in-law William F. Beebe was named president of the company. The University of Michigan graduate and decorated Navy veteran had joined the firm as head of production after World War II. In 1979 the company added a new Canadian subsidiary called Holland Hitch Western, as well as a manufacturing plant in Texas.

ACQUISITION OF HOLLAND METALCRAFT IN 1981

In 1981 a joint venture with Holland businessman Louis Padnos was formed to acquire a local manufacturer of screw machine products called Holland Metalcraft, which had been one of the firm's suppliers. In 1985 the company's headquarters moved from 10th street to Ottawa Avenue in Holland, and the firm began working with Unisys to upgrade its computer operations and integrate them onto a central server.

In 1989 Holland Hitch formed a joint venture with AFE in France to produce steel castings, and the following year Holland Transtrade was founded to make and distribute products in Malaysia, while a new manufacturing plant was opened in Germany. By this time one of the world's leading makers of fifth wheels and other coupling devices for the heavy truck industry, the firm had 1,100 employees and estimated annual sales of $100 million.

In 1991 The Binkley Company of Warrenton, Missouri, was acquired. Binkley was a leading manufacturer of landing gear products for trailers as well as tandem sliders, steel racking systems, and other rolled metal products. T.E DeBlase would remain president of the firm, which employed 450 at two plants in Missouri and a third in Arkansas. Binkley became the fourth division of what was known as the Holland Group, the others being Holland Hitch USA, Holland Hitch Canada, and Holland Hitch International. The company was headed by William Beebe's son-in-law Richard Muzzy, Jr.

During the early 1990s sales continued to grow, with the firm's customers including all of the major heavy-duty truck and trailer manufacturers like Freuhauf, Mack, Freightliner, and Volvo-White, as well as the U.S. government. By 1993 the company, which had 14 manufacturing sites in the U.S., Canada, Europe, Malaysia, and Australia, had begun to export products to China.

In early 1997 the Holland Group bought the Delphos Axle division of bankrupt Fruehauf Trailer Corp. for $14.4 million plus the cost of leftover inventory. The company would subsequently market its line of axles under the Holland ProPar brand name.

KEY DATES

1910: Safety Release Clevis Company is formed in South Dakota to make plow hitches.

1920: The company relocates to Holland, Michigan, and becomes known as Holland Hitch.

1935: Henry Ketel and Henry Geerds revive the firm after bankruptcy.

1956: The company opens a warehouse in California.

1963: New plants built in South Carolina and Ontario, Canada.

1969: Holland Hitch Forwarding Co. is founded and a German sales office is added.

1981: Holland Metalcraft is purchased.

1991: The Binkley Company of Missouri is acquired.

1999: Neway Anchorlok International of Muskegon, Michigan, is purchased.

2002: The company is restructured; the South Carolina plant and the Anchorlok brake line are sold.

2004: Simplex brand of fifth wheels is acquired from Consolidated Metco.

NEWAY ANCHORLOCK PURCHASED IN 1999

In 1999 the firm bought Neway Anchorlock International, Inc., of Muskegon, Michigan, a 50-year old manufacturer of air suspensions for trucks, trailers, and motorhomes. Neway, which employed 510 in Muskegon, also made brakes and valves.

Pressure on truck fleet operators to cut costs inspired a number of improvements to Holland Group products during this era, including the first "low-lube" fifth wheel, introduced in 1999, which utilized a polyurethane coating that rendered it 90 to 95 percent lubrication free. In 2000 the firm's new Holland In-Cab Air Release System allowed drivers to uncouple trailers directly from the cab, and the company also debuted an electronic lock indicator that could verify that a trailer had been correctly attached. The firm was looking toward further improvements as well, including integrating the fifth wheel and a truck's suspension into a single unit to save weight and improve performance.

Trailer and hitch sales were slowing, and in 2001 the Holland Group began a major restructuring to cut costs. The firm's Binkley and Neway subsidiaries were merged with Holland USA, which was headquartered in Muskegon. About 50 employees were relocated there, with ten others shifted to Holland. The engineering departments of these units also began working together, which led to the development of new products like the CB4000 Air-Ride Suspension System, which was easier to adjust, lighter, and more durable than previous designs.

Restructuring continued in early 2002 with the sale of the Anchorlok brake and Neway suspension control valve product lines to Haldex of Sweden. The $21.5 million deal gave Haldex plants in Mexico and Grand Haven, Michigan, that employed 235 and accounted for $50 million in annual revenues. In November the Holland Group also closed its Denmark, South Carolina, fifth wheel manufacturing plant. The facility's operations were moved to other sites and some of its staff of 44 were offered jobs elsewhere.

In 2003 the company introduced the FW-17 fifth wheel, the lightest and most durable model it had produced to date, which featured a new locking and release mechanism. A new suspension for buses and motorhomes was introduced as well, as were pintle hooks and draw bars for lighter-duty vehicles.

In 2004 Holland Group CEO Richard Muzzy took on the added title of board chairman, while 30-year company veteran Samuel A. Martin was named president and chief administrative officer. As executive vice president, Martin had overseen the firm's restructuring efforts. That September, the company also purchased the Simplex fifth wheel line from Consolidated Metco, Inc.

In early 2005 the Holland Group revamped its aftermarket parts service and delivery procedures. All U.S. parts would ship from either Holland or Wylie, Texas, with no minimum order required, and a new Web page for aftermarket sales was later added. In the fall the firm also introduced a new series of pintle hooks that were lighter and more durable than previous models.

Nearly a century after it first began marketing an agricultural plow hitch, the Holland Group had become the leading maker of fifth wheels and related hitching products for the heavy trucking industry. Through strategic acquisitions the firm was also a manufacturer of suspension systems for trucks, buses, and motorcoaches, as well as a producer of a variety of rolled metal products.

Frank Uhle

PRINCIPAL SUBSIDIARIES

Eurohitch GmbH (Germany); FWF France (50%); Holland Eurohitch Ltd. (United Kingdom); Holland Europe GmBH (Germany); The Holland Group, Inc. (Mexico);

Holland Hitch of Australia Ltd.; Holland Hitch of Canada Ltd.; Holland International; Holland Transtrade Far East (Malaysia); Holland Transtrade Thailand Co. Ltd.; Holland USA, Inc.; Nippon Holland, Ltd. (Japan).

PRINCIPAL COMPETITORS

ArvinMeritor, Inc.; Fontaine International; The Jost Group.

FURTHER READING

"Bankrupt Truck Trailer Maker Disposing of Business," *Associated Press Newswires*, February 19, 1997.

Cullen, David, "Getting Together," *Fleet Owner*, May 1, 2002.

Dlugopolski, Stephanie, "Holland Hitch Goes the Distance," *Holland Sentinel*, February 14, 1993.

Gwozdz, Tim, "Streamlined Holland USA Strategically in the Driver's Seat," *MiBizWest*, December 29, 2003.

"Haldex Agrees to Acquire Holland Group Units," *Trailer/Body Builders*, January 1, 2002.

Harvey, Robert E., "Holland Orders Mainframe, Software from Unisys," *Metalworking News*, August 7, 1989, p. 12.

"Holland Fifth Wheel Technology Enters the Cab," *Fleet Equipment*, December 1, 2000, p. 70.

"Holland Firm Buys Muskegon Manufacturer," *Grand Rapids Press*, June 15, 1999, p. B8.

"Holland Group Joins Divisions," *Grand Rapids Press*, December 23, 2001, p. A16.

"Holland Hitch Buys Competitor," *Grand Rapids Press*, May 22, 1991, p. B5.

"Holland's Low-Lube Fifth Wheel," *Fleet Equipment*, March 1, 2001, p. 46.

Radigan, Mary, "William F. Beebe," *Grand Rapids Press*, May 1, 2005, p. F3.

"What's New in Fifth Wheels," *Fleet Owner*, November 30, 1999.

Intres B.V.

Postbus 150
Hoevelaken,
Netherlands
Telephone: (+31 033) 253 29 11
Fax: (+31 033) 253 22 99
Web site: http://www.intres.nl

Cooperative
Incorporated: 1964 as Topkring
Employees: 515
Sales: EUR 994 million ($1.4 million) (2005)
NAIC: 423220 Home Furnishing Merchant Wholesalers; 423210 Furniture Merchant Wholesalers; 424320 Men's and Boys' Clothing and Furnishings Merchant Wholesalers; 424330 Women's, Children's, and Infants' Clothing and Accessories Merchant Wholesalers

■ ■ ■

Intres B.V. is one of the Netherlands' leading cooperative retail services companies. Formed originally as part of the cooperative purchasing movement of the country's independent retail community, Intres (which stands for International Retail Support Services) has developed a full range of retail support services, including developing store formats and concepts that are then franchised to its members. Intres' services include purchasing and logistics support, cooperative marketing, centralized payment services, information, and trade fair operation, among others. Intres operates through a number of sector-specific divisions.

The Intres Mode/Textiel division supports clothing and textile retailers and has developed several store formats, including more than 130 Livera stores, the Netherlands' leading lingerie and bathing suit retail network, as well as the First Lady, Lindessa, First/Man, and Jambelle store formats. Intres' Sports division operates under Intersport, with 117 stores, and Coach, with 46 stores. Intres Wonen serves the furniture (Woonsfeer, Woonflair, City Meubel, Studio, Woonfacet, Runner, Garant Meubel, among others), home textiles (Lin-O-Lux, Style d'Or, WSW/Nachtwacht, Shop in Shop Compact, Berg en Berg, and others), bed (Sleepy Belgie, Slaapgilde, Morgana Slaapkamers), and kitchen (Kitchenworld) markets. Intres also serves the bookstore and media markets with the Blz and Libris store formats through its Intres Media division. Altogether, the company counts more than 1,400 members operating nearly 2,100 stores. The group's total turnover of more than EUR 2.1 billion ($3 billion) in 2005 placed Intres among the Netherlands' top four retail groups. Intres' own revenues totaled nearly EUR 1 billion ($1.4 billion) in 2005.

PURCHASING COOPERATIVE MOVEMENT IN THE EARLY 20TH CENTURY

Intres stemmed from the development of the retail purchasing cooperative movement in the early 1920s. A particularly European phenomenon, especially in the Netherlands and Germany, the purchasing cooperatives were formed by small, independent retailers as a means of grouping their buying needs, thereby obtaining better prices from wholesale suppliers. The purchasing

companies typically were formed by members of the
same retail sector, and were especially popular in the
textile, furniture, and clothing sectors. As the movement
grew in popularity, a growing number of purchasing
groups began to operate on a larger, often regional and
even national scale.

Two of the earliest parts of the later Intres appeared
shortly after World War I, with the establishment of
both Onderling Behand and Noord Nederland in 1918.
The two groups grew strongly through the difficult
economic climate of the 1920s, and into the 1930s the
purchasing movement often meant the survival of many
of the country's retailers.

The end of World War II brought a new boom to
the purchasing movement. A number of new companies
appeared during this time, such as Beco, formed in 1949
and Ceniko, created in 1950. A number of existing
groups also merged during the postwar period to form
larger companies. In this way, Onderling Behang merged
with Maninko in 1952; in 1972, Onderling Behang
changed its name to Obema.

By then, the country's rising prosperity—and the
appearance of new retailing rivals—during the postwar
era had begun to influence a transformation of the
purchasing movement. These companies originally were
founded to serve more or less as middlemen for their
retailer members, essentially functioning as wholesalers,
but in the member's interest. Yet the appearance of new
large-scale retail groups and the growth of the country's
department store chains brought a new threat to the
small retail store sector. Facing rising competition, more
and more of the country's smaller retailers joined the
cooperative buying movement. At the same time, the
buying groups began developing a wider range of
services, such as transport and other logistics operations,
the development of common advertising operations, and
a growing range of financial services.

The purchasing groups also began moving toward
consolidation of the market, creating a smaller number
of larger groups capable of offering a wider number of
services to their members, as well as presenting a

competitive front against the country's fast-growing
large-scale distribution groups. The consolidation of the
movement began in earnest in the early 1960s. The
modern Intres began to emerge during this period, starting with the merger in 1964 of Noord-Nederland with
another group, Ingo. Both companies were specialized in
the textiles market—a retail sector that remained at the
core of Intres' operations into the next century. The new
company, called Topkring, set up its headquarters in
Hoevelaken in 1968. Topkring quickly attracted a
number of other purchasing groups in the country, such
as Dicos, Union, Hercon, and others.

MERGING FOR STRENGTH IN
THE LATE 20TH CENTURY

Mergers remained a driving force behind Topkring's
growth through the 1970s and into the 1980s. Although
many of the company's additions remained within the
textile sector, the consolidation of the purchasing
cooperative movement gave Topkring the opportunity to
extend its range of services to other retail sectors. In
1976, the group entered the furniture market through
its merger with purchasing group Ceniko, at which point
the company took on the new name of Topkring-Ceniko.

The 1970s and 1980s also marked Topkring's
transition from purchasing cooperative to full-scale retail
support services group. A major part of this development came through the group's efforts to convince its
members of the need to create common store formats
and store brands. Although the group met with resistance
from its typically and traditionally independent
membership, Topkring nonetheless succeeded in launching a number of highly successful store formats. These
included Livera, which became one of the first in the
Netherlands to provide specialized retail sales of lingerie
and bathing suits. Livera went on to become the leader
in that retail category in the Netherlands. As more and
more members signed on to the group's formats, Topkring's retail network spread across the country, presenting as a strong rival to the growing number of nationally
and even internationally operating chain store formats.
The development of these formats also allowed Topkring
to deepen its range of services, developing a full-featured
franchising operation, with the group aiding its retailer
members in choosing and purchasing new store locations, and the like.

The 1980s and 1990s marked a new era of
competition for the retail purchasing cooperatives. The
country's retail chain groups were forced to slow their
rapid growth as a result of a growing saturation of the
various retail markets. Unable to continue to grow
through new store openings, the retail chains increas-

1964: Topkring is formed through the merger of two Netherlands purchasing cooperatives, Noord-Nederland and Ingo.

1976: Topkring merges with Ceniko, becoming Topkring-Ceniko.

1988: The company takes over the Intersport sporting goods network in the Netherlands; the company name is shortened again to Topkring.

1992: The company merges with Obema, founded as Onderling Behang in 1918, one of the earliest Dutch purchasing cooperatives; Intres is formed as a holding company for the combined operations.

1997: The company merges with Beco, a retail support group specializing in furniture and home furnishings.

2000: The company restructures into four main divisions; the Engering-Forster group is acquired.

2003: The Coach Holland B.V. sporting goods retail network is acquired; the decision to refocus on ten core retail brands is announced; a cooperation agreement is formed with Kopgroep, adding the Berg & Berg retail format.

2005: The company opens the first Intersport megastore and launches a re-styling of the Livera lingerie format.

ingly turned to a franchise model, signing up a growing number of independent retailers. Faced with a direct threat to their own area of operations, the retail purchasing cooperatives launched a new wave of consolidations.

Topkring not only sought to combine with similar cooperatives, it also used the consolidation of the cooperative movement as an opportunity to expand its range of retail offerings. This led the company into the sporting goods sector in 1988, when it agreed to merge with the Intersport network. The leading sporting goods group in the Netherlands, Intersport had been created in 1968 by purchasing cooperatives from ten countries, including the Netherlands. Intersport Nederland became part of the Hobo-faam/Retailnet group and later grew into a chain of 220 stores. As part of Topkring, and later Intres, Intersport remained associated with the larger Switzerland-based INTERSPORT International Corp-

oration. By the mid-2000s, the larger Intersport network spanned more than 30 countries, with nearly 5,000 stores and a total turnover of more than EUR 7.7 billion.

Following the addition of the Intersport network, Topkring shortened its name, dropping the "Ceniko." By the early 1990s, Topkring sought to consolidate its operations with one of the other large-scale Dutch retail services cooperatives. The company began talks with rival group Nederland; the two parties were unable to reach an agreement, however, and instead Nederland joined with another group, Samen Sterk, to form Euretco in 1992. By then, Topkring had found a more willing partner in Obema. Following the merger, a new holding company was formed to oversee the group's operations, called Intres—taken from International Retail Support Services.

STREAMLINING FORMATS FOR THE NEW CENTURY

Intres turned toward the start of the 21st century as one of the Netherlands' retail powerhouses, overseeing a network of more than 1,500 retailers across the Netherlands. Through the decade, the company continued to expand its range of retail store formats. The group also entered a new retail sector, that of bookstore operations under the Blz and Libris names. These stores later expanded their ranges to embrace the wider media category, including sales of software, CDs, and DVDs.

The consolidation of the Netherlands' retail support cooperatives market continued through the end of the 1990s and into the 2000s. In 1997, for example, the company merged with Beco, which had by then grown into a leading specialist in the furniture and home furnishings sectors. Intres further extended its home furnishings operations with the takeover of Engering-Forster, a group of 17 retailers focused on the bedding and household textiles sectors, in 2000. The following year, Intres added the Burmann group of high-end linen retailers, representing ten stores. By then, the company had completed its restructuring into four divisions, Intres Mode/Textiel, Intres Wonen, Intres Sport, and Intres Media.

Other acquisitions followed into the middle of the decade. In 2002, the company added the Biggie Best Interiors group, followed by the takeover of sporting goods group Coach Nederland B.V. in 2003. In that year, the company completed a larger-scale merger with Centurion, originally established in 1932, which represented 140 women's and men's clothing stores. Not all of Intres' activities led to expansion of the company's own operations. In 2006, for example, the company spun off its Fedac Accountants & Adviseurs unit into a merger with Alfa-groep. In this way, Intres strengthened the range of financial services for its retailer members.

In addition to mergers, Intres sought out an increasing number of partnerships, such as a cooperation agreement with CombiFoto Nederland, formed in 2000, the Eurobrands partnership, formed with department store group Peek & Coppenburg in 2001, and a cooperation agreement with Kop-groep and its 20 Berg & Berg furniture home textiles, reached in 2003.

As it turned toward the mid-decade, Intres began taking steps to streamline and update its list of retail formats. In 2003, the company announced its plans to refocus its retail portfolio around ten core formats— Livera, Firstlady, First/Man, Runner, Lin-O-Lux, Berg & Berg, Kitchenworld, Intersport, Coach, and Libris. The phasing out of the group's other format was expected to be accomplished only over a period of several years, however. As part of the brand refocusing effort, Intres launched a new Intersport "megastore" format in 2005, while converting its five Active Life stores to the Intersport format. In that year, the company also began rolling out a re-styling effort for the Livera format. As one of the Netherlands' top-four nonfood retail groups, Intres remained one of the backbones of the Netherlands' independent retail sector.

M. L. Cohen

PRINCIPAL SUBSIDIARIES

Berg & Berg Holding B.V. (33%); Bouchier Groep B.V.; Coach Nederland B.V.; Coach Sports Venlo B.V.; IFS B.V.; Intres Belgium N.V. (Belgium); Intres Participaties B.V.; J. Burmann Beheer B.V.; RetailConnect B.V. (30.5%); RetailPay B.V., (50%); Valcom ApS (Denmark).

PRINCIPAL COMPETITORS

Euretco B.V.

FURTHER READING

"Berg & Berg en Intres Wonen Gaan Samenwerken," *Franzine+,* August 2003.

"Beter resultaat Intres," *De telegraaf,* April 27, 2004.

"Flinke Groei Inkooporganisatie Intres," *De telegraaf,* April 25, 2002.

"Fusie Centurion en Intres," *MKB-Net,* July 5, 2003.

"Iets Meer Omzet Winkels Intres," *Reformatorisch Dagblad,* May 10, 2005.

"Intres Introduceert Shop in Shop Compact," *Franzine+,* April 2005.

"Kop-groep en Intres Wonen Ontwikkelen Franchiseformule," *Franzine+,* April 18, 2002.

"Retailer INTRES Acts As an Information Center for Members and Suppliers," *Intentia Fashion Newsletter,* No. 2., 2004.

"Winkeliers Hebben Problemen Bij Zoeken Opvolger," *Reformatorisch Dagblad,* April 26, 2001.

John Dewar & Sons, Ltd.

1700 London Road
Glasgow, Lanarkshire, Scotland G32 8XR
United Kingdom
Telephone: (44) 0141-551-4000
Fax: (44) 0141-551-4030
Web site: http://www.dewars.com

Wholly Owned Subsidiary of Bacardi & Company Ltd.
Incorporated: 1846
Employees: 204
Sales: $129.5 million (2006 est.)
NAIC: 312140 Distilleries

■ ■ ■

John Dewar & Sons Ltd. produces Dewar's White Label, the best-selling blended Scotch whisky in the United States and one of the top brands worldwide. The firm's other offerings include the premium Dewar's 12-Year and Dewar's Signature, five single malt scotches, and two William Lawson blended whiskies. The company is owned by the privately held Bacardi & Company Ltd. of Bermuda.

BEGINNINGS

Dewar's origins date to the mid-19th century. Founder John Dewar was born in 1805 in the small village of Dull, near Aberfeldy, Scotland, where he grew up on a farm. After an apprenticeship as a joiner, he moved in his early 20s to Perth, where he began working for his uncle's wine and spirits wholesaling firm. He became a partner in 1837 but in 1846 decided to go into business on his own and began blending whisky from several different producers to give it a mellower flavor. Dewar was one of the first to sell his beverage in a glass bottle with the brand name embossed on the front, rather than in a ceramic container.

One of Dewar's ten children, John A. Dewar, began working for the firm in 1871, and in 1879 he was made partner at the age of 23. The following year the senior Dewar died, and John A. inherited the business. The son was a skilled blender of whisky as well as a talented businessman, and he began to build up the company his father had founded.

In 1881 Dewar's 17-year-old brother Tommy joined the firm, and in 1885 he was made a partner in John Dewar & Sons. That same year the firm began distribution to London, where whisky had traditionally sold poorly next to spirits like brandy, rum, and gin. Tommy Dewar had a knack for marketing, and though he arrived in town with introductions to only two men, one of whom was dead and the other bankrupt, he made a splash by bringing a kilt-wearing bagpiper to the 1886 London Brewer's Exhibition. To capitalize on its new notoriety and to emphasize the whisky's heritage, the firm soon began using a depiction of a traditionally-clad Scotch Highlander on its labels.

In 1886 Dewar's whisky won a medal at the Edinburgh Exhibition, which was the first of many such awards it would receive over the years, and in 1888 the firm began exclusively supplying top catering firm Spiers and Pond, whose customers included railways, hotels, and music venues.

COMPANY PERSPECTIVES

Whether you're in the mood for the perfectly balanced blend that "never varies" (Dewar's White Label) or full flavour and smoothness without compromise (Dewar's 12), Dewar's has something truly unique for every discerning Scotch whisky drinker.

In 1891 the company was the recipient of some unanticipated free publicity in the United States when the wealthy Scottish steel magnate Andrew Carnegie gave a small keg of Dewar's to President Benjamin Harrison. When he was blasted in the press for not supporting American-made products, the Dewar's name appeared in papers around the country and orders for the firm's whisky began rolling in.

In 1892 Tommy Dewar began a two-year sales trip to 26 countries around the world. The journey resulted in contracts with 32 new sales agents and the publication of *Ramble 'Round the Globe,* an account of his travels that was spiced with the pithy sayings ("Dewarisms") he was becoming known for.

In 1893 Queen Victoria awarded a Royal Warrant to John Dewar & Sons, which officially recognized the firm as a supplier to the crown, and in 1895 the company established a U.S. office in New York. Three years later Dewar's commissioned the first-ever motion picture advertisement for a beverage, which was produced by the Edison Company and projected onto the roof of a building in New York's Herald Square. A few years later the company would also make films that documented the process of blending its whisky.

ABERFELDY DISTILLERY OPENS IN 1898; WHITE LABEL SCOTCH DEBUTS

Dewar's had traditionally purchased whisky for its blends from other producers, but in 1898 the company opened a distillery of its own in the small village of Aberfeldy. The custom-built facility consisted of a long row of buildings that allowed for continuous distillation, with barley coming in at one end and casks of whisky going out the other. The distillery utilized water from the River Tay and was positioned on a train line to the firm's headquarters in Perth. Soon after it opened the company introduced Dewar's White Label Scotch, which was a blend of ten whiskies with the Aberfeldy variety at its heart, created by renowned whisky blender A. J. Cameron.

In 1900 the increasingly prominent Dewar brothers were both elected to the British Parliament. Tommy, who had begun serving as Sheriff of London in 1897, represented the Conservative party, while brother John was a Liberal. A year later Tommy Dewar was knighted by King Edward VII, who also granted Dewar's its latest royal warrant. (It would receive one from each successive monarch.) Both Dewar brothers would ultimately be granted the status of Lords. The colorful Tommy Dewar, whose observations included statements like "a teetotaller is one who suffers from thirst instead of enjoying it," soon became the third Briton to purchase an automobile.

International expansion continued in the 20th century, with sales offices added in Sydney and Melbourne, Australia, and Calcutta, India in 1902. In 1908 the firm's new office, Dewar House, was opened in London's Haymarket, and three years later the company erected the largest mechanical neon sign in Europe on the Thames embankment. The 80 foot tall advertisement showed the firm's Scotch Highlander mascot "bending an elbow" with a glass of Dewar's.

In 1915 John Dewar & Sons merged with the large whisky-blending firm of James Buchanan to form Buchanan-Dewars. The company's new partner had been founded in London in 1884 and produced the popular Black and White brand.

In 1920 the United States prohibited the sale of alcoholic beverages, which put a damper on sales, but the company continued to grow, and between 1919 and 1923 bought a total of six distilleries to supply whisky for its blends, including facilities in Ord, Parkmore, Pultney, and Aultmore.

MERGER WITH DCL IN 1925

In 1925 Buchanan-Dewars merged with the publicly traded Distillers Company Ltd. (DCL). Created in 1877 by the merger of six distillers, DCL had grown over the next half-century to become Britain's leading spirits conglomerate. Following the subsequent acquisition of the John Walker distilling company (makers of Johnnie Walker scotch), Dewar's parent company would own the three leading blended whisky producers, and it continued to acquire other major names like White Horse Distillers over time.

In 1929 John A. Dewar died, leaving an estate worth some £4.5 million, and less than a year later his younger brother Tommy also passed away, leaving £5 million. The firm had recently recorded profits of more than a million pounds per annum.

The repeal of U.S. prohibition in 1933 returned Dewar's whisky to that major market, but with the start of World War II in late 1939 the British government

KEY DATES

1846:	John Dewar begins blending whisky in Perth, Scotland.
1880:	Ownership of firm passes to sons John A. and Tommy Dewar.
1898:	Aberfeldy distillery opens.
1915:	Merger with whisky blending firm of John Buchanan.
1925:	Distillers Company, Ltd., acquires Buchanan-Dewars.
1942:	Production sharply curtailed during World War II.
1961:	New bottling facility opens in Perth.
1969:	Dewar's Profiles advertising campaign debuts.
1972:	Rebuilding and expansion of Aberfeldy distillery completed.
1986:	Dewar's White Label becomes top-selling whisky in United States.
1986:	Distillers Co. and Dewar acquired by Guinness in hostile takeover.
1998:	Dewar's sold to Bacardi; operations combined with Wm. Lawson Distillers.
1999:	Dewar's brand relaunched with $20 million advertising campaign.
2000:	Bottling plant in Glasgow modernized; visitor's center opens at Aberfeldy.

ordered distilleries to produce only one-third of their previous year's production to conserve barley. The company was forced to lay off its sales force as it rationed orders at home and abroad, and production at the Aberfeldy distillery was later halted for a time. With the war's end in 1945, production began to return to normal levels.

In 1954 the company renamed its aged Victoria Vat brand of scotch Ancestor, which would go on to become one of Dewar's best-known brands. In 1961 new production facilities were opened in Perth, and during the 1960s the firm began to rebuild and expand its Aberfeldy distillery, completing the work in 1972.

In 1966 the company won a Queen's Award for Export Achievement, and in 1969 it began running print advertisements that featured photographs of celebrities under the heading "Dewar's Profiles." Playing off the phonetic spelling of the firm's name ("Doers"), the ads spotlighted their subjects' achievements with black-and-white photographs that featured a small whisky bottle in color.

By the early 1980s some 95 percent of Dewar's output was exported, with about half going to the United States. In the United Kingdom, where sales were dominated by the Bells brand, Dewar's had only a 1–2 percent market share, and in 1982 the firm shut down its internal marketing unit there and turned sales over to the firm of Hedges and Butler, who would sell it in part through 8,000 public houses aligned with Bass.

DEWAR'S BECOMES TOP U.S. WHISKY IN 1986

While Dewar's sales had tripled between 1960 and 1980, U.S. exports had increased fourfold during the same period, and in 1986 Dewar's became the top-selling whisky in the United States. In the fall of that year DCL successor United Distillers was acquired by the Guinness Beverage Group in a hostile takeover, after which the firm's international marketing offices were combined with those of James Buchanan and Company, John Walker and Sons, White Horse Distillers, William Sanderson and Sons, and Pimm's.

In 1987 the Dewar's trademark was secretly transferred from Guinness to Schenley Industries, a U.S.-based spirits distributor owned by Meshuklam Riklis. Schenley had been distributing Dewar's in the United States since 1936, and the whisky accounted for half of that firm's total profits. The company later claimed the move was made to combat lower-priced parallel imports of Dewar's from other countries. Though Riklis (who owned a 5 percent stake in Guinness) had been given the trademark for free, a short time later the brewing giant paid him $480 million to buy it back, along with his distribution network and the right to sell Dewar's in the United States.

In 1996 the company celebrated its 150th anniversary with a special bottling of whisky and the launch of a Web site that featured games based on the life of Tommy Dewar. The company's whisky continued to be the top brand in the United States, accounting for some 1.5 million cases of the 9.4 million total sold there during the year.

DEWAR'S JOINS BACARDI FAMILY IN 1998

In 1998 the proposed merger of Guinness and Grand Metropolitan to form Diageo plc came under scrutiny from U.S. and European trade regulators, and, to clinch the deal, in March John Dewar & Sons was sold to Bacardi & Co. along with the Bombay Sapphire gin brand for a total of $1.4 billion. Dewars' value was put at nearly three-fourths of the total.

The firm's new owner had a colorful history of its

own, having been founded in 1862 in Cuba and then moving to Bermuda in 1960 after Castro's revolution. Bacardi rum was the world's top selling spirit, and the company was the world's largest family-owned alcoholic beverage maker.

Following the acquisition, John Dewar was combined with earlier Bacardi purchase William Lawson Distillers Ltd. to form John Dewar & Sons, Ltd., which would be based in Glasgow. A smaller distillery, Royal Brackla, was purchased at this time as well and folded into the company. Diageo would bottle Dewar's through mid-2000, after which time this function would be taken over by Bacardi.

The Dewar's name had lost much of its luster in recent years due to Guinness' focus on the Johnnie Walker and B brands, which had stronger global sales. In October 1999 Bacardi relaunched the firm's whisky with new label graphics and new advertising targeted at younger drinkers. The $20 million ad campaign updated the "Dewar's Profiles" series and also used new ads depicting the familiar Scottish Highlander in various modern settings, such as shirtless, with a surfboard and sunglasses.

DEWAR'S 12 INTRODUCED IN 2000

In 2000 the premium Dewar's 12-Year Old Scotch brand was introduced to strong sales, and other deluxe variations followed including a 15-year blended malt. Less than two years after the Bacardi acquisition, the company had gone from ranking eighth in global whisky sales to fifth, with sales of Dewar's rising to 3.5 million cases per year and Lawson's to 1.1 million. In addition to its continuing U.S. sales leadership, Dewar's was also ranked near the top in several other countries including Spain and Greece. The Lawson brand was popular in France, Spain, Portugal, and Mexico.

In the spring of 2000 the firm opened a new £2 million visitor's center at the Aberfeldy Distillery. Dubbed Dewar's World of Whisky, it would play host to some 30,000 visitors per year. The year 2000 also saw completion of the company's £8.5 million refurbishing of a Glasgow bottling plant which had been closed for 13 years. When the Diageo bottling contract ended in June it began packaging Dewar's and Lawson's whiskies.

In late 2000 two shipping containers of Dewar's 12-year-old scotch were stolen from a dock in Scotland. The 24,000 bottles lost were valued at nearly $1 million. Dewar's subsequently joined a coalition of spirits makers that were working to combat similar thefts.

In 2003 the firm's sales declined by 10 percent, from 84.2 million pounds to 75.7 million pounds, due to poor results in France, Spain, and Venezuela. A year later Dewar's signed Scottish actor Sean Connery to appear in ads for Dewar's 12-Year Old Scotch. The 74-year-old former James Bond star would deliver the new slogan, "Some age, others mature."

The company celebrated its 160th anniversary in 2006. Dewar's was operating distilleries in Aberfeldy, Craigellachie, Brackla, Aultmore, and MacDuff to produce whisky for its blends, as well as limited-edition single malt scotches.

More than a century and a half after its namesake began blending whisky in Perth, Scotland, John Dewar & Sons, Ltd. continued to produce fine distilled beverages. The firm's flagship brand, Dewar's White Label, was the best-selling whisky in the United States and also popular in other countries around the world. With the backing and distribution muscle of new owner Bacardi, the company appeared well-positioned for many more years of success.

Frank Uhle

PRINCIPAL SUBSIDIARIES

William Lawson Distillers; John Dewar & Sons Co. (United States).

PRINCIPAL COMPETITORS

Diageo plc; Pernod Ricard SA; Fortune Brands, Inc.; Brown-Forman Corporation; Constellation Brands, Inc.

FURTHER READING

Bain, Julie, "Dewar's Raises Glass to a New Spirit of Wealth," *Scotland on Sunday,* April 23, 2000.

Benady, David, "Double Boost for Bacardi," *Marketing Week,* July 2, 1998, pp. 29–31.

Blackwell, David, "Raw Victorian Enterprise Finely Distilled," *Financial Times,* December 16, 1997, p. 19.

"Blend into the Background," *Herald,* September 4, 2004, p. 1.

Brown, Gordon, *The Whisky Trails,* London: Prion Books Ltd., 1993.

Cruickshank, Jim Watt, and Dani Garavelli, "Whisky Producers Gang Up on Hijackers," *Sunday Times,* November 25, 2001.

"Curriculum Vitae," *Off-Licence News,* January 16, 1998, p. 28.

Elliott, Stuart, "A Face Lift Is Planned for 'Dewar's Profiles,'" *New York Times,* July 25, 1991.

"Following Their Controversial Takeover of Distillers, Guinness Are Centralising the Company's Overseas and Marketing Operations in Hammersmith and Disposing of Five Central

London Buildings," *Estates Gazette,* November 22, 1986.

Gibbs, Geoffrey, and Mary Brasier, "Guinness Brand Name in Secret Switch to US," *Guardian,* January 16, 1987.

Lyons, William, "Dewar's Suffers 10 Per Cent Drop," *Scotsman,* August 8, 2003, p. 24.

Masterson, Victoria, "Dewar's Prospers on Bacardi Distribution," *Scotsman,* October 21, 1999, p. 24.

McGookin, Stephen, "Whisky Galore on the Net," *Financial Times,* August 8, 1996.

Morton, Tom, "Tommy Dewar, the First Whisky Baron to Sell Thirsty Americans a Dream—and a Dram," *Scotsman,* March 31, 1998, p. 27.

Powell, Robert, "Bacardi Raises Sales of Dewar's," *Herald,* February 26, 2000, p. 23.

Willman, John, "A Rolls by Any Other Name," *Financial Times,* April 4, 1998, p. 9.

Katokichi Company Ltd.

■

5-18-37 Sakamoto-cho
Kanonji,
Japan
Telephone: (81) 0875 56 1100
Fax: (81) 0875 56 1109
Web site: http://www.katokichi.co.jp

Public Company
Incorporated: 1956 as Katokichi Suisan Co., Ltd.
Employees: 3,590
Sales: ¥339.8 billion $2.82 billion (2005)
Stock Exchanges: Tokyo
Ticker Symbol: 2873
NAIC: 311412 Frozen Specialty Food Manufacturing; 311330 Confectionery Manufacturing from Purchased Chocolate; 311511 Fluid Milk Manufacturing; 311712 Fresh and Frozen Seafood Processing

■ ■ ■

Katokichi Co., Ltd., is one of Japan's leading processed foods companies. The company holds the number two spot for processed and frozen seafood, and also ranks number two in the pre-cooked and frozen rice segments. Founded as a frozen shrimp producer in the late 1950s, Katokichi has since expanded its range to include a large variety of foods and beverages, including noodles, curries, pouch-style and other ready-to-eat foods, bottled mineral water, and other consumer-sector products. The company is also a major producer of sushi ingredients for the consumer retail market. Katokichi is also a major

supplier to the food service market, with a product list including fried, breaded and frozen seafood and vegetables, rice, noodles, eggs and egg products, poultry and beef products, sushi ingredients, and pre-cooked dishes, among others. Katokichi has maintained a production presence in mainland China since the early 1990s; the company also operates production subsidiaries in Thailand and Indonesia.

While food production accounts for the majority of the company's revenues, Katokichi has diversified into the restaurant sector, operating nearly 450 bars, including 32 English-style pubs. The company also operates a number of hotels, including Hotel Reoma no Mori, the Kanonji Grand Hotel, and the Marugame Grand Hotel. The company's also operates several entertainment and leisure venues such as the Kume Country Club and the Yubara Country Club, and the New Reoma World amusement park. Katokichi is listed on the Tokyo Stock Exchange and is led by founder and chairman Yoshikazu Kato. In 2005, the company posted revenues of ¥339.8 billion, or $2.82 billion.

FROZEN FISH FOR THE FIFTIES

Katokichi was founded by Yoshikazu Kato in 1956 in order to produce and distribute frozen fish in Japan's Kanonji City region. Kato was just 20 years old at the time, yet had already worked for some five years as a fisherman. In that capacity, Kato formed a number of business principles, and especially an understanding of the need to change and adapt to the continuing market changes. Kato's summed up his business philosophy this way: "Continually be aware of risk, and view change as

COMPANY PERSPECTIVES

Our company's basic philosophy is to "serve society through the company's prosperity." By the company growing, responding to the needs of the era and the people, we are able to accomplish our mission in society. We think that this is, in fact, the real value of a business enterprise.

a challenge." Backed by this philosophy, Kato transformed his company from a small frozen seafood producer to one of Japan's top processed food companies.

Katokichi Suisan Co. was formally launched at the beginning of 1957. The company's first product was frozen shrimp. From the start, the export market formed a major part of the company's business. By 1962, Katokichi had recognized the opportunity to expand into the processed foods category, launching exports of frozen fried shrimp. The growing company, which shorted its name to Katokichi Co. in 1964, moved to new quarters in Kanonji in 1966. This moved enabled the company to expand its range of production, adding frozen vegetables to its seafood line.

In the early 1970s, Katokichi's spirit of adapting to the changing market enabled it to recognize the growing demand for prepared and processed foods amid the rapid industrialization and growing financial clout of the Japanese economy. In 1971, the company opened a new factory, in Yamamoto, dedicated to the production of processed foods including pork dumplings and breaded fish and meat products. The success of these lines led the company to move its headquarters once again in 1976. The company remained committed to its Kanonji roots, however.

Katokichi grew externally in 1980, through a merger with Omiya Kensetsu Kogyo Company, which was also headquartered in Kanonji. By the end of that year, the company had also completed a restructuring, adding a new subsidiary, Katokichi Shokuhin. By then, too, the company had two new factories, in Zentsuji and Tadotsu.

Katokichi went public in 1984, listing its stock on the Osaka Stock Exchange's secondary section. Two years later, the company added its listing to the Tokyo Stock Exchange as well. The company grew again the following year, launching its first diversification effort by adding a hotel management wing. Also in 1987, Katokichi's strong growth led to the shift of the company's share listing to the main boards of both the Tokyo and Osaka exchanges. The company also expanded into restaurant operations, with such holdings as the Murasaki and Hiikiya restaurant groups, both operators of traditional Izakaya-style restaurants. Other later holdings added to the company's growing leisure and entertainment portfolio included golf courses, including the Kume and the Yubara country clubs, and the New Reoma World amusement park.

RICE REVOLUTION IN THE NINETIES

The company stepped up its investments in the late 1980s. Importantly, the company entered the market for prepared noodles—one of the fastest-growing Japanese food categories—with the opening of a new frozen noodle factory in Naka Tado in 1988. In that year also, Katokichi extended its hotel management interests into the general real estate development market, adding a new subsidiary, Eiwa General Lease Company.

Katokichi added a new production facility in 1991, in Ayakamai, in the Kagawa Prefecture. However, the company had already recognized an opportunity for international expansion. In 1987, the company entered Hong Kong, launching subsidiary K and T Foods, which built a food processing factory, and also received a license to operate in the restaurant sector. The company then formed a joint venture with Café de Coral Group, the largest fast-food restaurant operator in the Hong Kong market, to open a fast-food restaurant featuring authentic Japanese cuisine in 1989. That year, Katokichi also began doing business in Thailand, where it set up a joint venture with Nichimen Corp. to produce processed frozen foods, and especially tiger shrimp.

The opening of the Chinese economy in the early 1990s provided the company with its next international expansion opportunity. In 1993, Katokichi founded the joint venture Weidongri Comprehensive Foodstuff Co. LTd., in Shandong. The move into China not only provided the company with lower operating costs, it also placed it closer to the rapidly developing Chinese market for shrimp and other fish and seafood products. Katokichi quickly expanded its Chinese operations beyond seafood, however. By the end of the 1990s, the company had opened more than ten subsidiaries and affiliated companies in China producing a wide variety of food items, ranging from fresh and processed seafoods to dumplings, crab pastes and sushi toppings, to fried chicken. Into the mid-2000s, the company continued to shift its most labor-intensive food production operations to the Chinese mainland, where labor costs were approximately one-twentieth the cost of the same resources in Japan.

An important moment in Katokichi's development came in the mid-1990s when the Japanese government

KEY DATES

1956: 20-year-old fisherman Yoshikazu Kato establishes Katokichi Suisan Co., Ltd., a frozen fish processing company in Kanonji, Japan, and begins producing frozen fish products.

1961: Katokichi launches production of frozen fried shrimp.

1971: The company adds a new factory in Yamamoto and diversifies its product line.

1984: Katokichi lists stock on the Osaka and Tokyo (1986) stock exchanges.

1987: First international operation begins with a food production subsidiary in Hong Kong.

1989: Katokichi forms a shrimp production joint venture in Thailand.

1993: A joint venture operation is established in Shandong Province, China.

1997: The company enters the healthy foods market with the acquisition of Green Food Company.

2002: Katokichi acquires Qingdoa Aska Foods as part of its plan to expand export operations to the United States and Europe.

2004: The company acquires Japanese instant noodle producer Kanebo Ltd.

2006: The company celebrates its 50th anniversary.

began taking steps to liberalize the all-important Japanese rice market. As the country's staple food—and a major agricultural crop—Japanese rice had enjoyed heavy protection from the government, especially in the form of tight restrictions on imports. These restrictions, however, created an artificial market for domestic rice, confronting consumers with high rice prices. A disastrous harvest in the early 1990s, however, forced the government to allow emergency imports of rice. This opened the breach for the legislation governing the rice market.

Katokichi recognized the opportunity to enter the market with a high-quality domestic rice sold at low prices. The company established its own rice factory in Niigata Uonuma, a region noted for its high-quality rice, in 1994, and by the following year had begun marketing its frozen, pre-cooked domestic rice at a significant discount compared to its competitors. The passage of the new Staple Foods Law at the end of 1995, which, among other provisions, required the government to stockpile rice as a hedge against future shortages, further boosted the domestic rice market, provid-

ing a ready customer for Katokichi.

In response, the company moved to deepen its rice operations, adding a new polishing factory in 1996. In that year, also, Katokichi built another new plant in Niigata Uonuma, for the production of long shelf-life rice in sterilized packaging. At the same time, Katokichi developed a highly efficient production system. These and other investments in the rice sector quickly paid off for the company, as it grew rapidly into the country's number two rice supplier by the early 2000s. Katokichi's rice operations were also quite profitable, despite the company's discount price formula, and by the early 2000s the company's gross profits on its rice operations outpaced the industry average.

EYES ON EXPORTS IN THE NEW CENTURY

True to the founder's vision, Katokichi remained on the lookout for new industry trends. In 1997, the company acquired a stake in Green Foods Company, one of Japan's pioneering producers of so-called healthy foods—the nation's fastest growing food segment at the turn of the century. Katokichi also continued to expand its production capacity, buying up frozen foods specialist KS Frozen Foods Co. in 2000.

Katokichi's continued expansion of its Chinese operations enabled it to develop a new strategy targeting the export market. The company's focus fell especially on the United States, but also on the European market. In support of this strategy, the company began construction of a new Shandong Province plant, completed in 2002, and acquired Qingdao Aska Food Co., also based in Shandong, a producer of eel and shrimp for sushi. Following that acquisition, the company launched a ¥250 million upgrade of the Qindao plant.

Katokichi's international focus also included expansion of food sales in the Chinese market. At the end of 2002, the company formed a partnership with Long Fong Foods Co., a leading producer and distributor of frozen foods in China. The partnership enabled Katokichi to distribute its own chicken and seafood products through Long Fong's distribution network. The move was part of the company's target to distribute as much as 50 percent of its China-based production to the Chinese market by the late 2000s, compared to just 10 percent in 2002.

Katokichi also attempted to expand its restaurant operations onto the mainland, forming a partnership with Ringer Hut Co., which operated a string of noodle restaurants. After opening two loss-making test restaurants in 2002, the partners agreed to terminate their partnership in 2003.

Despite this setback, Katokichi's overall operations remained in exemplary health, contrasting sharply with much of the rest of the Japanese food sector, which had been hit hard by a deepening recession at the turn of the century. Its competitors' difficulties opened new opportunities for Katokichi. In 2004, for example, the company became the leading candidate to take over struggling Kanebo Ltd. That acquisition added a crucial new category to Katokichi's operations, instant noodles, one of the largest food categories in Japan. By 2006, Katokichi's 50-year record of "viewing change as challenge" had enabled the company to become one of Japan's food industry leaders.

M.L. Cohen

PRINCIPAL SUBSIDIARIES

Meicheng Brother Co., Ltd. (China); P.T. Khome Foods (Indonesia); P.T. Sekar Katokichi (Indonesia); Qingdao Aska Food Co., Ltd. (China); Qingdao Katokichi Foods Co., Ltd. (China); Seafresh Katokichi Co., Ltd.; Thailand Seafresh Katokichi Co., Ltd.; Weidongri Comprehensive Foodstuffs Co., Ltd. (China); Weifang Kaijia Foodstuffs Co., Ltd. (China); Yantai Xinxing Foods Co., Ltd. (China); Zhoushan Katoka Foods Co., Ltd. (China).

PRINCIPAL COMPETITORS

Maruha Corporation; Nichirei Corporation; QP Corp.; Air Water Inc.; Toyo Suisan Kaisha Ltd.; Taiyo Nippon Sanso Corp.; Snow Brand Milk Products Company Ltd.; Kyokuyo Company Ltd.

FURTHER READING

"Japan's Katokichi Teams up with Chinese Frozen Food Company," *AsiaPulse News*, November 6, 2002.

"Japan's Katokichi to Develop China as US, European Export Base," *AsiaPulse News*, June 10, 2002.

"Katokichi Co. Ltd. Announces Business and Capital Alliance with China-based Company," *Reuters Key Development*, March 15, 2006.

"Katokichi Ordered to Recall Frozen Spinach from China," *Japan Weekly Monitor*, June 17, 2002.

"Katokichi Prime Candidate for Acquisition of Kanebo's Noodles Biz," *Jiji*, September 3, 2004.

"Katokichi to Boost Production for US, Europe Next Year," *Japan Weekly Monitor*, November 26, 2001.

"Katokichi to Open Japanese Restaurant Chain in Hong Kong," *Japan Economic Newswire*, May 31, 1989.

"Ringer Hut, Katokichi to Terminate JV in China," *Jiji*, September 19, 2003.

Kobrand Corporation

134 East 40th Street
New York, New York 10016
U.S.A.
Telephone: (212) 490-9300
Fax: (212) 867-7916
Web site: http://www.kobrandwine.com

Private Company
Founded: 1944
Employees: 200
Sales: $116.8 million (2004 est.)
NAIC: 424820 Wine and Distilled Alcoholic Beverage
Merchant Wholesalers

■ ■ ■

Based in a Midtown Manhattan townhouse in New York City, Kobrand Corporation is a privately owned marketer of wines and spirits that serves as the exclusive agent for many fine European wines. In addition, the firm owns many of the brands in its portfolio. Kobrand's wine offerings includes products from California, France, Hungary, Italy, New Zealand, Portugal, and Spain. Spirits include Alize, made from passion fruit, vodka, and cognac; Café Boheme, a French vodka and coffee liqueur; the Delamain line of cognac; Guyot fruit liqueurs; Larressingle armagnac, similar to cognac; and Depax Blue Cane Amber Rhum, a premium rum. Kobrand is owned by the three daughters of the firm's founder, Rudolph C. Kopf.

POST-PROHIBITION ROOTS

Kopf was born in the borough of Queens in New York City and graduated from the University of Columbia's Business School in 1927. At the time, the United States was still engaged in what many called the "great experiment," the prohibition on the consumption of any alcoholic beverage. Already proven to be a dismal failure, Prohibition would not be repealed until President Franklin Roosevelt took office in 1933. It was in that year that Kopf started a wine and spirits department at New York's famed Macy's department store. Under his guidance, it became known as one of the best shops in the country and Kopf established himself as an industry force. In 1944, at the age of 38, he struck out on his own and formed his own wine and spirits marketing company, which he called the Kobrand Corporation. He set up shop in the Empire State Building, a stone's throw from Macy's. Although light on money, Kopf was well connected, having established relationships in the wine and spirits business around the world.

Kopf's big break came in 1945 when he lined up his first major wine brand to represent, Maison Louis Jadot, which was established in France in 1859. Kopf flew across the Atlantic to make a personal appeal to Louis Auguste Jadot, the third generation owner of the Burgundy vineyard that was well regarded for the wines it produced. The two men already knew one another because Kopf had once arranged to sell some of Jadot's wine under a private label for Macy's. Kopf reportedly told Jadot when they met, "I have little money. But I have courage." Jadot was won over, granted U.S.

marketing rights to Kobrand and established a relationship that would extend to the next generations of both families.

With the Jadot business in hand, Kopf's next notable achievement was landing a spirits brand: Beefeater Gin. Little known outside of England, Beefeater Gin was a favorite before-dinner drink of Kopf. He liked it well enough to secure the importing rights in 1946. Kopf then worked to make it a highly successful brand in the United States. It soon numbered among the top-20-selling brands of spirits each year. Beefeater became a reliable source of income for Kobrand for almost 40 years. A third key brand acquisition in another important category, champagne, took place shortly after the Beefeater deal, when Kopf secured the marketing rights to Taittinger Champagne, whose heritage reached back to the 1730s.

With the Jadot, Beefeater, and Taittinger brands anchoring the portfolio, Kobrand enjoyed steady growth for the next 20 years. It was prosperous enough that in 1965 Kopf was able to acquire a five-story townhouse on 40th Street on Manhattan's east side to relocate Kobrand's headquarters. In wines, the firm focused on French brands until 1978, when it began to market the Italian wines of Michele Chiarlo in the United States. Kopf's relationship with Jadot in the meantime remained strong, even after Louis Jadot died in 1962 at the age of 62. Kopf worked with Jadot's successor, Andre Gagey, who was put in charge of the winery until Jadot's 20-year-old son and only child, Louis-Alain, was ready to assume control. Unfortunately, the young man died in an auto accident at the age of 23, and because neither Jadot's widow nor his four daughters were interested in running the business, Gagey remained in charge.

KOPF ACQUIRES FRENCH WINERY: 1985

Gagey was over 60 years of age when Kopf inquired about the future at Jardot in the early 1980s, and broached the possibility of buying the business for his three daughters: Patricia Colagiuri, Sue Mueller, and Brenda Helies. The Jardot family agreed to the offer, but because it would be the first time that foreigners acquired

a Burgundian winery the deal needed government approval. The sale finally closed in January 1985, and while ownership changed hands, Gagey remained in charge of the business and, after gaining permission from Kopf, groomed his son to succeed him. Kopf would not live to see the young man join Jadot, however. In 1985 Kopf died at the age of 80, only a few months after the Jadot deal was completed. His three daughters shared in the ownership of Kobrand.

Also in 1985 Kobrand acquired its first stake in a California company, Napa Valley's Sequoia Grove Vineyards. A year later, Kobrand turned its attention to Northern California's Sonoma County, forming a joint venture with Taittinger called Domaine Carneros to establish a new winery, the first in the Carneros district to focus exclusively on the premium sparkling wine category. Kobrand added further to its California interests in 1987 when it reached a marketing agreement with Cakebread Cellars, a Napa Valley winery started by former photographer Jack Cakebread in 1973.

Aside from the fine wine category, in 1986 Kobrand introduced Alize, a blend of cognac and passion fruit juices new to the U.S. market. The following year Kobrand gained the exclusive rights to market the port products of Portugal's venerable Taylor, Fladgate & Yeatman, S.A., whose heritage dated to the 1690s. The year 1987 also marked the end of the relationship with Beefeater Gin. The brand was sold and a new firm, Buckingham Wile Co. assumed marketing chores at the start of 1988. The loss of Beefeater, which had U.S. sales in the $60 million range, was a blow to Kobrand, but the firm countered by continuing to build its portfolio of wine and spirit brands.

In 1988 Kobrand added another major port producer, Fonseca-Guimaraens, established in Portugal in 1822. Also in that year, Kobrand began representing Sonoma Valley's St. Francis Vineyards, a winery established in 1979 that had established a reputation for its Merlots and other fine wines. Kobrand also turned its attention to a new country, Chile, which was beginning to gain a reputation for producing excellent wines. In 1989 Kobrand began importing wine from Vina Undurraga.

The late 1980s also brought some uneasiness to the Kobrand operation. The Kopf daughters were reportedly offered $148 million by United Kingdom-based Allied Lyons for Kobrand and the French American Vinters, the holding company for Jadot and the family's other French wine interests. According to *Wine Spectator,* "Longtime Kobrand and Jadot managers felt betrayed after rumors circulated that the sisters came very close to selling. ... When news of the negotiations leaked, it annoyed the sisters so much, says Sue Mueller, that they

KEY DATES

1944: Rudolph C. Kopf founds Kobrand.

1965: Kobrand moves into a Midtown Manhattan townhouse.

1978: The firm imports its first Italian wines.

1985: Kopf dies, after securing the company for his three daughters.

1988: A marketing agreement with Beefeater Gin is severed after 40 years.

1995: The firm begins distributing Benziger Family Winery products.

2004: Blue Alize is introduced.

broke off the talks." The sisters maintained that while they felt obligated to consider such a large offer, they were never serious about selling their interests. Indeed, after passing on a chance to sell the business, the sisters backed an ongoing expansion of Kobrand and the French American Vinters business.

Kobrand added to its portfolio on several fronts in the early 1990s. It acquired the rights to the cognacs produced by Delamain & Co., another French firm with deep roots, reaching back to the 1760s. In 1992 Kobrand tried a new approach in its French business, joining forces with the owners of Fortant de France to develop varietal wine in the South of France. Traditionally, the French believed that soil and climate combined to give a wine its unique character. To maintain the wine industry based on this philosophy, the French in 1935 passed what became known as the AOC laws, which covered almost all of France's most famous wines. These regulations set geographical limits on regions and vineyards, determined which grape varieties were permitted to be used in a region, established the minimum amount of alcohol in the wine, set the maximum yield permitted per hectare, and codified other traditional aspects of viticulture and vinification. Kobrand and its partner looked to a region of France not covered by the AOC laws because it had never produced excellent wine. They convinced small growers to replant with classic varietals and restrict their yields, and to follow other techniques to improve quality. From these grapes a number of new quality wines were produced and then marketed in the United States by Kobrand.

During this period, Kobrand was also building up its portfolio of Italian wines, a move that had begun in 1986 when the wines of Azienda Fratelli Pighin were added. In the late 1980s and early 1990s Kobrand added

a host of brands, making the firm a major marketer of Italian wines. These labels included Sassicala, Ornellaia, Terriccio, Spalletti, and Chiehe Chiarlo.

Kobrand did not neglect its interest in California and French wines, however. In 1995 the firm landed an exclusive sales and marketing contract with Sonoma Valley's Benziger Family Winery, producer of award-winning wines since its founding in the early 1980s. Another important sales and marketing agreement followed in 1996 with the addition of Joseph Phelps Vineyards of Napa Valley to the fold. In 1997, Jadot acquired Chateau des Jacques of Moulin-a-Vent in the Beaujolais district of France. It included 67 acres of vineyards, dedicated to the growing of Gamay grapes, used in the making of Beaujolais wines. In 2001 Jadot added the 86-acre vineyard Chateau de Bellevue, located in the Morgon region of France. Kobrand also improved its portfolio of Italian wines in 2001, acquiring the rights to Vino Nobile di Montepulciano of Calvano, and the "Super Tuscan" lines of Cabreo and Sette Ponti.

Kobrand looked to other emerging wine countries as well. In 2001 the firm became the U.S. distributor of New Zealand's Craggy Ranger Winery. Established in the 1980s, the vineyards produced its first wines with the 1999 vintage. In 2002 Kobrand became involved in the Hungary wine business, acquiring an interest in G.I.A. Winery, founded in 1993 by international wine figure Tibor Gal, who was intent on proving that Hungary was capable of growing the kind of grapes that could produce quality wines. He introduced a wine brand that bore his name, which Kobrand introduced in the United States in 2004. Unfortunately, Gal died in a car crash in South Africa in February 2005.

NEW CENTURY: POPULARITY OF COGNAC

Kobrand was also enjoying success in spirits in the late 1990s and into the new century. Although it had been selling Alize since 1986, the cognac-based drink benefitted from the rising popularity of cognac, especially among African-Americans. In the early 1990s the category was in trouble as cognac's consumers, generally white and wealthy, were growing older and dying off. On the other hand, cognac had always enjoyed niche appeal with African-Americans as a mixer with other spirits, and it gained popularity with hip-hop artists like Tupac Shakur, who made references in their songs to the most popular brands of cognac, such as Hennessy. Hip-Hop fans began drinking cognac as well, which led to a wider cultural appeal. Alize was a favorite of Shakur before his death from a drive-by shooting in 1996. His song, "Thug Passion," referred to his favorite drink, Alize Red Passion with Hennessy.

Taking advantage of the boost given to Alize by Shakur and other hip-hop artists, Kobrand introduced Alize Cognac, minus the fruit juices, in 2000. When the blue cocktail rage hit clubs and bars in the early 2000s, Kobrand in 2004 introduced Alize Bleu, a different combination of cognac, vodka, passion fruit, and other fruit juices. In addition to marketing to the hip-hop crowd, Kobrand's efforts naturally touched the urban market, which included a high percentage of gays and lesbians. Kobrand actively courted this market. It became the corporate sponsor of many popular gay and lesbian performers, many of whom incorporated the drink into their shows. In New York's hit drag show, "Kiki and Herb," for example, the Kiki character, lamenting the loss of youth and the monotony of breakfast, recounted, "I can't tell you how much better my life has been since I discovered passion fruit in the morning, ladies and gentlemen. There is nothing better than a little Alize to kick-start your day. Thank God I am not a diabetic." The line was both an inside joke the audience appreciated as well as a product pitch. Kobrand also used more traditional approaches to marketing Alize Bleu. In 2005 it began airing animated commercials featuring an animated character, "Lady in Bleu," which aired on cable television channels.

Kobrand became involved in a new spirit category in 2006: rum. Long regarded as a downscale product, rum had been making strides in recent years, especially in the premium category. Before the marketplace became cluttered, as was the case with premium vodka, a number of companies were rushing out high-end rum products to establish market share before the inevitable shakeout. Kobrand's bid was Depaz Blue Cane Amber Rhum, introduced in June 2006 at select outlets in New York City before making its way to other major cities.

Ed Dinger

PRINCIPAL SUBSIDIARIES

French-American Vinters.

PRINCIPAL COMPETITORS

Sidney Frank Importing Co., Inc.; Schieffelin & Somerset Company; Diageo North America.

FURTHER READING

Hein, Kenneth, "Cognac Is In the House," *Brandweek,* September 22, 2003, p. 28.

———, "Kobrand Puts Passion Into Promotion of Alize Bleu," *Brandweek,* May 3, 2004, p. 14.

Howard, Theresa, "Alize, Take Me Away!" *Brandweek,* April 12, 1999, p. 20.

Mansson, Per-Henrik, "Americans in Burgundy," *Wine Spectator,* November 15, 1998.

Quittner, Jeremy, "Selling Is A Drag," *The Advocate,* April 24, 2001, p. 38.

Lands' End, Inc.

1 Lands' End Lane
Dodgeville, Wisconsin 53595
U.S.A.
Telephone: (608) 935-9341
Toll Free: (800) 356-4444
Fax: (608) 935-4260
Web site: http://www.landsend.com

Wholly-Owned Subsidiary of Sears, Roebuck and Co.
Incorporated: 1963 as Lands' End Yacht Stores
Employees: 7,550
Sales: $2.2 billion (2004 est.)
NAIC: 448110 Men's Clothing Stores; 44812 Women's
Clothing Stores; 448130 Children's & Infants'
Clothing Stores; 448150 Clothing Accessories
Stores; 448190 Other Clothing Stores; 454110
Electronic Shopping & Mail-Order Houses

■ ■ ■

Lands' End, Inc., is perhaps best known as a marketer of traditionally styled, casual clothing, available through catalogs known for their folksy, chatty style. The company's emphasis on quality merchandise and customer service has made it a leader in the mail-order marketing field. Manufacturing is farmed out to hundreds of contractors in the United States and abroad. Based in rural Wisconsin, Lands' End has grown steadily since its inception as a seller of sailing equipment for racing boats. By the late 1990s, the company was marketing clothing for children and products for the home, in addition to its tailored clothing for men and women. Lands' End quickly developed a reputation for e-commerce excellence and became the country's largest online apparel merchant. Its web site sets the standard for technical innovation. The company's acquisition by Sears, Roebuck extended the brand's presence to 870 Sears stores. Lands' End also has 17 of its own outlets.

YACHTING ORIGINS

Lands' End got its start in 1963 when Gary Comer, a successful advertising copywriter with Young & Rubicam, who had long pursued a love of sailing in his spare time, decided to pursue his long-standing dream of opening his own business. Comer quit his job of ten years, and with $30,000 in initial funds started a company that made sails and sold other marine hardware. The company set up shop in a storefront at 2317 North Elston Avenue, along the Chicago River in the city's old tannery district.

In 1964, Comer produced a catalog offering Lands' End's goods through the mail. The first booklet, entitled "The Racing Sailors' Equipment Guide," was printed in black-and-white, had 84 pages, and featured a variety of technical-looking sailing implements on its cover. A printer's error, however, resulted in the company's name being rendered "Lands' End," with the apostrophe in the wrong place. Since Comer could not afford to have the piece reprinted, he decided to simply change the name of the business to correspond with the brochure.

Lands' End began filling orders from its basement. The company shipped out orders the day they were received, and unconditionally guaranteed all that it sold. In a subsequent catalog, Comer put his copywriting skills to work in an innovative, customer-friendly format. The text in the Lands' End publications, rather than being dry, technical, and brief, had a casual, engaging, informative, and sympathetic air. Customers were put at ease reading it and came to feel that they had developed a personal relationship with the company that had produced the catalog and the items that filled it. Comer is credited with originating the concept of the "magalogue," in which pictured items for sale are surrounded and cushioned by appealing text and illustrations.

FROM SAILING EQUIPMENT TO CLOTHING

Lands' End's customers began to look to the company for more than just technical sailing gear, and many felt comfortable writing to the company to ask about purchasing foul weather gear and duffel bags. In response, Lands' End added a small clothing section to the catalog, featuring rainsuits, canvas luggage, shoes, sweaters, and some other clothing. The catalog's name was accordingly altered to simply the "Lands' End Catalogue." Items sold in the clothing portion of the catalog soon became the company's most profitable offerings.

Throughout the 1960s, Lands' End continued to sell sailing equipment and related items through its catalog. In 1970, Lands' End's mail order business had grown large enough to merit computerization of its inventory and sales operations. Lands' End made its first foray into the world of manufacturing something other than sailing equipment in 1973, when the company began to make its own duffle bags. The next year, Lands' End also began to market its own brand of rainsuit, a two-piece outfit worn by sailors in foul weather. In 1975, the company came out with its first all-color catalog, which featured 30 pages of sailing equipment and two full pages of clothing. By the following year, the company had decided to shift its emphasis to the sale of clothing and canvas luggage, and the quotient of non-nautical

equipment had risen to include eight pages displaying duffel bags, and three pages of clothing, including a men's chamois-cloth shirt.

In the spring of 1977, Lands' End issued its first catalog that paid serious attention to clothing, with 13 out of 40 pages dedicated to dry goods. In addition, the company introduced its own line of soft luggage, called Square Rigger. Following these innovations, sales for the year reached $3.6 million. After 1977, Lands' End phased out the sailing equipment aspect of its operation altogether, retaining the rugged, reliable, and traditional nature that sailing implied, and applying it to a broader variety of clothing. In 1978, the company introduced its first button-down Oxford-cloth shirt, heralding the move to offerings of solid, conservative, basic clothing upon which it would build its future.

Lands' End also began to shift its operations from its Chicago base to a small town in rural Wisconsin called Dodgeville. Comer chose this location for his growing enterprise because, as he noted in a piece of promotional literature, "I fell in love with the gently rolling hills and woods and cornfields and being able to see the changing seasons." In addition to the intangible spiritual benefits of life on the land, the move enabled Lands' End to ultimately locate the bulk of its operations in the middle of a cornfield in rural Wisconsin, an area in which costs were extremely low. The company began this shift when it moved its Chicago warehouse to an empty garage in Dodgeville in 1978.

Lands' End's operations were also shifting in another significant way during this time, as the company moved from filling orders by mail to filling orders by phone. The company had brought its first toll-free 800-number online, and operators were standing by to take customer calls by the middle of 1978. With this shift, the company had incorporated another point of contact with the customer into its operation, and it stressed politeness and customer service in its operators, a continuation of the message it strove to portray in its catalog. Calls were answered within a ring and a half, and operators were permitted to chat with customers for as long as it took to make a sale.

Lands' End continued the process of transferring operations to Dodgeville in 1979, opening an office in a pre-existing strip mall while it broke ground for an office building and an accompanying 33,000-square-foot warehouse in a Dodgeville industrial park. The following year, the company moved into its new space on "Lands' End Lane." By this time, the clothing section of its catalog had grown further, and the 800-number service had been expanded to accommodate customers 24 hours a day. Interested in gaining more control over the quality of the clothes it sold, the company began to

KEY DATES

1963: Company is founded in Chicago as a mail order catalog for sailors.
1970: Inventory and sales functions are computerized.
1973: Company manufactures duffle bags.
1978: Lands' End begins selling button-down Oxfords and gets a toll-free number.
1979: Company completes its move to Dodgeville, Wisconsin.
1981: A national advertising campaign is launched.
1986: Sales exceed $200 million; the company becomes a Delaware corporation.
1987: Shares trade on the New York Stock Exchange; children's clothing is introduced.
1999: Lands' End introduces 3-D virtual modeling on its Internet site.
2002: Sears Roebuck acquires Lands' End.
2003: Selected Lands' End merchandise appears in 870 Sears stores.

recruit employees who were knowledgeable about fabric and the manufacture of clothing.

In addition to its new facilities in Dodgeville, Lands' End also opened an outlet store in Chicago, just one block from its original location, to sell the goods that made up excess inventory if catalog sales of a particular item were not as brisk as expected. Further physical expansion took place the following year, in 1981, when Lands' End began work on a 40,000-square-foot addition to its warehouse in Wisconsin. The company also broke ground on a plant to manufacture its own line of soft luggage in West Union, Iowa.

NATIONAL ADVERTISING CAMPAIGN IN 1981

To further support its burgeoning sales and reputation, Lands' End embarked on a national advertising campaign in 1981. The purpose of this effort was to make customers aware of the Lands' End business philosophy, and associate its name with service, value, and quality. The company used the expression "direct merchant" to describe its relationship, as a manufacturer and distributor, with the customer.

In the next year, Lands' End followed up this effort with a significant investment in computerization, as the company introduced online customer sales and ordering to speed up processes. Efficient use of computers was a keystone of Lands' End's program for success, and soon computer systems enabled operators to provide customers with a wealth of information at the touch of a finger.

In addition, Lands' End continued to expand its warehouse facilities as it started construction on an additional 126,000-square-foot warehouse across the street from its original Dodgeville facilities. Moving into this facility in 1983 required the unloading of 8,000 boxes of goods so that the company's new automated sorting system could be made operational. By this time, a nationwide boom in mail-order shopping was beginning to take off, and Lands' End saw its sales and earnings start to grow.

In an effort to exploit Americans' increasing willingness to shop by phone using their credit cards, Lands' End introduced a line of fancier clothing for men and women in 1983, under the name Charter Club. Instead of cotton and wool, these products were manufactured from Italian silks and other luxury fabrics. This line soon had its own catalog of offerings.

In 1984, Lands' End passed another landmark on the way to becoming a full-fledged manufacturer when its logo was registered as a U.S. trademark. By the following year, demand for Lands' End goods had increased to the point where the company was able to begin issuing monthly as opposed to seasonal catalogs. In addition, Lands' End broke ground on yet another warehouse addition.

In 1986, Lands' End discontinued its Charter Club line of dressier clothing, despite the fact that it was profitable, in an effort to maintain the company's culture and focus on solid, traditional, no-nonsense clothes. "When they started shooting photographs of models in London, I said, 'That's it, enough'," Comer later told *Fortune.* His conception of the company was more straightforward. "I picked things that I liked, and over the years people interested in the same sorts of things gathered around," he said, explaining Lands' End's growth.

PUBLIC IN 1987

By 1986, growth had brought Lands' End profits of more than $14 million on sales topping $200 million. At that point, after several years of phenomenal advances, the company sold stock to the public for the first time, offering 1.4 million shares at $30 apiece. In the following year, shares of Lands' End began to be traded on the New York Stock Exchange, as the company racked up earnings of about $15 million.

Also in 1987, in response to customer requests,

Lands' End introduced a line of children's clothing. Within a year it had yielded sales of almost $15 million. By 1988, Lands' End had built up a loyal core of catalog shoppers. The company shipped nine million booklets a month, full of homey straight talk about classic casual clothing, for a total of 80 million pieces mailed a year. To take the orders generated by this promotional literature, Lands' End also spent heavily on technology to improve its customer service, adding new sorting, packaging, and sewing equipment (for alterations). In addition, the company broke ground on an additional phone center in a town about 30 miles from Dodgeville, Cross Plains, Wisconsin. With this facility, Lands' End planned to add 100 new employees to its payroll.

At the end of the year, the company also opened a small retail outlet in Dodgeville to sell its clothes. Although Lands' End had no intention of branching out from the mail order business into conventional retail, the company had discovered that people felt so at home with the places and people depicted in the Lands' End catalog that they frequently got in their cars and drove to Dodgeville on vacation to see the place for themselves. After customers began wandering into Lands' End's corporate offices looking to buy turtlenecks and sweat-shirts, the company opened a small store to serve them. Additional Lands' End outlet stores followed, offering overstock items to the public.

COMPETITION HEATS UP

After a blockbuster year in 1988, Lands' End's revenues had nearly doubled in the span since its first stock offering, rising to $456 million for the fiscal year ending in January 1989. Two months later, however, the company was forced to announce its sharpest drop in earnings ever. Although sales had continued to grow, costs had grown at a much steeper rate. Confident that sales would continue strongly after 1988, the company had amassed a large inventory of merchandise. When sales slowed, it was forced to send out a large number of additional catalogs in an attempt to win new customers. This campaign proved to be extremely costly, adding about $2 million to the company's promotional budget. This cost promised to rise further as the post office implemented a 17 percent hike in third class mailing rates.

In addition, Lands' End found itself hurt by the stodgy reputation of its merchandise, as competition in the catalog sales field heated up. In particular, the company lost ground to Eddie Bauer, a marketer of rugged outdoor gear, as well as to L.L. Bean. Lands' End needed to update and freshen its offerings without alienating old customers who appreciated the company's solid, traditional goods.

The company's outdated offerings continued to damage its profitability throughout the start of 1990, and it posted a two-thirds drop in profits in the first quarter of that year. Concerned that Lands' End and its rival L.L. Bean might have grown so large that they had glutted the market for their type of merchandise, industry watchers predicted further declines at the company.

In response to its falling profits, Lands' End began to increase the amount of new merchandise in its catalog. Whereas the previous two years' catalogs had offered first 8 percent and then 11.5 percent new items, as much as 18 percent of the products in 1990's catalogs were new introductions. Among the additions were sunglasses, children's swimsuits, and clothing and bedding for infants. The company also began to market "Mom Packs," combinations of merchandise packed together to be presented as Mother's Day gifts. In addition, Lands' End introduced three new specialty catalogs: Button-downs and Beyond, which featured tailored clothing for men; Coming Home with Lands' End, with products for the bed and bath; and in August 1990, a separate catalog just for children called Kids. Also in 1992, the company created its corporate sales unit. This unit distributed five catalogs per year to corporations that regularly purchased gifts for clients and employees.

Lands' End also began its first attempt to expand its market beyond the borders of the United States. In typical company style, Lands' End encouraged its customers to become part of this new push, asking them to send in the names of their relatives who lived overseas. The company first began to mail a catalog to potential customers in the United Kingdom, and eventually opened a U.K. phone center and distribution facility in the fall of 1993. By the late 1990s, the company was publishing catalogs for 175 countries, with prices converted to the English pound, the German mark, and the Japanese yen. Moreover, it introduced three international subsidiaries, Lands' End Japan, K.K., Lands' End Direct Merchants UK Limited, and Lands' End GmbH in Germany.

RESTRUCTURING

During this time, the saturation of the catalog sales market had a major effect upon Lands' End's profitability. Although sales continued to increase, gross profit margins dropped. The 1990s saw the company acquire and then divest two subsidiaries—Territory Ahead, Inc., and MontBell America, Inc.—as well as liquidate Willis & Geiger, its outdoor clothing and accessories division. Lands' End made further reductions in early 1999, restructuring the company and eliminating 10 percent of its salaried jobs and closing three of its

19 outlet stores. These efforts streamlined the company to help it maintain its competitive edge. Management changes also ensued. In 1998 President and CEO Michael J. Smith resigned and was replaced by David F. Dyer. Company founder Gary C. Comer remained as chairman of the board.

Lands' End faced the future armed with several new retailing concepts to enhance its operations. In 1997 the company opened its first Inlet Store, described by its designers as "a catalog come to life." The Inlet Store prototype, in Richfield, Minnesota, featured a central area decorated in warm, residential tones, designed to overcome resistance some customers had to catalog shopping. In a comfortable homelike atmosphere, the "catalog-in-a-store" provided sales and sizing assistance, returns, alterations, and monogramming services. Along the perimeter of the Inlet Store were Lands' End overstocked and discontinued items. After the prototype's successful launch, the company began converting its existing outlet stores to Inlet Stores.

INTERNET INNOVATIONS

Lands' End also hoped to enhance its operations via the Internet, and it launched a web site for that purpose. In 1998 management reported that the Internet was still an insignificant but potentially valuable portion of their $1.2 billion business, serving as another venue for already-established customers. Visitors to the Lands' End site could peruse and purchase from an online catalog that allowed various views of an article of clothing, additional information about the clothing, and side-by-side views of various articles of clothing. The online shopping experience, in contrast to the company's phone order rules against "upselling," offered the customer the opportunity to add accessories to their purchases. The Internet site was continuously updated, while discontinued and out-of-stock items were quickly removed from the site. From Lands' End perspective, the online site represented a savings in catalog distribution costs, rather than a means of increasing client base.

However, a 1999 innovation drew media attention, when Lands' End became one of the first to provide 3-D apparel modeling for women. At www.landsend.com, online shoppers could key in their personal measurements, and their own personal 3-D apparel model would appear onscreen, helping the customer better determine whether the clothing suited him. *Computerworld* magazine characterized the 3-D process as "cool" and fun, noting that "according to retail experts, it's seen as one of the most promising ways to convert online browsers to online buyers." Oxford Express was another new feature of the Lands' End Website in 1999. With this feature, customers could select sizes, fabrics, styles, collars, and cuffs, and a depiction of the shirt appeared on screen, ready to order. Still, Lands' End expected the major portion of its business to be conducted through traditional catalog sales well into the next century.

Prospects for the newly restructured Lands' End remained strong. Its reputation for quality and its steady course of business growth ensured that it was rigged for competitive sailing in increasingly competitive seas. The cataloger was working to reduce inventory levels while updating styles. Less popular colors were removed as trendy items such as Polartec fleece jackets were added.

In fiscal 2000, Land's End posted revenues of $1.3 billion; online sales made up 10.5 percent of the total. The press was raving about Lands' End's Internet offerings, which seemed to be adding revolutionary new capabilities every year. The virtual model was relaunched in the fall of 2000, and was soon accompanied by the recommendations feature My Personal Shopper. Two years later, the web site began offering the ability to order custom tailored chinos. Developed with Emeryville, California software provider Archetype Solutions Inc., the custom-ft program helped keep inventories and returns low: orders were passed off to a contractor in Mexico and shipped directly to consumers. *Catalog Age* noted that Lands' End was still addressing the monumental task of integrating its online and telephone ordering systems.

Revenues reached a record $1.6 billion in the fiscal year ended February 1, 2002. The Internet accounted for one-fifth of sales. Net income of $67 million was nearly double the previous year's figure.

ACQUIRED BY SEARS IN 2002

Sears Roebuck and Co. acquired Lands' End for $1.84 billion in June 2002. Lands' End founder Gary Comer sold his majority shareholding in the transaction. *Catalog Age* called it the "Deal of the Century." Sears added a selection of Lands' End clothing to its 867 full lines stores in a bid to revive its traditionally weak apparel sections. At the same time, the in-store placements promised to raise Lands' End's brand awareness while adding a new bricks-and-mortar sales channel (though the company did already have 14 outlet stores). Though Sears' clothing tended to attract budget-hunters, the department store's Craftsman tools and Kenmore appliances attracted a similar demographic to Lands' End's relatively affluent customer base.

David Dyer left Lands' End in August 2003 (he later became CEO of Tommy Hilfiger Corporation), after which it was overseen by three executives who had followed the company to Sears. One of them, Mindy

Meads, was promoted to president and CEO of Lands' End in early 2004. Formerly in charge of Sears' apparel merchandising and design, she had 11 years' experience with Lands' End before it was integrated into Sears.

Sears' direct-to-customer revenues, most of which were provided by Lands' End, slipped 8 percent in fiscal 2004. Lands' End later cut about 400 jobs as a cost-controlling measure. Sears CEO Alan Lacy countered those who questioned the benefits of its great multi-channel experiment. He told analysts that Lands' End's total business rose more than 20 percent compared to the previous year (if direct sales were flat at $1.6 billion, the addition of the retail business would bring total revenues to roughly $2 billion). Sears had introduced the brand to millions of new customers since rolling it out to all of its stores in September 2003, and it had already accounted for $400 million of the year's in-store sales.

Department store giant Kmart Holding Corp. merged with Sears in March 2005; the new Sears Holdings Corporation had been formed as a parent company to both. Lands' End CEO Mindy Meads left the company a few months after the Kmart-Sears merger. Insiders told *Crain's Chicago Business* that sales had been flat for three years. Sears was experimenting with installing dedicated Lands' End boutiques inside its department stores (the goods had previously been sold alongside its other clothing lines). In 2006 a temporary "Lands' End Summer Shop" appeared in a Super Kmart in New York's affluent Hamptons community in 2006; at mid-decade, this was the brand's only presence in Kmart.

Elizabeth Rourke
Updated, Shannon and Terry Hughes; Frederick C. Ingram

PRINCIPAL COMPETITORS

Eddie Bauer, Inc.; L.L. Bean, Inc.

FURTHER READING

Berg, Eric N., "Standout in the Land of Catalogues," *New York Times,* December 8, 1988.

Berner, Robert, "Sears-Lands' End: The Seams May Show; Can Sears Avoid Cannibalizing the Cataloger's Business While Not Alienating Its Upscale Clientele? This Deal May Not Be a Perfect Fit," *Business Week Online,* May 16, 2002.

Bremner, Brian, "Lands' End Looks a Bit Frayed at the Edges," *Business Week,* March 19, 1990.

Buechner, Maryanne Murray, "Recharging Sears: Hooking Up with Lands' End, the Old Store Buys Into a New Idea: Multichannel Retailing. Will It Work?," *Time,* May 27, 2002, pp. 46ff.

Caminiti, Susan, "A Mail-Order Romance: Lands' End Courts Unseen Customers," *Fortune,* March 13, 1989.

Chandler, Susan and Becky Yerak, "Showdown Over Lands' End in Kmart, Sears Cost CEO Her Job," *Chicago Tribune,* August 5, 2005.

Chiger, Sherry, "A Match Made in... ," *Multichannel Merchant,* September 1, 2005.

Cotlier, Moira, "Case Study: Lands' End (Customer Service, Part 1)," *Catalog Age,* February 2001, p. 51.

Drickhamer, David, "A Leg Up on Mass Customization: Software Enables Lands' End Customers to Be Particular about Their Pants," *Industry Week,* September 2002, p. 59.

Gellers, Stan and Jessica Pallay, "Lands' End Ends at Kmart," *Daily News Record,* July 3, 2006, p. 2.

Higgins, Kevin T., "Opportunity Calls," *Marketing Management,* Winter 1997, pp. 4-8.

Jones, Sandra, "Saving Sears Apparel Biz; Will Lands' End's Pricey Polartec Be a Hit?," *Crain's Chicago Business,* November 25, 2002, p. 1.

——, "What's In Store for Lands' End? Store-Within-Store Being Tested, But How Long Will Sears Keep Brand?," *Crain's Chicago Business,* September 19, 2005, p. 2.

King, Julia, "3-D Images May Spur Web Buys," *Computerworld,* May 24, 1999, p. 1.

"Lands' End to Restructure, Cut Jobs and Close Stores," *Direct Marketing,* February 1999, p. 8.

Miller, Paul and Mark Del Franco, "Deal of the Century," *Catalog Age,* June 1, 2002.

Moin, David, Evan Clark, and Kristin Larson, "Sears Hooks Lands' End for $1.9B," *WWD,* May 14, 2002, p. 3.

Nathans, Aaron, "Fears of An Identity Crisis for Lands' End at Sears," *New York Times,* December 25, 2004, p. C5.

Odell, Patricia, "Welcome to the Party," *Direct,* June 1, 2002.

Podmolik, Mary Ellen, "Jury Is Still Out on Sears' New Lands' End Wardrobe," *Crain's Chicago Business,* January 26, 2004, p. 13.

Schwadel, Francine, "Lands' End Stumbles as Fashion Shifts Away from Retailer's Traditional Fare," *Wall Street Journal,* April 27, 1990.

"Sears Satisfied with Lands' End Business," *Daily News Record,* February 2, 2004, p. 7.

"The Solid Ground Under Lands' End; Balmy Weather May Be Wilting the Catalog Retailer's Share Price These Days, But Recent Strategy Shifts Look Like They'll Pay Off," *Business Week Online,* December 7, 2001.

Wagner, Mitch, "From the Top—Michael J. Smith, President and CEO, Lands' End," *Internetweek,* September 14, 1998, p. 22.

Wilson, Marianne, "Lands' End Captures Catalog Experience," *Chain Store Age,* March 1997, pp. 140-41.

Young, Vicki M., "Dyer to Exit as President of Lands' End," *WWD,* August 4, 2003, p. 23.

——, "Focus on New Shores: Sears Said Shopping Its Lands' End Division," *WWD,* March 15, 2005, p. 1.

Littleton Coin Company Inc.

1309 Mount Eustis Road
Littleton, New Hampshire 03561-3734
U.S.A.
Telephone: (603) 444-3571
Toll Free: (800) 645-3122
Fax: (603) 444-0121
Web site: http://www.littletoncoin.com

Private Company
Incorporated: 1945 as Littleton Stamp Company
Employees: 380
Sales: $84 million
NAIC: 452998 All Other Miscellaneous Stores Retailers
(Except Tobacco Stores)

■ ■ ■

Based in the small town of Littleton, New Hampshire, Littleton Coin Company Inc. is a privately owned coin dealer, serving coin collectors from around the world through catalogs and the Internet. The company offers a wide variety of coins, from U.S. pennies of the early 1800s costing $55 to ancient Roman gold coins with a price tag of more than $10,000. Littleton also sells rare coins, which have been out of circulation for an extended period of time, were part of small mintages, or possess an abnormality. The 1856 Flying Eagle cent, one of the rarest of all U.S. coins, can be purchased from Littleton for $21,900. The company also deals in U.S. paper money, including Confederate notes, and money from dozens of companies around the world. In addition, Littleton sells coin collecting books and videos albums,

coin holders, display frames, magnifiers, other supplies, and a variety of gifts and novelties; and operates several collector clubs for U.S. coins, world money, and ancient coins. The company also buys coins and paper money, having spent more than $200 million since 1945. Littleton is owned and operated by its founder Maynard Sundman and his son David. Another son, Don Sundman, heads a sister company, Mystic Stamp Company of Camden, New York.

FOUNDER DEVELOPS PASSION FOR STAMPS: 1927

Maynard Sundman was born in Bristol, Connecticut, in 1915, the son of a salesman. At the age of 12, in 1927, he was visiting a friend. Rain forced them inside, and to bide the time his friend brought out his stamp collection. Sundman was enthralled and when his parent came to bring him home, all he could talk about were the stamps. According to his recollections 75 years later, he never stopped talking about stamps. He soon sent away for a selection of stamps from one of the companies that advertised in the popular magazine *American Boy.* However, more than the stamps themselves, Sundman became fascinated by the stamp company ads and mail-order operations in general. He was constantly sending away for free offers and catalogs, disappointed on days that brought no mail. In high school he began nurturing the dream of starting up his own mail-order stamp company. Shortly before high school graduation, in May 1935, he wrote to the H. E. Harris Stamp Company, the largest stamp wholesaler in the world. In his letter to request a wholesale catalog, Maynard wrote that he had saved $400 in order to start his own business and wanted

COMPANY PERSPECTIVES

We've been making collecting fun and easy for collectors since 1945. Our goal is to provide collectors with the largest selection of coins and paper money in the widest range of grades, along with useful collector supplies and accessories—all of it backed with friendly, knowledgeable and dependable service.

to know if he could make a "good start." Receiving encouragement from the wholesaler, Sundman set up shop in his parents' home and launched the Maynard Sundman Stamp Company, placing his first ad in the "Trading Post" section of *Stamps Magazine,* giving away several foreign postage stamps—charging two cents for shipping—as a way to build a customer mailing list.

Sundman's stamp company slowly grew, and soon he hired four women to assist him in fulfilling orders, with his parents also chipping in. After a year he was established enough to receive credit from H.E. Harris Company. After four years he was meeting with Henry Ellis Harris himself, the most influential man in the stamp business. Harris had launched his own company at the age of 14, by 18 was traveling to Europe to cultivate contacts, and was still just 37 years of age when he summoned young Sundman to his Boston offices. There he offered a partnership arrangement in which Sundman would receive a line of credit, help with marketing and advertising, and access to the name of customers responding to Harris's own advertising. For his part, Sundman was to put up $3,500 in good faith money. With the help of his father, Sundman raised the money and joined forces with Harris, becoming the fourth of what would become known as the "Big Five" stamp companies, all of which relied on Harris as their stamp supplier. Another of the big five would be the Mystic Stamp, a name suggested by Harris because he had always been fascinated by the name of the Mystic River.

SUNDMAN ENTERS ARMY: 1941

Harris became Sundman's active mentor and business partner, reviewing the ads Sundman placed in such publications as *Boys Life, Tip Top Comics,* and *Young America.* Sundman also relied on Harris's printing services. In 1941 Sundman also gained a life partner, marrying Fannie Kasper, who shared his enthusiasm for the stamp business. Their mutual dream of running a stamp company would have to be put on hold, however,

when shortly before the United States became involved in World War II in December 1941 Maynard was called to active duty in the army. He served with a military police company for the next four years and had to liquidate his stamp inventory. While he was away, his wife worked as a dress buyer and built up their savings account to more than $4,000, money they planned to use to start a fresh mail-order company, one that did not rely on his parents' kitchen table. Moreover, they wanted to set up shop in a small New England town. Hearing about New Hampshire's North Country, he dispatched Fannie to take the train to visit the communities in the area. She was immediately won over by the small shoe-and-lumber-mill town of Littleton, not only because of its mountain setting and friendly residents, but also the town's unusually large post office, a major asset to a mail-order operation. In time, this post office would have to hire extra people to process the extra mail that would be addressed to the town's new stamp company.

With the war over, Sundman was discharged in the fall of 1945, and within a matter of days Fannie was showing him Littleton. They soon rented a pair of rooms above the Tilton Opera Block for office space and secured a one-room apartment. They called the new business the Littleton Stamp Company, a name not embraced by Harris but one that connoted the quality the Sundmans wished to convey: small town honesty. The first ads were placed in December, and with four employees, operations began in earnest in January 1946. The Littleton Stamp Company began to enjoy steady growth. In the spring of 1947 Sundman took the first step toward the coin and paper money business when he began offering foreign banknotes.

By the fall of 1950, employment at Littleton had grown tenfold, from four to 40, and the company was about to enjoy even stronger growth, due primarily to Sundman's innovative approach to advertising. Taking advantage of the public's morbid fascination with Adolf Hitler, he developed an ad that offered as a premium a set of Bohemia-Moravia stamps that featured ten different pictures of Hitler. More importantly, Sundman did not limit himself to advertising in the usual publications that carried stamp ads, instead turning to newspapers and comic books to attract a host of new customers. To meet demand Sundman had to hire 20 new full-time employees in 1950 and 1951, during which time he exhausted the world's supply of the Hitler stamps. Also remarkable was Sundman's ability to keep his new advertising strategy from gaining the notice of his rivals, who were mostly located in the Northeast. The campaign was rolled out from West to East, so that it escaped the attention of the other stamp companies; not so H.E. Harris, who could not help but notice Littleton's rising sales at a time when the industry itself was in a slump

KEY DATES

1945: Littleton Stamp Company founded by Maynard Sundman.
1954: Name changed to The Little Stamp & Coin Company.
1972: David Sundman joins father.
1974: Sundman buys Mystic Stamp Company, which later buys Littleton's stamp inventory.
1985: David Sundman assumed presidency.
1999: Company moves into new 65,000-square-foot headquarters.
2005: Addition of 20,000 square feet added to the headquarters.

because of the Korean War. After learning what Sundman had been up to, he passed on the information to the other members of the "Big Five," who soon began to emulate the Littleton strategy. Maynard was far from pleased with Harris's indiscretion, leading to a temporary breach between the long-time partners. It would be repaired, however, as Maynard realized that he could not keep his national advertising a secret for much longer, and he took pleasure in having secured thousands of new customers in the previous two years.

Maynard had long recognized the compatibility of stamp and coin collecting and had made some periodic banknote and coin offers. In 1954 he formally expanded into the coin business, changing the company's name to The Littleton Stamp & Coin Company. He scraped by, but lacked a reliable coin supplier, and that changed in 1960 when a young Montreal dealer named Max Yas sent Maynard a list of coin sets and single coins he had available. Sundman bought the entire inventory, thus establishing a prosperous relationship between the two men that would last 25 years.

The coin business proved successful enough that in 1964 Littleton hired its first full-time buyer. Also in that year, the company emerged as the largest postal customer in the region. To keep pace with business Littleton moved its 70 employees into newly leased facilities, replacing the offices that had taken up the entire third floor of the Opera Block, as well as three additional offices the company had been forced to rent in a building across the street.

While the Maynards were busy growing the stamp and coin business, they were also raising three sons: David, born in 1948, Rick in 1950, and Don in 1954. Their father would instill in them the love of collecting

and the thrill of discovering rarities. He brought home bags of coins for the boys to sort through, giving them 10 percent of the book value of any rare coin they found. By the time he graduated from high school David had become something of an expert in cataloging coin characteristics, or "attributing." Upon graduation from Gettysburg College with a degree in history, he hoped to join the family business, but his father thought it wiser that the young man first gain business experience elsewhere. So, David spent the next two years working as an assistant supervisor for a small retail fashion chain. In the meantime, Littleton moved into a newly constructed headquarters, a 19,000-square-foot facility to accommodate the firm's 90 employees and the mailing of more than 300,000 catalogs each year. David Sundman finally joined his father in August 1972.

MYSTIC STAMP COMPANY ACQUIRED: 1974

A second son, Rick, joined Littleton in 1974, and was instrumental in growing the coin business, especially in the area of coin shows, although he would eventually strike out on his own to pursue other business interests. The youngest son, David, would carry on the father's interest in stamps. He had been a child with an entrepreneurial spirit. At the age of 12 he borrowed $1,000 from his father to start an aquarium and tropical fish retail business, running it out of his bedroom. In about 18 months he was able to pay off the loan. In 1974 Maynard Sundman was presented with an opportunity to purchase his old-time rival, the Mystic Stamp Company, but he said he would only do so if Don agreed to run it. The youngest agreed and took over as president, despite being just 19 years of age. In about a year he succeeded in tripling sales at Mystic.

By the mid-1970s Littleton was doing more business in coins than in stamps and the gap continued to grow. In the 1980s Littleton sold its stamp inventory to Mystic, which under the leadership of Don Sundman had emerged by the end of the decade as the United States's largest stamp company. After selling off its stamps, Littleton shortened its name to Littleton Coin Company. In 1985, the 70-year-old Maynard Sundman turned over the presidency of Littleton to David, but he was hardly ready for retirement and continued to come into the office every day.

The 1980s was a period of intense interest in coins as a form of speculative interest. Littleton established its own investment division to participate, and although it was able to make money, the unit was ultimately shut down. The disreputable nature of the trade, in which the quality of coins were regularly misrepresented, did not hold much appeal to the Sundmans, who would ban the use of the word "investment" in their sales material. "When you promise something, you want it to be true," David Sundman told the *Philadelphia Inquirer* in 1992. "What we promise is people are going to have fun. That's something we can deliver." In the meanwhile, many of the silver dollars and other U.S. coins that enjoyed a spectacular rise in value in the 1980s came to a crash by the end of the decade, worth little more than they had been 20 years earlier.

UNPRECEDENTED GROWTH: 1990 AND BEYOND

By the early 1990s, Littleton was doing more than $10 million a year in business and employing a work force of 125. The company continued to send out coins to potential customers on an approval basis, requiring no down payment or credit card number, trusting that the coins would either be bought or returned. It was an old-fashioned, small town way of doing business, but it continued to be a successful formula. By the same token, Littleton hired experts to refine its operation and brought in talented managers in specialized areas to drive growth. As a result, from 1990 to 1995, when the company turned 50 years old, Littleton enjoyed the strongest five-year period of growth in its history.

Most of the business had come from U.S. coins, but now the company began paying greater attention to money from around the world, from recent years and antiquity. Nevertheless, some of the most exciting moments for the company in the late 1990s involved large caches of U.S. coins. Littleton, for example, acquired the 23,000-coin collection of a deceased New York City subway clerk, Morris Moscow. Each day at work from the 1940s to the 1960s, he sorted through the change, stashing interesting finds in tan Transit Authority envelopes, some of which would not be opened for 40 years or more. Littleton acquired an even greater hoard—over 1.7 million Indian Head pennies, Liberty Head nickels, and Buffalo nickels—collected by an anonymous man in the Midwest who stashed them in canvas bags and 55-gallon drums hidden in the walls of his house. In 1999 Littleton bought 8,261 silver dollars minted from the legendary Comstock Lode of the 1850s, which had been sitting in a bank vault for the past 26 years. In the year 2000 Littleton was again in the news and enhancing its reputation when it helped a New Hampshire man sell a $20 gold certificate, issued during the Civil War and redeemable from the U.S. treasury for $20 in gold. The oversized bill had been passed down in a family through a relative who had been a New York

banker, spending several decades in a leather pouch tucked in a desk drawer. The fourth-generation owner finally decided to have it appraised along with some other coins and 19th-century paper money that came to him. One dealer gave a value of $1,100 for the entire collection, while a second offered a $2,000 estimate. The owner sensed that the dealers had spotted something of value in the collection and he sought out Littleton, which immediately informed him that the gold certificate was extremely rare. When Littleton auctioned it off, the note fetched the owner $220,000 and the company praise for its honesty.

Business continued to grow for Littleton in the new century. The company moved into a new modern 65,000-square-foot headquarters, the largest in the United States dedicated to coin and paper money collecting. It became a minor tourist attraction for visitors from around the world, who came to take a company tour. In 2005, Littleton added another 20,000 square feet to increase operations and warehouse space. Now 90 years old, Maynard Sundman was on hand for the groundbreaking ceremony.

Ed Dinger

PRINCIPAL OPERATING UNITS

U.S. Coins; U.S. Paper Money; Rare Coins; Ancient Coins; World Money.

PRINCIPAL COMPETITORS

American Gold Exchange, Inc.; Legend Numismatics; National Gold Exchange.

FURTHER READING

Franklin, Amy, "Old West Coins Emerge from Vault," *Wisconsin State Journal*, April 24, 1999, p. 8B.

"Man Finds $20 Heirloom Worth $250,000," *Florida Times Union*, November 27, 2000, p. A4.

O'Traynor, Michael, *A Descent Boldness: The Life Achievement of Maynard Sundman at Littleton Stamp & Coin Company,* Littleton, New Hampshire: Littleton Coin Press, 1995, 330 p.

"Rare Coins Roar Back into Circulation," *Daily News* (Los Angeles, New York), July 24, 1997, p. N2.

Stecklow, Steve, "Firm Reflects Small-Town Virtues," *Philadelphia Inquirer*, July 21, 1992, p. A01.

Tirrell-Wysocki, David, "Littleton Firm Hits Jackpot with Old Coin Cache," *Associated Press*, November 16, 1998.

Mandom Corporation

**5-12 Juniken-cho
Chuo-ku
Osaka-shi, OSK 540-8530
Japan
Telephone: (81) 06 6767 5001
Fax: (81) 06 6767 5044
Web site: http://www.mandom.co.jp**

Public Company
Incorporated: 1927 as Kintsuru Perfume Corporation
Employees: 2,054
Sales: ¥47.92 billion ($422.55 million) (2006)
Stock Exchanges: Tokyo
Ticker Symbol: 4917
NAIC: 325620 Toilet Preparation Manufacturing

■ ■ ■

Mandom Corporation is an Osaka-based manufacturer and distributor of hair care, skin care, perfumes and deodorants, and other personal care products, including cosmetics. The company has traditionally specialized in serving the men's personal care market, and is one of Japan's leaders in that segment through its top-selling brands Gatsby and Lucido. Mandom also produces hair care, beauty products and cosmetics for women under the Lucido L and Simplicity brands. Other company brands include professional hair care and other products under Dr. Renaud; the Japanese license for distribution of the Guinot brand; hair care brands Formulate, Aristia, and Direction Refilia; the women's cosmetics brand

courrèges; and international brands Pixy, Pucelle, Miratone, and Johnny Andrean.

Founded in 1927, Mandom launched its first international operation in 1959, with a production partnership in the Philippines. The company has since expanded its range of operations to include manufacturing and distribution subsidiaries in China and Indonesia, and sales and distribution subsidiaries in Taiwan, Korea, Hong Kong, Singapore, and Malaysia. Asia region sales account for approximately 25 percent of group sales, which neared 48 billion ($422 million) in 2006. Mandom is listed on the Tokyo Stock Exchange. The founding Nishimura family continues to lead the company, as represented by Motonobu Nishimura, president and chairman of the board.

PRE-WAR PERFUME ORIGINS

Mandom Corporation was founded in 1927 by Shinpachiro Nishimura as Kintsuru Perfume Corporation. Named after a highly fragrant flower also known as the Japanese Stone Orchid, the company soon established its name among Japan's cosmetics and hair care industry. The launch of the company's Tancho Tique "hair control" stick in 1933 provided the company with its first major commercial success. Also known as the Tancho Stick, the pomade remained highly popular among Japanese men for decades, and continued to be featured as a company mainstay into the next century. The success of that product also encouraged the company to focus its growth efforts specifically on the men's care sector.

The company's importance in the Japanese market

was underscored following the war when Shinpachiro Nishimura was named as the president of the Kinki Cosmetic Industry Association in 1949. By the end of the 1950s, the company had launched its first effort to expand beyond Japan. In 1958, the company reached a technical agreement with a partner in the Philippines, with production beginning soon after. By 1959, the popularity of the Tancho Tique led the company to change its name to Tancho Corporation.

The next generation of the Nishimura family took over the leadership of the company in 1961, when Hikoji Nishimura was named company president. Founder Shinpachiro Nishimura died in 1966. Under the second generation of family leadership, which also included future company president Ikuo Nishimura, Tancho continued to explore international expansion. The next step in that direction came in 1969, when the company started up a joint venture in Indonesia. PT Tancho Indonesia, later wholly owned by the company, became the Tancho's primary international manufacturing center for its growing international sales effort.

This effort was further boosted in 1970 when the company launched a new line of highly successful men's care products, called Mandom. The launch of the new line, which took its name from a combination of the words "Human" and "Freedom" was backed by an innovative advertising campaign featuring Charles Bronson. The ad campaign became the first of a long series of Japanese ads to feature top Hollywood stars. The highly successful launch also inspired Tancho to change its name again, to Mandom Corporation, in 1971.

The following year, Mandom teamed up with French dermatological cosmetics developer Doctor Louis Raymond Renaud, founding the Japan Doctor Renaud Cosmetics Company to launch the brand for the Japanese market. That subsidiary, which changed its name to Piacelabo in the mid-1990s, later opened up its own salons, and began marketing a range of dermatological cosmetics, in addition to the Dr. Renaud brand.

In the meantime, Mandom itself had continued its strong growth, backed by the construction of a new factory at Fukusaki in 1976. The expanded production also encouraged Mandom to take over its own distribution operations, and by the end of the decade the company had put its own sales force into place. The shift to direct sales was initially aided by Mandom's launch of another highly successful line of men's care products, called Gatsby. That line went on to become the company's flagship brand.

1980–1993: MEDIUM-TERM PLANNING STRATEGY

Despite the success of the Gatsby brand, the shift to direct retail sales had proved disastrous for the company. By 1980, the company had been forced to abandon the direct sales model, returning to wholesale distribution. Even having taken this action, Mandom found itself in financial difficulty at the beginning of the 1980s. The period saw a change in command, with Hikoji Nishimura becoming company chairman, and Ikuo Nishimura being named as company president.

In order to pull itself out of its financial problems, Mandom instituted a new corporate culture, in which employees were asked to contribute to the management process. As part of that effort, the company launched the first of a long series of medium-term plans. These plans established specific areas of focus within the company's management and operations, as well as establishing strategic objectives over periods generally ranging from two to three years. The first medium-term plan, which spanned from 1982 to 1987, sought to restructure the group's management and corporate culture, which also included a redesign of the company's logo and a revitalization of the company's brand family. Later medium-term plans included product extensions, the group's initial public offering, international growth objectives, and the like.

Backed by the new planning process, Mandom soon returned to its former healthy growth through the 1980s and into the 1990s. The company made its first effort to enter the women's cosmetics market in 1984, with the launch of the Pucelle My Lip line. The company also extended the Gatsby brand family, backed by the construction of a new production facility at its Fukusaki site, which was designed specifically for the manufacture of aerosol products. The new site also enabled the company to add men's deodorants to its range of products.

Mandom went public in 1988, selling shares on the Tokyo exchange's over-the-counter market. The public offering boosted the company's next international growth effort, with the creation of a joint venture in Singapore in 1988. That subsidiary later became wholly owned by the company. The following year, Mandom added a

KEY DATES

1927: Shinpachiro Nishimura founds the Kintsuru Perfume Corporation to produce personal care items for the Japanese market.

1933: The company finds its first major commercial success with the launch of its Tancho Tique "hair control" stick.

1958: The company makes its first move into the international market with a cooperation agreement in the Philippines.

1959: The Kintsuru Perfume Corporation becomes the Tancho Corporation.

1969: Tancho launches a joint venture in Indonesia, which becomes a major company manufacturing center.

1971: After the successful launch of Mandom men's care brand family, the company becomes the Mandom Corporation.

1982: Mandom initiates its first medium-term plan as part of a change in management culture.

1988: The company enters Singapore through a joint venture as part of international expansion effort and begins trading shares on Tokyo exchange's over-the-counter market.

1996: Mandom establishes a production and distribution joint venture in mainland China.

2003: Company shares are listed on the Tokyo Stock Exchange's primary market.

2005: The company launches its eighth medium-term plan with a goal of establishing Mandom and Lucido as flagship global brands.

ing a marketing joint venture in Hong Kong, which later became known as Sunwa Marketing Co. In an extension to its Japanese operations, Mandom acquired the domestic distribution rights to fast-growing French hair care brand Guinot in 1993. In that year, the company's Indonesian operation went public, with a listing on the Jakarta stock exchange.

NEW LEADERSHIP IN THE NEW CENTURY

The next generation of the Nishimura family took over as head of the company in 1995, when Motonobu Nishimaura became company president. Mandom continued to build up its international network. This included a full-scale entry into the mainland Chinese market with the founding of a joint venture manufacturing and distribution unit in Zhongshan city in 1996. By the end of the decade, the company had also added distribution subsidiaries in Malaysia and in South Korea. The late 1990s also saw the launch of a number of new product lines, including the System E/O line of skin care treatment for women, and Michiko London, a brand family specifically destined for the convenience store circuit.

Into the early 2000s, Mandom continued to seek out new product markets. The company launched the Gatsby range of men's hair coloring products in 2001, becoming the first in Japan to market hair coloring specifically for men. The success of this range soon spilled over into other Asian markets—highly influenced by Japan's bouyant consumer culture—and by the end of 2001, the company had launched hair coloring manufacture at its plants in China and Indonesia, as well as in Japan. The Gatsby line and the Lucido brand were launched internationally in 2002. The success of its men's hair coloring products, in the meantime, encouraged the company to develop a range for the women's market as well. This led to the launch of the Lucido L Prism hair coloring range in 2003.

Into the middle of the decade, the company's growth was backed by a shift of its shares, first to the Tokyo exchange's secondary market in 2002, and then to its main board in 2003. The increase in capital became part of the company's new medium-term objectives, established as part of its eighth mid-term plan launched in 2005. Under the new plan, Mandom now set an objective to expand its international presence still further, especially by establishing the Gatsby and Lucido brands as its flagship global brands.

At the same time, Mandom continued to seek out new product areas. Into the mid-2000s, the company had developed a line of paper-based toiletry items, such

sales and distribution subsidiary in Taiwan, then, in 1990, entered Thailand, establishing the Mandom Thailand joint venture. By then, the company had a new strong-selling brand, Lucido, launched in 1989. The new cosmetic line was among the first in Japan to boast a fragrance-free formulation. The success of that line led the company to launch a fragrance-free women's brand, Lucido L, in 1993.

Mandom began building a new headquarters in the early 1990s which was completed in 1993. The company also expanded its Fukusaki factory with a facility dedicated to tube filling. At the same time, the company added a formal presence in the Philippines, establishing a joint venture there in 1992. Meanwhile, Mandom took its first step toward the Chinese market, establish-

as face and hand wipes. The effort to build this category hit a snag in mid-2005, however, when the company was forced to pull advertising for a facial wipe that had come under criticism for its racist content. Nonetheless, Mandom could look forward to its continuing success as one of Japan's most popular brands. At the same time, the company had succeeded in establishing a strong international presence. By 2006, foreign sales accounted for some 25 percent of the group's total sales.

—*M.L. Cohen*

PRINCIPAL SUBSIDIARIES

Beaucos Corporation; Guinot Japan Corporation; Mandom Business Service Corporation; Mandom Corporation Latin America Imp.E Exp. Ltda; Mandom Corporation(Singapore) Pte Ltd.; Mandom Corporation (Thailand) Ltd; Mandom Korea Corporation; Mandom Philippines Corporation; Mandom Taiwan Corporation; Mandom (Malaysia) Sdn. Bhd.; Piacelabo Corporation; Pt Mandom Indonesia Tbk; Sunwa Marketing Co.,Ltd. (Hong Kong); Zhongshan City Rida Fine Chemical Co., Ltd. (China).

PRINCIPAL COMPETITORS

Sunstar Inc.; Kao Corporation; Shiseido Company Ltd.; Sankyo Company Ltd.; Eisai Company Ltd.; Kanebo Ltd.; Taiyo Nippon Sanso Corporation; Yakult Honsha Company Ltd.; Kose Corporation.

FURTHER READING

"Cosmetic Company Mandom Indonesia Plans Expansion," *AsiaPulse News*, February 8, 2006.

"Cosmetic Maker Scraps Commercial With Expression Mocking Blacks," *Kyodo News International*, June 14, 2005.

"Mandom Achieves Record High Sales," *Cosmetics & Toiletries & Household Products Marketing News In Japan*, August 25, 2003.

"Mandom Corporation," *Soap & Cosmetics*, February 1999, p. 65.

"Mandom Sells Cosmetics in Hong Kong," *Cosmetics & Toiletries & Household Products Marketing News In Japan*, August 25, 2002.

"Mandom's Gatsby Brand A Strong Seller in Convenience Stores," *Innovative New Packaging in Japan*, March 25, 2001.

"New Products in System E/O Series from Mandom," *Cosmetics & Toiletries & Household Products Marketing News In Japan*, January 25, 2001.

MARSHFIELD CLINIC.

Where the future of medicine lives

Marshfield Clinic Inc.

1000 North Oak Avenue
Marshfield, Wisconsin 54449
U.S.A.
Telephone: (715) 387-5511
Toll Free: (800) 782-8581
Fax: (715) 387-5240
Web site: http://www.marshfieldclinic.org

Not-For-Profit Company
Founded: 1916
Employees: 6,400
Sales: $2.2 billion (2005)
NAIC: 541690 Other Scientific and Technical Consulting Services.

■ ■ ■

A not-for-profit corporation based in Marshfield, Wisconsin, Marshfield Clinic Inc. is among the United States' largest private multidisciplinary group medical practices, and the largest in the state of Wisconsin. Marshfield employs more than 720 physicians practicing 86 medical specialties, supported by more than 6,000 other employees. It operates 41 regional medical centers and other facilities in 35 northern, central, and western Wisconsin communities, and also serves much of Michigan's Upper Peninsula. Marshfield owns and operates its own health maintenance organization, Security Health Plan, which covers more than 115,000 people through a network of 26 affiliated hospitals. Through more than 1,200 hospitals, clinics, and other healthcare sites, Marshfield also conducts a number of outreach

services programs, such as regional blood banking, off-site physician consultation, mobile echocardiography, and orthotics/prosthetics services. Marshfield Laboratories provides testing services for Marshfield operations as well as for clients across the United States, performing more than 20 million tests each year.

The Marshfield Clinic Education Foundation offers fully accredited residency programs for recent medical school graduates in dermatology, internal medicine, medicine and pediatrics, pediatrics, surgery, and transitional year. Many of Marshfield's physicians hold clinical teaching appointments from the University of Wisconsin-Madison medical school. In addition, Marshfield is involved in research through the Marshfield Clinic Research Foundation, focusing on such areas as rural and agricultural health and safety, human genetics, epidemiology, and biomedical informatics. Another Marshfield research vehicle is the National Farm Medicine Center, devoted to the exploration of the impact of rural and agricultural life on health and safety, such as the effects chemicals used in farming may have on the rural population. Because Marshfield is a non-profit organization, all earnings are invested in the clinic operation and Security Health Plan.

EARLY 20TH CENTURY ROOTS

The leader among Marshfield's founding physicians was Karl W. Doege, who was raised in Thorp, Wisconsin. Originally a school teacher, he graduated in 1890 from the medical school of what is now known as Case Western Reserve University, based in Cleveland. While taking the train home he was told by a conductor that

Marshfield would be an ideal place for a young doctor to begin a practice. It was good advice, given that Marshfield was a relatively young town, established less than 20 years earlier, and was a nexus of railroad lines and the home to Upham Mills, one of Wisconsin's largest lumber mills. Doege soon settled here and began practicing medicine. By 1915 Marshfield boasted 15 physicians, one of which was Doege's assistant, Walter G. Sexton, the son of a local pharmacist. Doege had encouraged the young man to seek a medical education at Johns Hopkins. Following his graduation in 1911 and a Baltimore residency, Sexton was persuaded by Doege to return home to join his practice. Well regarded as a surgeon, Doege also enjoyed a strong working relationship with other Marshfield physicians, including Dr. Hansford Milbee, who had been practicing in town since 1901 and was strong on diagnosis and treatment, and Milbee's young protégé, Dr. Victor Mason, who set up his practice next door to Mason, above the Sexton family's drug store. Mason was also a skilled surgeon, his services in high demand around the state. Early in 1915 Doege broached the idea of a group practice with Sexton and Mason, one in which each participating doctor focused on his area of expertise. Mason told Milbee of the idea and the men began meeting for further discussions.

In April 1916 the four men formally invited the other Marshfield physicians to join them in a group practice and two accepted: Dr. William Hipke, the oldest of the group at 51, who would become the group's eye, ear, nose, and throat specialist; and Dr. Roy P. Potter, who had come to town six years earlier to work with a physician who subsequently died and elected to remain and practice on his own. Potter became the group's first radiologist. Thus, Marshfield Clinic set up shop over the drugstore with Doege serving as the first president. Four more physicians joined the group by 1920, at which point Marshfield formalized the arrangement, establishing it as a charitable trust. Two years later, Marshfield moved into a new building. Under the terms of the trust, each participating physician paid a fee and received one vote at the organization's annual meeting, although they received no equity. In 1924 Marshfield was established enough that the University of Wisconsin included it as part of its first medical preceptor program. Soon the clinic began educating the school's medical students through the program, and in 1928 Marshfield and local St. Joseph's Hospital received approval to maintain a rotating internship program.

Marshfield soon began to experience some turnover in its ranks. Only in his 40s, Mason died in December 1929. Koege passed away three years later and was replaced as president by Milbee, who in turn died in August 1934. Potter became president, and despite persistently poor health, he would lead Marshfield for many years and not fully retire from the practice of medicine until 1959 when he was 80 years old. He would live to be 89.

Marshfield enjoyed steady growth for the first 35 years, bringing in new physicians and adding capabilities, but the entry of the United States into World War II in late 1941 almost led to the dissolution of the group practice three years later. Not only had several of the physicians been called away to serve in the military, medical supplies were scarce due to the war and the clinic was overcrowded. A building addition was sorely needed, but construction was impossible because all available steel had been commandeered for military purposes. Nevertheless, Marshfield managed to hold on and in the post-war years resumed its growth.

RESEARCH FOUNDATION ESTABLISHED: 1959

In the 1940s the clinic provided $400 to Dr. Stephen Epstein, a German refugee, to begin dermatology research; this would eventually lead to the creation of a formal research foundation. With Epstein spearheading the effort, the Marshfield Clinic Research Foundation was established in 1959, focusing on farm health and safety issues. In that year, the foundation also received its first federal grant to study Farmer's Lung disease. A few years later work on organic dust toxic syndrome and maple bark disease was added.

By the mid-1950s Marshfield employed more than two-dozen physicians in some 16 specialties. The size of the staff would triple over the next decade, leading to the addition of three more floors to the clinic building in 1956, but Marshfield quickly outgrew this space as well. Because the downtown location made further expansion difficult, Marshfield looked to construct an entirely new facility where Saint Joseph's Hospital was

KEY DATES

1916: Marshfield Clinic is founded.
1926: Clinic building is completed.
1959: Marshfield Clinic Research Foundation is established.
1977: The first satellite clinic opens.
1986: The Security Health Plan begins.
1997: The Laird Center for Medical Research opens.
2005: Biomedical Informatics Research Center is established.

located in the outskirts of town. In 1975 a new 212,000-square-foot facility was opened.

The extra space was used to accommodate the 135 physicians on Marshfield's staff. It would also be put to good use in supporting Marshfield's health maintenance organization, founded in 1971 as the Greater Marshfield Community Health Plan, the first HMO in the state of Wisconsin. It was a joint venture with St. Joseph's Hospital and Blue Cross & Blue Shield United of Wisconsin. The plan expanded in the 1970s, as did Marshfield's clinic, which began opening satellite operations. The first came in 1977 after the city of Mosinee, Wisconsin, had pressed Marshfield to open a clinic practice in the community to replace a public health service (PHS) office that was unable to procure doctors. A year later, sites were opened in Greenwood and Stanley, which had similar problems with their PHS offices. Marshfield's expansion was also aided in 1978 when the state government allowed the organization to self-insure for professional liability.

Growth on a number of fronts continued in the 1980s. Satellite clinics opened in several communities, as start-up operations, mergers with local physician groups, or through the purchase of an existing practice. The Greater Marshfield Community Health Plan ran into trouble in the 1980s, caused by a new computerized claims-processing system that was plagued with problems. This resulted in the HMO losing more than $1 million in 1986. Blue Cross and the hospital wanted to exit the business, and so in 1986 Marshfield took sole control, reorganizing the HMO as Security Health Plan. Marshfield continued to hired more physicians and add new practices, leading to major additions to the main clinic building in both 1984 and 1989. In addition, Marshfield's clinical research efforts expanded. In 1981 the National Farm Medicine Center was established as a program of the Marshfield Clinic Research Foundation.

Funded by local contributions, private foundations, as well as the federal government, the Center studied such topics as cancer control among farmers, suicides in the rural population, and the prevention of child farm accidents. Two years later the Community Clinical Oncology Program was established.

In 1991 the Marshfield Epidemiologic Research Center was established to conduct population-based and other epidemiologic research in such areas as infectious diseases, antibiotic resistance, and the prevention of diabetes and obesity. During the early 1990s, Marshfield was responsible for the discovery of short tandem repeat polymorphisms, markers used to resolve population structure. It was a major advance in the study of human genetics. In 1994 Marshfield formed the Center for Medical Genetics, which developed a map of the human genome. To keep pace with its varied research activities, Marshfield opened the Laird Center for Medical Research, dedicated in 1997. In the meantime, Marshfield Clinic continued to add practices and open new satellite sites in Wisconsin during the 1990s.

BLUE CROSS SUES MARSHFIELD: 1994

Security Health Plan also enjoyed strong growth and proved so successful that it prompted former partner Blue Cross & Blue Shield United of Wisconsin to file an antitrust suit against Marshfield in February 1994. Blue Cross contended that it was unable to compete in central and northern Wisconsin because Marshfield controlled so many physicians it was unable to find enough health providers who were willing to participate in a Blue Cross HMO, except at artificially high rates because of Marshfield's backing. The insurer further charged that Marshfield's virtual monopoly in these markets eliminated incentives to practice quality medicine and that the organization was able to overcharge patients and insurers. Before opting for litigation, Blue Cross, which had decided to reenter the central and north Wisconsin markets, had tried for three years to make an arrangement with Marshfield to use its physicians, but the two sides failed to reach an accommodation. The ensuing court case was keenly watched by all parties in the healthcare field, holding the potential to undermine other rural physician networks or the building of new ones. In January 1995 a jury sided with Blue Cross and found damages of $16.2 million, which because it was an antitrust case were tripled to $48.6 million. Marshfield appealed the verdict to the 7th U.S. Circuit Court of Appeals in Chicago, which agreed that Marshfield impeded competition by illegally dividing markets with a regional HMO, the North Central Health Protection Plan, but the court did not find that Marshfield was an illegal monopoly as Blue Cross contended and, as a result, the damage award was overturned. The matter then worked its way to the U.S. Supreme Court, which in March 1996 opted not to review the appeals court decision. Upon this news, Marshfield's president, Richard Leer, portrayed the Supreme Court's refusal to take the case as an important decision for the future of health care, claiming, "Health care providers can continue to develop integrated health delivery systems in rural areas. It is a victory for the residents of central and northern Wisconsin and for rural America." Marshfield's legal woes did not end just yet, however. It also had to contend with consumer civil suits that arose out of the Blue Cross litigation. A settlement in which Marshfield admitted no guilt was finally reached in October 1997.

INTO THE 21ST CENTURY

Finally free of legal entanglements, Marshfield was able to grow its multifaceted operations into the new century. A second genetic research center, the Personalized Medicine Research Center, was established in 2001 to pursue research on how an individual genetic profile can be tailored to detect, prevent, and treat diseases. This program and the Center for Medical Genetics were then merged in 2004, creating the Center for Human Genetics. Moreover, Marshfield launched a fifth research center, the Biomedical Informatics Research Center, added in 2005 to pursue work in the field of medical informatics, the use of structures and algorithms, via computers, to improve health care. In the meantime, in 2003, the original clinic operation continued to grow, leading to another addition to the clinic building, completed in 2003.

Ed Dinger

PRINCIPAL DIVISIONS

Marshfield Clinic Research Foundation; Marshfield Clinic Education Foundation; Marshfield Laboratories; Security Health Plan.

PRINCIPAL COMPETITORS

Blue Cross & Blue Shield United of Wisconsin.

FURTHER READING

Barnett, Alicia Ault, "Don't Fence Us In," *Hospitals & Health Networks,* May 5, 1995, p. 36.

Cole, Jeff, "Clinic at Marshfield Grows Into Medical Conglomerate," *Milwaukee Sentinel,* June 17, 1992, p. 1D.

"High Court Won't Review Clinic Monopoly Case," *Wisconsin State Journal,* March 29, 1996, p. 8B.

"Marshfield Clinic Settles Lawsuit Accusing It Of Aiding Overcharges," *Wisconsin State Journal,* October 21, 1997, p. 8B.

Slomski, Anita J., "Is This Group An Illegal Doctor Monopoly?," *Medical Economics,* September 26, 1994, p. 64.

Martell and Company S.A.

BP 21, 7 Pl. Edouard Martell
Cognac,
France
Telephone: (+33 05) 45 36 33 33
Fax: (33 05) 45 36 33 99
Web site: http://www.martell.com

Wholly Owned Subsidiary of Pernod Ricard S.A.
Founded: 1715
Employees: 400
Sales: EUR 178.14 million ($222.66 million) (2006 est.)
NAIC: 312130 Wineries; 424820 Wine and Distilled Alcoholic Beverage Merchant Wholesalers

■ ■ ■

Martell and Company S.A. represents the oldest cognac brand, with a history stretching back to 1715. In the mid-2000s, Martell is also one of the fastest-growing brands in the Pernod Ricard group. In the 2005–06 year alone, Martell's sales grew by some 11 percent. Much of the company's growth comes from early entry into the Asian region, and especially China, with a cognac-drinking population estimated at some 200 million. Martell's share of the Chinese market is estimated to reach 24 percent. Nonetheless, the United Kingdom remains the brand's primary export market in terms of volume, followed by the United States, where the cognac market has been boosted by its embrace by the rap/hip hop music scene.

The travel/duty-free market is also a major market for the company's cognac sales. Martell's cognac brands include its traditional VS (Very Special) and VSOP (Very Superior Old Pale), Extra, and Cordon Bleu varieties. The company also has been developing new cognac labels, including the high-end Noblige, positioned above the VSOP label, launched in 2006. At the same time, in November 2005, Martell has re-launched its oldest label, XO, with a new blend of "eaux de vie" (literally "waters of life"). Martell and Company also serves as the umbrella for two other cognac houses, Bisquit, founded in 1819, the leading cognac brand in Belgium and the number three in France; and Renault, traditionally sold almost entirely in the Scandinavian market, where it claims a 45 percent share of the premium quality cognac market. Martell itself is part of Ricard Pernod's Champagnes Mumm Perrier-Jouët business unit, formed at the beginning of 2006, and led by former Martell & Co. chairman and CEO Lionel Breton.

FOUNDING A COGNAC DYNASTY IN 1715

The practice of distilling heated or "burnt" wine originated as a means of preserving wine for the long transport by Dutch traders. The resulting alcoholic beverage was called *brandewijn* (literally "burnt wine"), which later became more widely known by its English variant, brandy.

In France, one particular region, centered around the village of Cognac along the Charente river, became particularly prized for the quality of its brandy. Cognac, which was also a major producer of sea salt, used for preserving fish, had by then long been involved in

COMPANY PERSPECTIVES

Founded 1715. Since then, Martell has carefully preserved the integrity and reputation of the cognacs that bear its name, remaining loyal to the inspired and independent spirit of its founder: Jean Martell.

international trade, starting as early as the 5th century. The region's soil proved especially beneficial for the growth of certain types of grapes, especially the Champagne white wine variety. The region's wine trade started from around the 11th century, and grew in popularity especially with the developing brandy trade. Indeed, while the region's grapes produced an inferior quality wine, they proved excellent for distillation. In contrast to most brandy distillates, which were generally flavored with aromatic herbs to make them more palatable, the Cognac region's grapes provided a distillate that was immediately drinkable, if crude.

Cognac's true fame stemmed from the development of the double-distillation method, invented by one Marron seigneur de la Croix, later known as the Chevalier de la Croix-Marron, who retired from military service to his property in Segonzac, in the heart of the Cognac region, in 1610. Croix-Marron came up with the idea of reheating the brouillis, which was then distilled a second time. According to legend, the inspiration for the new method came from a nightmare during which the devil, in an attempt to steal Croix-Marron's soul, had him boiled. When that failed, the devil declared that he would have Croix-Marron's soul by boiling him a second time. Croix-Marron made the connection with his wine—and after experimenting with heating times, succeeded in creating a whiskey considered by many to be the finest in the world.

Yet this quality was not discovered until more than a decade from when Croix-Marron produced his first batch of double-distilled brandy and delivered two casks of the beverage to the monastery at Renorville. One of the casks was stored away and only tapped on the occasion of a visit to the monastery by the Bishop of Saintes some 15 years later. The monks discovered that a significant part of the brandy had evaporated, while, at the same time, the normally colorless brandy had taken on an amber hue. The resulting brandy proved to have gained smoother, more subtle palate than typical brandies. The discovery of the effects of wood-barrel aging played a key role not only in the development of the cognac industry, but in the wine and whiskey industries as well.

Whereas the Croix-Marron property continued to produce cognacs into the 21st century, the development of the region's major cognac houses began only at the beginning of the 18th century. The first of these was created in 1715, when Jean Martell came to the village of Cognac and built his own distillery on the banks of the Charente river. Born in Jersey, in 1694, Martell was marked by the region's reputation as a center of the European smuggling trade. Nonetheless, Martell himself established a successful and legal trading house in Cognac, trading a variety of items, such as groceries, seeds, and knitted goods. Martell also married into two of Cognac's leading brandy-producing families. Martell himself entered the trade, at first exporting non-aged brandies, and by the early 1720s the company was shipping more than 40,000 barrels each year. Germany was an important early market for the company, although by then the United Kingdom was already Martell's top customer.

Although Martell initially shipped young brandies, he also began developing his own cellars, allowing his brandy to age. Before long, Martell's brandies became recognized for their distinctive flavor and qualities. This was due to the company's preference for the use of grapes from the Borderie subregion, as well as its insistence on the use of Tronçais oak, as opposed to Limousin oak, for its casks. Martell's choice of establishing his warehouses along the river also proved beneficial to the quality of his brandies, with the dampness of the air further introducing a smoothness to the flavor.

COGNAC SPECIALIST IN 1815

Martell soon became the leading producer of brandy in the Cognac region. By 1783, the special nature of the Cognac brandy had led to the creation of a new brandy category, called cognac. During this period, the cognac makers also began developing a classification system for the different types of cognacs. As such, an XO cognac was required to have aged at least five years. The VSOP (Very Superior Old Pale) had a four-year minimum aging requirement, while the VS (Very Superior) was aged just two years. Other categories also were created, such as the Extra Perfection, with an average age of 35 years, and the Louis XIII, with an average age of 50 years. The use of English in the region's labeling system also reflected the English-speaking origins of the leading cognac houses, which by then included Martell's chief rival, Hennessy.

England also remained the primary market for brandy, and for cognac in particular. Martell took steps to solidify its own sales to the United Kingdom, signing an exclusive agreement with England's Matthew Clark in 1810. The Clark company helped build Martell's

KEY DATES

1715: Jean Martell, a native of Jersey, Channel Islands, founds a trading house in Cognac, France, and begins sales and exports of cognac.

1815: The Martell family decides to focus exclusively on cognac, adding its own distillery and vineyards, and adding warehouses and cellars.

1868: Martell begins developing an international distribution network, including markets in the Far East.

1919: The ultra-high-end Martell Cordon Bleu label is launched.

1964: The Jules Robin cognac house and its brandy-producing subsidiary Briand is acquired.

1988: Seagram acquires Martell; the Augier Robin Briand subsidiary is created.

2002: Pernod Ricard acquires Martell as part of its acquisition of part of Seagram's drinks portfolio.

2006: Martell becomes the cornerstone of Pernod Ricard's new luxury products division, Martell Mumm Perrier-Jouët.

position in the United Kingdom, and by the late 20th century, Martell claimed some 40 percent of the total brandy market in the United Kingdom.

As it developed its cognac house, the Martell family maintained its other trading activities into the early 19th century. By 1815, however, the company had decided to concentrate solely on the production of cognac. Martell then began investing in expanding its infrastructure, adding warehouses and new cellars, buying vineyards and building its own distillery operations. Nonetheless, the company continued purchasing from the region's vineyards, building up a network of some 2,500 grape growers. The company's expanded cellars also gave it a broader and broader assortment of eaux-de-vie—that is, distillates aged for a greater or lesser period. These were then blended, as much as 3,000 times to produce the final blend, which was then aged further before being labeled. The company's growing stock of eaux-de-vie enabled it to develop a new cognac label in 1819, Martell Extra.

Whereas exports had played an important part in

Martell's business from its origins, the company's international activities took off in the late 19th century. From 1868, Martell began developing new export markets, including the British-dominated Chinese and Hong Kong markets. Toward the end of the century, Martell also developed a new labeling system, in addition to the standard labeling, using stars to further distinguish the quality levels of its cognacs.

A new cognac joined the Martell family in 1912, when the company, then under Eduoard Martell, developed the Cordon Bleu. That cognac remained a key fixture in the company's cognac portfolio, and became prized worldwide by cognac connoisseurs.

NEW OWNERS IN 1988

The Martell company continued to develop its international reputation throughout the 20th century; the group's cognac was served at the signing of the Armistice of 1918 and was served on the first voyage of the *Queen Mary* in 1936, among other notable events. Martell also continued to expand its holdings in the Cognac region, which had received the AOC (*appellation d'origine controlé*) in 1938. Throughout this time, the company, known as J & F Martell, remained controlled by the Martell family—and then by the Firino-Martell family.

In 1964, Martell deepened its presence by acquiring another noted cognac house, Jules Robin. Founded in 1782, that company had been the first cognac producer to ship its cognac in bottles, instead of in casks. The use of bottles enabled the company to develop its own labels—and inspired other cognac makers to follow suit. The Robin purchase also brought Martell the Briand brandy brand. Martell also went public, listing its shares on the Paris Stock Exchange.

The 1970s marked an important period for Martell. The arrival of a new generation, led by René Firino Martell and Patrick Firino Martell, into the group in the late 1960s had important consequences for the company. Firino-Martell immediately set out to boost the group's presence in the Asian region, establishing through the 1970s a strong distribution network. In this way, Martell positioned itself as a pioneer in the region's cognac market, enabling the company to capture a leading position in markets such as Malaysia, Singapore, Thailand, and Hong Kong. By the 1990s, the group successfully expanded this leadership into the fast-growing mainland China market.

Martell sought another means of cementing its brand—in part in reaction to the growing restrictions on alcoholic beverage advertising in the late 1970s and 1980s. In 1984, the company launched its own leather goods line. Martell then expanded that range into the retail sector, launching its first stores in the mid-1980s, including a store in New York City in 1987.

By then, however, Martell was faced with the growing consolidation of the global drinks market. The development of a small number of large-scale groups placed the independent houses under enormous pressure. This became particularly true for Martell as it saw most of its major rivals, including Hennessy and Courvoisier, align themselves with the major drinks groups.

By 1987, Martell had chosen to ally itself with the Seagram group, which bought out the Firino-Martell family's 40 percent share in the company. Martell soon found itself the target of a takeover battle, as Grand Met (later Diageo) attempted to wrest control of the cognac brand. In the end, Seagram acquired full control of Martell. Patrick Firino Martell nonetheless remained with the company through the end of the 1990s.

Following its acquisition by Seagram, Martell was expanded with the addition of Seagram's existing cognac brand, Augier Frères, founded in 1643 and part of Seagram since 1966. Augier was placed under Martell, and merged with its Robin and Briand operations to form a new subsidiary, Augier Robin Briand.

FAST-GROWING COGNAC LEADER IN THE NEW CENTURY

Martell's tenure under Seagram proved disappointing, however. By the early 2000s, the company's sales volume had dropped by more than one-third. The company's market share had slipped dramatically, dropping back from number two cognac brand worldwide to just number four. Described as "dusty," the company's operations had also become overstaffed and inefficient, amassing an enormous surplus.

New life for Martell came in the early 2000s, when Seagram, in the process of merging its media interests with Vivendi to form Vivendi Universal, decided to sell off its drinks portfolio. France's Pernod Ricard teamed up with Diageo to launch a bid worth $7 billion in 2000. Initially, neither group appeared interested in acquiring Martell, announcing that the cognac producer,

along with a number of other Seagram brands, was to be placed in a new company to be sold separately. By the time the purchase agreement was completed at the end of 2001, however, Pernod Ricard had agreed to acquire Martell as well.

The decision proved fortuitous for Pernod Ricard. After a somewhat painful restructuring of Martell's operations, the company's cognac sales took off again: The brand achieved impressive year on year sales growth into the mid-2000s, including an 11 percent boost in sales volume in the 2006 year. Martell's strong position in the Asian region, and especially in the fast-growing Chinese market, accounted for a significant part of the group's newfound expansion. At the same time, the U.S. rap/hip hop culture's adoption of cognac as a status-symbol drink of choice also had helped the company recover much of its lost ground in that country. By January 2006, Martell had become a cornerstone of Pernod Ricard's new luxury products division, Martell Mumm Perrier-Jouët. After nearly 300 years, Martell remained one of the world's leading cognac brands in the new century.

M. L. Cohen

PRINCIPAL COMPETITORS

Bourbon; Rémy Cointreau; Société Jas Hennessy and Co.; Moët Hennessy Diageo; SMV Paris; Castel Frères; Rémy Martin and Cie S.A.; Bacardi Martini France.

FURTHER READING

"A la Découverte de Martell et de Ses Cognacs Exceptionnels," *Entreprendre*, Autumn–Winter 2005.

Bates, Joe, "Unlocking the Secrets of Cognac," *Vineyards and Historic Distillery*, September 2, 2005.

Jarrad, Kyle, "A Walk in Cognac Country," *International Herald Tribune*, February 6, 2004.

May, Clifford D., "The Seduction of Cognac," *American Spectator*, November 2005.

"Pernod Ricard Mise sur le Champagne et le Cognac pour Devenir No1 Mondial," *Agence France Presse*, May 25, 2006.

The Maschhoffs, Inc.

7475 State Route 127
Carlyle, Illinois 62231-3103
U.S.A.
Telephone: (618) 594-2125
Web site: http://www.themaschhoffs.com

Private Company
Incorporated: 1991
Employees: 525
Sales: $3 billion (2005)
NAIC: 112210 Hog and Pig Farming

■ ■ ■

Based in Carlyle, Illinois, The Maschhoffs, Inc., is one of the largest family-owned pork production companies in the United States. The company maintains a herd of about 110,000 sows, a large number of which are raised by contract growers, small Midwest farmers located in seven states that Maschhoffs calls its "production partners." The state-of-the-art operation raises hogs from weaning to finishing, prepared for sale to meat packers.

The Maschhoffs use a closed-herd system that produces its own replacement females rather than bringing them in from the outside. In this way, the risk of disease is reduced, the health of the herd is optimized, and the mortality rate is lowered. Moreover, a closed-herd enjoys higher feed efficiency, a greater growth rate, and a lower cost of production, resulting in more consistent cash flow and greater profitability. Maschhoffs has also been in the forefront of the pork industry in the use of artificial insemination, the latest in feed

technology, improved environmental safeguards, and better confinement configurations that improve the well-being of the herd and also result in more efficient pork production. Each year Maschhoffs sends well over two million finished hogs to market, delivering them to packing plants owned by Cargill in Beardstown, Illinois, and Ottumwa, Iowa. The company is run by brothers Ken Maschhoff and Dave Maschhoff, the former serving as chief executive officer and the latter as chief operating officer.

FOUNDING FAMILY: FARMING SINCE THE 1800S

The Maschhoff family has been farming in the Carlyle area since the mid-1800s. Raising hogs was a normal practice for all family farms at the time and a profitable sideline. In 1956 Wayne Maschhoff, the father of Ken and Dave, began farming with his father, Ben, who kept ten hogs. According to a company profile in *Top Producer*, Ben told the youngster, "I don't know if you want to raise hogs, but we've been keeping records and we make most of our money on hogs." Wayne took the advice and bought five sows. He was not alone among farmers raising hogs, however. Illinois and neighboring states like Iowa became major hog producers, but unlike many family farmers, he was quick to adopt new rearing methods, whether they were developed by others or invented by himself. At the same time, he continued to grow grain.

Wayne Maschhoff was also keen on carrying on the family farm tradition and groomed his sons from an early age to learn the life and love it. They were not

---

COMPANY PERSPECTIVES

We believe in Progressive Farming...Family Style.

---

only given plenty of chores but also responsibilities at an early age. "I was running a tractor in the field 1-2 miles away from home when I was 7 years old," Ken Maschhoff recounted for trade publication *National Hog Master*. "Dad put seatbelts on the tractor and bolted a block of wood on the clutch so I could push the clutch in." The brothers also learned how to give shots to baby pigs and to dock their tails. The area of hog production that especially appealed to Ken were the buildings, the hog barns, and machine shops. As a youngster he helped his father construct new hog buildings by hauling off concrete forms in his Radio Flyer wagon. When he became a teenager he and his friends—including Steve Quick, who would one day become the production coordinator at Maschhoffs—helped local farmers construct barns and other facilities. He then enrolled at Southern Illinois University at Carbondale to study animal industries, and during his freshman year designed an 857-foot-long hog barn that he would later erect on the Maschhoff family farm. New barn designs were important, as well as fascinating to him, because of new feeding systems and waste disposal methods. "I think hogs were almost the by-product of wanting to build— you had to put hogs in there to make it pay for itself," he told *National Hog Master*.

Dave Maschhoff and Steve Quick also graduated from Southern Illinois University at Carbondale. After college the brothers went to work on the family farm and were still in their 20s in 1979 when they made 50-50 partners with their parents and began to essentially run the operation. In that year Quick joined the operation as well, initially helping them with construction and the running of the farm's hog and grain operations. The brothers' wives at this stage handled the bookkeeping chores. Wayne Maschhoff explained to *Top Producer* why he was so willing to step aside: "I saw too many farm boys stifled by their fathers. I wanted my boys to keep growing."

The Maschhoff family farming business soon reached a crossroads. It had to expand to survive, but the price of land was escalating, making grain production quite expensive. The brothers decided that the only option, if they were going to remain on the farm, was to abandon grain cultivation and focus on their hog operation, which at this stage numbered 150 sows. It was no given that they would survive as hog producers, however,

because according to *Top Producer,* 90 percent of the farmers raising hogs in 1977 would be out of the business 25 years later.

HERD OF 2,400 BY 1996

Following in the footsteps of their father, the Maschhoff brothers used the latest production methods to grow their herd and maximize their profits, and they were not afraid to bring in consultants to help them with herd and health nutrition management. They also incorporated financial and management planning into the business. In 1991 the herd numbered 700 sows and the brothers bought out their parents. Like other Illinois producers, they were independent operators with no contracts with packers. The Maschhoffs grew the herd to about 2,400 sows by 1996, when they faced another watershed moment. At the time, according to *National Hog Farmer,* "Contract hog production was concentrated in the Southeast. Midwestern producers didn't favor the idea, because it was viewed as a sign of failure that you couldn't make it on your own." Nevertheless, the Maschhoffs decided to pursue contract production, reaching its first deal in December 1996 with a neighbor to finish some hogs. It proved to be a wise decision. Because the contractor provided the equipment, the use of production contracts reduced capital requirements and produced a higher return on investment. As a result Maschhoffs were able to make better use of the company's financial resources and grow the business at a faster clip than before, as the size of their herd began to double every 18 months.

Pork prices fell in 1998, creating difficult conditions for hog producers, especially those who had expanded too quickly. A large number of producers, as a result, were forced out of business. The Maschhoffs responded to the situation by price hedging and adhering to a strict budget. Having weathered the storm, the company was able to resume its growth, spurred by the addition of scores of new production partners. The company was also able to successfully negotiate another price dip in 2002.

The Maschhoffs' sow herd totaled 8,000 in 1998, a number that would grow to more than 50,000 in five years, more than half of which were company owned. The number of production partners, who were located throughout Illinois, Iowa, Indiana, and Kentucky, reached 125.

To accommodate the rapid growth of its herd, the Maschhoffs built a new 10,000-sow pod in 2002. A year later it bought 43,000 finishing spaces from Alden, Iowa-based Heartland Pork Enterprises and another 23,000 finishing spaces from Chandlerville, Illinois-based Triple

KEY DATES

1979: Ken and Dave Maschhoff become partners in their parents' farm.
1991: The Maschhoff brothers buy out their parents.
1996: The Maschhoffs begin contract production.
2003: New corporate headquarters opens.
2005: The Maschhoffs acquire the Land O'Lakes swine unit.

Edge Pork. These facilities were then converted to accommodate the Maschhoffs' wean-to-finish system.

To remain competitive, the company also invested $2.5 million in 2003 to retrofit two of its barns, each capable of holding 3,600 hogs, to serve as a research farm, where the company could perform realistic on-farm production research. For example, the farm had 120 specialized pens that featured a computerized feed delivery system, allowing researchers to determine exactly how much of a feed formulation was delivered to a particular pen on any given day. In this way, the hogs could be weighed and optimum feed formulations developed. Other areas of interest included pig stocking density, feeder types, meat quality, and the DNA typing of sires and dams. In general the research resulted in small tweaks to the Maschhoffs' hog production system, but those changes in relationship to a large production system resulted in major cost savings. In addition, the company took a long-range approach, exploring questions that might not pay practical dividends for several years.

Another sign that the Maschhoffs had reached a new level in scale was the 2003 opening of its new 20,000-square-foot office complex located outside of Carlyle, which replaced the company's overcrowded headquarters. More than just a place to house administrative functions, the new building served a public relations function. It included a 140-seat conference center where not only employees could meet but also contract growers, agricultural groups, and state officials.

LAND O'LAKES ACQUISITION: 2005

The Maschhoffs' growth had been accomplished incrementally, depending on the addition of production partners and a few acquisitions of production facilities, but in early 2005 the company doubled in size overnight when it bought the swine production assets of Land

O'Lakes Inc., Minnesota's highly successful dairy cooperative. The Maschhoffs herd numbered 55,000 sows while Land O'Lakes managed 60,000 sows on farms in Illinois, Missouri, Iowa, and Oklahoma. Over the years Land O'Lakes had become involved in the grain business to produce cattle feed, and it was a natural extension for the company to also begin selling feed for hogs as well as poultry. To increase profits from its grain, Land O'Lakes turned to hog production, which in theory could convert a low-margin commodity like grain into higher-margin meat.

The cooperative was not as adept at the swine business as it was in dairy and it began losing money on hogs in the late 1990s. The co-op's membership, especially dairy farmers on both coasts, grew increasingly disgruntled about covering the losses of a hog production operation in the middle of the country. By the start of the new century Land O'Lakes began looking to reduce its exposure to hogs, and finally in the spring of 2004 the pressure from membership was strong enough that management promised to exit the hog business, as well as the egg business, as soon as possible in order to focus on core operations. In June 2004 Land O'Lakes hired an investment banking firm to help in divesting the swine unit.

The Maschhoffs bided their time when the Land O'Lakes swine business came onto the market, waiting patiently while other producers made their bids, eventually had second thoughts and backed off. By the time Maschhoffs became involved, Land O'Lakes had lost its bargaining leverage. Needing to make a deal quickly, the company came to a reasonable accommodation with the Maschhoffs in 2005, although the terms of the transaction were not made public. By joining forces with the 12th largest hog-producing operation (Land O'Lakes), Maschhoffs, which had ranked No. 13, now became the seventh largest hog producer in the United States. Maschhoffs also picked up modern facilities and experienced employees and contractors.

In a matter of ten years, Maschhoffs had enjoyed extraordinary change, the operation growing from 2,400 sows and a handful of employees to a herd of 110,000 and hundreds of employees. While the meat industry was rapidly consolidating, with meat packers like Smithfield Foods and Cargill launching their own brands to challenge their own customers, such as Sara Lee and Kraft, Maschhoffs had no plans for vertical integration. "We have a niche. We know how to raise hogs and we've done that very well," Julie Maschhoff, Ken's wife and head of public relations, told *AgriNews*. Her husband added, "The thing about a packing house is, you've got to develop a brand, and that isn't something easily done." In the near-term, at least, the company was likely to pursue opportunities to grow its herd through acquisitions, explore international growth, and perhaps seek ways to diversify the business beyond hogs.

Ed Dinger

PRINCIPAL SUBSIDIARIES

Maschhoff Pork Farms Inc.; Maschhoff West LLC.

PRINCIPAL COMPETITORS

Smithfield Foods, Inc.; Premium Standard Farms, Inc.; Seaboard Farms Inc.

FURTHER READING

Egerstrom, Lee, "Land O'Lakes to Sell Hog Production Firm," *Saint Paul Pioneer Press,* February 16, 2005.

Smith, Rod, "Deals Restructure Beef, Pork Sectors," *Feedstuffs,* February 21, 2005, p. 1.

"Take the Leap From Good to Great," *Top Producer,* August 11, 2005.

Vansickle, Joe, "Blueprint For Success," *National Hog Farmer,* May 15, 2004.

———, "Building Barns and People," *National Hog Farmer,* May 15, 2006.

Williams, Nat, "Family Owned Operation Produces One-Million Hogs a Year," *AgriNews,* February 9, 2004.

Maytag Corporation

2000 North M-63
Benton Harbor, Michigan 49022-2692
U.S.A.
Telephone: (269) 923-5000
Fax: (269) 923-5443
Web site: http://www.maytag.com

Division of Whirlpool Corporation
Incorporated: 1925 as Maytag Company
Employees: 20,870
Sales: $4.9 billion (2005)
NAIC: 335224 Household Laundry Equipment Manufacturing; 335221 Household Cooking Appliance Manufacturing; 335222 Household Refrigerator and Home Freezer Manufacturing

■ ■ ■

Maytag Corporation, purchased by Whirlpool Corporation in 2006, manufactures washers, dryers, refrigerators, ranges, cooktops, irons, freezers, wall ovens, microwaves, disposers, dishwashers, central heating and cooling, and water heaters. In 2005, its Home Appliances business segment was responsible for over 95 percent of company sales. Its products are sold under the Maytag, Amana, Hoover, Jenn-Air, and Magic Chef brand names. Whirlpool secured its position as the leading home appliance manufacturer in the United States after its acquisition and integration of Maytag. A well-known and successful company since the late 1800s, Maytag will continue to operate as a brand of Whirlpool.

ORIGINS

Maytag Company was started by Frederick Louis Maytag and three partners in 1893 to produce threshing-machine band cutters and self-feeder attachments. The company soon began to produce other pieces of farm machinery, not all of it top quality: its corn husker, called the Success, caused the partners many problems because of its poor quality, and farmers often called Maytag out to their fields to fix the Success. When Maytag bought out his partners in 1907, he had learned his lesson; a Maytag product would always be dependable.

Maytag built his first washer in 1907, to bring his agricultural-equipment company through the slow-selling season as well as to fill a need for home-use washing machines. Home washing machines were already on the market, but Maytag wanted to make them more efficient. His first washer, called the Pastime, revolutionized washing. It had a cypress tub with a hand crank that forced the clothes through the water and against corrugated sides. The washer was a hit, and Maytag continued to improve on it. In 1911 he brought out the first electric washing machine, and in 1914 he introduced the gas-engine Multi-Motor for customers without access to electricity. The first aluminum washer tub was brought out in 1919, and the Gyrofoam, the first washer to clean with only water action, rather than friction, entered the marketplace in 1922. This revolutionary washer was the first with an agitator at the bottom of the tub instead of the top. This change allowed for the elimination of friction. Sales of this machine pushed Maytag, previously the 38th-largest U.S. washing machine company, into first place.

At this juncture, the farm-implement portion of the business was discontinued. L. B. Maytag, son of the founder, became president of the company in 1920. Under his direction the company began to market nationally. In 1925 Maytag incorporated and was listed on the New York Stock Exchange. In 1926 another Maytag son, E. H. Maytag, assumed the presidency and held the position until his death in 1940. Over the next several years, a number of interesting attachments were offered on washers. A butter churn and a meat grinder were two options offered to buyers. By 1927 Maytag had produced one million washers.

During the Great Depression, Maytag held its own; the company even made money. At his father's death in 1940, Fred Maytag II, grandson of the founder, took over the presidency. During World War II, the company made only special components for military equipment. In 1946 production of washers started up again, and in 1949 the first automatic washers were produced in a new plant built for that purpose. In 1946 Maytag began marketing a line of ranges and refrigerators made by other companies under the Maytag name. During the Korean War the company again produced parts for military equipment, although washer production continued.

PREMIUM BRAND IN POSTWAR YEARS

During the 1950s the appliance industry grew rapidly. Maytag first entered the commercial laundry field at this time, manufacturing washers and dryers for commercial self-service laundries and commercial operators. During these years full-line appliance producers began targeting Maytag's market. Full-line operators—such as General Electric, Whirlpool, and Frigidaire—provided washers and dryers, refrigerators, stoves, and other appliances. Maytag was much smaller than the full-line producers. It limited itself to the manufacture of washers and dryers, which it marketed with ranges and refrigerators built by other companies, and established its reputation as a premium brand.

The ranges and refrigerators Maytag had been marketing with its washers and dryers were dropped in 1955 and 1960, respectively, but the company soon reentered the field with its own portable dishwasher and a line of food-waste disposers in 1968. When Fred Maytag II, the last family member involved in the company's management, died in 1962, E. G. Higdon was named president and George M. Umbreit became chairman and CEO.

By the late 1970s over 70 percent of U.S. households were equipped with washers and dryers. Laundry-equipment sales had peaked in 1973 and the lifetime of such equipment was 10 to 12 years—often longer for Maytag. To help boost sales, prices became more competitive. Chairman Daniel J. Krumm, who had been elected president in 1972, set the company in a new direction in 1980 when he made the decision to make Maytag into a full-line producer, eventually selling a wide range of major appliances rather than just washers, dryers, and dishwashers.

FULL-LINE PRODUCER IN 1982

The expansion was effected by acquisition. The first purchase was Hardwick Stove Company in 1981, followed in 1982 by Jenn-Air Corporation, the leading manufacturer of indoor electric grills with stove-top vent systems. These products added a full line of gas and electric cooking appliances to the Maytag line and were sold under the Maytag umbrella. Maytag Company intended this diversification to increase its sales in both the new-home market as well as the replacement market; companies make bids to developers based on kitchen packages, not individual components. The larger replacement market had also changed: large chains selling several brands side by side dominated the market. Chairman Krumm felt the diversification was necessary despite the cyclical nature of the building industry.

The new strategy paid off. Consumers began to buy again, and Maytag's sales increased in all areas in 1983. In May 1986 the move toward becoming a full-line producer continued with the purchase of the Magic Chef group of companies in a $737 million stock swap. Magic Chef's Admiral brand gave Maytag a presence in the refrigerator and freezer sector. Besides Admiral refrigerators, Magic Chef also produced other home appliances under the names Toastmaster, Magic Chef, and Norge. The merger gave Maytag the fourth-largest share of the U.S. appliance market. It also brought vending machine manufacturer Dixie-Narco Inc., with its number one position in soft-drink vending equipment, into the fold.

The Magic Chef purchase also helped protect May-

KEY DATES

1893: Frederick Louis Maytag and three partners establish a company to produce threshing-machine band cutters and self-feeder attachments.

1907: Maytag buys out his partners and builds his first washing machine.

1911: Maytag launches his first electric washing machine.

1922: The Gyrofoam, the first washer to clean with only water action rather than friction, enters the marketplace.

1925: Maytag incorporates and lists on the New York Stock Exchange.

1949: The first automatic washers are produced.

1981: Maytag purchases Hardwick Stove Company.

1982: Jenn-Air is acquired.

1986: The move toward becoming a full-line producer continues with the purchase of the Magic Chef group of companies.

1989: Chicago Pacific Corp. is acquired.

1997: The Neptune high-efficiency front-loading washing machine is launched.

2001: Amana Appliances is purchased.

2006: Whirlpool Corporation completes its acquisition of Maytag.

tag from the threat of takeover. As the industry consolidated and other companies began to sell higher-priced appliances—Maytag's traditional forte—Krumm responded by moving into the medium-priced market. Magic Chef was Maytag's first step into that market.

The merger of Maytag and Magic Chef doubled Maytag's size and necessitated a restructuring. Maytag Company's name was changed to Maytag Corporation and three major appliance groups were formed: the Maytag appliance division, Magic Chef, and the Admiral appliance division (the Admiral division was consolidated into the other groups in 1988). Hardwick Stoves and Jenn-Air were included in the Maytag division. The president of Magic Chef remained as head of that division, which included Toastmaster—sold in 1987—Dixie-Narco, and Magic Chef air conditioning operations. The Admiral division included Norge and Warwick product lines, part of the old Magic Chef. Each division was given a great deal of autonomy. Other mergers within the industry during 1986 resulted in four companies—Whirlpool, General Electric, White Consolidated

Industries, and Maytag—controlling 80 percent of the industry.

By the late 1980s Krumm was ready to move Maytag into foreign markets. With the aim of being a European competitor before the unification of the European Economic Community in 1992, Maytag bought Chicago Pacific Corp. in early 1989 for $961 million. The primary reason for this purchase was Chicago Pacific's Hoover division. Hoover produced and sold high-quality washers, dryers, refrigerators, dishwashers, and other products primarily in Great Britain and Australia, but also in continental Europe. It also sold vacuum cleaners in the United States, a new product for Maytag. (Chicago Pacific also owned furniture operations, which Maytag sold later in 1989 to Ladd Furniture for $213.4 million.) Another reason for the Chicago Pacific purchase was to further ward off takeover. The $500 million debt the company assumed with the acquisition helped make the company less attractive to raiders. Meanwhile, 1989 also saw the debut of the first refrigerators bearing the Maytag brand.

RETRENCHMENT

Maytag's acquisitions spree led directly to a troubled period in the early 1990s. Profits declined each year from 1990 to 1992 as the company was hit hard by the recession and the increased competition that it engendered, and was further weakened by a continuing high debt load. The acquisition of Hoover was turning into a near-disaster as the European operations were in the red year after year, a situation made even worse in 1992 when Hoover Europe made a serious miscalculation in offering two free transatlantic airline tickets to anyone buying a Hoover product in the United Kingdom for as little as $165. More than 220,000 people responded to this almost-too-good-to-be-true deal, leading not only to a financial folly but also to a near public relations disaster when the company delayed getting tickets to people claiming them, as well as to litigation that continued for years to come. The fiasco led to the firing of three top executives at Hoover Europe, as well as Maytag being forced to take a $30 million charge in 1993 to cover the costs of the ill-fated promotion.

In the midst of these troubles, Krumm—the architect of the 1980s expansion—retired in late 1992, and was succeeded as chairman and CEO by Leonard A. Hadley, who had been company president. It did not take Hadley long to determine that it would be best in the long run if Maytag pulled back from its overseas ambitions and concentrated on putting its North American house in order. Hoover Europe alone had lost a total of $163 million from the date of its purchase by Maytag through 1994. In late 1994 Maytag sold its

Hoover Australia unit to Southcorp Holdings for $82.1 million in cash, resulting in an after-tax loss of $16.4 million. In the second quarter of the following year, Maytag sold Hoover Europe to Italian appliance maker Candy SpA for $164.3 million in cash, resulting in an after-tax loss of $135.4 million. Maytag retained the Hoover North America operation. Proceeds from these sales were largely used to pay down the company's long-term debt, which stood at just $488.5 million by 1996, compared to nearly $800 million in the early 1990s.

By 1996, Maytag was on the upswing. Although revenues of $3 billion were slightly lower than at the beginning of the decade in part due to the divestments of 1994 and 1995, the net income of $162.4 million represented a high point for the decade so far. That figure would have been even higher, if it were not for the $24.4 million restructuring charge the company took early that year in connection with the consolidation of its two separate major appliance operations into a single operation called Maytag Appliances, which was handed responsibility for all sales, marketing, manufacturing, logistics, and customer service functions for the Maytag, Jenn-Air, Admiral, and Magic Chef brands.

Freed from its overseas headache, Maytag also began to revitalize its appliance lines through record 1996 capital spending of $220 million, much of which went toward new product development and improvements in existing lines. Among new products introduced were washers and dryers tagged with a new brand: Performa by Maytag; these were priced lower than Maytag brand products but carried some of the Maytag cachet. On the high end of the scale, the company jumped onto the front-loading washer bandwagon with the March 1997 debut of the Neptune high-efficiency model. In the refrigerator arena—Maytag's weakest product line—a three-year, $180 million redesign effort culminated with the April 1997 introduction of a new generation of Maytag, Jenn-Air, Magic Chef, and Admiral models that had increased capacity, were quieter, included several pull-out features, and boasted of faster temperature recovery following the opening of the freezer or refrigerator door. Some of the credit for these innovations went to Lloyd D. Ward, whom Hadley had recruited from PepsiCo's Frito-Lay unit in early 1996 to become executive vice-president of Maytag and president of Maytag Appliances—and perhaps heir apparent to Hadley.

Despite the heavy investments in North America, Maytag had not entirely given up on overseas growth. Like numerous other companies in the mid-1990s, Maytag decided to move into the burgeoning Chinese market. It did so in September 1996 with an initial $70 million investment to set up a series of joint ventures with the Hefei Rongshida Group Corporation, the leading washing machine firm in China, marketing its products under the well-known RSD brand. Maytag initially teamed with Hefei Rongshida in the production and marketing of washing machines, but planned to extend the venture into refrigerators during a second phase.

Further evidence of the stronger financial position of Maytag came with the $93.5 million purchase of G.S. Blodgett Corp. in late 1997. The privately held Blodgett—which traced its origins to the Blodgett Oven Co. founded in Burlington, Vermont, in 1848—was a manufacturer of commercial ovens, fryers, and charbroilers for the food service industry, thus representing a logical extension of Maytag's product lines and customers. Blodgett was the company's first acquisition since that of Chicago Pacific in 1989.

The Maytag Corporation of the late 1990s was stronger than it had been in years. Through heightened new product introductions; strategic, manageable acquisitions; and selective overseas ventures the company was positioning itself for steady, profitable growth, while at the same time maintaining its reputation for quality.

CHANGES IN THE NEW MILLENNIUM

Despite the success of the late 1990s, problems were on the horizon for Maytag as it entered the new millennium. Falling profits brought on by a slowing economy, increased competition, and high costs forced the company into action. Maytag began to implement a $100 million cost-cutting reorganization program that included plant closures and employee layoffs. At the same time, chairman and CEO Lloyd Ward resigned suddenly, citing differences with the company board concerning Maytag's strategic direction. Leonard Hadley came out of retirement and took over until Ralph Hake was named CEO in 2001.

Hake immediately set plans in motion to get Maytag back on track. He shuttered unprofitable businesses and continued cutting costs including moving various plant operations to Mexico where labor was cheaper. On the acquisition front, the company added Amana Appliances to its arsenal in 2001. Even with these efforts, sales continued to fall well into 2004 and high material costs ate into company profits.

As early as 2000, takeover talks began to surface as changes in the company's corporate bylaws allowed for an easier acquisition process. Sure enough, Maytag announced in May 2005 that Triton Acquisition Holding Company, an investment group led by Ripplewood Holdings LLC, had made an offer to take the company private in a $1.13 billion leveraged buyout. The company's share prices rose nearly one dollar upon news of the deal, and Whirlpool Corporation swooped in with a $1.62 billion offer including the assumption of $977 million in debt. Whirlpool had outbid Ripplewood by nearly 43 percent and had sweetened the deal by offering to pay Triton a $40 million termination fee if the Whirlpool/Maytag deal went through. It also offered to pay Maytag $120 million if the deal failed to meet regulatory guidelines and an additional $15 million to retain certain Maytag employees.

Triton chose not to raise its bid for Maytag, paving the way for Whirlpool to complete its purchase. The acquisition cleared regulatory hurdles and in March 2006, Whirlpool completed its acquisition of Maytag and secured its position as one of the world's top manufacturers of home appliances. The company began the integration process immediately with Whirlpool management heading up the combined company in Benton Harbor, Michigan. Nearly 4,500 positions were cut as manufacturing facilities in Iowa, Illinois, and Arkansas were consolidated into Whirlpool's plants in Ohio.

Whirlpool was optimistic about its future with the Maytag brand. Still, as an independent company, Maytag was finished. Former CEO Hadley made his feelings about the acquisition and Maytag's performance known in a June 2006 interview. "I'm extremely disappointed with what has been happening in the last five years. Just extremely disappointed," he stated. "I can't tell you how it hurts. That was my life for 40 years." Indeed, Maytag Corporation had a long run as a venerable appliance manufacturer in the United States. While economic changes, shifts in consumer demand, and heightened competition got the better of Maytag Corporation, Maytag brand appliances would no doubt remain in stores for years to come under Whirlpool's watchful eye.

Vera A. Emmons
Updated, David E. Salamie; Christina M. Stansell

PRINCIPAL COMPETITORS

AB Electrolux; LG Electronics Inc.

FURTHER READING

"At 80, Maytag Feels 'Terrific,'" *Appliance Manufacturer,* November 1987, p. 28.

Barboza, David, "Maytag's Chief Executive Resigns, Citing Differences," *New York Times,* November 10, 2000.

Berman, Dennis K., "Ripplewood Won't Raise Maytag Bid; Whirlpool Closes In," *Wall Street Journal,* August 22, 2005, p. A3.

Bremner, Brian, and Mark Maremont, "Maytag's Foreign Fling Isn't Much Fun After All," *Business Week,* September 4, 1989, pp. 32–33.

Bulkeley, William M., "Wring in the New: Washers That Load from Front Are Hot," *Wall Street Journal,* April 29, 1997, pp. A1, A5.

Byrne, Harlan S., "Maytag Corp.: Hope for Growth Lies in European Operations," *Barron's,* May 25, 1992, pp. 35–36.

———, "The Predator or the Prey?," *Barron's,* March 3, 1997, pp. 22, 24.

———, "Remaking Maytag," *Barron's,* August 21, 1989, pp. 12–13.

David, Gregory E., "Breaking the Spell," *Financial World,* May 10, 1994, pp. 34, 36.

Dubashi, Jagannath, "Taken to the Cleaners," *Financial World,* August 4, 1992, p. 28.

"Former Maytag CEO Hadley Reacts to Sale," *AFX Asia,* June 24, 2006.

Geisi, Steve, "Maytag Revs $35M in Product Noise," *Brandweek,* February 17, 1997, pp. 1, 6.

———, "Spin-Cycle Doctor," *Brandweek,* March 10, 1997, pp. 38–40.

Gold, Howard, "Maytag Steps Out," *Forbes,* December 17, 1984, p. 96.

Hallinan, Joseph T., "Whirlpool Raises Maytag Bid Again," *Wall Street Journal,* August 9, 2005.

Hannon, Kerry, "Damned If You Do ...," *Forbes,* March 20, 1989, p. 201.

Harris, John, "Wake Up, Maytag Man!," *Forbes,* November 13, 1989, pp. 308, 310.

Hill, Andrew, and Michael Cassell, "Candy Pulls Hoover Away from the Mangle," *Financial Times,* May 31, 1995, p. 21.

Hillinger, Charles, "Washdays, Birthdays: Maytag Notes 80 Years," *Los Angeles Times,* May 8, 1987.

Hoover, Robert, and John Hoover, *An American Quality Legend: How Maytag Saved Our Moms, Vexed the Competition, and Presaged America's Quality Revolution,* New York: McGraw-Hill, 1993, 239 p.

"In Pursuit of Quality," *Appliance Manufacturer,* November 1987, p. 38.

Kelly, Kevin, Fred Guterl, and Roon Lewald, "Can Maytag's Repairman Get Out of This Fix?," *Business Week,* October 26, 1992, pp. 54–55.

"Maytag: Wizard of White Goods," *Dun's Business Month,* December 1985, p. 34.

Quintanilla, Carl, "Lloyd Ward Puts a New Spin on Maytag," *Wall Street Journal,* November 26, 1996, pp. B1, B8.

Remick, Norman C., Jr., "Maytag: A China Connection," *Appliance Manufacturer,* February 1997, p. G16.

The Spirit of Maytag: 100 Years of Dependability: 1893–1993, Newton, Iowa: Maytag Corporation, 1993.

Upbin, Bruce, "Global, Schmobal," *Forbes,* March 10, 1997, pp. 64, 66.

Wee, Heesun, "Maytag Is Cleaning Up Its Act," *BusinessWeek Online,* May 17, 2002.

McBride plc

McBride House, Penn Road
Beaconsfield, HP9 2FY
United Kingdom
Telephone: (44) 01494 607050
Fax: (44) 01494 607055
Web site: http://www.mcbride.co.uk

Public Company
Incorporated: 1927 as Robert McBride
Employees: 4,208
Sales: £537.1 million ($1.01 billion) (2005)
Stock Exchanges: London
Ticker Symbol: MCB
NAIC: 325620 Toilet Preparation Manufacturing;
325611 Soap and Other Detergent Manufacturing;
325612 Polish and Other Sanitation Good
Manufacturing

■ ■ ■

McBride plc is Europe's leading manufacturer of private-label household and personal care products. The company produces a wide range of laundry and dishwashing detergents, cleaning products, air fresheners, as well as soap, shampoo, toothpaste, deodorant, shaving cream, nail care, and skin care products. McBride's products are sold through nearly every major distribution group in Europe under supermarkets' house brands, and under a variety of smaller and discount brands. McBride is also a contract manufacturer for a number of branded products, including Colgate toothpaste, among others. Based near Manchester, England, McBride oper-ates six factories in the United Kingdom, three factories in both France and Belgium, and one factory each in Spain, Poland, and Italy. The company also has sales subsidiaries in the Czech Republic, Hungary, and Russia. Household products account for the largest part of group sales, generating more than 82 percent of McBride's £537 million ($1.01 billion) sales in 2005. Since the early 2000s, McBride has succeeded in boosting its share of foreign sales, primarily in continental Europe, which account for nearly 58 percent of group sales. McBride is organized into three core divisions: McBride U.K.; McBride Continental Europe (CE), covering Austria, Belgium, France, Germany, Italy, the Netherlands, Portugal, Spain, and Switzerland; and McBride International, including Poland, Czech Republic, Hungary, Central and Eastern Europe, the Nordic States, and markets beyond Europe. Formerly the personal products division of BP, McBride is listed on the London Stock Exchange. Miles Roberts is company chief executive.

FOUNDED IN MANCHESTER IN 1927

McBride Plc was formed by the 1993 buyout of the Consumer Products Division of BP, when the British petroleum giant adopted a new strategy of focusing on its core operations. The Consumer Products Division was based on a number of acquisitions made by BP after the division was created in the late 1970s. The most prominent and one of the earliest of these acquisitions was of Robert McBride PLC in 1978.

Robert McBride had founded the company in 1927

as a producer and distributor of bleach and other cotton and textile processing chemicals to the Lancashire textile industry. McBride launched his company in North Manchester; under son Reg McBride, the company moved to nearby Middleton in 1945. The company then launched its first consumer products sales, bottling bleach for delivery to local grocers.

McBride launched its expansion into a wider category of household cleaning products and detergents under the next generation of the McBride family to lead the company. Under Terry McBride, the company grew strongly through the 1960s. A major part of the company's expansion came through its developing operations in supplying the private label market. The rapid growth of the supermarket sector in the United Kingdom in the 1960s, and the emergence of a small number of large-scale regional and national supermarket groups, had introduced the demand for products that could be packaged and marketed under the supermarkets' own names and brands. In order to supply this market, McBride invested in plastic blow-molding equipment in the 1960s, allowing the company to produce its own bottles for a growing line of products. By the end of the

decade, the company had added production of dish-washing liquids, fabric conditioners, and the like. By the beginning of the 1970s, company sales already topped £1 million.

McBride grew strongly through the following decade—by the end of the decade, the company's sales had grown more by more than 10 times. Fueling this growth was the company's public offering, made in 1973. Following its listing on the London Stock Exchange, McBride made its first acquisition, paying £77,000 to acquire domestic household products producer Wimsol Lanry, a part of the Jeyes Group. Later that year, the company's expansion took on greater steam with the acquisition of a 50 percent stake in Gretna Laboratories. Based in Burnley, near Middleton, Gretna further boosted McBride's private label product offering with its own list of toiletries and other soaps and personal care items. McBride completed the acquisition of Gretna before the end of 1975.

The new acquisitions helped boost McBride's production capacity at a time when private label goods were beginning to take off in the United Kingdom. This market was aided in part by the growing British recession during the 1970s and the after-effects of the Arab oil embargo earlier in the decade. By the end of 1977, McBride's sales had topped £9.4 million.

FORMING THE BP CONSUMER PRODUCTS DIVISION IN 1980

By then, too, McBride had begun receiving approaches from other groups eager to buy the fast-growing company. The company rejected most of these approaches, in large part because the prospective buyers were not able to guarantee the company's future continuity. In 1978, however, McBride received an offer from British Petroleum (BP). At the time, BP had begun developing a small household products operation as part of its recently created Nutrition division. BP also operated an industrial detergents division in Edinburgh, not far from McBride's Manchester base. McBride accepted BP's offer to acquire some 53 percent of its shares, valuing the company at more than £10 million.

Under BP, McBride grew quickly, as the petroleum giant tacked on a number of small family-owned companies to the Middleton-based private label household products group. Among the group's acquisitions into the early 1980s was that of Hugo House Beauty Products, based in Bradford, acquired by McBride for £2.75 million in 1983. By the end of that year, McBride's turnover had soared to £23.5 million.

Yet McBride by then formed just one part of BP's rapidly growing Consumer Products Division. In 1980,

KEY DATES

1927: Robert McBride founds a textile chemical supply business in North Manchester.

1945: The company launches its first consumer products sales, distributing bottled bleach to local grocers.

1960s: McBride installs blow-molding equipment and expands into private label production of household products and soaps and shampoos.

1973: McBride goes public with a listing on the London Stock Exchange.

1978: British Petroleum (BP) acquires McBride as the core of its new Consumer Products Division.

1980: BP acquires Belgium's Tensia, which is placed under McBride.

1987: McBride acquires Camille Simon, of the U.K., holder of the Surcare brand.

1993: BP sells McBride to a management buy-in backed by Lehman Brothers and Legal & General.

1995: McBride acquires Arco Iris to enter Spain.

1998: The company acquires Problanc in France and Intersilesia in Poland.

2004: McBride acquires full control of Aerosol Products Ltd., a joint venture established in 1999.

2006: The company buys the liquid products operations of Sanmex International for £7.5 million.

the company had extended this division to the European continent's private label market, buying Belgium's Tensia group. Tensia's mix of household and industrial detergents included soaps, aerosols, fabric softeners, toiletries, cosmetics, and other specialty products. The Tensia group, placed under McBride, extended BP's reach into Belgium, France, Italy, and Germany, adding nearly £94 million to the McBride's turnover

Soon after the Tensia purchase, McBride sold the German business. McBride then launched a larger restructuring of its European holdings. In 1986, the company split off Tensia's Italian operations into a new company, Italian General Detergents. That company grew in 1989 through the takeover of smaller private-label shampoo and hair care rival Kopfchemie SpA.

The Tensia name itself disappeared after McBride bought Yplon S.A., based in Belgium with operations in France. Following the Yplon purchase, McBride regrouped all of its operations in these two countries under the Yplon name. These included a factory producing liquid detergents in Moyaux, and another factory, based in Rosporden, producing aerosols. Both plants had been acquired by Tensia during the mid-1980s.

McBride had also been expanding in its U.K. home base during this time. The company became the first in England to launch a private label liquid detergent in 1986. The following year, the company bought another leading U.K. laundry detergents group, Camille Simon. First established in the 1860s as a West London laundry, that company had launched its own laundry soap, called Simon's Lessive Cleaning Extract of Soap, in 1898. Over the following decades, Camille Simon grew into a major U.K. washing powders producer, particularly through its Surcare brand of detergents for people with sensitive skin.

After adding Camille Simon, McBride growth continued with further acquisitions, including an aerosol factory in Hull and Crestol Ltd., a company producing shampoo and other hair care items based in Bradford. McBride's fast growing position in the U.K. private label market was further enhanced in 1988 when the company became the first to market with a new liquid laundry product combining detergent with fabric softener.

INDEPENDENT EUROPEAN LEADER FOR THE NEW CENTURY

Amid economic turmoil at the beginning of the 1990s, BP launched a new strategy, refocusing its operations on its core businesses. In 1993, an investment group led by Lehman Brothers and Legal & General led a management buy-in of BP's Consumer Product Division worth £275 million. For the takeover, the group brought in Mike Handley, a veteran of Cadbury Schweppes, Reckitt and Colman, and Rank Hovis McDougal, as the newly independent company's managing director. The company retained the McBride name in order to capitalize on its reputation as a leading private label supplier both in the United Kingdom and on the European continent. By 1995, McBride had returned to the London Stock Exchange, listing as McBride Plc.

In the meantime, McBride had launched a new expansion campaign. In 1994, the company acquired privately owned Longthorne Laboratories, a manufacturer of private label personal care products. This acquisition was followed by the purchase of another private label supplier, Albright & Wilson, which focused on powdered laundry detergents, bought in 1995 for £3.2 million.

McBride entered Spain that same year, buying Productos Quimicos Arco Iris S.A., which produced household products for the Spanish private label market. A relatively small company, the bulk of Arco Iris's operations were in the production of bleach. Following the acquisition, however, McBride launched an expansion of the business, investing some £5 million and extending its product range to include a variety of liquid cleaning products, including detergents and dishwashing liquids.

Acquisitions remained a major part of the group's growth strategy through the end of the decade. In 1998, for example, the company acquired U.K.'s Globol, a producer of home fragrance and odor neutralizer products for both the private label and name-brand contract manufacturing markets. Also that year, McBride boosted its operations in France, acquiring private labels supplier Problanc S.A. and its subsidiary Sodichlor, and entered the Netherlands through the acquisition of that country's Grada.

McBride then entered Poland, buying Intersilesia, which manufactured liquid household and personal care products for both the private label and minor brand segments. Alongside the fast-growing private label market, the minor brand sector represented another attractive growth market for McBride. While the company's private label products were generally restricted to a single customer, the production of minor brands—that is, smaller brands owned by McBride itself—allowed the company to market the same product across a variety of customers and markets. Another advantage of McBride's minor brand operations was that they permitted retailers on the European continent to sell products with the well-regarded "Made in U.K." label. Featured among McBride's minor brand family were the popular Surcare and Brio brands, both of which were marketed across the U.K. and throughout Europe.

McBride briefly entered the market for over-the-counter medicines, buying Wrafton Laboratories in 1999. The company sold that business, however, in 2001, preferring to return its focus to its household and personal care lines. These were boosted that same year when the company became the first to market a soluble liquid laundry detergent sachet product, called the Brio Actipod, meant as a bridge between tablet and liquid detergents. In the meantime, the company had expanded its aerosol operations, forming the Aerosol Products Ltd. joint venture in 1999. In 2004, the company bought out its partner in that venture, Nichol Beauty. Aerosol Products held the number two spot in the U.K. aerosol-filling market.

By 2006, McBride had created an empire generating nearly £540 million ($1.1 billion) in revenues, with operations throughout Europe and sales to more than 40 countries. The company remained on the lookout for new expansion opportunities, such as its April 2006 purchase of Sanmex International's household liquids division for a total of £7.5 million. With the European private label sector's expansion expected to remain steady through the end of the 2000s, McBride looked forward to a bright future as market leader.

M. L. Cohen

PRINCIPAL DIVISIONS

McBride U.K.; McBride Continental Europe (CE); McBride International.

PRINCIPAL SUBSIDIARIES

Aerosol Products Ltd; Intersilesia McBride Polska Sp. Z.o.o. (Poland, 85%); McBride B.V. (The Netherlands); McBride Euro Finance Ltd; McBride Hungary Kft (Hungary); McBride S.A. (Belgium); McBride S.A. (Spain); McBride S.A.S. (France); McBride S.p.a. (Italy); McBride s.r.o. (Czech Republic); OOO McBride Russia; Problanc S.A.S. (France); Robert McBride Ltd; Vitherm S.A.S. (France).

PRINCIPAL COMPETITORS

Nestle S.A.; Procter and Gamble Co.; Unilever; Johnson & Johnson; E. Merck; Sanofi-Aventis; L'Oreal S.A.; Rhodia; Sara Lee/DE International B.V.; Bolton Group B.V.; Smith and Nephew plc.

FURTHER READING

"The Big Brands Go Begging in Europe," *Business Week*, March 21, 2005.

Hunt, Julian, "It's a Marketing Coup as Co-op Gets Laundry Pouches on Sale," *Grocer*, February 17, 2001, p. 4.

"McBridge Goes Globol," *European Cosmetic Markets*, December 1998, p. 485.

"McBride in Search of a New Suitor," *Soap Perfumery & Cosmetics*, December 2000, p. 7.

"McBride Sales Continue to Rise," *European Cosmetic Markets*, May 2000, p. 175.

Roberts, Patricia, "Clued-Up Mike Has the Answers," *Manchester Business*, November 30, 2004.

"Supermarket Market Remains Challenging, Says McBride,"
Manufacturing News, July 6, 2006.

Watson, Elaine, "House Proud: Own Label Supplier McBride
Attributes Its Market-Leading Position to Innovative
Product Development and Strong Customer Service,"
Grocer, January 31, 2004, p. 32.

Meiji Dairies Corporation

1-2-10 Shinsuna
Koto-ku
Tokyo, 136-8908
Japan
Telephone: (05) 653-0300
Fax: (05) 653-0400
Web site: http://www.meinyu.co.jp

Public Company
Incorporated: 1917 as Boso Condensed Milk
Employees: 12,684
Sales: $6.7 billion (2005)
Stock Exchanges: Tokyo Nagoya
Ticker Symbol: 2261
NAIC: 311511 Fluid Milk Manufacturing; 311512 Creamery Butter Manufacturing; 311514 Dry, Condensed, and Evaporated Dairy Product Manufacturing; 311520 Ice Cream and Frozen Dessert Manufacturing

∎ ∎ ∎

Meiji Dairies Corporation, formerly known as Meiji Milk Products Company Ltd., is Japan's leading dairy products manufacturer. The company introduced condensed milk to Japanese consumers in 1917 and its product arsenal evolved to include products such as yogurts, cheeses, ice creams, and various nutraceutical and health foods.

EARLY HISTORY

Milk was not a popular beverage in pre-1917 Japan, but a growing awareness of its nutritional value and an ap-

preciation of the storage convenience of unopened cans helped make the launch of condensed milk in Japan feasible.

With the participation of the Meiji Sugar Manufacturing Company, Boso Condensed Milk Co., Ltd., was founded in the closing months of World War I. Japan had risen to the status of a world power, and the resulting increase in contact with Western nations had begun to weaken the resistance of the Japanese public toward departures from traditional dietary customs and habits.

However, within months of the launch, a postwar recession began to slow the economy. It took several years for condensed milk to gain general acceptance. Recovery was gradual until the late 1920s, when a period of rapid industrialization took hold. As workers from rural areas flocked to the new factory sites, the mood was again favorable for acceptance of new products and changes in dietary habits.

From the invasion of Manchuria in the early 1930s until the end of World War II, Japan was preoccupied with the production and use of munitions. Despite wartime difficulties in transporting goods, Boso continued to make gains.

MERGERS AND DIVERSIFICATION: 1940 THROUGH THE POSTWAR YEARS

When it merged with the Tokyo Confectionery Company in 1940, Boso changed its name to Meiji Milk Products Company, Limited. The company then began to diversify, adding a line of chocolate, candy, gum, snack foods, and other confections, and Meiji grew quickly.

In 1949, Meiji was able to strengthen its position through a merger with Japan Dairy Products and three other companies. The following year, Meiji took over the Imagame factory from the Hokkaido Dairy Farm Association and also bought the Tokyo Dairy Industry and the Shoman Milk Company. A merger in 1951 brought Asahi Milk Products into the Meiji group.

Although most of the companies Meiji had acquired through these mergers were primarily milk producers, the need for continuing diversification had become a significant factor in planning for the future. The use of condensed milk as a dietary supplement for infants set the stage for development of a line of infant formula and baby food, and the postwar baby boom created a ready market.

In the 1950s, as ice cream became popular, Meiji decided to specialize in a high-grade product and eventually introduced "Lady Borden"—to this day an upscale market leader. Meiji's agreement with the Borden Company, an American food company, was the first of a number of business relationships Meiji has maintained profitably with foreign companies.

The next logical step was to introduce frozen foods for individual consumers in the grocery market and in institutional quantities for restaurants, hospitals, and other large organizations. Foods such as pizza, pilaf, frozen rice, and fried entrees were consistently strong sellers, along with puddings and other desserts, margarine, and creams.

NEW PRODUCT DEVELOPMENT IN THE 1980S AND EARLY 1990S

At this time, new products were developed in-house, for the most part. Meiji's research-and-development department explored fermentation processes and worked to develop more efficient technologies for 70 years. One of Meiji's most successful products was Meiji Infant Soft Curd FK-P, an infant formula popular in Japan and many other countries. Another, Meiji Bulgaria Yogurt LB51, was the leading yogurt in Japan.

The growing interest in health foods over the previous several decades not only spurred yogurt sales but also led to the development of other products, such as popular bottled yogurt drinks. Meiji established a subsidiary, Health Way, Inc., to develop and market new health-related foods.

The market for dairy foods fluctuated from time to time, with factors such as the rise and fall of the birth rate, but in general the market was a growing one; the market for cheese in particular appeared to be rising steadily. Through an agreement with Borden, Meiji imported natural cheese and manufactured and marketed processed cheese in Japan.

Branching out into nonfood products and services was also profitable for Meiji. After manufacturing animal feeds for a number of years, the company started raising livestock, and it also manufactured veterinary medicines.

One of Meiji's research-and-development sites, the Meiji Institute of Health Science, was instrumental in adding a line of pharmaceutical products to the company's wares. Among their products were antibiotics, enzymes, and agricultural chemicals. Other products, such as an anticancer drug using lactic acid bacilli, were under development. A Meiji vaccine was proven effective when tested against B-type hepatitis in 1985.

Meiji also capitalized on the time-saving services that were important to Japanese consumers. Nice Day, Inc., a Meiji subsidiary, operated a shop-at-home service for supplies related to child-rearing. Another specialized in home delivery of foods, and still another provided communication services for users of personal computers. Real estate was another interest the company developed during the 1980s.

But the main focus of Meiji's efforts in the early 1990s continued to be its original interest: the food market. In aspiring to become a major general food manufacturer, the company worked with several others overseas. For example, Meiji had an agreement with the England and Wales Milk Marketing Board, a major British dairy organization, to work together to develop new yogurt-related products and technology. Working with the American company Abbott Laboratories

KEY DATES

1917: The company introduces condensed milk to Japanese consumers.

1940: Boso Condensed Milk Co., Ltd. merges with Tokyo Confectionery Company; Boso changes its name to Meiji Milk Products Company, Limited.

1949: Meiji merges with Japan Dairy Products and three other companies.

1951: Asahi Milk Products is acquired.

1985: The company develops a Hepatitis B vaccine.

1991: The New Zealand Dairy Board is commissioned to produce all of Meiji's powered milk.

2001: The company changes its name to Meiji Dairies Corporation.

provided Meiji with the technology to produce new nutritional products. In 1991, the company commissioned the New Zealand Dairy Board to produce all of its powdered milk, which was then exported to Thailand.

In addition to marketing its products to domestic and overseas food outlets, Meiji also established its own chain of franchised food stores. Meiji's innovation, diversification, and strong marketing were expected to move the company in the direction it had chosen, and it was fast becoming a major, comprehensive food supplier.

LOOKING TO THE NEW MILLENNIUM

The company undertook several joint ventures and established new subsidiaries throughout the remainder of the 1990s. In 1994, Meiji Dairy Australia Pty. Ltd. was created. That same year, Guadong M&F Yang Tang Dairy Products Co. Ltd. was created as a joint venture to manufacture ice cream. In 1997, another company was created to oversee the manufacture of ice cream in Indonesia. In 1999, Meiji formed a business alliance with Coca-Cola Japan.

Meiji remained busy on the product front as well. Some of the company's new items included Oolong So-Cha tea in 1994, Clean Pit AZ throat spray in 1995, the Subesube Miruru baby skin care product and the VAAM sports drink in 1996, the MEINYU precipitation hepatitis B vaccine in 1997, and a new line of drinking yogurt in 1998.

Meiji entered the new millennium as Japan's leading dairy manufacturer. The company adopted a new corporate moniker—Meiji Dairies Corporation—in 2001 and also moved company headquarters to a different location in Tokyo. The Tohoku plant went online in August 2000, and the Kyushu facility was operational in May 2002. A new milk product, Meiji Oishii Gyunyu, was launched in June 2002.

The company's business strategy of diversifying its product line appeared to pay off. The company had become the leading seller of commercial milk in Japan in 1998 and the largest dairy products manufacturer in 2000 based on sales and profits. While sales remained relatively flat from 2000 to 2004 due to a slowdown in consumer spending, net income was on the rise. In fact, in fiscal year 2002, the company reported its net profit had increased by 93.5 percent over the previous year. In 2005, Meiji set plans in motion to open a new natural cheese plant in Memuro in the prefecture of Hokkaido. The plant was slated to be Japan's largest natural cheese facility.

Japan was plagued with an over-capacity of milk during this time period due to hot and wet summers that left dairy cows munching on lush grasses and farmers with more milk then they could sell. In fact, in one week during 2006, over 1,000 tons of milk were destroyed. In response to the crisis, Meiji began to look for ways to utilize the surplus, including turning the milk into methane for use in the generation of electricity.

Meiji would face challenges in the coming years and the company was prepared to meet them head on. Domestic competition as well as competition from imports forced the company to adopt strategies to increase profits while strengthening its brand name. Meiji also viewed several factors including the falling birthrate and aging society in Japan, the globalization of the industry, and growing consumer awareness of food safety as major components in Japan's changing dairy industry. The company believed these factors would produce future growth opportunities.

Christina M. Stansell

PRINCIPAL SUBSIDIARIES

Asahi Broiler Co., Ltd.; Chubu Meihan Co., Ltd.; Chugoku Meihan Co., Ltd.; Fresh Network Systems Co., Ltd.; Hokkaido Meihan Co., Ltd.; Kanazawa Meihan Co., Ltd.; Kantora Logistics Co., Ltd.; K.C.S. Co., Ltd.; Kinki Meihan Co., Ltd.; Kyushu Meinyu Hanbai Co., Ltd.; Meiji Agris Co., Ltd.; Meiji Dairy Products Co., Ltd.; Meiji Feed Co., Ltd.; Meiji Kenko Ham Co., Ltd.; Meiji Oils and Fats Co., Ltd.; Meiji Techno-Service Inc.; Nice Day Co., Ltd.; Nihon Kanzume, Co., Ltd.; Ohkura Pharmaceutical Co., Ltd.; Okinawa Meiji Milk Products Co., Ltd.; Osaka Hosho Milk Products Co., Ltd.; Pampy Foods Inc.; Shikoku

Tokai Meiji Co., Ltd.; Tohoku Meihan Co., Ltd.; Tokyo Meihan Co., Ltd.; Tokyo Meiji Foods Co., Ltd.; Tokyo Milk Transportation Co., Ltd.

PRINCIPAL COMPETITORS

Ezaki Glico Co., Ltd.; Morinaga & Co., Ltd.; Snow Brand Milk Products Co., Ltd.

FURTHER READING

Lewis, Leo, "Hot Summers Make Milk Boil Over," *Times*, March 28, 2006.

"Meiji Dairies 2006 Company Profile Edition 1: SWOT Analysis," *Just-Food*, July 2006.

"Meiji Dairies to Cut Workforce by 10 Pct Over 3 Yrs," *Jiji Press English News Service*, March 4, 2003.

"Meiji Dairies' Group Net Profit Up 93.5 Pct in FY '02," *Jiji Press English News Service*, May 20, 2003.

"Meiji Dairies Plans New Natural Cheese Plant," *Jiji Press English News Service*, October 7, 2005.

Sakashita, Yoku, "Cutting Fixed Costs Vital to Meiji Dairies," *Nikkei Weekly*, August 15, 2005.

Milliken & Co.

920 Milliken Road
Spartanburg, South Carolina 29308
U.S.A.
Telephone: (864) 503-2020
Fax: (864) 503-2100
Web site: http://www.milliken.com

Private Company
Incorporated: 1890 as Deering-Milliken & Co.
Employees: 11,000
Sales: $3.00 billion (est. 2005)
NAIC: 313210 Broadwoven Fabric Mills; 313111 Yarn Spinning Mills; 314110 Carpet and Rug Mills; 314121 Curtain and Drapery Mills; 314129 Other Household Textile Product Mills; 325612 Polish and Other Sanitation Good Manufacturing; 541710 Research and Development in the Physical Sciences and Engineering Sciences

■ ■ ■

Milliken & Co. is one of the largest privately owned textile and chemical manufacturing companies in the world. For decades Milliken & Co. has been the clear industry leader in technology and research and, to many observers, in quality and services as well. Chairman Roger Milliken, grandson of company founder Seth Milliken, has been recognized as a giant of the textile industry since his ascension to the company's chairmanship in 1947. The two characteristics that have defined Roger Milliken's reign are his commitment to research and technological innovation and his commitment to

secrecy regarding company matters. The former is best illustrated by the more than 2,000 patents held by Milliken & Co. on inventions ranging from computerized dyeing equipment to color-enhancing chemicals. The latter is reflected by the fact that most of the company's shareholders, predominantly Milliken family members and friends, do not have access to financial information. The company operates 60 facilities across the globe and manufacturers more than 38,000 different products related to fabrics and chemicals. In fact, Milliken & Co. claims that people touch Milliken products more than 50 times in an average day.

19TH-CENTURY ORIGINS

Milliken & Co. first appeared as Deering-Milliken & Co., a general store and selling agent for textile mills, in 1865. Deering-Milliken was a Portland, Maine–based partnership formed by Seth Milliken and William Deering. The company moved its base of operations from Maine to New York a few years later. Soon after that, Deering left the company for Chicago, where he formed the Deering Harvesting Machinery Company (now Navistar). Seth Milliken continued to operate under the Deering-Milliken name as a selling agent for woolen mills in New England. In the 1860s, he was selling for 16 different mills. Deering-Milliken made its first southern contact in 1884, when it began its long-standing and successful connection with Pacolet Manufacturing Company, headed by Captain John Montgomery of Spartanburg, South Carolina.

From his vantage point as part owner, sales agent, and factor (purchasing and procurement aide) for textile mills in both New England and the South, Milliken was able to determine when a mill was struggling financially, and much of Deering-Milliken's early growth sprang from the acquisition of these concerns. In 1890 Deering-Milliken & Co. was incorporated. Under Seth Milliken, the company eventually acquired interests in at least 42 mills, helping develop the textile industry in the southern United States by financing local manufacturing firms. Seth Milliken died in 1920 and was succeeded by his son Gerrish Milliken, who had joined the company in 1916. During Gerrish Milliken's tenure as head of Deering-Milliken, the company's primary role was that of sales agent and factor for southern mills.

The company's lasting tendencies toward free-flowing cash investment and technological farsightedness were already evident during the Gerrish Milliken era. For example, by keeping debt low and capital liquid during the Great Depression, Deering-Milliken was able to acquire controlling interest in several mills that faced bankruptcy while heavily indebted to Deering-Milliken. In addition, Gerrish Milliken recognized early on the potential importance of manmade fibers. He acquired the gigantic Judson mill in Greenville, South Carolina, and tested rayon, a new fiber, there.

WORLD WAR II SPURS
RESEARCH AND DEVELOPMENT

The onset of World War II created great demand for new, more durable textiles. Deering-Milliken was among a handful of companies that led the industry in the development of synthetics for military use. Mills that sold their goods through Deering-Milliken were commissioned by the War Production Board to produce a variety of fabrics and yarns to meet government specifications. In 1944 Deering-Milliken was designated to build a mill that would process a new manmade fiber for military tire cord. The DeFore mill, built on the Seneca River near Clemson, South Carolina, was the first windowless textile mill equipped with complete air-clearing and air-cooling systems; it set the plant standard for years to come. Throughout the war years, demand also continued to grow for the company's New England–produced worsteds and woolens, and more

southern mills were purchased.

Gerrish Milliken died in 1947, and his son Roger Milliken took charge of the company. Gerrish Milliken, Jr., and Minot Milliken, two other grandsons of Seth Milliken, also were given official positions in the company. Roger Milliken began to shift the company's emphasis away from commission selling toward its own manufacturing. Eight new mills were built between 1940 and 1953. The first mill Roger Milliken built was the Gerrish Milliken Mill, in Pendleton, South Carolina. In addition to weaving Orlon and nylon, this plant, along with two others, doubled as a cattle farm.

By the mid-1950s, Deering-Milliken & Co. was the third largest textile chain in the United States. About 19,000 workers were employed by the company, ranging geographically from New England through the South.

In 1956 the company became entangled in one of the ugliest and most drawn-out affairs in the history of labor relations, a case that continues to be studied by experts in labor law. On September 6, 1956, workers in Darlington, South Carolina, ignoring Roger Milliken's threats of a plant shutdown, voted to bring in the Textile Workers Union of America to represent them. The textile industry historically had been hostile to organized labor—15 percent to 20 percent of the industry had union representation by the mid-1970s—and Roger Milliken had been among the most vocal of union opponents. Milliken made good his threat, and the Darlington plant was closed. In 1962 the National Labor Relations Board ruled that the closing constituted an unfair labor practice, but this decision was reversed by a federal appeals court. The case was ultimately decided by the Supreme Court, which ruled that a plant could not be closed to discourage union activity at other company locations. It was not until 1980, after 24 years of litigation and negotiation over a formula for calculating back pay, that the case was finally settled. The company agreed to pay a total of $5 million to the 427 workers still alive and the survivors of the 16 workers who had died since 1956.

Originally, the mills controlled by Deering-Milliken were separate corporations, some of which had outside shareholders. By the end of the 1950s, Roger Milliken had succeeded in buying out all of them, integrating them into a single corporate entity. The year 1958 marked the opening of Deering-Milliken's gigantic research facility in Spartanburg, located on a 600-acre complex that became the company's headquarters. From this facility, the most sophisticated in the textile industry, flowed a steady stream of new fabrics and processing techniques. It was here that "durable press" and "soil release," important advancements in polyester treatment, were developed through irradiation.

KEY DATES

1865: Deering-Milliken & Co. is established.

1890: Deering-Milliken & Co. incorporates.

1944: The company is designated to build a mill that would process a new manmade fiber for military tire cord.

1947: Roger Milliken takes charge of the company.

1956: The company becomes entangled in one of the ugliest and most drawn-out affairs in the history of labor relations.

1958: Deering-Milliken's 600-acre research facility in Spartanburg opens.

1965: European expansion begins.

1978: Deering is removed from the company name.

1980: The labor relations case of 1956 is settled.

1987: A subsidiary is established in Japan.

1989: The U.S. Department of Commerce awards Milliken the Malcolm Baldrige National Quality Award.

2004: Increased competition forces the closure of two South Carolina plants.

2005: Roger Milliken turns 90 and remains company chairman.

NEW PRODUCTS, POLICIES

Under Roger Milliken's leadership, Deering-Milliken continued in its role as industry groundbreaker into the 1960s. In the early 1960s Milliken began to question the conventional thinking of most textile executives regarding inventories. Traditionally, manufacturing and marketing were treated as separate functions, often resulting in excessive inventories. Milliken commissioned a study that indicated an inverse relationship between inventory size and profits. This led Milliken to keep tighter control of inventory by adjusting the rate of production. Deering-Milliken began its European operations in 1965, opening mills and offices in England, France, and Belgium.

In 1967 Deering-Milliken eliminated 600 mid-level management jobs in a consolidation to cut overhead. Deering-Milliken was among the trailblazing companies in the 1960s, however, in producing double-knit fabrics. Toward the end of the decade, the company unveiled one of its most important inventions, Visa. Visa is a fabric finish that resists stains and is used on a wide variety of products, including clothing and tablecloths. The original irradiation process for making Visa has been replaced by a chemical process. The development

of Visa strongly reaffirmed the company's position as a leader in developing patented fabric finishes. It also produced huge profits.

For decades, Roger Milliken has been an active force in conservative politics. Milliken demonstrated the depth of his right-wing convictions in 1967, when, after viewing a television documentary on UNICEF aid to communist-governed countries sponsored by Xerox, he quickly had all Xerox copiers removed from company offices. Company executives routinely received subscriptions to conservative publications. By the late 1980s, however, the company began using Xerox machinery again, and Xerox was its major copier supplier in 1991.

In 1978 the name Deering was finally removed from the company, more than a century after company founder Deering's departure. The year also marked the 25th anniversary of a Milliken & Co. tradition known as the breakfast show. Each year, retail store buyers and other industry professionals were invited to a Broadway-style musical revue featuring big-name performers and staged at a major New York venue. The breakfast show had a run of 13 performances, nine actually at breakfast and four at cocktail hour, and was seen by more than 30,000 people annually. The show was essentially a glamorous advertisement for Milliken products and featured Phyllis Diller, Cyd Charisse, Ray Bolger, and Bert Parks, among others.

RISING TIDE OF IMPORTS: 1980

The first half of the 1980s was difficult for the textile industry. One reason was the doubling of textile imports between 1980 and 1985. During that period, Milliken & Co. closed seven plants, reducing its total to 55 in North Carolina, South Carolina, and Georgia, and a quarter of its workforce was laid off. These circumstances led Roger Milliken to depart from his general policy of avoiding the press. He began speaking out in favor of protectionist policies, recommending limiting the growth rate of imports to the growth rate of the U.S. market. By 1991 58 percent of the fabric and apparel sold at retail in the United States was imported. Milliken & Co. also was hurt during this period by Milliken's refusal to adjust to the trend among U.S. consumers toward wearing natural fibers. He believed that because synthetics required less labor, a shift in emphasis was not practical.

In 1984 Roger Milliken survived a helicopter crash. Some who knew him believe that this event brought about a new willingness to deal with the public. He began assuming leadership roles in a number of industry organizations, most notably the Crafted with Pride in U.S.A. Council. Milliken's increased public involvement resulted in his being named Textile Leader of the Year in 1986, the first such honor awarded by *Textile World,* an industry magazine.

Despite Milliken's objections to textile imports, between 1985 and 1989 Milliken & Co. purchased 1,500 modern Japanese looms, and in 1989 the company bought 500 more from Belgium, because U.S. weaving machinery manufacturers no longer existed. These looms were able to detect defects, stop themselves, and then start up again on their own. In 1987, the company fought fire with fire, establishing a subsidiary in Japan. This operation imported commercial (mostly modular) carpet until 1991, when Milliken brought its first Japanese manufacturing plant on line.

During the late 1980s Milliken & Co. began to show signs of moving toward diversification. The company opened a second chemical plant in 1988 in Blacksburg, South Carolina. The plant made Millad, a clarifying agent for polypropylene products. The company's first chemical plant had been opened in Inman, South Carolina, in 1963. It made chemical products used in the textile manufacturing process, as well as chemical additives for paint, crayons, markers, plastics, and other products.

TQM LEADS TO AWARDS AND ACCOLADES

Roger Milliken named 17-year company veteran Dr. Thomas Malone president in 1984. In response to the competitive challenges of the 1980s, the duo borrowed ideas from several management philosophies to create what soon came to be known as the "Milliken Quality Process." In the early 1980s, for example, they embraced the principles of Total Quality Management (TQM) espoused by Philip Crosby. Known as Pursuit of Excellence (POE), this program flattened the organization via the creation of relatively autonomous teams of "associates," not employees. By 1984, the company had increased its quality and simultaneously reduced its costs.

Having implemented this internal strategy, the company turned outward in a quest for customer satisfaction in the late 1980s. For this stage of Milliken's transformation, the company looked to management guru Tom Peters. In fact, the textile manufacturer implemented his theories so successfully that Peters dedicated his book, *Thriving on Chaos,* to Roger Milliken. The company "cherry-picked" dozens of other modern management concepts to create its own strategy. In 1989, the U.S. Department of Commerce recognized Milliken's achievements by awarding it the Malcolm Baldrige National Quality Award. (Ironically, that year's other winner was Xerox, the company that Roger Mil-

liken had shunned more than 20 years earlier because of his rigid political beliefs.)

Instead of resting on its laurels, Milliken established a new set of quality, customer satisfaction, and innovation goals. Its ongoing quest has earned it an astounding array of awards, including the European Quality award (1993), *Textile World's* "Best of the Best" (1993), and the Warren Featherbone Foundation Award for American Manufacturing Excellence (1996), to name just a few. The company even succeeded in turning a crisis, a devastating fire that destroyed the La Grange, Georgia, plant in January 1995, into yet another citation. Milliken not only rebuilt the mill in less than six months, it also managed to keep most of the factory's 700 associates employed during the interim by transferring them to the company's British plant. These heroic efforts earned the 1995 Model Mill award.

There is but one visible chink in the Milliken & Co. armor. A struggle over future control of the company developed during the late 1980s as Roger Milliken entered his mid-70s. The family of Joan Milliken Stroud, Roger Milliken's late sister, owned about 15 percent of the company and indicated that it resented its lack of input on company decisions. The Stroud family had sued Milliken and his board of directors at least three times by 1989 in attempts to win shareholders' information and input. When the Strouds threatened to sell their stock, Milliken countered by making new rules that require approval by 75 percent of the voting power before the company can be sold and handpicking a new, self-perpetuating board dominated by outside directors and managers. Roger Milliken, Gerrish Milliken, Jr., and Minot Milliken controlled about 50 percent of the company common stock. It has been suggested that they stymied the Stroud family's attempts to sell their stock because it was their wish to keep the company private. Nevertheless, in December 1990 the *Daily News Record* reported that the Stroud family had sold "a small amount of Milliken stock" to Erwin Maddrey and Bettis Rainsford, executives of Delta Woodside Industries Inc. The two investors hinted at the possibility of purchasing the remainder of the Stroud faction's stock.

In the late 1990s, Milliken became embroiled in corporate espionage lawsuits brought on by competitors NRB Industries and Johnston Industries. NRB filed suit in 1997, claiming the company had hired spies to gain corporate information. The suit was settled in January 1998 and the terms were not disclosed. Johnston Industries filed a similar suit in 1998 and Milliken continued to deny any wrongdoing. The suit was settled out of court.

MILLIKEN IN THE NEW MILLENNIUM

Roger Milliken remained firmly at the helm of the company in the early years of the new millennium as chairman. His passion for politics remained evident as he continued to speak out against U.S. trade policies. He claimed these policies were causing Americans to lose their jobs, increasing the trade deficit, and threatening the United States' position as the most technologically advanced country across the globe. As foreign competition—especially from Asia—continued to increase, the company was forced to shutter two plants in South Carolina in 2004. Milliken's public relations director echoed the chairman's sentiments in an October 2003 *Knight-Ridder/Tribune Business News* article. "The [American] industry is being decimated by imports from the Far East, primarily from China." The article went on to report that Asian markets exported more textiles to the United States than Mexico, leaving the concept that the North American Free Trade Agreement would secure the jobs of those working on the continent open for debate.

In 2004 and 2006, Milliken was named to *Fortune*'s "100 Best Companies to Work For" list, coming in 16th and 38th, respectively. During this time period, the company continued to launch new products and develop new chemicals including StainSmart, a product that made fabrics stain repellent. StainSmart was used in school uniforms, tuxedos, and clothing used in the medical industry. Milliken remained dedicated to preserving the environment as well and was named an "Environmental Champion" by the U.S. Environmental Protection Agency and McGraw-Hill Publishing.

Among textile industry insiders, Milliken & Co. has for generations been associated with quality products and services—quality usually achieved through foresight and innovation. Roger Milliken was, arguably, among the most important individuals in the textile industry during the 20th century and continued to be recognized for his accomplishments into the 21st century. The success of Milliken & Co. in the future depended in large part on the company's ability to continue with its steady technological and organizational advancement with or without a Milliken at the helm. In October 2005, Chairman Milliken turned 90 years old and the company would not release details regarding his successor. According to an October 2005 *Knight-Ridder/Tribune Business News* article, Milliken had once claimed, "I'm going to keep on doing what I'm doing. I'm going to die in the saddle, fighting for American manufacturing supremacy."

Robert R. Jacobson
Updated, April Dougal Gasbarre; Christina M. Stansell

PRINCIPAL COMPETITORS

Burlington Industries Inc.; E. I. du Pont de Nemours and Company; Shaw Industries Inc.

FURTHER READING

Andrews, Mildred Gwin, *The Men and the Mills*, Macon, Ga.: Mercer University Press, 1987.

Caulkin, Simon, "The Road to Peerless Wigan," *Management Today*, March 1994, pp. 28–32.

Christiansen, Laurence A., Jr., "There's Been Nothing Like It!," *Textile World*, September 1995, p. 13.

Cline, Damon, "U.S. Risks Allowing Manufacturing Sector to Erode, Milliken CEO Warns," *Knight-Ridder/Tribune Business News*, September 25, 2002.

Clune, Ray, "Delta Execs Not Now Buying Milliken Stock," *Daily News Record*, December 27, 1990, p. 9.

Davis, Kathleen, "Milliken & Co. Denies Spy Charge," *Spartanburg Herald-Journal*, December 1, 1998, p. B3.

DuPlessis, Jim, "90-Year-Old Magnate Holds Company's Reins," *Knight-Ridder/Tribune Business News*, October 24, 2005.

———, "Textile Firm Milliken & Co. to Lay Off 260 Employees in South Carolina," *Knight-Ridder/Tribune Business News*, October 14, 2003.

Furukawa, Tsukasa, "Milliken Unit to Build Carpet Plant in Japan," *Daily News Record*, October 5, 1990, p. 3.

"How Roger Milliken Runs Textiles' Premier Performer," *Business Week*, January 19, 1981.

Isaacs, McAllister III, "Define Excellence: Milliken & Co.," *Textile World*, June 1996, pp. 64–66.

Kalogeridis, Carla, "Milliken in Motion: A Pursuit of Excellence," *Textile World*, December 1990, pp. 42–46.

Konrad, Walecia, "How Milliken's Tightly Knit Empire Could Unravel," *Business Week*, May 28, 1990, p. 27.

Lappen, Alyssa A., "Can Roger Milliken Emulate William Randolph Hearst?," *Forbes*, May 29, 1989.

Lloyd, Brenda, "Thoroughly Modern Milliken; One of the Grand Old Names in American Textile Is at the Forefront of a High-Tech Revolution," *DNR*, May 22, 2006.

"Mind Your Ts and Qs," *Management Today*, March 1994, p. 3.

Orr, Susan, "Spartanburg, S.C., Textile Company Named One of the Country's Best Employers," *Knight-Ridder/Tribune Business News*, January 9, 2006.

Ostroff, Jim, "AAMA Convention Urged to Steer New Course of Business or Sink," *Daily News Record*, April 30, 1996, pp. 6–7.

Petersen, Melody, "Lawsuits by Rivals Accuse Textile Maker of Corporate Espionage," *New York Times*, October 13, 1998.

"Textile World's 1994 Leader of the Year: Dr. Thomas J. Malone," *Textile World*, October 1994, pp. 34–41.

Whaley, Peggy, "Milliken & Company: Covering All Bases," *Textile World*, April 2004.

Montblanc International GmbH

Hellgrundweg 100 22525
Hamburg,
Germany
Telephone: (49) 40 84 001 0
Fax: (49) 40 84 001 320
Web site: http://www.montblanc.com

Division of Compagnie Financiere Richemont
Incorporated: 1908 as Simplo Filler Pen Company
Sales: $226 million (2005)
NAIC: 339941 Pen and Mechanical Pencil Manufactur-
ing; 316993 Leather Goods, Small Personal,
Manufacturing; 334518 Watches and Parts (Except
Crystals) Manufacturing; 339910 Jewelry and
Silverware Manufacturing

■ ■ ■

Montblanc International GmbH manufactures one of
the world's leading brands of luxury writing instruments.
Its Montblanc pens have been sold around the world
since the early 20th century. Montblanc specializes in
very expensive pens and controls an estimated half the
global market for pens that cost more than $100. The
company also makes other luxury goods such as men's
and women's jewelry, desk accessories, leather goods,
watches, and perfume. Montblanc products are widely
distributed through retail establishments around the
world, and also sold through Montblanc boutiques. Sales
from its boutiques account for about a third of the
company's total volume. Montblanc has been owned
since 1977 by the British tobacco and luxury goods

company Alfred Dunhill Ltd. In 1998, its parent became
part of the wide stable of luxury brands owned by the
Swiss firm Compagnie Financiere Richemont.

AN AUSPICIOUS LAUNCH

Montblanc International began as the joint business
venture of three German entrepreneurs. Claus-Johannes
Voss ran a stationery shop in Hamburg, Alfred Nehemias
was a Hamburg banker, and the third partner, August
Eberstein, was an engineer operating out of Berlin. These
three began making pens in 1906, and in 1908
incorporated a company in Hamburg, called the Simplo
Filler Pen Company. Simplo Filler took a name imply-
ing that its pens could be filled simply. In the era of
fountain pens, advances in pen filling methods
represented a technological cutting edge. A hundred
years later, it is difficult for us to grasp what a huge
advance the modern fountain pen was over its
predecessor. For centuries, writing by hand was
accomplished with a pen cut from a reed or a quill
(feather), which had to be constantly dipped in ink. In
the late 18th century, pens were manufactured from
wood, with a metal nib. Although these were an
improvement over the quill, as the metal nib held ink
for a longer time, writers were still hampered by needing
to have an open bottle of ink at hand. In the late 19th
century, various inventors came up with systems that
combined the ink and pen in one instrument. An
American insurance agent, Lewis Edson Waterman, is
credited with the first modern ink-feeding system, which
he patented in 1884. By 1906, when Montblanc began,

pen manufacturers used many different filling mechanisms, all vying with each other for ease of use. Hamburg's Simplo Filler was one of a new breed of pen manufacturers who grew quickly because of the great utility of their products. German competitors included Pelikan and Fendograph, while Parker, Sheaffer, Waterman, and Wahl Eversharp dominated the U.S. market. France, Italy and England also had thriving fountain pen industries at this time.

Simplo Filler's first pens were called "Simplizissimus," and in 1909 the brand name became "Rouge et Noir" (Red and Black). Rouge et Noir were black pens with a red six-pointed star on the cap. By 1910, the company had offices in Paris, Barcelona, and London, and the business depended heavily on export. That was also the year the company adopted the brand name "Montblanc." The company did business under this name, although it did not officially change its name to Montblanc until some years later. Mont Blanc is a famed snow-covered peak in the Alps, the highest point in Europe, and the name was said to represent the height of quality promised by Simplo's pens. In 1913, the company began making its pens with a white, six-pointed star logo on the cap. This adaptation from the Rouge et Noir model was meant to graphically depict the top of Mont Blanc. In 1919, the company opened its first Montblanc Boutique to sell its pens in Hamburg.

After World War I ended, the company took the name Simplo Füllfeder GmbH. It made a range of pens, not all luxury, yet its advertising continued to feature the peak of Mont Blanc, with its implied promise of lofty quality. The company introduced its most enduring model in 1924. This was the Montblanc Meisterstück (Masterpiece), a top-of-the-line pen with a large engraved nib and other fine details. The Meisterstück was a status pen, though the company also made more everyday models. By the mid-1920s, Simplo Füllfeder was selling its pens in more than 60 countries, and supporting its sales with international advertising.

RECOVERING AFTER WORLD WAR II

The worldwide recession set off by the stock market crash in the United States in 1929 hit Simplo Füllfeder hard. In 1932, the company began selling a line of economy pens, which revived its fortunes somewhat. That year the firm changed its name, becoming Montblanc-Simplo GmbH. Along with its economy pens, Montblanc also continued to produce fine writing instruments in the 1930s, including Meisterstück pens with a new advanced piston filling system. Montblanc made a significant acquisition in 1935, buying a leatherware company. For the first time, Montblanc branched out from producing writing instruments and began making leather desk accessories.

During World War II, the German company was severely damaged. Its manufacturing facilities were bombed, and many records were lost. Montblanc was forced to rebuild. By the mid-1940s, Montblanc was back in production, with a new factory in Denmark as well as in Germany. The postwar years were difficult for fountain pen manufacturers in general, as ball point pens became popular worldwide. Ball points had been in production before World War II, but first became widely used during the war. After the war, dozens of ball point companies sprang up, and the price of pens dropped dramatically. Montblanc's more expensive pens were in a different world altogether from cheap plastic ball points, so competition from makers such as Bic was not direct. However, the writing instruments market was definitely different in the 1950s and 1960s than it had been in the heyday of the fountain pen in the 1920s.

Despite changed conditions, Montblanc maintained its brand profile, and came out with some of its best-selling pens in the postwar years. It debuted the "140" series of Meisterstück pens in 1948, a line which proved an enduring favorite. Other pens in the 1950s also did well in the export market. While continuing to make pens for the luxury market, Montblanc produced a wide range of pens in the 1960s and 1970s, with some meant to be introductory or "junior" models to its higher-priced pens.

In 1977, Montblanc was bought by the British firm Alfred Dunhill Ltd. Dunhill had been a long-time minority shareholder in Montblanc. Dunhill was known for luxury leather goods and tobacco. Under Dunhill's

KEY DATES

1906: Three founders begin manufacturing pens.
1908: The company is incorporated in Hamburg.
1910: The Montblanc brand name is introduced.
1932: The company's name is changed to Montblanc-Simplo.
1977: Montblanc is bought by Alfred Dunhill Ltd.
1992: Montblanc North America is founded; the company buys a leather goods firm.
1993: Montblanc, under Dunhill, becomes part of Vendome.
1997: Montblanc begins selling watches.
1998: Vendome is folded into Compagnie Financiere Richemont, its parent company.
2004: Montblanc's CEO becomes chief of the parent firm, Richemont.

management, Montblanc dropped its lower-priced pen lines and began to concentrate solely on the upper echelons of the market.

REVITALIZING THE LUXURY MARKET

Montblanc was a fortunate survivor of the postwar decades, when many European fountain pen makers went out of business. Its German competitor Soennecken expired in 1967, and another German maker, Kaweko, closed in 1970. Faber-Castell, another German writing instrument manufacturer, changed its focus to pencils and art supplies, closing its fountain pen division in 1975. Many French, Italian, and U.S. fountain pen manufacturers also went out of business in the 1960s and 1970s. Montblanc adopted a wise strategy in the mid-1970s when it was bought by Dunhill. Its specialization in the luxury market allowed the company to not only hang on but finally to prosper quite nicely.

In the 1980s, when computers became ubiquitous, fountain pens did not fade away but went through something of a rebirth. Montblanc hung steady in the luxury market, continuing to make its distinctive big, black Meisterstück pens and other models. Montblanc exported its pens to the United States through a distributor, Koh-I-Noor, in the 1980s, and then set up a North American distributor on the East Coast in 1992. The company marked 1986 as a year of revitalization, when fountain pen sales began to surge. Expensive pens were particularly valued by business executives. In the 1920s, a Montblanc pen had been a dignified business tool. In the 1980s and after, a Montblanc was more of a business status marker. A contract could be signed with an ordinary ball point just as well, but certain users found it more elegant and impressive to ink their deals with a pricey fountain pen.

The growth of the luxury pen segment intensified in the early 1990s. In 1990, Montblanc opened a stand-alone boutique, its first since the 1920s, in Hong Kong. Over the next decade, the company opened almost 300 more independent Montblanc boutiques. The fountain pen industry as a whole grew in double digits, so that by 1992, the niche in total was worth twice what it had been in 1986. Montblanc did extensive advertising as it mopped up the high end of the market. By 1992, Montblanc accounted for half of all sales of pens in the $100-and-up range with some pens selling for well over $100. A popular Meisterstück model retailed in the U.S. for $345 in the early 1990s, while some special edition Montblanc pens sold for $3,000 or more. Montblanc was by then part of a consortium of luxury goods companies that was formed when its parent, Dunhill, merged with Cartier in 1993 to form a new firm called Vendome. Vendome was itself owned by Compagnie Financiere Richemont. Vendome's brands included Montegrappa pens and some writing instruments made by Dunhill and Cartier. Montblanc's sales figures were not broken out, but Vendome's writing instruments division had sales of $290 million by 1994, an increase of more than 10 percent over the previous year.

Montblanc capitalized on the new popularity of luxury fountain pens with worldwide advertising and special edition pens. Montblanc raised its prices over the late 1980s into the early 1990s, so that by 1995 it was charging roughly twice what it had in 1985. Yet Montblanc's production costs had not risen at the same rate, meaning its pens were increasingly profitable. While Montblanc charged a lot for its pens, some of the limited editions rose sharply in value within a few years, so that collectors were paying even more for them. The company sometimes made special custom orders for pen collectors. A gold and diamond-studded Meisterstück, for example, sold for about $120,000, giving Montblanc the crown for world's most expensive pen.

With such success with its pens in the 1990s, Montblanc repeated a plan it had first tried in the 1930s, and branched out into leather accessories. Montblanc acquired the German leather goods company Seeger in 1992, and soon began selling pen holders, organizers, business card holders and other desk accessories, as well as fine writing paper. Montblanc also opened more boutiques. It opened six in the U.S. alone in 1996. Other stores opened across Europe and Asia.

EXPANDING THE BRAND

With the great success of its pens in the 1980s and 1990s, Montblanc began a serious campaign to expand its brand into other luxury goods beginning in the late 1990s. Montblanc had sold leather desk accessories early in its history and then again when it acquired Seeger in the early 1990s. In 1995, Montblanc began selling its own brand of luggage. The next year, the company added jewelry, and in 1997, Montblanc watches hit the market. Its jewelry line was aimed at men, and consisted of cuff links, as well as key rings and money clips. Montblanc was developing into what was termed a lifestyle brand, encompassing a range of products associated with a well-to-do manner of living. In 2001, Montblanc introduced its first perfume, a men's fragrance called Presence. The scent was made through a licensing agreement with Cosmopolitan Cosmetics/Intercosmetics Inc., a division of the Wella Group. A year after the men's scent debuted, Montblanc brought out a women's counterpart, called Presence d'une Femme. Montblanc was able to sell a wide range of goods in part because of the success of its stand-alone boutiques. Though Montblanc was best known for its pens, shoppers in its stores could be easily exposed to the other product lines. Though its pens, especially the thick, heavy Meisterstück, had long been a primarily masculine item, by the early 2000s, some 40 percent of purchasers in Montblanc's boutiques were women. They might enter the store to buy a pen as a gift for a man, but could be enticed to buy something else more feminine for themselves.

While Montblanc was venturing into new product lines, its parent company was also going through some changes. Vendome, which had been a partly-owned division of Compagnie Financiere Richemont, ceased to exist as a separate company in 1998. That year, Richemont acquired the remaining 30 percent of the company it did not already own, and Vendome ceased trading on the London and Luxembourg stock exchanges where it had previously been listed. This led to some changes in management structure, but Montblanc remained an important cog in the larger Richemont machine. Richemont's pen sales, which included Montegrappa as well as Montblanc, rose almost 20 percent over 1999, and this steep rise was attributed mostly to the expanding product line at Montblanc. In the early 2000s, Richemont piled up debt and was plagued by losses attributed to shifts in currency, especially the falling value of the dollar. In 2004, Montblanc's chief executive, Norbert Platt, moved up to become CEO of Richemont. By that time, Richemont had righted itself from its earlier slump, and sales were rising sharply.

Montblanc continued to bring out new offerings in the mid-2000s. After introducing a men's jewelry line in 1996, in 2005 the company came out with its first line of women's jewelry. By that time, the company was spending about $4 million annually on advertising. As the company drew more female customers, its advertisements changed from simply showing the product—be it pen or watch—to showing a female model. "I'm successful; I'm cultured," is the message the new ads sent, according to the president of Montblanc's North American division, quoted in *Brandweek* (October 3, 2005). In 2006, Montblanc's advertising went even farther in this direction, showing not only female models but featuring women's high fashion. The company partnered with young fashion designers and ran ads in women's magazines, showing models wearing Montblanc jewelry, a Montblanc watch, and a dress by the designer. The white star logo and the tag line "Signature Style" was all that tied these ads to Montblanc's history as a maker of writing instruments. The strategy to differentiate into a host of luxury goods under the Montblanc brand seemed to be paying off handsomely. Richemont's chief executive referred to Montblanc as one of the conglomerate's "star brands" in an interview with *WWD* (June 9, 2006). Sales had grown again by close to 20 percent over 2005, with about a third of sales coming through the roughly 300 Montblanc boutiques. As the company entered its second century, it had made a key transition, from pen manufacturer to purveyor of a range of luxury goods.

A. Woodward

PRINCIPAL COMPETITORS

A.T. Cross Company; Lamy GmbH; Sanford L.P.

FURTHER READING

Julie Bosman, "Venerable Maker of Pens Turns to Young Designers," *New York Times,* August 7, 2006, p. C6.

Canedy, Dana, "In Retailing, Biggest Gains Come from Big Spenders," *New York Times,* December 12, 1996, p. A1.

Collins, Glenn, "Montblanc Expands on Gertrude Stein to Suggest that Sometimes a Pen Is More than a Pen," *New York Times,* July 27, 1995, p. D9.

Conti, Samantha, "Richemont Sets Sales Record," *WWD,* June 9, 2006, p. 17.

Costello, Brid, "Montblanc's Femme Fragrance," *WWD,* June 21, 2002, p. 7.

Cowell, Alan, "Still Pricier Fountain Pens Gain Cachet and Profit," *New York Times,* May 10, 1995, p. D3.

Dragoni, Giorgio and Fichera, Giuseppe, eds., *Fountain Pens: History and Design,* Milan: Arnoldo Mondadori Editore S.p.A., 1997.

Elliot, Stuart, "Creative Agencies that Feel at Home in the Global Village Are Writing their Own Tickets," *New York Times,* September 30, 1994, p. D17.

Erano, Paul, *Fountain Pens Past & Present,* Paducah, KY: Collector Books, 1999.

Fallon, James, "Dunhill, Cartier Merger Okayed," *Daily News Record,* September 8, 1993, p. 14.

———, "Richemont Realigns Staff for Luxe Focus," *WWD,* November 23, 1999, p. 2.

Garbarine, Rachelle, "Remember Fountain Pens?," *New York Times,* April 23, 2000, p. NJ9.

"Happy Days Return," *WWD,* June 11, 2004, p. 1.

Langley, Alison, "'Mr. Cartier' Retiring from Swiss Parent Group," *New York Times,* May 7, 2003, p. W1.

———, "Swiss Maker of Luxury Goods Suffers from Currency Shifts," *New York Times,* June 6, 2003, p. W1.

Levine, Joshua, "Pen Wars," *Forbes,* January 6, 1992, p. 88.

O'Loughlin, Sandra, "Montblanc Pens Story for Jewelry," *Brandweek,* October 3, 2005, p. 10.

"Richemont Appoints CEO, Post 15% Increase in Sales," *WWD,* September 17, 2004, p. 17.

Rothstein, Edward, "Pens May Not Be Mightier than PC's, But Reports of their Death Are Greatly Exaggerated," *New York Times,* January 22, 1996, p. D5.

"Sales, Operating Profits Are Strong at Richemont," *WWD,* November 18, 2005, p. 9.

Underwood, Elaine, "Prestige Pens for a Paperless Era," *Brandweek,* July 1, 1996, p. 28.

"Vendome Luxury Group Becomes Part of Richemont," *WWD,* March 30, 1998, p. 2.

The Morgan Crucible Company plc

Quadrant 55-57 High Street
Windsor, Berkshire SL4 1LP
United Kingdom
Telephone: (44) (01) 753 837 000
Fax: (44) (01) 753 850 872
Web site: http://www.morgancrucible.com

Public Company
Incorporated: 1890
Employees: 9,500
Sales: £745.7 million (2005)
Stock Exchange: London
Ticker Symbol: MGCR
NAIC: 423690 Other Electronic Parts and Equipment Merchant Wholesalers; 327124 Clay Refractory Manufacturing; 327125 Nonclay Refractory Manufacturing; 442299 All Other Home Furnishings Stores

■ ■ ■

Based near London, The Morgan Crucible Company plc is a leading industrial manufacturing enterprise. Morgan is organized into four global business units (GBUs). Its Technical Ceramics GBU is engaged in the manufacture of industrial ceramics products. Thermal Ceramics concentrates on insulation and refractory products, such as high temperature insulating refractory bricks and refractory monolithics. The company's Crucibles GBU, formerly named Morgan Molten Metal Systems, manufactures crucibles, furnaces, and other products used by foundries. Finally, Morgan's Carbon

GBU makes carbon brush and related components, including graphite powder, body armor, and components used for space exploration.

ONE-HORSE START: 1856–1899

According to excerpts from *Battersea Works 1856-1956*, an early history published by Morgan Crucible, the company's origins date back to 1850s London where five brothers, the Morgans, ran a hardware and druggist sundries business. Crucibles—pot-shaped containers in which metal or glass can be melted—were among the items the brothers sold. A monumental development occurred when the brothers attended the Great Exhibition of 1851, an international exhibition in London's Hyde Park that intended to promote and expand industrial design. It was there that the Morgans saw an American crucible from New Jersey-based Joseph Dixon and Co.

Acting on their belief that the American crucible was superior to those that England imported from Germany at the time, the brothers arranged to become Joseph Dixon's exclusive British importers. Initial success prompted the Morgans to buy manufacturing rights to the American crucible in 1856. A tiny factory was purchased in Battersea, powered by a solitary horse for grinding clay and consisting of a small brick kiln, mill, house, and dilapidated out-buildings. Led by William Morgan, the brothers swiftly improved the buildings and added a new kiln.

The Morgans' fledgling enterprise managed to survive its first year, with the brothers initially drawing a collective weekly salary of £8. This amount eventually rose to about £40 by early 1857, when the company adopted the name Patent Plumbago Crucible Co. Within five years the enterprise claimed that its crucibles were used by English, Australian, French, Indian, and Russian mints, the arsenals of Brest and Toulon, and the Royal Arsenal of Woolwich.

By this time the brothers retired their trusty horse, which was replaced by two horizontal 35-horsepower engines. Similar mechanical upgrades continued through the late 1880s, helping the company to further its growth. The re-named Morgan Crucible Co. then rested on the strength of 150 workers and enjoyed a reputation for being the world's largest crucible manufacturer. The company's products received numerous awards at international exhibitions and were coveted by competitors, some of whom were sued for copyright infringement.

Morgan Crucible became a public limited company in 1890, with Chairman Octavius Vaughan Morgan and Edward Vaughan Morgan among the firm's first board of directors. Another charter member of the board, Samuel Arthur Peto, later succeeded Morgan to become the company's second chairman. The company became a pioneer in the area of profit-sharing, as sales of shares were limited to employees.

INITIAL CHALLENGES OF A NEW CENTURY: 1900–1949

At the turn of the twentieth century, Morgan ventured into the manufacture of carbon brushes. Initial experiments led to the formation of a dedicated research group, dubbed the "Z Department," in the fall of 1904. Orders eventually were received from the likes of AEG and Siemens, and cities throughout the world soon used the brushes for their railway and tram systems.

Morgan's brush products evolved so that by 1910 the company had formed the Morganite Brush Company Inc., an overseas branch office in New York that became profitable in short time. By 1912 Morgan offered several different kinds of brush products, including Carbon,

Copper Morganite, Electro-graphitic, Hard Morganite, and Morganite.

World War I created great demand for Morgan's products. For example, in September 1916 alone the firm received orders for 500,000 brushes. However, the company quickly focused on controlling costs and rebuilding its export business in order to survive in the difficult post-war economic climate. Even so, brush and crucible sales dropped to half of what they had been during the war, prompting wage and workforce reductions.

Despite these difficulties, Morgan continued to grow. Doulton and Co.'s crucible operation was acquired in 1919, and by 1925 Morgan was reaping record profits. That year the company moved ahead with construction of a new plant in Long Island, New York, for its U.S. operation. This came as no surprise, as the American automotive industry proved to be a key market during the 1920s.

During the 1930s the Great Depression forced Morgan Crucible to seek new opportunities. This led to the firm's foray into battery carbon production in 1931. Throughout the 1930s the company continued to venture into new areas, from furnaces to radio resistors.

Like many other manufacturers, Morgan Crucible benefitted from military-related production during World War II. By the end of March 1940 the company's sales totaled £2.47 million, an increase of £500,000 from the previous year. The Battersea plant in central London managed to escape destruction, although production was spread out to plants in North Staffordshire and Worcester to minimize risk.

During the war the company's U.S. operation was renamed Morganite Inc. As American males joined the war effort in large numbers, the plant faced serious labor shortages. By hiring female workers, Morganite saw its workforce swell by 1,100, but the enterprise still contended with a six-month order backlog. Additional expansion in 1944 included new operations in Canada, Australia, and South Africa.

In 1946 the company broke a 60-year tradition when it issued shares of stock to outside investors; a limited number of "A" shares were offered to the public, while a larger pool of "B" shares were reserved exclusively for employees. That year, the company created a staff college that prospective executives could attend during working hours.

After the war, Morgan faced a number of challenges, namely material and labor shortages. In his annual speech to shareholders Morgan Crucible Chairman P. Lindsay indicated that issues such as these were additional hardships for a management team that was already fatigued

KEY DATES

1856: After acquiring manufacturing rights to an American-made crucible, the five Morgan Brothers purchase a factory in Battersea, starting their own crucible enterprise in the United Kingdom.

1890: Morgan Crucible becomes a public limited company.

1946: After a 60-year practice of issuing stock only to employees, a class of shares is made available to the public.

1961: A reorganization effort results in domestic operations transferred to three wholly owned subsidiaries: Morganite Carbon Ltd., Morganite Crucible Ltd., and Morganite Electroheat Ltd.

1969: With representatives in 80 countries, Morgan consists of 25 U.K. subsidiaries and 15 overseas companies.

2003: A reorganization initiative results in the adoption of a new operational structure.

2006: Morgan celebrates its 150th anniversary and its 60th year on the London Stock Exchange.

and overloaded. However, conditions soon improved. By 1947 the company had reestablished relations with pre-war customers throughout Europe and exports had surpassed 1938 levels.

Competition from other domestic manufacturers started to increase by the end of the decade, in step with Europe's post-war recovery. The company continued to expand and diversify. A new subsidiary named Morgan Refractories Ltd. was formed in November of 1948 to produce specialized refractories. In fact, by the end of the 1940s Morgan had extended its product lineup well beyond crucibles and carbon brushes to include many specialized items.

In the July 20, 1949, issue of *The Times*, Chairman P. Lindsay noted the many applications of the company's products, explaining: "corrosive liquids are contained in carbon tanks and flow through carbon pipes; increasing interest is being taken in carbon linings for blast furnaces; carbon collectors are standard equipment on trolley-buses, cranes, and many locomotives; carbon contacts are in use for electrical control and signal devices; in freeing the harbours of Europe from the debris of sunken ships carbon electrodes have formed part of the underwater cutting equipment; carbon clutch rings,

pump seals, and Reservoil bearings will be found on most road vehicles; in domestic apparatus also, such as vacuum cleaners, fans, and clocks, Reservoil oil retaining bearings find their essential use."

GROWTH & EXPANSION: 1950–1989

As the 1950s dawned Morgan Crucible contended with a number of challenges, including inflationary pressure. Uncontrollable cost increases occurred in areas from building construction and transportation to fuel and power. However, progress continued. By 1950 the company had formed a centralized research and development department to coordinate the efforts of the parent organization and its growing subsidiary base. Construction of a new research lab was well underway by 1951, and the company had acquired a large factory in Cheshire for Morgan Refractories.

Strong production and sales led to record group trading profits in 1955, and the company moved forward with a number of new ventures late into the decade. In 1958 a new factory was erected to produce a non-metallic heater element named Crusilite. The company also became involved in production and research related to sintered alumina products. In addition, through a venture with A.E.I.-John Thomson Nuclear Energy Co. Ltd. called Nuclear Graphite Limited, Morgan produced high-quality graphite for use in nuclear power plants. The company also was involved in making other components for nuclear reactors. In 1959 Morgan drew approximately 40 percent of its sales from overseas, down from about 45 percent in 1958. This was reflected in the company's movement into markets such as Japan, Brazil, and Mexico.

A number of important changes took place during the 1960s. Morgan began the decade with a new chairman, A.L. Stock, who succeeded P. Lindsay upon his retirement. On the international front, existing operations were expanded in Canada and South Africa.

Significantly, in April of 1961 the Morgan Crucible Co. Ltd. ceased to be a traded entity. A reorganization effort saw the company's domestic operations transferred to three wholly owned, trading subsidiaries: Morganite Carbon Ltd., Morganite Crucible Ltd., and Morganite Electroheat Ltd. Other subsidiaries within the Morgan Crucible Group included Morganite Research & Development Ltd., Morganite Exports Ltd., Morganite Resistors Ltd., Morgan Refractories Ltd., Morgan-Mintex Ltd., Graphite Products Ltd., and the Ship Carbon Company of Great Britain Ltd. Beyond these enterprises were twelve international subsidiaries.

Morgan's growth continued into the mid-1960s. In

1963 Morgan-Borel S.A., a new Swiss subsidiary, was formed in partnership with Borel S.A. Steatite and Porcelain Products, an industrial ceramics firm based in the United Kingdom, was acquired in 1964. In order to provide more efficient and effective service, a new enterprise was established in 1965 to handle the technical services and sales needs of seven Morgan companies. A 26 percent stake in plastic moldings firm Bettix was purchased in 1966, and the remaining shares were acquired later in the decade.

While a company advertisement in 1969 used the tagline "Morgan—a name to remember," literally recalling the name of every Morgan enterprise was a virtually impossible task. By this time Morgan had evolved into a massive enterprise, with annual sales of £25 million, of which 46 percent came from international operations. The Morgan empire relied on the strength of representatives in 80 different countries and included 25 subsidiaries in the United Kingdom and 15 overseas companies. These various enterprises all fell under one of three main divisions: Thermic, Carbon, or Electronics.

The early 1970s ushered in difficult times in the form of a sluggish economy, both in the United Kingdom and the United States. This, in turn, had a negative impact on world trade and contributed to a drop in Morgan's profits. Another factor was the major expense involved in transferring operations from the Battersea plant to new locations.

Due to space constraints, the original 11-acre Battersea location purchased by the five Morgan brothers was no longer suitable for the growing enterprise. Preparations to relocate had begun in 1967, and a new 40-acre location in Morriston, South Wales, was selected as a replacement. By the mid-1970s Morgan had moved its carbon brush operations to Morriston, and crucible manufacturing was transitioned to a location in Worcester.

There were other positive developments during the 1970s. Copeland and Jenkins, as well as the Park Royal Porcelain Co., were acquired in 1971, and Morgan began producing small aluminum oxide boxes that integrated circuit manufacturers used to protect silicon chips—a critical component in the growing world market for electronics, namely calculators and computers.

During the early 1980s Dr. Bruce Farmer was named as Morgan Crucible's chief executive. He assumed the role of group managing director in 1983, succeeding John Gilbert upon his retirement. Farmer, who had joined Morgan in 1981, went on to lead the company for 14 years.

The 1980s were marked by a flurry of acquisitions. In 1980 the company acquired Cleveland, Ohio-based

Franklin Oil, a producer of lubricants for metalworking. Franklin was added to a Morgan division that included the industrial lubricant producer, Rocol. Another U.S. acquisition followed in 1981, when Hydrotex Industries, a manufacturer of petroleum-based products used for engine protection and plant maintenance, was purchased for $35 million. On the carbon front, Union Carbide's Greenville, South Carolina-based carbon seal operations were acquired by Morganite Inc. in 1984. Two years later Morgan obtained another Union Carbide enterprise, National Electric Carbon, for £23 million. The £20 million purchase of General Electric's Carbon Products division followed in 1988.

The 1980s also saw the company expand in the area of technical ceramics. After the Morgan companies in this area were merged and renamed Matroc midway through the decade, a series of U.S. acquisitions began, starting with New Jersey-based Duramic Products Inc. in 1985. Cleveland, Ohio-based Vernitron, along with its U.K. subsidiary, followed two years later. The acquisition of a New Bedford, Massachusetts-based company named Alberox took place in 1988.

Morgan also boosted its thermal ceramics business during the 1980s. Thermal Ceramics Industries, which had operations in Girard, Illinois, and Canon City, Colorado, was purchased for £7.2 million in 1984. In addition, Morgan acquired the Insulating Products Group in 1987 for £37 million.

A SHARPER FOCUS: 1990– PRESENT

The 1990s brought more acquisitions that expanded Morgan's business across its key operating areas. In January 1990 Manville International's thermal ceramics and electronics operations were acquired for £50.9 million. The following year GTE's Wesgo was acquired, along with Rhode Island-based Carbon Technologies and Pennsylvania-based Fulmer. Midway through the decade, Pennsylvania-based Pure Carbon was acquired in a $30 million deal.

In addition to these acquisitions, Morgan entered into a 50/50 joint venture with Japan's Nippon Steel Chemical in 1997, establishing a new company called Shinnikka Thermal Ceramics Corp. to produce ceramic fiber. Headquartered in Tokyo, the new venture's manufacturing operations were located in Sakai. Shinnikka sought to take advantage of projected ceramic fiber demand in the near and Middle East, as well as Southeast Asia.

During the mid-1990s Morgan faced falling demand for ceramics from semiconductor companies; economic woes in Japan, Germany, and France; as well as weak demand from the U.S. nuclear power and defense sectors. Against this backdrop the company cut costs and focused more on its carbon and ceramics businesses. In 1998 Morgan put its specialty materials division, which included aerospace coatings and lubricants, up for sale. The following year it sold product lines that included scales and radiation monitors for mobile equipment and forklifts. In 1999 Morgan also announced that it would trim 1,100 jobs from its workforce as part of a $33 million cost reduction initiative.

Morgan began operating in its third century in 2000. By this time the company's ceramics arm included products used by the telecommunications, medical, aerospace, and semiconductor industries, as well as alumina ceramics used in personal and automotive body armor. Growth in the ceramics sector included the acquisition of New Hampshire-based Performance Materials Inc.

Morgan reorganized in 2003, at which time a new operational structure was chosen. The company continued to shed non-core operations, including its consumer and automotive businesses, and consolidated nine global business units into six. In addition to streamlining its organizational chart, the company made efforts to implement a new performance-based culture and put more of an effort on commercialization. Research and development programs were simplified and placed back in the hands of individual business units.

Morgan sold its Magnetics unit for £300 million in late 2005. That same year, regional headquarters for Morgan Thermal Ceramics Shanghai Ltd. were established in Pudong, China. At this time Morgan claimed 55 percent of the global market for refractory fiber, as well as 40 percent of the world firebrick market.

The year 2006 was marked by two special milestones in Morgan Crucible's history. Led by Chairman Lars Kylberg and CEO Warren Knowlton, the company celebrated its 150th anniversary. In addition, the enterprise also was recognized for its 60th year of trading on the London Stock Exchange.

When the Morgan brothers formed their fledgling crucible business at Battersea with one horse in 1856, it would have been virtually impossible for them to envision the massive industrial giant it would become. Moving forward, the company's prospects for celebrating a 200th birthday seemed attainable.

Paul R. Greenland

PRINCIPAL SUBSIDIARIES

Carl Nolte Söhne GmbH and Co. K.G. (Germany); Dalian Morgan Refractories Limited (China; 70%);

Elettrolitica Del Basso Nera SpA (Italy); Grupo Industrial Morgan S.A. de C.V. (Mexico); Morgan Advanced Ceramics Inc. (United States); Morgan Advanced Ceramics Ltd.; Morgan Advanced Materials and Technology Inc. (United States); Morgan Korea Ltd. (South Korea; 93.2%); Morgan Rekofa GmbH (Germany); Morganite do Brasil Industrial Ltda.; Morganite Electrical Carbon Ltd.; Morganite Krug SA Industrial and Comercio Ltda (Brazil); Morganite Luxembourg S.A.; Morganite South Africa Pty. Ltd.; Murugappa Morgan Thermal Ceramics Ltd. (India; 51%); National Electrical Carbon B.V. (Netherlands); National Electrical Carbon Products Inc. (United States); Shanghai Morgan Matroc Technical Ceramics Company Ltd. (China; 90%); Shinnika Thermal Ceramics Corporation (Japan; 50%); Thermal Ceramics Deutschland GmbH & Co. K.G. (Germany); Thermal Ceramics de France S.A.; Thermal Ceramics Italiana S.r.l. (Italy); Thermal Ceramics South Africa Pty. Ltd.; Morgan Electro Ceramics Ltd.; Morganite Crucible Ltd.; Thermal Ceramics (U.K.) Ltd.; Thermal Ceramics Inc. (United States); W. Haldenwanger Technische Keramik GmbH and Co. K.G (Germany).

PRINCIPAL DIVISIONS

Technical Ceramics; Thermal Ceramics; Crucibles; Carbon.

PRINCIPAL COMPETITORS

Dixon Ticonderoga Company; Le Carbone Lorraine Company; Tokai Carbon Company Ltd.

FURTHER READING

"1,100 Jobs to Go at Morgan Crucible," *ECN—European Chemical News*, March 29, 1999.

"Bicron Buys Product Lines from U.K. Firm," *Crain's Cleveland Business*, December 20, 1999.

"British Ceramics Maker Morgan Crucible to Sell Specialty Materials Division," *Knight Ridder/Tribune Business News*, September 16, 1998.

"Company Meeting, Morgan Crucible Company, Continued Expansion, Increase of Capital," *Times*, August 7, 1946.

"Company Meeting, Morgan Crucible Company, War Economy and Future Trade," *Times*, July 21, 1945.

"Company Meeting, The Morgan Crucible Co., Ltd., Internal Financing of Development Projects, Four-Year £1,000,000 Plan, Ambitious Research Organization, Mr. P. Lindsay on Factors Affecting Trade," *Times*, September 5, 1950.

"Company Meeting, The Morgan Crucible Co., Ltd., Marked Improvement in Output, Unique Range of Products, Mr. P. Lindsay on Industrial Prospects," *Times*, September 3, 1951.

"Dr. Bruce Farmer," *Materials World*, June 1999.

"Interim 2004 Morgan Crucible Company plc Earnings Presentation—Final," *Fair Disclosure Wire*, August 4, 2004.

"Morgan Crucible Buy Stake in Bettix," *Times*, April 2, 1966.

"Morgan Crucible Buys US Group for £2.6m," *Times*, January 9, 1980.

"Morgan Crucible Expands in US," *Times*, July 23, 1981.

"Morgan Crucible Form Swiss Company," *Times*, December 16, 1963.

"Morgan Crucible Group Form New Company," *Times*, March 29, 1965.

"Morgan Crucible in $10m Deal," *Times*, May 1, 1984.

"Morgan Crucible to Set Up China Headquarters in Pudong," *Asia Africa Intelligence Wire*, October 31, 2005.

"Morgan Crucible Limited, Mr. P Lindsay on Expansion of Activities," *Times*, August 12, 1947.

"Morgan Crucible to Buy Rest of Bettix," *Times*, September 4, 1968.

"NSC, Morgan Tie Up in Ceramic Fiber," *Comline Chemicals & Materials*, April 7, 1997.

"Processing and Technologies, Body Armor from Morgan," *High Tech Ceramics News*, November 2000.

"The Morgan Crucible Company, Plans for Further Development, National Obstacles to Progress, Volume of Sales Maintained, Mr. P Lindsay on the Factors Affecting Profits," *Times*, July 20, 1949.

"The Morgan Crucible Company Limited, Export Business Continues to Prosper, Contribution to Nuclear Power Development, Trade Enters Period of Readjustment," *Times*, July 1, 1958.

"The Morgan Crucible Company Limited, Group Reorganisation Scheme, Mr. A.L. Stock on Proposed New Structure," *Times*, July 29, 1960.

"The Morgan Crucible Company Limited, High Level of Production and Sales, Record Group Trading Profit, Mr. P. Lindsay Reviews the Year," *Times*, June 28, 1955.

"The Morgan Crucible Company Limited, Opportunities for Expansion Actively Pursued, Strengthening of Oversea Organization, Mr. P. Lindsay's Tribute to Staff," *Times*, July 7, 1959.

"The Morgan Crucible Company Limited, Results Reflect Sales Expansion, Speedy Recovery of Morganite Resistors, Decentralization Policy Continues, Mr. A.L. Stock on Trading and Outlook," *Times*, July 5, 1960.

Wilson, Andrew. "Two-year View on Morgan Crucible as Order Book Begins to Fill," *Times*, November 4, 1972.

Morinda Holdings, Inc.

333 West River Park Drive
Provo, Utah 84604-5787
U.S.A.
Telephone: (801) 234-1000
Toll Free: (800) 445-2969
Fax: (801) 234-1001
Web site: http://www.tahitiannoni.com

Private Company
Incorporated: 1995
Employees: 1,164
Sales: $500 million (2005 est.)
NAIC: 311421 Fruit and Vegetable Canning

∎∎∎

Morinda Holdings, Inc., is a Provo, Utah–based holding company doing business through subsidiary Tahitian Noni International, Inc., which produces and markets noni juice in distinctive, dark-colored bottles. A one-liter bottle is priced around $40. Other products using noni include high-protein drinks, tea, jam, soft chews, raspberry chocolate cremes, skin care creams, appetite suppressants, a women's multivitamin, herbal extract combinations, and skin, body, and hair care items.

The company also offers health supplements for horses and dogs, as well as apparel, drinkware, and gift items promoting noni juice and the Tahitian Noni International brand. In addition, Morinda operates three restaurants under the Tahitian Noni Café banner in the United States, three units in Japan, and single opera-

tions in São Paulo, Brazil, and Munich, Germany. Noni is the hard, knobby, fist-size green fruit of the tropical Indian Mulberry plant, formally known as *morinda citrifolia,* hence the Morinda company name. For thousands of years natives of the South Pacific have used the tree and its fruit for medicinal purposes. Since its founding in 1996, Tahitian Noni International has popularized noni juice around the world, touting the drink's ability to boost a person's immune system, supply antioxidants, increase energy, and improve physical performance levels.

The company is careful about the health claims its makes, however, having been accused by the attorneys general of several states of violating consumer protections laws, a matter that resulted in a fine and a voluntary compliance agreement. However, celebrities—the likes of Arnold Schwarzenegger, John Travolta, Danny Glover, and football player Terrell Owens—have no such hesitations, and have opined freely about the wonders of noni juice. The vast majority of scientists, on the other hand, have remained skeptical. Morinda does not sell its wares through grocery stores, relying instead on independent distributors and a multilevel marketing plan in the vein of Amway, in which distributors recruit new distributors and share in their commissions. As they move up the sales levels of the organization, their titles change from Coral to Jade to Pearl, and so on, with the highest designation called the Black Pearl. It is a method that has pushed Morinda's annual revenues to the $500 million level in less than a decade. The company maintains manufacturing operations in the United States, Tahiti, Japan, and China, and sales offices in more than 30 countries.

COMPANY PERSPECTIVES

We are dedicated to improving the lives of our customers by producing the most innovative, highest-quality noni-based products possible.

FOUNDER'S TRIP TO TAHITI IN 1993

Food scientist John Wadsworth is credited as the founder of Morinda. He started out at Brigham Young University as a predentistry student, but his enjoyment of a food science course changed his mind and instead he earned a degree in food science and economics. He went to work for nutritional products companies, and according to the *Salt Lake Tribune* helped to develop products for Utah-based network marketing companies. By 1993 he and a partner, Stephen Story, were running an independent health-food research and development operation, working out of his garage. According to one account, reported by *Forbes* in 2004, Wadsworth "heard from a neighbor just back from Tahiti about a strange fruit that supposedly performed medical miracles." He located some of the noni juice his neighbor talked about, tried it on a friend with diabetes to no effect, but then gave it for a month to some elderly people suffering from arthritis and was pleased with the results. Believing he had found something that could support a business, Wadsworth searched out a supply of noni fruit, traveling to the island of Nuka Hiva, some 1,000 miles north of Tahiti. Here, according to *Forbes,* "He and two translators camped in a one-room hut for three days. He finally stumbled upon an entire valley of the stuff on the last day." He told the magazine, "It was a vision that changed my life."

Utah Business offers a different, somewhat less romantic, version of Morinda's heritage. Wadsworth told the publication, four years before his *Forbes* interview, "I heard there was this fruit in Tahiti called noni that helped relieve the symptoms of diabetes. I was interested in it, and was able to set up a study with a [Type I] diabetic." When the subject failed to respond Wadsworth dismissed noni as a viable health supplement: "The juice tasted horrible, terrible, and I thought it was a joke, so I just put it aside." A short time later, however, he decided to play a joke on a colleague with a head cold, giving him the foul-tasting juice to relieve his symptoms. To Wadsworth's surprise, his colleague reported that the elixir had relieved his arthritis, renewing Wadsworth's interest in noni juice. According to this

account, he recruited Story and together they studied the juice, which they learned helped to alleviate arthritis, Type II diabetes, autoimmune deficiencies, and other conditions. Morinda's company information maintains that Wadsworth learned about noni from the work of Dr. Ralph Heinicke, a biochemist once employed by Dole in the mid-1950s to research pineapple enzymes. In the process he discovered the beneficial properties of noni, which he claimed activated an alkaloid he called xeronine, and in turn xeronine allowed for an increased flow of amino acids by opening cell membranes. Because the presence of xeronine was so minute, Heinicke said it was almost undetectable. This explanation had to be taken on faith, something that reputable scientists were not willing to extend to Heinicke. One told *Forbes,* "Heinicke is in his own universe."

FORMING THE COMPANY IN 1995

According to *Utah Business,* "After three years of testing, production development and formulating a flavor system to enhance the otherwise daunting taste, Tahitian Noni Juice was ready for distribution." It was also reported that Heinicke helped in the flavor formulation. At any rate, the juice remained barely tolerable to drink, but with health claims in hand, Wadsworth and Story tried to interest health-food-marketing companies but found no takers. "Everybody was laughing at it, saying it would never happen," Wadsworth told *Utah Business.* Finally their persistence paid off when they were able to convince brothers Kerry and Kim Asay, who together ran a Utah supplements business called Nature's Sunshine Products, Inc., to start a company to distribute noni juice. As they had done with Nature's Sunshine, the Asay brothers looked to implement a multilevel marketing plan to sell the product. In late 1995, Kerry and Kim Asay, Wadsworth, Story, and Kelly Olsen, another network marketing veteran recruited by Wadsworth, formed Morinda and subsidiary Tahitian Noni International.

A Los Angeles bottling plant was engaged to produce noni juice in 1996 and the new company began advertising the product and its perceived benefits. In the first month the company sold $40,000 worth of the juice and by the end of the year sold nearly $6.6 million. The pace continued in 1997 when U.S. sales totaled $10 million. The international market also established itself, contributing another $23 million in revenues.

However, Morinda in its advertising was making medical claims that it could not back up scientifically, leading the attorneys general in Arizona, California, New Jersey, and Texas to file suit against the company, which they claimed was engaged in false advertising and marketing the juice as a drug, rather than a food, without U.S. Food and Drug Administration approval. Morinda

KEY DATES

1993: John Wadsworth begins researching noni
fruit.
1995: Morinda Holdings is founded.
1997: The company begins selling noni juice.
2001: A new headquarters opens in Provo.
2003: The first Tahitian Noni Café opens.
2006: Record-setting sales and massive restructuring.

settled the matter in August 1998 without admitting any wrongdoing by agreeing to pay $100,000 and refrain from further advertising that alleged healing powers for noni juice. While Morinda became especially circumspect about the claims it made about noni juice, the same could not be said about the network of distributors who pitched the product privately or through their own web sites where noni was portrayed as a cure-all. Many doctors, in fact, believed that noni juice possessed actual medicinal value. For example, Dr. Steven Masley, who conducted research on nutrition and aging in Clearwater, Florida, told the *St. Petersburg Times* that he thought noni juice might be as beneficial as orange juice or ginseng, and knew patients who used the supplement, but, he added, "Some got better, some got drastically better, some got worse. That's part of the problem—you don't know what to use it for."

While there may have been concerns about the benefits of noni juice within the medical community, Morinda had no doubt that it had a product with global potential and as the 1990s came to a close the product was introduced in Mexico, Japan, and Hong Kong. According to press reports, Morinda recorded revenues of $289 in fiscal 1999.

With business booming, Morinda secured a steady supply of noni fruit in 2000 by striking a deal with the government of French Polynesia, best known for the island of Tahiti, to be the company's exclusive source for the fruit. In addition, Morinda agreed to build a state-of-the-art processing plant, which would open in 2005, as well as a museum. Sales were so strong, growing to $360 million in 2000, that a year later Morinda opened a new 150,000-square-foot headquarters in Provo. The company also was ranked No. 26 by *Inc.* magazine's 2001 list of the 500 fastest growing private companies in the United States.

Not content merely to sell juice, Morinda began branching out to offer new products, many of which made use of the entire noni plant. Early product launches included a protein drink mix and skin care products,

followed in 2003 by the introduction of Tahiti Trim Plan 40, a weight-management program aimed at women over 40, as well as a new line of single-serve, ready-to-drink noni beverages in a variety of flavors. In 2004 Morinda came out with a myriad of products, including a fiber supplement, a seed oil for dry and irritated skin, a noni-based body cleansing tea, a multivitamin, and different concentrated noni fruit extracts blended to promote healthy hearts, mental clarity, calmness and relaxation, and endurance. Also in 2004, Morinda introduced Equine Essentials, a noni-based liquid-based nutritional supplement for horses.

OPENING OF THE FIRST NONI CAFÉ IN 2003

In addition to product development, Morinda looked to expand the Tahitian Noni brand to restaurants. In October 2002, Kelly Olsen first conceived the idea of opening a café on the ground floor of the company's new headquarters in Tokyo. A concept was developed and in March 2003 the first Tahitian Noni Café opened in Tokyo. A second site opened in Fukuoka, Japan, in April 2005, followed later in the year by openings in Provo; São Paulo, Brazil; Nagoya, Japan; Atlanta, Georgia; and Dallas, Texas. In June 2006, a Munich, Germany, café opened.

Morinda also was becoming involved in areas unconnected to the noni plant. In March 2003 it acquired the international marketing rights to Stephen's Gourmet brand of hot cocoas, cider, and wassail. In that same month Morinda added Pure Fruit Technologies, L.L.C., a Las Vegas company that developed and marketed exotic fruit beverages offering health benefits. They included drinks made from the fruit of the mangosteen tree, the goji berry, the gac fruit, and seabuckthorn berries, all hailing from China and surrounding countries. Even further afield, Morinda produced a family film, *The Legend of Johnny Lingo,* released in 2003. Essentially a 90-minute product placement vehicle, it was a remake of a 1969 movie that tells the story of a boy washed up on a South Pacific island, where he becomes familiar with the native culture, falls in love—and learns how to make noni juice. While the film managed to achieve a theatrical release, it was panned by the few critics that reviewed it and did little business outside of the Christian and civic groups drummed up by the producers.

After ten years in business, Morinda topped $500 million in revenues in 2005, and worldwide the company's products realized $3 billion in volume. The company also enjoyed record-setting sales in the early months of 2006. Scores of new noni-based products, including a canine supplement and a new line of gourmet foods—teas, jams, and confections—using noni fruit as a base, were introduced in 2006. In addition, the company initiated a restructuring in 2006 to transfer support of the international operations from Provo to the field offices and local markets. As a result, about 130 people were laid off at the Utah headquarters.

Ed Dinger

PRINCIPAL SUBSIDIARIES

Tahitian Noni Café, Inc.; Pure Fruit Technologies, L.L.C.; Tahitian Noni International, Inc.; Stephen's International, L.L.C.

PRINCIPAL COMPETITORS

Ocean Spray Cranberries, Inc.; POM Wonderful L.L.C.; Welch Foods Inc.

FURTHER READING

Beebe, Paul, "Tahitian Noni Lays Off 130 in Provo," *Salt Lake Tribune,* May 27, 2006.

Beers, Heather, "Show Me the Noni," *Utah Business,* November 2000, p. 41.

Nealy-Brown, J., "Noni Juice: Magical Elixir or Trendy Nostrum," *St. Petersburg Times,* July 5, 2001, p. 1B.

Neill, Richard, "South Sea Bubble," *Daily Telegraph* (London, U.K.), September 3, 2005.

Smillie, Dirk, "Tale of the South Pacific," *Forbes,* May 24, 2004, p. 178.

Smith, Virginia A., "In the Stinky Noni Fruit, Many Claim All Kinds of Cures," *Philadelphia Inquirer,* July 15, 2005.

Nevamar Company

—■—

8339 Telegraph Road
Odenton, Maryland 21113-1397
U.S.A.
Telephone: (410) 551-5000
Toll Free: (800) 638-4380
Fax: (410) 519-2072
Web site: http://www.nevamar.com

Wholly Owned Subsidiary of Panolam Industries International, Inc.
Founded: 1939 as National Plastic Products Company
Employees: 1,600
Sales: $378 million (2003)
NAIC: 326130 Laminated Plastics, Plate, Sheet, and Shape Manufacturing

■ ■ ■

A subsidiary of Panolam Industries International, Inc., Nevamar Company is an Odenton, Maryland-based manufacturer of decorative, protective laminate products. They are used for countertops, tabletops, wall panels, interior doors, furniture, and other applications. Nevamar offers high pressure laminates, featuring a plastic substrate molded at pressures as high as 2,000 pounds per square inch; specialty laminates that may be chemical resistant or fire resistant, offer static dissipation, are suitable for signage, or engineered to meet other specific needs, such as a special grade for rail cars and buses; thermofused melamine panels, for use in furniture, cabinets, and doors; and metal laminates to provide a polished and brushed color finish and other distinctive looks in furniture and interiors. Navamar products are manufactured at four plants. The company maintains six distribution centers in the United States and sells its products around the world through a network of independent distributors.

COMPANY FOUNDED: 1939

Nevamar was founded in 1939 as the National Plastic Products Company by the Winer family in Baltimore, Maryland, owners of a cabinetmaking business who were one of the first to make use of high-pressure, plastic-based laminating technology to produce veneers for cabinet surfaces. In 1943, they moved their fledgling operation to Odenton, in central Maryland, a town that had been built around the Washington, Baltimore and Annapolis Railroad. Odenton had enjoyed its heyday during World War I when the railroad's owners convinced the government to establish Camp Meade in the area. With the end of the war and the rise of the automobile, WB&A struggled, as did Odenton, which fared even worse during the Great Depression of the 1930s when the railroad went bankrupt. The Winers were able to move the National Plastic operation into the abandoned WB&A car shops, revitalize the area economy, and in effect turn Odenton into a company town. During the war years, National Plastic focused on the production of war materials, but with the end of hostilities in 1945 the company turned its attention to consumer products.

National Plastic trademarked the Nevamar name for its laminates in 1946, but it also became involved in other forms of plastic production, including filaments

COMPANY PERSPECTIVES

With a widely respected brand for high style, durability and customized solutions, Nevamar is firmly positioned as a one of the top manufacturers of decorative laminates, specialty laminates and TFM panels in North America.

made from such polymers as polyolefin and nylon, as well as molded products and extrusions. In addition to Nevamar laminates, the company made paint brush bristles, doll hair, textiles, and even hula hoops. By the start of the 1960s National Plastic was doing about $20 million in annual sales.

WINER FAMILY SELLS: 1961

In August 1961 the Winer family sold the business to a 50-50 joint venture formed by textile producer J.P. Stevens and Enjay Chemical Co., a division of Humble Oil & Refining, which a decade later would become known as Exxon. The oil company was interested in National Plastic's extruded fiber technology, but by the end of the 1960s all of National Plastic's assets were sold, save the Nevamar business. National Plastic was one of about 15 companies competing in laminates and was hardly a major force in the field, barely breaking even and very much directionless. Exxon managers were assigned to the company on a two-year basis and, as a result, the business stagnated.

Permanent members of National Plastic's management team decided to take matters into their own hands in 1969, forming a study group to develop a ten-year plan. It soon became apparent that the company was devoting too many resources on commodity items that were price dependent. Larger rivals could simply use their scale to produce laminates at a price National Plastic could not hope to match. The group decided that the company needed to play to its strength: product design. Instead of producing cheap laminates for the residential market, the plan was to focus on more expensive, better designed laminates for the commercial market. Not only would the company gain a competitive edge, one not dependent on size, it would also improve profit margins.

In the 1960s and early 1970s, National Plastic developed a number of dimensional finishes. Some of the most innovative designs were Fossil, which offered a look similar to fossilized artifacts; a Fresco Finish that had a natural wood grain look; Glaze, reminiscent of

vitreous china; Slate Finish, the industry's first sculptured laminate, which gave the appearance of quarried slate; and Leather, a pattern that offered a three-dimensional leather appearance. In the mid-1970s National Plastic introduced a number of natural patterns, including Butcher Block; Registered Cane and Classic Cane, providing a woven look; Natural Cork; Registered Leather; Blue Denim; and Natural Finish Woods.

National Plastic was enjoying success with its ten-year plan when Exxon decided to focus on its core business and sell the laminate business. Three National Plastic executives—Herb Scher, Charles Jackson, and Norman Roux—decided to make their bid for the company and tried to drum up financial backing from Goldman Sachs & Co. Instead, another backer emerged in Chagrin Valley Corporation (CVC), a new Cleveland investment group on the lookout for a company to buy. Their offer of $12 million was accepted by Exxon, but the man they wanted to run the company, which would assume the Nevamar name, was Roux, who decided to stay with Exxon. Instead, a CVC partner, John W. Cullen, was dispatched to run Nevamar on a temporary basis. He would act as the company's chief executive for more than a dozen years.

A graduate of both Duke University and Harvard University, Cullen brought a rich and varied business background to Nevamar. He had worked for a pair of innovative companies: the famous consulting firm of McKinsey & Co., and International Management Group, the pioneering sports management business founded by visionary Mark H. McCormack. Cullen was experienced in promoting team work and problem solving, skills that would be put to the test. Nine of Nevamar's executives had been given a piece of the business by CVC, including Scher and Jackson. Rather than come in and insist on putting his stamp on the company, Cullen was content to promote a group effort in building the business.

A little more than a year after breaking away from Exxon, Nevamar found itself short of cash due to the $5 million purchase of a new laminate press and $3 million spent to acquire a General Electric laminate unit, Textalite. Nevamar was able to secure a loan from the Farmers Home Administration, the mandate of which was to help rural companies of less than 500 employees. However, in terms of employment, Nevamar barely qualified. According to Warfield's magazine, "To convince Farm's Home officials that Nevamar was suitably bucolic, Vice President for Finance C. Gordon McBee drove them from the airport to Odenton by every back road and cow pasture he could find."

Nevamar resumed its efforts to build up its commercial business. To do this the company courted

KEY DATES

1939: The company is founded as National Plastic Products Company by the Winer family.
1943: Production is moved to Odenton, Maryland.
1946: The Nevamar name is trademarked.
1961: The Winers sell their company to a partnership of the J.P. Stevens company and a division of Humble Oil & Refining.
1978: Chagrin Valley Corporation acquires the company.
1990: International Paper acquires Nevamar.
1995: Micarta business is acquired by Nevamar.
2003: The Odenton plant closes.
2006: Nevamar is acquired by Panolam Industries International, Inc.

designers, forging relationships that over the long-term would allow Nevamar to anticipate the kind of patterns the commercial market would want, highly important because a year or two lead time was necessary in introducing a new pattern. It was from talking to designers that Nevamar began to understand their customers wanted something they could not quite put into words. The company distilled it down to the idea of "visual texture," a laminate that was smooth to the touch yet looked textured and could be produced in a range of colors.

Nevamar technicians went to school on the way the brain perceives texture and then used computers to generate laminate patterns that met the need for visual textures, resulting in what it call the Matrix Pattern. It was a true breakthrough that would result in a standard category for all laminate manufacturers. First, Nevamar had to iron out the engraving process, creating a proprietary process to accomplish the task, and find the right protective overlay to protect the pattern from abrasion. The standard paper overlay resulted in a milky appearance, but this problem was solved with the development of a patented coating, ARP Surface, that relied on microscopic particles of aluminum oxide.

The Matrix line secured Nevamar's place in the laminate industry as a true innovator. Moreover, the product was a hit, and basic laminates soon accounted for 80 percent of the company's revenues. The rest of the business came from specialty products, "thick sheets." Not content with being overly dependent on basic laminates, Nevamar began looking for new products and in 1981 decided there was an opportunity to challenge

DuPont and its Corian product, which since the 1960s had enjoyed a virtual monopoly. It was a moldable material that was ideal for kitchen and bathroom countertops as well as shower surrounds. It was an attractive business for Nevamar because it was high-end and it could be sold to the same customers that bought the company's laminates. Corian's main drawbacks were that it came in just one width and offered little more than white as a color. Nevamar devoted four years and spent as much as $20 million to develop its own product, which it introduced in 1985 as Fountainhead. Priced similarly to Corian, it came in a variety of widths, patterns, and colors. As it turned out, many fabricators remained committed to Corian, forcing Nevamar to develop its own fabricator network.

INTERNATIONAL PAPER ACQUIRES BUSINESS: 1990

CVC had cashed out in 1984, selling the business to the New York venture capital firm of Clayton & Dublier Inc., which by 1988 was ready to take its profit. Cullen and his management team thought about engineering another buyout, backed by Kohlberg & Co., but in the end decided against the move. Three suitors came calling, and in May 1990 the offer made by International Paper was accepted. International Paper picked up a company with $140 million in annual sales and brand name recognition—overall, a nice complement to International Paper's Masonite and Polrey subsidiaries. For its part, Nevamar hoped to take advantage of International Paper's deep pockets and marketing reach to grow its business overseas. In addition to its lone manufacturing plant, Nevamar operated 20 distribution centers.

Under new ownership, Nevamar continued to develop innovative products. The company introduced Hallmark Laminates, which offered a unique luminescent effect and could be applied both horizontally and vertically. Nevamar also brought out its LamMates line of thermalfused melamine panels.

In 1995 Nevamar benefitted from the resources of its parent company, when International Paper acquired the Special Materials Division of Westinghouse Electric Company, known as Micarta, a Nevamar rival in the high-pressure laminate field and a company with its own rich history. Micarta was founded in 1905 by George Westinghouse, an inventor who had made his reputation and fortune on the railcar air brake, but had also became involved in electric power and other fields, and developed into one of America's great industrialists. In his search for electrical insulating materials, Westinghouse purchased the rights to an insulating sheet that used shellac to fuse mica to paper, and trademarked the product as Micarta. While Micarta would serve its purpose as an electrical insulating material, still used today in such applications as the space shuttle, the Westinghouse company would soon take the business in new directions. In the 1910s it developed a way to bond a decorative sheet to regular paper, creating an early decorative laminate. The engineer responsible for the product was quick to leave Westinghouse to become a competitor. He founded the Formica Corporation, and was so successful that Formica became, to the general public, a generic term for laminate countertops. The Micarta division, meanwhile, continued to be a force in the laminate field and after World War II focused on decorative laminates for use in furniture and housing.

International Paper folded Micarta into the Nevamar operations. By this point Nevamar's Maryland plant was operating at full capacity, and it welcomed the addition of Micarta's plant located in Hampton, South Carolina, which was able to take on more work.

International Paper decided to exit the laminates field in 2002, selling its entire Decorative Products Division to Kohlberg & Co. The assets were packaged into a new corporate entity called Nevamar Company. They included ten manufacturing sites that produced laminates as well as particleboard, man-made veneer, and foam-based graphics, and insulation products. Kohlberg sold the non-laminate assets and in 2003, after 60 years in operation, the Odenton, Maryland, plant was closed, although the company would continue to maintain its corporate headquarters in Odenton. The high-pressure laminate production done in Maryland was moved to Hampton, South Carolina, where Nevamar was able to negotiate a package of tax reductions, wage concession, and other concessions that Odenton and the State of Maryland were unable to match.

Ownership of Nevamar changed hands again in 2006 when Panolam Industries International, Inc., the North American market leader in the decorative laminate panel industry, acquired the business. Nevamar was an ideal fit for Panolam, which added a strong brand name to its stable and beefed up its distribution network. For Nevamar it marked the beginning of a new chapter in its history, as it looked to find its place with a new corporate parent.

Ed Dinger

PRINCIPAL COMPETITORS

Armstrong Holdings, Inc.; Formica Corporation; Pergo AB.

FURTHER READING

Goldstein, Stephen, "Paper Firm Buys Nevamar Corp.," *Washington Times,* March 27, 1990, p. 3.

Hopkins, Jamie Smith, "Odenton, Md., Laminate Maker Nevamar to Close Plant," *Baltimore Sun,* October 3, 2003.

Keiger, Dale, "Surface Tension," *Warfield's,* December 1, 1990, p. 51.

Wachter, Paul, "Laminate Manufacturer Chooses Hampton, S.C. Plant Over Odenton, Md., Plant," *State (Columbia, S.C.),* November 30, 2003.

Orkla ASA

Karenslyst alle 6
Oslo, 0278
Norway
Telephone: (47) 22 54 40 00
Fax: (47) 22 54 44 90
Web site: http://www.orkla.com

Public Company
Incorporated: 1991
Employees: 19,575
Sales: NOK 55 billion ($8.11 billion) (2005)
Stock Exchanges: Oslo
Ticker Symbol: ORK
NAIC: 422410 General Line Grocery Wholesalers;
422420 Packaged Frozen Food Wholesalers; 422430
Dairy Product (Except Dried or Canned) Wholesalers; 422440 Poultry and Poultry Product Wholesalers; 422450 Confectionery Wholesalers; 422460
Fish and Seafood Wholesalers; 422990 Other
Miscellaneous Nondurable Goods Wholesalers;
421990 Other Miscellaneous Durable Goods
Wholesalers

■ ■ ■

Orkla ASA is a leading manufacturer of branded
consumer goods, specialty materials, and financial
investments based in Norway. With a history dating
back to the 17th century, Orkla provides a wide variety
of products and services, ranging from frozen pizza and
seafood to metals and specialty chemicals. The company
also owns one of the largest equity portfolios in Norway.
Its Specialty Materials business segment is comprised of
Elkem, one of the world's largest suppliers of metals and
materials; Sapa, a leading aluminum producer; and Borregaard, which offers specialty chemicals, fine chemicals,
and ingredients. The company's Branded Consumer
Goods segment—comprised of Orkla Foods, Orkla
Brands, and Orkla Media—accounted for nearly 55
percent of total revenues in 2005. Orkla sold its media
group in 2006 in a $1.2 billion deal.

ORKLA INDUSTRIER A/S: 1904–85

The original firm of the present-day Orkla ASA
conglomerate traces its roots back to the first pyrite
mining operations conducted at Løkken Verk, Norway
(south of Trondheim near the Orkla River), which began
in 1654. In the succeeding years, a smelting industry
grew up around the mines in the area, and after a period
of disuse, in 1904 the Løkken Verk mines were reopened
by the newly formed Orkla Industrier. For the next 40-
plus years, Orkla focused on developing its mining
businesses. In the years following World War II, however,
Orkla Industrier began building up an ever widening
investment portfolio of other companies and in 1958
established an important joint venture with the Unilever
Group (makers of "All" detergent, among other products)
to manufacture detergents and personal products—a
relationship that was still in place in 1997. In 1981,
Orkla extended its strategy to diversify beyond its
original mining businesses by purchasing its first
newspaper publisher.

INTERNATIONAL DIRECTORY OF COMPANY HISTORIES, VOLUME 82   259

COMPANY PERSPECTIVES

Orkla seeks to achieve growth and long-term value creation in its industrial activities by creating competitive advantages based on: a competent organization and a sound corporate culture in which learning and empowerment are key elements; specialized and clearly differentiated products; and strong and leading market positions.

BORREGAARD A/S: 1918–85

In 1986 Orkla agreed to merge with Borregaard A/S, a major Norwegian chemicals company, to form a new entity, Orkla Borregaard A/S. Borregaard traced its roots back to 1918, when a partnership of Norwegian business interests had acquired the British firm The Kellner Partington Paper Pulp Co., Ltd., itself founded in 1889. A manufacturer of pulp and paper in Norway, Sweden, and Austria, Kellner Partington had fueled its growth through a combination of British capital and Austrian technology. Rechristened Borregaard, the new firm began establishing a reputation as one of the world's foremost producers of pulp and paper, with production facilities in several countries and international sales.

In 1938, Borregaard entered the chemicals business when it began using sugar compounds found in the byproducts of wood pulp production as the raw material for the production of ethanol (used in alcohol and as a solvent). In 1960, it began expanding its chemicals and consumer products, and in 1962 and 1967 it extended its pulp byproduct chemicals manufacturing applications from ethanol to vanillin and lignin, respectively. Although by the mid-1970s Borregaard still owned one of the two largest wood pulp mills in Norway, in the early 1980s it made the radical leap from using pulp as its primary raw material to the production of fine chemicals that used nonpulp-based applications from the specialized fields of advanced chemicals manufacture.

The reason for the shift was plain: demand for Borregaard's traditional wood processing products had begun to fade, and it was forced to begin unloading its international production facilities. In 1979, for example, it sold its Borregaard Osterreich AG subsidiary for NOK 84 million; then in 1983 it sold a 6 percent interest in its stock to food and beverages group Nora Industrier A/S, only to purchase back a 42 percent interest in Nora a year later. In 1985, Borregaard and Nora turned to each other's shares again: in a so-called demerger, Borregaard gained a 45 percent share in Stabburet-Nora—a Norwegian fresh and wholesale grocery company—in exchange for half a million shares of its own stock. Borregaard's overhaul of its historical identity as an old-line paper and pulp producer was about to enter a new phase.

ORKLA BORREGAARD A/S: 1986–91

Borregaard's merger with Orkla in 1986 began the most important stage in its transformation into a high-tech global chemicals maker. As Borregaard's businesses were integrated into Orkla's corporate structure, Orkla's management undertook a major restructuring of the Borregaard fold to bring it in line with the new global markets for advanced chemicals products. Meanwhile, Orkla could add to its traditional brand-name consumer goods, media, and investments businesses Borregaard's wood processing, chemical products, hydroelectric power generation, forestry, and engineering operations.

In 1987, Orkla Borregaard closed its Løkken Gruber mining operations and a year later merged with four Norwegian firms: Johan Norlie A/S, Berskaug A/S, parsley producer Persilfabriken A/S, and real estate firm Orkla Eiendom A/S. To further bolster its new consumer and media orientation, it acquired Ostlandske Fryserier A/S's cold storage plant in Brummunddal, Norway, in 1988 and map publisher Planforlaget in early 1989. During 1989 and 1990 Orkla Borregaard enhanced its position in the chemicals industry with the purchase of increased interests in the chemicals firms Elkem and Dyno Industrier, the acquisition of a Swedish firm's international lignin operations, and the formation of a joint venture with the Eni Group of Italy to produce vanillin, synthetic vanillin, raw materials, and derivative products.

NORA INDUSTRIER A/S: 1969–91

Less than five years after Orkla's monumental merger with Borregaard, the company moved again to expand its product lines and market share through a major acquisition: on January 1, 1991, Orkla Borregaard and Nora Industrier were united through an exchange of stock to form Orkla A/S. Nora Industrier had been formed in 1978 from the consolidation of several Oslo breweries with roots going back to the 1820s. Within a few years, it had become Norway's leading supplier of beer and carbonated soft drinks, fortified by holdings in the Norwegian food market.

Within five years of its founding Nora had acquired holdings in a brewery, a mineral water producer, and a glassmaker and merged operations with a fourth firm. In 1984 alone it bought another brewery (A/S Lillehammer Bryggeri) and a health drink maker (Vitaminveien 6),

KEY DATES

1654: The first pyrite mining operations begin at Løkken Verk, Norway.

1904: The Løkken Verk mines are reopened by the newly formed Orkla Industrier.

1958: The company establishes a joint venture with the Unilever Group to manufacture detergents and personal products.

1981: Orkla purchases its first newspaper publisher.

1986: The company merges with Borregaard A/S.

1987: Orkla Borregaard closes its Lokken mining operations.

1991: Orkla Borregaard and Nora Industrier merge to form Orkla A/S.

1995: Procordia Foods and Abba Seafood AB are purchased.

2005: Elkem and Sapa are acquired.

2006: The company sells Orkla Media.

established a real estate firm, and began acquiring a 47 percent interest in Helly-Hansen A/S, a major Norwegian manufacturer of men's and women's clothing founded in 1877. Between 1986 and 1988 Nora merged with yeast makers Gjaer A/S and Idu Gjarfabrikken A/S, chemicals producer Oslo Kjemiske Industri A/S, seed supplier Norsk Froforsyning A/S, flour mill Bjolsen Valsemolle A/S, and beverage maker Hamar Bryggeri, among others. In 1987 Nora moved closer to Orkla's product sphere by gaining a substantial ownership stake in six Nordic industrial bakeries and becoming a majority shareholder in the new bakery industry group Bakers A/S. By 1995 the Nora unit within Orkla A/S would be one of the largest suppliers of foods and ingredients to the Norwegian grocery trade, catering, bakery, and food manufacturing industries. In 1988 it merged its breweries and mineral water companies with beverage maker Ringnes Frydenlund, creating a single beverage division and a major new force in the Norwegian beverage market.

Ringnes had been founded as Ringnes Bryggeri (brewery) by Amund and Ellef Ringnes in 1876. Among its landmark products were Vørterol (1903), "recommended by 400 doctors"; the first bottles of a popular new soft drink named Solo (1934); the first Coca-Cola sold in Norway (1938), the first Heineken beer produced in Norway (1975), and the introduction of the market-leading Ringnes brand of beer itself. With Ringnes leading its beverage markets, Nora let Hamar Bryggeri's bot-

tling pact with Pepsi expire in 1987, and in 1989 and 1990 acquired ten companies, from mineral water producer Narvik Minneralvann A/S and food producer Danish Fancy Food A/S to brewer Tou A/S and health food producer Elfas Helsekost A/S.

ORKLA A/S: 1991–94

Until the Nora merger, Orkla Borregaard for all its rapid growth had remained primarily a Norwegian company with scattered businesses in Denmark. Its holdings in Sweden—the largest segment of the Scandinavian market—were almost nonexistent. With Nora anchoring Orkla's industry-leading consumer brands group, however, Orkla A/S entered the 1990s poised to become a broadly positioned Scandinavian firm ready to expand into Europe and beyond. Its specific long-term goal was to reduce its dependence on Norwegian sales to less than half of annual revenues, and toward that end in 1991 Orkla Beverage joined in a Polish joint venture to gain a foothold in the newly opened Iron Curtain market and two years later established Ringnes Beer Ltd. of Poland.

Orkla's late 1980s campaign to restructure Borregaard into a global high-tech chemicals firm continued in the early 1990s with the erection of a new fine chemicals plant in Norway and the acquisition of Daishowa Chemicals of the United States and industrial ethanol producer Kemetyl AB of Sweden in 1991. In 1993, it added the lignin operations of Finland's Metsä-Serla and the Italian and Chinese diphenol (used in the production of vanillin) plants of Italy's EniChem Synthesis in 1994. In addition, the EniChem deal—which was expected to net Orkla NOK 500 million in 1995—gave Orkla's new Borregaard Synthesis unit control of the Norwegian firm EuroVanillin, the second-largest vanillin producer in the world.

Orkla also focused intently on its media empire. In 1991 Orkla Media bought three Norwegian newspapers, and in November the Norwegian government awarded Netcom GSM A/S, a mobile telecommunications company owned by Orkla Communications, the go-ahead to provide cell phone services to Norway's central region beginning in late 1992. Then in 1993, in a joint venture with Norske Egmont Orkla, the company acquired a 50 percent stake in Hjemmet Mortensen group, the market leader in the Norwegian magazine business. It followed this with the purchase of interests in the Norwegian newspaper *Bergens Tidende* and six Polish newspapers in 1993. In 1994, Orkla Media acquired the newspapers *Drammens Tidende og Buskeruds Blad* and *Varden* and gained a stake in the newspaper *Fjordenes Tidende*. Finally, in its critical food segment, Orkla scooped up Swedish biscuit maker Goteborg Sex

AB, Finnish biscuit maker Quintillion, and grocery wholesaler R.N. Glossiest of Sweden. Concentrating on the consumer food market, it bought out the remainder of Bakers A/S and sold half its interest in clothier Helly-Hansen before repositioning its household products, biscuits/snacks, and chocolate/confectionary units under one roof: Orkla Brands.

PROCORDIA, ABBA, PRIPPS, RINGNES—AND COCA-COLA: 1995–96

Orkla's activities in the food industry in the early 1990s paled in comparison to its third major acquisition in a decade: the purchase in April 1995 of Procordia Foods and Abba Seafood AB from Swedish car maker Volvo for $578 million. The deal, however, would not only make Orkla a $1.6 billion corporate colossus with annual food sales twice the size of current levels. Volvo also agreed to enter into a joint venture with Orkla to create a new beverage industry leader out of the two companies' flagship bottlers, Pripps (Sweden's largest brewery) and Ringnes (Coca-Cola's largest Norwegian bottler), respectively. The new Pripps Ringnes AB would make Orkla the number one beer, carbonated soft drink, and water products company in Norway and Sweden and, through Pripps Ringnes's stake in Oy Hartwall Ab and Baltic Beverage Holdings, the market leader in beer sales in, respectively, Finland and the Baltic/St. Petersburg, Russia.

Orkla's CEO Jens P. Heyerdahl told interviewers that the magnitude of the Volvo acquisition/merger would improve Orkla's ability to stave off foreign competition for its nearby markets. Although Heyerdahl had helped to defeat Norway's proposed membership in the European Union (EU) in 1994, the Procordia/Abba/Pripps Ringnes deal demonstrated that he wanted to position Orkla to enter the European market he had once scorned by way of Sweden, an EU member since 1994. Because the new venture, Pripps Ringnes, would effectively control 82 percent of the Norwegian beer market, 60 percent of the Swedish soft drink market, and 95 percent of Norway's market for bottled water, however, the second phase of the Volvo-Orkla deal had to wait upon the approval of both the EU and Norway and Sweden's antitrust agencies. The anchor of the Volvo-Orkla food deal, Procordia AB, had been formed by the Swedish government in 1969 as Statsforetag, and in its two-decade-plus existence had branched from beverage sales into foods, pharmaceuticals, media services, hotels, tobacco, engineering, and development. By the end of 1990 it had sales of SEK 36.6 billion and 45,000 employees and maintained subsidiaries and affiliated companies in Denmark, Spain, the United

Kingdom, Japan, the Netherlands, France, the United States, and Switzerland. By the time Volvo assumed direction of the company, however, Procordia was, as the *Wall Street Journal* characterized it, "only moderately profitable," and thus Volvo was unable to get prospective international buyers outside of Scandinavia to make compelling bids.

By September 1995, the EU and the Swedish government's antitrust agency had granted Orkla permission to absorb Procordia and Abba in exchange for several concessions: Orkla could no longer prevent the Swedish food company ICA from marketing its own private-label juices and jams, and Orkla itself would refrain from producing private-label juices and jams in Sweden for three years. More importantly, Orkla agreed to sell Hansa Bryggeri, the second-largest brewer in Norway, in 1996 to ease competitors' antitrust anxieties.

Almost as soon as the deal was finalized, however, Orkla faced a major obstacle. As part of its 42-year-old bottling and distribution contract with Pripps, the Coca-Cola Company—whose products accounted for 35 percent of Pripps Ringnes's total sales—was entitled to renegotiate its Pripps contract, and it quickly submitted a new contract in which Pripps would not only be required to focus exclusively on Coke's products but also sell Coke the Pripps line of soft drinks that it marketed along with Coke's products. Pripps's management rejected Coke's demands, calling them "corporate imperialism," and in December 1995 Coke dropped Pripps as its sole supplier for the Swedish market, citing Pripps's new management (i.e., Orkla) and the company's "weak" performance. Pripps countered that its Swedish sales had grown 10 percent annually in each of the past eight years, but the damage was already done. In December, union members of a Pripps bottler in Norway stopped production of Coke products in sympathetic protest even though Pripps's Norwegian operations were unaffected by the terminated Swedish contract.

Unaccustomed to such unrest in its foreign operations, in July 1996 Coca-Cola terminated its Norwegian bottling and sales agreements as well, forcing Orkla's new Pripps Ringnes venture to lay off 1,400 workers. With Coke determined to set up its own bottling and sales operations in Scandinavia, Coke and Orkla agreed on a $166 million severance package that would temporarily extend the historic Coke-Pripps collaboration until the beginning of 1999. Orkla was now free to promote its own soft drink products (such as Mozell and Farris) over Coca-Cola's, and with 60 to 65 percent market share in the Swedish and Norwegian soft drinks market it hoped to be able to compete against Coke's new Scandinavian soft drink machine.

GLOBAL AT LAST: 1996–97

If Orkla's new beverage operations were in tumult, the expansion of its chemicals businesses proceeded at a more orderly pace. By the mid-1990s, an ever more substantial portion of Borregaard's sales were coming from Asia. It was the majority owner of a fine chemicals company for the manufacture of crop pesticide products in China's Jiangsu province, had established a laboratory for technical customer support in Singapore, and maintained sales offices in Singapore, Japan, and mainland China. In May 1996, Borregaard LignoTech and China's Kaishantun Chemical Fibre Pulp Mill signed an agreement to jointly produce lignin-based products (primarily for additives to concrete) through a new joint venture in northeast China, and a year earlier Orkla had opened a new lignin plant outside Seattle. As the century drew to a close, Borregaard had successfully made the transition from a basic paper and pulp supplier to a niche producer of vanillin and intermediates to a diversified global producer of a full range of chemicals for the construction, agricultural, and pharmaceuticals industries.

Orkla's campaign to become an even larger presence in the European media market also advanced in the mid-1990s. In mid-1996, for example, Orkla Media signed a letter of intent with the Hersant Group, a French media giant, to take over Hersant's controlling interest in the Polish newspaper publishing company Presspublica, which owned the national daily *Rzeczpospolita* and the newspaper's printing company Warszawa Print. The deal brought to nine the number of local and regional Polish dailies owned by Orkla Media, not counting its printing facilities in northern and southern Poland. With the Presspublica acquisition, improved advertising revenues in its Norwegian newspaper businesses, and cost reductions in its magazine segment, Orkla Media's profits edged upward in mid-1996.

Between 1995 and 1997, Orkla wrestled with the problems and opportunities presented by the Procordia/Abba/Pripps Ringnes merger of 1995. In early 1996 beer and soft drink sales in Sweden fell in part because of high Swedish alcohol taxes, which drove consumers to buy private beer imports. Under a European Union deadline, Orkla finally sold brewery Hansa Bryggeri to a group of investors in December 1996 to meet the terms of the 1995 Pripps Ringnes merger, and to consolidate its new Abba Seafood business in September 1996 Orkla sold its German seafood operations and mackerel and shrimp factories in Sweden and reduced its interest in Abba's Danish mussel factory. By intentionally focusing on fewer products and markets, a leaner Abba Seafood promised to offer Orkla increased long-term profitability.

Productivity improvements, a new 20-year extension of its detergent/personal products agreement with Unilever, Sweden's reduction of its value-added tax (VAT) on food, price increases for Orkla's Swedish grocery products, the reorganization of its Swedish fruit and berry production operations, and improved versions of its Omo and Blenda detergent brands—all contributed to an increase in Orkla's consumer-branded products segments in 1996. From operating revenues of NOK 15.47 billion in 1990, Orkla's revenues had risen to NOK 21.53 billion by 1995. As the day drew near when identical, truly "Nordic" brands could be marketed in every Scandinavian country, in 1996 Orkla reached its long-sought goal of 50 percent or more non-Norwegian sales.

ORKLA IN THE NEW MILLENNIUM

Orkla made several important moves in the early years of the new millennium to strengthen its operating structure while increasing profits. In an attempt to bolster its consumer goods business segment, the company began a joint venture with Carlsberg A/S in 2000 in which the two companies combined their brewing operations to form Carlsberg Breweries. Orkla retained a 40 percent interest in the newly formed company but arguments over business strategies led Orkla to sell its shares back to Carlsberg in 2004 in a $3.3 billion deal. That same year, the company acquired SladCo, a Russian manufacturer of chocolate, biscuits, and confectionary products. Finnish company Chips was purchased the following year.

Orkla's next big purchase came in 2005 when it added Elkem, a specialty metals group, to its arsenal. Orkla had been battling for control of Elkem ASA with U.S.-based Alcoa—owner of 46 percent of Elkem—since 1998. In the end Alcoa retreated, leaving Orkla free to complete its acquisition. The overall process however, proved costly to the company. Longtime Orkla employee and CEO Finn Jebsen was ousted during the bidding process, criticized for failing to reveal that the company would have to bid on Swedish aluminum group Sapa AB as part of its bid for the remaining shares of Elkem. In the end, Orkla paid approximately $1.16 billion for Elkem and $290 million for Sapa. Dag J. Opedal was named president and CEO in 2005.

When the dust settled on the deal, Elkem, Sapa, and Borregaard became part of Orkla's Specialty Materials group. The company planned to strengthen this group by looking for growth opportunities in the renewable energy sector. Orkla also planned to shore up Elkem profits in primary aluminum by constructing a new anode factory in Mosjoen, by strengthening its partnership with Alcoa, and by securing its electricity supplies until 2020 through a contract with Vattenfall. To improve Sapa's bottom line, the company looked to organic growth as well as geographical expansion.

The company made a major change in its Branded Consumer Goods segment when it decided to sell Orkla Media, which at the time was the fifth largest media group in Scandinavia. Mecom Group plc of the United Kingdom paid $1.2 billion for the media unit in 2006. Orkla planned to use the proceeds to focus on its core industrial businesses.

Orkla's strategy at this time was also included a focus on innovation, operational improvements, and structural development as a means of growth. Company management was aware that the industries it operated in were constantly changing and as such, planned to take advantage of opportunities that would strengthen the company's overall structure and profitability. While Orkla ASA had indeed achieved conglomerate status on a global scale, only time would tell how its acquisitions and the sale of its Orkla Media group would affect its long-term profitability.

Paul S. Bodine
Updated, Christina M. Stansell

PRINCIPAL OPERATING UNITS

Orkla Foods; Orkla Brands; Elkem; Sapa; Borregaard.

PRINCIPAL COMPETITORS

BASF AG; Kraft Foods Inc.; Nestlé S.A.

FURTHER READING

Alperowicz, Natasha, "Nordic Chemical Sector Reshuffles," *Chemical Week,* June 21, 1995, p. 25.

"Beer Maker Is Sold to a Group of Investors," *New York Times,* December 31, 1996.

Bergsli, Camilla, "Orkla Says to Reinvest Media Money in Core Areas," *Reuters News,* July 25, 2006.

Braude, Jonathan, "Mecom Seals Orkla Media Purchase," *TheDeal.com,* July 26, 2006.

Carnegy, Hugh, "Hansa Bryggeri Sold," *Financial Times,* December 31, 1996.

——, "Investment Gains Lift Orkla at Eight Months," *Financial Times,* October 4, 1996.

"European Digest—Mecom Acquires Orkla Media," *Media and Marketing Europe,* July 28, 2006.

Frank, Robert, and Stephen D. Moore, "Coca-Cola Seen Resuming Talks over Bottler," *Wall Street Journal,* December 11, 1995.

Johnson, Greg, "World Watch," *Los Angeles Times,* June 20, 1996, p. D4.

Koza, Patricia, "Carlsberg Marriage Goes Flat," *TheDeal.com,* February 20, 2004.

Markiewicz, Tadeusz, "Orkla to Snap Up Rzeczpospolita," *Warsaw Voice,* June 2, 1996.

McIver, Greg, "Coca-Cola Sets Scandinavia's Drinks Market Fizzing," *Financial Times,* June 25, 1996.

Moore, Stephen, "Volvo to Sell Food Unit to Orkla, Set up Beverage Joint Venture," *Wall Street Journal,* April 4, 1995, p. A16.

Nicholas, George, "Orkla Ousts Chief amid Bid Row," *Financial Times,* January 26, 2005, p. 32.

Nordli, Jan-Frode, "NetCom Gets Norway's 2nd GSM Mobile Phone Franchise," *Newsbytes News Network,* November 8, 1991.

"Norway Orkla Unit, Coca Cola to End Cooperation," *Wall Street Journal,* January 28, 1997, http://www.wsj.com

"Norway's Orkla Finally Wins Control of Elkem," *Financial Times,* March 23, 2005.

"Orkla Names Replacement for Ousted Chief," *Associated Press Newswires,* June 1, 2005.

"Orkla Pre-tax Up 18.6%," *Financial Times,* June 7, 1996.

"Orkla to Make Offer For All Sapa Shares," *Platt's Metals Week,* January 17, 2005.

"Orkla Will Keep and Actively Promote the Development of Elkem, Sapa, and Borregaard," *Hugin Press Release,* October 17, 2005.

"Pacts Will Be Terminated with Unit of Volvo, Orkla," *Wall Street Journal,* June 20, 1996.

"Sweden Approves Orkla Purchase," *Wall Street Journal,* September 15, 1995.

"Sweden's Pripps Loses Coca-Cola Franchise, Dealing Blow to Orkla," *Wall Street Journal Interactive,* December 1, 1995.

"Union at Norwegian Bottler Threatens Production Halt," *Wall Street Journal,* December 5, 1995.

"Volvo Sells Food Firms," *Automotive News,* April 10, 1995.

"Volvo to Sell Food Unit to Orkla, Set Up Beverage Joint Venture," *Wall Street Journal,* April 4, 1995.

Ormet Corporation

380 Southpointe Boulevard
Southpointe Plaza II
Suite 200
Canonsburg, Pennslyvania 15317
U.S.A.
Telephone: (724) 820-1800
Toll Free: (800) 331-6950
Fax: (724) 820-1810
Web site: http://www.ormet.com

Private Company
Incorporated: 1956 as Orlin Revere Metals Corporation
Employees: 2,000
Sales: $467 million (2005 est.)
NAIC: 331312 Primary Aluminum Production

■ ■ ■

Ormet Corporation is a privately owned manufacturer of alumina and primary aluminum whose headquarters are located in Canonsburg, Pennsylvania. Ormet's specialty alumina materials are used in aluminum production as well as abrasives, refractories, ceramics, and electrical insulation as a fire retardant. Ormet maintains manufacturing operations in Burnside, Louisiana; Hannibal, Ohio; and Terre Haute, Indiana. The company also operates Bens Run Recycling Facility in Friendly, West Virginia, and the Burnside Bulk Marine Terminal in Darrow, Louisiana, which provides import and export services for such bulk commodities as coal, coke, ores, cement, fertilizers, and minerals.

LAUNCHED AS JOINT VENTURE: 1956

Because of the Korean War, the United States in 1950 offered an assistance program to encourage companies to become involved in primary aluminum production. Two companies interested in entering the field were Olin Mathieson Chemical Corporation and Revere Copper and Brass, Inc., (founded by Revolutionary War patriot Paul Revere in 1801). During World War II Olin had managed a government aluminum production plant, and Revere was an aluminum fabricator. Both companies ran into difficulties in financing their own primary aluminum operations, which were costly endeavors. Instead, they decided to join forces and in August 1956 established a joint venture called Orlin Revere Metals Corporation, which was later shortened to Ormet Corporation. The new company issued $16 million in common stock and raised another $15 million in 25-year bonds, split equally between Olin and Revere. A further $200 million in funding was borrowed from banks and insurance companies at rates approved by the corporate parents. According to the structure of the joint venture agreement, Ormet was confined to the production of primary aluminum as long as Revere and Olin were the sole shareholders. Moreover, Ormet was required to sell 66 percent of its production to Olin and 34 percent to Revere, and Olin and Revere were required to buy it.

In 1957 Ormet began construction on a mill and reduction plant in Hannibal, Ohio, and an aluminum plant in Burnside, Louisiana, both of which opened a year later. Also in 1958 Ormet opened the Burnside Bulk Marine Terminal Division. Ormet became the first company to join Alcoa, Kaiser, and Reynolds as producers of primary aluminum and more companies, spurred by government incentives, were to follow. Ormet proved to be a money-losing affair initially. The U.S. government had overestimated the amount of aluminum the country required, leading to a glut in production. On the military front, there was less need for aircraft that relied heavily on aluminum, superseded by missiles, which needed heat-resistant and more durable metals. The aluminum industry found new applications which helped to alleviate the situation, including the introduction of the aluminum can, aluminum foil for packaging, and use of aluminum in high-voltage wire, railroad boxcars, and mobile homes. Nevertheless, the aluminum industry was generally depressed through the 1960s.

By the mid-1960s, Ormet was able to produce about 360 million pounds of aluminum per year, but despite having opened only a few years earlier, the Hannibal plant was in need of upgrading to make it a more cost-effective producer. As a result, in December 1964 Olin and Revere forged a new agreement to create the Olin Revere Realty Company, the purpose of which was to provide land, buildings, and equipment for Ormet.

OLIN SELLS STAKE: 1974

The Olin and Revere ownership arrangement remained intact until 1974 when Olin, displeased with Ormet's performance, sold its half interest to Consolidated Aluminum Corporation, a subsidiary of Swiss aluminum, chemicals, and packaging company Alusuisse Lonza Holding Ltd. Revere's ownership stake was reduced to 34 percent, in proportion to the amount of metal it received from Ormet. Ormet would become a millstone around the neck of Revere, along with other unprofitable units, and it could not cope with a recession in the early 1980s. In 1982 it filed for Chapter 11 bankruptcy protection, and emerged in 1985. A year later it was bought out by private investors, who began to sell off the assets. Not only did Revere want to cut its losses, Consolidated wanted to sell its share of Ormet, which was struggling to be competitive. At the close of 1985

the Burnside alumina plant was shuttered, putting more than 240 people out of work, because alumina could be bought cheaper elsewhere.

While Revere was working on its reorganization plan, Ormet hired a new president, E. Emmett Boyle. "The only way for Ormet to continue was for someone to buy it," he told *Ceramic Industry* in 1993. "So I commenced a leverage buyout in the fall of 1985." Born in 1937, Boyle was a seasoned veteran of the aluminum industry. After earning a mechanical engineering degree from Youngstown University and working as a design and development engineer at McDonnell Aircraft corporation, he went to work for Kaiser Aluminum and Chemical Company in 1965 and worked his way up through the ranks before coming to Ormet. He also earned a master's degree in industrial systems engineering from Ohio University in 1970.

Boyle, his management team, and a group of investors formed Ohio River Associates, Inc., to acquire Ormet. The deal was on the verge of completing the sale when the Hannibal plant was hit with a strike by 1,500 members of the United Steelworkers, delaying the transaction until September 1986. With the strike continuing, the Hannibal plant was run by a skeleton crew of less than 300 people, a number that included supervisors from the decommissioned Burnside plant. The strike finally ended in early 1989 with the steelworkers agreeing to much-needed concessions in wages and benefits. In return, Boyle pledged that every dollar the workers gave up the company would return in the form of preferred stock and profit sharing over the course of three years. The Hannibal plant was reopened, but because about half the smelting operation had been put out of commission, Boyle had to borrow nearly $14 million to restart the company.

Fortunately aluminum prices were on the rebound, allowing Boyle to begin making capital investments, mostly at the Hannibal facility. In addition the Burnside alumina production plant was reopened. In just the first 18 months after buying the company, Boyle and his group invested more in modernization and other improvements than Revere and Consolidated had done in 20 years. By 1993 Ormet invested more than $70 million in capital improvements, all drawn from profits rather than borrowed. In addition, the company had paid back $21 million to the workers when the agreed three-year period came to a close in 1992.

CONSOLIDATED ASSETS ACQUIRED: 1994

Because of its strong turnaround, Ormet was able to pursue a long-term strategy of expanding beyond basic

KEY DATES

1956: The company is founded as a joint venture between Olin Mathieson Chemical Corporation and Revere Copper and Brass.

1958: The Hannibal, Ohio, plant opens.

1974: Olin sells his interest to Consolidated Aluminum Corporation.

1986: R. Emmett Boyle heads a management-led buyout of Ormet.

1994: Ormet acquires assets from Consolidated Aluminum.

2004: Ormet declares Chapter 11 bankruptcy.

2005: The company exits bankruptcy.

aluminum products to add value-added operations and promise greater profits. The company was able to achieve this objective in 1994 when it acquired several operations owned by its former corporate parent, Consolidated Aluminum. Ormet added the Bens Run Recycling facility located in Friendly, West Virginia, to recycle aluminum for the Hannibal plant or third parties; an aluminum coating and foil production operation in Jackson, Tennessee; a rolling mill in Hannibal; and a lamination plant in Iuka, Mississippi, that made aluminum backed with paper or plastic for use as gift wrap, food and drug packaging, and insulation material. These assets comprised subsidiary Ormet Aluminum Mill Products Corp. The company's other holdings formed Ormet Primary Aluminum Corp.

In 1995, Ormet took another step in adding value-added products when it began construction on the Velveflow Cast House, a $15 million plant to produce thixotropic billet, a semi-solid material that could be used in certain automobile components and was also used in the complex joints of such sporting equipment as mountain bikes, snowmobiles, and water craft. Another line of business added through acquisition was the 1997 purchase of Terre Haute, Indiana-based Specialty Blanks, Inc., maker of industrial aluminum alloy blanks used by cookware, lighting, and cylinder makers. The company also sold products to the automotive and aerospace markets for use in making wheels.

Ormet looked to increase its diversification by continuing to invest in capital improvements as well as external growth in the second half of the 1990s. At Burnside the company installed one of the largest cranes on the Mississippi River in 1996. That year also saw the advent of the Ormet Railroad Corporation, a shortline

railroad formed when the company bought a 13-mile stretch of railroad track from the Hannibal rolling mill to Powhatan, Ohio. Ormet bought a majority interest in Formcast, Inc., in 1997. Formcast was a Denver, Colorado-base semi-solid metal caster, the addition of which complimented Ormet's Velvetflow billet business. Ormet also added to its recycling capabilities in 1997, acquiring SPL Recycling LLC and Vortex Corporation. In 1999 Ormet's Formcast unit acquired Buhler North American Casting Development Center from Buhler A.G,. a Swiss manufacturer of die casting machines. Other investments in the late 1990s included the start of a truck fleet to serve customers within 300 miles of the Jackson plant, which also added continuous casting to its operations. In addition, in 1999 Ormet launched a $30 million upgrade of the Burnside Alumina Plant.

A downturn in the economy led to poor business conditions in 2000, ushering in a period of tough times for Ormet. By the end of the year about 200 hourly employees were laid off at the Hannibal plant. Almost all were recalled a few weeks, but this proved to be put a brief respite for the company and its employees. Complicating matters were negotiations with the United Steelworkers union that became protracted after the labor contract at the Hannibal plant expired in May 1999. Ormet was not alone in feeling the pinch. The aluminum industry as a whole suffered from the poor economy, a slump in the manufacturing of aluminum goods, depressed metal prices, overseas competition, and high energy costs. Moreover, Ormet was hit hard by escalating health-care costs.

In late 2001 Ormet decided to once again shutter the Burnside Alumina plant, a move completed in February 2002, because it was again cheaper to buy alumina than to produce it. Several months later Ormet restructured its management ranks. One of those moves included the creation of a separate position of president, filled by Michael Williams, a former U.S. Steel Corp. manager who had been with Ormet since 1999. Williams assumed some of Boyle's responsibilities to allow the CEO and chairman to focus on long-term strategic decisions. In November 2002, Boyle told *American Metal Market,* "During my 40 years in the aluminum business, I have never seen the U.S. industry in more trying times." Indeed, a number of aluminum smelters had gone out of business, part of a longer-term trend. In 1978 there had been 34 U.S. companies involved in the business, but that number had since dwindled to 13.

Alumina prices rebounded in 2003, prompting Ormet to reopen the Burnside facility. The company also decided to focus on its primary aluminum and mill products businesses. As a result in November 2003, Ormet sold its laminaton division in Iuka to Packaging

Dynamics Corp. and was in the market to divest other non-core assets. By the end of the year the company also decided to cut back on mill production at the Hannibal site because alumina prices were so high, electing instead to sell on the open market the alumina Burnside produced that Hannibal would have consumed in making the primary metal.

During this time Ormet was still trying to negotiate a new labor contract and meeting with lenders in an effort to crawl out from under $225 million in debt, which the company was hoping to convert to equity. When those talks broke down, Ormet elected in February 2004 to file for Chapter 11 bankruptcy protection.

Ormet submitted a reorganization plan with the bankruptcy court in September 2004. It called for the New York-based private equity fund MatlinPatterson Asset Management to support the plan with a $30 million infusion of cash, in the process making it the company's largest shareholder. A few weeks later, as the plan of reorganization was expected to receive court approval, Boyle resigned from the company, saying that the timing was right for such a move.

Ormet finally exited Chapter 11 bankruptcy protection in April 2005 with Michael Williams serving as CEO. While the company possessed a clean balance sheet and a new line of credit, its future remained uncertain. In July 2005 Ormet retained a financial advisor, Jefferies and Company, Inc., to consider any offers to buy the company or other strategic arrangements. While Ormet was not sold, in November 2005 it divested some assets, exiting the milled products business. What remained was the Burnside operations and the Hannibal Reduction plant. The restructuring of the company included a relocation of its corporate headquarters from Wheeling, West Virginia, to Canonsburg, Pennsylvania, in 2006.

More changes occurred in 2006. In April, Williams resigned, replaced as president and CEO by Ken Campbell, a former executive at ICF Kaiser as well as Railworks, and HQ Global. A short time later labor talks resumed with the United Steelworkers union, and in July 2006 a contract agreement was finally reached.

Ed Dinger

PRINCIPAL SUBSIDIARIES

Ormet Primary Aluminum Corporation.

PRINCIPAL COMPETITORS

Alcan Inc.; Alcoa Inc.; Norsk Hydro ASA.

FURTHER READING

"The Aluminum Glut," *Barron's National Business and Financial Weekly,* October 16, 1961, p. 1.

Brennan, Terry, "Ormet Goes Bankrupt," *Daily Deal,* February 2, 2004.

"Buyout Considered for Ormet Corp.," *Baton Rouge State Times,* January 9, 1986, p. 3-B.

Foster, Kevin, "Ormet Shuts Two Potlines, Cites Alumina 'Imbalance,'" *American Metal Market,* December 24, 2003, p. 1.

Hatflich, Frank, "Williams Appointed President In Executive Shuffle," *American Metal Market,* November 27, 2002, p. 1.

Hoddeson, David A., "White Hot Potlines," *Barron's National Business and Financial Weekly,* May 31, 1965, p. 3.

Janeway, Patricia A., "Ormet Enhances the Stakes in Specialty Aluminas," *Ceramic Industry,* January 1993, p. 32.

Lamb, Michele R., "Ormet Aluminum Has Something to Prove," *Metal Center News,* November 1997, p. 48.

"Ormet Hopes to Emerge From Chapter 11 by Year-End," *Platt's Metals Week,* February 2, 2004, p. 4.

Petry, Corinna C., "Ormet Eggs in Many Baskets—Diversifications," *American Metal Market,* November 27, 1997.

The PBSJ Corporation

5300 West Cypress Street, Suite 200
Tampa, Florida 33607
U.S.A.
Telephone: (813) 282-7275
Toll Free: (800) 477-7275
Fax: (813) 282-9767
Web site: http://www.pbsj.com

Employee Owned Company
Founded: 1960
Employees: 3,900
Sales: $521 million (2005)
NAIC: 541330 Engineering Services; 541310 Architectural Services; 541320 Landscape Architectural Services; 541370 Surveying and Mapping (Except Geophysical) Services; 541620 Environmental Consulting Services; 541618 Other Management Consulting Services

■ ■ ■

The PBSJ Corporation is a holding company whose wholly owned subsidiaries provide a wide variety of engineering, planning, and construction management services to over 3,000 public and private clients. Post, Buckley, Schuh and Jernigan, Inc. (PBS&J) is one of the largest engineering design firms in the United States and provides most of the corporation's engineering, architectural, and planning services. The other major unit, PBS&J Construction, manages the building of infrastructure projects. Recent projects include conducting environmental impact studies, consulting on intel-

ligent transportation systems, emergency preparedness and homeland security, managing the removal of debris after forest fires and hurricanes, and planning development of recycled water programs. The company has more than 75 offices from California to Puerto Rico.

LAYING THE FOUNDATION: 1960–70

In 1959, Howard M. "Budd" Post was a young engineer working for the Florida State Road Department. Toward the end of the year, William Graham, a prominent South Florida dairyman, approached him with a job offer. Graham had decided to convert some 3,000 acres of pastureland owned by his family into a residential community and wanted Post to come work for his land development company. Post suggested Graham hire an engineering firm where two of Post's best friends worked instead, but the dairyman was not interested in dealing with a big company. Post then said perhaps he should form an engineering company to do the work and Graham accepted the offer.

Post quickly met with those two good friends, George G. Mooney and Robert P. Schuh, and a top sanitary engineer, John D. Buckley, who also worked at the engineering firm Post had recommended to Graham. As their wives played bridge in another room, the four men decided to form a new company, with each of them contributing $125 to create $500 in working capital. On Leap Year Day, February 29, 1960, Bob Schuh became the first full-time employee of the new firm, Robert P. Schuh & Associates, with an office in Hialeah, near Miami. The company's first project was the design

COMPANY PERSPECTIVES

The success of our firm is a direct result of continuing to live our strong company culture and staffing all of our offices with passionate professionals who are focused on the needs of our clients. Our journey continues to be focused and guided by a series of standards that have established how we conduct our business and build professional relationships, now and in the future. Mission: To provide professional services to our clients through technical excellence and innovation. Core Values: belief in the virtues of integrity, hard work and loyalty; relentless in the pursuit of quality and excellence; honor our promises and contracts; belief in open, honest, respectful communications; actively support our professions; and personally invest in our communities.

of Miami Lakes, the first planned "new town" in Florida, on the pastureland owned and developed by the Graham family. Later that year, Post joined Schuh, and the firm was briefly named Post & Schuh.

Before 1961 ended, the other two partners left their day jobs to join the company full time and changed the firm's name to Post, Buckley, Mooney & Schuh. The four founders set as their goal "to provide high quality services to the diverse clients who need them." One of their first decisions was to create a full-service engineering company. Although each of the founders was a civil engineer, he brought an area of specialization to the company. Post handled transportation (highway and bridge) engineering. Buckley dealt with sanitary and environmental work. Mooney managed general civil engineering assignments. Schuh was responsible for project administration as well as participating in transportation assignments. Each project was under the direct supervision of one of the principals, an approach the men found effective in marketing their services.

Over the next few years, the company made other important decisions. One was to develop a balance between public and private sector clients. In 1962, the firm billed $83,000 in fees, including work for its first public clients. Among its projects that year were a hotel project on Grand Bahama Island and school drainage and road design projects in Dade County, Florida. The firm was also appointed town engineers for Miami Springs and county engineer for Monroe County, two local relationships that would last for decades.

One of the founders' most significant decisions was made in 1963, when they initiated the Post, Buckley, Mooney & Schuh Employees Trust, a pioneering profit-sharing program. The partners wanted to hire people passionate about excellent work and customer service, and they saw the Trust as a means of motivating and retaining key employees.

By the middle of the decade, the company had opened its first branch office, in the Florida Keys (Monroe County), and hired Alex M. Jernigan to strengthen the firm's marketing capabilities. Another civil engineer, Jernigan had worked for the development company on the Miami Lakes project. At the end of 1969, the company had grown to four offices in South Florida. It had 140 employees and billings of $5 million. Jernigan was named a principal when Mooney retired for health reasons, and the company marked its tenth anniversary by changing its name to Post, Buckley, Schuh & Jernigan, Inc. For the next several decades the firm was referred to by its full name, but by 2005 was known as PBS&J.

STATEWIDE EXPANSION: 1971–80

Although the company had concentrated on building its business locally, in 1971, PBS&J was ranked 220th among the nation's top design firms by *Engineering News-Record*. During the 1970s, PBS&J strategically expanded throughout Florida.

Florida's economy was flourishing, as tourists, retiree "snowbirds," year-round residents, Cuban immigrants, and new businesses flocked to the state. In 1960, Florida was the tenth most populous state; by 1980, it ranked seventh. Most of the population lived along the coasts, and these areas saw record growth during this period. Central Florida was also growing. Walt Disney World opened in 1971, just outside of Orlando, and in its first two years, more than 20 million people visited the park. (That was 40 times the number of tourists coming to all of Florida in 1950.) Some 50 miles away, around Cape Canaveral, the country's space program generated new jobs, new homes, and new industry. All of this growth required feasibility studies, transportation and water treatment, and wastewater systems, as well as environmental impact studies. During the decade, PBS&J opened offices in carefully selected areas of the state: Dunedin (1972); the Tampa Bay area (1973); Orlando (1974); Fort Myers (1975); and Tallahassee (1976). It also established its first office outside the state, in Atlanta, Georgia, in 1973.

As the firm expanded physically, it was also changing organizationally. In 1973, the Trust established a holding company, PBSJ Corporation, monitored by a

KEY DATES

1960: Robert P. Schuh & Associates is incorporated in Miami, Florida.
1961: Company's name is changed to Post, Buckley, Mooney & Schuh.
1963: Founders create an employee trust, enabling employees to buy into the firm.
1970: Firm renamed Post, Buckley, Schuh & Jernigan, Inc.
1973: The PBSJ Corporation is incorporated.
1977: Construction management services are added.
1980: Architectural services are added.

board of directors consisting of officers and key employees. Within a year it added a stock ownership plan to the Trust, offering certain employees the option to buy stock in the company. Principal associates could buy up to 2.5 percent and senior associates up to 10 percent. (Post, Buckley, Schuh, and Jernigan gave up their controlling interests during the 1980s, and in 2003, all employees could buy shares.) In 1975, Walter Revell, who came to PBS&J in 1968, was named president, the first non-founder to hold that position.

The company weathered the recession of 1974–75, which significantly slowed construction in the state. Then, in 1976, the firm was selected general consultant for the $1.1 billion Miami Metrorail project. In 1977, the company added construction management services to its portfolio and landed the contract for construction engineering and inspection for the 37 bridges connecting U.S. Highway 1 through the Florida Keys. By the end of the decade, PBS&J had grown to 15 offices with 499 employees and annual revenues of $16.5 million.

MOVING BEYOND FLORIDA: 1981–90

PBS&J had 20 years of experience in, and a reputation for, meeting challenges related to improving infrastructure systems in ecologically sensitive locations. It was time to expand beyond Florida, focusing on areas facing similar challenges. Following that strategy, the company went after more international business. It created an international division and won contracts for projects that included transit studies for Santiago, Chile, a $50 million renovation of an airport in Honduras, and a $250 million highway in Dominican Republic. Within a year, international accounts contributed 10 percent of annual revenues. The company continued to diversify,

adding architectural services in 1980.

PBS&J began by opening offices in four more states that had infrastructure and environmental needs similar to Florida: South Carolina, Texas, Tennessee, and New Jersey. In 1983, James Glass, who had been with the company for 20 years, was named president. The company continued to open new offices, primarily in the Southeast. It also was able to expand services and geographic reach through acquisitions, such as HOH Associates, a Denver company known for its land planning of complete communities, and through joint ventures, including one on the Los Angeles Metro Rail, followed by the opening of the company's first office in California. In 1987, PBS&J reorganized the corporate structure from geographic divisions to four service lines: Environmental, Planning and Development, Transportation, and Construction.

The office in Charlotte, North Carolina, which opened in 1988, provided a good example of how the firm planned its expansions. PBS&J spend three and a half years marketing its services in the state before setting up an office. Originally the company thought it would select Raleigh, but there were already a number of transportation engineering firms operating there. According to a 1991 article in the *Business Journal Serving Charlotte and the Metropolitan Area,* they chose Charlotte instead, because of its aggressive transportation program, which was supported by a $100 million bond issue, and for its proximity to South Carolina, where PBS&J was doing a lot of work. "The firm didn't get any of the bond money set aside for three or four major projects, but it did win other projects that might not have been ordered if the bonds had not been issued," PBS&J's regional transportation manager explained.

In 1988, the firm was selected to be general consultant for the Florida Turnpike, with broad responsibility for a multi-million dollar turnpike expansion plan. In 1990, the company had 31 offices, 1,050 employees, and annual revenues of $79.4 million.

BUILDING A NATIONAL ORGANIZATION: 1991–99

The recession in the first years of the decade meant local and state governments had less money to spend on transportation, water and wastewater projects. At the same time, the engineering industry was changing through consolidation, client demands for "one-stop" shopping, and moves to integrate design and construction services. PBS&J took several steps to counter the tightening in its traditional markets, and the resulting increased competition. The firm expanded its international efforts, which had focused on Latin

America, with projects such as a World Bank assignment to design a new town for coal miners in Siberia. It also created national divisions to help clients effectively use emerging technologies, such as designing and managing intelligent transportation and transit systems.

Most critically, the firm expanded through strategic acquisitions, to become a national entity. PBS&J selected companies that contributed to geographic and technical diversification—increasing PBS&J's presence in new or existing markets and/or adding to the firm's technical capabilities. For example, Church Engineering of Nevada, acquired in 1992, provided PBS&J access to that state and the Rocky Mountain region. Coastal Environmental Services, acquired in 1996, added to PBS&J's biostatistics, ecological risk assessment, and watershed management capabilities. To reflect its geographic range, the company designated four regions—East, Florida, Central, and West—to complement its technical service lines of Transportation, Environmental, Civil, and Construction.

PBS&J more than doubled the number of employees during this period. Many of its corporate initiatives at this time focused on increasing communications and building a common corporate culture throughout the organization. The company held encounter groups and workshops to define the corporate mission and instituted a Program Manager Training program, a work sharing/cross-region initiative, an employee recognition awards program, and a corporate-wide employee intranet. In 2000, the firm had 60 offices, 2,400 employees, and annual revenues of $241 million.

PBS&J continued to grow through acquisitions, adding six by mid-decade, and to invest in its employees. In 2002, the company established PBS&J University to oversee its training and development activities. Employees could improve professional, technical and management/leadership skills through classroom training, web-based instruction and on-the-job mentoring programs. The Trust changed its employee stock ownership plan (ESOP) to allow all employees to purchase shares and the company established a Corporate Diversity Advisory Council. In 2003 and 2004, *CE News* magazine ranked PBS&J among the top ten best engineering firms to work for.

INTERNAL CHALLENGES: 2005 AND BEYOND

Early in 2005, John Zumwalt III was named chairman while continuing to serve as chief executive. Todd Kenner was appointed president. Together, these two men represented 48 years of experience with the 45-year-old company and exemplified its efforts to develop and promote employees within the organization. In less than two months they were notifying the Securities and Exchange Commission that an internal inquiry was underway after the company's audit committee discovered accounting irregularities and misappropriation of company assets. Shortly thereafter, the chief financial officer and treasurer (a 20-year employee) resigned, along with two subordinates, voluntarily turning over homes, bank accounts and other assets. The fraud involved inflating the overhead rate on various projects (the costs of rent, insurance, and other non-project-specific expenses). According to a 2006 article in the *St. Petersburg Times,* this resulted in the over-billing of about 3 percent on more than $1 billion worth of work.

PBS&J notified its clients immediately and committed to making full restitution to those effected. The company also created a new position, chief ethics and compliance officer, and began reviewing all of its contracts. With little long-term debt, a large line of credit and positive case flow, the company remained financially strong and functioning.

In mid-2006, the organization announced it had been selected, with the firm Skidmore, Owings & Merrill, in a partnership to transform Fort Belvoir, in Virginia, under the military base realignment and closure legislation. It also began moving the corporate offices from Miami to Tampa.

Ellen D. Wernick

PRINCIPAL SUBSIDIARIES

Post, Buckley, Schuh & Jernigan, Inc. (PBS&J); PBS&J Construction Services; Seminole Development Corporation; PBS&J Caribe Engineering, C.S.P (Puerto Rico); Post, Buckley International, Inc.

PRINCIPAL COMPETITORS

AECOM Technology Corporation; CH2M HILL Cos.; HDR; The Louis Berger Group; Parsons Brinckerhoff Inc.; URS.

FURTHER READING

Boyd, Christopher, "Hot Exports: Architects, Engineers," *Florida Trend,* July 1993, pp. 34–36.

Building the Future: The Heritage of PBS&J, Miami: PBS&J, 2005.

Christensen, Dan, "Millions Gone Missing," *Miami Daily Business Review,* May 12, 2005.

Engel, Clint, "Engineers Build on City's Bustle," *Business Journal Serving Charlotte and the Metropolitan Area,* April

15, 1991, p. 20.

Jackson, Kim M., "PBS&J." *Hydrocarbon Processing,* January 2002, p. 72.

Kirzan, William G., "Diversified Firms Are Chomping at Market," *Engineering News-Record,* April 5, 1993, p. 34.

Kohn, David, "FlaDOT Ends Tie with Consultant," *Engineering News-Record,* August 25, 1988, p. 10.

"Largest Military Base Transformation Under BRAC 2005 Now Underway," PBS&J press release, July 26, 2006.

Miller, Steve, "ESOP Fables (Employee Stock Ownership Plans)," *Top Producer,* December 4. 2005.

Miracle, Barbara, "As We Change, So Do They: Beholden to Their Clients, Florida's Professional Service Firms Reflect the Times," *Florida Trend,* July 1993, p. 38.

Moss, Bill, and Kati Kairies, "Consultant's DOT Ties Still Lucrative," *St. Petersburg Times,* October 10, 1990, p. 1B.

Nickell, David, "Luis Ajamil: Post, Buckley, Schuh & Jernigan," *South Florida Business Journal,* December 14, 1987, p.68.

"PBS&J Chairman Retires, Zumwalt and Kenner Receive New Appointments," PBS&J Press release, February 3, 2005.

"PBS&J Grows with Florida," *Engineering News-Record,* December 15, 1983, p. 30.

"PBS&J Resumes Bidding on New Contracts for Texas and Florida Departments of Transportation," PBS&J press release, July 11, 2006.

Thorner, James, "A Fresh Start for Firm in Tampa," *St. Petersburg Times,* June 30, 2006, p. 1D.

Whitefield, Mimi, "Profile of Post Buckley Schuh & Jernigan," *Miami Herald,* July 13, 1981, Bus. Sec., p. 19.

Perini Corporation

---

73 Mount Wayte Avenue
Framingham, Massachusetts 01701
U.S.A.
Telephone: (508) 628-2000
Fax: (508) 628-2357
Web site: http://www.perini.com

Public Company
Incorporated: 1918 as B. Perini and Sons Inc.
Employees: 2,400
Sales: $1.7 billion (2005)
Stock Exchanges: New York American
Ticker Symbol: PCR
NAIC: 23331 Manufacturing and Industrial Building Construction; 23332 Commercial and Institutional Building Construction

■ ■ ■

Consistently ranked among the top 50 contractors in the United States by *Engineering News Record* magazine, Perini Corporation services the public and private sectors in general contracting, construction management, and design-build services from its world headquarters in Framingham, Massachusetts. Perini has built some of the America's most intriguing and challenging structures, including the Massachusetts Turnpike Extension—the largest highway contract awarded in the 1960s—the Trump Taj Mahal Casino Resort in Atlantic City, New Jersey, the Paris Casino Resort and the Egyptian-themed Luxor Hotel and Casino in Las Vegas, Nevada, and the expansion of the La Guardia Airport in New York. Perini

Corporation is organized into three operating business segments: Building Operations; Civil Operations; and Management Services. The majority of the company's clients are from the hospitality, gaming, corrections, health care, sports, entertainment, and education industries.

EARLY HISTORY

Perini Corporation grew out of the hard work of Italian immigrant Bonfiglio Perini. In 1892, five years after he emigrated from Gotolengo, Italy, where he had been a stone mason, Bonfiglio Perini won contracts to build waterworks projects in the eastern United States. One of his first large contracts was a 20-mile bluestone wall in the Catskill Mountains of New York, which historian Bob Steuding praised in *Constructor* as "a majestic project when you think about it, a giant piece of sculpture." Bonfiglio Perini also built one of the nation's first hot-mixed asphalt highways in 1917 in Rhode Island. In 1918 Bonfiglio Perini brought his sons officially into his business by incorporating the company as B. Perini & Sons, Inc. On Bonfiglio Perini's death in 1924, four of his ten children took control of the company. Louis Perini acted as president, Joseph as treasurer, Ida as secretary, and Charlie, the youngest, eventually became vice-president of equipment. They continued their father's tradition of hard work, setting new paving records in 1930 on the Boston-Worcester Turnpike, their first million-dollar contract.

A POSTWAR PERIOD OF GROWTH

In the 1950s the company name changed to Perini Corporation. This decade was a period of tremendous growth for the company—especially internationally. Perini built the world's largest uranium ore concentrator for Consolidated Denison Mines Ltd. in Ontario, Canada. To secure the company's growth as a large-scale contractor, Louis Perini developed path scheduling—a way of routing project needs—to ensure project efficiency. Louis "was an absolute demon when it came to productivity," his son David Perini told *Constructor.* He was "always looking for a way to do things faster and better." The company quest for efficiency and productivity effected Perini's engineers. By the 1950s, entry-level engineers were prepared for future leadership roles in the company by a 36-month training program that gave them experience in all aspects of construction. The training program, David Perini noted in *Constructor,* was "probably the most important program in the company, because these young engineers are the feedstock, the people who will lead Perini one day." The program continued into the 1990s.

Perini Corporation offered stock to the public in 1961. The company continued its reputation as a large-scale contractor throughout the 1960s, building the 750-foot-high Prudential Center in Boston, the world's tallest building outside of New York at the time, and the Calima Hydroelectric Project in Colombia, South America, which was a 3 million cubic-yard earthfill dam with 35,000 feet of tunnel.

In 1972 the third generation of Perinis assumed control of the company when David Perini took over his father Louis's position as president and chairman. David was well prepared to assume the role; he joined the firm as assistant to general counsel in 1962 after finishing his law degree at Boston College, and served as vice-president, general counsel, and vice-chairman before taking over the top position. Even though David had gained much academic knowledge, Louis served as his role model. "Dad ate and slept the construction business," David told *Constructor.* David remembered that the *Engineering News Record* wrote that "more than a little bit of the heart went out of the construction industry" when Louis Perini passed away. In 1991 the U.S. Army Corps of Engineers Historical Foundation posthumously honored Louis as one of the top contractors in the engineering and construction industry.

Under David Perini's control, Perini concentrated on growth. The company outgrew the second-floor Framingham storefront headquarters that it had occupied since the 1920s and moved to the company's old equipment shops, which it transformed into a modern office building that included a courtyard and sun deck along the Sudbury River. Perini expanded its business operations through investing and acquiring interest in other companies. After the 1974 merger of a Perini-owned Canadian pipeline subsidiary with Wiley Oilfield Hauling, Ltd., Perini gained control of 74 percent of Majestic Contractors Ltd., a Canadian pipeline construction company. This company built section two of the Trans-Alaska Pipeline, which consisted of 82 miles of heavy pipe built above ground and 67 below. In the same year, Perini acquired Mardian Construction Co. of Phoenix, Arizona. After a troubled venture in open-highway construction, the company began in the 1980s to focus on acquiring firms whose specialties, such as civil works and large-scale urban construction, meshed well with the existing Perini businesses. "Most kinds of construction require a certain degree of specialization. It's generally not a good idea to work in someone else's backyard," Kirchenberger noted in the *Providence Business News.* Perini acquired R. E. Dailey & Co. of Detroit, Michigan, in 1980, and Loomis Construction Co. of New Mexico in 1984.

RESTRUCTURING REAL ESTATE ACTIVITIES

In the 1980s, Perini took steps to reorganize its real estate activities. In 1984 the company made its real estate investment division a separate entity called Perini Investment Properties Inc. Perini Corporation and Perini Investment Properties Inc. were autonomous organizations trading under different names on the American Stock Exchange, but David Perini served as chairman

KEY DATES

1892: Bonfiglio Perini wins contracts to build waterworks projects in the eastern United States.

1917: Perini builds one of the nation's first hot-mixed asphalt highways in Rhode Island.

1918: Perini incorporates the company as B. Perini & Sons, Inc.

1961: Perini Corporation goes public.

1980: R. E. Dailey & Co. of Detroit, Michigan, is acquired.

1984: Loomis Construction Co. of New Mexico is purchased.

1993: The company sells its shares of Majestic Contractors, Ltd.

2000: Perini initiates a $40 million recapitalization plan.

2003: James A. Cummings Inc. is acquired.

2005: Perini adds Cherry Hill Construction Inc. and Rudolph and Sletten Inc. to its arsenal.

and major stockholder for each. By the mid-1980s, Perini's real estate activities were confined to its wholly owned subsidiary, Perini Land and Development Company, which owned and managed commercial, residential, and industrial properties. As early as 1957, Perini had begun its investment in developmental property with 5,500 acres in West Palm Beach, Florida. By 1988 Perini Land and Development Company had developed 35 percent of West Palm Beach with housing, commercial development, and entertainment facilities. The Villages of Palm Beach Lakes, a 1,400-acre property holding 4,000 residences, offices, retail shops, golf courses, and more than 7,000 people, "has become one of the most profitable projects" for the company, according to the *Palm Beach Post.* Throughout the early and mid-1980s, David Perini told the *Business Worcester,* "our real estate development operations made the major contribution to our overall results." Perini's real estate profits peaked in 1987 due to ten consecutive years of record earnings in Perini Land and Development Company's five real estate markets: Arizona, California, Florida, Georgia, and Massachusetts. Its holdings in Florida contributed the most toward profits.

Perini Land and Development Company ensured the appeal of their real estate through unique marketing techniques. Eager to attract buyers in Golden Gateway Commons, its eight-year-old condominium project in San Francisco, California, Perini Land and Development Company hired the Mulhauser and Young advertising agency to craft a fresh approach. Starting with a new name and logo, Mulhauser and Young promoted the 1,254-unit project as a neighborhood. The most influential aspect of the marketing campaign, however, was a direct mail campaign that included cans of spaghetti, a bar of chocolate in the shape of the new logo, and a shopping bag that listed the neighborhood shopping attractions. Moreover, Perini Land and Development Company advertised in the real estate and business sections of the Sunday *San Francisco Examiner and Chronicle* and the western edition of the *Wall Street Journal,* instead of the traditional trade and consumer press.

Perini's real estate success slowed in late 1988 as the real estate industry slumped, and by the early 1990s this portion of the company accounted for only 5 percent of corporate revenues. However, as the company incurred losses in its real estate investments, the company's construction divisions began to report record earnings. The construction business grew to be the most significant contributor to profits in the early 1990s. Reacting to this shift in trends, Perini consolidated its general construction divisions into the Perini Building Company Inc. in December 1991 to further penetrate the nationwide building market. The consolidation was designed to allow Perini to take advantage of its name recognition; until that time Perini's acquisitions had acted independently. The Loomis, Mardian, and R. E. Dailey companies were united into the Perini Building Company in name, but continued to operate from their existing offices. Eastern U.S. Division headquarters are located in Framingham, Massachusetts, Western U.S. Division headquarters in Phoenix, and Central U.S. Division headquarters in Detroit. Perini gathered the construction division's executive, administrative, and operational functions into the corporate structure, which centralized decision-making and project allocation.

Perini reorganized its heavy construction division in that same period. The heavy construction division had extensive experience in building mass transit systems like the San Francisco Bay Area Rapid Transit system, and in building infrastructure projects like the Tunnel and Reservoir Plan in Chicago. Perini targeted the infrastructure market for growth into the year 2000 because, according to materials published by the company, "over 40 percent of the nation's bridges are rated deficient, and roughly the same percentage of highway miles are in poor or fair condition." Anticipating the need for future efficiency, Perini divided the heavy construction division into two operating entities, the Metropolitan New York Division and the U.S. Heavy Division. The Metropolitan New York Division handled contracts in New York and other large eastern cities, such as Baltimore and Washington, D.C., while the U.S. Heavy Division was responsible for work throughout the rest of the United States.

Perini International's projects made significant contributions to Perini earnings beginning in 1985. The international division has worked in 20 countries, primarily on the construction of U.S. embassies. The division has erected U.S. embassy buildings in Zaire, Gabon, Brazil, and Paraguay. In 1992 the division continued to build for the U.S. Department of State in Djibouti and Venezuela, for the U.S. Air Force in Egypt, and for the National Oil Company in Morocco. The division also began efforts to expand into new overseas markets, focusing initially on Mexico and Latin America.

JOINT VENTURES LEAD TO GROWTH

A source of past success and future growth for Perini was the joint venture. Forming joint ventures was one way that Perini has diversified its operations, won large infrastructure contracts, built its reputation, and shared its financial risk. Executive vice-president of construction Thomas Dailey said in *Perini: Second Century* that Perini's "shared sense of purpose has enabled our joint venture partnerships to be successful, and to contribute to our growth and reputation." Perini began working with other firms beginning in the 1890s, and relationships forged during World War II allowed the company to expand into Australia, Canada, India, and South America. Some projects that Perini contributed to through joint ventures were the Trans-Alaskan Pipeline, the North River Water Pollution Control Project in New York City, and the Trump Taj Mahal Casino Resort.

In 1988 Perini sought further growth through a joint venture in the hazardous waste cleanup market. The company joined with Ashland Technology and Versar Inc. to form Perland Environmental Technologies Inc., which provides scientific, environmental engineering and construction services for hazardous-waste management and cleanup. Perini controlled 90 percent of Perland Environmental Technologies in 1991. That year Perland won a $19 million award to work on the New Bedford harbor Superfund site in Massachusetts. Perland positioned itself to take advantage of the market growth by seeking out projects that would expand its expertise. It has worked on soil stabilization, incineration, and groundwater treatment at Superfund sites in Michigan. Perini expected Perland to contribute significantly to profits, noting that the hazardous waste-cleanup market grew 15 percent in the early 1990s, and that the company expected the market to expand to $5 billion per year by 2000.

In the early 1990s company management, anticipating Perini's future growth, initiated a plan called Mission 2000 to attempt to anticipate the company's needs in the year 2000. Teamwork between company divisions, subsidiaries, trade organizations, and through joint venture partnerships was cited as "a prerequisite for success." Allying Perini with companies whose specialties enhance Perini's work helped the company remain competitive. Given the goal of working with companies that work in similar fields, Perini sold its share of the pipeline company, Majestic Contractors, Ltd., in early 1993 because Majestic's core business did not mesh well with Perini's other divisions. The resultant divisions and subsidiaries could all work together through internal joint ventures. One such internal joint venture between the Eastern U.S. Building Division and the U.S. Heavy Division allowed Perini to work on a $190 million project at the Deer Island residuals treatment facility in Boston, which included building sludge and gas storage tanks.

Perini's competitiveness, noted David Perini in a company publication, would be enhanced by the company's participation in public/private ventures, which included prisons, health centers, sports arenas, and toll roads. Public/private ventures were projects which traditionally had been paid for with taxes but were increasingly being funded by private investors. Project development vice-president Robert Band explained in a company publication that "public/private ventures leverage future revenues generated by projects such as toll roads, lease-back prisons and sports arenas, and present them as the credit in the financial transaction." Tolls, rent monies, and ticket sales supplement or even replace tax dollars in these projects. Band called Perini's public/private venture approach, which included project design, finance arrangement, and a guaranteed maximum construction cost, "the project delivery system of the future." The company used this approach when it built the Somerset County Prison in Pennsylvania, which allowed the state to lease the prison for 20 years instead of purchasing it outright.

In addition to securing its reputation through new projects and joint ventures, Perini was concerned with maintaining a company supportive of its employees' needs. Concerned about the rights of nonsmokers in the mid-1980s, Perini constructed smoking lounges that had large fans to draw out smoke to accommodate its employees who smoked. Vice-president of human resources Douglas Mure said that "we were ahead of the game," when the Environmental Protection Agency declared passive smoke a carcinogen. Perini emphasized safety as well as health by giving an annual President's Award for safety. The company also employed a retired Occupational Safety and Health Administration (OSHA) inspector to inspect facilities weekly and paid foremen to go to safety meetings. "If they come to [the meetings], have no recordable injuries for the week, pass a safety inspection and give their crews a 'tool-box talk' on safety, they win a $50 bond," according to the *Rochester Business Journal.*

Even though Perini regarded itself as a family-owned business, it recognized the advantages of employee ownership in a company. In 1992 the company revised its all-cash bonus plan for top executives and operating management to include 60 percent common stock and 40 percent cash. The cash savings would be invested in company growth and the stock awards would "promote stock ownership among many employees," vice-president of finance James Markert relayed to the *Wall Street Journal.* The adjustment would affect about 100 of the company's 2,000 employees.

Anticipating growth into Perini's second century of business, the company planned to double its construction operations by expanding its work in infrastructure, environmental and general building markets. The company decided to stay in the real estate business but to reduce its level of investments. In his 1992 message to stockholders, David Perini focused on Perini's reputation. He noted that "a company and its reputation are like a building. They take much longer to build than to demolish. Build your image and reputation and do nothing to damage your good name."

REVERSAL OF FORTUNE

The late 1990s proved to be challenging for the company as various real estate investments turned sour, which left profits faltering. In 1999, the company reported a net loss of $16.04 per share. In 2000, Perini initiated a $40 million recapitalization plan that increased its net worth to $38 million, allowing it to focus on its core construction operations.

The company's fortunes began to turn around and in 2002, the company reported its third highest net income in its history—$23.1 million—due in part to the completion of several projects in the hospitality and gaming industries. Perini Management Services had a good year as well and secured U.S. government contracts to update embassy locations across the globe. Perini also benefited from contracts related to the rebuilding of Iraq and Afghanistan. Other new contracts included the construction of Glendale Arena in Phoenix, Arizona; hotel expansion in Atlantic City; new Hard Rock hotels in Tampa and Hollywood, Florida; the Chumash Casino & Resort in Santa Ynez, California; and the Pala Hotel & Casino in Pala, California.

While the company was experiencing growth, especially in its building operations segment, it did face challenges brought on by an overall economic slowdown in the United States and its company's exposure to losses related to its involvement in Boston's "Big Dig" project—this multi-billion dollar tunnel project routed Interstate 93 under downtown Boston and is known as one of the most controversial and expensive public works projects in the United States.

Nevertheless, Perini forged ahead with its growth plans. The company expanded its foothold in the southeastern United States in 2003 by purchasing James A. Cummings Inc., a builder of educational, municipal, and commercial developments. Two years later, the company added Cherry Hill Construction Inc. and Rudolph and Sletten Inc. to its arsenal. The latter, a California-based building contractor and construction management company, had $700 million in annual revenues at the time of the deal.

Perini appeared to be on track for future success with a construction backlog of nearly $7.9 billion at the end of 2005. By focusing on healthcare facilities and casino projects, Perini had carved out a coveted niche in that sector of the industry. During 2005, the company landed several lucrative contracts including the MGM Project City Center, a $3.4 billion urban complex covering 66 acres located between the Bellagio and the Monte Carlo casino resorts in Las Vegas. The project included a 4,000-room hotel tower, casino, convention center, showroom, 500,000 square feet of retail and restaurants, three boutique hotels, and several residential towers. Perini also secured a $1.28 billion contract to work on The Cosmopolitan Resort and Casino located on the Las Vegas strip adjacent to the Bellagio Hotel and Casino. This project included the construction of two high-rise hotel and condo hotel towers 600 feet tall.

Sara and Tom Pendergast
Updated, Christina M. Stansell

PRINCIPAL SUBSIDIARIES

Perini Building Company; Perini Civil Construction; Perini Management Services Inc.; James A. Cummings Inc.; Cherry Hill Construction; Rudolph and Sletten Inc.

PRINCIPAL COMPETITORS

Clark Enterprises Inc.; The Turner Corporation; Washington Group International Inc.

FURTHER READING

Caffrey, Andrew, "Heard in New England: Perini's Cleanup of Balance Sheet Can Hoist Builder's Stock, Bulls Say," *Wall*

Street Journal, March 8, 2000.

DuPont, Dale K., "Construction Firm Buys Broward, Fla.–Based Builder," *Knight-Ridder/Tribune Business News,* December 20, 2002.

Fortin, Frank, "Perini Has Deep Roots in State," *Providence Business News* (Rhode Island), September 12, 1988.

Herring, Ben L., "Perini: Quality Construction Since 1892," *Constructor,* December 1990, pp. 63–65.

"Perini Corp.: Cash Bonus Plan Revised to Consist of 60% Stock," *Wall Street Journal,* March 19, 1992, p. C15.

"Perini Corp. Completes Acquisition of Jessup-Based Cherry Hill Construction," *Daily Record,* January 25, 2005.

"Perini Corporation Completes Acquisition of Rudolph and Sletten, Inc.," *Business Wire,* October 4, 2005.

Perini: Second Century, Vols. 1–2, Framingham, Mass.: Perini, 1992.

Phelps, Richard, "Perini Posts Big Numbers," *Business Worcester,* June 13, 1988.

Regan, Keith, "150 Top Public Companies: Perini Corp., Roll of the Dice," *Boston Business Journal,* May 7, 2004, p. S10.

Robbins, Jonathan, "Perini Loses $17.9M in '85; Outlook Appears Brighter for '86," *Middlesex News* (Framingham, Mass.), February 22, 1986.

Saef, Scott, "Linstroth to Leave Perini Co.," *Palm Beach Post,* April 9, 1988.

Weinberg, Neil, "Perini Returning Construction Group to Corporate Fold," *Middlesex News* (Framingham, Mass.), July 10, 1992.

Young, Jill, "Chocolate Logos, Spaghetti in Recipe to Market Condos," *San Francisco Business Times,* February 15, 1988.

Pick 'n Pay Stores Ltd.

PO Box 23087, Claremont
Cape Town, 7735
South Africa
Telephone: (27) 21 658 1000
Fax: (27) 21 683 2514
Web site: http://www.picknpay.co.za

Public Company
Incorporated: 1968
Employees: 34,484
Sales: ZAR 35.08 billion ($4.48 billion) (2006)
Stock Exchanges: Johannesburg
Ticker Symbol: PIK
NAIC: 445110 Supermarkets and Other Grocery (except Convenience) Stores; 445210 Meat Markets; 445292 Confectionery and Nut Stores; 445299 All Other Specialty Food Stores; 551112 Offices of Other Holding Companies

■ ■ ■

Pick 'n Pay Stores Ltd. is South Africa's leading food, clothing, and general merchandise retailer. The Cape Town–based company has long been a champion of "consumer sovereignty," focusing primarily on the discount retail market. Pick 'n Pay operates through a number of retail formats, including 14 Pick 'n Pay hypermarkets and 106 Pick 'n Pay supermarkets. The company also operates the Pick 'n Pay Pantry convenience store format, as well as franchise grocery operations under the Pick 'n Pay Family format; more than 130 Score retail stores throughout South Africa, as

well as in Botswana and Swaziland; and a small number of stores in Namibia.

In addition, the company owns the Franklins supermarket group in Australia. In June 2006, Pick 'n Pay expanded its South African presence again with the acquisition of Fruit & Veg City, which operates nearly 90 company-owned and franchised stores throughout South Africa. The company also has extended its range of customer services with the creation of the Go Banking joint venture with Nedbank. Listed on the Johannesburg Stock Exchange, Pick 'n Pay remains controlled by founder and Chairman Raymond Ackerman, and Sean Summers serves as CEO. In 2006, the company's revenues are expected to top ZAR 35 billion ($4.4 billion).

SOUTH AFRICA'S RETAIL REVOLUTIONARY IN 1967

Raymond Ackerman was born in 1931 into one of South Africa's leading retailing families—father Gus Ackerman had founded the Ackermans department store chain in 1916. Raymond Ackerman studied commerce at the University of Cape Town under noted economist W.H. Hutt. Hutt's ideas, particularly his philosophy of "customer sovereignty," were to have a lasting impact on the young Ackerman.

Having graduated from University, Ackerman went to work for his father's business as a trainee manager in 1951. Ackerman's first position with his father's company, however, was as a store greeter. In this way Ackerman's father hoped to instill the importance of politeness for the store's customers, while also helping

COMPANY PERSPECTIVES

OUR MISSION: We serve. With our hearts we create a great place to be. With our minds we create an excellent place to shop. OUR VALUES: We are passionate about our customers and will fight for their rights. We care for, and respect each other. We foster personal growth and opportunity. We nurture leadership and vision, and reward innovation. We live by honesty and integrity. We support and participate in our communities. We take individual responsibility. We are all accountable.

Ackerman overcome his shyness. Ackerman later worked for two years in the company's distribution warehouse.

By then, Ackermans had been bought by department store rival Greatermans, based in Johannesburg (and which reportedly took its name from its ambition to be greater than Ackermans). Raymond Ackerman was offered a new position at Greatermans, and served as manager at a series of small-town stores into the mid-1950s. The introduction of the first American-styled self-service supermarkets in the early 1950s inspired Greatermans to expand into food retailing as well. The company added a supermarket to its Springs store, placing Ackerman in the store as assistant manager.

The experience proved a life-altering one for Ackerman, who found his true calling in food retailing. Persuaded by the potential of the supermarket format in South Africa, Ackerman encouraged Greatermans to launch its own supermarket format, called Checkers, in 1955. Two years later, Ackerman and wife Wendy traveled to the United States to study the supermarket sector more closely. There, Ackerman took a decidedly hands-on approach, working for some six months in nearly every area of the supermarket operation—from stocking shelves to serving in the butcher section. During his U.S. trip, Ackerman also met up with Bernard Trujillo, the so-called "Pope of Modern Distribution," who held that customer sovereignty represented an "enlightened form of self-interest." Trujillo became, alongside Gus Ackerman and Hutt, another major influence in Ackerman's rapidly evolving retail philosophy.

Upon returning to South Africa, Ackerman set out to build the Checkers chain. Yet Ackerman ran into a great deal of resistance from the Greatermans board, which saw the company as a department store group, not a supermarket company. While lacking a free hand to develop the Checkers format—and especially to implement his own retail philosophy—Ackerman nonetheless succeeded in expanding the chain from just five stores at the beginning of the 1960s to more than 85 by 1965. In that year, Ackerman shared an award—as the Outstanding Young South African—with Gary Player. Indeed, by then, the Checkers chain not only had become a leading supermarket group in South Africa, it also had begun to outpace Greatermans itself.

The success of Checkers, however, led to soured relations between Ackerman and the Greatermans board. As Ackerman himself told the *Sunday Times,* "It reached a point where there was a jealousy factor. It was like the tail wagging the dog." The situation came to a head in 1966 with the death of Gus Ackerman, who had served as a director at Greatermans. Within two weeks, Raymond Ackerman found himself fired from Greatermans, given just two weeks' severance pay.

Yet Ackerman soon turned this setback into a new opportunity. In early 1967, Ackerman returned to Cape Town and negotiated to acquire four small stores, called Pick 'n Pay, from Jack Goldin (who then founded the Clicks retail group in 1968). Now the owner of his own stores, Ackerman was able to put his retail philosophy fully to the test and set out to become "the housewives friend." A key component in Ackerman's formula was his insistence on discount pricing, enabling him to undercut his competitors. In order to pay for the stores, Ackerman invested most of his own money, while raising the remainder of the funding from a small group of shareholders. By 1968, however, the company had gone public, listing its stock on the Johannesburg Stock Exchange.

Success came quickly—by the end of its first year, Pick 'n Pay Stores Ltd. had already topped ZAR 5 million in sales, turning a profit of more than ZAR 300,000. By the following year, the company had doubled its sales. Pick 'n Pay's success, however, caught the attention of rivals Checkers and OK Bazaars (which had introduced the self-service supermarket format to South Africa in the early 1950s). The two companies started a price war in order to slow the growth of Ackerman's chain.

Instead, Ackerman leapt at an opportunity to acquire a new store in Port Elizabeth, allowing the company to enter the Eastern Cape market. The move forced Checkers and OK Bazaars to choose between expanding the price war they had launched, or withdrawing. In the end, Pick 'n Pay's rivals chose the latter, and the Cape Town company began its ascension to becoming South Africa's leading retail group.

KEY DATES

1967: Raymond Ackerman buys four stores in Cape Town and establishes a discount supermarket format.
1968: Pick 'n Pay Stores Ltd. goes public with a listing on the Johannesburg Stock Exchange.
1975: Pick 'n Pay launches South Africa's first hypermarket.
1984: After opening a store in Brisbane, Pick 'n Pay is forced to exit the Australian market; Boardman's hardware store chain is acquired.
1994: A new corporate culture and structure is developed following an extended strike by employees; the Family franchise supermarket format is launched.
2002: The company purchases Franklins retail group in New South Wales, Australia.
2006: The company acquires Fruit & Veg City, with nearly 90 stores throughout South Africa.

HYPERMARKET PIONEER IN 1975

Pick 'n Pay quickly captured the attention of South Africa's financial community as well. By the end of the decade, the company had begun receiving praise from the financial press, and soon was named to the *Sunday Times'* Top 100 companies list. Ackerman's commitment to consumer sovereignty remained a major component of the group's success, helping to guide its operations. In this way, the company started to take on the wholesale sector, dominated by a number of government-backed cartels that had helped maintain artificially high prices on most goods sold in the country, including basic food items. Ackerman found ways to skirt the high prices, often imposed by the South African government itself. A notable example of this came early in the 1970s when Ackerman took the company's entire treasury to buy a warehouse full of cigarettes. When the government imposed price increases on new cigarette imports, Pick 'n Pay was able to sell its stock of cigarettes at a substantial discount.

Pick 'n Pay continued to expand beyond the Cape Town region. Its move into the important Johannesburg market was met with resistance, however. The company's own survival appeared at stake, after a suspicious fire destroyed its first Johannesburg store, in Blackheath. Ackerman also blamed the fire as the cause of his mother's death. As Ackerman told the *Financial Mail:* "This was a devastating event, not just because it could

have caused the demise of the fledgling Pick 'n Pay chain, but because it probably also contributed to the death of my mother. She had warned me that the company was growing too quickly and she died while reading the account of the fire in the newspaper."

Yet Ackerman seemed only the more determined to impose his retailing vision on the South African market. In 1973, the company announced that it would be building the country's first "hypermarket." The new large-scale format, which combined department store offerings with supermarket operations, had been developed in France by the growing Carrefour department store group—the leaders of which had also been inspired by Trujillo's retail ideas. Pick 'n Pay opened the doors of its first hypermarket in 1975, smashing all previous sales records.

With Pick 'n Pay's rise to the top of South Africa's retail scene in full swing, Ackerman next attempted to expand the company's format into a new market, entering Australia with a highly successful store in Brisbane in the early 1980s. Yet the company's attempt to open a second store in Melbourne in 1984 became caught up in the growing international resistance to South Africa's apartheid policies. Ironically, Pick 'n Pay itself had long served as a model anti-apartheid group—indeed, the company had long been a champion of South Africa's own anti-apartheid movement. Long before the end of apartheid, the company's management had been fully integrated, with some 50 percent of all management positions held by black South Africans.

Forced to withdraw from Australia, the company licked its wounds by expanding its South African retail presence, acquiring the Boardman's hardware chain in 1984. The purchase helped raise the company's profile, and boost sales to more than ZAR 2 billion by 1986—more than doubling sales in just three years. The company continued to build the Pick 'n Pay chain as well, and by the end of the decade, the company operated more than 100 stores throughout the country.

SOUTH AFRICAN RETAIL LEADER IN THE NEW CENTURY

Despite its progressive policies, Pick 'n Pay was again caught by the political environment as apartheid came to an end. In 1994, the company found itself faced with a strike by its employees. Yet Ackerman turned this crisis into an opportunity for renewed corporate growth. The company worked out a new trade union agreement, but, perhaps of more importance, set into place a new corporate culture to guide its entry into the new century. At the same time, the company established a new organizational structure, based on two core divisions:

Retail, which took over the various Pick 'n Pay formats, as well as the Family franchise store format launched in 1994, and others; and Group Enterprises, which took over the company's acquisition of a majority stake in the predominantly rural-based Score supermarket group, as well as other retail businesses. Increasingly, Pick 'n Pay also targeted international expansion, adding stores in the neighboring markets of Botswana, Swaziland, and Namibia. The company also briefly entered Tanzania, but sold its holdings there in 2002.

Instead, the company targeted a re-entry into the Australian market, buying up struggling retailer Franklins there. The purchase brought the company more than 50 stores under the Franklins and No Frills formats, primarily in the New South Wales market. Despite the continuing losses of its Franklin division into the mid-decade, in 2006, Pick 'n Pay reaffirmed its intention to maintain its Australian presence.

Pick 'n Pay in the meantime continued to expand its presence in South Africa, with a steady stream of its new store openings. The company also maintained its commitment to customer service, launching in 2005 a partnership with Nedbank to launch GO Banking, an in-store banking service that featured checking and savings accounts customers could literally buy off the shelf. The following year, the company expanded its South Africa retail presence yet again, agreeing to acquire Fruit & Veg City, a chain of nearly 90 stores throughout South Africa. After nearly 40 years, Pick 'n Pay remained true to its philosophy of customer sovereignty—and continued to reap its rewards.

M. L. Cohen

PRINCIPAL SUBSIDIARIES

Boxer Fresh Meats (Pty.) Ltd.; Boxer Holdings (Pty.) Ltd.; Boxer Superstores (Pty.) Ltd.; Franklins Pty. Ltd. (Australia); Franklins Supermarkets Pty. Ltd. (Australia); Fresco Supermarket Holdings Pty. Ltd. (Australia); Guardrisk Insurance Company Ltd.; InterFrank Group Holdings Pty. Ltd. (Australia); KwaZulu Cash & Carry (Pty.) Ltd.; Mfolozi Properties (Pty.) Ltd.; Pick 'n Pay (Gabriel Road) (Pty.) Ltd.; Pick 'n Pay Franchise Financing (Pty.) Ltd.; Pick 'n Pay Garages (Pty.) Ltd.; Pick 'n Pay Insurance Company Ltd.; Pick 'n Pay International Ltd. (U.K.); Pick 'n Pay Namibia (Pty.) Ltd. (Namibia); Pick 'n Pay Retailers (Pty.) Ltd.; Score Supermarkets (Botswana) (Pty.) Ltd.; Score Supermarkets (Swaziland) Ltd.; Score Supermarkets (Trading) (Pty.) Ltd.; Score Supermarkets Operating Ltd.; The Blue Ribbon Meat Corporation (Pty.) Ltd.

PRINCIPAL COMPETITORS

Shoprite Holdings Ltd.; Spar Group Ltd.; Woolworths Holdings Ltd.; Massmart Holding Ltd.

FURTHER READING

Ackerman, Raymond, *Hearing Grasshoppers Jump: The Story of Raymond Ackerman,* Johannesburg: David Phillips Publishers, 2001.

Barron, Chris, "Diary of a Retail Revolutionary," *Sunday Times* (South Africa), November 11, 2001.

Gilmour, Chris, "The Champion of Consumer Sovereignty," *Financial Mail,* March 10, 2006.

———, "The Original," *Financial Mail,* March 10, 2006.

"Pick 'n Pay Clarifies Its Position in Australia," *Cape Business News,* May 29, 2006.

"Pick 'n Pay Expands into the Eastern Cape in Response to Growth," *East Cape News,* November 21, 2003.

"Pick 'n Pay Lifts Profit on Price Reduction Policy," *Africa News Service,* October 20, 2004.

"Pick 'n Pay Reins in Costs to Lift Earnings 20 Percent," *Africa News Service,* April 20, 2005.

"Pick 'n Pay to Acquire Fruit & Veg," *Sunday Times* (South Africa), June 13, 2006.

"Pick 'n Pay to Build Nine New Supermarkets," *Africa News Service,* May 26, 2005.

Thomas, Stafford, "Pick 'n Pay and Nedbank Go Banking," *Retail Banker International,* May 19, 2005, p. 5.

Pilot Pen Corporation of America

60 Commerce Drive
Trumbull, Connecticut 06611
U.S.A.
Telephone: (203) 377-8800
Fax: (203) 377-4024
Web site: http://www.pilotpen.us

Wholly Owned Subsidiary of Pilot Corporation
Incorporated: 1970
Employees: 85 (est.)
Sales: $200 million (2005 est.)
NAIC: 339941 Pen and Mechanical Pencil Manu-
facturing

■ ■ ■

Pilot Pen Corporation of America is the U.S. subsidiary of Pilot Corporation, Japan's oldest and largest writing instrument manufacturer. In addition to its headquarters in Trumbull, Connecticut, Pilot Pen maintains an assembly and distribution facility in Jacksonville, Florida, and a distribution operation in Guadalajara, Mexico.

The company's product offerings include a variety of ball point, roller ball, gel, and fountain pens, as well as styli, mechanical pencils, markers, and highlighters. They are sold under such trademarks as VBall, Dr. Grip, Razor Point, Vanishing Point, Precise, EasyTouch, Nel-Gel, G2, and Varsity. Pilot Pen also sells high-end pens under the Namiki name, manufactured in Japan, and ranging in price from $35 for a ball point pen to $8,500 for an Emperor Collection fountain pen. On the other end of the spectrum, Pilot Pen develops new technolo-gies, licensed to other companies, including magnetic drawing panels, which can be written on and erased with an eraser bar; thermal transfer ribbon, used by the garment industry to print clothing labels; and a counting pen that keeps track of checked-off items, used by contractors and others.

PARENT COMPANY'S EARLY 20TH CENTURY ORIGINS

Pilot Corporation was founded by Ryosuke Namiki. Born in Japan in 1880, Namiki graduated from Tokyo Mercantile Marine and then became a professor there after a stint as a merchant ship's chief engineer. As part of his work he made drawings for ship designs using technical pens. He began making improvements to the instruments, and in 1909 he received a patent on a non-clogging drafting pen. He then turned his attention to developing a durable gold nib point to improve fountain pens. After almost six years of effort, Namiki perfected a process for making pen nibs, with gold and an iridium alloy, that were especially suited to the writing of Japanese characters and script. In 1915, with the financial backing of several friends, he quit his professorship to launch a small Tokyo-area factory to produce the nibs. A year later he expanded beyond nibs and began producing complete fountain pens. In 1918 he took on a partner, Masao Wada, a friend and classmate, and the business was incorporated as the Namiki Manufacturing Company Ltd., capitalized with ¥200,000. In keeping with the company's nautical roots, they chose "Pilot" (a helmsman or a licensed seaman who guides ships in and out of harbors or through dangerous waters) as a trade name. The company's logo depicted the letter "p" in the middle of a circular buoy.

In 1925 Namiki Manufacturing introduced lacquer pen bodies. For decades fountain pen bodies had been made from ebonite, a vulcanized sulfur and rubber compound that had replace ebony. While the material was inexpensive and durable, ebonite's glossy black surface eventually faded after exposure to sun and the elements. Namiki Manufacturing added raw lacquer to the ebonite to create a patented laccanite process, which produced a permanent glossy black surface, one resistant to scratching and fading. The company soon used the new surface to create decorations to distinguish its pens from the wares of foreign competitors. Given Japan's 1,000-year tradition of maki-e, a lacquer art form, it was not surprising that the company began hiring lacquer artists to decorate the pens. With an impressive selection of sample pens, Namiki and Wada set off on a worldwide tour to show their pens to enthusiastic buyers. Within the year, Namiki Manufacturing opened branches in Shanghai, Singapore, London, and New York. Merchants who carried the pens included Tiffany's in New York, Asprey in London, and Cartier in Paris. In 1927 legendary English retailer Alfred H. Dunhill, best known for his tobacco pipes, smoking supplies and luxury goods, began to carry Namiki pens at the Paris store he had opened three years earlier. Dunhill soon secured the distribution rights to Namiki maki-e-decorated pens and pencils in several countries under the Dunhill Namiki label, and then in 1930 became the distributor of all Namiki products worldwide except in Japan, China, and the United States.

U.S. SUBSIDIARY FORMED: 1972

In 1938 Namiki Manufacturing changed its name to Pilot Pen Co., Ltd. With the advent of World War II, business was disrupted and the Dunhill relationship came to an end. After the war Pilot Pen rebuilt its business, resumed producing decorative lacquer pens, and in 1961 added a mass-market line with the production of ballpoint pens. The company launched a subsidiary in Brazil in 1953 and opened in an office in Europe in 1967 that several years later became The Pilot Pen

Europe GmbH. Pilot Pen Corporation of America was established in 1972.

The new American operation acted as a distributor, possessing no manufacturing capabilities. It enjoyed modest growth in its first three years, building annual sales to the $1 million level. Then, in 1975, the parent company hired the national sales manager of rival Bic Pen Co., Ronald Shaw, to become the U.S. national sales manager. He would drive the growth of the stateside subsidiary for the next three decades.

Born Ronald Schurowitz in 1938, Shaw grew up in Miami, Florida, the son of a uniform company driver and salesman. He graduated from the University of Miami, where he majored in radio, television, and film. He worked as a radio announcer and became an aspiring stand-up comedian, and was talented enough to provide the opening act for the likes of Dean Martin, Liberace, Connie Francis, and Dean Martin, working in nightclubs from the Catskills to Miami. Although in his early 20s, Shaw was already married and the rigors of the road, the late hours, and the unsteady work of the entertainment business did not mesh with family life. Thus, in 1961 he began looking for a regular job, answered a newspaper ad from Bic and beat several dozen other applicants for the sales position. The trained entertainer proved well suited to sales, and quickly distinguished himself. In 1969, at the age of 30, Shaw became Bic's national sales manager, the youngest in the industry to hold that post.

When Shaw left Bic for Pilot Pen in 1975, he was joining a company that was little known by U.S. consumers, and he faced the daunting challenge of virtually building a brand from scratch. He recognized that one of the company's products, the extra-fine point Razor Point pen, had potential as a mass market product that could establish the Pilot Pen brand. At the time, the Razor Point was marketed as a technical writing instrument for professionals, such as architects and engineers, but Shaw believed that the judicious use of advertising could successfully pitch the fine-point pen to general consumers who would appreciate its attributes. However, as Shaw explained to *Industry Week* in a 2002 profile, "Conventional thinking wouldn't have worked. If we had gone to the consumer and simply said that our pen wrote longer or smoother without leaking, we'd be merely parroting the timeworn claims of our competitors. I knew we had to market the product a different way, and humor was the route I took."

First, however, Shaw would have to find the $75,000 he determined he needed to pay for the advertising. He flew to Japan for the first time in order to make a personal appeal to the chairman of the parent company. It proved to be an eye-opening experience for Shaw,

KEY DATES

1918: Namiki Manufacturing Company is founded in Japan.
1938: Namiki changes its name to The Pilot Pen Co., Ltd.
1972: Pilot Corporation of America is formed.
1975: Ronald Shaw joins the company.
1986: Shaw is named president of Pilot.
1993: Shaw is named CEO.
1995: The Jacksonville, Florida, operation is launched.
2001: The Jacksonville expansion is completed.
2004: Shaw's heir apparent, Dennis Burleigh, is named COO.

who began to learn Japanese customs by repeatedly breaching them. He refused an offer of tea and a chance to sit, insisting that he would like to make his presentation as soon as possible. Once ushered into the chairman's office, Shaw again brushed aside the usual courtesies to begin making his case for a marketing budget. As Shaw wrote later about the experience, the chairman "listened carefully, nodding his head and smiling and looking as if he could not be more pleased. I assumed I was doing great and would definitely close the deal. At the end of my presentation, he stood up, expressed profuse admiration for my intentions, and said, 'Shaw-San, this is a wonderful plan. Now, go back to America and sell enough pens so that you have enough profits to afford to do this advertising!' Needless to say, I felt deflated."

Back in the United States, Shaw gambled, taking out a $75,000 bank loan to back the Razor Point ad campaign. The resulting humorous ads caught the attention of consumers, who at the time were accustomed to serious, uninspired pen ads. One of the first print ads showed a woman on a couch conversing with her psychiatrist. The headline read, "Is It Sick to Love a Pen?" In the copy the psychiatrist tells her that loving a pen is "perfectly normal, as long as it's a Pilot Pen." Shaw also put his background as a performer to good use—and saved money—by appearing in some of the early television spots. The campaign worked, the Razor Point became a hit with general consumers, and after a year Pilot Pen's sales doubled to $2 million dollars. Not insignificantly, Shaw was able to repay the bank loan.

Over the next decade, sales steadily climbed as Pilot Pen continued to pursue a lighthearted approach to its advertising. In the 1980s the company enjoyed a successful relationship with comedian Rodney Dangerfield, the perennially downtrodden man unable to gain respect from the world. The running gag in the two-year radio and print campaign was that people, such as a bank teller, would borrow his Pilot Pen and refuse to give it back. Pilot Pen also found another way to promote its brand: tennis. In 1982 Shaw was asked to sponsor a Challenger Series tennis tournament to be held in New Haven, Connecticut. Called the Pilot Pen Open, the event was backed by the company for ten years. Shaw also spent money on a California tournament, the Pilot Pen Classic.

SHAW NAMED PRESIDENT: 1986

Pilot Pen sales reached $31 million in 1982, and a year later the company moved into a new headquarters building in Trumbull. Sales continued to increase at a steady clip, totaling $49 million in 1986, the same year that Shaw was promoted from executive vice president—a title he received in 1978—to president of Pilot Pen. By this time well versed in the ways of Japanese business, he was entrusted to run the U.S. subsidiary without a Japanese national on hand to keep watch. Allowed to make his own decisions, he continued to grow the business, and his relationship with the parent company was so solid that in 1992 he became only the sixth American to ever be elected to serve on the board of directors of a Japanese company. A year later he received the additional title of chief executive officer of the U.S. subsidiary.

Pilot Pen added manufacturing capabilities in June 1995 when it opened a $5 million, 90,000-square-foot plant in Jacksonville, Florida, which also included packaging and distribution operations. It was backed by $500,000 in city and state funds, an investment that paid off for the community as Pilot Pen soon added a $4.5 million 50,000-square-foot expansion and bought 7.8 acres of adjacent land to accommodate further growth. Pilot Pen steadily added the domestic production of pens, including the New EasyTouch line. It was also distributing the Namiki line of limited editions pens, introduced to the U.S. market in 1994, four years after their debut in Japan.

By this stage Pilot Pen was generating sales in the $135 million range, ranking as the fourth largest pen manufacturer in America. It continued to build the brand through cost-effective advertising relying on humor. Shaw was also a mainstay, serving as the company pitchman. In 1998 he was featured in a new 30-second television spot that took place on a troubled airplane. A stewardess sent from the cockpit cries that she needs a pilot. Shaw rises from his seat, introduces himself as the

CEO of Pilot Pen, and offers her a pen. Pilot Pen was also again promoting its brand through the sponsorship of tennis. In 1996 the company became the title sponsor for New Haven's then Volvo International tennis tournament, notable because it served as a tune-up for the prestigious U.S. Open held in New York, the last of the sport's four annual Grand Slam events, and was televised around the world. The alliance proved mutually beneficial, especially after the tournament became a women's event. In 2002 Pilot Pen extended the sponsorship arrangement through 2008.

Every year under Shaw's leadership, Pilot Pen increased sales, reaching the $200 million level in the 2000s. Along the way, the company introduced a number of new pens to the U.S. retail market, as well as promotional products for advertising purposes and specialized new products designed to be sold through licensing agreements with corporate partners. Products created through this New Business Development initiative included 18-karat gold and platinum jewelry, produced using pen-manufacturing technology; magnetic panels and the chalkless blackboard; thermal transfer ribbon; and the counting pen. New Business Development also created unique use pens that could, for example, apply and remove nail polish or apply silver traces to repair electronic circuit boards. With the rise in use of personal digital assistants (PDAs) and tablet PCs, the company also created special writing instruments for use with handheld and other computer devices. To support Pilot Pen's increasing number of product lines, which included conventional pens such as the VBall Grip rolling ball pen, the ergonomic Dr. Grip pen, and the new "gel" pen brands, the company completed a

$10 million expansion to its Jacksonville facility, adding another 120,000 square feet.

Shaw reached retirement age in 2003 and a year later began grooming his successor, Dennis Burleigh, who became executive vice-president in 2004 and chief operating officer in 2005. He was slated to succeed Shaw as president and CEO in May 2007.

Ed Dinger

PRINCIPAL COMPETITORS

Société Bic; Faber-Castell AG; Newell Rubbermaid Inc.

FURTHER READING

Berdon, Caroline, "Fond Farewells," *Office Product International,* June 2006, p. 30.

Brewer, Geoffrey, "Take My Pen—Please!" *Sales & Marketing Management,* February 1994, p. 11.

Dawkins, Pam, "New Haven, Conn., Tennis Tournament Raised Pilot Pen's Profile," *Connecticut Post,* August 16, 2001.

Kane, Courtney, "Pilot Pen Tries Out A Campaign That Doesn't Star Its President," *New York Times,* August 21, 2001, p. C5.

Mathis, Karen Brune, "Pilot Making Its Mark," *Florida Times Union,* September 18, 1996, p. B-4

———, "Pilot Pen CEO Set to Write New Chapter," *Florida Times Union,* March 23, 2005, p. F1.

Shaw, Ron, "A Tale of Brashness and Japanese Boards," *Directors & Boards,* Spring 2002, p. 49.

Teresko, John, "From Stand-Up to Boardroom," *Industry Week,* March 2002, p. 20.

Proeza S.A. de C.V.

Avda Constitucion 405 Pte
Centro Monterrey,
Mexico
Telephone: (52) 81 8369 7000
Fax: (52) 81 8342 8691
Web site: http://www.proeza.com.mx

Private Company
Incorporated: 1974 as Proeza (Promotora de Empresas Zano)
Employees: 3,000
Sales: $6.1 billion (2005 est.)
NAIC: 551112 Offices of Other Holding Companies; 111310 Orange Groves; 311411 Frozen Fruit, Juice, and Vegetable Processing; 336370 Motor Vehicle Metal Stamping; 541512 Computer Systems Design Services

■ ■ ■

Proeza S.A. de C.V.—the name stands for Promotora de Empresas Zano—is a Monterrey, Mexico-based holding company with diversified interest in the production of automotive parts and fruit and fruit juices and the operation of foundries. The company is also active in the information technology (IT) services market.

Proeza's main subsidiary is Metalsa, which also makes up the core of the group's Automotive Division. Metalsa is a major supplier of structural steel components for automobiles and trucks, include side rails, light truck chassis, fuel systems and a number of die-stamped parts. Metalsa produces primarily for the North American

automotive market, and operates a plant in Roanoke, Virginia, in addition to its factories in Apodaca and San Luis Potosi in Mexico. Metalsa has also announced plans to add factories in San Antonio, Texas, and in Saltilla, expected to be operational as early as 2006.

Proeza also operates the Ogihara Proeza Mexico (OPM) joint venture, which produces stamped tools for the automotive industry. Proeza also controls fruit juice processor Citrofrut, the centerpiece of its Juice and Fruits Division, and operates its own citrus groves in Veracruz and San Luis Potosi through subsidiary Imdecit, as well as nursery and research facilities thru Procigo. Proeza's Foundries Division consists of the joint-venture Proeza-GREDE, formed with the United States's GREDE, which began production in 2001; the company also produces complex modular iron parts through Teknik.

In the mid-2000s, Proeza beefed up its interest in technology, forming its Proeza IT division. This company provides supply chain management, enterprise solutions and related services in Monterrey, Mexico City, Guadalajara, and also operates an office in Maryland. While Proeza itself remains a private company controlled by the founding Zambrano family, the company has formed a partnership with U.S. auto parts manufacturer Tower Automotive, giving Tower a 40 percent stake in Proeza. Enrique Zambrano Benitez is Proeza's managing director, while founder Guillermo Zambrano acts as company chairman.

METALWORKS IN 1956

Guillermo Zambrano founded a metalworking business in Monterrey in 1956 called in Manufacturas Metalicas

COMPANY PERSPECTIVES

Our mission is to create, transform and develop innovative-oriented companies, thereby contributing to the progress of society and the development of our people. We are an international group whose development is supported by creativity and innovation, seeking always to raise our customers, shareholders and employees expectations. Our Group operates globally with automotive, agricultural equipment as well as service businesses and exports to all five continents. We invest in products, processes and services research and development, in order to offer innovative solutions to our customers. We are committed to the communities where we operate, through the creation of new jobs and environmental support, thus contributing to its economical and social development.

Monterrey (Metalsa). Zambrano's originally focused the group's operations on Mexico's construction industry. By the early 1960s, however, Metalsa had shifted its focus to the automotive business. This transition was made possible by the group's alliance with the A. O. Smith company. Smith, which had been manufacturing automotive frames since the late 1890s, assisted Metalsa in developing its own automotive frame capacity. While Metalsa went on to develop a range of automotive products, the company's frames production for both the automotive and light truck markets remained its core product line. The relationship between Metalsa and Smith remained a strong one through the end of the century, and ended only when Smith, which held 40 percent of Metalsa, exited the automotive business altogether in 1997.

Zambrano continued to develop other business interests—as well as becoming a noted breeder of thoroughbred horses. In 1974, Metalsa was regrouped under a new holding company, Promotora de Empresas Zano, or Proeza. Metalsa was then the cornerstone of Proeza's newly created automotive division. In 1982, Manufacturas Metalicas Monterrey formally changed its name to Metalsa. Two years later, Proeza's metals interests expanded with the creation of Teknik, which specialized in the production of cast iron components. Teknik's production targeted various markets, including the agricultural market.

Proeza's automotive division continued to drive the company's growth through the 1980s. The company

shifted its production to a new facility in Apodaca in 1985. In 1988, Metalsa acquired automobile components manufacturers Premecna and Kuhlpre. As a result, Metalsa added a new factory in San Luis. Proeza boosted its presence in the North American automotive market the following year through the creation of a tool and die joint venture, Perfek, in partnership with world-leading toolmaker Miyazu Seisakusho and the Sumitomo Corporation. Proeza's partnership with the two Japanese companies lasted into the beginning of the 2000s. In the meantime, the company had developed another partnership, with Belgian plastic fuel tank system producer Solvay. That partnership resulted in the creation of the Prolvay joint venture in 1991, with a factory in Puebla.

Proeza had also begun building a business presence in an entirely different field: the fruit and vegetable juice processing industry. Proeza's interests included Impulsora de Desarrollo Citricola (Imdecit), and Promotoro Citricola del Golfo (Procigo). Both companies were created in 1989, with the former acting as a research and development in order to improvement the quality of the country's citrus stock, and the latter operating nurseries in order to supply trees and consulting services for the country's citrus and fruit growers. In 1994, Proeza acquired Cycosa, which operated a citrus fruit processing facility in San Luis Potosi. Following that acquisition, Cycosa was merged with two other companies: Alver, a citrus fruit processor based in Veracruz, founded in 1969, and Jucosa—originally Jugos Concentrados—which had established fruit juice processing operations in Montemorelos, in 1959. The newly merged operation was then named Citrofrut.

Following the creation of Citrofrut, Proeza launched a new restructuring of its operations again. This led to the creation of the strategic business units in 1996: Automotive, which remained Proeza's largest division; Fruits and Juices; and Businesses in Development. The latter division anticipated Proeza's entry into the technology sector at the turn of the century.

HIGH TECH AND CHANGING PARTNERS IN THE NEW CENTURY

By the late 1990s Zambrano was joined by son Enrique Zambrano Benitez, who took up the role of the company's managing director and spearheaded a fresh diversification effort for the new century. In 1998, the company developed a new 10-year strategy, which targeted an expansion of the group's operations at an international level, while also identifying new diversification areas.

The first new directions were identified in 1998,

KEY DATES

1956: Guillermo Zambrano founds Manufacturas Metalicas Monterrey (Metalsa) in order to produce metal parts for the construction industry.

1960: Metalsa forms a partnership with A. O. Smith and transitions to producing automotive frames and other components.

1974: Zambrano creates Proeza as a holding company for Metalsa and other holdings, including fruit juice processing units Jucosa, founded in 1959, and Alver, founded in 1969.

1982: Manufacturas Metalicas Monterrey changes its name to Metalsa.

1984: Proeza expands into cast iron production with Teknik.

1988: Metalsa acquires the Premecna factory in San Luis and forms the Perfek joint venture with Miyazu Seisakusho.

1991: The company forms its Prolvay joint venture with Solvay.

1994: Proeza merges fruit juice and citrus orchard operations into Citrofrut.

1997: A.O. Smith sells the automotive division to Tower Automotive, which agrees to a new partnership with Metalsa.

1998: Metalsa buys Tower's plant in Roanoke, Virginia.

2002: Citrofrut acquires Fruitalamo in Veracruz.

2004: Metalsa launches a new factory in San Antonio, Texas.

2006: Metalsa announces plan to build a new factory in Saltilla, Mexico, and a possible new factory in China or India.

Proeza had also begun developing its operations in the high-technology market. The company operations by then included Servidata, created in 1976 to provide IT services, including systems integrations and supply chain management systems. Into the turn of the century, Proeza began exploring interests in other technology sectors. Proeza established a new operation, called Datasat, which used satellite technology to offer wireless asset tracking services. The company made an attempt to deepen its entry into the telecommunications market, through subsidiary Astrum Comunicaciones. That company was awarded two satellite transmission concessions in 2002. In 2004, Proeza combined its technology operations, including Astrum, DataSat and Servidata, into a new subsidiary, Proeza IT, and targeted the market based in Monterrey.

Citrofrut continued to show strong growth into the 2000s, emerging as a major force in the region's fruit juice market. The company expanded its presence in 2002, with the acquisition of Frutalamo, a citrus fruit processor based in Veracruz. At the same time, Citrofrut expanded beyond citrus fruits, adding a facility for the processing of tropical fruit juices.

Despite the growth of its other operations, Proeza's automotive division remained its driving force into the new century. Following A.O. Smith's decision to exit the automotive industry, Proeza took the opportunity to buy back the 40 percent Smith held in its Mexican partner in 1997, paying $70 million. Proeza then began looking for a new partner, turning to Tower Automotive, which had bought Smith's automotive division. As part of the new partnership, Tower bought a 40 percent stake in Metalsa, paying $120 million outright—and up to $45 million more, depending on the group's earnings.

The partnership with Tower enabled Proeza to put into place the other prong of its long-term strategy, that of establishing an international base. In 2000, Metalsa bought out Tower's heavy-truck rail manufacturing plant based in Roanoke, Virginia, paying $55 million.

That year, Proeza forged a new partnership, merging the Perfek joint venture into a new joint venture with Japan's Ogihara, a major automotive components producer. The new company took on the name of Ogihara Proeza Mexico (OPM) following the completion of the merge in 2000.

Proeza continued to boost its international operations into the mid-2000s. In 2004, the company announced its interest in establishing a new plant in San Antonio, Texas, in support of the new Toyota factory scheduled to begin production there in 2006. Proeza also announced that it would begin construction of a new factory in Saltilla, to transfer part of its frames production from its main Apodaca plant. At the same

when the company created two new strategic business units, Proeza Foundries and Proeza IT. Proeza began looking for partners for the former, resulting in the creation of a joint venture with the United States' GREDE Foundries, in 1999. The new company, ProezaGrede, launched construction of a new $65 million iron foundry in 2000, near Monterrey. The first phase of the project called for a production capacity of 70,000 metric tons. At the same time, Proeza announced plans to expand the ProezaGrede site to as much as 200,000 metric tons.

time, the company indicated that it was considering adding a factory in either China or India, in order to expand its operation to these market. Proeza appeared to have hit on a winning formula with its diversified group of businesses.

M.L. Cohen

PRINCIPAL SUBSIDIARIES

Citrofrut S.A. de C.V.; Metalsa S de RL; Ogihara Proeza Mexico, S. De R.L. De C.V.; Proeza Automotriz S.A. de C.V.; Proeza IT S.A. de C.V.

PRINCIPAL DIVISIONS

Automotive; Juice and Fruits; Foundries; Information Technology.

PRINCIPAL COMPETITORS

Magna International Inc.; Lear Corporation; PACCAR Inc.; Toyota Motor Manufacturing North America Inc.; Tower Automotive Inc.; V and M do Brasil S.A.

FURTHER READING

"Confirma Metalsa Planta para Saltillo," *Vanguardia*, February 14, 2006.

Couretas, John, "People Power: Tower Automotive and Affiliate Metalsa See Energized Work Force Fueling the Future," *Automotive News*, August 3, 1998, p. 30.

Hendricks, David, "Toyota Plant's Expansion Key to Luring Manufacturing Jobs," *San Antonio Express*, July 13, 2004.

"Monterrey-based Grupo Proeza," *Mexico Business Monthly*, January 2000.

"Proeza, Grede Begin Construction on Mexican Foundry," *Modern Casting*, December 2000, p. 14.

"SLIM Technologies Launches Partnership with Proeza TI by Providing Supply Chain Design Solution to Grupo Altex," *Business Wire*, May 24, 2005

"US Slowdown Hurts Mexican Supplier," *Autoparts Report*, March 15, 2001.

Wrigley, Al, "Metalsa Frame Drive Spurs Mexican Steel," *American Metal Market*, July 30, 1997, p. 2.

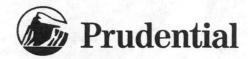

Prudential Financial Inc.

---

751 Broad Street
Newark, New Jersey 07102
U.S.A.
Telephone: (973) 802-6000
Toll Free: (800) 346-3778
Fax: (973) 802-4479
Web site: http://www.prudential.com

Public Company
Incorporated: 1873 as Widows and Orphans Friendly
    Society
Employees: 39,418
Total Assets: $568 billion (2006)
NAIC: 524113 Direct Life Insurance Carriers; 524114
    Direct Health & Medical Insurance Carriers;
    524126 Direct Property & Casualty Insurance Car-
    riers; 524298 All Other Insurance Related Activi-
    ties; 525990 Other Financial Vehicles; 523930
    Financial Planning Services

■ ■ ■

Prudential Financial Inc. is one of the largest diversified
financial institutions in the world and, based on total assets, one of the largest insurance companies in North
America. Along with its life insurance and annuities
business, The Prudential Insurance Companies of
America, the company also operates in asset management, securities brokerage, real estate brokerage, and
relocation services. In 2001, Prudential completed the
process of demutualization, by converting to public
ownership; the company then adopted its current

moniker. The company's assets in June 2006 were $568
billion.

19TH CENTURY ORIGINS

A Yale dropout named John F. Dryden established the
forerunner of Prudential in 1873, naming it the Widows
and Orphans Friendly Society. Two years later, influenced
by the British Prudential Assurance Company, Dryden
changed his company's name to The Prudential Friendly
Society (the company settled on its current name in
1877). When Dryden visited British Prudential at this
time, he was impressed by several key elements, including the British company's offering of low-cost industrial
insurance for laborers; the fact that agents collected
premiums each week from customers at home; and that
the company served not the wealthy or middle class, but
the working class. Unable to find backers in his native
New England or New York to build the company he
envisioned, Dryden crossed the Hudson to Newark,
New Jersey, and convinced several Newark citizens to
purchase $30,000 of capital stock.

The first prospectus of the company succinctly set
forth its aims: Relief in sickness and accident for people
of meager means, pensions for old age, adult and infant
burial funds—all goals which corresponded closely to
the needs of the diverse ethnic groups then immigrating
to the United States. Yet the company's first directors
failed to recognize Dryden's vision or organizational
talents. As a result, Newark real estate broker Allen L.
Bassett was installed as president. His tenure was short-
lived, however, and Noah Blanchard, a tanner, took the
helm. In 1881, when Blanchard died, the directors finally

COMPANY PERSPECTIVES

Prudential Financial's distinctive rock logo and Prudential's name are among the most enduring brands in U.S. corporate history. The company's long history is a testament to the quality it has provided its customers. In addition to the level of service, Prudential Financial is today recognized for the breadth of products and services it provides and continues to be a recognized company of quality financial services at home and abroad.

elected John Dryden president by one vote. He served in that position for 30 years. During those years, he led Prudential to several major innovations and established a corporate culture that marked Prudential for generations.

Under Dryden's leadership, Prudential enjoyed explosive growth. In 1885, it reported 422,671 policies in force; by 1905 it had 6.49 million. Assets grew from $1.03 million in 1885 to $102.38 million in 1905. Prudential expanded to neighboring states, and, in 1909, opened its first international branch in Toronto, Canada. In 1896, the company's advertising department created Prudential's long-standing logo and slogan: the Rock of Gibraltar accompanied by the words, "The Prudential has the strength of Gibraltar." Both were chosen to express the solidity of the products the company offered. The company's image was further bolstered by the outcome of a New York state legislative committee investigation under Senator William W. Armstrong in 1905. While the major companies of the day became targets of the investigation into violation of customer interests, Prudential emerged relatively unscathed.

When Dryden died in 1911, his son, Forrest Dryden, followed him as president. Under Forrest's leadership, the company continued its rapid growth.

MUTUALIZING AND SURVIVING

However, control of the company became and remained a problem during Forrest Dryden's term. Its huge resources and conservative investment philosophy made Prudential's assets look appealing to potential purchasers. Tired of fending off corporate suitors and raiders, the board took its first steps to make the company mutual and sell the company to its policyholders.

Later in Forrest's tenure, World War I drained the company with its heavy claims. Then, as a result of the 1918–19 influenza pandemic, Prudential paid over $20 million for flu-related deaths. Shortly afterward, Forrest Dryden brought scandal to the firm because of a conflict of interest he had due to certain stocks he held. By the time he resigned in 1921, company totals exceeded $5.6 billion, an increase of $3.6 billion in ten years. Corporate assets rose from $259 million in 1911 to $830 million in 1922. Edward D. Duffield became Prudential's next president.

During Duffield's term, Prudential stayed much the same. While the company innovated by offering group insurance coverage to home office staff in 1924 and started group health in 1925, the Great Depression strangled most growth. Mortgages valued at $1.5 billion in 1931 bottomed at $787 million in 1935, even though the value of policies in force grew $1.5 billion between 1930 and 1935. In 1938, when Duffield died suddenly, he left a company still tremendously successful, but no longer a leader in the industry.

Franklin D'Olier followed Duffield as president. While D'Olier recognized the problems Prudential faced with its conservative managerial corps, he never succeeded in attending to them. A larger crisis demanded his attention: Hitler's actions in Europe and the U.S. commitment to World War II. D'Olier helped organize the New York regional civil defense and later served on the Strategic Bombing Survey Commission. However, in 1942, Prudential finally converted to a mutual company, completing the process started in 1915, and, in 1928, it entered the market for major medical coverage, group credit insurance, and group insurance in multiple employer-collective bargaining units. The group sales department was the brainchild of Edmund Whittaker, an actuary who had joined the company in 1928, and who conceived of actuaries as the "engineers of insurance."

A NEW ERA OF DECENTRALIZATION

In 1946 Prudential entered a new era. Carroll M. Shanks took office as Prudential's seventh CEO. At 40, he was the youngest president since Dryden. Shanks had joined Prudential in 1932 and was known for his unorthodox methods. During his 15 years as president, he remade the company, leading Prudential into a bold decentralization that stunned the industry.

Within months of Shanks taking office, resignations or early retirements were announced down to the level of middle management. Next, in 1948, he opened regional home offices across the nation, each with its own senior vice-president in charge and with total responsibility for the region. Newark retained the corporate senior officers, actuaries, and evaluation and

KEY DATES

1873: John F. Dryden establishes the Widows and Orphans Friendly Society.

1877: The company changes its name to The Prudential Insurance Company of America.

1896: Prudential's advertising department creates its long-standing Rock of Gibraltar logo.

1942: Prudential converts to a mutual company.

1967: Prudential surpasses the Metropolitan as the world's largest insurance company.

1970: The company enters the property and casualty insurance business.

1976: Hanbro Life Assurance Ltd. of Britain is acquired.

1981: Bache investment and brokerage house is purchased; George L. Ball is named chairman and CEO of Pru Bache.

1991: Ball resigns from Pru Bache as losses total more than $250 million amid lawsuits relating to selling real estate limited partnerships.

1997: Prudential is assessed a $35 million fine and forced to pay restitution to 10.7 million policyholders for its part in a churning scandal.

2001: The company completes the demutualization process and changes its name to Prudential Financial Inc.

2003: The U.S. operations of Skandia Insurance Co. Ltd. are acquired.

2006: Prudential buys Allstate Financial's annuity business.

staff departments, but each vice-president handled local sales, investments, general management, and issues from policy to claims.

The reorganization dealt with many of the company's problems. It attacked the excessive specialization that separated workers and stymied activity; it cut the many levels between the president and operating employees; it eliminated layers of red tape and provided new opportunities for energetic and creative managers. Each regional home office occupied a striking modern office building that dominated its city and told the region that Prudential had arrived in style and strength. Quickly the regional home offices helped Prudential establish a new national presence. Corporate policy called for the regional office to invest its dollars in the local community. With the inception of each of the eight home regional offices, Prudential's sales jumped and investment income rose sharply. In 1948, the first regional sales office in Los Angeles boosted revenue in that region by 20 percent. Group pension sales totaled $44 million in 1945, and, by 1955, exceeded $194 million; group life sales exceeded $589 million in 1949, a record for both Prudential and the industry.

As regional leaders exercised their autonomy, they created a multitude of new products, many tailor-made to their regional markets. Shanks adapted the best innovations to the national scene. Prudential set up employee security programs that combined group life and health insurance. In addition, it changed major medical insurance in the 1950s when it revised the method for computing the deductible. The company also underwent internal change. In 1951 Prudential's district agents voted to go on strike, the first formal job action by a white collar union in the nation. The American Federation of Labor led the workers for three months as they negotiated for improvements and succeeded in obtaining recognition of the union as their bargaining agent.

INVESTMENT STRATEGIES

Under Shanks, Prudential also revised its investment strategies. Shanks consistently looked for niches where Prudential could risk a small amount yet increase its average return much above that of its competitors. In 1950 the Prudential began buying common stocks and, by 1964, had 3 percent of its assets in stock on which it realized $75 million in capital gains. The strategy was successful; by 1962, the life insurance industry averaged a return of 4.4 percent on all invested assets. Prudential averaged 4.7 percent, producing an additional $60 million in income for the company. After 1958, Prudential ceased to buy bonds in the market and instead negotiated separate loans with corporations for higher rates on which the corporations received more rapid, less costly, and more flexible financing. In 1956, Shanks created a commercial and industrial loan department to seek out small business loans.

When Shanks retired in 1960, the Prudential board named Louis R. Menagh, Jr., as chief executive officer. At 68 one of the oldest to win the post, Menagh had worked his way to the top from a position as clerk. Menagh retired in October 1962, and the board named Orville E. Beal president. Beal had headed the regional home office in Minneapolis, Minnesota, and was committed to Shanks' bold vision.

In 1964, Beal led Prudential in selling its first group variable annuity policy. These annuities were invested entirely in common stocks and were thus a much more attractive hedge against inflation than prior annuities based on bonds, mortgages, and similar investments. In 1967, Prudential surpassed the Metropolitan as the world's largest insurance company; total Met assets amounted to $23.51 billion while Prudential announced $23.6 billion. In 1968, it established PIC Realty Corporation as a wholly owned subsidiary that owned and leased commercial real estate through joint ventures with established real estate developers. Prudential shared additional profits as a principal in real estate development.

Beal stepped down in 1968, the same year the company abandoned its original pay-by-the-week policies, closing an important chapter in the company's history. He turned his leadership role over to Donald MacNaughton, who led the company through some of its most expansive innovations. MacNaughton particularly addressed issues of corporate social responsibility. When Newark suffered terribly after one of the worst urban riots in U.S. history, MacNaughton pledged to use Prudential's resources to help with the problems of urban centers and gave $50 million to Newark. He convinced the insurance industry to pledge $1 billion in help to U.S. cities, an amount later increased to $2 billion. In his nine years as CEO, MacNaughton developed an array of new products for the company and plunged it into the international marketplace, well ahead of most of the competition. In 1969, Prudential celebrated total assets of over $25 billion; when MacNaughton retired in 1978 reported assets were $35.8 billion.

OPPORTUNITIES AMID INFLATION AND STAGFLATION

When the New Jersey legislature revised insurance laws in 1967, it broadened the operations of life insurance companies, permitting them to offer fire and casualty coverage, individual variable annuity plans, direct investment in real estate, investment management services, mortgage investing, and to own or lease business or communication equipment. Prudential took advantage of these new opportunities; inflation was corroding the paychecks of U.S. workers and fewer customers wanted policies that pledged fixed payments. Instead Prudential aimed its sites at the new middle-class consumer, aiming to meet all their insurance needs.

In 1970 Prudential entered the property and casualty insurance business. Unable to secure the necessary state licenses, and without a sufficiently large body of trained and certified agents, the company contracted with Kemper Insurance to provide "shell" companies in 26 states. Homeowners insurance policies had traditionally

been written for three to five years, and corporate profits suffered from inflation. Instead, Prudential wrote all its policies at current rates. To minimize losses, it carefully selected the geographic regions it entered. However, the retraining costs of certifying 30,000 agents were great. By 1972, Prudential dropped its contract with Kemper and continued in the casualty and fire field through its subsidiary Prudential Property and Casualty Insurance Company.

MacNaughton continued the search for higher returns in a period of inflation and stagflation. In 1973 Prudential formed Prudential Reinsurance Company, insuring other insurance companies against extraordinary losses. In 1974 Prudential purchased CNA Nuclear Leasing, renaming it Prudential Lease. In its first year, contracts grew by 88 percent and returned 16 percent on equity. Prudential Reinsurance gave Prudential its first entrance into the international market.

In 1976 Prudential acquired Hanbro Life Assurance Ltd. of Britain and entered the European Common Market. MacNaughton developed many more product lines between 1973 and 1978. PIC Realty Canada, Ltd., owned and developed property in Canada. Prudential Health Care Plan operated health maintenance organizations. Pru Capital Management provided administration and management services to Prulease. Le Rocher, Compagnie de Reassurance, wrote reinsurance in Europe. Pru Funding offered long-term loans and operation leases for Prulease. Pru Supply contracted to supply fossil fuels or other inventories. Prudential General Insurance Company provided group casualty and property protection, and Pru Service Participacos, a wholly owned Brazilian subsidiary, provided services to another Brazilian property and casualty company.

MacNaughton retired in 1978 and was succeeded by Robert Beck, who had joined Prudential in 1951 as an agent. Beck attacked the problem of the continuing lapse rate on life insurance policies by entering new markets. The company formed Dryden and Company and Gibraltar Casualty Company to sell coverage of unusual and difficult insurance risks to the surplus lines market. Prudential also formed additional subsidiaries to market group and commercial property and casualty insurance. In 1979 Prudential signed with Sony Corporation to form Sony-Prudential to sell life insurance in Japan. Beck also led Prudential in another investment opportunity; PRUCO formed a subsidiary, P.G. Realty, to purchase, sell, and operate farmlands in Nebraska. Later, other subsidiaries were formed to operate farm lands in Florida.

Beck's most controversial acquisition came when he purchased the Bache investment and brokerage house in 1981. With Bache, Prudential could sell money market funds, mutuals, tax shelters, real estate partnerships, as well as stocks and bonds, all hedges against inflation. Prudential-Bache hired George L. Ball, former president of E.F. Hutton & Company, as its chair and CEO. Ball, a Wall Street star known for his aggressive and innovative tactics as a broker, led the brokerage firm on an expensive, but ultimately failed effort to break into the top levels of Wall Street investment banks for the next nine years.

UNPRECEDENTED GROWTH AND SCANDAL

Throughout the 1980s, Prudential continued to search for ways to maximize income from its investments. In 1981, the company formed Property Investment Separate Account, a vehicle to enable pension funds to invest in real estate. It also developed several successful investment initiatives: SMALLCO invested in firms under $200 million, and MIDCO in firms between $75 and $460 million in capital. Beck led Prudential in a continued effort to diversify, opening health maintenance offices in Oklahoma; Atlanta, Georgia; and Nashville, Tennessee. New life insurance subsidiaries were formed in Texas, Arizona, and Illinois. The company also formed the Mircali Asset Management firm to manage global investments for other institutions.

In September 1986, Robert Beck retired. His successor as CEO and chairman of the board, 54-year-old Robert C. Winters, had joined Prudential in 1953. Winters took over after several decades of unprecedented growth in the company. Prudential's assets had more than doubled since 1978. After many years of spinning off a seemingly endless line of subsidiaries and holding companies, the company took time to evaluate and integrate the gains of earlier years. A new corporate strategy needed to be articulated to make sense out of the period of expansion, one that gave form to future plans.

In 1987 the company reorganized its Prudential Realty Group into four new firms: Prudential Property Company, Prudential Acquisition and Sales Group, Prudential Mortgage Capital Company, and the Investment Service Group. Prudential offered its customers virtually every variety of insurance known, both for individuals and groups. That year, it acquired Merrill Lynch Realty and Merrill Lynch Relocation Management and offered customers a nationwide system of real estate brokers. Prudential sold its shares in Sony-Prudential to Sony. It formed a Prudential Life Insurance Company Ltd. in Japan, which offered a full range of individual life policies. Other subsidiaries were formed or acquired to sell policies in Spain, Italy, South Korea, and Taiwan.

The October 1987 panic on the market cost Prudential $1 billion in paper value and marked at least a temporary end to runaway leveraged buyouts (LBOs) and massive mergers and acquisitions. The managers at Prudential had made millions for the company in the heady days of LBOs. From one financial package put together to help sell a company, Prudential earned $200 million on an investment of $650 million.

There was, however, a negative side to the boom years of the market. Many of the sophisticated financial packages Prudential crafted were initially tax havens for its customers. When the 1986 tax reform act eliminated the rationale for the many tax shelters, customers quickly abandoned them. In addition, the packages designed by the financiers were often so sophisticated that neither the customers nor the agents marketing the devices could understand them, and many of the innovations tried by Prudential faltered. Prudential pumped $2.4 billion into Bache Group, for example, with continual losses. In 1989, a difficult year for Prudential, Bache lost $48 million. In November 1990, Prudential-Bache announced that it was cutting back on its investment banking operation by about two-thirds, having made the decision to reorganize the firm to focus on its strengths in the retail brokerage business. In early 1991, with losses totaling more than $250 million and amid lawsuits relating to selling real estate limited partnerships, Ball resigned. Hardwick Simmons, former president of Shearson's Private Client Group, took over leadership of Prudential Securities Inc., renamed as part of its restructuring.

During Simmons's first year in charge of Pru Securities, the firm launched an aggressive ad campaign and enjoyed record earnings. In 1993 profits reached nearly $800 million. Yet Simmons had also to deal with the private lawsuits of angry investors who had lost hundreds of millions of dollars in limited partnerships sold by Pru Securities brokers, several potentially damaging class action suits, and an SEC investigation. The cause of his trouble: some $6 billion of limited partnerships sold in the 1980s to more than 100,000 investors valued at only a fraction of their original selling price. In response to the negative publicity, Prudential retreated behind a shield of secrecy, but with probes into the limited partnerships by state securities regulators expanding, the company accepted various settlements, including public censure in 1992. Prudential remained under scrutiny for the next several years for "churning," inducing policy holders to trade up to more expensive policies without explaining the costs. The investigation, concluded in 1996, and involving regulators from 45 states, assessed Prudential a $35 million fine and set up a restitution plan for 10.7 million policyholders. The settlement, approved by a New Jersey district court judge in 1997, led to an eventual payment in excess of $2 billion.

The problems at Prudential Securities coincided with a downturn in profits for the brokerage firm. Profits at Prudential Mortgage dropped, too, with a decline in mortgage lending activity and a rise in interest rates. Sales of life insurance to individuals diminished as well. Prudential's reinsurance business and property and casualty units had been hard hit by several natural disasters, including Hurricane Andrew. In 1994 insurance operations lost $907 million as a result of the Northridge, California, earthquake. The board took advantage of Winters's retirement in late 1994 to bring in new "outsider" management in an attempt to resolve its problems. Arthur Ryan came from Chase Manhattan, where he had overseen the marketing of mutual funds and insurance. Before that, he had led a large sales operation at Control Data. With $300 billion in assets, Prudential also began to take steps to boost efficiency, bringing in Coopers & Lybrand, McKinsey, Deloitte & Touche, and other consultants. It announced plans to shed its reinsurance and mortgage units and to liquidate its $6 billion real estate portfolio. Real estate divestitures began in 1997 with the sale of the company's property management unit and its Canadian commercial real estate business. The following year, it sold Prudential Center complex in Boston.

THE MOVE TO GO PUBLIC IN 2001

In 1998, Ryan went before New Jersey's insurance commissioner to lobby for passage of a law that would allow a mutual insurance company to sell shares to the public. Under Ryan's plan, the company would change its corporate structure so that it could raise money by selling stock. Detractors of the plan, such as the insurance director for the Consumer Federation of America, argued that it would enrich management via stock options, while causing policyholders to lose out in the form of lower dividends. In 1999, in preparation for becoming a stock-owned firm, Prudential undertook another reorganization, dividing its businesses into international, institutional, and retail units. The firm's life, property/casualty, mutual fund, and investment products fell within the retail unit, while group life, 401(k) and other employee benefit products became part of the institutional unit.

To focus on insurance and financial products, Prudential divested some of its business, including healthcare operations, which it proposed to sell to Aetna for $1 billion. In late 1998, it had announced its intention to pull out of unprofitable Medicare markets, dropping coverage for about 20 percent of its seniors in the SeniorCare program by refusing to renew Medicare-risk contracts in northern and southern California; Maryland; Washington, D.C.; New York; New Jersey; and parts of Florida. Also in 1999, Prudential began rapid global expansion; early that year, it opened a mutual fund company with Mitsui Trust & Banking Co. in Japan, acquired a license to open an office in Poland, and launched new insurance companies in Argentina and the Philippines.

Prudential ranked as the largest life insurer in terms of assets in the United States in 1998. It placed second in net premiums written that year and occupied sixth place in annuity sales during the preceding three years. About 55 percent of the company's earnings came from the sale of insurance, which grew by 21 percent in 1998, while 45 percent came from its investment and securities businesses. As it approached the 21st century, Prudential faced competition not only from a host of domestic giants, including Citigroup, MetLife, and Merrill Lynch, but from the overseas financial service titans as well.

PRUDENTIAL IN THE NEW MILLENNIUM

The company completed its demutualization process in 2001. Prudential went public on the New York Stock Exchange and launched one of the largest public offerings ever in the industry on December 13 of that year. The IPO raised more than $3 billion. At this time, the company adopted the Prudential Financial Inc. moniker, making The Prudential Insurance Company of America one of its subsidiaries.

Meanwhile, Prudential remained busy on the acquisition front. In 2000, it gained full ownership of Prudential-Mitsui Trust Investments Co., its joint venture with Mitsui Trust & Banking. It also strengthened its foothold in the auto insurance market with the purchase of THI Holdings Inc., and set plans in motion to purchase an interest in Japan's Kyoei Life Insurance Company Ltd. In 2002, it acquired a 50 percent stake in Oppenheim Funds Trust GmbH and Oppenheim Investment Management International.

Prudential made several divestitures at this time as well. It sold its personal automobile and homeowners lines to Liberty Mutual Group Inc., and its brokerage division to Wachovia Securities. Prudential retained a 38 percent stake in Wachovia Securities, which became the third-largest brokerage firm in the United States after the deal.

The company restructured operations in the early years of the new millennium, focusing on three main divisions: Insurance, Investments, and International

Insurance and Investments. It also pledged to cut nearly $600 million in expenses and achieve 12 percent return on equity (ROE)—a measure used to analyze operating performance—by 2005. In addition, Prudential continued to seek out strategic acquisitions that would increase its competitive advantage. In 2003, the company added the U.S. operations of Skandia Insurance Co. Ltd. to its arsenal in a $1.2 billion deal that secured its position as one of the top ten annuity companies in the United States. One year later, it added Cigna Corp.'s retirement and investment products division to its portfolio. In 2006, Prudential acquired Allstate Financial's variable annuity business for $591 million. The company stood as the third-largest provider of adviser-sold variable annuity products in the United States upon completion of the purchase.

With revenues and profits on the rise, Prudential's actions over the past several years appeared to have paid off. The company achieved 12.4 percent ROE in 2005, exceeding its goal set back in 2001. Arthur Ryan was firmly at the helm of Prudential as chairman, CEO, and president and the company remained optimistic about its future, believing it was on the path to success in the years to come.

Thomas J. Heed
Updated, Carrie Rothburd; Christina M. Stansell

PRINCIPAL DIVISIONS

Insurance; Investment; International Insurance and Investments.

PRINCIPAL COMPETITORS

AXA Financial Inc.; Citigroup Inc.; MetLife Inc.

FURTHER READING

Barker, Robert, "The Right Price for the New Pru," *BusinessWeek,* December 3, 2001.

Carr, William H. A., *From Three Cents a Week ... The Story of the Prudential Insurance Company of America,* Englewood Cliffs, N.J.: Prentice Hall, Inc., 1975.

Eichenwald, Kurt, "Prudential-Bache Chief Quits After Big Losses," *New York Times,* February 14, 1991, p. D1.

Fifty Years the Prudential: The History of a Business, Charged with Public Interest, Newark, N.J.: Prudential Insurance Company of America, 1927.

Fuhrmans, Vanessa, "Prudential Agrees to Buy Cigna Unit," *Wall Street Journal,* November 18, 2003.

Hawkins, Chuck, "Pru Securities Isn't Secure Yet," *Business Week,* September 7, 1992, p. 82.

Miller, Theresa, "Pru's Focus on Distribution," *Best's Review Life/Health Edition,* February 1999, p. 49.

"Prudential Closes on Acquisition of Allstate Financial's Variable Annuity Business," *Best's Insurance News,* June 1, 2006.

"Prudential Launches Biggest IPO in Insurance Industry," *Bestwire,* December 13, 2001.

Sheehan, Robert, "That Mighty Pump, Prudential," *Fortune,* January 1964.

Sommer, Jeff, "Prudential Buys Skandia Unit," *New York Times,* May 4, 2003.

Spiro, Leah Nathans, "What Does Prudential Really Owe?," *Business Week,* February 2, 1998, p. 117.

Treatser, Joseph B., "Prudential Insurance Raises $3.03 Billion in Initial Public Offering," *New York Times,* December 13, 2001.

Retail Ventures, Inc.

3241 Westerville Road
Columbus, Ohio 43224
U.S.A.
Telephone: (614) 471-4722
Fax: (614) 478-2253
Web site: http://www.retailventuresinc.com

Public Company
Incorporated: 1991 as Value City Department Stores,
    Inc.
Employees: 18,000
Sales: $2.91 billion (2006)
Stock Exchanges: New York
Ticker Symbol: RVI
NAIC: 448210 Shoe Stores; 448190 Other Clothing
    Stores; 452990 All Other General

∎ ∎ ∎

Retail Ventures, Inc., formerly known as Value City
Department Stores, Inc., is a retailer of value-priced apparel, footwear, and other merchandise through three
main operating segments: Value City, DSW, and Filene's
Basement. The 113 stores of its Value City chain are
unique in offering a huge array of discounted goods in a
vast space. Stores are typically between 80,000 and
100,000 square feet, about three times larger than most
other off-price competitors. Items at Value City retail
for at least 30 to 40 percent below regular department
store prices. The stores sell men's, women's, and
children's apparel, housewares, sporting goods, and other
items. Much of the merchandise is purchased directly

from manufacturers, and other goods are bought as
overstock or from liquidations of other merchants. The
stores offer leading brands as well as moderate and
budget-priced lines.

Retail Ventures also runs a chain of discount shoe
stores called DSW Shoe Warehouse. Its roughly 200
stores sell brand-name shoes at low prices. The company
also operates the more upscale Massachusetts-based
discount chain Filene's Basement. Retail Ventures was
formerly an operating division of Schottenstein Stores
Corporation (SSC), a private firm run by members of
the Schottenstein family. Schottenstein Stores was well
known as a liquidator, specializing in buying up failing
regional department stores. Retail Ventures is still
controlled by the Schottenstein family.

EARLY YEARS

The precursor of Retail Ventures Inc., Value City
Department Stores, was spun off from Schottenstein
Stores Corporation (SSC) in 1991. SSC began as a single
store in Columbus, Ohio, opened by Ephraim Schottenstein in 1917. Schottenstein's family emigrated from
Lithuania and settled in Columbus in the late 1800s.
Ephraim was apparently in the clothing business as early
as 1909, and soon after he opened his store, E.L. Schottenstein Department Store. Ephraim Schottenstein had
four sons, Saul, Alvin, Leon, and Jerome, and a daughter,
Selma. The children all grew up working in the family
store. One brother in particular, Jerome, was credited
with orchestrating much of the growth of the corporation in later years. By the time Jerome was a teenager,
he was taking trips to New York and making buying

COMPANY PERSPECTIVES

Our pledge ... To our customers, our associates, our vendors and business partners ... to our shareholders and our neighbors ... we will support the mission statement of each of our retail brands with integrity, honor, and enthusiasm.

decisions for the store. Jerome became an executive in Schottenstein Stores in 1946. By the early 1950s, the Schottenstein retail empire encompassed only the original Schottenstein store and several furniture stores. At that time the company began to get involved in the liquidation business, bidding on the merchandise of failing area stores. From liquidating merchandise, the company moved to acquiring bankrupt businesses. In 1963, Schottenstein Stores acquired a failing store in Dayton, Ohio, called Concord City, and the next year it bought another struggling store, Elyria City, in Elyria, Ohio. Then in 1966 the Schottenstein family acquired a store named Value City, in Independence, Ohio. The family business continued to buy up bankrupt stores, and it gave them all the Value City name. This name conveyed the prime message of the stores, which was to sell at budget prices.

A LEGENDARY LIQUIDATOR

Jerome Schottenstein became president of Schottenstein Stores Corp. in 1972. He went on to become an almost legendary figure in retailing: he was expert at buying liquidated merchandise, and equally astute at turning around failing stores. The Value City chain grew in the 1970s by taking over floundering regional chains and reopening them profitably. Some were closed and reopened under the Value City name, while others SSC funded and gave management assistance in exchange for a percentage of the business. SSC turned around bankrupt chains such as Valley Fair/Widmann in New Jersey and Levine's in Texas. Most of the company's operations centered in the Midwest, in relatively small towns within 250 miles of Columbus. The company owned extensive real estate in and around Columbus, Ohio, where the firm was headquartered.

However, Jerome Schottenstein sometimes roamed far afield in looking for juicy liquidations. In the early 1980s he bought and sold the discontinued product line of flamboyant and bankrupt car maker John DeLorean. Schottenstein also sold overstocked Fiat cars. He was involved in the operation of an air freight company in Singapore, though he had never been to Singapore. While most of the Value City stores operated in relatively small towns such as Lima, Ohio, Schottenstein Stores Corp. also bought chains in big cities, such as Wieboldt's in Chicago.

In the early 1980s, Schottenstein Stores was still tightly controlled by the Schottenstein family. The Value City chain had grown to around 35 stores, and it pulled in about $250 million annually. The company's furniture division, Value City Furniture, was one of the leading furniture retailers in the country. SSC also ran a chain of lawn and garden stores in the Philadelphia area; a drug and beauty aid chain; a chain of auto supply stores, and it also had a 50 percent interest in two mall-based apparel chains, Silverman's and American Eagle. The entire Schottenstein retail enterprise was estimated to bring in $600 million a year.

PUBLIC IN 1991

The Value City chain expanded through the Midwest in the late 1980s. It opened nine stores in 1989, and then six more in 1990, bringing the total to 53 stores in 11 states. Sales and earnings rose annually in the late 1980s. Sales of $537.8 million in 1990 were over 25 percent higher than the year previous, and operating profits too rose more than 20 percent. In mid-1991, Schottenstein Stores Corp. announced that it would take its Value City division public, offering a 25 percent stake in the business. The money raised would be used to retire debt. Value City's initial public offering went over well. Off-price retailing was seen as a smart trend, and Value City found eager investors. The stock price quickly rose by almost 90 percent, and the company soon declared a two-for-one stock split. The Schottenstein family still owned three-quarters of the new company's stock, giving it controlling power, and Jerome Schottenstein led Value City as chairman. His son Jay was vice-chairman and chief operating officer.

Jerome Schottenstein died in March 1992 of cancer at age 66. His son Jay, then 37, became chairman and CEO of Value City Department Stores, Inc. Jay had worked for SSC since 1976, and had been vice-chairman since 1986. He had worked closely with his father, and been responsible for much of the day-to-day business. Under his leadership, the Value City chain continued to expand as anticipated. Amid a generally flat retailing environment, Value City posted sales and earnings gains, and the company continued to open new stores. In 1992 it acquired a chain of 15 Gee Bee stores based in Johnston, Pennsylvania. Gee Bee was a struggling chain picked up by SSC in 1990. Value City took over the stores and converted most of them into Value Cities. The Value City formula seemed to make it stand out

KEY DATES

1917: Ephraim Schottenstein opens first store.
1946: Jerome Schottenstein joins Schottenstein Stores as executive.
1966: Schottenstein Stores buys Value City store, and utilizes this name for subsequent purchases and resuscitations of bankrupt stores.
1991: Value City is spun off from Schottenstein Stores as a public corporation.
1992: Jerome Schottenstein dies; son Jay takes over as CEO of Value City.
2000: Value City buys Filene's Basement chain.
2003: Retail Ventures, Inc., becomes holding company for Value City, Filene's Basement, and DSW.

even as the market filled with other discount chains such as Marshall's, T.J. Maxx, and Filene's Basement.

A writer for *Discount Store News* described Value City stores in an October 5, 1992, article as "an off-price, value-driven mall, a collection of specialty stores, under one roof." The stores were so big, and with such a variety of merchandise, that they attracted shoppers from all income levels. While some of the goods were genuinely inexpensive, some of the bargains Value City offered were top-of-the-line brand name items including men's suits and raincoats. These sold for hundreds of dollars, which was still hundreds of dollars less than department stores charged. Thus it was not just consumers on tight budgets who were attracted to the stores. A native of Columbus familiar with the store described shopping there in a September 28, 1992, *Forbes* article as "more like a sport than ordinary shopping." He claimed it was currently trendy among the city's affluent to dig for bargains at Value City.

Given the success of its initial public offering (IPO) and its apparently excellent retailing strategy, the chain laid plans for major growth. Already by early 1993, the Value City chain boasted 79 stores and sales of around $870 million; management foresaw hitting the $1 billion mark soon. Over the next ten years, management planned to open a minimum of five to seven stores a year, and company planners expected sales to eventually hit $2 billion.

Yet by 1995 the story was a little different. Apparel, which accounted for about two-thirds of Value City's sales, was stagnant, and company analysts struggled to

come up with a corrective strategy. The company had problems getting a new distribution center up and running, the market was considered flat in any case, and exceptionally warm weather in the fall of 1994 further depressed apparel sales. This led to a steep drop in earnings. The company looked at ways to make its stores friendlier, to advertise more effectively, and to move more goods from the back room onto the selling floor. Company executives reiterated that Value City had a great retail strategy. The firm's senior vice-president told the *Daily News Record* on November 3, 1995, that the chain was depending on its buyers being "sharper and closer to need" in order to get Value City cooking again. Despite difficulties, the chain continued to expand, moving mostly eastward. It opened stores in Atlanta, Georgia, and Charlotte, North Carolina, in 1995, and in 1996 opened nine stores total, including stores in New Jersey and Washington, D.C. Though the chain had long been suited to smaller towns, it expanded in Chicago and in suburbs of Philadelphia and St. Louis. All the stores the chain opened were not the same. The merchandise mix was specifically targeted to certain buying groups. A Paramus, New Jersey, store, for example, was filled with pricier and more sophisticated goods, while others in less trendy urban markets were designated as "moderate" or "budget" stores. The chain's advancement continued as the firm bought struggling regional merchants. Its new Philadelphia stores, for instance, were remodeled from units of a chain called Clover.

By the late 1990s, Value City had grown to a chain of over 90 stores. However the growth had come at a cost. By 1997, Value City was in a slump that had lasted for many months and sent earnings spiraling down. Same-store sales growth was under 1 percent monthly, and inventory piled up. In late 1997 Value City hired a turnaround artist, Martin P. Doolan, to take over as president and chief executive, temporarily setting aside Jay Schottenstein and former president George Iacono. Doolan brought in a team of new executives, and set to work refocusing Value City's apparel buying. Some stores were slated for renovations, which included wider aisles, new carpeting and signs, and a way of grouping goods by category rather than brand name. The company also began offering more services to its customers, such as automated teller machines in the stores and promotional incentives to its store credit card holders, and upped the discount its employees received on purchases, from 10 to 20 percent.

By the fourth quarter of 1998, the company had survived its red-ink period. Doolan had refocused the store on branded goods, and he attributed that shift to the company's returning fortunes. What Doolan called "good brands" had grown over his tenure from 15 percent of sales to over 60 percent. Most stores were renovated. The chain had halted its new store openings for fiscal 1998, but resumed its expansion with several new openings in the Southeast in 1999. Sales for 1998 reached $1.16 billion, and the company also made a new acquisition, buying up a shoe retailer called Shonac Corporation in May. A year later, the picture looked even better. Earnings increased dramatically, and the firm made several more strategic acquisitions. Value City took over eight stores from the Crowley's chain, which was in bankruptcy proceedings, giving it five stores in Detroit and three in Connecticut. Later in 1999, Value City acquired the inventory of the bankrupt Starter Corporation, a maker of athletic outerwear. Value City also purchased a chain of 14 discount stores in the St. Louis area, Grandpa's, converting most of them to the Value City format.

In 2000, Value City paid $16.1 million in cash and stock for the Filene's Basement chain. Filene's Basement was a rival discounter which had had its IPO at the same time as Value City's. The Wellesley, Massachusetts-based chain had at first been quite successful, growing to over 50 stores. However, by 2000 Filene's Basement had started to shut its stores and enter bankruptcy proceedings. Value City intended to sell off one part of the purchase, a chain of warehouse stores called Aisle 3 that Filene's operated, and to revive Filene's under new management. Value City began reopening some of the shuttered Filene's within months of the purchase, and it claimed it could bring the chain back to profitability within a year. With steadily growing sales and a stabilized earnings picture, Value City in the early 2000s seemed to be furthering its earlier pattern of success. It continued to expand across the country, using its tested strategy of buying up other bankrupt regional chains.

American Eagle's chief operating office George Kobler was tapped to fill the newly created CEO position at Value City in December 2000. The Value City chain was having a more difficult year than Filene's and DSW, as high fuel prices kept shoppers at home.

In 2001 the Schottenstein family proposed buying DSW and Filene's from Value City through its Schottenstein Stores Corporation holding company in a deal worth $275 million ($75 million of it in assumed debt). However, the offer was scrubbed after a lawsuit by shareholders who felt the units were worth much more. *Forbes* magazine was highly critical of this deal as well as other arrangements it said enriched the Schottensteins at shareholders' expense. Kobler defended the deal, saying Retail Ventures on its own did not have the money to finance growth at the two subsidiaries.

Kolber's tenure was short-lived, however, as he was replaced by John Rossler in March 2002. Rossler had held a number of executive posts with Value City's DSW business.

NEW HOLDING COMPANY IN 2003

Reorganization came in October 2003 in the form of a new umbrella corporation called Retail Ventures, Inc., which became the holding company for three operating segments: Value City Department Stores LLC, Filene's Basement, and DSW.

Heywood Wilansky was named president and CEO of Retail Ventures in November 2004 after a stint as head of Filene's Basement. Jay Schottenstein remained the company's chairman. Wilansky had led Filene's in the early 1990s when it was a division of May Department Stores, and was credited with initiating a turnaround at the chain beginning in 2002. To lift flagging sales, he guided the chain to the less crowded, higher end of the off-price market, noted the *Daily News Record*. Filene's aggressively updating its offerings and in 2004 opened a very successful outlet in the ultra competitive fashion environment of Manhattan. Other stores were enlarged and given a more upscale look. By differentiating itself from its competitors, Filene's was able to raise sales from $280 million to $450 million in a couple of years. The Value City formula was also tweaked in 2004, scaling back the home departments.

DSW Shoe Warehouse's immediate parent, Shonac Corporation, was renamed DSW Inc. and spun off in a July 2005 IPO that netted $286 million. Retail Ventures retained 63 percent of shares and 93 percent of voting power, and continued to count DSW as a subsidiary. With proceeds from the sale, the company was able to pay down debt. By January 2006, DSW was overseeing 199 stores in 32 states, while Value City had 113 stores and Filene's Basement 27. Retail Ventures' restated revenues for the fiscal year ended January 28, 2006, were $2.9 billion, an increase of 6 percent. Unprofitable for years, its net loss exploded to $183 million. In April 2006 Retail Ventures announced it was restating results for the three years ended January 29, 2005, due to an error in deferred tax account balances; its previously reported net losses were correct, however. Still, the chain stores that comprised Retail Ventures were enjoying strong sales and growth, and in 2006 DSW opened four new outlets. Returning the corporate structure to profitability would be the challenge in the immediate future.

A. Woodward
Updated, Frederick C. Ingram

PRINCIPAL OPERATING UNITS

Value City Department Stores LLC; Filene's Basement; DSW Shoe Warehouse.

PRINCIPAL COMPETITORS

Federated Department Stores, Inc.; Payless ShoeSource, Inc.; Ross Stores, Inc.; The TJX Companies, Inc.

FURTHER READING

Arlen, Jeffrey, "Value City: Orchestrating Off-Price," *Discount Store News,* May 3, 1993, p. A18.

"At Value City, Off-Price Retailing Is the Tradition," *Discount Store News,* July 25, 1983, p. 22.

Buchanan, Doug, "AEO's Schottenstein Family Looks to Buy Value City Subsidiaries," *Pittsburgh Business Times,* July 20, 2001, p. 6.

"From Value City to Ann Taylor: Winners and Losers in This Year's New Issues," *WWD,* December 5, 1991, p. 20.

Gebolys, Debbie, "Value City Lays Out Its Plans for a Turnaround," *WWD,* December 10, 1997, p. 5.

Hogsett, Don, "Retail Ventures Boosts Margins, Pushes Home," *Home Textiles Today,* June 19, 2006, p. 18.

Koselka, Rita, "The Schottenstein Factor," *Forbes,* September 28, 1992, pp. 104–05.

Lisanti, Tony, "Value City a Sign of Retail Vitality," *Discount Store News,* October 5, 1992, p. 8.

Markowitz, Arthur, "SSC: Powerful Retailer Besides Liquidator," *Discount Store News,* July 11, 1983, p. 5.

Pallay, Jessica, "A Basement Ascends in New York City; The New Filene's Basement Is More Than an Underground Phenomenon," *Daily News Record,* November 15, 2004, p. 14.

Palmieri, Jean E., "Heywood Wilansky; CEO, Retail Ventures Inc.," *Daily News Record,* May 16, 2005, p. 24.

———, "Schottenstein Speaks Softly, But Carries a Big Pencil," *Daily News Record,* November 8, 1996, p. 4.

"Parent Takes Value City Public," *Discount Store News,* May 20, 1991, p. 1.

Phillips, Jeff, and Jackson, William, "Schottenstein Empire Passes to Son, Jay," *Business First-Columbus,* March 16, 1992, p. 1.

"Retail Ventures to Restate Some Past Results," *Dow Jones Corporate Filings Alert,* April 11, 2006.

Rurberg, Sidney; "Schottenstein: It's All in Knowing When to Cure, When to Pull the Plug," *WWD,* July 14, 1983, p. 6.

Ryan, Thomas J., "Crowley Milner Liquidating, Will Sell Eight Units to Value City," *Daily News Record,* February 8, 1999, p. 20.

———, "Kobler to Value City as CEO," *WWD,* December 7, 2000.

———, "Rx for Sagging Sales: Customer-Friendly Stores and Prices," *Daily News Record,* November 3, 1995, p. 3.

Tatge, Mark, and Evan Hessel, "The Wasteland," *Forbes,* November 24, 2003, p. 92.

"Value City," *Fortune,* March 23, 1992, p. 109.

"Value City Aim: Absorb Gee Bee," *Discount Store News,* May 4, 1992, p. 1.

"Value City Chief Dead at 66," *Discount Store News,* April 6, 1992, p. 3.

"Value City Goes in the Black," *WWD,* October 12, 1998, p. 25.

"Value City Keeps Up the Pace," *Discount Store News,* November 18, 1996, p. 4.

"Value City Profits Soar 92.5%," *WWD,* November 30, 1999, p. 15.

"Value City to Acquire Filene's Basement for $16.1 Million," *Wall Street Journal,* February 4, 2000, p. B6.

Young, Vicki M., "Value City Completes Filene's Basement Deal," *WWD,* March 22, 2000, p. 11.

Russ Berrie and Company, Inc.

111 Bauer Drive
Oakland, New Jersey 07436
U.S.A.
Telephone: (201) 337-9000
Fax: (201) 405-7399
Web site: http://www.russberrie.com

Public Company
Incorporated: 1963
Employees: 1,220
Sales: $290.2 million (2005)
Stock Exchanges: New York
Ticker Symbol: RUS
NAIC: 339931 Doll and Stuffed Toy Manufacturing; 321999 All Other Miscellaneous Wood Product Manufacturing; 327112 Vitreous China, Fine Earthenware and Other Pottery Product Manufacturing; 339999 All Other Miscellaneous Manufacturing

■ ■ ■

Russ Berrie and Company, Inc., sells a wide variety of gift items, including stuffed animals, mugs, picture frames, figurines, and various home accessories through retailers located around the world. The company's brands include RUSS, Applause, Sassy, and Kids Line. Founded by a New Jersey toy salesman, the company saw its sales escalate dramatically after it went public in the early 1980s and began to acquire other gift makers. This growth through acquisition policy continued into the early years of the new millennium.

ORIGINS

The company that bears Russ Berrie's name was founded in 1963. Berrie himself had always had entrepreneurial leanings. As a child in the East Bronx he worked delivering Sunday newspapers and selling scorecards at baseball games. After attending the University of Florida, Berrie worked as a salesman and as a manufacturer's representative, and in 1963, he decided to strike out on his own. With $500, he rented a garage in Palisades Park, New Jersey, and launched his own firm, named after himself. Berrie intended to design, market, and distribute "impulse" gift items.

Berrie believed that the market for impulse gifts was ripe for expansion. Impulse gifts, items that shoppers did not seek specifically but noticed while in a store and purchased on a whim, were designed to be affordable and evoke an emotional response in the shopper. The classic impulse gift was an object such as a stuffed animal, a mug, or a cute figurine found in a gift and card store. Demand for these items had been growing in the early 1960s, and Berrie believed that they could be sold in all sorts of retail outlets, not just stationery and gift stores.

Berrie also chose this field because he felt that his experience in the toy industry would serve him well. He knew which products sold well and, through the contacts he had made, was able to purchase his merchandise directly from manufacturers. In his first year of business, Berrie himself was Russ Berrie and Company's sole employee. He handled all tasks, from selling products, to putting them in packages, to typing up invoices. At the end of the year, he had racked up $60,000 in sales.

In 1964, Berrie created his first line of manufactured

novelty items. Working with a designer, he came up with a line of stuffed animals and dubbed them "Fuzzy Wuzzies." In the following year, he supplemented the Fuzzy Wuzzie franchise with the "Bupkis Family," a group of soft, rubbery dolls. On the basis of the popularity of these products, sales for Russ Berrie and Company continued to grow throughout the company's first two years.

In 1966, Berrie formally incorporated his enterprise. Also that year, the company moved locations, trading up to a larger facility in Palisades Park, New Jersey, and adding to its workforce. In 1968, as the company shifted quarters again, moving to Elmwood Park, New Jersey, Berrie introduced Sillisculpts, small statues with messages inscribed on them, and these, too, became popular sellers.

EXPANSION

Berrie used the capital generated by sales of his first three product lines to finance further expansion of the company. Among his chief goals was the creation of a national sales force to sell his products to retailers. In 1968, the company hired its first full-time salesperson. This step allowed Russ Berrie & Company to promote its own products, rather than rely on manufacturers' representatives, who carried the goods of several different firms.

In 1971, as sales passed the $7 million mark, Russ Berrie and Company moved again, to a new corporate headquarters facility in Oakland, New Jersey. This location would become the center of the company's worldwide marketing and distribution businesses. In the following year, Russ Berrie and Company opened a second new facility, when a distribution center, in Santa Rosa, California, came on line. This was the first of a planned network of regional centers, each designed to fulfill warehousing, order processing, customer service, credit, and collections functions for accounts in a separate part of the country.

For its first ten years in business, Russ Berrie and Company concentrated on creating and designing its own products, and then contracted with manufacturers in the United States and abroad to produce them. Key to the company's success was the maintenance of a steady flow of ever-changing merchandise. Stores that sold Russ Berrie products needed a constant stream of seasonal, holiday, and everyday items to continually appeal to customers. In order to create these products and ensure that they tapped into current trends, Berrie inaugurated a product development department.

By 1973, however, dealings with manufacturers in Asia had become difficult, and Berrie decided to have his company take over the manufacturing of its products. Over the course of the next two years, the company purchased several manufacturing facilities, adding a stuffed animal factory in California, an injection molding factory in Florida, and another factory in Haiti. In addition, the company established a plastics factory in New Jersey and acquired a second plant in Florida. By 1977, Russ Berrie and Company had become a diversified producer and marketer of novelty goods, with a large number of different operations being run under the company's umbrella.

Such dramatic expansion in Russ Berrie and Company's activities, however, presented problems, as the company had, according to some critics, lost its focus. Berrie's expertise lay in sales and marketing, and he made sure to offer a wide variety of carefully selected products. As a manufacturer, however, Russ Berrie and Company was forced to abandon careful selection of products to market, in favor of keeping the machines in its factories running. As a result of its rapid expansion into manufacturing, Russ Berrie and Company found itself on the brink of bankruptcy. When Berrie realized that what his company did best was come up with ideas for novelty items, and market and sell them, not actually manufacture them, the company decided to withdraw from the production end of its business. In the mid-1970s, it began to shut down and sell its factories.

Following this decision, Berrie flew to the Far East and began to put into place structures for the manufacture of Russ Berrie products by others. In 1977, in Korea, the company set up the first of several satellite offices it would eventually open to facilitate production. Employees in this office were responsible for keeping tabs on items being manufactured for Russ Berrie and Company in the Far East. In this way, by hiring its own direct employees, the company hoped to avoid the difficulties of dealing with agents. Two years later, a second office, in Taiwan, was opened. Workers there oversaw

KEY DATES

1963: The company that bears Russ Berrie's name is founded.
1964: Berrie creates his first line of manufactured novelty items—Fuzzy Wuzzies.
1966: Berrie incorporates.
1968: The company hires its first full-time salesperson.
1979: Russ Berrie and Company establishes a subsidiary in the United Kingdom.
1984: The company goes public.
1985: Amram's Distributing Limited is acquired.
1987: Russ Berrie and Company enters the retail business for the first time when it buys the Fluf N'Stuf chain of 21 gift stores.
1992: The popularity of Trolls, one of the company's oldest products, escalates dramatically.
1996: Papel/Freelance is sold.
2002: Founder Russ Berrie dies; Sassy Inc. is acquired.
2004: The company purchases the Applause trademark.

the production of Russ Berrie goods in Taiwan and also took part in product development, helping to produce seasonal catalogues.

Also in 1979, Russ Berrie and Company established a subsidiary in the United Kingdom to serve customers there, as well as in the wider European market. The company set up a distribution center in Southhampton, England, which had a sales and support staff mirroring that of the company's American operations. With time, this facility was replaced with a larger one and distribution was expanded to cover Ireland, Holland, and Belgium. Russ Berrie and Company also set up agreements with independent distributors in other countries throughout Europe, guaranteeing that its products would achieve wide penetration of this market.

CONTINUING GROWTH

In the early 1980s, Russ Berrie and Company's sales continued to grow, and the company continued to expand its line of products. In fact, in 1982, the company was listed as one of the 500 fastest growing privately held firms in the United States by *Inc.* magazine. At this time, Russ Berrie and Company's sales force had grown to include 200 people. In a reorganiza-

tion of company activities, the firm split its operations into two units: Plush & Stuff, which sold stuffed animals, fabric dolls, and other soft items; and Gift/Expression, which was responsible for figurines, picture frames, greeting cards, magnets, mugs, and holiday ornaments and designs. With this new structure, each retail account was serviced by two salespeople, one from each division. In order to make this possible, Russ Berrie and Company hired a large number of new salespeople, doubling the size of its domestic salesforce.

By 1983, annual sales of Russ Berrie and Company products had exceeded $100 million. To keep track of the increased volume of products, the company installed a new computer system to oversee inventory and sales. Moreover, the company's MIS department was created for providing accurate data to managers, so that they could make decisions about which merchandise to select or discontinue.

Also in 1983, Russ Berrie and Company opened its Tri Russ International office in Hong Kong. Employees at this location were responsible for overseeing manufacturing in Hong Kong and also for providing sales and product support to all Russ Berrie and Company distributors around the world who did not have their own direct sales representative.

In 1984, Russ Berrie and Company sold stock to the public for the first time, as it was listed on the New York Stock Exchange. In the wake of this move, sales of the company's products started to grow rapidly. As a sign of this growth, Russ Berrie and Company opened two new warehouses to distribute its goods. One, in South Brunswick, New Jersey, serviced the eastern part of the United States. Another, in Petaluma, California, was designed to help move products from the Far East to other locations within the country most efficiently. Together, these two new facilities boasted 700,000 square feet of space, making the company's worldwide total of property owned more than 1.5 million square feet of space.

By 1985, Russ Berrie and Company sales had reached $204.6 million, and revenues more than doubled in just two years. At this time, the company embarked upon a program of rapid growth through acquisitions. In that year, Russ Berrie and Company bought Amram's Distributing Limited, which already functioned as the distributor for the company's products in Canada. Under the umbrella of the parent company, Amram's quickly expanded, until it had more than 60 salespeople peddling Russ Berrie and Company products to more than 6,300 retailers.

The following year, the company purchased two more firms in its industry: Freelance, Inc., and the Ef-fanbee Doll Company. In 1987, the company also bought Phil Papel Imports, Inc. The Freelance and Papel operations were amalgamated into one subsidiary, called Papel/Freelance, which was served by more than 100 salespeople. This division of the company distributed seasonal and everyday gifts, and was particularly well known for its beverage mugs. More than 20,000 retailers sold these goods throughout the United States, Canada, and the United Kingdom.

Also in 1987, Russ Berrie and Company entered the retail business for the first time, when it bought Fluf N'Stuf, a chain of 21 gift stores. Fluf N'Stuf outlets were located in regional malls throughout the East Coast of the United States. In this way, Russ Berrie and Company was able not only to sell its own goods, but to get an accurate picture of where demand for gift items was moving.

Also in 1987, Russ Berrie and Company became a licensee of the National Football League, with the right to sell products marked with the insignia of various NFL teams. At the end of the year, the company was given an award for its high sales of NFL products. Later, the company also began to market Major League Baseball merchandise.

As a result of its steady expansion through acquisition, Russ Berrie and Company reported pretax profits of $56 million in 1987. This figure was also enhanced by a boom in the demand for stuffed animals. The following year, however, the market for stuffed animals crashed, as the fad passed, and Russ Berrie and Company's profits plummeted to $23 million. Consequently, the price of the company's stock fell as well.

In the late 1980s, the company opened additional manufacturing supervision offices in Indonesia and Thailand, as these areas became locations of production for the company. In addition, Russ Berrie and Company expanded its distribution to areas of the former Soviet Union after the fall of the Berlin Wall in 1989. In time, its products and dolls were even featured in the Moscow airport gift shop.

NEW ACQUISITIONS

Russ Berrie and Company continued its expansion through acquisition in the early 1990s. In 1991, the company bought Bright of America, which produced place mats and stationery products sold primarily through big mass marketers, such as Wal-Mart and Kmart. In the wake of this purchase, Russ Berrie and Company began to utilize this company's manufacturing facility, located in West Virginia, to manufacture greeting cards and other paper products. Bright also ran a school fund-raising operation, in which schools purchased gift items for the students to resell in order to earn money for clubs and trips. During this time, Russ Berrie and Company also bought Weaver Werks, another gift producer, which specialized in popular and trendy items, such as cleverly packaged jelly beans and candy. The products of this subsidiary were added to the company's Papel/Freelance division.

In 1992, Russ Berrie and Company's fortunes got a lift, when the popularity of one of its oldest products, Trolls, first introduced in the 1960s, escalated dramatically. Although they had not been a big seller for many years, suddenly the company's trolls—squishy dolls with rubbery faces and hair that stood on end— were experiencing wild demand. To meet this clamor, Russ Berrie and Company's designers began to churn out hundreds of different troll products, and the company's Far Eastern suppliers raced to keep output high. By the end of the year, pushed by the troll fad, the company's earnings had soared to $300 million.

Flush with this success, Russ Berrie and Company expanded its product line even further in 1993, when it purchased Cap Toys, Inc., a Cleveland distributor of toys and candies. With this move, the company hoped to diversify its activities. Cap Toy products included the Stretch Armstrong and Spin Pops candies, which were supported through heavy advertising and were sold through many large retailers. With the addition of these products, the company's product line grew to more than 8,000. In 1994, OddzOn Products Inc. was acquired. With a strong record of success over the previous three decades and a solid franchise in the gift market, the company seemed assured of continued success as it moved into the late 1990s.

1995 AND BEYOND

With gift item sales on the rise, Russ Berrie and Company decided to sell its Papel/Freelance unit in order to focus on its core business in 1996. It also sold Cap Toys and OddzOn Products the following year. The cash from these sales would allow funding for future acquisitions. The company expanded its foothold in several international markets during this time period as well. Showrooms were opened in Hong Kong and South America and direct sales forces began selling Russ Berrie products in Germany and Spain. In 1999, Russ Australia Pty. Ltd. was formed in Sydney, Australia. That year the company adopted a new advertising slogan—"Make someone happy".

The company made several key purchases in the early years of the new millennium. In 2002, Russ Berrie and Company added Sassy Inc. to its arsenal in a $45 million deal. The addition of Sassy, a Michigan-based designer and manufacturer of baby and juvenile products, was expected to fuel future growth. It also launched its home and garden subsidiary that year. In 2004, the company acquired the rights to use the Applause Inc. trademark. Later that year, it purchased Kids Line L.L.C., a designer and distributor of juvenile bedding products, and sold its Bright of America subsidiary.

In December 2002, founder, chairman, and CEO Russ Berrie died unexpectedly after having a heart attack in his home. Often named by *Fortune* magazine as one of America's most generous philanthropists, Berrie was just 69 years old when he died. Josh Weston was named chairman and Berrie's widow, Angelica Berrie, took over as CEO. She stepped down in 2004 when former Toys 'R' Us executive Andrew Gatto assumed the position.

At the time of Gatto's arrival, Russ Berrie and Company stood well positioned with no debt and more than $60 million in free cash even as independent gift stores were seeing sales falter amid intense competition from the likes of Wal-Mart, Target, and other large stores. Gatto outlined part of his strategy in a July 2004 *Knight-Ridder/Tribune Business News* article. "The company will be far more open to externally fueled development. That will come in the form of relationships with the inventing and product development communities as well as the licensing community. That's a major change of direction for this company." In addition, Gatto planned to develop new brands for mass market and upscale department stores. Gatto's first licensing deal was with Wolverine Worldwide to produce its Hush Puppy hound doll.

As sales in the company's core retail gift business continued to falter in 2005, Russ Berrie and Company initiated a restructuring plan that included job cuts and other streamlining efforts to reduce costs. It planned to shutter sales and distribution operations in France, Germany, Belgium, and the Netherlands. Overall, company sales increased in 2005 due mainly to growth in its infant and juvenile division. The company's bottom line was not as positive, as it posted a net loss of $35.1 million for the year. Angelica Berrie, head of The Russell Berrie Foundation, decided to sell the foundation's 42 percent stake in Russ Berrie and Company in August 2006. Private investment firm Prentice Capital Management LP set plans in motion to acquire the stake. Prentice Capital Management would become the company's largest shareholder upon completion of the deal.

Elizabeth Rourke
Updated, Christina M. Stansell

PRINCIPAL SUBSIDIARIES

Russ Berrie U.S. Gift, Inc.; Russ Berrie & Co. (West), Inc.; Russ Berrie and Company Investments, Inc.; Russ Berrie and Company Properties, Inc.; Amram's Distributing Ltd.; Russplus, Inc.; Sassy, Inc.; Kids Line, L.L.C.; Kids Line Australia Pty. Ltd.; Tri Russ International (Hong Kong) Ltd.; Russ Consulting Service (Shenzhen) Co., Ltd.; Russ Berrie (U.K.) Ltd.; Russ Berrie (Holdings) Ltd.; Russ Berrie España, S.L.; Russ Berrie (Deutschland) GmbH; Russ Berrie (Österreich) GmbH; Russ Berrie France S.A.R.L.; Russ Berrie (Benelux) B.V.; Russ Berrie (Ireland) Ltd.; Russ Australia Pty. Ltd.

PRINCIPAL COMPETITORS

The Boyds Collection Ltd.; Enesco Group Inc.; Ty Inc.

FURTHER READING

Berrie, Russell, "Concentrate on Doing What You Do Best," *Baylor Business Review,* Fall 1994, pp. 2–5.

Morley, Hugh R., "Englewood, N.J., Toy Maker Dies at 69," *Knight-Ridder/Tribune Business News,* December 27, 2002.

"Russ Berrie Acquires Kid Line," *Furniture Today,* January 2005, p. 18.

"Russ Berrie Acquires Sassy for $45 Million," *Furniture Today,* October 2002, p. 24.

Toplis, Maggie, "Awakenings," *Financial World,* July 7, 1992, p. 66.

"A Toy Maker's Search for Cheer," *NJBIZ,* December 19, 2005, p. 4.

Verdon, Joan, "42 Percent of Berrie Changing Hands," *Knight-Ridder/Tribune Business News,* August 8, 2006.

———, "Gift Company Russ Berrie and Co. Charts New Course," *Knight-Ridder/Tribune Business News,* July 21, 2004.

———, "Gift Maker in Oakland, NJ, Winds Trademark for $7 Million," *Knight-Ridder/Tribune Business News,* October 16, 2004.

———, "Russ Berrie Will Cut Jobs, Shut Operations in Europe," *Knight-Ridder/Tribune Business News,* April 20, 2006.

Russell Corporation

3330 Cumberland Boulevard
Suite 800
Atlanta, Georgia 30339
U.S.A.
Telephone: (678) 742-8000
Fax: (678) 742-8300
Web site: http://www.russellcorp.com

Wholly Owned Subsidiary of Berkshire Hathaway Inc.
Incorporated: 1902 as Russell Manufacturing Company
Employees: 15,500
Sales: $1.435 billion (2005)
NAIC: 315211 Men's & Boys' Cut & Sew Apparel
Contractors; 315212 Women's, Girls', & Infants'
Cut & Sew Apparel Contractors; 31321 Broadwoven
Fabric Mills; 315191 Outerwear Knitting Mills;
313311 Broadwoven Fabric Finishing Mills

■ ■ ■

From humble origins in a small Alabama town in 1902, Russell Corporation has evolved into a leading authentic athletic and sporting goods manufacturer. The company sells athletic uniforms, apparel, athletic footwear, sporting goods and athletic equipment, and accessories in over 100 countries across the globe. Its brands include Russell Athletic, Jerzees, Spalding, Brooks, American Athletic, Huffy Sports, Mossy Oak, Cross Creek, Moving Comfort, Bike, Dudley, Discus, and Sherrin. Through its Spalding arm, Russell operates as the largest provider of basketball equipment in the world.

Conglomerate Berkshire Hathaway Inc. acquired Russell Corp. in 2006.

EARLY 20TH-CENTURY FOUNDING

Founder Benjamin Russell was only 25 when he bought six knitting machines from R.A. Almond in 1902. Russell, a struggling lawyer in Birmingham, Alabama, was anxious to return home to Alexander City and open his own business. With borrowed money, he incorporated Russell Manufacturing Company in 1902, remaining its president until he died in 1941. Russell's knitting machines, 12 sewing machines, and 12 employees were crammed into a 50 by 100 foot wooden building. Because of the lack of electricity, Russell Manufacturing Company relied on steam for power. At the end of the first year of production, the company was turning out 150 items of clothing per day. Though first year profits were disappointing, the entrepreneurial young owner envisioned his plant expanding into all aspects of the garment-making business.

Russell's dream was slowly realized, and profits grew steadily in the following years. Six years after opening his plant, Russell acquired spinning frames, allowing the company to produce its own yarn. Several years later, it could bleach its own cloth. Electricity came to the plant in 1912, and two years later a second yarn plant went into operation.

Demand for cloth and yarn shot up dramatically during World War I, during which time the company expanded and prospered. When the war ended, the ensuing recession left the company unaffected because

COMPANY PERSPECTIVES

From its beginnings in 1902, Russell Corporation has prided itself on the quality and value of its products—and on its commitment to its employees and the communities where it operates. Russell has long been a company that is able to take advantage of changes in the marketplace, changes in technology and changes in its products. Building on its heritage as an athletic company, Russell has become a global leader in the sporting goods industry with apparel and equipment for all levels of activity—from the playing fields of major colleges to the backyards of homes across the country.

the demand for yarn continued. In response, the company added workers and plants. Also at this time, the Russell Mill School was established for educating the children of employees as well as for adult programs. The company's fourth yarn plant began operation in 1921, and in early 1927 a weaving operation was installed. By the end of the year Russell Manufacturing Company could dye its own cotton and yarn, coming close to realizing Benjamin Russell's ambition of making his company a completely vertical or "fiber to fabric" operation.

MOVING INTO ATHLETIC WEAR AND SCREEN PRINTING

Until 1932, however, fabric still had to be sent to other U.S. plants for finishing. Despite the company's losses during the Great Depression, Benjamin Russell decided to expand his business. The worst year of the Depression, 1932, turned into a milestone year for the 30-year-old company; it acquired full finishing operations, thereby becoming one of the few fully vertical fabric factories in the world. That same year Benjamin Russell's son, Benjamin C. Russell, established an athletics division called the Southern Manufacturing Company. Its first products were football jerseys sold to a sporting goods distributor in New York. In 1938 the company's first screen printing developed for the printing of names, numbers, and designs on athletic uniforms. In 1960 the Southern Manufacturing Company was renamed the Russell Athletic Division. No one in 1932 would have guessed that this unobtrusive sideline would alter the company's identity from that of a domestic fabric manufacturer to a global leader in the sportswear industry.

Civilian textile manufacturing declined during World War II because of enormous government clothing contracts that strained the company. By war's end, machinery was badly in need of repair because replacement materials had been difficult to obtain during the war years. In addition the company's founder, Benjamin Russell, had died at the outset of World War II. His son Benjamin C. Russell took over the helm during the difficult but prosperous war years but died prematurely of pneumonia in 1945. Another Russell son, Thomas Dameron Russell, succeeded him at the helm. By the time he stepped down as president 23 years later, the company had become a leading manufacturer of athletic and leisure wear and exited the fashion clothing manufacturing business.

In the 1950s sporting and leisure wear had not yet caught on with the general public. With two domestic recessions, the company was hard hit by falling sales and growing competition, and expansion was temporarily impeded. Changes in the clothing industry, however, helped Russell rebound. By the early 1960s, T-shirts had become acceptable garb for both sexes. In the late 1960s the unisex trend in clothing strengthened while leisure clothing became popular in the early 1970s. These trends served to Russell's advantage. In 1966 a new sewing plant was established in Montgomery, Alabama (the first Russell plant to be built outside of Alexander City). Four years later, the Athletic Division had expanded so much that a separate plant became necessary. The company had gone public in 1963. The firm, whose name had been changed in 1962 to Russell Mills, Inc., would be a public stockholding company in which the Russell family and other insiders would continue to own approximately 32 percent of the stock.

MODERNIZATION AND EXPANSION

In 1968 Eugene C. Gwaltney became president of Russell Mills (which in 1973 would become the Russell Corporation). That year company sales stood at $51 million. During Gwaltney's term in office, plant expansion continued. The company's screen printing facilities were enlarged, and it acquired a yarn manufacturing plant in northeast Georgia in 1977. In the mid-1970s Russell opened a new distribution center in Alexander City. All operations at this ultramodern facility, such as storage retrieval, shipping, and goods reception, were fully automated and consolidated. At the same time, new buildings went up to house operations including data processing, personnel, and security. By 1981, with the consolidation of knitting into one plant, Russell could boast the most modern knitting facilities in the world. Expansion into Florida and south Alabama took

KEY DATES

1902: Russell Manufacturing Company is established.
1927: The company can dye its own cotton and yarn.
1932: Russell Manufacturing becomes one of the few fully vertical fabric factories in the world; athletics division Southern Manufacturing Company is formed.
1938: Screen printing is developed for the printing of names, numbers, and designs on athletic uniforms.
1960: Southern Manufacturing Company is renamed Russell Athletic Division.
1963: The company goes public as Russell Mills Inc.
1973: The company changes its name to Russell Corp.
1992: NuBlend is introduced in Russell's Jerzees line of sportswear.
1998: Russell launches a major restructuring.
2003: The Jagged Edge trademark, Bike Athletic Company, and Spalding Sports Worldwide Inc. are purchased.
2006: Berkshire Hathaway Inc. acquires Russell.

place after 1982, the year Eugene Gwaltney was elected chairman of the board and was succeeded as president by Dwight L. Carlisle.

In 1989 the Russell Corporation test and evaluation mill was constructed at a cost of $6 million. This was an innovative facility in which new machinery was evaluated before purchase, avoiding the interruptions in operations implicit in conducting tests during the production process. By 1990 the company owned and operated 13 sewing plants outside of Alexander City and employed 15,000 workers. Since 1976 sales revenues had increased by 13 percent annually. With the acquisition of two subsidiaries, Quality Mills in North Carolina and Cloathbond Ltd. in Scotland, in 1988 and 1989 respectively, the company had become a global contender in the sportswear industry.

According to market analysts, a key to the company's success was its aggressive technological modernization. In a five-year period ending in 1992, the company invested more than half a billion dollars in capital expenditures which translated into approximately 15 percent of annual sales—far higher than the industry's

average of 8 percent. In addition, the company spent at least 3 percent of sales revenues on print and television advertising. In both 1980 and 1990 Textile World cited Russell Corporation as the "Model Mill" of the year. Another reason for the company's success was research and development. In 1992 an innovative new material that prevented pilling, NuBlend, was introduced in Russell's Jerzees line of sportswear and won accolades from the leisurewear industry. Partly because NuBlend was the preferred fabric for screen printers, Russell held the top market share in the fleece screen printing business at 30 percent.

Under president and CEO John C. Adams, who succeeded the retiring Carlisle in 1991, approximately 80 percent of Russell Corporation's early 1990s sales were derived from its principal divisions: Athletic, Knit Apparel, Fabrics, and its major U.S. subsidiary, Cross Creek Apparel, Inc. (formerly Quality Mills). The company had become the top manufacturer of athletic uniforms in the nation. In 1992 Russell was awarded a five-year contract to serve as the exclusive producer and marketer of athletic uniforms for most Major League Baseball teams. The contract also stipulated that the company held the exclusive right to manufacture and market replicas of major league uniforms, T-shirts, and shorts. This put the company in an advantageous position in relation to its main rival, Champion, Inc., the supplier of uniforms to the NBA teams. The Knit Apparel Division produced the Jerzees brand of activewear, which had been introduced in 1983, and included T-shirts, fleece, knit shorts, and tank tops, which were sold to specialized retailers and large merchandisers such as Wal-Mart. Cross Creek produced the Cross Creek Pro Collection, featuring casual knit shirts and rugbys, which were sold mainly in golf pro shops, and Cross Creek Country Cottons, which were purchased by screen printers and embroiderers for resale. The remainder of Russell's revenues were derived from the Fabrics Division, which manufactured and marketed lightweight cotton material for sale to clothing manufacturers, and from its European subsidiary, Russell Corp. UK Ltd. in Scotland. This subsidiary had been acquired in 1989 under the name Cloathbond, Ltd.; it was a vertical establishment that manufactured and marketed a full line of Russell clothing, from the cotton fiber to the finished product, for the European market. This international expansion helped the company approach $1 billion in sales in the early 1990s. In 1992 alone, Russell's international sales increased 40 percent over 1991.

In April 1993 Gwaltney retired as chairman of Russell, ending a 41-year career at the company. Adams then served as chairman, president, and CEO. Later that year Russell paid $35 million to acquire The Game,

Inc., a maker of licensed sports headgear and apparel, with a leading position in the marketing of such products for colleges and universities. The name of the acquired entity was changed to Licensed Products Division in 1994. That year Russell acquired Fort Payne, Alabama-based Desoto Mills, a finisher/manufacturer and marketer of sports and casual socks under the Desoto Players Club, Athletic Club, Performance Club, and Player Performance brand names. Russell also acquired the trademarks and licenses of Chalk Line, Inc., in 1994, a year in which the company's revenues exceeded $1 billion for the first time.

MAJOR RESTRUCTURING NEAR THE END OF THE DECADE

Although sales and net income reached record levels in 1996, in part because of the impact of the Summer Olympics which were held in Atlanta that year, Russell's fortunes turned south in 1997 when both sales and net income fell. The decline was caused by intensifying competition as industry-wide over-capacity and price-cutting by rivals forced Russell to lower its own prices, all of which hurt the company's results. Particularly troubled was the Licensed Products Division, which Russell dissolved in 1997, dividing its operations among the other divisions. In 1997 Russell also ended its licensing deals with the professional football, basketball, and hockey leagues.

In early 1998, as the company's troubles continued, Adams retired; stepping in as chairman, president, and CEO was John "Jack" Ward, former CEO of the Hanes Group and senior vice-president of Sara Lee Corporation. Within months of Ward's arrival, Russell announced a major restructuring. Over a three-year period, the company planned to eliminate about 4,000 jobs, or 23 percent of its workforce; close about 25 of its 90 plants, distribution centers, and other facilities; and move most of the final assembly of garments abroad, to Mexico, Honduras, and elsewhere in the Caribbean basin. The company expected to take charges of $100 to $125 million during the restructuring period. Russell hoped these efforts would result in annual savings of $50-$70 million. Part of these funds would then be used to bolster the marketing and advertising of Russell's brands, including tripling the advertising budget to $25 million per year. Russell also established a second headquarters in Atlanta in February 1999, a move designed to make travel more convenient and to aid in recruiting efforts, particularly of marketing aces who did not relish the idea of living in the small town of Alexander City.

Finally, in January 1999 Russell reorganized into six strategic business units as part of its transformation from a manufacturing-driven organization to a consumer-oriented marketing corporation. Each of the units was self-contained, with full responsibility and accountability for results; each included such functional areas as manufacturing, sales, marketing, finance, information systems, and human resources. Three of the units centered around a major Russell brand: Russell Athletic, Jerzees, and Cross Creek. Fabrics and Services focused on quality woven fabrics, as well as housing some central service functions operating companywide. Russell Yarn was established as a supplier of yarn for the manufacture of Russell textiles and apparel. The International Division was charged with marketing all Russell branded products outside the United States and Canada; it conducted business in 50 countries in all.

Restructuring charges led Russell to post a fiscal 1998 net loss of $10.4 million on revenues of $1.18 billion. Results for the first half of 1999 also showed a net loss of $12.9 million but the restructuring had resulted in a decrease in selling, general, and administration costs of 13 percent. Russell had also increased its offshore apparel assembly to 55 percent of total capacity, a substantial increase from the 17 percent mark before the restructuring was launched. Russell had far to go before it could be considered fully turned around, but it appeared that the company was well on its way.

RUSSELL IN THE NEW MILLENNIUM

The company completed its restructuring process in 2001. When the dust settled, nearly all of its retail outlets had been shuttered, over 6,000 jobs had been cut, and most of its manufacturing operations had moved overseas. At the same time, Russell continued to seek out opportunities that would strengthen its operations. In 2000, Russell Corporation acquired the apparel operations of Haas Outdoors, Inc., which later became the Mossy Oak Apparel Company.

Russell celebrated its 100th anniversary in 2002. That year the company purchased Moving Comfort, a manufacturer of women's activewear. It added the Jagged Edge trademark to its holdings the following year, along with Bike Athletic Company and Spalding Sports Worldwide Inc. The Spalding deal gave Russell a foothold in the sporting goods market for the first time in its history. Russell continued its acquisition spree in 2004 by purchasing American Athletic Inc. (AAI), Huffy Corp.'s sports division, and Brooks Sports. It also secured an extended contract to provide Spalding and Huffy branded products to the National Basketball Association. In 2005, Russell landed a five-year licensing contract with Itochu Fashion System Co. to market the Spalding brand in Japan and also secured a deal to manufacture and market athletic apparel and footwear in China.

The company faced challenges in 2005 due to rising costs and falling sales. During Hurricanes Rita and Katrina, over 40 containers of Russell products were lost or destroyed and nearly 70 percent of the ports it used for shipping were closed. Amid intense competition and faltering profits, the company launched a restructuring plan much like the effort of the late 1990s. Russell continued shifting its manufacturing base overseas and cut a total of 2,300 jobs. In 2006, the company closed its Huffy manufacturing facilities and moved production overseas. It also merged its Moving Comfort brand into its Athletic Division.

Conglomerate Berkshire Hathaway Inc. made a $600 million play for Russell Corp. in early 2006. Berkshire, led by billionaire Warren Buffet, believed Russell would be a good fit with its Fruit of the Loom Inc. subsidiary. At the same time, Russell stood to benefit from Berkshire Hathaway's deep pockets. CEO Jack Ward commented on the deal in an April 2006 *Wall Street Journal* article claiming, "Russell will be better positioned against our world-wide competitors in all three segments of our business, and that includes apparel, sports equipment, and athletic shoes." Ward ended up opposing the deal, however, during the shareholder vote. He argued Russell's restructuring efforts would lead to stronger financial results in 2006 and 2007 and that a purchase was no longer necessary to secure the company's financial future. His sole vote did not sway shareholders and in the end, Berkshire Hathaway completed its purchase.

Sina Dubovoj
Updated, David E. Salamie; Christina M. Stansell

PRINCIPAL COMPETITORS

Gildan Activewear Inc.; NIKE Inc.; Sara Lee Branded Apparel.

FURTHER READING

"Berkshire to Buy Russell Corp.," *Wall Street Journal*, April 18, 2006, p. C3.

"Berkshire Hathaway Acquires Russell," *Apparel*, June 2006, p. 10.

Bernstein, Andy, "John Adams: The SGB Interview," *Sporting Goods Business,* September 22, 1997, pp. 26-27.

Ebenkamp, Becky, and Terry Lefton, "Russell Shows Some Muscle," *Brandweek,* May 10, 1999, p. 1.

Hagerty, James R., "Russell's New CEO Is Looking to Make Rivals Sweat: Stock Price Bulks Up on Plans for a Trimmer Athletic-Gear Company," *Wall Street Journal,* August 5, 1998, p. B4.

Herek, Matthew, "Russell Takes on a New Look With Spalding," *Sporting Goods Business,* May 2003, p. 14.

Kletter, Melanie, "Russell Restructures Amid Rising Costs," *WWD,* January 23, 2006, p. 2.

Leibowitz, David S., "Finding Value in Small Town America (Russell and Dean Foods' Stocks)," *Financial World,* February 2, 1993, p. 86.

Lloyd, Brenda, "Russell Benefits From Acquisitions, Cost Cuts," *Daily News Record,* April 26, 2004.

——, "Russell Corp. to Cut 4,000 Employees and Close 25 Facilities," *Daily News Record,* July 24, 1998, p. 1.

——, "Russell Sees Sales Hitting $1.1B, Increase in Earnings for Year," *Daily News Record,* April 28, 1994, pp. 5+.

McCurry, John, "Adams Retires, Russell Names Ward As CEO," *Textile World,* May 1998, pp. 24+.

——, "'New' Russell Stresses "'Global,'" *Textile World*, March 1999, p. 20.

Miller, Andy, "Russell Hopes to Score with Baseball Apparel," *Atlanta Constitution,* January 21, 1992, p. D1.

"Russell CEO Opposed Sale to Berkshire Hathaway," *Associated Press Newswires,* June 21, 2006.

"Russell Corp. Says It Will Cut 4,000 Jobs, Shift Work Abroad," *Wall Street Journal,* July 23, 1998, p. A6.

"Russell's All Star Line-up: Managing for the Distance; Russell Manufacturing Tops Technology Curve," *Textile World,* June 1990, pp. 40-64.

Smarr, Susan L., "Looking at the Big Picture," *Bobbin,* February 1990, pp. 60-64.

"TW's 1996 Leader of the Year: John C. Adams," *Textile World,* October 1996, pp. 36+.

Welling, Kathryn M., "Out of Fashion Buys: An Analyst Cottons Up to Selected Apparel Stocks," *Barron's,* July 9, 1990, pp. 12-13, 28-29, 50.

Safety-Kleen Systems Inc.

5400 Legacy Drive
Cluster II, Building 3
Plano, Texas 75024
U.S.A.
Telephone: (972) 265-2000
Toll Free: (800) 669-5740
Fax: (972) 265-2990
Web site: http://www.Safety-Kleen.com

Private Company
Incorporated: 1963
Employees: 5,000
Sales: $868 million (2004)
NAIC: 56292 Materials Recovery Facilities; 562211 Hazardous Waste Treatment and Disposal; 562219 Other Nonhazardous Waste Treatment and Disposal

∎ ∎ ∎

Safety-Kleen Systems Inc., formerly known as Safety-Kleen Corporation, is a leading provider of parts washers, industrial waste management, and oil recycling and re-refining services. The company has more than 400,000 customers including auto shops, government agencies, and corporations such as General Electric, Goodyear, and Chrysler. Safety-Kleen is the largest recovery and recycling company for used oil products in the United States refining nearly 160 million gallons of used motor oil each year. The company emerged from bankruptcy protection in 2003 as a private entity.

EARLY HISTORY

Safety-Kleen traces its roots to a Wisconsin inventor named Ben Palmer who designed the Safety-Kleen parts washer, a device that helped remove grease from auto parts. While working in his family's sand and gravel business during the 1950s, Palmer was inspired to come up with a safer means of cleaning automotive parts than the standard and somewhat dangerous method of washing parts in gasoline. In 1954 Palmer developed his first parts-washing device, a sink with a nonflammable fire cover placed on top of a barrel containing a parts-washing solvent. Palmer attached a hose and spigot to the sink, which was used to pump cleaning solution into the sink. Beneath the sink Palmer placed a screening filter, allowing the part-washing solvent, once screened, to be reused in a relatively dirt-free condition.

By 1959 Palmer had received an initial patent for his parts washer and sold a few of his machines to other gravel pit businesses. He then left his native Milwaukee area to market his invention in New Orleans and Chicago. With minimal sales success, Palmer, who was still assembling his own machines, returned to Milwaukee during the early 1960s. He leased his parts washers to local businesses and periodically serviced those machines, removing used solvent and adding a clean solution. By the mid-1960s Palmer had 100 customers.

In 1967 Gene Olson, a Wisconsin businessman, discovered one of Palmer's parts washers in a local service station and thought the under-marketed device represented a gold mine. Olson offered Palmer $100,000 for his Safety-Kleen business and the inventor accepted the offer. In order to make the business more profitable, Olson expanded service areas around the Milwaukee area, franchised his business to independent operators outside of Wisconsin, and established minimum service intervals. Marketing efforts, which boosted Safety-Kleen's customer base to 400, were not enough to keep the parts washer operation afloat and within a year the company was nearly bankrupt.

In 1968 Olson sold Safety-Kleen to Chicago Rawhide Manufacturing Company, an Elgin, Illinois–based manufacturer of automotive bearing shaft seals for the original equipment market. Chicago Rawhide, seeking to diversify into the automotive replacement market, paid Olson $25,000 in cash and assumed Safety-Kleen's $160,000 worth of debt. Donald W. Brinckman, a Chicago Rawhide vice-president who helped engineer the Safety-Kleen deal, became president and chief executive of the new Chicago Rawhide subsidiary.

In order to avoid competitor duplication of the Safety-Kleen washer, which held only a loose patent, and also to avoid unwanted competition in a yet developed market for parts washer services, Brinckman devised a marketing plan designed to quickly push Safety-Kleen into the national arena. The plan divided the country into seven regions for marketing purposes. Newly recruited regional managers were trained in the Minneapolis-St. Paul, Minnesota, area just a few months after Safety-Kleen was acquired in preparation for a national rollout of services. The managers leased service centers, rented trucks, hired route drivers and sales help, and established branch routes in a matter of weeks before moving on to their own respective regions. Following a similar formula in other major market areas, Safety-Kleen established a network of 130 branch facilities within three years.

The Safety-Kleen business—which literally created its own industry—was targeted to help sell Chicago Rawhide's replacement wheel seals by placement of route drivers throughout the United States and provision of a regular customer service that could become an inroad for selling seals. Safety-Kleen's initial activities included placement of its parts washer free of charge at an auto or retail repair business; it then collected a fee to remove and replace the dirty solvent.

Safety-Kleen was the first company to provide other companies with solvent disposal services, which became a major selling point. Seeking to avoid direct disposal of waste solvents, in 1969 Allan Manteuffel, a Safety-Kleen chemical engineer, began experimenting with ways to recycle used solvents. That same year Safety-Kleen purchased and began conversion of a former oil storage plant; by 1970 the company was processing solvents at its first recycling center.

GROWTH IN THE 1970S

Safety-Kleen entered the international arena in 1970 when it began establishing service routes in Canada. By October 1971 Safety-Kleen had placed 75,000 machines on 132 routes in 42 states and two Canadian provinces. That same year the company added a computerized control center in Elgin to manage customer records and automatically generate lists of needed service calls. The company also converted a second oil storage plant into a recycling center in Reedley, California. With annual sales topping $7.4 million in 1971, the company became profitable for the first time.

In 1972 Safety-Kleen began introducing allied products that its service representatives could regularly offer to established customers. Safety-Kleen's first allied product, an oil filter produced outside the company and offered exclusively by Safety-Kleen, debuted in September 1972 and was followed by a cream hand cleaner one year later. In December 1972 Safety-Kleen utilized trade magazines to launch the company's first major advertising drive, which targeted service station and automobile garage operators.

In 1973 Safety-Kleen established its first overseas operations and began to do business in England. That same year the company constructed a new Wisconsin parts cleaner production facility to replace a much smaller factory it had been leasing. In 1974 a recycling center in Clayton, New Jersey, opened.

The expansion of Safety-Kleen's business during the early 1970s drove the company to devise a branch system, with each branch encompassing several service and sales routes. Much like a franchise system without any required initial investment on the part of the branch manager, the branch system rewarded the success of individual branch operators by giving managers a stake in the company at a cost for route trucks and sales help. The branch manager was also responsible for sale representatives' commissions.

The Safety-Kleen formula for sales growth paid off

KEY DATES

1954: Ben Palmer develops his first parts-washing device.

1959: Palmer has received an initial patent for his parts washer and has sold a few of his machines to other gravel pit businesses.

1967: Gene Olson offers Palmer $100,000 for his Safety-Kleen business.

1968: Olson sells Safety-Kleen to Chicago Rawhide Manufacturing Company.

1970: The company processes solvents at its first recycling center; the company enters the Canadian market.

1974: Safety-Kleen is spun off as an independent company.

1983: The company lists on the New York Stock Exchange.

1998: Laidlaw Environmental Services acquires Safety-Kleen.

2000: The company files for Chapter 11 bankruptcy protection.

2003: The company emerges from Chapter 11 as Safety-Kleen Systems Inc.

and by 1974 the company had placed 125,000 washers and grown from a local work force of ten to an international operation with more than 700 employees. In October 1974 Safety-Kleen, which never delivered the seal sales expected of it, was spun off as an independent corporation. Brinckman was named president of Safety-Kleen and Russell A. Gwillim, president of Chicago Rawhide, assumed the position of chairman of Safety-Kleen. Four days after the spinoff, Safety-Kleen moved into its new Elgin headquarters, adjacent to the Chicago Rawhide office.

In December 1974 Safety-Kleen set up shop in Germany, but the language barrier resulted in recruiting problems and growth remained slow there throughout the 1970s. In 1975 Safety-Kleen opened recycling centers in Denton, Texas, and Lexington, South Carolina. The company's five recycling centers completed Safety-Kleen's national "closed loop" recovery system, which followed waste fluids throughout their existence and recovered them for re-use. The recycling centers began paying more than environmental dividends in 1973, following the onset of the OPEC Oil Embargo and the accompanying rise in gas prices and the cost of new solvent.

In 1976 Safety-Kleen opened a new, state-of-the-art recycling plant in Elgin and two years later began recycling immersion cleaner solvent. By the mid-1970s Safety-Kleen was processing more than 15 million gallons of used mineral spirits solvent annually, with 70 of every 100 gallons of solvent delivered to customers as recycled liquid.

During the mid-1970s Safety-Kleen introduced a number of allied products, including a powdered concrete floor cleaner that was the first company-made allied product, a wiper blade, a carburetor cold parts cleaner, an aerosol spray choke and carburetor cleaner, and a Safety-Kleen broom. In 1977 Safety-Kleen introduced a wheel seal cabinet service.

Safety-Kleen continued to target industrial customers, introducing a number of allied services during the mid-1970s. In 1976 the company introduced its immersion cleaner service, which cleaned gum-and-varnish encrusted automotive parts, and two years later Safety-Kleen debuted a customer-owned machine service (COMS). COMS—aimed at customers who originally purchased parts washers from Ben Palmer as well as customers who owned parts cleaning machines made by other firms—opened up industrial markets by providing a service for all sizes and brands of parts washers.

In 1978 Safety-Kleen entered the Australian market and two years later established a recycling center there. In April 1979 Safety-Kleen went public with an initial over-the-counter offering of 265,000 shares. Proceeds from the stock offering allowed Safety-Kleen to polish off its $4 million debt to Chicago Rawhide.

During the late 1970s Safety-Kleen began test marketing a restaurant filter cleaning business and in mid-1979, after establishing a regional restaurant filter cleaning business around the Elgin area, Safety-Kleen opened an automated filter cleaning plant in Elk Grove Village, Illinois; similar plants opened a year later in New Jersey and California. Overseas, U.K. parts washer placements nearly doubled in the late 1970s. In 1980 Safety-Kleen absorbed its chief U.K. competitor, Greaseater, Ltd., a two-year-old firm that had modeled its operations on Safety-Kleen's business.

Safety-Kleen entered the 1980s with more than six domestic recycling centers and more than 200 branch facilities, including more than 160 branches in the United States. By 1980 Safety-Kleen was the world's largest solvent recycler, processing more than 25 million gallons of mineral solvents a year. In addition, the company's recycling efforts had been expanded to include restaurant exhaust grease filters and Safety-Kleen route vans and trucks, which the company regularly rebuilt.

FOCUSING ON INDUSTRIAL MARKETS IN THE EARLY 1980S

Safety-Kleen's business profile shifted during the early 1980s as the industrial market replaced the automotive repair market as the company's targeted core business. The move toward the industrial market was encouraged in part by U.S. Environmental Protection Agency (EPA) regulations that took effect in 1980 and labeled used solvents as hazardous material. Fortunately for the company, its recycling process was recognized as a safe means of disposal of solvents.

By 1980 Safety-Kleen's German business was still losing money, so in April 1981 the German operation was sold to a local businessman who continued to provide Safety-Kleen services for customers as a licensee, paying the company royalties on his revenues. Australian operations flourished, though, and in 1981 a branch office was established in New Zealand.

In 1981 Safety-Kleen enhanced its service to restaurants with the introduction of its Fire-Shield restaurant filter. That same year the company began bulk solvent sales to industrial customers and launched a national collection and recycling business.

Safety-Kleen debuted its auto body shop buffing pad service following its 1980 acquisition of American Impacts Corporation, a service company that recycled buffing pads used in high-luster lacquer finishing. Safety-Kleen's sales—pushed upward by diversification and increased industrial sales—rose to $134.8 million in 1981 and the company made the "*Fortune* 1000" list.

In 1983 the company made a secondary public offering and was listed on the New York Stock Exchange. The following year Safety-Kleen entered Puerto Rico, after licensing Puerto Rico Oil Company (PROICO) to market Safety-Kleen services.

In November 1984 the U.S. Resource Conservation and Recovery Act was expanded to include small-quantity waste generators, which included thousands of Safety-Kleen customers. That same year the company debuted a plan to target dry cleaner businesses, especially small firms in need of help to comply with EPA regulations, which had made dry cleaner solvent a hazardous waste. The dry cleaner service, which included the collection, recovery, and recycling of dry cleaner solvent, was the company's first major experience handling hazardous waste through its branch system and helped to firmly establish Safety-Kleen as an environmental service company.

By 1985 the company had extended its operations to include the acquisition and recycling of large volumes of hazardous waste streams, which were collected and sent directly to recycling centers. The wastes from these customers were recycled and sold, or blended into fuels for industrial use. Safety-Kleen also prepared EPA-approved legal manifests for other companies, which made Safety-Kleen entirely responsible for the life span of the solvent it provided. In order to accommodate the increasing amounts of waste solvent it was handling, in 1985 Safety-Kleen established its first regional accumulation center for small-quantity-generator hazardous waste and within two years a dozen such accumulation centers were in place.

In 1985 Safety-Kleen introduced a paint refinishing service, providing businesses with a machine designed to clean paint spray guns and trap the solvent and paint residue. Like other closed loop solvent services, the paint refinishing service used the company's branch and recycling center system to collect, store, recycle, and produce clean solvent.

As a result of its foreign start-up experiences in Germany, Safety-Kleen resolved to enter non-English-speaking countries only through joint ventures. The first such venture, SOPIA, was created in 1985 through a 50/50 partnership with Primagaz Company, France's largest independent supplier of liquified gases. Within a few years SOPIA had established branches in France, Belgium, and Italy. In 1985 Safety-Kleen also began a test joint venture in Japan and a year later Safety-Kleen and the Spanish firm Armero-Johnsen created the Spanish joint venture CODISA. Through CODISA, Safety-Kleen entered Portugal in 1987.

EXPANSION IN THE MIDDLE TO LATE 1980S

Between 1985 and 1987 Safety-Kleen made three strategic acquisitions designed to expand its technological base and broaden the types of fluids the company could recycle. In 1985 the company acquired Custom Organics, a privately owned recycler of solvents and chemical wastes for the electronics industry. In 1986 Safety-Kleen enhanced its restaurant services through the acquisition of Phillips Manufacturing Company, a vapor-degreaser operation. One year later Safety-Kleen purchased McKesson Envirosystems, a solvent-refining company with plants in Kentucky, Illinois, and Puerto Rico. McKesson's ability to process flammable wastes provided Safety-Kleen with new inroads to industrial markets; it increased the company's ability to handle large quantities of wastes and produce supplemental fuels for cement kilns.

Capitalizing on its expanding capabilities, in 1987 Safety-Kleen launched its fluid recovery service, designed to remove and treat small and medium-sized quantities of industrial waste. The service included collection of

55-gallon drums of industrial fluid wastes, which were recycled or processed as part of the company's new supplemental fuels program. In 1987 Safety-Kleen also entered the oil recovery services business after the acquisition of the Canadian firm Breslube Enterprises, North America's leading re-refiner of lubricating oils. Like other Safety-Kleen businesses, the oil recovery service was designed to take advantage of the company's branch network in the collection of used oil, destined to be re-refined into lubricating oils or processed into industrial fuels.

In 1987 Safety-Kleen's revenues leaped 31 percent for the company's biggest percentage gain in 12 years. Net income rose 24 percent and Safety-Kleen became the first American company to post 17 straight years of earnings growth of more than 20 percent.

In 1988 Safety-Kleen entered Ireland after acquiring Greaseaters of Ireland (renamed Safety-Kleen of Ireland). One year later the company established joint ventures in Korea and Taiwan that solidified Safety-Kleen's foothold in the Pacific Rim area.

In 1988 Safety-Kleen sold its restaurant services business after it concluded that the operation no longer fit the company's emerging profile as an industrial waste handler. That profile was enhanced the following year through the acquisition of Solvents Recovery Service of New Jersey, Inc. (SRS), a processor of heavy-duty industrial solvent wastes.

In 1989 Safety-Kleen began construction of both a new re-refining oil plant in East Chicago, Indiana, and the company's first European solvent recycling plant in Dinnington, England. Record expenditures were allocated to expand the company's oil and solvent recovery services, and for the first time in 20 years Safety-Kleen's earnings, which rose only 8 percent in 1989, showed less than a 20 percent increase. Gwillim retired at the end of 1989 and Brinckman assumed the additional duties of chairman.

FOCUS ON INTERNATIONAL MARKETS

Safety-Kleen entered the 1990s seeking to expand its foreign operations and take advantage of the proposed unification of the European Economic Community. In 1990 Safety-Kleen reached agreements to acquire entire control of Safety-Kleen operations in Belgium, France, and Italy, and started licensee operations in Hong Kong, Israel, Singapore, and Taiwan. That same year Safety-Kleen acquired complete control of Breslube and purchased its German licensee's operation. In 1991 Safety-Kleen acquired Orm Bergold Chemie, Germany's largest solvent recycler. One year later Safety-Kleen

purchased Niemann Chemie, a leading provider of parts cleaner services to German automotive repair outlets, and acquired complete control of its Spanish licensee's business in exchange for the sale of Safety-Kleen's 50 percent ownership in Portuguese operations.

Safety-Kleen's nearly untarnished environmental record was smudged during the early 1990s after the company agreed to pay a $1.3 million settlement to the state of California, which had charged the company with 89 alleged violations of the state's hazardous waste laws. Safety-Kleen neither admitted to nor denied the charges. In 1992 a Safety-Kleen internal inspection found that the company had exceeded its authorized waste storage capacity and was illegally storing three million gallons of hazardous waste fluids at its Puerto Rico facilities. The company was later fined $1.4 million by the U.S. EPA.

In 1991 the company opened its new East Chicago oil recycling facility, billed as the world's largest re-refining plant, with a capacity to process more than 100 million gallons of oil annually. However, the oil recovery business, banking in part on an unrealized expectation that lubricating oils would join the federal government's list of hazardous wastes, met with a sluggish economy and a slow start.

Safety-Kleen was ranked among the *Fortune* 500 companies in 1991, despite the company's first-ever drop in annual earnings. The company's payout of two large EPA fines, as well as lower-than-anticipated oil re-refining sales, led to a second drop in earnings the following year. Between 1990 and 1992, then, Safety-Kleen's net income fell from $55 million to $45 million, despite continued record revenue totals.

In March 1993 John G. Johnson, Jr., a former Arco Chemical Company executive, was named president, while Brinckman remained chairman and chief executive. The company moved toward the close of 1993 predicting that its oil recovery services and European operations would be profitable by the end of that year. The company's plans beyond 1993 called for further expansion of European branches, which were expected to increase in number from 55 in 1993 to 75 or 80 by 1997. Looking toward the future, Safety-Kleen—with infrastructure in place to expand both at home and overseas, a near-spotless record of tremendous earnings growth, and still no nationwide competition in its home country—appeared likely to move back into record territory as it rolled into the remainder of the 1990s.

CHALLENGES IN THE FUTURE

The latter half of the 1990s and the early years of the new millennium would prove to be a challenging time for Safety-Kleen. CEO Jack Johnson abruptly left the company and former CEO Donald W. Brinckman was called in to take the helm. At this time, Safety-Kleen began to look for ways to increase shareholder value. Its steady growth and position in the industry made it an attractive suitor for companies looking to expand into the waste services business. Sure enough, the company soon found itself in the middle of a takeover battle between Philip Services Corp. and Laidlaw Environmental Services Inc., owned by Laidlaw Inc. of Canada. In November 1997, industrial services company Philip Services made a friendly $1.97 billion bid for Safety-Kleen. Laidlaw then countered with a hostile bid of its own. Safety-Kleen's chairman and CEO Donald W. Brinckman commented on Laidlaw's hostile bid in a December 1997 *Oil Daily* article: "The ultimate objective of Laidlaw Environmental's offer is to allow Laidlaw Inc., the parent company, to deconsolidate and remove the liabilities and environmental exposure of Laidlaw Environmental from its financial statements." He went on to claim, "If their deal were consummated, these risks would be passed on to Safety-Kleen shareholders." Despite Brinckman's protests, shareholders voted to accept Laidlaw Environmental's $1.8 billion offer in March 1998. The merged company retained the Safety-Kleen name.

The benefits of the merger failed to reach fruition. Laidlaw decided to sell its stake in Safety-Kleen in 2000 but put its plans on hold as its stock price faltered. In March of that year, Safety-Kleen discovered accounting irregularities in previous financial statements and reported its findings to the U.S. Securities and Exchange Commission. Struggling under a $1.6 billion debtload, Safety-Kleen filed for Chapter 11 bankruptcy protection in June 2000. In response, Laidlaw filed a $6.5 billion claim against Safety-Kleen, hoping to recoup its investment. It was then forced to declare bankruptcy, leading Safety-Kleen to file its own claim against Laidlaw. The two companies eventually settled all claims against each other as part of their reorganization plans.

In 2001, Safety-Kleen restated its results for 1997, 1998, and 1999. Overall, earnings had been overstated by nearly $500 million. Four former Safety-Kleen executives including CEO Kenneth Winger, chief financial officer Paul R. Humphreys, controller William D. Ridings, and vice-president Thomas W. Ritter, Jr., were charged with accounting fraud in December 2002. The SEC settled its case with Safety-Kleen later that year.

As part of the company's restructuring plan, it sold its chemical services division and divested its environmental health and safety compliance and information management firm. Headquarters also were moved from South Carolina to Plano, Texas. In 2003, the U.S. Bankruptcy Court approved its reorganization plan and the company emerged from Chapter 11 as a private entity operating under the name Safety-Kleen Systems Inc.

In 2004, Ron Haddock was named chairman and Frederick J. Florjancic, Jr., was elected president and CEO. Under the new management team, Safety-Kleen appeared to be back on track. By December 2005, the company had reported five consecutive quarters of revenue and profit growth. It had signed a national contract with the U.S. Postal Service, secured a three-year renewal of its contract with Wal-Mart, and expanded its contract with Federal Express. It also completed a significant refinancing of its senior debt. Plans for the future included paying down remaining debt, increasing revenues and profits, and an eventual public offering. Florjancic commented on the company's post-bankruptcy/accounting scandal mood in a 2005 *Dallas Morning News* article: "The organization is walking taller, smiling more. Confidence is building. Success begets success, and those successes are becoming more frequent."

Roger W. Rouland
Updated, Christina M. Stansell

PRINCIPAL COMPETITORS

Industrial Services of America Inc.; MPW Industrial Services Group Inc.; Philip Services Corporation.

FURTHER READING

Bowman, Jim, *Waste Not: The Safety-Kleen Story,* Chicago, Ill.: J.G. Ferguson, 1989.

Chamberlain, Jennifer, "Whatever Happened to Safety-Kleen Systems," *Dallas Morning News,* December 18, 2005.

Cook, James, "What Have You Done for Me Tomorrow?," *Forbes,* February 19, 1990.

Dietrich, Kevin, "Four Former Safety-Kleen Executives Charged with Accounting Fraud," *Knight-Ridder/Tribune Business News,* December 13, 2002.

Fish, Dwight, "Kleanliness Is Next to Nothing on Earth," *Business People Magazine,* December, 1991, Sec. 1, p. 22.

Jackson, Cheryl, "Safety-Kleen Facility Refines Oil Recovery," *Chicago Tribune,* July 10, 1991, Sec. 3, pp. 1, 4.

"Laidlaw Outbids Philip in Deal for Safety-Kleen," *Engineering News-Record,* March 23, 1998.

"Laidlaw, Safety-Kleen Settle Their Disputes Through Mediation," *Wall Street Journal,* July 19, 2002.

Murphy, H. Lee, "Oil Recovery: Slippery Slope for Safety-Kleen," *Crain's Chicago Business,* June 22, 1992, p. 41.

Palmer, Jay, "Pay Dirt: Safety-Kleen, After a Mild Skid, on Track Again," *Barron's,* October 21, 1991, pp. 17–20.

"Safety-Kleen Rejects Laidlaw's Sweetened $1.76 Billion Hostile Bid," *Dow Jones Online News,* December 22, 1997.

Sherrod, Pamela, "Safety-Kleen Now Remains Only in CEO's Debt," *Chicago Tribune,* March 30, 1987, Sec. 4, p. 11.

Siklos, Richard, "Safety-Kleen Emerges a Sparkling Object of Desire," *Financial Post,* November 26, 1997.

Wells, Jennifer, "How Laidlaw CEO James Bullock Won a $2-Billion Takeover Fight for Waste-Management Giant Safety-Kleen," *Globe and Mail,* April 24, 1998.

Young, David, "Green's Also the Color of Money," *Chicago Tribune,* November 17, 1991, pp. 16–18.

Sanborn Map Company Inc.

—■—

1935 Jamboree Drive
Suite 100
Colorado Springs, Colorado 80920-5358
U.S.A.
Telephone: (719) 593-0093
Toll Free: (877) 368-7702
Fax: (719) 528-5093
Web site: http://www.sanmap.com

Wholly Owned Subsidiary of Daily Mail and General Trust plc
Incorporated: 1867 as the Sanborn Map and Publishing Company
Employees: 485
Sales: $36.3 million
NAIC: 511140 Database and Directory Publishers

■ ■ ■

The Sanborn Map Company Inc. is a leading provider of geographic information system and photogrammetric mapping products and services. The company's range of products and services include consulting, off-the-shelf products, analog, digital, and lidar data acquisition, photogrammetric mapping, and data conversion. Sanborn offers its products and services to government and commercial customers. The company is part of the DMG Information group of companies.

ORIGINS

The Sanborn Map Company was founded in 1866 by Daniel Alfred Sanborn, a young surveyor from Somer-ville, Massachusetts. Sanborn founded his company after preparing insurance maps of several cities in Tennessee for the Aetna Insurance Company in 1866. The Aetna experience together with a successful atlas he published on the city of Boston in 1867 led the young surveyor to see the importance of producing specialized maps for assessing fire insurance liability in cities and towns in the United States. Following his commission with Aetna, he established the D.A. Sanborn National Insurance Diagram Bureau in New York City. The company surveyed and mapped 50 towns in its first year, and by 1873, seven years later, it had surveyed more than 600.

The practice of fire insurance mapping began in London at the end of the 18th century as large fire insurance companies and underwriters began demanding accurate and detailed information about the buildings they were insuring. Between 1785 and 1820, insurance mapping arrived in the United States after the London based Phoenix Assurance Company began expanding its coverage to buildings in the West Indies, Canada, and the United States, where it financed surveys of several cities. Following the American Civil War, fire insurance mapping grew on an unprecedented scale, spurred by the rapid urbanization of American society. With western expansion, the construction of the transcontinental railroad, the industrial revolution, and waves of European immigrants, the nation became transformed from an agrarian to an urban society, heightening the demand for insurance mapping of the growing cities and towns. These sweeping economic and demographic changes attracted numerous surveyors and map publishers to the field. Between 1865 and 1900, local cartographic firms arose to map many cities in New Jersey, Missouri, Illinois, Michigan, Minnesota, and other cities in the East and Midwest. Many of these companies, however, survived only brief periods of commercial activity, or were acquired by Sanborn.

In 1876, the company incorporated under the name Sanborn Map and Publishing Company. In the years immediately prior to and after its incorporation, the company had already expanded its insurance mapping business throughout the United States. The growth stemmed both from acquisitions of other map companies and the Sanborn company's superior ability to produce detailed, comprehensive, and up-to-date maps that met the growing needs of the fire insurance industry. Following Sanborn's death in 1883, the company he founded continued to prosper, acquiring the Perris and Browne firm in 1899. With this acquisition, the company changed its name to the Sanborn Perris Map Company, Ltd, until 1902, when it became simply the Sanborn Map Company, the name it still holds today.

SANBORN COMPANY DOMINATES INSURANCE MAPPING INDUSTRY

The company relocated its headquarters office to Pelham, New York, in 1907, just a few miles north of New York City. Constructed on five acres of land, its publishing plant featured a 75,000-square-foot main building adorned on the outside with dozens of relief sculptures of ancient mapmakers. The Sanborn Map Company rapidly grew to become the country's largest and most successful mapping company. It employed numerous surveyors in each state in order to allow clients to incur major financial risks without having to personally inspect the properties. The mapmakers worked anonymously and without attribution; their names never appeared on the maps they created. Its most famous surveyor was Daniel Carter Beard, a naturalist, illustrator, author of books for boys, and one of the founders of the Boy Scouts of America. In his 1939 autobiography, Beard wrote of his work as a Sanborn surveyor. After joining the company in 1872, he "not only saw all those places I had heard about but I made maps of them, made

diagrams of all the homes in each town and city I visited. I took delight in putting into my records mention of real occupancy, genteel or disreputable. After four or five years of this work I knew a lot about our people, saints and sinners, rich and poor."

In 1905, the Sanborn company began standardizing its map producing system for accuracy and design. The standards were published in a surveyors' manual comprising more than 100 pages of detailed instructions, including sample maps and a comprehensive symbol key. The surveyors drew their maps at the scale of 50 feet to an inch, on sheets 21 by 25 inches, which were cross ruled in one-inch squares. The maps included considerable information, including the location and material composition of buildings within cities and towns, the location of water and gas mains, the strength of fire departments, and labeled most buildings by name. The maps were also color-coded to show building composition. The company also provided critical services to customers, often conducting surveys immediately after areas had been struck by natural or man-made disasters to note which buildings had survived and which had been lost. Sanborn expanded coverage to other cities each year and issued revised editions and paste-on correction slips for previously published maps and atlases. The company seems to have reached peak production in the early 1930s. By 1937, its maps depicted the homes of every street in more than 13,000 U.S. cities and towns.

The work of coloring the maps was done by individual artists, who painted on lithographs with the aid of waxed paper stencils at the company's Pelham, New York plant. Because orders of any single sheet rarely exceeded twenty, it was more economical to employ artists than to utilize printing for small orders. Sanborn issued maps as unbounded sheets for small cities and towns and in bound volumes for larger cities, each including approximately 100 plates. Thirty-nine volumes were produced for New York City alone. A loose-leaf atlas format was introduced around 1920, allowing for the replacement of outdated plates without having to reprint an entire volume.

The 1920s marked the golden era for the Sanborn Map Company. By 1920, Sanborn dominated the insurance mapping industry with only two or three relatively small competitors. During the decade, the company, with more than 1,000 employees, also expanded by setting up production facilities in Chicago and San Francisco. With its monopoly also came scrutiny from some of its clients who complained about the cost of Sanborn's products and services. The majority of the company's customers were members of national or regional underwriting associations, one of which—the

KEY DATES

1866: Daniel Alfred Sanborn founds the D.A. Sanborn National Insurance Diagram Bureau.

1867: The company incorporates under the name Sanborn Map and Publishing Company.

1899: Perris and Browne is acquired.

1902: The company changes its name to the Sanborn Map Company.

1907: Sanborn Map Company relocates its headquarters to Pelham, New York.

1950: The company publishes its last catalogue and downsizes operations.

1960: Sanborn Map Company begins diversifying into new markets.

1996: Environmental Data Resources acquires Sanborn.

1998: Sanborn acquires Lockwood Mapping Co.

1999: DMG Information acquires Sanborn with a buyout of Environmental Data Resources.

2000: Sanborn acquires Aero Dynamics Corp, Barton Aerial Technologies, Inc., and Williams Stackhouse.

2001: Sanborn acquires the assets of Analytical Surveys, Inc.

2005: Sanborn announces the acquisition of Space Imaging's North American Federal Civil and Commercial Solutions business unit.

National Board of Fire Underwriters (NBFU)—proved to be the most persistent in pressuring Sanborn to lower its costs. In 1914, the NBFU had formed a map committee to consider creating its own map publishing unit to compete with Sanborn. Although the map committee never entered the insurance mapping business despite repeated attempts, it nevertheless became a watchdog and kept the pressure on Sanborn for almost a half a century. Sanborn eventually bowed to a measure of NBFU control and supervision by granting the map committee two slots on its board of directors.

With the economic prosperity and building boom of the mid- to late-1920s, Sanborn profited by preparing numerous maps of new cities and towns and resurveying previously mapped areas. In areas that were experiencing tremendous growth, the company issued maps at six-month intervals. Nevertheless, the 1929 collapse of the stock market and the onset of the Great Depression of the 1930s curtailed Sanborn's business. With fire insurance sales lagging, companies again pressured the company to reduce the costs of its maps and services. Sanborn responded by offering cash discounts to subscribers and by lowering the cost of paste-on services for sheet maps concerning smaller cities and towns. After 1930, Sanborn also began issuing correction slips to update specific sections of map sheets. The correction slips enabled the company to reflect current changes without having to update entire map sheets.

DEMISE OF SANBORN INSURANCE CARTOGRAPHY

Sanborn's financial troubles continued throughout World War II largely because of U.S. government restrictions on new construction and on the production of maps. Like other map publishing firms, Sanborn survived the lean years primarily by producing maps for the U.S. military. The immediate post-war era continued to be difficult years for the company. To bolster declining sales, Sanborn issued maps for cities at reduced scales of one inch to 100 feet and one inch to 200 feet in comparison to its previous format of one inch to 50 feet. It also tried publishing small-size atlases.

By 1960, major changes in the fire insurance industry were rendering the company's maps largely obsolete. In a 1962 report, the NBFU Map Committee noted that there was a general consensus among companies that residential mapping was no longer essential. According to the report, however, business and industrial areas still warranted map service. The report proved to be overly optimistic as the market for Sanborn maps never recovered after World War II. In 1950, the company published its last catalog and downsized its operations, shutting down all of its offices except for the Pelham office. In 1967, Sanborn president, C.F. Donne, observed that since 1961 there had been no new catalog entries for insurance maps for distribution. Instead, the company shifted focus to revising existing atlases and graphics prepared on a custom basis for non-insurance clientele. These publications consisted largely of corrected, reduced-scale, photo-revision, black and white atlases covering approximately 150 cities and towns that the company issued after 1962 in spiral binding.

The demise of Sanborn cartography stemmed from a variety of factors, ranging from new and more efficient methods of determining insurance risk, to company mergers that allowed larger firms to maintain their own engineering divisions. On the whole, however, as the country grew at an exponential rate following the war, Sanborn could no longer keep pace or bear the expense of keeping the maps updated. The decreased demand for detailed locality information led the company to terminate the service before 1950. Moreover, the dramatic improvement in building construction, better fire codes, and new and enhanced fire protection methods also diminished the need for such comprehensive mapping information.

PERIOD OF TRANSITION AND RENEWAL

In response to these trends, in 1960, Sanborn began diversifying with a variety of new thematic map styles, such as noise abatement and land use maps. Between 1970 and 1983, the company entered the fields of geographic information systems (GIS), aerial photography, and photogrammetric mapping. With the use of computers, it began tax parcel mapping and produced land/building usage databases, entering the digital age.

In 1996, Environmental Data Resources, Inc. (EDR), national provider of environmental information, purchased Sanborn. After acquiring Sanborn, EDR digitized the original Sanborn collection, making it searchable through its website. DMG Information then acquired Sanborn with its buyout of EDR in 1999. With more financial backing, Sanborn embarked on a roll-up strategy to acquire local companies to establish a more national presence. The roll-up enabled the company to offer local services when it needed to, but provided the benefits of economies of scale and a national sales force. As a result, in 1998, Sanborn acquired the Lockwood Mapping Company of Rochester, New York. In 2000, Sanborn acquired a host of other companies, including Aero Dynamics Corporation of Charlotte, North Carolina; Barton Aerial Technologies, Inc. of Columbus, Ohio; and Williams Stackhouse of San Antonio, Texas. In 2001, Sanborn acquired the assets of the Colorado Springs office of the Indianapolis-based Analytical Surveys, Inc., a struggling digital map-maker founded in Colorado Springs 20 years earlier. By 2002, these various acquisitions had made the company into a leader in the GIS and photogrammetry industry fields with more than 350 GIS and mapping professionals employed in eight divisions nationwide and abroad.

In January 2004, the company won a major image-based GIS project in central California. The project, encompassing 1,450 square miles in the Monterey Bay area, involved producing a variety of photographic, contour data, as well as digital terrain and elevation models for the Association of Monterey Bay Area Governments, an organization dedicated to the planning and study of regional concerns affecting California's central coast. In August 2004, Sanborn and Pictometry, a provider of a patented information system and related software that captures georeferenced, digital aerial oblique, and orthogonal images, announced a strategic partnership. The agreement provided that the companies would market a combined product offering that included each firm's technical expertise to meet their client's mapping needs. Sanborn's mapping technology would enhance Pictometry's orthogonal imagery for clients needing guaranteed mapping accuracy. In turn, Pictometry would market Sanborn-certified orthophotography images to local, state, and federal government agencies, as well as to private business.

In March 2005, Sanborn announced the acquisition of Space Imaging's North American Federal Civil and Commercial Solutions business unit, a provider of a full range of geospatial services, from in-depth imagery analyses to customized software applications. Space Imaging developed the unit from a small group serving largely the West Coast to a national business reputed for its technical expertise in cartography, remote sensing, decision support systems, and geographic analysis. By combining customized software with in-house cartography, remote sensing, imagery processing, and database analysis, Sanborn was positioned to provide GIS solutions to disaster response, security and risk assessment, state and local governments, forestry and ecosystem resource management, air and ground transportation, and wild land fire management.

Bruce P. Montgomery

PRINCIPAL COMPETITORS

Rand McNally and Co.; DeLorme; Intergraph Corporation.

FURTHER READING

Engelhardt, Jim, "Kodak Partners for Aerial Imagery," *Geospatial Solutions*, March 2002.

Keister, Kim, "Charts of Change," *Historic Preservation*, May/June 1993.

Lieber, Tammy, "ASI Maps Out Future without Colorado Office," *Indianapolis Business Journal*, February 12, 2001.

Oswald, Dianne L., *Fire Insurance Maps: Their History and Application*, College Station, Tex.: Lacewing Press, 1997.

Ristow, Walter, *American Maps and Mapmakers*, Detroit: Wayne State University Press, 1985.

"Sanborn Acquires Space Imaging Business Unit," *Satellite News*, March 7, 2005.

"Sanborn Acquires Unit of Spacing Imaging," *Wireless News*, March 2, 2005.

Sanford L.P.

2707 Butterfield Road
Oakbrook, Illinois 60523
U.S.A.
Telephone: (708) 547-6650
Toll Free: (800) 323-0749
Fax: (708) 547-6719
Web site: http://www.sanfordcorp.com

Division of Newell Rubbermaid
Incorporated: 1857 as Sanford Manufacturing Company
Employees: 3,000
Sales: $1 billion (2006 est.)
NAIC: 339942 Lead Pencil and Art Good Manufacturing; 339941 Pen and Mechanical Pencil

■ ■ ■

Sanford L.P. is a division of Newell Rubbermaid and one of the world's leading makers of both fine and mass-market writing instruments. The company began as an ink manufacturer, established an important brand in mid-century with Sharpie permanent marking pens, and controls a variety of well-known pen, marker, and art supply brands. Sanford makes Accent highlighters, Expo dry erase markers, Prismacolor art markers and pencils, Grumbacher artist's paints and brushes, and the Foohy line of children's markers, colored pencils, pens, and erasers. Sanford also sells the Papermate line of low-end pens, Uni-ball ballpoints, and two lines of high-end pens and fountain pens, Waterman and Parker. Sensa and Rotring are two more lines of writing instruments in the Sanford stable. Sanford has manufacturing facili-

ties in Tennessee, Wisconsin, California, Canada, Mexico, and Thailand, and several locations in the United Kingdom, Europe, and Latin America. It sells its products worldwide.

A 19TH-CENTURY INK MAKER

Sanford started out in Worcester, Massachusetts, the project of two investors, Frederick W. Redington and William H. Sanford, Jr. They founded an ink and glue manufacturing company in 1857, known then simply as the Sanford Manufacturing Co. In 1866, the company moved west, leaving Massachusetts for the booming lakeside town of Chicago. Sanford's factory was damaged five years later in the notorious Great Chicago Fire, but it was quickly rebuilt. In 1885, the company acquired a patent on a "universal ink stand," a safe and clean container for opened ink. Sanford was a leading brand of what was then an all-important product. Business records and correspondence were all written with fountain pens in this era, and companies, schools, and organizations required constant supplies of fountain pen ink. The company also made other business essentials such as mucilage (rubber cement) and sealing wax. The company apparently did well, and when another fire destroyed its factory in 1899, Sanford had a new factory up and running a year later.

GROWTH AT MID-TWENTIETH CENTURY

Sanford continued to thrive as a privately owned ink manufacturer through the early 20th century. In 1940, the company changed its name from Sanford

Manufacturing to the Sanford Ink Company. In 1947, Sanford moved from downtown Chicago to a new, larger location in suburban Bellwood, Illinois. At that time, Sanford had just 100 employees. Annual sales were around $500,000. The company seems to have been quietly profitable. Ownership had dispersed into the hands of five families by the 1960s. The company primarily sold to wholesalers, who in turn sold Sanford products to what was then a still highly fragmented market of small office supply and stationery stores. The company's best-known product came out in 1964, the Sharpie marker. This was a fine-tipped felt pen that boasted indelible black ink. The Sharpie marker soon became ubiquitous, and was joined by a similar marker, the Rub-a-Dub, marketed specifically for laundry-marking clothing.

Five families held stock in the company, which was chaired in the 1960s by Charles Lofgren. Lofgren's son-in-law, Henry Pearsall, joined Sanford in 1969. At just 23 years old, Pearsall set to work in the purchasing department. Ten years later, Pearsall had risen to president of Sanford. Although Pearsall had married into the business, he evidently had a genuine knack for the writing instruments industry, and Sanford was admirably profitable under his leadership. Sanford kept its costs down by using its own inks in the pens and markers it sold. In addition, the company was clever at investigating many niche products. Sanford made markers for children, for artists, for people writing on transparencies for overhead projectors. It developed a special nonsmearing marker for use on the treated paper used in fax machines. Attention to the market allowed Sanford to grasp what customers wanted, and to bring out new products for many different needs.

With the company making money and expanding, Pearsall offered to buy out the other family members. In 1984, he put together $66 million with some other investors, and bought out his father-in-law and the other longstanding stockholders. Then a year later, in August 1985, Sanford went public, with an initial stock price of $17. The company was admired by Wall Street analysts for its double-digit return on equity. Sales in 1985 stood

at $69 million, with a profit of $4.9 million. By 1988, sales had risen to $102 million, and profit reached $17.6 million. In the late 1980s, two-thirds of Sanford's sales were from its lines of markers, while stamp pads, adhesives, and other writing instruments made up the remainder.

There were a few clouds on the horizon in the late 1980s, however. Sanford had paid $31 million in 1988 to acquire a Borden, Inc., subsidiary called Sterling Plastics Co. Sterling's sales were around $22 million annually, and its principal products were plastic storage boxes, school supplies, and desk accessories. This was perhaps a high price to pay for a unit that was not as spectacularly profitable as Sanford itself. By the late 1980s, the way office supplies were sold began to change. As the so-called big-box office stores like Staples spread, and other mass-marketers like Kmart and Wal-Mart became bigger purveyors of school and office supplies, the distribution picture changed. These large chain retailers were able to negotiate lower prices from their suppliers, and Sanford had to adapt. Then in 1991, Sanford employees went on strike. The company at that time employed 700 people total, with some 300 represented by a division of the Teamsters Union. When economic issues could not be settled, Sanford's workforce walked out. The short-lived strike impacted profits, and a few months later, in November 1991, Sanford announced that the company was being acquired by the consumer products company Newell Co.

NEWELLIZATION IN THE 1990S

Newell Co. began as Newell Manufacturing Co., Inc., a maker of curtain rods. Founded in 1902 in Ogdensburg, New York, it gradually expanded through the East Coast and Canada over the next 50 years. In 1962, Newell moved its headquarters to Freeport, Illinois, and for the next many years it acquired companies in a variety of industries. By 1992, the year the Sanford acquisition was finalized, Newell owned many prominent consumer brands, including Mirro cookware, Anchor Hocking housewares, and other hardware and so-called do-it-yourself products. The acquisition of Sanford was Newell's first venture into office supplies. Sanford president Henry Pearsall's rationale for the sale was that Newell had established expertise in dealing with the big discount retailers like Wal-Mart. These were becoming increasingly big players in Sanford's industry, and leaning on Newell's experience seemed a viable move. The sale went through as a stock swap valued at more than $686 million. Sanford then became a division of Newell.

Over the next three years, parent Newell almost doubled in size, with sales topping $2 billion. This was achieved through a string of acquisitions. The company

KEY DATES

1857: Sanford Manufacturing Company is founded in Massachusetts.
1866: Company headquarters are moved to Chicago.
1899: A new factory is built after the fire.
1940: The company name is changed to Sanford Ink Company.
1947: Headquarters are moved to suburban Bellwood, Illinois.
1964: Sanford debuts the Sharpie marker.
1984: Henry Pearsall buys out other family shareholders.
1985: Sanford goes public.
1991: Sanford is acquired by Newell.
2000: The Parker and Waterman brands are acquired from Gillette.

coined the term "Newellization" for the way it brought struggling companies into its fold, raised profit margins and shed underperforming segments. Newell had concentrated its acquisitions on companies that were not doing well, but Sanford was an exception. Its profit margins had long been stellar. Nevertheless, Newell made changes at Sanford. The new parent added to Sanford by grouping it with other acquisitions, such as the Eberhard Faber line of pencils and ballpoints. In 1994, sales of Newell's combined office products division had grown to $383 million, while Sanford's sales had been slightly more than $100 million five years earlier.

Sanford began building a new warehouse and distribution center in 1996, in Shelbyville, Tennessee. This gave the company a more centralized facility for its brands, which were reaching international markets. In 1999, parent Newell changed its name to Newell Rubbermaid when it bought Rubbermaid Inc. The biggest change for Sanford came in 2000, when Newell Rubbermaid paid $743 million for the pen business of the Gillette Co. Gillette owned two venerable fine pen lines, Parker Pen and Waterman, as well as the low-end line of Papermate pens and the Liquid Paper brand of typewriter correction fluid. These became part of Sanford.

Both Parker and Waterman were storied companies with 19th-century roots. They had been two of what was known as the "Big Four" pen manufacturers in the heyday of the fountain pen, from the early 20th century to around World War II. Parker Pen was founded in Janesville, Wisconsin, in 1889 by George Parker. Parker

was responsible for many advances in pen design, including the guaranteed ink-tight Jack Knife Safety pen. Parker Pen's signature product was the "Big Red," a popular and distinctive pen still valued by collectors. The L.E. Waterman Fountain Pen company was founded in New York at about the same time as Parker. Its founder was an insurance agent who had, out of frustration with a leaking pen, invented a new ink filling system that was the impetus for a new generation of writing instruments. Waterman led the world in fountain pen production around the turn of the 19th century, with strong sales in Europe as well as North America. With the introduction of ballpoint pens, which became widely available during World War II, the leading fountain pen makers began to suffer. Waterman closed its North American operations in the 1950s, confining its operations to Europe. It was then acquired by the Gillette Company, known principally for its disposable shaving razors, in 1989. Gillette also bought Parker in 1993.

Gillette had started out making disposable razors, but evolved by the 1990s into a diversified personal care products company with dozens of brands. Its pen brands, which were part of the company's stationery unit, seemed to not quite fit with the rest of Gillette's stable. Growth in the early 1990s was satisfactory, with Parker's sales increasing by 7 to 8 percent annually and reaching about $300 million. Parker was the leading pen in the $5-and-up range. Gillette spent some time trying to come up with marketing that would differentiate the Parker and Waterman brands. By the end of the 1990s, Gillette's stationery unit was clearly in decline. While sales were stagnant or declining, the unit saw a drop in profit of almost 90 percent over its fourth quarter in 1999, and rumors grew that Gillette would unload the unit. Although the cheap, disposable Papermate brand of ballpoints may have been a better fit with Gillette's overall line, the fine pen lines of Parker and Waterman suffered acutely. Rebecca Mann, writing about the brands for *Travel Retailer International* (December 2002) described Parker and Waterman as "all but dead in the water" at the time Sanford bought Gillette's stationery unit.

REPOSITIONING FOR GROWTH IN THE EARLY 2000S

Meanwhile, Sanford's parent Newell Rubbermaid was going through some difficult transitions. The company got a new chief executive, Joseph Galli, Jr., in 2001. The company had suffered earnings setbacks since the Rubbermaid acquisition two years earlier, and the company's leader vowed to cut costs and to redirect energy to some of Newell Rubbermaid's units. Galli singled out Sanford as one Newell Rubbermaid division that was ready for more growth. By the early 2000s, Sanford's combined brands held a global market share of close to 40 percent. The addition of Gillette's stationery brands was seen as adding to Sanford's robustness. With sales of around $1 billion by the early 2000s, a huge increase since a decade earlier, the unit was seen as one of the more hopeful spots in the Newell galaxy. And there was still room for growth. In 2001, Newell and Sanford management announced plans to gain a market share of 10 percent in the children's coloring market. This was a market long dominated by Crayola, then owned by Hallmark Cards, which controlled some 75 percent of the market share in children's coloring. Sanford launched a new marketing campaign, aiming to grab a bigger portion of this lucrative market.

The Parker and Waterman brands represented another area where Sanford could look to increase sales. The brands still had tremendous recognition, and fine writing instruments were beginning to enjoy something of a comeback. Sanford reissued some classic Parker and Waterman pens, such as the famous Parker 51, which had originally come out in 1939 to celebrate Parker's 51st anniversary. This sold well for Sanford, as did limited edition Waterman reissues. Sanford made a concentrated effort to bring its fine pens into distribution at duty-free shops and other so-called travel-retail outlets, where travelers frequently bought writing instruments as gifts.

The Rotring brand also attracted the interest of the travel-retail market. Rotring was a German company founded in 1928. It was best known for its Rapidograph drafting pens. These pens with ultra-fine points had been used by artists, architects, and draftsmen for years, but they faded somewhat as computers replaced hand drawing in these fields. Newell acquired the brand in 1998, where it became part of Sanford. The staid, quotidian Sharpie also had something of a surge in the 2000s. Sanford used the brand name to sponsor a Nascar race in 2001, and began its first national advertising for the markers the next year. Sharpie got much free publicity as well, when a San Francisco 49ers football player whipped a Sharpie out of his sock on the playing field, to autograph a ball he had just made a touchdown with. While the player's antics were deplored, Sharpie found itself in the news. Sales grew, and Sanford extended the product line to 34 different colors and 18 different tips over the next few years.

Nevertheless, cost-cutting measures, including factory closings and layoffs, came along with parent Newell Rubbermaid's search for a return to higher profits. While increasing its investment in a manufacturing plant in Thailand in 2004, some domestic plants closed. The plant in Bellwood, Illinois, where Sharpie markers had

long been produced, shut in 2004, as production moved to the Shelbyville, Tennessee, plant. In 2006, Sanford began shutting down a Santa Monica, California, plant that made Papermate pens. It closed two plants in Madison, Wisconsin, that same year. Production from the California and Wisconsin plants was moved to a large Sanford manufacturing facility in Maryville, Tennessee.

A. Woodward

PRINCIPAL COMPETITORS

Faber-Castell AG; Montblanc International GmbH; Sheaffer Pen Corporation.

FURTHER READING

Asawinipont, Nitida, "US Stationery Maker Plans Thai Hub," *Nation* (Thailand), May 13, 2004.

Cochran, Thomas N., "Sweet on Sanford," *Barron's,* July 31, 1989, p. 30.

Coleman, Calmetta Y., "Newell Builds Success from Diamonds in the Rough," *Wall Street Journal,* April 14, 1995, p. B4.

Ebenkamp, Becky, "Brand Builders," *Brandweek,* May 5, 1997, p. 17.

Erano, Paul, *Fountain Pens Past and Present,* Paducah, Ky.: Collector Books, 1999.

Fannin, Rebecca A., "Gillette Out to Differentiate Premium Pens," *Advertising Age,* November 18, 1996, p. 20.

Gallun, Alby, "Newell's New Colors," *Crain's Chicago Business,* June 4, 2001, p. 3.

Gallun, Alby, Greg Hinz, and Steve Daniels, "Another HQ Shoot-Out Shaping Up," *Crain's Chicago Business,* June 18, 2001, p. 1.

Johnsen, Michael, "Newell Adds Gillette Stationery Business to Brand Portfolio," *Drug Store News,* February 19, 2001, p. 32.

Kerfoot, Kevin, "Sanford Corporation Building New Facility in Shelbyville," *Tennessee Manufacturer,* November 1, 1996, p. 9.

Knowles, Francine, "250 Jobs to Go As Sharpie Moves Some Work," *Chicago Sun-Times,* January 8, 2004, p. 57.

Mann, Rebecca, "Indelible Ink," *Travel Retailer International,* December 2002, p. 50.

"Newell's Sanford Unit to Close Calif. Plant," *Plastics News,* April 24, 2006, p. 22.

Phalon, Richard, "'It Was a Friendly Deal,'" *Forbes,* August 5, 1991, pp. 52–53.

"Retractable Sharpie Pirating Permanent Marker Market," *DSN Retailing Today,* February 27, 2006, p. 24.

"Rubbermaid Will Close Madison Operation," *Wisconsin State Journal,* February 1, 2006, p. 23.

"Sanford-Newell Tie Is Approved," *New York Times,* February 15, 1992, p. 39.

"Sanford to Shut Down Facility in Wisconsin," *Plastics News,* January 9, 2006, p. 20.

Scott, Carlee R., "Newell Co. Plans to Acquire Sanford with Stock Swap," *Wall Street Journal,* November 25, 1991, p. A5.

Schlage Lock Company

1915 Jamboree Drive, Suite 165
Colorado Springs, Colorado 80920-5377
U.S.A.
Telephone: (719) 264-5300
Fax: (719) 264-5382
Web site: http://www.schlagelock.com

Wholly Owned Subsidiary of Ingersoll-Rand Company Ltd.
Incorporated: 1920 as Schlage Manufacturing Company
Employees: 800
Sales: $151 million (2005)
NAIC: 332510 Hardware Manufacturing

■ ■ ■

Schlage Lock Company is a leader in developing security devices for residential and commercial markets. Schlage Lock operates as part of Ingersoll Rand Security Technologies, a division of Ingersoll-Rand Company Limited, a global innovator and solutions provider featuring a portfolio of worldwide businesses, including refrigeration equipment, locks and security systems, construction equipment, industrial equipment, heavy equipment, and golf carts.

ORIGINS

The Schlage Manufacturing Company was founded in 1920 by Walter Reinhold Schlage, a German-born engineer and inventor renowned for creating the bored cylindrical lock. As a young boy, his father recognized his mechanical aptitude and worked to have his son admitted to the Carl Zeiss Optical Works in Jena, Germany. While an apprentice there, Walter Schlage learned drafting, applied mechanics, and engineering.

After four years Schlage graduated with a special award of merit and then traveled to London where he found work as an instrument maker for Hileger, Ltd. Following a one-year stint in England, he emigrated to the United States where he became employed with the Western Electric Company at age 23. During his nonworking hours, Schlage began experimenting with lock mechanisms and electrical switching ideas. One of the light switching mechanisms in use involved a two push-button style, where one button was pushed to turn on the lights and another was pushed to turn off the lights. Schlage was developing his own idea, however, for controlling room lights using the doorknob, which would alleviate any fumbling in the dark for light switches located on the wall. In 1909, he received his first patent for an invention that enabled a light switch to be switched on and off by turning the doorknob. Schlage followed this success in 1910 with a patented lock that operated by pushing and pulling on the knob. Pursuing his interest in electricity and mechanics, he received patents in 1911 and 1913 for developing an indicating push-button for an electrical door bell.

Schlage then returned his attention to door locks, patenting in 1916 the Throw-Lock concept, a lock that could be unlocked by tilting the knob. His interest in developing a more practical door lock led him to focus on two primary features. First, he believed that the entire lock structure had to be constructed out of sheet metal to compete with other lock manufacturers of the day. Second, the lock should be designed for ease of installment by merely boring two cylindrical holes into the door, one a cross bore, and the other, an edge bore. This design would have the advantage of being both more cost-effective for builders to purchase and easier to install. On April 12, 1920, Schlage applied for his first cylindrical door lock patent, which described a lock made out of assembling the knob, spindle, and latch retractor into one unit within a circular housing. He received his patent on May 22, 1923.

In 1920, Schlage left Western Electric and formed and incorporated the Schlage Manufacturing Company in San Francisco, California, where he also recruited three businessmen, C.P. Griffin, J. Thomkins, and J.H. Morgan, as his board of directors. The first board meeting was held on August 28, 1920. The three businessmen were the first owners of the company's capital stock, each with ten shares with a par value of $1.00 per share.

EARLY 20TH CENTURY: REFINING DESIGNS AND ACCELERATING PRODUCTION

Ever refining his lock design, Schlage filed a second patent for the locking push-button door lock on October 5, 1920. The patent described a cylindrical lock design with a locking mechanism operated by pushing a button in the center of the doorknob to lock and turning the interior knob to unlock. He received his patent for the locking push-button door lock on April 8, 1924. With improvements in his push-button design, Walter Schlage abandoned his previously patented Throw-Lock idea in 1921. The push-button design was the basis for his ninth application for a patent relating to door locks and became the mainstay of the company's business for years to come.

In 1922, the first Schlage board of directors approved the push-button design and in 1923 the company went into full-scale production of the new cylindrical lock with a push-button in the center of the doorknob. The company grew quickly from six employees and

several punch presses to 100 employees working two shifts producing almost 20,000 locks per month. In 1926, Schlage opened a new plant in San Francisco, and on December 20, 1927, he received another patent for a key-activated rotatable tumbler lock. The new design represented another step forward, as all previous Schlage locks were non-key operated.

Despite the opening of the new plant, the company, now known as the Schlage Lock Company, was overextended and operating at a deficit in 1926. Beset with financial difficulties, Schlage urgently appealed to Charles Kendrick, a local businessman and manufacturer, who agreed to make a substantial investment in the company. In 1927, Kendrick then became president of Schlage Lock Company, forming a prosperous alliance with the inventor Walter Schlage that served the company well in the years ahead. By 1929, Kendrick wiped out the deficit of more than $80,000, and netted $108,330 in 1928 against $81,157 in 1927 and a net loss of $85,585 in 1926. The company was seeing considerable success in marketing a new lock for households and offices, with a corresponding rise in profits.

In October 1929, the Schlage Lock Company's board of directors also voted to offer common stockholders the right to subscribe for new common treasury stock at $10 a share on a basis of one share for each ten shares held. The purpose of the stock sale was to raise new capital for purchase of machinery and other expenses with the aim of developing and manufacturing a new line of locks for office buildings, hotels, and other businesses. As a result of the stock offering, in December 1929, the company announced that it was signing contracts for new factory buildings, which were anticipated to increase plant capacity by a third. The company believed that it was an especially favorable time for expansion and that it would ensure the growing company's continued prosperity. Further, alluding to the 1929 stock market crash, a company spokesman was quoted in the December 16 issue of the *Wall Street Journal* as follows: "We are very glad to be able to do our bit in contributing to the efforts being made by Mr. Hoover to insure continued prosperity for 1930." Company officials placed the cost of aggregate expansion, including expenses for new construction and installation of new machinery, at between $50,000 and $100,000.

In March 1930, the company reported a steep decline in net profits from $95,319 in 1928 to just $42,337 in 1929. Earnings were affected by the collapse in the building industry and by the stock market crash, which drastically reduced the company's operations. Nevertheless, the Schlage Lock Company weathered the

KEY DATES

1920: Walter Reinbold Schlage founds Schlage Manufacturing Company.

1923: Schlage receives his first cylindrical door lock patent and the company goes into full production of the cylindrical door lock.

1924: Schlage receives a patent for the locking push-button door lock.

1946: Company founder Walter Schlage dies.

1965: Schlage Lock acquires Von Durbin Co.

1974: Ingersoll-Rand Company acquires Schlage Lock Company for approximately $84 million.

1986: Schlage Lock introduces the KeepSafer Security System, its first low-cost, wireless, easy-to-install home security system.

1996: The company splits its residential and commercial units.

1998: Schlage Lock unveils a new line of maximum security products.

1999: Schlage Lock acquires H.B. Inves Company.

2001: Schlage Lock launches new lines of plumbing fixtures in its Broadway Collection, and markets the new Schlage E-Bolt, an electronically controlled deadbolt lock.

2002: Schlage Lock acquires Kryptonite, enabling it to further diversify product offerings and increase sales.

2004: Schlage announces some work force cutbacks as it shifts production to Mexico and China.

financial crisis of the Great Depression, emerging as a more profitable company in the 1940s. In 1946, Walter Schlage died, leaving the company he founded in the hands of his successors, who steered the firm through more profitable times.

POSTWAR PROSPERITY

In 1958, a labor strike together with a slow building year lowered the company's net profits by about 10 percent from the preceding year, from $1,478,337 to about $1,330,000 in 1957. Nevertheless, an unexpected year-end sales increase helped to counter the effects of the six-week strike in the summer of 1957. The year 1958 also started out well, with the company anticipating a 10 percent boost in sales and earnings based on estimates that housing starts would be up a corresponding 10 percent from the previous year. With a strong

cash position, the company began looking to expand operations beyond its three San Francisco plants, which totaled 300,000 square feet and 1,600 employees. Despite its optimistic predictions, however, by April 1958, the company announced that about 900 of its 1,075 production workers would go on a four-day work week because of a reduction in business.

The company's declining business was short-lived, however, and by the early 1960s it had returned to profitability. In January 1962, Schlage Lock Company announced that it would build a $1.5 million addition to its San Francisco factory, enlarging the facility by 50 percent. The company further refined its position in the lock business by introducing the deadbolt lock with a strike frame reinforcer, a metal plate that improves the effectiveness of a lock. Schlage Lock also acquired a couple of companies, including the Von Durbin Co. in 1965, adding panic-door devices to its line of products, and the mortise lock manufacturing company, General Lock Company of Pontiac, Michigan, in the 1970s.

In August 1970, former company president Charles H. Kendrick died at the age of 93. Kendrick, a veteran of World War I and holder of the Silver Star, was a national vice-commander of the American Legion in the early 1920s. He later became a critic of the national organization for not taking a stronger stand against the Ku Klux Klan. He also criticized state Legion leaders for opposing socialist Eugene V. Debs's right to speak in San Francisco.

BECOMING A SUBSIDIARY OF INGERSOLL-RAND IN 1974

In 1974, New Jersey–based Ingersoll-Rand Company announced that it agreed to acquire the Schlage Lock Company in an exchange of stock valued at approximately $84 million. Under the agreement, the producer of diversified industrial machinery and equipment would exchange 965,145 shares of Ingersoll-Rand, or 1.23 percent of its shares, for each of Schlage's 784,673 outstanding shares. Schlage Lock would be a wholly owned subsidiary of Ingersoll-Rand and would continue to operate under its current management. In 1973, Schlage Lock had earnings of about $5 million and sales of $75 million.

At the time of its acquisition, Schlage Lock was a dominant player in the commercial lock business. Because Ingersoll-Rand believed that the lock-making firm relied too much on the construction business, with its periodic downturns, it pushed Schlage into the retail-residential market. As a result, Schlage Lock broke into the home security business, which by the mid-1980s represented more than half of the company's sales. In

1986, Schlage Lock introduced the KeepSafer Security System, its first low-cost, wireless, easy-to-install home security system.

Schlage's market timing rode the crest of an era of rising crime rates, which included increases in home break-ins from an estimated three million in 1985 to about 3.2 million in 1986. The home security business enabled the company to break out of a mature business into a profitable new growth niche. At the time, every American home had an average of 1.57 locks, but only 8 percent had home alarm systems. Schlage priced its KeepSafer alarm system below that of its competitors.

The system came with two wireless transmitters and two sensor sets that could be screwed or stuck onto doors or windows. The transmitters sent out a radio signal that tripped the alarm whenever a door or window frame was moved an inch or more. The system also included a personal access code that enabled only homeowners to program the system. Schlage introduced a more expensive SafeKeeper Plus, which came with more sensors and transmitters, in addition to a remote control unit for arming or disarming the system from outside the home. Schlage's main competitor for its home security device came from Black & Decker, which also offered two wireless systems. In the late 1970s, several other firms had tried and failed to mass-market home security devices, which proved to be too expensive and unreliable. With improved technology and lower prices, the home security market became a profitable new niche for the Schlage Lock Company.

CATERING TO RESIDENTIAL AND COMMERCIAL MARKETS INTO THE 21ST CENTURY

In 1995, the company introduced a line of premium-priced locks aimed at capturing a large piece of the $120 million custom-home market. Schlage Lock closed out 1994 with a 15 percent increase in sales and $350 million in revenues. With escalating concerns about crime during the 1990s, the lock industry experienced a corresponding boom in business. From the beginning, Schlage catered to the mid-priced residential and commercial markets, where it held a 40 percent market share by 1995. It successfully created brand awareness with a national cable advertising campaign that depicted Schlage as the "Doberman of Locks." The company's $3 million ad campaign featured people imitating barking dogs to keep intruders at bay. Schlage's new upscale locks, including the line called Mediterranean Designer Entrances, consisted of three designs under the names Capri, Corsica, and Cypress. The company also invested $3.5 million to produce a new lock that would not stain, tarnish, or allow burglars to jimmy it. The new

lock was designed and introduced to challenge the industry's top competitor, Pennsylvania-based Baldwin Hardware, which held a $50 million share of the market. Schlage saw its most profitable growth coming from the high-end residential market, but also had its eye on the growing market for smart locks, such as handheld computer-operated systems that allowed only select individuals to gain entry.

In February 1996, Schlage split its residential and commercial divisions. The company relocated its commercial division's administrative operations from San Francisco to its security plant in Colorado Springs, Colorado. The company's two separate divisions enabled it to sharpen the focus on its respective markets. In September 1996, *Professional Builder* magazine's 1996 brand use survey confirmed Schlage's leading position in the residential lock and hardware market with an estimated 63.9 percent of the nation's builders stating their preference for the company's products. The findings supported Schlage's business strategy of designing and making products for different markets with distinct needs.

In 1998, Schlage unveiled a new line of maximum security products. The Handleset was introduced in four designs with security features that protected against kick-in and other forced entry attacks. With the acquisition of the H.B. Inves Company in 1999 and Kryptonite in 2002, Schlage was able to further diversify product offerings and increase sales. In May 2001, Schlage continued efforts to broaden its market niches by launching new lines of plumbing fixtures in its Broadway Collection, which could be matched with an array of door hardware and decorative trim. The company also marketed the Schlage E-Bolt, an electronically controlled deadbolt lock that could be programmed to accept only specific keys. The system eliminated the need to rekey or replace locks due to tenant turnover or lost or stolen keys. The E-Bolt system enabled reprogramming of the intelligent deadbolt, which included accepting a new key and denying access by old keys within minutes.

In February 2004, Schlage announced the elimination of 150 temporary jobs at its Security plant in Colorado Springs with the prospect of many more layoffs within three years as the company shifted production to Mexico and China. Reflecting pressures of the global economy, the company claimed that it had to shift production of high-volume residential and commercial locks to foreign plants to reduce costs and remain competitive. Nonetheless, Schlage's position as a leading producer of locks and home security devices appears to assure its continuing profitability into the future.

Bruce P. Montgomery

PRINCIPAL DIVISIONS

Residential; Commercial.

PRINCIPAL COMPETITORS

ASSA ABLOY; Master Lock Company; STRATTEC.

FURTHER READING

"Builders Sold on Schlage," *Professional Builder,* September 1998.

"Builders Turn to Schlage for Security That Lasts a Lifetime," *Professional Builder,* September 1996.

"Charles H. Kendrick of Schlage Lock Co.," *Wall Street Journal,* August 5, 1970.

Ginsberg, Steve, "Keying on New Products: Schlage Tries to Pick Its Way into Locks for Custom Homes," *San Francisco Business Times,* February 3, 1995.

Greenberg, Manning, "Can Schlage Find the Key to Home Security?" *HFD—The Weekly Home Furnishings Newspaper,* April 13, 1987.

Heilman, Wayne, "Ingersoll-Rand to Move Lock Commercial Division Offices to Colorado," *Knight-Ridder/Tribune Business News,* March 18, 1996.

———, "Schlage Lock Sending Jobs Overseas; 150 Local Cuts Will Be First of Many More," *Gazette,* February 7, 2004.

"Ingersoll-Rand Plans $84 Million Purchase of Schlage Lock Co.," *Wall Street Journal,* January 25, 1974.

Panczyk, Tania D., "Schlage Locks in Ads," *AdWeek Midwest Edition,* May 7, 2001.

Paris, Ellen, "To Catch a Thief," *Forbes,* August 24, 1987.

"Schlage Lock Co.: Declares 10% Stock Dividend," *Wall Street Journal,* October 7, 1929.

"Schlage Lock Co. to Enlarge Plant," *Wall Street Journal,* December 16, 1929.

"Schlage Lock Cuts Workweek," *Wall Street Journal,* April 10, 1958.

"Schlage Lock Expects Upturn This Year," *Wall Street Journal,* January 28, 1958.

"Schlage Lock—Maximum Security Handleset," *National Home Center,* September 1, 1998.

"Schlage Lock: Urban Dread Set to a Catchy Beat," *AdWeek Midwest Edition,* August 5, 1996.

Schmidt, Joanna, "Schlage Lock Co. Features Dog and Senior Citizen in Television Ad Campaign," *Knight-Ridder/Tribune Business News,* July 13, 1993.

Smutko, Liz, "Deadbolts: Still a Top Security Seller," *Chilton's Hardware Age,* May 1995.

Sephora Holdings S.A.

65, Avenue Edouard Vaillant 92100
Boulogne-Billancourt,
France
Telephone: (33) 1 44 13 22 22
Fax: (33) 1 46 09 34 01
Web site: http://www.sephora.fr

Wholly Owned Subsidiary of LVMH Moët Hennessy Louis
Vuitton S.A.
Incorporated: 1969
Employees: 3,050
Sales: $827 million
NAIC: 424210 Drugs and Druggists' Sundries Merchant
Wholesalers; 424310 Piece Goods, Notions, and
Other Dry Goods Merchant Wholesalers; 424820
Wine and Distilled Alcoholic Beverage Merchant
Wholesalers; 424990 Other Miscellaneous
Nondurable Goods Merchant Wholesalers; 453998
All Other Miscellaneous Store Retailers (Except
Tobacco Stores)

■ ■ ■

Sephora S.A. is a world-leading specialist perfume
retailer, with more than 560 stores across Europe, in the
United States, and, since 2005, in China. Sephora
pioneered the limited assistance self-service concept in
the perfume sector, presenting a broad product range
encompassing many different brands, in a break from
the traditional single-brand retail focus. An increasing
share of Sephora's revenues, however, has come from the
development of its own private label, Sephora-branded

range. This line has captured consumer attention not
only from its low-pricing policy, but also for its launch
of such innovative products as makeup for legs, and
especially the launch of its StriVectin-SD, a hugely successful anti-wrinkle cream, launched in 2004. Another
key to Sephora's success in the mid-2000s has been the
addition of a wide range of beauty services, such as the
hair styling counter called "The Style Lounge" and
specialized service areas such as the Nail Bar, the Brow
Bar, and the Smile Bar, among others. Architects of the
company's turnaround have been chairman and CEO
Jacques Levy and European marketing director Natalie
Bader-Michel, who have also redesigned the group's
retail format. These changes have helped the company
end years of losses and post impressive revenue increases
at mid-decade. Sephora is a subsidiary of luxury goods
group LVMH Moët Hennessy Louis Vuitton S.A., which
owns many of the brands positioned on Sephora's
shelves. Sephora is the largest unit of LVMH's Selective
Retailing Division, which includes the sephora.com online sales site, DFS Galleria and Miami Cruiseline, and
the Bon Marché department store in Paris. In 2005, the
Selective Retailing division posted sales of EUR 3.65
billion ($4.3 billion).

SELF-SERVICE STARTUP IN 1969

Dominique Mandonnaud started out in business with a
single perfume store in Limoges, in France's Haute Vi-
enne region, in 1969. The French perfume and cosmetics market, as elsewhere in Europe, remained dominated
by a heavily service-based retail model, in which sales
staff generally received commissions based on sales. In
the case of department stores, which dominated the

COMPANY PERSPECTIVES

Sephora is a visionary beauty-retail concept founded in France in 1969 and acquired by Paris-based LVMH Moët Hennessy Louis Vuitton, the world's leading luxury products group, in 1997. Sephora's unique, open-sell environment features over 250 classic and emerging brands across a broad range of product categories including skincare, color, fragrance, makeup, bath & body, and haircare, in addition to Sephora's own private label. To build the most knowledgeable and professional team of product consultants in the beauty industry, Sephora developed "Science of Sephora." This program ensures that our team is skilled to identify skin types, have a knowledge of skin physiology, the history of makeup, application techniques, the science of creating fragrances, and most importantly, how to interact with Sephora's diverse clientele.

market for perfumes and cosmetics, sales staff typically represented a single brand. This retail model continued to dominate the perfume sector, despite the rise of self-service retailing elsewhere, especially in the grocery and supermarket sectors.

Yet through the 1970s, Mandonnaud increasingly sought a means to adapt the self-service format to perfume sales. In 1979, Mandonnaud made the leap, launching a new perfume store called Shop 8 in Limoges. The store was a distinct departure from the typical small perfume shop, providing a large and open selling space, and placing products within reach of customers. Mandonnaud's new store also featured an extended range of both perfumes and cosmetic brands. However, these products, rather than being grouped by brand, were arranged according to product family. In this way, brands were presented side by side on the store's shelves—in this way the new perfume store had more in common with the typical supermarket than with traditional perfume shops. The Shop 8 format was, at the time, nothing short of revolutionary in France's retail perfumery and cosmetics sector.

Mandonnaud continued to develop the Shop 8 format and its "assisted self-service" formula, while seeking to build a network of stores. By 1984, Mandonnaud had opened a total of four Shop 8 stores. By that year, too, Mandonnaud's company had come under control of fast-growing distribution group Promodes, then in

the midst of a large-scale expansion phase. The relationship with Promodes soon soured, however, as the distribution giant focused its efforts on the international expansion of its core food sector operations. By 1987, Promodes had separated itself from Shop 8. Nonetheless, Promodes maintained a hold over the perfume business, through convertible debt, which, if exercised, would have given Promodes the majority of voting rights.

Part of this debt was generated by Mandonnaud's first external expansion effort. In 1988, recognizing that retail success in France came first and foremost through the all-important Parisian market, Mandonnaud acquired a small chain of eight perfume stores in the French capital city. Mandonnaud quickly converted these shops to the Shop 8 format, and began making plans for further growth.

Yet Mandonnaud's relationship with Promodes proved an obstacle for these ambitions. Promodes refused to fund further growth in the small perfume chain, which had remained unprofitable through the 1980s. At the same time, Promodes set a high asking price for the company, making it impossible for Mandonnaud to purchase back the shares in the chain.

Mandonnaud approached a private equity group, Apax Partners, with a plan to back a buyout of the Shop 8 chain. That plan soon took on momentum after a visit from another private equity group, Astorg, part of Suez, which had become interested in the Shop 8 format. Mandonnaud approached both groups, suggesting that the two equity firms join together to back Mandonnaud in a buyout of the retail chain. Apax and Astorg agreed to back Mandonnaud's plans for the company's expansion. They also agreed to Mandonnaud's stipulations to set an exit date before Mandonnaud's 50th birthday, when he intended to retire.

BECOMING SEPHORA IN 1993

The buyout was completed in 1991, with Mandonnaud's holding vehicle, Altamir, maintaining majority control of the company. The three partners then set out to achieve an expansion plan calling for the opening of from three to five stores per year. Yet these plans quickly ran into difficulties, as the French economy entered a severe downturn. Instead, the company began seeking to acquire an existing perfume chain in order to achieve their growth objectives.

In the meantime, Mandonnaud had begun developing an expanded version of his assisted self-service format. In 1993, the company launched the new format under a new name, Mille et Un Parfums, with a first store in the Belle-Epine shopping mall in Val-de-Marne, near Paris. The new format featured not only a larger

KEY DATES

1969: Dominique Mandonnaud opens a perfume shop in Limoges.

1970: Boots plc of the United Kingdom opens its first perfume store in Paris.

1976: Boots and Nouvelles Galeries form a partnership to build Sephora perfume chain.

1979: Mandonnaud launches the Shop 8 "assisted self-service" retail perfume format.

1984: Promodes acquires control of Shop 8.

1988: Shop 8 acquires eight perfume stores in Paris.

1991: Mandonnaud, backed by two equity investment firms, buys out Shop 8.

1993: Shop 8 launches its new Mille et un Parfums retail format, then acquires the Sephora chain from Boots; Shop 8 becomes Sephora and rebrands stores.

1996: Sephora opens its flagship Champs Elysées store.

1997: Mandonnaud and investors sell Sephora to LVMH; Sephora acquires the 75-store Marie Jeanne-Godard perfume chain.

1998: Sephora opens its first store in New York City, launching an international expansion drive.

2003: Jacques Levy is appointed CEO and he leads the redevelopment of the Sephora format, including the rollout of an extended line of Sephora branded products.

mass market goods, and featuring only a limited self-service offering—had failed to find a market in France. After years of losses, the Sephora chain managed to turn a profit of just FRF 270,000 on revenues of FRF 606 million in 1992.

Shop 8, through Altamir, agreed to pay FRF 360 million ($61 million) for the Sephora chain in a deal completed in September 1993. The acquisition not only boosted Shop 8's total network to nearly 50 stores, it also gave the group a number of prime city center locations, including a presence in most of the major Parisian shopping streets. Following the purchase, Mandonnaud announced the company's intention to roll out the Mille et Un Parfum format across the entire chain, and at the same time, all of the stores, as well as the company itself, were rebranded under the Sephora brand name.

Sephora continued expanding its chain into the mid-1990s. By 1997, the company operated 54 stores throughout France, and controlled some 8 percent of the total French retail perfume market. By then, too, the company had innovated again, opening a new flagship store on the Champs-Elysées in Paris. Featuring 1,300 square meters of selling space, roughly triple the company's average store size, the new store served as the model for future group store developments.

Mandonnaud and partners prepared to exit their investments before Mandonnaud's birthday in 1997. The partners initially investigated a public offering. However, because Mandonnaud himself prepared to retire from the company's direction, the group instead opted to find a buyer for the company. This led the company to luxury products group LVMH Moët Hennessy Louis Vuitton, which was engaged in a major expansion of its holdings, while at the same time seeking to add a retail component to complement its designer label products. The deal was completed in July 1997, when LVMH agreed to pay the equivalent of EUR 344 million for Sephora.

FROM PERFUME TO BEAUTY CARE IN THE NEW CENTURY

Under LVMH, Sephora developed new and far more ambitious expansion plans. Almost immediately, the company more than doubled its number of stores, through the acquisition of the Marie Jeanne-Godard chain. That chain, rebranded under the Sephora name, added 75 stores and more than FRF 790 million in revenues, boosting Sephora's control of the French perfume market to 18 percent. By the end of 1997, Sephora's sales had already topped the FRF 2 billion.

Sephora turned to the international market, opening its first flagship store in New York City in 1998.

selling space than the company's other stores, but a more upscale, luxury-oriented interior and graphic design, as well.

The year 1993 marked a turning point for the company. The continued search for an acquisition target had brought the company into contact with the U.K.'s Boots PLC, which operated a chain of 38 Sephora-branded chain stores, largely in the Parisian region. That chain had been founded in 1970, when Boots opened a first store on Paris's Rue de Passy. By 1976, Boots had expanded the perfume business, launching the Sephora brand in partnership with department store group Nouvelles Galeries. That company became part of Boots PLC in 1979. Under Boots' control, the Sephora chain grew quickly, becoming the largest perfume specialist in the highly fragmented French market. Nonetheless, the chain, which had adopted a similar format to Boots's retail mix in the U.K.—blending high end items with

The company then began to target expansion into the European market. Italy became one of the company's first targets, and it began buying up a number of smaller chains in that country. The company's acquisitions in Italy included Kharys in 1998, the 46-store Laguna chain in 1999, and Boidi, a chain of 19 perfume stores in 2000. By 2005, Sephora operated more than 100 stores in Italy, including its Milan flagship location, opened that year.

Not all of Sephora's international expansion efforts proved successful—the company struggled to impose itself in both the United Kingdom and Spain. By 2006, the company had decided to exit the former altogether. In Spain, Sephora decided instead to team up with that country's major department store group, El Corte Ingles, in order to boost its presence. Meanwhile, in the United States, the company built up a national network of more than 150 stores. The company also entered a number of other markets, such as Japan in 1999, and Portugal and Greece in 2000. By the end of that year, Sephora had been transformed into an international giant with more than 460 stores.

Sephora's rapid growth had come at a price, however, as the company slipped into losses at the turn of the century. The company was forced to slow the pace of its new store openings, even as it entered a number of new markets, including the Czech Republic in 2002. At the same time, the company was forced to abandon its efforts to break into the Japanese markets, where its seven stores had met with relative indifference from consumers. By then, rumors had begun to circulate that LVMH intended to sell its flagging perfume retailer.

Instead, the company brought in new management in 2003, appointing former Staples International head Jacques Levy as Sephora's CEO. Levy, backed by European managing director Natalie Bader-Michel, initiated a revamping of the Sephora concept. Part of the group's revitalization effort centered on introducing an extensive line of private label products under the Sephora brand name. Featuring discounted prices, the Sephora brand quickly distinguished itself for its innovative products, such as the launch of makeup specially developed for use on the leg. In 2004, the company also launched its own anti-wrinkle cream, StriVectin-SD, which became a huge international best seller. That product was followed by the launch in 2005 of a full line of Sephora skin care items. As part of the continued effort to boost Sephora's sales, the company also rolled out an increasing range of in-store services, including hair styling centers and specialized service counters with monikers such as the Nail Bar, the Brow Bar, the Smile Bar, and the like. In another boost to the company's image, Sephora also stepped up the introduction of a growing number of new brands, many of which were imported from the United States and elsewhere, helping to position the company on the cutting edge of beauty fashions.

Sephora also renewed its international expansion drive. In 2004, the company boosted its presence in Eastern Europe, buying up the Empik perfume chain in Poland, then forming a partnership with leading Russian perfumery L'Etoile to bring the Sephora format to that market. Sephora next targeted the Chinese market, creating a joint venture with Shanghai Jahwa United, and opening three stores in Shanghai in 2005. By the beginning of 2006, Sephora had largely transcended its former image as a perfume specialist. Instead, the company had successfully re-established itself as a full-scale beauty care retailer, featuring a large assortment of perfumes, make up, and skin care items. In 2006, the steady success of the line of Sephora branded products led the company to announce its plans to emphasize the future development of the brand. One of the most dynamic parts of the LVMH empire, Sephora targeted further growth in the new decade.

M.L. Cohen

PRINCIPAL SUBSIDIARIES

Sephora Italia S.p.A.; Sephora Polska Sp zoo; Sephora Portugal Perfumeria Lda.; Sephora UK Ltd.; Sephora USA LLC.

PRINCIPAL COMPETITORS

Douglas Holding AG; Bath & Body Works, Inc.; Beauti-Control Cosmetics, Inc.; The Body Shop International PLC; The Boots Company PLC; Buth-Na-Bodhaige Inc.; Duane Reade, Inc.; Marionnaud SA; The Estée Lauder Companies Inc.

FURTHER READING

Christofari, Jean-Francois, "Sephora," *Marketing Magazine*, January 11, 1998.

Costello, Brid, Finn, Kristin, and Klepacki, Laura, "Sephora Rolls Out New Initiatives," *WWD*, February 18, 2004, p. 30.

Costello, Brid, "Sephora Steps Up Private Label," *WWD*, May 31, 2002, p. 10.

Epiro, Stephanie, and Costello, Brid, "Sephora Forging Ahead in Italy," *WWD*, March 8, 2005, p. 3.

Han Mui Ching, "LVMH's Sephora Leaps into China, Exits UK." *Cosmetics International*, April 8, 2005, p. 1.

Hernandez, Itaxso, "El Corte Ingles & Sephora in Spanish Joint Venture," *Cosmetics International*, February 25, 2005, p. 6.

Lihn, Pham, "Sephora Donne un Coup de Jeune a la Beaute," *Le Figaro*, April 8, 2006.

"'Moment of truth' Ahead for Sephora, says chief," *Cosmetics International*, November 21, 2003, p. 7.

Richards, Carla, "Sephora to Introduce Plethora of New Niche Brands in France," *Cosmetics International*, March 26, 2004, p. 9.

"Sales Soar at Sephora," *Cosmetics International*, January 27, 2006, p. 9.

"Sephora Launches Own Label Skin Care," *Cosmetics International*, April 22, 2005, p. 7.

Sheaffer Pen Corporation

301 Avenue H
Fort Madison, Iowa 52627
U.S.A.
Telephone: (319) 372-3300
Fax: (319) 372-7539
Web site: http://www.sheaffer.com

Wholly Owned Subsidiary of Bic USA Inc.
Incorporated: 1913 as W.A. Sheaffer Pen Company
Employees: 250
Sales: $38.6 million (est.)
NAIC: 339942 Lead Pencil and Art Good Manufacturing; 339941 Pen and Mechanical Pencil Manufacturing

■ ■ ■

The Sheaffer Pen Corporation is a leading maker of pens, particularly luxury fountain pens. The Sheaffer brand hails back to the early 20th century, and it remains one of the best known fine pen brands in the United States and abroad. The company was controlled by three generations of its founder's family until 1966, when it was bought by a conglomerate. Since then, Sheaffer has gone through several owners, and is now wholly owned by Bic USA Inc., itself a subsidiary of the French manufacturer Societé BIC. Sheaffer makes several lines of moderately priced pens, including its EVT, Sentinel, and Award brands, and its Sheaffer Gift Collection. It also makes several lines of fine pens, which sell for thousands of dollars. Its White Dot line is its storied luxury brand, and Sheaffer also sells luxury pens under the names Prelude, Agio, Javelin, Valor, and others. Sheaffer manufactures calligraphy pens and kits as well. Other lines include ballpoint pen refills; roller ball refills; highlighter refills; Skrip ink, in both bottles and cartridges; and erasers.

BUILDING A BETTER PEN

Sheaffer Pen Corp. was founded by Walter A. Sheaffer, an Iowa jeweler, in 1912. Sheaffer was born in Bloomfield, Iowa, in 1867, and brought up in the jewelry trade. He worked at jewelry stores in Iowa and Missouri as a teenager, and then at the age of 20 became a partner in his father's jewelry store in Bloomfield. Sheaffer then started his own jewelry store in Fort Madison, Iowa. He was fascinated by fountain pens, and he began experimenting in the back of his jewelry shop, trying to devise a better filling system. Fountain pens before the 1890s were usually filled with ink by means of a fragile glass dropper. This system was both inconvenient and messy, and several inventors had developed improvements on it by the turn of the century. Around the time Sheaffer was experimenting, pens were filled by various more or less complicated systems employing syringes, the vacuum principle, or buttons that sometimes had to be turned or pressed with a coin. Walter Sheaffer came up with a simple and elegant filling system that he patented in 1907. It employed a lever on the side of the pen, which, when depressed, caused ink to rise up from the ink bottle into the pen. Sheaffer's lever system was easy to use and clean, a big advantage, and the enclosed lever did not detract from the appearance of the pen. Sheaffer's pens were at first just a sideline, but in 1912, when he was in his mid-40s and the father of a family,

The Sheaffer brand today reflects who you are—it's your signature, a reflection of your personality, ambitions and image. Our fine writing instruments provide a welcome "escape" from the hectic pace of modern times, and our exciting range of fresh luxury finishes complements any attire or mood. Most importantly, we do all the of the above while continuing to provide the superior writing experience you expect!

he decided to risk all and go into pens full time. He raised $35,000 to enable him to manufacture his pens on a large scale. The company incorporated in 1913 as the W.A. Sheaffer Pen Co.

Sheaffer poured money into advertising the pens, which were cast as modern, big-city, big-business writing instruments. Growth was quick, and by 1917, when Sheaffer writing instruments were advertised as "For Uncle Sam's Fighting Boys," the company's annual pen production had reached 100,000 units. In the 1920s the company experimented with new plastics, then very much in vogue, and launched its own ink brand, Skrip, in 1922. Sheaffer always stood for quality, and one of Walter Sheaffer's maxims was that it was "better to sell one pen for $10 than ten pens for $1." The company introduced the Lifetime pen, a luxury model, in 1920, and in 1924 modified it to include a signature white dot on the cap. The White Dot line continued as the most high-priced and sought-after Sheaffer model, both in vintage pens and new releases. These sell in the 2000s for thousands of dollars. In 1928, Sheaffer took the company public on the New York Stock Exchange. By that time, the company had captured some 25 percent of the domestic pen market. Sheaffer was one of the so-called Big Four pen makers, along with Parker, Waterman, and Wahl Eversharp. Between 1913 and 1925, the company had grown some 2000 percent, while its rivals had to be satisfied with mere 400 percent growth.

THE DEPRESSION YEARS AND
THE BIRTH OF THE BALL POINT

In 1929, Sheaffer told the *Wall Street Journal* (December 20, 1929) that the past two months had been "the best in the history of his company," and that the "outlook was very bright." For many manufacturers, the impact of the October stock exchange crash and ensuing Great Depression was not felt for a few more months yet. Sheaffer Pen was a rarity in that it actually continued to

prosper as the Depression dragged much of the country down. Sheaffer claimed that the profit-sharing system he had instituted with his employees was responsible for the company's good fortune. Perhaps Sheaffer was also insulated from the worst effects of the Depression because much of its business was in luxury goods. Whatever the reason, Sheaffer saw significant sales gains in the 1930s (for example, sales of 50 percent greater in 1934 than 1933), and employees received bonuses regularly throughout the decade of the 1930s.

During World War II, pens sold well, as they were a popular gift for people in the armed forces. Sheaffer even had trouble keeping up with demand in 1942. The company also reconfigured some of its manufacturing during the war years, making artillery fuses and bomb components for the war effort. At the end of the war, Walter Sheaffer resigned the presidency of the company in favor of his son, Craig. Walter Sheaffer died in 1946. Craig Sheaffer ran the company until 1953, when he left to take a post in the Eisenhower administration as assistant secretary of commerce. His son Walter Sheaffer II then took the top job.

Sheaffer continued to prosper in the 1950s, coming out with several significant models. The Snorkel pen, which debuted in 1952, was a fountain pen with a revolutionary and much admired filling system. Sheaffer's PFM (the Pen for Men) came out in 1959, and was an enduring seller. Sheaffer had grown to three manufacturing plants in Fort Madison by 1950, as well as running a plant in Mount Pleasant, Iowa, and another in Canada. In 1951 the company consolidated the Fort Madison plants, spending $2.5 million to expand its production capacity and office space. Sales were about $25 million in 1952. The company was still doing well, though the pen market was changing drastically. Many new writing instrument companies had come into the market after World War II, most capitalizing on a recent invention, the ball point pen.

The earliest known patent for a ball point pen dates back to 1888. Though the idea was a good one in theory, ink at the time could not be made thick enough to work effectively in a ball point. Though several ball points were patented and manufactured in the 1910s and 1920s, mass production of ball points did not begin until 1935. Then two Hungarian brothers, Lazlo Joszef and Georg Biro, came up with their own ball point pen, which they patented in 1938. Their pen, colloquially known as the Biro, became a best-seller in England when it was introduced in 1943. The Eberhard Faber Pencil Co. bought the U.S. rights to the Biro in 1944. The new ballpoints could write for months without a refill. While the first models retailed in the U.S. in the high price range of from $12 to $18, by 1947, the market

KEY DATES

1907: Walter Sheaffer patents his lever filling fountain pen.

1912: Sheaffer abandons the jewelry business to manufacture pens full time.

1913: Company is incorporated as W.A. Sheaffer Pen Co.

1928: Sheaffer Pen is launched on the New York Stock Exchange.

1946: Founder Walter Sheaffer dies.

1966: Company is sold to conglomerate Textron.

1976: Textron combines Sheaffer with a stationery firm to form the Sheaffer Eaton division.

1987: Textron sells Sheaffer Eaton to Gefinor.

1997: Gefinor sells Sheaffer to Bic.

was flooded with cheap ball points that could be bought for less than $1. Sheaffer had been one of the Big Four pen companies, and its total competition was estimated at some 60 pen manufacturers in the early 1940s. By the close of the decade, three times that many companies had some stake in the writing instruments market. The *Wall Street Journal* (May 13, 1947) noted with some alarm that more pens were being produced per year in the U.S. than there were people.

Given these conditions, one fountain pen maker after another struggled or went out of business. Wahl Eversharp was bought by its competitor Parker in 1957, and ceased to exist by the end of the 1960s. A premier British pen maker, De La Rue, stopped making pens in 1958, and many other European makers went under around this time. Waterman USA (though not its British counterpart Waterman England) also collapsed, leaving only Sheaffer and Parker of the Big Four.

UNDER NEW OWNERS

Sheaffer was still a profitable company in the early 1960s. It made both ball point and fountain pens, and continued to emphasize quality rather than price as the major selling point. In 1966, Walter Sheaffer II, the founder's grandson, resigned the presidency to become chairman, and the company was run by a former Standard Packaging Corp. executive, John A. Keenan. A few months after the leadership change, the company announced that it was being acquired by Textron, Inc., for approximately $19 million. 1965 sales had reached over $30 million. Textron, with sales of $720 million, described itself as a diversified manufacturer, and in fact

it was considered the first modern conglomerate. Its interests were varied, from machine parts to defense to stationery.

In 1976, Sheaffer was combined with another Textron unit, the Massachusetts-based Eaton. Eaton had been acquired by Textron one year after Sheaffer, and it made typing paper and other writing paper. The new combined division was called Sheaffer Eaton, and its headquarters were in Pittsfield, Massachusetts. By the early 1980s, Textron had grown to a $3 billion behemoth. It made Bell helicopters, machine tools, ball bearings, industrial measuring devices, and many other mostly industrial products. While diversification was once thought to be a hedge against swings in the business cycle, the company was evidently unwieldy by the 1980s, with sales and profits sliding. The company took on some $800 million of debt in 1986 when it bought a Michigan machine tool company, Ex-Cell-O, and soon Textron began shedding some of its units. Sheaffer Eaton was one of the first to go.

In 1987, Sheaffer Eaton was acquired by a subsidiary of a Swiss merchant banking company, the Gefinor Group. Gefinor (USA) Inc. paid $135 million for the Textron unit, which at that time had sales of approximately $140 million. Its product lines included Sheaffer pens, Eaton stationery, At-A-Glance appointment books, and Duo-Tang report covers. Gefinor considered Sheaffer Eaton a strong brand with much potential for growth. Textron had clearly not been paying much attention to the unit, and the new European owners may have seen much more potential for fountain pens than the American conglomerate did. Sheaffer had staked out a position as a maker of fashion and luxury pens, a trend which was even stronger in Europe. Indeed, under Gefinor's wing, Sheaffer's luxury pens had rising sales. Its line of pens priced between $75 and $175 rose 25 percent in 1990. One of Sheaffer's most popular products in the early 1990s was a silver fountain pen and ball point pen set that retailed for almost $1,000. Sheaffer's product line included even more expensive pens, with a solid gold Masterpiece fountain pen selling for $4,000.

After ten years with Gefinor, Sheaffer was sold again, this time to the U.S. subsidiary of French manufacturer Bic S.A. Bic, founded by French baron Marcel Bich, had entered the ball point pen market in 1952 and made cheap, disposable pens a worldwide sensation. The company was also well known for its disposable razors and lighters. In 1997, Bic offered an undisclosed amount (but claimed to be less than $50 million) for what was then known as the Sheaffer Group. Sheaffer by that time did about $50 million in sales annually on its pens. While the overall pen market had gone up and down in the 1990s, fountain pen sales, particularly of high-end pens, were strong. Sheaffer was no longer associated with Eaton products, which had been sold earlier to Fox River Paper and Pratt & Austin. It focused on fine pens, some of which were made by hand by skilled artisans. These might retail for as much as $5,000. Bic's own high-end pen lines had not enjoyed strong sales, and the company wished to acquire Sheaffer's prestigious brands. The sale was complicated by a counter-offer by a group of Sheaffer executives. They claimed to have a right of first refusal of any buyout. Bic took the case to court and upped its offer by $2 million. The sale to Bic eventually went through. The sale of Sheaffer to Bic echoed the sale of another former "Big Four" American pen manufacturer, Parker, which was acquired by Gillette in 1993.

Under new ownership, Sheaffer seemed to do what it had always done well, which was to emphasize quality rather than price. Though its parent was known for some of the cheapest pens on the market, Sheaffer concentrated on its select customers for the prestigious White Dot and other high-end lines. Sheaffer launched a magazine called *Sphere* in 1999, which went to Sheaffer customers but contained no articles or advertising for Sheaffer pens. This was part of an overall strategy to position Sheaffer as an essential element in a luxurious lifestyle. Consequently, the magazine did not mention pens, but was filled with articles about travel, food, and fine design. Sheaffer marketing in the 2000s continued to emphasize the elegance and mystique of its pens. In 2005, the company began a push into a distribution channel it had entered previously and then let fall: duty-free shops in airports, border crossings, and cruise ships. Though pen technology had changed dramatically since 1913, Sheaffer managed to endure, not as an anachronism but as a luxury brand.

A. Woodward

PRINCIPAL COMPETITORS

A.T. Cross Company; Faber-Castell AG; Montblanc International GmbH.

FURTHER READING

Andrew, Jack, "Bic Completes Sheaffer Buy," *Financial Times*, October 21, 1997, p. 29.

"Bic Corp. Sues Sheaffer to Bar Sales to ABTS," *Wall Street Journal Europe*, August 27, 1997, p. 3.

"Bic Wins Time in Fight to Acquire Sheaffer," *New York Times*, August 28, 1997, p. D19.

Dragoni, Giorgio and Fichera, Giuseppe, eds. *Fountain Pens: History and Design*. Milan: Arnoldo Mondadori Editore, 1997.

"Fountain Pen Flood," *Wall Street Journal*, May 13, 1947, p. 1.

"Fountain Pens Point to a Sales Record," *New York Times*, January 6, 1958, p. 84.

Flack, Jo-Anne, "Lifestyle Push," *Marketing Week*, September 30, 1999, p. 72.

"John A. Keenan Named Sheaffer Pen President," *Wall Street Journal*, April 23, 1965, p. 18.

Kalita, S. Mitra, "Bic Agrees to Acquire Sheaffer in Bid to Enter Market for Higher-Priced Pens," *Wall Street Journal*, August 1, 1997, p. A9B.

Killingbeck, Chris, "Design Choice/Sheaffer Fountain Pen," *Marketing*, June 15, 2000, p. 13.

Morin, Stephen P., "Power Posts," *Wall Street Journal*, September 8, 1983, p. 1.

Neiss, Doug, "Sheaffer Eaton Moves Ahead," *HFD*, October 5, 1987, p. 94.

———, "Sheaffer Eaton to be Sold," *HFD*, July 27, 1987, p. 34.

"Pen Manufacturers' Sales Volume Running Well Ahead of 1941," *Wall Street Journal*, November 17, 1942, p. 6.

"Sell on Quality, Not on Price—Says Pen Head," *Wall Street Journal*, January 29, 1935, p. 3.

Semans-Herald, Sandy, "Writing a Note Can Cost More than Price of a Stamp," *Business First-Louisville*, August 12, 1991, p. 36.

"Sheaffer Move Marks New Focus on Travel-Retail Markets," *Duty-Free News International*, May 15, 2005, p. 50.

"Sheaffer Pen Sales Put at $25 Million; Net May Dip," *Wall Street Journal*, January 11, 1952, p. 11.

"Sheaffer Pen Sees 50% Gain in Fiscal '62 Profit," *Wall Street Journal*, January 5, 1962, p. 7.

"Sheaffer Pen to Build Plant Consolidating Three Units," *Wall Street Journal*, March 21, 1950, p. 14.

"Textron Agrees to Sell its Sheaffer Eaton Unit," *Wall Street Journal*, July 14, 1987, p. 1.

"Textron Proposes to Buy Assets of Sheaffer Pen," *Wall Street Journal*, September 24, 1965, p. 2.

"Textron Sells Sheaffer Eaton Division," *Boston Globe*, September 1, 1987, p. 35.

"Walter A. Sheaffer, II, Is Elected President of W.A. Sheaffer Pen," *Wall Street Journal*, February 6, 1953, p. 3.

"Walter Sheaffer, Manufacturer, 78," *New York Times*, June 20, 1946, p. 23.

Watts, Thomas S., "Rising Writer," *Wall Street Journal*, June 4, 1953, p. 1.

Spector Photo Group N.V.

Kwatrechtsteenweg 160
Wetteren,
Belgium
Telephone: (+32 09) 365 98 11
Fax: (32 09) 365 98 98
Web site: http://www.spectorphotogroup.com

Public Company
Incorporated: 1964 as DBM Color N.V.
Employees: 1,700
Sales: EUR 349.09 million ($420 million) (2005)
Stock Exchanges: Euronext Brussels
Ticker Symbol: SPEC
NAIC: 812921 Photo Finishing Laboratories (Except One-Hour); 443112 Radio, Television, and Other Electronics Stores; 443120 Computer and Software Stores; 443130 Camera and Photographic Supplies Stores; 453998 All Other Miscellaneous Store Retailers (Except Tobacco Stores)

■ ■ ■

Belgium's Spector Photo Group N.V. has established a major presence in the European digital media market through its two core divisions: Retail Group and Imaging Group. The company's Retail Group operates more than 165 stores under the Photo Hall (in Belgium and Hungary) and Hifi International (in Luxembourg and France) names. The group's retail offering focuses on consumer electronics and multimedia products, including cellular telephones, digital and analog cameras and accessories, computer products, and other audiovisual products. Belgium is the group's largest retail market, with 95 stores, followed by Hungary, with 52 company-owned stores. The Retail Group generated 55 percent of Spector Photo Group's total revenues of nearly EUR 350 million ($420 million) in 2005. Spector's Imaging Group, which is structured under subsidiary Photomedia N.V., offers analog and digital processing services both through retail and online channels. The company's core brand in this unit is its ExtraFilm mail-order and online film processing business, which directly serves customers in Belgium, the Netherlands, Luxembourg, France, Sweden, Norway, Denmark, Finland, Switzerland, Italy, and Australia, and, since 2006, Germany, Spain, the United Kingdom, and Austria. Through its web site, ExtraFilm is able to accept orders from around the world. Other brands include the group's business-to-business brands Spector and Kodak Images, limited to the Benelux market, and the business-to-business-to-consumer e-commerce brand Wisiti in Belgium and France. The Benelux market contributes 33.5 percent of this division's sales, while France adds 26 percent and the Scandinavian markets nearly 24 percent. Spector Photo Group is listed on the Euronext Brussels Stock Exchange, and is led by Chairman Luc Vansteenkiste and Managing Director Tonny Van Doorslaer.

BROTHERLY BEGINNINGS IN 1964

Brothers Georges and Jules de Buck, and their brother-in-law Jérôme Mussche, were already active in the photo business in the early 1960s, with each operating his own photo studio and store in Wetteren, in Belgium. The

COMPANY PERSPECTIVES

The mission of Spector Photo Group is to help consumers enjoy audiovisual experiences and to capture emotional moments in order to revive them and cherish them. In fulfilling its mission, Spector Photo Group will also create added value for its shareholders, its staff members and all other stakeholders, as well as for the community in which it operates.

Spector Photo Group has two core activities, each structured in a separate division: the Retail Group and the Imaging Group.

The overall strategy followed by Spector Photo Group involves retaining its two core activities within the group but developing each using separate tactics.

development of a consumer color film market in the early 1960s led the brothers to join together to invest in their own color processing facility. The new company, founded in 1964, took the initials of their family names to form DBM Color N.V.

As an early entrant in the color processing market, DBM grew quickly through the 1960s and 1970s, emerging as the Belgian leader in the sector. In the mid-1970s, the company began developing a new logo, the Spector bird, which began appearing in independent photo shops utilizing DBM Color's services. In 1977, the company formally launched the Spector brand name, which became the group's main business-to-business brand.

The next generation of the family took over the business in 1980, led by Johan Mussche. As a market leader in Belgium, the company began to target international expansion, while also seeking to expand its operations to provide direct consumer operations. The company's first move internationally came in 1982, when DBM Color began serving the Netherlands market. Later that same year, the company entered France with the creation of ExtraFilm France, in a joint venture with ExtraFilm in Sweden. That company, founded by Lennart Sjögren, had been a pioneer in the European mail-order film processing market, deriving its name from its policy of including an extra roll of film with each processed film order. The French ExtraFilm operation also enabled DBM Color to offer direct to consumers film processing services. DBM and ExtraFilm's partnership soon extended the ExtraFilm franchise to the Netherlands market as well. Back at home, DBM strengthened its

position with a new 24-hour film processing guarantee.

By 1986, DBM Color's sales had topped BEF 400 million. In that year, the company, which remained entirely family owned, brought in its first outside director, Tonny Van Doorslaer, who had been working for Kredietbank before joining DBM as its financial director. The addition of Van Doorslaer was part of the De Buck and Mussche family's effort to "de-familiarize" the family-owned business. Van Doorslaer quickly became a close ally and business partner to Johan Mussche, providing the financial structure for Mussche's strategic leadership.

The threat that a foreign company might buy Aalst-based Tecnocrome, DBM's chief Belgian rival, led it to acquire that company in 1988. This purchase was followed in 1989 by the acquisition of Fotronic, which acted as the importer of Noritsu-made minilabs for the Belgian market. The addition of Fotronic gave DBM further control of the Belgian film processing market, where its market share soon rose past 50 percent. By 1991, the company had extended its Noritsu minilab concession through the acquisition of Sacap, the Noritsu importer for the French market.

EUROPEAN BREAKTHROUGH IN 1990

By then, DBM had risen to the front ranks of the European film processing market. Over the preceding decade, DBM had continued to build up its relationship with ExtraFilm in Sweden. In 1990, ExtraFilm agreed to be acquired by DBM, a move that placed the Sjögren family as the company's majority shareholder. In 1992, the de Buck, Mussche, and Sjögren families, together with a number of other investors, pooled their shareholdings into a new company, Fotoinvest.

The acquisition of ExtraFilm led DBM to change its name, to International Photo Group in 1991. By then, too, the company had acquired a listed company, Promoinvest, which provided the company with a backdoor to its own listing on the Brussels Stock Exchange. Following the Promoinvest acquisition in 1991, the company launched a restructuring of its operations, shedding the noncore holdings of Promoinvest. The completion of the restructuring effort, which lasted through 1993, was marked by the adoption of a new company name, Spector Photo Group, that year.

Having multiplied its turnover by more than ten times (the company's sales topped BEF 4 billion in the early 1990s), Spector began to plot the next phase of its expansion. International growth remained a focus for the company. This led the group back to France in 1994, when it acquired French counterpart Racine. That

KEY DATES

1964: The DBM Color film processing laboratory is founded in Wetteren, Belgium.

1977: The Spector brand name is launched.

1982: DBM Color partners with Sweden's Extra-Film to launch the ExtraFilm France mail-order film processing business.

1988: DBM Color acquires Belgian rival Tecnocrome, solidifying its lead in the Belgian market.

1989: DBM Color acquires Fotronic, importer of minilabs for the Belgian market.

1990: DBM takes over ExtraFilm, and changes its name to International Photo Group.

1993: The company acquires publicly listed Promo-invest and changes its name to Spector Photo Group.

1994: The company acquires French counterpart Racine, the second largest independent photo processor in France.

1996: The company acquires Photo Hall (Belgium) and Photo Porst (Germany, Czech Republic, Hungary) consumer electronics retail operations from Interdiscount.

1998: Photo Hall acquires Hifi International in Luxembourg and goes public on the Brussels Stock Exchange.

2001: Spector divests the bankrupt Photo Porst in Germany and the Czech Republic and re-brands its Hungarian retail operations as Photo Hall.

2002: Spector takes back full control of Photo Hall.

2005: The company restructures into two core divisions, Retail Group and Imaging Group.

2006: Spector forms a click-through partnership with Google's Picasa photo service as part of a repositioning for the digital photo and multimedia markets.

company was the second largest player in the French film processing market and, like Spector, had remained an independent operation competing against integrated groups such as Kodak and Fuji.

Spector entered a new market in 1995, when it bought a 70 percent stake in Austria's Bilderland, part owned by Switzerland-based home electronics retailing cooperative Interdiscount Group. That same year, Spec-

tor formed a partnership with Interdiscount to extend the ExtraFilm service to Switzerland.

By then, Spector had begun exploring ways of extending its operations into the retail sector. The company's relationship with Interdiscount provided the group with the opportunity it sought. In 1996, Spector agreed to acquire much of Interdiscount's international holdings, including Belgian consumer electronics retailer Photo Hall, and its counterparts in Hungary (Föfoto) and Germany and the Czech Republic (Photo Porst). The company also took full control of both Bilderland and ExtraFilm Switzerland in that deal.

The acquisition of Photo Hall in particular helped transform the company into a leading retailer in the Benelux market. Photo Hall had been founded in 1933 in Blankeberge, on the Belgian coast. The company initially sold photographs to vacationers (still a rare luxury at the time) and quickly developed a chain of 20 shops along the coast. Photo Hall also entered the Brussels market, opening a chain of 12 photo studios specialized in children's portraits. Over the next decade, the company's operations increasingly focused on retail sales of cameras and equipment. Into the 1970s, the company expanded its range into the wider consumer electronics segment. Photo Hall was acquired by Interdiscount in two stages between 1986 and 1993.

MEETING THE DIGITAL CHALLENGE IN THE NEW CENTURY

Photo Hall quickly became the centerpiece of Spector's retail offering—all the more so because of the steady losses at the Photo Porst chain. The company expanded its Benelux operations, buying up Luxembourg consumer electronics retail leader Hifi International, which also operated in France. In that year, Spector launched Photo Hall in its own public offering, listing 54 percent of its shares on the Brussels Stock Exchange.

By then, Spector also had been developing its mail-order photographic processing operations. This division was boosted through the purchase of Maxicolor, a mail-order film processing firm serving the European market, in 1996. Also in that year, Spector became one of the first in Europe to launch an e-commerce digital photo processing site. In 1999, the company formed a new division for its e-commerce and digital processing operations, ahead of an expected boom in both the Internet and digital photography markets.

Spector stumbled, however, as it moved into the beginning of the 2000s. Continued losses in the group's operations in Germany had begun to hurt the group's overall performance. By 2001, the company was forced to sell its bankrupt retail operations in Germany. At the same time, the company decided to withdraw from the wholesale markets in both Germany and France. The company suffered more bad news that year when longtime leader Johan Mussche died after a long illness. His place was taken by longtime partner Van Doorslaer, and Luc Vansteenkiste was named company chairman.

Spector's restructuring continued into 2002, with the sale of its wholesale processing operation in Austria. The company also bought back 100 percent control of Photo Hall, removing its listing from the Brussels Stock Exchange. Following the bankruptcy of its German subsidiary, Spector decided to rebrand the Photo Porst retail chain in Hungary, which included 50 stores operated by Spector's Föfoto subsidiary and another 237 franchised shops, with the Photo Hall format. The rebranding also included a broadening of the Hungarian stores' product assortment, in line with the more than 3,500 items typically carried by a Photo Hall store.

Spector's retail operations became all the more important for the company into the mid-decade. The sudden boom in the digital photography market—and the concurrent rise of home photo printing systems—placed the group's own photo processing operations under pressure. As prices on digital cameras continued to drop into the mid-decade, Spector took steps to meet the challenges of the new market. In late 2005, the company restructured its operations into two core divisions, Retail Group and Imaging Group. The company by then had transferred its Swiss and French mail-order processing operations to its main lab in Wetteren, shutting down its facility in Munster, France.

At the same time, Spector began actively seeking out new partnerships to position itself at the center of the digital printing revolution. In January 2005, for example, the company announced an agreement with Fujifilm that placed ExtraFilm as the recommended printing group in Fujifilm's digital camera software bundle in the French, German, Spanish, and U.K. markets. In June of that year, the company launched its own software package enabling customers to create photo cards and albums for processing by ExtraFilm. Then in February 2006, the company reached a new market when it formed a partnership with Picasa, the digital photo service offered by Google, providing click-through service to ExtraFilm from Google's Belgian, French, Scandinavian, German, Italian, Netherlands, Swiss, and Spanish sites. Spector Photo Group appeared prepared to meet the challenges of the new digital photography revolution in the new century.

M. L. Cohen

PRINCIPAL SUBSIDIARIES

Alexander Photo S.A. (Luxembourg); DBM Color N.V.; Digital Photoworks Ltd. (Extra Film Australia); Edro Bvba Be; Extra Film A/S (Norway); Extra Film AB (Sweden); Extra Film AG (Switzerland); Extra Film Austria GmbH; Extra Film Belgium N.V.; Extra Film Denmark A/S; Extra Film Europe N.V.; Extra Film Finland Oy; Extra Film France S.A.; Extra Film Logistics AG (Switzerland); Extra Film Nederland B.V.; Filmobel N.V.; Flt S.p.A. (Italy); Föfoto Kft. (Hungary); Fotocoop N.V.; Fotronic S.A.; Hifi International S.A. (Luxembourg); Litto-Color B.V. (Netherlands); Litto-Color N.V. (Belgium); Litto-Color S.A.R.L. (France); Maxicolor France S.A.; Photo Hall France S.A.R.L.; Photo Hall Multimedia N.V.; Photo Holdings Ireland Ltd.; Photomedia N.V.; Spector Nederland B.V.

PRINCIPAL COMPETITORS

Dixons Group PLC; Valora Holding AG; AGFA-Gevaert AG; Intres B.V.; CeWe Color Holding AG; Photo-Me International PLC; Niedermeyer GmbH; Laboratoires Kodak; Valora Imaging; BAC Color B.V.; Fujicolor AB; FOTOLAB A.S.

FURTHER READING

Byl, Roeland, "Tonny Van Doorslaer: Te weinig sex-appeal?," *Trends,* June 13, 2002.

"Kodachrome Processing to Continue in Switzerland, Despite Lab Closing," *Photo Marketing Newsline,* December 8, 2004, p. 3.

Olah, Peter, "Photo Chain Gets Makeover," *Budapest Business Journal,* November 18, 2002.

"Spector gaat in zee met Google," *Digimedia,* February 13, 2006.

"Spector Intends to Acquire Shares of Litto-Color from Kodak," *Photo Marketing Newsline,* September 8, 2004, p. 2.

"Spector Photo Group Launches Pixbox Kiosk," *Digital Imaging Digest,* November 2002.

"Spector Photo Group: op tien jaar maal twintig!," *Crescendo,* May 1996.

"Spector Photo Group SA Announces Reorganization Plans," *Reuters Key Development,* October 26, 2005.

"Spector Photo Grp's ExtraFilm Teams with Google's Picasa," *ISEdb,* February 10, 2006.

"Spector Selects IBM for Digital Expansion Project," *DMEurope,* February 20, 2006.

"Wie zijn de eigenaars van Spector?," *Trends,* December 22, 2005.

Stage Stores, Inc.

10201 Main Street
Houston, Texas 77025
U.S.A.
Telephone: (713) 667-5601
Fax: (713) 663-9780
Web site: http://www.stagestoresinc.com

Public Company
Incorporated: 1988 as Specialty Retailers, Inc.
Employees: 13,304
Sales: $1.34 billion (2005)
Stock Exchanges: New York
Ticker Symbol: SSI
NAIC: 452110 Department Stores; 448140 Family
 Clothing Stores

■ ■ ■

Houston-based Stage Stores, Inc., was founded in 1988 as a private company and went public in 1996. The company is an apparel-retail chain operating more than 627 stores in small and mid-sized towns and communities in 31 states in the United States. The retail chain operates primarily under the Stage, Bealls, Palais Royal, and Peebles trade names to offer nationally recognized, moderately priced brand-name apparel, accessories, fragrances, cosmetics, and footwear for the entire family. Stage's stores have approximately 18,800 square feet of selling space and are mostly found in strip malls. Women's and juniors' clothing accounted for 39 percent of company sales in 2005; men's and young men's, 19 percent; children's, 12 percent; footwear, 12 percent;

and accessories, cosmetics, and home décor, 18 percent. The company successfully emerged from bankruptcy in 2001 and is focused on growth in small to mid-sized markets.

BEGINNINGS OF A NEW RETAIL CONCEPT: 1988–92

Stage Stores' operating history dates back to late 1988 when, through a leveraged buyout, the former management team of Palais Royal, Inc., Bain Capital Funds, and Acadia Entities formed a separate company—named Specialty Retailers, Inc. (SRI)—to acquire Palais Royal, a retail chain of 28 stores. Concurrently, SRI acquired Bealls Brothers, Inc., which operated 126 stores. Both Palais Royal and Bealls were family-owned, Houston-based apparel retailers that since the 1920s had built strong regional franchises in the central and southwestern United States. Palais Royal focused mainly on the operation of large stores in metropolitan markets while Bealls' business consisted primarily of smaller stores in rural markets. SRI's management team focused on integrating Palais Royal and Bealls and refined the retail concept that would differentiate the company from both department stores and specialty stores: SRI stores offered more convenience and customer service than were usually found in department stores, provided leading brand names of apparel, and made available a broader assortment of merchandise than could be found in specialty stores.

Palais Royal had relied on automation to improve operating efficiency, as evidenced by its early implementation of an automated personnel scheduling system, electronic point-of-sale cash registers, and a credit-application and behavioral-scoring system. SRI recognized the advances Palais Royal had made in automation and developed a retail concept that relied on efficient operating systems, advanced technology, centralized decision making, and tight control of operating expenses. In about 18 months SRI substantially completed the consolidation of Bealls' general and administrative functions into those of Palais Royal. Within three years, underperforming Bealls stores had been closed and the financial performance of the remaining Bealls stores had significantly improved. Expenses of acquisition and consolidation notwithstanding, SRI's net sales increased at a 3.5 percent compound annual rate to $447.14 million in 1991, from $403.9 million in 1988.

According to Kenneth R. Pybus' story in the *Houston Business Journal,* in 1992 SRI wanted to go public and "sought to raise $192 million in a dual debt and equity offering, but pulled back when the response was less enthusiastic than expected." Jim Marcum, vice-chairman and chief financial officer for Stage Stores, later commented that the filing was made "in anticipation of future growth. Because the future growth really hadn't been executed yet, they just felt you couldn't get the best valuation for the company," so they withdrew the filing. Undaunted, SRI focused on growth through additional acquisitions and consolidations of complementary apparel retailers, improved sales performance of acquired stores, and opened new stores, especially in small rural markets. In June 1992 the company acquired Colorado-based Fashion Bar, Inc., a family-owned business having 71 stores of which approximately 75 percent were comparable to Palais Royal and Bealls stores while the remainder were small specialty stores. Including Fashion Bar, as of June 26, 1992, SRI operated 230 stores—in Texas (141 stores), Colorado (66 stores), Oklahoma (nine stores), New Mexico (six stores), Alabama (three stores), California (three stores), and Wyoming (two stores).

When SRI reviewed its operations for the 1988–92 period, it could pinpoint the special features that distinguished Palais Royal and Bealls from other apparel retailers: namely, store size, layout, and location; merchandising strategy; customer service; operating systems and technology; and growth strategy.

The format and locations of the Palais Royal and Bealls stores offered a convenient and efficient shopping experience to customers. These stores, smaller than typical department stores yet larger than most specialty stores, accommodated apparel and accessories for an entire family. The stores were small enough for strategic locations in rural markets—where the company faced limited competition—or in convenient locations in outlying metropolitan areas. The company used a multimedia advertising approach to position its stores as the local destination for fashionable, brand-name merchandise. In the early 1990s consumers in small markets usually had been able to shop for branded merchandise only in distant regional malls. Consequently, SRI's merchandising strategy focused on the traditionally higher-margin merchandise categories of family apparel and accessories.

The company emphasized excellent customer service and promoted its private-label, credit-card program, which in 1991 included more than one million active accounts and contributed approximately 60 percent of net sales. Early in its history, Palais Royal had applied highly automated, integrated systems to reduce operating costs in labor-intensive areas, such as merchandising, credit, personnel management, accounting, and distribution. These proprietary systems increased sales per square foot, reduced markdowns, lowered overhead, increased efficiency, and allowed store personnel to focus on customer service and selling. Furthermore, automation allowed buyers to select and allocate merchandise according to the local demographics and sales trends of the various stores.

The company's successful experience in choosing complementary acquisitions and the timely consolidation of Bealls brought out several facts. First, many family-operated apparel retailers had healthy customer franchises but were underperforming due to lack of advanced systems and buying economies; second, gaining market share through acquisitions was generally more economical and offered greater opportunity for rapid growth than opening new stores.

EXTENDING THE SMALL-MARKET FRANCHISE: 1993–96

In order to eliminate the possibility of having Specialty Retailers, Inc., be identified as only a specialty retail chain, in 1993 SRI's board of directors formed Apparel

```
┌──────────────────────────────────────────┐
│                                          │
│             KEY DATES                    │
│          ━━━━━━━━■━━━━━━━━                 │
│                                          │
│  1988:  Specialty Retailers, Inc. (SRI) is formed to │
│         acquire Palais Royal, Inc.       │
│  1992:  SRI acquires Colorado-based Fashion Bar, │
│         Inc.                             │
│  1993:  SRI's board of directors forms Apparel Retail- │
│         ers, Inc. (ARI), which becomes the parent │
│         company of SRI.                  │
│  1994:  ARI acquires Beall-Ladymon, Inc. │
│  1996:  The company goes public and changes its │
│         name to Stage Stores, Inc.       │
│  1997:  C.R. Anthony Company is purchased. │
│  1999:  Stage reports a loss of $129 million for the │
│         year.                            │
│  2000:  The company files for Chapter 11 bankruptcy │
│         protection.                      │
│  2001:  Stage emerges from bankruptcy.   │
│  2003:  Peebles Inc. is purchased.       │
│  2006:  B.C. Moore & Sons Inc. is acquired; the │
│         company begins trading on the New York │
│         Stock Exchange.                  │
│                                          │
└──────────────────────────────────────────┘
```

Retailers, Inc. (ARI), which concurrently became the parent company of SRI. Management recognized the potential of a unique franchise in small markets and committed the company to several initiatives for bringing about the full realization of this potential. These initiatives included: recruitment of a new senior management team; expansion in new markets through store openings and strategic acquisitions; emphasis on customer service and aggressive promotion of ARI's proprietary card; continuing refinement of ARI's concept; and closure of unprofitable stores.

On July 1, 1993, Carl Tooker—who had 25 years of administrative experience in the retail industry—was chosen as ARI president to lead the company's growth; a year later he became chairman and chief executive officer. Tooker succeeded 70-year-old founding President Bernard Fuchs, who retired after having been in the retail industry since 1944.

During 1994, ARI approved The Store Closure Plan that provided for the closure of the 40 underperforming Fashion Bar stores that were part of a 1992 acquisition and did not seem good candidates for consolidation into ARI's evolving small-market strategy. The ARI board believed that the merchandising strategy and market positions of these stores—located in major regional malls within the Denver area—were not compatible with its

overall strategy. Then in late 1994 ARI initiated the series of acquisitions that became the backbone of its expansion into the small-market niche. The company purchased the 45 stores of Beall-Ladymon, Inc., and reopened the stores in the first quarter of 1995 under the Stage name. Where did that name come from? Fashion Bar had operated a small group of stores known as Stage Stores, which already had become part of ARI's operation. In 1996 ARI completed the closure of the other Fashion Bar Stores but kept the Stage name.

The results of the Beall-Ladymon acquisition confirmed the value of ARI's strategy for growth. The acquired stores posted an annual sales increase of 78 percent and a store-contribution margin more than twice that of the previous year. The company also opened 23 new stores. Total ARI sales increased 17.4 percent to $682.62 million in 1995, compared with $581.46 million in 1994. This increase was due in part to increased sales from 23 stores opened during 1994 and 1995. The increase, however, was partially offset by the effects of the Store Closure Plan and the 1995 devaluation of the Mexican peso, which negatively impacted sales at the six Bealls stores located on the Texas/Mexico border.

In keeping with its strategy of controlled geographic growth, ARI completed its second major entry into small markets with the June 1996 purchase of Uhlmans Inc., a privately held retailer with 34 locations in Ohio, Indiana, and Michigan—states where the company previously had no stores. These stores were similar in size and content to ARI's existing stores and were compatible with the company's retail concept. The company opened 35 new stores in the central United States and reported record sales of $776.55 million for 1996.

On October 25, 1996, more than four years after filing—and then withdrawing—an initial public offering (IPO) with the U.S. Securities and Exchange Commission, Apparel Retailers, Inc., changed its name to Stage Stores, Inc., completed another IPO by selling 11 million shares of common stock at $16.50 per share, and began to trade on the NASDAQ. In conjunction with its stepped-up expansion strategy, Stage Stores applied its small-market retail concept to micromarkets in communities with populations of from 4,000 to 12,000. The company capitalized on its favorable operating experience in scaling its store concept to an appropriate size of less than 12,000 square feet to operate in these small markets that generally had lower levels of competition as well as low labor and occupancy costs.

According to industry analysts David M. Mann and Ethan J. Meyers's December 1997 report on Stage Stores and the retail industry, during the last two decades, many small towns were experiencing "a resurgence as computer and communications technologies allowed professionals to live/work in small towns and improve their quality of life." Furthermore—due to the proliferation of electronic, computer, and print media—customers in small markets were generally as aware of current fashion trends and were as sophisticated as consumers in larger urban centers. National retailers, such as J.C. Penney and Sears, Roebuck & Co., had abandoned small towns in favor of locations in cities and large suburban malls; the majority of independent apparel retailers had been put out of business by the national discount retailers that still operated in small towns, but these discounters did not carry the depth of family-oriented, fashionable brand-name merchandise offered by Stage.

Mann and Meyers's analysis of the regional family apparel sector found that there were 22 companies operating more than 850 stores generating $2.3 billion. Within the relatively short span of less than ten years, Stage had recognized the latent opportunities in this market, noted the emergence of new lifestyles (for example, career women did not spend as much time shopping for the family as did the women of earlier decades), and developed a retail strategy based on convenient locations where all the family members of small communities could find nationally advertised, branded apparel.

GROWTH IN THE LATE 1990S

With the June 1997 purchase of C.R. Anthony Company (Anthony's), Stage Stores strengthened its position as the dominant branded-apparel retailer in small-town America. Anthony's consisted of 246 family-apparel stores located in small markets in 16 states; the largest concentration of stores was in Texas, Oklahoma, Kansas, and New Mexico. Approximately 87 percent of Anthony's stores were located in small markets and communities having populations generally below 30,000. During the 1997 calendar year, Stage converted 130 of the acquired locations to its format, primarily under the Stage and Bealls trade names; the other remaining 105 stores were converted and included in Stage's operation by the summer of 1998. The 11 Anthony's stores that were located in overlapping markets were closed.

Acquisition of the Anthony's stores gave Stage the opportunity to accelerate its expansion program in existing markets and to extend its presence in new markets. Both companies benefited from synergizing their administrative infrastructures, leading, for example, to cost savings on overhead and enhanced opportunities for increased revenue and gross margins. Sales for 1997 increased 38.2 percent to $1.07 billion from $776.55 million in 1996.

As mentioned previously, Stage Stores operated under three different store nameplates: Palais Royal, Bealls, and Stage. Both the Stage and the Bealls nameplates identified the company's small-market stores. The company kept the two nameplates because Bealls was so well known in its home states. The Palais Royal nameplate identified the company's larger-market stores located in suburban neighborhoods and high-traffic strip centers, mainly in the Houston and Galveston areas. Although these large stores generated a significant amount of cash, which the company applied mainly to continue expanding into small-market stores, their profit margins were lower than those of the smaller stores. Stage continued to focus its growth primarily on small markets and did not plan significant expansion of the Palais Royal stores.

On March 25, 1998, Stage Stores announced that the Office of the Comptroller of the Currency had granted the company preliminary approval of an application for a credit-card bank charter. Pending further approval by the FDIC and the completion of all remaining conditions, Chief Financial Officer James Marcum stated that the company felt "confident that we will begin to see the economic benefits of the bank by the end of the third quarter." At this period in its history, the company had more than two million active credit accounts and proprietary credit-card purchases accounted for approximately 51 percent of the company's sales. Final approval of the bank charter allowed Stage to maximize fees and rates, the majority of which were subject to limits set by each state.

In April 1998 Stage began trading on the New York Stock Exchange. Sales for the first quarter of fiscal 1998 (ending May 2) peaked at a record $272.2 million, a 42.1 percent increase from 1997 first quarter sales of $191.5 million. Shares of stock rose to the $44–$52 price range, compared with the $16.50 price per share when the company went public in October 1996.

During fiscal 1997 the company's store count almost doubled, going from 315 stores in 19 states to 606 stores in 24 states as of January 1998. Furthermore, Stage clearly demonstrated that it had the ability and wherewithal to successfully open and convert a significant number of stores. As the 21st century drew near, Stage Stores continued to implement its aggressive small-market growth strategy through organic store openings, strategic acquisitions, and efficient consolidations. In June 1998 the company gained a foothold in the Pacific Northwest through the acquisition of 15 Tri-North Department Stores in Montana, Nevada, Oregon, and Washington. Upon completion of the acquisition, Stage completely remodeled and re-merchandized the stores; they were opened under the Stage name and format in the early fall of 1998. For the near future, Stage identified six viable acquisitions of privately held companies having a total store count of 425. The company's total vision, however, encompassed 1,200 potential U.S. markets that met its criteria for remaining the store of choice for well known, national brand-name family apparel throughout America's small towns and communities.

OVERCOMING BANKRUPTCY IN THE NEW MILLENNIUM

Stage's success during the 1990s came to a screeching halt in 1999 when the company reported a loss of more than $129 million due in part to a slowdown in store sales. Chairman, President, and CEO Tooker left the company early that year, leaving former C.R. Anthony executive Jack Wiesner temporarily at the helm. James Scarborough was named president and CEO in 2000. By this time, the company was in financial turmoil, struggling under a burgeoning debtload of $600 million related to its aggressive acquisition and expansion program. Unable to pay some of its vendors, Stage was forced to file for Chapter 11 bankruptcy protection in June 2000.

Stage emerged from bankruptcy in August 2001, owned mostly by its creditors. As part of its restructuring plan, the company shuttered 249 unprofitable stores, developed new merchandising strategies, and made sure to keep inventory at acceptable levels. The reorganization appeared to pay off and Scarborough's optimism was evident as he claimed in an August 2001 *Journal Record* article, "We've gone from a train wreck a year ago to one of the most profitable retailers in the country."

Indeed, Stage had secured six quarters of sales growth by 2002. Buoyed by its recent success, the company decided it was time to once again expand its arsenal of stores. Its plans for the year included opening 13 new stores, remodeling 14 stores, relocating four stores, and increasing the size of five stores. In 2003, the company acquired Peebles Inc., a chain with 136 stores in the Mid-Atlantic, southeastern, and midwestern regions. Upon completion of the deal, Stage operated in 27 states with revenues topping out at $1.2 billion. By mid-2004, the company's store count had climbed to 518 locations.

Stage posted record sales of $1.34 billion in 2005, climbing 8.1 percent over the previous year's figures. The company opened 36 new stores during the year but was forced to close four locations due to damage from Hurricanes Katrina and Rita.

In keeping with Stage's strategy to increase its store count in small profitable markets, the company decided to add B.C. Moore & Sons Inc. to its portfolio in February 2006. The 78-store chain had a presence in Georgia, North and South Carolina, and Alabama. A total of 69 of these stores would be converted to the Peebles name. In addition, the company planned to open 39 new stores during 2006.

In March of that year, the company began trading on the New York Stock Exchange. Company management was confident that Stage's problems related to its bankruptcy filing in 2000 were a thing of the past. With a strong focus on its customers in small and mid-sized towns, Stage and its Bealls, Palais Royal, Peebles, and namesake stores appeared to be on track for success in the years to come.

Gloria A. Lemieux
Updated, Christina M. Stansell

PRINCIPAL SUBSIDIARIES

Specialty Retailers, Inc.; Specialty Retailers (TX) L.P.; SRI General Partner L.L.C.; SRI Limited Partner L.L.C.

PRINCIPAL COMPETITORS

J.C. Penney Company, Inc.; Target Corporation; Wal-Mart Stores, Inc.

FURTHER READING

Lloyd, Brenda, "Stage Purchase Expands Southeastern Presence," *DNR*, February 27, 2006, p. 4.

Mann, David M., and Ethan J. Meyers, *Stage Stores, Inc.*, New Orleans: Johnson Rice & Company L.L.C., pp. 1–4.

Palmeri, Christopher, "Stage Stores: Smelling Nice for Choir Practice," *Forbes*, August 25, 1997, p. 64.

"Profiles of Leadership: James Scarborough," *Chain Store Age*, April 2004.

Pybus, Kenneth R., "Retail Firm Ready to Go Public Again," *Houston Business Journal*, June 21, 1996, pp. 1–2.

"Stage Hires New CEO," *Journal Record*, August 9, 2000.

"Stage Stores Emerges from Bankruptcy," *Journal Record*, August 28, 2001.

"Stage Stores Inc. Files for Chapter 11, Plans to Close Some Stores," *Wall Street Journal*, June 2, 2000.

"Stage Stores Inc.: Initiating Coverage of Niche Retailer Thriving in Small-Town America," Chicago: EVEREN Securities, Inc. Equity Research, pp. 1, 3–8.

Wollam, Allison, "Platform Set for Stage Stores Comeback," *Houston Business Journal*, July 5, 2002, p. 2.

Steamships Trading Company Ltd.

P.O. Box 1
Hunter Street-Champion Parade
Port Moresby, N.C.D. 121
Papua New Guinea
Telephone: (+675) 322 0222
Fax: (+675) 321 1786
Web site: http://www.steamships.com.pg

Public Company
Incorporated: 1919 as Steamships Ltd.
Employees: 4,000
Sales: PGK 370.04 million ($126.66 million) (2005)
Stock Exchanges: Port Moresby Australian
Ticker Symbol: SST
NAIC: 311520 Ice Cream and Frozen Dessert Manufacturing; 312140 Distilleries; 325611 Soap and Other Detergent Manufacturing; 339999 All Other Miscellaneous Manufacturing; 421320 Brick, Stone, and Related Construction Material Wholesalers; 421390 Other Construction Material Wholesalers; 421710 Hardware Wholesalers; 444130 Hardware Stores; 483113 Coastal and Great Lakes Freight Transportation; 484110 General Freight Trucking, Local; 484121 General Freight Trucking, Long-Distance, Truckload; 484122 General Freight Trucking, Long-Distance, Less Than Truckload; 484230 Specialized Freight (Except Used Goods) Trucking, Long-Distance; 48832 Marine Cargo Handling; 531110 Lessors of Residential Buildings and Dwellings; 531120 Lessors of Nonresidential Buildings (Except Miniwarehouses); 551112 Offices of Other Holding Companies; 72111 Hotels (Except Casino Hotels) and Motels

■ ■ ■

Steamships Trading Company Ltd. is involved in a broad range of activities in Papua New Guinea. Originally an operator of merchant ships and stores, the venerable company is still active in the freight industry but also supplies the local population with power tools, hotel rooms, office space, soap, and liquor. Steamships owns the country's only manufacturer of ice cream (Laga Industries, makers of the Gala brand). The company's stock was the first one listed on the Port Moresby Stock Exchange. The Swire Group has a majority holding in Steamships, which is the largest non-mining company in Papua New Guinea.

ORIGINS

Steamships Trading Company Limited was started in 1919 when retired sea captain Algernon Sydney Fitch (born 1881) left his Tasmanian apple farm to lead a £5,000 salvage operation to recover a grounded barge called the *Southern Cross*. Unfortunately, this was lost in towing by the small, coal-powered SS *Queenscliffe*, which had been built in 1855. In 1924 the company listed shares on the Sydney Stock Exchange and launched a trading venture connecting Port Moresby with Papua New Guinea's isolated outposts. The first cargo was 25 coconut fiber sacks, about 15 pounds of tobacco, and a case of condensed milk.

Fitch originally traded out of his house in Port Moresby. A branch store was opened on Samarai Island in 1926; within a few years it was doing about £50,000 a year in business. Trading was difficult in the global recession but by the mid-1930s, the enterprise had grown to a chain of several stores. The company acquired a coconut plantation in 1935.

Operations were suspended during World War II, and the company's Cosmopolitan Hotel in Samarai was torched due to a scorched earth policy. The company promptly set out to restore its retail operations after the war.

POSTWAR REBUILDING

Steamships founder Fitch retired in 1952 to be succeeded by 20-year company veteran E.V. Crisp. In the same year, Steamships became the Papua New Guinea agent for a new service being launched by the China Navigation Company of Hong Kong. This was the beginning of a long association with China Navigation's parent, the London-based Swire Group. Swire bought a small interest in Steamships in the early 1960s.

The 1962 acquisition of Collier Watson (NG) Limited included the company's first stores and plantations beyond Papua New Guinea (PNG). Over the years, however, it tended to invest exclusively in domestic enterprises. Also in 1962, Steamships reentered the hotel business for the first time since World War II by buying a stake in the Lamington Hotel.

The company's subscribed capital exceeded £1 million in 1964. During the year, E.V. Crisp stepped down as head of the company and was succeeded by H.D. Underwood. The company was diversifying in the mid-1960s. The Brown River Timber Company was acquired and sheet metal fabrication and industrial gas plants were established. Steamships also continued its traditional activities, buying coffee plantations and opening the Melanesian Hotel in Lae. Steamships became a Coca-Cola bottler in 1967.

Steamships sold several unprofitable rubber plantations in 1979. Within a couple of years, turnover exceeded PGK 100 million, and profits reached a record

PGK 4 million in 1981. Steamships then employed 5,000 people, about 11 percent of them expatriates. In the first half of the decade, Steamships landed a massive contract to provide logistics for the Ok Tedi gold and copper mine, while opening PNG's largest department store in the relatively isolated community of Tabubil.

In the mid-1980s, Steamships' ownership came to be dominated by two groups: John Swire and Sons Investment Ltd., which raised its holding to 33.3 percent, and Goroka-based Collins and Leahy Investments Limited, which acquired another third interest. Lean years followed, particularly in the freight and steel fabrication divisions, while hotels were flat in spite of the creation of a new marketing office to promote tourism.

Steamships rounded out the decade with new investments. It was a partner in a new toothpaste plant built in PNG by Colgate Palmolive in 1987. In 1988, Steamships acquired the bankrupt Papua New Guinea Shipping Corporation (PNG Shipping), which was active in trading with Australia.

LATE 20TH-CENTURY REORGANIZING

PNG's national economy was upended by political turmoil after rioting at a copper mine in Bougainville in the late 1980s. Following the unrest, Steamships reevaluated the strategic fit of its various holdings. PNG was reducing tariffs on imported goods, making Steamships more vulnerable to foreign competition in some manufactured products such as soap.

Steamships divested its bottling operations to an Australian affiliate of Coca-Cola for PGK 27 million (AUD 36 million) in 1991. The next year, it bought the retail and hardware stores of rival Burns Phillip (BP) for AUD $24 million. BP's retail business dated back 100 years.

According to the *Australian Financial Review* much of Steamships' hotel business was tied to the mining industry. In the early 1990s the company had about 3,000 employees.

The company was a dealer for Honda and Mitsubishi autos and in 1993 acquired New Guinea Motors Ltd., the Isuzu and Land Rover dealership for PNG. Steamships also bought out Laurabada Shipping Ltd.

Chris Pratt led the company through the last half of the 1990s. Toward the end of the decade, Steamships sold the Smuggler's Inn in Madang while building a new hotel at Boroko (Round House). The coastal shipping fleet was augmented with the purchase of a couple of new vessels.

<table>
<tr><td colspan="2"><h2>KEY DATES</h2></td></tr>
</table>

1919:	Sea captain Algernon Sydney Fitch comes out of retirement in an unsuccessful attempt to salvage a grounded barge.
1924:	Steamships lists on the Sydney Stock Exchange; Fitch operates a trading route from Port Moresby.
1926:	The first branch store is opened.
1942:	Operations are suspended during World War II.
1952:	Steamships becomes the Papua agent for Swire Group's China Navigation Company.
1962:	Collier Watson (NG) Limited is acquired, adding the first stores and plantations outside PNG; Steamships buys its first hotel interest since World War II.
1964:	Brown River Timber Company is acquired; a metal and timber fabrication plant is established.
1965:	Steamships builds an industrial gas factory; buys Korfena Coffee Plantations.
1967:	Lae's Melanesian Hotel is opened; the company begins bottling Coca-Cola.
1979:	Two rubber plantations are sold.
1980:	Steamships merges with diversified manufacturer New Guinea Industries Ltd., buys ANG Timbers, and adds to its hotel interests.
1981:	Turnover exceeds PGK 100 million; the company has 5,000 employees.
1986:	Swire and Collins and Leahy each amass one-third of shares.
1988:	Steamships acquires PNG Shipping Corporation.
1991:	The soft drink bottling operations are divested.
1992:	The retail and hardware business of rival Burns Philip is acquired.
1993:	Auto dealer New Guinea Motors Ltd. is acquired.
1999:	Steamships is the first company listed on the Port Moresby Stock Exchange.
2005:	The company buys out a liquor and soap joint venture, and acquires Mitre Hardware; the Merchandise division is divested.

FIRST ON POMSOX IN 1999

Steamships was the first company listed on the Port Moresby Stock Exchange (POMSoX), which opened in 1999. Its shares continued to trade on the Australian Stock Exchange. Steamships was PNG's leading enterprise outside of the mining industry.

The workforce was being composed of an increasing percentage of the native population over the years. By 2003, only 70 of Steamships' 4,000 employees were expatriates.

In 2003 the company exited the car rental business it had been operating in affiliation with Hertz Rent-A-Car. It also left the Kwikshop convenience store partnership with Mobil Oil Limited. The company's traditional shipping business was thriving, bolstered by renewed offshore drilling.

Steamships was operating in a difficult economic environment, with the local interest rate (16 percent) more than twice that in Australia, its managing director John Dunlop told the *PNG Post-Courier*. Dunlop, in charge for four years, was replaced by David Cox in 2004.

The company's Coral Sea Hotels unit added another property in 2004, buying the Ela Beach Hotel from Kumul Hotels Ltd. The next year saw the division renovating other hotels and leasing some new apartments.

STABILITY IN 2005

In May 2005, Steamships' shareholders voted to acquire its sister company Collins & Leahy. The company also acquired virtually all the remaining shares of Melanesian Soap Products. A Transport division was subsequently created from the Shipping division.

In October 2005, the company sold its Merchandise division to City Pharmacy Ltd. for nearly PGK 20 million. This included the well known Stop 'n' Shop chain of stores.

The Hardware unit acquired Mitre Hardware from Collins & Leahy in early 2005. At the end of the year, Steamships bought out its partners in the Trade Winds Liquor joint venture, whose facility was rebuilt after being destroyed in a fire in 2004.

Revenues were PGK 370 million in 2005; consolidated profit rose 173 percent to PGK 40.2 million. Steamships benefited from the country's strong, stable economy led by demand for PNG's minerals, particularly copper. Inflation had dropped considerably.

There still remained considerable challenges to doing business in PNG, bemoaned Steamships' 2005 annual report. International telecommunications services were expensive and broadband Internet access was lacking. The country's shipping, transportation, and power infrastructure also needed updating.

Frederick C. Ingram

PRINCIPAL SUBSIDIARIES

Bird of Paradise Hotel Ltd.; Coral Sea Hotels Ltd.; Five Star Packaging Ltd. (68%); Goroka Soft Drinks Ltd. (68%); Henganofi Hotel Ltd.; Kavieng Port Services Ltd. (60%); Lae Port Services Ltd. (51.5%); Laga Industries Ltd. (68%); Laurabada Properties Ltd.; Laurabada Shipping Services Ltd.; Madang Port Services Ltd. (60%); Melanesian Soap Products Ltd.; Monier (PNG) Ltd.; Monier Allied Products Ltd.; North Solomons Stevedoring Ltd. (50%); Pacific Novelty Products Ltd. (68%); Papua New Guinea Shipping Corporation Ltd.; PNG Mainport Liners Services Ltd.; Port Services PNG Ltd. (51.5%); Progressive Traders Ltd.; Steamships Ltd.; Tanubada Food Processors Ltd. (88%); Trade Winds Liquors Ltd.; Windward Apartments Ltd.

PRINCIPAL DIVISIONS

Hardware; Hotels; Shipping, Transport; Manufacturing; Property.

PRINCIPAL COMPETITORS

MBf Carpenters Limited; P&O PNG Ltd.

FURTHER READING

Adamson, Graeme, "Top of the Stocks Defeat the Odds," *Australian Financial Review,* August 27, 1992, p. 36.

Bromby, Robin, "Britons Storm the Bridge As Trader Changes Course; Steamships Turns Page on PNG History," *The Australian,* December 6, 1999, p. 37.

Callick, Rowan, "Fallout from PNG Share Raid," *Australian Financial Review,* June 4, 1996, p. 25.

———, "Last of the Big Traders," *Australian Financial Review,* September 21, 1992, p. 51.

———, "PNG Group Urges More Local Involvement for Job Creation," *Australian Financial Review,* December 16, 1987, p. 29.

———, "PNG Minister the Mastermind in Share Raids," *Australian Financial Review,* June 3, 1996, p. 23.

Dougherty, Bridget, "Acquisition Helps Steamships," *Australian Financial Review,* March 30, 1988, p. 26.

Flynn, Matthew, "Swire Box Service First," *Lloyd's List International,* November 11, 1997.

"Hotel to Be Renovated," *PNG Post-Courier,* June 21, 2004, p. 38.

Killen, Heather, "Collins Issue to Buy Slice of Steamships," *Australian Financial Review,* May 21, 1986, p. 26.

Mengel, N., "PNG Retail Operation Is Sold Off," *Courier-Mail,* June 23, 1992.

Mitchell, Sue, "Coca-Cola Buys Steamships' PNG Business," *Australian Financial Review,* May 22, 1991, p. 24.

Tapakau, Eric, "Steamships Face Winds of Change," *PNG Post-Courier,* December 16, 2003, p. 31.

The Strober Organization, Inc.

———— ■ ————

Pier 3, Furman Street
Brooklyn, New York 11201
U.S.A.
Telephone: (732) 819-7049
Fax: (718) 246-3070
Web site: http://www.strober.com

Wholly Owned Subsidiary of Pro-Build Holdings Inc.
Founded: 1912
Employees: 1,200
Sales: $1 billion (2005 est.)
NAIC: 444190 Other Building Material Dealers

■ ■ ■

Based in Brooklyn, New York, the Strober Organization, Inc., is a leading building supplies provider to builders, contractors, and remodeling professionals, shying away from the do-it-yourself market dominated by the likes of Home Depot and Lowe's. Strober operates more than 90 locations under the Strober Building Supply Center and The Contractor Yard names, located in 15 states along the East Coast and as far west as Ohio and Mississippi. Name-brand products offered include lumber, plywood, gypsum and drywall, roofing, millwork products, acoustical products, masonry, flooring products, insulation, siding, windows and skylights, kitchen and bath cabinets and sinks, hardware, and power tools. In addition, the Strober Organization includes U.S. Components, a Mt. Holly, New Jersey-based company with three manufacturing plants producing roof, floor, and wall trusses.

Strober also is involved in a joint venture, Architectural Wall Systems L.L.C., which distributes Dryvit exterior wall systems, Tremco Sealants, Windlock Tools, and Driangle Foam Shapes. Strober is part of Pro-Build Holdings Inc., the United States' largest professional building materials supplier, which in turn is a subsidiary of Fidelity Capital, the business development component of mutual fund company Fidelity Investments. Strober's chief executive officer, Frederick M. Marino, also heads Pro-Build, which was established in 2006 by Fidelity to acquire professional materials dealers in midwestern and western states.

STROBER'S FOUNDING AS FAMILY BUSINESS IN 1912

The Strober Organization grew out of a single building supply store founded in Brooklyn in 1912. It was not until the third generation, under Eric D. Strober, that the business began to expand. He was just 20 years old and a recent graduate of Boston University when he took over for his late father. For another decade the business remained a single location, mostly serving the New York City roofing market. Starting in 1972 Strober began broadening its product lines to attract increased business from building subcontractors and remodelers, as well as some do-it-yourself customers. The company also added two more locations by 1980. In 1981 the company prepared for even greater growth when it raided the ranks of competitor L&W Supply Corp. to bring in seven managers to serve as the foundation of a talented young staff.

Over the next five years Strober added another six

COMPANY PERSPECTIVES

Since 1912 the Strober Organization, Inc., has been assisting builders, remodelers and contractors in both the residential and commercial markets.

---

building supply centers. In 1986 the business was divided into five regions, New York City, which included the top-selling, flagship location in Brooklyn; Long Island; New York's Hudson Valley; New Jersey; and New Haven. Strober took advantage of central buying power and focused on a market that offered some predictability. It also offered extra customer service, such as providing customers with a detailed computer printout of all the materials a job required. Strober was able to build sales to $77.9 million in 1985 and $92.4 million in 1986, while net income during this period increased from $3.4 million to $5 million. Far from satisfied, the company looked to opportunities in New England, Pennsylvania, and Washington, D.C., as well as the enlargement of some of its centers. To help finance these aims, the company went public in November 1986, making an initial public offering (IPO) of stock at $12 a share, netting some $11 million. The Strober family maintained a slight controlling interest, and all told, the company's top 11 officers held 82 percent of the stock.

Following the offering, the company took out a $5 million key-man life insurance policy on Eric Strober as well as a $15 million term life insurance policy. The officers and directors of the company also took out another $20 million in life insurance on his life. In addition, the company adopted a provision that in the event of Strober's death the company was obligated to purchase shares from the Strober family in the amount of $15 million or the amount of the life insurance policy, if that was less. In this way, the family was guaranteed a buyer and the top officers would gain control of the business without fear of a hostile takeover attempt. These were far from unusual provisions, all spelled out in the prospectus for the IPO. Because Eric Strober was in good health in his mid-40s, these arrangements seemed to be nothing more than the kind of careful planning a company could expect from its lawyers. Instead, they would soon come into play.

ERIC STROBER'S MYSTERIOUS DEATH: 1988

In October 1987 Strober arranged its first acquisition since going public 11 months earlier, agreeing to pay

$22 million to East Hartford, Connecticut–based General Building Supply Co. It was a move that would add two locations in Strober's existing market, $43 million in annual sales, and provide a kitchen and bath operation that could be introduced to Strober's other nine locations. These showrooms could then be used to attract some do-it-yourself repair and remodeling business. The deal closed in January 1988, and by all accounts Eric Strober, who had headed the acquisition effort, was quite pleased. A short time later, on the afternoon of January 26, 1988, he paid a visit to his lawyer and a director of the company, David W. Bernstein, at a midtown Manhattan office building. He left to use the men's room and minutes later was found dead in the courtyard 22 floors below. The initial finding of the medical examiner was suicide.

According to the *Wall Street Journal,* "Police detectives who investigated Mr. Strober's death believe he took the metal top off a trash can in the men's room and went into the service area at the end of the hall. The service area has two freight elevators and a thick, opaque window. The window was nailed shut. 'Our final determination agreed with the finding of the medical examiner that Mr. Strober committed suicide by smashing out the window and leaping to his death.'"

A few days after Strober's death, Bernstein was named the company's new chairman and President Gary F. Kulick assumed the additional role of chief executive officer. Over the next several months the company considered some offers to buy the business but nothing came of them. It also had to contend with a softening in residential and commercial construction in the Northeast, which began to affect earnings. However, management was fighting with the insurance companies, which were attempting to avoid paying off the policies taken out on the life of Eric Strober. The company maintained that his death was the result of an accident, insisting that he had no reason to kill himself, while the insurers claimed it was suicide, something that was always difficult to prove.

According to the *Wall Street Journal,* "The insurers suggest an organized-crime link to Mr. Strober's death. They contend that Mr. Strober committed suicide rather than face possible prosecution and disgrace in an investigation by the federal Organized Crime Strike Force in Brooklyn." The link was to one of Strober's customers, Cambridge Drywall & Carpentry, a firm reported to have once been owned by Vincent DiNapoli, a "captain" in the Genovese crime family, who sold his share of the business to Larry Wecker when he went to prison. In 1982 DiNapoli was sentenced to five years in prison on labor racketeering charges, and in 1988 received another 24-year sentence for racketeering

KEY DATES

1912: The company is founded as single store in Brooklyn, New York.
1962: The founder's grandson, Eric D. Strober, takes charge at age 20.
1986: The company is taken public.
1988: Eric Strober dies.
1997: Fidelity Ventures takes Strober private.
2003: Contractor Yard is acquired.
2006: Newly created Pro-Build Holdings becomes Strober's corporate parent.

charges that included, according to the *Wall Street Journal,* "a scheme to rig bids in the New York construction industry." On the day that he died Eric Strober was scheduled to have a dinner meeting with Wecker. According to Kulick, the meeting was set up in part to discuss how Wecker planned to take care of a $20,000 check that had been returned for insufficient funds. Kulick maintained that the insurers pursued the organized crime connection as a way to avoid paying the claims, telling the *Wall Street Journal,* "For $40 million, they'll do an awful lot."

Given that there was no suicide note and no discernible fingerprints from anyone, let alone Eric Strober, on the trash can that may have been used to break out the window from which he fell, the insurance companies had a difficult task in overcoming the law's presumption against suicide. It was no surprise that the two parties eventually reached an out-of-court settlement in November 1990. The company received $11.3 million on the $20 million worth of life insurance policies it took out, while the $20 million with the officers listed as beneficiaries was settled for an amount that was not publicly disclosed. There were no determinations regarding the circumstances of Eric Strober's death. Of the $11.3 million received, the company retained $2.8 million for corporate purposes and used the rest to purchase shares of the company held by the estate of Eric Strober.

The construction industry, hurt by a recession, continued to slump in the early 1990s, adversely impacting the Strober balance sheet. In fact, were it not for the insurance payment, the company would have suffered a $2.6 million net loss in 1990. The company was forced to cut costs by consolidating operations, closing two of its smaller facilities, one of which was located close to a newly opened Home Depot store in New Jersey. The other was closed to consolidate the New

Haven and Hartford, Connecticut, operations. Strober also saw a change in management in 1991 when Robert J. Gaites, who headed the New York City business, took over as CEO and Kulick assumed the chairmanship, a post he would hold only briefly. In January 1992 he died of a heart attack, and Gaites became chairman as well.

Sales bottomed out at $100 million in 1991 and slowly rose as the economy improved, reaching $105 million in 1992, $119 million in 1993, and $125.4 million in 1994, this despite a harsh winter in 1994. During this time, in 1992, Strober opened a very successful unit in Kingston, Pennsylvania, prompting management to consider further expansion in the state. A second Pennsylvania location was launched in November 1995 in the city of Bethlehem, giving Strober 11 units. Also in 1995, Strober moved its Farmingdale, New York, store to a larger site.

Although Strober had enjoyed some success, the company lacked the resources to spur further growth. In February 1996 the company retained Hill Thompson Capital Markets Inc. as a financial advisor to sort through options to maximize stockholder value, and it was clear that management was open to selling the business. A few months later, Strober agreed to acquire Rowley Building Products Corporation, a building material supply company with operations in five locations in the Hudson Valley of New York. The deal was scuttled, however, when Strober agreed in November 1996 to be sold to Fidelity Ventures for approximately $32 million. Although Fidelity planned to take a hands-off approach to the running of the business, the purchase agreement called for the installation of Frederick Marino, a Fidelity investor, as chairman and CEO. He was hardly a newcomer to the business, however, having served as the CEO of a Strober supplier, Marino-Ware Industries, a New Jersey company that manufactured steel framing products.

BEING TAKEN PRIVATE: 1997

The sale was completed in March 1997 and Strober was taken private. Marino did not hide his intention to grow Strober into the top professional lumberyard chain in the Northeast and wasted little time in pursuing that goal. After posting sales of $152 million from 11 yards in 1997, Strober began 1998 by acquiring the Bayport Lumber facility in Long Island and opened a pair of start-up yards in Leola, Pennsylvania, and Fishkill, New York. Then, in April 1998, it reached a tentative agreement to acquire New Jersey–based Haddonfield Lumber and doubled the size of Strober. Haddonfield owned 14 lumberyards in New Jersey, Pennsylvania, and Delaware, as well as three building material component plants, only one of which, U.S. Components, would be included in the deal completed eight months later. The result was a regional powerhouse boasting 19 yards in six states.

With the Haddonfield units in the fold, Strober posted revenues of $400 million in 1999. The company looked to add to those totals and expand southward in 2000 by acquiring Arkay Building Supply with two yards in Catonville and Gaithersburg, Maryland, that served the Baltimore and Washington, D.C., markets. However, this deal paled in comparison with Strober's next transaction, the 2004 purchase of the 26 units of North Carolina–based The Contractor Yard, a division of Lowe's Corporation that operated 26 locations in nine states: North Carolina, South Carolina, Virginia, Tennessee, Florida, Maryland, Ohio, Mississippi, and Georgia. With 71 yards, Strober became the seventh largest professional building supply dealer in the United States.

More acquisitions were to follow. In November 2004, Strober added another 19 yards in the mid-Atlantic region, 11 in Virginia alone, by acquiring Moore's Lumber and Building Supplies, based in Roanoke, Virginia. These yards would be folded into The Contractor Yard business. It was at this point that Strober organized its business into three principal subsidiaries: Strober Building Supply, The Contractor Yard, and U.S. Components. Contractor Yard grew further in 2005 with the purchase of Northlake Lumber, a yard that provided Contractor with a presence in both the northern and southern parts of the thriving Charlotte market.

In 2006 Strober's parent company, Fidelity Capital, pleased with its investment in the professional building materials business, looked to become a national player. It created Pro-Build Holdings Inc. and promptly purchased Lanoga Corporation, the country's third largest dealer of professional building materials. Doing business under a number of regional brands, Lanoga operated 320 centers in 24 midwestern and western states. Strober's Marino was made CEO and vice-chairman of Pro-Build and commented on the acquisition: "Lanoga's divisions are an excellent strategic fit with our current Strober divisions. Although the companies will continue to operate separately, this new relationship creates the opportunity for Pro-Build to provide nationwide coverage." Four months later, in June 2006, Pro-Build furthered its national aspirations by acquiring Tulsa, Oklahoma–based Hope Lumber, which operated 49 yards in nine southeastern and south central states.

Ed Dinger

PRINCIPAL SUBSIDIARIES

The Contractor Yard; Strober Building Supply; U.S. Components.

PRINCIPAL COMPETITORS

The Home Depot, Inc.; Lowe's Companies, Inc.

FURTHER READING

Alson, Amy, "Strober Building Solid Profits in Fragmented Supply Market," *Crain's New York Business,* May 11, 1987, p. 13.

Biederman, Marcia, "Chairman's Death Shakes Up Strober," *Crain's New York Business,* February 1, 1988, p. 2.

Gonzalez, Jason, "Fidelity to Buy Strober for $32 Million," *National Home Center News,* November 25, 1996, p. 6.

———, "Strober to Buy Haddonfield Lumber," *National Home Center News,* April 27, 1998, p. 3.

Machalaba, Daniel, "Strober Organization, Insurers Settle Claims Made After Death of Chairman," *Wall Street Journal,* November 12, 1990, p. A7A.

Moss, Linda, "Rebuilding Strober in a Down Market," *Crain's New York Business,* August 5, 1991, p. 15.

Penn, Stanley, "Did Eric Strober Commit Suicide? $40 Million Question," *Wall Street Journal,* June 19, 1989, p. 1.

Rice, Faye, "Soaring Sales, Stalled Stock," *Fortune,* November 9, 1987, p. 172.

Sumitomo Metal
Industries Ltd.

◾

5-33, Kitahama 4-chome
Chuo-ku
Osaka, 541-0041
Japan
Telephone: (06) 220-5111
Fax: (06) 223-0305
Web site: http://www.sumitomometals.co.jp

Public Company
Incorporated: 1935
Employees: 8,237
Sales: ¥1.23 trillion ($11.5 billion) (2005)
Stock Exchanges: Tokyo Osaka Nagoya Fukuoka Sapporo
Ticker Symbol: 5405
NAIC: 331221 Rolled Steel Shape Manufacturing; 331210 Iron and Steel Pipes and Tubes Manufacturing from Purchased Steel; 331111 Iron and Steel Mills; 332322 Sheet Metal Work Manufacturing

■ ■ ■

Sumitomo Metal Industries, Ltd. (SMI) is one of Japan's leading steelmakers. The company supplies steel sheets used in the automotive and electrical machinery industries, and pipes and tubes used in oil and natural gas drilling and pipelines. SMI also provides wheels, axles, and various other components used in trains in Japan. The company controls nearly 10 percent of all crude steel production in Japan, 50 percent of its domestic seamless pipe market, and 20 percent of the global seamless pipe market.

EARLY HISTORY

Sumitomo Metal Industries has its roots in the foundation of the Sumitomo group in copper mining in the late 16th century. Its origins as a modern company date from 1897, when Sumitomo Copper works was opened in Osaka, and as a steelmaker from 1901, when Sumitomo Steel works began operation.

Both openings represented a privatization of Japanese industry, established by the government after the Sino-Japanese War of 1894–95. The copper works were acquired from the Japan Copper Manufacturing Company, the steel works with the purchase of Japan Steel Manufacturing Company.

It was a slow start, however. The newborn steel industry was unable to compete internationally because its plants were small and inefficient, and it grew very little. This situation changed with World War I, when demand grew strong at home and abroad because of large steel orders for military use by the Allied powers and the temporary withdrawal of European steelmakers from the Japanese market. From 1914 Japan supplied the Allies with iron and steel while itself engaged in limited naval military action. Japanese industry, including Sumitomo Steel works, profited economically from World War I.

After the war, heavy industry suffered a recession, and demand fell. The lull was temporary, however. The government entered into extensive railway and public-works construction, and steel production quadrupled in the 1920s. Wartime investment in plant and equipment paid off. The relatively undeveloped Japan moved toward industrial independence, and heavy industries were established.

CATASTROPHE AND GOVERNMENT PROGRAMS LEAD TO GROWTH

Growth came in part from catastrophe. During the 1923 earthquake, 44 percent of Tokyo was burned to the ground, as was 26 percent of Yokohama. Substantial rebuilding followed, and the next two years were a boom period for the Japanese steel industry, which nonetheless was unable to meet domestic needs. Japanese iron and steel production in 1927 met about 60 percent of consumption. The industry was gaining on the problem, however, and the gains showed in a steady transformation of the Japanese economy. Heavy industry accounted for only 26 percent of the value of overall Japanese output in 1925, but 37 percent of its value five years later, when its share of output was still rising.

The 1930s were a time of continued expansion and diversification because of growth of the metal, machinery, and chemical industries. Heavy industry continued to outpace light industry. The number of metals factories more than doubled, and the number of workers quadrupled. During the 1930s the yen value of production grew by 800 percent. Japan became practically self-sufficient in production of rolling stock and in steel and steel products in general. The production-to-consumption ratio reached 103 percent for steel and 115 percent for steel products. Contributing to this increased ratio were the abandonment by the Japanese government of the gold standard with attendant freeing of money for investment, technical improvements, increased government spending on armaments, exploitation of the Manchurian resources newly acquired after the Japanese invasion of Manchuria, and development

of Manchukuo, the Japanese puppet state in Manchuria, as a center of heavy industry.

In 1935, the Sumitomo copper and steel works were merged to form Sumitomo Metal Industries, Ltd. Meanwhile, Japan, accustomed since 1914 to unusually high profits, had embarked on a course of economic imperialism with a view to keeping such profits flowing. Even so, only in 1936 did the military demand for steel become an important factor in keeping profits flowing. Until then the major steel users had been the construction industry and heavy industries such as shipbuilding, machinery, and the steel industry itself.

A program of government subsidy funded this growth, for example, the Subsidy Facility for Improvement of Ships of 1932-37. By this arrangement boats over 25 years old were scrapped, and subsidies were granted for replacement of up to half the number of ships scrapped. Heavy industry in general profited from such subsidization. Development of new products made of metals such as aluminum and magnesium contributed to growth in profits. During the early 1930s, heavy industries, including the chemical industry, showed profits for first time without concentration on military demand.

By 1937 the military was expanding its requirements. A five-year industry plan in March 1937 called for annual steel production of 6.5 million tons of steel by 1941, up from 5 million. Since the army wanted ten million tons produced, the option was given to export three million tons if there should be peace rather than war.

Japan went to war, first with China beginning in July 1937, and later with the Allies. Capital and labor were diverted to war industries. Government regulation of the economy increased, accompanied by continuous conflict between industry leaders and militarist-bureaucratic factions over who should control the new economic structure.

WARTIME BRINGS ABOUT CHANGES

The National Mobilization Law of March 1938 gave the government great authority over labor and working conditions, production, consumption and exchange of goods, control of property including confiscation, and business and industry in general. In 1941 this authority was expanded to cover virtually all aspects of business. Manufacturers, banks, and investment institutions were required to seek government permission for plant development and loans; thus savings were forced into investment in heavy industry. By the end of 1940 steel production was almost seven million tons. Industry was

KEY DATES

1897: Sumitomo Copper works opens in Osaka.

1901: Sumitomo Steel works begins operation.

1914: Japan begins to supply the Allies with iron and steel during World War I.

1935: Sumitomo Copper and Steel works merge to form Sumitomo Metal Industries, Ltd.

1953: Kokura Steel Manufacturing Company, Ltd., is acquired.

1959: The company divests its nonferrous metal processing unit.

1962: Japan becomes the world's fourth largest steel producer.

1982: SMI's steel tubes and pipes are considered among the world's best; the company is able to supply 30 percent of world demand for wheels for rolling stock.

1999: The company lands a contract with British Petroleum.

2002: Sumitomo Mitsubishi Silicon Corporation is formed.

2005: The company joins with Nippon Steel and Kobe Steel to strengthen their steel-supply capabilities.

seen increasingly as auxiliary to the military. Private profits were eliminated or severely curtailed. Industrialists were pitted against bureaucrats. The national debt, having tripled in five years, equaled national income.

In December 1940 a compromise was reached. Private enterprise was to be the basis of the new structure. There would be closer cooperation among the state, conservative elements in the armed forces, and representatives of the great financial interests that opposed the military extremists as well as their ultraconservative business counterparts.

Sumitomo's director general, Masatsune Ogura, was made minister without portfolio in April 1941, charged with the task of overall economic coordination. An industry-oriented general replaced a bureaucrat as head of the state planning board, and an admiral with close ties to shipbuilding interests became minister of commerce and industry.

Ogura had army ties, and Sumitomo industries, including Sumitomo Metal Industries, was in both light and heavy industry, whose interests did not always coincide. Thus he was well qualified to bring the armed forces closer to business and finance, and to bring light industry closer to heavy industry.

The changes resulted in a partnership between business and the military, a military-industrial complex. War was looming, and Japan wanted to be ready. In July 1941, a few months after Sumitomo's Ogura took on these responsibilities, the United States froze Japanese assets in the United States. So did the British throughout their empire, and the Dutch in the East Indies. The Sumitomo group contributed to the war effort through its mining, manufacturing, steelmaking, banking, and other enterprises and grew considerably during the war, from 40 firms to 135 and from ¥574 million in paid-in capital to ¥1.92 billion.

After the war, Sumitomo Metal Industries changed its name to Fuso Metal Industries, reverting to the name Sumitomo when the Allied occupation ended in 1952. The group, or *zaibatsu*, had been dissolved in February 1948, but was reconstituted in the 1950s as a *keiretsu*, a confederation of interrelated companies, with the role of the family greatly diminished.

POSTWAR GROWTH

By 1951 manufacturing was back to prewar levels, after a change in Allied policy, from punishment to encouragement, with a view to balancing Far Eastern power, especially in the wake of the fall of Nationalist China and the Korean War. During the Korean War, U.S. purchases in Japan helped Japanese industry develop and grow. The iron and steel industry was a leading factor. It had been a major source of Japan's military strength in World War II and was at first to be dismantled under the Allied occupation, except for what was needed to meet domestic needs. With the new policy it, too, was encouraged.

Sumitomo Metal Industries (SMI) shared in the 1950s growth, in 1953 acquiring Kokura Steel Manufacturing Company, Ltd., and entering into a long-term modernization program that included installing large blast furnaces and building new mills in coastal areas. In 1959 it divested its nonferrous metal processing unit, establishing it as a separate company, Sumitomo Light Metal Industries, Ltd.

In 1962 Japan became the world's fourth largest steel producer, outstripping France and the United Kingdom. Japan was producing nearly 30 million tons of steel a year, about four times its pre-1950 total and was second to the United States in continuous hot strip mill capacity. Larger blast furnaces were being built, and oxygen converters were being installed to reduce dependence on scrap-iron imports. Japan became the first country to use oxygen converters on a large scale, after they were used for the first time anywhere, in Austria in 1953.

New plants were built along the seacoast with furnaces of 1,200-ton to 2,000-ton capacity. The coastal location made it easier to receive raw materials and to ship manufactured products. The new plants accommodated the newer, larger ships built to haul raw materials more cheaply.

SMI kept pace with these national developments. Among Japanese steel producers, it was tied in third place with Nippon Kokan and Kawasaki, each with 11.5 percent of total production. Yawata Iron & Steel led with 18.5 percent; Fuji Iron & Steel had 17 percent. By 1976 SMI had built new processing plants and established a technical research institute. Its capacity for producing blister steel, low-carbon, semi-finished material formed by heating bar iron in contact with carbon in a cementing furnace, was 22.7 million tons a year.

By 1982 SMI's steel tubes and pipes, almost half its output, were considered among the world's best. The company was able to supply 30 percent of world demand for wheels for rolling stock. It had three affiliated companies in the United States and one each in Thailand and Saudi Arabia, plus offices in the United States, Brazil, Venezuela, West Germany, Australia, the United Kingdom, Iran, and Singapore.

Sales that year were ¥1.5 trillion, the third highest in Japan after Nippon Steel and Nippon Kokan. Besides tubes and pipes, SMI production was 31 percent steel plates, 7 percent steel wire, and the rest rolling stock, castings, forgings and other products.

In the mid-1980s, major Japanese steel producers, Sumitomo Metal, Nippon Steel, NKK, Kobe Steel, and Kawasaki Steel, were hurt by the rising yen. They closed six furnaces, sending 47,000 workers to other businesses or early retirement. As a result of the cuts, these companies once again became the world's most efficient steelmakers.

SMI's main lines were iron and steel in various semifabricated and fabricated forms, engineering services, titanium, electronics, chemicals, and energy. The company had more than 80 subsidiaries and affiliated companies and participated in several overseas joint ventures. In addition to Osaka and Tokyo, it had offices in 23 other Japanese cities, as well as offices in New York, Los Angeles, Chicago, Houston, Düsseldorf, Vienna, London, Sydney, Singapore, Mexico City, and Beijing.

In 1988 the Sumitomo group was one of six major *keiretsu*, with Mitsui, Mitsubishi, Sanwa, Fuyo, and Dai-Ichi Kangyo. Sumitomo Metal Industries was a leader of the Sumitomo group. SMI steel works were located in Osaka and four other cities, including two in Wakayama; laboratories were in Hyogo and Ibaraki.

In early 1990 the five largest Japanese steelmakers, faced with weak domestic demand, rising financing costs, and strong competition from mini-mills at home, and South Korean and Taiwanese steel producers abroad, cut more jobs. The five—SMI, Nippon Steel, NKK, Kobe Steel, and Kawasaki Steel—had invested heavily in automation and in the manufacture of higher-margin products such as stainless and coated steels. These investments were promising, but a less promising diversification was the move into microchip production and other nonsteel businesses. While SMI had invested least in these new fields, nine SMI affiliates had begun building semiconductor-manufacturing equipment.

The rising cost of raw material created a problem. Iron ore prices had risen 16 percent, and the cost of coking coal was up by 5 percent. Mini-mills, by contrast, were circumventing this problem by making steel out of scrap iron in small electric-arc furnaces. Scrap was available at bargain prices because new car sales had risen and old cars were scrapped proportionately.

One nonsteel diversification, SMI's investment in a U.S. computer firm, Lam Research, seemed more promising. By 1990 SMI owned a half million shares in Lam, which marketed and serviced Sumitomo's integrated-circuit technology in North America and Europe, while Sumitomo did the same for Lam's equipment in Japan. The company spent the majority of the early 1990s forging marketing agreements to bolster sales of its semiconductor and computer products.

THE FUTURE

During the mid-1990s, SMI launched a restructuring effort that included the elimination of several thousand jobs in order to cut costs. Meanwhile, the company continued to secure key partnerships to strengthen its steel business. LVT Corporation and British Steel plc joined forces with SMI in 1994 to form Trico Steel Co, a hot-rolled steel mill. Two years later, SMI and Mitsui & Co. formed Indiana Precision Forge LLC to manufacture and market cold forged auto parts. In 1997, the company landed a British Petroleum contract with SMI to provide pipes used in the oil industry. The contract was extended in 1999 when the company became the leading supplier of pipes for British Petroleum.

The Asian currency crisis began taking its toll on Japan's steelmakers in 1997. As the construction industry slowed, demand for steel began to fall. As such, SMI made several moves to remain competitive including cutting capacity, shuttering and selling unprofitable businesses, and laying off additional workers. The company suffered significant losses in the late 1990s as a result of industry downturn.

Nevertheless, SMI entered the new millennium optimistic about its future. Sure enough, the company returned to profitability in 2000. Two years later it merged its silicon wafers business with that of Mitsubishi Materials Corporation to form Sumitomo Mitsubishi Silicon Corporation. It also combined its stainless steel operations with Nippon Steel to form Nippon Steel & Sumikin Stainless Steel Corporation. In 2005, SMI joined with Nippon Steel Corporation and Kobe Steel Ltd. to strengthen their steel supply capabilities. According to the terms of the partnership, Nippon Steel and Kobe Steel agreed to invest in East Asia United Steel Corporation, a joint venture between SMI and China Steel Corporation of Taiwan. The three companies joined again in 2006, taking preemptive measures to fend off any hostile takeover attempts that could threaten their lucrative partnerships. A new commercial code was expected to take effect in Japan in 2007 that would allow foreign entities to buy Japanese firms by buying shares of the company. By launching joint defense measures, the companies hoped to thwart any takeover attempts.

The company reported a loss in fiscal 2002 but secured profits the following year. Profits continued in 2004 and 2005 amid strong demand for steel. During 2005 the company revamped operations at its Wakayama Steel Works and Kashima Steel Works facilities, which allowed both plants to maintain high capacity utilization rates.

Hiroshi Tomono was named president in 2005. Under his leadership, the company continued to focus on its steel operations as well as new business ventures that would protect it from fluctuating demand in the industry. At the same time, SMI pledged to remain highly competitive in the industry by utilizing cutting-edge technology to provide environmentally friendly products. With a longstanding history in Japan's steelmaking industry, Sumitomo Metal Industries appeared to be on track for growth in the future.

Jim Bowman
Updated, Christina M. Stansell

PRINCIPAL SUBSIDIARIES

Kashima Kyodo Electric Power Company; Daiichi Chuo Kisen Kaisha; Sumitomo Metal Steel Products, Inc.; Sumikin Iron & Steel Corporation; Chuo Denki Kogyo Co., Ltd.; Sumikin Weld Pipe Company, Ltd.; Sumikin Steel & Shapes, Inc.; Wakayama Kyodo Power Company, Inc.; Sumimetal Mining Co., Ltd.; Sumikin Plant, Ltd.; Ring Techs Co., Ltd.; Shearing Kozyo, Ltd.; Sumikin Koka Co., Ltd.; Wako Steel Co., Ltd.; Ware House Industrial Co., Ltd.; Nippon Stainless Steel Kozai Co., Ltd.; Sumitomo Pipe & Tube Co., Ltd.; Sumikin Stainless Steel Tube Co., Ltd.; Sumikin Kikoh Company, Ltd.; Zirco Products Co., Ltd.; Drilltec Japan, Ltd.; Sumikin Kansai Industries, Ltd.; Kantoc Roll, Ltd.; Sumitomo Metal Plantec Co., Ltd.; Sumitomo Metals (Kokura), Ltd.; Nippon Steel & Sumikin Welding Co., Ltd.; Sumikin Precision Forge, Inc.; Umebachi Kogyo Co., Ltd.; Sumikin Recotech Co., Ltd.; Daishin Steel Wire Co., Ltd.; Sumikura Co., Ltd.; Sumitomo Metals (Naoetsu), Ltd.; Sumitomo Mitsubishi Silicon Corporation; Sumitomo Metal (SMI) Electronics Devices, Inc.; Sumikin Ceramics & Quartz Co., Ltd.; Sumitomo Metal Micro Devices, Inc.; Sumikin Molycorp, Inc.; S I Tec Co., Ltd.; Sumitomo Precision Products Co., Ltd.; Kyoei Steel Ltd.; Sumikin Bussan Corporation; East Asia United Steel Corporation; Sumitomo Titanium Corporation; Nippon Steel & Sumikin Stainless Steel Corporation; Sumitomo Metal Logistics Service Co., Ltd.; Kashima Antlers Football Club Co., Ltd.; Narumi China Corporation; Kashiwara Machine Manufacturing Co., Ltd.; Sumikin Kosan Co., Ltd.; Sumitomo Metal Technology, Inc.; Sumikin Recycling Co., Ltd.; Fuso Finance Co., Ltd.

PRINCIPAL COMPETITORS

JFE Shoji Holdings Inc.; Kobe Steel Ltd.; Nippon Steel Corporation.

FURTHER READING

Abrahams, Paul, "Japan's Steelmakers Forecast Downturn," *Financial Times*, November 10, 1997, p. 22.

A Brief History of Sumitomo, Tokyo: Sumitomo Corporation, 1990.

Gibney, Frank, *Miracle by Design: the Real Reasons Behind Japan's Economic Success*, New York: Times Books, 1982.

Guillain, Robert, *The Japanese Challenge*, Philadelphia: Lippincott, 1970.

Hall, Robert B., Jr., *Japan: Industrial Power of Asia*, Princeton: D. Van Nostrand, 1963.

"Japan's Steelmakers: Virtue Is its Own Reward," *Economist*, April 28, 1990.

Mitchell, Kate L., *Japan's Industrial Strength*, New York: Alfred A. Knopf, 1942.

Moulton, Harold G., with Junichi Ko, *Japan: An Economic and Financial Appraisal*, Washington, D.C.: Brookings Institution, 1931.

Nakamoto, Michiyo, "Sumitomo to Cut Jobs and Overcapacity," *Financial Times*, September 2, 1999.

Nakamura, Takafusa, *Economic Growth in Prewar Japan*, New Haven: Yale University Press, 1971.

"Nippon Steel, S'Tomo Metal, Kobe Steel Forge Steel Ties," *Jiji Press English News Service*, March 30, 2005.

Prestowitz, Clyde V., Jr., *Trading Places: How We Allowed Japan To Take the Lead,* New York: Basic Books, 1988.

Shimamura, Kazuhiro, "Japan Steel Firms Plan Defenses Against Takeovers," *Wall Street Journal*, March 30, 2006, p. A10.

"S'Tomo Metal Ind. Sees FY '99 Group Net Loss of 146 B. Yen," *Jiji Press English News Service*, March 7, 2000.

"S'Tomo Metal Ind. To Return to Black in FY '00," *Jiji Press English News Service*, November 22, 2000.

Watanabe, Mayumi, "Sumitomo Saves $11 Million from Nippon, Kobe Tie-Up," *Platt's Metals Week*, April 3, 2006, p. 12.

Sun-Maid Growers of California

13525 South Bethel Avenue
Kingsburg, California 93631
U.S.A.
Telephone: (559) 896-8000
Fax: (559) 897-2362
Web site: http://www.sunmaid.com

Cooperative
Incorporated: 1912 as California Associated Raisin
  Company
Employees: 550 (est.)
Sales: $253 million (2005)
NAIC: 311423 Dried and Dehydrated Food Manu-
  facturing

■ ■ ■

Sun-Maid Growers of California is the largest producer of raisins in the world. The firm's output is split about equally between packaged raisins bearing the Sun-Maid logo and those used as ingredients by the likes of cereal and baking companies. Sun-Maid also produces different varieties of dried fruits, including apricots, dates, and cherries, and licenses its name to companies that make derivative foods like bread, rolls, candy, and fruit juice. Structured as a cooperative, Sun-Maid is owned by its member-growers.

EARLY YEARS

The origins of Sun-Maid date to 1912, when a group of San Joachin Valley, California, raisin growers formed a cooperative organization called the California Associated Raisin Company (CARC). Raisins, made from grapes that were left in the sun to dry, had long been used around the world, but had become a cash crop in California only in the late 1800s. Growers had formed the organization to help combat low prices and fluctuating demand, following in the wake of earlier agricultural cooperatives like Sunkist and Welch's.

CARC was organized as a corporation under the laws of California and had capital stock worth $1 million, which both member-farmers and nonmembers could buy. The stock was held by a group of 25 trustees, many of whom were bankers or community leaders. Growers sold their raisins to CARC for a guaranteed price and then shared in any net profit, less a fee of one-quarter cent per pound to run the organization and pay a dividend to shareholders. CARC would take care of packaging the raisins and help promote their use around the country.

The prospect of guaranteed prices was appealing, and by the spring of 1913 the raisin cooperative had signed up 4,400 of the 6,500 raisin growers in California. CARC, headed by President Wylie M. Giffen and Treasurer James Madison, contracted with 16 of the 21 fruit packing companies in the area to process and pack the raisins for sale. Some disgruntled packers soon began to complain that the cooperative was a monopoly, but no action was initially taken by regulators.

The firm, meanwhile, had begun using marketing efforts like a "Raisin Train" that traveled eastward to Chicago bearing signs promoting its product. Deciding that a brand identity would be helpful as well, in 1915 the Sun-Maid name was created by advertising executive

COMPANY PERSPECTIVES

At Sun-Maid Growers, we try to embody these principles. Our core cooperative principles are: Member-growers gain through cooperation; Members share in the cooperative's marketing efforts; Economies of scale produce higher grower returns; Education and technical support assist growers in their own operations as a building block for success; and Members participate in governance through democratic process.

E. A. Berg, and the following year raisin boxes began to feature an illustration of a young girl with a red bonnet holding a tray of fresh grapes. The model, Lorraine Collett Peterson, worked part time for a packing company and was chosen for her fresh-faced beauty. She and other "Sun Maids" employed by the firm made personal appearances in red bonnets to promote the raisins, while the firm also used magazine and newspaper ads and issued a steady stream of recipe booklets and other materials, which helped increase Americans' consumption of raisins significantly. In 1915 the raisin cooperative also began to employ a national team of sales agents to pitch raisins directly to grocers, reducing the need for an outside distribution network.

In 1918 CARC, which had signed 88 percent of the state's raisin growers and was spending $400,000 per year on advertising, took another step toward vertical integration by opening a huge new plant near downtown Fresno to process and package raisins. It virtually eliminated the opportunities for outside packers, and the CARC's near-monopoly finally caught the attention of federal regulators, who in 1920 sued the raisin cooperative for violating antitrust laws. Two years later a consent decree was signed that allowed the cooperative to continue operating with some modifications to its structure, and the federal Capper-Volstead Act was signed, which exempted agricultural cooperatives from most antitrust laws.

CARC BECOMES SUN-MAID RAISIN GROWERS IN 1922

In 1922 CARC's name was changed to Sun-Maid Raisin Growers of California, reflecting the success of its national branding efforts. It was suffering from financial woes, however, and after first seeking additional funding, in 1924 Sun-Maid declared bankruptcy and was restructured. The industry also was experiencing serious problems with "night riders" forcing nonmember growers to join Sun-Maid through intimidation, as well as disloyal members refusing requests to cut back on production, which caused an oversupply that drove prices down. As members began to quit, Sun-Maid's debts mounted, and in 1927 the organization issued $5 million worth of bonds. When raisin prices bottomed out a year later, the cooperative declared bankruptcy and its assets were taken over by creditors. Only 32 percent of California raisin growers were now members of the organization.

In 1930 the cooperative's bank debts were paid off with loans from the federal government, and ownership of Sun-Maid was returned to its members. The firm's sales force was subsequently let go, and distribution of raisins was taken over by a network of 100 food brokers around the United States. In 1934 the cooperative began offering to buy raisins from nonmembers to boost output.

In 1942 some of Sun-Maid's continuing debt to the federal government was paid by transferring several properties to it, though the large Fresno processing facility was retained. Later that same year, the H.J. Heinz Company took over national distribution of raisins for the cooperative.

In 1952 Sun-Maid terminated its contract with Heinz and returned to selling through food brokers. By the end of the decade, about 40 percent of the U.S. raisin crop was handled by the organization. Sales of raisins had grown during the 1950s, and in 1961 the firm broke ground on a new $12 million plant in Kingsburg, California, which would replace the Fresno facility. Completed in 1964, it had 5.5 acres of floor space and could accommodate a line of raisin-filled trucks ten abreast at its inspection stations. It would employ 600. In addition to raisins sold to consumers in the familiar red Sun-Maid box, the firm was producing nearly an equal amount for sale to bakeries and other food companies for use in their products.

Over time the original Sun-Maid logo had received several minor alterations to keep up with the times, and in 1970 it was modified to feature a large yellow circle with bursting sun rays behind the familiar "maid." Considered one of the most recognizable advertising logos in existence, it was credited with helping make Sun-Maid the leading brand of raisins in the world, with millions of children taking lunches to school each day that included a small red box of raisins.

1972–78: HARD YEARS FOR RAISIN GROWERS

Like any agricultural producers, raisin growers were always at the mercy of the weather, and in the 1970s

KEY DATES

1912: California Associated Raisin Company is formed by raisin growers.

1915: Sun-Maid brand is created.

1918: A new packing plant is opened in Fresno.

1922: The firm becomes known as Sun-Maid Raisin Growers of California.

1928: Sun-Maid declares bankruptcy, and is taken over by creditors.

1930: A federal loan pays off the banks, and the growers take back ownership.

1942: H.J. Heinz Company begins distribution of Sun-Maid raisins.

1952: Distribution by the Sun-Maid broker network resumes.

1964: A new packing plant opens in Kingsburg, California.

1970s: Spring freeze and late summer rains cause massive crop losses.

1980: A licensing unit is formed to sell the Sun-Maid brand to bakeries and other firms. Improved harvesting and processing methods are introduced.

1998: Membership in the Sun-Diamond cooperative ends; additional dried fruits are added.

2006: New digitally animated commercials featuring the "Sun-Maid Girl" debut.

they suffered several difficult years. In 1972 a spring freeze devastated the crop, resulting in the smallest yield since the beginning of the century, and between 1976 and 1978 heavy rain at harvest time caused more losses, with close to 75 percent of the crop destroyed in the latter year.

There were also difficulties with labor during this era. In 1975 the Agricultural Labor Relations Act was signed by California Governor Edmund Brown, but it failed to fully rein in problems that included boycotts of Sun-Maid raisins by Cesar Chavez's United Farm Workers of America.

In 1980 an umbrella marketing organization called Sun-Diamond Growers was founded by Sun-Maid, Diamond Walnut Growers, and Sunsweet Prune. Packaging of the firm's products also was evolving during this time, with new concepts including a resealable can that was introduced during the year.

The firm began to license its brand to bakeries in 1980, with Sun-Maid raisin bread soon available on shelves around the country. In 1982 a new unit, Sun-Maid Brand Licensing, was formed to facilitate more such agreements. Sun-Maid also would operate a quality assurance program that inspected manufacturing and distribution facilities. By mid-decade, Sun-Maid raisin bread was being made in the United States, Canada, Holland, and the United Kingdom.

In 1983, the year that original Sun-Maid Lorraine Collett Peterson died at age 90, the California raisin market was hit hard by surpluses brought on by overproduction and other grapes being converted to raisins due to falling wine sales. Prices fell from $1,200 a ton two years earlier to $500 a ton, and many farmers went bankrupt.

In 1986 the company's fortunes received a boost when the "dancing raisins" commercial series debuted, featuring claymation raisins dancing to the Motown hit, "I Heard It Through the Grapevine." It was produced by the state-sponsored California Raisin Advisory Board, and although it boosted raisin sales for a time, it also served to dilute the impact of Sun-Maid's brand identity.

In 1990 Sun-Maid began using laser sorting technology to improve quality, and in 1994 the firm received a patent for a new "dried-on-the-vine" production and harvesting method its growers had developed. Two other patents were received in 1995, one for a trellising system related to the 1994 patent, and the other for a new method of processing that retained higher amounts of natural grape sugars so raisins could remain tender during baking, which were marketed as Sun-Maid Baking Raisins. The firm also licensed its name to Ferrara Pan Candy Company, which began producing chocolate-coated Sun-Maid raisins. They would compete in stores and at movie theater concession counters with the well-known Nestlé Raisinets brand.

In 1995 Dole Food Company sold its California dried fruit operations to Sun-Diamond Growers Cooperative for $100 million, three-fourths of which was put up by Sun-Maid. A year later Sun-Diamond was banned from participating in government agriculture programs for three years after it was convicted of giving gifts to former U.S. Agriculture Secretary Mike Espy, who had resigned in 1994. In 1997 the U.S. Agriculture Department signed agreements with the four cooperatives that made up Sun-Diamond, allowing them to continue participating in government programs if they established a corporate code of conduct and ethics, instituted employee training programs, and improved rules for travel and entertainment expenses. Each would have to supply quarterly reports and submit to unannounced audits.

In 1998 Sun-Diamond was dissolved, with Sun-Maid once again taking over the work of processing and promoting raisins. At the same time a new state agency, the California Raisin Marketing Board, took on the promotional duties of the former California Raisin Advisory Board, which had been shuttered in 1994.

1999: EXPANSION OF FRUIT OFFERINGS

Sun-Maid had begun offering other dried fruit products, including currants and fruit mixes in addition to raisins, and in 1999 dried apricots, figs, cherries, and apples were added, as well as mixed fruit blends. The firm also had begun to sell grape alcohol for commercial use. Recognizing the more varied product offerings, the word "raisin" was dropped from its name and the organization became simply Sun-Maid Growers of California. The cooperative had 1,200 members.

In 1999 the company partnered with Simon & Schuster unit Little Simon, which published the *Sun Maid Raisins Play Book.* A collectible Sun-Maid doll was also made available. Sales for 1999 hit $221.7 million, with licensed products adding another $100 million. During the year Sun-Maid was fined $887,000 as a result of a lawsuit claiming it had wrongly collected crop insurance for rain-damaged raisins, then bought some back at a discount and reconditioned them to sell at full value.

In 2000 new product licenses included Honey Raisin Bran Muffin Mix and Oatmeal Raisin Cookie Mix and Sun-Maid fruit bars. The company also introduced more new packaging options, including a 12-ounce resealable foil container that stood on end. In 2001 Fast Fruit Packs debuted, in Natural, Yogurt, and Raisin Crunch versions.

By the early 2000s the organization had made a number of structural changes, including retaining some earnings for reinvestment, rather than giving them all back to growers. Its tax-exempt status was also shed, and its bylaws changed. Raisin growers were once again facing hard times brought on by oversupply, and in 2002 the Sun-Maid board of directors voted to support a proposal banning replanting of vineyards that had been pulled out for three years. Farmers who participated in the effort would get extra raisins to sell from the cooperative in compensation. Growers also were suggesting new methods to dispose of extra raisins as well, including as cattle feed or in ethanol fuel.

In late 2002 an agreement was signed with Cinnabon, Inc., to license that firm's cinnamon bread to bakeries. In 2003 A. Lassonde, Inc., licensed the Sun-Maid brand for a line of fruit juices in Canada that would include grape, cranberry, and blueberry blend flavors. The firm also bought the former International Raisins facility in Selma, California, during the year for $1 million. It would be used to receive, store, and inspect raisins, employing 20. Sun-Maid had once owned the property some 60 years earlier.

In 2004 the company added a variety of dried tropical fruits like pineapple, papaya, and mango, as well as Mixed Jumbo Raisins, which combined the standard Thompson variety with large Red Flame and California Golden types.

Raisin growers had a good year in 2005, with Sun-Maid reporting record net sales of $253 million for a crop of about 200 million pounds. Growers received a $200-per-ton premium over the field price set in 2004. The latest technical advancement, mechanized harvesting, had been used for about 40 percent of the total.

In 2006 the Sun-Maid girl received another makeover from the firm's new ad agency of McCann Erickson, this time becoming a digitally animated, talking cartoon character in advertisements that explained how raisins were made from nothing but "grapes and sunshine." The firm budgeted about $7 million for advertising during the year, up from the typical amount of $4 million to $6 million, with ads running in the United States as well as in foreign markets like France and Japan. About 70 percent of Sun-Maid's sales came from the United States, with most of the rest from Canada, Japan, the United Kingdom, Germany, and Scandinavia.

In April 2006 Sun-Maid's growers and the members of a similar organization called the Raisin Bargaining Association voted to continue to fund the California Raisin Marketing Board for another five years. The board was charged with promoting California-grown raisins and sponsoring research, with growers assessed $16.20 per ton. Shipments had risen by nearly 24 percent since 1999.

Nearly 100 years after its founding, Sun-Maid Growers of California was adhering to its mission of processing and marketing raisins and other dried fruit for its member-growers. Although its power had diminished from the early years when more than 80 percent of raisin growers were members, the cooperative's well-known trademark guaranteed its presence on store shelves and in school lunches, and its products appeared certain to remain in favor as healthy eating trends continued to grow in popularity.

Frank Uhle

PRINCIPAL SUBSIDIARIES

Sun-Maid Licensed Products.

PRINCIPAL COMPETITORS

Raisin Bargaining Association; Lion Raisins, Inc.; Sunshine Raisin Corporation; American Raisin Packers, Inc.; Caruthers Raisin Packing Co., Inc.; American Dried Fruit Company; Del Rey Packing Company; Fresno Cooperative Raisin Growers, Inc.; National Raisin Company; Sun-Beam Raisin Company; Sunset Raisin and Nut; West Coast Growers, Inc.

FURTHER READING

"Ag Dept Reaches Agreements with Fruit, Nut Coops," *Reuters News,* March 6, 1997.

Arnold, Roxanne, "State Farmers Harvest Bitter Financial Woes," *Los Angeles Times,* December 23, 1984, p. A1.

"Banks Cancel Sun-Maid Debt," *Los Angeles Times,* May 30, 1932, p. 10.

"Cinnabon and Sun-Maid Partner to Launch Cinnabon Cinnamon Bread," *Food Institute Report,* December 9, 2002, p. 2.

Kirkpatrick, David D., "Snack Foods Become Stars of Books for Children," *New York Times,* September 22, 2000.

Ledbetter, Les, "Demise of Labor Board Perils Agriculture Truce in California," *New York Times,* February 18, 1976.

"New Order for Raisin Industry," *Los Angeles Times,* September 26, 1926, p. F10.

Paris, Ellen, "Growing Pains," *Forbes,* June 30, 1986, p. 92.

Pollock, Dennis, "Fresno, Calif. Judge Orders Panel to Arbitrate Raisin Field Price Dispute," *Knight-Ridder/Tribune Business News,* January 27, 2001.

———, "Kingsburg, Calif.–Based Raisin Cooperative Shows Off Machinery," *Knight-Ridder/Tribune Business News,* December 7, 2003.

———, "Raisin Growers Recap the Season," *Fresno Bee,* December 4, 2005, p. B1.

———, "Raisin Panel Weighs Proposal on Glut," *Knight-Ridder/Tribune Business News,* October 11, 2002.

———, "Sun-Maid Celebrates 85 Years As Raisin Cooperative," *Knight-Ridder/Tribune Business News,* December 3, 1997.

———, "Sun-Maid Growers Told to Embrace Stiff Competition," *Knight-Ridder/Tribune Business News,* December 2, 2001.

———, "Sun-Maid Remade," *Fresno Bee,* March 15, 2006.

"Raisin Industry Tells of Its Losses from Rains," *New York Times,* September 28, 1982, p. A17.

"Raisin Sales Plan Changed by Growers," *Los Angeles Times,* November 18, 1952, p. 23.

"Reorganize Sun-Maid," *Los Angeles Times,* May 21, 1925, p. A8.

Reyes, Sonia, "Sun-Maid Branches Out," *Brandweek,* January 17, 2000, p. 12.

"Sun-Maid Now Safe from Receivership," *Los Angeles Times,* August 19, 1929, p. 2.

"Sun-Maid Raisin Growers to Purchase Selma, Calif. Storage Facility, Hire 20," *Fresno Bee,* September 6, 2003.

"Sun-Maid Settles Crop Insurance Case for $887,085," *Reuters News,* April 14, 1999.

"Sun-Maid Turns Over Plants to Government," *Los Angeles Times,* April 17, 1942, p. 15.

"What's Ahead for Sun-Maid and Dole?," *Food Institute Report,* April 17, 1995.

Woeste, Victoria Saker, *The Farmer's Benevolent Trust: Law and Agricultural Cooperation in Industrial America 1865–1945,* Chapel Hill: University of North Carolina Press, 1998.

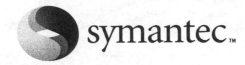

Symantec Corporation

20330 Stevens Creek Boulevard
Cupertino, California 95014-2132
U.S.A.
Telephone: (408) 517-8000
Fax: (408) 517-8186
Web site: http://www.symantec.com

Public Company
Incorporated: 1982
Employees: 16,000
Sales: $4.1 billion (2006)
Stock Exchanges: NASDAQ
Ticker Symbol: SYMC
NAIC: 51121 Software Publishers

■ ■ ■

Symantec Corporation is one of the largest software companies in the world providing content and network security software to individual consumers and businesses. Its products are used in virus protection, intrusion detection, and remote management applications. The company also provides security assessment, consulting, and security management services. During 2005, Symantec completed its $11 billion acquisition of Veritas Software Corporation. Symantec operates facilities in 40 countries across the globe—nearly half of fiscal 2006 revenues was generated outside of the United States.

ORIGINS

Symantec was founded in 1982 by 34-year-old Dr. Gary Hendrix, a prominent expert in natural language processing and artificial intelligence. He brought together a group of Stanford University researchers in the field of natural language processing to form the company, which had various ideas for innovative software, including a database program. The enterprise's initial funding was a National Science Foundation grant. When that grant ran out, Hendrix obtained financing from venture capital firms that were interested in investing in the field of artificial intelligence, even though the company in 1983 was still far from creating a product.

In 1984 Symantec was acquired by another, even smaller computer software start-up company, C&E Software, founded by Dennis Coleman and Gordon E. Eubanks, Jr., and headed by Eubanks. The merged company retained the name Symantec, and 38-year-old Eubanks became its chief executive officer. Eubanks, formerly a nuclear submarine commander, had studied computer engineering at the Naval Post-Graduate School in Monterey, California. For his master's thesis, Eubanks had developed an innovative microcomputer tool for the CPM operating system called EBASIC. At the time of the merger, C&E Software also was working on a database program, but the different fields of expertise of the two companies complemented each other. Whereas Symantec's founders were strong in high-technology innovation, C&E had more experience writing tight computer code and working out program bugs. The merger received significant support from venture capitalist John Doerr, who went on to become a member of the board of directors. Doerr was the first to see the potential in the merger and helped bring it about through his urging and financial backing.

Symantec shipped its first major product, Q&A for

COMPANY PERSPECTIVES

Symantec's commitment to corporate responsibility stems from our dedication to earning the trust of our stakeholders. Integrity matters in everything we do, and that includes the policies and practices that guide how we operate in the global marketplace.

the IBM-compatible PC, in 1985. Q&A was a flat-file database program and was one of the few database management software packages for personal computers that used natural language query, based on an internal vocabulary of nearly 600 words. In order to obtain lists or statistics based on a data file, the user types in queries as ordinary English sentences instead of as arcane commands (hence the name Q&A for the process of question and answer). The use of natural language query in this product was a significant step in making computers more user-friendly. Symantec's sales for 1985 totaled $1.4 million.

EXPANSION THROUGH PRODUCT OFFERINGS AND ACQUISITIONS: 1985–89

Despite the modest success of Q&A, it soon became clear that the product would not be able to compete with the major personal computer database program on the market, Ashton-Tate's dBase, or Lotus Development Corp.'s spreadsheet program Lotus 1-2-3. Although innovative, Q&A managed to bring in only $8 million in sales in its first two years combined, which was far short of its expectations. Eubanks realized that the market had changed in such a way that Symantec could no longer be a one-product company relying solely on Q&A like other, established software companies, such as Ashton-Tate, Lotus Development, or WordPerfect Corp. Thus Symantec took the strategic move of broadening its product base, particularly in specialty niche software categories.

To take advantage of such software developments of other, smaller firms, Symantec formed its Turner Hall Publishing division to publish third-party software. In October 1985, Turner Hall introduced Note-It, a notation utility for Lotus 1-2-3. Of more significance, Eubanks decided that the company would expand its product offerings through acquisitions of other software companies. This involved not only obtaining a company's products but also retaining the company's programmers (in order to continue to develop new

products in the given category) and its marketing staff (who had established client relationships).

At the same time, Eubanks decided to structure Symantec's organization into complete teams for each product. This involved establishing product groups consisting of all the functions of product development, quality assurance, marketing, documentation, and technical support. Subsequently, when other companies were acquired by Symantec, product autonomy was maintained. This way, employees of acquired companies who were accustomed to working in small companies were able to maintain a sense of the small company culture.

Symantec began its acquisition campaign in 1987. In January that year Symantec acquired Breakthrough Software, located in Novato, California. Breakthrough had developed Time Line, the leading project management program for the IBM-compatible PC. In July Symantec acquired Living Videotext, based in nearby Mountain View, California. Living Videotext was the developer of ThinkTank, a presentation graphics program for the Macintosh, and Grandview, an information management program for the PC. In September Symantec acquired Think Technologies of Bedford, Massachusetts. Think had developed THINK C and THINK Pascal, both programming language compilers for the Macintosh, and InBox, an electronic-mail system.

As a result of these acquisitions Symantec's sales doubled between 1987 and 1988, to reach $19.6 million. The number of employees likewise nearly doubled, to reach 180 in 1988, with 90 percent of the acquired companies' employees staying on. Direct sales representatives increased from 20 to 45. The portion of Symantec's sales to large corporations rose from 18 percent to about 35 percent in 1988. Symantec's existing products also benefited from the acquisitions through the ability to provide complementary software package combinations.

For a relatively small company, managing such acquisitions was not easy. Sales doubled, but Symantec suffered net losses due to the costs of the acquisitions. Although product management was kept separate, the acquired companies' finance, administration, personnel, and public relations functions all had to be merged. The restructuring was complicated by the loss of top managers. The founders of acquired companies Videotext and Think Technologies decided to leave Symantec. Of more significance, in 1988 Chief Financial Officer Michael Perez and Vice-President of Business Development Spencer Leyton both left the company. Eubanks proceeded to reorganize the company to reduce the number of top executives and give more authority to middle managers. These management and financial difficulties all contributed to the postponement of an initial public offering (IPO), which Symantec had originally planned for May 1988.

After six years of losses, Symantec finally became profitable in 1988, or fiscal year 1989 (ending March 31, 1989). On June 23, 1989, the company made its IPO. A stock split went into effect in September 1991. By November of that year the stock price was five times higher than it was when it went public, and it was selling at 64 times earnings. The high stock price supported Symantec's acquisitions, which were usually bought in exchange for Symantec stock.

Meanwhile, Q&A continued to be successful in its own smaller market of flat-file database programs. Flat-file databases, in contrast to relational database programs, require all the data to be in a single file. In fiscal 1989, Q&A accounted for one-third of Symantec's $50 million in revenues. In 1991 Q&A was the leader in the $60 million flat-file database market.

ACQUISITIONS CONTINUE IN THE LATE 20TH CENTURY

Symantec made its biggest acquisition at the time in August 1990 when it purchased the highly successful Peter Norton Computing Inc. of Santa Monica, California. Norton Computing became a pioneer in DOS-based utilities software with its introduction of The Norton Utilities in 1982. This software package historically has been the market leader in PC utilities software. Utilities are programs that perform functions such as backing up and compressing files, checking for viruses, and restoring lost data. The acquisition gave Symantec a 34 percent share of the $410 million utilities market.

The purchase also helped Symantec, whose utility products were more heavily weighted toward the Macintosh platform, expand into the PC utilities market. Peter Norton, the founder and owner of the acquired company, was given one-third of Symantec's stock, worth about $60 million, and a seat on Symantec's board of directors. The acquired company became a division of Symantec and was renamed Peter Norton Computing Group. Most of Norton Computing's 115 employees were retained. The merger also helped Norton Computing regain the market share it was losing to competitors, especially Central Point Software. Norton Computing's revenues tripled between June 1990 and September 1991, and by November it appeared to have regained the market lead over Central Point. Norton Computing's merger with Symantec has since been cited as one of the most successful acquisitions in the software industry.

Symantec made three more acquisitions in 1991. In June it acquired Leonard Development Group, which had developed GreatWorks, an integrated applications program for the Macintosh. In August it acquired Zortech Inc., a developer of cross-platform C++ programming language compilers. Zortech had been the first company to introduce a C++ compiler for microcomputers. Symantec's acquisition of Zortech, with 32 employees for $10 million in stock, thus brought the company into the business of object-oriented programming and multiple platforms. Also in 1991 Symantec acquired Dynamic Microprocessor Associated Inc., which had developed pcANYWHERE, the leading remote control communications software product for personal computers.

Even during the recession of the early 1990s, which was especially severe in California, Symantec continued to grow. Revenues increased from $75 million in fiscal 1990 to more than $116 in fiscal 1991, and the number of its employees increased by 28 percent between June 1990 and June 1991.

Symantec also expanded in Europe. The company opened a European manufacturing facility outside Dublin, Ireland, in October 1991. The facility subsequently began supporting Symantec's customers outside North America. In May 1991, Symantec began selling Norton Utilities and certain other software packages in the Soviet Union through three official distributors. To combat rampant software piracy in Russia, Symantec also offered after-sale services and technical support to registered users. Taking a more active role in international distribution, Symantec acquired its exclusive distributor in the United Kingdom, Symantec U.K., in March 1992. By 1994 Symantec had a network of more than 150 partner companies worldwide and had produced more than 120 translated versions of various software products into different foreign languages.

Symantec moved toward becoming a significant provider of programming tools for corporate software developers when it acquired two more companies in June 1992 for a total of about $2.1 million. The acquired companies were Whitewater Group of Evanston, Illinois, a developer of object-oriented programming tools and a provider of a collection of graphics libraries, and Multi-Scope Inc. of Mountain View, California, a developer of innovative debugging programs for the DOS, Windows, and OS/2 platforms. In 1992 only 5 percent of Symantec's sales were in programming languages software, but Symantec hoped to expand its market by offering programming tools that could be used for multiple computer platforms.

In late 1992 Symantec officers were sued by rival software company Borland International Inc. over Symantec's hiring of former Borland vice-president Eugene Wang. Borland charged that Wang had passed on trade secrets via electronic mail to Symantec CEO Eubanks before leaving Borland. This was the first legal case in which a high-level executive had been implicated based on electronic-mail messages as evidence, and thus the case attracted a great deal of attention even outside the software industry. Eubanks and Wang were cleared of all charges in 1996.

The next major product category that Symantec pursued was business project management software. In the early 1990s this was seen as one of the fastest-growing software areas. Symantec introduced Guide Line, an easy-to-use project scheduling software, and provided improved versions of Time Line, a leading project management software package.

To expand in other areas of business software, Symantec made its largest acquisition since Norton Computing, purchasing Contact Software International Inc. for $47 million in exchange for 2.7 million in common shares. Contact Software, which had sales of about $20 million, was the maker of Act!, the leading contact management database program for executives and sales staffs.

The acquisition also boosted Symantec's sales, which had been flat for the first nine months of fiscal 1993. In addition, Symantec finally centralized the separate marketing activities of each of its four product groups at its Cupertino, California, headquarters in 1993 in order

to be more efficient. Product development, though, remained autonomous.

Despite forays into different software categories, Symantec remained dedicated to utilities programs ever since gaining that market's leadership with the acquisition of Norton Computing. In 1992 utility programs accounted for about 65 percent of revenues, whereas applications programs, such as Q&A, accounted for only 30 percent. In October 1993 Symantec acquired Certus International Corp. of Cleveland, Ohio, which had developed antivirus and security software for the PC. In the fall of 1993, Symantec acquired Fifth Generation Systems Inc. of Baton Rouge, Louisiana, a developer of DiskLock, FastBack, Safe, and other software utilities for various platforms. Both companies, while remaining in their respective locations, were administratively merged into the Peter Norton Computing Group in Santa Monica, which in 1992 accounted for 75 percent of Symantec's revenues. Finally, in the spring of 1994, Symantec made a $60 million bid to acquire its leading competitor in utilities programs, Central Point Software of Beaverton, Oregon, whose 1993 revenues were estimated at $80 million. The two companies combined held 60 percent of the $440 million market for utilities software, but competition had forced prices and profits down.

Symantec's latest major strategic move was to broaden its product offerings to include software for client/server systems and local area networks. Despite its dominance in the field of software utilities, the market was shrinking as the leading supplier of PC operating system software, Microsoft, was increasingly combining utilities into later versions of its DOS operating system. Microsoft, however, was less dominant in the field of network software. Thus Symantec purchased the Net-Distributor Pro product and other technology from Trik Inc. in 1993. To aid its product development technology, in January 1994 Symantec acquired the Rapid Enterprises division from DataEase International Inc., based in Shelton, Connecticut, for $7.5 million. Rapid Enterprises had been developing a fourth-generation software development tool for client/server applications. These tools helped Symantec to revise its existing software products so as to be able to run on enterprise-wide networks. Symantec began offering a line of network utilities in early 1994 and later combined them in a common management program, Norton Administrator for Networks. These programs permit central monitoring and execution of utilities functions on a number of computers over a network. Symantec also planned to redesign the product foundations for better integration when used over wide area networks, but its competition was tougher in this field.

GROWTH AT THE END OF THE 20TH CENTURY AND BEYOND

During 1997, Symantec filed suit against competitor McAfee Associates, claiming the company had used Symantec and Norton software codes in several of its programs. McAfee countered with a $1 billion defamation suit. The companies settled in 1999, but the terms were kept confidential. Meanwhile, Symantec forged ahead with its growth plans. In 1998, the company acquired Intel Corp.'s antivirus software division, including its licensed Intel systems management technology. Symantec also purchased IBM's antivirus business. Eubanks left the following year to head up a new enterprise software company. IBM executive John W. Thompson was named CEO and became the first African American to lead a major U.S.-based software company.

Thompson was immediately charged with the task of securing Symantec's position in the corporate network security industry. He sold the company's Internet Tools division and the Visual Café product line, as well as the ACT software line. He then orchestrated several acquisitions including the $975 million purchase of Axent Technologies, a producer of firewall technology; L-3 Network Security; and Seagate's Network Storage Management Group.

The company continued its growth-through-acquisition strategy throughout the early years of the new millennium. In fact, between February 2000 and February 2006, Symantec purchased more than 25 companies. Thompson's strategy appeared to pay off as revenues increased by nearly 30 percent in 2003 and 2004. By late 2004, the firm had set the stage for its largest acquisition to date and one of the largest software mergers at the time. In December, Symantec made a $13 billion play for Veritas Software Corp., the leading provider of information storage software. News of the merger sent Symantec share prices plummeting by 32 percent in just one week, a signal that the investment world did not think the pairing of the two companies was a good fit. At the same time, Microsoft Corporation announced plans to enter the antivirus and corporate security markets in the near future, making the software giant Symantec's largest competitor. Despite analyst and investor dissent, shareholders approved the Veritas acquisition in June 2005. By now, the value of the all-stock deal had fallen to just under $11 billion due to Symantec's faltering share price. One month later, Symantec and Veritas officially joined forces and formed the fourth largest software company in the world based on revenue.

Thompson's next big task was combining the two companies—a process that proved tricky at first. The company reported in November 2005 that it had overstated its revenue forecast for 2006 and by July 2006, its share price was at its lowest point in three years. With intense competition nipping at its heels, Symantec reorganized its sales force, invested heavily in marketing, and also revamped training procedures for employees and resellers. Only time would tell, however, if the Veritas purchase would pay off. Indeed, a July 2006 *Wall Street Journal* article reported, "Mr. Thompson concedes that making the combined company work may be the biggest challenge he has faced at Symantec, but he says he is moving aggressively and is confident he will succeed."

Heather Behn Hedden
Updated, Christina M. Stansell

PRINCIPAL SUBSIDIARIES

AXENT (EMEA) Ltd.; BindView Development Corporation; DataCenter Technologies N.V.; Delrina Corporation; Ejasent, Inc.; Invio Software, Inc.; Jareva Technologies, Inc.; Kvault Software Ltd.; Precise Software Solutions, Inc.; Sygate Technologies L.L.C.; Symantec (Australia) Pty. Ltd.; Symantec (Canada) Corporation; Symantec (Japan), Inc.; Symantec Australia Holding Pty. Ltd.; Symantec Cyprus Ltd.; Symantec Financing Ltd.; Symantec Holdings Ltd.; Symantec Information Technology (Beijing) Ltd.; Symantec International Ltd.; Symantec Israel Ltd.; Symantec Ltd.; Symantec Security Services Holding Ltd.; Symantec STDL Ltd.; Symantec Technology Services GmbH; Symantec UK (Limited); Symantec US Holdings L.L.C.; The Kernel Group Inc.; VERITAS Operating Corporation; VERITAS Software Corporation; VERITAS Software International Holding Ltd.; VERITAS Software (Beijing) Co., Ltd.; VERITAS Software Asia Pacific Trading PTE Ltd.; VERITAS Software Global L.L.C.; VERITAS Software GmbH; VERITAS Software India PVT. Ltd.; VERITAS Software Holdings Ltd.; VERITAS Software International Ltd.; VERITAS Software Investment Company; VERITAS Software Technology Corporation; W. Quinn, Inc.

PRINCIPAL COMPETITORS

CA Inc.; McAfee Inc.; Microsoft Corporation.

FURTHER READING

Bowen, Ted Smalley, and Jai Sigh, "Symantec on Prowl Again: Eyes Relationships with DataEase and Fifth Generation," *PC Week,* August 30, 1993, p. 6.

Cunningham, Cara A., "Symantec Makes Play for Tools with Acquisition of Two Firms," *PC Week,* June 15, 1992, pp. 147–48.

Flynn, Laurie J., "Shareholders Approve Symantec-Veritas Software Merger," *New York Times,* June 25, 2005.

Grimes, Ann, "Symantec Says It Will Purchase Three Small Security Companies," *Wall Street Journal,* July 18, 2002.

Heinlein, Susan W., "Gordon Eubanks Jr.: Intense Drive and Focus Distinguish Symantec Corp. Leader," *Business Journal-San Jose,* pp. S7–S8.

———, "Symantec: The Pride and the Passion," *Business Journal-San Jose: Software Magazine,* September 1991, p. 14.

Lacy, Sarah, and Steve Hamm, "'I Can't Wait to Compete'; As Symantec's Chief Finalizes His Deal for Veritas, War with Microsoft Looms," *Business Week,* March 21, 2005.

Lyons, Daniel J., "Stumbling Blocks Put Symantec's IPO on Hold," *PC Week,* September 5, 1988, p. 133.

Morrissey, Jane, and Karen D. Moser, "Symantec's REI Acquisition Fuels Enterprise Push," *PC Week,* January 10, 1994, pp. 107–8.

"Norton Gets a Bit Less Secure," *Business Week,* December 12, 2005.

Pitta, Julie, "Talk to Your Computer," *Forbes,* July 23, 1990, pp. 281–82.

Rebello, Kathy, "This Boss Measures 6.0 on the Richter Scale," *Business Week,* April 20, 1992, pp. 96–98.

Schoenberger, Karl, "I.B.M. Veteran Finds a Challenge at Symantec," *New York Times,* November 19, 2000, p. 4.

Shaffer, Richard A., "Symantec's Little Hits," *Forbes,* November 25, 1991, p. 196.

Vara, Vauhini, "Symantec Finds Diversifying Slow to Pay Off," *Wall Street Journal,* July 20, 2006, p. B1.

Tamron Company Ltd.

1385 Hasunuma, Minuma-ku
Saitama,
Japan
Telephone: (81) 048 684 9111
Fax: (81) 048 683 8282
Web site: http://www.tamron.co.jp

Public Company
Incorporated: 1952 as Taisei Kogaku Kogyo Co., Ltd.
Employees: 3,672
Sales: ¥59.61 billion ($557.6 million) (2005)
Stock Exchanges: Tokyo
Ticker Symbol: 7740
NAIC: 333314 Optical Instrument and Lens Manufacturing

■ ■ ■

Tamron Company Ltd. is leveraging its position as a world-leading manufacturer of camera and binocular lenses to transform itself into a major opto-electronics producer. The Japanese company's Photographic Products division produces camera lenses, zoom lenses, and interchangeable lens systems, as well as medium-range cameras. This division accounts for less than 20 percent of group sales, however, as a result of the company's launch of its Optical Components division, which produces lenses for digital still cameras, camcorders, and, since 2005, cellular telephone-based cameras. The Optical Components division is Tamron's fastest growing, accounting for nearly 70 percent of group sales.

Tamron has further extended its range into the broader opto-electronics field, forming its Commercial/Industrial-use Optics division, which produces lenses used in closed-circuit television systems, surveillance systems, image processing and projection systems, as well as high-precision molds, injection-molded parts and components, and other optical devices and systems. The broadening of the group's product lines has enabled the company nearly to double its sales since the beginning of the 2000s. Tamron operates three production facilities in Hirosaki, Namioka, and Owani, in Japan, and a fourth facility in Foshan, China. Approximately 31 percent of the company's sales, which neared ¥60 billion ($560 million) in 2005, come from outside Japan, with the Asian region accounting for 16 percent of group revenues. Nearly half of the company's revenues come from a single customer, Sony EMSC Corporation. In addition, the company operates sales and distribution subsidiaries in the United States, Germany, France, Hong Kong, and Shanghai. Tamron is listed on the Tokyo Stock Exchange. Morio Ono is president and CEO.

LENS MOUNT INNOVATOR IN 1959

Tamron was founded in 1950 by Takeyuki Arai as Taisei Kogaku Kogyo (Taisei Optical Equipment Manufacturing) in Urawa-city. The company launched production of camera and binocular lenses that year, then formally incorporated in 1952. Much of the group's development of optical equipment was led by Uhyone Tamura, an optics designer, under whom the company launched its breakthrough product, the first interchangeable lens system for single-lens reflex (SLR) cameras, in 1957.

COMPANY PERSPECTIVES

Corporate Philosophy: With its firm commitment to developing high-quality, innovative and technologically advanced products that satisfy customer needs, Tamron is securing a leading position in the worldwide optical industry. Our primary objective is to sustain strong corporate growth based on a high level of customer satisfaction achieved by providing superior products at the right price, thus also contributing to the prosperity of our shareholders and employees. We at Tamron are advancing with our corporate philosophy to guide our mission.

The company also introduced a high-performance lens that year, the 135 millimeter F4.5 lens. Tamura's efforts for the company were rewarded with the creation of a new brand name, Tamron, based on Tamura's name and introduced in 1959.

In that same year, the company had cemented its international status with the debut of the T-mount, a universal interchangeable mounting system that could be adapted to nearly every existing camera. Invented by Arai himself, the T-mount represented something of a revolution for the camera industry, and especially for professional photographers. Instead of being required to invest in a complete set of lenses for each camera they owned, photographers were able to use a single set of lenses on a variety of cameras. Backing up the launch of the T-mount, the company moved to a new headquarters and production plant in Hasunuma, Omiya-city in 1959.

Taisei innovated again at the beginning of the 1960s, becoming the first to develop a mass-produced zoom lens, featuring a range between 95 and 205 millimeters, in 1961. The introduction of large-scale production techniques helped to reduce the cost of zoom lenses, bringing them within the budgets of the mass of hobbyist photographers. As such, Taisei played an important part in the great photography boom of the 1960s. Photography rapidly became a popular hobby worldwide, before becoming a ubiquitous consumer product.

Taisei remained focused on the higher-end, high-quality market, a commitment underscored by the group's entry into the production of high-precision lenses and prisms in 1966, including lenses for the television broadcasting industry. In that year, as well, the company introduced its own lens testing platform and a new generation of its interchangeable lens systems, called the

Adapt-a-Matic, which also offered automatic aperture control. The rising popularity of the Tamron brand prompted the company to adopt the name as its own in 1970. By then, Tamron had opened a new factory, in Hirosaki, where it expanded its product range to include lenses for photocopying machines, as well as its SLR camera lenses and television camera lenses. Later in the decade, Tamron launched its latest innovation, the Adaptall lens, which included a quick-focus system, among other features.

INTERNATIONAL SALES GROWTH BEGINNING IN 1979

The growing popularity—and then dominance—of Japanese camera brands on the international market offered new sales opportunities for Tamron. The company's lens mounting systems and their adaptability to a wide variety of camera models and brands found strong demand worldwide. To support its growing international sales, Tamron opened its first overseas sales office, Tamron Industries Inc., in the United States in 1979. In that year, the company also launched a new lens line, the Super Performance series. The SP series represented the company's high-end, and high-performance, range, and remained a top-seller for the company into the 2000s.

Tamron also began producing lenses and zoom lenses for the growing new video camera market. In 1981, for example, the company launched a new 6X zoom lens. Production of these and other company products was assured by the expansion of the company's Hirosaki factory in 1981. By 1983, the company's video camera lens line had been expanded with a new integrated video camera lens.

Tamron also continued to build up its international sales network, adding new sales and distribution subsidiaries in Germany and Hong Kong in 1982. In Japan, meanwhile, the company had begun an effort to diversify its operations beyond lens production. In 1984, for example, the company established a new optics subsidiary, Optech Tamron Company, with a site in Namioka-machi. Optech Tamron was later merged into Tamron in 1991.

Meanwhile, in 1985, Tamron added precision molding capacity, establishing subsidiary Tamron Fine-Giken Company. The company boosted its moldings business in 1986 with the creation of a new factory in Owani-machi. As support for this expansion, Tamron went public, listing its shares on the over-the-counter (OTC) market of the Tokyo Stock Exchange in 1984.

By 1985, the company's diversification effort had led to the launch of a new product, the Fotovix film

KEY DATES

1950: Takeyuki Arai founds a company for the production of lenses for cameras and binoculars in Urawa-city, Japan.

1952: The company incorporates as Taisei Kogaku Kogyo (Taisei Optical Equipment Manufacturing) Company.

1957: The company introduces the first interchangeable SLR lens system.

1959: The company launches the T-mount universal lens adapter system and adopts the Tamron trademark.

1970: The company name is changed to Tamron Company.

1979: Tamron establishes its first overseas subsidiary in the United States.

1982: The company sets up its first European subsidiary in Germany, and opens a sales subsidiary in Hong Kong.

1984: Tamron goes public with a listing on the Tokyo Stock Exchange's OTC market.

1985: The company diversifies into precision molding through subsidiary Tamron Fine-Giken, and launches the Fotovix film video processor system.

1992: A subsidiary is founded in Mexico.

1995: The company adds a sales subsidiary in the United Kingdom; a majority stake is acquired in Zenza Bronica Co., a maker of medium-format SLR cameras established in the 1950s.

1997: The company establishes a manufacturing plant in Foshan, China.

2003: The company launches its first digital camera lenses.

2005: Tamron introduces the first lenses for cellular telephones; a new subsidiary is added in Shanghai.

video processor. This product enabled the transfer of photographs and slides to videotape (and later to DVD) and remained a popular product until it was discontinued at the start of the 21st century. Tamron also continued to develop new lenses, such as the Vari-Focal lens, for use in closed-circuit television systems, introduced in 1986. By 1989, the company had launched a new ½-inch Vari-Focal lens with a 6 to 12 millimeter range.

FOCUS ON DIGITAL FOR THE NEW CENTURY

Tamron opened a new subsidiary in Mexico in 1992. The company also released a new SLR zoom lens that year, the SP AF35-105 mm F2.8. The company increasingly targeted the compact, lightweight zoom lens segment, launching the AF28-200 mm F3.8-5.6 that year as well. Both lenses were well received and won industry awards.

Tamron extended its European presence in 1995, adding a sales subsidiary in the United Kingdom. In that year, as well, Tamron moved into the production of cameras for the first time, when it acquired 75 percent of Japanese camera maker Zenza Bronica Co. Ltd. Founded in the 1950s by Zenzaburo Yoshino, that company initially focused on camera design, launching the Bronica Z, based on Nikon lenses, in 1958. The success of that model helped establish Bronica as a top-selling maker of medium-format SLR cameras. Tamron continued to release new Bronica models through the end of the decade, including the well-received Rangerfinder RF645, introduced in 2001. The company also acquired full control of Bronica in 1998, merging the camera-maker into its own operations.

Tamron set up a new distribution subsidiary in Hong Kong in 1997, in support of the launch of the company's first foreign manufacturing plant, which opened in Foshan, China, that same year. The company also established a new sales subsidiary in France in 2000. The expanded manufacturing, sales, and distribution operations helped support the company's continuing rollout of new products at the start of the 21st century, including the latest in the award-winning SP series, such as the AF28-200mm Super XR F/3.8-5.6 Aspherical [IF] Macro, launched in 2001, and the AF28-300mm Ultra Zoom XR F/3.5-6.3 LD Aspherical [IF] Macro, launched in 2002.

Yet the emergence of digital camera technologies in the early 2000s, and the rapid expansion of the digital camera market in both the professional and consumer markets, placed Tamron under pressure. In response, the company began developing its own line of digital camera lenses, launching its first "DI" series lens in 2003. The company's efforts were quickly rewarded, as its DI line began tallying up a series of international awards.

The emergence of the digital photography era also encouraged Tamron to adopt a new strategy into the mid-2000s, with a focus on enhancing the group's optical technologies, and in developing new capacity in optics-linked electronics technologies. An example of this was the 2005 launch of the company's first line of camera lenses specifically developed for the booming mixed-used cellular telephone market, including the market's smallest camera lens—at just eight millimeters. In support of the surging demand for new generation lenses, Tamron opened a new subsidiary in Shanghai in 2005. Tamron had successfully navigated the transition to the digital era and appeared certain to maintain its position as a worldwide reference in precision optics.

M. L. Cohen

PRINCIPAL SUBSIDIARIES

Tamron Europe GmbH (Germany); Tamron France EURL; Tamron Industries (Hong Kong) Ltd.; Tamron Optical (Shanghai) Co., Ltd. (China); Tamron Optical (Foshan) Co., Ltd. (China); Tamron USA, Inc.

PRINCIPAL COMPETITORS

Canon Inc.; 3M Co.; Olympus Corporation; Northrop Grumman Corporation Electronic Sensors and Systems Division; Nikon Corporation; Citizen Watch Company Ltd.; Hoya Corporation; Magna Donnelly Corporation; JENOPTIK AG; BelOMA; Bausch and Lomb Inc.

FURTHER READING

Ayers, Michael, "Take a Trip with Tamron," *Photo District News,* October 2005, p. S20.

Keppler, Herbert, "Tamron Breaks the 28-200mm Close Focusing Barrier," *Popular Photography,* November 1996, p. 15.

Stensvold, Mike, "Tamron Zooms," *Petersen's Photographic,* October 1985, p. 6.

"Tamron: Optical Experts with 50+ Years of Experience," *Advanced Imaging,* July–August 2003, p. 46.

"Tamron Zooms," *Petersen's Photographic,* April 1994, p. 56.

"Top Camera Lens Makers in Japan Boost Production As Global Demand Grows," *AgenceFrancePresse,* April 8, 2003.

Tchibo GmbH

Überseering 18 22297
Hamburg,
Germany
Telephone: (49) (0)40 6387 0
Fax: (49) (0)40 6387 2600
Web site: http://www.tchibo.com

Wholly Owned Subsidiary of Tchibo Holding AG
Incorporated: 1949
Employees: 12,796
Sales: EUR 4 billion (2005)
NAIC: 311920 Coffee and Tea Manufacturing; 454113
    Mail-Order Houses; 454390 Other Direct Selling
    Establishments; 722213 Snack and Nonalcoholic
    Beverage Bars

■ ■ ■

Tchibo GmbH operates Germany's top chain of coffee shops. The parent company, Tchibo Holding AG, also controls Beiersdorf AG. Tchibo claims to be the largest purveyor (by value) of roasted coffee in several European countries, including Germany, Austria, Poland, the Czech Republic, and Hungary. In addition to more than 1,300 coffee shops of its own, Tchibo also sells its beans through the Internet, mail order catalogs, and via a "store-within-a-store" program at roughly 50,000 bakeries, drugstores, and supermarkets. Awareness of the Tchibo brand among Germans is reportedly 99 percent.

A defining feature of the company's business model has been the consumer goods its coffee shops started carrying in the early 1970s. Updated on a weekly basis

(every Wednesday), these impulse-oriented offerings have included items as diverse as tennis racquets and lingerie (the latter of which has spawned a small chain of intimate apparel stores in Germany). Tchibo has also pitched mobile phones and airline tickets. The combination of coffee and well-priced, quality nonfood items keeps customers coming back, and helps the company weather the ups and downs of the coffee and consumer goods markets.

ORIGINS

Tchibo was formed in 1949 by Max Herz and Carl Tchilling-Hiryan. Its mission was to sell coffee by mail. The brand is said to be a contraction of Tchilling's name with the Bohne, the German word for "bean."

Tchibo opened its first coffee shop in 1955. By 1958, the company's Gold Mocca brand was Germany's top-selling coffee. A long-running series of television ads helped sustain the brand's momentum though the 1960s. Around 1963, the company began establishing outlets in existing bakeries, the beginnings of its "shop-within-a-shop" concept.

Tchibo opened a new coffee roasting facility in Hamburg in 1964. Max Herz died the next year; management of the company remained in the family, led by his son, Günter Herz.

BRINGING NONFOOD ITEMS
INTO THE BUSINESS MODEL

Tchibo Café Service was established in 1972 to supply the office and food service market. (It would become an

COMPANY PERSPECTIVES

Established by Max Herz in 1949, the name Tchibo has stood for freshness and quality in the coffee market for over 50 years. The original mail-order coffee company has grown into a multinational enterprise, active in many more sectors than just traditional coffee retailing. Over the years, Tchibo has consistently expanded its range and number of sales channels. Its strong brands guarantee variety and quality worldwide. The Tchibo GmbH is a wholly-owned subsidiary of Tchibo Holding AG, which leads and manages the Tchibo Group's portfolio of company participations and stakeholdings.

independent subsidiary of Tchibo Holding AG in 1994.) The company was finding novel ways to connect with customers. It launched what would become a popular consumer goods program with a cookbook, which sold 250,000 copies within a week. Tchibo soon moved on to items such as watches and shirts.

Tchibo bought a minority holding in Beiersdorf AG, maker of Nivea skin care products, in 1977. The company diversified further in 1980 when a controlling interest in Reemtsma Cigarettenfabrik GmbH was acquired. The moves helped counter slowing domestic coffee sales.

According to Britain's *Financial Times,* the German coffee market contracted by a quarter in the early 1980s. At the time, Tchibo had 500 of its own shops and a presence in another 8,000 independent bakeries. Total revenues were roughly DEM 2.3 billion, with one-fifth of sales coming from the consumer goods program, which had expanded to sports equipment (even surfboards) and discounted electronics, much to the ire of certain specialist retailers and stereo manufacturers.

HOLDING COMPANY STRUCTURE IN 1988

Tchibo Frisch-Röst-Kaffee AG was renamed Tchibo Holding AG in 1988. The coffee business was transferred to the subsidiary Tchibo Frisch-Röst-Kaffee GmbH (later called Tchibo GmbH).

Tchibo International was formed in 1991 to take the brand to new countries. Tchibo soon had 600 coffee shops across Europe, including the former East Germany, where Tchibo promptly built a leading position following reunification of East and West. The first Russian

outlet opened in St. Petersburg in 1994. In addition to the shops, new roasting facilities were established in Hungary and Poland. In the Czech market, Tchibo began by contracting roasting to a local company (Balirny Jihlava) while supplying its own packaging equipment.

Tchibo's range of coffee products expanded notably around 1992. Previously focused on whole beans, it added vacuum-packed ground coffee, which proved instantly successful. So was its new instant coffee, sold under the Picco brand.

The marketing of non-food items was refined in the mid-1990s. Henceforth, the line-up of about two-dozen products would be changed every week, organized around themes such as "Beach" or "Office." The novelty kept customers coming back, while accelerating their purchasing decisions. An official told Britain's *In-Store* that demand for more products than the coffee shops could carry was what initially prompted the rotation of stock.

ACQUISITION STRATEGY LAUNCHED IN 1996

Tchibo launched an aggressive acquisition strategy around 1996. It acquired control of rival Eduscho coffee group in 1997. Eduscho brought with it a number of facilities in Eastern Europe.

Tchibo was also becoming an early adopter of the Internet as a sales channel for consumer goods as well as coffee. Within a few years, its site was established as Germany's second leading e-commerce destination after www.amazon.de.

After losing DEM 209 million at the unit in 1997, Tchibo closed 200 underperforming coffee shops to restore the coffee division to profitability. Parent company Tchibo Holdings AG ended the 1990s with sales of about DEM 19 billion (EUR 10 billion; $9 billion).

New sales territories breached in 2000 included England and Romania. The mail order catalog program was extended to Switzerland, followed two years later by the country's first Tchibo shops. The Netherlands was entered in 2004.

A weekly magazine was launched to support the consumer merchandise program in 2000. It had a circulation of about one million and featured general interest articles and a television schedule. According to the *European Retail Digest,* the company was soon counting more than 850 coffee shops and 48,000 "shop-in-shop" placements; a quarter of the latter included non-coffee merchandise as well.

A CHANGE OF LEADERSHIP IN 2001

Günter Herz resigned as Tchibo's chief executive in 2001 after 35 years at the helm. The move was said to be a result of differences in opinion with the rest of the family-controlled board over the company's future direction. Günter Herz and his sister Daniela left the company a couple of years later.

The board decided to ditch cigarettes in favor of cosmetics. Reemtsma, maker of the West, Davidoff, and Peter Stuyvesant brands, was sold to Imperial Tobacco Group Plc in 2002 for about $5 billion. Tchibo Holdings had increased its holding in Beiersdorf AG to 30 percent in 2001 and 49.9 percent by 2003. The next year, it attained a majority 50.46 percent interest.

Italian-style espresso drinks were becoming a worldwide phenomenon and Starbucks, the American popularizer of the trend, had its first stores in Germany by 2002. For its part, Tchibo was upgrading the Vienna roasting facility it had acquired with the Eduscho purchase.

In 2004, the coffee business, Tchibo Frisch-Röst-

Kaffee GmbH, was renamed Tchibo GmbH. Tchibo was active on many fronts. The French catalog *l'Homme Moderne* was acquired in the same year. Tchibo began selling O2 mobile phones in its stores through its Tchibo Mobilfunk joint venture. It was also bringing its store-within-a-store concept to Britain via a successful partnership with the Somerfield grocery chain.

An instant coffee packaging plant was opened in Russia in 2004. However, the next year Tchibo shut down its Budapest roasting facility to spare the expense of upgrading the facilities there.

Tchibo brought out a new home coffee machine in 2005. Called the Cafissimo, it was billed as a single machine capable of different brewing methods. An instant coffee called Dueccino was also introduced.

By this time, the company had more than 1,300 coffee shops. It claimed to be the largest purveyor of roasted coffee (by value) in several European countries, including Germany, Austria, Poland, the Czech Republic, and Hungary.

Tchibo's coffee and retail business reached EUR 4 billion in revenues in 2005. It had about 13,000 employees, two-thirds of them in Germany. The parent company Tchibo Holding AG, which included a majority interest in Beiersdorf, reported total revenues of EUR 8.8 billion and 30,000 employees.

Tchibo was expanding sales of lingerie, which it had offered in its coffee shops, into a new series of stand-alone lingerie boutiques in Germany. However, slower consumer spending in the country made international growth a priority, officials told *Frankfurter Allgemeine Zeitung*.

Frederick C. Ingram

PRINCIPAL COMPETITORS

Kraft Foods Inc.; Melitta Unternehmensgruppe Bentz KG; Nestle S.A.; Sara Lee Corporation.

FURTHER READING

Addy, Rod, "Giving Cabinet Approval: Tchibo's Non-Food Units Built Into 120 Somerfield Stores' Grocery Aisles Are Profiting Both Parties," *Grocer,* March 5, 2005, p. 36.

Braude, Jonathan, "Speculation High on Tchibo's Next Move," *Daily Deal (New York),* March 7, 2002.

Clausen, Sven, "Tchibo Chief Executive Quits," *Financial Times (London),* January 11, 2001, p. 28.

"Coffee Marriage: Tchibo and Eduscho Join Forces," *Tea & Coffee Trade Journal,* January 1, 1997, p. 68.

Davies, John, "A Storm in a Coffee Cup," *Financial Times (London),* December 1, 1983, p. 9.

Hosea, Maeve, "Kaffee Culture: Themed Stock and Espresso Are All in a Day's Work for Tchibo UK Managing Director David Haimes," *In-Store,* March 2004, pp. 18f.

Korner, Manfred, "Tchibo: A Wind of Change," *Tea & Coffee Trade Journal,* November 1, 1994, pp. 66f.

——, "Tea & Coffee in Germany: Old & New Cultures Thrive," *Tea & Coffee Trade Journal,* November 20, 2002, pp. 47ff.

Leuffen, Julia, "Tchibo to Boost Lingerie Business," *Financial Times (London),* October 14, 2005, p. 26.

McCabe, Jane, "Tchibo: Custom Roaster Shops Throughout Europe," *Tea & Coffee Trade Journal,* March 1, 1992, pp. 36f.

Mehta, Manik, "Eduscho and Tchibo Approach Vacuum-Packs," *Tea & Coffee Trade Journal,* September 1992, pp. 45f.

——, "Tchibo's Growth Fueled by Acquisitions: Profits Increase Despite Fierce Competition," *Tea & Coffee Trade Journal,* September 1, 1997, p. 40.

——, "Tchibo Ready to 'Play'," *Tea & Coffee Trade Journal,* September 1, 1995, pp. 62f.

Schubert, Siri, "Starbucks Meets The Sharper Image," *Business 2.0,* March 2006, p. 50.

"Tchibo Determined to Grow Abroad (Tchibo Sucht Sein Heil im Ausland)," *Frankfurter Allgemeine Zeitung,* May 23, 2006.

"Tchibo Earning Money Again with Its Coffee Shops (Tchibo Verdient mit Seinen Kaffeeladen Wieder Geld)," *Frankfurter Allgemeine Zeitung,* June 4, 1999, p. 20.

"Tchibo Shuts Down Coffee Roasting Facilities in Hungary," *Hungarian News Agency,* January 6, 2005.

"Tchibo to Take on Nestle in Espresso Machine Market," *AFX.COM,* February 7, 2005.

"Trademark Challenge," *East European Business Law,* April 1, 1994.

Zaharia, Silvia and Petra von Strombeck, "Key Success Factors of Tchibo's Multi-Channel Strategy in German Retailing," *European Retail Digest,* December 2002, p. 46.

Teekay Shipping Corporation

Bayside House
Bayside Executive Park
West Bay Street & Blake Road
PO Box AP-59212
Nassau,
Bahamas
Telephone: (242) 502-8820
Fax: (242) 502-8840
Web site: http://www.teekay.com

Public Company
Incorporated: 1973 as the Teekay Shipping Group
Employees: 5,500
Sales: $1.96 billion (2005)
Stock Exchanges: New York
Ticker Symbol: TK
NAIC: 483111 Deep Sea Freight Transportation; 483211 Inland Water Freight Transportation

■ ■ ■

Teekay Shipping Corporation (TK), with the world's largest and most modern fleet of mid-sized oil tankers, is a leading transporter of crude oil and petroleum products. Ten percent of the world's oil passes through TK's ships at some point. TK expanded its reach in the late 1990s through a number of strategic acquisitions and entered the liquefied natural gas (LNG) business in 2004 through an affiliate that was soon spun off. As of December 2005, TK's fleet consisted of 145 vessels (including 17 newbuildings on order) with a total cargo capacity of approximately 13.6 million tons of oil and 2.2 million cubic meters of liquefied natural gas. These ships provide transportation services to major oil companies, oil traders, and government agencies. Incorporated in the Marshall Islands and headquartered in the Bahamas, Teekay has principal operating offices in Vancouver and a presence in 14 countries around the world. Two trusts hold about 40 percent of Teekay shares.

GETTING INTO THE SHIPPING BUSINESS

Jens Torben Karlshoej's lifelong passion for the sea and ships probably began with visits to the harbor when he was a child in Denmark. Although he came from a farming family, he left the land and went to work for a small Danish shipping company. Then, in his early 20s, Karlshoej emigrated to the United States. During the 1960s and early 1970s he held a progression of increasingly responsible jobs with shipping companies in New York and Los Angeles.

In 1973 Karlshoej struck off on his own, founding the Teekay Shipping Group in New York, incorporating it in Liberia, and using his initials to give the company its name. His strategy was for the company to manage and operate a range of tankers, but to charter the vessels from independent ship owners, not to own them.

Major oil companies, whether private or state-owned, as well as independent ship owners, transported crude oil and other petroleum products under two types of contract: short-term contracts, including "spot charters," which were for a single voyage, or long-term "time charters." New York was one of the shipping centers where tanker chartering occurred, with brokers

COMPANY PERSPECTIVES

Energy powers industries, fuels transportation systems and improves the quality of our lives. Our customers face the challenge of moving oil and gas from where it is produced to where it is consumed. At Teekay, it is our job to ship that oil and gas anywhere in the world. It is our promise to provide our customers with a safe and reliable service. Teekay Shipping is committed to being an essential marine link in the global energy supply chain, serving the world's leading oil and gas companies. We connect our customers' upstream oil and gas production with their downstream refining and distribution, positioning us as the marine midstream company.

(and sometimes ship owners and charterers) working around the clock to transact business.

When the oil market collapsed, however, Karlshoej closed up his New York operation and moved to the West Coast. In 1975 he established an affiliated company, Palm Shipping Inc., which concentrated on chartering medium-sized tankers for Pacific routes. Tankers came in various sizes, for certain types of trips and cargoes. A charterer usually wanted the largest possible vessel for the cargo that would meet port and canal dimension restrictions for the route. Karlshoej chartered medium-sized tankers (75,000–115,000 deadweight tonnage), referred to in the industry as "aframax." These vessels typically made medium- and short-haul trades of less than 1,500 miles and carried crude oil or petroleum products. They were smaller than the Suezmax size of approximately 115,000 to 200,000 dwt used for long- and medium-haul crude oil trades and bigger than the Panamax vessels used to transport petroleum products in short- to medium-haul trades.

The West Coast was a tough market to break into. California refiners favored smaller ships to import crude oil and were hesitant to go with an unknown company. However, Karlshoej persuaded them to consider a larger tanker, and within a year he had time-chartered his first ship, *White Peony*, an aframax owned by Takebayashi of Japan. The ship was chartered to Palm Shipping at $1.35 dwt per month, which came to $3,800 a day. By 1977 Karlshoej was operating two Norwegian vessels as well. That year, Captain James Hood, a Scotsman who left school to go to sea at age 16, joined Karlshoej to run the operational side of the business. Palm Shipping's all-chartered fleet quickly grew from 16 to 18 ships.

In 1979 Karlshoej founded another affiliated organization, Viking Star Shipping, Inc., to buy and own tankers to provide a reliable source of high-quality vessels to support Palm's chartering activities. His timing was poor, as the market began to slide in 1980, and Viking Star made no purchases.

FROM CHARTERER TO OWNER

In 1985 Palm Shipping signed a deal with Japanese ship owner Sanko Steamship to charter 12 of Sanko's aframax vessels on a two-year timecharter. The transaction was a major coup for Karlshoej and happened because Sanko, which had been the most powerful aframax operator in the world, was shaky and Karlshoej was offering three months' hire up front. As Jim Hood remembered it in a 1996 *Seatrade Review* article, "It was not exactly a vibrant market. Taking those ships was at once an act of faith and the grasping of an opportunity." Because there was not enough business on the Pacific routes, Palm Shipping extended operations into the Atlantic. "You took what you could get and ran with it," Hood said. Later that year Karlshoej bought his first ship paying $3.9 million for the *Golden Gate Sun,* a ten-year-old aframax. The purchase made Viking Star Shipping a shipowner, finally. This time Karlshoej's timing was right, as the market began to turn.

The Sanko timecharter gave the Teekay Shipping Group controlled tonnage and credibility. In an improving market, it was suddenly a big player. Shell Oil saw Teekay's power as a threat and offered Sanko more money to charter ten of the tankers when Teekay's leases expired. Without even letting Karlshoej make a counterbid, Sanko agreed to the Shell offer.

Karlshoej was amazed, to say the least. After all, his financing flexibility had allowed Sanko to keep going some five months before it went bankrupt. Suddenly left out in the cold, Teekay could have gone under. Instead, Karlshoej vowed revenge and went on a building spree, ordering some 30 vessels over the next six years at a cost of $1.4 billion. "The newbuilding run was driven by Torben's conviction that massive aframax replacement would be needed and that newbuilding prices would not come down," Hood told *Seatrade Review.* Karlshoej bet the company on that vision, ordering ships first from Hyundai in South Korea and then from a variety of yards, including 3 Maj in Yugoslavia and Imabari and Onomichi in Japan. The Onomichi yard created a design to Karlshoej's specifications, the 100,000 dwt Onomax, which would become the backbone of Karlshoej's fleet. The first of these vessels, the *Palm Star Orchid,* was delivered in 1989. For the fiscal year that ended in April 1989, the Teekay group had net income of $54.7 million on revenue of $200.9 million.

```
┌─────────────────────────────────────────────────┐
│                                                   │
│              KEY DATES                            │
│                   ■                               │
│ ─────────────────────────────────────────────    │
│                                                   │
│ 1973:  Torben Karlshoej forms Teekay Shipping     │
│         Group (TK) using chartered tankers.       │
│ 1975:  Karlshoej forms Palm Shipping Inc. to      │
│         charter mid-size tankers in the Pacific.  │
│ 1977:  Captain James Hood heads operations as     │
│         chartered fleet reaches 18 ships.         │
│ 1979:  Karlshoej forms Viking Star Shipping,      │
│         Inc., to buy tankers.                     │
│ 1985:  Palm Shipping charters a dozen tankers,    │
│         expands to Atlantic; Karlshoej buys       │
│         first ship, the Golden Gate Sun.          │
│ 1989:  Palm Star Orchid is first of 30 vessels    │
│         delivered in six-year buying spree; group │
│         revenues are $200 million.                │
│ 1991:  Operational headquarters moved from        │
│         California to Vancouver.                   │
│ 1992:  Nagazaki Spirit lost in fatal collision;   │
│         Karlshoej passes away a month later.      │
│ 1993:  New CEO James Hood restructures company    │
│         in face of falling revenues, $1 billion   │
│         debt.                                      │
│ 1995:  TK goes public, raising $139 million.      │
│ 1998:  Bjorn Moller becomes CEO after James       │
│         Hood retires; Australian Tankerships      │
│         acquired.                                  │
│ 2001:  Ugland Nordic Shipping AS acquired.        │
│ 2003:  Navion AS acquired.                        │
│ 2004:  LNG market entered through acquisition of  │
│         Spain's Naviera F. Tapias S.A. while      │
│         total sales exceed $2 billion.            │
│ 2005:  LNG business spun off in successful        │
│         initial public offering.                  │
│                                                   │
└─────────────────────────────────────────────────┘
```

ON THE BRINK OF DISASTER: 1990–92

Company revenues continued to climb at the beginning of the decade, first as a result of the run up after the Gulf War and then as more ships were delivered or purchased secondhand and put into service. In 1991 Karlshoej moved his operations from Long Beach, California to Vancouver, British Columbia, in part to protect it from potential liabilities under the new U.S. oil spill legislation, but primarily to take advantage of new tax laws in Canada, where headquarters of foreign companies were not taxed on their worldwide business operations. However, even as he made the move, the situation was worsening.

Overcapacity in the tanker market caused freight

rates and newbuilding prices to sink. On top of that, the yen, in which the company had most of its contracts, strengthened. Although Viking Star's fleet had increased from an average of 18 vessels in 1989 to 46 in 1992, the Teekay group was heavily in debt, owing nearly $1 billion. During 1992 Karlshoej renegotiated the debt repayments and sold the company's 50 percent interest in Baltimar Overseas Limited. Then, in September 1992, one of Viking Star's tankers collided with a container ship, resulting in the deaths of 20 crew members. The ship, the *Nagazaki Spirit*, was declared a total loss. A month later, on October 3, Torben Karlshoej died in his sleep of an apparent heart attack, at age 51. In columns in trade papers and in letters to the editor, Karlshoej was honored for his integrity and vision.

Lloyd's Shipping Economist credited Karlshoej with leaving two legacies. "The first was a leading position in a competitive market, based upon a high standard of operations and modern vessels." The second was a towering debt.

Amid speculation about the future of the Teekay group, Jim Hood was named president and chief executive officer of Teekay Shipping Ltd., the parent company. Under a contingency plan Karlshoej set up shortly before his death, a four-member executive board took over the company's operations. The board included Karlshoej's elder brother, Axel; shipowner Thomas Hsu; shipbroker Shigeru Matsui; and Arthur Coady, Teekay's general counsel.

NEW LEADERSHIP

Hood replaced Karlshoej's flair with a more cautious, financially focused approach, but he faced severe challenges. In the fiscal year ending March 31, 1993, revenues dropped to $337.4 million from $416.1 million the year before. Even after Viking Star raised more than $37 million by selling vessels, the group had a loss of $47.5 million. The global recession finally had hit the tanker freight market, depressing rates, especially those for spot chartering, on which Teekay concentrated. A time charter equivalent rate of $19,270/day the year before dropped to $13,722/day. Added to this was the company's heavy dependence on yen-dominated debt, which resulted in a $77.9 million foreign exchange loss.

The company's structure was in keeping with Karlshoej's passion for privacy. Teekay reported its activities through Viking Star Shipping, Inc., its holding company. Teekay operated and managed the Viking Star–owned fleet, while Palm Shipping Inc. handled chartering activities. Each vessel was owned by a separate Teekay subsidiary, as was common in the industry, which was built with commercial bank mortgages to one-ship companies. Teekay also owned 50 percent of Viking Consolidated Shipping Corp., which owned three ships on long-term charter to a big Japanese company.

Under Hood, Palm became a subsidiary of Viking Star, and the company restructured. Ultimate ownership rested in two trusts set up by Karlshoej before he died. Cirrus Trust owned 100 percent of Viking Star's common stock and JTK Trust held 100 percent of the redeemable preferred stock. The company's advisory board oversaw the trusts, the ultimate beneficiaries of which were charitable organizations.

In the year after Hood become president, Viking Star sold six ships, postponed building of two others, renegotiated some of its debt, refinanced 15 of its vessels, and, in a significant move for this very private company, privately placed $175 million in notes backed by its ships. These measures more than doubled the company's liquidity by early 1994, but it still faced long-term debt of more than $900 million.

To raise money, the Teekay group announced in March that it would take its ship owning company, Viking Star, public, issuing 13.5 million shares, about 27 percent of the company. Hoping to raise $250 million, the company planned to use the proceeds to build replacements for its older vessels and to repay some of its debt. Viking Star's prospectus eased speculation about the company's liquidity. The low-profile company reported net income of $4.3 million for the nine months ending January 31, 1994, on revenues of $264.2 million. Within a month, however, the company postponed the offering, when share prices dropped ten percent as interest rates started to rise.

A SINGLE, PUBLIC COMPANY IN 1995

By July 1995, the Teekay group was ready to go ahead with a public offering, though on different terms. To begin with, the shares were no longer for Viking Star Shipping, Inc. In March, Hood restructured the group, merging the ship owning and ship management companies into a single entity. Viking Star acquired Teekay Shipping Ltd. and then reverted to the group name, Teekay Shipping Corporation. In a July 1995 article, *Lloyd's List* speculated that the change was due to market criticism about the earlier plan to leave the management of the fleet in private hands. Teekay issued fewer shares (6.9 million) at a higher price of $21.50 a share and raised $138.7 million. The bulk of the proceeds was used to pay down debt from previous newbuilding and Hood's more recent purchases of secondhand vessels. The company also sold its older ships, including the *Golden Gate Sun,* the first ship Karlshoej had bought.

Taking the company public appeared to mark the turning point for Teekay. Within a year a study by U.S. investment bank Lazard Freres reported that Teekay "was well positioned to benefit from better conditions projected for the aframax sector over the next three years." Those conditions included the strong growth in oil imports to Asia, the potential market in China, and the firming of the oil industry cycle.

According to *Lloyd's Shipping Economist,* the Teekay group had four operational strengths: fleet age, vessel uniformity, regional targeting, and in-house servicing. Because of its remarkable ship building program, the company had a youthful fleet, with an average age of under eight years during the last half of the decade. This compared with an average age of more than 13 years for the world oil tanker fleet and more than 12 years for the world aframax tanker fleet. Teekay believed that its modern fleet gave it a significant advantage, with higher fuel efficiency and lower operating costs, important considerations in an industry with increasingly stringent operating and safety standards. The large fleet also was fairly homogeneous in size, with many vessels being identical sister ships. That uniformity made it possible for Teekay to substitute vessels, giving it greater flexibility in accommodating changes on short notice.

The company had targeted the Indo-Pacific basin when it moved to the West Coast in 1975 and developed a significant presence and long-term relationships in an area that underwent explosive and sustained economic growth. That region, with the Red Sea on one border and the west coast of the United States on the other, encompassed the Arabian Gulf, Indonesia, and Australia—three major oil exporting regions—and the company derived approximately 90 percent of total revenues from its operations there.

That regional concentration contributed to the final operational plus, Teekay's ability to meet its needs inhouse. Through its wholly owned subsidiaries, the company was able to operate independently, providing all of the operations, ship maintenance, crewing, technical support, shipyard supervision, insurance, and financial management services required to support its fleet.

For example, the company recruited staff through its offices in Glasgow, Manila, Sydney, and Mumbai and used two specially configured tankers to train the 24 to 29 crew members needed for each of its vessels. It also operated a cadet program to develop future senior officers and provided additional training for newly hired seamen and junior officers at its training facilities in the Philippines. The company budgeted about $1 million to educate crews to Teekay's standards, two to three times as much as the competition spent. "Cost is not the only thing to consider. We need quality people. You can't compromise on ship safety," the manager of technical training told *LSM* in a 1994 article.

ENTERING THE FPSO MARKET IN 1997

Aframax freight rates were historically high as the new year began, with owners averaging $25,226 per day, according to *Fairplay.* This resulted from the growing importance of short-haul crude, and Teekay's net income rose 46 percent to $42.6 million for the fiscal year. Teekay claimed its fleet utilization was almost 70 percent, due to the availability of back haul cargoes from the West Coast. Recognizing the high risk involved in its spot trades strategy, Teekay began exploring the possibility of converting some of its tankers for the floating production, storage, and off-loading (FPSO) market. Chief operating officer Bjorn Moller told the company's annual meeting, "During the past year we have stepped up our efforts to develop new projects where we can lever our strengths into related business opportunities, an example being offshore marine."

At the beginning of 1998, Teekay announced an eight-year contract to provide a FPSO vessel to Apache Energy Ltd. and the acquisition of Australian Tankerships Pty. Ltd., a shipping subsidiary of Australian Petroleum Pty. Ltd. which brought with it the servicing of Caltex Petroleum's oil transportation requirements. In March, Jim Hood retired as president and CEO, replaced by Bjorn Moller. Moller, who came to the company in 1985, had been chief operating officer since 1997. Shortly after that, the company announced plans to order at least two new aframax tankers and to sell seven million shares of common stock.

During the 1990s Teekay Shipping survived near disaster by its careful financial policies, reputation for safety, and quality customer service. It changed from a highly secretive, wholly private company to a popular public corporation, reorganizing from a group of affiliated companies into a single entity. Although economic problems in Asia and 94 aframax vessels under construction might cause concern in the next few years, Teekay appeared well positioned to withstand a period of reduced rates.

TK expanded its reach in the late 1990s through a number of strategic acquisitions. Bona Shipholding was acquired in 1999, bringing TK into the Norwegian market for the first time.

ENTERING THE SHUTTLE TANKER MARKET IN 2001

TK began offering shuttle tankers in 2001 when it acquired a 56 percent interest in Norway's Ugland Nordic Shipping AS. The company was also forming a ship management joint venture with BHP Billiton.

Revenues plunged to $783 million in 2002; net income of $53 million was but a sixth of that in 2001. The year 2003 was a watershed for the company. Buoyed by acquisitions and recovery in the energy industry, TK's revenues doubled in 2003 to $1.6 billion and net income of $177 million was more than three times the previous year's figure.

After a couple of quiet years TK had bolstered its shuttle presence with the April 2003 acquisition of Norway's Navion AS. Navion's shuttle fleet included 27 vessels, eight of them owned. These were later combined with UNS's fleet into the Teekay Navion Shuttle Tankers business unit.

TK entered the market for transporting liquefied natural gas (LNG) through the $1 billion April 2004 acquisition of Naviera F. Tapias S.A. This unit was renamed Teekay Shipping Spain S.L. The LNG market required specialized vessels and allowed for fees of up to three times that of conventional oil tankers. TK Spain was also one of the leading suppliers of petroleum shipping in the country.

At the same time, the oil industry was clearly in full swing. An insatiable appetite for oil in fast-burning economies such as China and India was increasing the demand for TK's services to unprecedented levels. Its rates were reaching record highs, more than $100,000 in some instances, Moller told *Investor's Business Daily* (average rates were closer to $50,000).

TK's fleet had tripled in a few years to nearly 160 ships. Most were the double-hulled variety. The older, single-hulled type was being phased out over concerns about spills. *Investor's Business Daily* noted this resulted in huge backlogs among shipbuilders, and made TK's available spot fleet all the more attractive.

TK stepped up its in-chartering of vessels from other tanker operators when the cost of new vessels began to rise around the end of 2004 due to the increase in tanker rates. Having ordered earlier than its competitors, it had plenty of new ships under construction—$1 billion worth, Moller told the *Wall Street Transcript* in March 2005.

TK's liquefied natural gas business, Teekay LNG Partners L.P., was spun off in 2005. Its successful initial public offering raised $132 million. Federal tax law had been changed to allow mutual funds to invest Teekay LNG's type of corporate structure, which was a master limited partnerships.

Total sales slipped about 10 percent to just under $2 billion in 2005, and net income fell 25 percent during the year to $571 million. TK had more than 5,000 employees and was continuing to grow. In 2006, the company was planning a new joint venture with a unit of Petroleum Geo-Services ASA to expand its FPSO business.

While there appeared no slowdown in sight in the world's energy demands, TK was prepared in case of a market downturn, Moller told the *Wall Street Transcript.* Its contracts from its fixed business had grown to the extent that they could carry the company even if the spot market dried up.

Ellen D. Wernick
Updated, Frederick C. Ingram

PRINCIPAL SUBSIDIARIES

Navion Offshore Loading AS (Norway); Navion Shipping Ltd. (Marshall Islands); Norsk Teekay AS (Norway); Norsk Teekay Holdings Ltd. (Marshall Islands); Single Ship Companies (Australia); Single Ship Companies (Spain); Single Ship Limited Liability Companies (Marshall Islands); Teekay Chartering Limited (Marshall Islands); Teekay Lightering Services LLC (Marshall Islands); Teekay LNG Partners LP (Marshall Islands; 68%); Teekay Marine Services AS (Norway); Teekay Navion Offshore Loading Pte Ltd. (Singapore); Teekay Nordic Holdings Inc. (Marshall Islands); Teekay Norway AS; Teekay Shipping (Canada) Ltd.; Teekay Shipping Ltd.; Teekay Shipping Spain SL; Ugland Nordic Shipping AS (Norway).

PRINCIPAL OPERATING UNITS

Teekay Tanker Services; Teekay Navion Shuttle Tankers; Teekay Gas & Offshore; Teekay Marine Services.

PRINCIPAL COMPETITORS

Aframax International Pool; General Maritime Corporation; Knutsen OAS Shipping AS; Malaysian International Shipping Corporation.

FURTHER READING

Bate, Alison, "The Newcomers," *Westcoast Shipping,* May 1997, p. 20.

Brady, Joe, "Analyst Ranks Teekay Shipping as a Good Buy," *Tradewinds,* April 26, 1996, p. 8.

Brewer, James, "Teekay Looking to Branch Out into New Areas," *Lloyd's List,* September 4, 1997.

"Company Interview: Bjorn Moller, Teekay Shipping Corporation," *Wall Street Transcript,* March 7, 2005.

"Down … But Not Out," *Lloyd's Shipping Economist,* December 1994, p. 22.

Elliott, Alan R., "Teekay Shipping Co. Nassau, Bahamas; Demand for Fuel Gives Shipping Firm a Lift," *Investor's Business Daily,* October 26, 2004, p. A6.

Gray, Tony, "Teekay Orders Two Aframaxes," *Lloyd's List,* May 15, 1998.

———, "Teekay President Hood Hands Over Reins," *Lloyd's List,* February 6, 1998, p. 2.

"Lazard Freres Study Lifts Teekay Spirits," *Lloyd's List,* April 30, 1996.

Lillestolen, Trond, "Teekay Faces Challenge After Founder's Death," *Tradewinds,* October 9, 1992, p. 6.

"Mutual Funds Laud LNG Shipping IPO," *Investment Dealers' Digest,* May 9, 2005.

"Profile: Modest Man of the Moment," *Seatrade Review,* October 1996, p. 13.

Shinkle, Kirk, "New America Spotlight: Owner of Oil Tankers Rides the High Tide," *Investor's Business Daily,* March 4, 2004, p. A7.

Smith, Leigh, "It's Business as Before at Teekay," *Lloyd's List,* October 19, 1992.

"Teekay Boss Fondly Recalls His Roots as an Ordinary Seafarer," *Europe Intelligence Wire/Lloyd's List,* March 15, 2005.

"Teekay Builds on Founder's Legacy," *LSM,* December 1994, p. 63.

"Teekay Prospers Again," *Fairplay,* February 6, 1997, p. 18.

"Teekay Puts Money Where Its Mouth Is," *Tradewinds,* March 4, 1994, p. 1.

"Teekay Sets Offer Price," *Lloyd's List,* July 21, 1995.

"Teekay Share Issue Capital Tagged for New Aframaxes," *Tradewinds,* March 31, 1994, p. 7.

"Teekay Shipping Acquires Australian Tanker Operation," *Worldwide Energy,* January 1998.

"Teekay Shipping Corp Outlook Revised to Positive by S&P," *Business Wire,* April 16, 1998.

"Written-Down Single Hull Tankers Are Not for Sale, Declares Teekay," *Europe Intelligence Wire,* December 12, 2003.

Tootsie Roll Industries, Inc.

———— ■ ————

7401 South Cicero Avenue
Chicago, Illinois 60629
U.S.A.
Telephone: (773) 838-3400
Fax: (773) 838-3564
Web site: http://www.tootsie.com

Public Company
Incorporated: 1922 as Sweets Company of America
Employees: 2,200
Sales: $487.7 million (2005)
Stock Exchanges: New York
Ticker Symbol: TR
NAIC: 311330 Confectionery Manufacturing from Purchased Chocolate

■ ■ ■

Tootsie Roll Industries, Inc., is one of the largest candy companies in the United States, with headquarters in Chicago and operations in Illinois; Massachusetts; Tennessee; Wisconsin; Mexico City, Mexico; and Concord, Ontario. Best known for producing the candies that bear the company name—the chewy, chocolate cylinders in the distinctive brown, white, and red wrappers—the company has manufactured and sold confectionery products for more than 100 years. In addition to the famous Tootsie Roll, the company manufactures lollipops and hard candy under the brand names Tootsie Roll Pops, Caramel Apple Pops, Charms, Blow Pops, and Blue Razz, as well as Mason Dots, Zip-A-Dee-Doo-Da-Pops, and chocolate covered cherries under the Cel-

la's trademark. In 2004, the company made the largest acquisition in its history, integrating Concord Confections of Toronto, Canada, a market leader in the bubble gum category, and thereby gained ownership of the Dubble Bubble brand and Razzles, Cry Baby, and Nik-L-Nip candies.

EARLY HISTORY

The genesis of the company that has been a familiar part of the American cultural landscape for nearly a century can be traced to the Brooklyn kitchen of a newly arrived immigrant from Austria, Leo Hirshfield. In 1896, after having already developed such successful products as Bromangelon, a jelling powder that would later serve as the prototype for modern day gelatins, Hirshfield concocted a thick, chewy chocolate mixture, which he divided into bite-size rolls, wrapping each piece with paper to keep it clean and sanitary. The hand wrapping—believed to be an industry first—enabled Hirshfield's product, named "Tootsie Roll" after his daughter Clara "Tootsie" Hirshfield, to stand out among the competitor's candy-counter offerings, which were sold by the scoop out of large barrels or jars. The new penny candy was an instant success with the children in Hirshfield's Brooklyn neighborhood. He soon realized that he would need more capital to promote and expand his candy business to meet the growing demand. To that end, he merged his operation with a local candy manufacturer, Stern & Staalberg, just a year later. Sales continued to boom, and by 1922 the company, renamed Sweets Company of America, was listed on the New York Stock Exchange.

The Great Depression put a temporary halt to the

COMPANY PERSPECTIVES

We believe that the differences among companies are attributable to the caliber of their people, and therefore we strive to attract and retain superior people for each job. We believe that an open family atmosphere at work combined with professional management fosters cooperation and enables each individual to maximize his or her contribution to the company and realize the corresponding rewards. We do not jeopardize long-term growth for immediate, short-term results. We maintain a conservative financial posture in the deployment and management of our assets. We run a trim operation and continually strive to eliminate waste, minimize cost and implement performance improvements. We invest in the latest and most productive equipment to deliver the best quality product to our customers at the lowest cost. We seek to outsource functions where appropriate and to vertically integrate operations where it is financially advantageous to do so. We view our well known brands as prized assets to be aggressively advertised and promoted to each new generation of consumers. We conduct business with the highest ethical standards and integrity.

remarkable growth of the young company. It was during this period, though, that William Rubin, a box manufacturer whose family would control Tootsie Roll for the better part of the century, quietly began purchasing shares in the Sweets Company of America. As the nation's economy improved, Tootsie Roll began to receive more orders; by 1938, the company was ready to expand again, opening up a modern, 120,000-square-foot facility in Hoboken, New Jersey. With the help of such innovations as the conveyor belt, which ushered in the era of mass production, the company again enlarged its operating facilities, adding 40,000 square feet to the plant in 1941.

While the World War II economy forced many candy companies to suspend production, it proved quite a boon for Tootsie Roll. Highly valued for its "quick energy" properties and its ability to stay fresh for long periods of time, Tootsie Rolls were included in G.I. rations. While the company's involvement in the war effort, to be sure, resulted in gains on its balance sheet, it also contributed largely to the company's enduring status as an American icon. Frederick Arnold, in his

autobiography of his days as a World War II fighter pilot, *Doorknob Five Two*, told, for instance, how he carried Tootsie Rolls with him on every mission, rewarding himself with a segment after each completed stage. This ritual proved a lifesaver when his plane was shot down over the Sahara; stranded in a stone quarry for three days, he sustained his energy with his Tootsie Rolls, and after he was taken in by a native tribe who shared their raw dog meat with him, he returned the favor by giving them a Tootsie Roll segment and a cigarette.

POSTWAR EXPANSION

With the postwar boom in the U.S. economy and the increased availability of raw materials such as sugar and cocoa, Tootsie Roll was able to take full advantage of the competitive edge it had gained. Under the direction of William Rubin—who by 1948 had worked his way up to the post of company president—Tootsie Roll continued to expand. With Rubin's appointment came a stronger focus on the marketing and advertising efforts of the company. In 1950, he came up with a *Life* magazine ad that became a rich part of company lore; surrounded by the words "Sweet!, Popular! And Wholesome!" was pictured a beaming 18-year-old woman who embodied those adjectives, Rubin's daughter and future company president, Ellen Gordon. In the 1950s, while continuing to advertise in magazines, newspapers, and on the radio, the company also put some of its advertising dollars into the fledgling medium of television, becoming the first regular advertiser on classic children's programs such as the *Howdy Doody Show* and the *Mickey Mouse Club*.

Under Rubin's leadership, the company experienced 15 consecutive years of record growth and opened up a second operating plant in Los Angeles to accommodate the ever increasing demand of its customers. In 1962, Melvin Gordon took over chief executive duties, and the company continued along this pattern of growth, with net earnings nearly tripling during the first six years of the decade. In 1966, the company changed its name to Tootsie Roll Industries, Inc., and opened a large midwestern plant in Chicago's South Side, which would later become company headquarters. By 1970, both the Hoboken and Los Angeles operations had been consolidated in Chicago to facilitate both distribution and production. From this more central location, goods could be shipped more efficiently throughout the United States, and such fundamental commodities as corn syrup, a product of the midwestern corn refineries, could be more easily obtained. Starting in the late 1960s, the company also began exploring foreign markets, establishing a subsidiary in Mexico, where the candy became known as "Tutsi." Encouraged by its success

---

KEY DATES

1896: Austrian immigrant Leo Hirshfield invents the Tootsie Roll.

1917: The name of the company is changed to Sweets Company of America; the company begins to advertise nationally.

1922: Sweets Company of America is registered with the New York Stock Exchange.

1931: The Tootsie Pop is invented.

1938: Sweets Company moves from New York City to a larger plant in Hoboken with conveyor belt systems for mass production.

1942: The candy is included in World War II rations to give troops "quick energy."

1966: The company's name is changed to Tootsie Roll Industries, Inc.

1968: Tootsie Roll expands operations to include the Philippines and other areas of the Far East.

1978: Ellen Gordon is named president of Tootsie Roll Industries, Inc.

1985: Company acquires chocolate covered cherry manufacturer Cella's Confections.

1988: Tootsie Roll acquires the Charms Company and becomes the world's largest lollipop producer.

1993: The company acquires brands from Warner-Lambert Company, including Junior Mints, Sugar Daddy, Sugar Babies, and Charleston Chew.

2000: O'TEC Industries and Andes Candies join Tootsie Roll and production of Fluffy Stuff Cotton Candy begins.

2004: Tootsie Roll acquires Dubble Bubble bubble gum producer Concord Confections of Toronto, Canada.

---

south of the border, Tootsie Roll, after negotiating a licensing agreement in the Philippines in 1969, branched into Canada in 1971.

Tootsie Roll also looked towards acquisitions as a means of expanding. In 1972, the company purchased the Mason and Bonomo division of the Candy Corporation of America, adding such established brand names as Mason Dots, Mason Licorice Crows, and Mason Mints, as well as Bonomo Turkish Taffy and Bonomo Sour Balls, to its repertoire. The decade was not without its

hardships, though. In 1974, a 600 percent increase in sugar prices, combined with a similar rise in cocoa prices, forced the company to reexamine the size and price of some of its products. "We had to take a hard look at things," Ellen Gordon—Melvin's wife and, at the time, a company director—explained in a *Chicago Tribune* article, noting that "we had to make some pieces smaller and increased the price of other items, but that was true of the entire industry." While Nestlé raised its prices that year, Hershey reduced the size of its chocolate bars.

Having proven her business savvy in her ten years with the company, serving as a director responsible for managing outside investments and the pension fund, Ellen Gordon joined her husband at the top of the management team, taking over as president in 1978. In 2006, the married team of Chairman and CEO Melvin Gordon and President and COO Ellen Gordon controlled 80 percent of the company's voting power. After guiding the company through the cocoa-sugar crisis, they were faced with a challenge that would again test their management skills: the Tylenol crisis of 1982. At the outset of that year's Halloween candy-buying season, traditionally the company's most profitable period, seven Chicago area people died after taking Extra Strength Tylenol capsules, causing many parents throughout the country to worry that their children's trick-or-treat candy might be poisoned. While sales for the candy industry as a whole suffered in the wake of the Tylenol scare, Tootsie Roll—already known for its public service announcements to the media to promote safe Halloween candy giving—recorded a slight increase in sales, and, just two years later, sales jumped almost 20 percent. The Gordons, in a 1985 *Chicago Tribune* article, cited two primary factors behind the rebounding sales figures: first, an increase in distribution through the sale of more products in stores that already carried the Tootsie Roll line and the introduction of products in stores that did not; and second, the development of new products, such as the "foot of Tootsie," a larger version of the original Tootsie Roll. Halloween would remain the largest selling period and major focus of marketing efforts.

During the 1980s, Tootsie Roll strengthened its position in the candy market through key acquisitions. In 1985, the company purchased Cella's Confections, Inc., a New York–based manufacturer of chocolate-covered cherries, putting "Tootsie squarely into an adult market," according to the *Chicago Tribune* writer Gormon, by adding "changemakers"—the small, foil-wrapped candies often offered at check-out counters—to their product line. Three years later, the company invested another $65 million on the acquisition of the Charms Company, a purchase which enabled Tootsie Roll to gain a virtual lock on the lollipop market. Such additions, according to Pat Magee of *Candy Industry,* were successful due to the Gordons' focus on acquiring companies "that will fit well into their own philosophy of candy making, their own marketing methodology." Magee noted that the company added "snap and pizzazz to the companies that they buy," primarily by "upgrade-[ing] the packaging." Also during this time, Ellen Gordon invested $10 million in a manufacturing modernization program and a new, sophisticated computer system was installed.

As the company moved into the late 1980s and early 1990s, "Tootsie on Roll," became a familiar phrase within business circles, aptly describing the company's continued growth in spite of the recessionary environment. Net sales rose more than 80 percent between 1987 and 1990, while net profits increased 75 percent during the same period. As Malcolm Berko stated in an *Akron Beacon Journal* column, the company appeared "nearly impervious to economic cycles." Berko noted that "since 1979, Tootsie Roll's dividends have increased three-fold, sales have tripled, book value has jumped five-fold, net profit margins have doubled while sales sweetened from $60 million to $220 million" in 1991.

A primary factor behind the success of Tootsie Roll was undoubtedly the distinctive quality of its products. While customers were inundated with the multitude of shapes, sizes, and colors of the various chocolate bars and other sweets offered in the candy aisle, the trademark packaging of Tootsie Roll products stood as something of an American classic. That the company's products achieved the status of a "national institution" was due in no small part to the creativity of its television advertising. One especially successful commercial initiated in the 1970s featured a young boy asking a venerable Mr. Owl, "How many licks does it take to get to the center of a Tootsie Pop?" After taking three licks, Mr. Owl bit into the candy and concluded that three licks was all it took. Tens of thousands of children, however, actually wrote the company with their own answers—usually between 800 to 2,000 licks, according to company reports. The ad was still prompting responses in the 1990s, when two American soldiers, stationed in the Middle East during Operations Desert Shield and Desert Storm, concluded that it took a little over 1,600 licks to reach the Tootsie Roll center.

Noting that the company was a mainstay on *Forbes'* honor roll of small companies and *CFO* magazine's list of America's strongest companies, analysts pointed to Tootsie Roll's efficient style of management. "People ask us how we can compete against the giant candy corporations," stated Melvin Gordon in an interview with *Midway* reporter Jack Klobucar. Gordon explained, "we wonder how they can compete against us. We can make

decisions on the spot; we have hands-on management that's impossible in most billion-dollar companies." One of the strategies behind the Gordons' successful company was their hands-on, "vertical" style of management. As Melvin Gordon explained in an interview with *Compass Readings'* Jane Ammeson, "We try to be vertical wherever we can. We have our own sugar refinery, probably the only candy manufacturer in the world with its own. We have our own printing press and rebuild our own machinery in-house. We bought our own advertising agency. We even make the sticks for the Tootsie Roll Pops." By maintaining control over these services, Midway's Klobucar observed, "they not only reduce operating costs but also reinforce their independence—a commodity almost as precious as chocolate."

Many analysts expected Tootsie Roll to continue its consistent pattern of growth through the 1990s, based on the company's plans for further acquisitions and more foreign expansion. In 1993, the company obtained Warner-Lambert's chocolate and caramel brands—Junior Mints, Charleston Chew, Pom Poms, Sugar Babies and Sugar Daddy's—for an estimated $81 million. The new brands "were a natural to join the Tootsie family," Ellen Gordon told *Snack Food's* Wendy Kimbrell. "We have, while keeping the nostalgia and general look of the products, designed new packaging for the some of the Warner-Lambert products, so they fit better with our existing line," Gordon noted. Analysts regarded the strategy as successful: sales from the new brands contributed to the company's 6 percent increase in total sales for 1993. Moreover, Tootsie Roll's record sales figures for the first nine months of 1994 were achieved principally as a result of the Warner-Lambert brands.

With the 1993 passage of the North American Free Trade Agreement (NAFTA), which promised to relax trade restrictions between the United States and its neighboring countries of Canada and Mexico, Tootsie Roll was expected to place more emphasis on its operations to the north and south. In an interview for Snack Food magazine, Ellen Gordon predicted more intense competition as a result of NAFTA, commenting, "there's no doubt about it—Mexican candies will come into the U.S. and American candies will go down into Mexico." Nevertheless, as her husband was quick to add, Tootsie Roll had "unique products down there. Tutsi has been advertised in a major way ever since it started in Mexico in 1968 on Televisa, the nation's largest TV network."

TOOTSIE ROLLS ON INTO THE NEW MILLENNIUM

In 2000, Tootsie Roll acquired O'TEC Industries and began to manufacture Fluffy Stuff Cotton Candy as well as the thin chocolate mints known as Andes Candies. In

2004, the company made the largest acquisition in its history, integrating Concord Confections of Toronto, Canada, a market leader in the bubble gum category. Concord Confections' products were sold primarily under the Dubble Bubble brand but also included Razzles, Cry Baby, and Nik-L-Nip candies.

Sales in 2005 reached $488 million, an increase of $68 million over 2004, and a new record for the company. Highlights for the company included the continued integration of Concord Confections. Under the leadership of the married team of CEO and COO, the company's long-term strategy focused on state-of-the-art operations and low cost production of major product lines. Another key component of the company's strategy was the pursuit of growth through expanding distribution of existing brands and new product introductions. In August 2000, in an interview with *Candy Industry* Ellen Gordon said "We do see ourselves as innovators. Innovation is coming up with a new way of doing things—be it in technology, ingredients, or marketing. We are developing new ways of doing things all the time."

Tootsie, Charms, and Concord products are sold in Canada and over 75 other countries in Europe, Asia, and South and Central America. In 2005 the company was recognized by *Business Ethics* magazine as one of the 100 Best Corporate Citizens. Tootsie showed no signs of slowing down and continued to target for acquisition companies that would complement its product line.

Jason Gallman
Updated, Suzanne Clark York

PRINCIPAL SUBSIDIARIES

Andes Candies Inc.; Cambridge Brands Inc.; Charms LLC; Concord (GP) Inc.; Concord Brands, Ltd. (Canada); Concord Canada Holdings ULC; Concord Confections Holdings USA, Inc.; Concord Confections, Ltd. (Canada); Concord Partners LP; JT Company, Inc.; The Sweets Mix Company, Inc.; Tootsie Roll of Canada Ltd.; Tootsie Roll Worldwide Ltd; Tootsie Rolls–Latin America; TRI de Latinoamerica S.A. de C.V.; Tutsi S.A. de C.V. (Mexico); World Trade & Marketing Ltd.

PRINCIPAL COMPETITORS

The Hershey Company; Nestlé S.A.; Mars Inc.

FURTHER READING

Amire, Roula, "Innovation and Quality Keep Tootsie Roll on Top," *Candy Industry,* August 2000, p. 24.

Ammeson, Jane, "Tootsie Roll's Sweet Taste of Success," *Compass Readings,* December 1989, pp. 32–37.

Barko, Malcolm, "A Sweet Deal for Long-Term Investors," *Akron Beacon Journal,* August 4, 1991.

Bettner, Jill, "Sticky Business," *Forbes,* February 13, 1984, p. 112.

Blades, John, "Tootsie's on a Roll," *Chicago Tribune,* December 6, 1990.

Boas, Nancy, "How Sweet It Is," *Across the Board,* December 1984.

Driscoll, Mary, and Maile Hulihan, "America's Strongest Companies," *CFO,* April 1991, p. 17.

Gorman, John, "Tootsie Roll Turns Chocolate into Gold," *Chicago Tribune,* June 24, 1985, Sec. 4, p. 1.

Jargon, Julie, "Tootsie Rut," *Crain's Chicago Business,* December 20, 2004, p. 3.

Kichen, Steve, "The Best Small Company Honor Roll," *Forbes,* November 11, 1994, p. 264.

Kimbrell, Wendy, "Way to Grow," *Snack Food,* May 1994, p. 22.

Klobucar, Jack, "How Sweet It Is: Tootsie Roll Industries Posts Record Sales," *Midway,* May 1986, p. 24.

Lappen, Alyssa A., "Tootsie Rolling in Money," *Forbes,* January 21, 1991.

Magee, Patricia, "Ellen Gordon Reaches 'Top of the Mountain,'" *Candy Industry,* September 1985.

Marcial, Gene G., "A Nibble at Tootsie Roll," *Business Week,* April 18, 2005.

Merrion, Paul, "Tootsie Rolling Downhill," *Crain's Chicago Business,* May 23, 1994, p. 46.

———, "Tootsie Roll to Stay in the Family, Owners Say," *Crain's Chicago Business,* May 9, 2005, p. 4.

Moore, Anne, "Focus: Influential Families: Gordon," *Crain's Chicago Business,* October 17, 2005, p. 34.

Morris, Kathleen, "Tootsie Roll: Cashing In on Closet Candy Eating," *Financial World,* January 21, 1992, p. 16.

Ryan, Nancy, "Tootsie on a Roll in *Forbes* Magazine Survey," *Chicago Tribune,* October 29, 1991.

Tiffany, Susan, "Tootsie Roll Keeps Rolling in the Riches," *Candy Industry,* June 1993.

Wilkinson, Stephen, "The Practical Genius of Penny Candy," *Working Woman,* April 1989.

Transaction Systems
Architects, Inc.

224 South 108th Avenue
Omaha, Nebraska 68154-2684
U.S.A.
Telephone: (402) 334-5101
Fax: (402) 390-8077
Web site: http://www.tsainc.com

Public Company
Incorporated: 1975 as Applied Communications Inc.
Employees: 1,674
Sales: $313.24 million (2005)
Stock Exchanges: NASDAQ
Ticker Symbol: TSAI
NAIC: 511210 Software Publishers; 541511 Custom
    Computer   Programming   Services;   334113
    Computer   Terminal   Manufacturing;   334111
    Electronic Computer Manufacturing; 334119 Other
    Computer Peripheral Equipment Manufacturing

■■■

Transaction Systems Architects, Inc., (TSA) develops software for processing electronic payments. The company's customers include large banks and retailers. TSA's electronic funds transfer (EFT) software is used in transactions involving automated teller machines, point-of-sale terminals, wire transfers, home banking, and credit and debit cards. Originally developed around proprietary computers systems made by Tandem (later absorbed by Compaq and Hewlett-Packard), TSA has since embraced open standards. Diversification was achieved through acquisitions, giving the company greater market reach and positioning it in burgeoning markets, such as e-commerce. Annual revenues swelled during the expansion, rising from approximately $70 million in 1992 to nearly $300 million six years later. A falloff in Y2K-related business ensued, however, followed by a period of slow growth. Nevertheless, TSA has remained well positioned in the center of the global trend toward more electronic processing of payments. Two-thirds of the company's revenues are derived from outside the United States.

ORIGINS

TSA's corporate roots stretch to the origins of one of its subsidiaries, Nebraska-born Applied Communications Inc. Applied Communications was founded in 1975 by computer programmer James Cody and two colleagues. The entrepreneurs had developed electronic funds transfer software for banks, marking their entry into a nascent yet soon-to-burgeon industry. Point-of-sale (POS) systems that enabled card-based, electronic payments were introduced in the early 1980s to accommodate consumer preferences for using credit and debit cards instead of cash or checks. Prior to the development of automated POS systems, card-based transactions generally were processed manually, using paper-based systems to obtain authorization from card-issuing banks. As the volume of credit and debit card transactions increased, however, a more sophisticated method of authorization was needed. Card-issuing banks, with the backing of VISA and MasterCard, offered financial incentives to promote the development and use of POS-related technologies, which spawned the creation of electronic payment systems that improved accuracy,

COMPANY PERSPECTIVES

TSA's solutions are positioned at the heart of the growing electronic payments market. TSA's solutions are highly differentiated in large-scale, complex technology environments, and have been proven in most demanding environments. TSA licenses its solutions based on product features, transaction volume and term, and also sells complimentary services and product maintenance. As TSA's customers' systems grow, TSA benefits. With its leading market position and business model, TSA is uniquely positioned to benefit from the generational shift away from paper to electronic payments. TSA's customers process over 65 billion electronic payment transactions per year and growing. TSA's investment in technology, customer support and expertise help drive its strong customer retention, and ensure that TSA will be a long-term beneficiary of the shift from paper to pulse.

reduced costs, increased efficiency, and reduced credit card abuse and fraud. Cody and his partners were early developers in this field, entering when the technology was raw and the use of such technology was a relatively novel alternative, rather than obligatory, as electronic-based systems later would be. Although Applied Communications was marketing a product whose time was yet to come, the company did well early on, with its software making enough of an impression on bankers to overcome the less than reassuring appearance of Cody, who on one sales visit sold the company's software while wearing mismatched shoes.

By the time electronic-based systems had started to become commonplace, Applied Communications was prepared to take advantage of a market that had caught up to its pioneering technology. The company went public in 1983 to gain the financial resources to expand and began doing so aggressively, particularly overseas. Until 1982, Applied Communications had never made an effort to cultivate international business and, consequently, collected only a fraction of its revenues from foreign sales. Although the company had not made itself known to the global marketplace, overseas businesses had heard of Applied Communications. The company's marketing staff began receiving a growing number of unsolicited inquiries about its software in 1982, prompting an organized pursuit of overseas business and the establishment of an international distribu-

tion unit, ACI Ltd. (ACIL). Much of Applied Communications' growth during the decade was derived from the concerted, international effort to market its software for automated teller machines (ATMs) and POS systems, contributing to a more than sixfold increase in the company's workforce between 1982 and 1989. Applied Communications was awarded the President's "E" Award for excellence in exporting in 1987 and by 1989 was selling its software in 29 countries. By the end of the decade, international sales accounted for more than half of the company's revenue.

OWNERSHIP CHANGES

Midway through the company's decade-long expansion overseas, Applied Communications became the target of a much larger suitor. The demand for its technology had increased exponentially since the company's founding, repositioning the software developer from the fringe of the mainstream market to the center of attention. U S West was interested in Applied Communications' expertise, and it purchased the company in 1986. Life as a subsidiary of a much larger parent gave the company voluminous financial support, but freedom was the expense. U S West, not surprisingly, was pursuing its own objectives and enlisted the assistance of Applied Communications to achieve those objectives, directing the company to develop telephone company systems.

The redirection of Applied Communications' focus ran counter to the company's original focus, an alteration that a third company, Tandem Computers Inc., found disturbing. The reason for Tandem's anxiety, and the company's eventual intervention into the relationship between U S West and Applied Communications, hinged on one of the fundamental aspects of Applied Communications' success. Early in its corporate life, Applied Communications had allied itself to Tandem's technology, programming its software to run on the computer manufacturer's hardware, which was used by an overwhelming majority of banks. Under U S West's ownership, however, Applied Communications' focus had shifted, provoking Tandem to respond. "We didn't see [Applied Communications] flourishing under U S West ownership," explained a Tandem official, "so we decided to acquire them to protect our joint customer base." The acquisition, completed in 1991, gave Tandem control of Applied Communications and ACIL for slightly less than $60 million.

The change in ownership returned Applied Communications' focus to the banking industry. Virtually all of the company's software was designed to run exclusively on the computers made by its new parent company, but despite the strong synergy between the two companies, Tandem professed no desire to own Ap-

KEY DATES

1975: Applied Communications is formed to market electronic funds transfer (EFT) software.

1982: International distribution unit ACI Ltd. is formed.

1983: Applied Communications goes public.

1986: Phone giant U S West acquires Applied Communications.

1989: International sales account for more than half of revenue.

1991: Tandem Computers Inc. buys Applied Communications for about $60 million.

1993: Transaction Systems Architects, Inc., is formed to facilitate a management buyout of Applied Communications; U.S. Software is acquired.

1995: Transaction Systems Architects (TSA) goes public; the company begins an acquisition spree.

1998: TSA invests in smart cards and home banking.

2000: Business falls off suddenly as Y2K preparations end.

2005: S2 Systems is acquired; TSA is reorganized around the ACI Worldwide business unit.

2006: Electronic Payment Systems AG is acquired.

plied Communications on a long-term basis. By 1993, after two-and-a-half years of control, Tandem decided to sell Applied Communications, explaining that its subsidiary was sufficiently profitable to operate on its own. Under the terms of the agreement, Tandem sold Applied Communications and ACIL, which had moved to London in 1992, to a management-led group for $80 million.

EXPANSION FOLLOWING INDEPENDENCE IN 1993

Leading the group of senior executives who purchased Applied Communications was William E. Fisher, the individual who guided the company during its new-found independence. Fisher, who received his MBA from the University of Nebraska, had joined Applied Communications in 1987 and held a number of different titles, including president of financial systems, senior vice-president of software and services, executive vice-president, and chief operating officer. When Tandem bought the company from U S West in 1991, Fisher was named chairman and chief executive officer, the same offices to which he was appointed when a new company was formed to facilitate the management-led buyout from Tandem. Transaction Systems Architects, Inc., (TSA) was formed as ACI Holding, Inc., in November 1993 and the acquisition of Applied Communications and ACIL occurred the following month, completed on the last day of 1993.

During its last full year as a Tandem subsidiary, Applied Communications had generated more than $70 million in revenue, ranking it as the world's largest supplier of electronic funds transfer software programmed for Tandem computers. In the years ahead, however, the company's business would be far less dependent on the success of Tandem ATM and POS hardware. "As we look forward," Fisher said, "we know our future is open systems." Independence provided Fisher with the opportunity to develop software for other platforms, such as Microsoft Corp.'s NT operating system, as well as Unix and IBM operating systems. Although the company continued to regard its software partnership with Tandem as its mainstay business and continued to develop software for its longtime associate, the ability to diversify its product line to run on other vendors' computers opened numerous avenues for growth. It was Fisher's task to take advantage of these opportunities during the fast-paced growth of the middle and late 1990s.

After seven years of operating under the corporate umbrella of a parent company, TSA did not wait long to express its independence. Four days after the buyout from Tandem was completed, Fisher acquired U.S. Software Inc. (USSI), headquartered near Omaha, Nebraska, in Crater Lake, Iowa. Founded three years before TSA acquired it, USSI provided software solutions to the financial and payment card industries, developing its software products at a facility in Victoria, Texas. TSA's purchase of USSI signaled the beginning of an acquisition campaign that diversified TSA's product line and expertise beyond the capabilities of its core subsidiary, Applied Communications. The middle and late 1990s witnessed the rapid growth of electronic commerce around the globe, as card-based transactions proliferated and new areas of opportunities, such as home banking, emerged. To keep pace with technological advances surrounding it, TSA sought to accelerate its own technological development through the fastest means possible: by acquiring companies with expertise in emerging areas of growth. The company's motto was "it's an electronic world, we move the money," underscoring its intention to involve itself in as many as possible of the billions of card-based transactions that were completed annually.

Before TSA began to strategically position itself through acquisitions, the company filed for an initial public offering (IPO) in January 1995. The IPO of 2.75 million shares at $15 per share was completed the following month, giving the company the means to reduce its debt. Six months later, in August, TSA returned to Wall Street for additional cash from investors, completing a second sale of stock that netted the company $22 million. Fisher explained: "We had a strong IPO, and our underwriters thought we could have sold more shares. We decided to go back to the market in order to strengthen up our balance sheet a bit, as well as have some cash for acquisitions."

Financially invigorated after two stock offerings, the company turned its attention to the expanding markets and emerging industries in the "electronic world." Fisher was looking for acquisition candidates that could extend TSA's market reach and found one in late 1995. In October 1995 TSA acquired a German software firm named M.R. GmbH. Three more acquisitions—TXN Solution Integrators, Grapevine Systems, Inc., and Open Systems Solutions, Inc.—followed in 1996. By this point, more than 60 percent of the largest U.S. banks and nearly 25 percent of the 500 largest banks worldwide used software designed by TSA.

Revenues had more than doubled from the total generated under the auspices of Tandem, yet the majority of the company's business was derived from its BASE24 product line, programmed for Tandem computers. (In 1997 Tandem was acquired by Compaq Computer Corporation, which was itself acquired by Hewlett-Packard Co. five years later.) Applied Communications, responsible for the BASE24 software, still represented TSA's mainstay business, but the acquisitions were giving the company expertise in complementary and promising areas. One of these new market niches centered on "smart" cards, or plastic cards programmed with a particular monetary value that could be used at ATMs and elsewhere like a debit card. TSA established a name for itself in the smart card market with two acquisitions, the August 1998 purchase of Smart Card Integrators Ltd., a London-based technology developer for systems such as Modex and Visa Cash, and the November 1998 acquisition of Media Integration B.V., a Dutch smart card systems developer. Also in 1998, the company strengthened its presence in the market for home banking software, convinced that the practice of paying bills and transferring money from a consumer's home computer would develop into a widespread trend.

By the end of the 1990s, TSA stood as a strategically diversified, global company, marketing its products in 68 countries. For the immediate future, revenues were projected to increase 25 percent annually and earnings were expected to increase 35 percent. Based on this forecast, there was justifiable optimism for the company's success during the early 21st century, optimism expressed not only by TSA executives but also by stock analysts. "These guys don't get a lot of press," remarked one analyst in reference to TSA, "but they are a really well-positioned company." Despite rising revenues and earnings, however, the company's stock was not performing as well as some analysts believed it should, prompting several industry pundits to characterize TSA as a "sleeper" yet to be discovered by the investing public. "The company hasn't been given credit for the type of business it runs," explained an analyst at Lehman Brothers. Considering that the company was a direct beneficiary of lucrative trends in electronic commerce, the secrecy of its success appeared to be nearing its end.

REORGANIZING AFTER Y2K

Y2K conversions had been a major source of business as the company approached the year 2000. Unfortunately, there was a sudden falloff in sales after these preparations were completed. Revenues (as later restated) were about $300 million in 2000 and 2001, when the company posted a rare loss of $80 million.

TSA turned its attention to growing its e-commerce business, led by the InSession unit, although the volume of transactions completed through the Internet was still relatively low. MessagingDirect Ltd., a Canadian provider of software for presenting bills and financial statements, was acquired in October 2000 in an all-stock deal worth about $50 million.

Early in 2000, TSA was reorganized into six new business units: Consumer Banking; Corporate Banking e-Payments; Internet Infrastructure; Internet Banking; Electronic Commerce; and the new Health Claims Transaction Processing and Management unit. The aim was to make it easier to appropriate resources to lines with different needs; however, the grouping only lasted a few years. Consumer Banking remained by far the largest unit, accounting for 70 percent of revenues.

TSA continued to win important new banking clients, such as BB&T Co., which in 2003 chose TSA's new BASE24-es system, an open source product, for its nearly 2,000 ATMs in the Southeast. The company's existence was becoming complicated on the regulatory front, however. It restated three years of revenues during an SEC inquiry; faulty guidance from its former auditor, the defunct Arthur Anderson & Co., was blamed. The company's new chairman, Gregory Duman, resigned; he had been CFO at the time of the errors, which reportedly involved a few transactions with an electronic payments company in Utah.

Former Chairman and CEO Fisher had left the company in May 2001 after returning from retirement the previous year. Greg Derkacht became the company's next permanent chief executive in January 2002.

Revenues slipped slightly to $292 million in fiscal 2004. Although net income tripled to $46.7 million, Jana Partners L.L.C. was openly calling for a sale of the company. Jana was a hedge fund in San Francisco that held nearly 5 percent of TSA's shares and was notorious for strong-arming companies. Management refused to sell the company. Philip G. Heasley, formerly an executive with U.S. Bancorp and Bank One Corp., was hired as TSA's CEO in 2005 to help guide it through this situation.

S2 Systems Inc., a Plano, Texas–based company, was acquired for $35 million in the summer of 2005. Although only one-tenth the size of TSA, S2 brought with it a couple of large banks as well as a significant number of retail customers.

The company was reorganized along line and staff functions into a single operating unit in October 2005. IntraNet Worldwide and InSession Technologies were absorbed into the ACI Worldwide business unit, which had accounted for more than three-quarters of revenues in the previous 12 months.

The company was looking to grow internationally, in Latin America and especially Asia, Heasley told *American Banker*. It announced that it was buying Frankfurt, Germany's Electronic Payment Systems AG in May 2006 in a deal worth $36 million. The new acquisition led the market in a country that was said to have the third largest volume of electronic transactions in the world, behind the United States and the United Kingdom. It also had a fragmented banking industry ripe for third-party software sales, an analyst told *American Banker*. By this time, international sales accounted for two-thirds of TSA's revenues, which were $313 million in the fiscal year ended September 30, 2005 and were expected to rise to between $348 million and $360 million in fiscal 2006.

Jeffrey L. Covell
Updated, Frederick C. Ingram

PRINCIPAL SUBSIDIARIES

ACI Worldwide Inc.; InSession, Inc.; ACI Worldwide (Japan) K.K.; Applied Communications Inc. U.K. Holding Limited; IntraNet Worldwide, Inc.; Messaging-Direct Company (Canada).

PRINCIPAL DIVISIONS

Product; Americas; Europe, Middle East and Africa (EMEA); Asia/Pacific (A/P); Software as a Service.

PRINCIPAL OPERATING UNITS

ACI Worldwide.

PRINCIPAL COMPETITORS

eFunds Corporation; Fair Isaac Corporation; S1 Corporation.

FURTHER READING

Bills, Steve, "Heasley Gets His Chance in Hot Seat," *American Banker*, March 14, 2005, p. 1.

"Developer of ATM Technology Grows with New Products, Acquisitions," *Knight-Ridder/Tribune Business News*, February 24, 1998.

"Exporting Pays Off," *Business America*, July 3, 1989, p. 14.

Iida, Jeanne, "Tandem to Sell Software Unit to Its Senior Management," *American Banker*, November 16, 1993, p. 17.

Jennings, Robert, "Transaction Systems Architects Files for 2.75M-Share IPO to Retire Debt," *American Banker*, January 18, 1995, p. 19.

Jordon, Steve, "Founder Is Leaving As CEO of Omaha, Neb., Software Provider," *Omaha World-Herald*, May 3, 2001.

———, "Investors Punish Omaha, Neb., Software Firm After Accounting Disclosure," *Omaha World-Herald*, August 16, 2002.

———, "Omaha, Neb.–Based Software Firm Reports Questionable Accounting; Chief Resigns," *Omaha World-Herald*, August 15, 2002.

Larson, Virgil, "Acquisition to Boost TSA's 2006 Profits," *Omaha World-Herald*, July 1, 2005.

"Major Payment Systems Manufacturer Is in Play," *Electronic Payments Week*, March 1, 2005.

Marjanovic, Steven, "Payment Processor Drafts Former CEO to Stop Skid," *American Banker*, May 31, 2000, p. 14.

———, "A Software Sleeper May Awaken in '99," *American Banker*, December 7, 1998, p. 32.

McLean, Bethany, "Cashing In on Plastic," *Fortune*, November 25, 1996, p. 218.

Norris, Melinda, "Omaha, Neb., ATM Technology Firm to Buy Milwaukee ATM Services Company," *Knight-Ridder/Tribune Business News*, December 3, 1998.

Shim, Grace, "Omaha, Neb.–Based Financial Transaction Software Firm to Buy Canadian Firm," *Omaha World-Herald*, October 27, 2000.

"Tandem to Buy Rest of ACI," *Supermarket News*, December 6, 1993, p. 21.

Tracey, Brian, "Transaction Systems of Omaha, Neb., Acquires Two Companies," *Knight-Ridder/Tribune Business News*, September 3, 1998.

———, "Transaction Systems Raises $60M with Second Public Offering of Year," *American Banker*, August 14, 1995, p. 16.

"Transaction Systems Buying Intranet Inc.," *American Banker,* April 29, 1998, p. 15.

"Transaction Systems Closes on Dutch Deal," *American Banker,* December 4, 1998, p. 23.

"TSA Forms New Business Units," *EFT Report,* March 22, 2000.

"TSA Is Having Success with Software, Hopes for Same in SEC Investigation," *ATM & Debit News,* August 21, 2003, p. 1.

Wade, Will, "Software Vendor Has Deal to Enter Germany," *American Banker,* May 15, 2006, p. 17.

Refrigeration at its best.

Victory Refrigeration, Inc.

110 Woodcrest Road
Cherry Hill, New Jersey 08003
U.S.A.
Telephone: (856) 428-4200
Fax: (856) 428-7299
Web site: http://www.victory-refrig.com

Wholly Owned Subsidiary of Aga Foodservice Group plc
Founded: 1944
NAIC: 333415 Air-Conditioning and Warm Air Heating Equipment and Commercial and Industrial Refrigeration Equipment Manufacturing

∎∎∎

For more than half a century, Victory Refrigeration, Inc., a subsidiary of the United Kingdom's Aga Foodservice Group plc, has been manufacturing commercial refrigeration equipment for the food service industry. High-end products include blast chillers, both reach-ins and roll-ins, that are used to cool food as quickly as possible to prevent possible contamination; rapid thaw refrigerators; a wide range of regular, extra wide, and shallow depth refrigerators; a similar array of storage freezers; dual temperature refrigerators and freezers; undercounter refrigerators; a variety of display and merchandiser refrigerators; modular proofers for baked goods; and warming cabinets. Victory also offers its "Value Line" of equipment, including regular size refrigerators; refrigerators with clear front panels; compact undercounter refrigerators; refrigerators combined with sandwich, salad, pizza, and general food

preparation tables; merchandisers with glass doors; bottle coolers; and reach-in freezers. All told, Victory offers 1,800 different models, sold around the world through a network of distributors. The company maintains its headquarters in Cherry Hill, New Jersey, close to Philadelphia, Pennsylvania.

WORLD WAR II-ERA ROOTS

Victory was begun in 1944 in Philadelphia by a pair of sheet metal specialists named Ray Constantini and Tony D'Angelis. Like many companies at the time it drew its name from war-related words like "Allied" and "Victory." In fact, the business was very much part of the war effort. The metal shop served the Philadelphia Naval Shipyard, the country's first naval shipyard and one that reached its peak of activity during World War II, employing 40,000 people, while building more than 50 ships and repairing nearly 600 others. Constantini and D'Angelis had both been employed at the shipyard and now, working out of a garage, they supplied the Navy with a variety of fabricated stainless steel products, including sinks, worktables, and lockers.

When the war came to an end, work at the shipyard fell off dramatically, forcing Constantini and D'Angelis to seek out a new source of customers. They found it in Philadelphia's fast-growing foodservice industry. With the war at an end, the U.S. economy, after a brief recession, began to boom. Servicemen returned home, got married, moved to the new suburbs, and began to raise the Baby Boom generation. They also sought out entertainment as never before and that meant eating out. Not only did a large number of restaurants, diners,

COMPANY PERSPECTIVES

■

With a broad and flexible product line, exclusive features, unsurpassed quality, and excellent service, Victory Refrigeration has earned a reputation for "Refrigeration at its best."

and coffee shops open for business, pizza parlors proliferated and many of today's fast food restaurant chains began to take root. All of them required commercial refrigeration equipment, fashioned from stainless steel, and the Victory metal shop evolved into Victory Refrigeration to meet that growing need and became an industry pioneer. The business soon outgrew its space and in 1954 the company moved to the Philadelphia suburb of Plymouth Meeting, Pennsylvania, where it opened a 125,000-square-foot plant. Here, Victory continued to build a reputation as an innovator, introducing such features as self-closing doors, urethane foamed-in-place insulation, and top-mounted, "plug box" refrigeration systems.

Victory operated as an independent company until 1973 when it was acquired by McGraw-Edison Co. and folded into that corporation's group of foodservice equipment subsidiaries. The lineage of McGraw-Edison reached back to the great inventor Thomas Edison and his company, Thomas A. Edison Inc., manufacturer of office dictation machines and automated teaching equipment. In 1957 it was acquired by McGraw Electric Co., which had been established by Max McGraw who, as a teenager in Iowa around the turn of the century, was an electrical contractor. McGraw moved beyond wiring houses and hooking up door bells when he bought a Chicago toaster manufacturer in 1926 and formed McGraw Electric Co. to make appliances. The company grew through a series of acquisitions, including such divergent businesses as Edison and foodservice equipment companies. By the mid-1960s sales approached $500 million for McGraw-Edison, which was producing high voltage electrical equipment, components, and systems, as well as such appliances as toasters, air conditioners, blenders, clothes washers, and power drills. With Victory Refrigeration added to the fold, along with other acquisitions, McGraw-Edison was generating more than $1 billion in sales. Under McGraw-Edison, Victory, in 1977, expanded its product offering, introducing its line of food processing products. These included rapid thaw cabinets, blast chillers, and blast freezers.

McGraw-Edison was just one of several changes in ownership that Victory would experience in the final decades of the century. McGraw-Edison experienced an erosion in earnings in the 1970s and decided to exit its consumer businesses. At the end of the decade it took on considerable debt to acquire locomotive manufacturer Studebaker-Worthington. Then, in 1980, to help pay down its accumulated debt, McGraw-Edison divested its foodservice group, including Victory Refrigeration, selling it to Bastian International Holdings, a New York City-based company with a pair of subsidiaries: BIH Foodservice Inc. and Bastian-Blessing Foodservice Equipment Co. Victory would be part of the Bastian family for five years.

NEW JERSEY MOVE: 1989

In 1985 assets of the two subsidiaries were sold to Hussman Corp., a unit of IC Industries Inc., formerly known as Illinois Central Industries, the holding company for the Illinois Central Railroad, founded in 1962. With the rail industry struggling, the company diversified into a number of areas, including aerospace, real estate, and consumer goods such as Whitman Chocolates. To reflect its move away from the railroad industry and a new focus on consumer goods and services, the company changed its name to Whitman corporation in 1988. Hussman manufactured gas stoves and refrigeration equipment for the food service industry, making Victory a natural fit. While part of Hussman, Victory moved to Cherry Hill, New Jersey, when it opened a new 250,000-square-foot plant in 1989. By this time, however, Whitman was looking to sell Hussman's foodservice equipment assets, as well as other businesses, in order to focus on consumer products. Whitman attempted to sell Hussman assets to Japan's Sanyo Electric Co. Ltd. and other others, but, displeased with the offers generated, briefly pulled it off the block. Finally an acceptable offer of $62.5 million was received from Middleby Corp. in May 1989 and the business, including Victory, was sold.

Based in Morton Grove, Illinois, Middleby grew out of Middleby Marshall Oven Co., a company with a heritage that dated back to the 1800s when bakery supply company owner Joseph Middleby and engineer John Marshall got together and began making custom designed movable ovens. One hundred years later the company made a name for itself with its patented conveyor ovens that could bake pizzas in one-third the time as a conventional oven, making it the ideal choice for such pizza chains as Pizza Hut and Domino's. In the late 1980s the company looked to expand into other types of foodservice equipment, such as electric food mixers. By acquiring Hussman, Middleby picked up four business lines with recognizable foodservice industry

KEY DATES

1944: Victory is founded as a metal shop in Philadelphia, Pennsylvania.
1954: The company moves to Plymouth Meeting, Pennsylvania.
1973: McGraw-Edison Co. buys the company.
1980: Bastian International Holdings acquires Victory.
1989: Victory is sold to Middleby Corp. and moves to Cherry Hill, New Jersey.
1997: Victory is acquired by a management-led investor group.
1999: The company is acquired by Glynwed International PLC.
2001: Glynwed becomes Aga Foodservice Group.

brands: Southbend, maker of heavy duty cooking equipment; Toastmaster, which produced cooking and warming equipment for the foodservice industry (a separate company, Toastmaster, Inc., produced consumer products under the same brand name); Seco (Southern Equipment), manufacturer of holding and serving systems; and Victory refrigeration.

Middleby was soon displeased with the Hussman transaction, however. After Middleby was unable to gain satisfaction from Hussman's management, in May 1990 it took Hussman to court, alleging fraud and breach of contract and asking for $30 million in damages. At the heart of the matter was the financial state of Southern Equipment, which Middleby maintained Hussman's executives had said prior to the sale was a profitable business. Afterwards, when it finally received copies of financial statements, Middleby learned that Southern Equipment had lost money in 1989. As a result, Middleby, which had planned on selling the unit for $15 million, was only able to find a buyer at less than $8. Moreover, the lawsuit charged, according to the *Chicago Sun-Times,* that "Hussman officials failed to disclose the deterioration of Victory's customer base and its bad relations with some of its remaining customers." One Hussman executive called the lawsuit "a crock of banana oil." A jury thought otherwise and in October 1992 awarded Middleby $27 million, an amount later set aside by a judge due to a technicality. In the end, the two parties agreed to an out-of-court settlement of $19.5 million in 1993.

For many years, Victory had operated as a stand-alone business with the framework of a large corporation.

Middleby was much smaller and took a greater interest in growing the business. Victory had been concentrating on contracts and high end of dealers, but now took steps to serve the entire foodservice market. In addition, the company retired the Raetone brand, which it had been using for less expensive, basic products. Now the Victory name was carried by the full gamut of the company's products. Victory also placed more emphasis on customer service, a move that would go along way to restoring the company's image with disgruntled customers. Victory also took steps to improve its manufacturing processes and the shortening of the lead time required to have Victory equipment installed. The company also expanded into a new area in 1993 when it produced a merchandiser for Coca-Cola USA and gained entry to the beverage equipment industry. In addition, two years later Victory introduced a new line of specification products.

TAKEN INDEPENDENT: 1997

In 1996 Victory was generating sales of about $40 million, but by this point Middleby was looking to concentrate on its core cooking and warming equipment divisions and to beef up its international business. In November 1996, the company announced that it was selling Victory to a management-led investment group. The deal was completed in early 1997, and for the first time in more than 20 years Victory was an independent company. It was an arrangement that would be short lived, however, as the business was soon put up for sale and considered by a number of suitors. In July 1999 a United Kingdom engineering conglomerate, Glynwed International PLC, paid $24.5 million for Victory.

A few years prior to the Victory acquisition Glynwed was comprised of such divisions as Foundry Products, Metal Services, Steels & Engineering, Tubes & Fittings, Plastics and Properties, and Consumer Products. Then, in 1997, the company began a reorganization that one year later left it with just two core divisions: Pipe Systems and Consumer & Foodservice Products. Through the Falcon Catering Equipment subsidiary Glynwed had become the United Kingdom's largest foodservice equipment maker. It became even larger in 1998 when it acquired Williams Refrigeration, the leading U.K. commercial refrigeration company. The purchase of Victory was a good fit for Glynwed because it provided a foothold in the United States, and the capabilities of Victory and Williams complemented one another. Williams could make use of Victory's North American distribution network, while Victory could take advantage of William's superior technology in blast chillers and cold rooms. Moreover, Glynwed could sell Williams products in the United States under the Victory brand and Victory products in the United Kingdom under the Williams name.

In 2001 Glynwed made an even greater commitment to its foodservice equipment and consumer businesses by selling its pipe systems division. The company subsequently changed its name to Aga Foodservice Group. Under its new corporate parent, Victory continued to introduce products. A new line of glass door merchandisers, the VM Series, was introduced in 2000. In 2002 Victory brought out its new Big Top Salad/Sandwich Refrigerator line of worktop refrigerators. A pair of new product lines, Deep Well Bottle Coolers and Modular Proofers, were added in 2004. The company also introduced three models of a refrigerated mobile bar caddy. Moreover, Victory was improving the quality of its products, enough that in 2005 it was able to double the standard one-year industry guarantee to two years. The products simply needed less service, and in order to make this a marketing advantage, the company touted what it called its V2E Pledge. With a well respected brand name and backed by a supportive corporate parent, Victory appeared well positioned to enjoy steady growth for years to come.

Ed Dinger

PRINCIPAL COMPETITORS

Sanyo Electric Co., Ltd; Maytag Corp; Ingersoll-Rand Co.; United Technologies Corp.

FURTHER READING

"All Circuits Humming: McGraw-Edison Could Generate Peak Earnings This Year," *Barron's National Business and Financial Weekly,* May 6, 1968, p. 13.

Dresser, Guy, "Victory Is Cool For Glynwed As Shares Soar," *Birmingham Post,* July 6, 1999, p. 17.

Dzierwa, Richard, "A Victory to Savor," *Appliance,* June 1992, p. M11.

Lowe, Frederick H., "Customer Sues Whitman Subsidiary," *Chicago Sun-Times,* May 15, 1990, p. 49.

Solomon, Steve, "Paring Down the Debt at McGraw-Edison," *Institutional Investor,* October 1980, p. 201.

Vivartia S.A.

3 Kerkyras Street, Tavros
Athens,
Greece
Telephone: (30) 210 349 4000
Fax: (30) 210 349 4040
Web site: http://www.delta.gr

Public Company
Incorporated: 1968 as Delta Dairy S.A.
Employees: 13,000
Sales: EUR 872 million ($1.1 billion) (2005)
Stock Exchanges: Athens
Ticker Symbol: DELTK
NAIC: 551112 Offices of Other Holding Companies

■ ■ ■

Vivartia S.A. is the new name for Greece's leading dairy and processed foods group, resulting from the merger of dairy products leader Delta Holdings, including subsidiaries Goody's and General Frozen Foods, with baked and snack food leader Chipita S.A. As such, Vivartia operates four primary divisions: Dairy & Drinks (43 percent of sales); Bakery & Confectionery (32 percent); Frozen Foods (9 percent); and Food Services & Entertainment (16 percent). Vivartia's brand family includes beverage brands Delta, Life, and Milko; baked goods and snack brands including 7 Days pastries and breads and the Extra brand of savory snacks; Chips Stars potato chips, as well as the Molto, Finetti, Bake Rolls, Spinspan, and Nova brands. The company's flagship frozen food brand is Uncle Stathis, and its restaurant operations include the Goody's fast-food restaurant chain and the Flocafe chain of coffee bars. Vivartia is not only a dominant food group in Greece, it is also one of the country's top ten industrial companies, and among the top 20 largest corporations in the country. Vivartia also ranks 35th among Europe's processed foods groups. In addition to its Greek operations, Vivartia is active throughout the Balkans region, with extensive operations in Eastern Europe as well. The company also operates joint ventures in Mexico, Egypt, Portugal, and Nigeria. The company's products reach more than 30 countries, including the United States and Canada. Dimitris Daskalopoulos, from Delta Holdings, has been named company chairman, and Spyros Theodoropoulos of Chipita is Vivartia's CEO. The company retains a listing on the Athens Stock Exchange. Combined sales for the company topped EUR 872 million ($1.1 billion) in 2005.

FOUNDING GREECE'S DAIRY GIANT IN 1952

Born in 1923, Aristides Daskalopoulos entered the dairy business in 1952. Initially, Daskalopoulos made yogurt and fresh milk available to his customers in the Athens area. The company's bid to expand was launched in 1962, when Daskalopoulos acquired land in Tavros, a small town in the suburbs of Athens. The company built a new headquarters, including a large-capacity milk processing facility, in Tavros, and moved its operations there in 1965. The new facility also allowed the company to begin the production of pasteurized milk and dairy products for the first time. In 1968, the company incorporated under a new name, Delta Dairy S.A.

COMPANY PERSPECTIVES

The Vision to Create One Company. A company with significant scale in the European market, increased capabilities for further innovation and product development, the financial resources to exploit opportunities for geographic expansion world-wide and the persevering ambition for consistent growth and results.

Delta grew steadily through the 1970s, and by the end of the decade claimed the position as the leading dairy products group in the country. In 1979, Delta launched production of ice cream as well and rapidly built up market share; by 1980, the company had taken the leadership in the ice cream segment as well.

The Greek dairy industry nonetheless remained highly competitive. The high level of competition was due in large part to the country's geography and the need to ensure supply to the many Greek islands. At the same time, Greece's popularity as a tourist destination meant that the total population, especially in areas such as Crete, often swelled by several times during peak periods. Part of Delta's success was its ability to adapt to the specific factors of the market, putting into place a strong logistics and distribution platform that enabled the company to achieve standardized pricing on a national level. Delta's investment in new packaging technologies also played an important role in its continued success.

In 1987, for example, the company introduced a new generation of packaging for its milk products, enabling the company to expand its line of products as well. The new packaging struck a chord with Greek consumers and quickly resulted in a doubling in sales for the company. By 1989, Delta had begun to extend its range into new food and beverage categories, launching a line of Life-branded fruit juices that year.

Delta went public in 1990, listing its shares on the Athens Stock Exchange in an offering that raised some EUR 44 million. The public offering enabled Delta to develop its first international growth strategy, targeting the nearby Balkans region market, just then emerging from decades of Communist domination, before expanding sales to the greater Eastern European area, and to Western Europe as well. Delta's early investment in the Balkans, in particular, enabled it to grab a leading share of the milk and fruit juice markets in much of the region. The company also emerged as a strong player in

the ice cream market in the region, backing up its presence with the construction of a factory in Bulgaria in 1992.

DIVERSIFICATION DRIVE IN THE LATE 20TH CENTURY

In the early 1990s, Delta began targeting more diversified food offerings. As part of this effort, the company sought out partnerships with other groups. The most notable of these came in 1993, when the company formed a partnership with European foods giant Danone, selling 20 percent of its stock to Danone in exchange for the larger company's technology and the right to produce and market a number of Danone brands to the Greek market.

The following year, Delta expanded into the frozen foods segment. As part of this effort, the company first took over the frozen foods group Froza. After revamping that company's production facilities, Delta bought a 51 percent stake in another major Greek frozen foods company, Uncle Stathis. Founded in 1969, that company launched the Uncle Stathis brand of frozen fruits and vegetables that same year. A pioneer in the Greek frozen foods sector, the Uncle Stathis brand remained a market leader into the 1990s. In 1991, the company went public, listing its shares on the Athens Stock Exchange. Following its acquisition by Delta, the company was merged into Froza, and the larger group took on a new name, General Frozen Foods. The Uncle Stathis brand remained the company's flagship brand.

Delta meanwhile invested heavily into the middle of the decade in order to boost its production and prepare itself for the next phase of its international growth. In 1994, the company spent nearly EUR 53 million to build a new automated yogurt production facility, including its own research and development laboratory. That investment was followed by the completion of an automated milk and fruit juice production facility, built at a cost of EUR 50 million. By then, Delta had announced an investment program of nearly EUR 300 million in order to position itself as one of Europe's most modern dairy producers.

Having achieved a strong sales position in the Balkans region, Delta's international strategy led the company to establish its own operations in much of this market. In 1996, the company began building a series of new production facilities, especially ice cream production units, in the Balkans, as well as elsewhere in the Eastern European market. The company built a plant in Romania in 1996, and added a new ice cream factory in Serbia in 1998. The company also added to its operations in Bulgaria, buying up a majority stake in that country's Vitalact in 1997.

KEY DATES

1952: Aristides Daskalopoulos founds a dairy and yogurt production company in Athens.

1965: The company opens a new large-capacity milk pasteurization plant in Tavros, a suburb of Athens.

1968: The company incorporates under the name Delta Dairy S.A.

1969: The Uncle Stathis frozen fruit and vegetable company is founded.

1973: Chipita S.A., a producer of savory snacks, is founded.

1975: Goody's fast-food restaurant chain is founded.

1979: Delta Dairy becomes the leading dairy group in Greece.

1990: Delta lists shares on the Athens Stock Exchange and launches an international expansion drive.

1991: Uncle Stathis goes public on the Athens Stock Exchange.

1994: Chipita goes public on the Athens Stock Exchange.

1999: Delta restructures as Delta Holdings, with two subsidiaries, Delta Dairy and Delta Ice Cream.

2001: Delta and Chipita form an international distribution partnership.

2002: Delta acquires Vigla S.A., expanding into cheese production.

2005: Delta agrees to sell Delta Ice Cream to Nestlé.

2006: Delta and Chipita merge to form Vivartia.

GREEK FOODS GIANT FOR THE NEW CENTURY

Delta's successful diversification and international expansion led the company to restructure its operations in 1999. In that year, the company transformed itself into a holding company, spinning off its two primary divisions as two separate companies, Delta Dairy and Delta Ice Cream. As part of the restructuring, Danone exchanged its 20 percent stake in Delta for a 30 percent stake in Delta Dairy. The newly restructured Delta targeted further diversification, targeting a vertical integration of its operations. In 1999, for example, the company set up its own state-of-the-art dairy farm, with 500 cows. The new facility enabled the company to produce milk with higher protein levels, with a lower risk of bacterial contamination.

Delta's vertical integration drive soon turned toward the opposite end of the supply chain, targeting an entry into retail sales. In 1999, the company joined a group of investors in the buyout of rival ice cream producer Dodoni Ice Creams S.A. Delta's initial stake of nearly 25 percent gave the company an interest in Dodoni's chain of gelataria "scoop shops" and cafes. The following year, Delta moved into restaurant operations proper, acquiring a 20 percent stake in the Goody's fast-food chain. Founded in 1975, Goody's had grown into Greece's leading fast-food restaurant and coffee bar operator. In 2000, Delta raised its stake in Goody's to more than 60 percent.

Aristides Daskalopolous died in 2000; the company remained controlled by the family, however, with son Dimitris taking over as company chairman and CEO. The young Daskopolous continued the company's rapid expansion into the mid-decade. In 2001, the company formed a partnership with Chipita S.A., Greece's major snack and baked goods group, as part of both companies' efforts to expand into the southern European market.

Delta itself entered a new market in 2002, buying up Cyprus's Charalambides Dairies. The acquisition gave the company control of the country's largest and oldest dairy producer. Also in that year, Delta placed Delta Ice Cream S.A. on the Athens Stock Exchange, in the first step of the later sale of that operation. In December 2005, Delta agreed to sell its stake in Delta Ice Cream to Nestlé S.A. By then, too, the company had ended its longstanding partnership with Danone, buying back the French group's shareholding.

Instead, Delta continued to explore new markets. The company entered the production of cheese, and especially feta cheese, with the purchase of Vigla S.A. in 2003. That acquisition gave Delta the position of market leader in the packaged Greek cheese sector, with a 20 percent market share.

As it prepared for the next phase in its growth, Delta adopted a new management structure in 2004, splitting its chairman and CEO functions. Dimitris Daskalopolous remained as chairman, and the CEO spot was taken over by Justin Jenk. The new management structure proved short-lived, however.

By the end of 2005, Delta had strengthened its relationship with Chipita. This led the two companies to announce their intention to merge their operations to form a new company, Vivartia, by July 2006. Chipita had been founded in 1973 as a producer of corn chips and other savory snacks, and grew into a market leader by the mid-1980s. In 1986, the company's leadership was taken over by Spiros Theodoropoulos, who took full control of the company by the end of the decade. Theodoropolous then led Chipita on a diversification drive, launching production of a new product line of mini-croissants. In 1993, Chipita bought a leading competitor, Konstantinos Arabatzis S.A. Bakery and Confectionery, which was renamed for its popular brand name, Snacky.

Chipita went public in 1994, listing on the Athens Stock Exchange. The company built new production facilities for the production of potato chips, as well as expanding its production of savory snacks. The company also added chocolate-covered snacks in 1995, under the Choco brand name. In another highly successful launch, the company introduced its Bake Rolls line of packaged pastries.

Chipita began an international expansion effort in the mid-1990s, building production facilities in Bulgaria and Portugal in 1996, while also forming a number of production and distribution joint ventures, such as in Egypt that year. By the beginning of the next decade, Chipita had added facilities in Mexico, in partnership with PepsiCo, and had acquired a presence in Russia through the purchase of Saint Petersburg–based Eldi and Krasnoselskaya. Further expansion came in 2002, when the company added operations in Italy. The company then expanded its effort to break into the Western European markets with the purchase of a 51 percent stake in Germany's Food & Snack.

The merger of Chipita and Delta was completed in large part by July 2006. The combined company adopted its new name, Vivartia. Dimitris Daskalopolous became the new company's chairman, and Spiros Theodoropoulos became the company's CEO. With combined sales of EUR 872 million ($1.1 billion), Vivartia had emerged as Greece's leading food, beverage, and restaurant group, as well as one of the country's ten largest industrial corporations, and had positioned itself as the leading player in much of the southern European market. Ranked 35th among Europe's leading food groups, Vivartia had established a firm basis for its future in the ever-growing European Union.

M. L. Cohen

PRINCIPAL SUBSIDIARIES

Balkan Restaurants S.A. (Bulgaria); Chipita Belgrade S.A. (Serbia 92.75%); Chipita Bulgaria S.A.; Chipita Czech Ltd.; Chipita Foods Bulgaria EAD; Chipita Germany GmbH; Chipita Hungary Kft.; Chipita International AE; Chipita Italia S.p.A.; Chipita Participations Ltd. (Cyprus); Chipita Poland Sp. z.o.o.; Chipita Romania S.R.L.; Chipita Slovakia Ltd.; Chipita St. Petersburg ZAO (Russia); Delta Dairy S.A.; Delta Food Holdings Ltd. (Cyprus); Delta Food Participation & Investments Ltd. (Cyprus); Endeka S.A.; Eurofoods Hellas S.A.; General Frozen Foods S.A.; Goody's S.A. (71.05%); Hellenic Food Service S.A. (87.06%); Pagrati Restaurants S.A.; Paralias Café–Patisseries S.A. (82.59%); Saranda S.A. (95.26%); Vigla S.A.

PRINCIPAL COMPETITORS

FAGE S.A.; Prehrambena Industrija Vindija dd Varazdin; Mevgal Dairy Product Industry; Union of Agricultural Cooperatives of Larissa-Tirnavos-Agia Larissa; Pinar Sut Mamulleri Sanayii A.S.; Tyras S.A.; Dodoni S.A.; Kolios S.A.; Agno S.A.; Imlek AD.

FURTHER READING

"Absorbing Times in Greece," *Food Trade Review,* January 2006, p. 55.

"Arla, Delta Link Up for Better Med Sales," *Dairy Industries International,* March 2001, p. 9.

Christiansen, Suzanne, "The Little Cow That Could," *Dairy Industries International,* December 2005, p. 30.

"Dairy Group Delta Holdings Has Agreed to Buy Nestlé's Condensed Milk Operations in Greece," *Dairy Industries International,* May 2006, p. 6.

"Delta Holdings Ends Partnership with Danone Group," *Athens News Agency,* February 15, 2005.

Hope, Kerin, "Slowly, Slowly Path to Profit," *Financial Times,* December 13, 2000, p. 5.

Kammerer, Roy, "Delta Holdings to Merge with Chipita International, Forming Greece's Largest Food Company," *AP Worldstream,* December 19, 2005.

"Licked," *Financial Times,* July 10, 2001, p. 23.

"Nestle Inks Deal to Acquire Greece's Delta Ice Cream," *Quick Frozen Foods International,* January 2006, p. 89.

"Nestlé Moves to Acquire 100% Delta Ice Cream," *just-food.com,* June 23, 2006.

Volga-Dnepr Group

Usacheva Street 35
Building 1 119048
Moscow,
Russia
Telephone: (07) (495) 755 7836
Fax: (07) (495) 2442879
Web site: http://www.voldn.ru

Private Company
Incorporated: 1990 as Volga-Dnepr Airline Company
Employees: 1,636
Sales: $487 million (2005 est.)
NAIC: 481111 Scheduled Passenger Air Transportation;
481112 Scheduled Freight Air Transportation;
481212 Nonscheduled Chartered Freight Air
Transportation; 484230 Specialized Freight (Except
Used Goods) Trucking, Long-Distance; 488190
Other Support Activities for Air Transportation

■ ■ ■

Volga-Dnepr Group is the world leader in outsized air cargo. The company is closely associated with the giant Antonov An-124 freighter, but also operates more conventional cargo aircraft; the group's AirBridge Cargo unit provides scheduled air freight services using Boeing 747s. Another unit operates a small passenger service. A number of businesses have sprung up around the airlines, offering trucking, aircraft maintenance, and insurance services.

POST-SOVIET ORIGINS

The Volga-Dnepr Airline Company was formed as one of Russia's first joint stock companies in August 1990. It was the country's first private cargo airline. The company took its name from two rivers linking Russia and the Ukraine; this was appropriate, as Volga-Dnepr's operation was based around an aircraft that was the product of both countries. Though it used other types from the start, Volga-Dnepr would be closely associated with the formidable Antonov An-124, the first of which arrived by the end of 1991.

Under the Soviet system, aircraft were designed by one company and built at one or more separate factories, while engines were sourced from yet another facility. The Antonov An-124 Ruslan freighter was designed by the Antonov Design Bureau in Kiev. Engines were also made in the Ukraine; the plane itself was assembled at sites including OAO Aviastar's facility in Ulyanovsk, Russia. The above-named companies were all original shareholders in Volga-Dnepr. The organizer of the enterprise and its first president was Alexey Isaikin, a retired lieutenant colonel from the Soviet Air Force.

The An-124 had an interesting history. Developed beginning in the 1970s, it broke numerous world records for carrying payloads. However, military orders eventually fell off and production was canceled in 1989 after only 25 examples of the aircraft had been completed.

The An-124 soon found a commercial niche, however. There was no other readily available plane anywhere in the world that could match its 120-ton capacity. The Soviet Air Force was willing to part with a few of the planes in order to raise cash.

The world's outsized cargo market, according to the company, was then valued at $42 million a year. The work typically involved one-off shipments of equipment too large to fit in most freighters, including large aerial towers, aircraft fuselages and engines, and machinery for oil and other industries. Such large items previously had to be moved by surface transport.

In September 1991, Volga-Dnepr formed a London-based joint venture with HeavyLift Cargo to pitch the An-124's capacities to the world outside the former Soviet Union. This partnership would last ten years.

Volga-Dnepr was based at Ulyanovsk-Vostochny airport. Its first flight under its own flag took place in March 1992. The destination was Sofia, Bulgaria.

Volga-Dnepr flew its first humanitarian mission on behalf of the United Nations in 1994. Response to wars, natural disasters, and the like would provide an enduring source of business over the years.

NEW VENTURES IN 1994 AND 1995

A trucking unit was created in 1994, allowing for door-to-door delivery. In December that year, Volga-Dnepr launched scheduled service between Moscow and Tientsin, China, using an Ilyushin Il-76. However, this was suspended in 1998 during the Asian financial crisis.

Other new ventures went more smoothly. The group's maintenance unit was certified to provide maintenance on certain Antonov and Ilyushin aircraft types in March 1995. The next year, Volga-Dnepr opened maintenance line stations in the United Arab Emirates and Shannon, Ireland. The New Insurance Company was also set up in 1995.

Volga-Dnepr Airlines participated in an international off-road race. It was chosen to haul participants' vehicles from Paris to Russia for the Master Rally-97 Marathon Paris-Moscow-Baikonur-Ulan Bator. This showcased new proprietary equipment allowing the carrier to pack 40 vehicles inside an An-124. Volga-Dnepr's own two-level loading system ultimately was able to fit more than 50 conventional passenger cars inside the plane.

A small, scheduled passenger service between Ulyanovsk and Moscow was launched in November 1996 using a small Yak-40 regional jet. This was later expanded with summertime flights to the Black Sea. Over the next ten years, this unit grew to six aircraft, one of them configured as a business jet.

In 1996, British Petroleum hired Volga-Dnepr to carry equipment to a remote mining project in Colombia, which lacked suitable roads. The airlift from the port of Barranquilla to the El Yopal oilfield was a challenging undertaking that help helped cement Volga-Dnepr's international reputation, noted *Airliner World*.

Business increased steadily in the mid-1990s. Revenues exceeded $100 million in 1996. The group had 873 employees and was carrying about 40,000 metric tons of outsized freight annually on its seven An-124s, which accounted for about 90 percent of the company's revenues.

GROUP FORMED IN 2001

A U.S.-based unit, Volga-Dnepr–Unique Air Cargo, Inc., was established in Houston in 2000. The next year, the group ended its association with HeavyLift Cargo Airlines in order to handle its own marketing of the An-124. (HeavyLift later merged with Air Foyle and became the agent for Antonov Airlines.)

Revenues fell following the loss of the HeavyLift connection, from about $140 million in 2000 to $99.5 million in 2001. The group had about 1,000 employees. By this time, the entire outsized cargo market had grown to more than $200 million. This was still a mere sliver of the larger air cargo market, which Volga-Dnepr was already planning to penetrate, according to *Air Cargo World*.

The company's various subsidiaries were organized under the new "Volga-Dnepr Group" in 2001. A Moscow-based managing company was formed to oversee the various elements, which included maintenance, trucking, and insurance operations.

According to *Airliner World*, Volga-Dnepr was the first civilian carrier to fly into Afghanistan following the fall of the Taliban regime in December 2001. It made

KEY DATES

1990: Volga-Dnepr Airline Company is formed.
1991: A joint venture is formed with HeavyLift Cargo Airlines.
1994: Volga-Dnepr flies its first United Nations mission.
2000: A U.S. subsidiary is established in Houston.
2001: The HeavyLift Cargo partnership ends; Volga-Dnepr is reorganized into group structure.
2004: AirBridge Cargo scheduled air freight service is launched using Boeing 747s.
2006: Ruslan International partnership is formed with Antonov Airlines.

hundreds of flights to the area over the next year, carrying a diverse array of supplies into the country. Revenues nearly doubled in 2002 to $193.6 million.

Volga-Dnepr was estimated to have a 45 percent share of the $500 million outsize cargo market, according to the U.S.-based *Journal of Commerce*. Its nearest rival was Antonov Airlines of the Ukraine, while Russia's Polet Cargo Airlines made up the remainder. These operators had a lock on the market since there were no similar aircraft available in the West. While a freighter version was in the works for the giant A380 that Airbus was developing, it was being designed to haul conventionally packaged cargo, not massive, oversized items.

SCHEDULED SERVICE LAUNCHED IN 2004

In 2004, Volga-Dnepr entered the scheduled cargo market in China for a second time. The Chinese economy was booming; the new service capitalized on Russia's strategic location as a bridge between Asia and Europe. The scheduled operation was branded "AirBridge Cargo" (ABC) to differentiate it from Volga-Dnepr's charter trade. ABC operated the Boeing 747, which was the largest American-made commercial freighter, and was guided by executives from U.S. cargo line Atlas Air, Inc. The initial flight was routed Beijing-Novosibirsk-Luxembourg. Stops in Krasnoyarsk, Russia; Tianjin, China; and Frankfurt, Germany, were soon added; trans-polar service to New York City was envisioned for the future.

Revenues reached $308.6 million in 2004; the company posted a $12 million loss. In 2005, profits

were estimated at $5.1 million on revenues of $487 million. An initial public offering was being planned for 2007.

In 2006 Volga-Dnepr formed a partnership with Antonov Airlines after it, too, broke off an arrangement with Britain's Air Foyle HeavyLift. The venture was dubbed Ruslan International. Ironically, one of its first contracts came from NATO.

PREPARING FOR THE FUTURE

Volga-Dnepr's ten An-124s made up nearly half of the number in commercial service anywhere in the world. The group had another ten Soviet-made aircraft and two Boeing 747s. It was putting newer, quieter engines on its Il-76 airliners, a Soviet transport workhorse that had been banned from Europe and the U.S. due to noise restrictions.

Volga-Dnepr had also been arranging the development of a new version of the AN-124 *Ruslan* featuring updated engines and avionics. A company official told *Airliner World* that planned production of three planes a year was expected to begin around 2020. By this time, Volga-Dnepr was aiming to have become a leading integrated logistics provider or "cargo supermarket."

Frederick C. Ingram

PRINCIPAL SUBSIDIARIES

AirBridge Cargo; Managing Company Volga-Dnepr-Moscow; NIK Insurance Company; Passenger Operations; Volga-Dnepr Airline Company; Volga-Dnepr China Company; Volga-Dnepr International Educational Center; Volga-Dnepr Ireland Ltd.; Volga-Dnepr-Leasing; Volga-Dnepr UK Ltd.; Volga-Dnepr—Unique Air Cargo Inc. (U.S.); Volga-Trucks.

PRINCIPAL COMPETITORS

Antonov Airlines; Atlas Air, Inc.; CargoLux Airlines International S.A.; HeavyLift Cargo Airlines Ltd.; KLM Cargo; Polet Cargo Airlines.

FURTHER READING

Barnard, Bruce, "A Breed Apart: Russian and Ukraine Companies Use Archaic Planes, Western Ideals to Corner Heavy-Lift Airfreight Market," *Journal of Commerce*, June 2, 2003, pp. 32ff.

"Big Profit in Heavy Freight," *American Shipper*, June 1, 1997, p. 72.

"The Bigwide World of 'Impossible' Logistics Solutions: Few, If Any, Cargo Airlines Have Had Quite as Much Impact on the World of Aviation as Volga-Dnepr Over the Past 15 Years," *Air Cargo World*, September 2005, pp. 1Aff.

Bingley, Paul, and Richard Maslen, "A Tale of Two Rivers: The Story of the Volga-Dnepr Group," *Airliner World*, March 2006, pp. 44–48.

Conway, Peter, and Paul Page, "Volga-Dnepr's Global Cargo Project," *Air Cargo World*, March 2001, p. 28.

Daly, Kieran, "Volga-Dnepr Learns a New ABC; Company President Sees Activity Tripling Over Next Decade, as 747s Are Added Gradually to Its New Freight Operation," *Flight International*, December 9, 2003, p. 27.

Donoghue, J.A., "Little Big Airline Shop," *Air Transport World*, November 1999, p. 93.

Hooson, Ben, "Taxes Weigh Down Air Carrier," *Moscow Times*, March 15, 1997.

Humphries, Conor, "Cargo Giant Plans London IPO, Urges Improvements," *St. Petersburg Times* (Russia), April 14, 2006.

Karp, Aaron, "Simple as ABC: Volga-Dnepr's Latest Cargo Project Is a 747 Freighter Operation That's Carrying Profits Between Asia and Europe," *Air Cargo World*, January 2005, pp. 20ff.

Keane, Angela Greiling, "Russia Bridges Cargo Service: Volga-Dnepr Subsidiary Opens First Scheduled All-Cargo Service with Beijing-Luxembourg Flight," *Traffic World*, May 31, 2004.

"Russian-Ukrainian Partnership to Provide An-124s for NATO Duty," *Flight International*, March 28, 2006.

Turney, Roger, "Russian Launch: Volga-Dnepr Latest Project Cargo Is to Make Itself a Scheduled Heavyweight with Air Bridge Cargo," *Air Cargo World*, January 2004, pp. 12ff.

"Two Years On and ABC Is Flying High," *International Freighting Weekly*, April 10, 2006.

"Volga-Dnepr and Antonov Join Forces for Heavylift," *Flight International*, July 18, 2006.

"Volga-Dnepr Is Fully Russian Now," *Kommersant*, April 27, 1999, p. 5.

Wah Chang

1600 N.E. Old Salem Road
Albany, Oregon 97321
U.S.A.
Telephone: (541) 926-4211
Toll Free: (888) 926-4211
Fax: (541) 967-6990
Web site: http://www.wahchang.com

Wholly Owned Subsidiary of Allegheny Teledyne Inc.
Incorporated: 1916
Employees: 1,100
Sales: $265 million (2005 est.)
NAIC: 212299 All Other Metal Ore Mining; 325199 All Other Basic Organic Chemical Manufacturing; 332312 Fabricated Structural Metal Manufacturing; 333516 Rolling Mill Machinery and Equipment Manufacturing; 331491 Nonferrous Metal (Except Copper and Aluminum) Rolling

∎ ∎ ∎

Wah Chang produces reactive and refractory metals and alloys and chemicals. Its products include corrosion-resistant metals, such as hafnium, niobium, titanium, vanadium, and zirconium that are used in commercial airliners, MRIs, rockets, satellites, orthopedic implants, and nuclear fuel. Its zirconium and hafnium industrial chemicals include such products as zirconium basic carbonate, a drying agent in antiperspirants and paints. Wah Chang also offers analytical laboratory services, photomicrographs of metals, and aerospace fabrication, and maintains an aerospace machine shop to design

products for that industry. It operates metals plants in Alabama, Oregon, and Pennsylvania, and a laboratory in Illinois.

1916–1967: BICOASTAL GROWTH AS A GOVERNMENT CONTRACTOR

In 1916, Dr. K. C. Li founded the Wah Chang Corporation, an international tungsten ore and concentrate trading company, in New York state. Li was a mining engineer who had earned worldwide recognition as the leading authority in mining and processing tungsten ores. He came from a family that owned an antimony and tungsten mining operation in China.

According to company literature, Li chose the name Wah Chang, which means "great development," to indicate the promising future he saw for the world in metals. The first symbol of the company's name in Chinese represents a tree copiously covered with blossoms. The second character denotes two suns, or radiance greater than that which humans have known previously. Li, who envisioned his company contributing "intellectual brilliance that would lead to great progress for all people," remained actively involved in the company until his death in 1961.

During the 1920s and 1930s, Wah Chang increased the scope of its operations beyond importing and exporting raw materials to become an international engineering firm. In the 1940s, it expanded into the reduction and refining of all types of tungsten ores and also began to produce tungsten and molybdenum mill products.

Immediately prior to World War I, Wah Chang developed an ongoing relationship with the United States government. During the war, the company supplied almost 100 percent of the nation's antimony needs with metal that it obtained from the Far East. Wah Chang later helped the United States build its stockpile of tungsten, tin, and antimony and became allocating agent for all the tungsten that defense forces used during World War II.

In 1955, Wah Chang moved into the reactive metal field by producing the first high-purity titanium sponge in the United States at the government's Bureau of Mines station in Nevada. In early 1956, the Atomic Energy Commission contracted with Wah Chang to run the U. S. Bureau of Mines zirconium plant in Albany, Oregon, to develop high-purity zirconium for use in the Navy's nuclear program.

Wah Chang purchased land and built a second plant on a 45-acre site in Albany, Oregon, in 1956, and in 1957 the company began production there of zirconium, using chemical and high heat processes to separate the zircon and the silica in zircon silicate sand, and producing reactor- and commercial-grade zirconium sponge and hafnium as a side-product. Beginning in 1959, Wah Chang partnered with Boeing to develop niobium alloys for rocket engines and satellites. In the early 1960s, the Atomic Energy Commission's aircraft nuclear propulsion project fueled demand for columbium products, and Wah Chang installed additional production facilities for this material at its Albany plant.

1967–1989: DRAMATIC GROWTH FOLLOWED BY TWO DECADES OF CHALLENGES

In 1967, Teledyne Inc. purchased the Wah Chang facilities, infusing capital and management experience into the company. During the decade that followed, Wah Chang expanded niobium production to meet needs for rocket nozzle skirt extensions, satellite orbit thrusters, MRI equipment, and particle accelerators. Commercial nuclear application of zirconium and hafnium also grew as Wah Chang supplied material for nuclear power plants. As a result, Wah Chang experienced an average growth rate of more than 20 percent per year during the early 1970s, becoming the world's largest production facility for zirconium and hafnium metals, niobium and tantalum alloys, and a leading research center for refractory metals.

The company also made advances in the area of employee safety, instituting a major safety awareness campaign beginning after 1974, a year in which one on-the-job injury occurred for every five workers. By 1976, the number of injuries at the company had dropped to 1 for every 13 workers, and by 1983, Wah Chang was experiencing one-fifth of the statewide average lost-time accident rate for manufacturing industries. By 2006, fewer than one in 20 workers experienced an on-the-job injury, a number that translated to less than half the rate of other facilities in the same industry classification.

The 1980s were a strong decade overall for Wah Chang; superalloy demand was high as aviation engine and airframe makers were making a lot of products for assembly or were stockpiling inventory. In the early 1980s, Wah Chang still occupied its original 45-acre site in Albany, Oregon, but its facilities covered an additional 65 acres and included 130 buildings and seven operating divisions. It had a virtual monopoly on the free-world production of zirconium and produced twice as much as its sole domestic competitor, Westinghouse's Western Zirconium.

However, the company's production capacity had been stagnant from about 1972, and in 1982, as the specialty metals industry overall hit a slump, French zirconium producer Cezus, walked off with about 40 percent of the world market for that metal. (By 1989, Cezus was responsible for 45 percent of world zirconium production, Western Zirconium 25 percent, and Wah Chang 30 percent.) This, plus a dive in specialty metals prices, led Wah Chang to take action. In 1982, it joined forces with Mitsui and Ishizuka Research to form Zirconium Industry, which produced zirconium sponge using a simplified process to separate the hafnium from the zirconium sand at a new plant in Japan beginning in 1983.

Another challenge facing Wah Chang beginning in 1982 arose over the disposal of the radioactive sludge produced as a by-product of the zirconium refining process at its Albany plant between 1967 and the late 1970s. This waste contained elevated levels of radium, uranium, and thorium. Wah Chang had been storing

KEY DATES

1916: Dr. K. C. Li founds the Wah Chang Corporation in New York State.

1956: Wah Chang remodels its Albany, Oregon, facility.

1957: The company starts to manufacture commercial quantities of zirconium sponge.

1961: Li dies.

1967: Teledyne, Inc., purchases Wah Chang.

1982: Wah Chang joins with Mitsui and Ishizuka Research to form Zirconium Industry.

1998: Allegheny Teledyne purchases Oregon Metallurgical Corporation of Albany, Oregon.

2000: Lynn D. Davis becomes president of Oremet-Wah Chang.

2001: The company closes its titanium sponge manufacturing facility in Albany, Oregon.

the sludge in large ponds adjacent to an old channel of the Willamette River about 400 feet from the river's main stem. The company proposed stabilizing the sludge by raising dykes around it, covering the face of the structures with riprap, and covering the sludge with plastic, clay, and rock. However, the Oregon Energy Facility Siting Council ordered it to move the sludge about a mile from its plant and three miles from Albany to the state's first radioactive waste disposal site.

Wah Chang financed a study that showed that radioactive levels in the sludge were too low to be hazardous, but the Siting Council rejected the company's request to take the study into evidence. Wah Chang, in response, appealed the Council's order to move the sludge to the State Supreme Court. However, in the end, Wah Chang removed 100,000 cubic yards of sludge and about 2,000 cubic yards of radioactive material between 1991 and 1993 at a cost of about $10 million, and in 1997, another 1,500 cubic yards of sludge. Groundwater remedies were curtailed in 1997.

Meanwhile, in 1989, a similar discovery of 16,000 tons of radioactive material containing thorium and radium at the company's former smelting and refining plant in Glen Cove, New York, again raised the specter of long-term environmental issues for the company. Former employees of the plant came forward to talk about their health problems in a 1989 *New York Times* article. "We used to joke about the contamination, saying, 'I'm not putting my hands in that powder, I don't know what's in it,'" one employee was quoted in the

article. He continued, "'Now I wonder how big a joke it was. I hope the joke isn't on us.'"

The abandoned Glen Cove property, added to EPA's Superfund list, contained nine dilapidated buildings, more than 150 chemical and processing tanks, 200 drums of waste chemicals, and thousands of barrels, containers, and boxes containing ore residue. New York State's Department of Health responded by working with Glen Cove officials to take medical histories of former plant employees to determine whether they had been exposed to radiation or hazardous chemicals or metals. The Department's initial assessment of the site was that it posed no danger to the public because thorium is a low emitter of radiation. However, it continued to monitor the area and to take soil and air samples, as well as to study local creek and fish life.

1990–2006: INDUSTRY SLUMPS LEAD TO REDIRECTION

The timing of the Glen Cove discovery could not have been worse for Wah Chang. In the early 1990s, as Pentagon spending ended, jet engine manufactures and other superalloy users worked hard to reduce their inventories, and from 1990 to 1995, the metals industry went into a steep decline. Observers attributed the industry's worst slump ever to three factors: the end of the Cold War, which led to a glut of low-priced titanium from the former Soviet Union onto the world market; the Gulf War, which triggered worldwide recession; and airliner deregulation, which resulted in "a very undisciplined purchasing pattern" for commercial transports, the single largest end market for titanium, according to a 1998 *American Metal Market Supplement* article.

Wah Chang's parent company Teledyne merged with Allegheny Technologies to become Allegheny Teledyne Inc. (ATI) in 1996. ATI responded to rising demand for specialty metals from 1995 to 1998 by acquiring Oregon Metallurgical Corporation (Oremet) of Albany, Oregon, in 1998. Oremet, an integrated titanium producer, had been founded, like Wah Chang, in 1956, and had collaborated with Wah Chang several times in the 1990s.

Soon after, due to increased competition in the titanium industry, ATI consolidated Wah Chang and Oremet. The consolidation entailed 88 layoffs at both Oremet and Wah Chang, which together became a part of ATI's specialty metals division. This division also consisted of Allegheny Ludlum, producer of stainless steel and other specialty metals; Allvac, producer of superalloys and other metals, including titanium; International Hearth Melting, producer of titanium and zirconium; Rodney Metals, manufacturer of high performance alloys; Rome Metals, a finishing facility for flat-rolled products; and Titanium Industries, distributor and processor of titanium mill products.

In 1998 and 1999, titanium shipments again dropped off as the commercial aircraft industry reduced inventory. Under the leadership of Lynn D. Davis, appointed president of Wah Chang in 2000, the company slightly altered its course. Davis knew Wah Chang well; he had joined company in 1977 after earning masters degree in metallurgical engineering and had spent time as Oremet's company's executive vice-president and general manager.

INTO THE 21ST CENTURY

In 2001, Wah Chang began to focus on high-value products such as precision rolled strip, nickel-based and cobalt-based alloys and superalloys, premium titanium, and high-purity niobium alloys. ATI invested $50 million on expanding Allvac and Wah Chang and also built an energy co-generation plant that year to reduce its annual energy bill. Also in 2001, Wah Chang closed its titanium sponge manufacturing plant in Albany, Oregon, leaving Titanium Metals Corporation of Denver as the only domestic titanium sponge producer. Wah Chang continued to produce titanium ingot, slab, and mill products, using the low-priced sponge available for purchase on open market.

A strike led by the United Steelworkers of America idled the Wah Chang plant in 2001 after the union that represented the company's work force rejected a new labor contract. The dispute continued for seven months, during which time ATI's Wah Chang hired temporary workers; it ended when both sides approved a new six-year labor agreement in early 2002.

After the strike, the company returned to business as usual, continuing its focus on high-value products for the medical, chemical, energy, and other industries. One of its ventures entailed adapting a zirconium-niobium alloy originally designed for use in nuclear reactor tubes to knee and hip joint implants. In another venture, Wah Chang agreed to supply the specialized alloys for the magnets and walls of the new fusion reactor, the International Thermonuclear Experimental Reactor, being built in France. With the number of zirconium applications having grown from a small number in the 1960s to thousands by 2006, the future looked brilliant for Wah Chang.

Carrie Rothburd

PRINCIPAL COMPETITORS

Millenium Chemicals Inc.; OM Group Inc.; Titanium Metals Corporation; Precision Castparts Corporation; RTI International Metals Inc.

FURTHER READING

Haflich, Frank, "Titanium Industry Looks for Soft Landing," *American Metal Market Titanium Supplement*, October 8, 1998.

"Minor Metals," *Metals Week*, January 17, 1983, p. 8.

Saslow, Linda, "Old Plant is Linked to Health Threats," *New York Times*, June 11, 1989, p. 18.

"Teledyne Soil, Groundwater Clean-up Pared in Washington" *Superfund Week*, April 18, 1997.

"Teledyne Wah Change is Fighting to Continue its Waste Disposal Procedures," *Nucleonics Week*, August 19, 1982, p. 8.

"The Young Will Carry On," *Albany Democrat-Herald*, March 5, 1961, p. 13.

WAZ Media Group

Friedrichstrasse 34-38
Essen, 4512
Germany
Telephone: (49) (201) 804-0
Fax: (49) (201) 804-1644
Web site: http://www.waz-mediengruppe.de

Private Company
Incorporated: 1948 as Westdeutsche Allgemeine Zeitungsverlagsgesellschaft E. Brost und J. Funke
Employees: 16,000
Sales: EUR 2 billion ($2.5 billion) (2005)
NAIC: 51111 Newspaper Publishers; 51112 Periodical Publishers; 323110 Commercial Lithographic Printing; 513112 Radio Stations; 49211 Couriers

■ ■ ■

WAZ Media Group (WAZ) is Germany's second-largest newspaper publisher headquartered in Essen. The company's flagship publication *Westdeutsche Allgemeine Zeitung (WAZ)* achieves an average circulation of 580,000 copies in southwest Germany's Ruhr region, its core market. WAZ publishes three other major newspapers in the same area: *Neue Ruhr Zeitung/Neue Rhein Zeitung, Westfälische Rundschau* and *Westfalenpost.* Together they reach approximately 2.9 million readers in Germany's most populous state North-Rhine Westphalia. The company also controls three regional newspapers in Thuringia. WAZ is a major player in the newspaper markets of southeastern Europe, including Hungary, Bulgaria, Romania, Serbia and Croatia, and holds a 50 percent stake in Austria's largest newspaper *Krone Zeitung.* In addition to 38 daily newspapers, the company publishes more than 100 popular magazines and trade journals, over 130 free advertising journals and roughly 250 customer magazines for corporate clients. WAZ runs its own printing facilities and distribution networks, is involved in radio broadcasting, online services, direct marketing, and postal services and has its own school for journalists. The company is owned by the heirs of Erich Brost and Jakob Funke, the two journalists who founded *Westdeutsche Allgemeine* after World War II.

A NONPARTISAN NEWSPAPER IN POSTWAR GERMANY

Three years after Germany's defeat in World War II, the cluster of cities that formed the Ruhr region—Bochum, Bottrop, Castrop-Rauxel, Dortmund, Duisburg, Essen, Gelsenkirchen, Gladbeck, Herne, Mülheim, Oberhausen, Recklinghausen, Wanne-Eickel, Wattenscheid and Witten—still carried the scars of severe destruction from almost 2000 bombing raids. Still under the British Military Administration, Germany's most important industrial center slowly came back to life. The British had launched two newspapers after the war: *Die Welt* with national coverage and Essen-based *Neue Ruhrzeitung* geared to the Ruhr region. Written by German journalists, their content was still under British control. In 1946 a number of licenses were issued to German newspaper publishers with close ties to the main political parties.

In 1948 Erich Brost, at that time editor-in-chief of

COMPANY PERSPECTIVES

There remains much to be written about the future of the newspaper, but one thing is clear: the new paper must be a clever synthesis of very old tradition, perhaps even be rediscovered, but also truly modern. The newspaper is unique in localities and regions. Even advertising is seen here less as advertising than as a source of information about what is on offer today, what is new in town. A new focus for newspapers will have to be set here, because young people, too, not so *au fait* with newspapers, demand more information from their immediate surroundings.

the Essen-based *Neue Ruhrzeitung,* which was sympathetic to the Social Democratic Party, was approached by the British administration if he was interested in founding the first nonpartisan newspaper in the Ruhr region. Brost, an experienced journalist with a social-democratic background who had barely managed to escape the Nazis and worked for the British Broadcasting Corporation (BBC) during his exile in England, agreed. He hooked up with Jakob Funke, a journalist about his age who worked for the German news agency *Deutsches Nachrichtenbüro* in the same office building. Funke had learned the art and craft of making a newspaper from scratch at the Essen-based *Essener Anzeiger,* where he finally became editor-in-chief in the late 1920s. After the Nazis had shut the newspaper down in 1941, Funke served as a reporter in Belgrad during the war. He was an excellent organizer and had all the local connections necessary to get a new business venture off the ground under conditions of extreme adversity and scarcity.

On April 3, 1948, the first issue of *Westdeutsche Allgemeine Zeitung* (in short *WAZ*) was published. In a programmatic piece which appeared on the front page of the first issue, publisher and editor-in-chief Brost outlined his editorial principles. Although a Social Democrat by heart, he had internalized the idea that news reporting should not be influenced by a particular worldview during his exile years in England. *WAZ,* the first nonpartisan newspaper in the British zone, intended to keep its reporting as objective as possible, was to participate in the creation of a socially oriented democratic order based on the rule of law in Germany and Europe, and to take into account and reflect the particular interests of the Ruhr region's population. News articles were supposed to be short and to the point,

as well as easy to read and understand by everyone. News reporting was strictly differentiated from opinion pieces.

After years of censored reporting and party propaganda during the Nazi era people were starving for information that was not colored by any ideology. The editorial concept outlined by Brost quickly gained the approval of the Ruhr population. However, producing a newspaper and delivering it to its readers in the postwar era was an adventurous undertaking. *Westdeutsche Allgemeine* started out in Bochum, where Brost shared an office in the back of the building with his secretary and another employee at the site of Laupenmühlen & Dierichs, a commercial printing company. Co-owner Dr. Paul Dierichs became a *WAZ* shareholder for a number of years while a large part of it was printed on the only rotation printing machine with enough capacity to handle the print run of 250,000 to 300,000.

Not only food was still rationed, paper was too. In the beginning *Westdeutsche Allgemeine* came out three times a week with content and advertising crammed into four to six pages. Editors worked in a room missing a wall; a large wooden board set on a stack of bricks served as a desk. Manuscripts were written on scrap paper and trainees had to bring their own typewriter if they wanted to be hired. The local editorial team in Duisburg had to go across the street to the central train station to use the bathroom. Mostly women delivered the paper on foot or bicycle to its readers in the Ruhr cities where one half to two thirds of all housing units was destroyed and part of the population lived in basements and other improvised spaces. Beginning in September 1949 *WAZ* was published Monday through Friday. Two months later the British Administration lifted the licensing requirement for newspaper publishing.

BUILDING A REGIONAL NEWSPAPER EMPIRE

With the free market came immediate competition, for example from *Essener Allgemeine Zeitung,* one of the well-known pre-war newspapers. When *Essener Allgemeine* launched a Sunday edition in the summer of 1950 to attract new readers, *WAZ* followed suit. The battle was won when *WAZ* acquired the competitor, including 38,000 additional subscribers, four years later. By that time the Ruhr population had far outgrown pre-war numbers, due to the influx of refugees from the lost German territories in East Prussia who found work in the booming coal and steel industries, and to the beginning baby boom. Thanks to the aggressive marketing approach of sales manager Albert Lümmen the readership of *Westdeutsche Allgemeine* grew even faster than the Ruhr population. The increasing purchasing power of

KEY DATES

1948: Nonpartisan newspaper Westdeutsche Allgemeine Zeitung is established in Bochum.

1953: Company headquarters are moved to Essen.

1975: WAZ takes over daily newspaper *Westfälische Rundschau.*

1976: Essen-based *Neue Ruhr Zeitung / Neue Rhein Zeitung* is acquired.

1977: Advertising journal subsidiary Anzeigenblattgesellschaft WVW is founded.

1978: WAZ Group is formed.

1986: WAZ Group buys a 10 percent share in private TV station RTL+.

1987: The company acquires a 45 percent share in Austrian tabloid *Kronen-Zeitung.*

1990: Radio broadcasting holding Westfunk is established and a majority share in Hungarian publisher PLT acquired.

1991: WAZ Group takes over a customer magazine publisher and three regional newspapers in Thuringia.

1996: Bulgarian publisher 168 hours is acquired and online service Cityweb is launched.

1998: WAZ buys shares in Croatian publisher Europa Press Holding.

2000: Munich-based TV-magazine *Gong* is taken over.

2001: WAZ establishes commercial courier services and expands into Serbia and Romania.

2003: The company obtains major newspaper shares in Montenegro and Macedonia.

2005: WAZ Media Group sells its stake in RTL Group.

almost five million people combined with their hunger for new clothing, new furniture and new household appliances resulted in soaring advertising revenues from consumer goods manufacturers and department stores. In 1953 *WAZ* headquarters were moved to a brand-new office building in Essen. In 1958, ten years after its foundation, *Westdeutsche Allgemeine's* distribution covered the whole Ruhr region with 24 local editions. No other newspaper in Germany had as many subscribers as *WAZ* did.

The onset of the 1960s marked the beginning of a series of takeovers of ten local competitors by WAZ. The acquisition of the Recklinghausen branch of *West-*

deutsche Rundschau, one of WAZ's remaining major competitors, in the early 1970s pushed sales over the mark of half a million sold newspapers. Finally, in 1975 *WAZ* acquired a majority share in Dortmund-based *Westfälische Rundschau* and took over *Neue Ruhrzeitung / Neue Rheinzeitung (NRZ)* headquartered in Essen the following year. Besides its nonpartisan flagship publication, the publishers of *WAZ* also had control over the two major regional newspapers with a Social Democratic orientation.

CONQUERING NEW MARKETS UNDER NEW LEADERSHIP

Cofounder Jakob Funke died in 1975 at age 73. Under his leadership the WAZ publishing house had emerged from a single-publication start-up to a regional newspaper empire that included numerous local and four regional newspapers as well as several modern office buildings and printing facilities. After his death he was replaced by Günther Grotkamp, an experienced lawyer who had earned the respect and trust of the Funke family after he joined WAZ in 1960 and who worked closely with Jakob Funke up until his death. Grotkamp was considered the architect of the WAZ Group which was formed in 1978 to incorporate the acquired publishing houses into the company. The editorial departments of the four major newspapers the company owned in the Ruhr region retained their independence while production, the acquisition of advertising clients, marketing and administration were centralized. This business model proved to be very successful and became known as the WAZ Model.

When Erich Brost retired from his active role in the business in 1978, he was succeeded by Erich Schumann, another business lawyer who left a successful practice in Bonn to become the second executive director of WAZ Group. A strategic thinker by heart, Schumann envisioned WAZ Group expanding beyond the world of print media and across the German border. In a bold move Brost and his wife Anneliese adopted Schumann in the mid-1980s while their son Martin—who in Brosts opinion was not suitable to succeed him—was paid a cash settlement. In 1986 Grotkamp married Petra Funke, the youngest of the three Funke daughters. Under the leadership of Grotkamp and Schumann WAZ Group greatly expanded its activities into other print media, such as popular and customer magazines, advertising and trade journals. WAZ also conquered newspaper markets in eastern Germany and southeastern Europe and ventured into electronic media.

International expansion began in 1987 when the company acquired a 45 percent share in Austrian tabloid *Neue Kronen-Zeitung.* One year later followed a second acquisition in Austria with a 45 percent share in Kurier AG Vienna. After the Berlin Wall fell in 1989, Grotkamp and Schumann took a trip to East Germany to get an idea of the newspaper market there and to scout out new business opportunities. In 1990 they acquired two newspapers in the state of Thuringia: *Thüringische Landeszeitung* and *Thüringer Allgemeine*. When their attempt to take over *Ostthüringer Nachrichten*—a third newspaper in the same state—encountered strong political resistance, they bought out the whole editorial staff and founded *Ostthüringer Zeitung* instead. With an investment of roughly $200 million in new printing facilities and other infrastructure, the WAZ Model was established there too. During the 1990s WAZ Group became a dominant force in southeastern Europe where the company acquired major newspaper interests in Hungary, Bulgaria, and Croatia.

WAZ Group's activities in the emerging electronic media markets began in 1986 with the acquisition of a 10 percent share in commercial TV channel RTL+, launched in 1984 by Luxembourg-based Compagnie Luxembourgeoise de Télédiffusion (CLT) and the German Bertelsmann group's film and TV production subsidiary UFA. WAZ Group began to feed regional TV programming from the Ruhr, produced in the newly established TV production subsidiary Westfilm Medien GmbH, to the station. When CLT and UFA merged in 1997, WAZ Group traded its share in RTL TV and its own TV production arm for a 20 percent stake in Bertelsmann's BWTV-Holding which owned half of CLT-UFA as well as shares in more than 40 German and European TV and radio stations. The deal was financed through the sale of WAZ Group's majority share German paper manufacturer Holtzmann & Cie valued at about $300 million. When CLT-UFA merged with British Pearson TV in 2000, WAZ' share converted into a 7.4 percent stake in the newly formed RTL Group.

In 1990 the radio broadcasting holding Westfunk was established as an umbrella for the ten regional radio stations WAZ Group acquired an interest in. Unfortunately, this business branch continued to produce losses. Online Service Cityweb was launched in 1996. To reflect its expanded range of activities, the company was renamed WAZ Media Group in 1997.

GENERATION CHANGE, MISSED DEALS AND LEGAL BATTLES

In 1995 WAZ cofounder Erich Brost died at age 91. By that time WAZ Media Group had become Germany's third largest publishing house. Five years later Günther Grotkamp retired from the business. The Funke and Brost families hired two additional top managers to head the group. Grotkamp was succeeded by Lutz Glandt

and Detlef Haaks, two experienced media managers. Bernd Nacke became the second manager who represented the Brost family together with Erich Schumann. In 2002 Bodo Hombach became managing director of the WAZ Group as a possible predecessor of Erich Schuman. Hombach, a former minister in Gerhard Schröder's Social Democratic administration who later headed the European Union–led Balkan Stability Pact, used his excellent connections in the Balkans to advance WAZ Group's further expansion in Serbia, Rumania, Montenegro, and Macedonia.

As the new millennium arrived WAZ Group seemed ready to cease new growth opportunities. According to the company's policy, launching new publications was too expensive and risky. Consequently, WAZ Group's top management was on the lookout for takeover candidates. Unfortunately, when major stakes in two large German newspaper publishers became available, WAZ missed out. When the media empire of Leo Kirch crumbled in 2002, his 40 percent stake in Germany's largest newspaper publisher Axel Springer Verlag was put up for sale. Some WAZ managers viewed the deal as an excellent growth opportunity, but not all shareholders agreed. Despite the fact that a EUR 200 million loss in 2001 made Springer shares much less attractive for investors, majority shareholder Friede Springer was not interested in a publisher with close ties to the Social Democrats as a major shareholder in her conservatively oriented company. Although a hostile takeover was seen as potentially winnable, WAZ decided against it. Only a few months later Süddeutscher Verlag, publisher of the national daily newspaper *Süddeutsche Zeitung*, approached WAZ and other potential investors to consider buying a stake in the company which had slipped into the red in 2001. A deal was finally sealed with Stuttgart-based Südwestdeutsche Medien Holding—not WAZ.

In the summer of 2005 WAZ sold its stake in RTL Group to Bertelsmann for roughly EUR 530 million. The money was intended to boost WAZ Group's funds to enhance its position in the consolidating newspaper markets. However, only a few months later it became apparent that a full-fledged family war had broken out over this issue. All but one party among the company's shareholders agreed to cash out, since they had helped fund the acquisition with their private money in the first place. This led to the most serious conflict among WAZ owners in the company's history.

It had been the desire of the founders that all major decisions be approved unanimously by all shareholders. Designed to keep the balance between the Brost and Funke family branches, each of whom owned half of the company, this rule had caused much friction between the two families when it came to strategic decisions. Petra and Günther Grotkamp fiercely resisted the wish of the other shareholders to withdraw any cash from the business generated by the RTL sale. They were also strongly opposed to changes in the legal structure of the family-owned business such as the transformation of WAZ Group into a publicly traded corporation. So far, the company's cash flow had been sufficient to finance most of its growth and bank debt was minimal.

When the rest of WAZ shareholders took a large sum out of the business in September 2005 without her approval, Petra Grotkamp went to court. At the end of 2005 it looked as if the decision about WAZ Group's future structure could be determined by a court ruling. At the same time, the Funke family had not yet appointed the managers who were to succeed Lutz Glandt and Detlef Haaks. Yet, with Schumann and Grotkamp in their late 70s, it was only a matter of time until a new manager generation would take over WAZ leadership.

PREPARING FOR AN UNCERTAIN FUTURE

Meanwhile, WAZ Group was taking steps to meet the many challenges on the horizon. Thanks to growing competition for advertising revenues from Internet marketplaces and the lingering economic stagnation in Germany, newspapers suffered severe losses in advertising revenues—and WAZ newspapers were no exception. The company reacted with a number of measures. Distribution in the Ruhr region was reorganized and brand teams were formed to work on the strategic positioning and marketing controlling of the group's flagship publications. *Westdeutsche Allgemeine* received a face-lift and invested in a massive campaign to sign up new readers. A new editor-in-chief was hired while seven local editorial offices were shut down. Part of the local content was moved from the print version to the Internet. In the future, a central news desk was to be set up to bundle the information streams and mobile editorial units were intended to create closer contact with readers. Whether these measures were sufficient to consolidate revenues was up in the air.

Another possible problem child was Austrian tabloid *Kronen-Zeitung,* where a disagreement between 84-year-old founder, owner and editor-in-chief Hans Dichand about his successor and connected issues resulted in another lawsuit. The atmosphere between the two sides was tense, as if the disturbing market trends were not enough. Although the paper still yielded healthy profits, they had declined sharply a few years running, according to *Frankfurter Allgemeine Zeitung.* Readership was aging along with the editorial team and the paper's content and design had grown more and more old-fashioned.

Another looming uncertainty was the expected launch of very low-priced or even free newspapers in Germany, which would break loose a new round of fierce competition. To successfully compete in such an environment or to launch its own version of a low-priced compact tabloid for young urban readers, WAZ Group needed more capital. It could come from selling the two 12.5 percent stakes the Funke and Brost families held in German direct mail empire Otto Versand valued at well over one billion Euro. For the time being, WAZ Group focused on the new market that opened up when it was announced that the German Post Office monopoly for delivering letters would end. Using its comprehensive distribution network in the Ruhr region, the company, whose courier services subsidiary WPS Westdeutsche Post Service GmbH already served local clients such as Essen's city government in 2005, announced plans to launch a national mail delivery service together with the publishers Springer and Holtzbrinck in 2006.

Evelyn Hauser

PRINCIPAL SUBSIDIARIES

Westdeutsche Allgemeine Zeitungsverlagsgesellschaft E. Brost & J. Funke GmbH u. Co.; Zeitungsverlag Ruhrgebiet GmbH & Co. Essen KG; Zeitungsverlag Niederrhein GmbH & Co. Essen KG; Zeitungsverlag Westfalen GmbH & Co. KG Essen-Dortmund; Westfalenpost GmbH und Co. Verlags KG; OTZ Ostthüringer Zeitung Verlag GmbH & Co. KG; Thüringer Allgemeine Verlag GmbH & Co. KG; Krone-Verlag GmbH & Co. Vermögensverwaltung KG (Austria; 50%); Kurier Zeitungsverlag und Druckerei GmbH (Austria; 49.4%); Verlagsgruppe Pannon Lapok Társasága (PLT) (Hungary; 51%); Pressegruppe 168 Stunden EgmbH (Bulgaria; 51%); Zeitungsverlag Politika AD (Serbia; 550%); Westdeutsche Zeitschriften-Verlag GmbH & Co. KG; WVW Westdeutsche Verlags- und Werbegesellschaft mbH & Co. KG; SZV Spezial-Zeitschriftengesellschaft mbH. & Co. Verlag KG; Westfunk GmbH & Co. KG; Westdeutsche Zeitungs- und Zeitschriftenvertriebs-Ges. E. Brost & J. Funke GmbH u. Co.; Cityweb Online GmbH; Korneli-Werbung GmbH & Co. KG; WPS Westdeutsche Post Service GmbH; Journalistenschule Ruhr GmbH.

PRINCIPAL COMPETITORS

Axel Springer AG; Burda Holding GmbH. & Co. KG; Gruner+Jahr AG & Co.; Heinrich Bauer Verlag KG; Verlagsgruppe Georg von Holtzbrinck GmbH.

FURTHER READING

Benoit, Bertrand, "WAZ War of Words with Springer Escalates," *Financial Times,* August 27, 2002, p. 24.

"Die WAZ kauft sich in Europa's groesstes Rundfunkunternehmen ein," *Frankfurter Allgemeine Zeitung,* July 2, 1997.

"Dispute Between WAZ Shareholders Intensifies," *Europe Intelligence Wire,* October 24, 2005.

"Germany's WAZ Buys HVG, Most Popular Hungarian Weekly," *Hungary Business News,* June 16, 2003.

Hanfeld, Michael, "Dichand bleibt," *Frankfurter Allgemeine Zeitung,* February 16, 2005, p. 42.

"Irritationen in der WAZ-Gruppe über Hombach," *Frankfurter Allgemeine Zeitung,* October 31, 2001, p. 28.

Jakobs, Hans-Jürgen, "Mut zur Lücke," *Süddeutsche Zeitung,* August 19, 2004, p. 15.

Karle, Roland, "Die WAZ sieht sich nicht als Couponschneider," *HORIZONT,* April 9, 1998, p. 48.

"Major German Publishers Start Up Rival to Deutsche Post," *Europe Intelligence Wire,* November 9, 2005.

WAZ—50 Prägende Jahre: 1948–1998, Essen, Germany: Westdeutsche Allgemeine Zeitung, 1998, 162 p.

"WAZ Could Sell Stake in Otto," *Europe Intelligence Wire,* September 2, 2005.

"WAZ Experiences Unexpected Difficulties with Business in Eastern Europe," *Europe Intelligence Wire,* November 2, 2004.

"WAZ Family Owners Continue to do Battle," *Europe Intelligence Wire,* December 16, 2005.

"WAZ Group Wins Case Against German Cartel Office," *Europe Intelligence Wire,* June 25, 2004.

Welcome Wagon
International Inc.

———■———

245 Newton Road
Plainview, New York 11803-4316
U.S.A.
Toll Free: (800) 77 WELCOME
Web site: http://www.welcomewagon.com

Wholly Owned Subsidiary of Move, Inc.
Founded: 1928
Employees: NA
Sales: $50 million (2005 est.)
NAIC: 541870 Advertising Material Distribution
Services

■ ■ ■

Believed by many people to be a volunteer organization, Plainview, New York–based Welcome Wagon International Inc. is, in fact, a marketing company. Traditionally, Welcome Wagon's paid representatives, almost entirely women, have visited new families in a community (or brides-to-be, new mothers, and girls reaching their 16th birthday), bearing a gift basket filled with coupons and promotional items—bottle openers, pens, yardstick, etc.—provided by local merchants, who pay to be part of the basket in the hope of attracting new customers. The best of the Welcome Wagon ladies made their pitches so naturally that most newcomers never suspected they were being pitched to. However, times change, and since 1998, when the home visits came to an end, Welcome Wagon has done its marketing for local businesses through the Welcome Wagon Gift Book and through the company's web site, where

new homebuyers can check out promotional offers in their community and request the gift book. This contemporary version of the housewarming gift not only includes coupons and other offers but also articles, tips, and home design and insurance records. Welcome Wagon distributes about two million copies of the gift book each year. To produce the product, the company maintains in own in-house printing operations, as well as a research department to compile homeowner data. Welcome Wagon is a subsidiary of Move, Inc., primarily an online real estate listing company.

FOUNDING THE COMPANY IN 1928

Welcome Wagon was founded in 1928 in Memphis, Tennessee, by an advertising man, Thomas Winston Briggs. Born in Memphis in the late 1880s, he was the son of a dairy owner and helped with the business until he was 22. Then, at the age of 22, he married and went to work in Houston for his father-in-law, James O. Jones, a longtime newspaperman. Jones had launched a business to produce special advertising pages that could be distributed as extra editions of newspapers. Briggs thought the idea would also work in Memphis and moved there to start his own firm, Thomas W. Briggs Enterprises. He was correct, the business prospered, and soon he had 300 people working for him and some 100 newspapers as customers. His inspiration for Welcome Wagon came from a chance comment made by a business associate while they were driving home one evening. The man was describing the difficulties a friend had encountered in moving to a new city where he had just been transferred: "He'll probably have to begin his civic

COMPANY PERSPECTIVES

Welcome Wagon has a variety of products, designed to help our customers—our partners—build their businesses. Each year, we reach out to almost 2 million new homeowners with our flagship product, the Welcome Wagon Gift Book. We know who the home-buying family is, what they want and how to reach them.

and social life all over from scratch." Briggs was always a civic-minded person—who would later charter a foundation to carry on his philanthropic endeavors—but he was also an advertising man. Not only did he think it would be neighborly to welcome newcomers to Memphis, he did not see why he could not do it on behalf of his clients.

Briggs fleshed out his idea to greet newcomers by harkening back to frontier days, when boosters of small towns sometimes greeted passing wagon trains with gifts and supplies in the hope of convincing them to stay and join the community. They made their visits in Conestoga wagons, leading Briggs to call his fledgling operation Welcome Wagon. He never showed up at anyone's door with a gift basket, however. From the start, he considered that task suitable for "the ladies." According to the *New York Times,* he "built up a staff by recruiting what marketers today would call empty-nesters, church ladies and local influencers, creating what the company says became the country's largest female sales force—a harbinger of companies and brands like Avon, Tupperware and Mary Kay."

Welcome Wagon caught on quickly and began spreading across the country. In the first half of the 1940s the company had to contend with rationing imposed by the government during World War II. Unable to get enough gas and tires, the Welcome Wagon ladies had to walk, ride bicycles, go on horseback, or make use of a horse and buggy to pay their visits. In time, the morale boost provided by Welcome Wagon, which included 600 branches by 1944, persuaded the government to give the company gas ration coupons. For its work during the war years, Welcome Wagon received the Army and Navy E Awards for quality and service, and citations from the Treasury Department and the Red Cross.

Having established a solid reputation and recognition that would extend around the world, Welcome Wagon was well positioned to take advantage of the

postwar population boom, as servicemen returned home, got married, the baby boom generation took shape, and countless families moved into the new suburbs. Invariably a Welcome Wagon lady would be there soon after they moved in to greet them and offer them a gift basket courtesy of the fine merchants, dentists, doctors, and plumbers in town. The business thrived, allowing Briggs in 1953 to buy a 17-story building at 685 Fifth Avenue in New York City to serve as the corporate headquarters.

DEATH OF FOUNDER IN 1964

In the early 1960s Briggs began making plans to take the Welcome Wagon concept to Europe, but this idea never came to fruition. In March 1964 he died at the age of 77, and Welcome Wagon was sold to an employee, Rosanne Beringer, who served as president and chairman of the company. Welcome Wagon established a presence in the United Kingdom and in 1967 expanded to Australia. The business of home visitation in the United States was reaching its peak around this time, as Welcome Wagon, employing 6,000 hostesses representing 100,000 sponsors in some 2,200 communities, made 1.5 million visits each year.

In larger cities, in particular New York City, the Welcome Wagon ladies were no longer warmly welcomed by the people they visited, however. The reasons given were the impersonal nature of cities and an urbanite's general distrust of strangers. "City dwellers just don't believe you're not selling something," one Welcome Wagon hostess told the *New York Times* in 1967. "In the suburbs, mention Welcome Wagon and the door flies open." In addition, an increasing number of women in the city held jobs and were not available to receive the hostess, and evening calls were often not appreciated. As a result, the *New York Times* reported that by the fall of 1967 there were just two Welcome Wagon hostesses in Manhattan, two in Brooklyn, three in Queens, and five Bronx hostesses who were folded into the Westchester County operation. Welcome Wagon also had difficulty tracking down the names of city newcomers, having to resort to paying for lists. In addition, whereas in the suburbs there was a waiting list of women interested in becoming hostesses, in New York City the company had to resort to running ads on local radio.

In October 1968 Welcome Wagon was sold to FAS International, parent company of Famous Artists Schools, Inc., provider of home study courses for commercial art, photography, writing, and other subjects. The purchase price was $16 million, including $12.4 million in cash and another $3.6 million in convertible notes. FAS's ownership of Welcome Wagon was short-lived, however. In order to pay down debt, FAS sold Welcome Wagon to the Gillette Company in July 1971 for a reported

KEY DATES

1928: The company is founded by Thomas W. Briggs in Memphis, Tennessee.

1953: The company moves its headquarters to New York City.

1964: Briggs dies.

1968: FAS International acquires Welcome Wagon.

1971: Gillette acquires the company.

1995: CUC International acquires the company.

1998: Home visits come to an end.

2001: Move, Inc., acquires Welcome Wagon.

2004: Welcome Wagon moves its headquarters to Plainview, New York.

2006: The company launches a revamped web site, offering a local business directory.

$7.6 million. Gillette's chief executive officer and chairman saw Gillette as more than just a razor manufacturer, fancying it a diversified consumer products company. Under his leadership the company became involved in areas such as personal grooming products like shampoo and hair coloring, as well as small electronics, such as digital watches and calculators, and even smoke alarms and fire extinguishers. Gillette used Welcome Wagon as a way to test new products by including them in the gift baskets. Like many of the acquisitions made during this period, Welcome Wagon did not fit in well with Gillette, and in 1978 it was sold to members of Welcome Wagon's management team, which took the company private.

By the time Welcome Wagon changed hands for the fourth time since the death of its founder, the company had clearly peaked. Hostesses had an increasingly hard time finding women at home during the day, and a growing number of people were reluctant to let the hostesses into their homes. By 1988 the number of communities with Welcome Wagon operations fell to 4,500. By the mid-1990s the total fell to 2,000, and of that only 1,400 were deemed active representatives. The number of annual house calls also dipped to 500,000. Moreover, Welcome Wagon had to contend with competing welcoming services, such as Getting to Know You, established in 1962 in Great Neck, New York, which produced a directory of local businesses filled with coupons.

SOLD TO CUC INTERNATIONAL: 1995

In 1995 Welcome Wagon was purchased for $20 million by CUC International Inc., a publicly traded company based in Stamford, Connecticut, which offered discount coupon programs, fund-raising programs, and other services, including home shopping, travel, insurance, dining, and home improvement. CUC bought a company in Welcome Wagon that had seen its business erode steadily with the years, generating about $18 million in sales each year. CUC hoped to beef up the number of hostesses to 3,000, improve training, and increase home visits to 650,000 within the first year. The company had no interest in pursuing New York City and other major cities, instead targeting high-growth parts of the country, like Texas and Florida. CUC was initially drawn to Welcome Wagon as a way to market one of its products, Privacy Guard, a credit history service, but CUC came to believe that Welcome Wagon could be used to provide niche marketing for a variety of products and services. Hence, Welcome Wagon, which at one time turned down the business of weight-loss programs and vitamin companies, now opened up the gift baskets to any reputable company, as well as CUC services. With offerings from regional and national companies added to the mix, Welcome Wagon was drifting away from its longtime formula of introducing newcomers to local merchants and professionals.

In December 1997 CUC merged with HFS Inc., owner of real estate brokerages Century 21 and Coldwell Banker, the Avis car rental agency, and a number of hotel chains, to form Cendant Corporation. Several months later, however, Cendant ran into trouble because of a $100 million overstatement of earnings that resulted not only in a loss of investor confidence, but shareholder lawsuits alleging fraud. In the wake of Cendant's stock losing three-quarters of its value, a major shakeup was announced at Welcome Wagon, although management insisted the changes were not connected to the difficulties encountered by the parent company. In the autumn of 1998 Welcome Wagon announced that home visits would cease at the end of the year and all but about 500 hostesses would be dismissed. The ones kept would be retrained to sell ads as Welcome Wagon began shifting to direct marketing through the mail. Whatever role the difficulties at Cendant may have played in the changes at Welcome Wagon, the home visits had been growing impractical. The number of married mothers working full time, according to Census Bureau statistics, had increased steadily from 17 percent of households in 1969.

Late in 1998, Cendant acquired Getting to Know You and merged it with Welcome Wagon. While the better known Welcome Wagon name was kept, the operation was centered around the address and coupon book developed by Getting to Know You for more than 40 years. In 1999 the company made 1.4 million mailings. In addition to the local address book, Welcome Wagon introduced a Pre-Move Planner, a mailing that helped merchants make contact with new homeowners before they moved. Welcome Wagon also made more use of the Internet both to attract new customers and increase distribution of its products.

Welcome Wagon again changed owners in February 2001, when Homestore.com acquired Cendant's Move.com unit, which included Welcome Wagon. Homestore subsequently changed its name to Move, Inc. A company spokesperson explained to the *New York Times,* "We saw their business as fitting in nicely with ours, especially in terms of the Internet and e-mail." The Welcome Wagon material was mailed to new home buyers only, not to renters. The average new homeowner was a valued marketing demographic: 38-year-old married adult with household income of $71,300. The newcomers among them were highly coveted because they were open to seeking out new relationships with merchants, service providers, professionals, and others. Coupons used by Welcome Wagon people, advertisers found, were more likely to result in regular customers than other types of coupons.

In 2004, Welcome Wagon moved its headquarters to Plainview, New York, and continued to refine its new business model, especially the incorporation of Internet capabilities. In July 2006 the company launched a revamped web site that offered a local business directory. In addition to special offers and local pages, the site of-

fered consumer reviews, dynamic mapping of business locations, as well as articles and tips on home and gardening and living well.

Ed Dinger

PRINCIPAL COMPETITORS

Yellow Book USA; Valpak Direct Marketing Systems, Inc.

FURTHER READING

Hays, Constance L., "Welcome Wagon to Make Its Visits Via Post Office," *New York Times,* October 12, 1998, p. A15.

Meier, Peg, "After Corporate Acquisition, Welcome Wagon Rolls Back on the Streets," *Star-Tribune Newspaper of the Twin Cities,* July 29, 1995, p. 1E.

Rejnis, Ruth, "The Horn of Plenty Is a Wicker Basket," *New York Times,* October 8, 1972, p. R1.

Robbins, Kevin, "Welcome Wagon Is Rolling to a Stop After 70 Years," *Commercial Appeal,* October 11, 1998, p. A1.

Strugatch, Warren, "This Time, Welcome Wagon Is New in Town," *New York Times,* October 31, 2004, p. 14LI.6.

"Thomas W. Briggs Dies at 77; President of Welcome Wagon," *New York Times,* March 3, 1964, p. 35.

"Welcome Wagon Stalls in New York," *New York Times,* September 1, 1967, p. 39.

Whitaker, Barbara, "Just Neighbors Being Friendly? Not Exactly," *New York Times,* May 19, 1996, p. 3.

Whitehall Jewellers, Inc.

———■———

155 North Wacker Drive
Chicago, Illinois 60606
U.S.A.
Telephone: (312) 782-6800
Fax: (312) 782-8299
Web site: http://www.whitehalljewellers.com

Wholly Owned Subsidiary of WJ Holding Corporation
Incorporated: 1895
Employees: 2,880
Sales: $319.63 million (2006)
NAIC: 448310 Jewelry Stores

■ ■ ■

Whitehall Jewellers, Inc., is a leading American specialty retailer of fine jewelry, primarily gold and diamonds, which owns and operates 386 stores in 38 states across the country. Under the names of Whitehall Company Jewellers, Lundstrom Jewelers, and Marks Brothers Jewelers, the company runs stores in upscale city and suburban shopping malls. Whitehall reported a string of consecutive sales records and earnings in the 1990s. Much of its success was due to its ability to take advantage of the highly seasonal aspect of jewelry sales. The company's rapid growth continued until the economy began to slow in 2000. A couple of years later, an accounting scandal was uncovered that resulted in the firing of its CFO and cost Whitehall millions of dollars in legal fees and restitution as its stock price plummeted. A new strategy of focusing on the higher end of the market failed to pull the company out of the

red, and Whitehall was bought out by an affiliate of Prentice Capital Management and Holtzman Opportunity Fund in 2006.

EARLY HISTORY

Marks Brothers Jewelers began its long history in 1895, when a retail jewelry store opened in the center of downtown Chicago. In 1903 Hugo Marks acquired the store from his uncle Ben Roth and began running it with his brother Al as Marks Bros. Jewelers.

Émigrés from Eastern Europe, the brothers welcomed the growing middle and upper classes of the city that were inclined to spend their money on high-quality, elegant diamonds, watches, rings, earrings, and fashionable hat pins. Within a very short time, Marks Brothers Jewelers had garnered a reputation as one of the most reliable and trustworthy jewelers in the city of Chicago, with some of the finest diamonds in the entire Midwest.

During the early years of the 20th century, and through the end of World War I, Marks Brothers Jewelers developed its reputation as a first-rate jeweler. At that time, Chicago was a city that provided ample opportunity to satisfy the ambition of entrepreneurs yearning for success. The railroads had made Chicago hog-butcher to the world, and families such as Kraft and Hormel made their fortunes from the stockyards on the south side of the growing metropolis. The families that managed this new wealth spent their money on items that indicated their status in society, such as diamond-studded tie pins and gold brooches, to highlight the dresses of women attending gala winter balls. The prosperity of the city was also shared by the growing middle class, who also frequented Marks Brothers Jewelers and purchased items for special occasions, such as diamond engagement rings. By 1919, the company had not only established and solidified its reputation as a jeweler, but had also laid a firm financial foundation for its continuation into the future.

The "Roaring Twenties," as they were called in the United States, had a particularly load roar in Chicago. The Volstead Act, which prohibited the production, sale, and consumption of alcoholic beverages, was a godsend to gangsters who illegally distributed beer, wine, and hard liquor to customers in "speakeasies" (private membership clubs). The ownership of these clubs and the territories they were located in generated bitter and violent battles between the gangsters for the large amounts of cash involved. In addition, many individuals in Chicago were making large sums of money speculating on the stock market, and there seemed no end to the growing wealth in the city. Many of these individuals who had made large sums of money legally and illegally bought their diamonds at Marks Brothers Jewelers.

Although the stock market crash of October 1929 sent the entire U.S. economy into a downward spiral, Marks Brothers Jewelers was able to survive this difficult period. Sales dropped dramatically, of course, and the company was forced to lay off many of its employees, but the brothers were able to gather together their family in order to run and operate the store themselves. As the Great Depression continued throughout the decade of the 1930s, sales at the company remained stagnant. Yet a glimmer of more profitable times was just around the corner.

WORLD WAR II AND THE POSTWAR PERIOD

Even before the beginning of World War II, the country's economy began to improve. President Franklin Delano Roosevelt implemented a comprehensive national program to place the United States on a wartime production schedule, with the manufacture of materials for troops that would be sent overseas to fight the Axis Powers of Germany and Japan. The resurgence of American manufacturing and production stimulated the economy and lifted the country out of the throes of the Depression. As a result, employment rose and people were paid comfortable wages. No longer worried about putting food on the table, people were able to spend more money on luxury items, such as marriage bands and diamond rings. Gradually, with the revitalization of the economy, specialty retailers like Marks Brothers Jewelers benefited from the increase in consumer purchasing power.

Marks Brothers Jewelers rode the wave of postwar American economic prosperity. Employment was high, wages were increasing, and America was the undisputed economic leader of the free world. All of these developments meant that many more American citizens were doing better than they had ever done before, and were able to pursue leisure activities and buy luxury items like no time in the past. This meant higher sales for Marks Brothers Jewelers, especially as more and more young couples decided that expensive diamond rings and gold wedding bands were necessities for their weddings.

Marks Bros. had five stores by 1946, making it the largest chain in downtown Chicago. The business passed to three children of Hugo Marks in 1948, and they were responsible for extending the franchise as far as Rodeo Drive in Beverly Hills.

Throughout the 1950s and 1960s, Marks Brothers Jewelers prospered, albeit unobtrusively. Still managed and run by family members, the company was run as a relatively small but highly regarded operation, with a modest-sized, long-term staff that was knowledgeable about diamonds and fine jewelry. A loyal customer base that grew steadily over the two decades was also a significant factor.

The company began to open a few stores in shopping malls as the phenomenon grew in the 1960s. By the time the decade had come to an end, Marks Brothers Jewelers had increased its revenues dramatically since the end of World War II.

GROWTH AND EXPANSION

The jewelry specialty retail business changed significantly during the 1970s, as companies which had traditionally operated as one-store retailers began to expand their business by establishing new stores in different parts of one city or by expanding into different cities altogether. Thus although a well-known company might have its flagship store in downtown New York, it would begin to open stores in Chicago and Los Angeles, for example, and also take advantage of the enormous demographic

KEY DATES

1895: Original jewelry store opens in Chicago.
1903: Hugo Marks of Eastern Europe acquires the store from his uncle, runs it with his brother Al.
1948: Hugo Marks's children take over the shop, begin opening branches.
1979: Fourth generation of family management arrives with Hugh and Matthew Patinkin; company has nine stores.
1990: New management has opened 100 new stores in malls across the country.
1996: Marks Brothers Jewelers goes public, raises $52 million in initial public offering.
1998: Jewel Box chain of 36 stores in the Southeast acquired.
1999: Marks Brothers renamed Whitehall Jewellers Inc., has more than 250 stores.
2001: Shares move from NASDAQ to the New York Stock Exchange.
2002: Accounting scandal emerges.
2005: Hugh Patinkin dies suddenly and is succeeded as CEO by Robert Baumgardner.
2006: Prentice Capital Management and Holtzman Opportunity Fund acquire Whitehall.

changes that led to the creation of the suburban "mall." This latter development changed the jewelry retail business forever, since many companies decided at this time to rent mall space in order to attract the growing and affluent middle class that was moving to the suburbs.

Marks Brothers Jewelers did expand its operations during the 1970s, and gradually opened nine additional stores in various sections of downtown Chicago. However, there was no serious consideration of expanding company operations farther than the city limits. This attitude changed in 1979 with the arrival of a new and younger management team. Hugh Patinkin became chairman, president, and CEO, while his brother Matthew Patinkin assumed the position of executive vice-president of store operations, and John Desjardins was brought on board to act as executive vice-president of finance and administration. By this time, the company had a dozen stores: the Whitehall Co. Jewellers brand had been added. The company's first Lundstrom Jewelers store opened in Florida soon after.

Throughout the 1980s, the new management team implemented a comprehensive strategy to expand and

improve company operations. Rejecting the trend toward developing high-volume superstores that sold diamonds and jewelry, such as Service Merchandise, Marks Brothers Jewelers remained faithful to its own brand of a unique, small store concept. What this meant was that the size of a Marks Brothers store averaged around 800 square feet, but could be as small as 400 square feet, while the average size of most jewelry stores averaged 1,500 square feet. In addition, management at Marks Brothers decided to locate new company stores in center court locations in malls. The center court location provided the company with a high profile, and the small store concept helped keep rent and operating costs to a minimum. By the beginning of 1990, the new management team had opened 100 new stores in malls across the country.

The impressive expansion achievement of Marks Brothers was not done through an acquisition strategy but by a detailed and careful analysis that resulted in choosing prime mall locations one by one. Most of these new stores were opened under the names of either Whitehall Company Jewellers or Lundstrom Jewelers. The modus operandi of the management team was to first open a Whitehall Company Jewellers store, and later open a Lundstrom Jewelers store, an upscale rendition of the Whitehall store in regard to its merchandise, in the same mall. In this way management minimized competition, and customers were not usually aware of the fact that the parent company, Marks Brothers, operated the two stores.

In 1995, the company continued its aggressive growth strategy by opening 14 additional stores, and in 1996 there were 19 new store openings. Most of these stores were located in two new locations, San Diego, California, and Orange County, California. The success of these stores, especially in an extremely competitive environment where upscale merchandise and elegant surroundings were of utmost importance, was largely based on the knowledge and effectiveness of a highly trained sales force.

PUBLIC IN 1996

To make certain these stores were a success, management decided to clean house and rid the company of nearly 10 percent of its sales force that was not meeting company standards. With all the pieces in place, the company was ready to take the next major step in its expansion strategy, namely, make the change from a private to a public company. In May 1996, Marks Brothers Jewelers went public with a stock offering that garnered over $52 million to fuel its continued expansion.

By the end of fiscal 1997, the company was operating 188 stores in 24 states, all under the names of Whitehall Company Jewellers, Lundstrom Jewelers, and the Marks Brothers Jewelers Company. Traditionally having sold its wares to more affluent customers, management also decided to upgrade merchandise in all of its stores. Diamond jewelry comprised most of each store's inventory at approximately 60 percent, while gold represented about 20 percent and gemstones about 15 percent of the inventory respectively. The company's focus on selling more diamond jewelry was related to its goal of attracting an aging baby-boomer market that would grow dramatically during the next 10 years. The company had discovered that some of the top items sold to this demographic group included a $7,000 pear-shaped diamond ring, a $3,000 trillion-cut diamond ring, and a $6,000 diamond solitaire ring. Even more exciting for the company was the discovery that items selling at over $1,500 accounted for approximately 25 percent of sales at its Lundstrom and Whitehall stores, while items selling at over $3,000 accounted for 12 percent of sales.

Marks Brothers Jewelers had grown so rapidly in such a short period of time that it was then the fourth largest mall jeweler in the country, and the sixth largest jewelry retailer overall. Zales, Sterling Jewelry, and Service Merchandise were the company's prime competitors in the malls, while Helzberg Diamond rounded out the general competition. Only two of these companies, Zales and Sterling, continued to expand their operations. Zales, which operated more than 1,000 stores, had initiated a major marketing effort to capture new customers and intended to open nearly 200 new stores in the near future, and Sterling, having just gone through a period of consolidation, was also concentrating on opening new stores in malls throughout the United States. Service Merchandise was closing 60 of its stores, and Helzberg Diamond only opened 10 new stores during fiscal 1997.

With a growing trend toward consolidation in the industry, and the lack of new competitors on the horizon, Marks Brothers Jewelers was well situated to take advantage of the growing market demand from aging and affluent baby boomers for luxury items such as diamonds, jewelry, and gemstones. The family business that once regarded growth with suspicion was positioned to become one of the most prominent jewelry retailers in America. The company's expansion continued in 1998 with the $22 million purchase the Jewel Box chain, which had three dozen stores in the Southeast.

Marks Brothers Jewelers Inc. was renamed Whitehall Jewellers Inc. in early 1999. Its ticker symbol also changed, from MBJI to WHJI. By this time, it had 264 stores in 30 states. The company's share price more than tripled over the course of the year as a buoyant economy spurred impulsive consumer spending. Revenues rose 32 percent to $315.4 million in the fiscal year ended January 2000.

As consumer spending began to slow in 2000, Whitehall's share price fell to pre-boom level. Nevertheless one investment banker called this a "solid bargain" due to the company's history of profitability.

Actually, a major slowdown was around the corner. The 2001 calendar year saw Whitehall drastically scaling back growth plans and closing stores. However, in November of the year, its shares migrated from the NASDAQ to the New York Stock Exchange.

CRISIS AND NEW OWNERSHIP

Though *National Jeweler* proclaimed Whitehall had appeared to have "weathered the storm" by mid-2002, in fact, the worst was yet to come. By the end of calendar 2003, Whitehall would be under investigation by both the SEC and federal prosecutors. The crisis began with a $30 million lawsuit filed by Capital Factors Inc., a unit of Union Planters Corporation, against Whitehall and 13 other companies (including rival gem giant Friedman's Inc.) over charges it was defrauded by jewelry wholesaler Cosmopolitan Gem Corporation.

Whitehall fired a couple of executives including its chief financial officer—never a reassuring sign for investors. It also restated financials for a couple of years due to inventory valuation adjustments. A number of shareholders groups sued the company and several of its officers alleging misrepresentation of the company's finances.

One lawsuit and the federal investigations were resolved in September 2004. Former CFO Jon Browne pleaded guilty to bank and wire-fraud conspiracy charges, while Whitehall agreed to pay $15 million in restitution to defrauded parties and $350,000 in penalties to the government (it also spent at least $22 million more on related expenses). Whitehall also agreed to include more outside directors on its board. The class action suit by shareholders remained to be settled.

While these suits were playing out in the courts, Whitehall changed its strategic course. The company had launched an e-commerce site around September 2002. It was also seeking to compete in the more lucrative, more upscale parts of the market. This cut into margins as old merchandise was marked down and resulted in revenues slipping 3 percent to $334 million in fiscal 2004.

Hugh Patinkin died in March 2005 of an apparent heart attack. He was succeeded as CEO by Lucinda M.

Baier, who had formerly been involved with the credit card business at Sears, Roebuck and Co. A few months later, the company hired Beryl Raff for the top spot but she resigned the post even before the announcement made the trade papers to return to the jewelry division of J.C. Penney Co. Inc. The shock of her resignation chopped more than two-thirds off of the company's already record low share price in one day, noted *National Jeweler*. The stock was delisted from the NASDAQ during the year.

Robert L. Baumgardner, formerly head of Tiffany & Co.'s Little Switzerland unit, was next to take up the mantle of CEO in November 2005. One of his top priorities was scrambling for capital. The company had also announced plans to close 77 unprofitable stores.

Two investment groups wrested for control of Whitehall. In March 2006, the team of Prentice Capital Management LP and Holtzman Opportunity Fund L.P. won the bidding over Newcastle Partners, L.P. Whitehall then became a subsidiary of WJ Holding Corporation, ending its ten years as a public company. Whitehall then had roughly 300 stores and about 2,880 employees. Revenues for the fiscal year ended January 31, 2006, were $319.6 million; the company posted a staggering net loss of $84 million (in addition to the $19 million it had lost in the previous two years).

Thomas Derdak
Updated, Frederick C. Ingram

PRINCIPAL SUBSIDIARIES

WH Inc. of Illinois; Whitehalljewellers.com LLC.

PRINCIPAL COMPETITORS

Friedman's Inc.; Helzberg Diamonds; J.C. Penney Co. Inc.; Sterling Jewelers Inc.; Zale Corporation.

FURTHER READING

Andrews, Gregg, "Whitehall Jewellers Appears to Have Weathered the Storm," *National Jeweler*, May 16, 2002, p. S18.

Asare, Sophia, and Rob Bates, "Whitehall Agrees to Buyout Offer," *Jewelers Circular Keystone*, March 2006, p. 39.

Baeb, Eddie, "Slow Sales Squelch Whitehall Expansion: Jeweler Says Impulse Buying Dips," *Crain's Chicago Business*, August 7, 2000, p. 26.

———, "Sparkle Gone, Whitehall Cuts Growth Plans: Jewelry Chain Aims to Buy When Economy Rebounds," *Crain's Chicago Business*, June 18, 2001, p. 34.

Bray, Chad, "Whitehall to Avoid Prosecution," *Wall Street Journal*, September 29, 2004, p. B3.

Countryman, Andrew, "Chicago-Based Whitehall Jewellers Fires Chief Financial Officer," *Chicago Tribune*, December 12, 2003.

———, "Jewelry Giant Whitehall to Settle Probe for $13 Million," *Chicago Tribune*, September 29, 2004.

Donahue, Peggy Jo, "Teaching a New Generation of Consumers the Value of Quality," *Jewelers Circular Keystone*, March 1997, p. 62.

Elliot, Stuart, "Marks Brothers Jewelers," *New York Times*, June 4, 1997, p. C8(N).

Frischknecht, Donna, "Marks Brothers Jewelers: On Your Mark, Get Set, Grow," *Supersellers*, January 1997, p. 21.

Gallun, Alby, "Whitehall Jewellers to Move HQ to 125 S. Wacker Dr.," *Chicago Business*, July 12, 2006.

Gomelsky, Victoria, "Friedman's and Whitehall Embroiled in SEC Investigations," *National Jeweler*, January 1, 2004, p. 1.

Guy, Sandra, "Whitehall Jewellers Names New CEO: Troubled Company Announces Rejected Takeover Offer," *Chicago Sun-Times*, November 3, 2005, p. 67.

———, "Whitehall Jewellers Shifting Focus to Upscale Customers," *Chicago Sun-Times*, August 27, 2004, p. 72.

———, "Whitehall Jewellers Turns to Former Sears Exec," *Chicago Sun-Times*, December 2, 2004, p. 65.

———, "Whitehall's Product Change Proves Costly in 2004," *Chicago Sun-Times*, April 15, 2005, p. 67.

———, "Whitehall to Split Its Stock," *Chicago Sun-Times*, December 15, 1999.

"Jewelry Execs Say Securities Plaintiffs' Claims Fail," *Corporate Officers and Directors Liability Reporter*, August 23, 2004.

Jones, Sandra, "Fund Sees Jewel in Whitehall; SEC Probe, CEO's Death Lead to Changes in Jewelry Firm's Board," *Crain's Chicago Business*, July 25, 2005, p. 3.

Law, Glenn, "Raff Resigns from Whitehall, Returns to Penney," *National Jeweler*, October 16, 2005.

"Majority of Securities Claims Against Jewelry Execs Survive Dismissal," *Securities Litigation & Regulation Reporter*, February 23, 2005.

"N.D. Ill. Consolidates Securities Suits Against Jeweler, Execs," *Securities Litigation & Regulation Reporter*, August 11, 2004.

Podmolik, Mary Ellen, "Marks Buys 36 Jewel Box Stores," *Chicago Sun-Times*, June 23, 1998, p. 43.

"Quality Diamonds," *Jewelers Circular Keystone*, June 1997, p. 402.

Shabelman, David, "Whitehall, Newcastle Duck and Weave," *TheDeal.com*, January 13, 2006.

Shor, Russell, "Auction Houses vs. Luxury Retailers: Myth & Reality," *Jewelers Circular Keystone*, January 1997, p. 134.

Shuster, William George, and Stacy King, "Jewelers As Store Designers," *Jewelers Circular Keystone*, November 1996, p. 86.

Thompson, Michael, "Time Is Money," *Jewelers Circular Keystone*, October 1997, p. 111.

"Whitehall Jewellers Expansion," *Wall Street Journal*, June 18, 1999.

"Whitehall Jewellers Fires Its Chief Financial Officer," *New York Times,* December 12, 2003, p. 4.

"Whitehall Jewellers, Inc.: Executive Is Said to Violate Policy and Placed on Leave," *Wall Street Journal,* November 24, 2003.

"Whitehall Names New CEO, Plans to Close 77 Stores," *National Jeweler,* November 2, 2005.

Zacks, Mitchell, "Market Overreacts, Makes Whitehall a Solid Bargain," *Chicago Sun-Times,* September 3, 2000, p. 49.

Xilinx, Inc.

—■—

2100 Logic Drive
San Jose, California 95124-3400
U.S.A.
Telephone: (408) 559-7778
Fax: (408) 559-7114
Web site: http://www.xilinx.com

Public Company
Incorporated: 1984 as Xilinx, Inc.
Employees: 3,295
Sales: $1.73 billion (2006)
Stock Exchanges: NASDAQ National Market
Ticker Symbol: XLNX
NAIC: 334413 Semiconductor and Related Device
     Manufacturing; 511210 Software Publishers

■ ■ ■

Xilinx, Inc., designs and develops advanced programmable logic devices and related software development systems. It is the world's leading supplier of programmable logic devices. In essence, the company's customized chips sequentially order the logic that tells sophisticated electronic gear the order in which its functions are to be performed. The company is credited with launching the "fabless" trend by outsourcing its manufacturing from the start.

Xilinx bolted to the forefront of its industry during the late 1980s and early 1990s through breakthrough product innovations. Following a dramatic slowdown in the telecommunications industry in the tech bust, the company has benefitted as its ever more powerful, cost-effective, and energy-efficient chips have found their way into new applications such as mobile electronics.

FOUNDED 1984

Xilinx was founded in 1984 by Ross Freeman and Bernard Vonderschmitt. Freeman and Vonderschmitt were both working as chip engineers at Zilog Corp. prior to joining in the Xilinx venture. Zilog, a subsidiary of oil behemoth Exxon Corp., was a developer of integrated circuits and related solid-state devices and had numerous technological innovations to its credit. It was there that Freeman came up with the idea that would soon make Xilinx larger than Zilog. He wanted to design a computer chip that effectively acted as a blank tape, allowing the user to program the chip himself rather than having to purchase a preprogrammed chip from the manufacturer.

Freeman was on the cutting edge of changes that were beginning to occur in the semiconductor industry. Prior to the mid-1980s, most computer chip manufacturers were interested almost solely in mass-market chips that could be produced in large volumes and sold for big profits. For several years that strategy was profitable for U.S. chipmakers, who dominated the global semiconductor market. When low-cost foreign manufacturers, particularly in Japan, began competing for market share, traditional manufacturers, including Zilog, suffered in what eventually became a commodity industry. At the same time, chip consumers began demanding increasingly specialized chips that could be used for specific applications.

Few big chip producers were excited about the prospects of chasing the market for application-specific circuits. Serving those customers meant designing and manufacturing many different chips, each of which would be sold to much smaller markets and at a lower total profit in comparison with mass-market chips. Because of the reluctance of chip makers to cater to their needs, consumers of application-specific circuits also were frustrated. Besides having to pay a relatively high price for customized chips, they were usually forced to endure costly problems related to defects in their chips. Specifically, if the semiconductor had a flaw or if the customer's chip requirements suddenly changed, the customer would have to wait for several weeks or even months for a new chip. Such a holdup could cost millions of dollars if an entire project was stalled while waiting for the new semiconductor.

Freeman realized that there might be a better way of meeting the need for application-specific circuits. His idea was to develop a sort of blank computer chip that could be programmed by the customer, thus minimizing risks associated with faulty chips and allowing much greater flexibility for companies designing equipment that incorporated the chips. The technology became known as "field programmable gate array," or FPGA. Freeman, who was a vice-president and general manager at Zilog at the time, approached his superiors and suggested that the development of FPGA devices could be a viable new avenue for Zilog. However, he was unable to convince executives at Exxon, who controlled more than $100 billion in assets, to chase a totally unexplored market that was worth perhaps only $100 million at the time.

Confident of the practicality of his concept, Freeman left his post at Zilog and began developing the first FPGA chip. He joined forces with another Zilog expatriate, Bernard Vonderschmitt. The 60-year-old Vonderschmitt also had been working as a vice-president and general manager at Zilog. Prior to that he had served 20 years at RCA, where he had headed the solid-state division. Their combined brainpower and management experience allowed them to attract several million dollars of venture capital, which they used to design the first commercially viable field programmable gate array.

In February 1984 they incorporated the venture as Xilinx. It was combined with their research and development limited partnership several months later, and in April 1990 the company was converted to a Delaware corporation. Xilinx began selling its first product in November 1985.

Xilinx's FPGA was based on the company's patented Logic Cell Array technology. The company's system basically consisted of an off-the-shelf programmable chip and a software package that could be used to program and tailor the chip for specific needs. The technology was based on the arrangement of gates (the lowest level building block in a logic circuit) in complex formations called arrays; as the number of gates increased, the more complex were the functions that the semiconductor could perform. The advantage of Xilinx's system was that the software allowed the customer to program the gates and arrays, in a manner analogous to a connect-the-dots puzzle, to perform any number of different functions. Also integral to the success of the system was a small family of advanced standard semiconductors, which were manufactured for Xilinx under license by Seiko Epson in Japan.

Xilinx's FPGA systems ultimately lived up to Freeman's original vision, providing greater flexibility for equipment manufacturers and minimizing problems caused by traditional chip manufacturing methods. The company's first products offered less complexity (i.e., fewer gates) than non-field-programmable devices available at the time. By late 1987, after injections of venture capital amounting to more than $18 million, Xilinx was offering a new generation of FPGA chips that, with 9,000 gates, could compete technologically with all but the most advanced non-field-programmable products. The result was that in 1987, after marketing its products for little more than one year, Xilinx was generating revenues at an annualized rate of nearly $14 million.

MARKET GROWTH AND COMPANY SUCCESS

As Xilinx was earning respect for its FPGA technology, the market for application-specific circuits continued to grow during the late 1980s and into the 1990s. The result was that the market for FPGA chips surged, contributing to rapid revenue and profit growth at Xilinx. Indeed, sales rose to nearly $30.5 million in 1988 (fiscal year ended March 30, 1989) before rising to

about 30 percent of its output overseas. More than half of its revenues were attributable to its popular XC3000 family of FPGA systems, but Xilinx had a stream of products in its development pipeline. The company sold nearly $100 million worth of its products in 1990, and its base of 3,500-plus customers grew to include big names like Apple Computer, IBM, Compaq Computer, Hewlett-Packard Co., Fujitsu, Sun Microsystems, and Northern Telecom. To keep pace with demand, Xilinx moved into a 144,000-square-foot plant in San Jose, California.

Although Xilinx rapidly increased sales and profits in the late 1980s and early 1990s, it also ceded much of its market share. Indeed, after Xilinx had invented its niche and controlled 100 percent of the FPGA market during the mid-1990s, other companies began offering competing technology that rapidly eroded Xilinx's dominance. By the early 1990s, in fact, Xilinx was controlling only about 65 percent of the total FPGA market. It had succeeded, though, in pressuring many of its earliest competitors out of the business, despite the fact that some of them had access to much more funding. By 1993 only a few companies were seriously vying for market share. The largest was Actel, which had introduced its first product in 1988 and by 1993 was serving about 18 percent of the market. The distant third-place contender was Altera Corporation, which sold technology similar to FPGA systems.

Despite loss of market share, high demand allowed Xilinx to boost revenues to $135 million in 1991 (fiscal year ended March 30, 1992) and then to $178 million in 1992. Part of that growth resulted from Xilinx's jump into the market for EPLDs (EPROM technology-based complex Programmable Logic Devices), which effectively offered higher performance and higher density per chip, and were designed to complement FPGA devices. By 1993 Xilinx was capturing more than $250 million in annual revenue and generating net income of $41.3 million. In addition, market growth for FPGA chips was expected to intensify in the mid-1990s.

To take advantage of market expansion, Xilinx introduced a completely new line of FPGA products in 1994: the XC5000 family of FPGA chips and software. The XC5000 line was developed to cater to the market for low-end gate array products. Specifically, XC5000 chips were designed to offer a cost-effective alternative to high-volume non-field-programmable gate array products, thus giving Xilinx access to a new spectrum of the market for application-specific circuits. Xilinx followed the introduction of the XC5000 family with other new products, including the XC3100L and XC4000L. Both new families of FPGA chips were designed to complement low-power applications, which boosted Xil-

KEY DATES

1984: Former engineers from Exxon's Zilog subsidiary form Xilinx to produce new programmable logic chips.
1987: Annualized revenues reach $14 million.
1988: Company makes first profit as sales exceed $30 million.
1989: AMD buys a 20 percent holding in Xilinx, which goes public.
1996: Revenues exceed $500 million in 1995/96 fiscal year; company has 1,000 employees.
1998: Virtex series offers industry's first million-gate FGPA.
2000: Revenues exceed $1 billion in 1999/2000 fiscal year.
2002: Xilinx posts loss in tech slowdown; IBM contracts to manufacture some chips for hybrid processor.
2004: Toshiba signs on as chip producer as IBM contract ends; Seiko and UMC continue as suppliers.
2005: Sales exceed $1.5 billion; company has about 3,000 employees.

$50 million in 1989. Xilinx posted its first surplus—a net income of $2.92 million—in 1988 and went on to generate profits of $6 million in 1989. Unfortunately, Freeman died in 1989. Vonderschmitt took the reins as president and chief executive.

Xilinx was aided during the late 1980s by a partnership with Monolithic Memories Inc. (MMI), which in 1987 signed a deal with Xilinx that gave MMI royalties and free patent rights to manufacture Xilinx's products. In return, MMI supplied capital to Xilinx. The arrangement provided needed funding to bring Xilinx's products to market and sustain its research and development initiatives. Soon after signing the deal, though, MMI was purchased by American Micro Devices, Inc. Xilinx became uncomfortable with the new arrangement, partly because American Micro was one of its competitors. So, in 1989 Vonderschmitt convinced American Micro to buy 20 percent of the company at a 10 percent premium and dissolve the original agreement. In search of new funding, Xilinx went public with a stock offering on the NASDAQ over-the-counter exchange.

With cash from the stock sale, Xilinx continued to grow. By late 1990 the company was selling its products throughout the United States, but was also shipping

inx's access to manufacturers of increasingly popular low-power devices like portable computers and related peripheral devices, portable and wireless communication gear, and digital cameras.

New products and healthy growth in demand for existing FPGA chips helped Xilinx to boost its sales to $335 million in 1994, a record $59.28 million of which was netted as income. Likewise, revenues rose to about $550 million in 1995 (fiscal year ended March 30, 1996). By that time, Xilinx was employing more than 1,000 workers in offices throughout North America, Asia, and Europe. The company was selling more than 40 varieties of programmable logic products and related software applications and continued to be firmly entrenched as the leader in its industry niche.

Early in 1996 Vonderschmitt stepped down as chief executive of the company he had co-founded. Vonderschmitt remained as chairman of the board for another seven years and passed away in 2004.

Control of the company went to Willem P. "Wim" Roelandts. The 51-year-old Roelandts had worked for 28 years at Hewlett-Packard Co., serving as senior vice-president and managing the company's Computer Systems Organization, among other posts. He was known as a seasoned high-tech industry veteran and was chosen to lead Xilinx into a "new era of growth," according to Vonderschmitt.

A new line of high-end FPGAs called Virtex came out in 1998. Offering the industry's first million-gate FPGA, the series gave Xilinx a perceived technological edge over its rivals. Xilinx and Altera each held a little more than 30 percent of the PLD market in 1999, according to *Electronic Business,* although Altera was then a bit larger. Over the next several years, Xilinx would greatly expand its market share with its new products, while Altera's would remain static. Xilinx posted net income of $127 million on revenues of $614 million in the fiscal year ended March 28, 1998. It had about 1,400 employees.

TECH BUST AND RECOVERY

Xilinx's revenues just exceeded $1 billion in the fiscal year ended March 31, 2000. Unfortunately, the PLD (programmable logic devices) market would be nearly halved in the tech and telecom slowdown. Xilinx was burdened with millions in excess inventory. Though revenues were up to $1.7 billion in the 2000–01 fiscal year, net income slipped from $653 million to $36 million.

Eight years of legal wrangling came to an end in 2001 when Altera agreed to pay Xilinx $20 million to settle a patent infringement dispute. The two also agreed on a moratorium on intellectual property suits between the companies for the next five years.

At the time, both were reeling from the tech slowdown. Xilinx lost $113 million on revenues of $1 billion in 2002. However, new markets were opening for PLDs. Designers had typically used the flexible PLDs in prototypes, while switching to ASICs (application-specific integrated circuits) for mass production. The increasing complexity of smart phones and other multi-function electronic devices made them ideally suited for PLDs—once their price of these chips came down enough to make them practical for high-volume applications. Xilinx's new CoolRunner chips were compact and energy efficient, making them suited for portable systems.

Roelandts told *Forbes* that FPGAs would soon change the way computers were designed. Xilinx supplied the chips to a new web server from newly-formed Wincom that did away with the microprocessor, which was once the central feature of any computer system. FPGAs, which performed tasks in parallel, could perform some repetitive jobs more quickly than the traditional CPU. A number of third parties were designing add-on products with Xilinx's FPGAs to make traditional processor-based computers run many times faster.

Xilinx worked with IBM Microelectronics to build a hybrid system that teamed the Virtex-II FPGA with IBM's PowerPC microprocessor. In 2002, IBM contracted to manufacture the Virtex chips itself, the first time it had entered a volume production agreement for an outside party. Japan's Toshiba Corp. took over this manufacturing in 2004 after the arrangement with IBM lapsed. Xilinx chips continued to be produced by Seiko in Japan as well as Taiwan's United Microelectronics Corp. (UMC).

Xilinx commanded the PLD market with a 50 percent share, according to *Electronic Business.* Its revenues were $1.7 billion in the fiscal year ended April 1, 2006, while net income had climbed to $354 million. Altera was still its only close rival. Xilinx had grown to employ about 3,000 people.

Not all of Xilinx's growth had been organic. Acquisitions included that of San Jose programming company LavaLogic, bought from Canada's TSI Telsys Corp. in 2000. Santa Clara's Hier Design, Inc., which made software for designing FPGAs, was purchased in 2004. Next, Xilinx bought AccelChip, Inc., a producer of software for designing digital signal processing systems, in January 2006 for $19.6 million.

Dave Mote
Updated, Frederick C. Ingram

PRINCIPAL SUBSIDIARIES

Xilinx Asia Pacific Ptd. Ltd. (Singapore); Xilinx Hong Kong Ltd.; Xilinx Ireland; Xilinx Limited (United Kingdom); Xilinx K.K. (Japan).

PRINCIPAL COMPETITORS

Altera Corporation; Lattice Semiconductor Corporation.

FURTHER READING

Arnold, Bill, "Slugfest," *Electronic Business,* August 1999, p. 77.

Autry, Ret, "Xilinx," *Fortune,* August 27, 1990, p. 81.

Barrett, Larry, "Xilinx Decides to Move Away from Specialty Chip Market," *Silicon Valley/San Jose Business Journal,* August 9, 1996.

Dennis, Ann, "Xilinx Triples Three-Volt Product Offerings," *Business Wire,* December 18, 1995.

Druce, Chris, "Xilinx Makes Historic $100m Manufacturing Deal with IBM," *Electronics Weekly,* March 6, 2002, p. 2.

Edwards, John, "No Room for Second Place: Xilinx and Altera Slug It Out for Supremacy in the Changing PLD Market," *Electronic Business,* June 2006, pp. 30ff.

Ghosheh, Vallee, "Xilinx Targets Gate Array Market with New XC5000 FPGA Family," *PR Newswire,* November 28, 1994.

Goldman, James S., "With Just Two Xs They Pack a Punch," *Business Journal-San Jose,* August 12, 1991, p. 1.

Hayes, Mary, "Xilinx Leads, Actel Gains," *Business Journal-San Jose,* May 3, 1993, p. 1.

Kaus, Danek S., "On-Site Waste Consultant Helps Xilinx Double Its Recycling," *Silicon Valley/San Jose Business Journal,* May 31, 2002.

Koland, Cordell, "Xilinx Founder Opens "Gate" to New Chip Market Horizon," *Business Journal-San Jose,* October 19, 1987, p. 10.

Lammers, David, "Xilinx's Bernard Vonderschmitt Dead at 80—EE Entrepreneur Drove Fabless Business Model," *Electronic Engineering Times,* June 14, 2004, p. 1.

Lyons, Daniel, "Chipping Away," *Forbes,* April 14, 2003, p. 206.

Manners, David, "Managing to Succeed," *Electronics Weekly,* June 18, 1997, p. 14.

Morrison, Gale, "Xilinx, Altera Call Truce," *Electronic News,* July 23, 2001, p. 1.

Nass, Richard, "Programmable Logic Fills the Bill for Portable Applications," *Portable Design,* July 2002, pp. 20ff.

Seither, Mike, "Xilinx Appoints Hewlett-Packard Executive as New CEO," *Business Wire,* January 11, 1996.

Souza, Crista, "Finding Partners in Prosperity—Aiming to Better Serve Its Customers, Xilinx Is Improving Inventory Management and Production Flow by Ceding More Control to Its IC Packaging Partners," *EBN,* April 29, 2002, p. 29.

Sperling, Ed, "Logical Outcome: PLD Maker Xilinx Has Gained Market Share in a Down Market, But the Future Remains Hazy," *Electronic News,* June 3, 2002, pp. 2f.

Sutherland, Lani, "Corporate Profits for Xilinx," *Business Wire,* February 25, 1994.

———, "Xilinx Announces Record Results," *Business Wire,* October 11, 1990.

Xilinx Corp. *Xilinx; About the Company,* San Jose: Xilinx, 1995.

Index to Companies

American Factors, Ltd. *see* Amfac/JMB Hawaii L.L.C.

American Family Corporation, III **187–89** *see also* AFLAC Inc.

American Family Publishers, **23** 393–94

American Feldmühle Corp., **II** 51; **21** 330

American Financial Group Inc., III **190–92; 48 6–10 (upd.)**

American Fine Wire, Inc., **33** 248

American First National Supermarkets, **16** 313

American Fitness Centers, **25** 40

American Fitness Products, Inc., **47** 128

American Flange, **30** 397

American Flavor & Fragrance Company, **9** 154

American Flyer Trains, **16** 336–37

American Foods Group, 43 23–27

American Football League, **29** 346

American Foreign Insurance Association *see* AFIA.

American Freightways Corporation, **42** 141

American Fructose Corp., **14** 18–19

American Fur Company, **25** 220

American Furniture Company, Inc., 21 **32–34**

American Gaming and Electronics, Inc., **43** 461

American Gas & Electric *see* American Electric Power Company.

American General Corporation, III **193–94; 10 65–67 (upd.); 46 20–23** **(upd.)**

American General Finance Corp., 11 **16–17**

American Girl, Inc., 69 16–19 (upd)

American Golf Corporation, 45 22–24

American Gramaphone LLC, 52 18–20

American Graphics, **23** 100

American Greetings Corporation, 7 **23–25; 22 33–36 (upd.); 59 34–39** **(upd.)**

American Grinder and Manufacturing Company, **9** 26

American Hardware & Supply Company *see* TruServ Corporation.

American Hawaii Cruises, **27** 34

American Health & Life Insurance Company, **27** 47

American Healthcorp Inc., **48** 25

American Healthways, Inc., 65 40–42

American Heritage Savings, **II** 420

American Hoechst Corporation *see* Hoechst Celanese Corporation.

American Home Mortgage Holdings, **Inc., 46 24–26**

American Home Patients Centers Inc., **46** 4

American Home Products, I 622–24; 10 **68–70 (upd.)** *see also* Wyeth.

American Home Publishing Co., Inc., **14** 460

American Home Shield *see* ServiceMaster Inc.

American Home Video, **9** 186

American Homestar Corporation, 18 **26–29; 41 17–20 (upd.)**

American Homeware Inc., **15** 501

American Hospital Association, **10** 159

American Hospital Supply Co., **III** 80; **11** 459, 486; **19** 103; **21** 118; **30** 496; **53** 345

American Hydron, **25** 55

American I.G. Chemical Corporation *see* GAF Corporation.

American Improved Cements *see* Giant Cement Holding, Inc.

American Independent Oil Co. *see* Aminoil, Inc.

American Industrial Properties *see* Developers Diversified Realty Corporation.

American Information Services, Inc., **11** 111

American Institute of Certified Public **Accountants (AICPA), 44 27–30**

American Institutional Products, Inc., **18** 246

American Insurance Group, Inc., **73** 351

American International Airways, Inc., **17** 318; **22** 311

American International Group, Inc., III **195–98; 15 15–19 (upd.); 47 13–19** **(upd.)**

American Isuzu Motors, Inc. *see* Isuzu Motors, Ltd.

American Italian Pasta Company, 27 **38–40; 76 18–21 (upd.)**

American Janitor Service, **25** 15

American Jet Industries, **7** 205

American Kennel Club, Inc., 74 17–19

American Knitting Mills of Miami, Inc., **22** 213

American La-France, **10** 296

American Land Cruiser Company *see* Cruise America Inc.

American Lawyer Media Holdings, Inc., **32 34–37**

American Learning Corporation, **7** 168

American Light and Traction *see* MCN Corporation.

American Lightwave Systems, Inc., **10** 19

American Limousine Corp., **26** 62

American Linen Supply Company *see* Steiner Corporation.

American Locker Group Incorporated, **34 19–21**

American Lung Association, 48 11–14

American Machine and Foundry Co., **7** 211–13; **11** 397; **25** 197

American Machine and Metals, **9** 23

American Machine and Tool Co., Inc., **57** 160

American Machinery and Foundry, Inc., **57** 85

American Maize-Products Co., 14 **17–20**

American Management Association, 76 **22–25**

American Management Systems, Inc., **11 18–20**

American Materials & Technologies Corporation, **27** 117

American Media, Inc., 27 41–44; 82 **10–15 (upd.)**

American Medical Association, 39 **15–18**

American Medical Disposal, Inc. *see* Stericycle, Inc.

American Medical Holdings, **55** 370

American Medical International, Inc., **III 73–75**

American Medical Optics, **25** 55

American Medical Response, Inc., 39 **19–22**

American Medical Services, **II** 679–80; **14** 209

American Medicorp, Inc., **14** 432; **24** 230

American Melamine, **27** 317

American Merchandising Associates Inc., **14** 411

American Metal Climax, Inc. *see* AMAX.

American Metals and Alloys, Inc., **19** 432

American Metals Corporation *see* Reliance Steel & Aluminum Company.

American Micro Devices, Inc., **16** 549

American Modern Insurance Group *see* The Midland Company.

American Motors Corp., I 135–37

América Móvil, S.A. de C.V., 80 5–8

American MSI Corporation *see* Moldflow Corporation.

American Multi-Cinema *see* AMC Entertainment Inc.

American National Can Co., **IV** 175

American National General Agencies Inc., **III** 221; **14** 109; **37** 85

American National Insurance Company, **8 27–29; 27 45–48 (upd.)**

American Natural Snacks Inc., **29** 480

American Oil Co., **7** 101; **14** 22

American Olean Tile Company, **III** 424; **22** 48, 170

American Optical Co., **7** 436; **38** 363–64

American Overseas Airlines, **12** 380

American Pad & Paper Company, 20 **18–21**

American Paging, **9** 494–96

American Paper Box Company, **12** 376

American Patriot Insurance, **22** 15

American Payment Systems, Inc., **21** 514

American Petrofina, Inc., **7** 179–80; **19** 11

American Pfauter, **24** 186

American Pharmaceutical Partners, Inc., **69 20–22**

American Phone Centers, Inc., **21** 135

American Pop Corn Company, 59 **40–43**

American Port Services (Amports), **45** 29

American Power & Light Co., **6** 545, 596–97; **12** 542; **49** 143

American Power Conversion **Corporation, 24 29–31; 67 18–20** **(upd.)**

American Premier Underwriters, Inc., **10 71–74**

American Prepaid Professional Services, Inc. *see* CompDent Corporation.

American President Companies Ltd., 6 **353–55** *see also* APL Limited.

American Printing House for the Blind, **26 13–15**

AMOR 14 Corporation, **64** 95

Amorim Investimentos e Participaço, **48** 117, 119

Amorim Revestimentos, **48** 118

Amoskeag Company, 8 32–33

Amot Controls Corporation, **15** 404; **50** 394

AMP, Inc., II 7–8; 14 26–28 (upd.)

Ampacet Corporation, 67 27–29

Ampad Holding Corporation *see* American Pad & Paper Company.

AMPAL *see* American-Palestine Trading Corp.

AMPCO Auto Parks, Inc. *see* American Building Maintenance Industries, Inc.; ABM Industries Incorporated.

Ampco-Pittsburgh Corporation, 79 26–29

Ampeg Company, **48** 353

AMPEP, **III** 625

Ampersand Ventures, **73** 227–28

Ampex Corporation, 17 18–20

Amphenol Corporation, 40 34–37

Ampol Petroleum Ltd., **III** 729; **27** 473

Ampro, **25** 504–05

AMR *see* American Medical Response, Inc.

AMR Combs Inc., **36** 190

AMR Corporation, 28 22–26 (upd.); 52 21–26 (upd.)

AMR Information Services, **9** 95

Amram's Distributing Limited, **12** 425

AMRE, **III** 211

AMREP Corporation, 21 35–37

Amro *see* Amsterdam-Rotterdam Bank N.V.

Amrop International Australasia, **34** 249

AMS *see* Advanced Marketing Services, Inc.

Amsbra Limited, **62** 48

Amscan Holdings, Inc., 61 24–26

Amsco International, **29** 450

Amserve Ltd., **48** 23

AmSouth Bancorporation, 12 15–17; 48 15–18 (upd.)

Amstar Corp., **14** 18

Amstar Sugar Corporation, **7** 466–67; **26** 122

Amsted Industries Incorporated, 7 29–31

Amsterdam-Rotterdam Bank N.V., II 185–86

Amstrad plc, III 112–14; 48 19–23 (upd.)

AmSurg Corporation, 48 24–27

AMT *see* American Machine and Tool Co., Inc.; American Materials & Technologies Corporation.

Amtech *see* American Building Maintenance Industries, Inc.; ABM Industries Incorporated.

Amtech Systems Corporation, **11** 65; **27** 405

Amtel, Inc., **10** 136

Amtrak *see* The National Railroad Passenger Corporation.

Amtran, Inc., 34 31–33

AmTrans *see* American Transport Lines.

Amurol Confections Company, **58** 378

Amvac Chemical Corporation, **47** 20

Amvent Inc., **25** 120

AMVESCAP PLC, 65 43–45

Amway Corporation, III 11–14; 13 36–39 (upd.); 30 62–66 (upd.) *see also* Alticor Inc.

Amy's Kitchen Inc., 76 26–28

Amylin Pharmaceuticals, Inc., 67 30–32

ANA *see* All Nippon Airways Co., Ltd.

Anacomp, Inc., **11** 19

Anaconda Aluminum, **11** 38

Anaconda Co., **7** 261–63

Anadarko Petroleum Corporation, 10 82–84; 52 27–30 (upd.)

Anadex, Inc., **18** 435–36

Anaheim Angels Baseball Club, Inc., 53 41–44

Anaheim Imaging, **19** 336

Analex Corporation, 74 20–22

Analog Devices, Inc., 10 85–87

Analogic Corporation, 23 13–16

Analysts International Corporation, 36 40–42

Analytic Sciences Corporation, 10 88–90

Analytical Nursing Management Corporation (ANMC) *see* Amedisys, Inc.

Analytical Science Laboratories Inc., **58** 134

Analytical Surveys, Inc., 33 43–45

Analytico Food BV *see* Eurofins Scientific S.A.

Anam Group, 23 17–19

Anarad, Inc., **18** 515

Anaren Microwave, Inc., 33 46–48

Anchor Bancorp, Inc., 10 91–93

Anchor Brake Shoe, **18** 5

Anchor Brewing Company, 47 26–28

Anchor Corporation, **12** 525

Anchor Gaming, 24 36–39

Anchor Hocking Glassware, 13 40–42

Anchor Motor Freight, Inc., **12** 309–10

Anchor National Financial Services, Inc., **11** 482

Anchor National Life Insurance Company, **11** 482

Andenne Bricolage BVBA, **68** 64

Anders Wilhelmsen & Co., **22** 471

Andersen, 68 23–27 (upd.)

Andersen Consulting *see* Accenture Ltd.

Andersen Corporation, 10 94–95

Andersen Worldwide, 29 25–28 (upd.)

Anderson Animal Hospital, Inc., **58** 354

The Anderson-DuBose Company, 60 32–34

Anderson Exploration Ltd., **61** 75

Anderson, Greenwood & Co., **11** 225–26

Anderson Packaging, Inc., **64** 27

Anderson Testing Company, Inc., **6** 441

Anderson Trucking Service, Inc., 75 27–29

The Andersons, Inc., 31 17–21

Andlinger & Co., **60** 132

Andreas Christ, **26** 243

Andreas Stihl AG & Co. KG, 16 22–24; 59 44–47 (upd.)

Andrew Corporation, 10 96–98; 32 38–41 (upd.)

Andrew Jergens Company *see* Kao Brands Company

Andrews Group, Inc., **10** 402

Andrews Kurth, LLP, 71 31–34

Andrews McMeel Universal, 40 38–41

Andrews Office Supply and Equipment Co., **25** 500

Andritz AG, 51 24–26

Andronico's Market, 70 10–13

Andrx Corporation, 55 25–27

Anfor, **IV** 249–50

Angele Ghigi, **II** 475

Angelica Corporation, 15 20–22; 43 28–31 (upd.)

Angelo's Supermarkets, Inc., **II** 674

ANGI Ltd., **11** 28

AngioDynamics, Inc., 81 26–29

Angle Steel, **25** 261

Anglian Water Plc, **38** 51

Anglo-Abrasives Ltd. *see* Carbo PLC.

Anglo-American Clays Corp., **IV** 346

Anglo American Industrial Corporation, **59** 224–25

Anglo American PLC, IV 20–23; 16 25–30 (upd.); 50 30–36 (upd.)

Anglo-Canadian Telephone Company of Montreal *see* British Columbia Telephone Company.

Anglo-Celtic Watch Company, **25** 430

Anglo Company, Ltd., **9** 363

Anglo-Dutch Unilever group, **9** 317

Anglo Energy, Ltd., **9** 364

Anglo-Iranian Oil Co., **7** 141

Anglo-Lautaro Nitrate Corporation, **9** 363

Anglo-Persian Oil Co., **7** 140

Anglovaal Industries Ltd., **20** 263

Anheuser-Busch Companies, Inc., I 217–19; 10 99–101 (upd.); 34 34–37 (upd.)

ANI America Inc., **62** 331

Anker BV, 53 45–47

ANMC *see* Amedisys, Inc.

Ann Street Group Ltd., **61** 44–46

Anne Klein & Co., **15** 145–46; **24** 299; **40** 277–78; **56** 90

Annecy Béøn Carrières, **70** 343

Anneplas, **25** 464

Annie's Homegrown, Inc., 59 48–50

AnnTaylor Stores Corporation, 13 43–45; 37 12–15 (upd.); 67 33–37 (upd.)

Annuaires Marcotte Ltd., **10** 461

Anocout Engineering Co., **23** 82

aQuantive, Inc., 81 30–33

ANR Pipeline Co., 17 21–23

Anritsu Corporation, 68 28–30

Ansa Software, **9** 81

The Anschutz Company, 12 18–20; 36 43–47 (upd.); 73 24–30 (upd.)

Ansco & Associates, LLC, **57** 119

Ansell Ltd., 60 35–38 (upd.)

Ansell Rubber Company, **10** 445

Anselmo L. Morvillo S.A., **19** 336

Ansett Australia, *see* Air New Zealand Limited.

Ansoft Corporation, 63 32–34

Belden CDT Inc., 19 43–45; 76 49–52 (upd.)

Beldis, 23 219

Beldoch Industries Corp., 17 137–38

Belgacom, 6 302–04

Belgian Rapid Access to Information Network Services, 6 304

Belglas, 16 420; 43 307

Belgo Group plc, 31 41

Belize Electric Company Limited, 47 137

Belk, Inc., V 12–13; 19 46–48 (upd.); 72 26–29 (upd.)

Bell and Howell Company, 9 61–64; 29 54–58 (upd.)

Bell Aerospace, 24 442

Bell Aircraft Company, 11 267; 13 267

Bell Atlantic Corporation, V 272–74; 25 58–62 (upd.) see also Verizon Communications.

Bell Canada Enterprises Inc. see BCE, Inc.

Bell Canada International, Inc., 6 305–08

Bell Communications Research see Telcordia Technologies, Inc.

Bell Fibre Products, 12 377

Bell Helicopter Textron Inc., 46 64–67

Bell Helmets Inc., 22 458

Bell Industries, Inc., 47 40–43

Bell Laboratories see AT&T Bell Laboratories, Inc.

Bell Microproducts Inc., 69 63–65

Bell Mountain Partnership, Ltd., 15 26

Bell-Northern Research, Ltd. see BCE Inc.

Bell Pharmacal Labs, 12 387

Bell Resources, III 729; 10 170; 27 473

Bell Sports Corporation, 16 51–53; 44 51–54 (upd.)

Bell System, 7 99, 333; 11 500; 16 392–93

Bell Telephone Manufacturing, II 13

Bellcore see Telcordia Technologies, Inc.

Belle Alkali Co., 7 308

Belleek Pottery Ltd., 71 50–53

Bellofram Corp., 14 43

BellSouth Corporation, V 276–78; 29 59–62 (upd.)

Bellway Plc, 45 37–39

Belmin Systems, 14 36

Belmont Savings and Loan, 10 339

Belo Corporation see A.H. Belo Corporation

Beloit Corporation, 14 55–57

Beloit Tool Company see Regal-Beloit Corporation.

Beloit Woodlands, 10 380

Belron International Ltd., 76 53–56

Bemis Company, Inc., 8 53–55

Ben & Jerry's Homemade, Inc., 10 146–48; 35 58–62 (upd.); 80 22–28 (upd.)

Ben Bridge Jeweler, Inc., 60 52–54

Ben E. Keith Company, 76 57–59

Ben Franklin Retail Stores, Inc. see FoxMeyer Health Corporation.

Ben Franklin Savings & Trust, 10 117

Ben Hill Griffin, III 53

Ben Myerson Candy Co., Inc., 26 468

Ben Venue Laboratories Inc., 16 439; 39 73

Benair Freight International Limited see Gulf Agency Company

Benchmark Capital, 49 50–52

Benchmark Electronics, Inc., 40 66–69

Benchmark Tape Systems Ltd, 62 293

Benckiser Group, 37 269

Benckiser N.V. see Reckitt Benckiser plc.

Benderson Development Company, 69 120

Bendick's of Mayfair see August Storck KG.

Bendix Corporation, I 141–43

Beneficial Corporation, 8 56–58

Beneficial Finance Company, 27 428–29

Beneficial Standard Life, 10 247

Benefit Consultants, Inc., 16 145

Benefits Technologies, Inc., 52 382

Benelli Arms S.p.A., 39 151

Benesse Corporation, 76 60–62

Bénéteau SA, 55 54–56

Benetton Group S.p.A., 10 149–52; 67 47–51 (upd.)

Benfield Greig Group plc, 53 63–65

Benguet Corporation, 58 21–24

Benihana, Inc., 18 56–59; 76 63–66 (upd.)

Benjamin Moore and Co., 13 84–87; 38 95–99 (upd.)

Benjamin Sheridan Corporation, 62 82

Benlee, Inc., 51 237

Benlox Holdings PLC, 16 465

Benn Bros. plc, IV 687

Bennett Industries, Inc., 17 371–73

Bennett's Smokehouse and Saloon, 19 122; 29 201

Bennigan's, 7 336; 12 373; 19 286; 25 181

Benpres Holdings, 56 214

BenQ Corporation, 67 52–54

Bensdorp, 29 47

Benson & Hedges, Ltd. see Gallaher Limited.

Benson Wholesale Co., II 624

Bentalls, 37 6, 8

Bentex Holding S.A., 48 209

Bentley Laboratories, 22 360

Bentley Mills, Inc., see Interface, Inc.

Bentley Motor Ltd., 21 435

Bentley's Luggage Corp., 58 370

Bentoel, PT, 62 97

Benton International, Inc., 29 376

Benton Oil and Gas Company, 47 44–46

Bentwood Ltd., 62 342

Benwood Iron Works, 17 355

Bercy Management see Elior SA.

Beresford International plc, 24 335; 27 159

Beretta see Fabbrica D' Armi Pietro Beretta S.p.A.

Bergdorf Goodman Inc., 52 45–48

Bergen Brunswig Corporation, V 14–16; 13 88–90 (upd.) see also AmerisourceBergen Corporation.

Berger Associates, Inc., 26 233

Berger Bros Company, 62 31–33

Berger Manufacturing Company, 26 405

Bergerat Monnoyeur see Groupe Monnoyeur.

Berges electronic GmbH, 56 357

Beringer Blass Wine Estates Ltd., 22 78–81; 66 34–37 (upd.)

Berisford International plc see Enodis plc.

Berjaya Group Bhd., 67 55–57

Berk Corp., 52 193

Berkeley Farms, Inc., 46 68–70

Berkey Photo Inc., see Fuqua Industries, Inc.

Berkley Dean & Co., 15 525

Berkley Petroleum Corporation, 52 30

Berkline Corp., 17 183; 20 363; 39 267

Berkshire Hathaway Inc., III 213–15; 18 60–63 (upd.); 42 31–36 (upd.)

Berkshire Partners, 10 393

Berkshire Realty Holdings, L.P., 49 53–55

Berleca Ltd., 9 395; 42 269

Berlex Laboratories, Inc., 66 38–40

Berli Jucker, 18 180–82

BerlinDat Gesellschaft für Informationsverarbeitung und Systemtechnik GmbH, 39 57

Berliner Kindl Brauerei, 75 334

Berliner Stadtreinigungsbetriebe, 58 25–28

Berliner Verkehrsbetriebe (BVG), 58 29–31

Berlitz International, Inc., 13 91–93; 39 47–50 (upd.)

Berman Brothers Fur Co., 21 525

Berman Buckskin, 21 525

Bernard C. Harris Publishing Company, Inc., 39 51–53

Bernard Chaus, Inc., 27 59–61

Bernard Warschaw Insurance Sales Agency, Inc., 55 128

Bernardin Ltd., 30 39

Berndorf Austria, 44 206

Berndorf Switzerland, 44 206

Berner Nut Company, 64 110

Bernheim-Meyer: A l'Innovation see GIB Group.

The Bernick Companies, 75 62–65

Bernie Schulman's, 12 132

Bernina Holding AG, 47 47–50

Berrios Enterprises, 14 236

Berry Bearing Company, 9 254

The Berry Company see L. M. Berry and Company

Berry Petroleum Company, 47 51–53

Berry Plastics Corporation, 21 57–59

Berryhill Nursery see Monrovia Nursery Company.

Bert L. Smokler & Company, 11 257

Bertelsmann A.G., IV 592–94; 43 63–67 (upd.)

Bertelsmann Music Group, 52 428

Bertolini's Authentic Trattorias, 30 329

Bertram & Graf Gmbh, 28 45

Bertucci's Corporation, 16 54–56; 64 51–54 (upd.)

Berwick Offray, LLC, 70 17–19

Berwind Corp., 14 18

Beryl Corp., 26 149

Charles R. McCormick Lumber Company, **12** 407

Charles Revson Inc. *see* Revlon Inc.

Charles River Laboratories International, Inc., 42 66–69

The Charles Schwab Corporation, 8 94–96; 26 64–67 (upd.); 81 62–68 (upd.)

Charles Scribner's Sons, **7** 166

The Charles Stark Draper Laboratory, Inc., 35 90–92

Charles Vögele Holding AG, 82 63-66

Charlesbank Capital Partners LLC, **44** 54

Charleston Consolidated Railway, Gas and Electric Company, **6** 574

Charley Brothers, **II** 669

Charley's Eating & Drinking Saloon, **20** 54

Charlie Browns, **24** 269–70

Charlotte Russe Holding, Inc., 35 93–96

Charming Shoppes, Inc., 8 97–98; 38 127–29 (upd.)

Charoen Pokphand Group, 62 60–63

Charrington United Breweries, **38** 76

Chart House Enterprises, Inc., 17 85–88

Chart Industries, Inc., 21 107–09

Charter Club, **9** 315

Charter Communications, Inc., 33 91–94

Charter Consolidated, **IV** 23, 119–20; **16** 293; **49** 234

Charter Corp., **III** 254; **14** 460

Charter Golf, Inc. *see* Ashworth, Inc.

Charter Medical Corporation, **31** 356

Charter National Life Insurance Company, **11** 261

Charter Oak Capital Partners, **58** 88

Charter Oil Co., **II** 620; **12** 240

Charterhouse Japhet, **24** 269

ChartHouse International Learning Corporation, 49 87–89

Chartwell Associates, **9** 331

Chartwell Investments, **44** 54

Chartwell Land plc, **V** 106; **24** 266, 269

Chas. H. Tompkins Co., **16** 285–86

Chas. Levy Company LLC, 60 83–85

The Chase Manhattan Corporation, II 247–49; 13 145–48 (upd.) *see* J.P. Morgan Chase & Co.

Chateau Communities, Inc., 37 76–79

Chateau St. Jean, **22** 80

Chateau Souverain, **22** 80

Chateau Ste. Michelle Winery, **42** 245, 247

Chateaux St. Jacques, **24** 307

Chatham Steel Corporation *see* Reliance Steel & Aluminum Company.

Chatham Technologies Inc., **38** 189

Chatillon *see* John Chatillon & Sons Inc.

Chattanooga Gas Company, Inc., **6** 577

Chattanooga Gas Light Company, **6** 448; **23** 30

Chattanooga Medicine Company *see* Chattem, Inc.

Chattem, Inc., 17 89–92

Chatto, Virago, Bodley Head & Jonathan Cape, Ltd., **31** 376

Chautauqua Airlines, Inc., 38 130–32

CHC Helicopter Corporation, 67 101–03

Check Express, **33** 4–5

Check Point Software Technologies Ltd., **20** 238

Checker Auto Parts *see* CSK Auto Corporation.

Checker Holding, **10** 370

Checker Motors Corp., **10** 369

Checkers Drive-In Restaurants, Inc., 16 95–98; 74 79–83 (upd.)

CheckFree Corporation, 81 69–72

Checkpoint Systems, Inc., 39 77–80

Checkport Schweiz AG *see* Swissport International Ltd.

The Cheesecake Factory Inc., 17 93–96

Cheetham Salt Ltd., **62** 307

Chef Boyardee, **10** 70; **50** 538

Chelan Power Company, **6** 596

Chelsea GCA Realty, Inc., **27** 401

Chelsea Milling Company, 29 109–11

Chelsfield PLC, 67 104–06

Cheltenham & Gloucester PLC, 61 60–62

Chem-Nuclear Systems, Inc., **9** 109–10

Chemcentral Corporation, 8 99–101

Chemdal Corp., **13** 34; **59** 31

Chemed Corporation, 13 149–50

Chemfab Corporation, 35 97–101

ChemFirst, Inc., **27** 316

Chemgas Holding BV, **41** 340

Chemgrout, **26** 42

Chemi-Trol Chemical Co., 16 99–101

Chemical Banking Corporation, II 250–52; 14 101–04 (upd.)

Chemical Grouting Co. Ltd., **51** 179

Chemical Process Co., **7** 308

Chemical Waste Management, Inc., 9 108–10

Chemicon International, Inc., **63** 353

Chemie Linz, **16** 439

Cheminor Drugs Limited, **59** 168

Chemische Werke Hüls GmbH *see* Hüls A.G.

Chemise Lacoste, **9** 157

ChemLawn, **13** 199; **23** 428, 431; **34** 153

Chemonics Industries–Fire-Trol, **17** 161–62

Chemonics International–Consulting, **17** 161–62

Chemquest Sdn Bhd, **57** 292, 294–95

Chemviron Carbon. S.A. *see* Calgon Carbon Corporation.

Cheney Bigelow Wire Works, **13** 370

CHEP Pty. Ltd., 80 63–66

Cherokee Inc., 18 106–09

Cherry-Burrell Process Equipment, *see* United Dominion Industries Limited.

Cherry Hill Cheese, **7** 429

Cherry Lane Music Publishing Company, Inc., 62 64–67

Cherry-Levis Co., **26** 172

Chesapeake and Ohio Railroad *see* CSX Corporation.

Chesapeake Corporation, 8 102–04; 30 117–20 (upd.)

Chesapeake Microwave Technologies, Inc., **32** 41

Chesapeake Paperboard Company, **44** 66

Chesapeake Utilities Corporation, 56 60–62

Cheshire Building Society, 74 84–87

Chesebrough-Pond's USA, Inc., 8 105–07

Chessington World of Adventures, **55** 378

Chester Engineers, **10** 412

Cheung Kong (Holdings) Limited, IV 693–95; 20 131–34 (upd.) *see also* Hutchison Whampoa Ltd.

Chevignon, **44** 296

Chevrolet, **9** 17; **19** 221, 223; **21** 153; **26** 500

Chevron U.K. Ltd., **15** 352

ChevronTexaco Corporation, IV 385–87;19 82–85 (upd.); 47 70–76 (upd.)

Chevy's, Inc., **33** 140

Chevy's Mexican Restaurants, **27** 226

ChexSystems, **22** 181

Cheyenne Software, Inc., 12 60–62

CHF *see* Chase, Harris, Forbes.

Chi-Chi's Inc., 13 151–53; 51 70–73 (upd.)

CHI Construction Company, **58** 84

Chi Mei Optoelectronics Corporation, 75 93–95

Chiasso Inc., 53 98–100

Chiat/Day Inc. Advertising, 11 49–52 *see also* TBWA/Chiat/Day.

Chiba Gas Co. Ltd., **55** 375

Chiba Mitsukoshi Ltd., **56** 242

Chibu Electric Power Company, Incorporated, V 571–73

Chic by H.I.S, Inc., 20 135–37

Chicago and North Western Holdings Corporation, 6 376–78

Chicago and Southern Airlines Inc. *see* Delta Air Lines, Inc.

Chicago Bears Football Club, Inc., 33 95–97

Chicago Blackhawk Hockey Team, Inc. *see* Wirtz Corporation.

Chicago Board of Trade, 41 84–87

Chicago Bridge & Iron Company N.V., 82 67-73 (upd.)

Chicago Cutlery, **16** 234

Chicago Faucet Company, **49** 161, 163

Chicago Flexible Shaft Company, **9** 484

Chicago Medical Equipment Co., **31** 255

Chicago Mercantile Exchange Holdings Inc., 75 96–99

Chicago Motor Club, **10** 126

Chicago Musical Instrument Company, **16** 238

Chicago National League Ball Club, Inc., 66 52–55

Chicago O'Hare Leather Concessions Joint Venture Inc., **58** 369

Chicago Pacific Corp., **III** 573; **12** 251; **22** 349; **23** 244; **34** 432

Chicago Pizza & Brewery, Inc., 44 85–88

Fox Paine & Company L.L.C., **63** 410, 412

Fox Ridge Homes, **70** 208

Fox-Vliet Drug Company, **16** 212

Foxboro Company, **13** 233–35

Foxconn International, Inc. *see* Hon Hai Precision Industry Co., Ltd.

FoxMeyer Health Corporation, **16** 212–14

Foxmoor, **29** 163

Foxx Hy-Reach, **28** 387

Foxy Products, Inc., **60** 287

FP&L *see* Florida Power & Light Co.

FPA Corporation *see* Orleans Homebuilders, Inc.

FPK LLC, **26** 343

FPL Group, Inc., **V** 623–25; **49** 143–46 (upd.)

FR Corp., **18** 340; **43** 282

Fracmaster Ltd., **55** 294

Fragrance Corporation of America, Ltd., **53** 88

Fragrance Express Inc., **37** 271

Framatome SA, **19** 164–67

Framingham Electric Company, **12** 45

Franc-Or Resources, **38** 231–32

France-Loisirs, **IV** 615–16, 619

France Quick, **12** 152; **26** 160–61; **27** 10

France Télécom Group, **V** 291–93; **21** 231–34 (upd.)

Franchise Associates, Inc., **17** 238

Franchise Business Systems, Inc., **18** 207

Franchise Finance Corp. of America, **19** 159; **37** 351

Francis H. Leggett & Co., **24** 527

Franciscan Vineyards, Inc., **34** 89; **68** 99

Francisco Partners, **74** 260

Franco-American Food Company *see* Campbell Soup Company.

Franco-Américaine de Constructions Atomiques, **19** 165

Francodex Laboratories, Inc., **74** 381

Frank & Pignard SA, **51** 35

Frank & Schulte GmbH, *see* Stinnes AG.

Frank Dry Goods Company, **9** 121

Frank H. Nott Inc., **14** 156

Frank Holton Company, **55** 149, 151

Frank J. Zamboni & Co., Inc., **34** 173–76

Frank Russell Company, **46** 198–200

Frank Schaffer Publications, **19** 405; **29** 470, 472

Frank W. Horner, Ltd., **38** 123

Frank's Nursery & Crafts, Inc., **12** 178–79

Franke Holding AG, **76** 157–59

Frankel & Co., **39** 166–69

Frankenberry, Laughlin & Constable, **9** 393

Frankford-Quaker Grocery Co., **II** 625

Frankfurter Allgemeine Zeitung GmbH, **66** 121–24

Franklin Assurances, **III** 211

Franklin Brass Manufacturing Company, **20** 363

Franklin Coach, **56** 223

Franklin Container Corp., **IV** 312; **19** 267

Franklin Corp., **14** 130; **41** 388

Franklin Covey Company, **11** 147–49; **37** 149–52 (upd.)

Franklin Electric Company, Inc., **43** 177–80

Franklin Electronic Publishers, Inc., **23** 209–13

The Franklin Mint, **69** 181–84

Franklin Mutual Advisors LLC, **52** 119, 172

Franklin National Bank, **9** 536

Franklin Plastics *see* Spartech Corporation.

Franklin Research & Development, **11** 41

Franklin Resources, Inc., **9** 239–40

Franklin Sports, Inc., **17** 243

Frans Maas Beheer BV, **14** 568

Franz Inc., **80** 122–25

Franzia *see* The Wine Group, Inc.

Frape Behr S.A. *see* Behr GmbH & Co. KG.

Fraser & Neave Ltd., **54** 116–18

Fray Data International, **14** 319

Frazer & Jones, **48** 141

FRE Composites Inc., **69** 206

Fred Campbell Auto Supply, **26** 347

Fred Meyer Stores, Inc., **V** 54–56; **20** 222–25 (upd.); **64** 135–39 (upd.)

Fred Sammons Company of Chicago, **30** 77

Fred Schmid Appliance & T.V. Co., Inc., **10** 305; **18** 532

Fred Usinger Inc., **54** 119–21

The Fred W. Albrecht Grocery Co., **13** 236–38

Fred Weber, Inc., **61** 100–02

Fred's, Inc., **23** 214–16; **62** 144–47 (upd.)

Freddie Mac, **54** 122–25

Fredelle, **14** 295

Frederick & Nelson, **17** 462

Frederick Atkins Inc., **16** 215–17

Frederick Bayer & Company, **22** 225

Frederick Gas Company, **19** 487

Frederick Manufacturing Corporation, **26** 119; **48** 59

Frederick's of Hollywood Inc., **16** 218–20; **59** 190–93 (upd.)

Fredrickson Motor Express, **57** 277

Free-lance Uitzendburo, **26** 240

Free People LLC *see* Urban Outfitters, Inc.

Freedom Airlines, Inc. *see* Mesa Air Group, Inc.

Freedom Communications, Inc., **36** 222–25

Freedom Group Inc., **42** 10–11

Freedom Technology, **11** 486

Freeman Chemical Corporation, **61** 111–12

Freeman, Spogli & Co., **17** 366; **18** 90; **32** 12, 15; **35** 276; **36** 358–59; **47** 142–43; **57** 11, 242

Freemans *see* Sears plc.

FreeMark Communications, **38** 269

Freeport-McMoRan Copper & Gold, Inc., **IV** 81–84; **7** 185–89 (upd.); **57** 145–50 (upd.)

Freeport Power, **38** 448

Freeze.com LLC, **77** 156–59

Freezer Queen Foods, Inc., **21** 509

Freight Car Services, Inc., **23** 306

Freight Outlet, **17** 297

Freixenet S.A., **71** 162–64

Frejlack Ice Cream Co., **II** 646; **7** 317

Fremont Canning Company, **7** 196

Fremont Group, **21** 97

Fremont Investors, **30** 268

Fremont Partners, **24** 265

Fremont Savings Bank, **9** 474–75

French Connection Group plc, **41** 167–69

French Fragrances, Inc., **22** 213–15 *see also* Elizabeth Arden, Inc.

French Quarter Coffee Co., **27** 480–81

Frequency Electronics, Inc., **61** 103–05

Frequency Sources Inc., **9** 324

Fresenius AG, **56** 138–42

Fresh America Corporation, **20** 226–28

Fresh Choice, Inc., **20** 229–32

Fresh Enterprises, Inc., **66** 125–27

Fresh Fields, **19** 501

Fresh Foods, Inc., **29** 201–03

Fresh Start Bakeries, **26** 58

Freshbake Foods Group PLC, **II** 481; **7** 68; **25** 518; **26** 57

Freshlike, **76** 17

Fretter, Inc., **10** 304–06

Freudenberg & Co., **41** 170–73

Friction Products Co., **59** 222

Frictiontech Inc., **11** 84

Friday's Front Row Sports Grill, **22** 128

Friden, Inc., **30** 418; **53** 237

Fried, Frank, Harris, Shriver & Jacobson, **35** 183–86

Fried. Krupp GmbH, **IV** 85–89 *see also* Thyssen Krupp AG.

Friede Goldman Halter, **61** 43

Friedman, Billings, Ramsey Group, Inc., **53** 134–37

Friedman's Inc., **29** 204–06

Friedrich Grohe AG & Co. KG, **53** 138–41

Friendly Hotels PLC, **14** 107

Friendly Ice Cream Corporation, **30** 208–10; **72** 141–44 (upd.)

Friesland Coberco Dairy Foods Holding N.V., **59** 194–96

Frigidaire Home Products, **22** 216–18

Frigoscandia AB, **57** 300

Frimont S.p.A., **68** 136

Frisby P.M.C. Incorporated, **16** 475

Frisch's Restaurants, Inc., **35** 187–89

Frisdranken Industries Winters B.V., **22** 515

Frisk Int. Nv, **72** 272

Frito-Lay North America, **32** 205–10; **73** 151–58 (upd.)

Fritz Companies, Inc., **12** 180–82

Fritz Gegauf AG *see* Bernina Holding AG.

Fritz Schömer, **75** 56–57

Fritz W. Glitsch and Sons, Inc. *see* Glitsch International, Inc.

Frolich Intercon International, **57** 174

Fromagerie d'Illoud *see* Bongrain SA.

Fromageries Bel, **23** 217–19; **25** 83–84

Fromarsac, **25** 84

Frome Broken Hill Co., **IV** 59

Hongkong Electric Holdings Ltd., 6
498–500; 23 278–81 (upd.)
Hongkong Land Holdings Ltd., IV
699–701; 47 175–78 (upd.)
Honolua Plantation Land Company, Inc.,
29 308
Honshu Paper Co., Ltd., IV 284–85
Hood Rubber Company, 15 488–89
Hood Sailmakers, Inc., 10 215
Hoogovens see Koninklijke Nederlandsche
Hoogovens en Staalfabricken NV.
Hook's Drug Stores, 9 67
Hooker Corp., 19 324
Hooker Furniture Corporation, 80
143–46
Hooper Holmes, Inc., 22 264–67
Hoorcomfort Nederland B.V., 56 338
Hoosier Insurance Company, 51 39
Hoosier Park L.P., 29 118
Hooters of America, Inc., 18 241–43;
69 211–14 (upd.)
The Hoover Company, 12 250–52; 40
258–62 (upd.)
Hoover Group Inc., 18 11
Hoover Treated Wood Products, Inc., 12
396
HOP, LLC, 80 147–50
Hopkinsons Group see Carbo PLC.
Hopkinton LNG Corp., 14 126
Hopper Soliday and Co. Inc., 14 154
Hops Restaurant Bar and Brewery, 46
233–36
Hopwood & Company, 22 427
Horace Mann Educators Corporation,
22 268–70
Horizon Air Industries, Inc. see Alaska Air
Group, Inc.
Horizon Corporation, see MAXXAM Inc.
Horizon Group Inc., 27 221
Horizon Healthcare Corporation, 25 456
Horizon Holidays, 14 36
Horizon Industries, 19 275
Horizon Lamps, Inc., 48 299
Horizon Organic Holding Corporation,
37 195–99
Horizon/CMS Healthcare Corp., 25 111,
457; 33 185
Horizons Laitiers, 25 85
Hormel Foods Corporation, 18 244–47
(upd.); 54 164–69 (upd.)
Horn Venture Partners, 22 464
Hornbrook, Inc., 14 112
Horne's, 16 62
Horsehead Industries, Inc., 51 165–67
Horseshoe Gaming Holding
Corporation, 62 192–95
Horsham Corp. see TrizecHahn.
Horst Breuer GmbH, 20 363
Horst Salons Inc., 24 56
Horten, 47 107; 50 117, 119
Hortifrut, S.A., 62 154
Horton Homes, Inc., 25 216–18
Hoshienu Pharmaceutical Co. Ltd., 58
134
Hoshino Gakki Co. Ltd., 55 208–11
Hosiery Corporation International see
HCI Direct, Inc.
Hospal SA, 49 156

Hospira, Inc., 71 172–74
Hospital Central Services, Inc., 56
166–68
Hospital Corporation of America, III
78–80 see also HCA - The Healthcare
Company.
Hospital Cost Consultants, 11 113
Hospital Management Associates, Inc. see
Health Management Associates, Inc.
Hospital Products, Inc., 10 534
Hospital Specialty Co., 37 392
Hospitality Franchise Systems, Inc., 11
177–79 see also Cendant Corporation.
Hospitality Worldwide Services, Inc., 26
196–98
Hosposable Products, Inc. see Wyant
Corporation.
Hoss's Steak and Sea House Inc., 68
196–98
Host America Corporation, 79 202–06
Host Communications Inc., 24 404
Hot Dog Construction Co., 12 372
Hot Dog on a Stick see HDOS
Enterprises.
Hot Sam Co. see Mrs. Fields' Original
Cookies, Inc.
Hot Shoppes Inc. see Marriott.
Hot Topic, Inc., 33 202–04
Hotel Corporation of America, 16 337
Hotel Corporation of India, 27 26
Hotel Properties Ltd., 71 175–77
Hotel Reservations Network, Inc., 47 420
Hotels By Pleasant, 62 276
HotJobs.com, Ltd. see Yahoo! Inc.
HotRail Inc., 36 124
HotWired, 45 200
Houbigant, 37 270
Houchens Industries Inc., 51 168–70
Houghton Mifflin Company, 10
355–57; 36 270–74 (upd.)
Houlihan's Restaurant Group, 25 546
Housatonic Power Co., 13 182
House of Blues, 32 241, 244
House of Fabrics, Inc., 21 278–80
House of Fraser PLC, 45 188–91 see also
Harrods Holdings.
House of Miniatures, 12 264
House of Prince A/S, 80 151–54
House of Windsor, Inc., 9 533
Household International, Inc., II
417–20; 21 281–86 (upd.)
Household Rental Systems, 17 234
Housing Development Finance
Corporation, 20 313
Housmex Inc., 23 171
Houston Airport Leather Concessions
LLC, 58 369
Houston, Effler & Partners Inc., 9 135
Houston Electric Light & Power
Company, 44 368
Houston Industries Incorporated, V
641–44 see also Reliant Energy Inc.
Houston International Teleport, Inc., 11
184
Houston Oil & Minerals Corp., 11
440–41
Houston Pipe Line Company, 45 21
Hoveringham Group, III 753; 28 450

Hoving Corp., 14 501
Hovnanian Enterprises, Inc., 29 243–45
Howard B. Stark Candy Co., 15 325
Howard Flint Ink Company, see Flint Ink
Corporation.
Howard H. Sweet & Son, Inc., 14 502
Howard Hughes Corporation, 63 341
Howard Hughes Medical Institute, 39
221–24
Howard Hughes Properties, Ltd., 17 317
Howard Humphreys, 13 119
Howard Johnson International, Inc., 17
236–39; 72 182–86 (upd.)
Howard Research and Development
Corporation, 15 412, 414
Howard Schultz & Associates, Inc., 73
266
Howard, Smith & Levin, 40 126
Howden see Alexander Howden Group.
Howdy Company, 9 177
Howe & Fant, Inc., 23 82
Howe Sound Co., 12 253
Howmedica, 29 455
Howmet Corporation, 12 253–55
Hoyle Products, 62 384
Hoyt Archery Company, 10 216
HP see Hewlett-Packard Company.
HPI Health Care Services, 49 307–08
HQ Global Workplaces, Inc., 47 331
HQ Office International, see Office Depot
Incorporated.
HRB Business Services, 29 227
Hrubitz Oil Company, 12 244
HSBC Holdings plc, 12 256–58; 26
199–204 (upd.); 80 155–63 (upd.)
HSG see Helikopter Services Group AS.
Hsiang-Li Investment Corp., 51 123
HSN, 64 181–85 (upd.)
HSS Hire Service Group PLC, 45 139–41
HTH, 12 464
HTM Goedkoop, 26 278–79; 55 200
H2O Plus, 11 41
Hua Bei Oxygen, 25 82
Hua Yang Printing Holdings Co. Ltd., 60
372
Hub Group, Inc., 38 233–35
Hub Services, Inc., 18 366
Hubbard Air Transport, 10 162
Hubbard, Baker & Rice, 10 126
Hubbard Broadcasting Inc., 24 226–28;
79 207–12 (upd.)
Hubbard Construction Co., 23 332
Hubbell Inc., 9 286–87; 31 257–59
(upd.); 76 183–86 (upd.)
Huck Manufacturing Company, 22 506
Hudepohl-Schoenling Brewing Co., 18
72; 50 114
Hudson Automobile Company, 18 492
The Hudson Bay Mining and Smelting
Company, Limited, 12 259–61
Hudson Foods Inc., 13 270–72
Hudson Housewares Corp., 16 389
Hudson I.C.S., 58 53
Hudson Pharmaceutical Corp., 31 347
Hudson River Bancorp, Inc., 41 210–13
Hudson Software, 13 481
Hudson's see Target Corporation.

Little Caesar Enterprises, Inc., 7
278–79; 24 293–96 (upd.) *see also*
Ilitch Holdings Inc.
Little General, II 620; 12 179, 200
Little Giant Pump Company, *see*
Tecumseh Products Company.
Little League Baseball, Incorporated, 23
450
Little Leather Library, 13 105
Little Switzerland, Inc., 60 202–04
Little Tikes Company, 13 317–19; 62
231–34 (upd.)
Littleton Coin Company Inc., 82
201–04
Littlewoods Financial Services, 30 494
Littlewoods plc, V 117–19; 42 228–32
(upd.)
Litton Industries Inc., I 484–86; 11
263–65 (upd.) *see also* Avondale
Industries.
Litwin Engineers & Constructors, *see*
United Dominion Industries Limited.
LIVE Entertainment Inc., 20 347–49
Live Nation, Inc., 80 217–22 (upd.)
LiveAquaria.com., 62 108
Liverpool Daily Post & Echo Ltd., 49
405
Liverpool Mexico S.A., 16 216
Living Arts, Inc., 41 174
Living Videotext, 10 508
LivingWell Inc., 12 326
Liz Claiborne, Inc., 8 329–31; 25
291–94 (upd.)
LKQ Corporation, 71 201–03
Lledo Collectibles Ltd., 60 372
LLJ Distributing Company *see* Spartan
Stores Inc.
Lloyd Aereo de Bolivia, 6 97
Lloyd Creative Staffing, 27 21
Lloyd George Management, 18 152
Lloyd Instruments, Ltd., 29 460–61
Lloyd Italico, III 351
Lloyd Thompson Group plc, 20 313
Lloyd Triestino company, 50 187
Lloyd-Truax Ltd., 21 499
Lloyd's, III 278–81; 22 315–19 (upd.);
74 172–76 (upd.)
Lloyd's Electronics, 14 118
Lloyds Chemists plc, 27 177
Lloyds Life Assurance, III 351
Lloyds TSB Group plc, II 306–09; 47
224–29 (upd.)
LLP Group plc, 58 189
LM Ericsson *see* Telefonaktiebolaget LM
Ericsson.
LMC Metals, 19 380
LME *see* Telefonaktiebolaget LM Ericsson.
LNM Group, 30 252
Lo-Cost, II 609
Lo-Vaca Gathering Co., 7 553
Loblaw Companies Limited, 43 268–72
see also George Weston Limited.
Local Data, Inc., 10 97
Lockhart Corporation, 12 564
Lockheed Martin Corporation, I 64–66;
11 266–69 (upd.); 15 283–86 (upd.)
Locksmith Publishing Corp., 56 75
Lockwood Banc Group, Inc., 11 306

Lockwood Greene Engineers, Inc., 17 377
Lockwood National Bank, 25 114
Lockwood Technology, Inc., 19 179
Loctite Corporation, 8 332–34; 30
289–91 (upd.)
Lodding Engineering, 7 521
Lodestar Group, 10 19
Lodge Plus, Ltd., 25 430
LodgeNet Entertainment Corporation,
28 240–42
The Lodging Group, 12 297; 48 245
Loehmann's Inc., 24 297–99
The Loewen Group, Inc., 16 342–44;
40 292–95 (upd.) *see also* Alderwoods
Group Inc.
Loewenstein Furniture Group, Inc., 21
531–33
Loews Cineplex Entertainment Corp., 37
64
Loews Corporation, I 487–88; 12
316–18 (upd.); 36 324–28 (upd.)
LOF Plastics, Inc. *see* Libbey-Owens-Ford.
Loffland Brothers Company, 9 364
Logan's Roadhouse, Inc., 29 290–92
Loganair Ltd., 68 235–37
Logic Modeling, 11 491
Logica plc, 14 317–19; 37 230–33
(upd.)
Logicon Inc., 20 350–52
Logility, 25 20, 22
Logistics.com, Inc. *see* Manhattan
Associates, Inc.
Logistics Data Systems, 13 4
Logistics Industries Corporation, 39 77
Logistics Management Systems, Inc., *see*
Amoskeag Company.
Logitech International S.A., 28 243–45;
69 242–45 (upd.)
LOGIX Benelux, 74 143
Logo Athletic, Inc., 35 363
Logo 7, Inc., 13 533
Logon, Inc., 14 377
Lohja Corporation, 61 295
LoJack Corporation, 48 269–73
Lojas Americanas S.A., 77 240–43
Lojas Arapuã S.A., 22 320–22; 61
175–78 (upd.)
Loma Linda Foods, 14 557–58
Lomak Petroleum, Inc., 24 380
Lomas & Nettleton Financial
Corporation, III 249; 11 122
London & Hull, III 211
London & Midland Bank *see* Midland
Bank plc.
London & Overseas Freighters plc *see*
Frontline Ltd.
London & Rhodesia Mining & Land
Company *see* Lonrho Plc.
London and Scottish Marine Oil, 11 98
London & Western Trust, 39 90
London Assurance Corp., 55 331
London Brick Co., 14 249
London Brokers Ltd., 6 290
London Buses Limited *see* London
Regional Transport.
London Cargo Group, 25 82
London Central, 28 155–56
London Drugs Ltd., 46 270–73

London East India Company, 12 421
London Electricity, 12 443; 41 141
London Fog Industries, Inc., 29 293–96
London Insurance Group, III 373; 36
372
London International Group *see* SSL
International plc.
London Precision Machine & Tool, Ltd.,
39 32
London Records, 23 390
London Regional Transport, 6 406–08
London Rubber Co., 49 380
London Scottish Bank plc, 70 160–62
London South Partnership, 25 497
London Stock Exchange Limited, 34
253–56
London Transport, 19 111
Londontown Manufacturing Company *see*
London Fog Industries, Inc.
Lone Star Funds, 59 106
Lone Star Industries, 23 326; 35 154
Lone Star Steakhouse & Saloon, Inc.,
51 227–29
Lone Star Technologies, Inc., 22 3
Lonely Planet Publications Pty Ltd., 55
253–55
Long Distance Discount Services, Inc., *see*
LDDS-Metro Communications, Inc.
Long Distance/USA, 9 479
Long Island Bancorp, Inc., 16 345–47
Long Island Cable Communication
Development Company, 7 63
Long Island College Hospital *see*
Continuum Health Partners, Inc.
Long Island Lighting Company, V
652–54
Long Island Power Authority, 27 265
The Long Island Rail Road Company,
68 238–40
Long John Silver's, 13 320–22; 57
224–29 (upd.)
Long Lac Mineral Exploration, 9 282
Long Life Fish Food Products, 12 230
Long-Term Credit Bank of Japan, Ltd.,
II 310–11
Long Valley Power Cooperative, 12 265
The Longaberger Company, 12 319–21;
44 267–70 (upd.)
Longchamps, Inc., 38 385; 41 388
LongHorn Steaks Inc., 19 341
Longman Group Ltd., IV 611, 658
Longs Drug Stores Corporation, V 120;
25 295–97 (upd.)
Longview Fibre Company, 8 335–37; 37
234–37 (upd.)
Lonmin plc, 66 211–16 (upd.)
Lonrho Plc, 21 351–55 *see also* Lonmin
plc.
Lonza Group Ltd., 73 212–14
Lookers plc, 71 204–06
Loomis Armored Car Service Limited, 45
378
Loomis Fargo Group, 42 338
Loomis Products, Inc., 64 349
Loop One2, 53 240
Loose Leaf Metals Co., Inc., 10 314
Lor-Al, Inc., 17 10

Marine Bank and Trust Co., **11** 105
Marine Computer Systems, **6** 242
Marine Harvest, **56** 257
Marine Manufacturing Corporation, **52** 406
Marine Midland Corp., **9** 475–76; **11** 108; **17** 325
Marine Products Corporation, 75 247–49
Marine Transport Lines, Inc., **59** 323
Marine United Inc., **42** 361
Marinela, **19** 192–93
MarineMax, Inc., 30 303–05
Marinette Marine Corporation, **59** 274, 278
Marion Brick, **14** 249
Marion Foods, Inc., **17** 434; **60** 268
Marion Laboratories Inc., I 648–49
Marion Manufacturing, **9** 72
Marion Merrell Dow, Inc., 9 328–29 (upd.)
Marionet Corp., **IV** 680–81
Marionnaud Parfumeries SA, 51 233–35
Marisa Christina, Inc., 15 290–92
Maritime Electric Company, Limited, **15** 182; **47** 136–37
Maritz Inc., 38 302–05
Mark Controls Corporation, **30** 157
Mark Cross, Inc., **17** 4–5
Mark IV Industries, Inc., 7 296–98; 28 260–64 (upd.)
The Mark Travel Corporation, 80 232–35
Mark Trouser, Inc., **17** 338
Mark's Work Wearhouse Ltd. *see* Canadian Tire Corporation, Limited.
Markborough Properties, **V** 81; **25** 221
Market Development Corporation *see* Spartan Stores Inc.
Market Growth Resources, **23** 480
Market National Bank, **13** 465
Marketing Data Systems, Inc., **18** 24
Marketing Equities International, **26** 136
MarketSpan Corp. *see* KeySpan Energy Co.
Märklin Holding GmbH, 70 163–66
Marks and Spencer p.l.c., V 124–26; 24 313–17 (upd.)
Marks-Baer Inc., **11** 64
Marks Brothers Jewelers, Inc., 24 318–20 *see also* Whitehall Jewellers, Inc.
Marlene Industries Corp., **16** 36–37
Marley Co., **19** 360
Marley Holdings, L.P., **19** 246
Oy Marli Ab, **56** 103
Marman Products Company, **16** 8
The Marmon Group, Inc., IV 135–38; 16 354–57 (upd.); 70 167–72 (upd.)
Marmon-Perry Light Company, **6** 508
Marolf Dakota Farms, Inc., **18** 14–15
Marotte, **21** 438
Marpac Industries Inc. *see* PVC Container Corporation.
Marquam Commercial Brokerage Company, **21** 257
Marquette Electronics, Inc., 13 326–28
Marquis Who's Who, **17** 398

Marr S.p.A., **57** 82–84
Marriot Inc., **29** 442
Marriot Management Services, **29** 444
Marriott International, Inc., III 102–03; 21 364–67 (upd.)
Mars, Incorporated, 7 299–301; 40 302–05 (upd.)
Marsh & McLennan Companies, Inc., III 282–84; 45 263–67 (upd.)
Marsh Supermarkets, Inc., 17 300–02; 76 255–58 (upd.)
Marshall & Ilsley Corporation, 56 217–20
Marshall Amplification plc, 62 239–42
Marshall Die Casting, **13** 225
Marshall Field's, 63 254–63 *see also* Target Corporation.
Marshall Industries, **19** 311
Marshalls Incorporated, 13 329–31
Marshfield Clinic Inc., 82 209–12
Marship Tankers (Holdings) Ltd., **52** 329
Marstellar, **13** 204
Marstons, **57** 412–13
The Mart, **9** 120
Martank Shipping Holdings Ltd., **52** 329
Martek Biosciences Corporation, 65 218–20
Martell and Company S.A., 82 213–16
Marten Transport, **27** 404
Martha Lane Adams, **27** 428
Martha Stewart Living Omnimedia, Inc., 24 321–23; 73 219–22 (upd.)
Martin & Pagenstecher GMBH, **24** 208
Martin-Baker Aircraft Company Limited, 61 195–97
Martin Band Instrument Company, **55** 149, 151
Martin Bros. Tobacco Co., **14** 19
Martin Collet, **19** 50
Martin Dunitz, **44** 416
Martin Franchises, Inc., 80 236–39
Martin Gillet Co., **55** 96, 98
Martin Guitar Company *see* C.F. Martin & Co., Inc.
Martin Hilti Foundation, **53** 167
Martin Industries, Inc., 44 274–77
Martin Marietta Corporation, I 67–69 *see also* Lockheed Martin Corporation.
Martin Mathys N.V., *see* RPM Inc.
Martin Sorrell, **6** 54
Martin Theaters, **14** 86
Martin-Yale Industries, Inc., **19** 142–44
Martin Zippel Co., **16** 389
Martin's, **12** 221
Martindale-Hubbell, **16** 398
Martini & Rossi SpA, 63 264–66
Martinus Nijhoff, **14** 555; **25** 85
Martz Group, 56 221–23
Marubeni Corporation, I 492–95; 24 324–27 (upd.)
Maruetsu, **17** 124; **41** 114
Maruha Group Inc., 75 250–53 (upd.)
Marui Company Ltd., V 127; 62 243–45 (upd.)
Marusa Co. Ltd., **51** 379
Maruti Udyog Ltd., **59** 393, 395–97
Maruzen Co., Limited, 18 322–24
Maruzen Oil Co., Ltd., **53** 114

Marva Maid Dairy *see* Maryland & Virginia Milk Producers Cooperative Association, Inc.
Marvel Entertainment, Inc., 10 400–02; 78 212–19 (upd.)
Marvin H. Sugarman Productions Inc., **20** 48
Marvin Lumber & Cedar Company, 22 345–47
Marwick, Mitchell & Company, **10** 385
Marx, **12** 494
Mary Ann Co. Ltd., **V** 89
Mary Ellen's, Inc., **11** 211
Mary Kathleen Uranium, **IV** 59–60
Mary Kay Corporation, 9 330–32; 30 306–09 (upd.)
Maryland & Virginia Milk Producers Cooperative Association, Inc., 80 240–43
Maryland Medical Laboratory Inc., **26** 391
Maryland National Corp., **11** 287
Maryland National Mortgage Corporation, **11** 121; **48** 177
Maryland Square, Inc., **68** 69
Marzotto S.p.A., 20 356–58; 67 246–49 (upd.)
Masayoshi Son, **13** 481–82
The Maschhoffs, Inc., 82 217–20
Maschinenfabrik Augsburg-Nürnberg *see* M.A.N.
Masco Corporation, III 568–71; 20 359–63 (upd.); 39 263–68 (upd.)
Masco Optical, **13** 165
Mase Westpac Limited, **11** 418
Maserati *see* Officine Alfieri Maserati S.p.A.
Maserati Footwear, Inc., **68** 69
Mashantucket Pequot Gaming Enterprise Inc., 35 282–85
MASkargo Ltd. *see* Maladian Airlines System Bhd.
Masland Corporation, 17 303–05
Mason Best Co., **IV** 343
Masonite International Corporation, 63 267–69
Mass Rapid Transit Corp., **19** 111
Massachusetts Capital Resources Corp., **III** 314
Massachusetts Electric Company, **51** 265
Massachusetts Mutual Life Insurance Company, III 285–87; 53 210–13 (upd.)
Massachusetts Technology Development Corporation, **18** 570
Massachusetts's General Electric Company, **32** 267
Massey Energy Company, 57 236–38
MasTec, Inc., 55 259–63 (upd.)
Master Cellars Inc., **68** 146
Master Electric Company, **15** 134
Master Glass & Color, **24** 159–60
Master Lock Company, 45 268–71
Master Loom, **63** 151
Master Processing, **19** 37
Master Products, **14** 162
Master Shield Inc., **7** 116

McGraw Electric Company *see* Centel
Corporation.
The McGraw-Hill Companies, Inc., IV
634–37; **18** 325–30 (upd.); **51**
239–44 (upd.)
McGregor Corporation, **26** 102
McGrew Color Graphics, **7** 430
McHugh Software International Inc. *see*
RedPrairie Corp.
MCI *see* Manitou Costruzioni Industriali
SRL; Melamine Chemicals, Inc.
MCI WorldCom, Inc., V 302–04; **27**
301–08 (upd.)
McIlhenny Company, **20** 364–67
McIlwraith McEachern Limited, **27** 474
McJunkin Corporation, **63** 287–89
McKechnie plc, **34** 270–72
McKee Foods Corporation, **7** 320–21;
27 309–11 (upd.)
McKesson Corporation, I 496–98; **12**
331–33 (upd.); **47** 233–37 (upd.)
McKesson General Medical, **29** 299
McKinsey & Company, Inc., **9** 343–45
MCL Land *see* Jardine Cycle & Carriage
Ltd.
McLain Grocery, II 625
McLane America, Inc., **29** 481
McLane Company, Inc., **13** 332–34
McLaren Consolidated Cone Corp., **7** 366
McLean Clinic, **11** 379
McLeod's Accessories *see* Repco
Corporation Ltd.
McLeodUSA Incorporated, **32** 327–30
McLouth Steel Products, **13** 158
MCM Electronics, **9** 420
McMahan's Furniture Co., **14** 236
MCMC *see* Minneapolis Children's
Medical Center.
McMenamins Pubs and Breweries, **65**
224–26
McMoCo, **7** 187
McMoRan, **7** 185, 187
McMullen & Yee Publishing, **22** 442
MCN Corporation, **6** 519–22
McNeil Corporation, **26** 363
McNeil Laboratories *see* Johnson &
Johnson
MCO Properties Inc., *see* MAXXAM Inc.
MCorp, **10** 134; **11** 122
McPaper AG, **29** 152
McPherson's Ltd., **66** 220–22
McQuay International *see* AAF-McQuay
Incorporated.
McRae's, Inc., **19** 324–25; **41** 343–44
MCS, Inc., **10** 412
MCSi, Inc., **41** 258–60
MCT Dairies, Inc., **18** 14–16
MCTC *see* Medical Center Trading
Corporation.
McTeigue & Co., **14** 502
McWane Corporation, **55** 264–66
McWhorter Inc., **27** 280
MD Distribution Inc., **15** 139
MD Foods (Mejeriselskabet Danmark
Foods), **48** 35
MDC *see* Mead Data Central, Inc.
MDC Partners Inc., **63** 290–92
MDI Entertainment, LLC, **64** 346

MDP *see* Madison Dearborn Partners
LLC.
MDS/Bankmark, **10** 247
MDU Resources Group, Inc., **7** 322–25;
42 249–53 (upd.)
Mead & Mount Construction Company,
51 41
The Mead Corporation, IV 310–13; **19**
265–69 (upd.) *see also* MeadWestvaco
Corporation.
Mead Data Central, Inc., **10** 406–08 *see
also* LEXIS-NEXIS Group.
Mead John & Co., **19** 103
Mead Packaging, **12** 151
Meade County Rural Electric Cooperative
Corporation, **11** 37
Meade Instruments Corporation, **41**
261–64
Meadow Gold Dairies, Inc., II 473
Meadowcraft, Inc., **29** 313–15
MeadWestvaco Corporation, **76** 262–71
(upd.)
Means Services, Inc., II 607
Measurement Specialties, Inc., **71**
222–25
Measurex Corporation, **14** 56; **38** 227
Mebetoys, **25** 312
MEC *see* Mitsubishi Estate Company,
Limited.
MECA Software, Inc., **18** 363
Mecair, S.p.A., **17** 147
Mecalux S.A., **74** 183–85
MECAR S.A. *see* The Allied Defense
Group.
Mecca Bingo Ltd., **64** 320
Mecca Bookmakers, **49** 450
Mecca Leisure PLC, **12** 229; **32** 243
Meccano S.A., **52** 207
Mechanics Exchange Savings Bank, **9** 173
Mecklermedia Corporation, **24** 328–30
Meconic, **49** 230, 235
Medal Distributing Co., **9** 542
Medallion Pictures Corp., **9** 320
Medar, Inc., **17** 310–11
Medco Containment Services Inc., **9**
346–48
Medeco Security Locks, Inc., **10** 350
Medford, Inc., **19** 467–68
Medi Mart Drug Store Company *see* The
Stop & Shop Companies, Inc.
Media Arts Group, Inc., **42** 254–57
Media Exchange International, **25** 509
Media General, Inc., **7** 326–28; **38**
306–09 (upd.)
Media Groep West B.V., **23** 271
Media News Corporation, **25** 507
Media Play *see* Musicland Stores
Corporation.
MediaBay, **41** 61
**Mediacom Communications
Corporation**, **69** 250–52
Mediamark Research, **28** 501, 504
Mediamatics, Inc., **26** 329
MediaNews Group, Inc., **70** 177–80
MediaOne Group Inc. *see* U S West, Inc.
Mediaplex, Inc., **49** 433
Mediaset SpA, **50** 332–34
Media24 *see* Naspers Ltd.

Medic Computer Systems LLC, **16** 94; **45**
279–80
Medical Arts Press, Inc., **55** 353, 355
Medical Care America, Inc., **15** 112, 114;
35 215–17
Medical China Publishing Limited, **51**
244
Medical Development Corp. *see* Cordis
Corp.
Medical Development Services, Inc., **25**
307
Medical Device Alliance Inc., **73** 33
Medical Economics Data, **23** 211
Medical Equipment Finance Corporation,
51 108
Medical Indemnity of America, **10** 160
Medical Information Technology Inc.,
64 266–69
Medical Innovations Corporation, **21** 46
Medical Learning Company, **51** 200, 203
**Medical Management International,
Inc.**, **65** 227–29
Medical Marketing Group Inc., **9** 348
Medical Service Assoc. of Pennsylvania *see*
Pennsylvania Blue Shield.
Medical Center Trading Corporation, **70**
182
Medical Tribune Group, IV 591; **20** 53
Medicare-Glaser, **17** 167
Medicine Bow Coal Company, **7** 33–34
Medicine Shoppe International *see*
Cardinal Health, Inc.
Medicis Pharmaceutical Corporation, **59**
284–86
Medicor, Inc., **36** 496
Medicus Intercon International *see* D'Arcy
Masius Benton & Bowles, Inc.
Medifinancial Solutions, Inc., **18** 370
MedImmune, Inc., **35** 286–89
Medinol Ltd., **37** 39
Mediobanca Banca di Credito Finanziario
SpA, **11** 205; **65** 86, 88, 230–31
Mediocredito Toscano, **65** 72
Mediolanum S.p.A., **65** 230–32
The Mediplex Group, Inc., **11** 282
Medis Technologies Ltd., **77** 257–60
Medite Corporation, **19** 467–68
MEDITECH *see* Medical Information
Technology Inc.
Meditrust, **11** 281–83
Medline Industries, Inc., **61** 204–06
MedPartners, Inc. *see* Caremark Rx, Inc.
Medsep Corporation, **72** 265
Medtech, Ltd., **13** 60–62
Medtronic, Inc., **8** 351–54; **30** 313–17
(upd.); **67** 250–55 (upd.)
Medusa Corporation, **24** 331–33
Meekma Distileerderijen BV, **74** 42
Mega Bloks, Inc., **61** 207–09
The MEGA Life and Health Insurance
Co., **33** 418–20
MEGA Natural Gas Company, **11** 28
MegaBingo, Inc., **41** 273, 275
Megafoods Stores Inc., **13** 335–37
Megahouse Corp., **55** 48
MegaKnowledge Inc., **45** 206
Megasong Publishing, **44** 164
Megasource, Inc., **16** 94

Meggitt PLC, 34 273–76
MEGTEC Systems Inc., **54** 331
MEI Diversified Inc., **18** 455; **70** 262
Mei Foo Investments Ltd., **IV** 718; **38** 319
Meier & Frank Co., 23 345–47
Meierjohan-Wengler Inc., **56** 23
Meijer Incorporated, 7 329–31; **27** 312–15 (upd.)
Meiji Dairies Corporation, II 538–39; **82** 231–34 (upd.)
Meiji Mutual Life Insurance Company, III 288–89
Meiji Seika Kaisha Ltd., II 540–41; **64** 270–72 (upd.)
Meinecke Muffler Company, **10** 415
Meineke Discount Muffler Shops, **38** 208
Meis of Illiana, **10** 282
Meisel *see* Samuel Meisel & Co.
Meisenzahl Auto Parts, Inc., **24** 205
Meister, Lucious and Company, **13** 262
Meiwa Manufacturing Co., **III** 758
Mel Farr Automotive Group, 20 368–70
Melaleuca Inc., 31 326–28
Melamine Chemicals, Inc., 27 316–18
Melbourne Engineering Co., **23** 83
Melcher Holding AG *see* Power-One.
Meldisco *see* Footstar, Incorporated.
Melitta Unternehmensgruppe Bentz KG, 53 218–21
Mello Smello *see* The Miner Group International.
Mellon Financial Corporation, II 315–17; **44** 278–82 (upd.)
Mellon Indemnity Corp., **24** 177
Mellon-Stuart Co., I 584–85
Melmarkets, **24** 462
Meloy Laboratories, Inc., **11** 333
Melroe Company, *see* Clark Equipment Company.
The Melting Pot Restaurants, Inc., 74 186–88
Melville Corporation, V 136–38 *see also* CVS Corporation.
Melvin Simon and Associates, Inc., 8 355–57 *see also* Simon Property Group, Inc.
MEM, **37** 270–71
MEMC Electronic Materials, Inc., 81 249–52
Memco, **12** 48
Memorial Sloan-Kettering Cancer Center, 57 239–41
Memphis International Motorsports Corporation Inc., **43** 139–40
Memphis Retail Investors Limited Partnership, **62** 144
Memry Corporation, 72 225–27
The Men's Wearhouse, Inc., 17 312–15; **48** 283–87 (upd.)
Menasha Corporation, 8 358–61; **59** 287–92 (upd.)
Mendocino Brewing Company, Inc., 60 205–07
The Mennen Company, **14** 122; **18** 69; **35** 113
Mental Health Programs Inc., **15** 122

The Mentholatum Company Inc., 32 331–33
Mentor Corporation, 26 286–88
Mentor Graphics Corporation, 11 284–86
MEPC plc, IV 710–12
MeraBank, **6** 546
Meralco *see* Manila Electric Company.
MERBCO, Inc., **33** 456
Mercantile Bancorporation Inc., **33** 155
Mercantile Bankshares Corp., 11 287–88
Mercantile Credit Co., **16** 13
Mercantile Estate and Property Corp. Ltd. *see* MEPC PLC.
Mercantile Stores Company, Inc., V 139; **19** 270–73 (upd.)
Mercator & Noordstar N.V., **40** 61
Mercator Software, **59** 54, 56
Mercedes Benz *see* DaimlerChrysler AG
Mercer International Inc., 64 273–75
Merchant Bank Services, **18** 516, 518
Merchant Distributors, Inc., **20** 306
Merchant Investors *see* Sanlam Ltd.
Merchants & Farmers Bank of Ecru, **14** 40
Merchants Bank & Trust Co., **21** 524
Merchants Distributors Inc. *see* Alex Lee Inc.
Merchants Home Delivery Service, **6** 414
Merchants National Bank, **9** 228; **14** 528; **17** 135
Mercian Corporation, 77 261–64
Merck & Co., Inc., I 650–52; **11** 289–91 (upd.); **34** 280–85 (upd.)
Mercury Air Group, Inc., 20 371–73
Mercury Asset Management (MAM), **14** 420; **40** 313
Mercury Communications, Ltd., 7 332–34
Mercury Drug Corporation, 70 181–83
Mercury General Corporation, 25 323–25
Mercury Interactive Corporation, 59 293–95
Mercury International Ltd., **51** 130
Mercury Mail, Inc., **22** 519, 522
Mercury Marine Group, 68 247–51
Mercury Records, **13** 397; **23** 389, 391
Mercury Telecommunications Limited, **15** 67, 69
Mercy Air Service, Inc., **53** 29
Meredith Corporation, 11 292–94; **29** 316–19 (upd.); **74** 189–93 (upd.)
Merfin International, **42** 53
Merial, **34** 284
Meriam Instrument *see* Scott Fetzer.
Merico, Inc., **36** 161–64
Merida, **50** 445, 447
Meridian Bancorp, Inc., 11 295–97
Meridian Emerging Markets Ltd., **25** 509
Meridian Gold, Incorporated, 47 238–40
Meridian Healthcare Ltd., **18** 197; **59** 168
Meridian Industrial Trust Inc., **57** 301
Meridian Investment and Development Corp., **22** 189
Meridian Oil Inc., **10** 190–91

Meridian Publishing, Inc., **28** 254
Merillat Industries, LLC, 13 338–39; **69** 253–55 (upd.)
Merisant Worldwide, Inc., 70 184–86
Merisel, Inc., 12 334–36
Merit Distribution Services, **13** 333
Merit Medical Systems, Inc., 29 320–22
Merit Tank Testing, Inc., **IV** 411
Merita/Cotton's Bakeries, **38** 251
Meritage Corporation, 26 289–92
MeritaNordbanken, **40** 336
Meritor Automotive Inc. *see* ArvinMeritor Inc.
Merix Corporation, 36 329–31; **75** 257–60 (upd.)
Merkur Direktwerbegesellschaft, **29** 152
Merlin Gérin, **19** 165
Merpati Nusantara Airlines *see* Garuda Indonesia.
Merrell, **22** 173
Merrell Dow, **16** 438
Merriam-Webster Inc., 70 187–91
Merrill Corporation, 18 331–34; **47** 241–44 (upd.)
Merrill Gas Company, **9** 554
Merrill Lynch & Co., Inc., II 424–26; **13** 340–43 (upd.); **40** 310–15 (upd.)
Merrill Lynch Capital Partners, **47** 363
Merrill Lynch Investment Managers *see* BlackRock, Inc.
Merrill, Pickard, Anderson & Eyre IV, **11** 490
Merrill Publishing, **IV** 643; **7** 312; **9** 63; **29** 57
Merrimack Services Corp., **37** 303
Merry-Go-Round Enterprises, Inc., 8 362–64; **24** 27
Merry Group *see* Boral Limited.
Merry Maids *see* ServiceMaster Inc.
Merryhill Schools, Inc., **37** 279
The Mersey Docks and Harbour Company, 30 318–20
Mervyn's California, 10 409–10; **39** 269–71 (upd.) *see also* Target Corporation.
Merz Group, 81 253–56
Mesa Air Group, Inc., 11 298–300; **32** 334–37 (upd.); **77** 265–70 (upd.)
Mesa Petroleum, **11** 441; **27** 217
Mesaba Holdings, Inc., 28 265–67
Messerschmitt-Bölkow-Blohm GmbH., I 73–75
Messner, Vetere, Berger, Carey, Schmetterer, **13** 204
Mesta Machine Co., **22** 415
Mestek, Inc., 10 411–13
Met Food Corp. *see* White Rose Food Corp.
Met-Mex Penoles *see* Industrias Penoles, S.A. de C.V.
META Group, Inc., **37** 147
Metaframe Corp., **25** 312
Metal Box plc, I 604–06 *see also* Novar plc.
Metal-Cal *see* Avery Dennison Corporation.
Metal Casting Technology, Inc., **23** 267, 269

Milton Bradley Company, 21 372–75
Milton Light & Power Company, 12 45
Milupa S.A., 37 341
Milwaukee Brewers Baseball Club, 37 247–49
Milwaukee Cheese Co. Inc., 25 517
Milwaukee Electric Railway and Light Company, 6 601–02, 604–05
Milwaukee Electric Tool, 28 40
MIM Holdings, 73 392
Mimi's Cafés *see* SWH Corporation.
Minatome, IV 560
Mindpearl, 48 381
Mindport, 31 329
Mindset Corp., 42 424–25
Mindspring Enterprises, Inc., 36 168
Mine Safety Appliances Company, 31 333–35
The Miner Group International, 22 356–58
Minera Loma Blanca S.A., 56 127
Mineral Point Public Service Company, 6 604
Minerales y Metales, S.A. *see* Industrias Penoles, S.A. de C.V.
Minerals & Metals Trading Corporation of India Ltd., IV 143–44
Minerals and Resources Corporation Limited *see* Minorco.
Minerals Technologies Inc., 11 310–12; 52 248–51 (upd.)
Minerec Corporation, 9 363
Minerva SA, 72 289
Minerve, 6 208
Minet Group, III 357; 22 494–95
MiniScribe, Inc., 10 404
Minitel, 21 233
Minivator Ltd., 11 486
Minneapolis Children's Medical Center, 54 65
Minneapolis Steel and Machinery Company, 21 502
Minnehoma Insurance Company, 58 260
Minnesota Brewing Company *see* MBC Holding Company.
Minnesota Mining & Manufacturing Company, I 499–501; 8 369–71 (upd.); 26 296–99 (upd.) *see also* 3M Company.
Minnesota Power, Inc., 11 313–16; 34 286–91 (upd.)
Minnesota Sugar Company, 11 13
Minnetonka Corp., III 25; 22 122–23
Minntech Corporation, 22 359–61
Minn-Dak Farmers Cooperative, 32 29
Minolta Co., Ltd., III 574–76; 18 339–42 (upd.); 43 281–85 (upd.)
Minorco, IV 97; 16 28, 293
Minstar Inc., 11 397; 15 49; 45 174
Minton China, 38 401
The Minute Maid Company, 28 271–74
Minuteman International Inc., 46 292–95
Minyard Food Stores, Inc., 33 304–07
Mippon Paper, 21 546; 50 58
Miquel y Costas Miquel S.A., 68 256–58
Miracle Food Mart, 16 247, 249–50

Miracle-Gro Products, Inc., 22 474
Miraflores Designs Inc., 18 216
Mirage Resorts, Incorporated, 6 209–12; 28 275–79 (upd.)
Miraglia Inc., 57 139
Miramax Film Corporation, 64 282–85
Mirant, 39 54, 57
MIRAX Corporation *see* JSP Corporation.
Mircali Asset Management, III 340
Mircor Inc., 12 413
Mirror Group Newspapers plc, 7 341–43; 23 348–51 (upd.)
Misceramic Tile, Inc., 14 42
Misonix, Inc., 80 248–51
Misr Airwork *see* AirEgypt.
Misr Bank of Cairo, 27 132
Misrair *see* AirEgypt.
Miss Erika, Inc., 27 346, 348
Miss Selfridge *see* Sears plc.
Misset Publishers, IV 611
Mission Group *see* SCEcorp.
Mission Jewelers, 30 408
Mission Valley Fabrics, 57 285
Mississippi Chemical Corporation, 39 280–83
Mississippi Gas Company, 6 577
Mississippi Power Company, 38 446–47
Mississippi River Corporation, 10 44
Mississippi River Recycling, 31 47, 49
Mississippi Valley Title Insurance Company, 58 259–60
Missoula Bancshares, Inc., 35 198–99
Missouri Book Co., 10 136
Missouri Fur Company, 25 220
Missouri Gaming Company, 21 39
Missouri Gas & Electric Service Company, 6 593
Missouri Pacific Railroad, 10 43–44
Missouri Public Service Company *see* UtiliCorp United Inc.
Missouri Utilities Company, 6 580
Mist Assist, Inc. *see* Ballard Medical Products.
Mistik Beverages, 18 71
Misys PLC, 45 279–81; 46 296–99
Mitchel & King Skates Ltd., 17 244
Mitchell Energy and Development Corporation, 7 344–46
Mitchell Home Savings and Loan, 13 347
Mitchells & Butlers PLC, 59 296–99
MiTek Industries Inc., IV 259
MiTek Wood Products, IV 305
Mitel Corporation, 18 343–46
MitNer Group, 7 377
MITRE Corporation, 26 300–02
Mitre Sport U.K., 17 204–05
MITROPA AG, 37 250–53
Mitsubishi Aircraft Co., 9 349; 11 164
Mitsubishi Bank, Ltd., II 321–22 *see also* Bank of Tokyo-Mitsubishi Ltd.
Mitsubishi Chemical Corporation, I 363–64; 56 236–38 (upd.)
Mitsubishi Corporation, I 502–04; 12 340–43 (upd.)
Mitsubishi Electric Corporation, II 57–59; 44 283–87 (upd.)
Mitsubishi Estate Company, Limited, IV 713–14; 61 215–18 (upd.)

Mitsubishi Foods, 24 114
Mitsubishi Group, 7 377; 21 390
Mitsubishi Heavy Industries, Ltd., III 577–79; 7 347–50 (upd.); 40 324–28 (upd.)
Mitsubishi International Corp., 16 462
Mitsubishi Kasei Corp., 14 535
Mitsubishi Kasei Vinyl Company, 49 5
Mitsubishi Materials Corporation, III 712–13
Mitsubishi Motors Corporation, 9 349–51; 23 352–55 (upd.); 57 245–49 (upd.)
Mitsubishi Oil Co., Ltd., IV 460–62
Mitsubishi Rayon Co. Ltd., V 369–71
Mitsubishi Shipbuilding Co. Ltd., 9 349
Mitsubishi Trust & Banking Corporation, II 323–24
Mitsui & Co., Ltd., I 505–08; 28 280–85 (upd.)
Mitsui Bank, Ltd., II 325–27 *see also* Sumitomo Mitsui Banking Corporation.
Mitsui Group, 9 352; 16 84; 20 310; 21 72
Mitsui Light Metal Processing Co., III 758
Mitsui Marine and Fire Insurance Company, Limited, III 295–96
Mitsui Mining & Smelting Co., Ltd., IV 145–46
Mitsui Mining Company, Limited, IV 147–49
Mitsui Mutual Life Insurance Company, III 297–98; 39 284–86 (upd.)
Mitsui-no-Mori Co., Ltd., IV 716
Mitsui O.S.K. Lines, Ltd., V 473–76
Mitsui Petrochemical Industries, Ltd., 9 352–54
Mitsui Real Estate Development Co., Ltd., IV 715–16
Mitsui Toatsu, 9 353–54
Mitsui Trust & Banking Company, Ltd., II 328
Mitsukoshi Ltd., V 142–44; 56 239–42 (upd.)
Mity Enterprises, Inc., 38 310–12
Mizuho Financial Group Inc., 25 344–46; 58 229–36 (upd.)
MJ Pharmaceuticals Ltd., 57 346
MK-Ferguson Company, 7 356
MLC *see* Medical Learning Company.
MLC Ltd., IV 709; 52 221–22
MLH&P *see* Montreal Light, Heat & Power Company.
MLT Vacations Inc., 30 446
MM Merchandising Munich, 54 296–97
MMAR Group Inc., 19 131
MMC Networks Inc., 38 53, 55
MML Investors Services, III 286; 53 213
MMS America Corp., 26 317
MNC Financial *see* MBNA Corporation.
MNC Financial Corp., 11 447
MND Drilling, 7 345
MNet, 11 122
MNS, Ltd., 65 236–38
Mo och Domsjö AB, IV 317–19 *see also* Holmen AB

MOB, **56** 335
Mobil Corporation, IV 463–65; **7**
351–54 (upd.); **21** 376–80 (upd.) *see
also* Exxon Mobil Corporation.
Mobil Oil Australia, **24** 399
Mobil Oil Indonesia, **56** 273
Mobile America Housing Corporation *see*
American Homestar Corporation.
Mobile Corporation, **25** 232
Mobile Mini, Inc., 58 237–39
**Mobile Telecommunications
Technologies Corp., 18** 347–49
Mobile TeleSystems OJSC, 59 300–03
Mobilefone, Inc., **25** 108
MobileMedia Corp., **39** 23, 24
MobileStar Network Corp., **26** 429
Mochida Pharaceutical Co. Ltd., **II** 553
Mocon, Inc., 76 275–77
Modar, **17** 279
Mode 1 Communications, Inc., **48** 305
Modell's Sporting Goods *see* Henry
Modell & Company Inc.
Modeluxe Linge Services SA, **45** 139–40
Modem Media, **23** 479
Modern Controls, Inc. *see* Mocon, Inc.
Modern Food Industries Limited *see*
Hindustan Lever Limited
Modern Furniture Rentals Inc., **14** 4; **27**
163
Modern Handling Methods Ltd., **21** 499
Modern Merchandising Inc., **19** 396
Modern Times Group AB, 36 335–38
Modern Woodmen of America, 66
227–29
Modernistic Industries Inc., **7** 589
Modine Manufacturing Company, 8
372–75; **56** 243–47 (upd.)
Modis Professional Services *see* MPS
Group, Inc.
MoDo *see* Mo och Domsjö AB.
MoDo Paper AB, **28** 446; **52** 164
Modtech Holdings, Inc., 77 284–87
ModusLink Corporation *see* CMGI, Inc.
Moe's Southwest Grill, LLC, **64** 327–28
Moen Incorporated, 12 344–45
Moët-Hennessy, I 271–72 *see also* LVMH
Moët Hennessy Louis Vuitton SA.
Mogen David *see* The Wine Group, Inc.
The Mogul Metal Company *see*
Federal-Mogul Corporation.
Mohasco Corporation, **15** 102; **26**
100–01
Mohawk & Hudson Railroad, **9** 369
Mohawk Carpet Corp., **26** 101
Mohawk Industries, Inc., 19 274–76; **63**
298–301 (upd.)
Mohawk Rubber Co. Ltd., **V** 256; **7** 116;
19 508
Mohegan Tribal Gaming Authority, 37
254–57
Mojave Foods Corporation, **27** 299
Mojo MDA Group Ltd., **11** 50–51; **43**
412
Moksel *see* A. Moskel AG.
Mokta *see* Compagnie de Mokta.
MOL *see* Mitsui O.S.K. Lines, Ltd.
MOL Rt, 70 192–95
Molabe S.A. Espagne *see* Leroux S.A.S.

Moldflow Corporation, 73 227–30
Molerway Freight Lines, Inc., **53** 250
Molex Incorporated, 11 317–19; **14** 27;
54 236–41 (upd.)
Molfino Hermanos SA, **59** 365
Moliflor Loisirs, 80 252–55
Molinera de México S.A. de C.V., **31** 236
Molinos Nacionales C.A., **7** 242–43; **25**
241
Molinos Río de la Plata S.A., 61
219–21
Molins plc, 51 249–51
Moll Plasticrafters, L.P., **17** 534
Molloy Manufacturing Co., **III** 569; **20**
360
Mölnlycke AB, **36** 26
The Molson Companies Limited, I
273–75; **26** 303–07 (upd.)
Molson Coors Brewing Company, 77
288–300 (upd.)
Molycorp, **IV** 571; **24** 521
Momentum Worldwide, **73** 279
Momentus Group Ltd., **51** 99
Mon-Dak Chemical Inc., **16** 270
Mon-Valley Transportation Company, **11**
194
Mona Meyer McGrath & Gavin, **47** 97
MONACA *see* Molinos Nacionales C.A.
Monaco Coach Corporation, 31 336–38
Monadnock Paper Mills, Inc., 21
381–84
Monarch Air Lines, **22** 219
Monarch Casino & Resort, Inc., 65
239–41
The Monarch Cement Company, 72
231–33
Monarch Development Corporation, **38**
451–52
Monarch Foods, **26** 503
Mondadori *see* Arnoldo Monadori Editore
S.p.A.
Mondex International, **18** 543
Mondi Foods BV, **41** 12
Moneris Solutions Corp., **46** 55
Monet Jewelry, **9** 156–57
Money Access Service Corp., **11** 467
Money Management Associates, Inc., **53**
136
Monfort, Inc., 13 350–52
Monitor Dynamics Inc., **24** 510
Monitor Group Inc., **33** 257
Monk-Austin Inc., **12** 110
Monmouth Pharmaceuticals Ltd., **16** 439
Monnaie de Paris, 62 246–48
Monneret Industrie, **56** 335
Monnoyeur Group *see* Groupe
Monnoyeur.
Monogram Aerospace Fasteners, Inc., **11**
536
Monogram Models, **25** 312
Monolithic Memories Inc., **16** 316–17,
549
Monon Corp., **13** 550
Monongahela Power, **38** 40
Monoprix *see* Galeries Lafayette S.A.
Monro Muffler Brake, Inc., 24 337–40
Monroe Savings Bank, **11** 109

Monrovia Nursery Company, 70
196–98
Monsanto Company, I 365–67; **9**
355–57 (upd.); **29** 327–31 (upd.); **77**
301–07 (upd.)
Monsoon plc, 39 287–89
Monster Cable Products, Inc., 69
256–58
Monster Worldwide Inc., 74 194–97
(upd.)
Mont Blanc, **17** 5; **27** 487, 489
Montabert S.A., **15** 226
Montan TNT Pty Ltd., **27** 473
Montana Alimentaria S.p.A., **57** 82
Montana Coffee Traders, Inc., 60
208–10
Montana-Dakota Utilities Co., **7** 322–23;
37 281–82; **42** 249–50, 252
Montana Group, **54** 229
Montana Mills Bread Co., Inc., **61** 153
The Montana Power Company, 11
320–22; **44** 288–92 (upd.)
Montana Refining Company, **12** 240–41
Montana Resources, Inc., **IV** 34
Montaup Electric Co., **14** 125
MontBell America, Inc., **29** 279
Montblanc International GmbH, 82
240–44
Monte Paschi Vita, **65** 71–72
Montedison S.p.A., I 368–69; **24**
341–44 (upd.)
Montefina, **IV** 499; **26** 367
Montell N.V., **24** 343
Monterey Homes Corporation *see*
Meritage Corporation.
Monterey Mfg. Co., **12** 439
Monterey Pasta Company, 58 240–43
Monterey's Acquisition Corp., **41** 270
Monterey's Tex-Mex Cafes, **13** 473
Monterrey, Compania de Seguros sobre la
Vida *see* Seguros Monterrey.
Monterrey Group, **19** 10–11, 189
Montgomery Elevator Company *see*
KONE Corporation.
**Montgomery Ward & Co.,
Incorporated, V** 145–48; **20** 374–79
(upd.)
Montiel Corporation, **17** 321
Montinex, **24** 270
Montreal Engineering Company, **6** 585
Montreal Mining Co., **17** 357
Montres Rolex S.A., 13 353–55; **34**
292–95 (upd.)
Montrose Capital, **36** 358
Montrose Chemical Company, **9** 118, 119
Montupet S.A., 63 302–04
Monumental Corp., **III** 179
Moody's Corporation, 65 242–44
Moody's Investors Service, **III**
Moog Inc., **13** 356–58
Moog Music, Inc., 75 261–64
Mooney Aerospace Group Ltd., 52
252–55
Mooney Chemicals, Inc. *see* OM Group,
Inc.
Moonlight Mushrooms, Inc. *see* Sylvan,
Inc.
Moonstone Mountaineering, Inc., **29** 181

Mrs. Paul's Kitchens *see* Campbell Soup Company.

Mrs. Smith's Frozen Foods *see* Kellogg Company

Mrs. Winner's Chicken & Biscuits, **58** 324

MS&L *see* Manning Selvage & Lee.

MS-Relais GmbH *see* Matsushita Electric Works, Ltd.

MSAS Cargo International *see* Excel plc.

MSC *see* Material Sciences Corporation.

MSC Industrial Direct Co., Inc., 71 **234–36**

MSE Corporation, **33** 44

MSI Data Corp., **10** 523; **15** 482

M6 *see* Métropole Télévision S.A..

MSL Industries, **10** 44

MSNBC, **28** 301

MSP, Inc., **57** 231

MSR *see* Mountain Safety Research.

MSU *see* Middle South Utilities.

Mt. *see also* Mount.

Mt. Beacon Insurance Co., **26** 486

Mt. Goldsworthy Mining Associates, **IV** 47

Mt. Olive Pickle Company, Inc., 44 **293–95**

Mt. Summit Rural Telephone Company, **14** 258

Mt. Vernon Iron Works, **II** 14

MTA *see* Metropolitan Transportation Authority.

MTC *see* Management and Training Corporation.

MTel *see* Mobile Telecommunications Technologies Corp.

MTG *see* Modern Times Group AB.

MTM Entertainment Inc., **13** 279, 281

MTR Foods Ltd., 55 271–73

MTR Gaming Group, Inc., 75 265–67

MTS *see* Mobile TeleSystems.

MTS Inc., 37 261–64

MTV, **31** 239

MTV Asia, **23** 390

MTVi Group, **37** 194

Muehlens KG, **48** 422

Mueller Co. *see* Tyco International Ltd.

Mueller Furniture Company, *see* Haworth Inc.

Mueller Industries, Inc., 7 359–61; 52 **256–60 (upd.)**

Muench Woodworking, Inc., **68** 133

Muffler Corporation of America, **56** 230

Mulberry Group PLC, 71 237–39

Mule-Hide Products Co., **22** 15

Mullen Advertising Inc., 51 259–61

Mullens & Co., **14** 419

Multex Systems, **21** 70

Multi-Color Corporation, 53 234–36

Multi Restaurants, **II** 664

Multibank Inc., **11** 281

Multicanal S.A., **67** 200–01

Multicare Companies *see* NeighborCare, Inc.

Multicom Publishing Inc., **11** 294

Multiflex, Inc., **63** 318

Multilink, Inc., **27** 364–65

MultiMed, **11** 379

Multimedia Cablevision Inc. *see* Gannett Company, Inc.

Multimedia Games, Inc., 41 272–76

Multimedia, Inc., 11 330–32

Multimedia Security Services, Inc., **32** 374

Multiplex, **67** 104–06

MultiScope Inc., **10** 508

Multitech International *see* Acer Inc.

Multiview Cable, **24** 121

Mündener Gummiwerke GmbH, **68** 289

Munford, Inc., **17** 499

Munich Re (Münchener **Rückversicherungs-Gesellschaft** **Aktiengesellschaft in München), III** **299–301; 46 303–07 (upd.)**

Munising Woodenware Company, **13** 156

Munksjö, **19** 227

Munsingwear, Inc. *see* PremiumWear, Inc.

Munson Transportation Inc., **18** 227

Munster and Leinster Bank Ltd., **16** 13

Mura Corporation, **23** 209

Murata, **37** 347

Murdock Madaus Schwabe, 26 315–19

Murfin Inc., *see* Menasha Corporation.

Murmic, Inc., **9** 120

Murphey Favre, Inc., **17** 528, 530

Murphy Family Farms Inc., 22 366–68

Murphy Oil Corporation, 7 362–64; 32 **338–41 (upd.)**

Murphy-Phoenix Company, **14** 122

Murphy's Pizza *see* Papa Murphy's International, Inc.

Murray Inc., **19** 383

Murtaugh Light & Power Company, **12** 265

Muscatine Journal, **11** 251

Muse, Cordero, Chen, **41** 89

Musgrave Group Plc, 57 254–57

Music and Video Club, **24** 266, 270

Music-Appreciation Records, **13** 105

Music Corporation of America *see* MCA Inc.

Music Go Round, **18** 207–09

Music Man Co., **16** 202; **43** 170; **56** 116

Music Plus, **9** 75

Musical America Publishing, Inc., **22** 441

Musician's Friend, Inc. *see* Guitar Center, Inc.

Musicland Stores Corporation, 9 **360–62; 38 313–17 (upd.)**

Musicmatch, Inc. *see* Yahoo! Inc.

MusicNet, Inc., **53** 282

MusicNow, Inc. *see* Circuit City Stores, Inc.

Musitek, **16** 202; **43** 170

Muskegon Gas Company *see* MCN Corporation.

Muskegon Wire, **55** 305

Mutual & Federal, **61** 270, 272

Mutual Benefit Life Insurance **Company, III 302–04**

Mutual Broadcasting System, **23** 509

Mutual Gaslight Company *see* MCN Corporation.

Mutual Life Insurance Company of New **York, III 305–07**

Mutual Marine Office Inc., **41** 284

Mutual of Omaha, **III** 365; **25** 89–90; **27** 47

Mutual Papers Co., **14** 522

Mutual Savings & Loan Association, **III** 215; **18** 60

Muzak, Inc., 18 353–56

Muzzy-Lyon Company *see* Federal-Mogul Corporation.

MVC *see* Music and Video Club.

MVF *see* Mission Valley Fabrics.

MVR Products Pte Limited, **47** 255

MWA *see* Modern Woodmen of America.

MWH Preservation Limited **Partnership, 65 245–48**

MWI Veterinary Supply, Inc., 80 **265–68**

Mwinilunga Canneries Ltd., **IV** 241

MXL Industries, Inc., *see* National Patient Development Corporation.

Myanmar Brewery Ltd., **59** 60

Mycalkyushu Corporation *see* AEON Co., Ltd.

Myco-Sci, Inc. *see* Sylvan, Inc.

Mycogen Corporation, 21 385–87

Mycrom, **14** 36

Myer Emporium Ltd., **20** 156

Myers Industries, Inc., 19 277–79

Mylan Laboratories Inc., I 656–57; 20 **380–82 (upd.); 59 304–08 (upd.)**

Myojo Cement Co. Ltd., **60** 301

Myrna Knitwear, Inc., **16** 231

Myrurgia S.A., **60** 246

N

N.A. Woodworth, **III** 519; **22** 282

N. Boynton & Co., **16** 534

N.C. Cameron & Sons, Ltd., **11** 95

N.C. Monroe Construction Company, **14** 112

N.E.M., **23** 228

N.E. Restaurant Co. Inc. *see* Bertucci's Corpration.

N.F. Smith & Associates LP, 70 **199–202**

N.H. Geotech *see* New Holland N.V.

N.L. Industries, **19** 212

N M Electronics, **II** 44

N M Rothschild & Sons Limited, 39 **293–95**

N. Shure Company, **15** 477

N.V. *see under first word of company name*

N.Y.P. Holdings Inc., **12** 360

Na Pali, S.A. *see* Quiksilver, Inc.

Naamloze Vennootschap tot Exploitatie van het Café Krasnapolsky *see* Grand Hotel Krasnapolsky N.V.

Nabari Kintetsu Gas Company Ltd., **60** 236

Nabisco Brands, Inc., II 542–44 *see also* RJR Nabisco.

Nabisco Foods Group, 7 365–68 (upd.) *see also* Kraft Foods Inc.

Nabisco Holdings Corporation, **25** 181; **42** 408; **44** 342

Nabisco Ltd., **24** 288

Nabors Industries, Inc., 9 363–65

Nacamar Internet Services, **48** 398

Natomas Company, **7** 309; **11** 271

Natref *see* National Petroleum Refiners of South Africa.

Natrol, Inc., 49 275–78

Natronag, **IV** 325

NatSteel Electronics Ltd., **48** 369

NatTeknik, **26** 333

Natudryl Manufacturing Company, **10** 271

Natura Cosméticos S.A., 75 268–71

Natural Alternatives International, Inc., 49 279–82

Natural Gas Clearinghouse *see* NGC Corporation.

Natural Gas Corp., **19** 155

Natural Gas Pipeline Company, **6** 530, 543; **7** 344–45

Natural Gas Service of Arizona, **19** 411

Natural Ovens Bakery, Inc., 72 234–36

Natural Selection Foods, 54 256–58

Natural Wonders Inc., 14 342–44

NaturaLife International, **26** 470

Naturalizer *see* Brown Shoe Company, Inc.

The Nature Company, **10** 215–16; **14** 343; **26** 439; **27** 429; **28** 306

The Nature Conservancy, 28 305–07

Nature's Sunshine Products, Inc., 15 317–19

Nature's Way Products Inc., **26** 315

Naturin GmbH *see* Viscofan S.A.

Naturipe Berry Growers, **62** 154

Natuzzi Group *see* Industrie Natuzzi S.p.A.

NatWest Bancorp, **38** 393

NatWest Bank *see* National Westminster Bank PLC.

Naugles, **7** 506

Naumes, Inc., 81 257–60

Nautica Enterprises, Inc., 18 357–60; **44** 302–06 (upd.)

Nautilus International, Inc., **25** 40; **30** 161

Navaho Freight Line, **16** 41

Navajo LTL, Inc., **57** 277

Navajo Refining Company, **12** 240

Navajo Shippers, Inc., **42** 364

Navan Resources, **38** 231

Navarre Corporation, 24 348–51

Navigant International, Inc., 47 263–66

Navigation Mixte, **III** 348

Navire Cargo Gear, **27** 269

Navisant, Inc., **49** 424

Navistar International Corporation, I 180–82; **10** 428–30 (upd.) *see also* International Harvester Co.

NAVTEQ Corporation, 69 272–75

Navy Exchange Service Command, 31 342–45

Navy Federal Credit Union, 33 315–17

Naxon Utilities Corp., **19** 359

Naylor, Hutchinson, Vickers & Company *see* Vickers PLC.

NBC *see* National Broadcasting Company, Inc.

NBC Bankshares, Inc., **21** 524

NBC/Computer Services Corporation, **15** 163

NBD Bancorp, Inc., 11 339–41 *see also* Bank One Corporation.

NBGS International, Inc., 73 231–33

NBSC Corporation *see* National Bank of South Carolina.

NBTY, Inc., 31 346–48

NCA Corporation, **9** 36, 57, 171

NCB *see* National City Bank of New York.

NCC Industries, Inc., **59** 267

NCC L.P., **15** 139

NCH Corporation, 8 385–87

nChip, **38** 187–88

NCL Corporation, 79 274–77

NCL Holdings *see* Genting Bhd.

NCNB Corporation, II 336–37

NCO Group, Inc., 42 258–60

NCR Corporation, III 150–53; **6** 264–68 (upd.); **30** 336–41 (upd.)

NCS *see* Norstan, Inc.

NCS Healthcare Inc., **67** 262

NCTI (Noise Cancellation Technologies Inc.), **19** 483–84

nCube Corp., **14** 15; **22** 293

ND Marston, **III** 593

NDB *see* National Discount Brokers Group, Inc.

NDL *see* Norddeutscher Lloyd.

NE Chemcat Corporation, **72** 118

NEA *see* Newspaper Enterprise Association.

Nearly Me, **25** 313

Neatherlin Homes Inc., **22** 547

Nebraska Bell Company, **14** 311

Nebraska Book Company, Inc., 65 257–59

Nebraska Cellular Telephone Company, **14** 312

Nebraska Furniture Mart, **III** 214–15; **18** 60–61, 63

Nebraska Light & Power Company, **6** 580

Nebraska Power Company, **25** 89

Nebraska Public Power District, 29 351–54

NEBS *see* New England Business Services, Inc.

NEC Corporation, II 66–68; **21** 388–91 (upd.); **57** 261–67 (upd.)

Neckermann Versand AG *see* Karstadt AG.

Nedcor, **61** 270–71

Nederland Line *see* Stoomvaart Maatschappij Nederland.

Nederlander Organization, **24** 439

Nederlands Talen Institut, **13** 544

Nederlandsche Electriciteits Maatschappij *see* N.E.M.

Nederlandsche Handel Maatschappij, **26** 242

Nederlandsche Heidenmaatschappij *see* Arcadis NV.

Nederlandsche Kunstzijdebariek, **13** 21

N.V. Nederlandse Gasunie, V 658–61

Nedlloyd Group *see* Koninklijke Nedlloyd N.V.

NedMark Transportation Services *see* Polar Air Cargo Inc.

Neeco, Inc., **9** 301

Needham Harper Worldwide *see* Omnicom Group Inc.

Needlecraft, **II** 560; **12** 410

Needleworks, Inc., **23** 66

Neenah Foundry Company, 68 263–66

Neenah Printing, *see* Menasha Corporation.

NEES *see* New England Electric System.

Neff Corp., 32 352–53

Neff GmbH, **67** 81

NEG Micon A/S, **73** 375

Negromex, **23** 171–72

NEI *see* Northern Engineering Industries PLC.

Neico International, Inc., **67** 226

NeighborCare, Inc., 67 259–63 (upd.)

Neighborhood Restaurants of America, **18** 241

Neilson/Cadbury, **II** 631

Neiman Bearings Co., **13** 78

The Neiman Marcus Group, Inc., 12 355–57; **49** 283–87 (upd.)

Neisner Brothers, Inc., **9** 20

NEL Equity Services Co., **III** 314

Nelson Bros., **14** 236

Nelson Entertainment Group, **47** 272

Nelson Publications, **22** 442

Nelsons *see* A. Nelson & Co. Ltd.

NEMF *see* New England Motor Freight, Inc.

Neo Products Co., **37** 401

Neodata, **11** 293

Neopost S.A., 53 237–40

Neos, **21** 438

Neoterics Inc., **11** 65

Neozyme I Corp., **13** 240

Nepera, Inc., **16** 69

Neptun Maritime Oyj, **29** 431

Neptune Orient Lines Limited, 47 267–70

NER Auction Group, **23** 148

NERCO, Inc., 7 376–79

NES *see* National Equipment Services, Inc.

Nesco Inc., **28** 6, 8

Nescott, Inc., **16** 36

Nespak SpA, **40** 214–15

Neste Oy, IV 469–71 *see also* Fortum Corporation

Nestlé S.A., II 545–49; **7** 380–84 (upd.); **28** 308–13 (upd.); **71** 240–46 (upd.)

Nestlé Waters, 73 234–37

Net Investment S.A., **63** 180

NetApp *see* Network Appliance, Inc.

NetCom Systems AB, 26 331–33

NetCreations, **47** 345, 347

NetEffect Alliance, **58** 194

Netezza Corporation, 69 276–78

Netflix, Inc., 58 248–51

NETGEAR, Inc., 81 261–64

Netherlands Trading Co *see* Nederlandse Handel Maatschappij.

NetHold B.V., **31** 330

NetIQ Corporation, 79 278–81

NetLabs, **25** 117

NetMarket Company, **16** 146

NetPlane Systems, **36** 124

Netron, **II** 390

Newco Waste Systems *see* Browning-Ferris
Industries, Inc.
Newcor, Inc., 40 332–35
Newcrest Mining Ltd., **IV** 47; **22** 107
**Newell Rubbermaid Inc., 9 373–76; 52
261–71 (upd.)**
**Newfield Exploration Company, 65
260–62**
Newfoundland Brewery, **26** 304
Newfoundland Energy, Ltd., **17** 121
Newfoundland Light & Power Co. *see*
Fortis, Inc.
Newfoundland Processing Ltd. *see*
Newfoundland Energy, Ltd.
**Newhall Land and Farming Company,
14 348–50**
Newly Weds Foods, Inc., 74 201–03
Newman's Own, Inc., 37 272–75
Newmark & Lewis Inc., **23** 373
**Newmont Mining Corporation, 7
385–88**
Newnes, **17** 397
NewPage Corporation, **76** 270
Newpark Resources, Inc., 63 305–07
Newport Corporation, 71 247–49
**Newport News Shipbuilding Inc., 13
372–75; 38 323–27 (upd.)**
News & Observer Publishing Company,
23 343
**News America Publishing Inc., 12
358–60**
News Communications & Media Plc, **35**
242
**News Corporation Limited, IV 650–53;
7 389–93 (upd.); 46 308–13 (upd.)**
News Extracts Ltd., **55** 289
News International Corp., **20** 79
News of the World Organization
(NOTW), **46** 309
News World Communications, **73** 356
Newsco NV, **48** 347
Newsfoto Publishing Company, **12** 472;
36 469
Newspaper Enterprise Association, **7**
157–58
Newsquest plc, 32 354–56
Newth-Morris Box Co. *see* Rock-Tenn
Company.
Newton Yarn Mills, **19** 305
**NewYork-Presbyterian Hospital, 59
309–12**
Nexans SA, 54 262–64
Nexar Technologies, Inc., **22** 409
NEXCOM *see* Navy Exchange Service
Command.
Nexen Inc., 79 282–85
NexFlash Technologies, Inc. *see* Winbond
Electronics Corporation.
Nexity S.A., 66 243–45
**Nexstar Broadcasting Group, Inc., 73
238–41**
NeXstar Pharmaceuticals Inc., **54** 130
NeXT Incorporated, **34** 348
Next Media Ltd., 61 244–47
Next plc, 29 355–57
**Nextel Communications, Inc., 10
431–33; 27 341–45 (upd.)**
Nextera Enterprises, Inc., **54** 191, 193

NEXTLINK Communications, Inc., **38**
192
NextNet Wireless, Inc. *see* Clearwire, Inc.
**Neyveli Lignite Corporation Ltd., 65
263–65**
NFC Castings Inc., **68** 265
NFC plc, 6 412–14 *see also* Exel plc.
NFL *see* National Football League Inc.
NFL Films, 75 275–78
NFL Properties, Inc., **22** 223
NFO Worldwide, Inc., 24 352–55
NFT Distribution Limited, **61** 258,
260–61
NGC *see* National Grid Company.
NGC Corporation, 18 365–67 *see also*
Dynegy Inc.
NGI International Precious Metals, Ltd.,
24 335
NGK Insulators Ltd., 67 264–66
NH Hoteles S.A., 79 286–89
NHB Group Ltd. *see* MasterBrand
Cabinets, Inc.
NHK *see* Japan Broadcasting Corporation.
NHK Spring Co., Ltd., III 580–82
NI Industries, **20** 362
Ni-Med, **50** 122
Niagara Corporation, 28 314–16
Niagara First Savings and Loan
Association, **10** 91
**Niagara Mohawk Holdings Inc., V
665–67; 45 296–99 (upd.)**
Niagara of Wisconsin, **26** 362–63
Nice Day, Inc., **II** 539
Nice Systems, **11** 520
NiceCom Ltd., **11** 520
Nichido Fire and Marine Insurance Co.
see Millea Holdings Inc.
Nichii Co., Ltd., V 154–55
**Nichimen Corporation, IV 150–52; 24
356–59 (upd.)**
Nichimo Sekiyu Co. Ltd., **IV** 555; **16** 490
Nichirei Corporation, 70 203–05
Nichols Aluminum-Golden, Inc., **62** 289
Nichols-Homeshield, **22** 14
Nichols plc, 44 315–18
**Nichols Research Corporation, 18
368–70**
Nicholson File Co., **II** 16
Nicholson Graham & Jones, **28** 141
Nickelodeon, **25** 381
Nickerson Machinery Company Inc., **53**
230
Nicklaus Companies, 45 300–03
Nicolet Instrument Company, **11** 513
Nicolon N.V. *see* Royal Ten Cate N.V.
NICOR Inc., 6 529–31
Nidec Corporation, 59 313–16
Nielsen, **10** 358
Nielsen Marketing Research *see* A.C.
Nielsen Company.
Niesmann & Bischoff, **22** 207
Nieuw Rotterdam, **27** 54
NIF Ventures Co. Ltd., **55** 118
**Nigerian National Petroleum
Corporation, IV 472–74; 72 240–43
(upd.)**
Nigerian Shipping Operations, **27** 473
Nihon Keizai Shimbun, Inc., IV 654–56

Nihon Kohden Corporation, **13** 328
Nihon Lumber Land Co., **III** 758
Nihon Noyaku Co., **64** 35
Nihon Styrene Paper Company *see* JSP
Corporation.
Nihon Synopsis, **11** 491
Nihon Waters K.K., **43** 456
Nihron Yupro Corp. *see* Toto Ltd.
NII *see* National Intergroup, Inc.
**NIKE, Inc., V 372–74; 8 391–94 (upd.);
36 343–48 (upd.); 75 279–85 (upd.)**
Nikkei *see* Nihon Keizai Shimbun, Inc.
Nikkei Shimbun Toei, **9** 29
Nikkelverk, **49** 136
Nikken Global Inc., 32 364–67
**The Nikko Securities Company
Limited, II 433–35; 9 377–79 (upd.)**
Nikko Trading Co., *see* Japan Airlines
Company, Ltd.
Nikolaiev, **19** 49, 51
**Nikon Corporation, III 583–85; 48
292–95 (upd.)**
Nilpeter, **26** 540, 542
Niman Ranch, Inc., 67 267–69
**Nimbus CD International, Inc., 20
386–90**
9 Telecom, **24** 79
**Nine West Group Inc., 11 348–49; 39
301–03 (upd.)**
98 Cents Clearance Centers, **62** 104
99¢ Only Stores, 25 353–55
Ningbo General Bearing Co., Ltd., **45**
170
**Nintendo Co., Ltd., III 586–88; 7
394–96 (upd.); 28 317–21 (upd.); 67
270–76 (upd.)**
Nintendo of America, **24** 4
NIOC *see* National Iranian Oil Company.
Nippon Breweries Ltd. *see* Sapporo
Breweries Ltd.
Nippon Cable Company, **15** 235
Nippon Credit Bank, II 338–39
Nippon Del Monte Corporation, **47** 206
Nippon Densan Corporation *see* Nidec
Corporation.
Nippon Educational Television (NET) *see*
Asahi National Broadcasting Company,
Ltd.
Nippon Electric Company, Limited *see*
NEC Corporation.
**Nippon Express Company, Ltd., V
477–80; 64 286–90 (upd.)**
Nippon-Fisher, **13** 225
Nippon Foundation Engineering Co. Ltd.,
51 179
Nippon Gakki Co., Ltd *see* Yamaha
Corporation.
Nippon Global Tanker Co. Ltd., **53** 116
Nippon Gyomo Sengu Co. Ltd., **IV** 555
Nippon Hatsujo Kabushikikaisha *see*
NHK Spring Co., Ltd.
Nippon Helicopter & Aeroplane Transport
Co., Ltd. *see* All Nippon Airways
Company Limited.
Nippon Hoso Kyokai *see* Japan
Broadcasting Corporation.
Nippon Idou Tsushin, **7** 119–20
Nippon Interrent, **10** 419–20

Norsk Hydro ASA, 10 437–40; **35** 315–19 (upd.)

Norsk Rengjorings Selskap a.s., **49** 221

Norske Skog do Brasil Ltda., **73** 205

Norske Skogindustrier ASA, **63** 314–16

Norstan, Inc., **16** 392–94

Norstar Bancorp, **9** 229

Nortek, Inc., **34** 308–12

Nortel Inversora S.A., **63** 375–77

Nortel Networks Corporation, **36** 349–54 (upd.)

Nortex International, **7** 96; **19** 338

North African Petroleum Ltd., **IV** 455

North American Aviation, **7** 520; **9** 16; **11** 278, 427

North American Carbon, **19** 499

North American Cellular Network, **9** 322

North American Coal Corporation, **7** 369–71

North American Company, **6** 552–53, 601–02

North American Dräger, **13** 328

North American Energy Conservation, Inc., **35** 480

North American InTeleCom, Inc., **IV** 411

North American Light & Power Company, **12** 541

North American Medical Management Company, Inc., **36** 366

North American Mogul Products Co. *see* Mogul Corp.

North American Nutrition Companies Inc. (NANCO) *see* Provimi

North American Philips Corporation, *see* Philips Electronics North America Corp.

North American Plastics, Inc., **61** 112

North American Rockwell Corp., **10** 173

North American Site Developers, Inc., **69** 197

North American Systems, **14** 230

North American Training Corporation *see* Rollerblade, Inc.

North American Van Lines *see* Allied Worldwide, Inc.

North American Watch Company *see* Movado Group, Inc.

North Atlantic Energy Corporation, **21** 411

North Atlantic Laboratories, Inc., **62** 391

North Atlantic Packing, **13** 243

North Atlantic Trading Company Inc., **65** 266–68

North British Rubber Company, **20** 258

North Broken Hill Peko, **IV** 61

North Carolina Motor Speedway, Inc., **19** 294

North Carolina National Bank Corporation *see* NCNB Corporation.

North Carolina Natural Gas Corporation, **6** 578

North Carolina Shipbuilding Co., **13** 373

North Central Financial Corp., **9** 475

North Central Utilities, Inc., **18** 405

North East Insurance Company, **44** 356

North Eastern Bricks, **14** 249

The North Face, Inc., **18** 375–77; **78** 258–61 (upd.)

North Fork Bancorporation, Inc., **46** 314–17

North New York Savings Bank, **10** 91

North of Scotland Hydro-Electric Board, **19** 389

North Pacific Group, Inc., **61** 254–57

North Pacific Paper Corp., **IV** 298

North Ridge Securities Corporation, **72** 149–50

North Sea Ferries, **26** 241, 243

North Sea Oil and Gas, **10** 337

North Shore Gas Company, **6** 543–44

North Shore Land Co., **17** 357

North Star Communications Group Inc., **73** 59

North Star Container, Inc., **59** 290

North Star Egg Case Company, **12** 376

North Star Marketing Cooperative, **7** 338

North Star Mill, **12** 376

North Star Steel Company, **18** 378–81

North Star Transport Inc., **49** 402

North Star Tubes, **54** 391, 393

North Star Universal, Inc., **25** 331, 333

North State Supply Company, **57** 9

North Supply, **27** 364

The North West Company, Inc., **12** 361–63

North-West Telecommunications *see* Pacific Telecom, Inc.

North West Water Group plc, **11** 359–62 *see also* United Utilities PLC.

Northbridge Financial Corp., **57** 137

Northbrook Corporation, **24** 32

Northbrook Holdings, Inc., **22** 495

Northcliffe Newspapers, **19** 118

Northeast Petroleum Industries, Inc., **11** 194; **14** 461

Northeast Savings Bank, **12** 31

Northeast Utilities, **V** 668–69; **48** 303–06 (upd.)

Northeastern New York Medical Service, Inc., **III** 246

Northern Animal Hospital Inc., **58** 355

Northern Arizona Light & Power Co., **6** 545

Northern California Savings, **10** 340

Northern Dairies, **10** 441

Northern Drug Company, **14** 147

Northern Electric Company *see* Northern Telecom Limited.

Northern Energy Resources Company *see* NERCO, Inc.

Northern Engineering Industries Plc *see* Rolls-Royce Group PLC.

Northern Fibre Products Co., **I** 202

Northern Foods plc, **10** 441–43; **61** 258–62 (upd.)

Northern Illinois Gas Co., **6** 529–31

Northern Indiana Power Company, **6** 556

Northern Indiana Public Service Company, **6** 532–33

Northern Infrastructure Maintenance Company, **39** 238

Northern Leisure, **40** 296–98

Northern Light Electric Company, **18** 402–03

Northern National Bank, **14** 90

Northern Natural Gas Co. *see* Enron Corporation.

Northern Pacific Corp., **15** 274

Northern Pacific Railroad, **14** 168; **26** 451

Northern Pipeline Construction Co., **19** 410, 412

Northern Rock plc, **33** 318–21

Northern Star Co., **25** 332

Northern States Power Company, **V** 670–72; **20** 391–95 (upd.) *see also* Xcel Energy Inc.

Northern Stores, Inc., **12** 362

Northern Sugar Company, **11** 13

Northern Telecom Limited, **V** 308–10 *see also* Nortel Networks Corporation.

Northern Trust Company, **9** 387–89

Northfield Metal Products, **11** 256

Northgate Computer Corp., **17** 196

Northland *see* Scott Fetzer Company.

Northland Cranberries, Inc., **38** 332–34

Northland Publishing, **19** 231

NorthPrint International, **22** 356

Northrop Grumman Corporation, **I** 76–77; **11** 363–65 (upd.); **45** 304–12 (upd.)

NorthStar Computers, **10** 313

Northwest Airlines Corporation, **I** 112–14; **6** 103–05 (upd.); **26** 337–40 (upd.); **74** 204–08 (upd.)

Northwest Engineering Co. *see* Terex Corporation.

Northwest Express *see* Bear Creek Corporation.

Northwest Industries *see* Chicago and North Western Holdings Corporation.

Northwest Linen Co., **16** 228

Northwest Natural Gas Company, **45** 313–15

Northwest Outdoor, **27** 280

Northwest Telecommunications Inc., **6** 598

NorthWestern Corporation, **37** 280–83

Northwestern Engraving, **12** 25

Northwestern Financial Corporation, **11** 29

Northwestern Flavors LLC, **58** 379

Northwestern Manufacturing Company, *see* Crane Co.

Northwestern Mutual Life Insurance Company, **III** 321–24; **45** 316–21 (upd.)

Northwestern National Bank, **16** 71

Northwestern National Life Insurance Co., **14** 233

Northwestern Public Service Company, **6** 524

Northwestern States Portland Cement Co., **III** 702

Northwestern Telephone Systems *see* Pacific Telecom, Inc.

Norton Company, **8** 395–97

Norton Healthcare Ltd., **11** 208

Norton McNaughton, Inc., **27** 346–49

Norton Opax PLC, **IV** 259; **34** 140

Norton Professional Books *see* W.W. Norton & Company, Inc.

Norton Simon Industries, **22** 513

Quad Pharmaceuticals, Inc. *see* Par Pharmaceuticals Inc.

Quail Oil Tools, **28** 347–48

Quaker Alloy, Inc., **39** 31–32

Quaker Fabric Corp., 19 337–39

Quaker Foods North America, II 558–60; **12** 409–12 (upd.); **34** 363–67 (upd.); **73** 268–73 (upd.)

Quaker State Corporation, 7 443–45; **21** 419–22 (upd.) *see also* Pennzoil-Quaker State Company.

QUALCOMM Incorporated, **20** 438–41; **47** 317–21 (upd.)

Qualcore, S. de R.L. de C.V., **51** 116

Qualipac, **55** 309

QualiTROL Corporation, **7** 116–17

Quality Assurance International, **72** 255

Quality Aviation Services, Inc., **53** 132

Quality Bakers of America, **12** 170

Quality Chekd Dairies, Inc., 48 337–39

Quality Courts Motels, Inc. *see* Choice Hotels International, Inc.

Quality Dining, Inc., 18 437–40

Quality Food Centers, Inc., 17 386–88

Quality Inns International *see* Choice Hotels International, Inc.

Quality Markets, Inc., **13** 393

Quality Oil Co., II 624–25

Quality Paperback Book Club (QPB), **13** 105–07

Quality Products, Inc., **18** 162

Quality Systems, Inc., 81 328–31

Qualix S.A., **67** 347–48

Quanex Corporation, 13 422–24; **62** 286–89 (upd.)

Quanta Computer Inc., 47 322–24

Quanta Display Inc., **75** 306

Quanta Services, Inc., 79 338–41

Quanta Systems Corp., **51** 81

Quanterra Alpha L.P., **63** 347

Quantex Microsystems Inc., **24** 31

Quantronix Corporation *see* Excel Technology Inc.

Quantum Chemical Corporation, 8 439–41

Quantum Computer Services, Inc. *see* America Online, Inc.

Quantum Corporation, 10 458–59; **62** 290–93 (upd.)

Quantum Health Resources, **29** 364

Quantum Marketing International, Inc., **27** 336

Quantum Offshore Contractors, **25** 104

Quantum Overseas N.V., **7** 360

Quantum Restaurant Group, Inc., **30** 330

Quarex Industries, Inc. *see* Western Beef, Inc.

Quark, Inc., 36 375–79

Quarrie Corporation, **12** 554

Quebec Credit Union League, **48** 290

Québéc Hydro-Electric Commission *see* Hydro-Quebec.

Quebecor Inc., 12 412–14; **47** 325–28 (upd.)

Queen City Broadcasting, **42** 162

Queens Isetan Co., Ltd. *see* Isetan Company Limited.

Queensborough Holdings PLC, **38** 103

Queensland Alumina, **IV** 59

Queensland and Northern Territories Air Service *see* Qantas Airways Limited.

Queensland Mines Ltd., III 729

Quelle Group, V 165–67 *see also* Karstadt Quelle AG.

Quesarias Ibéricas, **23** 219

Quest Aerospace Education, Inc., **18** 521

Quest Diagnostics Inc., 26 390–92

Quest Education Corporation, **42** 212

Quest Pharmacies Inc., **25** 504–05

Questa Oil and Gas Co., **63** 408

Questar Corporation, 6 568–70; **26** 386–89 (upd.)

Questor Management Co. LLC, **55** 31

Questor Partners, **26** 185

The Quick & Reilly Group, Inc., 20 442–44

Quick Pak Inc., **53** 236

Quicken.com *see* Intuit Inc.

Quickie Designs, **11** 202, 487–88

Quidel Corporation, 80 300–03

The Quigley Corporation, 62 294–97

Quik Stop Markets, Inc., **12** 112

Quiksilver, Inc., 18 441–43; **79** 342–47 (upd.)

QuikTrip Corporation, 36 380–83

Quill Corporation, 28 375–77

Quillery, **27** 138

Quilmes Industrial (QUINSA) S.A., 67 315–17

Quilter Sound Company *see* QSC Audio Products, Inc.

Quimica Geral do Nordeste S.A., **68** 81

Química y Farmacia, S.A. de C.V., **59** 332

Quimicos Industriales Penoles *see* Industrias Penoles, S.A. de C.V.

Quincy Family Steak House, II 679; **10** 331; **19** 287; **27** 17, 19

Quiñenco S.A., **69** 56–57; **70** 61–62

Quintana Roo, Inc., **17** 243, 245; **25** 42

Quintel Communications, Inc., **61** 375

Quintex Australia Limited, **25** 329

Quintiles Transnational Corporation, 21 423–25; **68** 308–12 (upd.)

Quintron, Inc., **11** 475

Quintus Computer Systems, **6** 248

Quixote Corporation, 15 378–80

Quixtar Inc. *see* Alticor Inc.

Quixx Corporation, **6** 580

The Quizno's Corporation, 42 295–98

Quoddy Products Inc., **17** 389, 390

Quotron Systems, Inc., **IV** 670; **9** 49, 125; **30** 127; **47** 37

Quovadx Inc., 70 243–46

QVC Inc., 9 428–29; **58** 284–87 (upd.)

Qwest Communications International, Inc., 37 312–17

QwikSilver II, Inc., **37** 119

R

R&B Falcon Corp. *see* Transocean Sedco Forex Inc.

R&B, Inc., 51 305–07

R&D Systems, Inc., **52** 347

R&O Software-Technik GmbH, **27** 492

R&S Home and Auto, **56** 352

R&S Technology Inc., **48** 410

R. and W. Hawaii Wholesale, Inc., **22** 15

R-Anell Custom Homes Inc., **41** 19

R-B *see* Arby's, Inc.

R-Byte, **12** 162

R-C Holding Inc. *see* Air & Water Technologies Corporation.

R.B. Pamplin Corp., 45 350–52

R.C. Bigelow, Inc., 49 334–36

R.C. Willey Home Furnishings, 72 291–93

R.E. Funsten Co., **7** 429

R.G. Barry Corp., 17 389–91; **44** 364–67 (upd.)

R.G. Dun-Bradstreet Corp. *see* The Dun & Bradstreet Corp.

R. Griggs Group Limited, 23 399–402; **31** 413–14

R.H. Donnelley Corporation, **61** 81–83

R.H. Macy & Co., Inc., V 168–70; **8** 442–45 (upd.); **30** 379–83 (upd.)

R.H. Stengel & Company, **13** 479

R.J. Reynolds, **I** 261, 363; **II** 544; **7** 130, 132, 267, 365, 367; **9** 533; **13** 490; **14** 78; **15** 72–73; **16** 242; **21** 315; **27** 125; **29** 195; **32** 344 *see also* RJR Nabisco.

R.J. Reynolds Tobacco Holdings, Inc., 30 384–87 (upd.)

R.J. Tower Corporation *see* Tower Automotive, Inc.

R.K. Brown, **14** 112

R.L. Crain Limited, **15** 473

R.L. Manning Company, **9** 363–64

R.L. Polk & Co., 10 460–62

R-O Realty, Inc., **43** 314

R.P.M., Inc., **25** 228

R.P. Scherer Corporation, I 678–80

R.R. Bowker Co., **17** 398; **23** 440

R.R. Donnelley & Sons Company, IV 660–62; **38** 368–71 (upd.)

R.S.R. Corporation, **31** 48

R.S. Stokvis Company, **13** 499

R. Scott Associates, **11** 57

R-T Investors LC, **42** 323–24

R. Twining & Co., **61** 395

R.W. Beck, **29** 353

R.W. Harmon & Sons, Inc., **6** 410

RABA PLC, **10** 274

Rabbit Software Corp., **10** 474

Rabobank Group, 26 419; **33** 356–58

RAC *see* Ravenswood Aluminum Company; Roy Anderson Corporation.

Racal-Datacom Inc., 11 408–10

Racal Electronics PLC, II 83–84

Race Z, Inc. *see* Action Peformance Companies, Inc.

Rachel's Dairy Ltd., **37** 197–98

Racine Hidraulica, **21** 430

Racine Threshing Machine Works, **10** 377

Racing Champions *see* Action Performance Companies, Inc.

Racing Champions Corporation, 37 318–20

Racing Collectables Club of America, Inc. *see* Action Performance Companies, Inc.

Racket Store *see* Duckwall-ALCO Stores, Inc.

Rheinbraun A.G., **73** 131

Rheinische Metallwaaren- und Maschinenfabrik AG, **9** 443–44

Rheinische Zuckerwarenfabrik GmbH, **27** 460

Rheinmetall Berlin AG, 9 443–46

Rhenus-Weichelt AG *see* Schenker-Rhenus AG.

RHI AG, 53 283–86

RHI Entertainment Inc., **16** 257

Rhino Entertainment Company, 18 457–60; **70** 276–80 (upd.)

RHM *see* Ranks Hovis McDougall.

Rhodes Inc., 23 412–14

Rhodia SA, 38 378–80

Rhône Moulage Industrie, **39** 152, 154

Rhône-Poulenc S.A., I 388–90; **10** 470–72 (upd.)

RhoxalPharma Inc., **69** 209

Rhymney Iron Company, **31** 369

Rica Foods, Inc., 41 328–29

Ricardo Gallo *see* Vidrala S.A.

Riccar, **17** 124; **41** 114

Riccardo's Restaurant, **18** 538

Riceland Foods, Inc., **27** 390

Rich Products Corporation, 7 448–49; **38** 381–84 (upd.)

Rich's Inc., **9** 209; **10** 515; **31** 191

Richard A. Shaw, Inc., **7** 128

Richard D. Irwin Inc. *see* Dow Jones & Company, Inc.

Richard Ginori 1735 S.p.A., **73** 248–49

Richard R. Dostie, Inc. *see* Toll Brothers Inc.

Richards & O'Neil LLP, **43** 70

The Richards Group, Inc., 58 300–02

Richardson Company, **36** 147

Richardson Electronics, Ltd., 17 405–07

Richardson Industries, Inc., 62 298–301

Richardson-Vicks Company *see* The Procter & Gamble Company

Richardson's, **21** 246

Richfood Holdings, Inc., 7 450–51; **50** 458

Richland Co-op Creamery Company, **7** 592

Richman Gordman Half Price Stores, Inc. *see* Gordmans, Inc.

Richmond American Homes of Florida, Inc., **11** 258

Richmond Carousel Corporation, **9** 120

Richmond Cedar Works Manufacturing Co., **12** 109; **19** 360

Richmond Corp., **15** 129

Richmond Paperboard Corp., **19** 78

Richmond Pulp and Paper Company, **17** 281

Richton International Corporation, 39 344–46

Richtree Inc., 63 328–30

Richway, **10** 515

Richwood Building Products, Inc., **12** 397

Richwood Sewell Coal Co., **17** 357

Rickards, Roloson & Company, **22** 427

Rickel Home Centers, **II** 673

Ricky Shaw's Oriental Express, **25** 181

Ricoh Company, Ltd., III 159–61; **36** 389–93 (upd.)

Ricola Ltd., 62 302–04

Ricolino, **19** 192

Riddarhyttan Resources AB *see* Agnico-Eagle Mines Limited.

Riddell Inc., **33** 467

Riddell Sports Inc., 22 457–59; **23** 449

Ridder Publications *see* Knight-Ridder, Inc.

Ride, Inc., 22 460–63

Ridge Tool Co., **II** 19

Ridgewell's Inc., **15** 87

Ridgewood Properties Inc., **12** 394

Ridgway Co., **23** 98

Ridley Corporation Ltd., 62 305–07

Riedel-de Haën AG, **22** 32; **36** 431

The Riese Organization, 38 385–88

Rieter Holding AG, 42 315–17

Riggs National Corporation, 13 438–40

Right Associates, **27** 21; **44** 156

Right Management Consultants, Inc., 42 318–21

Right Source, Inc., **24** 96

RightPoint, Inc., **49** 124

RightSide Up, Inc., **27** 21

Rijnhaave Information Systems, **25** 21

Rike's, **10** 282

Riken Corp., **10** 493

Riken Kagaku Co. Ltd., **48** 250

Riklis Family Corp., 9 447–50

Rinascente S.p.A., 71 308–10

Ring King Visibles, Inc., **13** 269

Ring Ltd., **43** 99

Ringier America, **19** 333

Ringköpkedjan, **II** 640

Ringling Bros., Barnum & Bailey Circus, **25** 312–13

Ringnes Bryggeri, **18** 396

Rini-Rego Supermarkets Inc., **13** 238

Rini Supermarkets, **9** 451; **13** 237

Rinker Group Ltd., 65 298–301

Rio de Janeiro Refrescos S.A., **71** 140

Rio Grande Industries, Inc., **12** 18–19

Rio Grande Servaas, S.A. de C.V., **23** 145

Rio Sportswear Inc., **42** 269

Rio Sul Airlines *see* Varig, SA.

Rio Tinto plc, 19 349–53 (upd.) **50** 380–85 (upd.)

Riocell S.A. *see* Klabin S.A.

Riordan Freeman & Spogli, **13** 406

Riordan Holdings Ltd., **10** 554; **67** 298

Ripley Entertainment, Inc., 74 273–76

Ripotot, **68** 143

Riser Foods, Inc., 9 451–54; **13** 237–38

Risk Management Partners Ltd., **35** 36

Risk Planners, **II** 669

Ritchie Bros. Auctioneers Inc., 41 331–34

Rite Aid Corporation, V 174–76; **19** 354–57 (upd.); **63** 331–37 (upd.)

Rite-Way Department Store, **II** 649

Riteway Distributor, **26** 183

Rittenhouse Financial Services, **22** 495

Ritter Co. *see* Sybron Corp.

Ritter Sport *see* Alfred Ritter GmbH & Co. KG.

Ritter's Frozen Custard *see* RFC Franchising LLC.

Ritz Camera Centers, 18 186; **34** 375–77

The Ritz-Carlton Hotel Company, L.L.C., 9 455–57; **29** 403–06 (upd.); **71** 311–16 (upd.)

Ritz Firma, **13** 512

Riunione Adriatica di Sicurtà SpA, III 345–48

Riva Group Plc, **53** 46

The Rival Company, 19 358–60

Rivarossi, **16** 337

Rivaud Group, **29** 370

River Boat Casino, **9** 425–26

River City Broadcasting, **25** 418

River Metals Recycling LLC, **76** 130

River North Studios *see* Platinum Entertainment, Inc.

River Oaks Furniture, Inc., 43 314–16

River Ranch Fresh Foods—Salinas, Inc., **41** 11

River Thames Insurance Co., Ltd., **26** 487

Riverdeep Group plc, **41** 137

Riverside Chemical Company, **13** 502

Riverside Furniture, **19** 455

Riverside Insurance Co. of America, **26** 487

Riverside National Bank of Buffalo, **11** 108

Riverside Press, **10** 355–56

Riverside Publishing Company, **36** 272

Riverwood International Corporation, 11 420–23; **48** 340–44 (upd.)

Riviana Foods, 27 388–91

Riviera Holdings Corporation, 75 340–43

Riyadh Armed Forces Hospital, **16** 94

Rizzoli Publishing, **23** 88

RJMJ, Inc., **16** 37

RJR Nabisco Holdings Corp., V 408–10 *see also* R.J Reynolds Tobacco Holdings Inc., Nabisco Brands, Inc.; R.J. Reynolds Industries, Inc.

RK Rose + Krieger GmbH & Co. KG, **61** 286–87

RKO *see* Radio-Keith-Orpheum.

RLA Polymers, **9** 92

RMC Group p.l.c., III 737–40; **34** 378–83 (upd.)

RMH Teleservices, Inc., 42 322–24

Roadhouse Grill, Inc., 22 464–66

Roadmaster Industries, Inc., 16 430–33

Roadmaster Transport Company, **18** 27; **41** 18

RoadOne *see* Miller Industries, Inc.

Roadstone-Wood Group, **64** 98

Roadway Express, Inc., V 502–03; **25** 395–98 (upd.)

Roanoke Capital Ltd., **27** 113–14

Roanoke Electric Steel Corporation, 45 368–70

Robbins & Myers Inc., 15 388–90

Robeco Group, **26** 419–20

Roberds Inc., 19 361–63

Robert Allen Companies, **III** 571; **20** 362

Robert Benson, Lonsdale & Co. Ltd. *see* Dresdner Kleinwort Wasserstein.

Robert Bosch GmbH, I 392–93; **16** 434–37 (upd.); **43** 317–21 (upd.)

Saffery Champness, **80** 324–27
Saffil Ltd. *see* Dyson Group PLC.
Safilo SpA, **40** 155–56; **54 319–21**
SAFR *see* Société Anonyme des Fermiers
Reúnis.
Saga *see* Sociedad Andina de Grandes
Almeneces.
Saga Communications, Inc., **27 392–94**
Saga Petroleum ASA, **35** 318
Sagami Optical Co., Ltd., **48** 295
Sagamore Insurance Company, **51** 37–39
The Sage Group, **43 343–46**
Sagebrush Sales, Inc., **12** 397
Sagebrush Steakhouse, **29** 201
SAGEM S.A., **37 346–48**
Saginaw Dock & Terminal Co., **17** 357
Sagitta Arzneimittel, **18** 51; **50** 90
Sahara Casino Partners L.P., **19** 379
Sahara Las Vegas Corp. *see* Archon
Corporation.
SAI *see* Stamos Associates Inc.
Sai Baba, **12** 228
Saia Motor Freight Line, Inc., **6** 421–23;
45 448
Saibu Gas, **IV** 518–19
SAIC *see* Science Applications
International Corporation.
SAIC Velcorex, **12** 153; **27** 188
Saiccor, **IV** 92; **49** 353
SalesLink Corporation *see* CMGI, Inc.
Sainco *see* Sociedad Anonima de
Instalaciones de Control.
Sainrapt et Brice, **9** 9
Sainsbury's *see* J Sainsbury PLC.
St. Alban Boissons S.A., **22** 515
St. Andrews Insurance, **III** 397
Saint-Gobain *see* Compagnie de Saint
Gobain S.A.
Saint-Gobain Weber *see* Weber et Broutin
France.
St. Ives Laboratories Inc., **36** 26
St Ives plc, **34 393–95**
St. James Associates, **32** 362–63
St. James's Place Capital, plc, **71
324–26**
The St. Joe Company, **31 422–25**
St. Joe Corporation, **59** 185
St. Joe Gold, **23** 40
St. Joe Minerals Corp., *see* Flour
Corporation.
St. Joe Paper Company, **8 485–88**
St. John Knits, Inc., **14 466–68**
St. JON Laboratories, Inc., **74** 381
St. Jude Medical, Inc., **11 458–61; 43
347–52 (upd.)**
St. Laurent Paperboard Inc., **30** 119
St. Lawrence Cement Inc., *see* Holnam
Inc.
Saint Louis Bread Company, **18** 35, 37;
44 327
St. Louis Concessions Inc., **21** 39
St. Louis Music, Inc., **48 351–54**
St. Louis Post-Dispatch LLC, **58** 283
St. Luke's-Roosevelt Hospital Center *see*
Continuum Health Partners, Inc.
St. Martin's Press, **25** 484–85; **35** 452
St. Mary Land & Exploration
Company, **63 345–47**

St. Michel-Grellier S.A., **44** 40
St. Paul Bank for Cooperatives, **8
489–90**
St. Paul Book and Stationery, Inc., **47** 90
St. Paul Fire and Marine Insurance Co. *see*
The St. Paul Companies, Inc.
The St. Paul Travelers Companies, Inc.,
III 355–57; **22** 492–95 (upd.); **79**
362–69 (upd.)
St. Paul Venture Capital Inc., **34** 405–06
St. Regis Paper Co., **10** 265; **12** 377
salesforce.com, Inc., **79 370–73**
Saipem S.p.A. *see* ENI S.p.A.
SAirGroup, **29** 376; **33** 268, 271; **37** 241;
46 398; **47** 287
SAirLogistics, **49** 80–81
Saison Group, **V** 184–85, 187–89; **36**
417–18, 420; **42** 340–41
Sakae Printing Co., Ltd., **64** 261
Sako Ltd., **39** 151
Saks Fifth Avenue, **15** 291; **18** 372; **21**
302; **22** 72; **25** 205; **27** 329; **50**
117–19; **57** 179–80
Saks Holdings, Inc., **24 420–23**
Saks Inc., **41 342–45 (upd.)**
Sakura Bank *see* Sumitomo Mitsui
Banking Corporation.
Salant Corporation, **12 430–32; 51
318–21 (upd.)**
Sale Knitting Company *see* Tultex
Corporation.
Salem Broadcasting, **25** 508
Salem Carpet Mills, Inc., **9** 467
Salem Sportswear, **25** 167
Salick Health Care, Inc., **53 290–92**
Salient Partners & Pinnacle Trust Co., **70**
287
Salim Group, **18** 180–81
Salinas Equipment Distributors, Inc., **33**
364
Sallie Mae *see* SLM Holding Corp.;
Student Loan Marketing Association.
Sally Beauty Company, Inc., **60 258–60**
Salmon River Power & Light Company,
12 265
Salomon Brothers Inc., **28** 164
Salomon Inc., **II** 447–49; **13** 447–50
(upd.)
Salomon Smith Barney, **30** 124
Salomon Worldwide, **20** 458–60 *see also*
adidas-Salomon AG.
Salon Cielo and Spa *see* Ratner
Companies.
Salon Plaza *see* Ratner Companies.
Salt River Project, **19 374–76**
Salton, Inc., **30 402–04**
Salvagnini Company, **22** 6
The Salvation Army USA, **32 390–93**
Salvatore Ferragamo Italia S.p.A., **62
311–13**
Salzgitter AG, **IV 200–01**
SAM *see* Sociedad Aeronáutica de
Medellín, S.A.
Sam & Libby Inc., **30** 311
Sam Ash Music Corporation, **30 405–07**
Sam Goody, **9** 360–61; **63** 65
Sam Levin Inc., **80 328–31**
Sam's Club, **40 385–87**

Samancor Ltd., **IV** 92–93
Samaritan Senior Services Inc., **25** 503
Samas-Groep N.V., **47** 91
Sambo's, **12** 510
Samcor Glass *see* Corning Inc.
Samedan Oil Corporation, **11** 353
Sames, S.A., **21** 65–66
Samick Musical Instruments Co., Ltd.,
56 297–300
Samim, **IV** 422
Sammy Corp., **54** 16; **73** 291
Samna Corp., **6** 256; **25** 300
Sampoerna PT, **62** 96–97
Sampson's, **12** 220–21
Samson Technologies Corp., **30** 406
Samsonite Corporation, **13 451–53; 43
353–57 (upd.)**
Samsung-Calex, **17** 483
Samsung Display Co., Ltd., **59** 81
Samsung Electronics Co., Ltd., **14**
416–18; **41 346–49 (upd.)**
Samsung Group, **I 515–17**
Samuel Austin & Son Company, *see* The
Austin Company.
Samuel Cabot Inc., **53 293–95**
Samuel Meisel & Company, Inc., **11**
80–81; **29** 509, 511
Samuel, Son & Co. Ltd., **24** 144
Samuels Jewelers Incorporated, **30
408–10**
San Antonio Public Service Company *see*
City Public Service.
San Diego Gas & Electric Company, **V**
711–14 *see also* Sempra Energy.
San Diego Padres Baseball Club L.P., **78
324–27**
San Francisco Baseball Associates, L.P.,
55 340–43
San Francisco Maillots, **62** 228
San Francisco Mines of Mexico Ltd., **22**
285
San Gabriel Light & Power Company, **16**
496; **50** 496
San Giorgio Macaroni Inc., **53** 242
San Jose Water Company *see* SJW
Corporation.
San Miguel Corporation, **15** 428–30; **57**
303–08 (upd.)
San Paolo IMI S.p.A., **63** 52–53
Sanborn Hermanos, S.A., **20 461–63**
Sanborn Manufacturing Company, **30** 138
Sanborn Map Company Inc., **82
321–24**
The Sanctuary Group PLC, **69 314–17**
Sandals Resorts International, **65
302–05**
Sandcastle 5 Productions, **25** 269–70
Sanders Associates, Inc., **9** 324
Sanders Morris Harris Group Inc., **70
285–87**
Sanderson Computers, **10** 500
Sanderson Farms, Inc., **15 425–27**
Sandia National Laboratories, **49
345–48**
Sandiacre Packaging Machinery Ltd., **51**
249–50
Sandoz Ltd., **I 671–73** *see also* Novartis
AG.

Scandinavian Airlines System, I 119–20
see also The SAS Group.
Scandinavian Broadcasting System SA, 53 325
ScanDust, III 625
Scania-Vabis see Saab-Scania AB.
ScanSource, Inc., 29 413–15; 74 295–98 (upd.)
Scantron Corporation, 17 266–68
Scarborough Public Utilities Commission, 9 461–62
Scaturro Supermarkets, 24 528
SCB Computer Technology, Inc., 29 416–18
SCEcorp, V 715–17 see also Edison International.
Scenic Airlines, Inc., 25 420, 423
Scenographic Designs, 21 277
SCG Corporation, 56 323
Schäfer, 31 158
Schaper Mfg. Co., 12 168
Schauman Wood Oy, IV 277, 302
Schawk, Inc., 24 424–26
SCHC, Inc. see Shoe Carnival Inc.
Scheels All Sports Inc., 63 348–50
Scheid Vineyards Inc., 66 276–78
Schein Pharmaceutical Inc., 13 77; 56 375
Schell Brewing see August Schell Brewing Company Inc.
Schenker Deutschland AG, 59 391
Schenker-Rhenus Ag, 6 424–26
Schenley Industries Inc., 9 449; 24 140
Schenley Distilleries Inc., 68 99
Scherer see R.P. Scherer.
Schering A.G., I 681–82; 50 418–22 (upd.)
Schering-Plough Corporation, I 683–85; 14 422–25 (upd.); 49 356–62 (upd.)
Schiavi Homes, Inc., 14 138
Schibsted ASA, 31 401–05
Schick Products, 41 366
Schick Shaving, 38 363, 365
Schick-Wilkinson Sword see Wilkinson Sword Ltd.
Schieffelin & Somerset Co., 61 323–25
Schindler Holding AG, 29 419–22
Schlage Lock Company, 82 330–34
Schlitz Brewing Co., I 255, 268, 270, 291, 600; 10 100; 12 338; 18 500; 23 403
Schlotzsky's, Inc., 36 408–10
Schlumberger Limited, III 616–18; 17 416–19 (upd.); 59 366–71 (upd.)
SchlumbergerSema see Atos Origin S.A.
Schmalbach-Lubeca-Werke A.G., 15 128
Schmermund Verpackungstechnik GmbH, 60 193
Schmid, 19 166
Schmitt Music Company, 40 388–90
Schneider National, Inc., 36 411–13; 77 374–78 (upd.)
Schneider S.A., II 93–94; 18 471–74 (upd.)
Schneiderman's Furniture Inc., 28 405–08

Schnitzer Steel Industries, Inc., 19 380–82
Schnoll Foods, 24 528
Schnuck Markets, Inc., 60 256; 63 129
Schober Direktmarketing, 18 170
Schoeller & Co. Bank AG, 59 239
Schoeller & Hoesch Group, 30 349, 352
Schoenfeld Industries, 16 511
Scholastic Corporation, 10 479–81; 29 423–27 (upd.)
Scholl Inc., 49 359, 380
Schöller, 27 436, 439
School Specialty, Inc., 68 335–37
School-Tech, Inc., 62 318–20
Schorghuber, 70 61
Schott Brothers, Inc., 67 337–39
Schott Corporation, 53 296–98
Schottenstein Stores Corp., 14 426–28
Schreiber Foods, Inc., 72 303–06
Schreiber Frères see Groupe Les Echos.
Schrock Cabinet Company, 13 564
Schroders plc, 42 332–35
Schroders Ventures, 18 345
Schroff Inc., 26 361, 363
Schubach, 30 408
Schubert & Salzer GmbH, 42 316
Schuck's Auto Supply see CSK Auto Corporation.
Schuff Steel Company, 26 431–34
Schuitema, II 642; 16 312–13
Schuler Chocolates, 15 65
Schuler Homes, Inc., 58 84
Schuller International, Inc., 11 421
Schultz Sav-O Stores, Inc., 21 454–56; 31 406–08 (upd.)
Schultz, Snyder & Steele Lumber Company, 61 254, 256
Schuykill Energy Resources, 12 41
Schwabe-Verlag, 7 42
Schwabel Corporation, 19 453
Schwan's Sales Enterprises, Inc., 7 468–70; 26 435–38 (upd.)
Schwartz Iron & Metal Co., 13 142
Schwarze Pumpe, 38 408
Schwebel Baking Company, 72 307–09
Schweitzer-Mauduit International, Inc., 52 300–02
Schweizerische Post-, Telefon- und Telegrafen-Betriebe, V 321–24
Schweizerische Ruckversicherungs-Gesellschaft see Swiss Reinsurance Company.
Schweppes Ltd. see Cadbury Schweppes PLC.
Schwinn Cycle and Fitness L.P., 19 383–85
The Schwinn GT Co., 26 185
Schwitzer, II 420
SCI see Service Corporation International; Société Centrale d'Investissement.
SCI 169 Rue de Rennes, 53 32
SCI Systems, Inc., 9 463–64
Scicon International, 14 317; 49 165
SciCor Inc., 30 152
Science Applications International Corporation, 15 438–40
Scientific-Atlanta, Inc., 6 335–37; 45 371–75 (upd.)

Scientific Communications, Inc., 10 97
Scientific Data Systems, 10 365
Scientific Games Corporation, 64 343–46 (upd.)
Scientific Materials Company, 24 162
Scientific Research Products, Inc. of Delaware, 60 287
Scioto Bank, 9 475
Scitex Corporation Ltd., 24 427–32
Scitor, 52 108
SCLC, Inc. see Shoe Carnival Inc.
SCO see Santa Cruz Operation, Inc.
The SCO Group Inc., 78 333–37
SCOA Industries, Inc., 13 260
Scopus Technology Inc., 38 431
SCOR S.A., 20 464–66
The Score Board, Inc., 19 386–88
Score Entertainment see Donruss Playoff L.P.
Score! Learning, Inc., 42 211
Scot Lad Foods, 14 411
Scotch House Ltd., 19 181
Scotia Securities, II 223
Scotiabank see The Bank of Nova Scotia.
Scotsman Industries, Inc., 20 467–69
Scott-Ballantyne Company see Ballantyne of Omaha, Inc.
Scott Communications, Inc., 10 97
Scott Fetzer Company, 12 435–37; 80 339–43 (upd.)
Scott Health Care, 28 445
Scott Holdings, 19 384
Scott Paper Company, IV 329–31; 31 409–12 (upd.)
Scott Transport, 27 473
Scotti Brothers, 20 3
Scottish & Newcastle plc, 15 441–44; 35 394–97 (upd.)
Scottish and Southern Energy plc, 13 457–59; 66 279–84 (upd.)
Scottish Amicable plc, 48 328
Scottish Brick, 14 250
Scottish Electric, 6 453
Scottish Inns of America, Inc., 13 362
Scottish Media Group plc, 32 404–06; 41 350–52
Scottish Mutual plc, 39 5–6
Scottish Nuclear, Ltd., 19 389
Scottish Power plc, 49 363–66 (upd.)
Scottish Radio Holding plc, 41 350–52
Scottish Sealand Oil Services Ltd., 25 171
Scottish Universal Investments, 45 189
ScottishPower plc, 19 389–91
ScottishTelecom plc, 19 389
The Scotts Company, 22 474–76
Scotty's, Inc., 22 477–80
The Scoular Company, 77 379–82
Scovill Fasteners Inc., 24 433–36
SCP Pool Corporation, 39 358–60
Screen Actors Guild, 72 310–13
Screg Group, see Bouygues S.A.
Scriha & Deyhle, 10 196
Scripps-Howard, Inc. see The E.W. Scripps Company.
The Scripps Research Institute, 76 323–25
Scrivner Inc., 17 180

Souriau, **19** 166

South African Airways Ltd., **27** 132 *see also* Transnet Ltd.

The South African Breweries Limited, I 287–89; **24** 447–51 **(upd.)** *see also* SABMiller plc.

South African Transport Services *see* Transnet Ltd.

South Asia Tyres, **20** 263

South Australian Brewing Company, **54** 228, 341

South Beach Beverage Company, Inc., **73** 316–19

South Bend Toy Manufacturing Company, **25** 380

South Carolina Electric & Gas Company *see* SCANA Corporation.

South Carolina National Corporation, **16** 523, 526

South Carolina Power Company, **38** 446–47

South Central Bell Telephone Co. *see* BellSouth Corporation.

South Central Railroad Co., **14** 325

South Coast Gas Compression Company, Inc., **11** 523

South Coast Terminals, Inc., **16** 475

South Dakota Public Service Company, **6** 524

South Florida Neonatology Associates, **61** 284

South Fulton Light & Power Company, **6** 514

South Jersey Industries, Inc., **42** 352–55

South of Scotland Electricity Board, **19** 389–90

South Overseas Fashion Ltd., **53** 344

South Sea Textile, **III** 705

South Wales Electric Company, **34** 219

South West Water Plc *see* Pennon Group Plc.

South Western Electricity plc, **38** 448; **41** 316

South-Western Publishing Co., *see* The Thomson Corporation.

Southam Inc., **7** 486–89

Southco, **II** 602–03; **7** 20–21; **30** 26

Southcorp Holdings Ltd., **17** 373; **22** 350

Southcorp Limited, **54** 341–44

Southdown, Inc., **14** 454–56

Southdown Press *see* PMP Ltd.

Southeast Bank of Florida, **11** 112

Southeast Public Service Company, *see* Triarc Companies, Inc.

Southeastern Freight Lines, Inc., **53** 249

Southeastern Personnel *see* Norrell Corporation.

Southern and Phillips Gas Ltd., **13** 485

Southern Australia Airlines, **24** 396

Southern Bank, **10** 426

Southern Bearings Co., **13** 78

Southern Bell, **10** 202

Southern Blvd. Supermarkets, Inc., **22** 549

Southern Box Corp., **13** 441

Southern California Edison Co. *see* Edison International.

Southern California Financial Corporation, **27** 46

Southern California Fruit Growers Exchange *see* Sunkist Growers, Inc.

Southern California Gas Co., **25** 413–14, 416

Southern Casualty Insurance Co., **III** 214

The Southern Company, **V** 721–23; **38** 445–49 **(upd.)**

Southern Cooker Limited Partnership, **51** 85

Southern Corrections Systems, Inc. *see* Avalon Correctional Services, Inc.

Southern Cotton Co., **24** 488

Southern Cross Paints, **38** 98

Southern Discount Company of Atlanta, **9** 229

Southern Electric PLC, **13** 484–86 *see also* Scottish and Southern Energy plc.

Southern Electric Supply Co., **15** 386

Southern Electronics Corp. *see* SED International Holdings, Inc.

Southern Equipment & Supply Co., **19** 344

Southern Financial Bancorp, Inc., **56** 342–44

Southern Foods Group, L.P. *see* Dean Foods Company.

Southern Forest Products, Inc., **6** 577

Southern Gage, **III** 519; **22** 282

Southern Graphic Arts, **13** 405

Southern Guaranty Cos., **III** 404

Southern Idaho Water Power Company, **12** 265

Southern Indiana Gas and Electric Company, **13** 487–89

Southern Minnesota Beet Sugar Cooperative, **32** 29

Southern National Bankshares of Atlanta, **II** 337; **10** 425

Southern National Corporation *see* BB&T Corporation

Southern Natural Gas Co., **6** 577

Southern Nevada Power Company, **11** 343

Southern Nevada Telephone Company, **11** 343

Southern New England Telecommunications Corporation, **6** 338–40

Southern Oregon Broadcasting Co., **7** 15

Southern Pacific Communications Corporation, **9** 478–79

Southern Pacific Rail Corp. *see* Union Pacific Corporation.

Southern Pacific Transportation Company, **V** 516–18

Southern Peru Copper Corp.,

Southern Peru Copper Corporation, **40** 411–13

Southern Phenix Textiles Inc., **15** 247–48

Southern Poverty Law Center, Inc., **74** 312–15

Southern Power Company *see* Duke Energy Corporation.

Southern Recycling Inc., **51** 170

Southern Science Applications, Inc., **22** 88

Southern States Cooperative Incorporated, **36** 440–42

Southern Sun Hotel Corporation *see* South African Breweries Ltd.; Sun International Hotels Limited.

Southern Telephone Company, **14** 257

Southern Union Company, **27** 424–26

Southern Video Partnership, **9** 74

Southern Water plc, **19** 389–91; **49** 363, 365–66

Southgate Medical Laboratory System, **26** 391

Southington Savings Bank, **55** 52

The Southland Corporation, **II** 660–61; **7** 490–92 **(upd.)** *see also* 7-Eleven, Inc.

Southland Mobilcom Inc., **15** 196

Southland Paper, **13** 118

Southland Royal Company, **27** 86

Southland Royalty Co., **10** 190

Southmark Corp., **11** 483; **33** 398

Southport, Inc., **44** 203

Southtrust Corporation, **11** 455–57

Southwest Airlines Co., **6** 119–21; **24** 452–55 **(upd.)**; **71** 343–47 **(upd.)**

Southwest Airmotive Co., **II** 16

Southwest Convenience Stores, LLC, **26** 368

Southwest Converting, **19** 414

Southwest Enterprise Associates, **13** 191

Southwest Forest Industries, **IV** 334

Southwest Gas Corporation, **19** 410–12

Southwest Hide Co., **16** 546

Southwest Property Trust Inc., **52** 370

Southwest Sports Group, **51** 371, 374

Southwest Water Company, **47** 370–73

Southwestern Bell Corporation, **V** 328–30 *see also* SBC Communications Inc.

Southwestern Bell Publications, **26** 520

Southwestern Electric Power Co., **21** 468–70

Southwestern Explosives, Inc., **76** 34

Southwestern Gas Pipeline, **7** 344

Southwestern Illinois Coal Company, **7** 33

Southwestern Public Service Company, **6** 579–81

Southwestern Textile Company, **12** 393

Southwire Company, Inc., **8** 478–80; **23** 444–47 **(upd.)**

Souza Cruz S.A., **65** 322–24

Souza Pinto Industria e Comercio de Artefatos de Borracha Ltda., **71** 393

Sovereign Corp., **III** 221; **14** 109; **37** 84

Soviba, **70** 322

Sovintel, **59** 209, 211

Sovran Financial, **10** 425–26

Sovran Self Storage, Inc., **66** 299–301

SovTransavto, **6** 410

Soyco Foods, Inc., **58** 137

SP Alpargatas *see* Sao Paulo Alpargatas S.A.

SP Pharmaceuticals, LLC, **50** 123

SP Reifenwerke, **V** 253

SP Tyres, **V** 253

Space Control GmbH, **28** 243–44

Space Craft Inc., **9** 463

Space Data Corporation, **22** 401

Titan Sports, Inc., **52** 192

Titanium Metals Corporation, 21 489–92

Titileist *see* Acushnet Company.

TITISA, **9** 109

Titmuss Sainer Dechert *see* Dechert.

TiVo Inc., 75 373–75

Tivoli Audio, **48** 85

Tivoli Systems, Inc., **14** 392

TJ International, Inc., 19 444–47

The TJX Companies, Inc., V 197–98; **19** 448–50 (upd.); **57** 366–69 (upd.)

TKR Cable Co., **15** 264

TKT *see* Transkaryotic Therapies Inc.

TL Enterprises, Inc., **56** 5

TLC Associates, **11** 261

TLC Beatrice International Holdings, Inc., 22 512–15

TLC Gift Company, **26** 375

TLO, **25** 82

TMB Industries, **24** 144

TMC Industries Ltd., **22** 352

TML Information Services Inc., **9** 95

TMNI International Inc., **70** 275

TMP Worldwide Inc., 30 458–60 *see also* Monster Worldwide Inc.

TMS, Inc., **7** 358

TMS Marketing, **26** 440

TMS Systems, Inc., **10** 18

TMT *see* Trailer Marine Transport.

TMW Capital Inc., **48** 286

TN Technologies Inc., **23** 479

TNI Funding I Inc., **70** 275

TNT Crust, Inc., **23** 203

TNT Freightways Corporation, 14 504–06

TNT Grading Inc., **50** 348

TNT Limited, V 523–25

TNT Post Group N.V., 27 471–76 (upd.); **30** 461–63 (upd.) *see also* TPG N.V.

Toa Medical Electronics Ltd., **22** 75

Toa Tanker Co. Ltd., **IV** 555

Toastmaster, **17** 215; **22** 353

Tobacco Group PLC, **30** 231

Tobacco Products Corporation, **18** 416

Tobias, **16** 239

Tobu Railway Co Ltd, 6 430–32

TOC Retail Inc., **17** 170

Tocom, Inc., **10** 320

Today's Man, Inc., 20 484–87

Todays Computers Business Centers *see* Intelligent Electronics, Inc.

The Todd-AO Corporation, 33 400–04 *see also* Liberty Livewire Corporation.

Todd Shipyards Corporation, 14 507–09

Toden Real Estate Company Inc., **74** 348

Todhunter International, Inc., 27 477–79

Todito.com, S.A. de C.V., **39** 194, 196

Toei Co. Ltd., **9** 29–30; **28** 462

Tofa, *see* Koç Holding A.S.

Tofte Industrier, **63** 315

Toftejorg Group, **64** 18

Tofutti Brands, Inc., 64 382–84

Togo's Eatery, **29** 19

Toho Co., Ltd., 28 461–63

Tohoku Alps, **II** 5

Tohoku Anritsu Co., Ltd. *see* Anritsu Corporation.

Tohokushinsha Film Corporation, **18** 429

Tohuku Electric Power Company, Inc., V 726–28

Tokai Aircraft Co., Ltd. *see* Aisin Seiki Co., Ltd.

The Tokai Bank, Limited, II 373–74; **15** 494–96 (upd.)

Tokai Kogyo Co. Ltd., **I** 615; **48** 42

Tokheim Corporation, 21 493–95

Tokio Marine and Fire Insurance Co., Ltd., III 383–86 *see also* Millea Holdings Inc.

Tokiwa shokai Ltd., **64** 261

Tokos Medical Corporation, **17** 306, 308–09

Tokushima Automobile Service Company Inc., **60** 272

Tokyo Broadcasting System, **7** 249; **9** 29; **16** 167

Tokyo City Finance, **36** 419–20

Tokyo Disneyland, **6** 176

Tokyo Electric Power Company, V 729–33; **74** 343–48 (upd.)

Tokyo Electronic Corp., **11** 232

Tokyo Gas and Electric Industrial Company, **9** 293

Tokyo Gas Co., Ltd., V 734–36; **55** 372–75 (upd.)

Tokyo Ishikawajima Shipbuilding and Engineering Company, **9** 293

Tokyo Maritime Agency Ltd., **56** 181

Tokyo Motors *see* Isuzu Motors, Ltd.

Tokyo Stock Exchange, **34** 254

Tokyo Telecommunications Engineering Corp *see* Tokyo Tsushin Kogyo K.K.

TOKYOPOP Inc., 79 415–18

Tokyu Corporation, V 526–28; **47** 407–10 (upd.)

Tokyu Department Store Co., Ltd., V 199–202; **32** 453–57 (upd.)

Tokyu Land Corporation, IV 728–29

Toledo Edison Company *see* Centerior Energy Corporation.

Toledo Milk Processing, Inc., **15** 449

Toledo Scale Corp., **9** 441; **30** 327

Toll Brothers Inc., 15 497–99; **70** 323–26 (upd.)

Tollgrade Communications, Inc., 44 424–27

Tom Brown, Inc., 37 389–91

Tom Doherty Associates Inc., 25 483–86

Tom Snyder Productions, **29** 470, 472

Tom Thumb, **40** 365–66

Tom Thumb-Page, **16** 64

Tom's Foods Inc., 66 325–27

Tom's of Maine, Inc., 45 414–16

Toman Corporation, **19** 390

The Tomatin Distillery Co., Ltd., **62** 347

Tombstone Pizza Corporation, 13 515–17

Tomcan Investments Inc., **53** 333

Tomen Corporation, IV 224–25; **24** 488–91 (upd.)

Tomkins-Johnson Company, **16** 8

Tomkins plc, 11 525–27; **44** 428–31 (upd.)

Tomlee Tool Company, **7** 535; **26** 493

Tommy Armour Golf Co., **32** 446–47

Tommy Bahama *see* Viewpoint International, Inc.

Tommy Hilfiger Corporation, 20 488–90; **53** 330–33 (upd.)

TomTom N.V., 81 388–91

Tomy Company Ltd., 65 341–44

Tone Brothers, Inc., 21 496–98; **74** 349–52 (upd.)

Tone Coca-Cola Bottling Company, Ltd., **14** 288; **47** 206

Tonen Corporation, IV 554–56; **16** 489–92 (upd.)

TonenGeneral Sekiyu K.K., 54 380–86 (upd.)

Tong Yang Cement Corporation, 62 366–68

Tonka Corporation, 25 487–89

Tonkin, Inc., **19** 114

Tony Lama Company Inc., **19** 233

Tony Roma's, A Place for Ribs Inc. *see* Romacorp, Inc.

Tony Stone Images, **31** 216–17

Too, Inc., 61 371–73

Toohey, **10** 170

Toolex International N.V., 26 489–91

Tootsie Roll Industries, Inc., 12 480–82; **82** 392–96 (upd.)

Top End Wheelchair Sports, **11** 202

Top Glory International Group Company, **76** 89–90

Top Green International, **17** 475

Top Tool Company, Inc., **25** 75

Topack Verpackungstechnik, **60** 193

The Topaz Group, Inc., 62 369–71

Topco Associates LLC, **60** 302–04

Topkapi, **17** 101–03

Toppan Printing Co., Ltd., IV 679–81; **58** 340–44 (upd.)

Topps Company, Inc., 13 518–20; **34** 446–49 (upd.)

Topps Markets, **16** 314

Tops Appliance City, Inc., 17 487–89

Tops Markets LLC, 60 305–07

TopTip, **48** 116

Tor Books *see* Tom Doherty Associates Inc.

Toray Industries, Inc., V 383–86; **51** 375–79 (upd.)

Torchmark Corporation, 9 506–08; **33** 405–08 (upd.)

Torfeaco Industries Limited, **19** 304

The Toro Company, 7 534–36; **26** 492–95 (upd.); **77** 440–45 (upd.)

Toromont Industries, Ltd., 21 499–501

Toronto and Scarborough Electric Railway, **9** 461

The Toronto-Dominion Bank, II 375–77; **49** 395–99 (upd.)

Toronto Electric Light Company, **9** 461

Toronto Maple Leafs *see* Maple Leaf Sports & Entertainment Ltd.

Toronto Raptors *see* Maple Leaf Sports & Entertainment Ltd.

US Industries Inc., **30** 231

US Monolithics, **54** 407

US 1 Industries, **27** 404

US Order, Inc., **10** 560, 562

US Repeating Arms Co., **58** 147

US Sprint Communications Company *see* Sprint Communications Company, L.P.

US Telecom, **9** 478–79

US West Communications Services, Inc. *see* Regional Bell Operating Companies.

USA Cafes, **14** 331

USA Floral Products Inc., **27** 126

USA Interactive, Inc., 47 418–22 **(upd.)**

USA Networks Inc., **25** 330, 411; **33** 432; **37** 381, 383–84; **43** 422

USA Security Systems, Inc., **27** 21

USA Truck, Inc., 42 410–13

USAA, 10 541–43; **62** 385–88 **(upd.)**

USANA, Inc., 27 353; **29** 491–93

USCC *see* United States Cellular Corporation.

USCP-WESCO Inc., **II** 682

Usego AG., **48** 63

USF&G Corporation, III 395–98 *see also* The St. Paul Companies.

USFL *see* United States Football League.

USFreightways Corporation, **27** 475; **49** 402

USG Corporation, III 762–64; **26** 507–10 **(upd.)**; **81** 404–10 **(upd.)**

USH *see* United Scientific Holdings.

Usinas Siderúrgicas de Minas Gerais S.A., 77 454–57

Usinger's Famous Sausage *see* Fred Usinger Inc.

Usinor SA, IV 226–28; **42** 414–17 **(upd.)**

USLD Communications Corp. *see* Billing Concepts Corp.

USM, **10** 44

USO *see* United Service Organizations.

Usource LLC, **37** 406

USPS *see* United States Postal Service.

USSC *see* United States Surgical Corporation.

USSI *see* U.S. Software Inc.

UST Inc., 9 533–35; **50** 512–17 **(upd.)**

UST Wilderness Management Corporation, **33** 399

Usutu Pulp Company, **49** 353

USV Pharmaceutical Corporation, **11** 333

USWeb/CKS *see* marchFIRST, Inc.

USX Corporation, IV 572–74; **7** 549–52 **(upd.)** *see also* United States Steel Corporation.

UT Starcom, **44** 426

Utag, **11** 510

Utah Construction & Mining Co., **14** 296

Utah Federal Savings Bank, **17** 530

Utah Gas and Coke Company, **6** 568

Utah Medical Products, Inc., 36 496–99

Utah Mines Ltd., **IV** 47; **22** 107

Utah Power and Light Company, 27 483–86 *see also* PacifiCorp.

UTI Energy, Inc. *see* Patterson-UTI Energy, Inc.

Utilicom, **6** 572

Utilicorp United Inc., 6 592–94 *see also* Aquilla, Inc.

UtiliTech Solutions, **37** 88

Utility Constructors Incorporated, **6** 527

Utility Engineering Corporation, **6** 580

Utility Fuels, **7** 377

Utility Line Construction Service, Inc., **59** 65

Utility Service Affiliates, Inc., **45** 277

Utility Services, Inc., **42** 249, 253

Utility Supply Co. *see* United Stationers Inc.

Utopian Leisure Group, **75** 385

UTStarcom, Inc., 77 458–61

UTV *see* Ulster Television PLC.

Utz Quality Foods, Inc., 72 358–60

UUNET, 38 468–72

UV Industries, Inc., **7** 360; **9** 440

Uwajimaya, Inc., 60 312–14

V

V.L. Churchill Group, **10** 493

VA Linux Systems, **45** 363

VA Systeme *see* Diehl Stiftung & Co. KG

VA TECH ELIN EBG GmbH, 49 429–31

VA Technologie AG, **57** 402

Vacheron Constantin, **27** 487, 489

Vaco, **38** 200, 202

Vaculator Division *see* Lancer Corporation.

Vacuum Metallurgical Company, **11** 234

Vacuum Oil Co. *see* Mobil Corporation.

Vadoise Vie, **III** 273

VAE AG, **57** 402

VAE Nortrak Cheyenne Inc., **53** 352

Vail Resorts, Inc., 11 543–46; **43** 435–39 **(upd.)**

Vaillant GmbH, 44 436–39

Val Corp., **24** 149

Val-Pak Direct Marketing Systems, Inc., **22** 162

Val Royal LaSalle, **II** 652

Valassis Communications, Inc., 8 550–51; **37** 407–10 **(upd.)**; **76** 364–67 **(upd.)**

ValCom Inc. *see* InaCom Corporation.

Valdi Foods Inc., **II** 663–64

Vale do Rio Doce Navegacao SA—Docenave, **43** 112

Vale Harmon Enterprises, Ltd., **25** 204

Vale Power Company, **12** 265

Valenciana de Cementos, **59** 112

Valentine & Company, *see* The Valspar Corporation.

Valentino, **67** 246, 248

Valeo, 23 492–94; **66** 350–53 **(upd.)**

Valero Energy Corporation, 7 553–55; **71** 385–90 **(upd.)**

Valhi, Inc., 19 466–68

Valid Logic Systems Inc., **11** 46, 284; **48** 77

Vality Technology Inc., **59** 56

Vallen Corporation, 45 424–26

Valley Bank of Helena, **35** 197, 199

Valley Bank of Maryland, **46** 25

Valley Bank of Nevada, **19** 378

Valley Crest Tree Company, **31** 182–83

Valley Deli Inc., **24** 243

Valley Fashions Corp., **16** 535

Valley Federal of California, **11** 163

Valley Fig Growers, **7** 496–97

Valley Media Inc., 35 430–33

Valley Milk Products LLC *see* Maryland & Virginia Milk Producers Cooperative Association, Inc.

Valley National Bank, **II** 420

Valley of the Moon, **68** 146

Valley-Todeco, Inc., **13** 305–06

Valleyfair, **22** 130

ValleyCrest Companies, 81 411–14 **(upd.)**

Vallourec SA, 54 391–94

Valmet Corporation, III 647–49 *see also* Metso Corporation.

Valmont Industries, Inc., 19 469–72

Valois S.A. *see* AptarGroup, Inc.

Valores Industriales S.A., 19 473–75

The Valspar Corporation, 8 552–54; **32** 483–86 **(upd.)**; **77** 462–68 **(upd.)**

Valtek International, Inc., **17** 147

Value America, **29** 312

Value City Department Stores, Inc., 38 473–75 *see also* Retail Ventures, Inc.

Value Foods Ltd., **11** 239

Value Giant Stores, **12** 478

Value House, **II** 673

Value Investors, **III** 330

Value Line, Inc., 16 506–08; **73** 358–61 **(upd.)**

Value Merchants Inc., 13 541–43

Value Rent-A-Car, **9** 350; **23** 354

ValueClick, Inc., 49 432–34

ValueVision International, Inc., 22 534–36; **27** 337

ValuJet, Inc. *see* AirTran Holdings, Inc.

Valvtron, **11** 226

VAMED Gruppe, **56** 141

Van Ameringen-Haebler, Inc., **9** 290

Van Camp Seafood Company, Inc., 7 556–57 *see also* Chicken of the Sea International.

Van Cleef & Arpels Inc., **26** 145

Van de Kamp's, Inc., **7** 430

Van der Moolen Holding NV, **37** 224

Van Dorn Company, **13** 190

Van Houtte Inc., 39 409–11

Van Kirk Chocolate, **7** 429

Van Kok-Ede, **II** 642

Van Lanschot NV, 79 456–59

Van Leer Containers Inc., **30** 397

Van Leer Holding, Inc., **9** 303, 305

Van Leer N.V. *see* Royal Packaging Industries Van Leer N.V.; Greif Inc.

Van Mar, Inc., **18** 88

Van Ommeren, **41** 339–40

Van Sickle, **IV** 485

Van Wezel, **26** 278–79

Van Wijcks Waalsteenfabrieken, **14** 249

Van's Aircraft, Inc., 65 349–51

Vance Publishing Corporation, 64 398–401

Vanderbilt Mortgage and Finance, **13** 154

Vanessa and Biffi, **11** 226

The Vanguard Group, Inc., 14 530–32; **34** 486–89 **(upd.)**

Wadsworth Inc., *see* The Thomspn Corporation.
WaferTech, **18** 20; **43** 17; **47** 385
Waffle House Inc., **14** 544–45; **60** 325–27 (upd.)
Wagenseller & Durst, **25** 249
Waggener Edstrom, **42** 424–26
The Wagner & Brown Investment Group, **9** 248
Wagner Castings Company, **16** 474–75
Wagner Spray Tech, **18** 555
Wagonlit Travel, **22** 128; **55** 90
Wagons-Lits, **27** 11; **29** 443; **37** 250–52
Wah Chang, **82** 415–18
Waha Oil Company *see* Natinal Oil Corporation.
AB Wahlbecks, **25** 464
Waitaki International Biosciences Co., **17** 288
Waitrose Ltd. *see* John Lewis Partnership plc.
Wakefern Food Corporation, **33** 434–37
Wako Shoji Co. Ltd. *see* Wacoal Corp.
Wal-Mart de Mexico, S.A. de C.V., **35** 459–61 (upd.)
Wal-Mart Stores, Inc., **V** 216–17; **8** 555–57 (upd.); **26** 522–26 (upd.); **63** 427–32 (upd.)
Walbridge Aldinger Co., **38** 480–82
Walbro Corporation, **13** 553–55
Walchenseewerk AG, **23** 44
Waldbaum, Inc., **19** 479–81
Walden Book Company Inc., **17** 522–24
Waldorf Corporation, **59** 350
Wales & Company, **14** 257
Walgreen Co., **V** 218–20; **20** 511–13 (upd.); **65** 352–56 (upd.)
Walk Haydel & Associates, Inc., **25** 130
Walk Softly, Inc., **25** 118
Walker & Lee, **10** 340
Walker Dickson Group Limited, **26** 363
Walker Digital, **57** 296–98
Walker Interactive Systems, **11** 78; **25** 86
Walker Manufacturing Company, **19** 482–84
Walkers Shortbread Ltd., **79** 464–67
Walkers Snack Foods Ltd., **70** 350–52
Walkins Manufacturing Corp., **III** 571; **20** 362
Walkup's Merchant Express Inc., **27** 473
Wall Drug Store, Inc., **40** 455–57
Wall Street Deli, Inc., **33** 438–41
Wallace & Tiernan Group, **11** 361; **52** 374
The Wallace Berrie Company *see* Applause Inc.
Wallace Computer Services, Inc., **36** 507–10
Wallace International Silversmiths, **14** 482–83
Wallin & Nordstrom *see* Nordstrom, Inc.
Wallis *see* Sears plc.
Wallis Arnold Enterprises, Inc., **21** 483
Wallis Tractor Company, **21** 502
Walnut Capital Partners, **62** 46–47
Walrus, Inc., **18** 446

Walsworth Publishing Company, Inc., **78** 445–48
The Walt Disney Company, **II** 172–74; **6** 174–77 (upd.); **30** 487–91 (upd.); **63** 433–38 (upd.)
Walter Bau, **27** 136, 138
Walter E. Heller, **17** 324
Walter Herzog GmbH, **16** 514
Walter Industries, Inc., **III** 765–67; **22** 544–47 (upd.); **72** 368–73 (upd.)
Walter Kidde & Co., **73** 208
Walter Wilson, **49** 18
Walter Wright Mammoet, **26** 280
Walton Manufacturing, **11** 486
Walton Monroe Mills, Inc., **8** 558–60
Wanadoo S.A., **75** 400–02
Wang Global, **39** 176–78
Wang Laboratories, Inc., **III** 168–70; **6** 284–87 (upd.)
WAP, **26** 420
Waples-Platter Co., **II** 625
Warbasse-Cogeneration Technologies Partnership, **35** 479
Warburg Pincus, **9** 524; **14** 42; **24** 373; **61** 403; **73** 138
Warburg USB, **38** 291
Warburtons Bakery Cafe, Inc., **18** 37
Ward's Communications, **22** 441
Wards *see* Circuit City Stores, Inc.
Waremart *see* WinCo Foods.
WARF *see* Wisconsin Alumni Research Foundation.
Waring and LaRosa, **12** 167
The Warnaco Group Inc., **12** 521–23; **46** 450–54 (upd.) *see also* Authentic Fitness Corp.
Warner Communications Inc., **II** 175–77 *see also* AOL Time Warner Inc.
Warner Electric, **58** 67
Warner-Lambert Co., **I** 710–12; **10** 549–52 (upd.)
Warner Roadshow Film Distributors Greece SA, **58** 359
Warners' Stellian Inc., **67** 384–87
Warrantech Corporation, **53** 357–59
Warrell Corporation, **68** 396–98
Warren Apparel Group Ltd., **39** 257
Warren Bancorp Inc., **55** 52
Warren Bank, **13** 464
Warren Frozen Foods, Inc., **61** 174
Warren, Gorham & Lamont, *see* The Thomson Corporation.
Warren Oilfield Services, **9** 363
Warren Petroleum, **18** 365, 367; **49** 121
Warrick Industries, **31** 338
Warrington Products Ltd. *see* Canstar Sports Inc.
Warrior River Coal Company, **7** 281
Warwick Chemicals, **13** 461
Warwick International Ltd., *see* Sequa Corporation.
Warwick Valley Telephone Company, **55** 382–84
Wasatch Gas Co., **6** 568
Wascana Energy Inc., **13** 556–58
Washburn Graphics Inc., **23** 100
The Washington Companies, **33** 442–45
Washington Duke Sons & Co., **12** 108

Washington Federal, Inc., **17** 525–27
Washington Football, Inc., **35** 462–65
Washington Gas Light Company, **19** 485–88
Washington Inventory Service, **30** 239
Washington Mutual, Inc., **17** 528–31
Washington National Corporation, **12** 524–26
Washington Natural Gas Company, **9** 539–41
The Washington Post Company, **IV** 688–90; **20** 515–18 (upd.)
Washington Public Power Supply System, **50** 102
Washington Railway and Electric Company, **6** 552–53
Washington Scientific Industries, Inc., **17** 532–34
Washington Specialty Metals Corp., **14** 323, 325
Washington Sports Clubs *see* Town Sports International, Inc.
Washington Steel Corp., **14** 323, 325
Washington Water Power Company, **6** 595–98 *see also* Avista Corporation.
Washtenaw Gas Company *see* MCN Corporation.
Wassall Plc, **18** 548–50
Wasserstein Perella Partners, **II** 629; **17** 366
Waste Connections, Inc., **46** 455–57
Waste Control Specialists LLC, **19** 466, 468
Waste Holdings, Inc., **41** 413–15
Waste Management, Inc., **V** 752–54
Water Engineering, **11** 360
Water Pik Technologies, Inc., **34** 498–501
Water Street Corporate Recovery Fund, **10** 423
The Waterbury Companies, **16** 482
Waterford Foods Plc, **59** 206
Waterford Wedgwood plc, **12** 527–29; **34** 493–97 (upd.)
Waterhouse Investor Services, Inc., **18** 551–53
Waterlow and Sons, **10** 269
Waterman Marine Corporation, **27** 242
The Waterman Pen Company *see* BIC Corporation.
Watermark Paddlesports Inc., **76** 119
Waterpark Management Inc., **73** 231
WaterPro Supplies Corporation *see* Eastern Enterprises.
Waters Corporation, **43** 453–57
Waterstone's, **42** 444 *see also* HMV Group plc.
Waterstreet Inc., **17** 293
Watkins-Johnson Company, **15** 528–30
Watney Mann and Truman Brewers, **9** 99
Watsco Inc., **52** 397–400
Watson & Philip *see* Alldays plc.
Watson Group, **55** 52
Watson-Haas Lumber Company, **33** 257
Watson-Marlow Bredel, **59** 384
Watson Pharmaceuticals Inc., **16** 527–29; **56** 373–76 (upd.)
Watson-Triangle, **16** 388, 390

Weston Resources, **II** 631–32
Westpac Banking Corporation, II
388–90; 48 424–27 **(upd.)**
WestPoint Stevens Inc., 16 533–36 *see*
also JPS Textile Group, Inc.
Westport Resources Corporation, 63
439–41
Westport Woman, **24** 145
Westvaco Corporation, IV 351–54; **19**
495–99 (upd.) *see also* MeadWestvaco
Corporation.
The Westwood Group, **20** 54
Westwood One, Inc., 23 508–11
Westwood Pharmaceuticals, **III** 19
Westworld Resources Inc., **23** 41
Westwynn Theatres, **14** 87
The Wet Seal, Inc., 18 562–64; **70**
353–57 (upd.)
Wet'n Wild Inc., **64** 94
Wetterau Incorporated, II 681–82
Wexpro Company, **6** 568–69
Weyco Group, Incorporated, 32 510–13
Weyerhaeuser Company, IV 355–56; **9**
550–52 (upd.); 28 514–17 **(upd.)**
Weyman-Burton Co., **9** 533
WFP *see* Western Forest Products Ltd.
WFS Financial Inc., 70 358–60
WFSC *see* World Fuel Services
Corporation.
WGBH Educational Foundation, 66
366–68
WGM Safety Corp., **40** 96–97
WH Smith PLC, 42 442–47 **(upd.)**
Wham-O, Inc., 61 390–93
Wharf Holdings Limited, **12** 367–68; **18**
114
Whatman plc, 46 462–65
Wheat, First Securities, **19** 304–05
Wheaton Industries, 8 570–73
Wheaton Science Products, 60 338–42
(upd.)
Wheatsheaf Investment, **27** 94
Wheel Horse, **7** 535
Wheel Restaurants Inc., **14** 131
Wheel to Wheel Inc., **66** 315
Wheelabrator Technologies, Inc., 6
599–600; 60 343–45 **(upd.)**
Wheeled Coach Industries, Inc., **33**
105–06
Wheeling-Pittsburgh Corporation, 7
586–88; 58 360–64 **(upd.)**
Whemco, **22** 415
Where Magazines International, **57** 242
Wherehouse Entertainment
Incorporated, 11 556–58
WHI Inc., **14** 545; **60** 326
Whippoorwill Associates Inc., **28** 55
Whirl-A-Way Motors, **11** 4
Whirlpool Corporation, III 653–55; **12**
548–50 (upd.); 59 414–19 **(upd.)**
Whirlwind, Inc., **7** 535
Whistler Corporation, **13** 195
Whitaker-Glessner Company, **7** 586
Whitaker Health Services, **III** 389
Whitbread PLC, I 293–94; **20** 519–22
(upd.); 52 412–17 **(upd.)**
Whitby Pharmaceuticals, Inc., **10** 289
White & Case LLP, 35 466–69

White Automotive, **10** 9, 11
White Brothers, **39** 83, 84
White Castle System, Inc., 12 551–53;
36 517–20 **(upd.)**
White Consolidated Industries Inc., 13
562–64
White Discount Department Stores, **16**
36
The White House, Inc., 60 346–48
White Miller Construction Company, **14**
162
White Mountain Freezers, **19** 360
White Mountains Insurance Group,
Ltd., 48 428–31
White-New Idea, **13** 18
White Oil Corporation, **7** 101
White Rock Corp., **27** 198; **43** 218
White-Rodgers, **II** 19
White Rose, Inc., 24 527–29
White Star Line, **23** 161
White Swan Foodservice, **II** 625
White Tractor, **13** 17
White Wave, 43 462–64
White-Westinghouse *see* White
Consolidated Industries Inc.
Whitehall Jewellers, Inc., 82 429–34
(upd.)
Whitewater Group, **10** 508
WhiteWave Foods Company *see* Dean
Foods Company.
Whitewear Manufacturing Company *see*
Angelica Corporation.
Whiting Petroleum Corporation, 81
424–27
Whitman Corporation, 10 553–55
(upd.) *see also* PepsiAmericas, Inc.
Whitman Education Group, Inc., 41
419–21
Whitman's Chocolates, **7** 431; **12** 429
Whitmire Distribution *see* Cardinal
Health, Inc.
Whitney Group, **40** 236–38
Whitney Holding Corporation, 21
522–24
Whitney National Bank, **12** 16
Whitney Partners, L.L.C., **40** 237
Whittaker Corporation, I 544–46; **48**
432–35 (upd.)
Whittard of Chelsea Plc, 61 394–97
Whittle Communications L.P., **IV** 675; **7**
528; **13** 403; **22** 442
Whittman-Hart Inc. *see* marchFIRST, Inc.
Whitworth Brothers Company, **27** 360
Whole Foods Market, Inc., 20 523–27;
50 530–34 **(upd.)**
Wholesale Cellular USA *see* Brightpoint,
Inc.
The Wholesale Club, Inc., *see* Wal-Mart
Stores, Inc.
Wholesale Depot, **13** 547
Wholesale Food Supply, Inc., **13** 333
Wholesome Foods, L.L.C., **32** 274, 277
Wholly Harvest, **19** 502
WHSC Direct, Inc., **53** 359
WHX Corporation, **58** 360
Whyte & Mackay Distillers Ltd., **V** 399;
19 171; **49** 152
Wicanders Group, **48** 119

Wicat Systems, **7** 255–56; **25** 254
Wicell Research Institute, **65** 367
Wichita Industries, **11** 27
Wickes Inc., V 221–23; **25** 533–36
(upd.)
Wicor, Inc., **54** 419
Widmer Brothers Brewing Company, 76
379–82
Wielkopolski Bank Kredytowy, **16** 14
Wiener Städtische, **58** 169
Wienerwald Holding, **17** 249
Wiesner, Inc., **22** 442
Wight Nurseries *see* Monrovia Nursery
Company.
Wilbert, Inc., 56 377–80
Wilbur Chocolate Company, 66 369–71
Wild by Nature *see* King Cullen Grocery
Co., Inc.
Wild Harvest, **56** 317
Wild Leitz G.m.b.H., **23** 83
Wild Oats Markets, Inc., 19 500–02; **41**
422–25 (upd.)
WildBlue Communications Inc., **54** 406
Wilderness Systems *see* Confluence
Holdings Corporation.
Wildlife Conservation Society, 31
462–64
Wildlife Land Trust, **54** 172
Wildwater Kingdom, **22** 130
Wiles Group Ltd. *see* Hanson PLC.
Oy Wilh. Schauman AB *see*
UPM-Kymmene
Wilhelm Weber GmbH, **22** 95
Wilhelm Wilhelmsen Ltd., **7** 40; **41** 42
Wilkins Department Store, **19** 510
Wilkinson, Gaddis & Co., **24** 527
Wilkinson Hardware Stores Ltd., 80
416–18
Wilkinson Sword Ltd., 60 349–52
Willamette Falls Electric Company *see*
Portland General Corporation.
Willamette Industries, Inc., IV 357–59;
31 465–68 **(upd.)**
Willbros Group, Inc., 56 381–83
Willcox & Gibbs Sewing Machine Co.,
15 384
Willetts Manufacturing Company, **12** 312
Willey Brothers, Inc. *see* BrandPartners
Group, Inc.
William B. Tanner Co., **7** 327
William Barnet and Son, Inc., **III** 246
William Benton Foundation, **7** 165, 167
The William Brooks Shoe Company *see*
Rocky Shoes & Boots, Inc.
William Byrd Press Inc., **23** 100
William Carter Company, **17** 224
William Cory & Son Ltd., **6** 417
William E. Pollack Government Securities,
II 390
William E. Wright Company, **9** 375
William Esty Company, **16** 72
William George Company, **32** 519
William Grant & Sons Ltd., 60 353–55
William Hewlett, **41** 117
William Hill Organization Limited, 49
449–52
William Hodges & Company, **33** 150

WVT Communications *see* Warwick
  Valley Telephone Company.
WWG Industries, Inc., **22** 352–53
WWT, Inc., **58** 371
WWTV, **18** 493
Wyandotte Chemicals Corporation, **18** 49
Wyant Corporation, **30** 496–98
Wycombe Bus Company, **28** 155–56
Wyeth, **50** 535–39 (upd.)
Wyeth-Ayerst Laboratories, **25** 477; **27** 69
Wyle Electronics, **14** 560–62; **19** 311
Wyly Corporation, **11** 468
Wyman-Gordon Company, **14** 563–65
Wymar, **76** 347
Wynkoop Brewing Company, **43** 407
Wynn's International, Inc., **33** 466–70
Wyse Technology, Inc., **10** 362; **15**
  540–42

X

X-Acto, **12** 263
X-Rite, Inc., **48** 443–46
XA Systems Corporation, **10** 244
Xaos Tools, Inc., **10** 119
Xaver Fendt GmbH & Co. KG *see*
  AGCO Corporation.
XCare.net, Inc. *see* Quovadx Inc.
Xcel Energy Inc., **73** 384–89 (upd.)
Xcor International, **15** 538; **53** 364–65
Xeikon NV, **26** 540–42
Xenell Corporation, **48** 358
Xenia National Bank, **9** 474
Xenotech, **27** 58
Xeron, Inc., **56** 62
Xerox Corporation, **III** 171–73; **6**
  288–90 (upd.); **26** 543–47 (upd.); **69**
  374–80 (upd.)
Xetra, **59** 151
Xiamen Airlines, **33** 99
Xilinx, Inc., **16** 548–50; **82** 435–39
  (upd.)
Xing Technology Corp., **53** 282
XM Satellite Radio Holdings, Inc., 69
  381–84
XMR, Inc., **42** 361
XP, **27** 474
Xpect First Aid Corp., **51** 76
Xpert Recruitment, Ltd., **26** 240
Xpress Automotive Group, Inc., **24** 339
XR Ventures LLC, **48** 446
XRAL Storage and Terminaling Co., **IV**
  411
Xros, Inc., **36** 353
Xstrata PLC, **73** 390–93
XTO Energy Inc., **52** 425–27
XTRA Corp., **18** 67
Xtra Limited New Zealand, **54** 355–57
Xuzhuo Liebherr Concrete Machinery Co.
  Ltd., **64** 241
Xynetics, **9** 251

Y

Yacimientos Petrolíferos Fiscales Sociedad
  Anónima *see* Repsol-YPF SA.
Yageo Corporation, **16** 551–53
Yahoo! Inc., **27** 516–19; **70** 372–75
  (upd.)
Yakima Products Inc., **76** 120

Yakovlev, **24** 60
Yale and Valor, PLC, **50** 134–35
Yamagata Enterprises, **26** 310
Yamaha Corporation, **III** 656–59; **16**
  554–58 (upd.); **40** 461–66 (upd.)
Yamaha Motor Co., Ltd., **59** 393, 397
Yamaha Musical Instruments, **16** 202; **43**
  170
Yamaichi Capital Management, **42** 349
Yamaichi Securities Company, Limited,
  II 458–59
Yamamotoyama Co., Ltd., **50** 449
Yamano Music, **16** 202; **43** 171
Yamanouchi Consumer Inc., **39** 361
Yamanouchi Pharmaceutical Co., Ltd., **12**
  444–45; **38** 93
Yamato Transport Co. Ltd., **V** 536–38;
  49 458–61 (upd.)
Yamazaki Baking Co., Ltd., **58** 380–82
Yanbian Industrial Technology Training
  Institute, **12** 294
Yangzhou Motor Coach Manufacturing
  Co., **34** 132
The Yankee Candle Company, Inc., **37**
  423–26; **38** 192
Yankee Energy Gas System, Inc., **13** 184
Yankee Gas Services Company, **48** 305
YankeeNets LLC, **35** 474–77
Yankton Gas Company, **6** 524
Yarmouth Group, Inc., **17** 285
Yasuda Fire and Marine Insurance
  Company, Limited, III 405–07
Yasuda Mutual Life Insurance
  Company, III 408–09; **39** 425–28
  (upd.)
The Yasuda Trust and Banking
  Company, Limited, II 391–92; **17**
  555–57 (upd.)
Yates-Barco Ltd., **16** 8
Yates Circuit Foil, **IV** 26
The Yates Companies, Inc., **62** 397–99
Yearbooks, Inc., **12** 472
Yeargin Construction Co., **II** 87; **11** 413
Yell Group PLC, **79** 472–75
Yellow Cab Co., **10** 370; **24** 118
Yellow Corporation, **14** 566–68; **45**
  448–51 (upd.)
Yellow Freight System, Inc. of Deleware,
  V 539–41
Yeo Hiap Seng Malaysia Bhd., **75**
  406–09
YES! Entertainment Corporation, **26**
  548–50
Yesco Audio Environments, **18** 353, 355
Yeti Cycles Inc., **19** 385
YGK Inc. *see* Cincinnati Gas & Electric
  Company.
Yhtyneet Paperitehtaat Oy *see* United
  Paper Mills Ltd.
YHS *see* Yeo Hiap Seng Malaysia Bhd.
YKK, **19** 477
YMCA of the USA, **31** 473–76
Ymos A.G., **IV** 53; **26** 83
YOCREAM International, Inc., **47**
  456–58
Yogen Fruz World-Wide, Inc. *see*
  CoolBrands International Inc.
Yokado Co. Ltd *see* Ito-Yokado Co. Ltd.

Yoko Sangyo Co., **64** 35
Yokohama Bottle Plant, **21** 319
The Yokohama Rubber Co., Ltd., V
  254–56; **19** 506–09 (upd.)
Yokohama Tokyu Deppartment Store Co.,
  Ltd., **32** 457
Yondenko Corporation, **60** 272
Yongpyong Resort Co., **61** 342
Yoosung Enterprise Co., Ltd., **23** 269
Yoplait S.A. *see* Sodiaal S.A.
The York Bank and Trust Company, **16**
  14; **43** 8
The York Group, Inc., **50** 540–43
York International Corp., **13** 569–71;
  22 6
York Research Corporation, **35** 478–80
York Safe & Lock Company, **7** 144–45;
  22 184
York Steak House, **16** 157
York Wastewater Consultants, Inc., **6** 441
Yorkshire Energies, **45** 21
Yorkshire Group, **61** 133
Yorkshire Television Ltd., **IV** 659
Yorkshire-Tyne Tees Television, **24** 194
Yorkshire Water Services Ltd. *see* Kelda
  Group plc.
Youbet.com, Inc., **77** 485–88
Young & Co.'s Brewery, P.L.C., **38**
  499–502
Young & Rubicam, Inc., **I** 36–38; **22**
  551–54 (upd.); **66** 375–78 (upd.)
Young & Selden, **7** 145
Young Broadcasting Inc., **40** 467–69
Young Chang Akki Company, **51** 201
Young Innovations, Inc., **44** 451–53
Young Readers of America, **13** 105
Young's Bluecrest Seafood Holdings
  Ltd., **81** 435–39
Young's Market Company, LLC, **32**
  518–20
Youngblood Truck Lines, **16** 40
Youngjin Pharmaceutical, **62** 221
Youngstown Sheet & Tube, *see* LTV
  Corporation.
Younkers, **76** 19 510–12; **383**–86 (upd.)
Your Communications Limited, **52** 372,
  374
Youth Centre Inc., **16** 36
Youth Services International, Inc., **21**
  541–43; **30** 146
Youthtrack, Inc., **29** 399–400
YPF Sociedad Anónima, **IV** 577–78 *see*
  also Repsol-YPF S.A.
Yside Investment Group, **16** 196
YTT *see* Yorkshire-Tyne Tees Television.
The Yucaipa Cos., **17** 558–62
Yue Yuen Industrial (Holdings) Ltd. *see*
  Pou Chen Corporation
Yugraneft, **49** 306
Yukon Pacific Corporation, **22** 164, 166
YUKOS, **49** 305–06 *see also* OAO NK
  YUKOS.
Yule Catto & Company plc, **54** 422–25
Yum! Brands Inc., **58** 383–85
Yutaka Co., Ltd., **55** 48
Yves Bertelin SAS., **72** 35
Yves Rocher *see* Laboratoires de Biologie
  Végétale Yves Rocher.

Index to Industries

Automotive

Beverages

Bio-Technology

Chemicals

Conglomerates

Construction

Engineering & Management Services

Entertainment & Leisure

Financial Services: Banks

Financial Services: Excluding Banks

Food Services & Retailers

Health & Personal Care Products

Health Care Services

Hotels

SINA Corporation, 69
SkillSoft Public Limited Company, 81
SmartForce PLC, 43
Softbank Corp., 13; 38 (upd.); 77 (upd.)
Sonic Solutions, Inc., 81
Specialist Computer Holdings Ltd., 80
SPSS Inc., 64
SRA International, Inc., 77
Standard Microsystems Corporation, 11
STC PLC, III
Steria SA, 49
Sterling Software, Inc., 11
Storage Technology Corporation, 6
Stratus Computer, Inc., 10
Sun Microsystems, Inc., 7; 30 (upd.)
SunGard Data Systems Inc., 11
Sybase, Inc., 10; 27 (upd.)
Sykes Enterprises, Inc., 45
Symantec Corporation, 10; 82 (upd.)
Symbol Technologies, Inc., 15
SYNNEX Corporation, 73
Synopsys, Inc., 11; 69 (upd.)
System Software Associates, Inc., 10
Systems & Computer Technology Corp., 19
T-Online International AG, 61
Tandem Computers, Inc., 6
TenFold Corporation, 35
Terra Lycos, Inc., 43
The Thomson Corporation, 34 (upd.); 77 (upd.)
3Com Corporation, 11; 34 (upd.)
The 3DO Company, 43
TIBCO Software Inc., 79
Timberline Software Corporation, 15
TomTom N.V., 81
Traffix, Inc., 61
Transaction Systems Architects, Inc., 29; 82 (upd.)
Transiciel SA, 48
Triple P N.V., 26
Tucows Inc. 78
Ubi Soft Entertainment S.A., 41
Unica Corporation, 77
Unilog SA, 42
Unisys Corporation, III; 6 (upd.); 36 (upd.)
United Business Media plc, 52 (upd.)
United Online, Inc., 71 (upd.)
United Press International, Inc., 73 (upd.)
UUNET, 38
VASCO Data Security International, Inc., 79
Verbatim Corporation, 14
Veridian Corporation, 54
VeriFone Holdings, Inc., 18; 76 (upd.)
Verint Systems Inc., 73
VeriSign, Inc., 47
Veritas Software Corporation, 45
Verity Inc., 68
Viasoft Inc., 27
Volt Information Sciences Inc., 26
Wanadoo S.A., 75
Wang Laboratories, Inc., III; 6 (upd.)
WebMD Corporation, 65
WebEx Communications, Inc., 81
West Group, 34 (upd.)
Westcon Group, Inc., 67

Western Digital Corp., 25
Wind River Systems, Inc., 37
Wipro Limited, 43
Wolters Kluwer NV, 33 (upd.)
WordPerfect Corporation, 10
Wyse Technology, Inc., 15
Xerox Corporation, III; 6 (upd.); 26 (upd.)
Xilinx, Inc., 16; 82 (upd.)
Yahoo! Inc., 27; 70 (upd.)
Zapata Corporation, 25
Ziff Davis Media Inc., 36 (upd.)
Zilog, Inc., 15

Insurance

AEGON N.V., III; 50 (upd.)
Aetna Inc., III; 21 (upd.); 63 (upd.)
AFLAC Incorporated, 10 (upd.); 38 (upd.)
Alexander & Alexander Services Inc., 10
Alfa Corporation, 60
Alleanza Assicurazioni S.p.A., 65
Alleghany Corporation, 10
Allianz AG, III; 15 (upd.); 57 (upd.)
Allmerica Financial Corporation, 63
The Allstate Corporation, 10; 27 (upd.)
AMB Generali Holding AG, 51
American Family Corporation, III
American Financial Group Inc., III; 48 (upd.)
American General Corporation, III; 10 (upd.); 46 (upd.)
American International Group, Inc., III; 15 (upd.); 47 (upd.)
American National Insurance Company, 8; 27 (upd.)
American Premier Underwriters, Inc., 10
American Re Corporation, 10; 35 (upd.)
N.V. AMEV, III
AOK-Bundesverband (Federation of the AOK) 78
Aon Corporation, III; 45 (upd.)
Arthur J. Gallagher & Co., 73
Assicurazioni Generali SpA, III; 15 (upd.)
Assurances Générales de France, 63
Atlantic American Corporation, 44
Aviva PLC, 50 (upd.)
Axa, III
AXA Colonia Konzern AG, 27; 49 (upd.)
B.A.T. Industries PLC, 22 (upd.)
Baldwin & Lyons, Inc., 51
Bâloise-Holding, 40
Benfield Greig Group plc, 53
Berkshire Hathaway Inc., III; 18 (upd.)
Blue Cross and Blue Shield Association, 10
British United Provident Association Limited (BUPAL), 79
Brown & Brown, Inc., 41
Business Men's Assurance Company of America, 14
Capital Holding Corporation, III
Catholic Order of Foresters, 24
China Life Insurance Company Limited, 65
ChoicePoint Inc., 65
The Chubb Corporation, III; 14 (upd.); 37 (upd.)

CIGNA Corporation, III; 22 (upd.); 45 (upd.)
Cincinnati Financial Corporation, 16; 44 (upd.)
CNA Financial Corporation, III; 38 (upd.)
Commercial Union PLC, III
Connecticut Mutual Life Insurance Company, III
Conseco Inc., 10; 33 (upd.)
The Continental Corporation, III
Debeka Krankenversicherungsverein auf Gegenseitigkeit, 72
The Doctors' Company, 55
Empire Blue Cross and Blue Shield, III
Enbridge Inc., 43
Engle Homes, Inc., 46
The Equitable Life Assurance Society of the United States Fireman's Fund Insurance Company, III
ERGO Versicherungsgruppe AG, 44
Erie Indemnity Company, 35
Fairfax Financial Holdings Limited, 57
Farm Family Holdings, Inc., 39
Farmers Insurance Group of Companies, 25
Fidelity National Financial Inc., 54
The First American Corporation, 52
First Executive Corporation, III
Foundation Health Corporation, 12
Gainsco, Inc., 22
GEICO Corporation, 10; 40 (upd.)
General Accident PLC, III
General Re Corporation, III; 24 (upd.)
Gerling-Konzern Versicherungs-Beteiligungs-Aktiengesellschaft, 51
Great-West Lifeco Inc., III
Groupama S.A., 76
Gryphon Holdings, Inc., 21
Guardian Financial Services, 64 (upd.)
Guardian Royal Exchange Plc, 11
Harleysville Group Inc., 37
HDI (Haftpflichtverband der Deutschen Industrie Versicherung auf Gegenseitigkeit V.a.G.), 53
HealthExtras, Inc., 75
Hilb, Rogal & Hobbs Company, 77
The Home Insurance Company, III
Horace Mann Educators Corporation, 22
Household International, Inc., 21 (upd.)
HUK-Coburg, 58
Irish Life & Permanent Plc, 59
Jackson National Life Insurance Company, 8
Jefferson-Pilot Corporation, 11; 29 (upd.)
John Hancock Financial Services, Inc., III; 42 (upd.)
Johnson & Higgins, 14
Kaiser Foundation Health Plan, Inc., 53
Kemper Corporation, III; 15 (upd.)
Legal & General Group plc, III; 24 (upd.)
The Liberty Corporation, 22
Liberty Mutual Holding Company, 59
Lincoln National Corporation, III; 25 (upd.)
Lloyd's, 74 (upd.)
Lloyd's of London, III; 22 (upd.)
The Loewen Group Inc., 40 (upd.)

Legal Services

Southern Poverty Law Center, Inc., 74
Stroock & Stroock & Lavan LLP, 40
Sullivan & Cromwell, 26
Troutman Sanders L.L.P., 79
Vinson & Elkins L.L.P., 30
Wachtell, Lipton, Rosen & Katz, 47
Weil, Gotshal & Manges LLP, 55
White & Case LLP, 35
Williams & Connolly LLP, 47
Wilson Sonsini Goodrich & Rosati, 34
Winston & Strawn, 35
Womble Carlyle Sandridge & Rice, PLLC, 52

Manufacturing

A-dec, Inc., 53
A. Schulman, Inc., 49 (upd.)
A.B.Dick Company, 28
A.O. Smith Corporation, 11; 40 (upd.)
A.T. Cross Company, 17; 49 (upd.)
A.W. Faber-Castell
  Unternehmensverwaltung GmbH & Co., 51
AAF-McQuay Incorporated, 26
AAON, Inc., 22
AAR Corp., 28
Aarhus United A/S, 68
ABB Ltd., 65 (upd.)
ABC Rail Products Corporation, 18
Abiomed, Inc., 47
ACCO World Corporation, 7; 51 (upd.)
Accubuilt, Inc., 74
Acme United Corporation, 70
Acme-Cleveland Corp., 13
Acorn Products, Inc., 55
Acushnet Company, 64
Acuson Corporation, 36 (upd.)
Adams Golf, Inc., 37
Adolf Würth GmbH & Co. KG, 49
Advanced Circuits Inc., 67
Advanced Neuromodulation Systems, Inc., 73
AEP Industries, Inc., 36
Ag-Chem Equipment Company, Inc., 17
Aga Foodservice Group PLC, 73
AGCO Corporation, 13; 67 (upd.)
Agfa Gevaert Group N.V., 59
Agrium Inc., 73
Ahlstrom Corporation, 53
Airgas, Inc., 54
Aisin Seiki Co., Ltd., III
AK Steel Holding Corporation, 41 (upd.)
AKG Acoustics GmbH, 62
Aktiebolaget Electrolux, 22 (upd.)
Aktiebolaget SKF, III; 38 (upd.)
Alamo Group Inc., 32
ALARIS Medical Systems, Inc., 65
Alberto-Culver Company, 36 (upd.)
Aldila Inc., 46
Alfa Laval AB, III; 64 (upd.)
Allen Organ Company, 33
Allen-Edmonds Shoe Corporation, 61
Alliant Techsystems Inc., 8; 30 (upd.); 77 (upd.)
The Allied Defense Group, Inc., 65
Allied Healthcare Products, Inc., 24
Allied Products Corporation, 21
Allied Signal Engines, 9

AlliedSignal Inc., 22 (upd.)
Allison Gas Turbine Division, 9
Alltrista Corporation, 30
Alps Electric Co., Ltd., 44 (upd.)
Alticor Inc., 71 (upd.)
Aluar Aluminio Argentino S.A.I.C., 74
Alvis Plc, 47
Amer Group plc, 41
American Axle & Manufacturing Holdings, Inc., 67
American Biltrite Inc., 43 (upd.)
American Business Products, Inc., 20
American Cast Iron Pipe Company, 50
American Greetings Corporation, 59 (upd.)
American Homestar Corporation, 18; 41 (upd.)
American Locker Group Incorporated, 34
American Power Conversion Corporation, 67 (upd.)
American Seating Company 78
American Standard Companies Inc., 30 (upd.)
American Technical Ceramics Corp., 67
American Tourister, Inc., 16
American Woodmark Corporation, 31
Ameriwood Industries International Corp., 17
Amerock Corporation, 53
Ameron International Corporation, 67
AMETEK, Inc., 9
AMF Bowling, Inc., 40
Ampacet Corporation, 67
Ampco-Pittsburgh Corporation, 79
Ampex Corporation, 17
Amway Corporation, 30 (upd.)
Analogic Corporation, 23
Anchor Hocking Glassware, 13
Andersen Corporation, 10
The Andersons, Inc., 31
Andreas Stihl AG & Co. KG, 16; 59 (upd.)
Andritz AG, 51
Ansell Ltd., 60 (upd.)
Anthem Electronics, Inc., 13
Apasco S.A. de C.V., 51
Apex Digital, Inc., 63
Applica Incorporated, 43 (upd.)
Applied Films Corporation, 48
Applied Materials, Inc., 10; 46 (upd.)
Applied Micro Circuits Corporation, 38
Applied Power Inc., 9; 32 (upd.)
AptarGroup, Inc., 69
ARBED S.A., 22 (upd.)
Arc International, 76
Arctco, Inc., 16
Arctic Cat Inc., 40 (upd.)
Ariens Company, 48
The Aristotle Corporation, 62
Armor All Products Corp., 16
Armstrong Holdings, Inc., III; 22 (upd.); 81 (upd.)
Artesyn Technologies Inc., 46 (upd.)
ArthroCare Corporation, 73
ArvinMeritor, Inc., 54 (upd.)
Asahi Glass Company, Ltd., 48 (upd.)
Ashley Furniture Industries, Inc., 35
ASICS Corporation, 57

ASML Holding N.V., 50
Astec Industries, Inc., 79
Astronics Corporation, 35
ASV, Inc., 34; 66 (upd.)
Atlas Copco AB, III; 28 (upd.)
Atwood Mobil Products, 53
AU Optronics Corporation, 67
Aurora Casket Company, Inc., 56
Austal Limited, 75
Austin Powder Company, 76
Avedis Zildjian Co., 38
Avery Dennison Corporation, 17 (upd.); 49 (upd.)
Avocent Corporation, 65
Avondale Industries, 7; 41 (upd.)
AVX Corporation, 67
B.J. Alan Co., Inc., 67
The Babcock & Wilcox Company, 82
Badger Meter, Inc., 22
BAE Systems Ship Repair, 73
Baker Hughes Incorporated, III
Baldor Electric Company, 21
Baldwin Piano & Organ Company, 18
Baldwin Technology Company, Inc., 25
Balfour Beatty plc, 36 (upd.)
Ballantyne of Omaha, Inc., 27
Ballard Medical Products, 21
Ballard Power Systems Inc., 73
Bally Manufacturing Corporation, III
Baltek Corporation, 34
Baltimore Aircoil Company, Inc., 66
Bandai Co., Ltd., 55
Barmag AG, 39
Barnes Group Inc., 13; 69 (upd.)
Barry Callebaut AG, 29
Bassett Furniture Industries, Inc., 18
Bath Iron Works, 12; 36 (upd.)
Beckman Coulter, Inc., 22
Beckman Instruments, Inc., 14
Becton, Dickinson & Company, 36 (upd.)
Behr GmbH & Co. KG, 72
BEI Technologies, Inc., 65
Beiersdorf AG, 29
Bel Fuse, Inc., 53
Belden CDT Inc., 76 (upd.)
Belden Inc., 19
Bell Sports Corporation, 16; 44 (upd.)
Belleek Pottery Ltd., 71
Beloit Corporation, 14
Bénéteau SA, 55
Benjamin Moore & Co., 13; 38 (upd.)
BenQ Corporation, 67
Berger Bros Company, 62
Bernina Holding AG, 47
Berry Plastics Corporation, 21
Berwick Offray, LLC, 70
Bianchi International (d/b/a Gregory Mountain Products), 76
BIC Corporation, 8; 23 (upd.)
BICC PLC, III
Billabong International Ltd., 44
The Bing Group, 60
Binks Sames Corporation, 21
Binney & Smith Inc., 25
bioMérieux S.A., 75
Biomet, Inc., 10
Biosite Incorporated, 73
BISSELL Inc., 9; 30 (upd.)

Varlen Corporation, 16
Varta AG, 23
Velcro Industries N.V., 19; 72
Ventana Medical Systems, Inc., 75
Verbatim Corporation, 74 (upd.)
Vermeer Manufacturing Company, 17
Vestas Wind Systems A/S, 73
Viasystems Group, Inc., 67
Vickers plc, 27
Victorinox AG, 21; 74 (upd.)
Vidrala S.A., 67
Viessmann Werke GmbH & Co., 37
ViewSonic Corporation, 72
Viking Range Corporation, 66
Villeroy & Boch AG, 37
Virco Manufacturing Corporation, 17
Viscofan S.A., 70
Viskase Companies, Inc., 55
Vita Plus Corporation, 60
Vitro Corporativo S.A. de C.V., 34
voestalpine AG, 57 (upd.)
Vorwerk & Co., 27
Vosper Thornycroft Holding plc, 41
Vossloh AG, 53
VTech Holdings Ltd., 77
W.A. Whitney Company, 53
W.C. Bradley Co., 69
W.H. Brady Co., 17
W.L. Gore & Associates, Inc., 14; 60
    (upd.)
W.W. Grainger, Inc., 26 (upd.); 68 (upd.)
Wabash National Corp., 13
Wabtec Corporation, 40
Walbro Corporation, 13
Walter Industries, Inc., 72 (upd.)
Washington Scientific Industries, Inc., 17
Wassall Plc, 18
Waterford Wedgwood plc, 12; 34 (upd.)
Waters Corporation, 43
Watts Industries, Inc., 19
Watts of Lydney Group Ltd., 71
WD-40 Company, 18
Weber-Stephen Products Co., 40
Weeres Industries Corporation, 52
Weg S.A. 78
Welbilt Corp., 19
Wellman, Inc., 8; 52 (upd.)
Weru Aktiengesellschaft, 18
West Bend Co., 14
Westell Technologies, Inc., 57
Westerbeke Corporation, 60
Western Digital Corp., 25
Wheaton Science Products, 60 (upd.)
Wheeling-Pittsburgh Corporation, 58
    (upd.)
Whirlpool Corporation, III; 12 (upd.); 59
    (upd.)
White Consolidated Industries Inc., 13
Wilbert, Inc., 56
Wilkinson Sword Ltd., 60
William L. Bonnell Company, Inc., 66
William Zinsser & Company, Inc., 58
Williamson-Dickie Manufacturing
    Company, 45 (upd.)
Wilson Sporting Goods Company, 24
Wincor Nixdorf Holding GmbH, 69
    (upd.)
Windmere Corporation, 16

Winegard Company, 56
WinsLoew Furniture, Inc., 21
The Wiremold Company, 81
WMS Industries, Inc., 15; 53 (upd.)
Wolverine Tube Inc., 23
Wood-Mode, Inc., 23
Woodcraft Industries Inc., 61
Woodward Governor Company, 13; 49
    (upd.)
Wright Medical Group, Inc., 61
Württembergische Metallwarenfabrik AG
    (WMF), 60
Wyant Corporation, 30
Wyman-Gordon Company, 14
Wynn's International, Inc., 33
X-Rite, Inc., 48
Xerox Corporation, 69 (upd.)
Yamaha Corporation, III; 16 (upd.)
The York Group, Inc., 50
York International Corp., 13
Young Innovations, Inc., 44
Zebra Technologies Corporation, 53
    (upd.)
Zero Corporation, 17
ZiLOG, Inc., 72 (upd.)
Zindart Ltd., 60
Zippo Manufacturing Company, 18; 71
    (upd.)
Zodiac S.A., 36
Zygo Corporation, 42

Materials

AK Steel Holding Corporation, 19
American Biltrite Inc., 16
American Colloid Co., 13
American Standard Inc., III
Ameriwood Industries International Corp.,
    17
Apasco S.A. de C.V., 51
Apogee Enterprises, Inc., 8
Asahi Glass Company, Limited, III
Asbury Carbons, Inc., 68
Bairnco Corporation, 28
Bayou Steel Corporation, 31
Blessings Corp., 19
Blue Circle Industries PLC, III
Bodycote International PLC, 63
Boral Limited, III
British Vita PLC, 9
Brush Engineered Materials Inc., 67
California Steel Industries, Inc., 67
Callanan Industries, Inc., 60
Cameron & Barkley Company, 28
Carborundum Company, 15
Carl-Zeiss-Stiftung, 34 (upd.)
Carlisle Companies Inc., 8; 82 (upd.)
Carter Holt Harvey Ltd., 70
Cemex SA de CV, 20
Century Aluminum Company, 52
CertainTeed Corporation, 35
Chargeurs International, 6; 21 (upd.)
Chemfab Corporation, 35
Cimentos de Portugal SGPS S.A.
    (Cimpor), 76
Cold Spring Granite Company Inc., 16;
    67 (upd.)
Columbia Forest Products Inc. 78

Compagnie de Saint-Gobain S.A., III; 16
    (upd.)
Cookson Group plc, III; 44 (upd.)
Corning Incorporated, III
CSR Limited, III
Dal-Tile International Inc., 22
The David J. Joseph Company, 14; 76
    (upd.)
The Dexter Corporation, 12 (upd.)
Dyckerhoff AG, 35
Dynamic Materials Corporation, 81
Dyson Group PLC, 71
ECC Group plc, III
Edw. C. Levy Co., 42
84 Lumber Company, 9; 39 (upd.)
ElkCorp, 52
Empire Resources, Inc., 81
English China Clays Ltd., 15 (upd.); 40
    (upd.)
Envirodyne Industries, Inc., 17
Feldmuhle Nobel A.G., III
Fibreboard Corporation, 16
Florida Rock Industries, Inc., 46
Foamex International Inc., 17
Formica Corporation, 13
GAF Corporation, 22 (upd.)
The Geon Company, 11
Giant Cement Holding, Inc., 23
Gibraltar Steel Corporation, 37
Granite Rock Company, 26
Groupe Sidel S.A., 21
Harbison-Walker Refractories Company,
    24
Harrisons & Crosfield plc, III
Heidelberger Zement AG, 31
Hexcel Corporation, 28
Holderbank Financière Glaris Ltd., III
Holnam Inc., 39 (upd.)
Holt and Bugbee Company, 66
Homasote Company, 72
Howmet Corp., 12
Huttig Building Products, Inc., 73
Ibstock Brick Ltd., 14; 37 (upd.)
Imerys S.A., 40 (upd.)
Imperial Industries, Inc., 81
Internacional de Ceramica, S.A. de C.V.,
    53
International Shipbreaking Ltd. L.L.C., 67
Joseph T. Ryerson & Son, Inc., 15
Lafarge Coppée S.A., III
Lafarge Corporation, 28
Lehigh Portland Cement Company, 23
Manville Corporation, III; 7 (upd.)
Material Sciences Corporation, 63
Matsushita Electric Works, Ltd., III; 7
    (upd.)
McJunkin Corporation, 63
Medusa Corporation, 24
Mitsubishi Materials Corporation, III
Nevamar Company, 82
Nippon Sheet Glass Company, Limited,
    III
North Pacific Group, Inc., 61
OmniSource Corporation, 14
Onoda Cement Co., Ltd., III
Otor S.A., 77
Owens-Corning Fiberglass Corporation,
    III

Pilkington plc, III; 34 (upd.)
Pioneer International Limited, III
PPG Industries, Inc., III; 22 (upd.); 81 (upd.)
Redland plc, III
Rinker Group Ltd., 65
RMC Group p.l.c., III
Rock of Ages Corporation, 37
Rogers Corporation, 80 (upd.)
Royal Group Technologies Limited, 73
The Rugby Group plc, 31
Schuff Steel Company, 26
Sekisui Chemical Co., Ltd., III; 72 (upd.)
Severstal Joint Stock Company, 65
Shaw Industries, 9
The Sherwin-Williams Company, III; 13 (upd.)
The Siam Cement Public Company Limited, 56
SIG plc, 71
Simplex Technologies Inc., 21
Siskin Steel & Supply Company, 70
Solutia Inc., 52
Sommer-Allibert S.A., 19
Southdown, Inc., 14
Spartech Corporation, 19; 76 (upd.)
Ssangyong Cement Industrial Co., Ltd., III; 61 (upd.)
Steel Technologies Inc., 63
Sun Distributors L.P., 12
Symyx Technologies, Inc., 77
Tarmac plc, III; 28 (upd.)
Tilcon-Connecticut Inc., 80
TOTO LTD., III; 28 (upd.)
Toyo Sash Co., Ltd., III
Tuscarora Inc., 29
U.S. Aggregates, Inc., 42
Ube Industries, Ltd., III
United States Steel Corporation, 50 (upd.)
USG Corporation, III; 26 (upd.); 81 (upd.)
Usinas Siderúrgicas de Minas Gerais S.A., 77
Vicat S.A., 70
voestalpine AG, 57 (upd.)
Vulcan Materials Company, 7; 52 (upd.)
Wacker-Chemie GmbH, 35
Walter Industries, Inc., III
Waxman Industries, Inc., 9
Weber et Broutin France, 66
Wienerberger AG, 70
Wolseley plc, 64
Zoltek Companies, Inc., 37

Mining & Metals

A.M. Castle & Co., 25
Aggregate Industries plc, 36
Agnico-Eagle Mines Limited, 71
Aktiebolaget SKF, 38 (upd.)
Alcan Aluminium Limited, IV; 31 (upd.)
Alcoa Inc., 56 (upd.)
Alleghany Corporation, 10
Allegheny Ludlum Corporation, 8
Alliance Resource Partners, L.P., 81
Alrosa Company Ltd., 62
Altos Hornos de México, S.A. de C.V., 42
Aluminum Company of America, IV; 20 (upd.)

AMAX Inc., IV
AMCOL International Corporation, 59 (upd.)
Amsted Industries Incorporated, 7
Anglo American Corporation of South Africa Limited, IV; 16 (upd.)
Anglo American PLC, 50 (upd.)
Aquarius Platinum Ltd., 63
ARBED S.A., IV; 22 (upd.)
Arcelor Gent, 80
Arch Mineral Corporation, 7
Armco Inc., IV
ASARCO Incorporated, IV
Ashanti Goldfields Company Limited, 43
Atchison Casting Corporation, 39
Barrick Gold Corporation, 34
Battle Mountain Gold Company, 23
Benguet Corporation, 58
Bethlehem Steel Corporation, IV; 7 (upd.); 27 (upd.)
BHP Billiton, 67 (upd.)
Birmingham Steel Corporation, 13; 40 (upd.)
Boart Longyear Company, 26
Bodycote International PLC, 63
Boliden AB, 80
Boral Limited, 43 (upd.)
British Coal Corporation, IV
British Steel plc, IV; 19 (upd.)
Broken Hill Proprietary Company Ltd., IV; 22 (upd.)
Brush Engineered Materials Inc., 67
Brush Wellman Inc., 14
Buderus AG, 37
Cameco Corporation, 77
Carpenter Technology Corporation, 13
Chaparral Steel Co., 13
Christensen Boyles Corporation, 26
Cleveland-Cliffs Inc., 13; 62 (upd.)
Coal India Ltd., IV; 44 (upd.)
Cockerill Sambre Group, IV; 26 (upd.)
Coeur d'Alene Mines Corporation, 20
Cold Spring Granite Company Inc., 16; 67 (upd.)
Cominco Ltd., 37
Commercial Metals Company, 15; 42 (upd.)
Companhia Siderúrgica Nacional, 76
Companhia Vale do Rio Doce, IV; 43 (upd.)
CONSOL Energy Inc., 59
Corporacion Nacional del Cobre de Chile, 40
Corus Group plc, 49 (upd.)
CRA Limited, IV
Cyprus Amax Minerals Company, 21
Cyprus Minerals Company, 7
Daido Steel Co., Ltd., IV
De Beers Consolidated Mines Limited/De Beers Centenary AG, IV; 7 (upd.); 28 (upd.)
Degussa Group, IV
Dofasco Inc., IV; 24 (upd.)
Earle M. Jorgensen Company, 82
Echo Bay Mines Ltd., IV; 38 (upd.)
Engelhard Corporation, IV
Eramet, 73
Falconbridge Limited, 49

Fansteel Inc., 19
Fluor Corporation, 34 (upd.)
Freeport-McMoRan Copper & Gold, Inc., IV; 7 (upd.); 57 (upd.)
Fried. Krupp GmbH, IV
Gencor Ltd., IV, 22 (upd.)
Geneva Steel, 7
Gerdau S.A., 59
Glamis Gold, Ltd., 54
Gold Fields Ltd., IV; 62 (upd.)
Grupo Mexico, S.A. de C.V., 40
Handy & Harman, 23
Hanson Building Materials America Inc., 60
Hanson PLC, 30 (upd.)
Harmony Gold Mining Company Limited, 63
Hecla Mining Company, 20
Hemlo Gold Mines Inc., 9
Heraeus Holding GmbH, IV
Highveld Steel and Vanadium Corporation Limited, 59
Hitachi Metals, Ltd., IV
Hoesch AG, IV
Homestake Mining Company, 12; 38 (upd.)
Horsehead Industries, Inc., 51
The Hudson Bay Mining and Smelting Company, Limited, 12
Hylsamex, S.A. de C.V., 39
IMCO Recycling, Incorporated, 32
Imerys S.A., 40 (upd.)
Imetal S.A., IV
Inco Limited, IV; 45 (upd.)
Industrias Penoles, S.A. de C.V., 22
Inland Steel Industries, Inc., IV; 19 (upd.)
Intermet Corporation, 32
Iscor Limited, 57
Ispat Inland Inc., 30; 40 (upd.)
Johnson Matthey PLC, IV; 16 (upd.)
JSC MMC Norilsk Nickel, 48
Kaiser Aluminum & Chemical Corporation, IV
Kawasaki Heavy Industries, Ltd., 63 (upd.)
Kawasaki Steel Corporation, IV
Kennecott Corporation, 7; 27 (upd.)
Kentucky Electric Steel, Inc., 31
Kerr-McGee Corporation, 22 (upd.)
Kinross Gold Corporation, 36
Klockner-Werke AG, IV
Kobe Steel, Ltd., IV; 19 (upd.)
Koninklijke Nederlandsche Hoogovens en Staalfabrieken NV, IV
Laclede Steel Company, 15
Layne Christensen Company, 19
Lonmin plc, 66 (upd.)
Lonrho Plc, 21
The LTV Corporation, I; 24 (upd.)
Lukens Inc., 14
Magma Copper Company, 7
The Marmon Group, IV; 16 (upd.)
Massey Energy Company, 57
MAXXAM Inc., 8
Meridian Gold, Incorporated, 47
Metaleurop S.A., 21
Metallgesellschaft AG, IV

Paper & Forestry

Publishing & Printing

Real Estate

Retail & Wholesale

Textiles & Apparel

Tobacco

Preston Corporation, 6
RailTex, Inc., 20
Railtrack Group PLC, 50
Réseau Ferré de France, 66
Roadway Express, Inc., V; 25 (upd.)
Royal Olympic Cruise Lines Inc., 52
Royal Vopak NV, 41
Ryder System, Inc., V; 24 (upd.)
Santa Fe Pacific Corporation, V
Schenker-Rhenus AG, 6
Schneider National, Inc., 36; 77 (upd.)
Securicor Plc, 45
Seibu Railway Company Ltd., V; 74 (upd.)
Seino Transportation Company, Ltd., 6
Simon Transportation Services Inc., 27
Smithway Motor Xpress Corporation, 39
Société Nationale des Chemins de Fer Français, V; 57 (upd.)
Société Norbert Dentressangle S.A., 67
Southern Pacific Transportation Company, V
Stagecoach Holdings plc, 30
Stelmar Shipping Ltd., 52
Stevedoring Services of America Inc., 28
Stinnes AG, 8; 59 (upd.)
Stolt-Nielsen S.A., 42
Sunoco, Inc., 28 (upd.)
Swift Transportation Co., Inc., 42
The Swiss Federal Railways (Schweizerische Bundesbahnen), V
Swissport International Ltd., 70
Teekay Shipping Corporation, 25; 82 (upd.)
Tibbett & Britten Group plc, 32
Tidewater Inc., 11; 37 (upd.)
TNT Freightways Corporation, 14
TNT Post Group N.V., V; 27 (upd.); 30 (upd.)
Tobu Railway Co Ltd, 6
Tokyu Corporation, V
Totem Resources Corporation, 9
TPG N.V., 64 (upd.)
Trailer Bridge, Inc., 41
Transnet Ltd., 6
Transport Corporation of America, Inc., 49
TTX Company, 6; 66 (upd.)
U.S. Delivery Systems, Inc., 22
Union Pacific Corporation, V; 28 (upd.); 79 (upd.)
United Parcel Service of America Inc., V; 17 (upd.)
United Parcel Service, Inc., 63
United Road Services, Inc., 69
United States Postal Service, 14; 34 (upd.)
USA Truck, Inc., 42
Velocity Express Corporation, 49
Werner Enterprises, Inc., 26
Wincanton plc, 52
Wisconsin Central Transportation Corporation, 24
Wright Express Corporation, 80
Yamato Transport Co. Ltd., V; 49 (upd.)
Yellow Corporation, 14; 45 (upd.)
Yellow Freight System, Inc. of Delaware, V

Utilities

AES Corporation, 10; 13 (upd.); 53 (upd.)
Aggreko Plc, 45
Air & Water Technologies Corporation, 6
Alberta Energy Company Ltd., 16; 43 (upd.)
Allegheny Energy, Inc., V; 38 (upd.)
Ameren Corporation, 60 (upd.)
American Electric Power Company, Inc., V; 45 (upd.)
American States Water Company, 46
American Water Works Company, Inc., 6; 38 (upd.)
Aquila, Inc., 50 (upd.)
Arkla, Inc., V
Associated Natural Gas Corporation, 11
Atlanta Gas Light Company, 6; 23 (upd.)
Atlantic Energy, Inc., 6
Atmos Energy Corporation, 43
Avista Corporation, 69 (upd.)
Baltimore Gas and Electric Company, V; 25 (upd.)
Bay State Gas Company, 38
Bayernwerk AG, V; 23 (upd.)
Bewag AG, 39
Big Rivers Electric Corporation, 11
Black Hills Corporation, 20
Bonneville Power Administration, 50
Boston Edison Company, 12
Bouygues S.A., 24 (upd.)
British Energy Plc, 49
British Gas plc, V
British Nuclear Fuels plc, 6
Brooklyn Union Gas, 6
California Water Service Group, 79
Calpine Corporation, 36
Canadian Utilities Limited, 13; 56 (upd.)
Cap Rock Energy Corporation, 46
Carolina Power & Light Company, V; 23 (upd.)
Cascade Natural Gas Corporation, 9
Centerior Energy Corporation, V
Central and South West Corporation, V
Central Hudson Gas and Electricity Corporation, 6
Central Maine Power, 6
Central Vermont Public Service Corporation, 54
Centrica plc, 29 (upd.)
Chesapeake Utilities Corporation, 56
Chubu Electric Power Company, Inc., V; 46 (upd.)
Chugoku Electric Power Company Inc., V; 53 (upd.)
Cincinnati Gas & Electric Company, 6
CIPSCO Inc., 6
Citizens Utilities Company, 7
City Public Service, 6
Cleco Corporation, 37
CMS Energy Corporation, V, 14
The Coastal Corporation, 31 (upd.)
Cogentrix Energy, Inc., 10
The Coleman Company, Inc., 9
The Columbia Gas System, Inc., V; 16 (upd.)
Commonwealth Edison Company, V
Commonwealth Energy System, 14

Companhia Energética de Minas Gerais S.A. CEMIG, 65
Connecticut Light and Power Co., 13
Consolidated Edison, Inc., V; 45 (upd.)
Consolidated Natural Gas Company, V; 19 (upd.)
Consumers Power Co., 14
Consumers Water Company, 14
Consumers' Gas Company Ltd., 6
Covanta Energy Corporation, 64 (upd.)
Dalkia Holding, 66
Destec Energy, Inc., 12
The Detroit Edison Company, V
Dominion Resources, Inc., V; 54 (upd.)
DPL Inc., 6
DQE, Inc., 6
DTE Energy Company, 20 (upd.)
Duke Energy Corporation, V; 27 (upd.)
E.On AG, 50 (upd.)
Eastern Enterprises, 6
Edison International, 56 (upd.)
El Paso Electric Company, 21
El Paso Natural Gas Company, 12
Electrabel N.V., 67
Electricidade de Portugal, S.A., 47
Electricité de France, V; 41 (upd.)
Electricity Generating Authority of Thailand (EGAT), 56
Elektrowatt AG, 6
The Empire District Electric Company, 77
Enbridge Inc., 43
ENDESA S.A., V; 46 (upd.)
Enersis S.A., 73
Enron Corporation, V; 46 (upd.)
Enserch Corporation, V
Ente Nazionale per L'Energia Elettrica, V
Entergy Corporation, V; 45 (upd.)
Environmental Power Corporation, 68
EPCOR Utilities Inc., 81
Equitable Resources, Inc., 6; 54 (upd.)
Exelon Corporation, 48 (upd.)
Florida Progress Corporation, V; 23 (upd.)
Florida Public Utilities Company, 69
Fortis, Inc., 15; 47 (upd.)
Fortum Corporation, 30 (upd.)
FPL Group, Inc., V; 49 (upd.)
Gas Natural SDG S.A., 69
Gaz de France, V; 40 (upd.)
General Public Utilities Corporation, V
Générale des Eaux Group, V
GPU, Inc., 27 (upd.)
Great Plains Energy Incorporated, 65 (upd.)
Gulf States Utilities Company, 6
Hawaiian Electric Industries, Inc., 9
Hokkaido Electric Power Company Inc. (HEPCO), V; 58 (upd.)
Hokuriku Electric Power Company, V
Hong Kong and China Gas Company Ltd., 73
Hongkong Electric Holdings Ltd., 6; 23 (upd.)
Houston Industries Incorporated, V
Hyder plc, 34
Hydro-Québec, 6; 32 (upd.)
Iberdrola, S.A., 49
Idaho Power Company, 12

Illinois Bell Telephone Company, 14
Illinois Power Company, 6
Indiana Energy, Inc., 27
International Power PLC, 50 (upd.)
IPALCO Enterprises, Inc., 6
ITC Holdings Corp., 75
The Kansai Electric Power Company, Inc., V; 62 (upd.)
Kansas City Power & Light Company, 6
Kelda Group plc, 45
Kenetech Corporation, 11
Kentucky Utilities Company, 6
KeySpan Energy Co., 27
Korea Electric Power Corporation (Kepco), 56
KU Energy Corporation, 11
Kyushu Electric Power Company Inc., V
LG&E Energy Corporation, 6; 51 (upd.)
Long Island Lighting Company, V
Lyonnaise des Eaux-Dumez, V
Madison Gas and Electric Company, 39
Magma Power Company, 11
Maine & Maritimes Corporation, 56
Manila Electric Company (Meralco), 56
MCN Corporation, 6
MDU Resources Group, Inc., 7; 42 (upd.)
Middlesex Water Company, 45
Midwest Resources Inc., 6
Minnesota Power, Inc., 11; 34 (upd.)
The Montana Power Company, 11; 44 (upd.)
National Fuel Gas Company, 6
National Grid USA, 51 (upd.)
National Power PLC, 12
Nebraska Public Power District, 29
N.V. Nederlandse Gasunie, V
Nevada Power Company, 11
New England Electric System, V
New Jersey Resources Corporation, 54
New York State Electric and Gas, 6
Neyveli Lignite Corporation Ltd., 65
Niagara Mohawk Holdings Inc., V; 45 (upd.)
NICOR Inc., 6
NIPSCO Industries, Inc., 6
North West Water Group plc, 11
Northeast Utilities, V; 48 (upd.)
Northern States Power Company, V; 20 (upd.)
Northwest Natural Gas Company, 45
NorthWestern Corporation, 37
Nova Corporation of Alberta, V
NRG Energy, Inc., 79
Oglethorpe Power Corporation, 6
Ohio Edison Company, V
Oklahoma Gas and Electric Company, 6
ONEOK Inc., 7
Ontario Hydro Services Company, 6; 32 (upd.)
Osaka Gas Company, Ltd., V; 60 (upd.)
Otter Tail Power Company, 18
Pacific Enterprises, V
Pacific Gas and Electric Company, V
PacifiCorp, V; 26 (upd.)
Panhandle Eastern Corporation, V
PECO Energy Company, 11
Pennon Group Plc, 45
Pennsylvania Power & Light Company, V

Peoples Energy Corporation, 6
PG&E Corporation, 26 (upd.)
Philadelphia Electric Company, V
Philadelphia Suburban Corporation, 39
Piedmont Natural Gas Company, Inc., 27
Pinnacle West Capital Corporation, 6; 54 (upd.)
PNM Resources Inc., 51 (upd.)
Portland General Corporation, 6
Potomac Electric Power Company, 6
Power-One, Inc., 79
Powergen PLC, 11; 50 (upd.)
PPL Corporation, 41 (upd.)
PreussenElektra Aktiengesellschaft, V
Progress Energy, Inc., 74
PSI Resources, 6
Public Service Company of Colorado, 6
Public Service Company of New Hampshire, 21; 55 (upd.)
Public Service Company of New Mexico, 6
Public Service Enterprise Group Inc., V; 44 (upd.)
Puerto Rico Electric Power Authority, 47
Puget Sound Energy Inc., 6; 50 (upd.)
Questar Corporation, 6; 26 (upd.)
RAO Unified Energy System of Russia, 45
Reliant Energy Inc., 44 (upd.)
Rochester Gas and Electric Corporation, 6
Ruhrgas AG, V; 38 (upd.)
RWE AG, V; 50 (upd.)
Salt River Project, 19
San Diego Gas & Electric Company, V
SCANA Corporation, 6; 56 (upd.)
Scarborough Public Utilities Commission, 9
SCEcorp, V
Scottish and Southern Energy plc, 66 (upd.)
Scottish Hydro-Electric PLC, 13
Scottish Power plc, 19; 49 (upd.)
Seattle City Light, 50
SEMCO Energy, Inc., 44
Sempra Energy, 25 (upd.)
Severn Trent PLC, 12; 38 (upd.)
Shikoku Electric Power Company, Inc., V; 60 (upd.)
SJW Corporation, 70
Sonat, Inc., 6
South Jersey Industries, Inc., 42
The Southern Company, V; 38 (upd.)
Southern Electric PLC, 13
Southern Indiana Gas and Electric Company, 13
Southern Union Company, 27
Southwest Gas Corporation, 19
Southwest Water Company, 47
Southwestern Electric Power Co., 21
Southwestern Public Service Company, 6
Suez Lyonnaise des Eaux, 36 (upd.)
TECO Energy, Inc., 6
Tennessee Valley Authority, 50
Tennet BV 78
Texas Utilities Company, V; 25 (upd.)
Thames Water plc, 11
Tohoku Electric Power Company, Inc., V
The Tokyo Electric Power Company, 74 (upd.)

The Tokyo Electric Power Company, Incorporated, V
Tokyo Gas Co., Ltd., V; 55 (upd.)
TransAlta Utilities Corporation, 6
TransCanada PipeLines Limited, V
Transco Energy Company, V
Trigen Energy Corporation, 42
Tucson Electric Power Company, 6
UGI Corporation, 12
Unicom Corporation, 29 (upd.)
Union Electric Company, V
The United Illuminating Company, 21
United Utilities PLC, 52 (upd.)
United Water Resources, Inc., 40
Unitil Corporation, 37
Utah Power and Light Company, 27
UtiliCorp United Inc., 6
Vattenfall AB, 57
Vereinigte Elektrizitätswerke Westfalen AG, V
VEW AG, 39
Viridian Group plc, 64
Warwick Valley Telephone Company, 55
Washington Gas Light Company, 19
Washington Natural Gas Company, 9
Washington Water Power Company, 6
Westar Energy, Inc., 57 (upd.)
Western Resources, Inc., 12
Wheelabrator Technologies, Inc., 6
Wisconsin Energy Corporation, 6; 54 (upd.)
Wisconsin Public Service Corporation, 9
WPL Holdings, Inc., 6
WPS Resources Corporation, 53 (upd.)
Xcel Energy Inc., 73 (upd.)

Waste Services

Allied Waste Industries, Inc., 50
Allwaste, Inc., 18
American Ecology Corporation, 77
Appliance Recycling Centers of America, Inc., 42
Azcon Corporation, 23
Berliner Stadtreinigungsbetriebe, 58
Brambles Industries Limited, 42
Browning-Ferris Industries, Inc., V; 20 (upd.)
Chemical Waste Management, Inc., 9
Clean Harbors, Inc., 73
Copart Inc., 23
E.On AG, 50 (upd.)
Ecology and Environment, Inc., 39
Industrial Services of America, Inc., 46
Ionics, Incorporated, 52
ISS A/S, 49
Kelda Group plc, 45
MPW Industrial Services Group, Inc., 53
Newpark Resources, Inc., 63
Norcal Waste Systems, Inc., 60
1-800-GOT-JUNK? LLC, 74
Pennon Group Plc, 45
Philip Environmental Inc., 16
Philip Services Corp., 73
Roto-Rooter, Inc., 15; 61 (upd.)
Safety-Kleen Systems Inc., 8; 82 (upd.)
Sevenson Environmental Services, Inc., 42
Severn Trent PLC, 38 (upd.)
Shanks Group plc, 45

Geographic Index

United States

Roanoke Electric Steel Corporation, 45
Robbins & Myers Inc., 15
Roberds Inc., 19
Robert Half International Inc., 18; 70 (upd.)
Robert Mondavi Corporation, 15; 50 (upd.)
Robert W. Baird & Co. Incorporated, 67
Robert Wood Johnson Foundation, 35
Roberts Pharmaceutical Corporation, 16
Robertson-Ceco Corporation, 19
Robinson Helicopter Company, 51
Rocawear Apparel LLC, 77
Roche Bioscience, 11; 14 (upd.)
Rochester Gas and Electric Corporation, 6
Rochester Telephone Corporation, 6
Rock Bottom Restaurants, Inc., 25; 68 (upd.)
Rock of Ages Corporation, 37
Rock-Tenn Company, 13; 59 (upd.)
The Rockefeller Foundation, 34
Rockefeller Group International Inc., 58
Rockford Corporation, 43
Rockford Products Corporation, 55
RockShox, Inc., 26
Rockwell Automation, 43 (upd.)
Rockwell International Corporation, I; 11 (upd.)
Rocky Mountain Chocolate Factory, Inc., 73
Rocky Shoes & Boots, Inc., 26
Rodale, Inc., 23; 47 (upd.)
ROFIN-SINAR Technologies Inc., 81
Rogers Corporation, 61; 80 (upd.)
Rohm and Haas Company, I; 26 (upd.); 77 (upd.)
ROHN Industries, Inc., 22
Rohr Incorporated, 9
Roll International Corporation, 37
Rollerblade, Inc., 15; 34 (upd.)
Rollins, Inc., 11
Rolls-Royce Allison, 29 (upd.)
Romacorp, Inc., 58
Ron Tonkin Chevrolet Company, 55
Ronco Corporation, 15; 80 (upd.)
Rooms To Go Inc., 28
Rooney Brothers Co., 25
Roper Industries, Inc., 15; 50 (upd.)
Ropes & Gray, 40
Rorer Group, I
Rose Acre Farms, Inc., 60
Rose Art Industries, 58
Rose's Stores, Inc., 13
Roseburg Forest Products Company, 58
Rosemount Inc., 15
Rosenbluth International Inc., 14
Ross Stores, Inc., 17; 43 (upd.)
Rotary International, 31
Roto-Rooter, Inc., 15; 61 (upd.)
The Rottlund Company, Inc., 28
Rouge Steel Company, 8
Rounder Records Corporation 79
Roundy's Inc., 14; 58 (upd.)
The Rouse Company, 15; 63 (upd.)
Rowan Companies, Inc., 43
Roy Anderson Corporation, 75
Roy F. Weston, Inc., 33

Royal Appliance Manufacturing Company, 15
Royal Caribbean Cruises Ltd., 22; 74 (upd.)
Royal Crown Company, Inc., 23
RPM, Inc., 8; 36 (upd.)
RSA Security Inc., 46
RTM Restaurant Group, 58
Rubbermaid Incorporated, III; 20 (upd.)
Rubio's Restaurants, Inc., 35
Ruby Tuesday, Inc., 18; 71 (upd.)
Ruiz Food Products, Inc., 53
Rural Cellular Corporation, 43
Rural/Metro Corporation, 28
Rush Communications, 33
Rush Enterprises, Inc., 64
Russ Berrie and Company, Inc., 12; 82 (upd.)
Russell Corporation, 8; 30 (upd.); 82 (upd.)
Russell Reynolds Associates Inc., 38
Russell Stover Candies Inc., 12
Rust International Inc., 11
Ruth's Chris Steak House, 28
RWD Technologies, Inc., 76
Ryan Beck & Co., Inc., 66
Ryan's Restaurant Group, Inc., 15; 68 (upd.)
Ryder System, Inc., V; 24 (upd.)
Ryerson Tull, Inc., 40 (upd.)
The Ryland Group, Inc., 8; 37 (upd.)
S&C Electric Company, 15
S&K Famous Brands, Inc., 23
S-K-I Limited, 15
S.C. Johnson & Son, Inc., III; 28 (upd.)
Saatchi & Saatchi, 42 (upd.)
Sabratek Corporation, 29
SABRE Group Holdings, Inc., 26
Sabre Holdings Corporation, 74 (upd.)
Safe Flight Instrument Corporation, 71
SAFECO Corporaton, III
Safeguard Scientifics, Inc., 10
Safelite Glass Corp., 19
Safeskin Corporation, 18
Safety Components International, Inc., 63
Safety 1st, Inc., 24
Safety-Kleen Systems Inc., 8; 82 (upd.)
Safeway Inc., II; 24 (upd.)
Saga Communications, Inc., 27
The St. Joe Company, 31
St. Joe Paper Company, 8
St. John Knits, Inc., 14
St. Jude Medical, Inc., 11; 43 (upd.)
St. Louis Music, Inc., 48
St. Mary Land & Exploration Company, 63
St. Paul Bank for Cooperatives, 8
The St. Paul Travelers Companies, Inc. III; 22 (upd.); 79 (upd.)
Saks Inc., 24; 41 (upd.)
Salant Corporation, 12; 51 (upd.)
salesforce.com, Inc. 79
Salick Health Care, Inc., 53
Sally Beauty Company, Inc., 60
Salomon Inc., II; 13 (upd.)
Salt River Project, 19
Salton, Inc., 30
The Salvation Army USA, 32

Sam Ash Music Corporation, 30
Sam Levin Inc., 80
Sam's Club, 40
Samsonite Corporation, 13; 43 (upd.)
Samuel Cabot Inc., 53
Samuels Jewelers Incorporated, 30
San Diego Gas & Electric Company, V
San Diego Padres Baseball Club LP 78
Sanborn Map Company Inc., 82
Sandals Resorts International, 65
Sanders Morris Harris Group Inc., 70
Sanderson Farms, Inc., 15
Sandia National Laboratories, 49
Sanford L.P., 82
Santa Barbara Restaurant Group, Inc., 37
The Santa Cruz Operation, Inc., 38
Santa Fe Gaming Corporation, 19
Santa Fe International Corporation, 38
Santa Fe Pacific Corporation, V
Sara Lee Corporation, II; 15 (upd.); 54 (upd.)
Sarnoff Corporation, 57
SAS Institute Inc., 10; 78 (upd.)
Saturn Corporation, 7; 21 (upd.); 80 (upd.)
Saucony Inc., 35
Sauder Woodworking Company, 12; 35 (upd.)
Sauer-Danfoss Inc., 61
Saul Ewing LLP, 74
Savannah Foods & Industries, Inc., 7
Sawtek Inc., 43 (upd.)
Sbarro, Inc., 16; 64 (upd.)
SBC Communications Inc., 32 (upd.)
SBS Technologies, Inc., 25
SCANA Corporation, 6; 56 (upd.)
ScanSource, Inc., 29; 74 (upd.)
SCB Computer Technology, Inc., 29
SCEcorp, V
Schawk, Inc., 24
Scheels All Sports Inc., 63
Scheid Vineyards Inc., 66
Schering-Plough Corporation, I; 14 (upd.); 49 (upd.)
Schieffelin & Somerset Co., 61
Schlage Lock Company, 82
Schlotzsky's, Inc., 36
Schlumberger Limited, III; 17 (upd.); 59 (upd.)
Schmitt Music Company, 40
Schneider National, Inc., 36; 77 (upd.)
Schneiderman's Furniture Inc., 28
Schnitzer Steel Industries, Inc., 19
Scholastic Corporation, 10; 29 (upd.)
School Specialty, Inc., 68
School-Tech, Inc., 62
Schott Brothers, Inc., 67
Schott Corporation, 53
Schottenstein Stores Corp., 14
Schreiber Foods, Inc., 72
Schuff Steel Company, 26
Schultz Sav-O Stores, Inc., 21; 31 (upd.)
Schwan's Sales Enterprises, Inc., 7; 26 (upd.)
Schwebel Baking Company, 72
Schweitzer-Mauduit International, Inc., 52
Schwinn Cycle and Fitness L.P., 19
SCI Systems, Inc., 9

W.B Doner & Co., 56
W.C. Bradley Co., 69
W. H. Braum, Inc., 80
W.H. Brady Co., 17
W.L. Gore & Associates, Inc., 14; 60 (upd.)
W.P. Carey & Co. LLC, 49
W.R. Berkley Corporation, 15; 74 (upd.)
W.R. Grace & Company, I; 50 (upd.)
W.W. Grainger, Inc., V; 26 (upd.); 68 (upd.)
W.W. Norton & Company, Inc., 28
Waban Inc., 13
Wabash National Corp., 13
Wabtec Corporation, 40
Wachovia Bank of Georgia, N.A., 16
Wachovia Bank of South Carolina, N.A., 16
Wachovia Corporation, 12; 46 (upd.)
Wachtell, Lipton, Rosen & Katz, 47
The Wackenhut Corporation, 14; 63 (upd.)
Waddell & Reed, Inc., 22
Waffle House Inc., 14; 60 (upd.)
Waggener Edstrom, 42
Wah Chang, 82
Wakefern Food Corporation, 33
Wal-Mart Stores, Inc., V; 8 (upd.); 26 (upd.); 63 (upd.)
Walbridge Aldinger Co., 38
Walbro Corporation, 13
Waldbaum, Inc., 19
Walden Book Company Inc., 17
Walgreen Co., V; 20 (upd.); 65 (upd.)
Walker Manufacturing Company, 19
Wall Drug Store, Inc., 40
Wall Street Deli, Inc., 33
Wallace Computer Services, Inc., 36
Walsworth Publishing Co. 78
The Walt Disney Company, II; 6 (upd.); 30 (upd.); 63 (upd.)
Walter Industries, Inc., II; 22 (upd.); 72 (upd.)
Walton Monroe Mills, Inc., 8
Wang Laboratories, Inc., III; 6 (upd.)
The Warnaco Group Inc., 12; 46 (upd.)
Warner Communications Inc., II
Warner-Lambert Co., I; 10 (upd.)
Warners' Stellian Inc., 67
Warrantech Corporation, 53
Warrell Corporation, 68
Warwick Valley Telephone Company, 55
The Washington Companies, 33
Washington Federal, Inc., 17
Washington Football, Inc., 35
Washington Gas Light Company, 19
Washington Mutual, Inc., 17
Washington National Corporation, 12
Washington Natural Gas Company, 9
The Washington Post Company, IV; 20 (upd.)
Washington Scientific Industries, Inc., 17
Washington Water Power Company, 6
Waste Connections, Inc., 46
Waste Holdings, Inc., 41
Waste Management, Inc., V
Water Pik Technologies, Inc., 34
Waterhouse Investor Services, Inc., 18

Waters Corporation, 43
Watkins-Johnson Company, 15
Watsco Inc., 52
Watson Pharmaceuticals Inc., 16; 56 (upd.)
Watson Wyatt Worldwide, 42
Watts Industries, Inc., 19
Wausau-Mosinee Paper Corporation, 60 (upd.)
Waverly, Inc., 16
Wawa Inc., 17; 78 (upd.)
Waxman Industries, Inc., 9
WD-40 Company, 18
The Weather Channel Companies, The 52
Weatherford International, Inc., 39
Webber Oil Company, 61
Weber-Stephen Products Co., 40
WebEx Communications, Inc., 81
WebMD Corporation, 65
Weeres Industries Corporation, 52
Wegmans Food Markets, Inc., 9; 41 (upd.)
Weider Nutrition International, Inc., 29
Weight Watchers International Inc., 12; 33 (upd.); 73 (upd.)
Weil, Gotshal & Manges LLP, 55
Weiner's Stores, Inc., 33
Weirton Steel Corporation, IV; 26 (upd.)
Weis Markets, Inc., 15
The Weitz Company, Inc., 42
Welbilt Corp., 19
Welcome Wagon International Inc., 82
The Welk Group Inc. 78
WellChoice, Inc., 67 (upd.)
Wellman, Inc., 8; 52 (upd.)
WellPoint Health Networks Inc., 25
Wells Fargo & Company, II; 12 (upd.); 38 (upd.)
Wells Rich Greene BDDP, 6
Wells' Dairy, Inc., 36
Wells-Gardner Electronics Corporation, 43
Wendy's International, Inc., 8; 23 (upd.); 47 (upd.)
Wenner Bread Products Inc., 80
Wenner Media, Inc., 32
Werner Enterprises, Inc., 26
West Bend Co., 14
West Coast Entertainment Corporation, 29
West Corporation, 42
West Group, 34 (upd.)
West Marine, Inc., 17
West One Bancorp, 11
West Pharmaceutical Services, Inc., 42
West Point-Pepperell, Inc., 8
West Publishing Co., 7
Westaff Inc., 33
Westamerica Bancorporation, 17
Westar Energy, Inc., 57 (upd.)
WestCoast Hospitality Corporation, 59
Westcon Group, Inc., 67
Westell Technologies, Inc., 57
Westerbeke Corporation, 60
Western Atlas Inc., 12
Western Beef, Inc., 22
Western Company of North America, 15
Western Digital Corp., 25

Western Gas Resources, Inc., 45
Western Publishing Group, Inc., 13
Western Resources, Inc., 12
The WesterN SizzliN Corporation, 60
Western Union Financial Services, Inc., 54
Western Wireless Corporation, 36
Westfield Group, 69
Westin Hotels and Resorts Worldwide, 9; 29 (upd.)
Westinghouse Electric Corporation, II; 12 (upd.)
Westmoreland Coal Company, 7
WestPoint Stevens Inc., 16
Westport Resources Corporation, 63
Westvaco Corporation, IV; 19 (upd.)
Westwood One, Inc., 23
The Wet Seal, Inc., 18; 70 (upd.)
Wetterau Incorporated, II
Weyco Group, Incorporated, 32
Weyerhaeuser Company, IV; 9 (upd.); 28 (upd.)
WFS Financial Inc., 70
WGBH Educational Foundation, 66
Wham-O, Inc., 61
Wheaton Industries, 8
Wheaton Science Products, 60 (upd.)
Wheelabrator Technologies, Inc., 6; 60 (upd.)
Wheeling-Pittsburgh Corporation, 7; 58 (upd.)
Wherehouse Entertainment Incorporated, 11
Whirlpool Corporation, III; 12 (upd.); 59 (upd.)
White & Case LLP, 35
White Castle System, Inc., 12; 36 (upd.)
White Consolidated Industries Inc., 13
The White House, Inc., 60
White Rose, Inc., 24
Whitehall Jewellers, Inc., 82 (upd.)
Whiting Petroleum Corporation, 81
Whitman Corporation, 10 (upd.)
Whitman Education Group, Inc., 41
Whitney Holding Corporation, 21
Whittaker Corporation, I; 48 (upd.)
Whole Foods Market, Inc., 20; 50 (upd.)
Wickes Inc., V; 25 (upd.)
Widmer Brothers Brewing Company, 76
Wieden + Kennedy, 75
Wilbert, Inc., 56
Wilbur Chocolate Company, 66
Wild Oats Markets, Inc., 19; 41 (upd.)
Wildlife Conservation Society, 31
Willamette Industries, Inc., IV; 31 (upd.)
William L. Bonnell Company, Inc., 66
William Lyon Homes, 59
William Morris Agency, Inc., 23
William Zinsser & Company, Inc., 58
Williams & Connolly LLP, 47
Williams Communications Group, Inc., 34
The Williams Companies, Inc., IV; 31 (upd.)
Williams Scotsman, Inc., 65
Williams-Sonoma, Inc., 17; 44 (upd.)
Williamson-Dickie Manufacturing Company, 14; 45 (upd.)
Wilmington Trust Corporation, 25